TOP INCOMES

Top Incomes

A Global Perspective

Edited by
A. B. ATKINSON
Nuffield College, Oxford
and
T. PIKETTY
PSE, Paris

OXFORD
UNIVERSITY PRESS

HC
79
.I5
T66
2010

OXFORD
UNIVERSITY PRESS

Great Clarendon Street, Oxford OX2 6DP

Oxford University Press is a department of the University of Oxford.
It furthers the University's objective of excellence in research, scholarship,
and education by publishing worldwide in

Oxford New York

Auckland Cape Town Dar es Salaam Hong Kong Karachi
Kuala Lumpur Madrid Melbourne Mexico City Nairobi
New Delhi Shanghai Taipei Toronto

With offices in

Argentina Austria Brazil Chile Czech Republic France Greece
Guatemala Hungary Italy Japan Poland Portugal Singapore
South Korea Switzerland Thailand Turkey Ukraine Vietnam

Oxford is a registered trade mark of Oxford University Press
in the UK and in certain other countries

Published in the United States
by Oxford University Press Inc., New York

© Oxford University Press 2010

British Library Cataloguing in Publication Data

Data available

Library of Congress Cataloging in Publication Data

Data available

Typeset by SPI Publisher Services, Pondicherry, India
Printed in Great Britain
on acid-free paper by
CPI Antony Rowe, Chippenham, Wiltshire

ISBN 978–0–19–928689–8

1 3 5 7 9 10 8 6 4 2

Preface

In Volume I, we assembled studies of top incomes covering ten OECD countries and focused on the contrast between continental Europe (France, Germany, the Netherlands, and Switzerland) and English-speaking countries (Australia, Canada, Ireland, New Zealand, the UK, and the USA). The present volume goes beyond this in several respects. Within Europe, the chapters in this volume cover both Nordic countries (Finland, Norway, and Sweden) and southern Europe (Italy, Portugal, and Spain). The Nordic countries have traditionally pursued more egalitarian policies and have typically lower levels of overall inequality. In contrast, overall inequality usually seems to rise as one moves further south in Europe. The chapters assembled here allow the reader to see whether the same geographical pattern is found at the top of the income distribution. Moreover, we can examine whether top income shares have risen in these countries in recent decades, as in the USA, or whether they have exhibited the relative stability found in a number of continental European countries.

A second important objective of the present volume is to widen the geographical coverage to include Asia (China, India, Indonesia, Japan, and Singapore) and Latin America, of which Argentina is the sole representative (we had hoped to include Brazil, but the data were not available at the time). Particular interest attaches to the impact of rapid growth in China and India on the top of the income distribution, and to the potential role of income taxation. The different growth history of Japan provides an interesting counterpoint. Indonesia and Singapore are contrasts of scale and post-colonial experience.

The series for top income shares in Volume I covered much of the twentieth century and are extended here in Chapter 13 to cover the early years of the twenty-first century. We have also extended the coverage back in time. One of the features of the chapters in this volume is that two go back to the nineteenth century: the data for Japan start in 1886 and those for Norway in 1875.

The book starts in Asia in Chapters 1 to 5, then comes to Argentina in Chapter 6, before turning to the Nordic countries in Chapters 7 to 9, and southern Europe in Chapters 10 to 12. In the final Chapter 13, we draw together the main findings from this volume and from Volume I. The data, covering twenty-two countries, and going back before the Second World War for all except three, provide a rich source of evidence about the long-run evolution of the upper part of the income distribution.

The project that has generated these two volumes is an unusual one in that it has no formal status and did not originate in a carefully planned research proposal to a funding agency. The chapters have been written by an informal network of academics, doctoral students, and members of research institutes and statistical offices. This network grew through a process of spontaneous diffusion rather than by any intelligent design. A number of the chapters enjoyed funding for the work on the particular country, and these are acknowledged in each case.

The informal nature of the project has meant that we have not sought to impose a rigid straitjacket on the format of the chapters, which in any case reflect the differing institutions and historical experiences of the countries. The chapters were written at different dates, and this means that some of the cross-country comparisons in individual chapters are based on earlier versions of the top income data for other countries. Those interested in exploring further cross-country comparisons are urged to look at the data collected in Chapter 13, which are the most recent at the time of completing this volume.

At the same time, the informality of the network has added to the pleasure of working with the authors, and we should like to thank warmly all seventeen for their cooperation in producing these volumes.

A. B. Atkinson and T. Piketty

Contents

List of Figures and Tables

FIGURES

TABLES

Contributors

Rolf Aaberge, Research Department, Statistics Norway; rolf.aaberge@ssb.no.

Facundo Alvaredo, University of Oxford, Manor Road Building, Manor Road, OX1 3UQ, Oxford, and CONICET; facundo.alvaredo@economics.ox.ac.uk.

Anthony B. Atkinson, Nuffield College, Oxford OX1 1NF; tony.atkinson@nuffield.ox.ac.uk.

Abhijit Banerjee, Department of Economics, MIT; banerjee@mit.edu.

Markus Jäntti, Swedish Institute for Social Research, Stockholm University, S-10961 Stockholm; markus.jantti@iki.fi.

Andrew Leigh, Research School of Social Sciences, ANU College of Arts and Social Sciences, Australian National University; http://econrsss.anu.edu.au/~aleigh/; andrew.leigh@anu.edu.au.

Chiaki Moriguchi, Northwestern University, Department of Economics, 2001 Sheridan Road, Evanston, IL 60208, USA; chiaki@northwestern.edu.

Thomas Piketty, Paris School of Economics, piketty@ens.fr; www.jourdan.ens.fr/piketty.

Elena Pisano, Department of Public Economics, University of Rome La Sapienza, Via del Castro Laurenziano n. 9—00161 Rome, Italy; elena.pisano@gmail.com or Elena.Pisano@uniroma1.it.

Nancy Qian, Department of Economics, Brown University; Nancy.Qian@brown.edu.

Marja Riihelä, Government Institute for Economic Research, PO BOX 1279, FI00101 Helsinki; marja.riihela@vatt.fi.

Jesper Roine, SITE, Stockholm School of Economics, PO Box 6501, SE-11383 Stockholm, + 46–8–7369000; Jesper.Roine@hhs.se.

Emmanuel Saez, University of California-Berkeley and NBER, Department of Economics, 549 Evans Hall #3880, Berkeley, CA 94720; saez@econ.berkeley.edu.

Risto Sullström, Government Institute for Economic Research, PO BOX 1279, FI-00101; risto.sullstrom@vatt.fi.

Matti Tuomala, University of Tampere, 3014 Tampereen yliopisto; matti.tuomala@uta.fi.

Pierre van der Eng, School of Management, Marketing and International Business, ANU College of Business and Economics, Australian National University; http:// ecocomm.anu.edu.au/people/pierre.vandereng; pierre.vandereng@anu.edu.au.

Daniel Waldenström, Research Institute of Industrial Economics, PO Box 55665, SE-102 15 Stockholm, Sweden; danielw@ifn.se.

1

Top Indian Incomes, 1922–2000

Abhijit Banerjee and Thomas Piketty

1.1 INTRODUCTION

This chapter presents series on top incomes and top wages in India between the years 1922 and 2000 based on individual tax returns data. We use tabulations of tax returns published each year by the Indian tax administration to compute the share of the top percentile of the distribution of total income, the top 0.5 per cent, the top 0.1 per cent, and the top 0.01 per cent. We do the same for the wage distribution. We do not go below the top percentile because incomes below this level are largely exempt from taxation in India.

Our series begin in 1922, when the income tax was created in India, and allow us to look at the impact of the Great Depression and the Second World War on inequality. We are particularly interested in the period starting in the 1950s, right at the beginning of India's experiment with socialism. This experiment was officially suspended in 1991 with the beginning of the liberalization process, which continued through the 1990s. One explicit goal of the socialist programme was to limit the economic power of the elite, in the context of a mixed economy. Our data offer us the opportunity to say something about the extent to which this programme, with all its well-known deficiencies, succeeded in its distributional objectives. This is important first, because it is a vital part of our assessment of this period. And second, because it offers a window into the broader question of the role of policy in affecting the distribution of income and wealth in a developing country. Given that much of the economic activity in these countries is outside the formal sector, it is not at all obvious that there is a lot that policy can affect.[1]

Our results are consistent with an important role for policy in shaping the distribution of income. In particular, we do find evidence of a substantial decline in the share of the elite during the years of socialist planning and a comparable

We are grateful to Tony Atkinson, Amaresh Bagchi, Gaurav Datt, Govinda Rao, Martin Ravallion, T. N. Srinivasan, Suresh Tendulkar, and two anonymous referees for useful discussions, to Sarah Voitchovsky for excellent research assistance, and to the MacArthur Foundation for financial support. A shorter version of this chapter was published as A. Banerjee and T. Piketty, 'Top Indian Incomes, 1922–2000', *World Bank Economic Review*, 19 (2005): 1–20.

[1] Especially tax policy.

recovery in the post-liberalization era. However the rebound seems to start significantly before the official move towards liberalization.

Given that these results are likely to be controversial, it is worth emphasizing that there are a number of obvious problems with using tax data, not the least because of tax evasion. We discuss these at some length in section 1.4. While we conclude that our results are probably robust, we do not intend them to be definitive. Our view is rather that they provide a point of departure on an important question about which very little is known, primarily because of data limitations. There are good reasons to suspect that the usual sources of information on income distribution in India—such as consumer expenditure surveys— are not particularly effective at picking up the very rich. This is in part because the rich are rare, and in part because they are much more likely to refuse to cooperate with the time-consuming and irksome process of being subjected to a consumer expenditure survey.[2]

While there is no hard evidence that the rich are indeed being undercounted in India (the Indian consumer expenditure surveys do not, for example, report refusal rates by potential income category), one reason to suspect that this is the case comes from what has been called the *Indian growth paradox of the 1990s*. According to the standard household expenditure survey conducted by the National Sample Survey (NSS), real per capita growth in India during the 1990s was fairly limited. Such a conclusion stands in sharp contrast with the substantial growth measured by national accounts statistics (NAS) over this same period. This puzzle has attracted quite a lot of attention during recent years[3] and it has been widely suggested that it might simply be that a very large part of the growth went to the very rich. However there has been no attempt to directly quantify this possibility.[4] Our data allow us to take a useful step in this direction. We are able to put bounds on the extent to which the growth gap can be explained simply in terms of undercounting the very rich. We conclude that it can explain between 20 per cent and 40 per cent of the puzzle. Although this is not negligible,

---

[2] See, e.g., Szekely and Hilgert (1999), who look at a large number of Latin American household surveys and find that the ten largest incomes reported in surveys are often not very much larger than the salary of an average manager in the given country at the time of survey. For a systematic comparison of survey and national accounts aggregates in developing countries, see Ravallion (2001).

[3] See, e.g., Datt (1999), Ravallion (2000), World Bank (2000), Sundaram and Tendulkar (2001). Recently released data from the 1999–2000 NSS round have revealed that NSS growth was larger than expected during the 1990s and that poverty rates did decline over this period, contrarily to what most observers believed on the basis of pre-1999–2000 NSS rounds (see Deaton and Drèze 2002 and Deaton 2003a, 2003b). However the overall NSS–NAS growth gap still appears to be substantial, even after this correction (see Table 1.2 below), and this substantial gap remains to be explained. The existence of a discrepancy between NSS and NAS statistics was already a subject of enquiry in India during the 1980s (see, e.g., Minhas 1988 and Minhas and Kansal 1990), but the gap observed during the 1990s appears to be substantially larger than during previous decades. For a broader, international perspective on the survey vs. national accounts debate, see Deaton (2003c).

[4] Sundaram and Tendulkar (2001) find that the NSS–NAS gap is particularly important for commodities that are more heavily consumed by higher income groups, thereby providing indirect evidence for the explanation based on rising inequality.

this leaves the bulk of the puzzle unaccounted for, largely because the share of the rich in total income is still relatively small. This suggests that there probably is some deeper problem with the way either the NSS or the NSO (which generates the NAS) collects its data.[5]

The rest of this chapter is organized as follows. Section 1.2 briefly outlines our data and methodology. Section 1.3 presents our long-run results. Section 1.4 discusses potential problems with this evidence. Section 1.5 uses this evidence to shed some light on the Indian growth paradox of the 1990s. Section 1.6 concludes.

1.2 DATA AND METHODOLOGY

The tabulations of tax returns published each year by the Indian tax administration in the 'All-India Income-Tax Statistics' (AIITS) series constitute the primary data source used in this chapter. The first year for which we have income data is 1922–3 while the last is 1999–2000.[6]

Due to the relatively high exemption levels, the number of taxpayers in India has always been rather small. The proportion of taxable tax units was around 0.5 per cent–1 per cent from the 1920s to the 1980s, and it rose sharply during the 1990s up to 3.5 per cent–4 per cent at the end of the decade, following the large increase in top nominal incomes (see Figure 1.1).[7] Therefore our long-run series cannot go below the top percentile.

---

[5] See Bhalla (2002) for a negative view of the NSS approach. For more balanced discussions of the relative merits of survey and national accounts aggregates in developing countries, see Ravallion (2001) and Deaton (2003c).

[6] All references to the relevant AIITS publications are given in Table 1A.1. Financial years run from 1 April to 31 March in India (1922–3 refers to the period running from 1 April 1922 to 31 March 1923, etc., and 1999–2000 to the period running from 1 April 1999 to 31 March 2000). Note also that AIITS publications always refer to assessment years (AY), i.e. years during which incomes are assessed, while we always refer to income years (IY) (IY=AY–1). For instance, AIITS 1923–4 contains the data on IY 1922–3, etc., and AIITS 1999–2000 contains the data on IY 1998–9. AIITS 2000–1 (IY 1999–2000) was not yet available when we revised this paper, and our IY 1999–2000 figures for top incomes were obtained by inflating the 1998–9 figures by the nominal 1999–2000/1998–9 per tax unit national income growth rate. This approximation probably leads us to underestimate top income growth. We did this because there was no large NSS round for 1998–9 so it was easier to make comparison with 1999–2000 as the end point.

[7] Throughout the chapter, 'tax units' should be thought of as individuals (all of our estimates have been obtained by summing up tax returns filed by individuals and those filed by 'Hindu undivided families' (HUF); the latter make less than 5% of the total in the 1990s, down from about 20% in the inter-war period). The total, theoretical number of tax units was set to be equal to 40% of the total population of India throughout the period (see Table 1A.1, col. (2)). This represents a rough estimate of the potential 'positive-income population' of India: this is lower than India's adult population (the 15-year-and-over population makes up about 60–5% of total population since the 1950s), but is very close to India's labour force (the labour force consists of about 40–5% of total population since the 1950s).

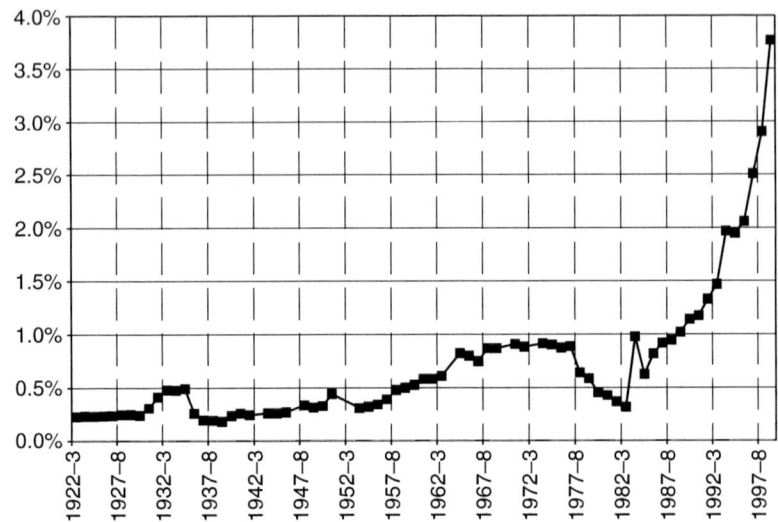

Figure 1.1 The proportion of taxable tax units in India, 1922–2000

Source: Authors' computations using tax returns data (see Table 1A.1, col. (4)).

The tabulations published in AIITS report the number of taxpayers and the total income reported by these taxpayers for a large number of income brackets. By using standard Pareto extrapolation techniques we computed for each year the average incomes of the top percentile (P99–100), the top 0.5 per cent (P99.5–100), the top 0.1 per cent (P99.9–100), and the top 0.01 per cent (P99.99–100) of the tax unit distribution of total income, as well as the income thresholds P99, P99.5, P99.9, and P99.99 and the average incomes of the intermediate fractiles P99–99.5, P99.5–99.9, and P99.9–99.99.[8]

To get a sense of the orders of magnitude, we report in Table 1.1 the results obtained for 1999–2000. There were almost 400 million tax units in India (396.4 million). Based on the national accounts statistics, the average income of those 400 million tax units was around Rs 25,000 per year ($3,000 in PPP terms).[9] To

---

[8] The Pareto law is given by $1–F(y)=(k/y)^a$ (where $1–F(y)$ is the fraction of the population with income above y, and $k>0$ and $a>1$ are the structural Pareto parameters). For a recent use of Pareto extrapolation techniques with similar tax return data, see Piketty (2003) and Piketty and Saez (2003). See also Atkinson (2007; chapter 4 in Volume I) and Dell (2007; chapter 9 in Volume I).

[9] Our average income series (see Table 1A.2, col. (7)) was set to be equal to 70% of national income per tax unit (the 30% deduction is assumed to represent the fraction of national income that goes to undistributed profits, non-taxable income, etc.; the national income series was taken from Sivasubramonian 2000, from whom we also took our population series). We also report in Table 1A.1 other income aggregates based on GDP and NAS household consumption (both taken from the World Bank's WDI database, from which we also extracted our CPI series, as well as the PPP exchange rate used in Table 1.1) and on NSS household consumption (computed from Datt 1997, 1999, for the 1956–98 series and Deaton and Drèze (2002: n. 24) for the corrected 1999–2000/1993–4 growth rate).

Table 1.1 Top Indian incomes in 1999–2000

Thresholds (1)	Income level (Rs) (2)	Income level (US$) (market exchange rate) (3)	Income level (US$) (PPP conversion factor) (4)	Fractiles (5)	Number of tax units (6)	Average income (Rs) (7)	Average income (US$) (market exchange rate) (8)	Average income (US$) (PPP conversion factor) (9)
				Full Population	396,400,000	25,670	596	2,968
P99	87,633	2,035	10,131	P99–99.5	1,982,000	98,842	2,295	11,427
P99.5	147,546	3,427	17,057	P99.5–99.9	1,585,600	216,929	5,038	25,079
P99.9	295,103	6,853	34,116	P99.9–99.99	356,760	590,488	13,713	68,264
P99.99	1,383,930	32,140	159,992	P99.99–100	39,640	4,034,289	93,690	466,392

Source: Table 1A.2 and Table 1A.3, row 1999–00. Amounts in $ have been computed by applying the average 1999–2000 market exchange rate (that is, 1$=43.06Rs) and the average 1999–2000 PPP conversion factor (that is, 1$=8.65Rs) to amounts in current 1999–2000 Rs.

belong to the top percentile (P99), which includes about 4 million tax units, one needed to make more than Rs 88,000 (around $10,000 at PPP). The average income of the bottom half of the top percentile (fractile P99–99.5, about 2 million tax units) was about Rs 99,000 (less than $12,000 at PPP). To belong to the top 0.01 per cent (about 40,000 tax units), one needs to make more than Rs 1.4 million ($160,000 at PPP), and the average income above that threshold was more than Rs 4 million ($470,000 at PPP).[10]

As in other countries, the top of India's income distribution appears to be very precisely approximated by the Pareto structural form.[11] On the other hand the estimates for the recent period are subject to sampling error: the AIITS tabulations were based on the entire population until the early 1990s (as in most OECD countries),[12] but they now seem to be based upon uniform samples of all tax returns. Although there is uncertainty about the new sampling procedure, the sampling rate seems to be sufficiently large to guarantee that the estimated trends for top income shares are statistically significant.[13]

AIITS publications also include tabulations reporting the amounts of the various income categories (wages, business income, dividends, interest, etc.) for each income bracket. In particular, AIITS offers separate tables for wage earners who are by far the largest subgroup. This allowed us to separate estimates for top wage fractiles, which we can compare to our top fractiles estimates for total income (see below).[14]

---

[10] In order to put these numbers in global perspective, one can note that India's 1999–2000 P99.99 threshold (about $160,000 in PPP terms) is located midway in between US 1998 P95 and P99 thresholds for 1998 (resp. $107,000 and $230,000; see Piketty and Saez (2003: table 1)), and that India's 1999–2000 P99.9 threshold (about $34,000 in PPP terms) is well below US 1998 P90 threshold ($82,000).

[11] In the same way as for other countries (see above for references), we checked that our extrapolation results are virtually unaffected by the choice of extrapolation thresholds used to estimate the structural parameters. Pareto coefficients are locally very stable in India, just as in other countries. Prior to the 1990s, the fraction of individuals subject to tax was less than 1%, and we used the lowest threshold available in order to estimate the top percentile threshold P99 (given that Pareto coefficients are in practice very stable, the resulting estimates appear to be as precise as estimates for thresholds P99.5 and above).

[12] Or on stratified samples with sampling rates close to 100% for top incomes.

[13] According to the tax administration statistics division, the sampling rate is about 1% and approximately uniform (no precise information about sampling design and rate is included in AIITS publications). Given India's large population, this implies that our estimate for the top 1% income share (8.95% of total income in 1999–2000) has a standard error of about 0.04%, and that our estimate for the top 0.01% income share (1.57% of total income in 1999–2000) has a standard error of about 0.08%. There is some evidence however that the sampling design is changing and that published tabulations are becoming more volatile by the end of the period. In particular, the tabulations for IY 1997–8 (AIITS 1998–9) contain far too many individual taxpayers above 1 million Rs, thereby suggesting that something went wrong in the sampling design during that year. The 1997–8 estimates were corrected downwards on the basis of 1996–7 and 1998–9 tabulations.

[14] Published wage tabulations for IY 1996–7 and 1997–8 appear to suffer from sampling design failures (top wages are clearly truncated in 1996–7, and they are too numerous in 1997–8), and our estimates for those two years were corrected on the basis of 1995–6 and 1998–9 data.

1.3 THE LONG-RUN DYNAMICS OF TOP INCOME SHARES, 1922–2000

Figure 1.2 illustrates the basic pattern of our findings. Our results show that income inequality (as measured by the share of top incomes) has followed a U-shaped pattern over the 1922–2000 period. The top 0.01 per cent income share was fluctuating around 2–2.5 per cent of total income from the 1920s to the 1950s. It then gradually fell from about 1.5–2 per cent of total income in the 1950s to less than 0.5 per cent in the early 1980s, and finally rose during the 1980s–1990s, back to 1.5–2 per cent during the late 1990s. What this means is that the average top 0.01 per cent income was about 150–200 times larger than the average income of the entire population during the 1950s. It went down to less than 50 times as large in the early 1980s, but went back to being 150–200 times larger during the late 1990s.

The exact turning point is also of some interest. We see that the decline in the share of the top 0.01 per cent is relatively rapid till 1974–5. Then it slows considerably but there is still a clear downward trend till 1980–1. Then it reverses: the trend is upwards throughout the 1980s, reaching a peak in 1988–9. Over the 1980s, the share of the top 0.01 per cent more than doubles—from less than 0.4 per cent to more than 0.8 per cent. But it then reverses once again, and by 1991–2 it is back below 0.6 per cent. Then it takes off and after 1995–6 remains in the 1.5–2 per cent range.

One also observes a similar (though less pronounced) U-shaped pattern for the top 1 per cent income share, which went from about 12–13 per cent during the 1950s to 4–5 per cent in the early 1980s to 9–10 per cent in the late 1990s (see Figure 1.4).

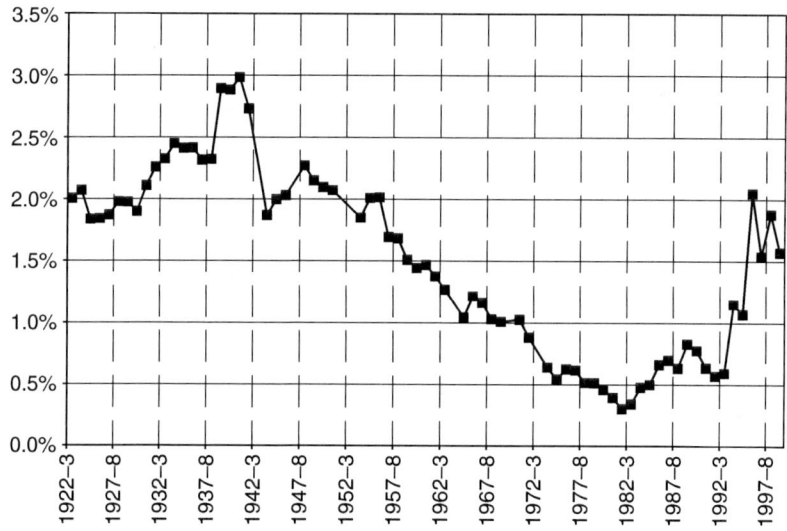

Figure 1.2 The top 0.01% income share in India, 1922–2000
Source: Table 1A.5, col. (4).

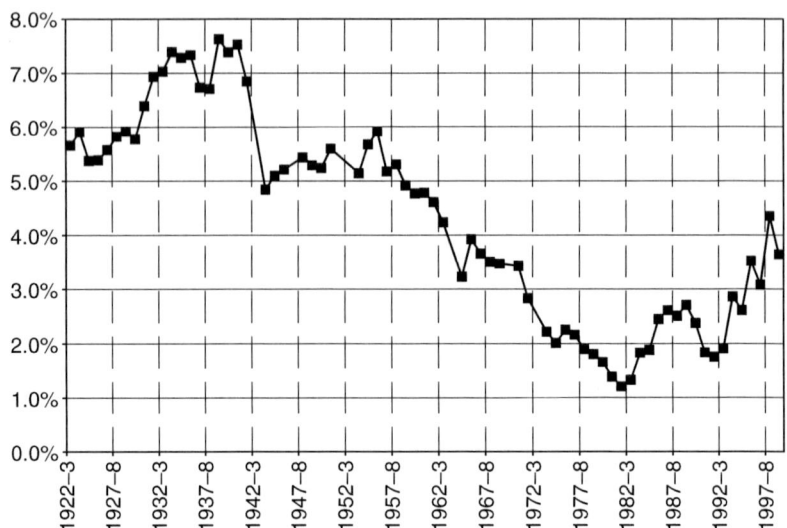

Figure 1.3 The top 0.1% income share in India, 1922–2000
Source: Table 1A.5, col. (3).

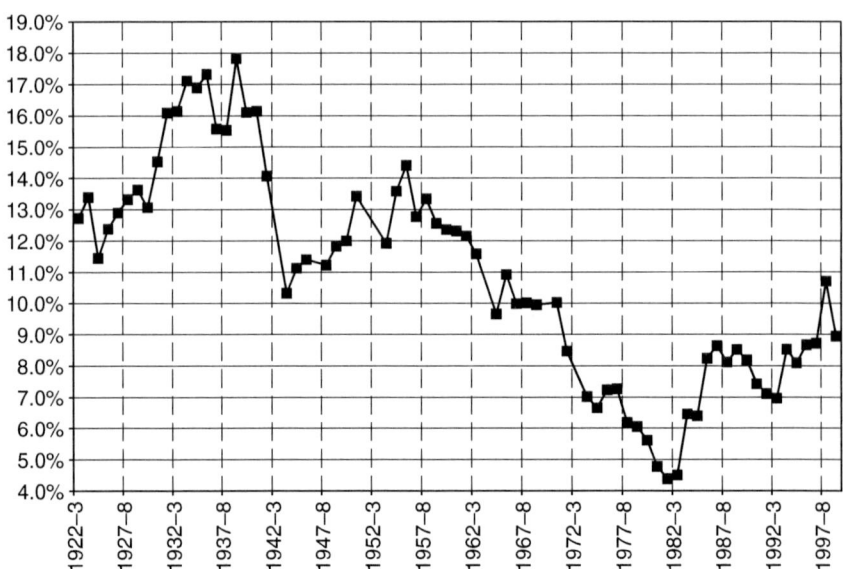

Figure 1.4 The top 1% income share in India, 1922–2000
Source: Table 1A.5, col. (1).

Once again the turning point seems to be around 1980–1, and over the 1980s, the share of the top 1 per cent also doubles. Then, as with the share of the top 0.01 per cent, there is a period of retrenchment that lasts till 1991–2, followed by a renewed upward movement.

The comparison of Figures 1.2 and 1.3 reveals another intriguing fact: While in the 1980s the share of the top 1 per cent increases almost as quickly as the share of the top 0.01 per cent, in the 1990s there is a clear divergence between what is happening to the top 0.01 per cent and the rest of the top percentile. To confirm that this is the case, we break up the top percentile into four groups: those between the 99th percentile and the 99.5th percentile, those between the 99.5th percentile and the 99.9th percentile, those between the 99.9th percentile and the 99.99th percentile, and those in the top 0.01 percentile. Table 1.2 reports what happened to each of these groups in the 1987–2000 period. We see that only those in the top 0.1 per cent enjoyed income growth rates faster than the growth rate of GDP per capita. This contrasts with what we see when we look at the period that includes the 1980s (see Table 1.3). For this period we see evidence of above-average growth for the entire top percentile.

While 1980–1 was clearly the year when the data series turn around, it is not possible to date the 'true' turnaround with quite so much precision, because the share of the rich is also affected by short-run, cyclical factors. It is possible that our data put the turning point in 1980–1 only because we have not made any allowances for the deep recession of 1979–80 and 1980–1, which hurt the rich. As a result, we see a sharp upward trend starting in 1981, even though perhaps what is really happening

Table 1.2 Top income growth in India during the 1990s: 1999–2000 vs. 1987–1988

	1999–2000 vs. 1987–8 (nominal growth)	1999–2000 vs. 1987–8 (real growth)
Household consumption/capita (NSS)	+242%	+19%
GDP/capita (NAS)	+337%	+52%
Household consumption/capita (NAS)	+304%	+40%
National income/tax unit (NAS)	+346%	+55%
Top income fractile P99–100 (tax returns)	+392%	+71%
Top income fractile P99.5–100 (tax returns)	+412%	+78%
Top income fractile P99.9–100 (tax returns)	+548%	+125%
Top income fractile P99.99–100 (tax returns)	+1009%	+285%
Top income fractile P99–99.5 (tax returns)	+331%	+50%
Top income fractile P99.5–99.9 (tax returns)	+317%	+45%
Top income fractile P99.9–99.99 (tax returns)	+393%	+71%
Top income fractile P99.99–100 (tax returns)	+1009%	+285%
Consumer price index	+188%	
Share of growth gap accounted for by P99–100		20.1%
Share of growth gap accounted for by P99.5–100		17.2%
Share of growth gap accounted for by P99.9–100		12.7%
Share of growth gap accounted for by P99.99–100		8.0%

Source: Authors' computations using tax return, NAS and NSS data (see Table 1A.2, Table 1A.3, and Table 1A.4, row 1999–2000/1987–8).

Table 1.3 Top income growth in India during the 1980s–1990s: 1999–2000 vs. 1981–1982

	1999–2000 vs 1981–2 (nominal growth)	1999–2000 vs 1981–2 (real growth)
Household consumption/capita (NSS)	+487%	+25%
GDP/capita (NAS)	+700%	+70%
Household consumption/capita (NAS)	+599%	+49%
National income/tax unit (NAS)	+688%	+68%
Top income fractile P99–100 (tax returns)	+1508%	+242%
Top income fractile P99.5–100 (tax returns)	+1747%	+293%
Top income fractile P99.9–100 (tax returns)	+2270%	+404%
Top income fractile P99.99–100 (tax returns)	+3980%	+767%
Top income fractile P99–99.5 (tax returns)	+992%	+132%
Top income fractile P99.5–99.9 (tax returns)	+1392%	+217%
Top income fractile P99.9–99.99 (tax returns)	+1698%	+282%
Top income fractile P99.99–100 (tax returns)	+3980%	+767%
Consumer price index	+370%	
Share of growth gap accounted for by P99–100		39.7%
Share of growth gap accounted for by P99.5–100		33.5%
Share of growth gap accounted for by P99.9–100		19.1%
Share of growth gap accounted for by P99.99–100		9.3%

Source: Authors' computations using tax return, NAS and NSS data (see Table 1A.2, Table 1A.3, and Table 1A.4, row 1999–00/1981–2).

in 1981–2 and 1982–3 is just a reversion to the pre-existing trend. Therefore rather than naming a single year, we date the turnaround to the early to mid 1980s.

The fact that the turning point is so early makes it hard to attribute it to the formal process of liberalization. Indeed, given the nature of our data, we cannot entirely rule out the possibility either that the driving factor was a shift in the global economic environment, or even that it was a part of the natural evolution of a mixed economy. However, the timing of the turnaround is also consistent with the view that there was a structural shift in the Indian economy in the early to mid 1980s. Delong (2001) and Rodrik and Subramanian (2004), based on macro time series data, date the acceleration in the growth rate of the Indian economy to the early to mid 1980s, rather than the early 1990s. They suggest that this may have to do with a shift of power within the ruling Congress Party towards a more technocratic/pro-business group associated with Rajiv Gandhi, who enters politics in 1981 following his brother's death, and becomes Prime Minister in 1984. Available macro series also show that the wage share in the private corporate sector has been declining in India since the early to mid 1980s (in contrast to the 1970s, when the profit share was declining),[15] which is again consistent with our turning point.

Also, while the turnaround was earlier, the data suggest a definite acceleration in the growth of the share of the top 0.01 per cent after 1991. Moreover this

---

[15] See Nagaraj (2000: figure 7) and Tendulkar (2003: table 14).

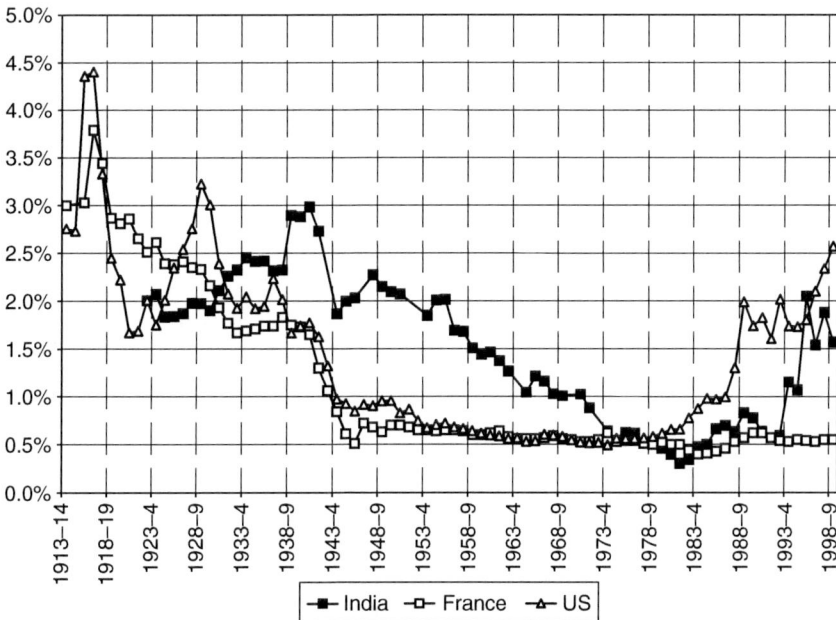

Figure 1.5 The top 0.01% income share in India, France, and the USA, 1913–2000

Source: Authors' computations using tax returns data (India: Table 1A.5, col. (4); France: Piketty (2003); US: Piketty and Saez (2003)).

contrasts with what we see in the case of the top 1 per cent, suggesting that what happened after 1991 was qualitatively different from what happened before, and even more biased in favour of the ultra-rich.

Finally, a tentative piece of evidence suggesting that what happened in India over this entire period was not simply a reflection of forces that were affecting countries all over the world. Figures 1.5, 1.6, and 1.7 compare what happened in India to the patterns obtained using similar data from France and the United States. During the 1950s–1960s, India was less egalitarian than either of these countries (they were actually quite similar at that time), in the sense that the top 0.01 per cent earned a substantially higher share of total income in India. Subsequently however, top income shares declined continuously in India during 1960s–1970s and fell below the Western levels during the early 1980s. The fact that the fall of top income shares occurred mostly during the 1950s–1970s in India (rather than during the inter-war period and the Second World War) seems consistent with the interpretation posited by Piketty (2003) and Piketty and Saez (2003) to explain the French and US trajectories. The shocks induced by the Great Depression of the 1930s and the Second World War were less severe in India,[16] while tax progressivity was extremely high in India during the 1950s–1970s, which might have induced a very large impact on capital concentration and

---

[16] Note that unlike in France, the USA, or the UK, top income shares were actually rising in India during the Great Depression of the 1930s. Top Indian nominal incomes do decline during the 1930s,

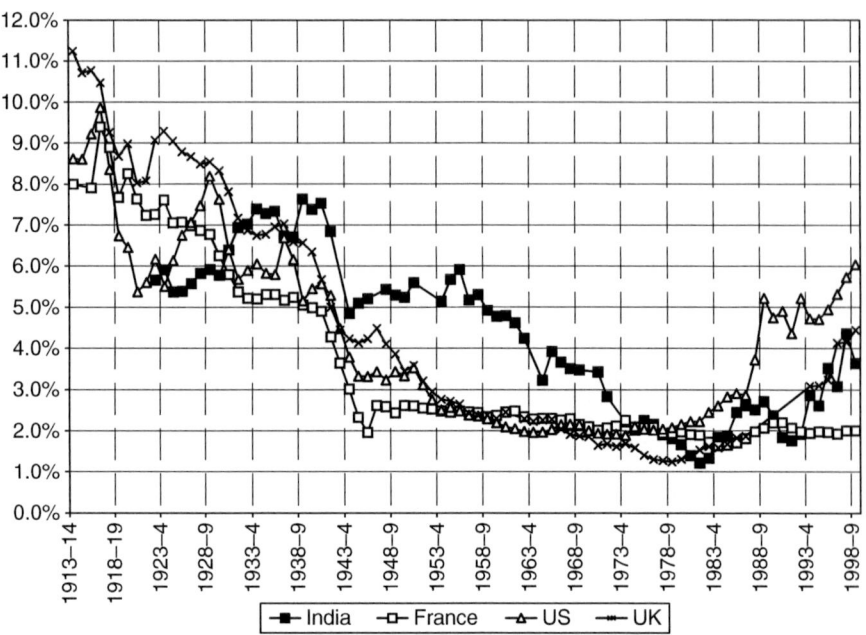

Figure 1.6 The top 0.1% income share in India, France, the USA, and the UK, 1913–2000

Source: Authors' computations using tax returns data (India: Table 1A.5, col. (3); France: Piketty (2003); US: Piketty–Saez (2003); UK: Chapter 13, Table 13A.2).

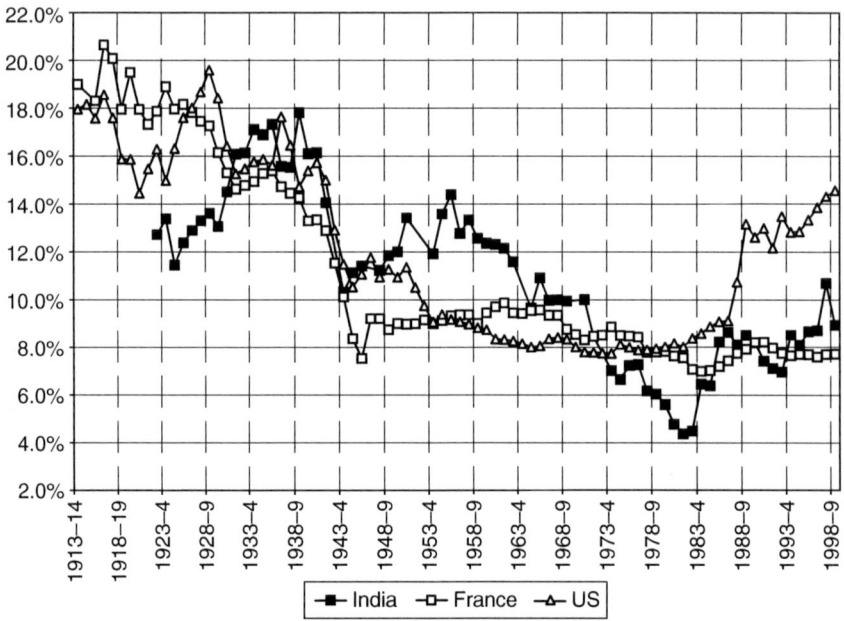

Figure 1.7 The top 1% income share in India, France, and the USA, 1913–2000

Source: Authors' computations using tax returns data (India: Table 1A.5, col. (1); France: Piketty (2003); US: Piketty–Saez (2003)).

pre-tax income inequality (even larger than in France or the USA). Available data do indeed seem to indicate that the fall in top shares observed during this period was primarily due to the fall of top capital incomes.[17]

Top income shares then went back up in India, following a pattern similar to the United States but not France, where the top shares remained fairly flat during the 1980s–1990s (the pattern in most other European countries is quite similar).[18] The share of the very rich in Indian incomes is currently much higher than in Europe. As we show below, the rise of top Indian incomes during the recent period was not due to the revival of top capital incomes (the rise of top wages did play a key role, like in the USA). Although our data do not allow us to identify precisely the causal channels at work, and in particular to isolate the impact of globalization, we note that the fact that the rise in income inequality was so much concentrated within top incomes seems more consistent with a theory based on rents and market frictions (see e.g. Banerjee and Newman 2003) than with a theory based solely on skills and technological complementarity (i.e. inequality rises in the south because low-skill southern workers are too low-skill to benefit from globalization; see e.g. Kremer and Maskin 2003).

1.4 MEASUREMENT ISSUES

Our presumption so far has been that what we have measured is the actual income share of the rich. There are a number of reasons why this may not be true. First, despite our best efforts, we were unable to discover the exact changes that occurred during the 1990s in the procedure for generating the samples used to create the tax tables. Our sense, from informal conversations with Indian tax officials, is that, at least in recent years, the procedure is more an informal attempt to sample randomly than a precise random sample. To the extent that this increases the risk of the data being clustered, the implication is that the within sample variance might overstate the precision of our data. While this remains a possibility, we take some consolation from the fact that the trends, for the most part, seem quite stable. While our results for single years or sets of years may reflect sampling variation, the fact that in every year between 1973–4 and 1992–3, the share of the top 0.01 per cent was less than 0.85 per cent (and in every year but two it was less than 0.7 per cent) and that in every year including and after 1995–6

but less rapidly than the national income and wage series computed by Sivasubramonian (2000). This probably reflects the fact that India had a very different position from France, the USA, or the UK in the world division of labour during the 1930s (Indian entrepreneurs might have benefited from the drop in world manufacturing output and raw prices).

[17] Unfortunately AIITS publications do not provide a complete set of tabulations broken down by income sources, so we were not able to study the point in greater detail.

[18] Top shares series recently constructed for Germany by Dell (2007; chapter 9 in Volume I) confirm that France is fairly representative of continental Europe. The UK appears to be intermediate between continental Europe and the USA: there was a rise in top shares since the early 1980s, but it was much less pronounced than in the USA (see Atkinson 2007; chapter 4 in Volume I).

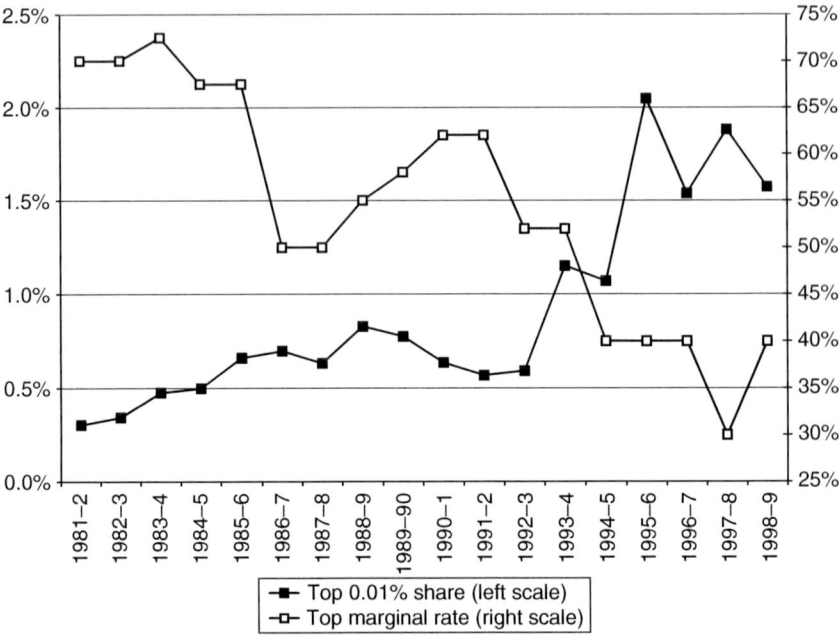

Figure 1.8 The top 0.01% income share and the top marginal income tax rate in India, 1981–2000

Source: Authors' computations using tax returns data (Table 1A.5) and tax return law.

it was greater than 1.5 per cent, seems much more robust. Moreover the intervening two years, 1993–4 and 1994–5, do show, as we might have hoped for, shares for the top 0.01 per cent that were between 0.7 per cent and 1.5 per cent.

A more serious problem is that the surge in top incomes may reflect improvements in the income tax department's ability to measure (and hence tax) the incomes of the wealthy. One reason for this may be that tax cuts in the early 1990s simply reduced the incentives for evading taxes among the wealthy. Note however that the overall decline in the top marginal rate, though non-monotonic, was quite moderate: the top marginal tax rate dropped from 50 per cent in 1987–8 to 40 per cent in 1999–2000 (see Figure 1.8). By comparison the change in the share of the top 0.01 per cent was enormous: It went up from 0.7 per cent in 1987–8 to over 1.5 per cent in 1999–2000. If this entire change is to be explained by a shift in tax rates, the implied elasticity would have to be enormous.

In particular, the implied elasticity would need to be much larger than what has been estimated in the USA following the Tax Reform Act of 1986. The current consensus in the USA seems to be that while short-run elasticities can be substantial,[19] the medium- and long-run elasticity of top taxable income with

---

[19] This reflected mostly income relabelling or changes in timing of exercise for bonuses or stock options.

respect to top tax rates is probably fairly modest. In particular, the rise in top income shares observed in the USA during the 1970–2000 period seems to reflect for the most part real economic change (rather than pure fiscal manipulation): top shares started rising much before TRA 1986, and the rise went on during the 1990s at an even higher pace, in spite of the 1993 rise in top tax rates.[20] It is also interesting to note that top income shares rose enormously in China during the 1986–2001 period (twice as fast as in India), in spite of the fact that top Chinese income tax rates have remained unchanged since the early 1980s (see Chapter 2). This again suggests that the rise of top incomes can be explained by non-tax structural factors (changing social norms, booming economy, international trade and globalization, etc.) rather than by tax changes and increased incentives to report top incomes.

Of course, the effect of tax changes in India could have been reinforced by spectacular improvements in the collection technology (and not only by increased incentives on the taxpayer side). There were, after all, a number of innovations in tax collection in the 1990s, such as the introduction of the 'one in six rule' (in 1998) that required everyone who satisfied at least one out of six criteria (owning a car, travel abroad, etc.) to file a tax return.

To further investigate this issue, we redid the exercise above exclusively for wages. Wages are clearly much less subject to tax evasion than non-wage incomes, since taxes are typically deducted at source and the employer has a strong incentive to report what he pays, since he gets to deduct the wages from his own taxes. Therefore if all that was happening was better collection, we would expect wage incomes to grow much more slowly than other incomes. To see if this is the case, we compare the evolution of top wages (see Table 1.4 below) with the evolution of top incomes (see Table 1.2). We find that top wages have increased essentially in step with top incomes during the 1990s. In fact, wage growth among the top percentile of the wage distribution rose by 81 per cent between 1987–8 and 1999–2000, while the corresponding figure was 71 per cent for the top percentile of the income distribution. This is consistent with the fact that the share of wages within the total income of the top percentile has increased somewhat during this period (from 28 per cent to 31 per cent). Although very top incomes are still mostly made of non-wage income, the wage part has increased during the 1990s.

Note that the view that there was 'real' increase in top incomes (and especially top wages) in India during the 1990s is also consistent with the evolution of the public sector salary scale. Following a succession of Pay Commissions, including the well-known Fifth Pay Commission, whose recommendations were implemented in 1997, the salaries of central government employees were raised sharply in India during the 1990s.[21] According to our computations (based upon published public sector salary scales), the Fifth Pay Commission alone can account for a substantial part of the rise in the number of top income tax payers in India

---

[20] See, e.g., Goolsbee (2000) and Piketty and Saez (2003).
[21] See, e.g., Kochar (2003).

Table 1.4 Top wage growth in India during the 1990s: 1999–2000 vs. 1987–1988

	1999–2000 vs. 1987–8 (nominal growth)	1999–2000 vs. 1987–8 (real growth)
Household consumption/capita (NSS)	+242%	+19%
GDP/capita (NAS)	+337%	+52%
Household consumption/capita (NAS)	+304%	+40%
National income/tax unit (NAS)	+346%	+55%
Top wage fractile P99–100 (tax returns)	+420%	+81%
Top wage fractile P99.5–100 (tax returns)	+492%	+105%
Top wage fractile P99.9–100 (tax returns)	+551%	+126%
Top wage fractile P99.99–100 (tax returns)	+955%	+266%
Top wage fractile P99–99.5 (tax returns)	+246%	+20%
Top wage fractile P99.5–99.9 (tax returns)	+470%	+98%
Top wage fractile P99.9–99.99 (tax returns)	+448%	+94%
Top wage fractile P99.99–100 (tax returns)	+955%	+266%
Consumer price index	+188%	

Source: Authors' computations using tax return, NAS and NSS data (see Table 1A.2, Table 1A.6, and Table 1A.7, row 1999–2000/1987–8).

between 1994 and 1997. Central government employees made up about 7 per cent of all income tax payers in India in 1994 (less than 500,000 central government taxpayers, out of a total of about 7 million taxpayers), and they made up almost 30 per cent of all taxpayers by 1997 (about 3.2 million central government taxpayers, out of a total of 11 million). According to these computations, out of the 4 million extra taxpayers recorded between 1994 and 1997, around 2.7 million (almost 70 per cent) were central government employees. The very top wage of the central government salary scale was 98,000 Rs (9,000 Rs per month) in 1994 (which was just a little bit above the P99.5 threshold), and it was raised to 360,000 Rs (30,000 Rs per month) in 1997 (which was well above the P99.9 threshold).[22] However it does not seem to be that public sector wage

[22] All our computations on public sector wages were made using the 1994 and 1997 (post-Fifth Commission) central government salary scales published in the 'Report of the 5th Central Pay Commission' ('Distribution of Filled Posts in Central Government and Union Territories in Different Scales of Pay, as on 31.3.1994', New Delhi: Government of India Press, 1997) and in the 'Gazette of India' (Special Issue, The First Schedule—Part A, 'Revised scales for posts carrying present scales in Group A, B, C and D', New Delhi: Government of India Press, 1997). In 1994, the central government scale ranked from scale 1 (9,000 Rs/month) to scale 62 (750 Rs/month), and all employees in scales 1 to 46 (approximately 500,000 employees) were subject to tax (i.e. had annual incomes over 28,000 Rs, which was the base exemption level in 1994, excluding all special deductions). In 1997, the (revised) scale ranked from scale S-34 (30,000 Rs/month, previously scale 1) to scale S-1 (2,550 Rs/month, previously scale 62), and all employees in (revised) scales S-34 to S-3 (i.e. approximately 3.2 million employees) were subject to tax (i.e. had annual incomes over 40,000 Rs, which was the base exemption level in 1997, excluding all special deductions). Note that these numbers only include central government employees strictly speaking, and that they would need to be scaled up substantially in order to take other government employees into account. In 1994, there were about 4 million central government employees, and the total number of workers employed by state governments,

increases were the primary driver behind the increase in inequality in the 1990s. Most of the rise in top Indian income shares actually took place before 1997, and it is likely that the revised scale put forward by the Fifth Commission was itself a response to the large rise in top private sector wages that had taken place in previous years.[23]

1.5 THE GROWTH PARADOX OF THE 1990S

Can the fact that the rich were getting richer help solve what has been called the Indian growth paradox of the 1990s? Table 1.2 illustrates this paradox: for the period 1987–2000, it compares the growth rate of average consumption as reported in the NSS, with the growth rate of average income and consumption from the national accounts (NAS), as well as the top incomes from the tax returns. The years 1987–8 and 1999–2000 were chosen because there were large rounds of the NSS surveys in those years, which makes our estimates of the NSS–NAS gap more precise.[24] To eliminate the effect of using different deflators, we first compare nominal growth performance, and then compute real growth performance by using the same deflator for all the series (namely, the CPI).

According to the NSS, real growth was fairly limited in India during the 1990s: per capita consumption increased by only 19 per cent in real terms between 1987–8 and 1999–2000. According to National Accounts (NAS), however, real growth was more than twice as large: both per capita GDP and national income increased by more than 50 per cent in real terms, and per capita household consumption increased by 40 per cent. This NSS–NAS gap is what has been called the Indian growth paradox and has been the subject of much discussion in recent years.[25]

Table 1.2 raises the possibility that the very large growth of top incomes during the 1990s might help solve this puzzle. The average income growth among the top percentile of the tax units was 71 per cent in real terms between 1987–8 and 1999–2000, which is substantially more than average growth according to the national

quasi-government bodies, and local bodies was about 3.5 times as large. In principle the Fifth Pay Commission revised scales also applied to these non-central government employees. Unfortunately we were unable to find the salary distribution for these employees (such a document apparently only exists for the central government).

[23] Such a view would be consistent with the fact the ceiling on private sector executive compensation was repealed as early as 1991.

[24] Intermediate NSS surveys were conducted between the two large surveys of 1987–8 and 1993–4 and between the two large surveys of 1993–4 and 1999–2000 but these were based on smaller samples, and are generally considered as less reliable. Note that we used the 1999–2000 per capita consumption estimates reported by Deaton and Drèze (2002), who implement a procedure for correcting the data for changes in the recall period (all surveys until 1993–4 were conducted with a thirty-day recall period, but the NSS has experimented with seven-day recall periods since then).

[25] See the references above. Real growth during the 1990s would be somewhat higher if one was to use the GDP deflator instead of the CPI, but the NSS–NAS gap would obviously not change.

accounts. Moreover, the higher one goes within the top percentile, the higher the growth (up to + 285 per cent for the top 0.01 per cent income fractile).

What fraction of the NSS–NAS gap can be explained by the huge growth performance of very top incomes? Let us assume that the NSS is unable to record any of the extra growth enjoyed by the top percentile (say the people in the top percentile do not report their extra growth to the NSS, or do not report anything at all). According to our calculations, the top percentile share in total consumption was around 8 per cent in 1987–8.[26] Since the average income of the top percentile increased by 71 per cent in real terms between 1987–8 and 1999–2000 according to the tax returns (as opposed to +19 per cent for average NSS consumption), this implies that NSS growth was 3.55 per cent less than what it would have been without the misreporting.[27] This implies that the growing incomes among the top percentile can explain at most 20.1 per cent of the total NSS–NAS gap (see Table 1.2).[28] This is significant, but leaves 80 per cent of the puzzle unexplained. The problem lies in the fact that almost all the extraordinary growth was among the top 0.1 per cent, and the weight of this group is simply not large enough to have an impact on aggregate statistics of the necessary magnitude. For the rise of inequality to explain fully the NSS–NAS gap, there would have to have been very high income growth at the bottom of the top percentile, and not simply among those in the top 0.1 per cent.

Top income growth can explain a larger proportion of the NSS–NAS gap if we start in the 1980s. For instance, under the same assumptions, the top percentile can explain almost 40 per cent of the cumulative NSS–NAS gap over the 1981–2000 period (see Table 1.3). This is because the bottom of the top percentile enjoyed rapid income growth in the 1980s (see Figures 1.2 to 1.4). The booming Indian elite of the 1980s–1990s seems too thin to explain all of the growth puzzle, but large enough to account for a non-negligible part of it.

1.6 CONCLUSION

Our results suggest that the gradual liberalization of the Indian economy did make it possible for the rich (the top 1 per cent) to substantially increase their share of total income. However, while in the 1980s the gains were shared by everyone in the top percentile, in the 1990s it was only those in the top 0.1 per cent who had big gains. The 1990s was also the period when the economy was opened. This suggests the possibility that the ultra-rich were able to corner most

---

[26] According to our estimates (computed with 70% of national income as the income denominator), the top percentile income share was 8.12% in 1987–8 (see Table 1A.5).

[27] $0.0812 \times (1.71/1.19-1) = 3.55$.

[28] $3.55/(1.40/1.19-1) = 20.1$. This is in a sense a lower bound, since we are using the 1987–8 top percentile share as our baseline for this computation, and the share was higher for later years.

of the income gains in the 1990s because they alone were in a position to sell what the world markets wanted.[29] It would be interesting to see whether in the coming years, as more and more people position themselves to benefit from the world markets, the share of the rich and the ultra-rich stops growing and even shrinks. For this and other reasons, we hope that this study will launch a trend towards more research (and better data) that focuses on the rich.

[29] The point is that one does not have to be rich on a global scale to be counted among the rich in India and even among the ultra-rich (see Table 1.1). Even those who got paid like an average American make it into the group of the ultra-rich.

APPENDIX 1A: TABLES OF SOURCES AND RESULTS

This appendix contains Table 1A.1 with details of the income tax sources, Table 1A.2 with the reference totals used, Tables 1A.3 to 1A.5 with results on income levels and shares, and Tables 1A.6 and 1A.7 on wage levels and shares.

Table 1A.1 References of official publications with India's income tax tabulations by income bracket, 1922–2000

Assessment Year	Exact name of publication	Publisher, place and year of publication	Table number
1922–3	'All India Income-tax Returns for the year…'	Central Board of Revenue, Superintendent Government Printing, Calcutta, 1924	Return IV
1923–4	'All India Income-tax Report and Returns for the year…'	Central Board of Revenue, Government of India Press, Calcutta, 1925	Return IV
1924–5	'All India Income-tax Report and Returns for the year…'	Central Board of Revenue, Government of India Central Publication Branch, Calcutta, 1926	Return IV
1925–6	'All India Income-tax Report and Returns for the year…'	Central Board of Revenue, Government of India Central Publication Branch, Calcutta, 1927	Return IV
1926–7	'All India Income-tax Report and Returns for the year…'	Central Board of Revenue, Government of India Central Publication Branch, Calcutta, 1928	Return IV
1927–8	'All India Income-tax Report and Returns for the year…'	Central Board of Revenue, Government of India Central Publication Branch, Calcutta, 1929	Return IV
1928–9	'All India Income-tax Report and Returns for the year…'	Central Board of Revenue, Government of India Central Publication Branch, Calcutta, 1930	Return IV
1929–30	'All India Income-tax Report and Returns for the year…'	Central Board of Revenue, Government of India Central Publication Branch, Calcutta, 1931	Return IV
1930–1	'All India Income-tax Report and Returns for the year…'	Central Board of Revenue, Government of India Central Publication Branch, Calcutta, 1932	Return IV

1931–2	'All India Income-tax Report and Returns for the year...'	Central Board of Revenue, Government of India Central Publication Branch, Calcutta, 1933	Return IV
1932–3	'All India Income-tax Report and Returns for the year...'	Central Board of Revenue, Government of India Press, New Delhi, 1934	Return IV
1933–4	'All India Income-tax Report and Returns for the year...'	Central Board of Revenue, Government of India Press, New Delhi, 1935	Return IV
1934–5	'All India Income-tax Report and Returns for the year...'	Central Board of Revenue, Government of India Press, Delhi, 1936	Return IV
1935–6	'All India Income-tax Report and Returns for the year...'	Central Board of Revenue, Government of India Press, Delhi, 1937	Return IV
1936–7	'All India Income-tax Report and Returns for the year...'	Central Board of Revenue, Government of India Press, Delhi, 1938	Return IV
1937–8	'All India Income-tax Report and Returns for the year...'	Central Board of Revenue, Government of India Press, Calcutta, 1939	Return IV
1938–9	'All India Income-tax Report and Returns for the year...'	Central Board of Revenue, Government of India Press, Calcutta, 1940	Return IV
1939–40	'All India Income-tax Report and Returns for the year...'	Central Board of Revenue, Government of India Press, Calcutta, 1941	Return IV
1940–1	'All India Income-tax Report and Returns for the year...'	Central Board of Revenue, Government of India Press, Calcutta, 1942	Statement 5
1941–2	'All India Income-tax Report and Returns for the year...'	Central Board of Revenue, Government of India Press, Calcutta, 1943	Statement 5
1942–3	'All India Income-tax Report and Returns for the year...'	Central Board of Revenue, Government of India Press, Calcutta, 1944	Statement 5
1943–4	Not available	Not available	N.a.
1944–5	'All India Income-tax Report and Returns for the year...'	Central Board of Revenue, Government of India Press, Calcutta, 1947	Statement 5
1945–6	'All India Income-tax Report and Returns for the year...'	Central Board of Revenue, Government of India Press, Calcutta, 1948	Statement 5
1946–7	'All India Income-tax Report and Returns for the year...'	Central Board of Revenue, Government of India Press, Calcutta, 1950	Statement 5
1947–8	Not available	Not available	N.a.
1948–9	'All India Income-tax Revenue Statistics for the year...'	Central Board of Revenue, Government of India Press, Calcutta, 1950	Statement 5
1949–50	'All India Income-tax Revenue Statistics for the year...'	Central Board of Revenue, Government of India Press, Calcutta, 1951	Statement 5

(continued)

Table 1A.1 Continued

Assessment Year	Exact name of publication	Publisher, place and year of publication	Table number
1950–1	'All India Income-tax Revenue Statistics for the year…'	Central Board of Revenue, Government of India Press, Calcutta, 1952	Statement 5
1951–2	'All India Income-tax Revenue Statistics for the year…'	Central Board of Revenue, Government of India Press, Calcutta, 1953	Statement 5
1952–3	'All India Income-tax Revenue Statistics for the year…'	Central Board of Revenue, Government of India Press, Calcutta, 1954	N.a.
1953–4	'All India Income-tax Revenue Statistics for the year…'	Central Board of Revenue, Government of India Press, Delhi, 1955	N.a.
1954–5	'All India Income-tax Revenue Statistics for the year…'	Central Board of Revenue, Government of India Press, Delhi, 1956	Statement 5
1955–6	'All India Income-tax Revenue Statistics for the year…'	Central Board of Revenue, Government of India Press, Delhi, 1957	Statement 5
1956–7	'All India Income-tax Revenue Statistics for the year…'	Central Board of Revenue, Government of India Press, Delhi, 1958	Statement 5
1957–8	'All India Income-tax Revenue Statistics for the year…'	Central Board of Revenue, Government of India Press, Delhi, 1959	Statement 5
1958–9	'All India Income-tax Revenue Statistics for the year…'	Central Board of Revenue, Government of India Press, Delhi, 1960	Statement 5
1959–60	'All India Income-tax Revenue Statistics for the year…'	Central Board of Revenue, Government of India Press, Delhi, 1961	Statement 5
1960–1	'All India Income-tax Revenue Statistics for the year…'	Central Board of Revenue, Government of India Press, Delhi, 1962	Statement 5
1961–2	'All India Income-tax Revenue Statistics for the year…'	Central Board of Revenue, Government of India Press, Delhi, 1963	Statement 5
1962–3	'All India Income-tax Revenue Statistics for the year…'	Central Board of Direct Taxes, Government of India Press, Delhi, 1964	Statement 5
1963–4	'All India Income-tax Statistics for the year…'	Central Board of Direct Taxes, Government of India Press, Delhi, 1965	Statement 5
1964–5	'All India Income-tax Statistics for the year…'	Directorate of Inspection, Delhi, 1966	Statement 5
1965–6	'All India Income-tax Statistics for the year…'	Directorate of Inspection, Delhi, 1967	Statement 5
1966–7	'All India Income-tax Statistics for the year…'	Directorate of Inspection, Delhi, 1968	Statement 5
1967–8	'All India Income-tax Statistics for the year…'	Directorate of Inspection, Delhi, 1969	Statement 5
1968–9	'All India Income-tax Statistics for the year…'	Directorate of Inspection, Delhi, 1971	Statement 5

1969–70	'All India Income-tax Statistics for the year…'	Directorate of Inspection, Delhi, 1972	Statement 5
1970–1	'All India Income-tax Statistics for the year…'	Directorate of Inspection, Delhi, 1972	Statement 5
1971–2	'All India Income-tax Statistics for the year…'	Directorate of Inspection, Delhi, 1973	Statement 5
1972–3	'All India Income-tax Statistics for the year…'	Directorate of Inspection, Delhi, 1974	Statement 5
1973–4	'All India Income-tax Statistics for the year…'	Directorate of Inspection, Delhi, 1975	Statement 5
1974–5	'All India Income-tax Statistics for the year…'	Directorate of Inspection, Delhi, 1976	Statement 5
1975–6	'All India Income-tax Statistics for the year…'	Directorate of Inspection, Delhi, 1977	Statement 5
1976–7	'All India Income-tax Statistics for the year…'	Directorate of Inspection, Delhi, 1978	Statement 5
1977–8	'All India Income-tax Statistics for the year…'	Directorate of Inspection, Delhi, 1979	Table 5
1978–9	'All India Income-tax Statistics for the year…'	Directorate of Inspection, Delhi, 1980	Table 5
1979–80	'All India Income-tax Statistics for the year…'	Directorate of Inspection, Delhi, 1981	Table 5
1980–1	'All India Income-tax Statistics for the year…'	Directorate of Inspection, Delhi, 1982	Table 5
1981–2	'All India Income-tax Statistics for the year…'	Directorate of Inspection, Delhi, 1983	Table 5
1982–3	'All India Income-tax Statistics for the year…'	Directorate of Inspection, Delhi, 1984	Table 5
1983–4	'All India Income-tax Statistics for the year…'	Directorate of Inspection, Delhi, 1985	Table 5
1984–5	'All India Income-tax Statistics for the year…'	Directorate of Inspection, Delhi, 1986	Table 4
1985–6	'All India Income-tax Statistics for the year…'	Directorate of Inspection, Delhi, 1987	Table 3
1986–7	'All India Income-tax Statistics for the year…'	Directorate of Income Tax, Delhi, 1988	Table 3
1987–8	'All India Income-tax Statistics for the year…'	Directorate of Income Tax, Delhi, 1989	Table 3
1988–9	'All India Income-tax Statistics for the year…'	Directorate of Income Tax, Delhi, 1990	Table 3
1989–90	'All India Income-tax Statistics for the year…'	Directorate of Income Tax, Delhi, 1991	Table 3
1990–1	'All India Income-tax Statistics for the year…'	Directorate of Income Tax, Delhi, 1992	Table 3
1991–2	'All India Income-tax Statistics for the year…'	Directorate of Income Tax, Delhi, 1994	Table 3
1992–3	'All India Income-tax Statistics for the year…'	Directorate of Income Tax, Delhi, 1994	Table 3
1993–4	'All India Income-tax Statistics for the year…'	Directorate of Income Tax, Delhi, 1995	Table 3
1994–5	'All India Income-tax Statistics for the year…'	Directorate of Income Tax, Delhi, 1996	Table 3
1995–6	'All India Income-tax Statistics for the year…'	Directorate of Income Tax, Delhi, 1997	Table 3

(*continued*)

Table 1A.1 Continued

Assessment Year	Exact name of publication	Publisher, place and year of publication	Table number
1996–7	'All India Income-tax Statistics for the year...'	Directorate of Income Tax, Delhi, 1999	Table 3
1997–8	'All India Income-tax Statistics for the year...'	Directorate of Income Tax, Delhi, 2000	Table 3
1998–9	'All India Income-tax Statistics for the year...'	Directorate of Income Tax, Delhi, 2001	Table 3
1999–2000	'All India Income-tax Statistics for the year...'	Directorate of Income Tax, Delhi, 2003	Table 3

Table 1A.2 Reference totals for tax units and income, India, 1922–2000

	(1) Population	(2) N.tax units	(3) N.tax returns	(4) (3)/(2)	(5) GDP/capita	(6) Hous. consump./capita (NAS)	(7) National income/tax unit	(8) Hous. consump./capita (NSS)	(9) CPI	(10) GDP/capita	(11) Hous. consump./capita (NAS)	(12) National income/tax unit	(13) Hous. consump./capita (NSS)	(14) Nat.Inc./capita real growth rate	(15) Inflation rate
	(millions)	(millions)	(millions)	(%)	(current Rs)	(current Rs)	(current Rs)	(current Rs)	(p(1999–00)/p(n))	(1999–2000 Rs)	(1999–2000 Rs)	(1999–2000 Rs)	(1999–2000 Rs)	(%)	(%)
1922-3	310.4	124.2	0.3	0.2			187		51.630			9,660			−9.2
1923-4	313.6	125.4	0.3	0.2			173		56.870			9,813		1.6	−1.2
1924-5	316.7	126.7	0.3	0.2			192		57.583			11,039		12.5	4.8
1925-6	319.9	128.0	0.3	0.2			188		54.965			10,333		−6.4	1.9
1926-7	323.2	129.3	0.3	0.2			185		53.933			9,990		−3.3	−3.3
1927-8	326.4	130.6	0.3	0.2			181		55.766			10,088		1.0	−1.7
1928-9	329.7	131.9	0.3	0.2			179		56.730			10,172		0.8	−3.7
1929-30	333.1	133.2	0.3	0.2			172		58.912			10,136		−0.4	−17.7
1930-1	336.4	134.6	0.4	0.3			135		71.575			9,663		−4.7	−17.7
1931-2	341.0	136.4	0.6	0.4			117		82.350			9,628		−0.4	−13.1
1932-3	345.8	138.3	0.7	0.5			111		87.693			9,770		1.5	−6.1
1933-4	350.7	140.3	0.7	0.5			104		93.778			9,755		−0.1	−6.5
1934-5	355.6	142.2	0.7	0.5			108		91.536			9,889		1.4	2.4
1935-6	360.6	144.2	0.4	0.3			106		89.748			9,505		−3.9	2.0
1936-7	365.7	146.3	0.3	0.2			110		88.709			9,730		2.4	1.2
1937-8	370.9	148.4	0.3	0.2			110		87.028			9,579		−1.5	1.9
1938-9	376.1	150.4	0.3	0.2			109		89.052			9,722		1.5	−2.3
1939-40	381.4	152.6	0.4	0.2			121		84.159			10,214		5.1	5.8
1940-1	386.8	154.7	0.4	0.3			130		82.646			10,740		5.1	1.8
1941-2	391.7	156.7	0.4	0.2			156		72.938			11,361		5.8	13.3
1942-3	396.3	158.5		0.0			221		53.807			11,902		4.8	35.6
1943-4	400.9	160.4	0.4	0.3			305		30.553			9,306		−21.8	76.1
1944-5	405.6	162.2	0.4	0.3			301		31.259			9,403		1.0	−2.3
1945-6	410.4	164.2	0.4	0.3			294		31.174			9,150		−2.7	0.3
1946-7	415.2	166.1		0.0			287		28.936			8,316		−9.1	7.7
1947-8	344.4	137.8	0.5	0.3			378		26.561			10,037		20.7	8.9
1948-9	350.0	140.0	0.4	0.3			385		22.976			8,836		−12.0	15.6
1949-50	355.0	142.0	0.5	0.3			397		22.569			8,950		1.3	1.8
1950-1	359.0	143.6	0.6	0.4			418		21.274			8,891		−0.6	6.1

(continued)

Table 1A.2 Continued

	(1) Population	(2) N.tax units	(3) N.tax returns	(4) (3)/(2)	(5) GDP/capita	(6) Hous. consump./capita (NAS)	(7) National income/ tax unit	(8) Hous. consump./capita (NSS)	(9) CPI p(1999–00) /p(n)	(10) GDP/ capita (1999– 2000 Rs)	(11) Hous. consump./ capita (NAS) (1999– 2000 Rs)	(12) National income/ tax unit (1999– 2000 Rs)	(13) Hous. consump./ capita (NSS) (1999– 2000 Rs)	(14) Nat.Inc./ capita real growth rate (%)	(15) Inflation rate (%)
	(millions)	(millions)	(millions)	(%)	(current Rs)	(current Rs)	(current Rs)	(current Rs)		(1999–2000 Rs)	(1999–2000 Rs)	(1999–2000 Rs)	(1999–2000 Rs)	(%)	(%)
1951–2	365.0	146.0		0.0			433		20.624			8,933		0.5	3.1
1952–3	372.0	148.8		0.0			418		23.081			9,644		8.0	–10.6
1953–4	379.0	151.6	0.5	0.3			448		21.221			9,501		–1.5	8.8
1954–5	386.0	154.4	0.5	0.3			409		26.756			10,945		15.2	–20.7
1955–6	393.0	157.2	0.5	0.3			408		25.299			10,320		–5.7	5.8
1956–7	401.0	160.4	0.6	0.4	334		479	221	22.371	7,464		10,712	4,941	3.8	13.1
1957–8	409.0	163.6	0.8	0.5	334		478	238	21.388	7,153		10,228	5,094	–4.5	4.6
1958–9	418.0	167.2	0.8	0.5	366		522	259	20.537	7,518		10,712	5,310	4.7	4.1
1959–60	426.0	170.4	0.9	0.5	377		535	258	20.638	7,786		11,051	5,327	3.2	–0.5
1960–1	434.0	173.6	1.0	0.6	405		574	275	20.686	8,386		11,879	5,687	7.5	–0.2
1961–2	444.0	177.6	1.0	0.6	420		589	281	20.330	8,541		11,976	5,707	0.8	1.8
1962–3	454.0	181.6	1.1	0.6	442		615		19.628	8,674		12,065		0.7	3.6
1963–4	464.0	185.6			496		689	292	19.067	9,457		13,130	5,565	8.8	2.9
1964–5	474.0	189.6	1.6	0.8	567		789	339	16.821	9,530		13,273	5,698	1.1	13.4
1965–6	486.0	194.4	1.6	0.8	582		809	359	15.364	8,940		12,431	5,523	–6.3	9.5
1966–7	495.0	198.0	1.5	0.7	646		891	395	13.865	8,959		12,360	5,479	–0.6	10.8
1967–8	506.0	202.4	1.8	0.9	740		1,029	427	12.264	9,074		12,617	5,240	2.1	13.1
1968–9	518.0	207.2	1.8	0.9	766		1,058	429	11.908	9,119		12,596	5,111	–0.2	3.0
1969–70	529.0	211.6			826		1,139	454	11.840	9,777		13,482	5,370	7.0	0.6
1970–1	541.0	216.4	2.0	0.9	845	696	1,181	465	11.266	9,525	7,843	13,302	5,244	–1.3	5.1
1971–2	554.0	221.6	2.0	0.9	885	733	1,223		10.929	9,670	8,014	13,366		0.5	3.1
1972–3	567.0	226.8			953	790	1,312	577	10.266	9,786	8,106	13,469	5,926	0.8	6.5
1973–4	580.0	232.0	2.1	0.9	1,133	931	1,580	680	8.779	9,947	8,170	13,870	5,974	3.0	16.9
1974–5	593.0	237.2	2.1	0.9	1,309	1,103	1,809		6.827	8,935	7,528	12,348		–11.0	28.6
1975–6	607.0	242.8	2.1	0.9	1,375	1,102	1,863		6.456	8,878	7,117	12,029		–2.6	5.7
1976–7	620.0	248.0	2.2	0.9	1,451	1,121	1,962		6.990	10,143	7,839	13,717		14.0	–7.6
1977–8	634.0	253.6	1.6	0.6	1,606	1,263	2,201	877	6.453	10,362	8,149	14,205	5,657	3.6	8.3
1978–9	648.0	259.2	1.5	0.6	1,704	1,344	2,304		6.294	10,726	8,458	14,500		2.1	2.5
1979–80	664.0	265.6	1.2	0.5	1,825	1,424	2,433		5.924	10,813	8,436	14,415		–0.6	6.3

Year															
1980–1	679.0	271.6	1.2	0.4	2,123	1,692	2,853	1,253	5.319	11,293	9,002	15,175		5.3	11.4
1981–2	692.0	276.8	1.0	0.4	2,447	1,903	3,257		4.703	11,506	8,947	15,319	5,894	0.9	13.1
1982–3	708.0	283.2	0.9	0.3	2,666	2,046	3,507		4.359	11,623	8,919	15,286		−0.2	7.9
1983–4	723.0	289.2	2.8	1.0	3,043	2,352	4,031	1,518	3.896	11,856	9,165	15,708	5,915	2.8	11.9
1984–5	739.0	295.6	1.8	0.6	3,318	2,538	4,381		3.597	11,934	9,131	15,760		0.3	8.3
1985–6	755.0	302.0	2.5	0.8	3,681	2,725	4,778		3.408	12,544	9,285	16,282		3.3	5.6
1986–7	771.0	308.4	2.8	0.9	4,027	3,002	5,184	1,978	3.134	12,620	9,409	16,248	6,200	−0.2	8.7
1987–8	788.0	315.2	3.0	0.9	4,481	3,291	5,749	2,156	2.881	12,909	9,479	16,562	6,210	1.9	8.8
1988–9	805.0	322.0	3.3	1.0	5,210	3,723	6,724	2,379	2.634	13,722	9,806	17,707	6,265	6.9	9.4
1989–90	822.0	328.8	3.7	1.1	5,890	4,084	7,606	2,605	2.481	14,611	10,131	18,870	6,463	6.6	6.2
1990–1	839.0	335.6	3.9	1.2	6,765	4,585	8,720	2,810	2.277	15,400	10,437	19,852	6,396	5.2	9.0
1991–2	856.0	342.4	4.5	1.3	7,636	5,207	9,805	3,348	1.999	15,267	10,410	19,603	6,692	−1.3	13.9
1992–3	872.0	348.8	5.1	1.5	8,579	5,777	10,958	3,441	1.788	15,343	10,332	19,597	6,154	0.0	11.8
1993–4	891.0	356.4	7.0	2.0	9,643	6,480	12,550	3,936	1.681	16,215	10,896	21,102	6,618	7.7	6.4
1994–5	908.0	363.2	7.1	1.9	11,122	7,280	14,640	4,312	1.526	16,969	11,107	22,335	6,579	5.8	10.2
1995–6	927.0	370.8	7.6	2.1	12,750	8,184	16,636	4,915	1.384	17,648	11,328	23,026	6,802	3.1	10.2
1996–7	943.0	377.2	9.5	2.5	14,443	9,540	18,710		1.270	18,344	12,116	23,763		3.2	9.0
1997–8	959.0	383.6	11.1	2.9	15,804	10,195	20,669	5,518	1.185	18,731	12,083	24,496	6,540	3.1	7.2
1998–9	975.0	390.0	14.7	3.8	18,078	11,501	23,872		1.047	18,922	12,038	24,986		2.0	13.2
1999–2000	991.0	396.4			19,562	13,304	25,670	7,362	1.000	19,562	13,304	25,670	7,362	2.7	4.7
1999–2000/ 1987–1988					4.37	4.04	4.46	3.42	2.88	1.52	1.40	1.55	1.19		
1999–2000/ 1981–1982					8.00	6.99	7.88	5.87	4.70	1.70	1.49	1.68	1.25		

Sources: Population and national income: Sivasubramonian (2000); GDP, household consumption (NAS) and CPI: World Development Indicators 2001 data base (World Bank); Household consumption (NSS): Datt (1997, 1999) and Deaton and Drèze (2002).

Table 1A.3 Top fractiles incomes levels in India, 1956–2000 (incomes are expressed in current Rs)

	P99–100 (1)	P99.5–100 (2)	P99.9–100 (3)	P99.99–100 (4)	P99–99.5 (5)	P99.5–99.9 (6)	P99.9–99.99 (7)	P99.99–100 (8)	P99 (9)	P99.5 (10)	P99.9 (11)	P99.99 (12)
1922–3	2,381	3,732	10,592	37,508	1,029	2,017	7,601	37,508	836	1,311	3,808	19,231
1923–4	2,311	3,613	10,190	35,714	1,008	1,969	7,354	35,714	820	1,283	3,735	18,453
1924–5	2,197	3,520	10,301	35,196	873	1,825	7,535	35,196	702	1,125	3,802	18,690
1925–6	2,328	3,626	10,130	34,603	1,029	2,000	7,411	34,603	839	1,307	3,785	18,444
1926–7	2,388	3,713	10,323	34,637	1,063	2,061	7,621	34,637	868	1,349	3,885	18,706
1927–8	2,410	3,760	10,534	35,787	1,060	2,066	7,728	35,787	863	1,347	3,919	18,859
1928–9	2,443	3,804	10,612	35,425	1,081	2,103	7,855	35,425	882	1,373	3,973	18,936
1929–30	2,248	3,528	9,933	32,685	968	1,926	7,405	32,685	787	1,234	3,829	17,261
1930–1	1,961	3,079	8,631	28,463	843	1,691	6,427	28,463	685	1,075	3,358	15,283
1931–2	1,882	2,934	8,111	26,421	830	1,639	6,077	26,421	676	1,054	3,232	14,304
1932–3	1,798	2,817	7,829	25,900	780	1,564	5,821	25,900	634	993	3,104	13,969
1933–4	1,780	2,781	7,689	25,505	780	1,553	5,710	25,505	635	991	3,069	13,709
1934–5	1,825	2,846	7,868	26,078	805	1,590	5,845	26,078	656	1,023	3,116	14,147
1935–6	1,835	2,842	7,769	25,597	828	1,611	5,788	25,597	677	1,048	3,120	13,812
1936–7	1,709	2,660	7,385	25,391	759	1,479	5,385	25,391	619	963	2,772	13,495
1937–8	1,711	2,662	7,384	25,582	760	1,482	5,362	25,582	620	964	2,904	13,294
1938–9	1,945	3,013	8,326	31,607	877	1,685	5,739	31,607	717	1,110	3,068	15,088
1939–40	1,955	3,092	8,962	34,991	818	1,624	6,070	34,991	662	1,047	3,036	16,042
1940–1	2,098	3,335	9,781	38,778	862	1,724	6,559	38,778	696	1,106	3,242	18,044
1941–2	2,191	3,527	10,663	42,564	854	1,744	7,119	42,564	685	1,103	3,334	19,917
1942–3												
1943–4	3,142	5,005	14,754	56,908	1,279	2,568	10,071	56,908	1,032	1,643	4,844	26,221
1944–5	3,348	5,293	15,332	60,073	1,403	2,783	10,361	60,073	1,135	1,795	5,200	27,082
1945–6	3,349	5,291	15,299	59,606	1,407	2,789	10,376	59,606	1,140	1,800	5,206	26,150
1946–7												
1947–8	4,245	6,837	20,539	85,816	1,653	3,411	13,286	85,816	1,326	2,136	7,145	33,820
1948–9	4,553	7,145	20,346	82,673	1,961	3,845	13,420	82,673	1,593	2,499	7,117	34,442
1949–50	4,760	7,417	20,778	83,082	2,102	4,077	13,856	83,082	1,713	2,670	7,479	34,846
1950–1	5,609	8,670	23,388	86,597	2,549	4,990	16,365	86,597	2,086	3,224	9,490	39,737

Year												
1951–2												
1952–3												
1953–4	5,339	8,430	23,037	82,778	2,247	4,778	16,400	82,778	1,856	2,992	9,600	37,790
1954–5	5,556	8,636	23,218	82,197	2,476	4,990	16,665	82,197	2,020	3,140	9,845	38,395
1955–6	5,877	9,095	24,131	82,180	2,658	5,336	17,681	82,180	2,174	3,365	10,412	39,596
1956–7	6,115	9,434	24,786	81,028	2,796	5,596	18,536	81,028	2,290	3,533	10,855	40,821
1957–8	6,378	9,813	25,373	80,446	2,943	5,922	19,254	80,446	2,413	3,713	11,282	41,850
1958–9	6,553	10,060	25,671	78,667	3,047	6,157	19,783	78,667	2,501	3,840	11,635	42,272
1959–60	6,619	10,109	25,543	77,281	3,128	6,251	19,794	77,281	2,574	3,932	11,677	41,715
1960–1	7,072	10,849	27,481	84,244	3,294	6,691	21,174	84,244	2,705	4,150	12,879	44,920
1961–2	7,160	10,946	27,176	81,036	3,375	6,889	21,191	81,036	2,776	4,244	13,104	44,063
1962–3	7,121	10,756	26,074	77,912	3,485	6,927	20,314	77,912	2,883	4,355	12,856	42,148
1963–4												
1964–5	7,618	11,024	25,492	82,357	4,211	7,407	19,173	82,357	3,556	5,146	13,826	43,080
1965–6	8,836	13,313	31,770	98,289	4,360	8,699	24,379	98,289	3,612	5,441	15,859	51,309
1966–7	8,901	13,501	32,652	103,613	4,302	8,713	24,767	103,613	3,552	5,387	16,036	51,888
1967–8	10,298	15,625	36,070	105,843	4,971	10,513	28,318	105,843	4,104	6,227	18,479	56,515
1968–9	10,526	15,901	36,765	106,656	5,151	10,685	29,000	106,656	4,135	6,817	19,285	56,254
1969–70												
1970–1	11,828	18,276	40,477	121,128	5,380	12,726	31,516	121,128	4,403	6,803	21,368	62,738
1971–2	10,358	15,444	34,652	107,641	5,273	10,642	26,543	107,641	4,389	6,544	17,926	50,914
1972–3												
1973–4	11,087	16,551	35,034	100,832	5,623	11,930	27,723	100,832	4,678	6,983	18,942	51,851
1974–5	12,028	17,244	36,385	97,844	6,812	12,459	29,556	97,844	5,777	8,283	20,500	55,455
1975–6	13,486	19,745	41,961	116,200	7,228	14,190	33,712	116,200	6,070	8,886	22,790	64,828
1976–7	14,260	20,384	42,413	120,749	8,136	14,877	33,708	120,749	6,630	10,344	23,559	62,706
1977–8	13,595	20,017	41,740	113,129	7,174	14,586	33,808	113,129	5,702	10,365	23,726	61,514
1978–9	13,927	19,945	41,588	118,213	7,908	14,534	33,074	118,213	6,475	10,121	23,100	61,389
1979–80	13,653	18,967	40,369	111,311	8,338	13,617	32,487	111,311	7,177	9,971	21,803	64,027
1980–1	13,630	18,834	39,690	112,687	8,427	13,619	31,580	112,687	7,272	10,048	21,521	62,971
1981–2	14,287	19,520	39,453	98,891	9,054	14,537	32,848	98,891	7,854	10,731	22,137	58,397
1982–3	15,803	21,925	46,707	120,377	9,681	15,730	38,521	120,377	8,338	11,568	25,026	75,296
1983–4	26,038	35,032	73,804	192,063	17,043	25,339	60,664	192,063	14,892	20,036	37,920	104,054
1984–5	28,001	39,226	82,447	218,454	16,777	28,420	67,336	218,454	14,384	20,150	46,370	116,071

(continued)

Table 1A.3 Continued

	P99–100 (1)	P99.5–100 (2)	P99.9–100 (3)	P99.99–100 (4)	P99–99.5 (5)	P99.5–99.9 (6)	P99.9–99.99 (7)	P99.99–100 (8)	P99 (9)	P99.5 (10)	P99.9 (11)	P99.99 (12)
1985–6	39,382	57,183	116,987	315,792	21,581	42,232	94,898	315,792	18,193	26,416	68,265	144,159
1986–7	44,800	66,715	135,420	361,637	22,885	49,538	110,285	361,637	19,061	28,386	78,641	180,974
1987–8	46,691	70,441	144,222	363,859	22,941	51,995	119,818	363,859	18,991	28,651	82,609	197,872
1988–9	57,293	85,827	182,253	557,193	28,760	61,720	140,593	557,193	23,888	35,784	95,133	269,775
1989–90	62,272	93,790	180,718	589,964	30,754	72,058	135,246	589,964	25,478	38,374	93,553	287,260
1990–1	64,731	90,059	160,196	554,137	39,402	72,525	116,425	554,137	33,255	49,744	62,419	273,884
1991–2	69,768	95,115	172,442	557,553	44,421	75,783	129,652	557,553	38,574	52,588	67,281	265,655
1992–3	76,319	105,333	209,611	649,042	47,304	79,264	160,785	649,042	40,842	56,369	96,319	372,766
1993–4	107,003	151,099	359,483	1,444,041	62,906	99,004	238,976	1,444,041	53,731	75,874	168,457	458,739
1994–5	118,486	170,320	382,798	1,565,554	66,653	117,200	251,380	1,565,554	56,456	81,153	183,753	550,353
1995–6	144,270	219,979	585,834	3,407,454	68,560	128,516	272,320	3,407,454	56,467	86,100	229,296	584,003
1996–7	163,179	241,932	576,276	2,877,818	84,426	158,346	320,549	2,877,818	70,470	104,479	258,770	646,416
1997–8	221,152	347,131	900,157	3,884,501	95,172	208,875	568,564	3,884,501	84,379	142,068	284,146	1,332,547
1998–9	213,587	335,257	869,367	3,751,628	91,916	201,730	549,115	3,751,628	81,493	137,208	274,427	1,286,966
1999–00	229,679	360,517	934,868	4,034,289	98,842	216,929	590,488	4,034,289	87,633	147,546	295,103	1,383,930
1999–2000/ 1987–1988	4.92	5.12	6.48	11.09	4.31	4.17	4.93	11.09	4.61	5.15	3.57	6.99
1999–2000/ 1981–1982	16.08	18.47	23.70	40.80	10.92	14.92	17.98	40.80	11.16	13.75	13.33	23.70

Source: Authors' computations using income tax returns data (All-India Income Tax Statistics, 1922–2000).

Table 1A.4 Top fractiles incomes levels in India, 1956–2000 (incomes are expressed in 1999–2000 Rs)

	P99–100 (1)	P99.5–100 (2)	P99.9–100 (3)	P99.99–100 (4)	P99–99.5 (5)	P99.5–99.9 (6)	P99.9–99.99 (7)	P99.99–100 (8)	P99 (9)	P99.5 (10)	P99.9 (11)	P99.99 (12)
1922–3	122,910	192,683	546,875	1,936,560	53,137	104,135	392,466	1,936,560	43,187	67,703	196,616	992,889
1923–4	131,411	205,482	579,514	2,031,062	57,339	111,974	418,231	2,031,062	46,660	72,960	212,388	1,049,438
1924–5	126,489	202,718	593,187	2,026,708	50,260	105,100	433,907	2,026,708	40,418	64,776	218,933	1,076,202
1925–6	127,935	199,292	556,802	1,901,954	56,577	109,915	407,340	1,901,954	46,123	71,849	208,070	1,013,797
1926–7	128,807	200,266	556,751	1,868,081	57,347	111,145	411,048	1,868,081	46,794	72,755	209,518	1,008,879
1927–8	134,385	209,670	587,414	1,995,698	59,100	115,234	430,938	1,995,698	48,144	75,115	218,556	1,051,673
1928–9	138,580	215,825	601,998	2,009,664	61,335	119,281	445,590	2,009,664	50,007	77,882	225,368	1,074,248
1929–30	132,428	207,813	585,191	1,925,509	57,043	113,469	436,267	1,925,509	46,340	72,719	225,597	1,016,873
1930–1	140,361	220,369	617,759	2,037,199	60,353	121,021	460,044	2,037,199	49,017	76,957	240,383	1,093,858
1931–2	154,955	241,581	667,932	2,175,730	68,328	134,993	500,399	2,175,730	55,681	86,809	266,162	1,177,900
1932–3	157,712	247,031	686,559	2,271,200	68,394	137,149	510,487	2,271,200	55,610	87,104	272,212	1,225,000
1933–4	166,932	260,756	721,065	2,391,820	73,107	145,679	535,426	2,391,820	59,520	92,974	287,832	1,285,637
1934–5	167,082	260,466	720,213	2,387,050	73,699	145,529	535,009	2,387,050	60,060	93,628	285,219	1,294,945
1935–6	164,687	255,078	697,219	2,297,251	74,297	144,542	519,438	2,297,251	60,735	94,070	280,043	1,239,607
1936–7	151,631	235,970	655,127	2,252,387	67,292	131,181	477,654	2,252,387	54,884	85,412	245,883	1,197,089
1937–8	148,892	231,678	642,592	2,226,384	66,106	128,949	466,615	2,226,384	53,920	83,901	252,716	1,156,923
1938–9	173,215	268,336	741,412	2,814,694	78,095	150,067	511,047	2,814,694	63,834	98,889	273,230	1,343,655
1939–40	164,521	260,192	754,270	2,944,786	68,849	136,672	510,880	2,944,786	55,722	88,125	255,466	1,350,059
1940–1	173,427	275,647	808,376	3,204,867	71,206	142,465	542,099	3,204,867	57,491	91,378	267,978	1,491,271
1941–2	159,775	257,287	777,757	3,104,547	62,264	127,170	519,224	3,104,547	49,956	80,445	243,178	1,452,725
1942–3												
1943–4	96,004	152,928	450,786	1,738,684	39,081	78,463	307,687	1,738,684	31,520	50,209	148,002	801,118
1944–5	104,648	165,450	479,268	1,877,826	43,846	86,995	323,872	1,877,826	35,492	56,113	162,545	846,577
1945–6	104,408	164,944	476,948	1,858,192	43,873	86,942	323,477	1,858,192	35,526	56,124	162,288	815,215
1946–7												
1947–8	112,744	181,587	545,546	2,279,373	43,900	90,597	352,899	2,279,373	35,220	56,725	189,770	898,298
1948–9	104,605	164,164	467,452	1,899,455	45,046	88,342	308,341	1,899,455	36,593	57,427	163,522	791,334
1949–50	107,422	167,402	468,952	1,875,089	47,441	92,015	312,715	1,875,089	38,668	60,259	168,805	786,447
1950–1	119,331	184,435	497,543	1,842,237	54,226	106,158	348,133	1,842,237	44,373	68,582	201,893	845,350

(continued)

Table 1A.4 Continued

	P99–100 (1)	P99.5–100 (2)	P99.9–100 (3)	P99.99–100 (4)	P99–99.5 (5)	P99.5–99.9 (6)	P99.9–99.99 (7)	P99.99–100 (8)	P99 (9)	P99.5 (10)	P99.9 (11)	P99.99 (12)
1951–2												
1952–3												
1953–4	113,292	178,893	488,882	1,756,642	47,692	101,395	348,020	1,756,642	39,392	63,500	203,731	801,960
1954–5	148,643	231,051	621,223	2,199,240	66,236	133,508	445,888	2,199,240	54,053	84,020	263,408	1,027,295
1955–6	148,677	230,099	610,483	2,079,083	67,254	135,003	447,306	2,079,083	54,999	85,119	263,421	1,001,744
1956–7	136,799	211,042	554,473	1,812,655	62,556	125,184	414,676	1,812,655	51,235	79,041	242,835	913,189
1957–8	136,402	209,868	542,669	1,720,548	62,935	126,668	411,793	1,720,548	51,611	79,409	241,293	895,080
1958–9	134,584	206,602	527,202	1,615,547	62,566	126,452	406,275	1,615,547	51,365	78,851	238,936	868,131
1959–60	136,597	208,638	527,159	1,594,948	64,555	129,008	408,515	1,594,948	53,125	81,143	241,001	860,933
1960–1	146,287	224,429	568,479	1,742,680	68,145	138,416	438,012	1,742,680	55,961	85,854	266,405	929,205
1961–2	145,569	222,533	552,475	1,647,440	68,604	140,048	430,812	1,647,440	56,434	86,271	266,397	895,797
1962–3	139,765	211,123	511,775	1,529,248	68,407	135,959	398,723	1,529,248	56,594	85,488	252,344	827,278
1963–4												
1964–5	128,135	185,431	428,790	1,385,308	70,838	124,591	322,510	1,385,308	59,810	86,555	232,562	724,644
1965–6	135,767	204,546	488,125	1,510,151	66,988	133,651	374,567	1,510,151	55,489	83,600	243,656	788,331
1966–7	123,420	187,197	452,729	1,436,632	59,643	120,815	343,407	1,436,632	49,247	74,695	222,345	719,448
1967–8	126,301	191,630	442,383	1,298,115	60,972	128,942	347,301	1,298,115	50,336	76,373	226,640	693,130
1968–9	125,339	189,342	437,790	1,270,021	61,335	127,230	345,319	1,270,021	49,238	81,173	229,643	669,861
1969–70												
1970–1	133,250	205,891	456,000	1,364,580	60,609	143,364	355,047	1,364,580	49,603	76,644	240,724	706,786
1971–2	113,206	168,787	378,713	1,176,400	57,625	116,306	290,082	1,176,400	47,970	71,523	195,913	556,435
1972–3												
1973–4	97,336	145,308	307,579	885,240	49,363	104,740	243,394	885,240	41,068	61,309	166,301	455,223
1974–5	82,114	117,722	248,394	667,966	46,506	85,054	201,775	667,966	39,440	56,543	139,950	378,584
1975–6	87,073	127,477	270,914	750,224	46,669	91,618	217,657	750,224	39,188	57,372	147,141	418,549
1976–7	99,674	142,482	296,462	844,032	56,867	103,987	235,621	844,032	46,344	72,303	164,673	438,315
1977–8	87,730	129,169	269,348	730,014	46,292	94,125	218,163	730,014	36,796	66,887	153,102	396,949
1978–9	87,661	125,544	261,775	744,088	49,777	91,487	208,184	744,088	40,759	63,708	145,406	386,413
1979–80	80,881	112,364	239,150	659,410	49,398	80,667	192,454	659,410	42,518	59,068	129,163	379,299
1980–1	72,505	100,185	211,133	599,435	44,826	72,448	167,988	599,435	38,681	53,448	114,482	334,973

Year												
1981–2	67,188	91,799	185,535	465,055	42,578	68,365	154,477	465,055	36,936	50,465	104,106	274,624
1982–3	68,885	95,571	203,592	524,714	42,199	68,566	167,912	524,714	36,345	50,425	109,084	328,208
1983–4	101,455	136,501	287,572	748,364	66,409	98,734	236,373	748,364	58,024	78,068	147,755	405,441
1984–5	100,724	141,099	296,573	785,804	60,348	102,230	242,214	785,804	51,741	72,482	166,800	417,519
1985–6	134,205	194,867	398,668	1,076,154	73,544	143,917	323,391	1,076,154	61,997	90,020	232,635	491,264
1986–7	140,409	209,094	424,429	1,133,425	71,724	155,261	345,651	1,133,425	59,741	88,966	246,474	567,202
1987–8	134,502	202,918	415,461	1,048,166	66,087	149,782	345,160	1,048,166	54,707	82,534	237,972	570,008
1988–9	150,884	226,028	479,970	1,467,390	75,739	162,543	370,256	1,467,390	62,909	94,239	250,537	710,464
1989–90	154,481	232,669	448,314	1,463,549	76,292	178,758	335,510	1,463,549	63,205	95,196	232,080	712,617
1990–1	147,360	205,021	364,688	1,261,498	89,699	165,104	265,042	1,261,498	75,706	113,242	142,097	623,500
1991–2	139,481	190,155	344,748	1,114,667	88,807	151,507	259,202	1,114,667	77,118	105,136	134,510	531,102
1992–3	136,488	188,378	374,868	1,160,748	84,598	141,756	287,547	1,160,748	73,041	100,810	172,256	666,654
1993–4	179,917	254,063	604,444	2,428,050	105,772	166,467	401,821	2,428,050	90,345	127,577	283,248	771,336
1994–5	180,767	259,846	584,010	2,388,467	101,688	178,805	383,515	2,388,467	86,131	123,810	280,340	839,639
1995–6	199,685	304,476	810,860	4,716,301	94,895	177,880	376,922	4,716,301	78,157	119,172	317,371	808,326
1996–7	207,253	307,276	731,925	3,655,103	107,229	201,114	407,127	3,655,103	89,503	132,699	328,662	821,010
1997–8	262,106	411,415	1,066,853	4,603,855	112,796	247,556	673,853	4,603,855	100,005	168,376	336,766	1,579,315
1998–9	223,561	350,913	909,965	3,926,823	96,209	211,151	574,758	3,926,823	85,298	143,615	287,242	1,347,065
1999–00	229,679	360,517	934,868	4,034,289	98,842	216,929	590,488	4,034,289	87,633	147,546	295,103	1,383,930
1999–2000/ 1987–1988	1.71	1.78	2.25	3.85	1.50	1.45	1.71	3.85	1.60	1.79	1.24	2.43
1999–2000/ 1981–1982	3.42	3.93	5.04	8.67	2.32	3.17	3.82	8.67	2.37	2.92	2.83	5.04

Source: Authors' computations using income tax returns data (*All-India Income Tax Statistics*, 1922–2000).

Table 1A.5 Top fractiles income shares in India, 1956–2000 (income shares are expressed as % of total income)

	P99–100 (1)	P99.5–100 (2)	P99.9–100 (3)	P99.99–100 (4)	P99–99.5 (5)	P99.5–99.9 (6)	P99.9–99.99 (7)	P99.99–100 (8)
1922–3	12.72	9.97	5.66	2.00	2.75	4.31	3.66	2.00
1923–4	13.39	10.47	5.91	2.07	2.92	4.56	3.84	2.07
1924–5	11.46	9.18	5.37	1.84	2.28	3.81	3.54	1.84
1925–6	12.38	9.64	5.39	1.84	2.74	4.25	3.55	1.84
1926–7	12.89	10.02	5.57	1.87	2.87	4.45	3.70	1.87
1927–8	13.32	10.39	5.82	1.98	2.93	4.57	3.84	1.98
1928–9	13.62	10.61	5.92	1.98	3.01	4.69	3.94	1.98
1929–30	13.07	10.25	5.77	1.90	2.81	4.48	3.87	1.90
1930–1	14.53	11.40	6.39	2.11	3.12	5.01	4.28	2.11
1931–2	16.09	12.55	6.94	2.26	3.55	5.61	4.68	2.26
1932–3	16.14	12.64	7.03	2.32	3.50	5.62	4.70	2.32
1933–4	17.11	13.37	7.39	2.45	3.75	5.97	4.94	2.45
1934–5	16.90	13.17	7.28	2.41	3.73	5.89	4.87	2.41
1935–6	17.33	13.42	7.34	2.42	3.91	6.08	4.92	2.42
1936–7	15.58	12.13	6.73	2.31	3.46	5.39	4.42	2.31
1937–8	15.54	12.09	6.71	2.32	3.45	5.38	4.38	2.32
1938–9	17.82	13.80	7.63	2.90	4.02	6.17	4.73	2.90
1939–40	16.11	12.74	7.38	2.88	3.37	5.35	4.50	2.88
1940–1	16.15	12.83	7.53	2.98	3.32	5.31	4.54	2.98
1941–2	14.06	11.32	6.85	2.73	2.74	4.48	4.11	2.73
1942–3								
1943–4	10.32	8.22	4.84	1.87	2.10	3.37	2.98	1.87
1944–5	11.13	8.80	5.10	2.00	2.33	3.70	3.10	2.00
1945–6	11.41	9.01	5.21	2.03	2.40	3.80	3.18	2.03
1946–7								
1947–8	11.23	9.05	5.44	2.27	2.19	3.61	3.16	2.27
1948–9	11.84	9.29	5.29	2.15	2.55	4.00	3.14	2.15
1949–50	12.00	9.35	5.24	2.10	2.65	4.11	3.14	2.10
1950–1	13.42	10.37	5.60	2.07	3.05	4.78	3.52	2.07
1951–2								
1952–3								
1953–4	11.92	9.41	5.15	1.85	2.51	4.27	3.30	1.85
1954–5	13.58	10.55	5.68	2.01	3.03	4.88	3.67	2.01
1955–6	14.41	11.15	5.92	2.01	3.26	5.23	3.90	2.01
1956–7	12.77	9.85	5.18	1.69	2.92	4.67	3.48	1.69
1957–8	13.34	10.26	5.31	1.68	3.08	4.95	3.62	1.68
1958–9	12.56	9.64	4.92	1.51	2.92	4.72	3.41	1.51
1959–60	12.36	9.44	4.77	1.44	2.92	4.67	3.33	1.44
1960–1	12.31	9.45	4.79	1.47	2.87	4.66	3.32	1.47
1961–2	12.15	9.29	4.61	1.38	2.86	4.68	3.24	1.38
1962–3	11.58	8.75	4.24	1.27	2.83	4.51	2.97	1.27
1963–4								
1964–5	9.65	6.99	3.23	1.04	2.67	3.75	2.19	1.04
1965–6	10.92	8.23	3.93	1.21	2.69	4.30	2.71	1.21
1966–7	9.99	7.57	3.66	1.16	2.41	3.91	2.50	1.16
1967–8	10.01	7.59	3.51	1.03	2.42	4.09	2.48	1.03
1968–9	9.95	7.52	3.48	1.01	2.43	4.04	2.47	1.01
1969–70								

1970–1	10.02	7.74	3.43	1.03	2.28	4.31	2.40	1.03
1971–2	8.47	6.31	2.83	0.88	2.16	3.48	1.95	0.88
1972–3								
1973–4	7.02	5.24	2.22	0.64	1.78	3.02	1.58	0.64
1974–5	6.65	4.77	2.01	0.54	1.88	2.76	1.47	0.54
1975–6	7.24	5.30	2.25	0.62	1.94	3.05	1.63	0.62
1976–7	7.27	5.19	2.16	0.62	2.07	3.03	1.55	0.62
1977–8	6.18	4.55	1.90	0.51	1.63	2.65	1.38	0.51
1978–9	6.05	4.33	1.81	0.51	1.72	2.52	1.29	0.51
1979–80	5.61	3.90	1.66	0.46	1.71	2.24	1.20	0.46
1980–1	4.78	3.30	1.39	0.40	1.48	1.91	1.00	0.40
1981–2	4.39	3.00	1.21	0.30	1.39	1.79	0.91	0.30
1982–3	4.51	3.13	1.33	0.34	1.38	1.79	0.99	0.34
1983–4	6.46	4.35	1.83	0.48	2.11	2.51	1.35	0.48
1984–5	6.39	4.48	1.88	0.50	1.91	2.59	1.38	0.50
1985–6	8.24	5.98	2.45	0.66	2.26	3.54	1.79	0.66
1986–7	8.64	6.43	2.61	0.70	2.21	3.82	1.91	0.70
1987–8	8.12	6.13	2.51	0.63	2.00	3.62	1.88	0.63
1988–9	8.52	6.38	2.71	0.83	2.14	3.67	1.88	0.83
1989–90	8.19	6.17	2.38	0.78	2.02	3.79	1.60	0.78
1990–1	7.42	5.16	1.84	0.64	2.26	3.33	1.20	0.64
1991–2	7.12	4.85	1.76	0.57	2.27	3.09	1.19	0.57
1992–3	6.96	4.81	1.91	0.59	2.16	2.89	1.32	0.59
1993–4	8.53	6.02	2.86	1.15	2.51	3.16	1.71	1.15
1994–5	8.09	5.82	2.61	1.07	2.28	3.20	1.55	1.07
1995–6	8.67	6.61	3.52	2.05	2.06	3.09	1.47	2.05
1996–7	8.72	6.47	3.08	1.54	2.26	3.39	1.54	1.54
1997–8	10.70	8.40	4.36	1.88	2.30	4.04	2.48	1.88
1998–9	8.95	7.02	3.64	1.57	1.93	3.38	2.07	1.57
1999–00	8.95	7.02	3.64	1.57	1.93	3.38	2.07	1.57

Source: Authors' computations using income tax returns data (*All-India Income Tax Statistics*, 1922–2000).

Table 1A.6 Top fractile wage levels in India, 1987–2000 (wages are expressed in current Rs)

	P99–100 (1)	P99.5–100 (2)	P99.9–100 (3)	P99.99–100 (4)	P99–99.5 (5)	P99.5–99.9 (6)	P99.9–99.99 (7)	P99.99–100 (8)	P99 (9)	P99.5 (10)	P99.9 (11)	P99.99 (12)
1987–8	22,860	32,470	43,262	80,942	13,250	29,772	39,075	80,942	11,238	15,962	25,901	47,310
1988–9	28,051	39,563	54,670	123,950	16,539	35,786	46,972	123,950	14,135	19,936	29,827	64,502
1989–90	29,933	42,456	58,197	133,071	17,411	38,521	49,877	133,071	14,841	21,049	31,240	68,131
1990–1	32,718	44,935	58,380	131,744	20,500	41,574	50,229	131,744	17,740	24,365	26,363	57,958
1991–2	36,956	48,712	63,142	158,045	25,199	45,104	52,597	158,045	22,230	29,301	26,922	71,978
1992–3	43,215	51,650	70,759	178,481	34,780	46,872	58,790	178,481	32,099	38,364	30,171	84,610
1993–4	42,126	63,482	144,468	487,871	20,770	43,236	106,312	487,871	17,203	25,924	72,935	151,514
1994–5	56,211	80,710	155,368	452,012	31,712	62,045	122,408	452,012	26,875	38,588	85,933	146,952
1995–6	64,379	93,558	180,337	532,192	35,199	71,864	141,242	532,192	29,660	43,104	97,135	164,540
1996–7	74,035	107,592	207,387	612,021	40,479	82,643	162,428	612,021	34,109	49,569	111,705	189,221
1997–8	81,439	118,351	228,126	673,223	44,526	90,908	178,671	673,223	37,520	54,526	122,876	208,143
1998–9	110,663	178,710	262,134	794,328	42,616	157,853	203,001	794,328	34,145	55,141	72,901	166,757
1999–00	118,962	192,113	281,794	853,903	45,812	169,693	218,226	853,903	36,706	59,277	78,369	179,263
1999–2000/ 1987–1988	5.20	5.92	6.51	10.55	3.46	5.70	5.58	10.55	3.27	3.71	3.03	3.79

Source: Authors' computations using income tax returns data (All-India Income Tax Statistics, 1922–2000).

Table 1A.7 Top fractile wage levels in India, 1987–2000 (wages are expressed in 1999–2000 Rs)

	P99–100 (1)	P99.5–100 (2)	P99.9–100 (3)	P99.99–100 (4)	P99–99.5 (5)	P99.5–99.9 (6)	P99.9–99.99 (7)	P99.99–100 (8)	P99 (9)	P99.5 (10)	P99.9 (11)	P99.99 (12)
1987–8	65,853	93,537	124,624	233,169	38,169	85,765	112,563	233,169	32,373	45,982	74,612	136,286
1988–9	73,874	104,190	143,974	326,427	43,557	94,244	123,702	326,427	37,226	52,503	78,552	169,868
1989–90	74,257	105,322	144,371	330,114	43,192	95,560	123,733	330,114	36,816	52,218	77,498	169,014
1990–1	74,482	102,295	132,904	299,915	46,669	94,643	114,347	299,915	40,386	55,467	60,017	131,943
1991–2	73,882	97,385	126,234	315,965	50,379	90,173	105,152	315,965	44,442	58,579	53,822	143,899
1992–3	77,286	92,370	126,546	319,196	62,201	83,826	105,140	319,196	57,406	68,610	53,959	151,316
1993–4	70,832	106,741	242,912	820,320	34,923	72,698	178,755	820,320	28,925	43,589	122,635	254,760
1994–5	85,757	123,134	237,035	689,606	48,381	94,659	186,750	689,606	41,001	58,871	131,102	224,195
1995–6	89,107	129,495	249,606	736,614	48,719	99,467	195,494	736,614	41,053	59,660	134,446	227,741
1996–7	94,032	136,652	263,401	777,325	51,412	104,965	206,299	777,325	43,322	62,958	141,877	240,328
1997–8	96,520	140,268	270,371	797,895	52,772	107,742	211,758	797,895	44,468	64,623	145,631	246,688
1998–9	115,830	187,055	274,375	831,422	44,606	165,225	212,481	831,422	35,740	57,716	76,306	174,544
1999–00	118,962	192,113	281,794	853,903	45,812	169,693	218,226	853,903	36,706	59,277	78,369	179,263
1999–2000/ 1987–1988	1.81	2.05	2.26	3.66	1.20	1.98	1.94	3.66	1.13	1.29	1.05	1.32

Source: Authors' computations using income tax returns data (All-India Income Tax Statistics, 1922–2000).

REFERENCES

Atkinson, A. B. (2007). 'Top Incomes in the United Kingdom over the Twentieth Century', in A. B. Atkinson and T. Piketty (eds.) *Top Incomes over the Twentieth Century: A Contrast between Continental European and English Speaking Countries.* Oxford: Oxford University Press.

Banerjee, Abhijit and Andrew Newman (2003). 'Inequality, Growth and Trade Policy', mimeo.

—— and Thomas Piketty (2004). 'Top Indian Incomes, 1922–2000', CEPR Discussion Paper.

Bhalla, Surjit (2002). *Imagine There is no Country: Poverty, Inequality and Growth in the Era of Globalization.* Institute for International Economics.

Datt, Gaurav (1997). 'Poverty in India 1951–1994: Trends and Decompositions', mimeo, The World Bank.

—— (1999). 'Has Poverty Declined since Economic Reforms', *Economic and Political Weekly*, 11–17 December.

Deaton, Angus (2003a). 'Adjusted Indian Poverty Estimates for 1999–2000', *Economic and Political Weekly*, 25 January.

—— (2003b). 'Prices and Poverty in India, 1987–2000', *Economic and Political Weekly*, 25 January.

—— (2003c). 'Measuring Poverty in a Growing World (or Measuring Growth in a Poor World)', NBER Working Paper 9822.

—— (2003d). 'How to Monitor Poverty for the Millennium Development Goals', forthcoming in *Journal of Human Development.*

—— and Jean Drèze (2002). 'Poverty and Inequality in India: A Re-examination', *Economic and Political Weekly*, 7 September.

Dell, F. (2007). 'Top Incomes in Germany throughout the Twentieth Century: 1891–1998', in A. B. Atkinson and T. Piketty (eds.) *Top Incomes over the Twentieth Century: A Contrast between Continental European and English Speaking Countries.* Oxford: Oxford University Press.

Delong, J. Bradford (2001). 'India since Independence: An Analytical Growth Narrative', mimeo, University of California, Berkeley.

Goolsbee, A. (2000). 'What Happens When You Tax the Rich? Evidence from Executive Compensation', *Journal of Political Economy*, April.

Kochar, Anjini (2003). 'Government, Schooling and Poverty: The Trickle-Down Benefits of Higher Schooling in India', mimeo, Stanford.

Kremer, Michael and Eric Maskin (2003). 'Globalization and Inequality', mimeo, Harvard.

Minhas, B. S. (1988), 'Validation of Large Scale Sample Survey Data: Case of NSS Estimates of Household Consumption Expenditure', *Sankhya*, Series B, 50(3), Supplement.

—— and S. M. Kansal (1990). 'Firmness, Fluidity and Margins of Uncertainty in the National Accounts Estimates of PCE in the 1980s', *Journal of Income and Wealth*, 12(1).

Nagaraj, R. (2000). 'Indian Economy since 1980? Virtuous Growth or Polarization?', *Economic and Political Weekly*, 5 August: 2831–9.

Piketty, Thomas (2003). 'Income Inequality in France, 1901–1998', *Journal of Political Economy*, 111: 1004–42.

—— and Emmanuel Saez (2003). 'Income Inequality in the United States, 1913–1998', *Quarterly Journal of Economics*, 118: 1–39.

Ravallion, Martin (2000). 'Should Poverty Measures Be Anchored to the National Accounts?', *Economic and Political Weekly*, 26 August–2 September.

—— (2001). 'Measuring Aggregate Welfare in Developing Countries: How Well do National Accounts and Surveys Agree?', mimeo, The World Bank.

Rodrik, Dani and Arvind Subramanian (2004). 'The Mystery of the Indian Growth Transition', mimeo, NBER.

Sivasubramonian, S. (2000). *The National Income of India in the Twentieth Century*, Oxford: Oxford University Press.

Sundaram, K. and Suresh D. Tendulkar (2001). 'NAS–NSS Estimates of Private Consumption for Poverty Estimation', *Economic and Political Weekly*, 13–20 January.

Szekely, Miguel and Marianne Hilgert (1999). 'What's Behind the Inequality We Measure: An Investigation Using Latin American Data', mimeo, Inter-American Development Bank.

Tendulkar, Suresh D. (2003). 'Organized Labour Market in India: Pre and Post Reform', mimeo, Delhi School of Economics.

World Bank (2000). *India: Policies to Reduce Poverty and Accelerate Sustainable Development*, Report No. 19471–IN.

2

Income Inequality and Progressive Income Taxation in China and India, 1986–2015

Thomas Piketty and Nancy Qian

2.1 INTRODUCTION

Current debates about policy reform in developing countries generally focus on improving the delivery of social services, the design of market-friendly economic institutions, the effectiveness of poverty reduction programmes, or the role of trade and market liberalization, and very rarely deal explicitly with tax reform and the need to develop modern income tax systems in those countries.[1]

This is unfortunate for at least three reasons. First, poor countries tend to rely excessively on highly distortionary tax instruments such as taxes on trade or indirect taxes on specific consumption goods. The gradual shift towards modern and transparent income and payroll tax systems is generally regarded as an important, efficiency-enhancing aspect of the modernization process.

Next, many developing countries need to raise more tax revenues in order to properly finance education and health investment, and income taxation can be part of the solution, especially in an international context characterized by sharp downward pressures on tariffs and various indirect taxes. In countries like China and India, in spite of very rapid growth, tax revenues are currently stagnating around 10–15 per cent of GDP, which is probably far too little. There is no example of a country in the West that has been able to develop a proper education and health system with total tax revenues around 10–15 per cent of GDP. Improving the efficiency of social services delivery is probably a good idea, but might well be illusory in case those services are not properly funded.

Finally, many developing countries have witnessed a sharp rise in income inequality during the recent period. Progressive taxation is probably one of the

We gratefully acknowledge financial support from the MacArthur Foundation. We are grateful to the Urban Household Income Survey Team of China's National Statistical Bureau (NSB) for helping us with the data, and to Ge Shozhong at the Shanghai Cai Jing University for sharing his expertise in China's tax system Wang Youjuan. We also thank Ye Jiang for excellent research assistance. A shorter version of this chapter was published as T. Piketty and N. Qian, 'Income Inequality and Progressive Income Taxation in China and India: 1986–2015', *American Economic Journal: Applied Economics*, 1(2) (2009): 53–63.

[1] See, e.g., the list of topics covered in World Development Reports over the past few years.

least distortionary policy tools available to keep the rise in inequality under control and to redistribute a bit more equally the gains from growth (it is less distortionary than more radical policy tools such as nationalization, minimum wages, or autarky). In India, the fact that many people did not benefit from the 5–6 per cent annual growth rates advertised by the government and felt left behind by 'shining India' probably played an important role in recent electoral outcomes.

In this chapter, we choose to focus on the case of progressive income taxation in China. Although a progressive individual income tax system has been in place in China since 1980, it has received very little attention so far, probably because the fraction of the population with income above the exemption threshold was negligible until the 1990s (less than 1 per cent). Using annual, 1986–2003, tabulations from urban household income surveys collected by China's National Statistical Bureau (NSB), we compute series on levels and shares of top incomes in China over this period, as well as series on theoretical numbers of taxpayers and total income tax receipts (based on actual tax law).[2] We also make projections about the evolution of the number of taxpayers and total receipts over the 2004–15 period, assuming constant income trends and income tax schedules.

One additional motivation for computing theoretical numbers of taxpayers and tax receipts is the fact that there is widespread presumption that official Chinese income tax law is not being applied very rigorously by tax authorities. In particular, many observers seem to believe that tax authorities make deals with large firms and autonomous regions or cities whereby the latter offer a lump-sum payment to tax authorities and their employees and residents are not subject to the official income tax schedule. Although at this stage there do not seem to exist detailed tabulations of income tax returns by income brackets or tax liability in China (such tabulations exist in most countries with an income tax system), we were able to use aggregate 1996–2003 income tax receipts series (broken down by wage income, business income, and capital income for 2000–3) and compare them with our theoretical series. It turns out that although there is some evidence that the law is not fully applied, actual receipts and theoretical receipts are reasonably close.

We were also able to compare our Chinese findings with similar series for India. Contrarily to its Chinese counterpart, the Indian tax administration has been compiling detailed tabulations of income tax returns every year since the creation of a progressive income tax in India (1922). As demonstrated in Chapter 1, the Indian tax returns tabulations can be exploited to study the long-run evolution of top income shares in India, and we use these results for the 1986–2001 sub-period as a comparison point for our Chinese series.

---

[2] A number of economists have used NSB's household surveys and have documented the rise in income inequality that took place in China during the 1990s (see, e.g., Chen and Wang 2001, Eckaus, Lester, and Qian 2003, and Ravallion and Chen 2003). However these works generally focus on poverty: they generally do not deal specifically with the top of the distribution and (most importantly) do not look at the issue of progressive income taxation. Chen and Wang (2001) show that income dispersion has increased at the top of the distribution (which is fully consistent with our findings) but do not mention the issue of income taxation. For more details on the NSB tabulations used in this study (these tabulations were designed explicitly to focus on top income brackets and to facilitate tax simulations), see section 2.2 below.

Our main conclusions are the following. First, our general conclusion is that progressive income taxation is about to become an important economic and political object in China and India, and that income tax reform should rank high on the policy agenda in these two countries. Due to high average income growth and sharply rising top income shares during the 1990s and early 2000s, progressive income taxation is starting to hit a non-negligible fraction of the population in both countries (as more and more workers pass the exemption threshold, following what happened in Western countries half a century ago) and to raise non-trivial tax revenues. According to our projections, the income tax should raise at least 4 per cent of Chinese GDP in 2010 (versus less than 1 per cent in 2000 and 0.1 per cent in 1990), in spite of the 20 per cent nominal rise in the exemption threshold that took effect in 2004. In the case where no further rise in exemption threshold occurs (which seems fairly unlikely), we predict that over 80 per cent of urban wage earners will be subject to tax by 2015, and that income tax revenues will well exceed 10 per cent of Chinese GDP (i.e. more than in a number of developed countries).

The fact that progressive income taxation is becoming an important policy tool has important consequences for China's ability to finance social spending and to keep under control the rise in income inequality associated with globalization and growth. Due to faster income growth, to lower bracket indexation, and to a higher fraction of wage earners in the labour force, the prospects for income tax development look better in China than in India. This potential is however limited by the fact that Chinese top wage earners are under-taxed relatively to top non-wage income earners.

The rest of the chapter is organized as follows. Section 2.2 briefly describes the NSB data used in this chapter. In section 2.3, we present our findings for the evolution of top income shares in China, and compare them to the Indian series of Banerjee and Piketty (2005 and Chapter 1). The results of our income tax simulations are presented and analysed in section 2.4. Section 2.5 offers some concluding comments.

2.2 DATA AND METHODOLOGY

The Chinese data used in this chapter come from the urban household income surveys collected by China's National Statistical Bureau (NSB). These surveys were designed so as to be representative of urban China. Between 13,000 and 17,000 households were being surveyed each year until 2002, up to 45,000–50,000 in 2002 and 2003 (see Table 2A.2). The micro-files for these surveys are unfortunately not available for all years,[3] and we asked NSB to provide us with annual, 1986–2003 tabulations based on the micro-files. We asked for two series of

---

[3] The micro-files for urban household surveys are available for researchers for years 1988 and 1995 only (see Eckaus, Lester, and Qian 2003).

tabulations: household tabulations and individual tabulations.[4] Household tabulations report for a large number of income brackets (and in particular a large number of top income brackets) the number of households whose total household income falls into that bracket, their average total income and household size, as well as their average income broken down by income sources (wage income, business income, capital income, and transfer income). Individual tabulations report for a large number of income brackets (and in particular a large number of top income brackets) the number of individuals whose individual income falls into that bracket, their average age, years of education, income, and household size, as well as their average income broken down by income sources. In practice, some forms of income cannot be properly attributed to a specific individual within the household (this is particularly true for transfer income and capital income), so that the total income aggregates reported in household tabulations are larger than in individual tabulations, and various adjustments are necessary when one uses the latter (see Tables 2A.2 and 2A.3). However the important advantage of individual tabulations is that China's income tax applies to individual income (rather than household income).

We used standard Pareto interpolation techniques to approximate the form of the Chinese household and individual distribution of income, and we then used these structural parameters to compute top fractiles incomes and to make income tax simulations.[5] The Chinese data appear to be very well approximated by a Pareto distribution (for any given year, Pareto coefficients are extremely stable within the top decile), although there is some presumption that top incomes are underestimated in the survey data (more on this below).[6]

We did not attempt to use similar tabulations from rural household surveys, but given that our focus is on top incomes and progressive income taxation this should not be too much of a problem: average rural income was in 2001 more than three times smaller than average urban income,[7] so that there are probably

---

[4] We also asked for 'age tabulations' (reporting for each age cell the relevant number of individuals, their average years of education and income, as well as their average income broken down by income sources).We did not use these tables here.

[5] For recent use of Pareto interpolation techniques, see, e.g., Piketty (2003) and Piketty and Saez (2003).

[6] The Pareto coefficients, as defined by the ratio between average income above a given threshold and the threshold (the definition of a Pareto distribution is that this ratio does not depend on the threshold), appear to be extremely low in China (around 1.2 in the late 1980s, up to around 1.4 in the late 1990s and early 2000s), much lower than in any country for which we have seen similar data. In the 1990s, similarly defined Pareto coefficients are around 1.7–1.8 in France and 2.3–2.4 in the USA. A higher Pareto coefficient means a fatter upper tail of the distribution (a coefficient equal to 1 means that there is nobody above the given threshold, i.e. the distribution is truncated) and generally implies higher top income shares. It should be noted that this definition of a Pareto coefficient follows Piketty (chapter 1 in Volume I), rather than the traditional definition, where the Pareto coefficient is the negative of the exponent of income in the expression for the cumulative distribution. One coefficient can be obtained from the other by the transformation $x/(x-1)$, but that used here has the intuitive appeal that, for a given mean income, inequality increases with the coefficient, whereas the reverse is true for the traditional coefficient.

[7] See Table 2A.1.

very few rural households and individuals in the national top decile, and even less so within the top incomes subject to progressive income taxation (agricultural income is exempt from the income tax and is being taxed separately).

All our series regarding India are from Banerjee and Piketty (Chapter 1), who used Indian income tax returns tabulations to estimate top income levels and national accounts to compute the average income denominator. Top income shares estimates based upon income tax returns are likely to be higher than estimates based on survey data (as the latter generally underestimate top incomes), but there is no obvious reason why the trends should not be comparable. Note also that the standard household surveys used by economists working on India (NSS surveys) can hardly be used to compute top income shares, as these are mostly expenditure surveys: except for particular years, and contrary to NSB surveys, NSS surveys contain no systematic information on incomes.[8]

2.3 TOP INCOME SHARES IN CHINA AND INDIA, 1986–2001

Did income inequality in China increase as much as in India during the 1990s? Before we look at our top income shares series, it is useful to recall one important difference between Chinese and Indian incomes during the past fifteen to twenty years. While real per capita GDP increased by almost 160 per cent in China between 1986 and 2001 (6.4 per cent per year), it increased by slightly more than 60 per cent in India (3.4 per cent per year) (see Figure 2.1). According to the best available PPP conversion factors at the time of writing, real per capita GDP was virtually identical in China and India in 1986 (less than 20 per cent larger in China), and it was almost twice as large in China as in India by 2001.[9] Note that the growth gap is even larger if we look at survey data rather than national accounts. While total 1986–2001 income growth is virtually the same in Chinese national accounts and household surveys, there exists a well-known 'growth paradox' in Indian statistics: real GDP per capita (as measured by Indian national accounts) has increased by 64 per cent between 1986 and 2001 (3.4 per cent per year), but real consumption per capita (as measured by NSS surveys) has increased by only 24 per cent (1.4 per cent per year).[10] According to official Chinese

---

[8] This important difference between China's NSB and India's NSS surveys has probably a lot to do with the fact that the Indian population includes a much higher fraction of independent workers with ill-defined income (including in the urban sector) and a much smaller fraction of formal wage earners than China (more on this below).

[9] See Table 2A.1.

[10] See Table 2A.1. This 'Indian growth paradox' has attracted a lot of attention from economists. Here we use as an end point the latest NSS figures corrected by Deaton (2003) on the basis of the 1999–2000 NSS round (we adjusted upwards this figure to make it comparable to other estimates available for 2001). Deaton's corrections did reduce the size of the gap between national accounts and NSS figures (until these corrections, there was basically no growth at all in the NSS during the 1990s), but the gap is still substantial. Banerjee and Piketty (Chapter 1) argue that the gap can be partly explained by the rise in top incomes in India during the 1990s (top incomes are not properly recorded in the NSS).

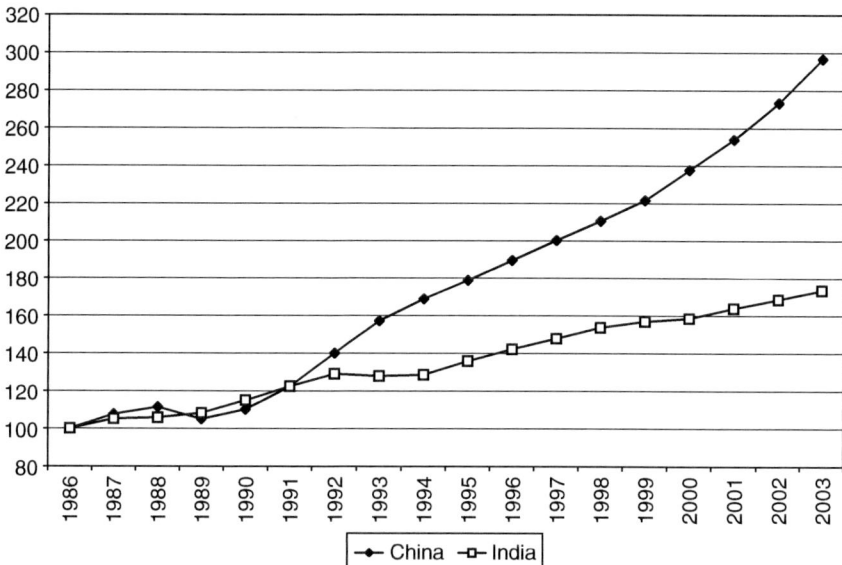

Figure 2.1 Real per capita GDP in China and India, 1986–2003 (1986 = 100)

Source: Author's computations using national accounts (see Appendix, Table 2A.1, col. (5) and (16)).

statistics, there exists no such growth paradox in China: real GDP per capita (as measured by Chinese national accounts) has increased by 154 per cent between 1986 and 2001 (6.4 per cent per year), and real per capita income (as measured by NSB surveys) has increased by 140 per cent (6.0 per cent per year).[11]

If we now look at the evolution of the top decile income shares in China over the same period, we find that income inequality has increased at a very high rate during the 1986–2003 period. According to our urban survey estimates, the top decile income share rose from about 17 per cent in 1986 to almost 28 per cent in 2003, i.e. by more than 60 per cent (see Figure 2.2). The levels are probably underestimated (during most of the period they are even lower than in the most egalitarian developed countries, e.g. Scandinavia), but the upward trend seems large and robust.

As we move up in the income hierarchy, the trend gets even bigger. For instance, the top 1 per cent income share more than doubled between 1986 and 2001, from slightly more than 2.6 per cent in 1986 to 5.9 per cent in 2003 (see Figure 2.3 and Table 2A.6). If we compare these results with those obtained for India,[12] we find

[11] Table 2A.1. Note that rural per capita income has increased much less rapidly than urban per capita income and national per capita GDP (both increased at approximately the same rate), but that this was almost exactly compensated by the rise in the urban population share.

[12] Banerjee and Piketty (Chapter 1) were only able to compute the income shares for the top percentile (and above) for India (and not the top decile), due to the low proportion of individuals subject to the income tax.

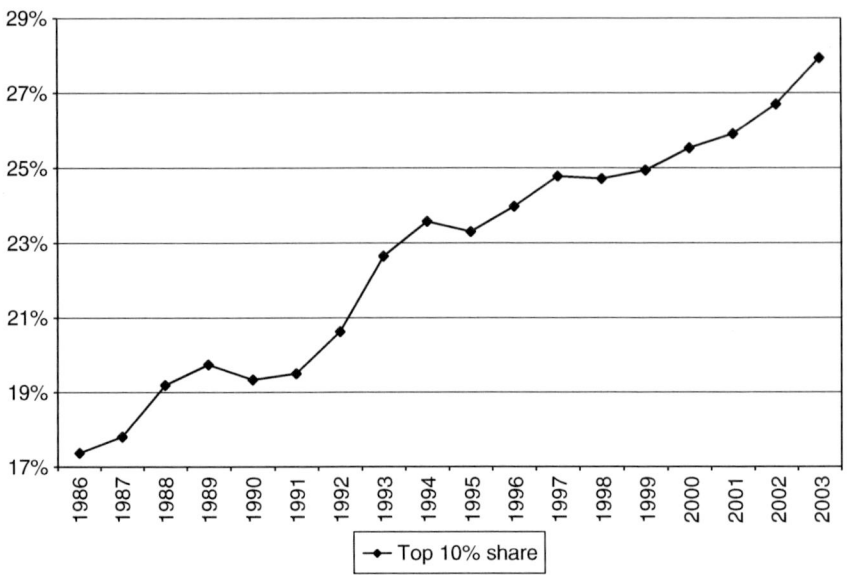

Figure 2.2 The top 10% income share in China, 1986–2003

Source: Author's computations using household surveys tabulations (Appendix, Table 2A.6, col. (1), ind. income).

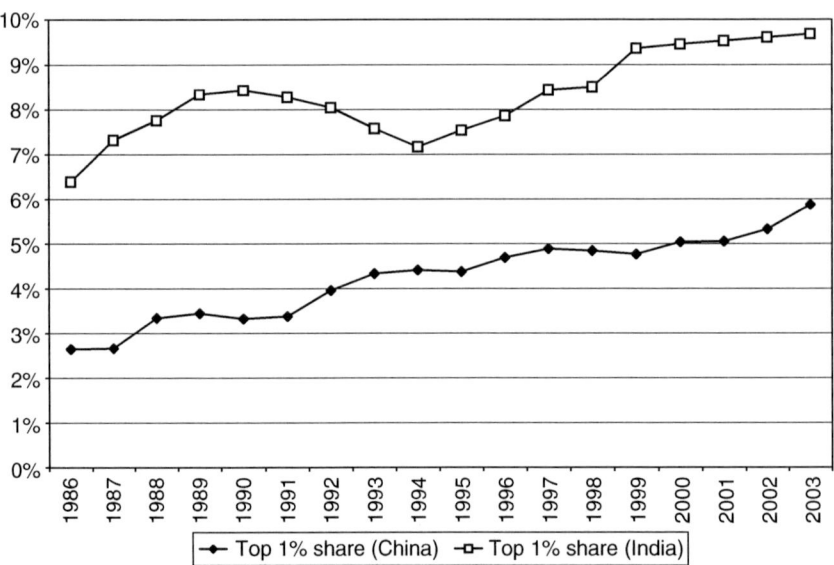

Figure 2.3 The top 1% income share in China and India, 1986–2003

Sources: China: author's computations using household surveys tabulations (Appendix, Table 2A.6, col. (4), ind. distribution); India: three-year moving average calculated from Table 1A.5, extrapolated linearly.

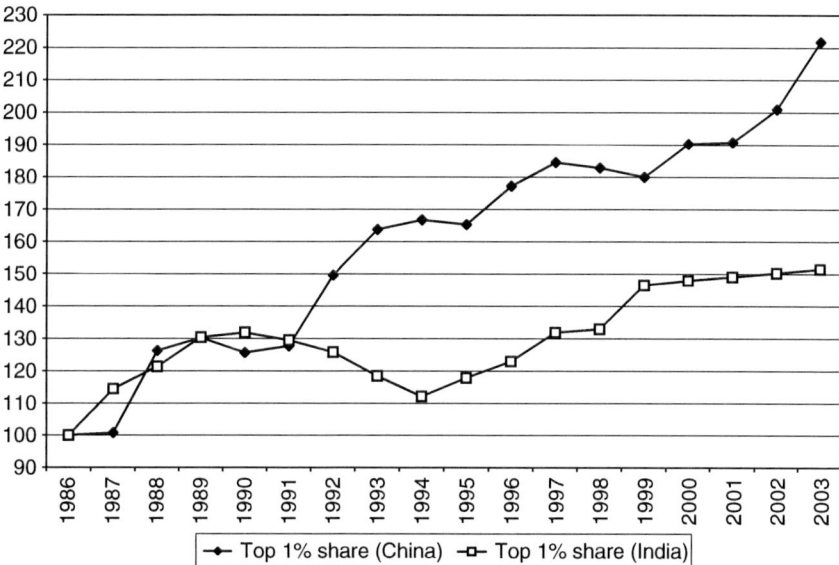

Figure 2.4 The top 1% income share, indexed to 100 in 1986, in China and India, 1986–2003

Sources: China: author's computations using household surveys tabulations (Appendix, Table 2A.5, col. (4), ind. distribution); India: three-year moving average calculated from Table 1A.5, extrapolated linearly.

that the levels are much lower in China than in India (the Chinese 2003 top 1 per cent share is still lower than the Indian 1986 top 1 per cent share), which again suggests that survey-based measures underestimate top incomes, but that the trend is substantially larger in China. The top 1 per cent income share has increased by more than 90 per cent in China between 1986 and 2001, and by less than 50 per cent in India (see Figure 2.4).

These results can be used not only to evaluate the prospects for progressive income taxation in China and India (see section 2.4 below), but also to shed some new light on the ongoing debate about globalization and the rise in inequality. Although our data do not allow us to identify precisely the causal channels at work, and in particular to isolate the impact of globalization, we note that the fact that the rise in income inequality was so much concentrated within top incomes in both countries seems more consistent with a theory based on rents and market frictions (see, e.g., Banerjee and Newman 2003) than with a theory based solely on skills and technological complementarity (i.e. inequality rises in the south because low-skill southern workers are too low-skill to benefit from globalization; see, e.g., Kremer and Maskin 2003), which would seem to imply more gradual shifts in the distribution. To the extent that the skill distribution is more unequal in India than in China (e.g. literacy rates are substantially higher in China), the skill-based theory would also seem to imply that income inequality should have risen more rapidly in India than in China, whereas we find the opposite (as far as the top 1 per cent income share is concerned).

2.4 PROGRESSIVE INCOME TAXATION IN CHINA AND INDIA, 1986–2010

Income Tax Schedules and Exemption Levels

We now come to the issue of progressive income taxation. Table 2.1 describes the evolution of Chinese income tax schedules during the 1980–2004 period.[13] In the pre-reform era, all workers worked for the state and paid an implicit tax from their wages. Expansion of the private sector by the market reforms decreased the government's ability to tax directly. Following other countries, China developed

Table 2.1 Progressive income tax schedules in China, 1980–2008

	Wage income			Business income (1980–2008) (no exemption)	
Exemption threshold		Tax schedules applying to wage income above exemption threshold (brackets and rates unchanged since 1980)			
Years	Annual income (yuans)	Brackets of annual income (yuans)	Marginal tax rate	Brackets of annual income (yuans)	Marginal tax rate
1980–1998	9,600	0–6,000	5%	0–5,000	5%
1999–2003	12,000	6,000–24,000	10%	5,000–10,000	10%
2004–2005	14,400	24,000–60,000	15%	10,000–30,000	15%
2006–2008	19,200	60,000–240,000	20%	30,000–50,000	20%
		240,000–480,000	25%	over 50,000	35%
		480,000–720,000	30%		
		720,000–960,000	35%		
		960,000–1,200,000	40%		
		over 1,200,000	45%		

Note: China's income tax applies to individual income (not to household income). The business income schedule applies to 'income from production and business operations derived by individual industrialists and merchants' and 'income from contracted or leased operation of enterprises and institutions'. Most forms of transfer income are exempt from the income tax. Capital income (interest, dividends, royalties, rent, etc.) has always been taxed at a flat 20% rate (with no allowance), although there are some exemptions (interest income on saving deposits and national debt is exempt from income tax). Agricultural income is excluded from the income tax (peasants are subject to a separate, indirect income tax based on average yields). The exemption thresholds for wage earners reported on this table are those applied in Beijing. The thresholds applied in other regions can be slightly different (e.g. in Shanghai the threshold was 9,600 yuans until 1993, 12,000 yuans in 1994–8, and 14,400 yuans in 1999–2003).

[13] Keeping track of all the changes in China's tax law is not an easy business, so unfortunately we cannot exclude the possibility that we missed some important changes. However to the best of our knowledge all parameters reported in Table 2.1 are accurate. Tax laws are enacted jointly by the National People's Congress and the Standing Committee of the National People's Congress. Some local tax regulations may be formulated at the provincial level. However, individual income tax brackets are set by the central government and it is illegal for regional governments to alter this although, in fact, some rapidly growing cities such as Shanghai and Shenzhen have on occasion increased the threshold above the centrally set threshold to alleviate the tax burden of their lower-income citizens.

an individual income taxation system, which officially began in 1980. In order to avoid negative public opinion, the deductible amount was set so high such that virtually no one had to pay income taxes in 1980.

However the striking fact is that China's income tax law has remained basically unchanged in nominal terms since its creation in 1980. The only major change is that the nominal exemption threshold for wage earners has been raised from 9,600 yuans per year in fiscal years 1980–98 to 12,000 yuans in 1999–2003 and 14,400 yuans since 2004. Also note that the Chinese income tax system treats wage income in a much more favourable manner than business income and capital income: while wage earners are subject to the progressive income tax only if their annual wage is large enough, all business and capital income earners are subject to the tax (with no exemption). Business income is taxed by applying graded progressive rates, while capital income is taxed at a flat 20 per cent rate. Many Western countries had a similar system when they first introduced income taxation (i.e. varying rates and deductions for different sources of income, with in general a large exemption for wages and little or no exemption for business and capital income), before gradually shifting to a more integrated system.[14]

In contrast to the Chinese income tax, the Indian income tax is a much older institution, since it was created in 1922 by the British. Moreover, it has always been an integrated system treating all income sources equally: Indian progressive tax schedules apply to total individual income, irrespective of where the income comes from. Another important difference is that the tax schedule has been changed almost constantly in India during the 1986–2004 period, resulting in a general decline in tax rates and a continuous increase in the exemption threshold (see Table 2.2).

From our perspective, the first important implication of these differing evolutions is that the exemption threshold (for wage earners) has increased less than inflation (and much less than nominal incomes) in China since 1986, while it increased approximately at the same rate as inflation in India, resulting in a massive increase in the proportion of the population subject to the income tax in China and a more modest increase in India (see Figures 2.5, 2.6, and 2.7). In China, the exemption threshold in 1986 (9,600 yuans) was about seven times larger than average individual urban income (1,394 yuans), so that less than 0.1 per cent of all wage earners were subject to the income tax in 1986. By 2003, the exemption threshold (12,000 yuans) has passed below average individual urban income (13,383 yuans), so that according to our estimates 44.1 per cent of all urban wage earners were subject to tax. In India, the exemption threshold has always been set around two to three times average income during the 1986–2001 period, and it is only because of the rise in top income shares that the proportion of the population subject to the income tax has increased somewhat during this period (from 0.7 per cent in 1986 to 3.8 per cent in 2001). This is an

---

[14] For instance, a similar schedular system existed in France when the income tax was put in place in 1914.

Table 2.2 Progressive income tax schedules in India, 1986–2008

1986–8

Brackets of annual income (Rs)	Marginal tax rate
0–15,000	0%
15,000–20,000	20%
20,000–25,000	25%
25,000–30,000	30%
30,000–40,000	35%
40,000–50,000	40%
50,000–70,000	45%
70,000–100,000	50%
over 100,000	55%

1989–91

Brackets of annual income (Rs)	Marginal tax rate
0–18,000	0%
18,000–25,000	25%
25,000–50,000	30%
50,000–100,000	40%
over 100,000	50%

1992–3

Brackets of annual income (Rs)	Marginal tax rate
0–22,000	0%
22,000–30,000	20%
30,000–60,000	30%
60,000–100,000	40%
over 100,000	50%

1994

Brackets of annual income (Rs)	Marginal tax rate
0–28,000	0%
50,000–100,000	20%
50,000–100,000	30%
over 100,000	40%

1995

Brackets of annual income (Rs)	Marginal tax rate
0–30,000	0%
50,000–100,000	20%
50,000–100,000	30%
over 100,000	40%

1996–7

Brackets of annual income (Rs)	Marginal tax rate
0–40,000	0%
40,000–60,000	20%
60,000–120,000	30%
over 120,000	40%

1998

Brackets of annual income (Rs)	Marginal tax rate
0–40,000	0%
40,000–60,000	15%
60,000–120,000	30%
over 120,000	40%

1999

Brackets of annual income (Rs)	Marginal tax rate
0–40,000	0%
40,000–60,000	10%
60,000–150,000	20%
over 150,000	30%

2000–4

Brackets of annual income (Rs)	Marginal tax rate
0–50,000	0%
50,000–60,000	10%
60,000–150,000	20%
over 150,000	30%

2005–6

Brackets of annual income (Rs)	Marginal tax rate
0–100,000	0%
100,000–150,000	10%
150,000–250,000	20%
over 250,000	30%

2007

Brackets of annual income (Rs)	Marginal tax rate
0–110,000	0%
110,000–150,000	10%
150,000–250,000	20%
over 250,000	30%

2008

Brackets of annual income (Rs)	Marginal tax rate
0–150,000	0%
150,000–300,000	10%
300,000–500,000	20%
over 500,000	30%

Note: India's income tax applies to individual income, not to household income (except for Hindu Undivided Families). The general principle is that all income sources are subject to the same tax rates (the progressive tax schedule applies to the sum of all individual incomes, whatever the source). There are however special exemptions for particular forms of interest income, transfer income, etc., as well as higher exemptions levels for women (Rs 180,000 in 2008) and individuals over 65 (Rs 225,000 in 2008). The tax schedules reported on this table also do not include 'temporary' tax surcharges (for instance, a 10% tax surcharge has been applied to all incomes above 60,000 Rs since 2000, so that the effective top rate is 33% rather than 30%). Finally note that in 1991 the 25% marginal rate was reduced to 20%.

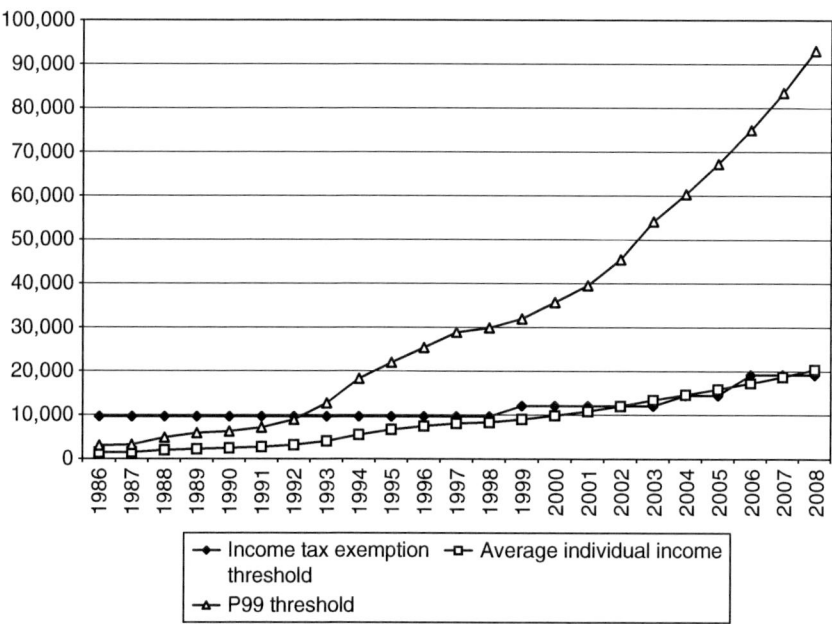

Figure 2.5 Income tax exemption threshold, average income, and P99 income threshold in China, 1986–2008 (current yuans)

Sources: Exemption threshold: Chinese tax law (Data Appendix, Table 2A.1); average income and P99 threshold: authors' computations using household surveys tabulations (Data Appendix, Table 2A.1, col. (10), and Table 2A.4, col. (15)).

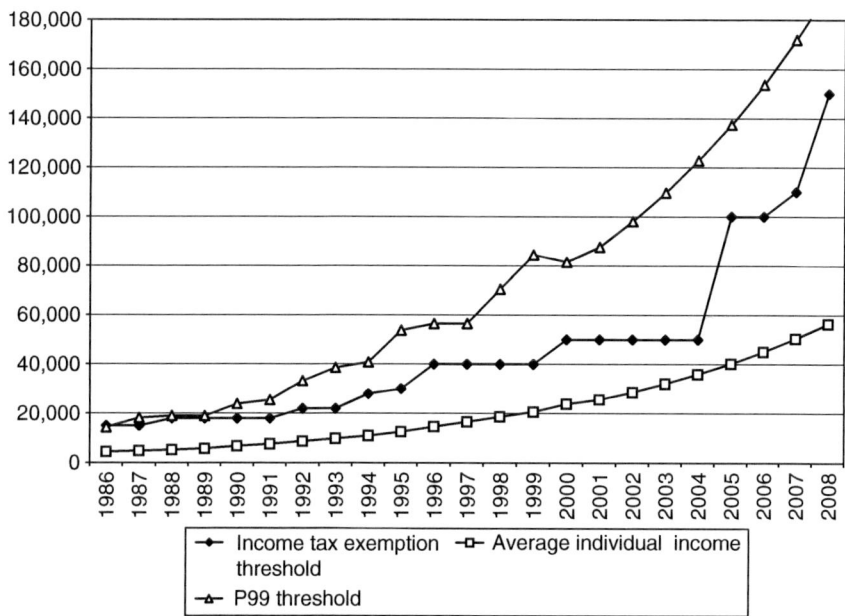

Figure 2.6 Income tax exemption threshold, average income, and P99 income threshold in India, 1986–2008 (current Rs)

Sources: Exemption threshold: Indian tax law (see Appendix, Table 2A.2); average income and P99 threshold: author's computations using income tax returns (see Chapter 1, Table 1A.2, col. (7), and Table 1A.3, col. (9)).

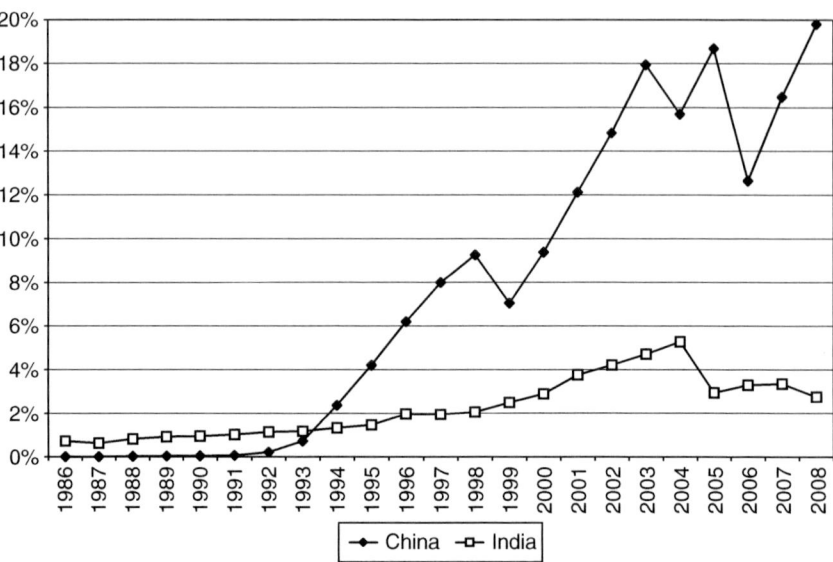

Figure 2.7 The fraction of the population subject to the income tax in China and India, 1986–2008

Sources: China: author's computations using household surveys tabulations (Appendix, Table 2A.7, col. (16)); India: three-year moving average calculated from Table 1A.2, extrapolated.

important rise from an historical perspective (the proportion of the population subject to the Indian income tax had been relatively stable around 0.5–1 per cent between the 1920s and the early 1990s), but this is clearly much less than in China.[15]

In other words, due to lower bracket indexation and higher real income growth, the Chinese income tax has become a mass tax during the 1990s, while it has remained an elite tax in India. Assuming that China's 2004 income tax law applies until 2010 (i.e. there is no further rise in the exemption threshold after 2004) and the income trends (both in average income and top income shares) continue after 2001 at the same rate as during the 1996–2001 period, our projections indicate that almost two-thirds of Chinese urban wage earners (over 200 million individuals) will be subject to the income tax by 2010, and over 85 per cent by 2015 (see Figure 2.8). As we shall see below, it is fairly likely that the exemption threshold will be increased again in order to keep this booming trend under control.

[15] The levels reported in Figure 2.7 are not strictly comparable, since the Chinese figure applies to urban wage earners, while the Indian figure applies to all tax units (i.e. adult individuals). Note however that the fraction of urban wage earners is fairly large in China: in 2003 total urban population (adults and children) was about 500 million, and the total numbers of urban wage earners was about 260 million (see Tables 2A.1 and 2A.3).

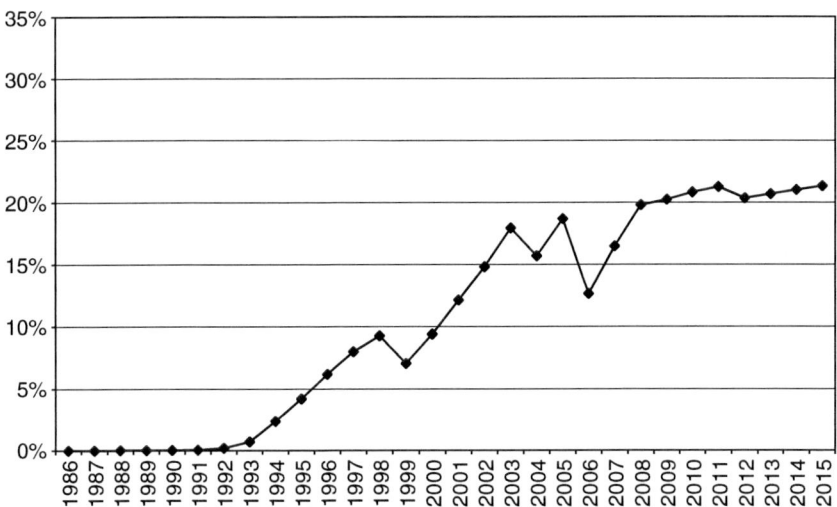

Figure 2.8 Projected fraction of the population subject to the income tax in China, 1986–2015
Authors' computations using household surrveys tabulation (Data Appendix, Table 2A.8, col. (16)).

Income Tax Revenues

One important question, however, is whether the Chinese income tax law is really being applied in practice: i.e. do all individuals who are supposed to be subject to the income tax according to the law really pay the income tax? Chinese tax laws are reasonably well documented, but there is almost no documentation of the actual implementation of these laws. Many observers in and outside China seem to believe that tax authorities make deals with large firms and autonomous regions or cities whereby the latter offer a lump-sum payment to tax authorities and their employees and residents are not subject to the official income tax schedule. We conducted a series of interviews with managers of six firms in Shanghai and several former employees of local tax ministries from another large city. We interviewed two large public sector firms (4,000–10,000 employees), two middle-sized private sector firms (a non-Chinese firm and a Chinese firm, 200–500 employees), and two small private sector Chinese firms (30–100). According to these firms, the amount of income tax deducted from salaries is determined by the tax bureau, which sends a representative to the firm once every couple of years. The duration is not set or announced ex ante. However, all the firms we met with had been visited by the tax bureau in the past three years. The visit entails an examination of the employment records and salaries. It is unclear whether the tax bureau determines an average tax rate for the firm on the basis of average wage only, or whether the full progressive schedule is really being applied. In many cases, all employees within a firm seem to share the same proportional tax liability. In other words, income taxation often seems to be progressive across firms, but not within firms.

Although this kind of anecdotal evidence is suggestive, one would obviously need systematic tabulations of taxpayers and effective tax rates by income brackets in order to better understand how income tax is really collected in China. Unfortunately, such tabulations by income brackets (similar to what is being published by the tax administration in India and other countries) are not available in China. There do not even seem to be any reliable statistics on the number of income tax payers in China, so we cannot compare our theoretical numbers of taxpayers with the actual numbers.[16] However we can use published statistics on aggregate income tax revenues and compare it to theoretical tax revenues in order to evaluate how strictly the law is being applied. We compiled from China Tax Yearbooks aggregate income tax revenues series for 1996–2003. Starting in 2000, published aggregate revenue statistics are broken down by income source (wage income, business income, capital income, and other income).[17] This very useful decomposition of tax revenues does not seem to be available prior to 2000. The comparison between actual tax revenues and theoretical tax revenues is given in Table 2.3. The theoretical tax revenues were computed by applying the relevant tax schedules to the individual distributions of wage income, business income, and capital income estimated from urban household income survey tabulations.

The first conclusion emerging from Table 2.3 is that actual income tax revenues are reasonably in line with theoretical tax revenues (as a first-order approximation), thereby suggesting that income tax collection in China is somewhat less chaotic and arbitrary than many observers tend to assume. In 1996, actual income tax receipts represented 0.28 per cent of GDP, and theoretical receipts 0.33 per cent of GDP; in 2003, actual income tax receipts represented 1.21 per cent of GDP, and theoretical receipts 1.13 per cent of GDP (cf. Table 2.3). If we look separately at receipts by income source for 2003, we find theoretical receipts on capital income were equal to 40 per cent of actual receipts (this reflects the fact that capital income is under-reported in surveys), and that the corresponding figure was over 120 per cent for business income and wage income. The latter figure could be interpreted as saying that

---

[16] Estimates according to which there were approximately 10–11 million income tax payers in China in 1997–8 have been published in the China Tax Yearbooks, but we were unable to find out what these numbers exactly refer to and how they were constructed. If they were true, these numbers would be substantially smaller than our theoretical estimates (about 25% of 200 million wage earners subject to income tax in 1997–8, i.e. approximately 50 million taxpayers; see Tables 2A.3 and 2A.7), which would seem to suggest that the law is not being applied properly. However the missing taxpayers might well have very low average tax liabilities, so it is hard to know how these figures should be interpreted (if the Chinese tax authorities were able to produce reliable estimates of the total number of taxpayers, they should also be able to break down this total number by income bracket or tax liability).

[17] 'Other income' includes small items such as 'author's remuneration' and 'property transferring income' (these income types are not properly recorded in income surveys, and we did not attempt to replicate the corresponding tax revenues).

Table 2.3 Simulated versus actual income tax revenues in China, 1996–2003

Actual income tax revenues

	Total receipts	Wage income receipts	Busines income receipts	Capital income receipts	Other receipts	Total receipts
			(billions current yuans)			(% GDP)
1996	19.3					0.28%
1997	26.0					0.35%
1998	33.9					0.43%
1999	41.4					0.51%
2000	66.0	28.3	13.3	19.0	5.5	0.74%
2001	99.6	41.1	16.0	34.8	7.7	1.02%
2002	121.1	56.1	18.5	38.4	8.0	1.15%
2003	141.7	74.1	20.0	38.2	9.3	1.21%
2004	173.6	94.0	24.6	44.5	10.5	1.37%
2005	209.4	116.2	29.6	51.4	12.2	1.65%

Simulated income tax revenues

	Total receipts	Wage income receipts	Busines income receipts	Capital income receipts	Other receipts	Total receipts
			(billions current yuans)			(% GDP)
1996	22.2	12.0	2.2	8.0		0.33%
1997	32.0	18.6	3.3	10.0		0.43%
1998	37.6	22.1	4.0	11.4		0.48%
1999	36.5	19.7	4.9	11.9		0.45%
2000	48.5	28.0	8.3	12.2		0.54%
2001	63.7	39.6	10.3	13.8		0.66%
2002	88.8	62.0	16.8	10.0		0.84%
2003	132.4	93.2	24.3	14.9		1.13%
2003b	213.3	131.4	34.3	38.2	9.3	1.82%

Ratio simulated/actual income tax revenues

	Total receipts	Wage income receipts	Busines income receipts	Capital income receipts	Other receipts	Total receipts
			(billions current yuans)			(% GDP)
1996	115%					
1997	123%					
1998	111%					
1999	88%					
2000	73%	99%	63%	64%		
2001	64%	96%	64%	40%		
2002	73%	110%	91%	26%		
2003	93%	126%	122%	39%		
2003b	151%	177%	172%	100%	100%	

Sources: Actual receipts: China Tax Yearbook, various issues (1997–2006); Simulated receipts: authors' computations using urban household surveys tabulations (see Table 2A.6).

Notes: Simulated receipts for 1996–2003 have been computed by applying the relevant tax schedule to the individual distribution of wage income, business income, and capital income estimated from urban household survey tabulations and reported in Tables 2A.3, 2A.4, and 2A.5. The 2003b estimates have been computed by inflating capital and other income so as to match actual tax receipts, and by inflating survey-based top decile wages and business incomes by 20%, so as to obtain a realistic Pareto coefficient for the wage distribution.

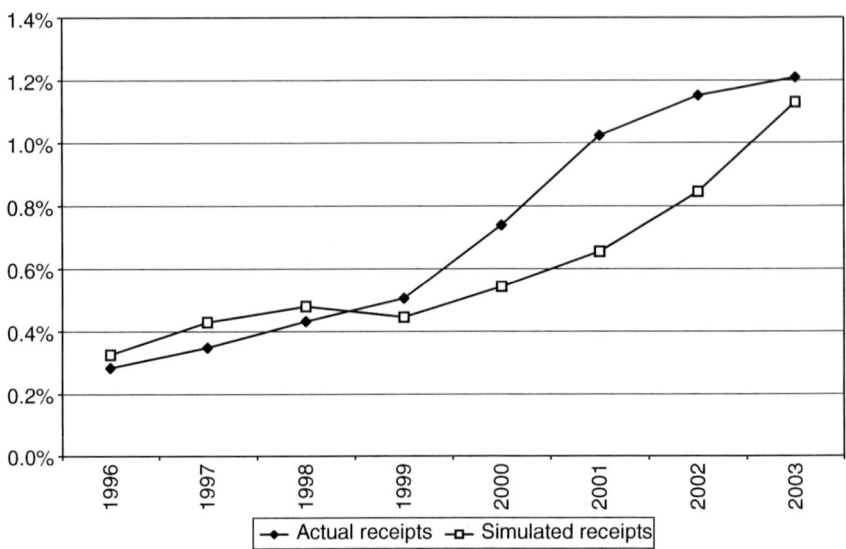

Figure 2.9 Simulated versus actual income tax revenues as a fraction of GDP in China, 1996–2003

Sources: Actual tax receipts from China Tax Yearbook; Simulated tax receipts were computed by applying income tax schedules to household survey income data (Data Appendix, Table 2A.3).

business income and wage income have an excellent reporting rate in household surveys, and that the tax law is reasonably well applied: almost all business income earners and wage earners who are supposed to pay the income tax do pay it and are charged the right rate.

Such an interpretation might be misleading, however. There are good reasons to believe that top business incomes and top wages are under-reported in NSB household surveys, in which case the fact that theoretical receipts (based upon under-reported top business incomes and wages) and actual receipts coincide merely reflects the fact that the collection rate is much less than 100 per cent. If we adjust top survey wages and business incomes so as to obtain reasonable Pareto coefficients for the distribution,[18] we find that theoretical receipts for wage and business income are equal to 170–80 per cent of actual receipts (see Table 2.3), i.e. the tax collection rate for wage and business income is less than 60 per cent. Although the problem is probably less severe than many observers tend to assume, these illustrative (and highly uncertain) computations suggest that there does exist a tax collection problem in China.

---

[18] In order to obtain Pareto coefficients in line with what we observe in the most egalitarian Western countries, NSB coefficients (and therefore top decile wages and business income) need to be raised by about 20%: the Pareto coefficient is around 1.4 in Chinese survey tabulations in the early 2000s, while it is at least 1.6–1.7 in Western countries. This is of course purely illustrative, as we have no reason to believe that the true Chinese Pareto coefficient is the same as in the West.

It is also interesting to note that actual receipts have increased at a significantly higher rate than theoretical receipts during the 1996–2001 period. One interpretation could be that tax collection has improved. Another interpretation is that household surveys underestimate not only the levels of top incomes, but also the upward trend in top income shares. In order to get a sense of the likely magnitude of this effect, we computed by how much the upward trend in top income shares needs to be scaled up in order to ensure that the trend in theoretical receipts does match the trend in actual receipts. We find that the 2001 top 1 per cent share should be scaled up by about 35 per cent relatively to the top 1 per cent share in 1996, which is substantial.

Although there is some uncertainty about the quality of tax collection and survey data, actual and theoretical tax receipts both show that income tax receipts (as a fraction of GDP) have increased substantially during the 1990s and 2000s. The contrast with India is particularly striking: while Indian income tax revenues have stagnated around 0.5–0.6 per cent of GDP during the 1990s, Chinese income tax revenues have been multiplied by more than 10, from less than 0.1 per cent of GDP in the early 1990s to over 1.2 per cent of GDP in 2003 (see Figure 2.10). The stagnation of Indian tax revenues reflects the fact that tax rates have been continuously reduced (see Table 2.2) and that the proportion of individuals subject to tax has increased only modestly (see Figure 2.7). The substantial rise in Chinese tax revenues reflects the facts that tax rates have remained the same (see Table 2.1) and that the proportion of individuals subject to tax has increased enormously (see Figure 2.7).

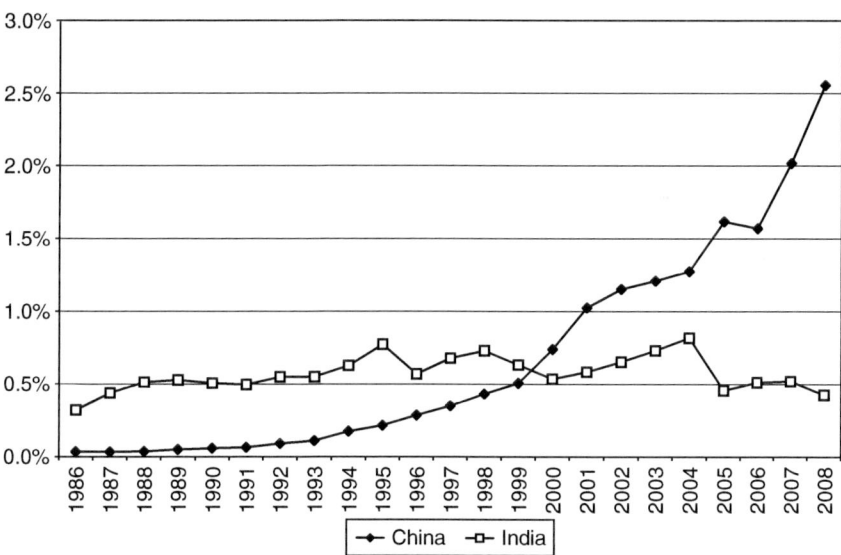

Figure 2.10 Income tax revenues as a fraction of GDP in China and India, 1986–2008

Sources: China: authors' computations using tax receipts data and houshold survey tabulations (Data Appendix, Table 2A.7, col. (15)); India: authors' computations using income tax returns data (sources listed in Chapter 1, Table 1A. 1).

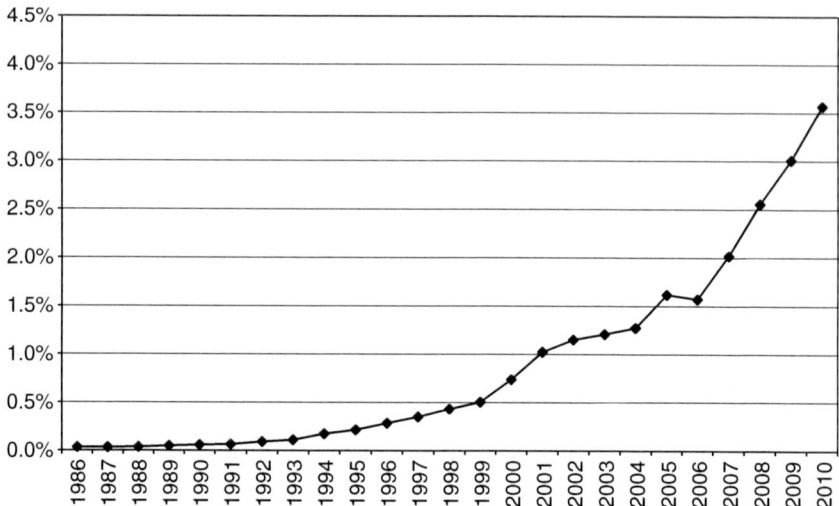

Figure 2.11 Projected income tax revenues (as a fraction of GDP), 1986–2010
Source: Authors' computations using household survey tabulations (Data Appendix, Table 2A.7, col. (15)).

Note that Chinese tax revenues would be substantially larger in the absence of a preferential tax treatment given to top wage earners over top business and capital income earners. We computed that if the business income tax schedule was applied to wage income as well, then Chinese income tax revenues in 2001 would be more than 3 per cent of GDP (instead of 1 per cent). Although this preferential tax treatment of wage income might raise serious political problems in the medium run (as independent workers feel more and more disadvantaged as compared to top wage earners in large firms), as it did in other countries where similar preferential tax treatment was applied, removing this legal provision is however unnecessary to ensure the growth of Chinese income tax revenues. Because of the phenomenal growth in average incomes (and even more so of top incomes), income tax revenues should make much more than 1 per cent of GDP in 2010. According to our projections, which are based on the assumption that tax law will not be changed after 2004 and that income trends will remain the same as in the 1996–2003 period, income tax revenues in China should make about 4.1 per cent in GDP by 2010 (see Figure 2.11).[19]

The assumption that the exemption threshold will not be raised in the short run does not seem unreasonable, given that the 2004 increase in the exemption threshold was fairly high (from 12,000 to 14,400 yuans, i.e. 20 per cent) and that inflation is currently very close to 0 per cent. Moreover our projected tax revenues

[19] We did not make similar projections for India, first because it depends a lot on how tax law will evolve (if exemption levels are increased as much as during the 1990s, then revenues won't increase very much), next because available income data are poorer than in China (we do not know much about incomes immediately below the current exemption threshold).

Table 2.4 Income tax revenue in historical and international perspective

	GDP/ capita (PPP 2001 $)	Total tax revenues (% GDP)	Income tax revenue (% GDP)	Income tax revenue (% total tax revenue)	% population subject to the income tax
United States 1914	6,700	8.2%	0.1%	1.2%	0.9%
United States 1950	13,300	20.7%	5.8%	28.0%	85.0%
United States 2000	36,100	31.8%	10.3%	32.4%	95.3%
France 1914	4,500	12.6%	0.1%	0.8%	1.7%
France 1950	7,400	25.5%	1.9%	7.5%	32.1%
France 2000	27,200	46.2%	7.3%	15.8%	90.0%
China 1990	1,800	15.2%	0.1%	0.4%	0.0%
China 2000	3,900	15.1%	0.7%	4.9%	9.4%
China 2015	10,300	23.3%	8.9%	38.2%	21.3%
India 1990	1,600	10.1%	0.5%	5.0%	0.9%
India 2000	2,200	9.1%	0.5%	5.9%	2.9%
India 2015	3,600	9.1%	0.5%	5.5%	2.9%

Sources: National accounts and tax statistics. USA: see Piketty and Saez (2003). France: see Piketty (2003). China: see this chapter. India: Chapter 1 and this chapter (total tax revenues for China and India 1990 and 2000 come from WDI database; the 2000–15 rise in total tax revenues is assumed to come solely from the income tax).

estimates should be viewed as a lower bound, first because we assumed that the survey-based trends and levels in top shares were not underestimated (in particular we did not make the adjustment reported in Figure 2.9), and next because we assumed that there would be no improvement in tax collection. In other words, there are good reasons to believe that the income tax will raise at least 4 per cent of GDP in China by 2010.

If this happens, then China will have gone through its fiscal revolution. As Table 2.4 illustrates, moving from an elite income tax raising less than 1 per cent of GDP to a mass income tax raising around 4–5 per cent of GDP is exactly the kind of process through which Western countries have gone during the 1914–50 period (when their income levels were similar to current Chinese levels). Although Indian income tax revenues will probably increase during the coming years, the prospects for India look less good, because of both lower income growth and higher bracket indexation. One reason why India faces more difficulties than China in making its income tax a mass tax might also be that the proportion of formal wage earners in the labour force is ridiculously low in India.[20]

Finally, note that according to our projections Chinese income tax revenues will exceed 10 per cent of GDP by 2015, with over 85 per cent of the urban workforce paying the income tax. This is again assuming fixed income trends, and most importantly no nominal change in income tax schedules until 2015, which seems very unlikely over such a long time period. As the income tax becomes

[20] See, e.g., Tendulkar (2003).

larger and starts hitting the majority of the population, it is likely that the Chinese authorities will need to start adjusting exemption thresholds and tax brackets in line with inflation and real growth.

2.5 CONCLUDING COMMENTS

One might be tempted to conclude from this chapter that the high growth performance of the Chinese economy is going to solve every problem, including the fiscal modernization problem, and that there is nothing else to worry about. We indeed found that due to high income growth and low bracket indexation, income tax revenues are currently booming in China, and that they should exceed 4 per cent of GDP by 2010 (assuming constant tax law and income trends). The prospects look much less promising in India, where the income tax will probably remain an elite tax (rather than a mass tax) in the coming years.

The main conclusion that we draw from this chapter, however, is that there is a lot policy makers and economists can do in order to improve the functioning and implications of progressive income taxation in countries like China and India. Given that income taxation is about to become something big, it is urgent to put income tax reform at the top of the policy agenda. For instance, China will not be able to under-index its exemption threshold forever, and the preferential tax treatment of wage earners will need to be addressed at some point. Next, there is clearly a problem with income tax collection in China (although our estimates suggest that it is less massive than is sometimes assumed). At the very least, China's tax authorities should start compiling and publishing detailed income tax tabulations by income bracket and tax liability (which every other country in the world with an income tax actually does), so that the tax collection problem can be properly evaluated and addressed.

APPENDIX 2A: TABLES OF SOURCES AND RESULTS

This appendix contains Table 2A.1 with details of the reference totals used, Tables 2A.2 and 2A.3 with summary statistics from the household surveys, Tables 2A.4 to 2A.6 with results on income levels and shares, and Tables 2A.7 and 2A.8 on the income tax simulations.

Table 2A.1 Reference totals for population, GDP, and survey income in China and India, 1986–2005

	China												India						
	(1)	(2)	(3)	(4)	(5)	(6)	(7)	(8)	(9)	(10)	(11)	(12)	(13)	(14)	(15)	(16)	(17)	(18)	(19)
				GDP/capita				Income/capita (NSB household survey)							GDP/capita			Consumption/capita (NSS household survey)	
	Population (millions)	GDP billions cur. yuans	CPI (1986 = 100)	(cur. yuans)	(2001 yuans)	(2001 PPP $)	Urban population (%)	Urban (cur. yuans)	Rural (cur. yuans)	Urban (2001 yuans)	Rural (2001 yuans)	Total (2001 yuans)	Population (millions)	CPI (1986 = 100)	(current Rs)	(2001 Rs)	(2001 PPP $)	(current Rs)	(2001 Rs)
1986	1,075	1,020	100	949	3,001	1,654	24.5%	927	424	2,932	1,340	1,730	739	100	3,318	11,934	1,380	1,655	5,954
1987	1,093	1,196	107	1,094	3,228	1,780	25.3%	1,016	463	2,996	1,364	1,778	755	106	3,681	12,544	1,450		6,200
1988	1,110	1,493	127	1,345	3,340	1,841	25.8%	1,212	545	3,010	1,354	1,781	771	115	4,027	12,620	1,459	1,978	6,210
1989	1,127	1,691	151	1,500	3,149	1,736	26.2%	1,369	602	2,873	1,263	1,685	788	125	4,481	12,909	1,492	2,156	6,265
1990	1,143	1,855	155	1,622	3,304	1,822	26.4%	1,549	686	3,156	1,398	1,862	805	137	5,210	13,722	1,586	2,379	6,463
1991	1,158	2,162	161	1,866	3,672	2,024	26.9%	1,738	709	3,420	1,394	1,940	822	145	5,890	14,611	1,689	2,605	6,463
1992	1,172	2,664	171	2,273	4,206	2,318	27.5%	2,129	784	3,938	1,450	2,134	839	158	6,765	15,400	1,780	2,810	6,396
1993	1,185	3,463	196	2,922	4,718	2,601	28.0%	2,673	922	4,316	1,488	2,279	856	180	7,636	15,267	1,765	3,348	6,692
1994	1,199	4,676	243	3,901	5,070	2,795	28.5%	3,706	1,221	4,816	1,587	2,507	872	201	8,579	15,343	1,774	3,441	6,154
1995	1,211	5,848	284	4,828	5,367	2,959	29.0%	4,459	1,578	4,957	1,754	2,684	891	214	9,643	16,215	1,875	3,936	6,618
1996	1,224	6,788	308	5,547	5,692	3,138	30.5%	4,991	1,926	5,122	1,977	2,935	908	236	11,122	16,969	1,962	4,312	6,579
1997	1,236	7,446	317	6,023	6,013	3,315	31.9%	5,379	2,090	5,369	2,086	3,134	927	260	12,750	17,648	2,040	4,915	6,802
1998	1,248	7,835	314	6,280	6,322	3,485	33.4%	5,754	2,162	5,792	2,177	3,382	943	283	14,443	18,344	2,121		
1999	1,258	8,191	310	6,512	6,649	3,666	34.8%	6,183	2,210	6,313	2,257	3,668	959	304	15,804	18,731	2,165	5,518	6,540
2000	1,267	8,934	312	7,049	7,133	3,932	36.2%	6,557	2,253	6,636	2,280	3,858	975	344	18,078	18,922	2,188		
2001	1,276	9,723	316	7,618	7,618	4,200	37.7%	7,113	2,366	7,113	2,366	4,154	991	360	19,562	19,562	2,261	7,362	7,362
2002	1,285	10,513	315	8,180	8,205	4,523	39.2%	8,054	2,740	8,078	2,748	4,835	1,008	391	21,900	20,126	2,327		
2003	1,294	11,721	322	9,056	8,905	4,909	40.7%	8,913	2,991	8,765	2,941	5,309	1,026	426	24,518	20,707	2,394		
2001/1986	1.19	9.53	3.16	8.03	2.54	2.54	1.54	7.67	5.58	2.43	1.77	2.40	1.34	3.60	5.90	1.64	1.64	4.45	1.24
	1.2%	16.2%	8.0%	14.9%	6.4%	6.4%	2.9%	14.6%	12.1%	6.1%	3.9%	6.0%	2.0%	8.9%	12.6%	3.3%	3.3%	10.5%	1.4%
2003/1996	1.06	1.73	1.04	1.63	1.56	1.56	1.33	1.79	1.55	1.71	1.49	1.81	1.09	1.53	1.76	1.15	1.15	1.71	1.12
	0.8%	8.1%	0.6%	7.3%	6.6%	6.6%	4.2%	8.6%	6.5%	8.0%	5.8%	8.8%	1.8%	8.8%	12.0%	2.9%	2.9%	11.3%	2.3%

Sources: China: Population and NSB household survey income: China Statistical Yearbook 2002 (SSB); GDP and CPI: World Development Indicators 2005 data base (World Bank); India: see Chapter 1, Table 1A.2). Incomes expressed in 2001 dollars have been converted into 2001 $ by applying the 2001 average PPP conversion factor (1$ = 1.814 yuans) (average 2001 exchange rate: 1$ = 8.270 yuans). Incomes expressed in 2001 Rs have been converted into 2001 Rs by applying the 2001 average PPP conversion factor (1$ = 8.65 Rs) (average 2001 exchange rate: 1$ = 43.16 Rs) (source: WDI).

Notes: Chinese data refers to calendar years, whereas Indian data refers to fiscal years (i.e. 1986 refers to 1985–6,..., and 2001 refers to 2000–1). The rows 2003/1996 and 2001/1986 provide interyear ratios and corresponding annual growth rates.

Table 2A.2 China's urban household income surveys (NSB), 1986–2003: summary statistics

	Household tabulations (all households)									Individual tabulations (all individuals with positive income)					
	(1)	(2)	(3)	(4)	(5)	(6)	(7)	(8)	(9)	(10)	(11)	(12)	(13)	(14)	(15)
						Income composition by source (% of total income)							Income composition by source (% of total income)		
	Sampling rate (1/.)	Number of observations (households)	Average household income (current yuans)	Average household size	Average individual income [=(3)/(4)]	Wage income	Property income	Transfer income	Business income	Number of observations (individuals)	Wage income	Average individual income (current yuans)	Property income	Transfer income	Business income
1986	5,579	12,437	3,523	3.8	927	83.2%	0.6%	15.4%	0.9%	23,584	1,394	100.0%	0.0%	0.0%	0.0%
1987	5,522	13,189	3,860	3.8	1,016	83.3%	0.6%	15.1%	1.0%	24,643	1,464	100.0%	0.0%	0.0%	0.0%
1988	5,785	13,761	4,363	3.6	1,212	78.8%	0.6%	19.3%	1.2%	24,054	1,963	88.9%	0.4%	9.6%	1.1%
1989	6,217	13,199	4,927	3.6	1,369	77.0%	0.9%	21.0%	1.2%	22,829	2,231	88.3%	0.4%	10.0%	1.3%
1990	6,306	13,681	5,422	3.5	1,549	77.6%	1.1%	20.4%	0.9%	23,691	2,438	89.5%	0.6%	8.9%	1.0%
1991	6,627	13,849	5,910	3.4	1,738	77.6%	1.1%	20.2%	1.0%	23,838	2,688	89.5%	0.6%	8.8%	1.1%
1992	5,773	16,890	7,025	3.3	2,129	74.2%	1.5%	16.5%	1.1%	29,607	3,152	85.8%	0.8%	4.6%	1.0%
1993	6,010	16,725	8,822	3.3	2,673	73.0%	1.6%	17.0%	1.2%	28,634	4,006	85.0%	0.9%	4.4%	1.2%
1994	6,322	16,889	11,859	3.2	3,706	72.0%	1.9%	18.4%	1.4%	27,728	5,462	85.7%	0.9%	4.2%	1.4%
1995	6,508	16,891	14,270	3.2	4,459	73.3%	2.0%	18.0%	1.4%	27,504	6,614	87.2%	0.9%	3.9%	1.5%
1996	6,898	16,900	15,971	3.2	4,991	72.7%	2.1%	18.1%	1.6%	27,508	7,407	86.7%	1.0%	3.9%	1.8%
1997	7,316	16,850	17,213	3.2	5,379	76.3%	2.4%	19.3%	2.1%	26,698	8,020	92.3%	1.1%	4.3%	2.3%
1998	7,895	17,000	17,837	3.1	5,754	74.9%	2.4%	20.5%	2.2%	26,326	8,274	92.2%	1.0%	4.3%	2.5%
1999	8,350	16,900	19,167	3.1	6,183	73.9%	2.2%	21.6%	2.3%	25,743	8,955	91.9%	1.0%	4.5%	2.7%
2000	8,762	16,900	20,327	3.1	6,557	70.7%	2.0%	23.9%	3.3%	23,761	9,825	90.4%	0.9%	4.7%	4.0%
2001	9,120	17,000	22,051	3.1	7,113	70.0%	2.0%	24.5%	3.4%	23,532	10,787	90.2%	0.9%	4.7%	4.3%
2002	3,645	46,028	24,162	3.0	8,054	73.5%	1.2%	26.8%	4.5%	69,222	11,958	89.6%	0.7%	4.2%	5.5%
2003	3,553	49,372	26,740	3.0	8,913	73.8%	1.6%	26.1%	5.2%	73,122	13,383	88.7%	0.8%	4.2%	6.3%

Source: Authors' computations using annual tabulations extracted from China's Urban Household Income Surveys (NSB), 1986–2003.

Note: The samples used by NSB urban household surveys are designed so as to be representative of urban China (with approximately uniform sampling rates). The implicit sampling rate was computed by using the demographic data reported in Table 2A.1. E.g. $3.8 \times 12{,}437 = 47{,}261$ individuals (with or without positive income, including children) are covered by the 1986 survey, and total urban population of China was equal to $24.5\% \times 1{,}075$ millions $= 264$ millions in 1986, hence a sampling rate equal to (1/.) 264 millions/47,261 $= 5{,}579$. Note that total income reported in household-level distributions is always 30–40% larger than total income reported in individual-level distributions (e.g., in 1986, $5{,}579 \times 12{,}437 \times 3{,}523 = 244$ billions yuans, while $5{,}579 \times 23{,}584 \times 1{,}394 = 183$ billions yuans). This is due to the fact that some forms of income cannot be attributed to a specific individual within the household (this is particularly true for transfer and property income; in 1986–1987, only wage income was individualized). The urban per capita income series was computed using household-level data (e.g., in 1986, $3{,}523/3.8 = 927$) and coincide with the urban per capita income series published in China Statistical Yearbook.

Table 2A.3 China's urban household income surveys (NSB), 1986–2003: total income aggregates

| | Household tabulations | | | | | Individual tabulations | | | | | | |
| | (1) | (2) | (3) | (4) | (5) | (6) | (7) | (8) | (9) | (10) | N. wage earners | N. bus. inc. earners |
Billions current yuans	Total income	Wage income	Property income	Transfer income	Business income	Total income	Wage income	Property income	Transfer income	Business income	(millions workers)	
1986	244.4	203.3	1.5	37.7	2.1	183.4	183.4	0.0	0.0	0.0	145.8	1.5
1987	281.1	234.2	1.6	42.5	2.9	199.2	199.2	0.0	0.0	0.0	160.0	2.0
1988	347.3	273.8	2.0	67.2	4.1	273.1	242.7	1.0	26.2	3.1	139.5	2.1
1989	404.3	311.3	3.5	84.9	4.8	316.6	279.5	1.3	31.7	4.0	139.6	2.1
1990	467.8	363.0	5.0	95.5	4.3	364.3	326.2	2.0	32.5	3.6	148.9	1.8
1991	542.4	421.1	6.2	109.5	5.6	424.7	380.2	2.5	37.3	4.7	156.6	2.1
1992	685.0	508.1	10.4	113.1	7.3	538.8	462.0	4.1	24.6	5.3	161.2	2.3
1993	886.8	647.4	14.6	151.0	10.9	689.4	586.2	6.4	30.3	8.3	161.6	2.7
1994	1,266.3	912.1	24.1	232.7	17.2	957.5	821.0	8.7	40.0	13.8	167.0	3.2
1995	1,568.6	1,149.1	31.1	282.9	21.4	1,183.8	1,031.7	10.8	45.9	17.9	173.7	3.2
1996	1,861.9	1,354.1	40.0	336.5	30.5	1,405.5	1,218.4	13.9	54.5	25.4	182.8	4.1
1997	2,121.9	1,619.0	50.0	409.0	43.9	1,566.6	1,445.2	17.7	67.7	35.9	201.9	5.5
1998	2,394.0	1,794.2	57.1	490.5	52.1	1,719.7	1,586.1	17.9	73.1	42.7	216.9	6.3
1999	2,704.9	1,999.0	59.5	585.2	61.2	1,924.9	1,768.4	18.8	86.5	51.2	223.2	6.8
2000	3,010.1	2,129.2	60.8	720.8	99.3	2,045.5	1,848.7	18.9	95.5	82.5	216.7	10.1
2001	3,418.9	2,393.7	69.0	838.4	117.9	2,315.1	2,087.9	20.5	107.7	99.1	221.9	10.9
2002	4,053.5	2,977.4	50.1	1,085.2	182.6	3,017.0	2,702.4	20.0	127.4	167.2	249.0	15.3
2003	4,690.3	3,463.2	74.3	1,225.5	242.4	3,476.6	3,084.2	27.4	145.1	219.9	258.8	18.1

Source: Authors' computations using annual tabulations extracted from China's Urban Household Income Surveys (NSB), 1986–2003.

Note: The total income aggregates reported on this table were computed using the series on sampling rates, number of observations, average income and income composition by source reported in Table 2A.2 (see example in the note to Table 2A.2). The numbers of wage earners and business income earners reported on this table were computed by dividing the relevant total income aggregate (household tabulation) by average individual income (average wage by wage earner and average business income by business income earner are approximately equal to average individual income by positive income earner, due to the fact that income composition shares do not vary very much by income bracket: business income is somewhat more prevalent both in low income brackets and high income brackets, and both effects approximately cancel out; for simplicity we assume strict equality): e.g, for 1986, 203.3 billions/1,394 = 145.8 millions wage earners.

Table 2A.4 Top fractiles incomes levels in China, 1986–2003 (household distribution)

Current yuans	P0-100 (1)	P90-100 (2)	P95-100 (3)	P99-100 (4)	P99.5-100 (5)	P99.9-100 (6)	P0-90 (7)	P90-95 (8)	P95-99 (9)	P99-99.5 (10)	P99.5-99.9 (11)	P99.9-100 (12)	P90 (13)	P95 (14)	P99 (15)	P99.5 (16)	P99.9 (17)
1986	3,523	6,577	7,463	9,869	11,214	16,794	3,183	5,691	6,861	8,525	9,820	16,794	5,377	6,102	8,163	8,870	12,019
1987	3,860	7,126	8,117	10,603	12,051	18,206	3,497	6,135	7,496	9,154	10,512	18,206	5,787	6,592	8,644	9,825	13,095
1988	4,363	8,240	9,445	12,925	14,743	19,554	3,932	7,035	8,575	11,106	13,541	19,554	6,493	7,599	10,520	12,006	16,544
1989	4,927	9,719	11,390	16,235	18,691	24,422	4,395	8,048	10,178	13,780	17,258	24,422	7,518	8,701	12,936	14,955	20,697
1990	5,422	10,697	12,546	18,106	20,730	28,026	4,836	8,849	11,156	15,482	18,907	28,026	8,238	9,661	14,459	16,830	22,601
1991	5,910	11,719	13,840	20,393	24,425	38,296	5,265	9,598	12,202	16,360	20,957	38,296	8,893	10,549	15,228	17,766	27,608
1992	7,025	14,793	17,877	27,774	33,538	52,433	6,162	11,709	15,402	22,010	28,814	52,433	10,745	12,989	20,285	24,348	37,415
1993	8,822	19,916	24,219	37,083	44,514	67,361	7,589	15,612	21,003	29,653	38,802	67,361	14,150	17,664	27,353	32,541	51,522
1994	11,859	27,716	33,812	51,671	60,127	84,362	10,097	21,621	29,347	43,215	54,068	84,362	19,517	24,281	39,493	48,388	66,094
1995	14,270	32,819	39,874	59,652	69,683	96,637	12,209	25,765	34,930	49,621	62,944	96,637	23,360	29,195	46,478	54,078	78,096
1996	15,971	37,171	45,226	68,658	80,714	110,747	13,616	29,115	39,368	56,602	73,206	110,747	26,314	32,618	52,220	62,084	90,099
1997	17,213	40,959	49,981	78,278	93,016	128,273	14,574	31,936	42,907	63,540	84,202	128,273	28,705	35,873	57,865	70,352	100,194
1998	17,837	42,435	52,154	82,151	98,688	138,349	15,103	32,717	44,654	65,613	88,773	138,349	29,766	36,618	60,371	72,000	113,345
1999	19,167	46,368	57,067	89,719	107,562	156,381	16,145	35,669	48,904	71,876	95,357	156,381	32,350	40,070	64,924	80,357	120,896
2000	20,327	49,701	60,733	93,669	110,864	158,301	17,063	38,669	52,499	76,475	99,004	158,301	35,118	43,537	69,680	85,650	123,450
2001	22,051	54,826	67,416	105,871	126,760	193,819	18,410	42,236	57,802	84,983	109,995	193,819	37,847	47,802	77,630	94,825	142,272
2002	24,162	62,262	77,707	126,797	155,209	255,955	19,929	46,817	65,435	98,385	130,022	255,955	41,565	53,570	89,225	110,686	176,029
2003	26,740	72,733	92,883	160,402	202,621	362,638	21,629	52,583	76,003	118,182	162,617	362,638	46,502	61,252	105,698	135,858	232,725
2001 yuans	P0-100 (1)	P90-100 (2)	P95-100 (3)	P99-100 (4)	P99.5-100 (5)	P99.9-100 (6)	P0-90 (7)	P90-95 (8)	P95-99 (9)	P99-99.5 (10)	P99.5-99.9 (11)	P99.9-100 (12)	P90 (13)	P95 (14)	P99 (15)	P99.5 (16)	P99.9 (17)
1986	11,140	20,798	23,600	31,212	35,465	53,110	10,067	17,996	21,698	26,958	31,054	53,110	17,006	19,297	25,815	28,050	38,008
1987	11,385	21,017	23,941	31,272	35,544	53,698	10,315	18,094	22,108	27,000	31,006	53,698	17,068	19,443	25,495	28,978	38,623
1988	10,837	20,468	23,462	32,106	36,623	48,574	9,767	17,475	21,301	27,588	33,636	48,574	16,129	18,877	26,132	29,824	41,096
1989	10,344	20,402	23,910	34,082	39,236	51,268	9,226	16,895	21,367	28,928	36,228	51,268	15,782	18,266	27,156	31,393	43,448
1990	11,045	21,790	25,555	36,880	42,226	57,086	9,851	18,025	22,724	31,535	38,511	57,086	16,779	19,679	29,452	34,282	46,036
1991	11,627	23,054	27,226	40,117	48,049	75,336	10,357	18,881	24,004	32,184	41,227	75,336	17,495	20,751	29,957	34,949	54,311

(continued)

Table 2A.4 Continued

2001 yuans	P0–100 (1)	P90–100 (2)	P95–100 (3)	P99–100 (4)	P99.5–100 (5)	P99.9–100 (6)	P0–90 (7)	P90–95 (8)	P95–99 (9)	P99–99.5 (10)	P99.5–99.9 (11)	P99.9–100 (12)	P90 (13)	P95 (14)	P99 (15)	P99.5 (16)	P99.9 (17)
1992	12,996	27,365	33,070	51,380	62,042	96,997	11,400	21,660	28,493	40,717	53,304	96,997	19,878	24,029	37,526	45,041	69,215
1993	14,242	32,153	39,101	59,870	71,866	108,752	12,252	25,205	33,909	47,874	62,645	108,752	22,844	28,518	44,161	52,536	83,181
1994	15,411	36,018	43,939	67,147	78,135	109,629	13,121	28,096	38,137	56,159	70,262	109,629	25,363	31,553	51,322	62,881	85,890
1995	15,864	36,484	44,327	66,313	77,464	107,429	13,573	28,642	38,830	55,162	69,973	107,429	25,969	32,455	51,668	60,117	86,818
1996	16,391	38,146	46,413	70,460	82,832	113,653	13,973	29,879	40,402	58,088	75,127	113,653	27,005	33,474	53,590	63,714	92,464
1997	17,182	40,886	49,893	78,139	92,852	128,045	14,548	31,880	42,831	63,427	84,053	128,045	28,654	35,809	57,762	70,227	100,017
1998	17,957	42,721	52,505	82,704	99,352	139,280	15,205	32,937	44,955	66,055	89,371	139,280	29,966	36,865	60,777	72,485	114,108
1999	19,572	47,347	58,271	91,613	109,832	159,682	16,486	36,422	49,936	73,394	97,370	159,682	33,033	40,916	66,295	82,053	123,448
2000	20,571	50,297	61,462	94,793	112,194	160,201	17,268	39,133	53,129	77,393	100,192	160,201	35,539	44,059	70,516	86,678	124,931
2001	22,051	54,826	67,416	105,871	126,760	193,819	18,410	42,236	57,802	84,983	109,995	193,819	37,847	47,802	77,630	94,825	142,272
2002	24,235	62,450	77,941	127,178	155,676	256,725	19,989	46,958	65,632	98,681	130,413	256,725	41,690	53,732	89,494	111,019	176,559
2003	26,294	71,521	91,336	157,730	199,246	356,598	21,269	51,707	74,737	116,214	159,908	356,598	45,727	60,232	103,938	133,595	228,848
2001/ 1986	1.98	2.64	2.86	3.39	3.57	3.65	1.83	2.35	2.66	3.15	3.54	3.65	2.23	2.48	3.01	3.38	3.74
	4.7%	6.7%	7.2%	8.5%	8.9%	9.0%	4.1%	5.9%	6.8%	8.0%	8.8%	9.0%	5.5%	6.2%	7.6%	8.5%	9.2%
2003/ 1996	1.60	1.87	1.97	2.24	2.41	3.14	1.52	1.73	1.85	2.00	2.13	3.14	1.69	1.80	1.94	2.10	2.47
	7.0%	9.4%	10.2%	12.2%	13.4%	17.7%	6.2%	8.1%	9.2%	10.4%	11.4%	17.7%	7.8%	8.8%	9.9%	11.2%	13.8%

Source: Authors' computations using annual tabulations extracted from China's Urban Household Income Surveys (NSB), 1986–2003.

Note: Due to a discontinuity in NSB methodology and sampling technique between 2001 and 2002 (large increase in sample size), we adjusted 2002/2001 income growth rates on the basis of average 2001/2000 and 2003/ 2002 observed rates.

Table 2A.5 Top fractiles incomes levels in China, 1986–2003 (individual distribution)

Current yuans	P0–100 (1)	P90–100 (2)	P95–100 (3)	P99–100 (4)	P99.5–100 (5)	P99.9–100 (6)	P0–90 (7)	P90–95 (8)	P95–99 (9)	P99–99.5 (10)	P99.5–99.9 (11)	P99.9–100 (12)	P90 (13)	P95 (14)	P99 (15)	P99.5 (16)	P99.9 (17)
1986	1,394	2,421	2,732	3,691	4,201	6,539	1,280	2,110	2,492	3,182	3,616	6,539	1,999	2,256	3,003	3,417	4,487
1987	1,464	2,607	2,920	3,905	4,350	6,802	1,337	2,293	2,673	3,461	3,737	6,802	2,150	2,392	3,200	3,112	3,942
1988	1,963	3,767	4,354	6,564	7,927	12,254	1,762	3,180	3,802	5,201	6,845	12,254	2,946	3,253	4,837	5,715	9,090
1989	2,231	4,404	5,226	7,694	9,059	12,521	1,989	3,582	4,609	6,329	8,193	12,521	3,361	3,931	5,862	6,924	10,411
1990	2,438	4,715	5,537	8,118	9,505	13,822	2,185	3,894	4,892	6,731	8,425	13,822	3,623	4,254	6,218	7,398	10,144
1991	2,688	5,243	6,215	9,095	10,627	16,355	2,404	4,272	5,495	7,562	9,195	16,355	3,978	4,667	7,086	8,163	11,534
1992	3,152	6,502	7,891	12,492	15,057	23,741	2,780	5,114	6,741	9,927	12,886	23,741	4,771	5,636	8,893	10,993	16,345
1993	4,006	9,073	11,083	17,378	20,684	29,869	3,443	7,062	9,510	14,073	18,388	29,869	6,410	7,890	12,653	15,539	23,606
1994	5,462	12,876	15,725	24,122	28,495	41,831	4,638	10,027	13,626	19,749	25,161	41,831	9,107	11,301	18,244	21,840	31,543
1995	6,614	15,412	18,860	28,959	33,903	46,050	5,636	11,964	16,336	24,015	30,866	46,050	10,842	13,440	22,012	27,019	37,361
1996	7,407	17,760	21,902	34,773	41,745	63,790	6,257	13,618	18,684	27,800	36,234	63,790	12,309	15,386	25,397	30,747	46,984
1997	8,020	19,875	24,566	39,209	47,105	72,176	6,703	15,184	20,905	31,312	40,837	72,176	13,603	17,208	28,860	34,615	53,039
1998	8,274	20,450	25,226	40,076	47,784	71,891	6,921	15,674	21,513	32,368	41,757	71,891	14,082	17,650	29,905	35,657	53,646
1999	8,955	22,333	27,492	42,703	50,839	76,218	7,468	17,174	23,689	34,567	44,494	76,218	15,510	19,441	31,959	38,048	57,042
2000	9,825	25,082	31,136	49,525	60,098	94,189	8,129	19,028	26,539	38,951	51,576	94,189	17,154	21,569	35,698	43,320	67,893
2001	10,787	27,950	34,689	54,509	65,948	102,635	8,880	21,210	29,734	43,070	56,776	102,635	18,878	24,216	39,529	47,824	74,428
2002	11,958	31,934	39,953	63,654	77,601	122,979	9,739	23,914	34,028	49,706	66,257	122,979	21,073	27,561	45,447	55,394	87,743
2003	13,383	37,386	47,522	78,604	97,474	160,702	10,716	27,250	39,752	59,735	81,667	160,702	23,858	31,793	54,179	67,171	110,690
2001 yuans	P0–100 (1)	P90–100 (2)	P95–100 (3)	P99–100 (4)	P99.5–100 (5)	P99.9–100 (6)	P0–90 (7)	P90–95 (8)	P95–99 (9)	P99–99.5 (10)	P99.5–99.9 (11)	P99.9–100 (12)	P90 (13)	P95 (14)	P99 (15)	P99.5 (16)	P99.9 (17)
1986	4,407	7,656	8,640	11,673	13,284	20,678	4,047	6,673	7,882	10,062	11,436	20,678	6,321	7,134	9,496	10,807	14,189
1987	4,318	7,688	8,612	11,519	12,829	20,062	3,944	6,765	7,885	10,209	11,021	20,062	6,341	7,056	9,437	9,180	11,627
1988	4,875	9,358	10,816	16,306	19,691	30,439	4,377	7,899	9,443	12,921	17,005	30,439	7,318	8,080	12,014	14,195	22,580
1989	4,683	9,245	10,971	16,151	19,016	26,283	4,176	7,519	9,676	13,286	17,200	26,283	7,056	8,252	12,305	14,536	21,856
1990	4,967	9,605	11,278	16,535	19,360	28,154	4,452	7,931	9,964	13,710	17,162	28,154	7,379	8,665	12,666	15,069	20,663
1991	5,288	10,315	12,226	17,891	20,906	32,174	4,730	8,404	10,810	14,876	18,089	32,174	7,826	9,182	13,940	16,058	22,691
1992	5,832	12,029	14,598	23,109	27,854	43,919	5,143	9,460	12,470	18,364	23,838	43,919	8,827	10,426	16,451	20,337	30,236
1993	6,468	14,648	17,894	28,057	33,394	48,223	5,559	11,402	15,353	22,720	29,687	48,223	10,348	12,738	20,429	25,087	38,112
1994	7,098	16,733	20,435	31,347	37,029	54,359	6,028	13,031	17,707	25,664	32,697	54,359	11,835	14,685	23,708	28,382	40,990
1995	7,352	17,134	20,967	32,193	37,689	51,193	6,266	13,300	18,160	26,697	34,313	51,193	12,052	14,941	24,470	30,036	41,534

(continued)

Table 2A.5 Continued

2001 yuans	P0–100 (1)	P90–100 (2)	P95–100 (3)	P99–100 (4)	P99.5–100 (5)	P99.9–100 (6)	P0–90 (7)	P90–95 (8)	P95–99 (9)	P99–99.5 (10)	P99.5–99.9 (11)	P99.9–100 (12)	P90 (13)	P95 (14)	P99 (15)	P99.5 (16)	P99.9 (17)
1996	7,602	18,226	22,477	35,685	42,841	65,465	6,421	13,975	19,175	28,530	37,185	65,465	12,632	15,790	26,064	31,554	48,217
1997	8,006	19,840	24,522	39,139	47,021	72,049	6,691	15,157	20,868	31,257	40,765	72,049	13,579	17,178	28,809	34,554	52,945
1998	8,329	20,588	25,396	40,346	48,106	72,375	6,967	15,779	21,658	32,586	42,038	72,375	14,177	17,769	30,107	35,897	54,007
1999	9,144	22,804	28,072	43,604	51,912	77,827	7,626	17,537	24,189	35,296	45,433	77,827	15,837	19,852	32,633	38,851	58,246
2000	9,942	25,383	31,510	50,119	60,819	95,319	8,227	19,256	26,858	39,418	52,195	95,319	17,360	21,828	36,127	43,840	68,708
2001	10,787	27,950	34,689	54,509	65,948	102,635	8,880	21,210	29,734	43,070	56,776	102,635	18,878	24,216	39,529	47,824	74,428
2002	11,994	32,030	40,074	63,845	77,835	123,349	9,768	23,986	34,131	49,856	66,456	123,349	21,137	27,644	45,583	55,560	88,007
2003	13,160	36,763	46,731	77,295	95,850	158,025	10,537	26,796	39,089	58,740	80,306	158,025	23,461	31,263	53,276	66,052	108,846
2001/ 1986	2.45	3.65	4.01	4.67	4.96	4.96	2.19	3.18	3.77	4.28	4.96	4.96	2.99	3.39	4.16	4.43	5.25
	6.1%	9.0%	9.7%	10.8%	11.3%	11.3%	5.4%	8.0%	9.3%	10.2%	11.3%	11.3%	7.6%	8.5%	10.0%	10.4%	11.7%
2003/ 1996	1.73	2.02	2.08	2.17	2.24	2.41	1.64	1.92	2.04	2.06	2.16	2.41	1.86	1.98	2.04	2.09	2.26
	8.2%	10.5%	11.0%	11.7%	12.2%	13.4%	7.3%	9.7%	10.7%	10.9%	11.6%	13.4%	9.2%	10.3%	10.8%	11.1%	12.3%

Source: Authors' computations using annual tabulations extracted from China's Urban Household Income Surveys (NSB), 1986–2003.

Note: Due to a discontinuity in NSB methodology and sampling technique between 2001 and 2002 (large increase in sample size), we adjusted 2002/2001 income growth rates on the basis of average 2001/2000 and 2003/2002 observed rates.

Table 2A.6 Top fractiles incomes shares in total income in urban China, 1986–2003

Household distribution	P90–100 (1)	P95–100 (2)	P99–100 (3)	P99.5–100 (4)	P99.9–100 (5)	P90–95 (6)	P95–99 (7)	P99–99.5 (8)	P99.5–99.9 (9)	P99.9–100 (10)
1986	18.7%	10.6%	2.8%	1.6%	0.5%	8.1%	7.8%	1.2%	1.1%	0.5%
1987	18.5%	10.5%	2.7%	1.6%	0.5%	7.9%	7.8%	1.2%	1.1%	0.5%
1988	18.9%	10.8%	3.0%	1.7%	0.4%	8.1%	7.9%	1.3%	1.2%	0.4%
1989	19.7%	11.6%	3.3%	1.9%	0.5%	8.2%	8.3%	1.4%	1.4%	0.5%
1990	19.7%	11.6%	3.3%	1.9%	0.5%	8.2%	8.2%	1.4%	1.4%	0.5%
1991	19.8%	11.7%	3.5%	2.1%	0.6%	8.1%	8.3%	1.4%	1.4%	0.6%
1992	21.1%	12.7%	4.0%	2.4%	0.7%	8.3%	8.8%	1.6%	1.6%	0.7%
1993	22.6%	13.7%	4.2%	2.5%	0.8%	8.8%	9.5%	1.7%	1.8%	0.8%
1994	23.4%	14.3%	4.4%	2.5%	0.7%	9.1%	9.9%	1.8%	1.8%	0.7%
1995	23.0%	14.0%	4.2%	2.4%	0.7%	9.0%	9.8%	1.7%	1.8%	0.7%
1996	23.3%	14.2%	4.3%	2.5%	0.7%	9.1%	9.9%	1.8%	1.8%	0.7%
1997	23.8%	14.5%	4.5%	2.7%	0.7%	9.3%	10.0%	1.8%	2.0%	0.7%
1998	23.8%	14.6%	4.6%	2.8%	0.8%	9.2%	10.0%	1.8%	2.0%	0.8%
1999	24.2%	14.9%	4.7%	2.8%	0.8%	9.3%	10.2%	1.9%	2.0%	0.8%
2000	24.5%	14.9%	4.6%	2.7%	0.8%	9.5%	10.3%	1.9%	1.9%	0.8%
2001	24.9%	15.3%	4.8%	2.9%	0.9%	9.6%	10.5%	1.9%	2.0%	0.9%
2002	25.8%	16.1%	5.2%	3.2%	1.1%	9.7%	10.8%	2.0%	2.2%	1.1%
2003	27.2%	17.4%	6.0%	3.8%	1.4%	9.8%	11.4%	2.2%	2.4%	1.4%

Individual distribution	P90–100 (2)	P95–100 (3)	P99–100 (4)	P99.5–100 (5)	P99.9–100 (6)	P90–95 (8)	P95–99 (9)	P99–99.5 (10)	P99.5–99.9 (11)	P99.9–100 (12)
1986	17.4%	9.8%	2.6%	1.5%	0.5%	7.6%	7.2%	1.1%	1.0%	0.5%
1987	17.8%	10.0%	2.7%	1.5%	0.5%	7.8%	7.3%	1.2%	1.0%	0.5%
1988	19.2%	11.1%	3.3%	2.0%	0.6%	8.1%	7.7%	1.3%	1.4%	0.6%
1989	19.7%	11.7%	3.4%	2.0%	0.6%	8.0%	8.3%	1.4%	1.5%	0.6%

(continued)

Table 2A.6 Continued

Individual distribution	P90–100 (1)	P95–100 (2)	P99–100 (3)	P99.5–100 (4)	P99.9–100 (5)	P90–95 (6)	P95–99 (7)	P99–99.5 (8)	P99.5–99.9 (9)	P99.9–100 (10)
1990	19.3%	11.4%	3.3%	1.9%	0.6%	8.0%	8.0%	1.4%	1.4%	0.6%
1991	19.5%	11.6%	3.4%	2.0%	0.6%	7.9%	8.2%	1.4%	1.4%	0.6%
1992	20.6%	12.5%	4.0%	2.4%	0.8%	8.1%	8.6%	1.6%	1.6%	0.8%
1993	22.6%	13.8%	4.3%	2.6%	0.7%	8.8%	9.5%	1.8%	1.8%	0.7%
1994	23.6%	14.4%	4.4%	2.6%	0.8%	9.2%	10.0%	1.8%	1.8%	0.8%
1995	23.3%	14.3%	4.4%	2.6%	0.7%	9.0%	9.9%	1.8%	1.9%	0.7%
1996	24.0%	14.8%	4.7%	2.8%	0.9%	9.2%	10.1%	1.9%	2.0%	0.9%
1997	24.8%	15.3%	4.9%	2.9%	0.9%	9.5%	10.4%	2.0%	2.0%	0.9%
1998	24.7%	15.2%	4.8%	2.9%	0.9%	9.5%	10.4%	2.0%	2.0%	0.9%
1999	24.9%	15.4%	4.8%	2.8%	0.9%	9.6%	10.6%	1.9%	2.0%	0.9%
2000	25.5%	15.8%	5.0%	3.1%	1.0%	9.7%	10.8%	2.0%	2.1%	1.0%
2001	25.9%	16.1%	5.1%	3.1%	1.0%	9.8%	11.0%	2.0%	2.1%	1.0%
2002	26.7%	16.7%	5.3%	3.2%	1.0%	10.0%	11.4%	2.1%	2.2%	1.0%
2003	27.9%	17.8%	5.9%	3.6%	1.2%	10.2%	11.9%	2.2%	2.4%	1.2%

Source: Authors' computations based on top fractiles incomes levels reported in Tables 2A.4 and 2A.5.

Table 2A.7 Simulating income tax receipts in China, 1986–2015 (I)

	(1)	(3)	(4)	(5)	(6)	(7)	(8)	(9)	(10)	(11)	(12)	(13)	(14)	(15)	(16)
	% urban wage earners subject to income tax	Total receipts	Wage income receipts	Business income receipts	Capital income receipts	Total receipts			Effective average tax rates				Adjusted simulations: Total receipts		adjusted % population subject to income tax
			(billions current yuans)					Wage earners			Business income earners		(billions cur. yuans)	% GDP	
						(% GDP)	P0–100	P90–100	P99–100	P0–100	P90–100	P99–100			
1986	0.0%	0.4	0.0	0.1	0.3	0.0%	0.0%	0.0%	0.0%	5.0%	5.0%	5.2%	0.3	0.0%	0.0%
1987	0.0%	0.5	0.0	0.1	0.3	0.0%	0.0%	0.0%	0.0%	5.0%	5.0%	5.2%	0.4	0.0%	0.0%
1988	0.1%	0.6	0.0	0.2	0.4	0.0%	0.0%	0.0%	0.2%	5.0%	5.2%	6.4%	0.5	0.0%	0.0%
1989	0.1%	1.0	0.0	0.2	0.7	0.1%	0.0%	0.0%	0.2%	5.1%	5.3%	6.9%	0.8	0.0%	0.0%
1990	0.2%	1.2	0.0	0.2	1.0	0.1%	0.0%	0.1%	0.3%	5.1%	5.4%	7.2%	1.1	0.1%	0.0%
1991	0.2%	1.6	0.1	0.3	1.2	0.1%	0.0%	0.3%	0.4%	5.2%	5.6%	7.6%	1.4	0.1%	0.1%
1992	0.8%	2.8	0.3	0.4	2.1	0.1%	0.1%	0.6%	1.5%	5.3%	6.3%	9.0%	2.4	0.1%	0.2%
1993	2.6%	4.4	0.8	0.6	2.9	0.1%	0.1%	1.6%	3.0%	5.6%	7.7%	10.7%	3.8	0.1%	0.7%
1994	8.4%	9.4	3.5	1.0	4.8	0.2%	0.4%	2.5%	4.9%	6.0%	9.2%	12.1%	8.2	0.2%	2.4%
1995	14.5%	14.5	6.8	1.4	6.2	0.2%	0.6%	3.3%	5.9%	6.6%	10.2%	12.7%	12.6	0.2%	4.2%
1996	20.3%	22.2	12.0	2.2	8.0	0.3%	0.9%	3.9%	7.0%	7.2%	11.1%	14.3%	19.3	0.3%	6.2%
1997	25.0%	32.0	18.6	3.3	10.0	0.4%	1.2%	3.9%	7.7%	7.6%	11.6%	15.1%	26.0	0.3%	8.0%
1998	27.8%	37.6	22.1	4.0	11.4	0.5%	1.2%	4.0%	7.8%	7.7%	11.7%	15.2%	33.9	0.4%	9.3%
1999	20.3%	36.5	19.7	4.9	11.9	0.4%	1.0%	3.6%	7.4%	8.0%	12.1%	15.7%	41.4	0.5%	7.0%
2000	25.9%	48.5	28.0	8.3	12.2	0.5%	1.3%	4.3%	8.6%	8.4%	12.7%	17.0%	66.0	0.7%	9.4%
2001	32.2%	63.7	39.6	10.3	13.8	0.7%	1.7%	5.0%	9.2%	8.7%	13.2%	18.1%	99.6	1.0%	12.1%
2002	37.9%	88.8	62.0	16.8	10.0	0.8%	2.1%	5.8%	10.2%	9.2%	14.1%	19.7%	121.1	1.2%	14.8%
2003	44.1%	132.4	93.2	24.3	14.9	1.1%	2.7%	6.9%	11.6%	10.0%	15.3%	22.6%	141.7	1.2%	17.9%
2004	37.1%	150.9	100.0	34.7	16.2	1.2%	2.5%	6.9%	11.9%	10.7%	16.0%	24.0%	161.5	1.3%	15.7%
2005	42.3%	207.1	139.9	49.4	17.8	1.5%	3.1%	7.6%	12.6%	11.3%	16.7%	25.2%	221.6	1.6%	18.7%
2006	27.5%	217.4	127.1	70.9	19.4	1.5%	2.5%	7.1%	12.5%	12.0%	18.0%	26.3%	232.6	1.6%	12.6%
2007	34.4%	301.9	179.6	101.1	21.2	1.9%	3.0%	7.9%	13.4%	12.8%	19.2%	27.3%	323.0	2.0%	16.5%

(continued)

Table 2A.7 Continued

	(1)	(3)	(4)	(5)	(6)	(7)	(8)	(9)	(10)	(11)	(12)	(13)	(14)	(15)	(16)
	% urban wage earners subject to income tax	Total receipts	Wage income receipts	Business income receipts	Capital income receipts	Total receipts		Wage earners			Business income earners		Adjusted simulations: Total receipts		adjusted % population subject to income tax
			(billions current yuans)			(% GDP)	P0–100	P90–100	P99–100	P0–100	P90–100	P99–100	(billions cur.yuans)	% GDP	
								Effective average tax rates							
2008	39.6%	413.7	247.2	143.3	23.2	2.4%	3.6%	8.7%	14.3%	13.4%	20.4%	28.1%	442.6	2.6%	19.8%
2009	46.0%	566.9	339.5	202.0	25.3	3.0%	4.4%	9.5%	15.1%	14.1%	21.4%	28.9%	606.5	3.2%	23.9%
2010	52.0%	773.8	459.8	286.2	27.7	3.8%	5.2%	10.3%	15.8%	14.8%	22.7%	29.6%	827.8	4.1%	28.2%
2011	57.3%	1,045.0	610.8	404.0	30.2	4.8%	6.0%	11.2%	16.4%	15.6%	24.0%	30.3%	1118.1	5.1%	32.4%
2012	61.6%	1,393.2	792.6	567.6	33.0	5.9%	6.8%	12.0%	17.0%	16.3%	25.1%	30.8%	1490.5	6.3%	36.3%
2013	66.4%	1,850.9	1,020.5	794.3	36.1	7.2%	7.7%	12.7%	17.7%	16.9%	26.2%	31.3%	1980.3	7.7%	40.7%
2014	70.8%	2,450.6	1,303.1	1,108.1	39.4	8.9%	8.6%	13.5%	18.5%	17.6%	27.1%	31.8%	2621.9	9.5%	45.3%
2015	74.9%	3,285.0	1,700.4	1,541.6	43.1	11.0%	9.8%	14.3%	19.3%	18.2%	28.0%	32.2%	3514.6	11.8%	49.9%

Source: Authors' computations based on top fractiles incomes levels reported in Tables 2A.3 and 2A.4 and on income tax schedules reported in Tables 2A.1. The simulation results (col. (1) to (13)) were computed assuming post-2003 nominal income trends and population trends similar to those observed during the 1996–2003 period, and unchanged tax law after 2008. Adjusted simulations results (col. (14) and (15)) were computed in the following way: for 1996–2001, adjusted simulation results are equal to actual receipts reported in Table 2.3; for 1986–96, adjusted simulation results were obtained by upscaling each income source tax simulation by the same adjusted/raw ratios as for 1996; for 2002–15, adjusted simulation results were obtained by upscaling each income source tax simulation by the same adjusted/raw ratios as for 2001.

Table 2A.8 Simulating income tax receipts in China, 1986–2015 (II)

	(1)	(3)	(4)	(5)	(6)	(7)	(8)	(9)	(10)	(11)	(12)	(13)	(14)	(15)	(16)
									Effective average tax rates				Adjusted simulations: Total receipts		adjusted
	% urban wage earners subject to income tax	Total receipts	Wage income receipts	Business income receipts	Capital income receipts	Total receipts	Wage earners			Business income earners					% population subject to income tax
			(billions current yuans)			(% GDP)	P0–100	P90–100	P99–100	P0–100	P90–100	P99–100	(billions cur.yuans)	% GDP	
1986	0.0%	0.4	0.0	0.1	0.3	0.0%	0.0%	0.0%	0.0%	5.0%	5.0%	5.2%	0.3	0.0%	0.0%
1987	0.0%	0.5	0.0	0.1	0.3	0.0%	0.0%	0.0%	0.0%	5.0%	5.0%	5.2%	0.4	0.0%	0.0%
1988	0.1%	0.6	0.0	0.2	0.4	0.0%	0.0%	0.0%	0.2%	5.0%	5.2%	6.4%	0.5	0.0%	0.0%
1989	0.1%	1.0	0.0	0.2	0.7	0.1%	0.0%	0.0%	0.2%	5.1%	5.3%	6.9%	0.8	0.0%	0.0%
1990	0.2%	1.2	0.0	0.2	1.0	0.1%	0.0%	0.0%	0.3%	5.1%	5.4%	7.2%	1.1	0.1%	0.0%
1991	0.2%	1.6	0.1	0.3	1.2	0.1%	0.1%	0.1%	0.4%	5.2%	5.6%	7.6%	1.4	0.1%	0.1%
1992	0.8%	2.8	0.3	0.4	2.1	0.1%	0.1%	0.3%	1.5%	5.3%	6.3%	9.0%	2.4	0.1%	0.2%
1993	2.6%	4.4	0.8	0.6	2.9	0.1%	0.1%	0.6%	3.0%	5.6%	7.7%	10.7%	3.8	0.1%	0.7%
1994	8.4%	9.4	3.5	1.0	4.8	0.2%	0.4%	1.6%	4.9%	6.0%	9.2%	12.1%	8.2	0.2%	2.4%
1995	14.5%	14.5	6.8	1.4	6.2	0.2%	0.6%	2.5%	5.9%	6.6%	10.2%	12.7%	12.6	0.2%	4.2%
1996	20.3%	22.2	12.0	2.2	8.0	0.3%	0.9%	3.3%	7.0%	7.2%	11.1%	14.3%	19.3	0.3%	6.2%
1997	25.0%	32.0	18.6	3.3	10.0	0.4%	1.2%	3.9%	7.7%	7.6%	11.6%	15.1%	26.0	0.3%	8.0%
1998	27.8%	37.6	22.1	4.0	11.4	0.5%	1.2%	4.0%	7.8%	7.7%	11.7%	15.2%	33.9	0.4%	9.3%
1999	20.3%	36.5	19.7	4.9	11.9	0.4%	1.0%	3.6%	7.4%	8.0%	12.1%	15.7%	41.4	0.5%	7.0%
2000	25.9%	48.5	28.0	8.3	12.2	0.5%	1.3%	4.3%	8.6%	8.4%	12.7%	17.0%	66.0	0.7%	9.4%
2001	32.2%	63.7	39.6	10.3	13.8	0.7%	1.7%	5.0%	9.2%	8.7%	13.2%	18.1%	99.6	1.0%	12.1%
2002	37.9%	88.8	62.0	16.8	10.0	0.8%	2.1%	5.8%	10.2%	9.2%	14.1%	19.7%	121.1	1.2%	14.8%
2003	44.1%	132.4	93.2	24.3	14.9	1.1%	2.7%	6.9%	11.6%	10.0%	15.3%	22.6%	141.7	1.2%	17.9%
2004	37.1%	150.9	100.0	34.7	16.2	1.2%	2.5%	6.9%	11.9%	10.7%	16.0%	24.0%	161.5	1.3%	15.7%

(continued)

Table 2A.8 Continued

	(1)	(3)	(4)	(5)	(6)	(7)	(8)	(9)	(10)	(11)	(12)	(13)	(14)	(15)	(16)
	% urban wage earners subject to income tax	Total receipts	Wage income receipts	Business income receipts	Capital income receipts	Total receipts		Wage earners			Business income earners		Adjusted simulations: Total receipts		adjusted % population subject to income tax
			(billions current yuans)			(% GDP)	P0–100	P90–100	P99–100	P0–100	P90–100	P99–100	(billions cur.yuans)	% GDP	
												Effective average tax rates			
2005	42.3%	207.1	139.9	49.4	17.8	1.5%	3.1%	7.6%	12.6%	11.3%	16.7%	25.2%	221.6	1.6%	18.7%
2006	27.5%	217.4	127.1	70.9	19.4	1.5%	2.5%	7.1%	12.5%	12.0%	18.0%	26.3%	232.6	1.6%	12.6%
2007	34.4%	301.9	179.6	101.1	21.2	1.9%	3.0%	7.9%	13.4%	12.8%	19.2%	27.3%	323.0	2.0%	16.5%
2008	39.6%	413.7	247.2	143.3	23.2	2.4%	3.6%	8.7%	14.3%	13.4%	20.4%	28.1%	442.6	2.6%	19.8%
2009	38.9%	526.1	298.8	202.0	25.3	2.8%	3.9%	9.1%	14.8%	14.1%	21.4%	28.9%	562.9	3.0%	20.2%
2010	38.4%	675.1	361.2	286.2	27.7	3.3%	4.1%	9.4%	15.3%	14.8%	22.7%	29.6%	722.3	3.6%	20.8%
2011	37.6%	872.3	438.1	404.0	30.2	4.0%	4.3%	9.9%	15.8%	15.6%	24.0%	30.3%	933.3	4.3%	21.3%
2012	34.5%	1,119.4	518.8	567.6	33.0	4.7%	4.5%	10.4%	16.2%	16.3%	25.1%	30.8%	1197.6	5.1%	20.3%
2013	33.7%	1,454.9	624.5	794.3	36.1	5.7%	4.7%	10.9%	16.7%	16.9%	26.2%	31.3%	1556.6	6.1%	20.7%
2014	32.9%	1,897.9	750.4	1,108.1	39.4	6.9%	5.0%	11.3%	17.3%	17.6%	27.1%	31.8%	2030.6	7.3%	21.0%
2015	32.0%	2,484.6	900.0	1,541.6	43.1	8.3%	5.2%	11.8%	18.0%	18.2%	28.0%	32.2%	2658.3	8.9%	21.3%

Source: Same computations as those reported in Table 2A.7, except that we now assume that the nominal income tax exemption threshold will be increased during the 2008–15 period at the same average annual rate as during the 2003–8 period (nominal tax brackets are however assumed to be unchanged; computations reported in Table 2A.7 assumed both unchanged exemption and unchanged brackets).

REFERENCES

Banerjee, A. and A. Newman (2003). 'Inequality, Growth and Trade Policy', mimeo.

—— and T. Piketty (2004). 'Top Indian Incomes, 1922–2000', CEPR Working Paper 4632.

—— —— (2005). 'Top Indian Incomes, 1922–2000', *World Bank Economic Review*, 19: 1–20.

Chen, S. and Y. Wang (2001). 'China's Growth and Poverty Reduction: Recent Trends between 1990 and 1999', mimeo, World Bank.

Deaton, A. (2003). 'Adjusted Indian Poverty Estimates for 1999–2000', *Economic and Political Weekly*, 25 January.

Eckaus, R., A. Lester, and N. Qian (2003). 'Income Inequality in a Transitional Economy: China as a Case Study', mimeo, MIT.

Kremer, M. and E. Maskin (2003). 'Globalization and Inequality', mimeo, Harvard.

Piketty, Thomas (2003). 'Income Inequality in France, 1901–1998', *Journal of Political Economy*, 111: 1004–42.

—— and Emmanuel Saez (2003). 'Income Inequality in the United States, 1913–1998', *Quarterly Journal of Economics*, 118: 1–39.

Ravallion, M. and S. Chen (2003). 'When Economic Reform is Faster than Statistical Reform: Measuring and Explaining Income Inequality in Rural China', mimeo, World Bank.

Tendulkar, S. (2003). 'Organized Labour Market in India: Pre and Post Reform', mimeo, Delhi School of Economics.

Wei, S. J. and Y. Wu (2001). 'Globalization and Inequality: Evidence from Within China', NBER Working Paper 8611.

3

The Evolution of Income Concentration in Japan, 1886–2005

Evidence from Income Tax Statistics

Chiaki Moriguchi and Emmanuel Saez

3.1 INTRODUCTION

Following the seminal work by Kuznets (1955), economists have devoted much effort to analysing the relationships between income inequality and economic growth.[1] Economics historians, in particular, have studied the evolution of income and wealth inequality during the process of industrialization in leading nations such as Britain or the United States (e.g. Soltow 1968, 1969; Williamson and Lindert 1985; Williamson 1985; Lindert 1986, 2000). Those studies, however, were often hampered by the absence of long-run homogeneous data to document inequality. To overcome this limitation, a number of recent studies have used income tax statistics to generate top income shares series for several European and Anglo-Saxon countries that provide the first consistent series of inequality measures that cover a large part of the twentieth century (Atkinson and Piketty 2007).

The primary objective of this chapter is to construct homogeneous and continuous top income shares series for Japan and study income concentration in Japan from long-run historical and comparative perspectives. The data for Japan are of particular interest, not only because Japan is the world's second largest economy after the United States today, but also because we can construct

We thank seminar participants at the NBER Japan Meeting, UC Berkeley, Columbia University, Harvard University US–Japan Relations Program, University of Tokyo, Hitotsubashi University, Keio University, Osaka University, Kyoto University, and Ohio State University for helpful discussions. In particular, we are grateful to Esther Duflo, Joseph Ferrie, Andrew Gordon, Laura Hein, Charles Horioka, Yasushi Iwamoto, Ryo Kambayashi, Anil Kashyap, Lawrence Katz, Wojciech Kopczuk, Ryoshin Minami, Joel Mokyr, Fumio Ohtake, Tetsuji Okazaki, Makoto Saito, Osamu Saito, Toshiaki Tachibanaki, Gail Triner, David Weinstein, and Hiroshi Yoshikawa for their comments and suggestions. A shorter version of this chapter was published as Chiaki Moriguchi and Emmanuel Saez, 'The Evolution of Income Concentration in Japan, 1886–2005: Evidence from Income Tax Statistics', *Review of Economics and Statistics*, 90(4) (November 2008): 713–34. Financial support from NSF Grant SES-0134946, the Alfred P. Sloan Foundation, and the Abe Fellowship Program is gratefully acknowledged.

[1] For recent work, see Forbes (2000), Barro (2000), and Banerjee and Duflo (2003).

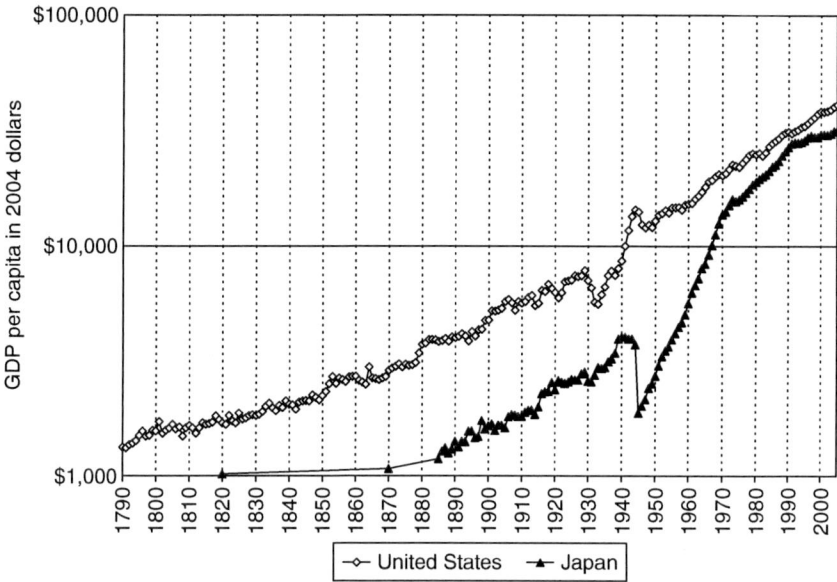

Figure 3.1. Real GDP per capita in Japan and the United States, 1790–2005

Sources: USA from Johnston and Williamson (2005) and National Accounts; Japan from Maddison (1995) and National Accounts.

top income shares series covering the full span of modern economic growth for Japan. Indeed, Japan's process of industrialization was compressed within a short time period. After the 1868 Meiji Restoration, the Japanese economy took off in the 1880s, and the nation underwent three phases of industrial revolution—from textiles, to heavy industries, to high technology industries—within less than 100 years. To illustrate this point, Figure 3.1 depicts the real GDP per capita in Japan, 1820–2005, against that in the United States, 1790–2005. Japan's GDP per capita in 1890 was at the level of US GDP per capita in 1790, or about $1,200 in 2004 dollars, which is roughly comparable to the GDP per capita of the less developed countries today. Japan had caught up quickly since then, and now has a GDP per capita only slightly lower than the United States. Real GDP per capita in Japan grew at the annual compound rate of 2.7 per cent in 1886–1940 and at 4.6 per cent in 1948–2005.

As the Japanese government introduced a comprehensive income tax system in 1887—a remarkably early date by international standards—we can trace the evolution of income concentration during the entire process of industrialization using the Japanese tax statistics.[2] Because the top income shares series compiled

---

[2] By contrast, the present comprehensive income tax was instituted in the United States in 1913, and in France in 1914, when the industrial revolution was already well under way in these countries.

so far for the Western countries span only part of their industrialization process, the Japanese data provide us with a unique opportunity to examine the relationship between income concentration and modern economic growth. To explore the causes of dynamic changes in income concentration and provide additional evidence, we also compile the series of top income composition, top estates and their composition, top wage income shares, and marginal tax rates for top wage income earners, all based on tax statistics.

We obtain three main findings. First, income concentration at the top 1 per cent income group in Japan was extremely high during the pre-Second World War period with some short-term fluctuations. Top income shares declined abruptly and precipitously during the Second World War and remained remarkably low for the rest of the twentieth century albeit with a sign of increase in the last decade. Our data thus indicate that the defining event for the evolution of income concentration in Japan was a historical accident, namely the Second World War, which was accompanied by large-scale government interventions, inflation, and war destruction.

Second, using income composition data, we show that the dramatic fall in income concentration at the top was primarily due to the collapse of capital income during the Second World War. Evidence from estate tax statistics confirms that top wealth holdings in fact declined drastically during the Second World War and continued to fall during the post-war occupation. We argue that the redistribution of assets and the transformation of institutional structure under the occupational reforms have prevented the re-concentration of income in the subsequent decades. Importantly, such redistributive policies, which certainly have affected the process of capital accumulation, were accompanied by one of the most impressive and sustained economic growths in modern history.

Third, according to our wage income data, wage income concentration also fell sharply during the Second World War. In contrast to the United States where wage income inequality has increased dramatically since 1970, top wage income shares in Japan have remained relatively low with only a modest increase since 1997. Comparing the Japanese and US data in more detail, we find that technological progress (i.e. skill-biased technological change) or tax incentives (i.e. the reduction in marginal income tax rates) alone cannot account for the divergent experience of the two countries. Instead we suggest institutional factors, most notably internal labour markets and collective bargaining structure, as important determinants of wage income concentration.

The rest of the chapter is organized as follows. Section 3.2 summarizes the preceding literature on income inequality in Japan. Section 3.3 describes the data and estimation methods. Section 3.4 presents our findings from the top income shares series, 1886–2005. Section 3.5 investigates the causes of the observed changes in income concentration, using top income composition and top estates series. Section 3.6 presents the top wage income shares series, 1929–2005, and offers comparative analysis of the USA and Japan. Section 3.7 provides comparative historical perspectives and concludes. The detailed description of our data and methods, as well as a complete set of results, are presented in Appendices 3A–3D.

3.2 INCOME INEQUALITY IN JAPAN PAST AND PRESENT

By international standards, Japan is widely perceived as a society with relatively low income inequality. Although comparing income statistics across nations has been difficult and should be interpreted with caution, recent OECD reports (Atkinson, Rainwater, and Smeeding 1995; Burniaux et al. 1998) and Japanese government studies (Nishizaki, Yamada, and Ando 1998; Kokumin Seikatsu-kyoku 1999) provide better comparative data. As Panel A of Table 3.1 shows, as of the late 1980s, Japan's Gini coefficient of the distribution of household income *before* tax and government transfers was one of the lowest among major industrial

Table 3.1 Income inequality in OECD countries

A. Income before tax and transfers

Country	Year	Gini coefficients
Ireland	1987	0.461
Sweden	1987	0.439
UK	1986	0.428
France	1984	0.417
USA	1986	0.411
Switzerland	1982	0.407
Germany	1984	0.395
Finland	1987	0.379
Canada	1987	0.374
Italy	1986	0.361
The Netherlands	1987	0.348
Japan	1989	0.317
Belgium	1988	0.273

Source: Nishizaki, Yamada, and Ando (1998).

B. Income after tax and transfers

Country	Year	Gini coefficients
USA	1986	0.347
Switzerland	1982	0.346
Ireland	1987	0.341
UK	1986	0.323
Italy	1986	0.321
France	1984	0.311
Canada	1987	0.305
Japan	1985	0.298
Sweden	1987	0.281
Germany	1984	0.277
The Netherlands	1987	0.266
Belgium	1987	0.260
Finland	1987	0.255

Sources: Kokumin Seikatsukyoku (1999: chapter 3);
Atkinson, Rainwater, and Smeeding (1995: table 4–10).

nations. When we consider the distribution of income *after* tax and government transfers, as one may expect, European welfare states ranked below Japan (see Panel B). In other words, one of the distinct characteristics of contemporary Japan is its low income inequality in the absence of government redistribution. Recently, however, there have been growing concerns among Japanese people that income inequality is on the rise. Most notably, in his widely read book, Tachibanaki (1998) declared Japan as an equal society a 'myth', generating much debate among scholars, government officials, and the general public.[3] When did Japan become the so-called equal society? And will Japan continue to be one as it enters the twenty-first century?

There is an extensive body of empirical work that examines the evolution of income inequality in Japan.[4] For the pre-Second World War period, the lack of household survey data has been a major obstacle in measuring income inequality. Shiomi et al. (1933) and Hayakawa (1951) instead used national and local income tax records to estimate the income distributions of all households in selected cities. Improving their methods and compiling comprehensive local income tax data, Minami (1995, 1998) estimated the income distributions of all households in Japan for selected years. Alternatively, Ono and Watanabe (1976) studied the long-run changes in income inequality, using several indirect measures such as urban–rural and intra-industry wage differentials. Otsuki and Takamatsu (1978) estimated the Pareto coefficients from 1887 to 1940 using the average and minimum household incomes based on the *Long-Term Economic Statistics* (Ohkawa, Shinohara, and Umemura 1974).

For the post-Second World War period, several types of household survey data became available. Wada (1975) estimated the income distributions during the 1950s combining the *Employment Status Survey* and the *Farm Household Economics Survey*. Mizoguchi and Takayama (1984) and Mizoguchi and Terasaki (1995) used the *People's Living Conditions Survey* to examine the changes in income inequality after 1962. For recent years, the income distribution of Japanese households can be estimated also from the *Family Income and Expenditure Survey* (e.g. Ohtake 2005) and the *Income Redistribution Survey* (e.g. Tachibanaki 2000). Because different surveys employ disparate sampling methods and income definitions, the resulting estimates of income inequality can differ considerably.

Figure 3.2 summarizes the long-run changes in income inequality, measured by the Gini coefficient, based on the above studies. Although the estimates in a given year differ across studies, they display fairly coherent time trends. Namely, (1) income inequality in Japan rose sharply from 1890 to 1940; (2) after the Second World War, it peaked around 1960, declined subsequently, and stabilized in the 1970s; and (3) there has been an increase in income inequality since the

---

[3] Tachibanaki (2005) is an English version of Tachibanaki (1998). See Ohtake (2005) for further analysis.

[4] For a comprehensive survey of income distributions in pre-Second World War Japan, see Terasaki (1986) and Minami (1995: chapter 1). For the post-Second World War period, see Mizoguchi and Takayama (1984: chapter 1), Mizoguchi and Terasaki (1995), and Yazawa (2004).

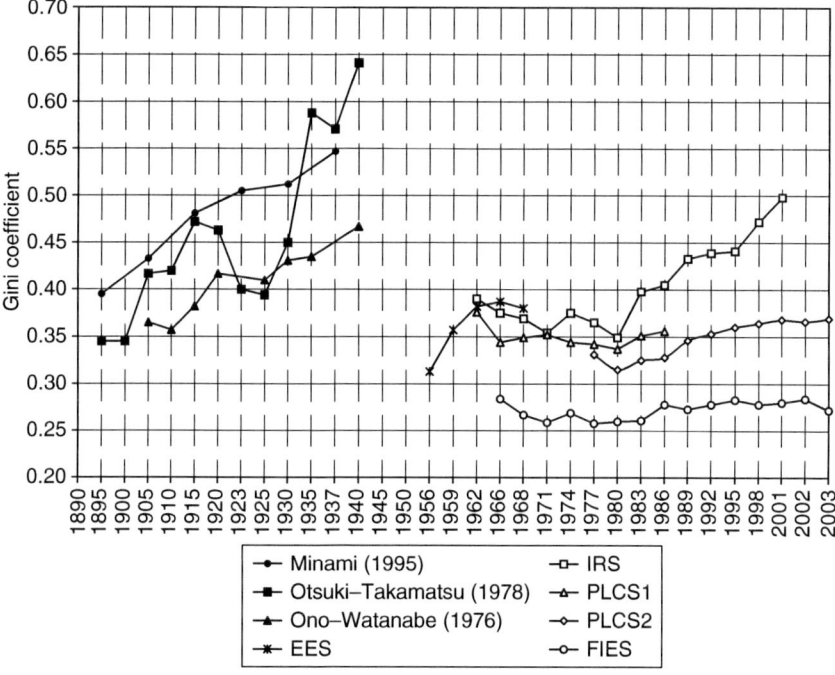

Figure 3.2 Change in income inequality in Japan, 1890–2003

Sources: Ono and Watanabe (1976: table 6); Otsuki and Takamatsu (1978: table 4); Minami (1995: table 6–4, series I & II); Wada (1975: 21); Tachibanaki (1998: table 3–1); Ohtake (2005: table 1–1).

Notes: Gini coefficient for income distribution (before tax and government transfers) of all Japanese households are reported; EES refers to Employment Status Survey; PLCS refers to People's Living Conditions Survey; FIES refers to Family Income and Expenditure Survey; and IRS refers to Income Redistribution Survey.

1980s, although scholars have disagreed over the extent of the increase and its causes.

It is important to note that not only there is no estimate between 1940 and 1955, but also Gini coefficients before 1940 and after 1955 in Figure 3.2 cannot be compared due to major data discontinuity. These limitations notwithstanding, the general consensus among historians based on mostly qualitative evidence is that income inequality dropped substantially between 1940 and 1955, presumably due to the Second World War or post-war occupational reforms, if not both (Mizoguchi and Terasaki 1995: 61). One of the objectives of this study, therefore, is to compile new data that enable us for the first time to compare the level of inequality between the pre- and post-Second World War periods and shed better light on the process of the alleged fall in income inequality. In addition, most of the pre-Second World War studies provide the estimates only for selected years that may or may not be representative. Furthermore, since most studies are concerned with the income distribution of all households, we know relatively little about high-income groups.[5] In particular, due to the problem of small sample and top coding, household surveys cannot be used for a study of high-income earners.

To fill these gaps in the literature, we construct continuous and homogeneous series of the top income shares, i.e. the shares of total income accruing to the upper groups of the income distribution, from 1886 to 2005. Although top income shares may not be an ideal measure of income inequality—as they do not reflect the shape of the bottom 95 per cent of the income distribution—they provide valuable information about the degree of income concentration that affects entrepreneurial incentives and capital accumulation process in a capitalist economy. Finally, because we employ the same methodology used in the recent high-income studies presented in Atkinson and Piketty (2007), we can compare our data with those of other industrial nations and offer a comparative historical analysis of income concentration.

3.3 DATA AND METHODOLOGY

In this section, we describe briefly the nature of data and the methods of estimation. A complete description can be found in the appendices to the chapter. Our estimates of top income shares are based on income tax return statistics published annually by the Japanese tax administration since the introduction of national income tax in 1887.[6] Typically, the statistics present the number of taxpayers, the amount of income reported by taxpayers, the amount of income tax paid, and the composition of the reported income, all by income brackets.

Income is defined as *gross income* before deductions of income and payroll taxes paid by individuals, but after employers' payroll taxes and corporate income taxes. It includes all income components reported in tax returns, namely, salaries and wages, bonuses, unincorporated business income, farm income, self-employment income, dividends, interest, rents, royalties, and other small items. Realized capital gains, however, are excluded from our definition of income for two reasons. First, capital gains were not taxed before 1947 in Japan and are thus missing entirely from the income tax statistics, and even after 1947, capital gains from land and stocks were only partially included in the statistics due to special treatments and exemptions. Second, in general, realized capital gains form a volatile component of income with large fluctuations as opposed to a steady source of annual income. Thus, in this study, we focus on the series that exclude capital gains.[7]

---

[5] For important exceptions, see Takahashi (1959), Yazawa (1992, 2004), and Miyamoto and Abe (1995: chapter 6).

[6] Japan Ministry of Finance, Tax Bureau, Shuzeikyoku Tokei Nenposho, 1887–1945, and Japan National Tax Administration, Kokuzeikyoku Tokei Nenposho, 1946–2002. For an overview of the Japanese income tax system, see Ishi (2001).

[7] We present results including reported realized capital gains in Appendix 3A.

Before 1950, the tax unit was 'family' defined as a married couple (or a single household head) with cohabiting dependants. Incomes of family dependants in a single household were aggregated for tax purposes. Starting in 1950, the tax unit became 'individual', whereby spouses were taxed separately on their incomes. To produce homogeneous series over the entire period, we estimate top income shares using the individual tax unit for the pre-1950 period. For most years before 1950, the statistics by income brackets provide a breakdown of income into the income of household head and the income of dependants. According to these data, the latter is very small relative to the former (less than 5 per cent of the former in general). Hence, we substitute household income for household head's income, which leads to a slight but minor upward bias in our estimates.

Thus, our top income groups are defined relative to the total number of adults (age 20 and above), in Japan in each year based on official population statistics. Because of high exemption points, only a small fraction of individuals filed income tax returns before 1947. For this reason, our analysis is necessarily restricted to the high end of income distribution. That is, we can estimate the income share for the entire period of 1886–2005 only *within* the top 1 per cent income group, while we also provide estimate of the top 5 per cent income share for sub-periods.[8]

As the top tail of the income distribution is well approximated by a Pareto distribution, we estimate the Pareto coefficient for each year using the tabulations of taxpayers by income brackets. We then use simple parametric interpolation methods to estimate the thresholds and average income levels of top income groups. As Table 3.2 presents, in 2005, the threshold income levels for the top 1 per cent and 0.1 per cent income groups in Japan were 13.8 million yen (or $125,000) and 34.2 million yen (or $311,000), respectively. The top 0.01 per cent income group in the same year consisted of roughly 10,000 individuals who earned more than 88 million yen (or $0.8 million), and their average income was almost 200 million (or $1.8 million).

We estimate a top income share by dividing the amount of income accruing to a top income group by total personal income computed from National Accounts for 1930–2005 and from *Long-Term Economic Statistics* (Ohkawa, Shinohara, and Umemura 1974) for 1886–1929.[9] The total and average real incomes per adult from 1886 to 2005 are reported in Table 3A.1 in Appendix 3A. We convert current income to real income in 2002 yen, using the CPI deflator from *Long-Term Economic Statistics* (Ohkawa, Shinohara, and Umemura 1967). Our top income shares estimates are reported in Table 3A.2 in Appendix 3A.

We estimate the composition of income accrued to the top 1 per cent group, using income composition statistics. For years in which composition data are

---

[8] We cannot extrapolate our top 5% income share estimates to the full period due to data limitations. See Table 3A.1 for the relevant information.

[9] Note that estimates for total personal income before 1930 are less reliable than after 1930, introducing potential biases in our estimates. See Appendix 3A for a discussion and a sensitivity analysis.

Table 3.2 Thresholds and average incomes for top income groups in Japan

Percentile threshold (1)	Income threshold (in 2005 yen) (2)	Income groups (3)	Number of tax units (adults age 20 and above) (4)	Average income in each income group (in 2005 yen) (5)
		Full Population	103,830,000	2,488,000
Top 10%	6,174,000	Top 10–5%	5,191,500	7,089,000
Top 5%	8,081,000	Top 5–1%	4,153,200	10,033,000
Top 1%	13,791,000	Top 1–0.5%	519,150	15,600,000
Top 0.5%	17,166,000	Top 0.5–0.1%	415,320	22,825,000
Top 0.1%	34,185,000	Top 0.1–0.01%	93,447	44,232,000
Top 0.01%	88,331,000	Top 0.01%	10,383	198,386,000

Notes: Computations are based on income tax return statistics and wage income tax statistics (see Appendix 3A). Income is defined as annual gross income before individual income taxes and employees' payroll taxes but excluding capital gains.

Top income groups are defined relative to adult population (age 20 and above) in Japan. 'Top 10–5%' refers to the bottom half of the top 10% income group, and 'Top 5–1%' refers to the Top 5% income group excluding the top 1%, etc.

Total income demonimator is defined as total personal income in Japan based on National Accounts.

Amounts are expressed in 2005 yen. The average exchange rate in 2005 was $1 = 110 yen.

reported by income brackets, we use a Pareto interpolation method to obtain the top 1 per cent estimates. For years in which only aggregate composition data are published, we use these data. Our top income composition series are reported in Table 3A.3 in Appendix 3A.

Next, we construct top estates series using estate tax return statistics published annually by the tax administration since 1905. Estates are defined as the sum of all properties (including real estates, household properties, business assets, stocks, bonds, deposits, cash, and other claims) net of debts and liabilities.[10] Top estate groups are defined relative to the total number of adult deaths in Japan in each year obtained from official population statistics. Due to the difficulty in estimating total assets in Japan, the top estate series are expressed in the level (as opposed to the share) in 2002 yen using the CPI deflator. Our top estates estimates are reported in Table 3B.1 in Appendix 3B.[11] We also provide estate composition series, 1926–2005, using aggregate estate composition data, which are presented in Table 3B.2 in Appendix 3B. Because estate compositions are not available by estate brackets, we cannot produce homogeneous series for top estate composition.

Finally, we compute top wage income shares using a similar methodology. For the post-war period, wage income data are compiled from the *Survey on Private Wages and Salaries* published by the tax administration annually since 1951.[12]

[10] Because estate value reported in the statistics is before standard deductions but after special tax reductions, our data underestimate the true estate value. See Appendix 3B for a discussion.

[11] Our top estates for 1905–57 are imprecisely estimated due to the difficulty in reconstructing estate statistics by actual (as opposed to fiscal processing) year, See Appendix 3B for a detailed discussion.

[12] Japan National Tax Administration, *Minkan Kyuyo no Jittai*, 1951–2002.

The survey covers virtually all regular employees in the private sector but excludes government employees. Wage income in our definition includes wages, salaries, bonuses, allowances, and taxable part of non-cash compensation, but excludes retirement benefits. Top groups are defined relative to the total number of regular employees in the private sector in Japan. Our estimates of the total wage income denominator are based on total salaries from National Accounts. For the pre-Second World War period, we use salary and bonus data reported in the income tax return statistics for the fiscal years 1930–45. Top groups are defined relative to the total number of regular employees in Japan. The total wage income denominators are based on total salaries and wages from National Accounts.[13] Table 3C.1 in Appendix 3C presents the number of wage income earners and total wage income from 1929 to 2005. Our estimates for top wage income shares for 1929–2005 are reported in Table 3C.2 in Appendix 3C. We also estimate marginal tax rates for the top wage income groups from 1951 to 2005. The estimates are made for an individual with a non-working spouse and two dependent children, assuming that all income is employment income. Our estimates include standard deductions but exclude local taxes and social insurance contributions. The marginal tax rates series are reported in Table 3C.3.[14]

Over the 120 years of our sample period, there are at least three major tax reforms, in addition to numerous revisions in income and estate tax laws. These changes potentially affect the comparability of our data across years. Therefore, to construct homogeneous series, we make a number of careful adjustments to the original data (see the appendices for a complete description). There are two major challenges in constructing the top income shares series that call for special attention.

First, after the introduction of an extensive withholding system (*gensen choshu seido*) in 1949, most individuals with only employment or pension income were no longer required to file self-assessed income tax returns. As a result, even though most income earners pay income taxes in Japan, only a minority of taxpayers file tax returns. Fortunately, as mentioned above, the Japanese tax administration publishes wage income tax statistics from the withholding system that include virtually all wage earners in the private sector. We thus use these data to complement the self-assessed income tax statistics to produce top income shares series.[15]

The second and perhaps more serious issue is tax erosion and evasion, that is, lawful and unlawful under-reporting of income by taxpayers. Because the self-assessed income tax statistics are by definition based on reported income, there is a concern that our data might reflect trends in tax avoidance and evasion rather than true changes in income inequality. For example, compared to wage income

---

[13] Due to data limitations, our estimates for 1929–44 are based on restrictive assumptions. See Appendix 3C for a detailed discussion.

[14] See Moriguchi (2008) for a more detailed study of the top wage incomes in Japan from 1951 to 2005.

[15] See Appendix 3A for a description of our method.

that is captured at source, farm income and business income in general are said to be subject to a higher degree of tax evasion. Furthermore, in an effort to avoid tax, employers often shift their compensation from cash to perquisites. Finally, in the post-war period, large parts of interest and dividend incomes are subject to special tax treatments and not included in the self-assessed income tax statistics. We discuss below these problems associated with tax avoidance and evasion, and provide a sensitivity analysis.

3.4 TOP INCOME SHARES IN JAPAN, 1886–2005

Historical Background

During the early Meiji period, Japan was predominantly a rural society based on agriculture and handicraft industry. After the fiscal reform that resulted in the Matsukata deflation in 1881–4, the Japanese economy began to modernize and grow in earnest (see Figure 3.1). Large-scale corporations in modern industries, such as railroads and textiles, were formed for the first time in the late 1880s. As a result, most historians regard 1886 as the starting year of the industrial revolution in Japan (Minami 1994; Miyamoto and Abe 1995: chapter 6). The proportion of employment in agriculture declined from 78 per cent in 1876 to 65 per cent in 1900; and fell further to 51 per cent in 1920, and 42 per cent in 1940 (NRUS 1959). After the Second World War, it declined even faster from 44 per cent in 1950, to 16 per cent in 1973, and 7.3 per cent in 1995.

To provide an overview of our sample period, Figure 3.3 depicts the average real income per adult and the CPI in Japan from 1886 to 2005. The average real income more than quadrupled from 1886 to 1938, the peak year in the pre-Second World War period. It grew particularly fast from 1887 to the end of the Sino-Japanese War (1894–95), during the First World War (1914–18), and during the period of military expansion (1932–8). Then the average income declined sharply towards the end of the Second World War (1939–45) that destroyed much of the nation's physical and human capital. The two world wars were accompanied by high inflation. In particular, Japan experienced hyperinflation in 1944–8 where consumer prices rose by 5,300 per cent during the period of four years. After the post-war US occupation (1945–52), the average real income recovered quickly, surpassing the 1938 level by 1959. During the period of high economic growth in 1955–73, real average incomes increased by a factor of six; this was one of the fastest sustained periods of economic growth in modern history. After the 1973 oil crisis, income grew at a slower pace in 1975–90. Since the collapse of the asset bubble in 1991, the average real income has declined for a decade. Except for the brief period during the oil crises, the inflation rate has been low throughout the post-1950 period in Japan.

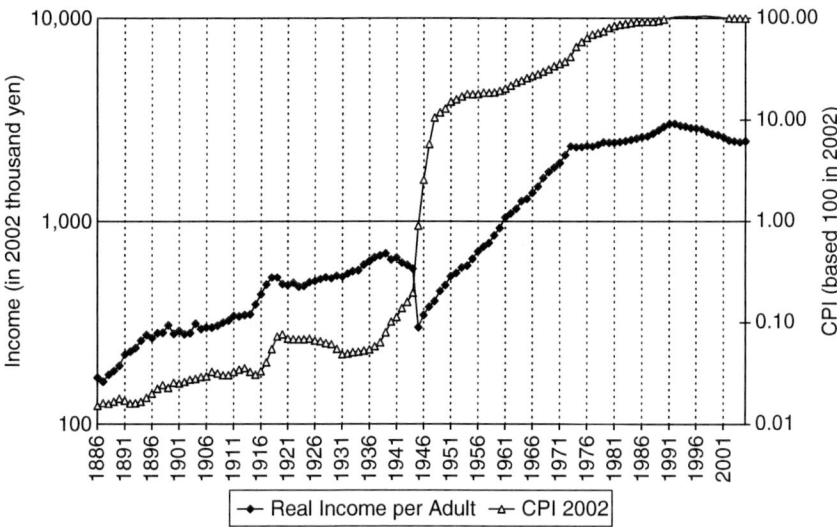

Figure 3.3 Average real income and consumer price index in Japan, 1886–2005
Source: Appendix Table 3A.1.

Trends in Top Income Shares

Figure 3.4 reports our estimates of the top 1 per cent income share from 1886 to 2005 and the next 4 per cent (denoted as 'top 5–1 per cent') income share for 1907–24, 1937–8, and 1947–2005. We first focus on the top 1 per cent income share series. Between 1886 and 1938, the top 1 per cent adult population in Japan received as much as 14 to 20 per cent of total personal income. The share, however, fell abruptly and precipitously from 1938 to 1945 from 20 per cent to 6.4 per cent, and remained relatively stable at around 8 per cent throughout the rest of the twentieth century. There are fairly large fluctuations in the top 1 per cent income share before the Second World War: after a steep fall in 1886–91,[16] it declined temporarily during the Sino-Japanese War (1894–5), the Russo-Japanese War (1904–5), the First World War (1914–18), and the Great Depression (1929–31), each time followed by an immediate recovery. As Figure 3.1 shows, the 1929 depression in Japan, in particular, was shorter and far milder than in the USA and other industrial countries (Moriguchi 2003). In terms of the long-run trend, the top 1 per cent income share was high throughout the initial stage of industrialization in 1900–38. Similarly, the extraordinary economic growth from 1950 to 1973 was accompanied by little change in the top 1 per cent income share. Finally,

---

[16] The estimates for early years are less reliable compared to later years due to larger measurement errors in assessing income by the tax administration. See Appendix 3A.

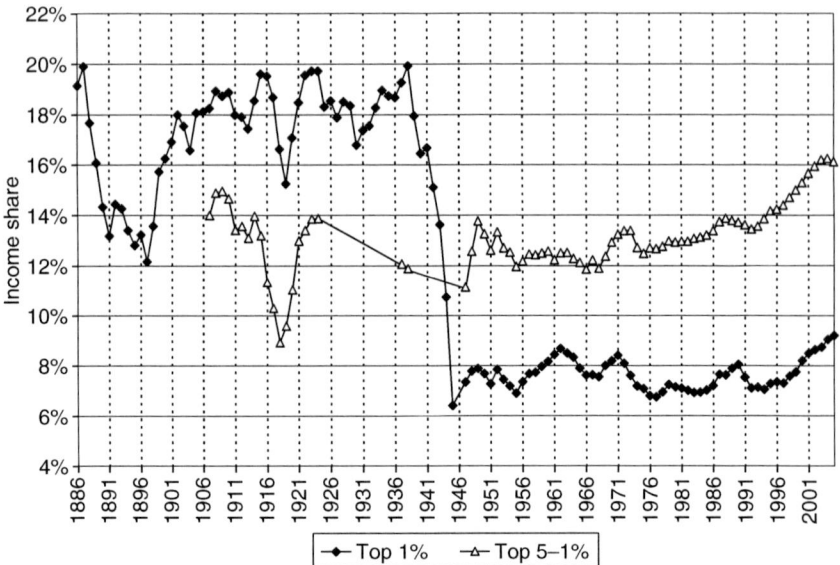

Figure 3.4 Top 1% and next 4% income shares in Japan, 1886–2005

Source: Appendix Table 3A.2.

Notes: Computations are based on income tax return statistics and wage income tax statistics (see Appendix 3A for details on the data and methods).

Groups are defined relative to the total adult population.

'Top 5–1%' denotes the top 5% excluding the top 1%.

For the top 5–1% group, estimates are not available for some years due to too few people filing income tax returns in these years.

consistent with the recent concerns over rising income inequality, we observe a steady increase in the top 1 per cent income share in Japan over the last ten years from 7.3 per cent in 1995 to 9.2 per cent in 2005. Although the 2005 number is still low by the pre-war standard, it is the highest level since the end of the Second World War.

The next 4 per cent income share series displays a substantially different pattern. During the pre-war period, although estimates are not available for some years, the share was consistently smaller than the top 1 per cent income share, where the next 4 per cent population received on average about 12 per cent of total income. By contrast, after 1947 it has been consistently and substantially larger than that of the top 1 per cent with a sharp increase in recent years from 13.5 per cent in 1992 to 16.1 per cent in 2005. The most striking difference is that the Second World War did not have much impact on the next 4 per cent income share. Figure 3.4 thus suggests that the income de-concentration phenomenon that took place during the Second World War was limited to *within* the top 1 per cent income groups.

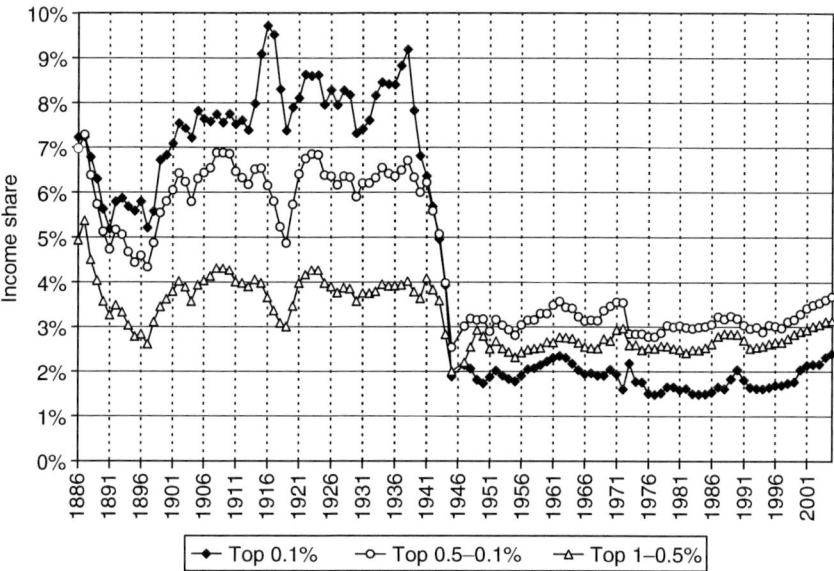

Figure 3.5 Decomposition of top 1% income share in Japan, 1886–2005

Source: Appendix Table 3A.2.

Notes: 'Top 0.5–0.1%' income group refers to the bottom 0.4% of the top 0.5% income group.
'Top 1–0.5%' income group refers to the bottom 0.5% of the top 1% income group.

Figure 3.5 demonstrates this point further by decomposing the top percentile into three subgroups: the top 0.1 per cent, the next 0.4 per cent ('top 0.5–0.1 per cent'), and the bottom half of the top 1 per cent ('top 1–0.5 per cent'). Although the three series exhibit similar overall patterns, the *higher* income group experienced the *earlier* and *larger* fall in their shares during the Second World War. While the share of the top 1–0.5 per cent group declined by 50 per cent (from 4.0 per cent to 2.0 per cent) in 1941–5, for the next 0.4 per cent group it fell by more than 60 per cent (from 6.7 per cent to 2.5 per cent) in 1938–45, and for the top 0.1 per cent group it fell by 80 per cent (from 9.2 per cent to 1.9 per cent) in 1938–45. The fall for the top 0.01 per cent income share is even more dramatic: it collapsed from 3.8 per cent to 0.6 per cent in 1938–45 and remained around the same level for the rest of the twentieth century with only a modest increase in the last several years (see Table 3A.2 in Appendix 3A and Figure 3.9). It offers a sharp contrast to the pre-Second World War period during which the top 0.01 per cent income share shows a positive trend, claiming an increasing share of total personal income.

Finally, to provide a comparative perspective, Figure 3.6 plots the top 0.1 per cent income share series in Japan with those in the United States and France, estimated respectively by Piketty and Saez (2003) and Piketty (2003), using the same methodology. The data indicate that the top 0.1 per cent income share in

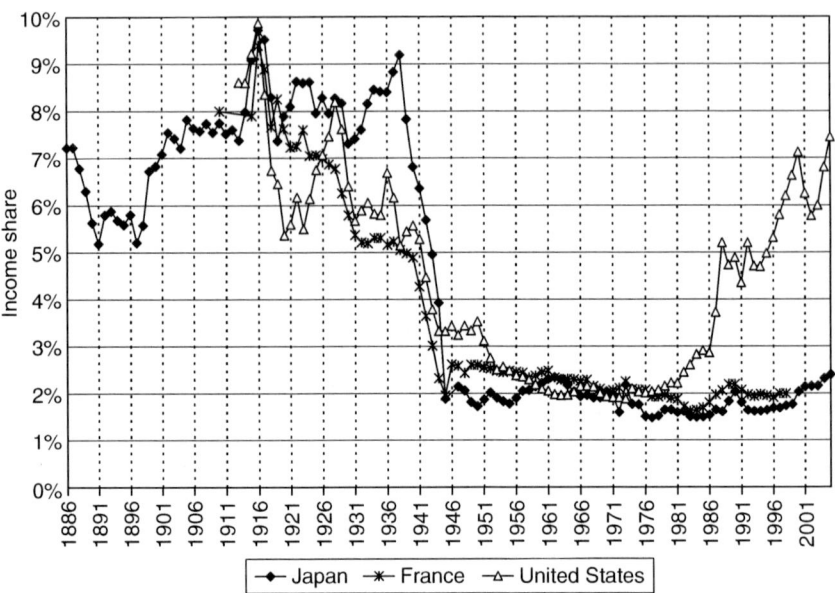

Figure 3.6 Top 0.1% income shares in Japan, the United States, and France
Sources: Japan, Appendix Table 3A.2; USA, Piketty and Saez (2003) updated to 2005; France, Piketty (2003).

Japan was roughly comparable to, if not higher than in, the United States or France during the inter-war period. Recall that the United States, in particular, was the world's uncontested technological leader by the 1920s where giant corporations in capital-intensive industries generated enormous fortunes (Chandler 1962). The top 0.1 per cent income shares in the United States and France declined roughly in three stages, first during the First World War, then during the Great Depression, and finally during the Second World War. Interestingly, by the 1960s, the shares in all three countries had converged to 2 per cent. The figure illustrates a sharp contrast in the evolution of income concentration between the United States, on one hand, and Japan and France, on the other hand, since the 1970s. While the top income shares in Japan and France have remained relatively low, the share in the United States has tripled in the last two decades, returning to the pre-Second World War level. In section 3.6, we explore the divergent experience of Japan and the United States using wage income tax statistics.

Trends in Top Income Composition

To better understand the mechanisms that led to the drastic decline in the top 1 per cent income share during the Second World War in Japan, we use composition data from the income tax statistics. In Figure 3.7, we decompose the top 1 per cent income share into five categories: (a) employment income (wages,

Figure 3.7 Top 1% income share and composition in Japan, 1886–2005

Source: Appendix Table 3A.3.

Notes: Computations based on income tax return statistics; see Appendix 3A.
Business income includes unincorporated business profits, farm income, and self-employment income.
Employment income includes wages, salaries, bonuses, and pensions.
Rental income includes rents from farm land, residential land, housing, and buildings, but excludes imputed rents.
For 1886 and 1900–45, estimates are based on aggregate income composition and thus imprecise.
For 1951–62, no estimates are available.
Most interest income in 1947–2005 and large part of dividends in 1965–2005 are missing from the statistics (see Appendix 3A for details).

salaries, bonuses, allowances, and pensions), (b) business income (profits from unincorporated businesses, farm income, and self-employment income), (c) rental income (from land and buildings, excluding imputed rents), (d) interest income (from bonds, deposits, and savings accounts, excluding returns on insurance policies), and (e) dividends (from privately held and publicly traded stocks). Immediate caveats are in order.

First, for 1886–1945, our estimates are based on the composition of total income reported in the income tax statistics. During this period, the series are not homogeneous as the fractions of adults filing tax returns fluctuated between 1 per cent and 4 per cent (see Table 3A.3 in Appendix 3A). Second, because almost all interest income has been either tax exempted or taxed separately and withheld at source since 1947, and so were a large part of dividends since 1965, these components were missing from the self-assessed income tax statistics (Iwamoto, Fujishima, and Akiyama 1995). Third, the introduction of the withholding system in 1949 probably reduced tax evasion of wage earners relative to others. We address these important issues below.

With these caveats in mind, we make the following observations from the top income composition data. First, throughout the 1886–1937 period, approximately 50 per cent of the top 1 per cent income consisted of capital income (i.e. rents, interest, and dividends). Within capital income, dividends steadily increased their share, while the share of interest income declined. Although not shown in Figure 3.7, within rental income, farm rents were a major component in the earlier years, but their share declined after 1915. Initially, the share of business income in the top 1 per cent income was higher than the share of employment income, but by 1930 the order was reversed. The decline of farm rents and the rise of employment income probably reflect the gradual shift from an agrarian economy with concentrated land ownership to an industrial economy with professional managers. Second, from 1937 to 1947, both the capital income and employment income components fell dramatically: right after the Second World War, the top 1 per cent income was almost entirely composed of business income. Third, since 1950, the share of employment income in the top 1 per cent income has increased steadily at the expense of business income. This trend is probably due to the further shift towards a highly industrialized economy with large corporations. Finally, as we discuss in more detail below, since the Second World War, capital income has become a less important component in the top 1 per cent income.

Evidence from Top Estates

Our income composition series suggest that capital income accrued to the top 1 per cent income group fell dramatically during the Second World War, never returned to the pre-war level, and was replaced by employment income. National Accounts show that total capital income in the economy, however, did recover, albeit gradually (see Figure 3A.3 in Appendix 3A). Then the fall in the top capital income must have been caused by a permanent decline in *wealth* concentration. In order to test this hypothesis, we turn to estate tax return statistics published annually since the introduction of estate tax in 1905.

Figure 3.8 plots the average sizes (in real 2002 yen) of the top 0.01 per cent estates and the bottom half of top 1 per cent estates ('top 1–0.5 per cent') from 1905 to 2005 in logarithmic scale. Recall that top estate groups are defined relative to the total number of adult deaths in each year. The top 0.01 per cent estates, namely, the 'very top' wealth holdings, correspond to the roughly top 100 decedents in 2005, whose average was about 5.3 billion yen or $48 million. By contrast, the average of the bottom half of top 1 per cent estates, namely, the 'moderately high' wealth holdings, was about 300 million yen or $2.7 million in the same year. According to the figure, both the top 0.01 per cent and 1–0.5 per cent estates increased substantially from 1905 to 1936. The top 0.01 per cent estates then declined precipitously by a factor of 140 from 1936 to 1949, and the

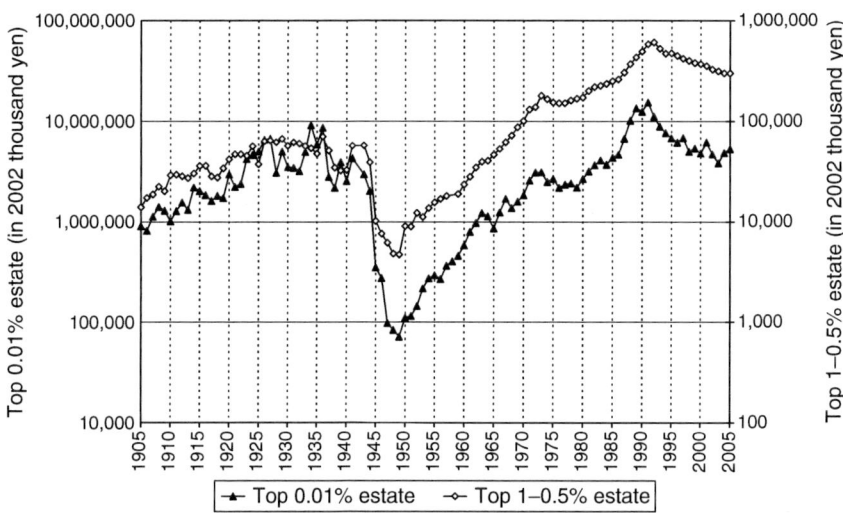

Figure 3.8 Top 0.01% estate and top 1–0.5% estate in Japan, 1905–2005

Source: Appendix Table 3B.1.

Notes: Computations based on estate tax return statistics.
The average estate levels (in 2002 yen) of the top 0.01% group and the bottom half of the top 1% are reported.
The 1905–57 estate levels are less precisely estimated than the 1958–2005 estate levels.
Due to special tax treatments, land values in estates are subject to considerable underestimates.
See Appendix 3B for details.

top 1–0.5 per cent estates declined by a factor of 18 during the same period. In contrast to top incomes, top estates not only fell dramatically in 1941–5 but also *continued* to fall during the initial four years of the post-war occupational reforms. Both estate levels grew rapidly during the high economic growth period of 1955–73, but they have been in decline since the burst of the asset bubble in 1991. While the level of the top 1–0.5 per cent estates surpassed the pre-Second World War peak by 1970, the level of top 0.01 per cent estates in 2005 is still smaller (in real terms) than in 1936 in spite of a tenfold increase in GDP per capita.[17]

When we compare the two series, the top 0.01 per cent estates were initially about 50 times larger than the bottom half of top 1 per cent estates, and by the 1930s, about 100 times larger. Because of the differential impacts of the Second World War and the post-war reforms on the two estate levels, however, by 1949 the former were only about 20 times larger than the latter. Moreover, this ratio has remained fairly constant from 1950 to 2005 despite the major changes in

[17] For the reason stated in an earlier footnote, our series probably underestimate true estate value. This problem is particularly serious concerning land due to low official valuation prices and special tax treatments. Because the share of land in total estate is higher in recent decades as shown below in estate composition data, our estimates probably suffer from greater downward bias in the more recent period. See Appendix 3B for a discussion.

Table 3.3 Top estates composition in Japan, 1935, 1950, and 1987

	Estate composition						
Year	Agricultural Land (1)	Residential Land (2)	Houses and Structures (3)	Business Assets (4)	Stocks (5)	Fixed Claim Assets (6)	Other Assets (7)
1935	22.5%	13.8%	8.4%	3.9%	25.9%	22.6%	2.9%
1950	11.8%	15.1%	37.3%	13.5%	4.8%	12.1%	19.7%
1987	20.6%	43.6%	3.7%	0.8%	10.2%	11.7%	9.5%

Notes: Computations based on estate tax return statistics (see Appendix 3B and Table 3B.2).
In 1935, 1950, and 1987, approximately top 9% of adult decedents filed estate tax returns.
Business assets include assets of unincorporated business and farm assets.
Fixed claim assets include bonds, cash, deposits, savings accounts, and other claims.
Other assets include household assets, pensions, life insurance, and other items.
Sum of all components in each year is 100%.

macroeconomic conditions during these years. In other words, there was a permanent decline in the level of the top wealth *relative to* the moderately high wealth after 1950.[18]

Table 3.3 presents estate compositions for selected years, 1935, 1950, and 1987, for which the fraction of adult decedents filing estate tax returns are constant at about 9 per cent.[19] Estates are decomposed into: (1) land (farm and residential land), (2) houses and structures, (3) business assets (unincorporated business assets and farm assets), (4) stocks, (5) fixed claim assets (bonds, cash, deposits, and savings accounts), and (6) other assets (including household properties, pension rights, and life insurances). The figure shows that the largest component of the top 9 per cent estates shifted from financial assets (stocks and fixed claim assets) in 1935 to movable properties (business assets, houses and structures, and household properties) in 1950, to real estate (predominantly residential land) in 1987. The share of stocks and fixed claims assets in the top estates declined sharply from 49 per cent in 1935 to 15 per cent in 1950, and then rose to 22 per cent in 1987. Namely, the share of financial assets in large estates in the midst of the bubble period was still less than half of that in 1935. Thus the top estate composition data provide additional evidence for our claim that the shares of dividends and interest in the top income collapsed during the Second World War and have not returned to the pre-war level to date.

To summarize, our top estates series suggest that a permanent reduction in the level of the top wealth relative to the moderately high wealth took place during

---

[18] It is important to note that top estates do not necessarily correspond to top capital incomes because the former are based on individuals who died in a given year, while the latter are based on all living individuals. The link between those two distributions can shift over time if the age distribution of decedents changes over time. That is why we examine the relative sizes between very high and moderately high estates in the same year to assess changes in wealth concentration.

[19] Table 3B.2 and Figure 3B.1 present aggregate estate compositions from 1925 to 2002. See Appendix 3B for details.

and immediately after the Second World War. This dramatic fall in wealth concentration at the top is not only consistent with our findings from the top income shares series, but also provides better insights as to why the precipitous decline in top income shares was concentrated *within* the top 1 per cent income group. The Second World War and the occupational reforms had a very large impact on the high end of wealth distribution, destroying much of the source of capital income. Because in general the share of capital income in total income increases with the size of income, top income earners probably suffered a disproportionately large loss of their income. In other words, our data suggest that the Second World War and the subsequent reforms probably had a lasting effect in wiping out high-income rentiers.

The Effects of Tax Evasion and Avoidance

In this section, we discuss what is known about the extent of tax evasion and avoidance in Japan, and provide sensitivity analysis to see whether our findings can be explained away by these phenomena.

The dramatic and seemingly permanent drop in income concentration after the Second World War could be explained by tax evasion only if the evasion among top income groups relative to the rest of the population increased dramatically during the Second World War and remained high ever since. One may assume that tax evasion must have been rampant during the war when labour and material shortages disrupted normal functioning of any administration. Yet, seeking additional sources for war finance, the government imposed various temporary taxes and intensified an effort to collect tax during the war. Not only the numbers of local tax offices and their personnel increased during the Second World War, but tax evasion was deemed highly unpatriotic (Japan National Tax Administration 1988). Second, it is unlikely that evasion was lower in the pre-war period when the tax administration was smaller and when most businesses did not compile systematic accounting records that the tax administration could examine. By contrast, after the Second World War, both the enforcement power and technology available for the tax administration were considerably expanded, and much economic transaction took place within large corporations or financial institutions with established accounting methods. For instance, it is widely believed that there is little tax evasion in Japan today concerning employment, dividend, and interest incomes, precisely because the sophisticated withholding system captures these incomes at source with the cooperation of corporate employers and financial institutions.

By contrast, tax evasion is considered to be substantially higher for business and farm incomes for which the withholding system does not apply.[20] According

---

[20] Not only Japan but most advanced countries face similar problems. For example, in the USA, the Internal Revenue Service also estimates that most income tax evasion takes place among small business owners.

to the estimate by Hayashi (1987), while nearly 100 per cent of employment incomes were captured, only 50 per cent of business income and 10 per cent of farm income were reported to the tax administration. However, both business and farm income components in the top income have been so small in recent years that it would require rates of evasion an order of magnitude higher than these estimated rates to generate the top income shares as high as in the pre-Second World War period. For example, if we assume that only 10 per cent of farm income and 50 per cent of business income are reported in 1999, then our estimate of the top 1 per cent income share would increase modestly from 7.8 per cent to 8.5 per cent.[21] In short, it is difficult to argue that the apparent permanent decline in income concentration was due to tax evasion or unlawful under-reporting of income.

In addition to tax evasion, individuals may shift their income using legal means and instruments to reduce tax payments. One such example is the usage of tax-exempted non-cash compensation in place of wages, which will be discussed in section 3.6. Another way is to take advantage of special treatments and tax favours. During the post-Second World War period, various tax privileges had been given to different components of capital income, most notably, interest and dividends. These measures effectively allowed taxpayers to pay tax separately at source at flat rates without filing tax returns. As a result, the self-assessed income tax statistics do not include these capital income components. Therefore, it is critical to evaluate the impact of the missing capital income components on our estimates of the top income shares.

The best available source for estimating the distribution of capital income by income group is the comprehensive household survey National Survey of Family Income and Expenditure (NSFIE).[22] In particular, the NSFIE in 1999 reports the holdings of various financial assets per household tabulated by the size of household head's income. We combine these asset distribution data and National Accounts data to estimate the shares of three capital income components missing from the tax statistics—interest, dividends, and the returns on life and other insurance policies—in total income for various top income groups. In Table 3.4, we compare our estimates from the income tax statistics in 1999 (in Panel B) with the estimates from the NSFIE in the same year (in Panel C). Three observations follow.

First, the estimated average incomes from the NSFIE coincide well with those from the tax statistics up to the top 1 per cent income group. For the top 0.5 per cent income group, the two estimates differ significantly, however. Because the NSFIE uses a representative sample (about 50,000 households) that contains few observations at the high end of income distribution, it is difficult to provide precise estimates for the top 0.5 per cent income group and above using NSFIE

---

[21] In 1999, business income and farm income represent 8.3% and 0.1% of reported incomes in the top 1% income group. With no evasion, they would represent 16.6% and 1%, respectively, and the top 1% income share would be approximately 9%, or 0.7 percentage point larger than our estimate.

[22] Statistics Bureau of Japan, *National Survey of Family Income and Expenditure* (Zenkoku Shohi Jittai Chosa). See Appendix 3D for a detailed discussion.

Table 3.4 Sensitivity analysis using the Japanese NSFIE data in 1999

Income groups (1)	Average income (in thousand yen) (2)	Fraction of capital income component to total individual income			
		Net interest income (%) (3)	Dividend income (%) (4)	Returns on insurance policies (%) (5)	All returns on liquid assets (%) (6) = (3) + (4) + (5)
A. National average from National Accounts					
All	2,805	1.9%	0.9%	4.3%	7.1%
B. Income tax statistics estimates					
Top 10–5%	7,530	0.0%	0.0%	0.0%	0.0%
Top 5–1%	10,601	0.0%	0.1%	0.0%	0.1%
Top 1–0.5%	16,276	0.0%	0.3%	0.0%	0.3%
Top 0.5%	32,754	0.0%	2.1%	0.0%	2.1%
Top 0.1%	67,662	0.0%	4.2%	0.0%	4.2%
C. NSFIE estimates (105,139 households)					
Top 10–5% (5,257 hlds.)	7,781	−0.4%	0.9%	5.2%	5.7%
Top 5–1% (4,206 hlds.)	10,381	0.5%	1.3%	4.6%	6.3%
Top 1–0.5% (526 hlds.)	14,391	1.9%	2.2%	4.5%	8.6%
Top 0.5% (526 hlds.)	22,958	1.3%	2.3%	3.8%	7.3%
Top 0.1%	n.a.	n.a.	n.a.	n.a.	n.a.

Notes: Computations based on the following three independent sources (see Appendix 3A).
National average in Panel A is based on total personal income in 1999 from National Accounts.
Estimates in Panel B are based on the self-assessed income tax return statistics in 1999. Income is defined as annual gross income reported in the tax returns, excluding capital gains. All returns on insurance policies, almost all interest income, and large part of dividends are not subject to comprehensive income tax and not reported in the self-assessed income tax returns.
Estimates in Panel C are based on the *National Survey of Family Income and Expenditure* in 1999. Net interest income is estimated based on the holdings of bonds, deposits, and loan trusts, net of liabilities. Dividend income is estimated based on stock holdings. Returns on insurance policies are estimated based on life and other insurance holdings.
The number of households in the NSFIE in each group is reported in column (1) of Panel C. Estimates for the top 0.5% group are based on 526 households and thus imprecise, and estimates for the top 0.1% group are not available due to too few households.

data. It is important to note that we find no systematic downward bias in estimating the average incomes using tax statistics compared to the NSFIE. The claim that the tax statistics are useless due to systematic under-reporting is thus not valid.

Second, according to Iwamoto, Fujishima, and Akiyama (1995), in recent decades, due to exemptions and separate taxation withheld at source, approximately 80 per cent of dividend income, over 99 per cent of interest income, and 100 per cent of the returns on insurance savings are not subject to progressive income tax and not included in the self-assessed income tax statistics. The NSFIE estimates indicate that, compared to the national average, the higher income group receives larger portions of their income as dividends but smaller portions of their income as interest or the returns on insurance policies. Furthermore, even in the NSFIE data, the three capital income components make up a very small portion of total income for the top income groups. For example, they respectively constitute 1.9 per cent, 2.2 per cent, and 4.5 per cent of total income for the bottom half of the top 1 per cent income group (the column 'top 1–0.5 per cent' in Panel C). Taken together, the table suggests that these components are not particularly concentrated at the top of the income distribution in today's Japan.

Third, Panel A shows that interest and dividends constitute only a small share (2.8 per cent) of total personal income in Japan. Even if we make the extreme assumption that all dividends and interest income go to the top 1 per cent income group, it would increase the top 1 per cent income share by 2.8 percentage points from 7.8 per cent to 10.6 per cent. Observe that this upper bound estimate is still substantially smaller than the pre-Second World War share of 16 per cent.

We provide similar sensitivity analysis for 1979–99, using the NSFIE data. Our results are reported in Table 3D.1 in Appendix 3D. Consistent with the estimates from the income tax statistics, the table shows that there is only a very modest increase in the top 5 per cent income shares during this period. The share of the three capital income components in total income for the top 5 per cent group was only moderately higher than the national average in 1979 and 1984, and was actually lower than the national average in 1989, 1994, and 1999. Therefore, fully incorporating the missing components would have only small effects (a slight increase in the 1980s and a slight decrease in the 1990s) on our estimates for the top income shares. In summary, adding back the missing capital income components would not change our main conclusion that the degree of income concentration fell drastically in Japan from the pre-war to post-war period.

3.5 UNDERSTANDING THE EVOLUTION OF INCOME CONCENTRATION

Using the income and estate tax statistics, we have documented that (1) income concentration in Japan was extremely high during 1886–1938 by both historical and international standards; (2) the drastic de-concentration of income at the top took place in 1938–45; (3) income concentration remained low for the next five decades with a sign of increase in the last ten years; (4) the size of top wealth relative to moderately high wealth declined sharply from 1936 to 1949 and stayed low, and (5) top income composition has shifted dramatically from capital and business incomes toward employment income over the course of the twentieth century. In this section, we explore the causes of the evolution of income concentration.

A High Level of Income Concentration in Pre-Second World War Japan

One of the merits of our data is that they allow a quantitative comparison of income concentration before and after the Second World War. Our findings strongly confirm the received view based largely on qualitative evidence that there was high concentration of income and wealth among the elite class in pre-war Japan.[23] Preceding studies suggest three major constituencies of the very rich: landlords, shareholders, and corporate executives.

First, there was a concentration of land ownership to a small number of 'absentee landlords' (*fuzai jinushi*) mostly in rural areas whose lands were cultivated by tenant farmers. Especially in the earlier years, landowners enjoyed social and economic privileges over their tenants. After the First World War, however, both the commercialization of agriculture and the rise of tenant unions led to lower rents and stronger tenant rights (Waswo and Nishida 2003: 14–17). As a result, large landowners began to diversify their assets and invest in financial and industrial assets. These observations are consistent with the substantive farmland rents component in the top 1 per cent income during 1886–1915 and its gradual decline thereafter in our income composition data.

Second, before the Second World War, large firms raised capital primarily from stock markets, and business ownership was heavily concentrated on a small number of individuals (as opposed to institutional) shareholders.[24] In addition, pre-war firms paid out high dividends to their shareholders. According to the study by Miyamoto and Abe (1995) based on corporate charters of fifty companies in the 1880s, on average 70 per cent of profit was distributed to shareholders as dividends (p. 276). Okazaki (1993) also finds that in the 1930s the average dividend to profit ratio at leading manufacturing firms was close to 70 per cent, while it was less than 50 per cent in the 1950s (p. 184).

Third, during the inter-war period, top management at large corporations received very high compensation. In addition to high monthly salary, they were

[23] Our data show that the top 1% income share increased only modestly from 1890 to 1940. By contrast, the preceding studies find a sharp increase in Gini coefficients during the same period (see Figure 3.2). Our findings are not necessarily contradictory, if the rise in inequality was driven by changes in the lower end of income distribution without changing the mean. For example, Mizoguchi and Terasaki (1995) attribute the rise primarily to a widening rural–urban income gap.

[24] For example, Okazaki (1999) finds that, in 1935, at the ten largest *zaibatsu* firms, the top ten shareholders held as much as 66% of total stocks (pp. 103–5).

rewarded with large year-end bonuses. According to Miyamoto and Abe (1995), the same fifty corporate charters stipulated that 10 per cent of profits be distributed as executive bonuses (p. 276).[25] At leading manufacturing firms, directors on average received 6 per cent of profit in the form of bonus in the 1930s, compared to just 2 per cent in the 1960s (Okazaki 1993: 184). At five leading electric power companies, executive bonus was 28 times larger than the average income in Japan in 1936, while in 1955 it was only 1.5 times larger (Minami 1995: 123). Moreover, before the Second World War, it was common practice for major shareholders to assume a position as corporate directors, which exacerbated income concentration.[26]

In a unique study using individual-level data, Yazawa (1992) examines the 5,000 highest income taxpayers in 1936 based on *Who's Who* that published their names, income tax paid, addresses, and occupational titles. He finds that, out of the top 5,000 income earners in 1936—which corresponds roughly to the top 0.01 per cent income group in our study—31 per cent were in retail business, 22 per cent were in manufacturing, 22 per cent were in finance, and 7 per cent had no occupation (pp. 155–9). He also shows that they were concentrated in metropolitan areas, such as Tokyo (45 per cent) and Osaka (25 per cent).[27] Only 2.2 per cent of them, however, were members of the aristocracy and merely 3.0 per cent were affiliated with *zaibatsu* holding companies, which indicates that the importance of aristocrats and *zaibatsu* families among the elite class should not be overstated (pp. 160–6).

Last but not least, the legal system in pre-war Japan proved favourable to the affluent class. Initially, both the 1886 income tax law and the 1905 estate tax law set extremely low marginal tax rates in which the highest statutory rates were 3 per cent and 1.8 per cent, respectively. Although the rates were increased subsequently, until the 1937 temporary tax increase law, top marginal tax rates for individual and corporate income taxes had remained low. In addition, the pre-war estate tax law endorsed primogeniture and allowed the first-born son (or a designated legal heir) to inherit entire family estates as a family head under preferential tax rates and high exemption points. In other words, with the minimum government intervention, rich families could accumulate their wealth over several generations before the Second World War.

Mechanisms of Income De-concentration in 1938–1945

Our data indicate that the top income shares fell precipitously during the Second World War, but not at all during the occupational reforms. We explore the two

[25] By contrast, paying bonus for rank-and-file employees was an exception rather than a norm in pre-war firms.

[26] For example, Okazaki (1999) finds that, at twenty leading manufacturing firms, the top ten shareholders held 23% of the director positions in 1935, while they held none after 1947 (pp. 103–5).

[27] Note that Yazawa's (1992) sample covers 26 major prefectures out of total 47 prefectures in Japan, under-representing rural prefectures (p. 149).

key questions in turn: how did the Second World War reduce the income concentration in such a short period of time, and why did the occupational reforms have such little impact?

The Second World War probably caused the drastic income de-concentration through three main channels: government regulations, inflation, and war destruction. Most importantly, with the promulgation of the 1938 National General Mobilization Act, the military government implemented a set of regulations that had profound impacts on shareholders, executives, and landlords (Hoshi 1998; Hoshi and Kashyap 2001: chapter 3; Okazaki 1993).

Dividends were regulated starting in 1939 where a dividend-to-equity ratio was capped at 8 per cent in 1940 and at 5 per cent by 1945, compared to the typical pre-war ratio of over 10 per cent. In addition, government pressure led to the decline in the number of shareholders holding director positions at major corporations after 1940 (Okazaki 1999: 108). The government also intervened in stock and bond markets to encourage the absorption of war bonds, reducing the returns on corporate shares and bonds. It regulated wages and salaries after 1939, standardizing wages across firms and industries. The government also mandated the establishment of works councils to empower blue-collar employees in 1938 and placed a ceiling on executive bonuses in 1940, compressing within-firm pay inequality. Finally, the government redistributed farmland from landlords to tenants starting in 1938, regulated rents and land prices after 1939, set up a two-tier price system for rice production in 1941 that rewarded tenants and penalized landlords, and revised land and house lease laws in 1941 to augment tenant rights (Waswo and Nishida 2003: 22–3). Although their goal was to stimulate food production, these measures reduced both land value and rental income of landlords. As Figure 3.7 shows, changes in different components of the top 1 per cent incomes coincide well with the timing of the corresponding wartime regulations, underscoring their importance in explaining the process of de-concentration.

Furthermore, to finance massive war effort, the government imposed increasingly heavy individual and corporate income taxes in 1937, 1938, 1940, 1942, 1944, and 1945 (Japan National Tax Administration 1988). The sharp increase in corporate income tax reduced after-tax profits, which in turn reduced dividends and bonuses paid out to shareholders and executives.[28] Moreover, despite the stringent controls, the price level began to surge after 1938 and rose dramatically towards the end of the Second World War (see Figure 3.3). The inflation probably played a major role in reducing the top estates, as it diminished the real value of fixed claim assets (e.g. bonds and deposits). It also contributed to the collapse of the top capital income by reducing interest income as well as rental income.[29]

---

[28] One may suspect that higher marginal income tax rates might have invited a higher degree of tax avoidance and evasion. Although we cannot deny this possibility, as discussed below, the government also intensified their effort to collect taxes during the Second World War.

[29] The 1941 land and house lease laws made it difficult for landlords to raise rents.

Finally, the Second World War brought about large-scale destruction of the nation's wealth, claiming 25 per cent of physical assets and 668,000 civilian casualties (Keizai Antei Honbu 1948). In particular, air raids on major Japanese cities by the Allied force between February and August 1945 probably had a devastating effect on the high-income earners who were concentrated in the metropolitan areas (Yazawa and Minami 1993: 366).[30] Note, however, that the late timing of the bombing implies that it could not have been a major reason for the income de-concentration that had started in 1938. In summary, the Second World War can be seen as a one-time shock that reduced income and wealth inequality in Japan through the combination of government regulations, inflation, and war destruction.

Impact of US Occupational Reforms in 1945–1952

Upon Japan's surrender in August 1945, the nation was placed under the indirect governance of the Supreme Commander for the Allied Powers until 1952. As preceding studies have emphasized, the post-war occupational reforms could potentially have a large effect in equalizing the income distribution (Yazawa and Minami 1993; Minami 1995). Three particularly powerful redistributive measures were implemented during this period.

First, the land reform in 1947–50 mandated landlords to sell their farmland to tenants, eliminating virtually all large- and medium-sized landowners. As a result, the percentage of land cultivated by tenants declined sharply from 46 per cent in 1941 to 9 per cent in 1955. Due to hyperinflation, compensation paid to landowners in real terms was a mere fraction of the land value. Second, to finance large deficits, the government imposed extremely heavy and highly progressive property tax (*zaisan zei*) from 1946 to 1951. The property tax affected approximately 13 per cent of all households in Japan in the initial year, and taxed away on average 33 per cent of their properties. For the top 5,000 households, more than 70 per cent of their properties were transferred to the government.

Third, under the dissolution of *zaibatsu* in 1946–8, not only ex- and current directors of *zaibatsu* firms were expelled, but also their stocks were confiscated and redistributed to a large number of employees and other investors at a market price. Consequently, these three measures transferred a significant amount of assets (i.e. land, stocks, and other household properties) from the higher to lower end of distribution. In addition, the hyperinflation in 1944–8 hit hard high-income rentiers. By contrast, farmers and small business owners who sold their products in underground markets were said to have earned substantive income in the immediate post-war years, explaining the surge of business income component in the top 1 per cent income in Figure 3.7.

---

[30] The bombing destroyed 51% of built-up area in Tokyo and 26% of that in Osaka (USSBS 1947: table 30).

Despite the emphasis placed on the importance of the occupational reforms in reducing income inequality in the literature, our data indicate that, although they affected the top estate levels, they had practically no impact on the top income shares. Namely, we find the Second World War, rather than the occupational reforms, to be the single most important event in reducing income concentration. Our finding may seem surprising at first, but the following observations indicate otherwise. First, our finding is consistent with the view that the occupational reforms were in many ways a *continuation* of the wartime policies (Okazaki and Okuno 1993; Noguchi 1995; Teranishi 2005). That is, the restrictions on landlord and shareholder rights, the adoption of progressive taxation, and the check on executive compensation had already begun during the Second World War, which probably had set off the process of income de-concentration well before the post-war democratization and demilitarization. As such, there was little room left for the occupational reforms in further reducing top incomes.[31] By contrast, our top estates series indicate that the reforms did have a large effect in reducing *wealth* concentration, whose implications will be discussed in next section.

Second, our finding is also consistent with the comparative evidence that indicates a universal role of the Second World War in reducing income concentration in such diverse countries as the United Kingdom, France, the United States, and Canada (Atkinson and Piketty 2007). Note that none of these countries was occupied after the Second World War and some did not even experience major war destruction in their homelands. But, without exception, the war was accompanied by large-scale government intervention in these countries.[32] In short, in the absence of quantitative evidence, the preceding studies have probably overstated the effect of the occupational reforms in equalizing income in Japan.

A Low Level of Income Concentration in Post-Second World War Japan

Perhaps the more challenging question is why the top income shares did not recover from the profound yet temporary shock of the Second World War in the decades that followed. Why did the degree of income concentration in Japan remain at the historic low reached in the late 1940s for the next fifty years? We argue that it was in this context that the occupational reforms played a critical role. By redistributing assets and reducing wealth (as opposed to income) concentration, they directly equalized the distribution of capital income in subsequent years. More importantly, deriving their origins from the wartime policies,

---

[31] It is also likely that some measures equalized income at the lower end of the distribution without changing the mean. For example, the land reform redistributed land primarily from middle-sized landowners to tenants, creating a large number of small-sized farmers. In such cases, we may not observe much change in the top 1% income share.

[32] By contrast, in Switzerland and Sweden which remained neutral during the Second World War, the data indicate a much smaller effect of the war on top income shares (Dell, Piketty, and Saez 2007; Roine and Waldenström 2006).

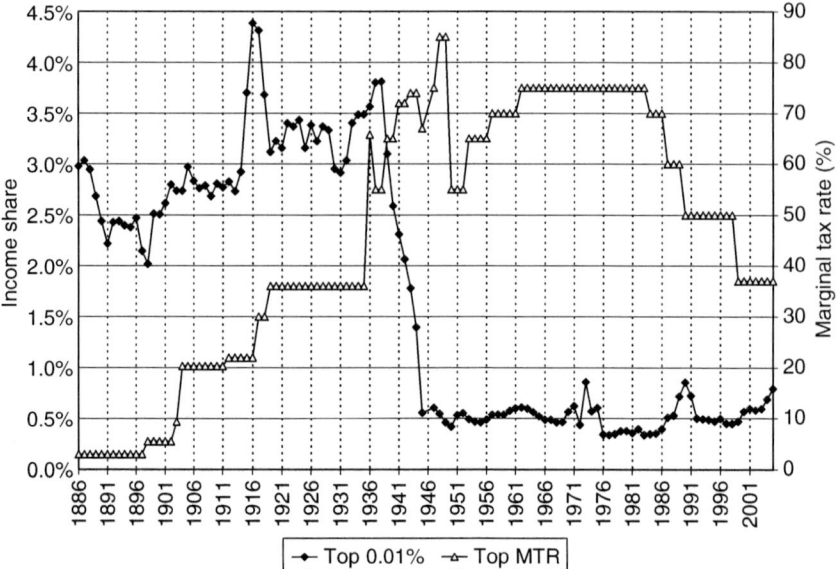

Figure 3.9 Top 0.01% income share and marginal tax rate, 1886–2005

Source: Appendix Tables 3A.1 and 3A.2.

Notes: 'Top 0.01%' refers to the top 0.01% income share.

'Top MTR' refers to the highest statutory marginal tax rates for individual income tax without taking deductions and exemptions into account.

the post-war reforms transformed many one-time measures into lasting ones, facilitating a structural change in the Japanese economy that probably prevented re-concentration of income during the ensuing period of high economic growth.[33]

First, the fiscal reforms in 1950 made progressive taxation a permanent feature of the Japanese tax system. Recall that the enormous fortunes that generated the high top 1 per cent income share in the pre-Second World War period had been accumulated at the time when progressive income tax hardly existed and capitalists could reinvest almost all of their incomes for further capital accumulation. As pointed out by Piketty (2003) in the context of France, the fiscal environment faced by Japanese capitalists after the Second World War, too, was vastly different. As Figure 3.9 shows, after a spike in 1938–49 caused by the combined effect of temporary tax increases and hyperinflation, the highest statutory marginal tax rate for individual income tax stayed at 60–75 per cent from 1950 until the 1988 tax reform. Tax rates on corporate income show similar trends. With respect to estate tax, the 1947 law abolished primogeniture and mandated the division of an

---

[33] Our findings thus lend support to the view that emphasizes the uniqueness of the post-Second World War Japanese economic system in contrast to the pre-Second World War system that was more market oriented (Okazaki and Okuno-Fujiwara 1993; Noguchi 1995; Teranishi 2005).

estate among the surviving spouse and children, and the 1950 law instituted highly progressive estate and gift taxes with top marginal tax rates in excess of 70 per cent. As a result, inter-generational transfers of large amounts of wealth became much more difficult after the Second World War. Progressive taxation probably hindered the re-accumulation of large wealth, resulting in more equal distribution of capital income.

Second, the seemingly permanent decline in the top capital income can be further attributed to measures specific to each capital income component. Since the introduction of the land and house lease laws in 1941 until their repeal in 1992, the government had heavily protected tenant rights, which depressed the supply of rental housing. As a result of both high home ownership rate and more equal land distribution, rental income became a less significant source of income for top income earners in the post-war period. As for interest income, the government expanded tax-exempted saving instruments for small asset holders from the 1960s until they were abolished in 1988. These measures had probably promoted wealth accumulation among the middle class, equalizing the distribution of interest income. With respect to dividend income, the emergence of the new corporate governance system, characterized by bank-centred debt finance and cross-shareholdings among affiliated companies, in the 1960s resulted in stable institutional shareholders and low dividend rates (Fukao 1995; Teranishi 1999). As a result, dividends too became less concentrated among top income groups after the Second World War.

Third, the changes in human resource management and collective bargaining structure in Japan probably compressed wage distributions within firms. As the so-called 'lifetime employment' became a hallmark of human resource management at large firms in the 1960s, most if not all management positions were filled by long-term employees promoted from within (Okazaki 1999). Moreover, after violent confrontations in 1945–55, most large firms in Japan were organized by single enterprise unions that represented both white- and blue-collar employees of the firms. By the 1970s, management regularly consulted with unions over personnel matters including wages and promotions (Morishima 1991; Moriguchi 2000; Kato and Morishima 2002). These changes probably resulted in smaller wage differentials between white- and blue-collar employees as well as more equitable executive compensation. We will turn to wage income tax statistics in the next section to examine these hypotheses more closely.

Finally, what is driving the recent increase in top income shares? It is too early to tell whether it is a temporary blip as in 1985–90, or a break from historical trends that signals the start of the 'post' post-Second World War era. Nonetheless it is worth noting that its timing coincides with another structural change that Japan has been undergoing since the 1990s which includes the decline of main bank system and cross-shareholding, an increasing pressure on lifetime employment practices, and major policy reforms concerning income tax and commercial laws.

3.6 TOP WAGE INCOME SHARES IN JAPAN, 1929–2005

Trends in Wage Income Concentration

In this section, we present our estimates of top *wage income* shares in Japan to investigate the role of employment income in the evolution of income concentration. Wage income in our definition includes wages, salaries, bonuses, and part of non-cash compensation, but excludes retirement benefits. For the pre-Second World War period, we use salary and bonus data reported in annual income tax statistics for fiscal years 1930–45 (corresponding to actual years 1929–44). For the post-war period, we use the results of statistical survey in the *Survey on Private Wages and Salaries* published annually by the tax administration since 1951. The survey covers all employees in the private sector who worked for the same employer throughout a year. Our estimates of the top 5 per cent and 1 per cent wage income shares series in Japan are shown in Figures 3.10 and 3.11.

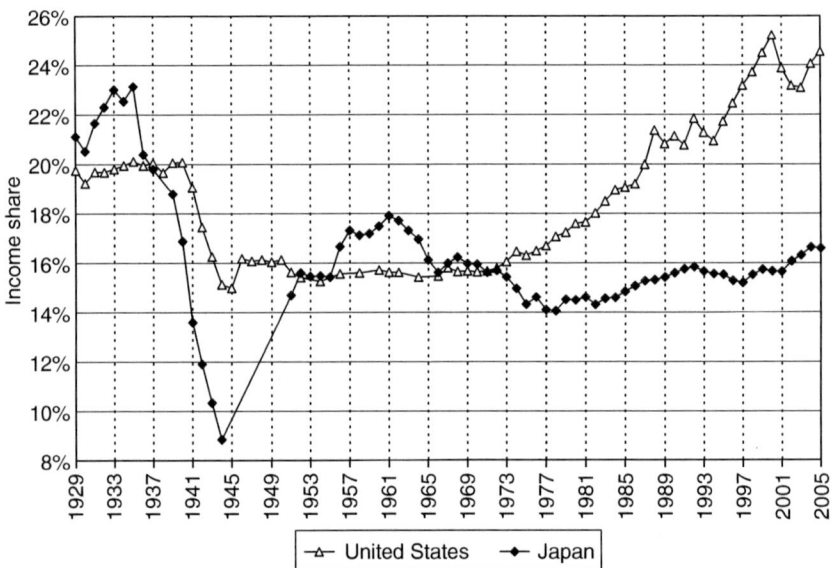

Figure 3.10 Top 5% wage income share in Japan and the United States, 1929–2005

Sources: Japan, Appendix Table 3C.2; USA, Piketty and Saez (2003: table IV, updated to 2005).

Notes: Computation based on income tax return statistics for 1929–44 and wage income tax statistics for 1951–2005; see Appendix 3C for details.

The 1929–44 estimates are less precise and not fully comparable to the 1951–2005 estimates.

Estimates for 1938 and 1945–50 are not available.

Wage income includes wages, salaries, allowances, and bonuses, but excludes retirement benefits and non-taxable part of noncash benefits.

Top wage income groups are defined relative to all regular employees for 1929–44 and all employees in the private sector for 1951–2005.

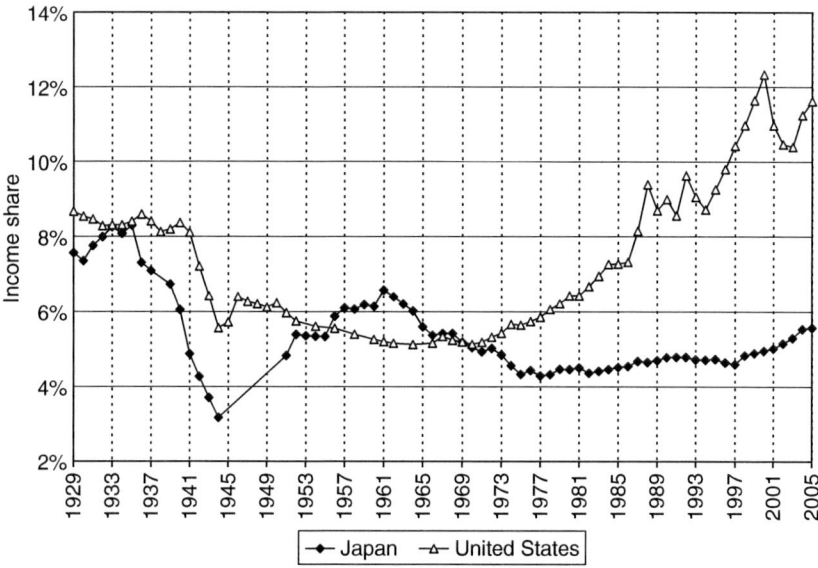

Figure 3.11 Top 1% wage income share in Japan and the United States, 1929–2005
Sources: Japan, Appendix Table 3C.2; USA, Piketty and Saez (2003: table IV, updated to 2005).

First, during 1929–35, Japan exhibited a high degree of wage income concentration where the top 5 per cent wage earners received more than 20 per cent of total wage income and the top 1 per cent received about 8 per cent of total wage income. As one might expect, the degree of wage income concentration is smaller than that of income concentration during the same period (8 per cent versus 16 per cent for the top 1 per cent group). High wage income inequality in Japan during the inter-war period can be explained by large intra- and inter-firm wage differentials. As discussed above, wages and bonuses paid to top management, white-collar employees, production workers, and unskilled labourers within the same firm were widely dispersed before the Second World War, resulting in high within-firm wage inequality (Showa Dojinkai 1960: 269, 263). In addition, with the growth of heavy industries with high capital intensity, productivity gap by industry as well as by firm size had widened since the First World War, resulting in substantial inter-firm wage differentials (Yasuba 1976).

Second, we observe a sharp decline in wage income concentration from 1935 to 1944, as the top 5 per cent wage income share fell from 23 per cent to 9 per cent and the top 1 per cent share from 8.9 per cent to 3.2 per cent. This 64 per cent decline in the top 1 per cent wage income share in 1935–44 is comparable to the 68 per cent decline in the top 1 per cent income share in 1938–45. According to our income composition data in Figure 3.7, the share of employment income in the top 1 per cent income remained fairly stable until 1940 and then dropped sharply in 1940–7. Therefore, we attribute the initial decline in wage income concentration in 1935–40 to the tightening of labour markets due to military expansion that compressed the wage distribution from below. The further decline in 1940–4 is probably due to the wartime regulations that capped executive bonuses and standardized wages across firms. Although the decline in income concentration was largely a capital income phenomenon, the data indicate that employment income also played an important role.

Third, in the post-war period, top wage income shares rose substantially from 1951 to 1961 (no estimates are available for 1945–50), and then declined gradually over the next two decades. The initial increase in the 1950s is consistent with our income composition data that show a recovery of the employment income component in the top 1 per cent income after the Second World War. It is worth noting that the trends in the top wage income shares parallel the trends in income inequality of all households documented by the preceding studies (see Figure 3.2). Minami (1998) attributes the rise in income inequality in the 1950s and its decline in the 1960s to Japan's transition from the chronic labour surplus before 1960 to the chronic labour shortage after 1960. Considering the top wage income shares, their decline in the 1960s and 1970s can be further attributed to the diffusion of the so-called 'Japanese-style' management, including lifetime employment, enterprise unionism with joint labour–management consultation, and corporate governance that places more weight on employee values than shareholder values (Gordon 1985; Aoki 1988). For example, by the end of the 1960s, executives at large firms were entirely promoted from within (Okazaki 1999). In sharp contrast to the pre-war period, bonuses were no longer paid disproportionately to top executives but distributed more equally among regular employees. In fact, the average ratio of bonus to total compensation has been 20 per cent to 30 per cent for both corporate executives and rank-and-file employees in recent years (see Hart and Kawasaki 1999; Kubo 2004).

Finally, the top 1 per cent wage income share has increased steadily since 1997 from 4.6 per cent to 5.6 per cent, confirming the public concern that wage inequality in Japan is rising. Although this trend is new, the extent of the increase is modest by historical standards.[34]

Comparative Analysis of Japan and the United States

To facilitate international comparison, we also plot the top wage income shares in the United States, estimated by Piketty and Saez (2003), in Figures 3.10 and 3.11.[35] The figures indicate that the top wage income shares were roughly

[34] A recent study by Moriguchi (2008) suggests that there is no major structural change in the determinants of top wage income shares before and after 1997.

[35] In addition to wages, salaries, and bonuses, US wage income includes stock options. In Japan, stock option was legalized in 1997, while various restrictions remained until the revision of the commercial law in 2002 (Naito and Fujiwara 2004: 255–60). As their usage has been limited in both the number of firms and the amount of stocks granted, inclusion of stock options would not change our Japanese estimates.

comparable between the two countries during 1929–35. Then wage income concentration in both countries fell sharply by the end of the Second World War. In contrast to Japan, however, US top wage income shares had remained low during the 1950s and 1960s. Japan and the United States exhibited the similar degree of wage income concentration at the end of the 1960s. The pattern of wage income concentration has sharply diverged between the two countries since the 1970s, however. While the top 1 per cent wage income share in Japan has been nearly constant at around 5 per cent from 1970 to 2005, the share in the United States has risen exponentially from 5 per cent to 12 per cent during the same period. Consequently, today, the United States exhibits a much higher degree of wage income concentration than in Japan.

One may question that the wage income concentration in Japan is seriously underestimated because Japanese companies make extensive use of tax-exempted non-cash compensation.[36] According to Abowd and Kaplan (1999), the inclusion of in-kind benefits and perquisites to the sum of salary, bonus, and stock options would raise total compensation for Japanese CEOs in 1988–96 by 32 per cent and for American CEOs by 10 per cent. This difference, however, is far too small to explain the huge gap in top wage shares between the USA and Japan.

What explains the diverging trends in wage income concentration between the two countries, then? Note that, by 1980, Japan had virtually caught up with the United States in both the level of income per capita and the stage of industrialization, as both countries entered the third industrial revolution characterized by high technology industries. Therefore, the comparative experience of the United States and Japan suggests that technology alone cannot account for the change in wage inequality. At the very least, elements other than technology—government policies, labour market institutions, demography, and social norms regarding pay inequality[37]—have to be taken into consideration. Although understanding the relative contributions of those elements is beyond the scope of this chapter, below we briefly examine the effect of income tax policies on wage inequality.

To assess the impact of income tax rates on wage income distribution, Figure 3.12 presents the top 0.1 per cent wage income share and the effective marginal income tax rates faced by this group in Japan (in Panel A) and the United States (in Panel B) from 1960 to 2005. In the United States, a number of influential studies, such as Lindsey (1987) and Feldstein (1995), have argued that the reductions in the top marginal tax rates since the 1970s—especially the sharp reduction in the late 1980s—were the key factor that drove up high wage incomes. According to their view, referred to as supply side theory, lower tax rates would increase reported incomes through higher labour supply and/or a

---

[36] Although all non-cash compensation is in principle taxable in Japan, expense account is fully exempted and company housing is partially exempted. See Appendix 3C.

[37] According to the ISSP Social Inequality III survey conducted in 1999, despite the higher income inequality in the United States than in Japan, 36% of 1,325 Japanese respondents strongly agreed with the statement, 'Differences in income in my country are too large', while only 23% of 1,272 US respondents strongly agreed with the same statement. These responses can be seen as an indication of lower tolerance to income inequality in Japan compared to the United States.

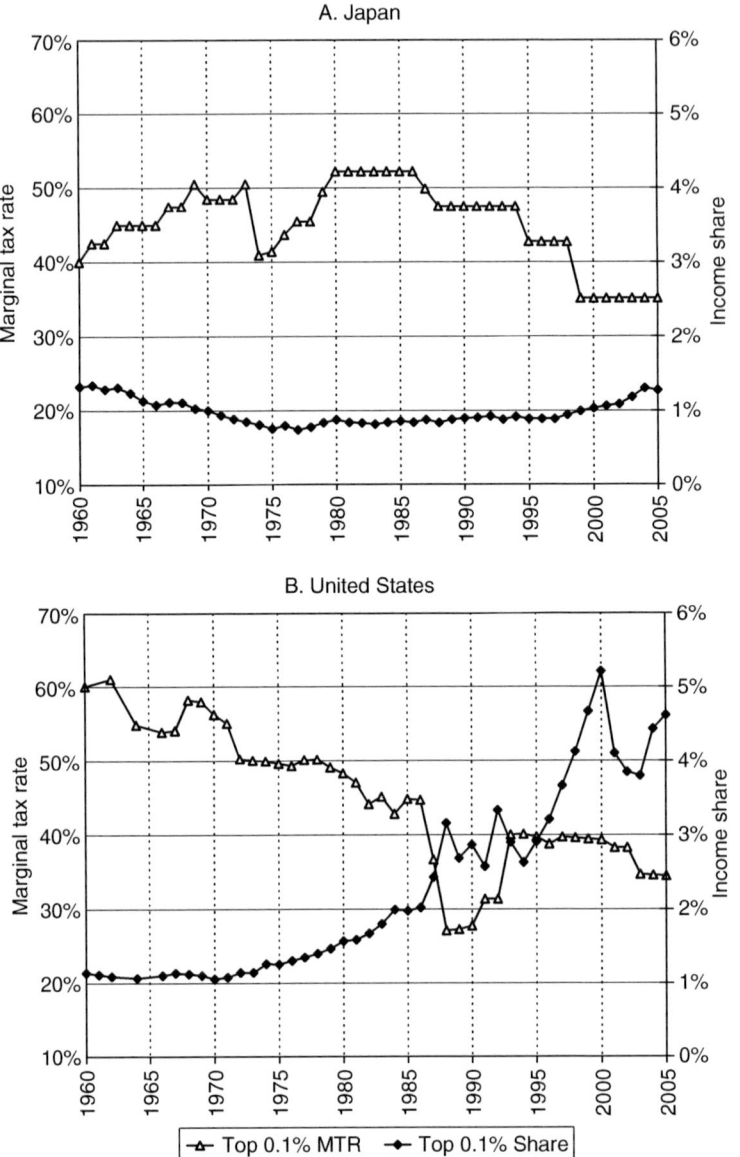

Figure 3.12 Top 0.1% wage income shares and marginal tax rates in Japan and the United States, 1960–2005

Sources: Japan, Appendix Table 3C.2 and computation by authors based on Table 3C3; USA, Saez (2004).

Notes: 'Top 0.1% MTR' refers to the effective marginal tax rate for the average tax payer in the top 0.1% wage income group with only wage income.

Marginal tax rate is estimated for an individual with non-working spouse and two dependent children.

Marginal tax rates in the USA are computed using micro tax return data and TAXSIM calculator.

Basic and dependent exemptions and employment income deductions are taken into account, but other non-standard tax reliefs and local income taxes are not included.

Social insurance contributions are defined as a fixed percentage of earnings up to the maximum earnings in both the US and Japan and therefore do not affect MTRs for the top 0.1% wage income earners. See Appendix 3C for details.

shift from tax-exempted forms of compensation to taxable compensation. Their conclusions have been challenged by subsequent studies and remain controversial (see Saez 2004 for an extensive survey). It is in this context that Japan's experience may offer a new insight. As shown in Panel A, the marginal tax rate faced by the top 0.1 per cent wage income earners in Japan has also declined by 20 percentage points between 1980 and 2005, the magnitude roughly comparable to that in the United States during the same period.[38] These reductions, however, have failed to generate supply side effects in Japan, at least until recently. The comparative experience of Japan and the United States thus also rules out tax incentives as the primary determinant of wage inequality. In case of Japan, highly developed internal labour markets, strong emphasis on firm-specific human capital, and the resulting absence of competitive markets for corporate executives might have played a key role in preventing the rise in wage inequality. By contrast, as Frydman (2005) documents, the inter-firm mobility of US executives has been increasing since the 1970s, indicating the presence of active labour markets and higher outside options for top managers in recent decades.

3.7 CONCLUDING REMARKS

In this chapter, we have studied the evolution of income concentration in Japan from 1886 to 2005 by constructing long-run series of top income shares and top wage income shares. To conclude our study, we re-evaluate Japan's historical experience from a comparative perspective.

According to our data, far from the egalitarian society that it is known for today, Japan was a nation with high income inequality during the first phase of industrialization. Although top income shares in Japan in the 1920s were extremely high by modern standards, they were roughly comparable to those of other industrial nations, such as Britain, the United States, France, Germany, and the Netherlands, during the same decade (Atkinson 2007a; Piketty and Saez 2003; Piketty 2003; Dell 2007; Atkinson and Salverda 2007). While most of these countries experienced a substantial decline in income concentration during the Great Depression, the impact of the Depression on the Japanese economy was far milder. As a result, even by international standards, Japan exhibited a high degree of income concentration on the eve of the Second World War: as of 1939, the top 1 per cent income earners received almost 20 per cent of total income in Japan, whereas the share was about 15 per cent in France, the United States, and Germany.

The top income shares in Japan then fell abruptly and dramatically during the Second World War and the impact of the war on top income shares was much

---

[38] The marginal tax rates in Japan and the USA exclude social security taxes and local income taxes. Including these components would not affect our comparative analysis. See notes in Figure 3.12 and Appendix 3C.

more pronounced in Japan than in the United States, or even Britain, France, and Germany. Our data indicate that this one-time income de-concentration process had a long lasting impact in Japan. We argue that the structural change of the economy after the Second World War transformed a temporary effect into a quasi-permanent one. In particular, we suggest that the fundamental changes in tax policies, corporate governance, and human resource management in the 1960s probably have prevented the re-concentration of income in Japan during the period of high economic growth. Although it is too early to say, a steady increase in top income shares in Japan over the last decade may well be a reflection of the ongoing structural change of the Japanese economy since the 1990s. This recent increase, however, is very modest compared with a dramatic increase in the income concentration in the USA and other Anglo-Saxon countries.

Finally, we draw two broader lessons from history. First, our data indicate that Japan achieved two 'economic miracles' before and after the Second World War under very different degrees of income concentration. Our findings thus cast doubt on simple relations between income inequality and economic growth often assumed in the literature, but instead suggest their complex relations to which specific institutional context matters (Banerjee and Duflo 2003). Second, according to the high-income studies, not only in Japan but in many leading industrial countries, income was once highly concentrated at the top. It was exogenous shocks such as the Great Depression and world wars, rather than endogenous technological or political process, that reduced income concentration in these countries. Consistent with the experience in many developing countries today, historical evidence underscores the difficulty of implementing drastic redistributive policies in the absence of a major exogenous impetus.

APPENDIX 3A: TOP INCOME SHARES

Definition of Income

Our primary data source is individual income tax return statistics published in *Annual Statistical Report* (*Zeimu Tokei Nenposho*) from 1887 by the Tax Bureau of Japan Ministry of Finance (*Shuzeikyoku*), renamed the National Tax Administration (*Kokuzeicho*) after 1947. Among other information, it publishes a table with the number of taxpayers residing in Japan, the amount of reported income, and the amount of income tax, by income brackets, which can be used to estimate top income shares. Note that the Tax Bureau's jurisdictional area was Japan proper and did not include colonies.

We define income as a gross income before deductions and payroll taxes paid by individuals, but after payroll taxes by employers and corporate income taxes. It includes employment income, business income, farm income, self-employment income, and capital income, but excludes realized capital gains as discussed below.

We refer to the year of the annual report (the year when income tax returns were processed and tax was paid) as 'fiscal year' which may be different from 'actual year' in which the income subject to taxation was earned. Because tax laws affect the nature and definition of the reported income in the income tax statistics, we first summarize the evolution of income tax laws in Japan. Unless noted otherwise, the following description is based on Japan National Tax Administration (1988), which provides detailed history of the Japanese income tax system from 1887 to 1987.

Income Tax Laws, 1887–2005

National-level individual income tax was first introduced in 1887 in Japan. During our sample period, there were three major income tax reforms in 1899, 1940, and 1947, and numerous minor revisions.

Under the 1887 income tax law, income was defined comprehensively to include capital income (interest, rents, and dividends), employment income (salaries, bonuses, benefits, and pensions), business and farm income, and other property income. It set a high exemption point (300 yen) and extremely low marginal tax rates (1.0–3.0 per cent) defined over five income brackets.

The 1899 law established income tax on three classes of income: corporate income, interest income, and individual income not included in the first two classes. Individual income tax during fiscal years 1899–1939 is thus often called 'Class III income tax'. It maintained the same exemption point (300 yen) and moderate tax rates (1.0–5.5 per cent) defined over twelve income brackets. Over the next two decades, income tax became increasingly progressive, with the highest marginal tax rate reaching 36 per cent by 1920. The tax rates were raised further by the temporary tax increase law in 1937 and the revised temporary tax increase law in 1938. Under the 1899 law, dividends and bonuses paid by corporations to individuals became non-taxable. From fiscal year 1920, however, 60 per cent of dividends and bonuses became taxable, and 80 per cent from 1937. We thus correct for missing dividends and bonuses, for the fiscal years 1899–1939.

The 1940 tax reform, in preparation for the wartime economy, established separate taxes on corporate income and individual income. Individual income was subject to both schedule tax and comprehensive tax. Under the schedule tax, income was taxed at different (flat) rates by income source (i.e. real estate, dividend and interest, self-employment, wage, forestry, and retirement incomes). In addition, comprehensive income tax was imposed on individuals' aggregate income above 5,000 yen with progressive tax rates that increased from 10 per cent to 65 per cent over twelve income brackets. We use the comprehensive income tax statistics in estimating top income shares for the fiscal years 1940–6.

The 1947 income tax reform, under the influence of US occupational authority, abolished the schedule tax and established a unified comprehensive income tax. Realized capital gains became taxable for the first time in 1947. The 1947 law also introduced an extensive withholding system (*gensen choshu seido*) for wage earners. As a result, for most wage earners, income tax was withheld at source, and they were no longer required to file self-assessed income tax returns (see Appendix 3C). The unified comprehensive income tax, culminating in the 1950 tax law, however, was soon replaced by the hybrid of comprehensive taxation, separate taxation withheld partially or wholly at source, and special exemptions in subsequent years. Under the hybrid system, instead of aggregating all incomes earned by an individual to apply a progressive tax rate, some incomes were taxed at flat rates separately from other incomes and some were tax exempted entirely (see below). Most important, separate taxation was introduced for interest income in 1951, for dividends in 1965, for part of real estate capital gains in 1969, which effectively gave substantial tax reduction to high-income earners. Capital gains from stocks had been tax exempted from 1953 to 1988, but were taxed separately after the 1988 reform. In addition, various tax privileges had been given to small-sized personal savings since 1963 until they were abolished by the 1988 tax reform.

Correspondence between Fiscal Years and Actual Years

In estimating top income shares series, it is important to know when the income reported in the tax statistics was actually earned. We first describe what the formal laws stipulated and then present our preferred specification based on how the laws were implemented. The following information is based on the tax codes reprinted in Japan National Tax Administration (1988).

For fiscal years 1887–98, the income tax law defined the income for tax purposes in year t as: for rents, farm income, and business income, the average of the incomes earned in previous three years (i.e. years $t–1$, $t–2$, $t–3$), and for interest, dividends, and employment income, projected income earned in the same year t. For fiscal years 1899–1925, all income except for farm income (which continued to be the average of previous three years) was defined as projected income earned in the same year. For fiscal years 1926–46, the law stated that the income reported for tax purposes should be based on the income earned in previous year $t–1$. Starting in fiscal year 1947, with the introduction of the withholding system for wage earners, income tax became a pay-as-you-earn system, and income tax paid in year t was based on the income earned in the same year.

In summary, according to the legal definition, (1) for fiscal years 1887–98, reported income in fiscal year t corresponds to a weighted average of incomes earned in years t, $t–1$, $t–2$, and $t–3$; (2) for 1899–1925, reported income in fiscal year t corresponds primarily to income earned in year t; (3) for 1926–46, fiscal year t corresponds to actual year $t–1$; and (4) for 1947–2005, fiscal year t coincides with actual year t.

In reality, however, we believe that it was difficult for the tax authority to obtain an accurate estimate of projected income in the absence of any withholding system during fiscal years 1887–1925. In addition, not all taxpayers filed an income tax return during this period. According to the laws, taxpayers were required to file a return and report the amount of income in April each year. A locally elected committee then examined individuals they deemed responsible for paying income tax, including those who did not file a return. The committee then determined the amount of income tax based both on the tax returns and their own enquiry. In fact, a large fraction of the people who paid income tax did not file a return (it was 48–78 per cent during 1903–25, the years for which data are available). Given this and the subsequent change in the 1926 law, we postulate that the committee was likely to rely on previous year's income as the best available estimate for projected income even before 1926, especially for those who did not file income tax returns. Thus, as our preferred specification, we assume that (1) for fiscal years 1887–1946, fiscal year t corresponds to actual year $t-1$; and (2) for 1947–2005, fiscal year t coincides with actual year t. Note that, due to the 1947 reform that adopted the pay-as-you-earn system, income earned in 1946 was not subject to progressive comprehensive income tax (it was subject to special tax), and hence we do not have data for 1946. The correspondence between fiscal years (in which tax was paid) and actual years (in which income was earned) is summarized in columns (1) and (2) of Table 3A.1.

To see if our estimates are sensitive to the specification of years, we also estimate top income shares series using the legal definitions. In doing so, based on income composition data, for fiscal years 1887–98, we place 50 per cent weight on income in year t and 50 per cent weight on the simple average of incomes in years $t-1$, $t-2$, $t-3$. For fiscal years 1899–1925, we place 100 per cent weight on income t, as farm income constituted a relatively small portion of total income. Figure 3A.4 plots the top 0.1 per cent income share series using the legal definitions ('formal law' series), along with our series ('preferred specification'). Except for years 1916–22, two series exhibit fairly similar levels and trends.

Tax Units

For fiscal years 1887–1949, the unit of income tax was 'family' defined as a married couple with dependants (e.g. children and old parents) or a single head of household with dependants. Incomes of cohabiting family members in a single household were aggregated for income tax purposes. Starting in fiscal year 1950, the unit of income tax became 'individual' whereby spouses are taxed separately on their incomes. The income tax statistics in 1950–2005 do not allow us to reconstruct household income. To produce homogeneous series over the entire period, we choose the individual as the tax unit. Fortunately, in fiscal years 1903–38 and 1949, the statistics provide a breakdown of total income into the income of household head and the income of dependants, by income brackets. According to these data, the latter is very small relative to the former (less than 5 per cent of the former in general). Hence, we substitute household income for household head's income, which leads to slight upward bias in our estimates.

Our top income groups are defined relative to the total number of adults, defined as 20 years old and above, in Japan (not including colonies). The total adult population, reported in Table 3A.1, is estimated as follows. First, we take the total population from Japan Statistics Bureau (2003: 32). Based on census data, the yearbook reports the estimated total population as of 1 January for years 1886–1919 and as of 1 October for years 1920–2005. Then we take the estimated population of people younger than 20 years old for years 1885–1920 from Ohkawa, Shinohara, and Umemura (1974: ii. 166–71).

Starting in 1920, the Japanese census, conducted every ten years, reports population by age.[39] We estimate the population of people younger than 20 years old in between census years by assuming its ratio to the total population changes linearly between census years. We define our total adult population series as the total population minus the population younger than 20 years old.

For the 1887–1949 period, we also computed top income shares using 'household' as the tax unit (the total number of households in Japan is obtained from Otsuki and Takamatsu 1982: table 1, p. 340). The results are not reported in the chapter, but available upon request. We found that the pattern of household top income shares is very similar to the pattern of individual top income shares, as the ratio of adults to households remained stable during 1885–1950 (it fluctuated between 2.65 and 2.95 with no trend).

Total Income Denominator

In order to obtain top income shares, we need to estimate the total income in Japan to be used as the denominator. This denominator should ideally be total personal income reported on tax returns *had* everybody been required to file an income tax return. As only a small fraction of households filed income tax returns before 1947, the income tax statistics cannot be used to estimate the denominator, and we must rely on National Accounts data.

System of National Accounts, 1930–2005

The System of National Accounts (SNA) in Japan has provided comprehensive estimates of national income since 1930. There are three partially overlapping series: (1) the old SNA, 1930–76, reported in Japan Statistics Bureau (1989: iii, section 13–5), (2) the 68SNA, 1955–98, reported ibid., table 3.6,[40] (3) the 93SNA, 1980–2005, reported ibid., table 3.24.[41] The SNAs are fairly detailed and provide the breakdown of personal income into the main components: wages and salaries, social contributions of employers and employees, personal capital income (dividends, net interest income, rents received), unincorporated business income (agricultural income, imputed rents of homeowners, and other business income).

Social contributions of employers and imputed rents are not part of the taxable individual income. Hence we define our personal income denominator as the sum of wages and salaries, employees' social insurance contributions, personal capital income, and unincorporated business income (excluding imputed rents). The old SNA does not report imputed rents separately from received rents for 1946–76. We have estimated imputed rents for the old SNA using the 68SNA, assuming that the fraction of imputed rents in total rents for 1946–55 is equal to the fraction from 68SNA in 1955, the first year the 68SNA becomes available. Similarly, the old SNA does not report a breakdown of social contributions between employees and employers. We assume that social contributions from 1930 to 1954 are divided as in year 1955. Social contributions were very small during that period, and therefore this imputation has a very small effect on our total income denominator.

---

[39] Available online at http://www.stat.go.jp/english/data/nenkan/zuhyou/y0207000.xls.
[40] Available online at http://www.stat.go.jp/english/data/chouki/index.htm.
[41] Available online at http://www.stat.go.jp/english/data/chouki/index.htm.

The 93SNA reports the returns on insurance funds separately, but this item was included in personal capital income in the old SNA and the 68SNA. We added back the returns on insurance funds to personal capital income for the 93SNA years to obtain consistent series even though the returns on insurance funds are not part of the taxable income.

Our personal income denominator is obtained from the 93SNA for the 1999–2005 period, the 68SNA for the 1955–98 period, and from the old SNA for the 1930–54 period, and then spliced together. The 93SNA and 68SNA personal income denominators are extremely close in 1998 (less than 1 per cent difference) so we do not make any correction to connect the 68SNA and 93SNA in 1998. The old SNA personal income denominator in 1955 is 4.4 per cent higher than the 68SNA in 1955. Therefore, in order to obtain homogeneous series, we have reduced old SNA personal income by 4.4 per cent so that the old SNA matches the 68SNA exactly in 1955. The old SNA does not provide estimates for 1945. Therefore, we have assumed, as in Maddison (1995), that real income in 1945 is one half of real income in 1944, based on estimates from other authors.

Personal Income Denominator, 1886–1930

We estimate the personal income denominator for the years 1886–1930 based on the series of personal disposable income in Japan proper in Ohkawa et al. (1974: i, table 8, column 9). Personal disposable income in 1930 is 11.5 per cent higher than the personal income denominator in the same year estimated above from the old SNA. Therefore, to obtain homogeneous series, we have reduced personal disposable income from 1886 to 1929 by 11.5 per cent.

It is important to note that total income estimates before 1930 are much less reliable than those after 1930, as no elaborate system of national accounts had existed. Although the estimates by Ohkawa et al. (1974) are considered most definite and reliable, there are three other national income estimates (reported in *Historical Statistics of Japan*, iii, table 13–3, pp. 344–9).

Yamada estimates from 1875 to 1948 are about 10 to 15 per cent percent higher than Ohkawa et al. estimates before 1900, comparable during the 1900–15 period, and about 10 to 20 per cent lower during 1915–30. Using Yamada estimates would have produced a more markedly increasing pattern of top income shares during the period 1885 to 1930 but would not have changed the conclusion that top income shares were much higher in the pre-Second World War period than in the post-war period.

Hijikata estimates from 1900 to 1937 are substantially (40 to 50 per cent) lower than Ohkawa et al. estimates during the 1900–20 period and somewhat (about 20 per cent) lower from 1920 to 1937. Thus Hijikata estimates would have led to even higher top income shares in the 1900–37 period and more declining pattern of top income shares over the 1900–37 period.

Finally, the Cabinet Bureau of Statistics series from 1887 to 1935 report substantially (about 40 per cent) higher estimates than Ohkawa et al. estimates in the 1887–95 period and then much (about 30 per cent) lower estimates in the period 1900–35. Those estimates are obtained directly from taxable income, however, and therefore the least appropriate as an independent denominator in our study.

Consumer Price Index, 1886–2005

We use a consumer price index (CPI) to deflate our nominal income series. Our CPI estimates for years 1886–1938 and 1946–50 are from Ohkawa et al. (1967: viii. 135, column 1). Estimates for 1938–46 are obtained from taking the ratios of real National Income to nominal National Income from *Historical Statistics of Japan*, p. 7, and pasted to the Okhawa estimates. For the 1950–2005 period, our CPI estimates are from *Japan Statistical Yearbook*. Then the pre- and post-1950 series are spliced together. The price index (with base 100 in 2002) is reported in Table 3A.1, column (9). The total real personal income denominator and average personal income per adult are reported in columns (7) and (8) in Table 3A.1.

Top Income Numerator

For the numerator, we estimate the income accrued to top income groups (e.g. top 0.01 per cent, 0.1 per cent, 0.5 per cent, 1 per cent, etc.), defined relative to the total adult population, as follows. Because the top tail of the income distribution is well approximated by a Pareto distribution, we estimate Pareto coefficients bracket by bracket for each year using the distribution tables in the income tax statistics. We employ the same parametric interpolation method, as in Piketty and Saez (2003), to estimate threshold income levels for the top income groups. We obtain the top income numerators for the respective top income groups simply by aggregating all incomes above the thresholds.

In almost all years up to the late 1970s, the top bracket contains fewer than the top 0.01 per cent individuals. For recent decades, however, the top bracket contains about the top 0.05 per cent individuals. We thus extrapolate within the top bracket assuming a constant Pareto parameter within the top bracket. Starting in 2005 (the latest year available), the tax administration made available a distribution table with much finer income brackets at the top.[42] According to these data, our extrapolation method within the top bracket in fact provides a fairly close (within 5 per cent) estimate for year 2005.

To produce homogeneous series, the income definition in the statistics has to be consistent across years. Below, we discuss major corrections we made to the original data to ensure consistency.

Combining Self-Assessed Income Tax Statistics and Wage Income Tax Statistics, 1951–2005

Our primary data source for the post-1947 period is the self-assessed income tax statistics that are summarized in *Annual Statistical Report*, 1947–2005, and published in more detail in the results of the sample survey for self-assessed income tax in the *Survey on Self-Assessed Income Tax* since 1963.[43] Due to the extensive and sophisticated withholding system, most individuals in Japan with only employment or pension income are not required to file self-assessed income tax returns. Typically, at the end of the year, there is an adjustment in the last amount withheld so that total tax withheld coincides exactly with total income tax due. As a result, although most income earners in Japan paid income taxes in 1951–2005, only 10–15 per cent of all adults filed tax returns each year. That is to say, a large number of income earners are missing from the self-assessed income tax statistics.

Fortunately, the Japanese tax administration also publishes wage income tax statistics that cover most private wage earners regardless of whether they filed tax returns. We use these statistics to complement the self-assessed income tax statistics. As described in Appendix 3C, the data include the distribution (by wage income brackets) of annual

---

[42] Available at: http://www.nta.go.jp/category/toukei/tokei/h17/hyouhon.htm.
[43] National Tax Administration (1963–2005), *Shikoku Shookuzei no Jittai*, which is available online for recent years at: http://www.nta.go.jp/category/toukei/tokei-e.htm.

wage income for virtually all employees in the private sector, but exclude government employees and retirees. We inflate the survey distribution by a uniform 10 per cent factor in order to account for the people not included in the wage income survey. This is equivalent to assuming that their income distribution is the same as that of private sector employees, which probably introduces a slight upward bias in our estimates.

We then combine the self-assessed income tax statistics and the wage income tax statistics to obtain a complete income distribution. The key difficulty is that those wage earners (1) who have income larger than 200,000 yen from other sources, (2) whose employment income exceeds 20 million yen, and (3) who receive wages from two or more employers during the year are required to file self-assessed income tax returns. Thus, before combining the wage income statistics and the self-assessed statistics, we have to subtract wage earners filing tax returns from the wage income survey. We use the income composition data from the self-assessed income tax statistics to do so.

Starting in 1963, the composition tables in the statistics present the number of wage earners (defined as taxpayers with any wage income) and the reported wage income, by income bracket. From those statistics, we estimate a distribution of wage income (by wage income brackets) for those wage income earners who filed tax returns. We obtain such a distribution by assuming that the ranking by total income and the ranking by wage income are the same. For example, in 2005, the self-assessed income tax statistics report that there are 40,035 filers in the top income bracket of incomes above 50 million yen. Those filers report on average 94.260 million yen. Among those 40,035 filers, 29,916 report some wage income, and the total wage income reported in the top bracket by those 29,916 wage earners is 1,227 billion yen. We assume that the top bracket of the wage income distribution contains 29,916 wage earners reporting on average 41.021 million yen (1,227 billion divided by 29,916) of wage income. We repeat this procedure for each bracket. We then need to estimate the wage income thresholds corresponding to those brackets. We proceed as follows. We first estimate the wage share in each bracket as the ratio of the average wage income in the bracket (41.021 million yen in the example given above) divided by the average total income in the bracket (94.260 million yen in the example given above). We then estimate the wage income thresholds corresponding to those brackets as the threshold for total income (50 million yen in the example given) times the mean of the wage share in the corresponding bracket and the bracket just below (in the example given above, these are the brackets 50 million and above, and 20 to 50 million yen respectively).

The above procedure generates a distribution of wage income by brackets for wage earners filing tax returns. We then subtract out this distribution from the wage income distribution based on the wage income tax statistics. This subtraction is done by assuming that the two distributions are Pareto distributed bracket by bracket. The resulting net distribution represents all wage income earners who did not file tax returns. Finally, we add this net distribution to the original self-assessed income distribution (using the same Pareto interpolation method) to obtain the final wage income distribution.

The key assumption underlying this method is that, among the self-assessed income tax return filers with positive wage income, the ranking by total income is identical to the ranking by wage income. If this assumption is not met, then our method would overstate the number of high wage filers in the final distribution and hence create small upward bias in our top income share estimates. For the analysis of income inequality, it would be extremely valuable if the tax administration produces aggregated tables that show the distribution of income earners regardless of whether a self-assessed income tax return was filed.[44]

---

[44] Currently, the administration does not compile such data even for internal purposes.

For years 1951–62, the self-assessed income tax statistics did not report wage income or the number of wage income earners by income brackets, but only in the aggregate. As a result, for these years, we first estimate top income shares by adding wage income earners from the wage survey to the self-assessed income tax statistics (without making the correction described above). We then correct top income share estimates for years 1951–62 by the ratio of estimates for 1963 with the correction applied to estimates for 1963 where the correction is not applied.

Removing Capital Gains, 1947–2005

For fiscal years 1887–1946, although never explicitly stated in the income tax laws, from the fact that no capital gains were reported in the composition data, we conclude that capital gains were not subject to individual income tax during this period. Since 1947, realized capital gains have become taxable, but they have been subject to special exemptions and separate taxation that changed over time (Ishi 2001: 143–4). Because (1) capital gains reported in the self-assessed income tax statistics are the taxable value after special exemptions and deductions[45] and (2) those capital gains whose tax was entirely withheld at source are not reported in the statistics, even after 1947, our data capture only part of realized capital gains.[46] To obtain consistent estimates, we remove capital gains from our data for the 1947–2005 period as follows.

We first compute the share of realized capital gains in each top income group using the income composition data by brackets and simple linear interpolation (as in Piketty and Saez 2003). Second, we subtract 80 per cent of the realized capital gain component from our top income share estimates. For example, if the top 1 per cent income share with capital gains is 6 per cent, and the share of capital gains is 50 per cent, we estimate the top 1 per cent income share as $6*(1-0.5*0.8)=3.6$ per cent. Removing 100 per cent of the capital gain component would bias the income shares downwards, as the ranking of taxpayers by income excluding capital gains is not necessarily equal to the ranking including capital gains. This issue also arises in the US study by Piketty and Saez (2003) and the Canadian study by Saez and Veall (2005). Using micro-data where it is possible to estimate income shares with and without capital gains, Saez and Veall (2005) conclude that the 80 per cent rule generates fairly accurate estimates.

---

[45] Based on the author's phone conversation with a Japan Tax Administration officer on 5 May 2006.

[46] Capital gains from stocks were taxed under comprehensive income tax in 1947–53, but were tax exempted in 1953–88 except for the cases involving large volume and frequent trading. From 1989 to 2005, capital gains from stocks are either taxed separately and withheld at source (and thus missing from our data) or taxed separately as part of self-assessed income tax (included in our data). In 2001–3, for capital gains from listed stocks held for more than 1 year, special deduction of 1 million yen was granted (thus under-reported in our data). Capital gains from bonds are not taxed throughout the 1947–2005 period. Capital gains from real estate (mostly land) were taxed under comprehensive income tax in 1947–68 after certain deduction, but for long-term capital gains (real estate held for more than three years), only 50% of the amount after deduction was taxed (thus under-reported in our data). From 1969 to 1975, long-term capital gains (real estate held for more than five years) were taxed separately at flat rates as part of self-assessed income tax. In 1976–88, part of long-term capital gains from real estate were taxed under comprehensive income tax. From 1989 to 2005, all long-term capital gains from real estate were taxed separately as part of self-assessed income tax, but with numerous special deductions and tax rates depending on the nature and usage of land (thus under-reported in our data).

Although we do not know if the 80 per cent rule applies also to the case of Japan, the following observation provides some assurance. If the correction factor is too large (such as excluding 100 per cent of realized gains), then when capital gains surge, the series excluding capital gains should dip. If the correction factor is too small, then when capital gains surge, the series excluding capital gains should rise. In Figure 3A.1, we present the top 0.1 per cent income share series with and without realized capital gains for the post-1947 period. It shows that the series without capital gains are fairly stable during the two periods of asset appreciation, first in the early 1970s and then in the late 1980s. This suggests that the 80 per cent rule for correcting capital gains is fairly adequate. To further improve our methodology, it would be necessary to have an access to individual micro-data in Japan.

According to Figure 3A.1, realized capital gains in fact had a large impact on the top 0.1 per cent income share during the two episodes of asset appreciation as well as in recent years. As noted above, however, capital gains reported in the self-assessed income tax statistics are subject to considerable underestimate. The series including full capital gains would thus display even larger spikes in the early 1970s and late 1980s. Nevertheless, the figure indicates that the impact of capital gains on the top shares tends to be short-lived, as capital gains in general are realized in a lumpy manner and do not constitute a source of steady annual income. We thus believe that the inclusion of capital gains would not change the *long-run* trends in the top income shares series. Furthermore, although we suspect that realized capital gains from land and stocks are much higher in the post-war period than in the pre-war period, it must be noted that the distributions of land and stocks were probably much more equal after the Second World War than before. Thus the inclusion of capital gains would not change our main finding that income concentration fell drastically from the pre-war period to the post-war period.

Erosion of Comprehensive Income Tax Base, 1950–2005

Soon after the introduction of the unified comprehensive income tax system in 1947–50, the Japanese government began to give special tax measures to various components of income (see Ishi 2001: chapter 8; Iwamoto, Fujishima, and Akiyama 1995). As a result, the erosion of comprehensive income tax base poses a potentially serious problem for us when using the income tax statistics. These special measures are: (1) full exemption from taxation (*hikazei*), (2) separate taxation at a flat rate with its tax entirely withheld at source (*gensen bunri kazei*), and (3) separate taxation at flat rate that is only partially withheld at source and requires self-assessed income tax returns (*shinkoku bunri kazei*). While income subject to (3) is included in the self-assessed income tax statistics, income subject to (1) and (2) is missing from these statistics.

According to the estimates by Iwamoto, Fujishima, and Akiyam (1995), before the 1988 reform, 70–80 per cent of total interest income was tax exempted under the tax privilege given to small-sized personal savings, 20 per cent was taxed separately and withheld at source, and only 0.3 per cent was subject to progressive comprehensive income tax. After the 1988 reform, only 20 per cent of total interest income was tax exempted, but almost 80 per cent was taxed separately and withheld at source, leaving less than 0.1 per cent of interest income under the comprehensive income tax. For dividend income, about 70 per cent was taxed separately and withheld at source, and 30 per cent was subject to comprehensive taxation throughout the 1980–2005 period.

Consequently, virtually all interest income and about 70 per cent of dividend income are missing from the income tax statistics in recent decades. Ishi (1979, 2001) has attempted to compute a comprehensive income base in order to assess the effect of tax erosion on taxes collected, using unpublished data obtained from the fiscal administration. In our chapter, we do not try to incorporate missing interest and dividend income directly in our estimates but rather assess the sensitivity of our estimates to those missing components using a wealth survey as described in Appendix 3D.

Imputing Missing Capital Income, 1898–1938

During fiscal years 1887–98, the income tax base was comprehensive, fully including dividends, interest, and bonuses. During fiscal years 1899–1920, dividend, bonuses, and part of interest income were excluded from Class III income and hence disappeared from the statistics. From August of 1920 to 1936, 60 per cent of dividends and bonuses were included in Class II income, 80 per cent from 1937 to 1939, and 100 per cent after 1940. Interest income was fully included again starting only in fiscal year 1940. These changes potentially create discontinuities in our data, especially for top income groups to which capital income constituted a large share.

First, for fiscal years 1921–39, we can recover missing dividends and bonuses from total reported dividends and bonuses in the Class III income tax statistics, because we know that a fixed percentage of dividends and bonuses are taxed (60 per cent in 1921–36 and 80 per cent in 1937–9). For fiscal years 1899–1920, no dividends or bonuses are reported, and therefore we have to rely on an alternative source to estimate dividends and bonuses. From fiscal years 1899–1939, corporate income was taxed separately as Class I income tax (we assume that for corporate income, fiscal year *t* corresponds to actual year *t*–1). For 1921–39, we can thus estimate corporate profits, using Class I income tax statistics, and total dividends and bonuses paid out to individuals, using Class III income tax statistics. During 1921–35, about 50 per cent of corporate profits were paid out as dividends and about 20 per cent of corporate profits were paid out as bonuses. For 1936–8, corporate profits were very high (around 12–15 per cent of the total personal income denominator), but dividends did not exceed 5 per cent of the total personal income. Therefore, we assume that 50 per cent of corporate profits were paid out as dividends in 1899–1920, up to 5 per cent of total personal income (the 5 per cent rule was binding during the high profit years 1915–18). We also assume that 20 per cent of corporate profits were paid out as bonuses in 1899–1920, up to 2 per cent of total personal income.

Second, we assume that 75 per cent of those missing dividends and bonuses go to the top 1 per cent income earners, 68 per cent to the top 0.5 per cent, 52 per cent to the top 0.1 per cent, 43 per cent to the top 0.05 per cent, and 27 per cent to the top 0.01 per cent. Those percentages are based on the relative composition of dividend income in top groups in the United States in 1916 in the analysis of Piketty and Saez (2003). We reluctantly use this assumption in the absence of the equivalent income composition data for Japan before 1947. Figure 3A.2 presents top 0.1 per cent income share series before and after the corrections for actual years 1898–1938. As the figure shows, our method smoothes most of the discontinuities in the raw data due to the capital income exclusions and seems therefore acceptable.

We have not made any correction for exempted interest income for fiscal years 1899–1939. From 1899 to 1919, only a small fraction of interest income (interest income from public bonds only) was excluded from Class III income tax. It was taxed separately at source (regardless of one's income level) as Class II income, and represented less than 1 per cent of the total personal income denominator. Starting in August of 1920, in addition to public bond interest, interest from bank deposits was also excluded from Class III income and moved to Class II income. As a result, the ratio of Class II income to the total personal income denominator jumped from less than 1 per cent to about 5 per cent in 1921. The total interest income reported in Class III income tax statistics, however, shows no break, implying that the top income earners did not have much bank deposit interest. Therefore, we assume that no correction is necessary for these interest income exclusions. In addition, for fiscal years 1913–39, for income less than certain amounts, 10 to 20 per cent of employment income was tax exempted and excluded from the Class III income statistics. Again, we do not correct for this exemption, as it was not a significant amount for top income earners.

Top Income Composition, 1886–2005

The composition of reported income by income source is published in the income tax statistics at the aggregate level for fiscal years 1887, 1901–46, and 1951–62, and by income brackets for fiscal years 1947–50 and 1963–2005. Using these data, we estimate the composition of the income accrued to the top 1 per cent income group. Although a finer decomposition can be done, we use five income categories: (1) employment income (wages, salaries, bonuses, and pensions), (2) business income (unincorporated business profits, farm income, and self-employment income), (3) rental income (rents from farmland, residential land, residential buildings, and business buildings), (4) interest income, and (5) dividends. Table 3A.3 reports the fraction of the people filing income tax returns and the composition of the top 1 per cent income.

For fiscal years 1887–1946, aggregate composition data are available in 1887 and 1901–46 (thus there is no estimate for actual years 1887–99 and 1946). The categories of income composition changed over the years. For fiscal years 1887 and 1901–39, the income from 'farmland (*tahata*)' includes both farm income from selling crops from the land (labelled 'owner cultivator (*jisaku*)') and rental income from leasing the land to tenants (labelled 'tenant (*kosaku*)').[47] For 1917–39, the breakdown of the farmland income is reported in the statistics. For 1887 and 1901–16, because no such breakdown is given, we estimate the amount of rental income included in the farmland income, using the ratio of rental income to the farmland income in 1917 (the first year for which the breakdown is available). For fiscal years 1901–39, we use the imputed value of dividends and bonuses in computing the income composition.

As the composition data by income brackets are not available before 1947, our estimate for the top 1 per cent income composition in 1886–1945 is simply the composition of the total income reported in the income tax statistics. Because the fraction of population filing income tax returns fluctuated from year to year depending on exemption points and the conditions of the economy, our top income composition series are not consistent over these years. In particular, between 1906 and 1925, relatively high fractions of adults (2.5 per cent to 4.6 per cent) filed income tax returns. If we assume that the share of capital income increases with income, our estimates for these years probably understate the share of capital income in the top 1 per cent income compared to other years.

For fiscal years 1947–50 and 1963–2005, the composition of the top 1 per cent income is estimated from composition data by income brackets, using a linear Interpolation method as in Piketty and Saez (2003). (We provide no estimates for 1951–62. For 1963–2005, we provide estimates only twice a decade.) Realized capital gains are removed as described above. It is important to note that, as explained earlier, almost all interest income after

---

[47] These definitions are explicitly stated for the first time in Japan Ministry of Finance (1938: 36, note 3-a).

1947 and large part of dividends after 1965 are taxed separately at source and thus missing from the income composition. In addition, the introduction of the withholding system for wage earners in 1949 probably reduced the degree of tax evasion in wage income, contributing to a sudden increase in the share of employment income in 1947–50. In order to assess these issues, we compare the composition of the top income based on the tax statistics with the composition of the total personal income based on National Accounts.

In Figure 3A.3, Panel A shows the composition of the top 1 per cent income, and Panel B shows the composition of the total personal income denominator estimated from National Accounts from 1930 to 2005. It is important to keep in mind that (1) imputed rents are excluded from the total personal income because they are not included in the income tax statistics; but (2) returns on insurance funds (which are not taxable and not included in income tax statistics) are included and distributed among the dividend and interest incomes in the total personal income. As mentioned above, we cannot separate the returns from insurance funds from dividends and interest except for recent years with the SNA98 series. The SNA98 data show that over half of dividends are actually earned through insurance funds. As a result, the total personal income estimated from National Accounts would show a larger fraction of capital income than the total income in income tax returns had everybody been required to file a tax return.

Comparing Panels A and B is nevertheless instructive. In 1930, the top 1 per cent income group received a far larger share of their income as dividends (33 per cent) than the national average (3 per cent), but they received smaller shares of income as interest income (2 per cent) and employment income (30 per cent) than the national averages (15 per cent and 45 per cent, respectively). Note that, as in the top 1 per cent income, the capital income component in total personal income declined sharply during 1937–47 from 20 per cent to less than 1 per cent. The dividend component in the total personal income had recovered to its pre-Second World War share by 1980, but the shares of interest and rental income components have remained relatively low. Finally, the employment income component in total personal income fell sharply in 1944–6 and then increased substantially from 1947 to 2005 at the expense of the business income component. But its rise during 1948–50 was much smaller than that in the top 1 per cent income share, indicating that the sudden increase in the latter is probably due to the introduction of the withholding system.

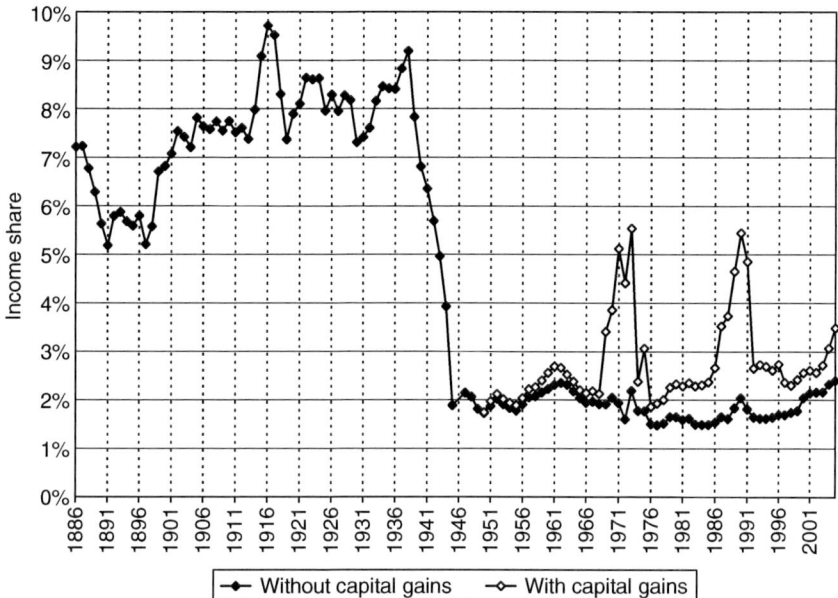

Figure 3A.1 Top 0.1% income share in Japan with and without capital gains

Sources: Series without capital gains, Appendix Table 3A.2; series with capital gains based on authors' computations.

Notes: Realized captal gains are not taxable and not included in the income tax return statistics in 1886–1945. In 1947–2005, only part of realized capital gains are reported in the statistics due to special tax treatments. See Appendix 3A for details.

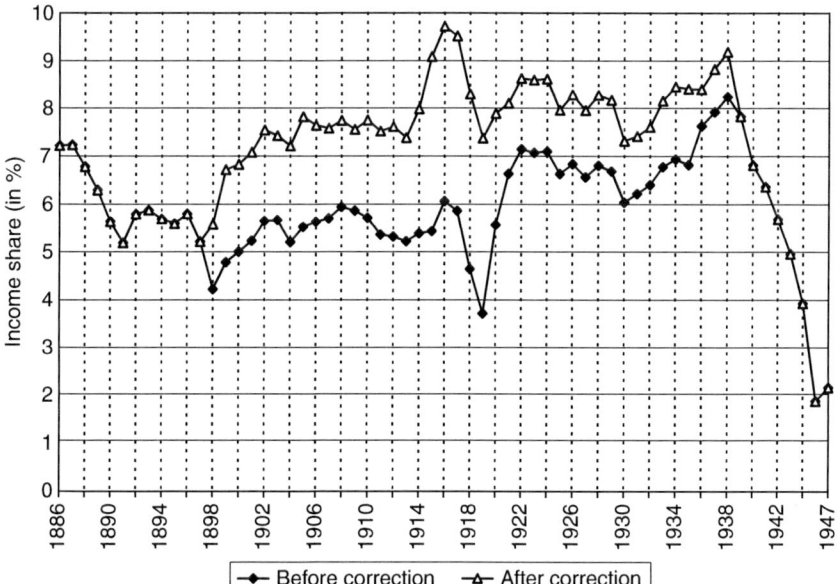

Figure 3A.2 Top 0.1% income share in Japan before and after correction, 1886–1947

Sources: Series after correction, Appendix Table 3A.2; series before correction based on authors' computations.

Notes: Dividends and bonuses are fully exempted from individual income tax in 1898–1919 and partially exempted in 1920–38. See Appendix 3A for the method of correction.

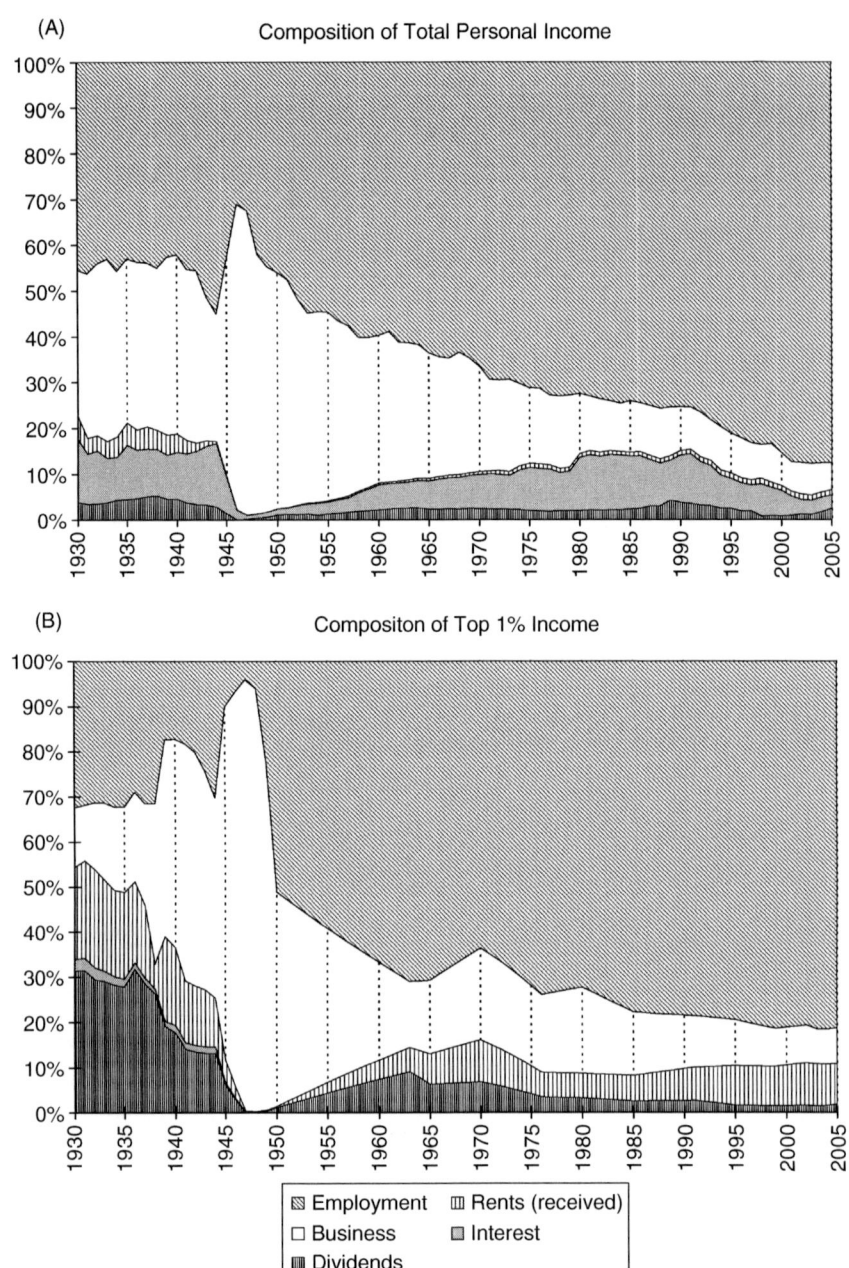

Figure 3A.3 Composition of total personal income and top 1% income, Japan 1930–2005

Notes: Panel A presents the composition of total personal income denominator based on National Accounts. Panel B presents the composition of top 1% income based on Appendix Table 3A.3. Imputed rents are excluded from rents in Panel A to be comparable to Panel B.

Returns on insurance policices are included in dividends and interest in Panel A.

All returns on insurance policies after 1947, almost all interest income after 1947, and large part of dividends after 1965 are not included in Panel B. See Appendix 3A for details.

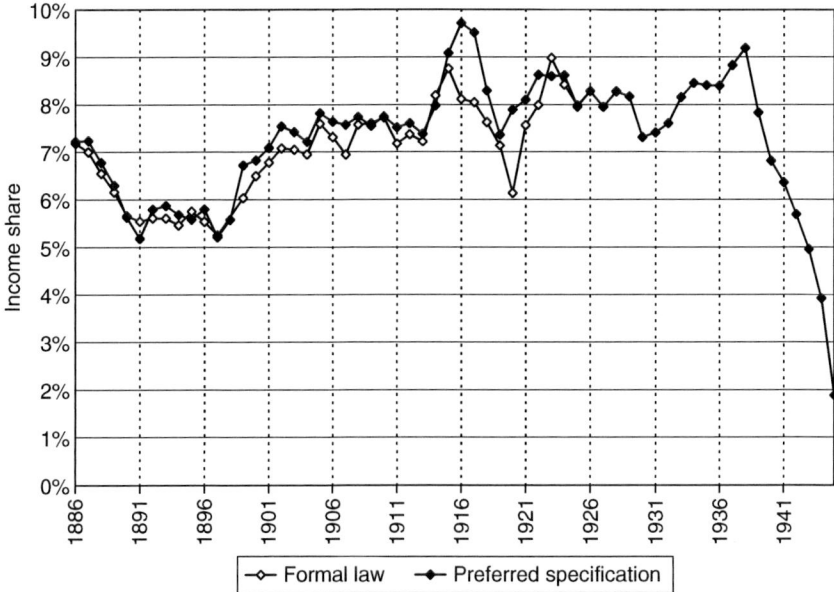

Figure 3A.4 Top 0.1% income share in alternative specification of years, Japan 1886–1945

Notes: 'Preferred Specification' series are from Appendix Table 3A.2; 'Formal Law' series are by authors' computation. In 'Formal Law' series, actual years are defined based on the income tax laws' stipulations. For the definition of 'Preferred Specification' series, see Appendix 3A.

Table 3A.1 Reference totals for population, income, inflation, and marginal tax rates, Japan, 1886–2005

(1)	(2a)	(2b)	(3)	(4)	(5)	(6)	(7)	(8)	(9)	(10)
	Years		Population and Tax units				Income		Inflation	MTR
Actual Year, (incomes earned in)	Fiscal Year (tax paid in)	Fiscal Year (Japanese Calendar)	Population ('000s)	Number of adults ('000s)	Number of tax returns ('000s)	(5)/(4) (%)	Total income (2002 billion yen)	Average income (2002 '000 yen)	CPI (2002 base 100)	Top Marginal Tax Rate (%)
1886	1887	20	38,541	21,853	118.6	0.54	3,708	170	0.0151	3.0
1887	1888	21	38,703	21,908	139.5	0.64	3,552	162	0.0161	3.0
1888	1889	22	39,029	22,054	115.6	0.52	3,867	175	0.0158	3.0
1889	1890	23	39,473	22,267	115.4	0.52	4,072	183	0.0168	3.0
1890	1891	24	39,902	22,471	115.9	0.52	4,363	194	0.0179	3.0
1891	1892	25	40,251	22,629	117.1	0.52	4,991	221	0.0171	3.0
1892	1893	26	40,508	22,734	124.1	0.55	5,186	228	0.0160	3.0
1893	1894	27	40,860	22,892	129.3	0.56	5,438	238	0.0161	3.0
1894	1895	28	41,142	23,011	134.7	0.59	5,943	258	0.0167	3.0
1895	1896	29	41,557	23,203	151.7	0.65	6,387	275	0.0182	3.0
1896	1897	30	41,992	23,405	172.8	0.74	6,222	266	0.0201	3.0
1897	1898	31	42,400	23,623	195.3	0.83	6,636	281	0.0224	3.0
1898	1899	32	42,886	23,884	288.6	1.21	6,754	283	0.0243	5.5
1899	1900	33	43,404	24,162	349.5	1.45	7,425	307	0.0229	5.5
1900	1901	34	43,847	24,399	406.3	1.67	6,808	279	0.0257	5.5
1901	1902	35	44,359	24,674	457.9	1.86	7,117	288	0.0251	5.5
1902	1903	36	44,964	25,000	507.9	2.03	6,928	277	0.0261	5.5
1903	1904	37	45,546	25,313	543.0	2.15	7,111	281	0.0274	9.4
1904	1905	38	46,135	25,630	580.5	2.27	8,021	313	0.0281	20.4
1905	1906	39	46,620	25,889	638.4	2.47	7,614	294	0.0291	20.4
1906	1907	40	47,038	26,110	702.4	2.69	7,827	300	0.0297	20.4
1907	1908	41	47,416	26,234	860.0	3.28	7,864	300	0.0328	20.4
1908	1909	42	47,965	26,452	930.4	3.52	8,079	305	0.0317	20.4

1909	1910	43	48,554	26,689	947.6	3.55	8,453	317	0.0305	20.4
1910	1911	44	49,184	26,947	964.5	3.58	8,738	324	0.0305	20.4
1911	1912	1	49,852	27,223	1,013.5	3.72	9,290	341	0.0328	20.4
1912	1913	2	50,577	27,528	707.9	2.57	9,342	339	0.0346	22.0
1913	1914	3	51,305	27,832	727.1	2.61	9,602	345	0.0357	22.0
1914	1915	4	52,039	28,137	718.2	2.55	9,760	347	0.0329	22.0
1915	1916	5	52,752	28,427	712.6	2.51	11,040	388	0.0308	22.0
1916	1917	6	53,496	28,732	771.0	2.68	12,513	436	0.0332	22.0
1917	1918	7	54,134	29,046	779.5	2.68	14,128	486	0.0408	30.0
1918	1919	8	54,739	29,341	1,079.8	3.68	15,488	528	0.0549	30.0
1919	1920	9	55,033	29,469	994.2	3.37	15,556	528	0.0730	36.0
1920	1921	10	55,963	29,937	1,168.2	3.90	14,618	488	0.0764	36.0
1921	1922	11	56,666	30,283	1,280.9	4.23	14,615	483	0.0700	36.0
1922	1923	12	57,390	30,639	1,400.5	4.57	15,192	496	0.0690	36.0
1923	1924	13	58,119	30,997	1,389.9	4.48	14,726	475	0.0683	36.0
1924	1925	14	58,876	31,369	1,432.3	4.57	15,022	479	0.0689	36.0
1925	1926	1	59,737	31,796	804.4	2.53	15,885	500	0.0698	36.0
1926	1927	2	60,741	32,298	732.2	2.27	16,380	507	0.0666	36.0
1927	1928	3	61,659	32,805	693.8	2.11	17,008	518	0.0656	36.0
1928	1929	4	62,595	33,323	700.5	2.10	17,653	530	0.0631	36.0
1929	1930	5	63,461	33,803	677.9	2.01	17,717	524	0.0617	36.0
1930	1931	6	64,450	34,350	569.0	1.66	18,521	539	0.0554	36.0
1931	1932	7	65,457	34,907	528.2	1.51	18,558	532	0.0490	36.0
1932	1933	8	66,434	35,449	569.6	1.61	19,515	551	0.0496	36.0
1933	1934	9	67,432	36,002	629.7	1.75	20,430	567	0.0511	36.0
1934	1935	10	68,309	36,491	679.3	1.86	20,914	573	0.0518	36.0
1935	1936	11	69,254	37,018	740.7	2.00	22,612	611	0.0531	36.0
1936	1937	12	70,114	37,499	815.2	2.17	23,754	633	0.0543	65.8
1937	1938	13	70,630	37,646	1,226.6	3.26	24,982	664	0.0585	55.0
1938	1939	14	71,013	37,921	1,404.0	3.70	25,666	677	0.0641	55.0
1939	1940	15	71,380	38,260	219.2	0.57	26,544	694	0.0802	65.0
1940	1941	16	71,933	38,686	266.0	0.69	25,016	647	0.1021	65.0
1941	1942	17	72,218	38,879	726.3	1.87	25,727	662	0.1137	72.0
1942	1943	18	72,880	39,275	878.6	2.24	24,509	624	0.1387	72.0

(continued)

Table 3A.1 Continued

(1) Actual Year (incomes earned in)	(2a) Fiscal Year (tax paid in)	(2b) Fiscal Year (Japanese Calendar)	(3) Population ('000s)	(4) Number of adults ('000s)	(5) Number of tax returns ('000s)	(6) (5)/(4) (%)	(7) Total income (2002 billion yen)	(8) Average income (2002 '000 yen)	(9) CPI (2002 base 100)	(10) Top Marginal Tax Rate (%)
1943	1944	19	73,903	39,867	1,053.9	2.64	24,277	609	0.1595	74.0
1944	1945	20	74,433	40,194	1,114.6	2.77	23,415	583	0.1960	74.0
1945	1946	21	72,147	38,999	343.3	0.88	11,690	300	0.9026	67.0
1946			75,750	40,988			14,104	344	2.56	
1947	1947	22	78,101	42,303	7,290.9	17.23	15,986	378	5.76	75.0
1948	1948	23	80,002	43,377	7,399.8	17.06	17,467	403	10.58	85.0
1949	1949	24	81,773	44,382	7,609.9	17.15	20,063	452	11.93	85.0
1950	1950	25	84,115	45,700	4,318.1	9.45	22,065	483	12.99	55.0
1951	1951	26	84,541	46,410			24,853	536	15.19	55.0
1952	1952	27	85,808	47,591			26,446	556	16.03	55.0
1953	1953	28	86,981	48,734			28,885	593	17.08	55.0
1954	1954	29	88,239	49,938			30,137	603	18.12	65.0
1955	1955	30	90,077	51,488			33,545	652	18.02	65.0
1956	1956	31	90,172	52,053			36,977	710	18.12	65.0
1957	1957	32	90,928	53,004			39,694	749	18.65	65.0
1958	1958	33	91,767	54,012			42,095	779	18.54	70.0
1959	1959	34	92,641	55,051			46,773	850	18.75	70.0
1960	1960	35	94,302	56,572			52,292	924	19.49	70.0
1961	1961	36	94,287	57,255			59,791	1,044	20.43	70.0
1962	1962	37	95,181	58,496			63,838	1,091	21.90	75.0
1963	1963	38	96,156	59,801			68,886	1,152	23.47	75.0
1964	1964	39	97,182	61,153			76,764	1,255	24.41	75.0

1965	1965	40	99,209	63,156	81,472	1,290	25.98	75.0
1966	1966	41	99,036	63,773	87,954	1,379	27.34	75.0
1967	1967	42	100,196	65,256	96,852	1,484	28.39	75.0
1968	1968	43	101,331	66,739	109,011	1,633	29.96	75.0
1969	1969	44	102,536	68,285	119,546	1,751	31.53	75.0
1970	1970	45	104,665	70,471	129,768	1,841	33.94	75.0
1971	1971	46	106,100	71,661	138,988	1,940	35.93	75.0
1972	1972	47	107,595	72,898	154,441	2,119	37.61	75.0
1973	1973	48	109,104	74,150	174,040	2,347	42.01	75.0
1974	1974	49	110,573	75,382	175,373	2,326	52.28	75.0
1975	1975	50	111,940	76,550	178,345	2,330	58.46	75.0
1976	1976	51	113,094	77,578	182,870	2,357	64.01	75.0
1977	1977	52	114,165	78,554	183,911	2,341	69.14	75.0
1978	1978	53	115,190	79,502	190,195	2,392	71.66	75.0
1979	1979	54	116,155	80,413	197,947	2,462	74.28	75.0
1980	1980	55	117,060	81,286	199,280	2,452	80.25	75.0
1981	1981	56	117,902	82,375	201,987	2,452	84.12	75.0
1982	1982	57	118,728	83,459	206,147	2,470	86.43	75.0
1983	1983	58	119,536	84,537	211,201	2,498	88.00	75.0
1984	1984	59	120,305	85,595	216,423	2,528	89.99	70.0
1985	1985	60	121,049	86,641	222,426	2,567	91.77	70.0
1986	1986	61	121,660	87,598	228,851	2,613	92.19	70.0
1987	1987	62	122,239	88,536	233,389	2,636	91.98	60.0
1988	1988	63	122,745	89,427	243,536	2,723	92.40	60.0
1989	1989	1	123,204	90,288	255,023	2,825	94.60	60.0
1990	1990	2	123,611	91,114	267,838	2,940	97.53	50.0
1991	1991	3	124,101	92,200	279,382	3,030	100.68	50.0
1992	1992	4	124,567	93,273	283,116	3,035	102.35	50.0
1993	1993	5	124,938	94,281	280,026	2,970	103.51	50.0
1994	1994	6	125,265	95,259	280,972	2,950	104.03	50.0
1995	1995	7	125,570	96,224	278,334	2,893	103.71	50.0
1996	1996	8	125,864	97,185	280,772	2,889	103.71	50.0
1997	1997	9	126,166	98,155	280,338	2,856	104.65	50.0

(continued)

Table 3A.1 Continued

	Years		Population and Tax units				Income		Inflation	MTR
(1)	(2a)	(2b)	(3)	(4)	(5)	(6)	(7)	(8)	(9)	(10)
Actual Year, (incomes earned in)	Fiscal Year (tax paid in)	Fiscal Year (Japanese Calendar)	Population ('000s)	Number of adults ('000s)	Number of tax returns ('000s)	(5)/(4) (%)	Total income (2002 billion yen)	Average income (2002 '000 yen)	CPI (2002 base 100)	Top Marginal Tax Rate (%)
1998	1998	10	126,486	99,142			274,392	2,768	104.54	50.0
1999	1999	11	126,686	100,039			270,310	2,702	103.82	37.0
2000	2000	12	126,926	100,970			269,971	2,674	102.47	37.0
2001	2001	13	127,291	101,642			264,609	2,603	100.91	37.0
2002	2002	14	127,480	102,175			257,286	2,518	100.00	37.0
2003	2003	15	127,687	102,724			255,669	2,489	99.70	37.0
2004	2004	16	127,776	103,281			254,820	2,467	99.70	37.0
2005	2005	17	127,757	103,830			258,324	2,488	99.39	37.0

Notes: Computation by authors: see Appendix 3A for details.

Actual year is the year in which income subject to taxation was earned, and fiscal year is the year in which tax returns were processed and income tax was paid.

Tax unit is defined as adult individual with age 20 and above.

Population estimates are based on Census data.

Number of tax returns are based on income tax return statistics.

Total income is based on personal disposable income from Ohkawa et al. (1974) for 1886–1930 and personal income from National Accounts for 1930–2005.

CPI is from Ohkawa et al. (1967) for 1886–1950 and *Japan Statistical Yearbook* for 1950–2005.

Top marginal tax rate is the highest statutory marginal tax rate from the National individual income tax stipulated by the law before exemptions and deductions.

Table 3A.2 Top income shares in Japan, 1886–2005

Year	Top 5% (1)	Top 1% (2)	Top 0.5% (3)	Top 0.1% (4)	Top 0.01% (5)	Top 5–1% (9)	Top 1–0.5% (10)	Top 0.5–0.1% (11)	Top 0.1–0.01% (12)	Top 0.01% (5)
1886		19.14	14.19	7.22	2.98		4.94	6.97	4.24	2.98
1887		19.89	14.52	7.24	3.03		5.38	7.28	4.20	3.03
1888		17.67	13.16	6.78	2.95		4.51	6.38	3.84	2.95
1889		16.07	12.03	6.30	2.68		4.04	5.74	3.61	2.68
1890		14.33	10.76	5.63	2.44		3.57	5.13	3.19	2.44
1891		13.19	9.92	5.19	2.22		3.27	4.74	2.97	2.22
1892		14.45	10.96	5.79	2.43		3.49	5.17	3.37	2.43
1893		14.27	10.94	5.87	2.44		3.33	5.06	3.44	2.44
1894		13.40	10.37	5.69	2.40		3.03	4.68	3.29	2.40
1895		12.82	10.03	5.59	2.38		2.79	4.44	3.21	2.38
1896		13.23	10.39	5.80	2.47		2.84	4.59	3.33	2.47
1897		12.16	9.55	5.21	2.15		2.62	4.33	3.07	2.15
1898		13.57	10.46	5.58	2.02		3.11	4.88	3.56	2.02
1899		15.72	12.27	6.72	2.51		3.45	5.55	4.21	2.51
1900		16.26	12.63	6.83	2.51		3.63	5.80	4.32	2.51
1901		16.93	13.14	7.09	2.62		3.80	6.05	4.47	2.62
1902		17.99	13.97	7.55	2.80		4.02	6.42	4.75	2.80
1903		17.55	13.66	7.43	2.74		3.89	6.23	4.69	2.74
1904		16.58	13.01	7.21	2.74		3.57	5.79	4.48	2.74
1905		18.07	14.13	7.82	2.97		3.94	6.31	4.85	2.97
1906		18.12	14.08	7.64	2.83		4.04	6.44	4.81	2.83
1907	32.25	18.26	14.12	7.58	2.76	14.00	4.13	6.54	4.82	2.76
1908	33.82	18.93	14.62	7.74	2.79	14.89	4.32	6.88	4.95	2.79
1909	33.71	18.74	14.43	7.56	2.68	14.96	4.31	6.88	4.87	2.68
1910	33.54	18.88	14.61	7.75	2.81	14.66	4.27	6.85	4.95	2.81
1911	31.40	17.99	13.98	7.52	2.77	13.41	4.01	6.46	4.75	2.77
1912	31.48	17.91	13.93	7.61	2.83	13.57	3.98	6.32	4.79	2.83
1913	30.56	17.45	13.56	7.38	2.73	13.11	3.90	6.17	4.65	2.73
1914	32.53	18.55	14.49	7.98	2.92	13.98	4.06	6.51	5.06	2.92

(continued)

Table 3A.2 Continued

Year	Top 5% (1)	Top 1% (2)	Top 0.5% (3)	Top 0.1% (4)	Top 0.01% (5)	Top 5–1% (9)	Top 1–0.5% (10)	Top 0.5–0.1% (11)	Top 0.1–0.01% (12)	Top 0.01% (5)
1915	32.79	19.60	15.63	9.09	3.70	13.19	3.98	6.54	5.39	3.70
1916	30.87	19.52	15.87	9.72	4.38	11.34	3.65	6.15	5.33	4.38
1917	28.98	18.68	15.32	9.52	4.31	10.30	3.36	5.80	5.20	4.31
1918	25.55	16.62	13.54	8.30	3.68	8.93	3.09	5.24	4.62	3.68
1919	24.83	15.25	12.24	7.37	3.12	9.58	3.01	4.87	4.25	3.12
1920	28.12	17.09	13.62	7.90	3.23	11.04	3.46	5.73	4.67	3.23
1921	31.47	18.48	14.51	8.10	3.15	12.99	3.98	6.40	4.95	3.15
1922	32.96	19.55	15.38	8.63	3.40	13.41	4.17	6.75	5.23	3.40
1923	33.58	19.72	15.45	8.60	3.37	13.85	4.27	6.85	5.23	3.37
1924	33.60	19.72	15.45	8.62	3.43	13.88	4.27	6.83	5.19	3.43
1925		18.32	14.34	7.96	3.16		3.98	6.38	4.80	3.16
1926		18.55	14.64	8.29	3.39		3.90	6.36	4.90	3.39
1927		17.89	14.12	7.96	3.22		3.77	6.17	4.73	3.22
1928		18.51	14.64	8.28	3.37		3.87	6.36	4.91	3.37
1929		18.35	14.51	8.17	3.33		3.85	6.33	4.84	3.33
1930		16.78	13.21	7.32	2.95		3.57	5.90	4.37	2.95
1931		17.38	13.62	7.42	2.92		3.76	6.20	4.50	2.92
1932		17.56	13.81	7.61	3.03		3.75	6.20	4.58	3.03
1933		18.28	14.48	8.16	3.40		3.79	6.32	4.76	3.40
1934		18.96	15.01	8.46	3.49		3.95	6.55	4.97	3.49
1935		18.74	14.83	8.41	3.49		3.91	6.42	4.93	3.49
1936		18.68	14.76	8.40	3.57		3.92	6.36	4.84	3.57
1937	31.34	19.26	15.33	8.83	3.80	12.07	3.94	6.50	5.03	3.80
1938	31.81	19.92	15.90	9.19	3.81	11.89	4.02	6.71	5.38	3.81
1939		17.95	14.16	7.83	3.10		3.79	6.33	4.73	3.10
1940		16.45	12.82	6.82	2.59		3.64	6.00	4.23	2.59
1941		16.67	12.58	6.36	2.31		4.09	6.22	4.05	2.31
1942		15.11	11.28	5.69	2.07		3.83	5.59	3.63	2.07
1943		13.63	10.04	4.96	1.78		3.59	5.08	3.18	1.78
1944		10.74	7.91	3.93	1.40		2.83	3.98	2.53	1.40
1945		6.43	4.42	1.89	0.56		2.01	2.54	1.33	0.56

Year										
1946										
1947	18.50	7.36	5.16	2.15	0.61	11.15	2.20	3.01	1.54	0.61
1948	20.37	7.79	5.24	2.06	0.55	12.58	2.55	3.18	1.51	0.55
1949	21.67	7.89	4.97	1.82	0.46	13.77	2.92	3.15	1.35	0.46
1950	20.96	7.69	4.90	1.73	0.42	13.27	2.79	3.17	1.31	0.42
1951	19.90	7.28	4.77	1.87	0.53	12.62	2.51	2.90	1.34	0.53
1952	21.19	7.85	5.18	2.02	0.55	13.34	2.68	3.16	1.47	0.55
1953	20.17	7.46	4.94	1.91	0.49	12.71	2.51	3.04	1.42	0.49
1954	19.73	7.20	4.76	1.83	0.47	12.53	2.44	2.93	1.37	0.47
1955	18.87	6.91	4.59	1.78	0.46	11.96	2.32	2.81	1.32	0.46
1956	19.55	7.37	4.94	1.90	0.49	12.18	2.43	3.04	1.42	0.49
1957	20.15	7.69	5.20	2.05	0.54	12.46	2.49	3.14	1.51	0.54
1958	20.17	7.74	5.23	2.08	0.54	12.43	2.51	3.15	1.54	0.54
1959	20.48	7.97	5.44	2.15	0.54	12.51	2.53	3.30	1.61	0.54
1960	20.75	8.17	5.51	2.22	0.58	12.57	2.66	3.29	1.64	0.58
1961	20.68	8.44	5.79	2.31	0.60	12.24	2.65	3.49	1.71	0.60
1962	21.19	8.68	5.91	2.35	0.61	12.51	2.77	3.57	1.74	0.61
1963	21.03	8.50	5.74	2.31	0.60	12.53	2.76	3.43	1.71	0.60
1964	20.62	8.33	5.59	2.18	0.56	12.29	2.74	3.41	1.61	0.56
1965	20.04	7.91	5.26	2.04	0.52	12.13	2.65	3.22	1.51	0.52
1966	19.47	7.62	5.07	1.94	0.49	11.85	2.55	3.13	1.45	0.49
1967	19.86	7.63	5.11	1.96	0.49	12.23	2.53	3.14	1.48	0.49
1968	19.45	7.56	5.05	1.91	0.46	11.89	2.51	3.13	1.45	0.46
1969	20.38	8.01	5.27	1.91	0.47	12.37	2.73	3.36	1.45	0.47
1970	21.13	8.19	5.50	2.05	0.57	12.94	2.69	3.46	1.48	0.57
1971	21.67	8.42	5.49	1.94	0.63	13.25	2.93	3.55	1.31	0.63
1972	21.49	8.10	5.14	1.60	0.44	13.39	2.96	3.54	1.16	0.44
1973	21.01	7.62	5.02	2.18	0.86	13.40	2.59	2.84	1.32	0.86
1974	19.93	7.20	4.61	1.78	0.57	12.73	2.60	2.83	1.21	0.57
1975	19.58	7.08	4.60	1.77	0.61	12.50	2.48	2.84	1.16	0.61
1976	19.52	6.81	4.28	1.51	0.34	12.71	2.52	2.78	1.16	0.34
1977	19.45	6.77	4.26	1.48	0.34	12.68	2.51	2.78	1.14	0.34
1978	19.74	6.96	4.39	1.52	0.35	12.78	2.57	2.86	1.18	0.35
1979	20.23	7.25	4.68	1.65	0.38	12.98	2.57	3.03	1.28	0.38
1980	20.10	7.16	4.65	1.65	0.38	12.94	2.51	2.99	1.28	0.38
1981	20.07	7.11	4.61	1.59	0.36	12.97	2.50	3.02	1.24	0.36

(continued)

Table 3A.2 Continued

Year	Top 5% (1)	Top 1% (2)	Top 0.5% (3)	Top 0.1% (4)	Top 0.01% (5)	Top 5–1% (9)	Top 1–0.5% (10)	Top 0.5–0.1% (11)	Top 0.1–0.01% (12)	Top 0.01% (5)
1982	19.99	7.02	4.60	1.62	0.40	12.96	2.42	2.98	1.23	0.40
1983	20.03	6.94	4.46	1.50	0.34	13.08	2.48	2.96	1.16	0.34
1984	20.09	6.95	4.48	1.49	0.35	13.14	2.48	2.98	1.15	0.35
1985	20.25	7.03	4.50	1.50	0.35	13.22	2.53	3.01	1.14	0.35
1986	20.60	7.21	4.59	1.54	0.40	13.39	2.62	3.05	1.14	0.40
1987	21.42	7.66	4.88	1.65	0.51	13.75	2.78	3.23	1.14	0.51
1988	21.52	7.63	4.79	1.62	0.53	13.89	2.84	3.17	1.09	0.53
1989	21.70	7.90	5.07	1.83	0.72	13.80	2.84	3.23	1.11	0.72
1990	21.78	8.05	5.22	2.04	0.86	13.73	2.83	3.18	1.18	0.86
1991	21.16	7.54	4.84	1.81	0.73	13.62	2.70	3.03	1.08	0.73
1992	20.58	7.12	4.60	1.65	0.50	13.46	2.52	2.96	1.15	0.50
1993	20.72	7.15	4.61	1.62	0.49	13.57	2.54	2.99	1.13	0.49
1994	20.93	7.07	4.50	1.62	0.49	13.87	2.57	2.88	1.13	0.49
1995	21.47	7.30	4.68	1.64	0.47	14.17	2.62	3.03	1.17	0.47
1996	21.61	7.36	4.71	1.69	0.50	14.25	2.66	3.01	1.20	0.50
1997	21.72	7.32	4.66	1.69	0.45	14.41	2.66	2.97	1.24	0.45
1998	22.30	7.59	4.85	1.74	0.45	14.72	2.74	3.11	1.29	0.45
1999	22.77	7.76	4.93	1.77	0.47	15.01	2.83	3.16	1.30	0.47
2000	23.52	8.22	5.32	2.04	0.57	15.30	2.90	3.28	1.47	0.57
2001	24.16	8.49	5.55	2.14	0.60	15.67	2.93	3.41	1.54	0.60
2002	24.60	8.65	5.64	2.16	0.58	15.95	3.01	3.48	1.57	0.58
2003	24.96	8.75	5.70	2.16	0.60	16.21	3.05	3.53	1.57	0.60
2004	25.29	9.04	5.92	2.32	0.69	16.25	3.12	3.60	1.63	0.69
2005	25.33	9.20	6.07	2.40	0.80	16.13	3.14	3.67	1.60	0.80

Notes: Computations by authors based on income tax return statistics and wage income tax statistics: See Appendix 3A for details.

Year refers to 'actual year' in Appendix Table 3A.1.

Income is defined comprehensively to include employment income, business income, farm income, and capital income, but capital gains are excluded.

Top groups are defined relative to adult population (age 20 and above) in Japan.

The total income denominator is defined as total personal income in Japan from National Accounts.

Top 5–1% refers to the top 5% income group excluding the top 1%.

Top 5% and 5–1% income share series are not estimated for those years in which the fractions of adults filing tax returns are too small.

Series are adjusted upward for years 1898–1938 to correct for non-taxable capital income components (see Appendix and Figure 3A.3).

Table 3A.3 Top 1% income share and composition in Japan, 1886–2005

Actual Year	Top 1% income share (%) (1)	Fraction population filing (%) (2)	% Composition of top 1% income				
			Dividends (3)	Interest (4)	Business income (5)	Employment income (6)	Rental income (7)
1886	19.14	0.54	17.88	7.98	36.28	17.45	20.41
1900	16.26	1.67	18.77	8.42	32.17	18.99	21.65
1901	16.93	1.86	20.01	8.63	29.76	18.63	22.97
1902	17.99	2.03	19.74	8.50	29.47	18.58	23.71
1903	17.55	2.15	18.83	9.17	30.05	16.45	25.50
1904	16.58	2.27	19.99	8.25	30.23	16.21	25.32
1905	18.07	2.47	20.34	7.47	29.81	18.20	24.19
1906	18.12	2.69	19.02	6.74	30.90	18.69	24.66
1907	18.26	3.28	18.26	6.27	32.32	17.88	25.28
1908	18.93	3.52	17.38	6.02	31.83	18.00	26.76
1909	18.74	3.55	17.17	5.96	31.23	19.33	26.31
1910	18.88	3.58	18.85	5.64	29.95	20.81	24.75
1911	17.99	3.72	20.07	5.03	28.92	21.08	24.90
1912	17.91	2.57	22.56	4.08	28.22	18.19	26.96
1913	17.45	2.61	21.86	3.77	27.61	18.13	28.63
1914	18.55	2.55	23.09	3.97	26.38	19.13	27.43
1915	19.60	2.51	27.61	3.67	25.43	20.58	22.72
1916	19.52	2.68	27.88	3.21	30.67	19.48	18.76
1917	18.68	2.68	28.73	2.61	34.28	18.03	16.35
1918	16.62	3.68	27.51	2.17	34.68	19.27	16.36
1919	15.25	3.37	29.67	2.02	30.00	19.19	19.12
1920	17.09	3.90	25.92	2.33	34.21	18.37	19.18
1921	18.48	4.23	23.66	2.48	35.39	19.14	19.33
1922	19.55	4.57	24.05	2.64	34.66	20.77	17.88
1923	19.72	4.48	25.23	2.83	32.82	22.36	16.77
1924	19.72	4.57	25.01	2.79	32.01	22.25	17.94

(continued)

Table 3A.3 Continued

Actual Year	Top 1% income share (%) (1)	Fraction population filing (%) (2)	% Composition of top 1% income				
			Dividends (3)	Interest (4)	Business income (5)	Employment income (6)	Rental income (7)
1925	18.32	2.53	25.56	0.71	29.33	22.44	21.95
1926	18.55	2.27	27.67	1.82	24.45	25.02	21.04
1927	17.89	2.11	28.71	2.12	21.00	26.88	21.29
1928	18.51	2.10	29.87	2.18	19.31	27.91	20.74
1929	18.35	2.01	30.28	2.30	16.48	29.72	21.21
1930	16.78	1.66	31.30	2.55	13.23	32.41	20.51
1931	17.38	1.51	31.36	2.75	12.35	31.89	21.65
1932	17.56	1.61	29.38	2.60	14.83	31.34	21.84
1933	18.28	1.75	29.04	2.23	17.15	31.39	20.18
1934	18.96	1.86	28.14	1.94	18.48	32.29	19.15
1935	18.74	2.00	27.81	1.71	18.89	32.31	19.28
1936	18.68	2.17	31.65	1.50	19.87	28.95	18.03
1937	19.26	3.26	28.46	1.29	22.61	31.50	16.14
1938	19.92	3.70	26.30	1.09	35.61	31.55	5.45
1939	17.95	0.57	19.11	1.09	43.83	17.29	18.68
1940	16.45	0.69	17.72	1.64	46.29	17.25	17.11
1941	16.67	1.87	14.11	1.42	52.66	18.20	13.61
1942	15.11	2.24	13.48	1.45	51.86	20.12	13.09
1943	13.63	2.64	13.20	1.46	48.59	24.20	12.54
1944	10.74	2.77	13.19	1.37	44.33	30.25	10.85
1945	6.43	0.88	6.05	0.59	78.15	10.05	5.16
1947	7.36		0.13	0.05	95.56	4.05	0.22
1948	7.79		0.13	0.03	93.69	6.00	0.15
1949	7.89		0.34	0.01	77.03	22.43	0.18
1950	7.69		1.13	0.00	47.49	51.13	0.26

1963	8.50	9.01	0.00	14.59	70.99	5.41
1965	7.91	6.21	0.00	16.14	70.80	6.85
1970	8.19	6.74	0.00	20.19	63.69	9.38
1976	6.81	3.45	0.00	17.20	73.92	5.42
1980	7.16	3.18	0.00	19.07	72.29	5.45
1985	7.03	2.50	0.00	14.08	77.78	5.64
1991	7.54	2.63	0.00	11.44	78.61	7.32
1995	7.30	1.62	0.00	10.25	79.43	8.69
1999	7.76	1.43	0.01	8.41	81.41	8.74
2002	8.65	1.56	0.01	8.40	80.60	9.41
2003	8.75	1.44	0.01	7.85	81.40	9.29
2004	9.04	1.55	0.01	7.85	81.50	9.09
2005	9.20	1.80	0.01	7.94	81.22	9.03

Notes: Computations based on income tax return statistics and wage income tax statistics; see Appendix 3A.

Business income includes unincorporated business profits, farm income, and self-employment income.

Employment income includes wages, salaries, bonuses, and pensions.

Rental income includes rents from farm land, residential land, housing, and buildings. For 1886 and 1900–45, composition estimates are based on aggregate income composition and thus imprecisely estimated.

In particular, for 1906–25, relatively high fractions of adults (2.5% to 4.6%) filed income tax returns.

For 1947–50 and 1963–2005, composition estimates are based on composition data by income brackets.

For 1951–62, no estimates are provided because only aggregate composition data are available.

Virtually all interest income after 1947 and large part of dividends after 1965 are not reported in income tax returns.

APPENDIX 3B: TOP ESTATES

Definition of Estate

We compile top estate series, using estate tax return statistics published in *Annual Statistical Report* (*Zeimu Tokei Nenposho*) from 1905 to 2005. Except for 1943, the statistics include a distribution table with the number of decedents who paid estate tax, the amount of estate, and the amount of tax, by estate brackets. The aggregate estate composition is also available starting in 1926, except for years 1942–3, but not by estate brackets.

In the tax statistics, estates are defined as the sum of all properties (real estate, houses, household properties, unincorporated business assets, farm assets, stocks, bonds, cash, deposits, tenant rights, intellectual property rights, pension rights, etc.) net of all debts and liabilities. As virtually all components of transferable wealth are included in the definition of estates for tax purposes, the statistics provide an accurate estimate of the value of net worth held by decedents. The value of estate reported in the estate tax statistics, however, is taxable value after standard deductions in 1905–52, and before standard deductions but after special reductions (especially with respect to real estate) in 1953–2005. As we discuss below, we correct for standard deductions but do not correct for special reductions.

Below, we refer to the year of the annual report (the year when estate tax returns were processed) as 'fiscal year' which may be different from 'actual year' in which the estate subject to taxation was transferred from an ancestor to heirs due to the ancestor's death. We first summarize the evolution of estate tax laws in Japan, based on the tax codes reprinted at the end of the annual reports in 1931 and 1950 as well as Ishi (2001: chapter 12), which summarizes post-war developments.

Estate Tax Laws, 1905–2005

The first estate tax law in Japan was promulgated in January 1905 and enforced in April 1905. During our sample period, there were three major reforms in estate tax laws in 1947, 1950, and 1958, and many minor revisions.

For fiscal years 1905–46, the Japanese estate tax law was based on a 'family system' (*ie seido*) defined by the old Civil Code. To maintain the family system, the law distinguished the inheritance of family estate (*katoku sozoku*), which we refer to as 'family inheritance', from ordinary inheritance (*isan sozoku*). Under family inheritance, a single heir succeeded to the entire family estate as a new family head (*koshu*) after the death or retirement (at age 60 or older) of the former family head. Commonly it was the first son who became a new family head, while if there was no son, a family head named a legal heir. By contrast, under ordinary inheritance, estate was transferred to heirs when a non-family head died or decided to give his or her estate to their heirs while alive. The estate was divided equally among children. If there were no children, then it went to a spouse. If there were no surviving children or spouse, then lineal ascendants inherited the estate.

The 1905 law set the exemption point of 1,000 yen for family inheritance and 500 yen for ordinary inheritance with progressive but extremely low marginal tax rates (i.e. 0.05–1.3 per cent for family inheritance and 0.1–1.8 per cent for ordinary inheritance) defined over twenty estate brackets. Gifts given to heirs within one year prior to the inheritance were aggregated to estates for tax purposes. Military personnel who died in war were exempted from estate tax. In 1926, the exemption point for family inheritance was increased to 5,000 yen and for ordinary inheritance to 1,000 yen.

Under the 1905 law, the inheritance tax statistics in fiscal years 1905–47 report the two forms of inheritance in separate tabulations. In estimating top estates, we aggregate the distributions of family inheritance and ordinary inheritance. The former is by far the dominant form of inheritance at the top of the estate distribution because non-family heads rarely owned large assets. We consider all forms of inheritance (not only those from deaths), because family inheritance due to retirement should be considered as an inter-generational transfer of wealth, and excluding it would lead us to underestimate the number of estates. We also include all ordinary inheritance cases, although excluding the cases not due to death would not change our series by much.

The 1905 law was superseded by the 1937 temporary tax increase law and the 1938 revised temporary tax increase law, both of which imposed additional tax on estates to increase wartime revenue. The 1940 estate tax law established highly progressive tax rates, while keeping the preferential treatment for family inheritance. As of 1946, the exemption point was 20,000 yen for family inheritance with marginal tax rates of 1.5–55 per cent defined over nineteen brackets. For ordinary inheritance, the exemption point was set lower (5,000 yen) and the tax rates higher (5.5–70 per cent).[48]

As part of the post-war democratization, the 1947 estate tax law abolished the distinction between family and ordinary inheritance and established a modern system of separate estate and gift taxes. It set the exemption point of 20,000 yen for estate tax with low marginal tax rates of 1.0–6.0 per cent.[49] The estate tax statistics continue to present tabulations by the size of estate under the 1947 law.

Under the 1950 estate tax law, following the recommendations by the Shoup Commission, Japan adopted inheritance tax based on cumulative amount of inheritance and gifts received by an heir (also known as 'accession tax'). As a result, for fiscal years 1950–7, distribution tables are based on the size of inheritances as opposed to estates. To provide homogeneous series, we convert inheritance statistics to estate statistics (see Appendix 3B). The 1950 law also changed fiscal year from accounting year (starting in April) to calendar year (starting in January). It set the exemption point of 200,000 yen and highly progressive tax rates of 25–90 per cent defined over eleven brackets.[50]

Finally, with the 1958 reform, Japan adopted a hybrid system of estate tax and inheritance tax. It initially set the very high exemption point of 1.8 million yen, resulting in the much smaller number of people filing estate tax returns. The statistics for fiscal years 1958–2005 are presented by the size of estates and hence are directly comparable to the statistics for 1905–49.

Correspondence between Fiscal Years and Actual Years

Estate tax statistics reported in fiscal year *t* are the estate tax returns *processed* in year *t*, and do not necessarily coincide with the returns filed for the deaths that took place in year *t*. In

[48] Japan National Tax Administration, *Annual Statistical Report* (1950: 280).
[49] Ibid. 279.
[50] Ibid. 278.

fact, due to delays in both filing and processing, before the Second World War, majority of the tax returns filed for the deaths in year *t* were probably processed in year *t* + 1, and some in even later years.[51] Thus, strictly speaking, the statistics in fiscal year *t* correspond to a weighted sum of the estate distributions in actual years *t*, *t* − 1, *t* − 2, etc.[52] Because the statistics in 1905–49 do not break down processed returns by the year of death but instead pool them in one distribution table, it is difficult to reconstruct the estate distribution corresponding to an actual year.

By contrast, starting in 1950, the distribution table in fiscal year *t* covers only the deaths taking place in the same year *t*, and separate aggregate statistics are reported for the tax returns processed in year *t* but filed in previous years. Furthermore, when there is a revision in estate tax laws in 1937, 1938, 1940, and 1947, annual reports in subsequent years publish separate estate distribution tables according to which version of law applies. For example, the 1937 statistics have two distribution tables, one for the '1905 law' estates (which reports the returns filed before 1937 but processed in 1937) and the other for the '1937 law' estates (which reports the returns filed and processed in 1937). In this case, we know for sure that the '1937 law' estates include only the deaths in 1937, while the '1905 law' estates consist primarily of the deaths in 1936 and 1935.

In the world of constant price, using the statistics in year *t* to estimate top estates in year *t* would result in smoother time series, as it amounts to taking a moving average over several years. During a period of high inflation, however, by placing a higher weight on current year than actually is, it would lead to a large upward bias in our estimates. Therefore, it is important to reconstruct an estate distribution for a given actual year as much as possible, exploiting the information based on legal changes. We determine the correspondence between actual and fiscal years as follows.

For actual years 1905–35, in the absence of better information, we assume that estate tax returns reported in fiscal year *t* + 1 correspond to the deaths in year *t* (which is a median year among *t* − 1, *t*, *t* + 1). We thus ignore the small number of returns reported in fiscal year 1905 and use only the 1906 statistics to estimate the 1905 distribution.

For actual year 1936, we add the distribution tables of the '1905 law' estates reported in fiscal years 1937–9. For actual year 1937, we add the '1937 law' estates reported in fiscal years 1937–40. For actual year 1938, we add the '1938 law' estates reported in fiscal year 1938 and 60 per cent of the '1938 law' estates reported in fiscal year 1939. For actual year 1939, we add 40 per cent of the '1938 law' estates reported in fiscal year 1939 and the '1938 law' estates reported in fiscal year 1940. The fractions 60 per cent and 40 per cent are chosen so that the total numbers of estates in 1938 and 1939 are approximately equal. Note that 1937 is the only year for which we can recover all and only deaths in 1937. Thus our 1937 estimate is most precise among all. By contrast, our respective estimates for 1938 and 1939 are imprecise, but the average of the 1938 and 1939 estimates should be fairly accurate.

For actual years 1940–5, we assume that the '1940 law' estates reported in fiscal year *t* + 1 correspond the deaths in year *t* − 1. We thus ignore very small number of the '1940 law' estates reported in 1940 in estimating the 1940 distribution. The distribution table is not available in fiscal year 1943, so we have no estimate for 1942.

For 1946, we add the '1940 law' estates reported in 1947–9. This may result in an overestimate, because we pool the statistics from three annual reports that include virtually

---

[51] This statement is based on tables in the annual reports in 1905–36 that provide the number of returns pending from previous fiscal years.

[52] As the law stipulates that estate tax is based on the value of estate at the time of deaths, we assume that the statistics sum up nominal estates across years without correcting for inflation. Late returns are subject to penalty or adjustment, which is imposed in addition to estate tax.

all the 1946 deaths as well as some deaths in 1944 and 1945. Given the hyperinflation in 1944–6, however, the effect of the extra returns from 1944 and 1945 on our 1946 estimate should be small.

For actual years 1947–9, we assume that '1947 law' estates reported in 1947–8 correspond to the deaths in 1947, that 70 per cent of the '1947 law' estates reported in 1949 correspond to the deaths in 1948, and that 30 per cent of the '1947 law' estates reported in 1949 and all the '1947 law' estates reported in 1950 and 1951 correspond to the deaths in 1949. We then inflate the numbers for 1949 by a factor 12/9 to adjust for the fact that the '1947 law' applied to only nine months during fiscal year 1949 (from April to December 1949) as the new law took effect in January 1950 and thereafter followed the calendar-year schedule. The 70–30 per cent split of the 1949 statistics between 1948 and 1949 is chosen so that the total numbers of estates in 1948 and 1949 are roughly equal. Although our respective estimates for 1948 and 1949 are imprecise, their average is fairly accurate.

For actual years 1950–7, the statistics in year *t* report the estates for deaths in year *t* that are processed by March of year *t* + 1. As a result, approximately 80 per cent of the deaths in year *t* are included in the statistics in year *t*. The remaining portion is reported, only at the aggregate level and not by brackets, in the statistics in the subsequent fiscal years. We assume that the distribution of estates reported in later fiscal years is the same as the distribution reported in fiscal year *t*, and we inflate the distribution in year *t* accordingly.

For fiscal years 1958–2005, with the introduction of the new hybrid system, the statistics in year *t* report the deaths in year *t* processed by June of year *t* + 1. Because the number of deaths in year *t* reported in later years becomes small (less than 10 per cent), we make no corrections.

Correcting for Standard Deductions, 1905–1952

For fiscal years 1905–52, distribution tables are presented by the taxable value of estate (or inheritance for 1950–2), namely the size of estate net of debts and *after* standard deductions. By contrast, for fiscal years 1953–2005, tables are presented by the size of estate net of debt and before standard deductions (but after special reductions). For fiscal years 1953–7, both the amounts of inheritance before and after deductions are reported. To obtain the true value of estates, we need to add back deductions for fiscal years 1905–52. Below, we describe deductions and our methods of correction.

For fiscal years 1905–14, there was no major deduction (only for funeral expenses), and we make no corrections. For fiscal years 1915–25, the deduction for family inheritance, called 'Section 3–2 deduction', was introduced. It allowed 1,000 yen deduction for estates below 3,000 yen and 500 yen deduction for estates below 5,000 yen. The statistics in these years are presented by the size of estate after the deduction. Therefore, we add back the Section 3–2 deduction for family inheritance, using the aggregate amount of Section 3–2 deductions. We then add together the distributions of family and ordinary inheritances using a standard Pareto interpolation method.

The 1940 law introduced 1,000 yen deduction per dependent family member. In 1942, the amount of dependent deduction was increased. For fiscal years 1940–6, the statistics report only the aggregate amount of dependent deductions. We compute the average deduction per estate from the aggregate data and add it back to the original tabulations.

The 1947 law abolished dependent family deductions and introduced a basic deduction of 50,000 yen per estate for estate tax purposes as well as per gift for gift tax purposes. We add back 50,000 yen per estate and gift to the original tabulations.

The 1950 law introduced four types of standard deductions: basic deduction (150,000 yen per heir), small amount deduction (30,000 yen per heir for inheritance smaller than certain size), spouse deduction (50 per cent deduction from the amount inherited), and minor deduction (small deduction for minors younger than 18 years old). The basic deduction was increased to 300,000 yen in 1952. We add back deductions of 180,000 yen per heir for years 1950 and 1951 and 330,000 yen per heir for 1952, which are the sum of the basic deduction and the small amount deduction for the respective years. We do not correct for the spouse and minor deductions because they are relatively small relative to the two other deductions according to the aggregate statistics.

For fiscal years 1953–2005, we make no corrections for these deductions as tabulations are presented in estates net of debts before deductions.

The Problem of Special Reductions, 1950–2005

In recent decades, the government has introduced various special tax treatments primarily for real estate to reduce the tax burden on heirs. Because the value of estate reported in the estate tax statistics is before standard deductions but after special reductions from these treatments,[53] our estimates are subject to a potentially large downward bias. There are two sources of the bias. First, the official valuation price for land is substantially lower than the market price. For example, according to Ishi (2001), the official price was about 40–60 per cent of market price in the 1980s (table 17.3). Second, if heirs can claim real estates of decedents as their residences or family business assets, then they may receive a large reduction in taxable value. For example, in 2005, up to 400 square metre of land, only 20 to 50 per cent of total real estate value is taxable.[54] As a result, our data underestimate the true value of estates especially when land is an important component of estates. If the share of land in top estates has increased over the post-war period as the composition data suggest, then our series in the recent decades may be subject to serious underestimation.

We do not try to correct for special reductions, however, for the following reasons. First, due to a complex and time-varying nature of special tax treatments concerning real estate, it is difficult to make an accurate correction. In addition, because we do not have estate composition data by estate brackets, we do not know the shares of land in the top 0.01 per cent and 1–0.5 per cent estates and their changes over time. Finally, we have little information about the valuation method and special treatments of real estate in the pre-Second World War period.

Converting Inheritance Statistics to Estate Statistics, 1950–1957

For all fiscal years except 1950–7, the unit of observation in the tax statistics is 'estate' defined as the properties owned by the decedent. For fiscal years 1950–7, the unit of observation switches to 'inheritance' defined as the properties received by an heir. As a result, tax statistics in 1950–7 report the number of heirs and the amount of inheritances ranked by brackets of inherited wealth. As the estate of a decedent is typically divided among multiple heirs, the inheritance statistics are not directly comparable to the estate statistics. In this study, we estimate series based on the estate unit.

To convert inheritance distributions to estate distributions, we simply assume that each decedent has 2.5 heirs and that estates are divided equally among heirs. The number, 2.5, is

[53] This information is based on the author's phone conversation with a Japan Tax Administration officer on 5 May 2006.

[54] Japan National Tax Bureau (2006), Heisei 18–nenbun: Souzokuzei no Aramashi (2006: Outline of Estate Tax), available online at: http://www.nta.go.jp/category/pamph/souzoku/h18sikata/index.htm.

taken from the average ratio of estate to inheritance in the 1958 statistics which simultan-eously report the number of estates (decedents) and the number of inheritances (heirs) for the first time. From the inheritance statistics, we estimate estate distributions by multi-plying the brackets by 2.5 (for example, the bracket 200,000 to 500,000 yen becomes the bracket 500,000 to 1,250,000 yen), and by dividing by 2.5 the number of inheritances in each bracket to obtain the number of estates.

Note that our estimates for 1950–7 are based on strong assumptions and have a larger margin of errors than in other years. Nevertheless, these estimates provide important evidence for the years immediately after the Second World War.

Construction of Top Estate Series, 1905–2005

We define top groups (e.g. top 1 per cent, top 0.1 per cent) relative to the total number of adult decedents in each year. The series of adult decedents in Japan is taken from the number of deaths by age groups published in *Japan Statistical Yearbook* for years 1985–2005 and in *Historical Statistics of Japan*, pp. 218–19, for years 1905–85. These series are reported in column (1) in Table 3B.1. The number of estate tax returns (after the adjustments described above) is reported in column (2). As column (3) indicates, the fraction of adult decedents filing the estate tax returns varies across years depending on exemption points and economic conditions, ranging from the high of 31 per cent in 1942 to the low of 1 per cent in 1958.

We estimate the average size of estate for various upper groups of the estate distribution, using a standard Pareto interpolation method. We convert the nominal value of estates to the real value, expressed in 2002 yen, using the CPI deflator (see Appendix 3A). Table 3B.1 displays our estimates of top estates series from 1905 to 2005. Unlike our top income shares, we do not attempt to estimate the shares of estates left by top decedents, because there is no simple way to compute the total amount of estates left by all decedents in each year, including those who did not file estate tax returns.

Estate Composition, 1925–2005

Estate composition data are available only at the aggregate level for fiscal years 1926–2005, except for years 1942–3. Because composition data by brackets are not reported, it is not possible to create homogeneous top estate composition series. In Table 3B.2 and Figure 3B.1, we present the decomposition of aggregate estates into eight categories: (1) agricul-tural land (i.e. farm land, forest land, and tenant right), (2) residential land (i.e. housing land and leasehold), (3) houses and structures, (4) business assets (i.e. machinery, goods, raw materials, intellectual property rights, account receivable, agricultural equipment, and farm products), (5) stocks (for both privately held and publicly traded companies), (6) fixed claim assets (i.e. public and corporate bonds, cash, deposits, savings accounts, and other claims), (7) other assets (which includes household properties, life insurance, pensions, and standing timber), and (8) debts (i.e. private debts and public obligation). Note that the sum of the first seven categories may exceed 100 per cent in Figure 3B.1, as we define estates net of debts to be 100 per cent. The composition estimates are based directly on the aggregate estates composition published in the annual reports. For simplicity, we assume that fiscal year t corresponds to actual year $t − 1$ for fiscal years 1926–46 and to actual year t for fiscal years 1947–2005 (because composition data are reported only for the returns filed under the new law after 1947). In other words, we do not use the complex specification of years we used for the top estate series.

Column (1) in Table 3B.2 reports the fraction of adult decedents filing estate tax returns (these numbers are different from those in column (1) in Table 3B.1 due to the different specification of years). Because the estate composition is sensitive to the fraction filing returns, and the fraction fluctuates substantially from year to year, it is difficult to see trends in estate composition from these series. For example, the fraction drops from 26.1

per cent in 1957 to 0.9 per cent in 1958 (due to the high exemption level under the 1958 law), which probably caused a sharp fall in the share of agricultural land, on one hand, and a large increase in the share of stocks.

To facilitate better comparison, Table 3.3 presents top estate compositions for selected years, 1935, 1950, and 1987, for which the fractions of adult decedents filing returns are comparable at around 9 per cent (9.0 per cent in 1935, 8.8 per cent in 1950, and 8.0 per cent in 1987). Estates before subtracting debts are defined to be 100 per cent. It shows that the largest component of top estates in Japan shifted from financial assets (stocks and fixed claim assets) in 1935 to movable property (business assets, houses and structures, and household properties) in 1950, to real estate (agricultural and residential land) in 1987. Note that, as discussed, if our data underestimate the true value of land compared to other estate components, then the share of financial assets in top estates in 1987 would be even smaller. Thus the top estate composition data provide additional support for our finding based on the top income shares series that, top capital income collapsed during the Second World War and has not returned to the pre-war level to date, despite the high economic growth in the post-war period.

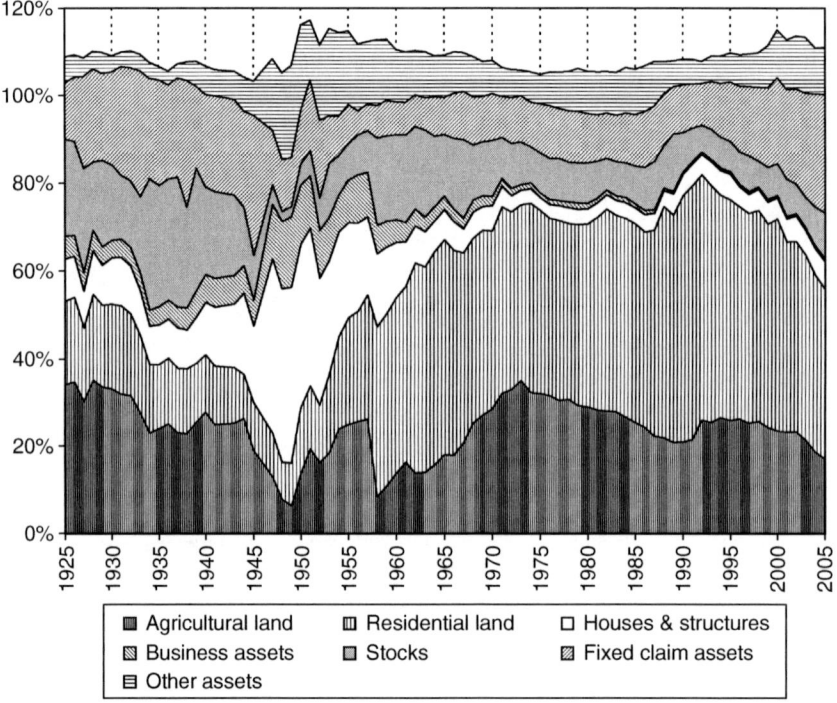

Figure 3B.1 Composition of aggregate estates in Japan, 1925–2005

Source: Appendix Table 3B.2.

Notes: Estimates are based on aggregate estate compositions in estate tax return statistics.

Total exceeds 100% because estates net of debts are defined to be 100%.

Business assets include assets of unincorporated business and farm assets.

Fixed claim assets include bonds, cash, deposits, savings accounts, and other claims.

Other assets include household assets, pensions, life insurance, and other items.

Because of changes in the fractions of decedents filing estate tax returns, compositions are not directly comparable across years.

See Appendix 3B for details and Table 3.3 for the comparison for selected years.

Table 3B.1 Levels of top estates in Japan, 1905–2005

Actual Year	# Adults decedents (age 20+)	# Estate tax returns	Fraction filing (2)/(1) (%)	Top 5%	Top 1%	Top 0.5%	Top 0.1%	Top 0.01%	Top 5–1%	Top 1–0.5%	Top 0.5–0.1%	Top 0.1–0.01%	Top 0.01%
						(in 2002 thousand yen)					(in 2002 thousand yen)		
	(1)	(2)	(3)	(4)	(5)	(6)	(7)	(8)	(9)	(10)	(11)	(12)	(13)
1905	569,672	23,712	4.16%		39,392	64,835	198,661	901,558		13,949	31,378	120,562	901,558
1906	543,109	28,616	5.27%		45,040	72,802	211,676	813,024		17,277	38,084	144,860	813,024
1907	566,733	36,175	6.38%	15,584	51,531	84,366	254,796	1,123,517	6,597	18,696	41,758	158,272	1,123,517
1908	548,334	39,237	7.16%	17,912	58,793	95,276	286,795	1,402,816	7,691	22,310	47,396	162,793	1,402,816
1909	575,094	32,028	5.57%	16,589	56,481	92,782	283,268	1,291,437	6,616	20,180	45,161	171,249	1,291,437
1910	558,154	47,374	8.49%	22,553	72,255	115,499	316,869	1,010,887	10,128	29,011	65,157	239,756	1,010,887
1911	544,055	48,742	8.96%	23,610	77,321	125,174	352,886	1,280,724	10,183	29,469	68,245	249,793	1,280,724
1912	548,046	47,512	8.67%	22,756	74,641	120,952	355,126	1,556,543	9,784	28,330	62,409	221,635	1,556,543
1913	536,993	44,678	8.32%	21,723	71,455	115,717	335,938	1,314,140	9,290	27,193	60,662	227,248	1,314,140
1914	573,534	38,228	6.67%	25,599	86,139	142,114	445,128	2,193,444	10,464	30,163	66,360	250,870	2,193,444
1915	564,966	39,494	6.99%	29,558	93,657	151,434	449,383	2,020,034	13,534	35,880	76,947	274,866	2,020,034
1916	623,196	47,784	7.67%	29,643	94,427	152,784	450,664	1,846,290	13,447	36,070	78,314	295,594	1,846,290
1917	627,640	38,810	6.18%	24,052	78,852	129,357	394,225	1,611,504	10,352	28,347	63,140	258,972	1,611,504
1918	805,793	55,695	6.91%	23,155	74,756	122,025	375,739	1,812,031	10,255	27,487	58,596	216,151	1,812,031
1919	679,934	89,488	13.16%	27,485	82,934	131,870	386,419	1,722,991	13,623	33,998	68,233	237,911	1,722,991
1920	762,101	137,236	18.01%	36,323	119,074	196,202	611,416	2,967,517	15,635	41,946	92,399	349,627	2,967,517
1921	668,956	130,990	19.58%	39,004	125,096	203,175	583,687	2,224,272	17,481	47,017	108,047	401,400	2,224,272
1922	678,237	124,684	18.38%	38,259	122,443	198,027	573,425	2,385,135	17,214	46,859	104,177	372,123	2,385,135
1923	698,548	111,840	16.01%	42,558	147,548	249,657	828,157	4,204,570	16,311	45,440	105,032	452,999	4,204,570
1924	670,083	123,347	18.41%	50,675	173,139	289,821	922,560	4,619,893	20,059	56,456	131,636	511,745	4,619,893
1925	642,982	55,684	8.66%		143,539	249,748	870,863	4,977,148		37,331	94,469	414,609	4,977,148
1926	619,940	80,104	12.92%	59,195	206,900	350,207	1,160,326	6,574,218	22,269	63,592	147,678	558,782	6,574,218
1927	648,975	129,086	19.89%	61,676	219,861	375,121	1,241,465	6,754,041	22,130	64,601	158,535	628,956	6,754,041
1928	669,274	103,160	15.41%	50,903	168,752	275,595	805,520	3,085,179	21,441	61,910	143,114	552,225	3,085,179
1929	680,466	97,308	14.30%	59,419	208,628	350,154	1,089,098	4,979,980	22,116	67,102	165,418	656,778	4,979,980
1930	659,662	83,424	12.65%	48,492	163,268	269,457	813,457	3,513,034	19,798	57,080	133,457	513,504	3,513,034
1931	698,288	90,670	12.98%	50,409	167,367	273,077	808,731	3,435,020	21,169	61,656	139,163	516,921	3,435,020
1932	661,659	86,854	13.13%	48,645	161,180	262,320	763,163	3,190,738	20,511	60,039	137,109	493,432	3,190,738
1933	681,678	88,183	12.94%	51,836	180,098	303,452	977,032	4,953,259	19,771	56,743	135,057	535,229	4,953,259
1934	711,414	89,302	12.55%	58,750	218,392	382,800	1,400,199	9,212,205	18,840	53,985	128,450	532,199	9,212,205

(continued)

Table 3B.1 Continued

| Year | # Adults Actual decedents (age 20+) | # Estate tax returns | Fraction filing (2)/(1) (%) | Top 5% | Top 1% | Top 0.5% | Top 0.1% | Top 0.01% | Top 5-1% | Top 1-0.5% | Top 0.5-0.1% | Top 0.1-0.01% | Top 0.01% |
| | | | | | | (in 2002 thousand yen) | | | | | (in 2002 thousand yen) | | |
	(1)	(2)	(3)	(4)	(5)	(6)	(7)	(8)	(9)	(10)	(11)	(12)	(13)
1935	675,407	60,615	8.97%	47,671	174,540	301,451	1,037,972	5,867,339	15,954	47,628	117,321	501,376	5,867,339
1936	727,603	88,670	12.19%	68,402	251,557	432,446	1,479,465	8,685,852	22,613	70,668	170,692	678,755	8,685,852
1937	704,060	92,998	13.21%	43,012	141,033	231,026	690,390	2,789,699	18,507	51,039	116,185	457,134	2,789,699
1938	768,112	69,350	9.03%	28,395	88,619	142,662	431,383	2,182,804	13,339	34,575	70,481	236,781	2,182,804
1939	769,360	68,364	8.89%	31,955	113,299	194,161	679,059	3,927,140	11,619	32,436	72,936	318,161	3,927,140
1940	739,777	77,478	10.47%	30,212	103,742	174,681	570,871	2,544,649	11,830	32,803	75,633	351,562	2,544,649
1941	714,781	148,649	20.80%	48,400	159,663	262,040	828,514	4,287,115	20,584	57,286	120,422	444,224	4,287,115
1942	748,709												
1943	769,258	170,180	22.12%	45,618	146,793	235,967	680,682	2,957,416	20,324	57,619	124,788	427,712	2,957,416
1944	798,830	125,523	15.71%	31,850	99,640	160,261	461,951	2,026,342	14,903	39,019	84,838	288,130	2,026,342
1945	1,363,345	191,638	14.06%	7,763	24,385	38,617	101,827	350,494	3,608	10,152	22,814	74,198	350,494
1946	869,315	270,172	31.08%	6,108	15,939	24,265	65,757	275,103	3,650	7,613	13,892	42,496	275,103
1947	726,363	107,956	14.86%	4,686	10,632	15,095	33,909	97,929	3,199	6,170	10,391	26,795	97,929
1948	640,123	122,240	19.10%	3,764	8,724	12,617	29,180	83,594	2,524	4,831	8,477	23,134	83,594
1949	629,361	150,834	23.97%	3,588	8,277	11,847	26,298	71,704	2,416	4,708	8,234	21,253	71,704
1950	630,765	37,229	5.90%	6,899	14,407	19,764	40,802	110,093	5,021	9,051	14,505	33,103	110,093
1951	594,257	51,678	8.70%	6,905	13,946	18,948	39,448	114,833	5,145	8,945	13,823	31,072	114,833
1952	569,367	21,565	3.79%		19,097	25,982	55,272	144,030		12,212	18,659	45,410	144,030
1953	595,400	12,138	2.04%		20,005	28,878	69,276	216,189		11,131	18,779	52,952	216,189
1954	567,040	16,443	2.90%		23,802	33,909	80,485	273,472		13,694	22,265	59,042	273,472
1955	562,344	19,839	3.53%		27,902	40,197	96,142	294,328		15,606	26,211	74,122	294,328
1956	599,844	23,100	3.85%		29,721	42,585	99,389	268,874		16,856	28,384	80,557	268,874
1957	635,827	26,585	4.18%		34,174	50,240	122,064	365,110		18,108	32,284	95,059	365,110
1958	581,735	5,296	0.91%			54,320	137,146	403,321			33,613	107,571	403,321
1959	591,577	6,749	1.14%			61,058	149,072	458,069			39,055	114,739	458,069
1960	618,324	9,146	1.48%		51,054	78,636	194,021	582,115		23,472	49,790	150,900	582,115
1961	615,040	11,316	1.84%		63,860	99,588	251,310	793,981		28,132	61,657	191,013	793,981
1962	636,949	9,428	1.48%		76,879	119,048	297,964	972,761		34,710	74,319	222,987	972,761
1963	605,286	11,253	1.86%		87,321	134,906	338,515	1,223,391		39,737	84,004	240,195	1,223,391

Year													
1964	612,370	10,404	1.70%	92,580	144,622	372,134	1,133,167		40,537	87,744	287,575	1,133,167	
1965	642,338	13,161	2.05%	97,174	147,776	344,552	859,992		46,571	98,583	287,281	859,992	
1966	619,868	9,238	1.49%	110,085	166,776	399,034	1,242,750		53,395	108,712	305,288	1,242,750	
1967	623,871	11,294	1.81%	131,925	201,489	498,842	1,693,012		62,361	127,151	366,157	1,693,012	
1968	636,652	14,524	2.28%	141,016	209,379	479,215	1,372,335		72,653	141,921	379,979	1,372,335	
1969	645,792	19,315	2.99%	168,872	250,106	557,592	1,585,821		87,638	173,234	443,345	1,585,821	
1970	666,723	24,479	3.67%	193,456	285,891	635,198	1,843,569		101,022	198,564	500,935	1,843,569	
1971	639,945	25,920	4.05%	249,332	367,274	829,692	2,584,884		131,390	251,669	634,671	2,584,884	
1972	640,574	30,191	4.71%	284,154	429,325	971,775	3,101,611		138,984	293,712	735,127	3,101,611	
1973	666,465	29,171	4.38%	343,481	506,656	1,100,018	3,118,922		180,306	358,315	875,696	3,118,922	
1974	671,039	32,879	4.90%		307,439	447,926	967,684	2,486,612		166,953	317,986	798,914	2,486,612
1975	666,391	14,186	2.13%		284,933	415,587	914,293	2,680,877		154,280	290,910	718,006	2,680,877
1976	670,510	15,567	2.32%		277,698	404,017	855,731	2,185,130		151,379	291,088	708,020	2,185,130
1977	659,717	17,358	2.63%		278,874	406,110	872,242	2,346,307		151,638	289,577	708,457	2,346,307
1978	667,058	19,677	2.95%		292,682	423,570	911,458	2,418,108		161,794	301,598	744,052	2,418,108
1979	663,373	22,144	3.34%		301,048	434,008	888,935	2,190,017		168,087	320,276	744,370	2,190,017
1980	698,060	26,315	3.77%		318,722	464,612	1,001,483	2,669,051		172,832	330,395	816,197	2,669,051
1981	696,931	31,017	4.45%		370,232	539,247	1,157,527	3,170,641		201,217	384,677	933,847	3,170,641
1982	690,132	35,328	5.12%		404,664	589,622	1,276,338	3,658,561		219,707	417,943	1,011,647	3,658,561
1983	719,124	38,826	5.40%	153,608	421,691	616,350	1,363,240	4,094,148	86,588	227,032	429,627	1,059,806	4,094,148
1984	720,529	42,323	5.87%	158,408	428,137	619,625	1,313,990	3,693,978	90,976	236,648	446,034	1,049,547	3,693,978
1985	733,797	47,270	6.44%	170,913	463,314	675,198	1,472,996	4,347,620	97,812	251,430	475,748	1,153,594	4,347,620
1986	749,125	50,857	6.79%	177,011	480,513	699,249	1,544,482	4,679,174	101,135	261,777	487,940	1,196,183	4,679,174
1987	735,429	57,992	7.89%	212,242	584,161	861,857	2,018,490	6,755,997	119,262	306,466	572,699	1,492,101	6,755,997
1988	769,676	50,204	6.52%	258,699	748,812	1,125,328	2,790,812	10,222,238	136,170	372,297	708,957	1,965,098	10,222,238
1989	778,517	41,521	5.33%	311,516	946,480	1,460,636	3,696,641	13,548,109	152,775	432,323	901,635	2,602,033	13,548,109
1990	805,350	48,220	5.99%	342,202	1,014,153	1,533,905	3,665,958	12,483,065	174,215	494,402	1,000,891	2,686,279	12,483,065
1991	814,604	56,480	6.93%	401,415	1,197,474	1,809,678	4,385,354	15,453,762	202,400	585,270	1,165,759	3,155,531	15,453,762
1992	839,909	46,032	5.48%	409,193	1,191,916	1,774,560	3,944,065	11,237,538	213,512	609,272	1,232,184	3,133,679	11,237,538
1993	868,210	44,268	5.10%	352,589	1,000,843	1,472,683	3,225,954	8,924,398	190,525	529,004	1,034,365	2,592,793	8,924,398
1994	864,048	38,880	4.50%	316,674	894,958	1,318,912	2,874,797	7,707,469	172,103	471,004	929,941	2,337,834	7,707,469
1995	909,318	42,814	4.71%	314,596	872,533	1,269,445	2,680,425	6,837,903	175,112	475,620	916,700	2,218,483	6,837,903
1996	884,329	40,929	4.63%	298,487	815,102	1,182,011	2,500,882	6,192,633	169,333	448,194	852,294	2,090,687	6,192,633

(continued)

Table 3B.1 Continued

Actual Year	# Adults decedents (age 20+)	# Estate tax returns	Fraction filing (2)/(1) (%)	Top 5%	Top 1%	Top 0.5% (in 2002 thousand yen)	Top 0.1%	Top 0.01%	Top 5–1%	Top 1–0.5%	Top 0.5–0.1% (in 2002 thousand yen)	Top 0.1–0.01%	Top 0.01%
	(1)	(2)	(3)	(4)	(5)	(6)	(7)	(8)	(9)	(10)	(11)	(12)	(13)
1997	909,812	41,223	4.53%		284,271	773,023	1,124,849	2,435,816	162,083	421,196	797,108	1,942,152	6,878,787
1998	922,486	41,490	4.50%		267,737	709,706	1,019,806	2,127,238	157,245	399,605	742,949	1,803,145	5,044,079
1999	971,827	42,185	4.34%		258,585	686,285	990,990	2,079,118	151,660	381,580	718,957	1,708,490	5,414,767
2000	952,505	40,217	4.22%		251,075	654,660	937,014	1,976,370	150,179	372,306	677,176	1,660,448	4,819,662
2001	961,722	37,903	3.94%		244,755	654,291	952,826	2,095,136	142,371	355,757	667,248	1,635,849	6,228,714
2002	984,349	44,378	4.51%		221,832	584,442	840,089	1,768,465	131,180	328,794	607,995	1,439,916	4,725,404
2003	1,006,976	44,409	4.41%		213,259	557,643	798,969	1,670,914	127,163	316,318	580,983	1,431,030	3,829,872
2004	1,021,197	43,495	4.26%		202,437	525,665	750,080	1,614,293	121,630	301,250	534,027	1,252,187	4,873,247
2005	1,035,418	45,126	4.36%		205,567	533,709	767,573	1,711,500	123,531	299,845	531,591	1,309,048	5,333,576

Notes: Computations by authors based on estate tax return statistics. See Appendix 3B for details.

Top groups are defined relative to the total number of adult decedents (age 20 and above).

Estates are defined as all properties owned by decedents before deductions net of debts.

The average size (as opposed to share) of estate for each top group is reported in 2002 thousand yen ($1 = 110 yen).

For the correspondence between actual and fiscal years, see Appendix 3B.

Due to the difficulty in reconstructing estate statistics for actual years, our estimate for each year in 1905–49 is imprecise, but their moving average is relatively accurate.

Because estates are before deductions but after special reductions, our data underestimate the true value of estates; see Appendix 3B for details.

For 1950–7, inheritance statistics are converted to estate statistics; see Appendix 3B for details.

Table 3B.2 Estate composition in Japan, 1925–2005

		% Estate composition							
Year	Fraction decedents filing returns % (1)	Agricultural Land (2)	Residential Land (3)	Houses & Structures (4)	Business Assets (5)	Stocks (6)	Fixed Claim Assets (7)	Other Assets (8)	Debts (9)
1925	9.6	34.1	19.1	9.6	5.2	22.2	12.9	5.9	−8.9
1926	15.3	34.6	19.4	9.4	4.7	21.5	14.7	5.1	−9.4
1927	19.9	30.2	16.9	8.4	4.2	23.7	21.1	4.2	−8.7
1928	15.4	35.1	19.6	9.9	4.6	15.6	21.3	4.0	−10.2
1929	14.3	33.5	18.7	9.1	4.1	19.7	19.9	4.7	−9.9
1930	12.6	33.0	19.4	10.6	3.9	17.2	21.3	3.7	−9.1
1931	13.0	31.9	20.1	11.1	4.1	14.6	24.9	3.3	−10.0
1932	13.1	31.6	18.7	10.9	4.1	15.3	25.8	3.9	−10.3
1933	12.9	27.6	17.7	10.3	4.0	17.4	28.7	3.8	−9.5
1934	12.6	23.0	15.7	8.8	3.6	29.9	23.0	3.7	−7.6
1935	9.0	24.0	14.8	9.0	4.2	27.6	24.2	3.1	−6.7
1936	14.0	25.0	15.2	8.9	4.2	27.6	21.6	3.1	−5.7
1937	16.8	23.0	14.8	9.3	4.7	29.6	22.6	3.2	−7.3
1938	19.5	22.8	14.9	9.0	4.9	23.0	28.9	4.2	−7.8
1939	6.7	25.4	13.6	10.5	6.0	27.9	18.8	5.7	−7.9
1940	10.5	27.7	13.2	11.9	6.3	20.0	21.1	6.6	−6.8
1941	20.8	24.9	13.5	13.5	6.5	19.7	21.8	6.1	−6.0
1944	15.7	26.3	10.1	18.6	6.3	13.3	21.9	7.8	−4.3
1945	14.1	18.9	11.1	17.5	5.9	10.2	31.9	7.9	−3.3
1947	17.0	13.0	10.0	39.8	12.4	4.4	12.5	16.4	−8.5
1948	28.7	7.8	8.5	39.6	15.4	2.3	11.8	19.9	−5.3
1949	30.9	6.3	9.8	40.2	16.0	2.4	11.2	21.0	−6.9
1950	8.8	13.7	15.1	37.3	13.5	4.8	12.1	19.7	−16.2
1951	6.4	19.4	14.4	36.0	11.9	5.8	16.2	13.7	−17.3
1952	3.6	16.2	13.2	28.9	10.8	7.4	17.7	17.3	−11.6
1953	1.7	18.4	18.0	26.0	9.8	12.3	10.9	20.0	−15.4
1954	2.3	23.9	21.3	23.8	8.5	9.0	8.9	19.2	−14.5
1955	2.8	24.9	24.4	21.7	9.7	8.3	8.9	16.9	−14.8
1956	3.2	25.5	25.3	20.1	11.0	9.1	5.5	15.3	−11.8
1957	3.5	26.1	28.4	17.8	10.1	9.5	6.0	14.4	−12.4
1958	0.9	8.4	38.9	16.6	6.4	20.0	7.4	15.1	−12.8
1959	1.1	10.9	39.4	15.2	5.9	19.5	8.0	14.2	−13.0
1960	1.5	13.8	40.2	12.5	5.2	19.3	7.5	12.0	−10.5
1961	1.8	16.3	40.2	10.1	4.4	20.0	7.4	11.6	−10.0
1962	1.5	13.9	47.9	8.4	3.9	18.7	7.3	10.2	−10.3
1963	1.9	14.0	46.9	7.9	3.4	19.8	7.4	10.6	−10.1
1964	1.7	15.7	48.7	7.0	3.2	16.0	9.0	9.4	−9.1
1965	2.1	18.0	49.1	6.9	3.1	14.0	8.5	9.7	−9.3
1966	1.5	17.9	46.8	6.6	2.8	16.1	10.3	9.5	−10.0
1967	1.8	20.7	43.4	5.5	2.5	17.9	11.0	9.0	−9.8
1968	2.3	25.2	42.2	6.0	2.7	12.5	10.9	9.2	−8.9
1969	3.0	27.0	42.2	5.5	2.4	12.3	10.4	8.0	−7.8
1970	3.7	28.5	40.6	5.8	2.2	12.8	10.6	7.7	−8.1
1971	4.1	32.0	42.5	4.8	1.7	9.3	9.4	6.7	−6.5

(continued)

Table 3B.2 Continued

		% Estate composition							
Year	Fraction decedents filing returns % (1)	Agricultural Land (2)	Residential Land (3)	Houses & Structures (4)	Business Assets (5)	Stocks (6)	Fixed Claim Assets (7)	Other Assets (8)	Debts (9)
1972	4.7	33.0	40.6	3.7	1.7	10.2	10.4	6.5	−6.0
1973	4.4	35.0	40.2	3.3	1.3	9.7	10.6	6.0	−5.9
1974	4.9	32.2	43.2	3.3	1.3	8.3	10.2	7.0	−5.5
1975	2.2	32.0	41.8	2.9	1.0	9.1	11.2	6.8	−4.9
1976	2.4	31.5	40.5	3.2	1.1	9.3	12.0	7.8	−5.4
1977	2.7	30.4	41.0	3.4	1.1	9.6	11.3	8.4	−5.4
1978	3.0	30.7	40.1	3.6	1.3	9.0	11.8	9.0	−5.6
1979	3.4	29.2	41.3	3.6	1.4	9.1	11.7	9.9	−6.2
1980	3.8	28.9	41.7	3.5	1.2	9.2	11.3	9.7	−5.6
1981	4.5	28.3	43.9	3.4	1.0	8.4	10.6	9.9	−5.5
1982	5.2	28.0	46.0	3.4	1.0	7.2	10.3	9.6	−5.5
1983	5.5	27.8	44.9	3.4	1.0	7.8	10.6	9.9	−5.4
1984	6.0	26.6	45.3	3.7	1.2	7.9	11.3	10.5	−6.4
1985	6.6	25.4	45.3	3.7	0.9	8.6	11.8	10.4	−6.1
1986	6.9	24.3	44.6	4.0	0.9	9.9	12.7	10.5	−6.8
1987	8.0	22.2	47.0	3.9	0.8	11.0	12.6	10.2	−7.9
1988	6.6	21.9	52.8	3.6	0.6	9.7	11.8	7.4	−7.8
1989	5.3	20.8	51.9	4.9	0.5	13.2	10.8	6.0	−8.0
1990	6.0	20.9	56.3	4.9	0.5	9.0	10.9	6.0	−8.4
1991	6.9	21.5	57.9	5.0	0.4	7.7	10.1	5.7	−8.3
1992	6.5	25.9	56.0	4.7	0.4	6.2	9.5	5.1	−7.9
1993	6.1	25.4	54.0	5.5	0.5	6.9	10.9	5.9	−9.1
1994	5.3	26.5	50.8	5.6	0.5	7.1	12.3	6.3	−9.1
1995	5.6	25.9	50.4	5.9	0.5	6.9	13.6	6.7	−9.8
1996	5.5	26.2	48.5	4.5	0.5	7.4	15.0	7.2	−9.4
1997	5.3	25.2	47.9	4.4	0.6	8.1	15.7	7.6	−9.5
1998	5.4	25.6	48.2	4.8	0.5	5.9	16.9	7.9	−9.8
1999	5.2	24.3	46.4	5.1	0.6	7.3	18.1	9.7	−11.5
2000	5.1	23.4	48.3	4.9	0.5	7.2	19.6	11.0	−15.1
2001	4.8	23.2	43.4	5.2	0.6	8.6	20.4	11.5	−12.8
2002	4.5	23.3	43.4	5.8	0.5	6.7	21.7	12.2	−13.7
2003	4.4	21.4	42.3	5.5	0.5	7.1	23.7	12.8	−13.4
2004	4.3	18.6	40.4	6.0	0.6	9.0	25.7	10.6	−10.9
2005	4.4	17.1	38.9	6.2	0.5	10.6	27.0	10.8	−11.1

Notes: Computations by authors based on aggregate estate tax return statistics. See Appendix 3B for details.
Estates net of debts are defined to be 100%.
Business assets include assets of unincorporate business and farm assets.
Fixed claim assets include bonds, cash, deposits, savings accounts, and other claims.
Other assets include household properties, pensions, life insurance, and other items.
Because the fraction of decedents filing estate tax returns fluctuates from year to year, estate compositions may not be directly comparable across years. See Table 3.3 for the comparison of top estate compositions for selected years.

APPENDIX 3C: TOP WAGE INCOME SHARES

In estimating top wage income shares, we use two different sets of statistics for the pre- and post-1950 period, as discussed below. As a result, our estimates for 1929–44 are less precisely estimated than the 1951–2005 estimates and two series are not fully homogeneous.

Top Wage Income Shares, 1951–2005

The National Tax Administration has annually published the statistics on wages and salaries in the results of the statistical survey of the actual status for salary in the private sector in the *Survey on Private Wages and Salaries* (*Minkan Kyuyo no Jittai*) since 1951.[55] The survey covers all employees in the private sector who worked for the same employer throughout a calendar year, but excludes temporary workers whose job duration is shorter than a year, regular employees who are hired mid-year, government employees, and retirees. Because the survey is based on the data filed by employers who are legally responsible for withholding tax at source for their employees, it provides accurate and detailed information on wages and salaries, often by firm size, industry, tenure, and sex. The statistics include a distribution table that reports the number of wage earners and the amount of annual wage income by wage income brackets, which we use to estimate top wage income shares.

Our definition of wage income includes wages, salaries, overtime pay, bonuses, and various allowances, but excludes retirement benefits and part of non-cash compensation. It is before subtracting employee's social insurance contributions and before including employer's social insurance contributions.[56] Although all non-cash compensation is in principle taxable, expense accounts for business purposes are fully exempted, and so is company housing if employees bear at least 50 per cent of its costs based on official valuation. Recreation or entertainment provided exclusively for executives is fully taxed, however. Stock option, which was legalized in 1997 and liberalized in 2002 in Japan, is in principle not taxed as wage income but taxed as capital gains at the point of exercise.[57] Thanks to the sophisticated withholding system with end-of-year adjustments, the tax statistics in fiscal year *t* report wages and salaries earned in the same year *t*. Therefore, fiscal year and actual year coincide for the wage income tax statistics in 1951–2005.

We again use a standard Pareto interpolation method to estimate top wage income shares. We define top groups (top 5 per cent and 1 per cent) relative to the total number of

---

[55] The first survey was conducted in 1949, but its sample differs from the subsequent surveys and its results were never published (National Tax Administration (1980), *Minkan Kyuuyo Jittai Chosa Sanjunen no Ayumi* (30-Year History of the Survey of Private Wages and Salaries)). We cannot locate the original 1950 and 1951 surveys. The data for 1951 are found in Takahashi (1959). The results of the statistical survey for recent years are available at http://www.nta.go.jp/category/toukei/tokei-e.htm.

[56] This information is based on the author's phone conversation with a Japan Tax Administration officer on 5 May 2006.

[57] For the definition of wage income and the detailed descriptions of exemptions and special treatments, see section 2 of National Tax Bureau (2004), *Heisei 16–nen 6–gatsu Gensen Choshu no Aramashi* (June 2004: Outline of Withholding Tax), available online at http://www.nta.go.jp/category/pamph/gensen/5151/01.htm.

regular employees, which excludes temporary as well as daily hired workers, in the private sector in Japan. The series for regular employees for 1951–2005 are obtained from *Historical Statistics of Japan*, table 19–7,[58] and are reported in column (2) in Table 3C.1. The number of employees in the wage income survey is reported in column (3). As shown in column (4), from 1951 to 2005, the coverage of the survey rose from 55 per cent to 97 per cent of regular employees in the private sector.

To obtain top wage income shares, we divide the amounts of wages and salaries accruing to top wage income groups by 90 per cent of total wages and salaries from National Accounts. The denominator is reported in column (7) in Table 3C.1, under the label 'total wage income'. To be consistent with our definition of wage income, total wages and salaries from National Accounts include employees' social insurance contributions and exclude employers' social insurance contributions. In recent years, where the coverage of the survey is almost complete for regular employees in the private sector, total wages reported in the survey are approximately 90 per cent of wages and salaries from National Accounts. Thus, we use the factor 90 per cent to correct for the exclusion of daily employees and government employees in the wage income survey. We present all values in real 2002 yen, using CPI. Our estimates for top 1 per cent and 5 per cent wage income shares for 1951–2005 are reported in Table 3C.2 and Figures 3.10 and 3.11.

Top Wage Income Shares, 1929–1944

For fiscal years 1930–45, the annual reports publish the data on salaries and bonuses as part of the composition tables in income tax statistics. The data include the numbers of taxpayers who received salaries and bonuses, respectively, and the amounts of salaries and bonuses they earned. The income tax statistics in fiscal years 1920–9 also report the amounts of salaries and bonuses but not the numbers of salary and bonus earners. We thus cannot use the data before 1929 to estimate top wage income shares. We assume that fiscal years 1930–45 correspond to actual years 1929–44 for the reasons described in Appendix 3A.

For the denominator, we take the total salaries (excluding employers' social insurance contributions) from the old SNA for 1930–44. For 1929, we extrapolate total salaries assuming that the fraction of salaries in total personal income is the same as in 1930.

We define top groups relative to the total number of regular employees. Although the tax statistics during the 1929–44 period do not exclude temporary workers, we use regular employees to be consistent with the 1951–2005 estimates. Moreover, naturally, most if not all top wage earners are regular employees. The total number of regular employees in Japan is estimated as follows. The total number of employees is reported in *Historical Statistics of Japan*, volume i, table 3–6, for years 1930, 1940, and 1947. For 1930, employees and family workers are not reported separately, thus we assume that the fraction of family workers to total employees in 1930 is the same as in 1940. We then estimate the total number of employees for years between 1930, 1940, and 1947, simply by linear interpolation. Finally, we estimate the number of regular employees for 1929–44, using the fraction of regular employees to total employees in 1953, the first year in which such information is available. These assumptions are restrictive, but our estimates are not very sensitive to these assumptions.

We make the following adjustments to the salaries and bonuses reported in the income tax statistics to recover the full value. For fiscal years 1930–9, the earned income credit allowed taxpayers to deduct 20 per cent of wage income for those with total income under

---

[58] Available online at http://www.stat.go.jp/english/data/chouki/19.htm.

6,000 yen and 10 per cent for those with total income between 6,000 and 12,000 yen. We therefore assume that the average deduction was 15 per cent and inflate the reported amount of salaries by a factor 1/0.85. For fiscal years 1940–5, the earned income credit is 10 per cent of wage income for those with total income below 10,000 yen. We assume that the average deduction is 8 per cent and inflate the reported salaries by a factor 1/0.92. Because, for fiscal years 1930–6, only 60 per cent of bonuses are taxable and reported in the statistics, we inflate bonuses by a factor 1/0.6. Similarly, for fiscal years 1937–9, as only 80 per cent of bonuses are reported in the statistics, we inflate bonuses by a factor 1/0.8. For fiscal years 1940–5, as 100 per cent of bonuses are reported, we make no adjustment.

The number of bonus earners in the income tax statistics is always smaller than the number of salary earners. We assume that all bonus earners also have some wage income, so that we can attribute all bonuses to all the taxpayers reporting positive salaries. Furthermore, we assume that those reporting salaries and bonuses on income tax returns represent the top wage income earners. This assumption does not necessarily hold, as individuals with large non-wage income and modest wage income also file tax returns, and may bias our estimates of top wage income shares downward.

Thus, from the aggregate statistics, we can compute the share of total wage income accruing to the tax return filers with positive wage income. To obtain the shares of wage income accruing to fixed fractions of wage earners (e.g. top 1 per cent and 5 per cent groups) using a standard Pareto interpolation method, however, we need at least two observations on the share of income and the fraction of employees per year. Because we have only one such observation per year, we proceed as follows.

For years 1929–44, on average about 3 per cent of regular employees filed income tax returns. This fraction changes over time. In particular, it falls sharply from 6.72 per cent in 1938 (fiscal year 1939) to 0.76 per cent in 1939 (fiscal year 1940), because of the large increase in the exemption level for comprehensive income tax under the 1940 law. We assume that the distribution of wage income did not change significantly from 1938 to 1939 and that the Pareto coefficient remained the same. Then we estimate the Pareto coefficient using the standard formula: $(1-1/a) = \{\log(\text{share of wage income in 1938})-\log(\text{share of wage income in 1939})\}/\{\log(\text{fraction of wage income filers in 1938})-\log(\text{fraction of wage income filers in 1939})\}$. The estimated coefficient is $a=2.76$. Assuming that the Pareto coefficient is constant for 1929–44, we compute the top 1 per cent and top 5 per cent income share for each year (which are reported in Table 3C.2). Because we use 1938 and 1939 to estimate the Pareto coefficient, by definition our top wage income shares in 1938 and 1939 are identical. Therefore, we exclude the 1938 estimates from Table 3C.2.

The assumption that the Pareto coefficient is constant across years 1929–44 is certainly restrictive. Our finding, a sharp decline in top wage income shares during this period, however, should be robust. The raw data clearly indicate that there was a large decline in wage income concentration during 1929–44: in the early 1930s, when 2 to 3 per cent of wage earners filed income tax returns, their wage income was more than 15 per cent of the total salaries from National Accounts; by contrast, in 1944, almost 5 per cent of wage earners filed income tax returns but their wage income was only about 9 per cent of all wages and salaries.

Marginal Tax Rates for Top Wage Income Earners, 1951–2005

We estimate marginal tax rates (MTRs) at the wage income thresholds for the top 10 per cent, 5 per cent, 1 per cent, 0.1 per cent, and 0.01 per cent groups (denoted as MTR at P90,

P95, P99, P99.9, and P99.99, respectively, in Table 3C.3) in 1951–2005 as follows. We assume that a taxpayer at each threshold income has only employment income and forms a household with a non-working spouse and two dependent children. To obtain net taxable income, we subtract basic, spouse, and two dependent exemptions and employment income deductions from the threshold wage income. Tax codes describing exemptions and deductions in each year are available in Japan National Tax Administration (1988) and OECD (1998–2005), *Taxing Wages*. We then use a standard tax schedule (that presents increasing marginal tax rates by income brackets) to obtain tax liability, from which we estimate MTR for a given taxable income level. Top MTR in Table 3C.3 is the highest statutory marginal tax rate according to the tax schedule after employment income deductions.[59]

To estimate the MTR for the average taxpayer in the top 0.1 per cent wage income group (presented in Figure 3.12, Panel A), we use the following method. First, we compute the MTR for the top 0.01 per cent group as: MTR Top 0.01 per cent = (MTR at P99.99 + Top MTR)/2, where a simple average is used as an approximation for the MTR for this group. We then compute the MTR for the top 0.1 per cent group as: MTR Top 0.1 per cent = {Income Share of Top 0.1–0.01 per cent Group * (MTR at P99.9 + MTR at P99.99)/2 + Income Share of Top 0.01 per cent Group * MTR Top 0.01 per cent} / {Income Share of Top 0.1 per cent Group}. This amounts to estimating MTR Top 0.1 per cent as the income-weighted average of MTR Top 0.01 per cent and MTR Top 0.1–0.01 per cent where MTR Top 0.1–0.01 per cent is computed using a simple average, (MTR at P99.9 + MTR at P99.99)/2.

Our marginal tax rates do not take into account social insurance contributions and local income taxes. In Japan, since their introduction in the early 1950s, social insurance taxes (for pensions and health insurance) have been determined as a fixed percentage of monthly earnings up to a maximum amount of monthly earnings set by law. The cap on monthly earnings has been set at around twice the average earnings of all insurers and revised periodically to adjust for inflation.[60] As a result, as in the USA, social insurance taxes hardly affect the top 1 per cent wage income earners in Japan.

For local income taxes (municipal and prefectural taxes) in Japan, local governments introduced a significant progressive income tax on the same income base as the national income tax since 1950 (Ishi 2001). Although the share of local income taxes in total income taxes (local and national combined) has grown over the 1950–2005 period, its progressivity has declined (the highest statutory marginal tax rates for local income has declined from 18 per cent in 1950 to 13 per cent in 2005.[61] Therefore, adding local MTRs to our national MTRs would probably magnify the decline in the marginal tax rates for top wage income earners in Japan during 1950–2005.[62]

In 2005, the share of local income taxes in total income taxes in Japan was 25 per cent, while the share of local income taxes in total income taxes (federal and state combined) in the USA is 22 per cent. The share of local income taxes in Japan is in fact comparable to the tax of high tax states such as California or New York. In short, the inclusion of social insurance contributions and local taxes would not affect our comparative analysis of Japan and the United States.

---

[59] In 2005, for example, for employment income over 10 million yen, 1.7 million yen plus 5% of the employment income can be deducted from taxable income, reducing MTR by 5%.

[60] See 'Tsuiseki Nenkin Kaikaku (Pension Reform)' published in Yomiuri Shimbun Online on 4 June 2004, at http://www.yomiuri.co.jp/atmoney/special/43/kaikaku53.htm and Kosei Hakusho (White Paper on Health and Welfare) in 1965 available online at http://wwwhakusyo.mhlw.go.jp/wpdocs/hpaz196501/b0163.html.

[61] The data on local tax rates in Japan, 1950–2005, are available at http://www.soumu.go.jp/czaisei/czaisei_seido/ichiran06_h17.html.

[62] See Moriguchi (2008) for MTR estimates incorporating local income taxes that confirms this point.

Table 3C.1 Reference totals for wage earners, wage income, and inflation, Japan, 1948–2005

| Years | | Regular Wage Earners | | | Wage Income | | Inflation |
(1a) Actual Year wage earned	(1b) Fiscal Year (tax paid)	(2) Number of employees ('000s)	(3) Number of tax returns ('000s)	(4) (3)/(2) (%)	(7) Total wage income (billions 2002 yen)	(8) Average wage income ('000s 2002 yen)	(9) CPI (2002 base 100)
1929	1930	9,821	336	3.42	7,911	806	0.062
1930	1931	10,009	302	3.02	8,791	878	0.055
1931	1932	10,197	274	2.69	8,969	880	0.049
1932	1933	10,385	291	2.81	8,996	866	0.050
1933	1934	10,573	322	3.05	9,190	869	0.051
1934	1935	10,761	353	3.28	9,971	927	0.052
1935	1936	10,949	384	3.51	10,135	926	0.053
1936	1937	11,137	425	3.82	10,828	972	0.054
1937	1938	11,326	655	5.78	11,450	1,011	0.059
1938	1939	11,514	774	6.72	12,053	1,047	0.064
1939	1940	11,702	89	0.76	11,806	1,009	0.080
1940	1941	11,528	102	0.89	11,012	955	0.102
1941	1942	11,355	243	2.14	12,150	1,070	0.114
1942	1943	11,181	325	2.90	11,662	1,043	0.139
1943	1944	11,007	444	4.03	12,986	1,180	0.159
1944	1945	10,834	532	4.91	13,459	1,242	0.196
1948	1948	11,006			6,904	627	10.58
1949	1949	10,729	1,410	13.14	7,225	673	13.93
1950	1950	10,928	5,114	46.80	9,532	872	12.99
1951	1951	11,835	6,463	54.61	11,104	938	15.19
1952	1952	12,275	6,838	55.70	12,846	1,046	16.03
1953	1953	14,340	6,939	48.39	14,870	1,037	17.08
1954	1954	14,800	7,625	51.52	15,439	1,043	18.12
1955	1955	15,370	8,219	53.47	16,486	1,073	18.02
1956	1956	16,660	8,745	52.49	18,813	1,129	18.12

(continued)

Table 3C.1 Continued

Years		Regular Wage Earners				Wage Income		Inflation
(1a)	(1b)	(2)	(3)	(4)		(7)	(8)	(9)
Actual Year wage earned	Fiscal Year (tax paid)	Number of employees ('000s)	Number of tax returns ('000s)	(3)/(2) (%)		Total wage income (billions 2002 yen)	Average wage income ('000s 2002 yen)	CPI (2002 base 100)
1957	1957	17,790	9,431	53.01		20,549	1,155	18.65
1958	1958	18,860	10,268	54.44		22,776	1,208	18.54
1959	1959	19,020	10,856	57.08		25,316	1,331	18.75
1960	1960	20,220	11,715	57.94		28,091	1,389	19.49
1961	1961	21,210	12,962	61.11		31,665	1,493	20.43
1962	1962	22,190	14,106	63.57		35,153	1,584	21.90
1963	1963	23,230	15,250	65.65		38,029	1,637	23.47
1964	1964	24,080	16,123	66.96		42,642	1,771	24.41
1965	1965	25,050	17,170	68.54		46,583	1,860	25.98
1966	1966	26,160	18,277	69.87		50,978	1,949	27.34
1967	1967	27,670	19,773	71.46		56,392	2,038	28.39
1968	1968	28,690	20,676	72.07		62,196	2,168	29.96
1969	1969	29,190	22,066	75.59		69,588	2,384	31.53
1970	1970	30,230	24,244	80.20		77,696	2,570	33.94
1971	1971	31,230	26,480	84.79		86,792	2,779	35.93
1972	1972	31,620	27,096	85.69		96,653	3,057	37.61
1973	1973	32,880	28,181	85.71		108,657	3,305	42.01
1974	1974	33,220	29,895	89.99		110,902	3,338	52.28
1975	1975	33,460	30,321	90.62		114,416	3,419	58.46
1976	1976	34,020	31,068	91.32		117,435	3,452	64.01
1977	1977	34,260	31,151	90.93		120,527	3,518	69.14
1978	1978	34,360	32,113	93.46		125,063	3,640	71.66
1979	1979	35,050	32,534	92.82		129,837	3,704	74.28
1980	1980	35,860	33,361	93.03		130,085	3,628	80.25
1981	1981	36,460	33,659	92.32		132,860	3,644	84.12

Year					
1982	36,920	33,996	92.08	136,637	3,701	86.43
1983	37,730	34,928	92.57	140,826	3,732	88.00
1984	38,260	35,306	92.28	145,394	3,800	89.99
1985	38,660	36,938	95.55	148,370	3,838	91.77
1986	39,320	37,287	94.83	153,379	3,901	92.19
1987	39,640	37,670	95.03	157,781	3,980	91.98
1988	40,540	37,918	93.53	165,970	4,094	92.40
1989	41,760	38,470	92.12	173,262	4,149	94.60
1990	43,160	39,307	91.07	181,689	4,210	97.53
1991	44,770	40,339	90.10	189,819	4,240	100.68
1992	45,890	41,247	89.88	195,086	4,251	102.35
1993	46,570	42,770	91.84	197,072	4,232	103.51
1994	46,900	43,726	93.23	201,399	4,294	104.03
1995	47,090	44,395	94.28	203,262	4,316	103.71
1996	47,540	44,895	94.44	207,393	4,362	103.71
1997	47,910	45,265	94.48	209,891	4,381	104.65
1998	47,500	45,446	95.68	206,707	4,352	104.54
1999	46,900	44,984	95.91	202,901	4,326	103.82
2000	46,840	44,939	95.94	207,231	4,424	102.47
2001	46,770	45,097	96.42	207,932	4,446	100.91
2002	46,040	44,724	97.14	198,802	4,400	100.00
2003	45,980	44,661	97.13	198,322	4,313	99.70
2004	46,080	44,530	96.64	197,278	4,281	99.70
2005	46,310	44,936	97.03	199,881	4,316	99.39

Notes: See Appendix 3C for details.

Due to the extensive withholding system for wage earners, actual years and fiscal years coincide for 1949–2002.

The number of employees is total number of regular employees in the private sector.

The number of tax returns is based on income tax statistics for 1929–1944, and *Survey on Private Wages and Salaries* for 1949–2005.

Wage Income is defined as wages, salaries, allowances, bonuses, and taxable part of noncash benefits, but excludes retirement benefits. Total wage income is defined as 90% of total wages and salaries from National Accounts.

Table 3C.2 Top wage income shares in Japan, 1929–2005

Year	Top 10% (1)	Top 5% (2)	Top 1% (3)	Top 0.5% (4)	Top 0.1% (5)	Top 0.01% (6)	Top 10–5% (7)	Top 5–1% (8)	Top 1–0.5% (9)	Top 0.5–0.1% (10)	Top 0.1–0.01% (11)
1929	23.20	21.11	7.57					13.54			
1930	24.37	20.51	7.35					13.16			
1931	24.06	21.65	7.76					13.89			
1932	24.20	22.30	8.00					14.31			
1933	24.19	23.01	8.25					14.76			
1934	25.77	22.55	8.08					14.46			
1935	26.84	23.14	8.30					14.84			
1936	26.47	20.39	7.31					13.08			
1937	26.49	19.80	7.10					12.70			
1938	27.00										
1939	27.41	18.78	6.73					12.05			
1940	26.85	16.88	6.05					10.83			
1941	26.67	13.60	4.88					8.73			
1942	26.17	11.91	4.27					7.64			
1943	25.01	10.34	3.71					6.63			
1944	24.43	8.85	3.17					5.68			
1951	25.08	14.70	4.83	2.98	0.97	0.19	8.50	9.87	1.85	2.01	0.79
1952	25.49	15.60	5.39	3.37	1.10	0.22	8.77	10.21	2.02	2.27	0.87
1953	25.24	15.46	5.35	3.36	1.12	0.22	8.61	10.11	2.00	2.23	0.91
1954		15.48	5.34	3.36	1.11	0.23	8.72	10.14	1.98	2.25	0.89
1955		15.43	5.34	3.34	1.10	0.22	8.77	10.09	2.00	2.24	0.89
1956		16.67	5.88	3.64	1.24	0.25	9.11	10.79	2.24	2.41	0.99
1957		17.31	6.10	3.79	1.29	0.25	9.53	11.21	2.31	2.50	1.04
1958		17.13	6.06	3.80	1.28	0.26	9.34	11.06	2.27	2.51	1.02
1959		17.18	6.19	4.04	1.32	0.25	9.31	11.00	2.15	2.72	1.07
1960		17.48	6.14	3.90	1.32	0.26	9.52	11.34	2.24	2.58	1.06
1961		17.91	6.58	4.23	1.34	0.26	9.50	11.33	2.35	2.89	1.08
1962		17.70	6.40	4.07	1.29	0.25	9.14	11.31	2.33	2.78	1.04
1963		17.31	6.20	3.90	1.31	0.27	9.36	11.11	2.31	2.59	1.04
1964		16.96	6.02	3.74	1.24	0.24	9.21	10.94	2.28	2.50	1.00
1965		16.12	5.59	3.43	1.13	0.23	8.89	10.53	2.16	2.30	0.91
1966		15.62	5.37	3.31	1.08	0.20	8.81	10.25	2.06	2.23	0.88
1967		16.00	5.42	3.37	1.11	0.22	9.08	10.58	2.05	2.26	0.90
1968		16.24	5.41	3.36	1.11	0.21	9.25	10.83	2.05	2.26	0.90
1969		15.98	5.18	3.21	1.03	0.19	9.26	10.79	1.97	2.18	0.83

1970	25.50	15.95	5.04	3.10	1.00	0.19	9.55	10.91	1.94	2.10	0.82
1971	25.19	15.63	4.93	2.99	0.94	0.18	9.57	10.70	1.94	2.05	0.76
1972	25.24	15.70	5.02	2.96	0.89	0.16	9.54	10.68	2.06	2.07	0.73
1973	24.91	15.44	4.85	2.81	0.85	0.16	9.47	10.59	2.04	1.96	0.68
1974	24.47	14.97	4.56	2.72	0.81	0.15	9.49	10.41	1.84	1.91	0.66
1975	23.54	14.33	4.33	2.57	0.75	0.13	9.20	10.00	1.76	1.82	0.62
1976	24.01	14.63	4.43	2.61	0.80	0.13	9.38	10.19	1.82	1.82	0.66
1977	23.36	14.11	4.29	2.54	0.74	0.13	9.25	9.82	1.76	1.79	0.61
1978	23.32	14.06	4.32	2.59	0.78	0.14	9.26	9.74	1.73	1.82	0.64
1979	23.92	14.53	4.47	2.69	0.84	0.16	9.40	10.06	1.78	1.86	0.67
1980	23.91	14.51	4.46	2.71	0.88	0.19	9.40	10.05	1.75	1.83	0.69
1981	23.92	14.62	4.50	2.72	0.84	0.16	9.30	10.12	1.79	1.88	0.68
1982	23.47	14.32	4.37	2.64	0.83	0.17	9.15	9.96	1.73	1.81	0.67
1983	23.78	14.57	4.42	2.66	0.82	0.16	9.21	10.15	1.75	1.85	0.66
1984	23.81	14.60	4.46	2.70	0.84	0.17	9.22	10.13	1.76	1.86	0.67
1985	24.30	14.85	4.51	2.73	0.86	0.17	9.45	10.33	1.78	1.87	0.69
1986	24.70	15.08	4.54	2.71	0.84	0.17	9.62	10.54	1.83	1.87	0.67
1987	25.08	15.28	4.68	2.79	0.88	0.17	9.80	10.60	1.89	1.91	0.71
1988	25.15	15.33	4.65	2.75	0.84	0.16	9.82	10.67	1.90	1.91	0.68
1989	25.32	15.43	4.70	2.78	0.88	0.17	9.90	10.73	1.92	1.91	0.71
1990	25.59	15.61	4.78	2.84	0.90	0.17	9.99	10.82	1.94	1.95	0.72
1991	25.78	15.76	4.79	2.87	0.91	0.18	10.01	10.98	1.91	1.97	0.73
1992	25.92	15.85	4.79	2.88	0.92	0.18	10.08	11.05	1.91	1.96	0.74
1993	25.70	15.66	4.72	2.83	0.88	0.17	10.04	10.94	1.90	1.95	0.71
1994	25.74	15.57	4.71	2.84	0.92	0.18	10.18	10.86	1.87	1.92	0.73
1995	25.76	15.54	4.73	2.85	0.89	0.17	10.23	10.80	1.89	1.96	0.72
1996	25.46	15.29	4.64	2.80	0.89	0.18	10.18	10.65	1.84	1.91	0.71
1997	25.42	15.21	4.60	2.78	0.89	0.18	10.22	10.61	1.82	1.89	0.71
1998	25.73	15.54	4.83	2.96	0.94	0.18	10.20	10.71	1.87	2.01	0.76
1999	25.89	15.73	4.89	3.00	1.00	0.21	10.16	10.84	1.89	2.01	0.78
2000	25.74	15.68	4.95	3.07	1.03	0.22	10.06	10.73	1.88	2.04	0.81
2001	25.68	15.66	5.01	3.12	1.06	0.24	10.02	10.65	1.89	2.06	0.83
2002	26.29	16.08	5.15	3.21	1.09	0.23	10.21	10.93	1.94	2.12	0.85
2003	26.56	16.32	5.29	3.34	1.18	0.27	10.24	11.03	1.95	2.16	0.91
2004	26.90	16.65	5.54	3.53	1.30	0.32	10.25	11.11	2.00	2.23	0.98
2005	26.77	16.61	5.57	3.55	1.27	0.30	10.17	11.04	2.02	2.28	0.97

Notes: Computations by authors based on income tax return statistics and wage income tax statistics; see Appendix 3C for details.
Wage income is defined as wages, salaries, allowances, and bonuses, excluding retirement benefits and non-taxable part of noncash benefits.
Top wage income groups are defined relative to all regular employees for 1929–1944 and regular employees in the private sector for 1951–2005.
Estimates are based on income tax statistics for 1929–44 and *Survey on Private Wages and Salaries* for 1951–2005.
The 1929–44 estimates are less precise than the 1951–2002 estimates and not fully comparable to the 1951–2005 estimates.

Table 3C.3 Wage income tax and marginal tax rates in Japan, 1951–2005

Year (1)	Basic Exemption per Tax Unit ('000 current yen) (2)	Exemption per Dependent ('000 current yen) (3)	Marginal Tax Rate at P90 (%) (4)	Marginal Tax Rate at P95 (%) (5)	Marginal Tax Rate at P99 (%) (6)	Marginal Tax Rate at P99.9 (%) (7)	Marginal Tax Rate at P99.99 (%) (8)	Top Marginal Tax Rate (%) (9)
						Marginal Tax Rates on Wage Income		
1950	25.0	12.0	30.0	33.0	43.0	48.0	53.0	55.0
1951	38.0	17.0	30.0	38.0	43.0	53.0	55.0	55.0
1952	50.0	20.0	21.3	30.0	40.0	50.0	55.0	55.0
1953	60.0	35.0	21.3	35.0	45.0	50.0	55.0	65.0
1954	67.5	38.8	21.3	30.0	40.0	50.0	55.0	65.0
1955	75.0	40.0	20.6	30.0	40.0	50.0	60.0	65.0
1956	80.0	40.0	12.0	18.0	25.0	35.0	40.0	70.0
1957	87.5	47.5	12.0	18.0	25.0	35.0	45.0	70.0
1958	90.0	50.0	13.5	18.0	25.0	35.0	45.0	70.0
1959	90.0	65.0	13.5	18.0	25.0	35.0	45.0	70.0
1960	90.0	70.0	9.0	18.0	25.0	40.0	45.0	70.0
1961	90.0	50.0	13.5	20.0	25.0	40.0	45.0	75.0
1962	97.5	50.0	13.5	20.0	30.0	40.0	50.0	75.0
1963	107.5	50.0	13.9	20.0	30.0	40.0	50.0	75.0
1964	117.5	57.5	15.0	20.0	30.0	40.0	50.0	75.0
1965	127.5	60.0	15.0	20.0	30.0	40.0	50.0	75.0
1966	137.5	67.5	15.0	20.0	30.0	45.0	50.0	75.0
1967	147.5	77.5	20.0	20.0	30.0	45.0	50.0	75.0
1968	157.5	95.0	17.3	21.1	29.4	46.0	55.0	75.0
1969	167.5	115.0	14.6	16.4	25.9	42.0	55.0	75.0
1970	177.5	135.0	12.6	15.2	22.8	42.0	55.0	75.0
1971	195.0	140.0	14.4	17.1	27.0	42.0	55.0	75.0
1972	200.0	155.0	16.4	19.1	28.8	46.0	55.0	75.0
1973	207.5	220.0	12.0	15.1	22.7	35.3	46.5	69.8
1974	232.5	260.0	12.8	16.8	24.3	37.8	45.0	67.5
1975	260.0	260.0	14.4	16.8	27.0	37.8	49.5	67.5
1976	260.0							

Year								
1977	290.0	290.0	14.4	16.8	27.0	41.4	49.5	67.5
1978	290.0	290.0	16.8	19.2	30.6	41.4	49.5	67.5
1979	290.0	290.0	16.8	19.2	30.6	45.0	54.0	67.5
1980	290.0	290.0	16.8	21.6	34.2	47.5	57.0	71.3
1981	290.0	290.0	19.2	24.3	36.1	47.5	57.0	71.3
1982	290.0	290.0	19.2	24.3	36.1	47.5	57.0	71.3
1983	290.0	290.0	19.2	24.3	36.1	47.5	57.0	71.3
1984	330.0	330.0	20.0	22.5	33.3	47.5	57.0	66.5
1985	330.0	330.0	22.5	27.0	38.0	47.5	57.0	66.5
1986	330.0	330.0	22.5	27.0	38.0	47.5	57.0	66.5
1987	330.0	330.0	22.5	27.0	38.0	47.5	52.3	57.0
1988	330.0	330.0	18.0	27.0	38.0	47.5	47.5	57.0
1989			18.0	27.0	38.0	47.5	47.5	57.0
1990			18.0	27.0	38.0	47.5	47.5	57.0
1991			27.0	27.0	38.0	47.5	47.5	47.5
1992			27.0	27.0	38.0	47.5	47.5	47.5
1993			27.0	27.0	38.0	47.5	47.5	47.5
1994			27.0	28.5	38.0	47.5	47.5	47.5
1995			18.0	19.0	28.5	38.0	47.5	47.5
1996			18.0	19.0	28.5	38.0	47.5	47.5
1997			18.0	19.0	28.5	38.0	47.5	47.5
1998	380.0	380.0	18.0	19.0	28.5	38.0	47.5	47.5
1999	380.0	380.0	18.0	19.0	28.5	38.0	47.5	47.5
2000	380.0	380.0	18.0	19.0	28.5	38.0	35.2	35.2
2001	380.0	380.0	18.0	19.0	28.5	35.2	35.2	35.2
2002	380.0	380.0	18.0	18.0	28.5	35.2	35.2	35.2
2003	380.0	380.0	18.0	18.0	28.5	35.2	35.2	35.2
2004	380.0	380.0	18.0	18.0	28.5	35.2	35.2	35.2
2005	380.0	380.0	18.0	18.0	28.5	35.2	35.2	35.2

Notes: Computations by authors based on wage income tax statistics; see Appendix 3C for details.

Marginal tax rates for a taxpayer with a non-working spouse and two dependent children are estimated, assuming all income is employment income.

Basic and dependent exemptions and employment income deductions are taken into account, but various non-standard tax reliefs are excluded.

Local income taxes and social insurance contributions are also excluded. Social insurance contributions are capped at about twice the average wage and therefore do not affect marginal tax rates above P99.

'Marginal tax rate at P90 (or P99.99)' refers to the marginal tax rate at the income threshold for the top 10% (or 0.01%) wage income group.

'Top marginal tax rate' refers to the highest statutory marginal tax rate net of employment income deductions.

APPENDIX 3D: SENSITIVITY ANALYSIS USING THE NSFIE DATA

The best available source for estimating the distribution of capital income by income group is the *National Survey of Family Income and Expenditure* (*NSFIE*).[63] NSFIE is conducted once in every five years and covers over 50,000 households, one of the largest and most comprehensive household surveys in Japan. Starting in 1979, the survey has reported the holdings of various financial assets per household by income class in its savings and liabilities section.[64] We compute top income shares and their income composition using NSFIE data, and compare these estimates with the income tax statistics estimates to evaluate the impact of the capital income erosion on our top income shares series.

Individual-Unit Estimates for 1999

In 1999, the NSFIE statistics report tabulations by the size of the household head's income (in addition to tabulations by the size of total household income).[65] We use these data to estimate top income shares and the composition of capital income, using individual as the unit of observation as in our series based on the income tax statistics. The NSFIE statistics present, by the size of household head's income, the average income of the household head and the average amount of financial assets owned by all household members by asset types, such as demand deposits, time deposits, insurance savings, securities (stocks, trust funds, public and corporate bonds), and liabilities. In our analysis, we divide the assets into three groups: (1) stocks, (2) returns on insurance policies, and (3) fixed claim assets net of liabilities (containing all financial assets except stocks and insurance savings).

We convert the asset holdings into capital income, using total capital income from personal income reported in National Accounts.[66] For example, to estimate dividend income, we take total dividends accrued to individuals from National Accounts and allocate them across households in proportion to the distribution of stocks by income class reported in the NSFIE. We then compute the share of each component in total income for top income groups. In doing so, we assume that the NSFIE represents all Japanese households and that all household assets reported in the survey belong to the household head. We make these extreme assumptions to generate an upper bound on our estimates.

In Table 3.4, we compare our income tax statistics results (in Panel B) with the estimates from the NSFIE (in Panel C) for the year 1999. Unlike income tax statistics, because NSFIE uses a representative sample, it contains few observations at the very high end of income distribution. As a result, we cannot provide accurate estimates for the top 0.1 per cent group and above with the 1999 NSFIE data.

---

[63] Statistics Bureau of Japan, *National Survey of Family Income and Expenditure* (Zenkoku Shohi Jittai Chosa). For the reliability of NSFIE compared to other household surveys, see Takayama et al. (1988).

[64] We cannot use 1969 and 1974 NSIFE data, because the sample in these years excludes households with professionals and managers.

[65] Table 24, available online at http://www.stat.go.jp/english/data/zensho/1999/menu.htm.

[66] As Hayashi, Ando, and Ferris (1988) demonstrate, capital income in the NSFIE is seriously under-reported and cannot be used. We thus use the asset holdings data to estimate capital income. According to Takayama et al. (1988), NSFIE data on assets, including stocks and bonds, are fairly accurate.

Table 3D.1 Sensitivity analysis using the Japanese NSFIE data, 1979–1999

Income Groups (1)	Income Share (2)	Fraction of Capital Income Component to Total Household Income			
		Net Interest Income (3)	Dividend Income (4)	Returns on Insurance Policies (5)	All Returns on Liquid Assets (6) = (3) + (4) + (5)
1979					
All	100.0%	6.2%	1.4%	3.0%	10.7%
Top 10–5%	8.8%	6.9%	2.2%	2.7%	11.8%
Top 5%	13.4%	8.4%	3.6%	2.5%	14.6%
1984					
All	100.0%	8.0%	0.8%	3.5%	12.4%
Top 10–5%	9.0%	9.1%	1.5%	3.2%	13.8%
Top 5%	13.4%	10.5%	1.9%	2.9%	15.4%
1989					
All	100.0%	7.4%	1.1%	5.2%	13.7%
Top 10–5%	9.0%	6.9%	1.4%	4.4%	12.6%
Top 5%	14.2%	5.8%	2.9%	4.2%	12.9%
1994					
All	100.0%	6.4%	0.8%	4.5%	11.7%
Top 10–5%	9.1%	5.1%	1.0%	3.9%	9.9%
Top 5%	14.2%	4.1%	1.3%	3.3%	8.7%
1999					
All	100.0%	1.9%	0.9%	4.3%	7.1%
Top 10–5%	9.3%	1.7%	0.7%	3.5%	6.0%
Top 5%	13.8%	1.7%	0.9%	3.1%	5.7%

Notes: Computations by authors based on the *National Survey of Family Income and Expenditure*; see Appendix 3D for details.

In contrast to Table 3.4, Panel C, the NSFIE estimates above are based on the household (as opposed to individual) unit.

Net interest income is estimated based on the holdings of bonds, deposits, and loan trusts, net of liabilities.

Dividend income is estimated based on stock holdings.

Returns on insurance policies are estimated based on the holdings of life and other insurance savings.

Estimates for above the top 5% groups are not available due to the problem of small sample and top coding in the NSFIE data.

Household-Unit Estimates for 1979, 1984, 1989, 1994, and 1999

From 1979 to 1999, the NSFIE statistics present tabulations by the size of the total household income (as opposed to household head's income). We use these data to compute top income shares and capital income composition, using household as the unit of observation. Note that, because the income shares are no longer based on the individual unit, the levels of the NSFIE estimates and the income tax statistics estimates are not directly comparable.[67] Instead, we can compare NSFIE estimates across years, using the

---

[67] See Atkinson (2007b) for a discussion of the link between individual and family-based income shares.

1999 NSFIE estimates as a benchmark. We compute the share of three capital income components in total income for top 5 per cent and 10 per cent income groups, using the same methodology as described above. Because the brackets of the NSFIE tabulations in earlier years are not as finely defined, the top bracket contains 2 per cent to 6 per cent of all households. Due to small sample and top coding, we cannot provide accurate estimates above the top 5 per cent groups with these data. The results are reported in Table 3D.1.

REFERENCES

Abowd, J. and S. Kaplan (1999). 'Executive Compensation: Six Questions That Need Answering', *Journal of Economic Perspectives*, 13(4): 145–68.

Aoki, M. (1988). *Information, Incentives, and Bargaining in the Japanese Economy*. Cambridge: Cambridge University Press.

Atkinson, A. B. (2007a). 'Top Incomes in the United Kingdom over the Twentieth Century', in Atkinson and Piketty (2007).

—— (2007b). 'Measuring Top Incomes: Methodological Issues', in Atkinson and Piketty (2007).

—— and T. Piketty (eds.) (2007). *Top Incomes from a Historical and International Perspective*. Oxford: Oxford University Press.

—— L. Rainwater, and T. Smeeding (1995). *Income Distribution in OECD Countries: Evidence from the Luxembourg Income Study*. Paris: OECD.

—— and W. Salverda (2007). 'Top Incomes in the Netherlands over the Twentieth Century', in Atkinson and Piketty (2007).

Banerjee, A. and E. Duflo (2003). 'Inequality and Growth: What Can the Data Say?', *Journal of Economic Growth*, 8(3): 267–99.

Barro, R. (2000). 'Inequality and Growth in a Panel of Countries', *Journal of Economic Growth*, 5(1): 5–32.

Burniaux, J., T. Dang, D. C. Fore, M. F. Förster, M. Mira D'Ercole, and H. Oxley (1998). *Income Distribution and Poverty in Selected OECD Countries*. Paris: OECD.

Chandler, A. (1962). *Strategy and Structure*. Cambridge, Mass.: MIT Press.

Dell, F. (2007). 'Top Incomes in Germany throughout the Twentieth Century: 1891–1998', in Atkinson and Piketty (2007).

—— T. Piketty, and E. Saez (2007). 'The Evolution of Top Income and Wealth Concentration in Switzerland over the Twentieth Century', in Atkinson and Piketty (2007).

Feldstein, M. (1995). 'The Effect of Marginal Tax Rates on Taxable Income: A Panel Study of the 1986 Tax Reform Act', *Journal of Political Economy*, 103(3), 551–72.

Forbes, K. (2000). 'A Reassessment of the Relationship between Inequality and Growth', *American Economic Review*, 90(4): 869–87.

Frydman, C. (2005). 'Rising through the Ranks: The Evolution of the Market for Corporate Executives, 1936–2003', Harvard University Ph.D. thesis.

Fukao, M. (1995). *Financial Integration, Corporate Governance, and the Performance of Multinational Companies*. Washington, DC: Brookings Institution.

Gordon, A. (1985). *The Evolution of Labor Relations in Japan: Heavy Industry 1853–1955*. Cambridge, Mass.: Harvard University Press.

Hart, R. and S. Kawasaki (1999). *Work and Pay in Japan*. Cambridge: Cambridge University Press.

Hayakawa, M. (1951). 'The Application of Pareto's Law of Income to Japanese Data', *Econometrica*, 19: 174–83.

Hayashi, F., A. Ando, and R. Ferris (1988). 'Life Cycle and Bequest Saving', *Journal of the Japanese and International Economies*, 2: 450–91.

Hayashi, H. (1987). 'Shotokuzei: Kinrou Shotoku to Shisan Shotoku' (Income Tax: Labor Income and Capital Income), in Hashimoto and Yomamoto (eds.) *Nihongata Zeisei Kaikaku (Japanese-Style Tax Reform)*. Tokyo: Yuhikaku.

Hoshi, T. (1998). 'Japanese Corporate Governance as a System', in Klaus J. Hopt, Hideki Kanda, Mark Roe, Eddy Wymeersch, and Stefan Prigge (eds.) *Comparative Corporate Governance: The State of the Art and Emerging Research*. Oxford: Oxford University Press.

—— and A. Kashyap (2001). *Corporate Financing and Governance in Japan*. Cambridge, Mass.: MIT Press.

Ishi, H. (1979). *Sozei Seisaku no Koka (Effects of Tax Policies)*. Tokyo: Tokyo Keizai Shinposha.

—— (2001). *The Japanese Tax System*, 3rd edn. New York: Oxford University Press.

Iwamoto, Yasushi, Yuichi Fujishima, and Norifumi Akiyama. 1995. 'Rishi Haito Kazei no Hyoka to Kadai' (Evaluating Interest and Dividends Taxation), *Finansharu Rebyu*, 35: 27–50.

Japan Ministry of Finance, Tax Bureau (1887–1945). *Shuzeikyoku Tokei Nenposho (Annual Statistical Report)* in Japanese.

Japan National Tax Administration (1946–2005). *Kokuzeikyoku Tokei Nenposho (Annual Statistical Report)* in Japanese, bilingual since 1999.

—— (1951–2005). *Minkan Kyuyo no Jittai (Survey on Private Wages and Salaries)* in Japanese.

—— (1963–2005). Shinkoku Shotokuzei no Jittai (*Survey on Self-Assessed Income Tax*) in Japanese.

—— (1988). *Shotokuzei Hyakunenshi (Hundred-Year History of Income Tax)*.

Japan Statistics Bureau (1949–2005). *Japan Statistical Yearbook*, bilingual.

—— (1989). *Historical Statistics of Japan*, bilingual.

Johnston, L. and S. Williamson (2005). 'The Annual Real and Nominal GDP for the United States, 1790–Present', Economic History Services, October 2005, at http://www.eh.net/hmit/gdp/.

Kato, T. and M. Morishima (2002). 'The Productivity Effects of Participatory Employment Practices', *Industrial Relations*, 41: 487–520.

Keizai Antei Honbu (1948). *Wagakuni Keizai no Senso Higai (Economic Damage of World War II in Japan)*. Tokyo: Keizai Antei Honbu.

Kokumin Seikatsukyoku (1999). *Shin Kokumin Seikatsu Shihyo (New People's Life Indicators)*. Tokyo: Okurasho Insatsukyoku.

Kubo, K. (2004). 'Executive Compensation in Japan and the UK', in Joseph Fan et al. (eds.) *Designing Financial Systems in East Asia and Japan*. London: Routledge Curzon.

Kuznets, S. (1955). 'Economic Growth and Economic Inequality', *American Economic Review*, 45: 1–28.

Lindert, P. (1986). 'Unequal English Wealth since 1670', *Journal of Political Economy*, 94: 1127–62.

—— (2000). 'Three Centuries of Inequality in Britain and America', in *Handbook of Income Distribution*. Amsterdam: North-Holland.

Lindsey, L. (1987). 'Individual Taxpayer Response to Tax Cuts: 1982–1984, with Implications for the Revenue Maximizing Tax Rate', *Journal of Public Economics*, 33: 173–206.

Maddison, A. (1995). *Monitoring the World Economy, 1820–1992.* Paris: OECD Press.

Minami, R. (1994). *The Economic Development of Japan*, 2nd edn. New York: St Martin's Press.

—— (1995). *Nihon no Keizai Hatten to Shotoku Bunpu* (*Japan's Economic Development and Income Distribution*). Tokyo: Iwanami Shoten.

—— (1998). 'Economic Development and Income Distribution in Japan: An Assessment of the Kuznets Hypothesis', *Cambridge Journal of Economics*, 22(1): 39–58.

Miyamoto, M. and T. Abe (eds.) (1995). *Keiei Kakushin to Kogyoka* (*Managerial Innovations and Industrialization*). Tokyo: Iwanami Shoten.

Mizoguchi, T. and N. Takayama (1984). *Equity and Poverty under Rapid Economic Growth: The Japanese Experience.* Tokyo: Kinokuniya.

—— and Y. Terasaki (1995). 'Kakei no Shotoku Bunpu Hendo no Keizai, Shakai oyobi Sangyo Kozoteki Yoin' (Economic, Social, and Industrial Factors Determining the Changes in Income Distribution of Households), *Keizai Kenkyu*, 46: 59–77.

Moriguchi, C. (2000). 'The Evolution of Employment Relations in U.S. and Japanese Manufacturing Firms, 1900–1960', NBER Working Paper No. 7939. Cambridge, Mass.

—— (2003). 'Implicit Contracts, the Great Depression, and Institutional Change: A Comparative Analysis of U.S. and Japanese Employment Relations, 1920–1940', *Journal of Economic History*, 63: 625–45.

—— (2008). 'Top Wage Incomes in Japan, 1885–2005', NBER Working Paper No. 14537. Cambridge, Mass.

—— and E. Saez (2008). 'The Evolution of Income Concentration in Japan, 1885–2005: Evidence from Income Tax Statistics', *Review of Economics and Statistics*, 90(4): 713–34.

Morishima, M. (1991). 'Information Sharing and Collective Bargaining in Japan: Effects on Wage Negotiation', *Industrial and Labor Relations Review*, 44: 469–85.

Naito, R. and S. Fujiwara (2004). *Stokku Opushon no Jitsumu* (*Practicing Stock Options*). Tokyo: Shoji Homu.

Nishizaki, F., Y. Yamada, and E. Ando (1998). *Nihon no Shotoku Kakusa: Kokusai Hikaku no Shiten kara* (*Income Inequality in Japan: An International Comparison*). Tokyo: Keizai Kikakucho Keizai Kenkyusho.

Noguchi, Y. (1995). *1940–nen Taisei* (*The 1940 System*). Tokyo: Toyo Keizai Shinpo.

NRUS (Nihon Rodo Undo Shiryo Kanko Iinkai) (1959). *Nihon Rodo Undo Shiryo* (*Historical Data of the Labor Movement in Japan*), x: *Statistics*. Tokyo: Nihon Rodo Undo Shiryo Kanko Iinkai.

OECD. Annual publication, 1998–2005. *Taxing Wages.* Paris: OECD.

Ohkawa, K., M. Shinohara, and M. Umemura (1967). *Choki Keizai Tokei*, viii: *Kakaku* (*Estimates of Long-Term Economic Statistics of Japan: Prices*). Tokyo: Toyo Keizai Shimposha.

—— —— —— (1974). *Choki Keizai Tokei*, i: *Kokumin Shotoku* (*Estimates of Long-Term Economic Statistics of Japan: National Income*). Tokyo: Toyo Keizai Shinposha.

Ohtake, F. (2005). *Nihon no Fubyodo* (*Inequality in Japan*). Tokyo: Nihon Keizai Shinbunsha.

Okazaki, T. (1993). 'The Japanese Firm under the Wartime Planned Economy', *Journal of the Japanese and International Economics*, 7: 175–203.

—— (1999). 'Corporate Governance', in T. Okazaki and M. Okuno-Fujiwara (eds.) *Japanese Economic System and its Historical Origins.* New York: Oxford University Press.

—— and M. Okuno-Fujiwara (eds.) (1993). *Gendai Nihon Keizai Sisutemu no Genryu* (*Historical Origins of the Japanese Economic System*). Tokyo: Nihon Keizai Shinbunsha.

Ono, A. and T. Watanabe (1976). 'Changes in Income Inequality in the Japanese Economy', in H. Patrick (ed.) *Japanese Industrialization and its Social Consequences.* Berkeley and Los Angeles: University of California Press.

Otsuki, T. and N. Takamatsu (1982). 'On the Measurement and Trend of Income Inequality in Prewar Japan', in *Papers and Proceedings of the Conference on Japan's Historical Development Experience and the Contemporary Developing Countries.* Tokyo: International Development Research Center of Japan.

Piketty, T. (2003). 'Income Inequality in France, 1901–1998', *Journal of Political Economy,* 111: 1004–42.

—— and E. Saez (2003). 'Income Inequality in the United States, 1913–1998', *Quarterly Journal of Economics,* 118: 1–39.

Roine, J. and D. Waldenström (2006). 'Top Incomes in Sweden over the Twentieth Century', SSE/EFI Working Paper Series in Economics and Finance No. 602.

Saez, E. (2004). 'Reported Incomes and Marginal Tax Rates, 1960–2000: Evidence and Policy Implications', in James Poterba (ed.) *Tax Policy and the Economy,* volume 18. Cambridge, Mass.: MIT Press.

—— and M. Veall (2005). 'The Evolution of High Incomes in Northern America: Lessons from Canadian Evidence', *American Economic Review,* 95(3): 831–49.

Shiomi, S. et al. (1933). *Kokumin Shotoku no Bunpai (Distribution of National Income).* Tokyo: Yuhikaku.

Showa Dojinkai (ed.) (1960). *Wagakuni Chingin Kozo no Shiteki Kosatsu (Historical Reflections on the Japanese Wage Structure).* Tokyo: Shiseido.

Soltow, L. (1968). 'Long-Run Changes in British Income Inequality', *Economic History Review,* 21: 17–29.

—— (1969). 'Evidence on Income Inequality in the United States, 1866–1965', *Journal of Economic History,* 29: 279–86.

Tachibanaki, T. (1998). *Nihon no Keizai Kakusa (Economic Inequality in Japan).* Tokyo: Iwanami Shoten.

—— (2000). 'Nihon no Shotoku Kakusa ha Kakudai shiteiruka? (Is Income Inequality in Japan Rising?)', *Nihon Rodo Kenkyu Zasshi,* 480: 41–51.

—— (2005). *Confronting Income Inequality in Japan.* Cambridge, Mass.: MIT Press.

Takahashi, Chotaro (1959). *Dynamic Changes of Income and its Distribution in Japan.* Tokyo: Kinokuniya Bookstore.

Takayama, N. (1992). *Sutokku Ekonomi (Stock Economy).* Tokyo: Toyo Keizai Shinposha.

—— et al. (1988). 'Zensho no Gaiyo to Deta no Ginmi' (Outline and Reliability of NSFIE Data), *Keizai Bunseki,* 116: 43–59.

Teranishi, J. (1999). 'Main Bank System', in T. Okazaki and M. Okuno-Fujiwara (eds.) *Japanese Economic System and its Historical Origins.* New York: Oxford University Press.

—— (2005). *Evolution of the Economic System in Japan.* Cheltenham: Edward Elgar.

Terasaki, Y. (1986). 'Senzenki no Shotoku Bunpu no Hendo: Tenbo' (The Evolution of Income Distribution before World War II: A Survey), *Nagasaki Daigaku Kyoyobu Kiyo: Jinbun Kagakuhen,* 26.

USSBS (United States Strategic Bombing Survey) (1947). *Effects of Air Attack on Japanese Urban Economy: Summary Report.* Washington, DC: Urban Areas Division.

Wada, R. (1975). 'Impact of Economic Growth on the Size Distribution of Income: The Postwar Experience of Japan', Working Paper, Geneva, International Labour Office.

Waswo, A. and Y. Nishida (eds.) (2003). *Farmers and Village Life in Twentieth-Century Japan.* London: Routledge Curzon.

Williamson, J. (1985). *Did British Capitalism Breed Inequality?* Boston: Allen & Unwin.

—— and P. Lindert (1985). 'Growth, Equality and History', *Explorations in Economic History*, 22: 341–77.

Yasuba, Y. (1976). 'The Evolution of Dualistic Wage Structure', in H. Patrick (ed.) *Japanese Industrialization and its Social Consequences.* Berkeley and Los Angeles: University of California Press.

—— (1992). 'Kogaku Shotokusha ni kansuru Senzen Sengo Hikaku' (Comparison of High-Income Earners before and after World War II), *Nihon Keizai Kenkyu*, 23: 146–85.

—— (2004). *Kindai Nihon no Shotoku Bunpu to Kazoku Keizai* (*Income Distribution and Family Economics in Modern Japan*). Tokyo: Tokyo Tosho Senta.

—— and R. Minami (1993). 'Dainiji Taisen Chokugo ni okeru Shotoku Bunpu no Byodouka Yoin' (Equalization Factors of the Income Distribution Immediately after World War II), *Keizai Kenkyu*, 44: 365–73.

4

Top Incomes in Indonesia, 1920–2004

Andrew Leigh and Pierre van der Eng

4.1 INTRODUCTION

According to the 2006 *Forbes* rich list, Indonesia's richest man, Sukanto Tanoto, and his family were worth US$2.8 billion (Doebele and Vorasarun 2006). Sukanto headed a group of Indonesia's forty richest with a combined net worth of US$22.3 billion, or about 19 million times Indonesia's average income of US$1,150. The richest forty Indonesians and their families hold about 6 per cent of the nation's wealth, a considerably larger share than in the United States. In contrast, academic literature on income distribution in Indonesia often indicated that income inequality has been relatively low as a consequence of 'pro-poor growth' policies pursued by its government (e.g. Ragayah 2005; Timmer 2004, 2005; World Bank 2005a). Such contrasting views are in part caused by significant difficulties in interpreting the available income and expenditure survey data for Indonesia (Cameron 2002).

Hence, whether income inequality in Indonesia has long been highly skewed, whether it is more skewed than elsewhere, and if so why, remain issues of debate. We aim to contribute to this debate on the basis of a methodology that establishes and analyses trends in the share of top income earners in a country's total income. Building on recent studies for other countries, employing under-explored historical data, and comparing our results with similar data for other countries, we

We are grateful to Anggito Abumanyu (Economic, Financial and International Cooperation Analysing Board BAPPEKI, Ministry of Finance of Indonesia) and Robert Pakpahan (Directorate General of Taxation, Ministry of Finance of Indonesia) for help in obtaining taxation data for recent years, to Anne Booth and Terry Hull for advice on constructing our population and income control totals, to Sophie Holloway and Stephen Gray for help obtaining survey data, to Alicia Paul and Michael Leigh for assistance with survey data definitions, to Gweneth Leigh for assistance in tabulating taxation data for the pre-war era, and to Daniel Suryadarma and Thee Kian Wie for advice on constructing our top tax rate series. Susanne Schmidt, Elena Varganova, and Yogi Vidyattama provided outstanding research assistance. Anthony Atkinson, Gavin Jones, Peter Lindert, Chikako Yamauchi, participants at the XIV International Economic History Congress, and a seminar at the Australian National University provided valuable comments on earlier drafts, as did Thomas Piketty and four anonymous referees. All errors are ours.

A shorter version of this chapter was published as Andrew Leigh and Pierre van der Eng, 'Inequality in Indonesia: What Can We Learn from Top Incomes?', *Journal of Public Economics*, 93(1–2) (2009): 209–12.

establish and analyse such trends for the first time for Indonesia, which is one of Asia's most populous countries and biggest economies. We offer an assessment of changes in the share of top income earners in Indonesia on the basis of income tax data for 1920–39 and 1990–2003, augmented by household income data from the country's national socio-economic survey for 1982–2004.

To preview our results, we find a significant increase in the income share of the richest households during the early 1920s, and again during the early 1930s. From the late 1930s until the early 1980s, top income shares fell (particularly the top 1 per cent share and above). Top income shares rose modestly in the 1980s, rose sharply in the late 1990s, and fell slightly in the early 2000s. Throughout the twentieth century, top income shares in Indonesia have been higher than in most other countries for which comparable data are available.

The remainder of this chapter is organized as follows. Section 4.2 outlines how this study relates to other academic studies that fall in three categories: income inequality in Indonesia, the long-term relationship between income inequality and economic growth, and changes in top incomes in other countries. Section 4.3 discusses the data and the methodology we used in this chapter, particularly the intricacies of the income tax data. Section 4.4 presents the results that the analysis of top incomes in Indonesia yields. Section 4.5 compares these results with top income shares in other countries, and presents some cross-national evidence on wealth concentration. The final section concludes.

4.2 CONTEXT

There are very few assessments of income distribution in colonial Indonesia. Booth (1988: 323–32) surveyed the available evidence and offered an assessment on the basis of the data on income tax that were published for 1920–39 in the annual statistical yearbooks for colonial Indonesia. These data differentiate between three groups of taxpayers—indigenous Indonesians, 'foreign Asians' (including ethnic Chinese, Indians, and Arabs), and Europeans—and allow for the calculation of average income in each group. Booth (1988: 333) found that 'the distribution of income between Indonesians revealed less glaring disparities than between ethnic groups'. However, the author used the income tax data at face value, without taking account of the ways in which they were collected and therefore of their shortcomings, such as the allowances for spouse and children or consequences of the f120 threshold (see section 4.3 below).[1]

For the 1950s, 1960s, and most of the 1970s, a lack of data impeded any analysis of changes in income distribution. The income tax system deteriorated and data on income tax revenues were only published in aggregated forms. The first information took the form of the national household survey (*Survei*

---

[1] The currency unit in colonial Indonesia was the guilder (f), which was renamed rupiah (Rp) after Indonesia's independence.

Sosial-Ekonomi Nasional, Susenas), which since 1964–5 included information on household expenditure and since 1978 also on household income. The Susenas household data have been used over and again to analyse expenditure inequality and, to a lesser extent, income inequality.

Cameron (2002) discussed the available data and noted that they generally indicated low degrees of inequality in household expenditure, with Gini ratios between 0.32 and 0.38. She also discussed the possible shortcomings of the Susenas data. For example, the surveys are often believed to be biased towards the urban poor. They also underestimate household expenditure on food (Surbakti 1995: 61) and non-food items, particularly durables such as televisions and cars. Such factors create a progressively increasing degree of underestimation of expenditure and income among the high-income households in the surveys.[2]

Cameron (2002: 12) noted that the Susenas household income data have hardly been used in the analysis of income distribution in Indonesia.[3] Compared to measuring expenditure, the measurement of income through household surveys contains a multitude of difficulties, as Deaton (1997: 26–32) explained. Cameron (2002: 15) concluded that very few studies offer a longer-term perspective on changes in income distribution and offered her estimates of the Gini ratio of per capita household income of 0.42 in 1984 and 0.43 in 1990. On the basis of the same source, Alatas and Bourguignon (2000: 159) estimated the Gini ratio of per capita household income of 0.38 in 1980 and 0.40 in 1996. Using much smaller samples of Indonesia's Family Life Survey, Fields et al. (2003: 73) estimated Gini ratios of household income distribution to be 0.56 in both 1993 and 1997.

Available studies of income and expenditure distribution in Indonesia tend to cover short-term changes and use different data configurations, indicators of inequality, and methods of decomposition that impede the comparability of the results. For those reasons, Cameron (2002) could not be conclusive about the degree of income inequality and changes in income distribution in the longer term. Hence, the low degree of inequality may be real, or due to shortcomings in the survey in capturing high-income households, or due to the fact that household expenditure tends to be more evenly distributed than income. Section 4.5

---

[2] The estimation of expenditure on consumer durables relies on the memory of a head of the household regarding spending during the year prior to the survey. For reasons that are unclear, low-income households tend to be less 'forgetful' than high-income households. On the whole, the degree of underestimation is illustrated by the fact that there has long been a substantial discrepancy between total household expenditure, estimated through Susenas, and total private consumption in the Indonesian national accounts, estimated as a residual after other main items of expenditure on GDP were accounted for (Hill 1996: 195). It is likely that the household income data from Susenas also suffer from underestimation. It is difficult to assess the possible degree of underestimation, as the Indonesian national accounts do not use the income-based approach, but Appendix 4E contains an approximation.

[3] An additional source of income data is contained in the National Labour Force Survey (*Survei Tenaga Kerja Nasional*, Sakernas), which collects information on wage incomes of employees since 1978. These have also hardly been used in assessments of wage income inequality in Indonesia, let alone changes in inequality over time.

will directly compare the available inequality estimates with our estimates of top income shares.

Interest in long-term trends in income distribution increased since Kuznets (1955), who hypothesized that, from low levels of living, economic growth first increases inequality, before it generates a more even distribution of income. Extensive debate exists on the historical consequences of industrialization during the nineteenth and twentieth centuries for the equality of income and wealth in Western countries, particularly the UK and the USA. This debate, and the evidence it yielded, indicate that inequality had indeed increased since the early nineteenth century, but that in the twentieth century pre-tax income inequality decreased until the 1970s. This was partly due to shifts in the progressivity of redistribution through government, and also to factor-market forces and economic growth (Lindert 2000).

Lindert and Williamson (2003) interpreted trends in income distribution between and within nations during 1500–2000 in the context of changes in relative factor prices, as the process of 'globalization' mobilized production factors around the world. For Indonesia, they hypothesized an increase in inequality during 1900–30, as the country's abundant land resources were mobilized for export production, raising land rents relative to wages. Implicitly, the mobilization of labour for export production since the 1970s should reverse the effect, as in other Asian countries where the mobilization of labour through labour-absorbing industrialization raised wages relative to the costs of capital and land. However, the authors noted instead—without referring to a specific source—that income in Indonesia became more concentrated in the top decile.

Such generalizations of long-term trends in income inequality enhance the pertinence of a closer study of the case of Indonesia. However, the available data for Indonesia—income tax data and national household surveys—contain limitations that impede an assessment of trends in inequality on the basis of conventional measures, such as Gini indices.

An alternative approach is the estimation of the share of top incomes in total income, which may suit the available data for Indonesia in principle. Increasing attention has been devoted to understanding long-term changes in top income shares. Beginning with the work of Piketty (2001) on France, there has been a renewed interest in using income taxation data to estimate the share of national income held by the rich. Long-run top incomes series have recently been estimated for more than a dozen developed countries, including Australia (Atkinson and Leigh 2007a), Canada (Saez and Veall 2005), Finland (Riihelä, Sullström, and Tuomala 2005), France (Piketty 2001, 2003, 2007; Landais 2007), Germany (Dell 2005, 2007), Ireland (Nolan 2007), Japan (Moriguchi and Saez 2008), the Netherlands (Atkinson and Salverda 2005), New Zealand (Atkinson and Leigh 2008), Spain (Alvaredo and Saez 2006 and Chapter 10), Sweden (Roine and Waldenström 2008 and Chapter 7), Switzerland (Dell 2005; Dell, Piketty, and Saez 2007), the United Kingdom (Atkinson 2005, 2007b) and the United States (Piketty and Saez 2003, 2006a). Piketty and Saez (2006b) and Leigh (2007, 2009) surveyed these papers, confirming the trends noted by Lindert (2000) for a greater range of countries, namely that top income shares in developed countries decreased during the first half of the twentieth century, and remained fairly flat during the 1950s and 1960s. Since the 1970s, top income shares in English-speaking countries have increased sharply, but there has been little change in top income shares in continental Europe.

Less work has so far been done on estimating top income shares in developing countries, with the exceptions of Argentina (Alvaredo 2007 and Chapter 6), urban China (Piketty and Qian 2006 and Chapter 2), and India (Banerjee and Piketty 2005 and Chapter 1). Since our focus is on Indonesia, we are most interested in understanding how top income shares in Indonesia compare with those in other Asian nations. Banerjee and Piketty (Chapter 1) used income taxation data to estimate top income shares for India during 1922–2000. They noted that the income share of top incomes decreased from the 1950s to the 1980s, before increasing again, and argued that this was consistent with economic policies in India. Using income tax data, Moriguchi and Saez (2008 and Chapter 3) found high top income shares in developing pre-war Japan, and significantly lower shares after the Second World War. Piketty and Qian (Chapter 2) used household survey data to estimate top income shares in urban China during 1986–2003, and noted increasing top income shares. They also assessed the revenue-raising potential of income taxation and its impact on mitigating after-tax income inequality.

The current chapter not only adds to this body of studies, it also offers an assessment of long-term changes in income distribution for Indonesia on the basis of data for 1920–39 and 1982–2004, and a comparison of trends in Indonesia with trends in other countries. The questions it seeks to answer are: do trends in top incomes substantiate the widely perceived long-term increase in income inequality in Indonesia, and is Indonesia different from other countries in this respect?

Since the rate of income tax avoidance is generally thought to be higher in developing countries, we use both income taxation data and the Susenas household survey data to analyse top income shares over the last two decades. As well as providing a check on our results, this also provides insights into the extent to which income tax data in developing countries can be relied upon for estimating top income shares.

4.3 METHODOLOGY FOR ESTIMATING TOP INCOME SHARES

Our estimates of top income shares in Indonesia are based on three sources: income taxation data compiled at the Ministry of Finance of colonial Indonesia for 1920–39, income taxation data from the Directorate General of Taxation of the Ministry of Finance of Indonesia for 1990–2003, and the Susenas household survey data for benchmark years between 1982 and 2004.

This section deals with the issues surrounding the use of taxation data first, before turning to the Susenas data.

Using Taxation Data to Estimate Top Income Shares

The general methodological issues surrounding the use of taxation data to estimate top income shares have been well canvassed by Atkinson (2007a). In essence, our approach involves using external control totals for both the adult population and total personal income, and interpolating top income shares using tabulated income taxation data. In Indonesia, as in other countries, those with incomes below a certain threshold were not liable for income tax. Our control totals are the total population that would have paid income tax if such thresholds did not apply, and the total personal income that would have been declared if such thresholds did not apply. We discuss tax evasion below.

Our first set of taxation data covers 1920–39. Until the enactment of the Income Tax Ordinance of 1920, the taxation system of colonial Indonesia was, as Mansury (1992: 13) described it, 'a mix of widely diverging statutes and provisions'. A tax on incomes in the trades and professions, or business tax (*bedrijfsbelasting*), was levied since 1839. The tax rate varied by income, but was paid by very few individual income earners and yielded only a very minor share of public revenue. In 1908, a general income tax was introduced, but only the net incomes of 'European' income earners were liable, while non-Europeans continued to be liable for the 1907 business tax on incomes in the trades and professions. The number of individuals assessed for income tax remained low— in 1919, still only 50,544 people were taxed.

The 1920 Income Tax Ordinance introduced a universal income tax for which in principle all individual income earners, regardless of ethnicity, as well as companies in colonial Indonesia were liable. This raised the number of individuals liable for income tax to 2.6 million in 1920 (22 per cent of all households). Provisional assessments for income tax started in 1920, but final assessments could take up to two years to be settled. Net incomes of less than ƒ120 were exempted from income tax. A revision of the income tax in 1935 increased the tax threshold to ƒ900 and also saw the introduction of a withholding wage tax, which employers deducted from the wages and salaries of their employees at a uniform rate of 4 per cent. Incomes higher than ƒ900 were also liable for income tax, but received an allowance for the withholding tax already paid.

The income taxation statistics were published annually in the statistical yearbooks of colonial Indonesia (see Appendix 4A). These tabulated net income into income bands, with the number of bands ranging between 23 and 91. Income tax was to be paid on all income and subject to a progressive scale, rising from 1 per cent on the minimum taxable income of ƒ120 to 25 per cent on incomes over ƒ180,000.

Although it is tempting to take these available data at face value, they harbour several problems. The following is a brief discussion of the main issues. First, persons living in the same household in Indonesia during this period were taxed jointly, as was the case under the tax system in the Netherlands at the time (see Atkinson and Salverda 2005). At the same time, heads of households could deduct set allowances for spouse and children from gross income. Hence, the income data represent net, pre-tax, taxable income.

Second, Huender and Meijer Ranneft (1926: 78–9) noted that non- and under-compliance was significant in the lower income bands. Reys (1925: 72–91) argued that taxable incomes in the lowest bands were significantly underestimated, simply because taxation authorities had no other data available to estimate income and base tax assessment on than the assessment of the previous year. Reys concluded that the cost of tax assessment and enforcing tax compliance was high in relation to the share of the income tax revenue from annual incomes between $f120$ and $f1,800$. Both studies proposed to raise the threshold to $f300$, respectively $f600$. Hence, there is a significant element of arbitrariness and underestimation in the numbers of income earners and their incomes in the lower income bands. In those bands, assessment of income tax liability was often a mere guess by village authorities, as non-European income earners with assessed incomes of less than $f1,200$ were not required to file income tax returns.

Third, farmers in Java liable for land tax (*landrente*) were exempted from income tax. This was also the case in other parts of the country, where the land tax was introduced during the 1920s–1930s, particularly Bali, Lombok, Sumbawa, South-East Kalimantan, and South-East Sulawesi. Consequently, most ethnic Indonesians were exempted from income tax, because they had income from land, not necessarily because they earned less than the threshold of $f120$ per year.

Fourth, the threshold was not adjusted for changes in the general level of prices until the revision in 1935. During the early 1920s, Indonesia experienced deflation after high price levels during the First World War, while during the early 1930s prices fell due to the impact of the international economic slump. Given that the income threshold and the income bands were not adjusted for price changes, deflation caused a reverse 'fiscal drag'. A large portion of income earners, who would otherwise have been taxed, fell below the threshold and were no longer liable for income tax. This effect was masked during the 1920s, when the number of income tax payers increased from 2.6 million in 1920 (22 per cent of households) to 4.1 million in 1930 (30 per cent of households). The effect was obvious during the 1930s, when the number of income tax payers decreased to a low of 2.3 million in 1938 (15 per cent of households).

Lastly, as noted in section 4.2, the data appear to distinguish between groups of income tax payers according to ethnicity. However, Fasseur (1994) explained that the distinction only served the purpose of determining which sets of private and family laws applied to individual cases involving people of different ethnic backgrounds. He also noted that from 1899, the distinction 'lost its purely racial connotation' (p. 40), as people would not necessarily be classified according to ethnic background. For example, all ethnic Japanese were classified as 'Europeans', Indo-Europeans could be classified as 'indigenous' or 'European', and ethnic Chinese could be classified as 'foreign Asians' or 'European'. Hence, by the 1920s, if not before, the distinction had no socio-economic basis. Under the 1920 Income Tax Ordinance, all income earners were subject to the same legislation for the purpose of income tax liabilities. The differences in average income between ethnic groups and the changes in income distribution may have been due to general factors which determine the distribution of income in all economies; particularly the distribution of human capital and advances in educational attainment.[4] In addition, the 1930 population census indicated that 66 per cent of the 'foreign Asians' and 71 per cent of the 'Europeans' had actually been born in Indonesia. It would therefore be more appropriate to regard all non-ethnic Indonesians as residents of colonial Indonesia, rather than 'foreigners'. Many became Indonesian nationals in the 1950s, after Indonesia became independent. For the purpose of comparing pre- and post-Independence data, we refrain from using the distinction of income tax payers according to 'ethnicity'.

More details on the taxation data for 1920–39 are provided in Appendix 4A. It should be noted that by developing country standards, the coverage of the income tax system in colonial Indonesia during this period, with a maximum of 4.1 million taxed income earners in 1930, was extraordinarily high. For example, Banerjee and Piketty (Chapter 1, Table 1A.1) note that the number of income tax returns in India—a much more populous nation—only passed 1 million in 1960–1. This may indicate that the income tax threshold in Indonesia was relatively low.

After Indonesia's independence, the land tax was abolished and all income earners became in principle liable for withholding wage tax and/or personal income tax. The total number of income tax assessments was still considerable, but decreasing—from 3.0 million in 1952 to 2.3 million in 1955 (Dris 1958: 433). This was most likely below the taxable capacity, as growing staff shortages, shortages of trained and experienced staff at the Ministry of Finance, and greater complexity of the accumulating new income tax regulations caused increasing delays in income tax assessments and payments, and new opportunities to evade tax obligations.

The number of self-employed people registered for personal income tax liability remained around 0.2 to 0.3 million during 1955–71, although by 1971 the number of effective taxpayers had approximately halved (Dris 1958: 433; Lent and Missorten 1967: 43; Oberndörfer, Avenarius, and Lerche 1976: 149). The total number of income tax payers, including withholding tax, decreased to just 0.6 million in 1971 or about 2.5 per cent of households (Lerche 1978: 300). By 1980, still only 1.2 million income earners paid income tax—or 4 per cent of households—of which only 0.2 million were self-employed (Asher 1997: 134). Hence, by the early 1980s, it was obvious that Indonesia's income tax system was 'plagued by uneven enforcement and compliance' (Asher 1997: 127) and underperforming in terms of maximizing tax revenues.

As part of a comprehensive package of tax reforms, a new income tax law was introduced in 1984. It integrated the personal and corporate income tax into a

---

[4] Scholte (1929: 4–5) noted that the average incomes of 'Europeans' were higher than in the Netherlands, due to the lower share of low-income groups.

single income tax law and simplified the income tax regulations considerably (Mansury 1992: 22–7; Asher 1997: 140–4; Uppal 2003: 1–29). The 1984 law introduced a new withholding tax, payable monthly by employers on wages and salaries of their employees, and also on gross dividends, interest payments, royalties, etc., and on estimated net incomes of a wide range of purchased services, including rentals and insurance premiums. Individual income earners engaged in business or self-employed, or with incomes higher than a specified non-taxable allowance (0.96 million rupiah from 1984, increasing gradually over time, plus allowances for dependants) were required to register for income tax and file tax returns.

The Income Tax Law was updated and revised in 1994 and 2000 (Siswanto 2003: 22–6). For example, in 1994, the principle of self-assessment of personal income tax liability was abandoned in favour of assessment by the tax authorities only. In 2000, five income bands were introduced, self-assessment was reintroduced, and the non-taxable allowance was drastically increased to 12 million rupiah from 2001, plus allowances for dependants. Withholding tax rates also changed marginally, but most principles remained the same.

The number of registrations for personal income tax increased from 0.3 million in 1984 to almost 0.7 million in 1988, where it stayed until 1991, when only half the registrants actually paid personal income tax (Asher 1997: 152–3; Mansury 1992: 209). Hence, non- and incomplete compliance were still significant. Including individuals assessed for withholding tax, the total number of actual income tax payers rose to 0.7 million in 1985, but was still only 1.4 million in 1989.

During the 1990s, the taxation authorities improved their tax registration capabilities and increased their efforts to enforce compliance. At the same time, the number of companies required to pay withholding tax on behalf of their employees increased. A sluggish adjustment of the non-taxable allowance caused 'fiscal drag' and also increased the number of income earners liable for income tax. The data we obtained from the Directorate General for Taxation indicate that the total number of individual income tax payers increased to 8.8 million in 1991 (22 per cent of households) and 20.7 million in 1997 (43 per cent of households), after which it stagnated until the increase to 23.7 million in 2002 (still 43 per cent of households), of which 23.0 million paid withholding tax and 0.7 million were personal income tax payers.

Although the withholding taxes were actually paid by a smaller number of companies, their number increased from about 51,900 in 1989 to 350,000 in 2003, requiring a greatly enhanced capacity and also greater capabilities of the taxation authorities. Employment at the Directorate General of Taxation and at the regional tax offices has indeed increased significantly during the 1990s. Despite this, non- and incomplete compliance remained a concern. Uppal (2003: 53–4) noted that in 1997, 56 per cent of individual taxpayers did not file income tax return forms. Although this percentage may have decreased as the tax office sought to increase compliance, a significant degree of non-compliance is likely to have remained.

Our second set of personal income taxation data for the period 1990–2003 was especially extracted for us at the Directorate General of Taxation of the Ministry of Finance in Jakarta in 2005. So far as we are aware, we are the first to use these particular data. Although 1989 was the first year for which the data were available in electronic format, the data for that year were not tabulated in a usable manner, so our analysis starts with the 1990 data. 2003 was the last year for which complete income tax data were available. The withholding tax data were not available in disaggregated form by individual wage earners, but only by companies paying the withholding tax obligations.

During 1990–2003, personal income taxation applied to wage, salary, and capital income, with earnings over the taxable threshold being subject to progressive tax rates in initially three bands, taxed at 10 per cent, 15 per cent, and 30 per cent, and five bands rising from 5 per cent up to 35 per cent since 2001. An advantage of 1990–2003 taxation data is that they are highly disaggregated. The number of bands into which earnings are divided ranges between 182 and 662. However, a disadvantage of these data is that we are only able to identify the very top taxpayers. In addition, since taxpayers with only salary income are not required to file a return, our results assume that all those with incomes in the top 0.5 per cent of the distribution file a return; either because they wish to seek deductions, or because they have other sources of income. Details of the 1990–2003 taxation data are provided in Appendix 4B.

Figure 4.1 shows the coverage of our two taxation series. For the pre-war years, the data cover the incomes of 15 to 30 per cent of the households, except for 1935–7 for which only the personal income tax data are available for about 2.5 per cent of households, not the withholding tax data. This share is lower than for the later period, but it should be reiterated that a large number of farming households were not liable for income tax, as noted above. The decrease after 1930 was caused by the fact that deflation, following the 1929 crisis, caused nominal incomes to fall below the *f*120 threshold.

For the period 1990–2003, Figure 4.1 shows the significant increase in the share of households paying income tax, mostly withholding tax. For this period, only data on households paying personal income tax data can be used, representing on average 0.9 per cent of households (see Appendix 4B).

For control purposes, we need to establish the total number of potential tax units. In both periods, married couples and their income-earning dependants were taxed jointly, which effectively defines the tax unit as a household. As noted above, farmers in parts of colonial Indonesia were excluded from income taxation. As there are hardly any data that allow us to identify income distribution among the farm households liable for land tax in order to add the top income-earning farmers to the income tax data, we opted to assume that the incomes of all farm households would have fallen below the cut-off incomes used to identify the top income earners. This is plausible, as by the 1920s, the size distribution of farm land was not heavily skewed in favour of large landholders (Van der Eng 1996: 142–52). For example, the only available quantitative information indicates that in 1925 the number of large holders of farmland in Java owning 18 hectares

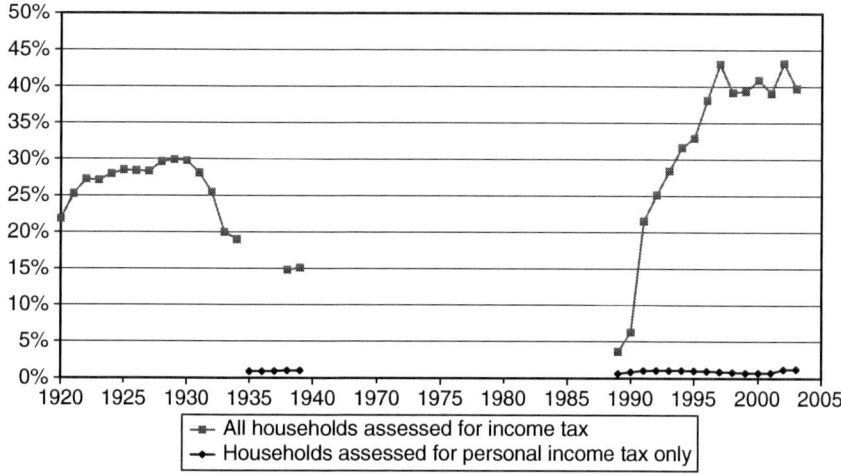

Figure 4.1 Share of households assessed for income tax as % of all households in Indonesia, 1920–2003

Sources: Tables 4A.1, 4B.1, 4C.2, 4C.3.

or more was 3,387, or just 0.06 per cent of the total number of landholders (Huender and Meijer Ranneft 1926: 203). Assuming that the net income of their land was the same as the Java average, 18 hectares would have generated an income of around ƒ3,000.[5] Hence, they would have been in the top 0.5 per cent of income earners, but they would have added less than 5 per cent to the total number of top 0.5 per cent income earners.

For the post-war years, we estimated the total number of households in Indonesia. For both periods we assumed that all households were earning an income. Details on the derivation of our population control totals are provided in Appendix 4C.

In using taxation data to estimate top income shares, our personal income control total aims to answer the question: if there had been no minimum threshold in the income taxation system and full tax compliance, how much income would have been declared? Estimates of total pre-tax household income do not exist for Indonesia for both 1920–39 and 1990–2003. For that reason we had to construct the best possible estimates of household earnings from wages, salaries, and capital on the basis of available National Accounts data. Details on the derivation of our income control totals are provided in Appendix 4D.

---

[5] Total value added in agriculture in Java was ƒ1,232 million (Polak 1943[1979]: 32–9), divided by 7.5 million hectares of farmland in Java (Van der Eng 1996: 285), times 18 hectares.

In short, for 1920–39, the estimates were based on estimates of total personal income in current prices from Polak (1979[1943]). It is very likely that Polak's estimates of total output were too low (Van der Eng 1992). The main reason for underestimation was that Polak had few data to make proper estimates of output or income in particularly small-scale industry and a range of services. The degree of underestimation of total output could be around 30 per cent, when compared with 'reflated' estimated gross domestic product (GDP) in constant prices (Van der Eng 2002a: 171–2). For that reason, the pre-war estimates of household income we used in this chapter have to be regarded as minimum estimates. This suggests that the income shares of top income earners may be somewhat lower than presented. At the same time, our implicit assumption that all land-tax-liable farm households had incomes below the cut-off incomes of the top income groups implies that the shares may be somewhat higher than presented. Both effects may cancel each other out.

The main problem for 1990–2003 was that Indonesia's National Accounts data do not employ the income approach to estimating GDP, only the output and expenditure approaches. Another problem is that the National Accounts data before the latest revision in 2000 are underestimated (Van der Eng 2005), which makes it difficult to use private consumption expenditure as a proxy of household income. For the purpose of this chapter, we estimated total pre-tax personal income on the basis of the data on disposable household income for benchmark years from Indonesia's Socio-Economic Accounts (BPS various years). These data are extensions of the improved official National Accounts data. They were interpolated on the basis of the official National Accounts data.

Using Household Survey Data to Estimate Top Earnings Shares

Given the noted limitations of the income tax data for 1990–2003, we also opted to use Susenas household survey data in our estimation of top shares, as far as they were available to us. We were able to obtain a relatively consistent income definition for twelve years between 1982 and 2004. The sample size was around 30,000 households for 1982–96, and around 80,000 households thereafter (sample sizes are listed in Appendix 4E). We are mindful of the possible shortcomings of the Susenas data, as noted in section 4.2.

When using survey data, we simply calculated the total employee earnings of all households, and then estimated the fractions of this income that are held by the richest 10 per cent, 5 per cent, 1 per cent, 0.5 per cent, 0.1 per cent, or 0.01 per cent of households. We assumed that the household samples were representative of the population, so that it was not necessary to use external control totals. For comparability with top incomes studies in other countries, we did not adjust household incomes for household size. Appendix 4E provides further details on our Susenas estimates.

4.4 TOP INCOME SHARES IN INDONESIA

Our estimated top income shares are presented in Table 4.1. We use taxation data to estimate the top 0.5 per cent share (and higher groups) from 1920–39. However, we are only able to reliably estimate the top 1 per cent share for 1921–39 and the top 5 per cent share for the years 1931–4. We also present survey-derived estimates for the top 10 per cent share (and higher groups) for 1982–2004, and taxation-derived estimates of the very highest groups from 1990–2003.

Figure 4.2 shows our estimate of the income share of the richest 1 per cent of households, combining taxation estimates for 1921–39 with survey estimates for 1982–2004. In 1921, the richest percentile group held 12 per cent of total income. We observe sharp increases in the share of the richest 1 per cent during 1921–3 and 1930–2. In both cases the increases may have been caused by significant reductions in the incomes of farm households relative to those of non-farm households, caused by drastic falls in the price of farm-produced export commodities, such as copra and rubber, in both the early 1920s and early 1930s. Most export commodities were produced by farmers outside Java who were not exempted from income tax. In the early 1920s, the price fall was in part a correction from a situation of very high commodity prices during and immediately after the First World War. The price fall in the early 1930s was a consequence of oversupply in and reduced access to commodity export markets, combined with increased competition from imported commodities, particularly rice. While high-income salary earners were to a degree shielded from the effects of these commodity price falls, small farmers had few choices to evade them, apart from returning to subsistence production. In 1933–4, the richest 1 per cent held 22 per cent of total income. By 1938–9, their share had fallen slightly to 20 per cent of total income.

We then have a four-decade break in our series. When we resume with the 1982 survey data, we find the income share of the richest 1 per cent to be lower—around 7 per cent (note that our income measure also differs, now being employee earnings). Over the next two decades, the top 1 per cent share fluctuated between 7 per cent and 16 per cent. From 1996 to 1998, the top percentile group's share rose from 10 per cent to 12 per cent, suggesting that the 1997–8 economic downturn increased the concentration of income at the top of the distribution.

Figure 4.3 focuses on the period 1982–2004, charting the top 1 per cent share against real GDP per capita. The rise in the top 1 per cent share in the late 1990s coincided with a fall in average per capita GDP, suggesting that part of the explanation may have been that the top 1 per cent were better able to withstand the 1997–8 economic downturn and its aftermath than the bottom 99 per cent.

Table 4.1 Top income shares in Indonesia, 1920–1939 and 1982–2004

Year	Using Pre-Independence Income Taxation Data									Using Post-Independence Income Taxation Data								Using Household Survey Data									100% – top marginal tax rate on personal income	100% – P99.5 MTR
	Top 10%	Top 5%	Top 1%	Top 0.5%	Top 0.1%	Top 0.05%	Top 0.01%	S0.1/S1	S1/S10	Top 10%	Top 5%	Top 1%	Top 0.5%	Top 0.1%	Top 0.05%	Top 0.01%	S0.1 in 1	Top 10%	Top 5%	Top 1%	Top 0.5%	Top 0.1%	Top 0.05%	Top 0.01%	S0.1/S1	S1/S10		
1920				6.92	3.70	2.73	1.39																				97.0	75
1921			11.82	10.08	5.54	4.15	2.21	0.47																			97.0	75
1922			14.28	11.53	5.35	4.04	1.69	0.37																			97.0	75
1923			14.81	11.99	5.69	4.06	1.93	0.38																			97.0	75
1924			14.42	11.62	5.67	4.01	1.97	0.39																			97.0	75
1925			14.19	11.42	5.65	4.30	1.91	0.40																			97.0	75
1926			15.00	12.08	5.97	4.24	2.04	0.40																			97.0	75
1927			15.52	12.41	5.98	4.30	1.94	0.39																			97.0	75
1928			16.38	13.04	6.14	4.45	1.93	0.37																			97.0	75
1929			16.71	13.31	6.32	4.45	1.92	0.38																			97.0	75
1930			16.64	13.08	5.87	4.02	1.67	0.35																			97.0	75
1931		30.57	20.03	15.65	6.77	4.53	1.78	0.34																			94.0	66
1932		32.62	21.13	16.57	7.02	4.62	1.74	0.33																			94.0	66
1933		32.83	21.55	17.01	7.18	4.68	1.72	0.33																			95.5	79
1934		31.82	21.51	17.02	7.22	4.69	1.68	0.34																			95.5	79
1935				15.82	6.81	4.45	1.60																				95.5	79
1936				15.99	6.93	4.52	1.63																				95.5	79
1937			14.64		6.56	4.38	1.69																				92.5	79
1938			19.80	15.84	7.24	4.90	2.00	0.37																			92.5	79
1939			19.87	15.83	7.03	4.68	1.83	0.35																				79
1940																												
1975																											53	
1976																											53	
1977																											53	
1978																											50	
1979																											50	

Year														
1980													50	
1981													50	
1982				32.64	20.85	7.17	4.60	1.80	1.21	0.58	0.25	0.22	50	85.0
1983													65	
1984													65	
1985													65	
1986													65	85.0
1987				36.48	24.12	7.99	4.68	1.23	0.61	0.28	0.15	0.22	65	
1988													65	
1989													65	75.0
1990		1.01	0.69	36.11	23.16	8.05	5.28	1.61	0.95	0.35	0.20	0.22	65	
1991		0.90	0.58										65	
1992		1.04	0.69										65	75.0
1993		1.02	0.66	39.94	26.07	9.10	5.85	2.04	1.33	0.38	0.22	0.23	65	
1994		1.02	0.67										70	
1995		0.89	0.55										70	85.0
1996		0.91	0.56	39.37	25.30	9.69	6.59	2.06	1.38	0.37	0.21	0.25	70	85.0
1997		0.94	0.59										70	
1998		0.80	0.54	36.22	24.92	12.42	9.87	5.93	4.93	2.17	0.48	0.34	70	85.0
1999		0.84	0.58	37.47	26.39	13.65	10.86	6.20	4.68	1.87	0.45	0.36	65	70.0
2000		1.05	0.78	38.45	27.25	13.82	11.11	6.94	5.29	2.25	0.50	0.36	65	85.0
2001		1.20	0.81	39.53	28.42	15.52	12.63	5.26	3.20	1.35	0.34	0.39	65	85.0
2002	1.47	1.26	0.75	36.38	23.40	10.47	7.93	4.05	3.21	1.58	0.39	0.29	65	85.0
2003	1.34	1.10	0.61	34.58	24.36	9.76	7.26	3.59	2.54	0.91	0.37	0.28	65	85.0
2004				34.76	22.03	8.46	5.89	2.12	1.29	0.47	0.25	0.24	65	
2005														
2006														

Note: Survey data are not available annually before 1998.

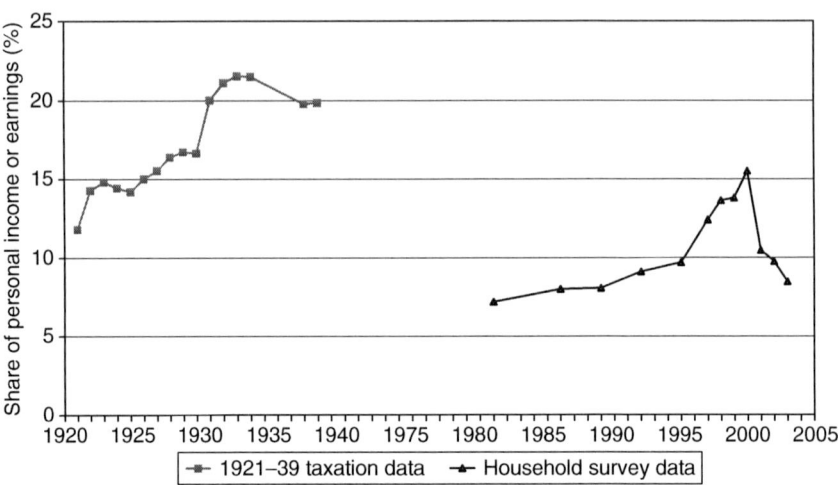

Figure 4.2 Income share of top 1% in Indonesia

Source: Table 4.1, column 4.

During 1996–2001, rapid inflation and currency depreciation eroded wage incomes in different sectors. Wages in private enterprises that were not heavily
affected by the crisis (e.g. the export sector that used domestic inputs, such as
agricultural exports) may have experienced a faster upward adjustment than
wages in the public sector and in private enterprises that were affected by the

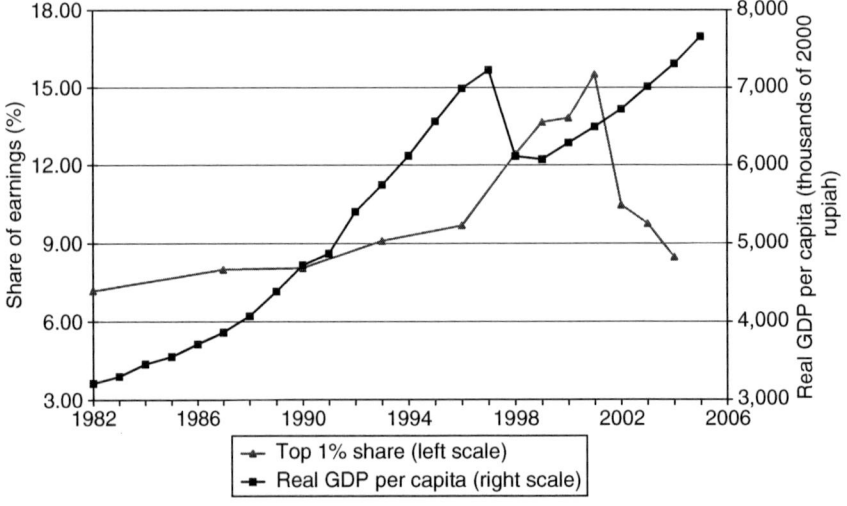

Figure 4.3 Top 1% share and average incomes

Sources: Top 1% share, Table 4.1, column 4; GDP per capita from Van der Eng (2008).

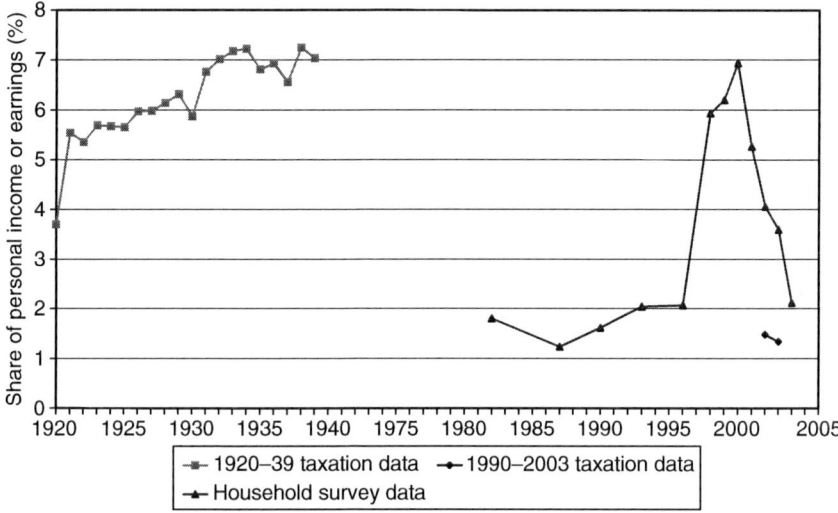

Figure 4.4 Income share of top 0.1% in Indonesia

Source: Table 4.1, column 6.

crisis (particularly the manufacturing export sector that depended on imported inputs), until the consequences of the crisis subsided after 2001.

Figures 4.4 and 4.5 show the income share of the richest 0.1 per cent and 0.05 per cent of the population, respectively. In these charts, we use both taxation and survey data for the post-war period. The income concept is not precisely the same in the two sources, being employee earnings in the survey data and taxable income in the tax data. Taxation data contain a much larger sample of the rich. However, in principle, both data sets may underestimate top incomes. In the case of survey data, this is typically thought to arise because high earners are under-represented in surveys (see, e.g., Groves and Couper 1998; Moore, Stinson, and Welniak 2000). In the case of taxation data, top incomes are generally thought to be downward biased because of under-reporting of income to the tax authorities. In practice, it is not clear which of these biases will be larger. For Argentina in 1997, Alvaredo (2007: appendix B4) finds 698 taxpayers with incomes over US$1 million, but no survey respondents with incomes in this range. At the very top of the Indonesian distribution, the same is true; the 2003 survey does not contain respondents with incomes over US$1 million, but the 2003 tax data contain seventy taxpayers with incomes over US$1 million.[6] However, when moving only slightly further down the distribution, we find the opposite: the cut-off for the top 0.01 per cent is higher in the survey data (874 million rupiah) than in the

---

[6] Our calculations are based on the average exchange rate for 2003, being US$1 = Rp 8,592.

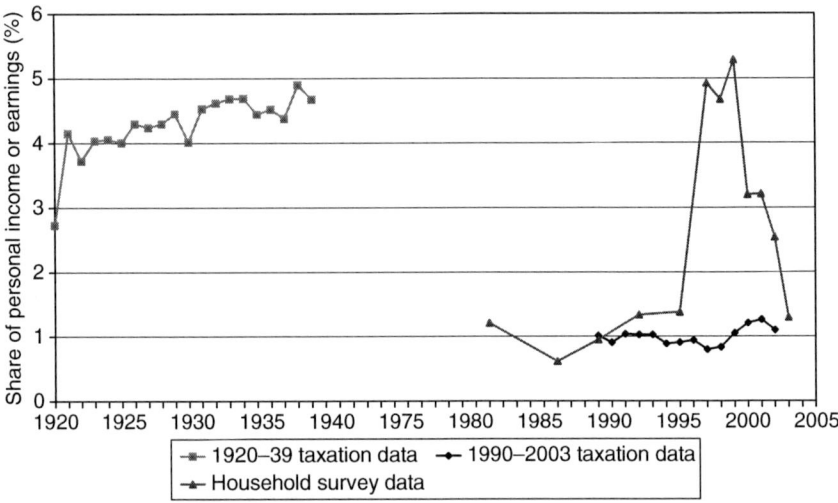

Figure 4.5 Income share of top 0.05% in Indonesia

Source: Table 4.1, column 7.

taxation data (816 million rupiah). We therefore opt not to follow Alvaredo's approach of combining tax and survey data.[7]

For the period 1920–39, we find that the income shares of the top 0.1 per cent increased during the 1920s and 1930s, but less sharply than the top 1 per cent. A similar pattern holds for the super-rich 0.05 per cent. A levelling at the very top appears to have occurred between 1939 and 1982; both the survey-derived and taxation-derived estimates indicate that the shares of the top 0.1 per cent and 0.05 per cent were lower in the early 1990s than the late 1930s. During the 1990s, the taxation and survey data both indicate a rise, but the magnitude of the increase is considerably larger in the survey data than in the taxation data.[8] Figures 4.4 and 4.5 also show an increase in top income shares from 1996 to 2000, followed by a fall in the early 2000s. The significant fluctuations in the survey data may be caused by the very low number of observations in the groups of top income

---

[7] Alvaredo (2007) also adjusts the Argentinean surveys so that the implied totals for aggregated wages, pensions, self-employment income, dividends, and rents match those in the national accounts. In the case of Indonesia, the national accounts do not use the income approach, only the production and expenditure approaches. In Appendix 4D, we outline our approximation of total household income on the basis of the Social Accounting Matrices. However, the income estimate cannot be disaggregated for the purpose of following Alvaredo's approach.

[8] Not only are top income shares higher in the survey estimates, it is also the case that income thresholds (in rupiah) are generally higher in the survey-derived estimates (Table 4E.4) than in the tax-derived estimates (Table 4B.2). Given that the income definition is narrower in the surveys, this is consistent with a substantial degree of tax under-reporting at the top of the distribution.

earners in the Susenas sample (ranging from 13 to 87 in the top 0.1 per cent and half as many in the top 0.05 per cent). However, it is worth noting that when we separately analyse the survey-derived estimates of the top 0.05 per cent share and the next 0.05 per cent share (i.e. P99.95–P100 and P99.90–P99.95), both series follow a similar trend, spiking upwards in the late 1990s. It should be noted as well that the income tax data, although they cover a much larger number of observations, only apply to those assessed for personal income tax, not all income tax paying households. This issue is discussed in detail in Appendix 4B.

Another approach is to estimate shares within shares, comparing the super-rich with the very rich. This has the benefit that it is not affected by our control totals. Figure 4.6 shows the share of the richest 1 per cent within the top 10 per cent, and the share of the richest 0.1 per cent within the top 1 per cent. We observe a slight decline in concentration within the top 1 per cent during the 1920s and 1930s, which is consistent with the earlier observation that the top 1 per cent share rose faster than that of the top 0.1 per cent. The S0.1/S1 concentration index shows a fall between 1939 and 1982. In 1939 the richest 1/1000th of households had about 35 per cent of the income held by the top 1/100th, compared with 25 per cent in 1982. During the late 1990s, both shares-within-shares measures rose sharply, before declining slightly in the early 2000s.

An advantage of the pre-war taxation data is that we are able to separate salary and non-salary income for the years 1935–9. Figure 4.7 shows the share of income from wages in 1935 and 1939. In general, the wage shares are high, though it

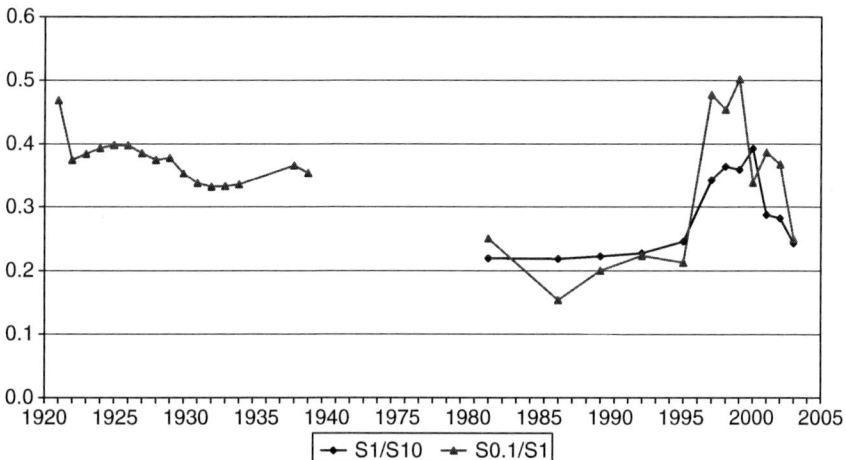

Figure 4.6 Shares within shares Indonesia

Notes: Taxation data for 1920–39; survey data for 1982–2005.
Sources: Authors' calculations, based on Table 4.1.

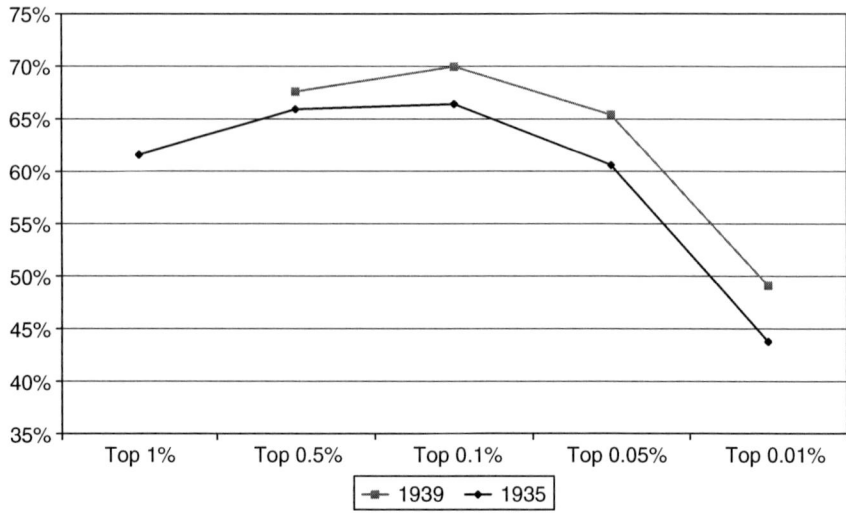

Figure 4.7 Share of income from wages in Indonesia, 1935 and 1939

Sources: Taxation data for 1935 and 1939.

should be recalled that most farmers are excluded from these statistics. For the richest 1 percentile group, about 70 per cent of income comes from wages, compared with about 40 per cent for the richest 0.01 per cent. The share of top incomes derived from wage earnings fell slightly from 1935 to 1939. But even in 1939, all but the richest 0.05 per cent derived a majority of their income from wages.

One factor that has been highlighted in studies of top incomes in developed nations is the negative relationship between top incomes and marginal tax rates (see, e.g., Saez 2004; Saez and Veall 2005; Atkinson and Leigh 2007b; Roine and Waldenström 2008). However, we are unaware of any attempt thus far to look at the effect of tax rates on top income shares in developing countries. Since the under-reporting of income to tax authorities is generally thought to be more of a problem in developing nations, one might expect that the elasticity of top income shares with respect to tax rates would be lower in the developing world. Figure 4.8 charts our estimates of the top 1 per cent share against the top marginal tax rate and the median marginal tax rate paid by the top 1 per cent (so far as we are aware, we are the first to construct such tax series for Indonesia).[9] Note that we are plotting the after-tax share—so if cutting top tax rates increased the share of

---

[9] The median marginal tax rates are calculated by taking the threshold incomes at the 99.5th and 99.95th percentiles (Appendix Tables 4A.2 and 4E.4), and checking the tax schedules for each year to determine the marginal rate at these incomes.

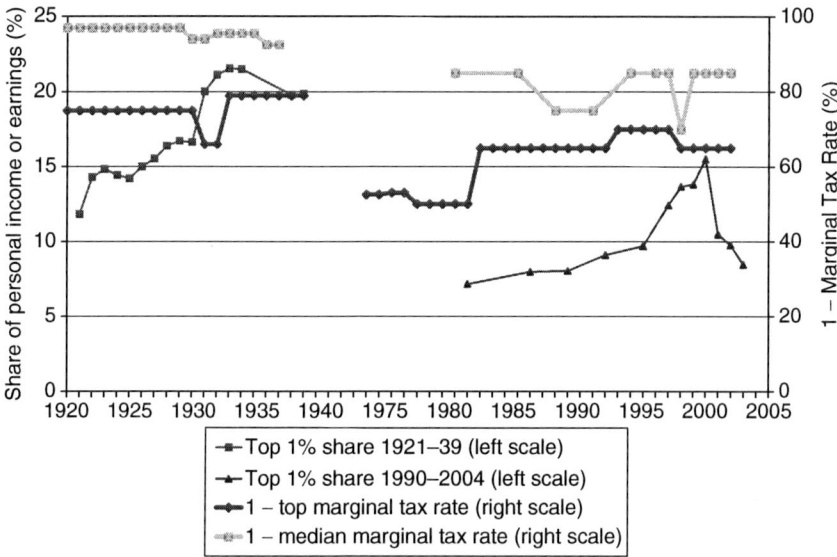

Figure 4.8 Top 1% share and after-tax share, Indonesia

Source: Table 4.2.

the rich, we would expect these lines to move together. Yet in contrast to studies that have focused on developed countries, there appears to be little evidence that an increase in the after-tax share (i.e. a reduction in the top tax rate) had the effect of boosting top income shares in Indonesia.

To test this more formally, we calculate the median marginal tax rates paid by the top 1 per cent group and the top 0.1 per cent group. We then regress top income shares on the after-tax share (based on the median marginal tax rate payable by that group). These results are shown in Table 4.2. Using either the top 1 per cent share or the top 0.1 per cent share as the dependent variable, we find no consistent evidence of a positive relationship between top incomes and the after-tax share. Using top income shares that are derived from taxation data (Panel A) we find a (counter-intuitive) negative relationship in three out of four specifications. Using top income shares that are derived from survey data (Panel B), the relationship is insignificant for the top 1 per cent share, negative for the top 0.1 per cent in the absence of a time trend, and positive for the top 0.1 per cent with a linear time trend. Although Panels A and B use a different income concept, we show in Appendix 4E that this has little impact on the estimated top income shares (at least for a year in which we have data on both). We therefore pool the data for 1920–2004 in Panel C, and find that the relationship between top income shares and the after-tax share is mostly positive (consistent with the findings for developed countries). However, the magnitude of the coefficient varies substantially across specifications.

Table 4.2 Tax rates and top incomes in Indonesia (endogenous rate)

	[1]	[2]	[3]	[4]
	Dependent variable is top 1% share		Dependent variable is top 0.1% share	
Panel A: 1920–1939 (tax-based top income shares)				
1 − Marginal Tax Rate	−1.289***	0.117	−0.455***	−0.172***
	[0.322]	[0.414]	[0.130]	[0.058]
Linear time trend	No	Yes	No	Yes
Observations	16	16	20	20
Panel B: 1982–2004 (survey-based top income shares)				
1 − Marginal Tax Rate	−0.034	−0.061	−0.152**	0.381*
	[0.106]	[0.084]	[0.057]	[0.182]
Linear time trend	No	Yes	No	Yes
Observations	12	12	12	12
Panel C: 1920–2004 (pooling data used in panels A and B)				
1 − Marginal Tax Rate	0.333***	0.033	0.091**	−0.163
	[0.111]	[0.126]	[0.038]	[0.106]
Linear time trend	No	Yes	No	Yes
Observations	28	28	32	32

Notes: Standard errors, corrected for autocorrelation using the Newey–West procedure with 8 lags, in square brackets. Marginal tax rate is the marginal rate payable by a taxpayer at the 99.5^{th} percentile (in the case of the top 1% share), and the marginal rate payable by a taxpayer at the 99.95^{th} percentile (in the case of the top 0.1% share).

While the results in Table 4.2 have the advantage that they use the median marginal rate paid by the income group, it is possible that this rate might be endogenous. To see this, suppose that some external factor caused the top 1 per cent share to fall, such that income at the 99.5th percentile slipped into a lower tax bracket. In this case, we might erroneously conclude that there was a negative causal relationship between the after-tax share and the top income share. In order to correct for this, we instrument for the (endogenous) marginal tax rate paid using the (exogenous) top marginal tax rate. This addresses the endogeneity problem, but suffers from the fact that there is only a weak relationship between the top rate and the rate paid—particularly in the pre-Independence era. This can be seen from the F-statistics in Table 4.3, which are often not statistically significant. However, even when the top rate is a good instrument (as in Panel C), the effects of tax rates on top income shares are mostly statistically insignificant. Overall, we interpret the results in Tables 4.2 and 4.3 as meaning that there is no systematic relationship between top marginal tax rates and top income shares in Indonesia.

Table 4.3 Tax rates and top incomes in Indonesia (IV specification)

	[1]	[2]	[3]	[4]
	Dependent variable is top 1% share		Dependent variable is top 0.1% share	
Panel A: 1920–1939 (tax-based top income shares)				
1 – Marginal Tax Rate	– 6.314	– 3.686	– 0.78	– 0.797
	[33.275]	[3.613]	[0.540]	[0.667]
Linear time trend	No	Yes	No	Yes
F-test on excluded instrument	0.02	1.45	2.87	3.39*
Observations	16	16	20	20
Panel B: 1982–2004 (survey-based top income shares)				
1 – Marginal Tax Rate	0.128***	– 1.053	– 0.196	– 0.145
	[0.013]	[3.905]	[0.112]	[0.852]
Linear time trend	No	Yes	No	Yes
F-test on excluded instrument	0.00	0.10	11.95***	1.13
Observations	12	12	12	12
Panel C: 1920–2004 (pooling data used in panels A and B)				
1 – Marginal Tax Rate	0.510**	1.526	0.148	– 0.367
	[0.200]	[1.953]	[0.089]	[0.347]
Linear time trend	No	Yes	No	Yes
F-test on excluded instrument	7.92***	1.41	5.65**	0.83
Observations	28	28	32	32

Notes: Standard errors, corrected for autocorrelation using the Newey–West procedure with 8 lags, in square brackets. Marginal tax rate is the marginal rate payable by a taxpayer at the 99.5th percentile (in the case of the top 1% share), and the marginal rate payable by a taxpayer at the 99.95th percentile (in the case of the top 0.1% share). This marginal tax rate is then instrumented using the top marginal tax rate. Our analysis is implemented using the *ivreg2* module in Stata (Baum, Schaffer, and Stilman 2007).

4.5 COMPARISON WITH OTHER ESTIMATES

In this section, we look at how our estimates compare with those for other countries. We approach the question in two ways. Our first approach simply uses available data to look for consistent patterns. Specifically, we take top income share estimates for all available countries and look at the relationship between those estimates and ours for Indonesia. Our second approach focuses on Argentina, India, Japan, and the United States, which allows us to chart and discuss the trends in more detail.

Table 4.4 shows the results from comparing Indonesian top income shares with those in seventeen other countries. For the purposes of this exercise, we focus on the top 1 per cent share. For Indonesia, we combine the tax-based estimate for

Table 4.4 Relationship between the income share of top 1% income earners in Indonesia and the income share of top 1% income earners in other countries

Country	Difference (Other country top 1% minus Indonesian top 1%)	Correlation	Number of common years	Common years
Argentina	5.456 [1.601]	−0.212	12	1932–2004
Australia	−5.242 [0.668]	0.666	26	1922–2003
Canada	−0.637 [0.424]	0.904	24	1921–2000
China (urban only)	−6.607 [0.746]	0.453	10	1987–2003
Finland	−5.952 [0.567]	0.859	8	1990–2002
France	−0.946 [0.852]	0.59	22	1921–1998
Germany	−3.654 [1.092]	0.504	17	1925–1998
India	−2.698 [0.317]	0.967	21	1923–1999
Ireland	−2.325 [0.434]	0.97	9	1939–2000
Japan	−0.302 [0.739]	0.717	26	1921–2002
The Netherlands	−1.6 [0.900]	0.633	23	1921–1999
New Zealand	−2.737 [0.611]	0.714	25	1922–2002
Spain	−2.416 [0.831]	0.689	10	1982–2002
Sweden	−5.863 [0.587]	0.905	17	1930–2004
Switzerland	−4.395 [1.876]	0.763	9	1933–1996
United Kingdom	0.467 [0.419]	0.923	8	1982–2000
United States	1.143 [0.710]	0.52	28	1921–2004
Mean	−2.253	**0.68**		

Sources: Top incomes series for Australia, Canada, France, Germany, Ireland, Japan, the Netherlands, New Zealand, Spain, Sweden, Switzerland, the UK, and the US are drawn from Leigh (2007), who makes minor adjustments to put the data on a consistent calendar year basis and account for series breaks. The original sources for Leigh's series are cited in section 4.2. In addition, we use data from Argentina (Alvaredo 2007, table 6, series adjusted for under-reporting where applicable), urban China (Piketty and Qian 2006, table A5, household distribution), Finland (Riihelä, Sullström, and Tuomala 2005, table 2, Gross income), and India (Banerjee and Piketty 2005, adjusted from tax year to calendar year basis). All series exclude capital gains, to the extent possible. These distributions are discussed in other chapters of this volume.

1921–39 with the survey-based measure for 1982–2004. Although the income concept in the two periods differs, we believe that they are sufficiently comparable so that pooling provides a more useful impression than separate analysis of both periods.

We estimate two summary statistics: the mean difference and the pair-wise correlation. Across the common years (which differ from country to country), the average top 1 per cent share in Indonesia is 2.3 points higher than the share in other countries for which top incomes have been estimated. In only three of the seventeen countries (Argentina, the United Kingdom, and the United States) is the mean top 1 per cent share higher than in Indonesia.

As has been documented in other studies (e.g. Piketty and Saez 2006b), top income shares in many countries follow a common path across the twentieth century—falling during the first half of the century, and rising (particularly in English-speaking countries) during the last quarter of the century. The estimated correlations in Table 4.4 reinforce this point, the mean correlation with the Indonesian top 1 per cent share being 0.650. The highest correlations are 0.967 with India (21 common observations) and 0.970 with Ireland (9 common observations). Given that the correlation with India is based upon more than twice as many data points as the correlation with Ireland, we conclude from this that trends in Indonesian top incomes most closely follow those in India. The lowest estimated correlations are with two other developing nations: Argentina and China. This suggests that trends in top income shares may have been more divergent among developing countries than in developed nations (although it is also possible that the apparent diversity merely reflects greater measurement error in developing country estimates). The results from Table 4.4 also suggest that it may be worth further exploring the relationship between top incomes in Indonesia and India.

We now turn to a more detailed comparison of Indonesian top income shares, focusing on four particular countries. For this purpose, we chose India and Japan, the two other Asian countries for which top income shares are available over a long time span, Argentina (the only Latin American country for which we were able to obtain long-run top income estimates), and the United States, since it provides a familiar benchmark for many readers. In the case of Argentina and the United States, the estimates are based on households, while the estimates for India and Japan are based on individuals. The estimates for India, Japan, and the United States are derived from taxation data, while those for Argentina are based upon both taxation and survey data.

Figure 4.9 compares the top 5 per cent share in Indonesia with that in Argentina, Japan, and the United States (the top 5 per cent share is unavailable for India). During the early 1930s, the top 5 per cent share was very similar in all three countries. In the 1980s and 1990s, the top vingtile share in Indonesia rose more rapidly than in Japan, though less rapidly than in the United States. In the early 2000s, the Indonesian top 5 per cent share fell; leaving it closer to the Japanese estimate than the United States estimate at the very end of the period. There are only two observations of the top 5 per cent share for Argentina, both significantly higher than for other countries in the same years.

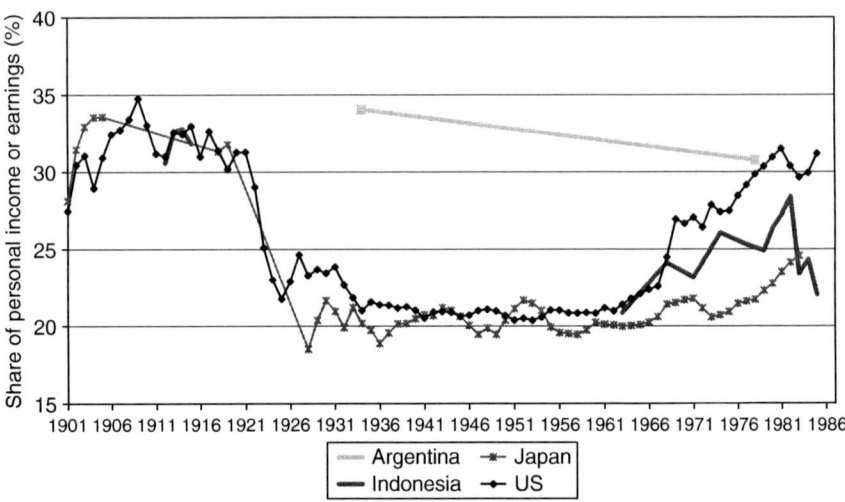

Figure 4.9 Income share of the top 5% in Argentina, Indonesia, Japan, and the United States

Sources: Argentina, Alvaredo (2007); Indonesia, authors' calculations; Japan, Moriguchi and Saez (2008); United States, Piketty and Saez (2003, 2006).

Figure 4.10 charts the top 1 per cent share. In Indonesia, India, and the United States, the series follows a similar trajectory, peaking in the 1920s or 1930s, falling in the middle decades of the twentieth century, and rising in the 1980s and 1990s (though not to the heights of the early decades). A similar pattern holds for Argentina, though the peak is in the 1940s. In the 1980s and 1990s, the share of the top percentile group was slightly higher in Indonesia than in India and Japan. The share of the richest 1 per cent in Indonesia was lower than that of Argentina and the United States during most of the twentieth century, although the level of top income inequality in Indonesia exceeded the level in both Argentina and the United States in the 1930s.

The high level of inequality in Indonesia in the 1930s is possibly caused by the fact that agricultural producers suffered from the downturn in the terms of trade of agricultural commodities *vis-à-vis* non-agricultural producers, as noted in section 4.4. In the United States, economic regulation and protection may to a degree have prevented a similarly sharp drop in agricultural incomes relative to non-agricultural incomes.

Our finding that top income shares in Indonesia are high—relative to other countries—may surprise some readers, as it contradicts the common 'growth with equity' understanding of Indonesia's growth experience since the 1960s. For example, a discussion of inequality in Indonesia's development experience in the

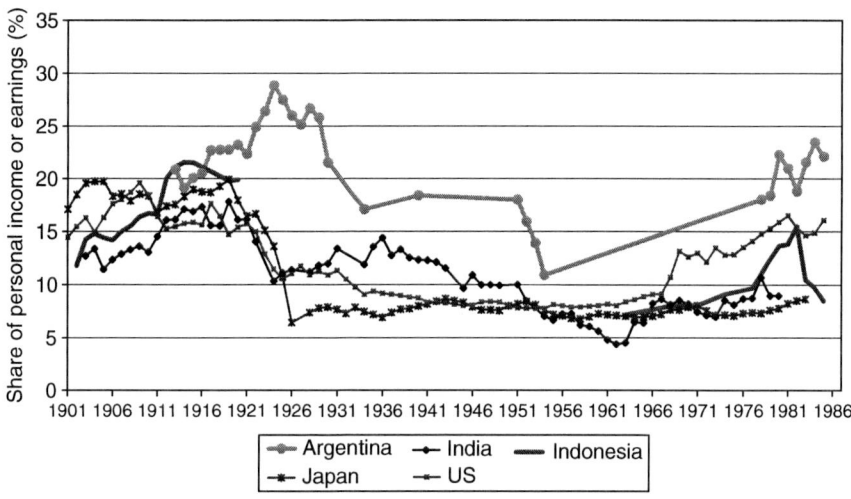

Figure 4.10 Income share of the top 1% in Argentina, India, Indonesia, Japan, and the United States

Sources: Argentina, Alvaredo (2007); India, Banerjee and Piketty (2005); Indonesia, authors' calculations; Japan, Moriguchi and Saez (2008); United States, Piketty and Saez (2003, 2006).

World Development Report 2006 used the phrase 'pro-poor' twelve times in two pages (World Bank 2005b: 126–7). Although our most recent estimates for Indonesia are based on surveys and taxation statistics, both data sources have some limitations for analysing top incomes. To buttress the foregoing conclusions, we therefore look briefly at wealth inequality, to see how the concentration of top wealth shares in Indonesia compares with other nations.

Population surveys on household wealth are a plausible source of information. In a comprehensive report on global wealth distribution, Davies et al. (2006) show data for twenty nations with comparable information on the distribution of wealth. Among these twenty countries, the top 10 per cent share is third highest in Indonesia (65 per cent), after only the United States (70 per cent) and Switzerland (71 per cent). A similar pattern emerges for the top 1 per cent of Indonesian wealth holders, who have 29 per cent of the nation's wealth, again surpassed only by the United States (32 per cent) and Switzerland (35 per cent).

A second way of analysing wealth inequality at the top end of the distribution is to use data from the *Forbes* rich lists. In 2006, for the first time, *Forbes* compiled a list of the richest Indonesians, covering the richest forty individuals and in some cases their families (Doebele and Vorasarun 2006). Table 4.5 compares these data to the forty richest Americans in the same year (from the *Forbes 400* rich list). In Indonesia, the richest forty held 6 per cent of the nation's wealth, while the richest

Table 4.5 Wealth inequality at the top of the distribution, 2006

	Indonesia	US
Wealth of richest 40 as a share of total national wealth	5.9%	1.1%
Distribution within richest 40:		
Top 4 / Top 40	39.1%	26.0%
Top 8 / Top 40	59.3%	37.8%
Top 20 / Top 40	85.5%	68.6%
Wealth per capita, US$2006 (exchange rate basis)	$1,686	$168,266

Sources: 2006 Forbes lists of the 40 richest individuals and families in Indonesia (Doebele and Vorasarun 2006) and the 40 richest individuals in the US (http://www.forbes.com/lists/). Wealth per capita is based upon figures for the year 2000 from Davies et al. (2006, Appendix V, table 1), scaled up by 1.17 to account for increases in the US CPI from 2000–2006.

forty Americans held 1 per cent of the nation's wealth. The same pattern holds *within* the top forty, a comparison that is unaffected by estimates of total national wealth. Of the total wealth held by the top forty, the richest four Indonesians held 39 per cent, while the richest four Americans held 26 per cent of the total wealth of the top 40. Similarly, the richest twenty held 85 per cent of top forty wealth in Indonesia, compared with 69 per cent in the United States.

4.6 CONCLUSION

Notwithstanding some major data problems, and continued shortcomings of the available data, we are able to offer several new insights into the long-term trends in income distribution in Indonesia during the twentieth century that allow us to address the questions that this chapter set out to answer.

The available evidence on trends in top incomes does not suggest that there has been a sustained long-term increase in income inequality in Indonesia. There was an increase in the top 1 per cent income share during the early 1920s and early 1930s, possibly caused by adverse changes in markets for agricultural commodities affecting farm incomes. But even during the rest of the 1920s, there was an increase, possibly associated with the fact that the 1920s was a period of significant economic expansion, largely based on the growth of commodity export production (Van der Eng 2002a). This increase may substantiate the inferences of Lindert and Williamson (2003). On the other hand, the share of the top 1 per cent decreased during the late 1930s, even though at that time the economic growth resumed vigorously, this time on the basis of the growth of import-substituting production.

For the period 1982–2004, which also was a period of high economic growth, we found that the income share of the top 5 per cent was lower than in the early 1930s. While the top 10 per cent in total income increased only slightly over the period 1982–2004, a more marked increase can be observed in the top 1 per cent share. Notably, the sharp economic contraction during 1997–8 was associated with a rise in the share of the very richest groups (top 1 per cent and above), but little change in the top 10 per cent share. Generally speaking, these findings accord with the interpretations of income inequality in Indonesia offered by e.g. Cameron (2002) and Timmer (2005). However, we should note that our findings and those of other studies are based on the same source: the household survey data.

Comparing top income shares in Indonesia with the available data for other countries, we find that Indonesian top income shares track Indian top income shares particularly closely. In terms of the level of top income shares, the top 1 per cent share in Indonesia has been higher than in most countries and years for which comparable data are available. The same is true of wealth concentration at the top of the distribution, which has been relatively unequal in Indonesia during recent years.

APPENDIX 4A: INCOME TAXATION DATA, 1920–1939

Our data are based on personal income taxation records for 1920–39 published by income bands in the annual reports and statistical yearbooks of colonial Indonesia: *Koloniaal Verslag*, 1922/3–1923/4, *Statistisch Jaaroverzicht voor Nederlandsch-Indië*, 1922–30, *Indisch Verslag*, 1931–40. The taxation data were revised in subsequent years, pending final assessments of tax obligations. Income earners with incomes over $f1,200$ were compelled to submit a tax return form that required time to be assessed (Reys 1925: 68). For that reason we use the latest data available. The sources only give net taxable income, after the deduction of set allowances for spouse and children from gross taxable income. Table 4A.1 shows the numbers of households assessed for income tax.

The published tables ordered taxpayers into various income bands, according to their taxable income. In 1920–9, the published tables show only the number of taxpayers within each income band. In these cases, we assume that the average earnings within each band are at the midpoint of the band, extrapolating for those in the top band. For example, in 1920, the top two bands are $f150,000$ and $f200,000$, so we assume that the average income of those in the second-top band is $f175,000$, and the average income of those in the top band is $f225,000$ (our results are not particularly sensitive to how we treat the top band). In 1930–9, such a correction is not necessary, since the tables show both the number of taxpayers within each band, and the total income earned within each band (a table for 1925 also shows total income, but it turns out to be based on the midpoint assumption). In 1935 and 1938–9, the tables separately identify wage and non-wage income.

As discussed in section 4.3, incomes of married couples and their income-earning dependants were taxed jointly. The exceptions to this rule were widows, divorced women, and women who held assets that were managed independently from those of their husbands. According to Reys (1925: 84) the share of women in the total of income tax payers was negligible. In instances where couples were separated, we assumed that they would have been living apart, and therefore will appear in separate households in the control totals.

As noted in section 4.3, there was a significant degree of non- and under-compliance in the lower income bands. Table 4A.2 shows the income cut-offs used in this study. Underestimation of incomes in the income bands up to $f1,200$ (below which income earners were not obliged to submit tax returns) may affect our estimates of top income shares. For this reason, we do not show estimates for income groups where the income cut-off for that group was below 150 per cent of mean personal income in the general population (estimated by dividing our control total for personal income by our control total for the number of households in the population).

Table 4A.1 Total income earners assessed for income tax, Indonesia, 1920–1939

Year	Withholding tax payers	Personal income tax payers	Total tax payers assessed for income tax
1920			2,648,640
1921			3,098,431
1922			3,377,760
1923			3,398,159
1924			3,544,376
1925			3,653,080
1926			3,683,578
1927			3,716,561
1928			3,934,933
1929			4,026,979
1930			4,057,698
1931			3,887,520
1932			3,574,353
1933			2,848,903
1934			2,748,721
1935		132,626	
1936		131,960	
1937		141,256	
1938	2,118,679	154,205	2,272,884
1939	2,198,770	157,415	2,356,185

Table 4A.2 Income cut-offs for given percentiles, Indonesia, 1920–1939 (guilders)

Year	Top 5%	Top 1%	Top 0.5%	Top 0.1%	Top 0.05%	Top 0.01%	mean income (based on control totals)
1920			1,958	7,862	11,529	27,091	483
1921		926	2,035	8,724	12,818	29,397	373
1922		1,220	2,915	9,519	13,012	26,969	337
1923		1,170	2,713	8,950	12,271	25,878	313
1924		1,281	2,822	9,252	13,103	28,482	336
1925		1,311	2,858	9,893	14,116	31,052	347
1926		1,480	3,166	10,364	14,589	35,425	364
1927		1,486	3,239	10,372	14,543	33,008	349
1928		1,523	3,397	10,664	14,686	32,765	337
1929		1,574	3,547	10,965	15,185	34,063	343
1930		1,594	3,556	10,528	14,583	30,761	330
1931	430	1,468	3,207	9,522	13,100	25,457	246
1932	372	1,201	2,636	7,978	10,728	20,160	191
1933	286	957	2,150	6,724	9,072	16,385	155
1934	245	867	1,976	6,355	8,521	15,321	143
1935			1,833	6,007	8,087	14,714	145
1936			1,777	5,900	7,937	14,520	140
1937			1,910	6,246	8,480	16,608	165
1938		904	2,109	7,021	9,653	19,697	174
1939		910	2,140	7,036	9,507	18,387	172

APPENDIX 4B: INCOME TAXATION DATA,
1990–2003

With the exception of 1966 and 1971 (Lent and Missorten 1967: 43; Lerche 1978: 298), we have been unable to locate any published tabulations of income taxpayers by income bands for Indonesia since the 1950s. (Both the 1966 and 1971 tabulations turned out to be unusable for our purposes.) However, we were fortunate in 2005 to be supplied with a unique tabulation of income taxpayers by grade of taxable income. These data were extracted for us from the electronic tax database of the Directorate General of Taxation, and are the only data available at the Directorate General.

The files supplied to us provided the number of taxpayers in each band, and the total taxable income of taxpayers in that band. The data are the result of online data submissions by the regional tax offices. Apart from non- or under-compliance, the low numbers of returns may indicate that data for 1990 were underestimated, because not all offices were online then. We were unable to check this. The 1989 data could not be used, since more than 99.9 per cent of the taxpayers were classified in the same income band (nonetheless, we show the summary statistics for 1989). The data only referred to net taxable income, after the deduction of set allowances for spouse and children from gross taxable income. Table 4B.1 shows the numbers of households assessed for income tax.

Our top income shares are estimated using midpoint interpolation, rather than Pareto extrapolation. We experimented with Pareto extrapolation, but found that the irregular size of the income ranges used in the taxation data meant that the Pareto index was imprecisely estimated. We therefore concluded that extrapolating outside the range of the available data was unlikely to provide accurate estimates of top income shares.

We were also supplied with data on withholding tax. However, this is not tabulated according to the wages of individuals, but according to the total income of the employees for which firms paid the withholding taxes. Since these data do not allow us to determine the distribution of earnings within the firm, we opted not to use them.

For the most part, Indonesian taxation laws require couples to file tax returns jointly (article 8 of the tax law). The two main exceptions are where the spouse's employer has already paid withholding tax, and where wife and husband are separated. Since we do not have any data on frequency with which the spouse's employer pays withholding tax, we do not make any adjustment for it. In instances where couples are separated, we assume that they will be living apart, and therefore will appear in separate households in the control totals.

Table 4B.1 Total income earners assessed for income tax, Indonesia, 1989–2003

Year	Withholding tax payers	Personal income tax payers	Total income tax payers
1989	1,156,891	244,091	1,400,982
1990	2,161,586	339,316	2,500,902
1991	8,360,557	424,572	8,785,129
1992	10,087,064	450,147	10,537,211
1993	*11,800,000*	460,223	12,260,223
1994	13,578,446	471,855	14,050,301
1995	14,565,973	467,303	15,033,276
1996	*17,400,000*	456,279	17,856,279
1997	20,262,393	434,849	20,697,242
1998	18,927,125	404,673	19,331,798
1999	19,541,043	380,796	19,921,839
2000	20,890,946	371,698	21,262,644
2001	20,488,669	391,210	20,879,879
2002	23,077,662	655,448	23,733,110
2003	21,771,865	709,787	22,481,652

Note: Numbers in italics are approximations.

Table 4B.2 Income cut-offs for given percentiles, Indonesia, 1990–2003 (million rupiah)

Year	Top 0.1%	Top 0.05%	Top 0.01%
1990		18.3	66.9
1991		19.9	79.6
1992		22.1	97.3
1993		25.7	117.3
1994		31.2	140.8
1995		39.1	159.2
1996		43.5	173.6
1997		46.1	190.9
1998		44.1	214.0
1999		47.4	254.2
2000		55.7	391.8
2001		89.0	748.8
2002	86.6	161.2	816.4
2003	105.9	188.8	774.2

APPENDIX 4C: POPULATION CONTROL TOTALS, 1920–2005

1920–1939

The population control totals had to be estimated, due to severe limitations in the available demographic data for colonial Indonesia, for which only the 1930 population census offers reliable data. The 1920 and 1930 population censuses do not offer estimates of households, so that their total number had to be estimated.

First, population numbers were estimated for Java and separately for the other islands for 1920–30. The 1930–9 population data are interpolations of 1930 and 1940 from Van der Eng (2002a). For 1920–30 Java, non-Indonesian population is taken from the 1920 population census, the administrative counts for 1925–7, and the 1930 population census, and interpolated with exponential growth rates. For Java, the Indonesian population 1920–30 is estimated, using 1920–7 growth rates for nineteen residencies (assuming that the 1920 data were the 'anchor' for the collection of the 1927 data). 1920–30 growth rates were used for four other residencies (Semarang, Kudus, Wonosobo, and Kedu, where the 1920–7 growth rate was negative and the 1927–30 growth rate was abnormally high). For 1920–30, Outer Islands non-Indonesian population is taken from the 1920 population census, the administrative counts for 1925 and 1927, and the 1930 population census, and interpolated with exponential growth rates. The Indonesian population is estimated, using 1920–7 growth rates for eighteen regions on the basis of the same reasoning as for Java above. For West Papua, 600,000 people were assumed in 1930, which was extrapolated assuming 1 per cent annual growth.

To estimate the number of households, we needed an indication of average household size. The 1920 and 1930 population censuses only identify the numbers of dwellings, which yields estimates of 4.6 people per dwelling in Java and 6.6 in the Outer Islands in 1920, and 4.6 people per dwelling in Java in 1930. These data may be used as proxies for average household size. The Java estimates appear acceptable, but the 1920 estimates for the Outer Islands seem too high. The only other sources are local surveys for consumption and expenditure surveys, summarized in Table 4C.1. Taken together, these surveys suggest a weighted average of 4.41 per household in both rural and urban Java. The 1961 population census also suggested an Indonesia-wide total of 4.41 people per household: 4.24 in Java and 4.82 in the Outer Islands (BPS 1963: 13–14).

We assumed all households in pre-war Indonesia to have comprised an average of 4.5 people. The estimated population totals were divided by 4.5 to yield the total number of income-earning households shown in Table 4C.2.

1990–2005

The estimates of the total number of households were based on the population census data for 1961, 1971, 1980, 1990, and 2000, and the inter-census survey of 1995. We used the 1961 and 1971 data for consistency checks. We interpolated the population totals from the census data and added population data for 2001–5. We then took the numbers of households for each census year, calculated the average number of people per household, interpolated these average numbers of people per household, and divided the total numbers of people for 1961–2005 by the average number of people per household to obtain annual estimates of the total number of households.

Table 4C.1 Overview of average household size in food consumption and expenditure surveys in Java, 1924–1961

Source	Sample size	Region	Year(s)	Av. hh size
Boeke (1926)	29 rural hh	Java (various parts)	1924–5	4.3
CKS (1928)	314 urban hh	Indonesia	1925	4.3
Ochse and Terra (1934: 59, 77)	30 farm hh	Kutawinangun (Kebumen, C.Java)	1932–3	6.7
CKS (1939)	95 labourers' hh	Jakarta	1937	4.6
Volksvoeding (1940: 42)	12 rural hh	Pacet (Cianjur, W.Java)	1938	4
Volksvoeding (1941)	100 rural hh	Gunungkidul (Yogyakarta, C.Java)	1938–9	5.5**
Postmus and Van Veen (1949: 264)	400 hh	Rengasdengklok (W.Java)	1939	4.2
Huizenga (1958: 112–148)	1,945 rural hh	Java	1939–40	4.7
Sato (1994: 90)	443 rural hh	Tasikmadu (Malang, E.Java)	1942	4
Sato (1994: 97)	345 rural hh	Tumut (Bantul, C.Java)	1942	5
Sato (1994: 103)	938 rural hh	Cimahi (Sukabumi, W.Java)	1942	5
Ibrahim and Weinreb (1957: 766–8)	50 urban hh	Jakarta	1953–4	5.9*
Bachtiar Rifai (1958: 39, 90)	806 rural hh	Pati (C.Java)	1956–7	4.2
ILO (1967: 27) = Ministry of Labour	2,639 urban hh	Jakarta	1957	4.3
ILO (1967: 27) = Ministry of Labour	2,180 urban hh	Surabaya	1958	4.3
ILO (1967: 27) = Ministry of Labour	123 rural hh	Wuryantoro (Solo, C.Java)	1958–9	4.9
Adyanthaya (1963: 11–12)	10,700 hh	Java (rural, throughout)	1958	4.3
Adyanthaya (1963: 11–12)	1,300 hh	Java (urban, throughout)	1958	4.8
Sukamto (1962), Wirjosudarmo (1964)	503 hh	Yogyakarta	1958	4.4
Lauw et al. (1962: 119)	46 rural hh	Pacet/Rengasdengklok (W.Java)	1961	4.4

* Children and other dependants included.
** Unusually high, according to the report.

Table 4C.2 Total number of households,
Indonesia, 1920–1939

1920	12,132,164
1921	12,265,765
1922	12,401,499
1923	12,539,414
1924	12,679,562
1925	12,821,994
1926	12,969,625
1927	13,122,109
1928	13,287,109
1929	13,456,353
1930	13,629,447
1931	13,834,123
1932	14,041,886
1933	14,252,784
1934	14,466,863
1935	14,684,172
1936	14,904,761
1937	15,128,678
1938	15,355,974
1939	15,586,701

Table 4C.3 Total number of households, Indonesia, 1971–2005

1971	24,322,589
1972	24,917,894
1973	25,528,406
1974	26,154,531
1975	26,796,684
1976	27,455,293
1977	28,130,798
1978	28,823,652
1979	29,534,317
1980	30,263,273
1981	31,140,668
1982	32,045,818
1983	32,979,691
1984	33,943,294
1985	34,937,672
1986	35,835,940
1987	36,759,990
1988	37,710,661
1989	38,688,822
1990	39,695,375
1991	40,809,866
1992	41,961,383
1993	43,151,390
1994	44,381,421
1995	45,653,084
1996	46,838,934
1997	48,065,457
1998	49,334,520
1999	50,648,103
2000	52,008,308
2001	53,416,089
2002	54,976,293
2003	56,590,330
2004	58,259,807
2005	59,982,945

APPENDIX 4D: INCOME CONTROL TOTALS, 1920–2003

1920–1939

As noted in section 4.3, the 1920–39 income control totals were based on estimates of personal income provided by Polak (1943[1979]: 70) for 'Indonesians', 'Europeans', and 'other Asians'. Polak's personal income data for the group of 'Indonesians' are based on a variety of estimates of incomes in different economic sectors, but are likely to have been underestimated, particularly for small-scale industry and a range of services. In essence, Polak used the income tax data to estimate these incomes for the groups of 'Europeans' and 'other Asians', albeit with various corrections, e.g. for non-compliance, to include some income not subject to income tax, and to exclude pensions. Polak added value added in farm agriculture and several other sources of income to approximate total income of the 'Indonesians'.

Table 4D.1 shows the estimates of total household income. 1920 is a rough estimate obtained by linking Polak's estimates of total income in 1921 to an estimate of 'reflated' gross domestic product (GDP) in constant prices (Van der Eng 2002a: 171). The estimates in Table 4D.1 are imperfect, in part because Polak's estimates are likely to be too low, in part because they only approximate disposable household income, and in part because Polak based them on population estimates that are not in line with our estimates used in Appendix 4C.

1980–2004

As noted in section 4.3, Indonesia's National Accounts do not disaggregate national income by sources of income, only by expenditure and output. Moreover, the National Accounts data are underestimated, as the successive rounds of revisions, the latest being in 2000, have shown (Van der Eng 2005). These revisions were based on the Input-Output (I-O) Tables, which were given much greater attention and where published with a significant delay, compared to the National Accounts data. For that reason the I-O Tables have been used as 'anchors' for National Accounts revisions.

The I-O Tables were also used as 'anchors' for Indonesia's System of Economic and Social Accounting Matrices and Extension (SESAME) for Indonesia (Keuning and Saleh 2000), which have been published as Social Accounting Matrices since the early 1980s. These accounts offer a fine disaggregation of total income by a variety of key socio-economic income groups, but not a disaggregation of income by size. The published accounts offer data on pre-tax disposable household income for 1980, 1985, 1990, 1993, 1995, 1998, 2000, and 2003 (BPS various years). These were interpolated with the help of National Accounts data in current prices, as follows.

First, the Social Accounting Matrices also offer revised estimates of total GDP, which are higher than in the National Accounts. The degree of underestimation of GDP was interpolated for each benchmark year, and the 1980–2003 series of the degree of

Table 4D.1 Total household income, Indonesia, 1920–1939 (million guilders)

1920	*5,870*
1921	4,587
1922	4,187
1923	3,927
1924	4,272
1925	4,452
1926	4,721
1927	4,585
1928	4,490
1929	4,623
1930	4,503
1931	3,417
1932	2,686
1933	2,217
1934	2,077
1935	2,130
1936	2,090
1937	2,503
1938	2,674
1939	2,685

Table 4D.2 Total pre-tax disposable household income, Indonesia, 1980–2004 (billion rupiah)

1980	31,172
1981	37,710
1982	42,314
1983	55,982
1984	65,740
1985	71,932
1986	76,365
1987	93,085
1988	111,928
1989	134,662
1990	158,545
1991	187,085
1992	210,384
1993	244,548
1994	310,805
1995	402,104
1996	438,717
1997	479,912
1998	671,984
1999	787,491
2000	988,484
2001	1,248,222
2002	1,461,546
2003	1,638,095
2004	1,881,756

underestimation was used to multiply the existing GDP series from the National Accounts with, to yield a new series of GDP in current prices.

Secondly, the shares of total pre-tax disposable household income in GDP were calculated for each benchmark year and these shares were interpolated. The 1980–2003 series representing the share of disposable household income in GDP was multiplied with the new GDP series in current prices, to yield the annual series of total disposable household income for 1985–2003. The 2003 share was used to estimate total disposable household income for 2004. The estimates in Table 4D.2 are firmly anchored to the official data of disposable household income for benchmark years.

APPENDIX 4E: USING HOUSEHOLD SURVEY DATA, 1982–2004

So far as we are aware, no other researchers have used the income variables from all available Susenas surveys. Most have argued that this is because the quality of data on income is inferior to the quality of data on expenditure. Whether or not this is true, it is almost certainly the case that for the very rich, ignoring savings will lead to large measurement errors when estimating inequality.

Generally speaking, there are two ways of measuring income in the Susenas.

(a) Approximately every three years, the Susenas contains an income module, which contains data on earnings from employment over the past month, from agricultural businesses over the past year, from non-agricultural businesses over the past quarter, and from other sources over the past month. In these years, the Susenas data files contain a variable with the English term *income*. However, because this variable follows a national accounting concept of income (e.g. it includes imputed rent for owner-occupiers), and not a Haig–Simons definition of income (i.e. the money value of the net increase over a period of time in a person's potential to consume), it is not suitable for our purposes. In some years (e.g. 1993, 1996), it is possible to create an income variable that includes earnings from employment, agriculture businesses, non-agricultural businesses, and other sources, but not imputed rent. However, this is not feasible for all years in which the Susenas includes an income module. Using this broader definition of income would substantially reduce the number of years for which we were able to estimate top income shares.

(b) In virtually all years, the Susenas contains questions on earnings. The question asks about cash earnings (*upah/gaji berupa uang*) and in-kind earnings (*upah/gaji berupa barang*). For comparability, we opt to use this simpler definition of income in our analysis, creating a measure of earnings that sums both cash and in-kind earnings. Note that in most cases, respondents were asked for their earnings over the past month, which implies that seasonal variations in income and the moment during the year when the survey is conducted may distort the estimated distributions, compared to a situation where households are asked about their annual income.

For 1999 and 2002, we used the core to calculate top shares, on the basis that this was more comparable with earlier and later years than using the income module. In calculating top shares, we sum earnings to the household level. Households with zero or negative earnings are ignored in the calculations.

Our data suggest that, for most years, average earned household income constituted between one-half and one-third of average household income from the National Accounts. By way of contrast, note that the ratio of the US wage bill to household income over the period 1917–2004 ranged between 0.62 and 0.95, with a mean of 0.79 (Piketty and Saez 2006a: tables A0 and B1). The lower share of wage income in Indonesia reflects the greater importance of self-employment earnings in developing nations than is the case in developed economies.

Although it is theoretically possible that self-employment income is distributed across households in a very different way from earned income, this appears not to be the case in practice. In Table 4E.2, we show estimates of top wage shares and top income shares, based on the 1996 Susenas, for which we are able to estimate both measures. The estimates are quite close, with the ratio of the two ranging between 0.87 and 1.00. In most cases, our estimated top shares are higher when based on earned income than on total income.

For comparison purposes, we also calculated three inequality measures, being the Gini coefficient, the mean log deviation, and the Theil index. We computed each of these measures for both earned income and expenditure (*rata-rata pengeluran rumah tangga*). As noted above, our top income share estimates follow the previous literature in not adjusting for household size, and treating each household as a single observation. Similarly, we do not make any adjustment for household size in these estimates (consequently, our expenditure Ginis do not perfectly match those in Cameron 2002).

These results are shown in Table 4E.3. In general, we do not observe strong trends in these measures, either upwards or downwards. For example, the Gini for earned household income ranges from 0.43 to 0.52, while the Gini for household expenditure is typically about 10 points lower, ranging from 0.32 to 0.40.

Micro-data from Susenas were obtained from the Australian Social Science Data Archive at the Australian National University (http://www.assda.anu.edu.au), and the Demography program at ANU. Two Susenas surveys were omitted from our analysis:

- Earned income data from the 1980 Susenas are so highly skewed (an apparent Gini of 0.85) that we formed the view that some incomes are probably monthly, and others are annual. We therefore decided not to use the survey.
- Earned income in the 2005 Susenas (core) appears to have been top-coded. The highest wage levels in the 2005 survey are about 100 times smaller than in the 2003 and 2004 surveys. We therefore opted not to use this survey.

We contacted Statistics Indonesia, and were told that it was not possible to obtain the micro-data for any Susenas surveys conducted prior to 1980. To the best of our knowledge, this chapter therefore incorporates all available Susenas income surveys.

Most Susenas codebooks (with English translations) are available at http://www.rand.org/labor/bps.data/webdocs/susenas/susenas_main.htm.

Table 4E.4 shows the income cut-offs used in this study.

Table 4E.1 Susenas summary statistics, 1982–2004 (households)

Year	Sample Size	Core or Income Module	Average Earned Household Income (Susenas)	Average Total Household Income (from appendices 4C and 4D)
1982	44,960	Core	754,979	1,320,423
1987	13,315	Module	1,203,789	2,532,249
1990	23,310	Module	1,430,713	3,994,037
1993	32,013	Module	2,211,095	5,667,217
1996	32,691	Module	2,886,196	9,366,504
1998	83,292	Core	4,581,106	13,620,969
1999	81,531	Core	5,881,665	15,548,283
2000	75,931	Core	6,880,478	19,006,261
2001	76,852	Core	9,563,413	23,367,910
2002	79,927	Core	11,255,366	26,585,031
2003	76,486	Core	12,364,493	28,946,561
2004	86,821	Core	13,422,218	32,299,389

Note: Sample sizes refer to the number of households with positive employee earnings.

Table 4E.2 Comparing top share estimates based on total income and earned income, Indonesia (1996 only)

	Top 10%	Top 5%	Top 1%	Top 0.5%	Top 0.1%
Based on total income	35.34	23.85	9.37	5.75	2.06
Based on earned income	39.37	25.30	9.69	6.59	2.06
Ratio	0.90	0.94	0.97	0.87	1.00

Sources: Authors' estimates, based on 1996 Susenas.

Table 4E.3 Susenas inequality estimates, 1982–2004

Year	Earned household income			Household expenditure		
	Gini	Mean Log Deviation	Theil	Gini	Mean Log Deviation	Theil
1982	0.45	0.38	0.37			
1987	0.43	0.35	0.32	0.34	0.19	0.21
1990	0.51	0.48	0.51	0.38	0.24	0.27
1993	0.5	0.48	0.47	0.39	0.25	0.29
1996	0.52	0.59	0.5	0.4	0.27	0.32
1998	0.46	0.4	0.49	0.34	0.19	0.22
1999	0.47	0.41	0.55	0.36	0.22	0.3
2000	0.47	0.41	0.54	0.32	0.18	0.2
2001	0.47	0.41	0.51	0.33	0.18	0.2
2002	0.46	0.39	0.44	0.36	0.22	0.27
2003	0.45	0.37	0.43	0.34	0.19	0.22
2004	0.44	0.34	0.38	0.35	0.21	0.25

Note: Expenditure data are not available in the version of the 1982 Susenas available to us.

Table 4E.4 Income cut-offs for given percentiles, Indonesia, 1982–2004 (million rupiah)

Year	Top 10%	Top 5%	Top 1%	Top 0.5%	Top 0.1%	Top 0.05%	Top 0.01%
1982	1.5	2.1	3.6	4.4	7.2	9.4	19.6
1987	2.4	3.1	5.1	6.4	10.8	12.5	20.4
1990	2.9	4.0	8.4	10.6	36.0	42.6	57.0
1993	4.6	6.4	13.0	18.0	32.3	39.0	71.7
1996	6.0	8.3	16.2	24.0	50.4	60.0	85.8
1998	8.5	11.4	24.0	33.0	76.5	135.2	600.0
1999	10.4	14.3	30.9	48.0	147.2	258.7	727.2
2000	12.4	16.8	37.2	52.8	196.1	260.8	743.3
2001	18.0	23.0	49.5	79.8	274.5	286.7	541.7
2002	21.6	29.4	57.6	84.0	180.0	240.0	759.6
2003	23.6	30.0	60.6	90.0	216.0	324.0	874.3
2004	25.2	34.8	69.6	97.0	194.4	258.0	492.0

REFERENCES

Adyanthaya, N. K. (1963). 'Report on the Labour Force Sample Survey in Java and Madura', *Ekonomi dan Keuangan Indonesia*, 14: 1–96.

Alatas, V. and F. Bourguignon (2000). 'The Evolution of the Distribution of Income during Indonesian Fast Growth: 1980–1996', unpublished paper, Research Project on Microeconomics of Income Distribution Dynamics. Washington, DC: Inter-American Development Bank and The World Bank.

Alvaredo, F. (2007). 'The Rich in Argentina over the Twentieth Century: From the Conservative Republic to the Peronist Experience and beyond 1932–2004', Paris School of Economics Working Paper 2007–02.

—— and E. Saez (2006). 'Income and Wealth Concentration in Spain in a Historical and Fiscal Perspective', CEPR Discussion Paper 5836. London: Centre for Economic Policy Research.

Asher, M. G. (1997). 'Reforming the Tax System in Indonesia', in W. Thirsk (ed.) *Tax Reform in Developing Countries*. Washington DC: The World Bank: 127–66.

Atkinson, A. B. (2005). 'Top Incomes in the UK over the Twentieth Century', *Journal of the Royal Statistical Society, Series A*, 168: 325–43.

—— (2007a). 'Measuring Top Incomes: Methodological Issues', in Atkinson and Piketty (2007: 18–42).

—— (2007b). 'Top Incomes in the United Kingdom over the Twentieth Century', in Atkinson and Piketty (2007: 82–140).

—— and A. Leigh (2007a). 'The Distribution of Top Incomes in Australia', *Economic Record*, 83: 247–61.

—— —— (2007b). 'The Distribution of Top Incomes in Five Anglo-Saxon Countries over the Twentieth Century'. Canberra: Australian National University, mimeo.

—— —— (2008). 'Top Incomes in New Zealand 1921–2005: Understanding the Effects of Marginal Tax Rates, Migration Threat, and the Macroeconomy', *Review of Income and Wealth*, 54(2): 149–65.

—— and T. Piketty (eds.) (2007). *Top Incomes over the Twentieth Century: A Contrast between Continental European and English Speaking Countries*. Oxford: Oxford University Press.

—— and W. Salverda (2005). 'Top Incomes in the Netherlands and the United Kingdom over the Twentieth Century', *Journal of the European Economic Association*, 3(4): 1–32.

Banerjee, A. and T. Piketty (2004). 'Top Indian Incomes, 1922–2000', CEPR Discussion Paper No. 4632. London: Centre for Economic Policy Research.

—— —— (2005). 'Top Indian Incomes, 1922–2000', *World Bank Economic Review*, 19: 1–20.

Baum, C. F., M. E. Schaffer, and S. Stillman (2007). 'ivreg2: Stata module for extended instrumental variables/2SLS, GMM and AC/HAC, LIML and k-class regression'. Available at http://ideas.repec.org/c/boc/bocode/s425401.html.

Boeke, J. H. (1926). 'Inlandsche Budgetten', *Koloniale Studiën*, 10: 229–334.

Booth, A. (1988). 'Living Standards and the Distribution of Income in Colonial Indonesia: A Review of the Evidence', *Journal of Southeast Asian Studies*, 19: 310–43.

BPS (1963). *Sensus Penduduk 1961 Republik Indonesia: Hasil Pendafteran Rumah-Tangga Bln. Maret 1961, Seluruh Indonesia* (Population Census 1961 Republic of Indonesia:

Results of Household Enumeration March 1961, Whole of Indonesia). Jakarta: Biro Pusat Statistik.

BPS (various years). *Sistem Neraca Sosial Ekonomi Indonesia* (The System of Socio-economic Accounts of Indonesia), 1990, 1993, 1998, 2000, 2003. Jakarta: Badan Pusat Statistik.

Cameron, L. (2002). 'Growth with or without Equity? The Distributional Impact of Indonesian Development', *Asian-Pacific Economic Literature*, 16(2): 1–17.

CKS (1928). 'Onderzoek naar Gezinsuitgaven in Nederlandsch-Indië Gedurende Augustus 1925 en het Jaar 1926', *Mededeelingen van het Centraal Kantoor voor de Statistiek No.60*. Weltevreden: Albrecht.

CKS (1939). 'Een Onderzoek naar de Levenswijze der Gemeentekoelies te Batavia in 1937', *Mededeelingen van het Centraal Kantoor voor de Statistiek No.177*. Batavia: Cyclostyle Centrale.

Davies, J. B., S. Sandstrom, A. Shorrocks, and E. N. Wolff (2006). 'The World Distribution of Household Wealth'. Helsinki: UNU WIDER. Available at http://www.wider.unu.edu/research/2006–2007/2006–2007–1/wider-wdhw-launch-5–12–2006/wider-wdhw-report-5–12–2006.pdf.

Deaton, A. (1997). *The Analysis of Household Surveys: A Microeconometric Approach to Development Policy*. Baltimore: Johns Hopkins University Press.

Dell, F. (2005). 'Top Incomes in Germany and Switzerland over the Twentieth Century', *Journal of the European Economic Association*, 3: 412–21.

—— (2007). 'Top Incomes in Germany throughout the Twentieth Century: 1891–1998', in Atkinson and Piketty (2007: 365–425).

—— T. Piketty, and E. Saez (2007). 'Income and Wealth Concentration in Switzerland over the Twentieth Century', in Atkinson and Piketty (2007: 472–500).

Doebele, J. and C. Vorasarun (2006). 'Indonesia's 40 Richest', 18 September. Available at http://www.forbes.com/lists/global/2006/0918/063.html. The ranking can be found at http://www.forbes.com/lists/2006/80/06indonesia_Indonesias-40–Richest_Rank.html.

Dris, M. D. (1958). 'Taxation in Indonesia', *Ekonomi dan Keuangan Indonesia*, 11: 404–528.

Fasseur, C. (1994). 'Cornerstone or Stumbling Block: Racial Classification and the Late Colonial State in Indonesia', in R. Cribb (ed.) *The Late Colonial State in Indonesia: Political and Economic Foundations of the Netherlands Indies 1880–1942*. Leiden: KITLV Press: 31–56.

Fields, G. S., P. L. Cichello, S. Freije, M. Menéndez, and D. Newhouse (2003). 'For Richer or for Poorer? Evidence from Indonesia, South Africa, Spain, and Venezuela', *Journal of Economic Inequality*, 1: 67–99.

Groves, R. and M. Couper (1998). *Nonresponse in Household Interview Surveys*. New York: Wiley.

Hill, H. (1996). *The Indonesian Economy since 1966: Southeast Asia's Emerging Giant*. Cambridge: Cambridge University Press.

Huender, W. and J. W. Meijer Ranneft (1926). *Onderzoek naar den Belastingdruk op de Inlandsche Bevolking* (Investigation into the Tax Burden on the Indigenous Population). Weltevreden: Landsdrukkerij.

Huizenga, L. H. (1958). *Het Koeliebudgetonderzoek op Java in 1939–40*. Wageningen: Vada.

Ibrahim, A. M. and W. F. Weinreb (1957). 'Penjelidikan Biaja Hidup di Djakarta', *Ekonomi dan Keunangan Indonesia*, 10: 738–95.

ILO (1967). *Household Income and Expenditure Statistics No. 1, 1950–1964*. Geneva: International Labour Office.

Keuning, S. J. and K. Saleh (2000). 'SAM and SESAME in Indonesia: Results, Usage and Institutionalization', in *Studies in Methods, Series F, No. 75/Vol. 2, Handbook of National Accounting: Household Accounting. Experience in Concepts and Compilation, vol. 2: Household Satellite Extensions*. New York: United Nations, Department of Economic and Social Affairs, Statistics Division: 355–97.

Kuznets, S. (1955). 'Economic Growth and Income Inequality', *American Economic Review*, 45: 1–28.

Landais, C. (2007). 'Les Hauts Revenus en France 1998–2006: une explosion des inégalités?', Paris School of Economics Working Paper.

Lauw Tjin Giok, I. Tarwotjo, Djokosaptono, and R. Rasidi (1962). 'A Study of the Nutritional Status of Two Economic Levels in Tjiwalen and Amansari Villages of West Java', in *Laporan Kongres Ilmu Pengetahuan Nasional Kedua, Djilid Kedua Seksi A-1*. Djakarta: MIPI: 113–44.

Leigh, A. (2007). 'How Closely do Top Income Shares Track Other Measures of Inequality?', *Economic Journal*, 117: F619–F633.

—— (2009). 'Top Incomes', in W. Salverda, B. Nolan, and T. Smeeding (eds.) *The Oxford Handbook of Economic Inequality*. Oxford: Oxford University Press: 150–76.

Lent, G. E. and W. Missorten (1967). 'Survey of Indonesia's Tax System', unpublished document, Fiscal Affairs Department. Washington, DC: International Monetary Fund. 16 November.

Lerche, D. (1978). *Steuersystem Indonesien* (Indonesia's Tax System). Munich: Weltforum Verlag.

Lindert, P. H. (2000). 'Three Centuries of Inequality in Britain and America', in A. B. Atkinson and F. Bourguignon (eds.) *Handbook of Income Distribution*. Amsterdam: Elsevier: 167–216.

—— and J. G. Williamson (2003). 'Does Globalization make the World more Unequal?', in M. D. Bordo, A. M. Taylor, and J. G. Williamson (eds.) *Globalization in Historical Perspective*. Chicago: University of Chicago Press: 227–70.

Mansury, R. (1992). *The Indonesian Income Tax: A Case Study in Reform of a Developing Country*. Singapore: Asian-Pacific Tax and Investment Research Centre.

Moore, J. C., L. L. Stinson, and E. J. Welniak (2000). 'Income Measurement Error in Surveys: A Review', *Journal of Official Statistics*, 16: 331–62.

Moriguchi, C. and E. Saez (2008). 'The Evolution of Income Concentration in Japan, 1886–2005: Evidence from Income Tax Statistics', *Review of Economics and Statistics*, 90: 713–34.

Nolan, B. (2007). 'Long-Term Trends in Top Income Shares in Ireland', in Atkinson and Piketty (2007: 501–30).

Oberndörfer, D., H. Avenarius, and D. Lerche (1976). *Steuersystem und Steuerverwaltung in Indonesien* (Tax System and Tax Administration in Indonesia). Stuttgart: Bundesministerium für wirtschaftliche Zusammenarbeit.

Ochse, J. J. and G. J. A. Terra (1934). *Geld- en Producten-Huishouding, Volksvoeding en -Gezondheid in Koetowingagoen*. Buitenzorg: Archipel.

Piketty, T. (2001). *Les Hauts Revenus en France au 20ème siècle*. Paris: Grasset.

—— (2003). 'Income Inequality in France, 1901–1998', *Journal of Political Economy*, 111: 1004–42.

—— (2007). 'Income, Wage and Wealth Inequality in France, 1901–1998', in Atkinson and Piketty (2007: 43–81).

Piketty, T. and N. Qian (2006). 'Income Inequality and Progressive Income Taxation in China and India, 1986–2015', CEPR Discussion Paper No. 5703. London: Centre for Economic Policy Research.

—— and E. Saez (2003). 'Income Inequality in the United States, 1913–1998', *Quarterly Journal of Economics*, 118: 1–39.

—— —— (2006a). 'Income Inequality in the United States'. Tables and Figures updated to 2004 in Excel format, http://emlab.berkeley.edu/users/saez/.

—— —— (2006b). 'The Evolution of Top Incomes: A Historical and International Perspective', *American Economic Review*, 96: 200–5.

Polak, J. J. (1979) [1943]. *The National Income of the Netherlands Indies, 1921–1939*. New York: Netherlands and Netherlands-Indies Council of the Institute of Pacific Relations. (Reprinted in P. Creutzberg (ed.) *Changing Economy in Indonesia*, v: *National Income*. The Hague: Nijhoff, 1979: 25–102.)

Postmus, S. and A. G. Van Veen (1949). 'Dietary Surveys in Java and East-Indonesia', *Chronica Naturae*, 105: 229–36, 261–8, 316–23.

Ragayah, H. M. Z. (2005). 'Income Distribution in East Asian Developing Countries: Recent Trends', *Asian-Pacific Economic Literature*, 19(1): 36–54.

Reys, R. J. W. (1925). *De Inkomstenbelasting der Inlanders en met Hen Gelijkgestelden in Nederlandsch Oost-Indië* (Income Tax of Native Indonesians and their Equals in the Netherlands East-Indies). The Hague: Nijhoff.

Riihelä, M., R. Sullström, and M. Tuomala (2005). 'Trends in Top Income Shares in Finland', VATT Discussion Papers 371. Helsinki: Government Institute for Economic Research.

Roine, J. and D. Waldenström (2008). 'The Evolution of Top Incomes in an Egalitarian Society: Sweden, 1903–2004', *Journal of Public Economics*, 92: 366–87.

Saez, E. (2004). 'Reported Incomes and Marginal Tax Rates, 1960–2000: Evidence and Policy Implications', in J. Poterba (ed.) *Tax Policy and the Economy*, vol. 18. Cambridge, Mass.: MIT Press.

—— and M. Veall (2005). 'The Evolution of High Incomes in Northern America: Lessons from Canadian Evidence', *American Economic Review*, 95: 831–49.

Sato, S. (1994). *War, Nationalism and Peasants: Java under the Japanese Occupation*. Sydney: Allen & Unwin.

Scholte, G. (1929). 'Eenige Bijzonderheden Betreffende Het Aantal Aangeslagenen in De Inkomstenbelasting en Hun Belastbaar Inkomen over het Jaar 1925' (Some Peculiarities about the Number of People Assessed for Income Tax and their Taxable Income for 1925), in *Mededeelingen van het Centraal Kantoor voor de Statistiek*, 69. Weltevreden: Landsdrukkerij.

Siswanto, B. (2003). 'Indonesia', in Y. Kitamura (ed.) *International Comparisons of Taxation in Developing Countries, 2003*. Tokyo: Keio University, Faculty of Business and Commerce: 1–40. Available at http://www.ic.keio.ac.jp/jjwbgsp/researchpapers.html.

Sukamto (1962). 'Laporan Penjelidikan Biaja Hidup untuk Daerah Istimewa Jogjakarta 1954–1960', in *Laporan Kongres Ilmu Pengetahuan Nasional Kedua, Djilid Kesembilan Seksi E-3*. Djakarta: MIPI: 331–78.

Surbakti, P. (1995). *Indonesia's National Socio-Economic Survey: A Continual Data Source for Analysis on Welfare Development*. Jakarta: Central Bureau of Statistics.

Timmer, C. P. (2004). 'The Road to Pro-Poor Growth: The Indonesian Experience in Regional Perspective', *Bulletin of Indonesian Economic Studies*, 40: 177–207.

—— (2005). 'Operationalizing Pro-Poor Growth: Country Study for the World Bank, Indonesia', unpublished manuscript, June. Available at http://siteresources.worldbank. org/INTPGI/Resources/342674–1115051237044/oppgindonesiaMay2005.pdf.

Uppal, J. S. (2003). *Tax Reform in Indonesia.* Yogyakarta: Gadjah Mada University Press.

Van der Eng, P. (1992). 'The Real Domestic Product of Indonesia, 1880–1989', *Explorations in Economic History,* 28: 343–73.

—— (1996). *Agricultural Growth in Indonesia: Productivity Change and Policy Impact since 1880.* New York: St Martin's Press.

—— (2002a). 'Indonesia's Growth Performance in the 20th Century', in A. Maddison, D. S. Prasada Rao, and W. Shepherd (eds.) *The Asian Economies in the Twentieth Century.* Cheltenham: Edward Elgar: 143–79.

—— (2002b). 'Bridging a Gap: A Reconstruction of Population Patterns in Indonesia, 1930–1961', *Asian Studies Review,* 26: 487–509.

—— (2005). 'Indonesia's New National Accounts', *Bulletin of Indonesian Economic Studies,* 41: 253–62.

—— (2008). 'The Sources of Long-Term Economic Growth in Indonesia, 1880–2007', Working Papers in Economics and Econometrics No. 499. Canberra: School of Economics, ANU College of Business and Economics.

Volksvoeding (1940). 'Patjet-Rapport: Onderzoek naar de Voeding en Voedingstoestand van de Bevolking te Patjet (Regentschap Tjiandjoer) in 1937–1939', *Mededeeling van het Instituut voor Volksvoeding No.2.* Batavia: Instituut voor Volksvoeding.

—— (1941). 'Goenoeng Kidoel-Rapport: Onderzoek naar de Voeding en Voedingstoestand der Bevolking in het Regentschap Goenoeng Kidoel (Djokdjakarta) in 1938–1941', *Mededeeling van het Instituut voor Volksvoeding No.5.* Batavia: Instituut voor Volksvoeding.

Wirjosudarmo, S. (1964). *Beberapa Penemuan pokok Penjelidikan Anggaran Belandja Keluarga di Daerah Istimewa Jogjakarta, Agustus 1958–Agustus 1959.* Yogyakarta: Gadjah Mada University.

World Bank (2005a). *Pro-Poor Growth in the 1990s, Lessons and Insights from 14 Countries: Operationalizing Pro-Poor Growth Research Program.* Washington, DC: World Bank.

—— (2005b). *World Development Report 2006.* Washington, DC: World Bank.

5

Top Incomes in a Rapidly Growing Economy

Singapore

A. B. Atkinson

5.1 INTRODUCTION

The economy of Singapore has grown rapidly. According to the estimates of Maddison (2003: 185), GDP per capita in PPP terms increased between 1959 and 2001 by a factor of 10. In 1959, GDP per capita in Singapore was around the world average; today it is more than three times the world average. Singapore was identified by the Commission on Growth and Development (2008) as one of thirteen 'success stories' of countries that have maintained high, sustained growth in the post-war period. The Singapore government has adopted distinctive policies, including state investment funds and a tripartite approach to labour relations. These policies are likely to have had implications not only for growth but also for the distribution of the benefits from that growth. In 1998 the UN Economic Commission for Asia and the Pacific commented:

Singapore has achieved enviable economic and social progress. Absolute poverty has been virtually eliminated. Income inequality has remained relatively stable. It thus makes an interesting study on how the fruits of growth have been more or less equally distributed. (1998: 131)

More recently, the Asian Development Bank (2007: 11) concluded that there was no evidence for Singapore of a Kuznets curve, where income inequality first rises

I am grateful to Salvatore Morelli and Thomas Piketty for helpful suggestions and to the Department of Statistics, Singapore, for kindly supplying a table from a publication that I had not been able to locate in the UK. I am solely responsible for the views expressed.

and than falls as a country develops. It is however possible that, as Singapore has become richer, it has joined those OECD countries that have seen rising income inequality as a result of globalization and technological change. Singapore's response to the 1997 financial crisis was again distinctive, and may have led to a rise in inequality. A study by the Singapore Department of Statistics found that income inequality had increased at the end of the 1990s and stated that 'widening income disparity was a reflection of globalisation and Singapore's transition to a knowledge-based economy' (2002: 7).

This chapter examines one aspect of the income distribution in Singapore— the shares of top incomes—using information published as a result of the administration of the income tax. Although tax data were used in earlier studies of developing countries (see, for example, Okigbo 1968), they have tended in recent years to be rejected as a source. In one sense, this is not surprising. Income taxes only cover a part, sometimes a very small part, of the population. The resulting data cannot provide a picture of the overall distribution. The income tax data reflect the specific features of the tax system, and are very much subject to avoidance and evasion. But, despite these weaknesses, the tax data have certain advantages. Most importantly, the tax data are typically available annually and for a long run of years. The data used in this chapter begin in 1947, when the personal income tax law was enacted, and cover, with a few exceptions, the entire period up to the present day. The series therefore starts in the colonial period, spans Independence and the separation from Malaysia, and goes right through to the modern Singapore economy. As far as I know, such a sixty-year time series—parallel to those for OECD countries (see Atkinson and Piketty 2007)—has not been constructed for Singapore. Rao and Ramakrishnan, for example, show the income tax distribution for 1966 (1980: 21), but do not assemble a time series of data. No one, as far as I know, has researched the colonial period in Singapore.

The income tax data cannot be employed on their own. The published distributions of taxpayers by income ranges have to be accompanied by external control totals for the total adult population and for total household income. The production of these control totals is described, along with the basic tax data, in section 5.2. This section also describes data on the distribution of earnings among contributors to the Central Provident Fund, which can be used to supplement the information contained in the income tax tabulations. The results for top income shares 1947 to 2005 are set out in section 5.3, together with evidence for the distribution of earnings covering the period 1965 to 2007. The interpretation of the findings in the light of the development of the Singapore economy is the subject of section 5.4. The results for Singapore are compared with those for the United Kingdom (the former colonial power) and for thirteen other countries in section 5.5. The main conclusions are summarized in section 5.6.

5.2 THE UNDERLYING DATA

Income taxation was employed in many British colonial territories, and the colonial administrators were required to publish detailed reports, which typically included information on the distribution of taxpayers by income range and total incomes.[1] Income tax was introduced into the colony of Singapore with effect from 1 January 1948.[2] The first *Report of the Income Tax Department*, published in 1950, gave details of the number of taxpayers assessed in 1948 by ranges of assessed income. The same information was published in annual reports (referred to as AR) for subsequent years and continues to the present day in the form of the Annual Reports of the Inland Revenue Authority of Singapore. The information is reproduced in the *Yearbook of Statistics, Singapore* (referred to as *YSS*), which began publication in 1967. From these sources, income tax data have been located for all income years apart from 1955 and 1992. The data sources are listed in Table 5A.1.

Income Tax Data

The income tax data show the number of taxpayers assessed by ranges of assessed income and the total amounts of assessed income per range. The number of ranges was typically ten and they extended up to many multiples of the mean: for example, in 1960 the first range started at 1.46 times the mean, and the top range at approximately 100 times the mean. No information is available on the sources of income by range.

The data reflect the administrative process by which they are produced. For example, the data refer to a 'year of assessment': e.g. in *YSS* 1969 there is information for the year of assessment 1967, which refers to 'assessments made during the period 1.1.67–31.12.68'. These figures are taken to refer to incomes during the year 1966 (see Rao and Ramakrishnan 1980: 21), referred to as income year (IY) 1966. In this case, the assessments are those made in the twenty-four months after the end of the income year, but in a few cases the figures are given only after twelve months. For example, the figures for the IY 1986 are given (in *YSS* 1989) only for assessments made during the period 1 January 1987 to 31 December 1987. The twelve-months figures may be different, particularly at the very top incomes: for example, for IY 1987, the shares were as follows:

---

[1] This chapter is an outgrowth of a larger project on top income shares in British colonies before and after independence. The income tax data for (Dutch) colonial Indonesia have been exploited by Leigh and van der Eng (2009 and Chapter 4) to provide estimates for 1920–39.

[2] Income taxation in Singapore was first administered by the Income Tax Department, created in 1947, which became the Inland Revenue Department following self-government in 1959. This was replaced in turn in 1992 by the Inland Revenue Authority of Singapore.

twelve-months assessment (*YSS* 1989: table 13.7)
share of top 10%   top 5%   top 1%   top 0.5%
33.9   25.5   10.0   6.3

twenty-four-months assessment (*YSS* 1990: table 13.7)
share of top 10%   top 5%   top 1%   top 0.5%
36.0   26.1   11.4   7.7

This needs to be taken into account when considering the estimates based on only twelve months (this applies to the seven years IY 1980 to IY 1986 inclusive, and to 1993).

The income tax was paid by non-resident as well as resident individuals. In what follows, attention is focused on Singapore residents. It is however interesting to note that in 1947, non-resident taxpayers accounted for 11 per cent of the total, and constituted 3 of the 11 people in the top tax bracket. By 2005, the percentage of non-resident taxpayers had fallen to 3 per cent, and they accounted for only 31 of the 2,121 people in the top tax bracket.

The income tax is levied on the tax unit, combining the incomes of husbands and wives, but the wife was allowed to elect for separate taxation. No information is given in the published tables about such separate elections. In what follows, I take the control total as the total number of adults, which means that the resulting estimates may overstate the top income shares among tax units. (It may be noted that this is different from the household approach adopted for Indonesia in the previous chapter.)

Use of income tax data is always open to the charge that the data take no account of tax avoidance and tax evasion. These are clearly important considerations. Since the control totals for income are based on National Accounts (see below), the estimates made here of the income *shares* understate the true top income shares to the extent that incomes are not declared. In this sense the estimates provide a lower bound. In the case of colonial Singapore, tax evasion was a concern. For example, in 1959 there was a commission of inquiry into the bank account of one citizen and 'the Income Tax Department leakage in connection therewith' (Colony of Singapore 1959). The Annual Report for 1960 announced that 'amendments to the Income Tax were introduced with a view to tightening up legislation against evasion of tax. The Comptroller is now given wider powers to obtain information and to have full and free access to all land, buildings and places, and all books and documents in the execution of his duties. The time limit for raising additional assessments is extended from six to twelve years' (State of Singapore 1963: 69). The present Inland Revenue Authority of Singapore devotes considerable resources to tax collection, and provides positive encouragement to tax compliance through emphasizing the role of taxes in financing key government services such as schools. It is therefore possible that compliance today is higher. If that is the case, today's top shares are closer to the true values. Any downward (upward) trend is therefore under (over) stated. The reader should therefore bear in mind that both the level and the trend of the estimated shares may be affected by tax non-compliance.

Interpolation

Since the basic data are in the form of grouped tabulations, and the intervals do not in general coincide with the percentage groups of the population with which we are concerned (such as the top 0.1 per cent), we have to interpolate in order to arrive at the shares of total income. Given that there is information on both the number of persons and the total income in the range, we use the mean-split histogram. The rationale is as follows. Assuming, as seems reasonable in the case of top incomes, that the frequency distribution is non-increasing, then restricted upper and lower bounds can be calculated for the income shares (Gastwirth 1972). These bounds are limiting forms of the split histogram, with one of the two densities tending to zero or infinity—see Atkinson (2005). Guaranteed to lie between these is the histogram split at the interval mean with sections of positive density on either side.

The ranges are in some cases quite broad, and the possible errors of interpolation need to be taken into account. For example, in 2005, taxpayers above $300,000 constituted 0.77 per cent of the adult population, and those above $200,000 were 1.59 per cent. (All dollars are Singapore dollars.) If we make no assumption about the distribution, then the 'gross' bounds for the share are from 13.05 to 13.39 per cent (these are calculated by assuming either that all incomes are equal to the mean for the range or that people are concentrated at the end points). If we assume that the frequency distribution is non-increasing (which rules out both of the bounds just described), then the restricted bounds are from 13.23 to 13.30, which are quite close. The mean-split histogram method gives a value for the share of the top 1 per cent of 13.28 per cent. In some years, however, the bounds are much wider apart. In view of this, I have not interpolated where the difference between the refined upper and lower bounds is more than 20 per cent. For example, in 2000, the refined lower bound for the share of the top 0.5 per cent was 8.6 per cent and the refined upper bound was 10.6 per cent, and no figure is used for this percentile group in this year.

In general, no extrapolation is made into the open upper interval, except in a few cases where the upper interval is close to one of the key percentages. Where the difference is less than 10 per cent, a simple Pareto extrapolation is used to calculate the share. For example, in 2001 and 2002, the top interval (above $1 million) contains 0.054 per cent of adults, and an estimate has been made of the share of the top 0.05 per cent. This has not however been done for 2005, when the top interval contained 0.075 per cent of adults.

Control Total for Population

The control totals for the adult population, defined as those aged 15 and over, have been taken from the demographic data in the *Yearbook of Statistics*. In 1991, the population estimates were revised downwards, reducing the estimated adult population for 1981 by 5.1 per cent. The figures for 1980 and earlier years have been reduced by this percentage.

For years where age composition is not available (prior to 1968 and for 1971 and 1973), the proportions of adult to total population were interpolated linearly and applied to estimates of the total population. The total population is available for census years (1947 and 1957), and then in the form of mid-year estimates from 1960; the remaining years are from Maddison (2003: 165), with 1948 and 1949 being interpolated. The resulting series is shown in Table 5A.2. As noted above, this overstates the number of tax units.

Control Total for Household Income

The construction of a control total for total household income (at current prices) proceeds here by first considering a measure of national income and then seeking to link total household income to national income.

In the case of national income, we can work backwards from 2005. For that year, current price GDP is estimated at $194,242 million (*YSS* 2007: table 5.1). As is recognized, a substantial part of GDP is generated by foreign companies and foreign individuals resident in Singapore. The Singapore Department of Statistics makes an estimate of 'Indigenous Gross National Income (GNI)' by subtracting the share of resident foreigners and resident foreign companies ($77,199 million) and adding net factor receipts of Singaporeans from the rest of the world ($31,722 million). The Indigenous GNI is some three-quarters of GDP. This percentage has fallen over the period since the Indigenous GNI series was introduced: for the first year, 1967, the percentage was 96.0. In what follows, the series for Indigenous GNI is used from 1967 to 2005, derived from successive issues of *YSS*. For the years 1960 to 1966, estimates are published only for GDP and a fixed percentage (96 per cent) has been taken of the *YSS* series.

It is not easy to obtain more than rough estimates for years before 1960. At the beginning of the period studied—the 1940s—the National Accounts were at best rudimentary. The estimates by Benham for the Federation of Malaya and Singapore combined are stated by him to 'involve a considerable amount of guesswork' (1951: 1). He goes on to say that 'separate estimates of national income for each territory would involve still more guesswork' (1951: 1), and it was not until 1959 that he attempted to make a first estimate for Singapore alone (relating to 1956). Maddison has made estimates of GDP (2003: 175), but these relate to constant purchasing power at 1990 international dollars.

Interestingly, the change over time from 1956 to 1960 is almost exactly the same as that in the current price GDP series, taking the Benham estimate for 1956 and the *YSS* figure for 1960.[3] The Maddison series is used to interpolate for the years 1957–9 and to extrapolate backwards to 1950. For the years 1947 to 1949, in the absence of other information, a growth rate of current price GDP per capita of 7.5 per cent per annum has been assumed. The resulting series is shown in Table 5A.2.

At the start of the period studied, expenditure by private households constituted a large proportion of national income: in the estimate for 1956 by Benham (1959), it was some 92.5 per cent. It seems reasonable to assume that total household income was of the same order. Later, estimates of total household income were smaller percentages of national income. The figures of Rao and Ramakrishnan (1980: 34) for employee plus property income are 79 per cent for 1966 and 73 per cent for 1975. Towards the end of the period, the results of the Household Expenditure Survey (HES) for 2003, when grossed up, give a figure of some 61 per cent (Khee and Liong 2005). The latter figure includes regular income from work, and income from investment, rentals, and other sources; it excludes imputed rent of owner-occupied accommodation.[4] We do not want to include imputed rent, but the survey amount may also be too low on account of under-reporting and differential non-response by upper income groups (and the omission of the institutional population). According to Rao, 'it must be accepted that there is considerable under-coverage (up to 15 per cent of GNP or 30 per cent of likely actual house-hold income) in the income data obtained by the HES' (2000: 144). In view of these considerations, I take a figure of 75 per cent of national income for recent years. To accommodate the fall from 92.5 per cent in 1956, the proportion is assumed to fall at the rate of 1 percentage point per year from 1956 to 1966, and then at a rate of half a percentage point per year until it reaches 75 per cent in 1981.

The resulting series for total household income is shown in Table 5A.2, together with mean income per adult. There is clearly a wide margin of error. In recent years, the error is likely to arise in the assumed percentage, rather than in the national income total. The correct percentage could be as much as a fifth higher (i.e. 90 per cent), although it is unlikely to be as much as a fifth lower (60 per cent). In the early years, the error is more likely to arise in the National Accounts total, rather than in the percentage. Use of the United Nations estimates for the 1950s, for example, would typically raise the control total by some 8 per cent, causing the estimated top shares to fall by 8 per cent. Overall, in these early years, a 20 per cent error in either direction seems quite possible, although it

---

[3] An alternative would be to use the figures given by the United Nations (1968: 147) for 1956 to 1966; these are typically some 8% higher than those used here.

[4] An important consideration in any overall distributional analysis is the role of housing policy, notably since the 1960s the provision of subsidized housing by the public sector (see Chia Siow Yue and Chen Yen Yu 2003: 19–20).

should be noted that, when account is taken of the (known) income of taxpayers, this means a variation of around a quarter in the income of non-taxpayers. It should also be noted that the use of total adult population, with an age cut-off of 15, may mean that the shares are overstated, which is a further reason for drawing a wide (lower) confidence interval.

Data on the Distribution of Earnings

The published income tax data for Singapore do not allow a distinction to be drawn between earned income and investment income. Information is however available since 1965 on the distribution of earnings obtained from the administrative records of the Central Provident Fund (CPF) Board. Under the Central Provident Fund Act, every employer is required to pay monthly contributions into this mandatory retirement savings scheme, so that the records provide good coverage of all employees in both the private and public sectors. (Employers, the self-employed, and unpaid family workers are excluded.) The earnings data have been described as follows:

The statistical measure of earnings is based on the concept of wages as income to the employee. The earnings data refer to all remuneration received before deduction of the employee's CPF contributions. Earnings data include basic wages and other regular payments like shift allowances, overtime payments, incentive payments and other monetary allowances. (Tan Yih Bin 1992: 1)

Distributions of employees by ranges of monthly earnings have been regularly published in the *Yearbook of Statistics, Singapore* (*YSS*), with typically some fifteen ranges. (The sources are listed in Table 5A.3.) The cumulative distributions have been interpolated linearly to give percentiles as percentages of the median. Since no information is published in *YSS* on the amounts per range, the bounds are simply the range interval, which means that the estimated percentiles are subject to considerable interpolation error. For example, in 1987, 64.4 per cent of workers had wages of $600 or more and 47.1 per cent had $800 or more, from which a median of $766.5 was interpolated, but it could lie anywhere between $600 and $800. The reader has therefore to be on guard against interpolation error.[5] At the same time, the results below do not suggest that this has led to any noticeable artificial volatility over time, and I believe that they are reasonably robust.

---

[5] For example, in that year, 11.7% of workers had wages of $2,000 or more and 7.6% had $2,500 or more, from which the top decile of $2,209 was interpolated. Combining this with the estimate for the median, we arrive at a figure showing the top decile as 288% of the median. But the grouped data are consistent, in extreme cases, with a top decile of $2,000 and a median of $800, giving a percentage of 250 or with a top decile of $2,500 and a median of $600, giving a percentage of 417.

5.3 TOP INCOME SHARES IN SINGAPORE

The estimated shares of top income groups in Singapore from 1947 to 2005 are given in Table 5.1. The percentile shares cover the following seven groups: top 10 per cent, 5 per cent, 1 per cent, 0.5 per cent, 0.1 per cent, 0.05 per cent, and 0.01 per cent. The results relate to individuals (aged 15 and over) and to assessed income before tax. The shares of all except the smallest group are graphed in Figure 5.1. The period between the two vertical lines is that when the assessments were based on twelve months rather than twenty-four months, and the top shares

Table 5.1 Top income shares in Singapore, 1947–2005

	10%	5%	1%	0.50%	0.10%	0.05%	0.01%
1947			10.94	7.72	3.34	2.31	0.99
1948			10.93	7.69	3.31	2.31	0.99
1949			10.38	7.40	3.24	2.26	0.92
1950			12.74	9.39	4.46	3.13	1.32
1951			14.79	11.21	5.79	4.28	2.12
1952			13.80	10.32	5.32	4.00	2.04
1953			12.49	9.17	4.48	3.32	1.68
1954			12.39	8.98	4.28	3.15	1.63
1955							
1956			12.42	8.72	3.68	2.49	0.98
1957			12.29	8.57	3.50	2.33	0.83
1958			11.70	8.06	3.17	2.07	0.74
1959			13.05	9.15	3.72	2.44	0.87
1960			10.97	7.72	3.15	2.12	0.80
1961			11.19	7.86	3.12	2.05	0.74
1962			11.07	7.69	3.04	1.99	0.75
1963			10.93	7.58	2.98	1.94	0.71
1964			12.62	8.65	3.37	2.20	0.84
1965			10.91	7.50	2.83	1.80	0.64
1966			10.36	7.06	2.61	1.63	0.55
1967			10.23	6.99	2.62	1.67	0.59
1968			10.63	7.44	3.06	2.09	0.92
1969		21.79	10.18	7.12	2.86	1.91	0.75
1970		22.87	10.77	7.51	2.99	2.01	0.82
1971		22.60	10.57	7.32	2.89	1.92	0.74
1972		23.22	10.80	7.50	3.08	2.07	0.85
1973		23.26	11.15	7.87	3.38	2.34	
1974	30.69	22.77	10.46	7.22	2.90	1.92	
1975	31.40	23.26	10.57	7.24	2.84	1.85	
1976	31.39	23.13	10.41	7.14	2.78	1.81	
1977	30.58	22.43	10.02	6.83	2.66	1.76	
1978	31.97	23.29	10.30	6.97	2.63	1.71	
1979	34.46	25.15	11.15	7.53	2.84	1.87	

1980	32.07	23.63	10.59	7.21	2.80	1.84	
1981	32.14	23.62	10.60	7.27	2.78		
1982	33.22	24.28	10.79	7.41	2.93		
1983	32.12	23.55	10.45	7.12	*2.81*		
1984	31.74	23.10	10.17	6.90			
1985	33.80	24.54	10.67	7.22			
1986	32.76	23.91	10.26	6.86	*2.60*		
1987	36.01	26.06	11.41	7.69	2.96	1.96	0.81
1988	33.95	24.57	10.72	7.24	2.76	1.86	0.76
1989	34.67	25.29	11.30	7.79	3.17	2.31	1.05
1990	35.04	25.50	11.22	7.65	2.99	2.18	0.79
1991	33.09	24.01	10.43	7.03	2.73	2.01	0.72
1992							
1993							
1994	30.41	22.16	10.02	6.87	3.11	2.19	
1995	30.18	21.93	9.84	6.67	3.05	2.11	
1996	30.91	22.47	9.99	6.76	3.09	2.04	
1997	30.79	22.64	10.31	7.06	3.27	2.15	
1998	32.64	24.11	11.10	7.62	3.53	2.34	
1999	36.28	27.01	12.78	8.94	4.24	2.88	
2000	38.06	28.28	13.26	9.39	4.43		
2001	43.87	32.50	15.07	10.58	4.74	*3.34*	
2002	43.53	32.19	15.06	10.70	4.95	*3.56*	
2003	41.36	30.63	14.24	10.02	4.51		
2004	38.92	28.91	13.60	9.63	4.36		
2005	37.36	27.92	13.28	9.46	4.29		

Notes. (1) Figures shown in italics are extrapolations into open upper interval.
(2) Estimates for 1980 to 1986 are based on 12 month rather than 24 month assessments.

may be expected on this account to be rather lower. The graph also indicates some of the main events in the recent history of Singapore.

The broad impression is that of stability over time—at least until the 1990s—a stability that is remarkable for a country that has seen its real income per head rise more than tenfold. It is true that there has been change. The commodities boom around 1950 saw the top shares in Singapore increase: that of the top 1 per cent rose from 10 per cent to 15 per cent. But the top shares subsequently fell back steadily over the colonial period, and by the time Singapore separated from Malaysia to become fully independent in 1965 there was little difference from the shares in 1947. There is no sign that Independence produced a marked change in top income shares. Nor did the distribution change as Singapore grew: the share of the top 1 per cent, the top 0.5 per cent, and the top 0.1 per cent were little different in 1996 from their values thirty years earlier.

Over a thirty-year period there was broad stability of the very top income shares. At the same time, there was some change lower down the distribution, below the top 1 per cent. The shares of the top 5 per cent and the top 10 per cent were higher in 1990 than in the 1970s; and they then fell back in the 1990s. It is

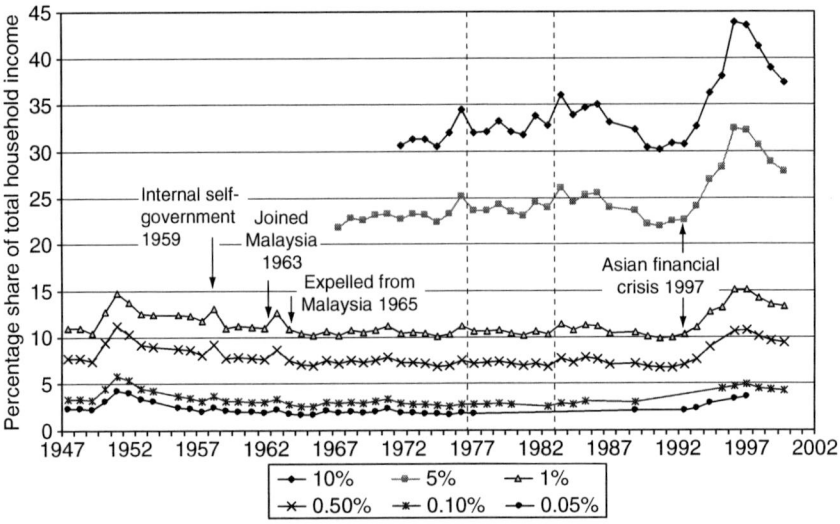

Figure 5.1 Top income shares in Singapore, 1947–2005

Source: Table 5.1.

interesting to compare these with the Gini coefficients for the entire distribution
of income summarized by Chia Siow Yue and Chen Yen Yu (2003: table 14). The
first observation cited is for 1966; the series then runs annually from 1972 to
1999. The Gini coefficients show a rise of about 4 or 5 percentage points between
the end of the 1970s and the end of the 1980s, a magnitude around the same as
the increase in the United States at that time.

Towards the end of the period, after a fall in the early 1990s, all top shares in
Singapore rose following the Asian financial crisis of 1997–8. From 1997 to 2002,
the share of the top 10 per cent went from 31 per cent to 44 per cent; the share
of the top 1 per cent went from 10 per cent to 15 per cent; the share of the top
0.5 per cent went from 7 per cent to over 10 per cent. In other words, the shares
increased to about 1.5 times their 1997 value. After 2002, these shares turned
down, but in 2005 were still well above their 1997 levels. At 9.5 per cent in 2005,
the share of the top 0.5 per cent was at a height comparable with that in the boom
at the start of the 1950s.

The different periods as they affected the share of the top 1 per cent are
summarized in Figure 5.2. This also shows a band of 20 per cent possible error.
As noted above, it seems possible that the control total for income in recent years
could be understated by as much as 20 per cent, causing the share to be overstated
by that amount. The resulting 2005 figure is marked with an X. For the early
years, the error in the National Accounts total could well be in either direction.
These are marked by + and − for 1947. As may be seen, the lower figure for
2005 lies within the +/− range for 1947, but the central value for 2005 lies (just)
above the 1947 range. The 2005 share of the top 1 per cent is higher than that

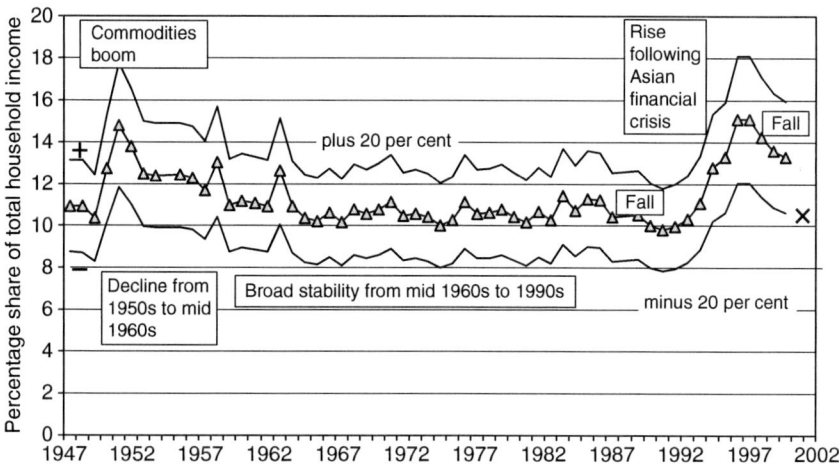

Figure 5.2 Share of top 1% in Singapore, 1947–2005

Source: Table 5.1.

in 1947 unless the National Accounts figure for 1947 is more than 20 per cent too high.

Shares within Shares

The uncertainties surrounding the control totals for income can be avoided if we look at the *shape* of the upper part of the distribution, as represented by the shares within shares. Figure 5.3 shows the share of the top 0.1 per cent within the total income of the top 1 per cent, and, from 1974, the share of the top 1 per cent within the total received by the top 10 per cent. For the earlier years, when less of the distribution was covered, we show the share of the top 0.01 per cent within the top 0.1 per cent (although it should be remembered that this is a very small group: around 1,300 taxpayers in the top 0.1 per cent in 1972, the last year shown).

The shares within shares show the same rise in the early 1950s, and this was followed by a fall to the mid 1960s. The fall was more marked than for the shares themselves, so that the distribution was less concentrated at the top in 1966 than in 1947. The ensuing period of broad stability was however similar. The share of the top 0.1 per cent in the top 1 per cent at the end of the 1980s was 26 per cent, a value little different from those observed in the mid 1960s. In contrast, the share of the top 1 per cent in the top 10 per cent was falling over this period; there was change in the distribution below the top percentile. At the end of the period, however, both showed increasing concentration: by 2005, the share of the top 0.1 per cent within

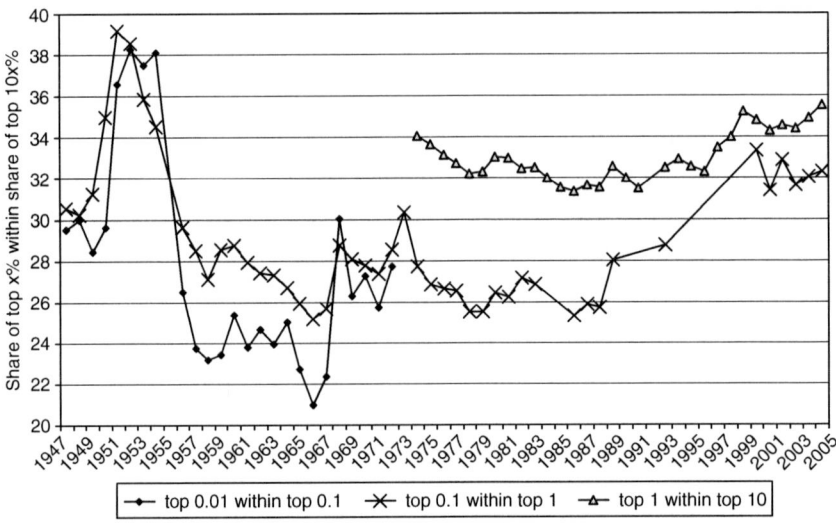

Figure 5.3 Shares within shares of top income groups in Singapore, 1947–2005
Source: Table 5.1.

the top 1 per cent had risen to 32 per cent, and a similar percentage point increase was recorded by the share of the top 1 per cent in the top 10 per cent.

The fact that the share of the top x per cent within that of the top 10x per cent is similar for the different values of x in Figure 5.3 indicates that the distribution is close to Pareto in form. The Pareto coefficients implied by these shares within shares are shown in Figure 5.4 for x = 0.1 and 1 (from 1974), as well as for x = 0.5 (from 1969). (The figures indicated by circles relate to India and are discussed in section 5.4.) At the end of the period, the coefficients were between 1.8 and 2.0. For much of the period, however, the coefficient based on the share of the top 0.1 per cent in that of the top 1 per cent has been in excess of 2.0, varying around 2.25. There was a definite rise and then fall in the Pareto coefficient. Interestingly, the fall in the coefficient (marking increased concentration) after the financial crisis in 1997 was not reversed after 2002—unlike the top income shares. Put another way, the top 1 per cent saw a fall in their income share between 2002 and 2005 of less than 2 percentage points, whereas the next 9 per cent saw a fall of 4.7 percentage points, or more than half the increase they had enjoyed between 1996 and 2002.

Upper Part of the Earnings Distribution

One of the elements driving the top income shares is the behaviour of the earnings distribution. The data from the CPF contributions allow us to estimate the upper percentiles as percentages of the median, and these are shown in

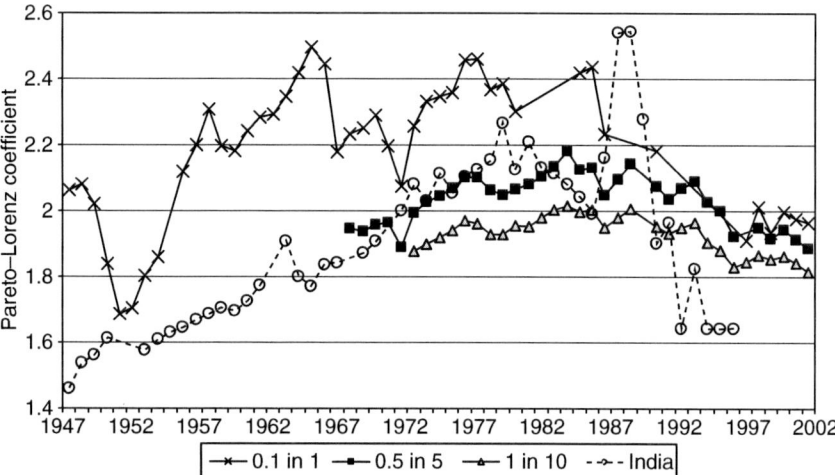

Figure 5.4 Pareto–Lorenz coefficients for Singapore (and India), 1947–2005

Source: Table 5.1 and shares of top 0.1 and 1 in Table 1A.5.

Figure 5.5. Since it was independent Singapore that introduced the Central Provident Fund, the estimates do not cover the colonial period: they start in 1965. As noted above, the figures are subject to interpolation error.

The estimates of top earnings percentiles in Figure 5.5 bear out the impression of stability in the middle part of the period. The top 5 (20) per cent earned more than 403 (191) per cent of the median in both 1971 and 1986. Earlier, in the 1960s there had been an increase in the upper percentiles: the top decile rose by over 5 per cent and the top quintile by over 10 per cent. (In this period, the income tax data do not reach down this far.) After 1987, we see a decline in the top decile and top vintile, both of which by the mid-1990s had fallen by more than 15 per cent; this resembles the falls observed in Figure 5.1 for the shares in total income of the top 10 per cent and top 5 per cent. The Gini coefficients calculated by Rao, Banerjee, and Mukhopadhaya (2003) using the CPF data, which start in 1974, show the Gini as falling from 46 per cent in 1987 to 43 per cent in 1988 and as maintained at that level until the mid 1990s. The fall was reversed after 1996. The data ranges do not allow the series in Figure 5.5 to be carried forward in all cases, but the upper quartile rose between 1996 and 2007 by more than 8 per cent.

The conclusion reached about the overall earnings distribution by Rao, Banerjee, and Mukhopadhaya was that 'there are some very stable income differentials among the workers/employees of Singapore' (2003: 216). As they note, however, a single summary measure conceals possibly divergent movements. It is also clear that the stability was a property of one period, as is illustrated in Figure 5.6, which shows the changes in the earnings percentiles (defined relative to the median) since 1970. Before 1987, the variation was contained within a band of ±5 per cent. In this respect, Singapore (solid

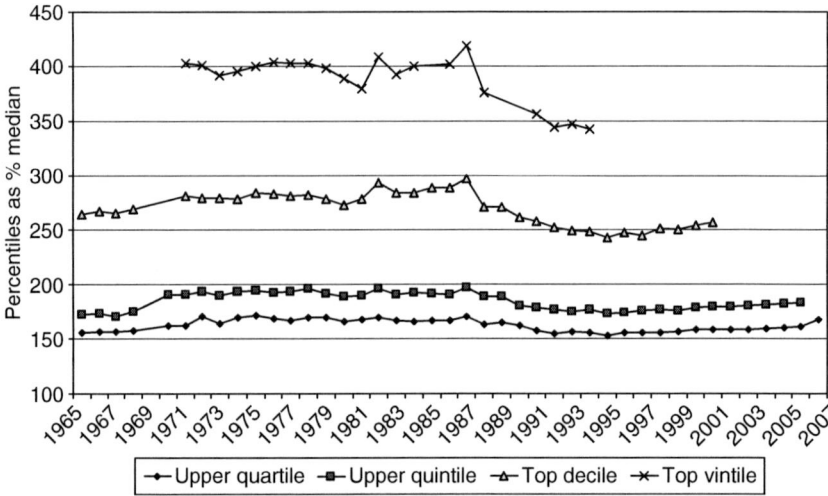

Figure 5.5 Earnings distribution in Singapore, 1965–2007
Source: Table 5A.4.

symbols) was similar to the United Kingdom, for which results are shown for comparison (hollow symbols). But after 1987 we see the fall of top percentiles in Singapore, of nearly 15 per cent for the top decile, followed by a rise starting after 1995. It is interesting to see that the rate of rise in recent years in Singapore is not dissimilar to that in the UK, where there has been a distinct fanning out of the upper part of the earnings distribution (Atkinson 2008).

Summary

The income tax data allow us to track the very top income shares in Singapore from 1947 through to the twenty-first century, covering first a colonial period, a short period as part of Malaysia, and then full independence from 1965. During the time as a colony, shares rose to a peak in 1951 and then declined over the 1950s. Following Independence there followed twenty-five years of broad stability at the very top. The 1990s saw a fall in top shares, but after 1996 they rose by around a half, and even if they have subsequently declined, they remain above earlier levels. The top percentiles of the earnings distribution were relatively stable up to 1987, and then fell, before starting an upward path after 1995. A first impression is that political events, such as Independence, have had little impact; much more potent have been economic events such as the commodities boom of 1950–1 and the Asian financial crisis. These are discussed in the next section.

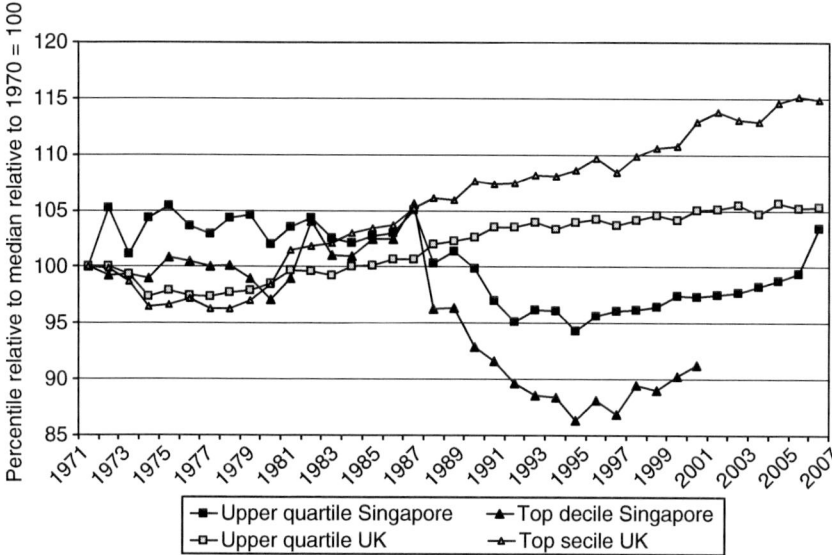

Figure 5.6 Changes in earnings percentiles relative to 1970: comparison of Singapore and UK
Source: Table 5A.4.

5.4 TOP INCOMES AND EARNINGS AND SINGAPORE'S ECONOMIC DEVELOPMENT

In considering the possible explanations for the behaviour of top income shares, in the case of Singapore we should begin with the impact of its remarkable economic growth.[6] Over the period studied in this chapter, Singapore has moved from having approximately average world income to having GDP per capita similar to that of Western Europe. It is often regarded as the archetypal Newly Industrializing Country, being labelled with Hong Kong, South Korea, and Taiwan as a member of the 'Gang of Four' or as an 'East Asian tiger'.

Growth and Structural Change

With its strategic position and natural harbour, Singapore developed in its colonial period not only as a base for British military operations but also as a centre for international commerce. As such, it was exposed to world economic conditions, notably the movements in commodity prices. Between 1948 and 1950, the price of rubber in US\$ doubled, and it rose by a further nearly

---

[6] In this summary of Singapore's economic development, I have drawn heavily on a number of sources, including Tan and Hock (1982) and Islam and Kirkpatrick (1986).

50 per cent between 1950 and 1951. From 1951, the rubber price then fell back, and by 1953 was little higher than in 1948.[7] Given the predominance of trading activity, these price movements are likely to have been at least one of the causes of the rise and then fall in top income shares in Singapore in the early 1950s.

The decline in both military and entrepôt activity meant that economic development had to be found elsewhere. The 1959 election platform of the People's Action Party (PAP) focused on industrialization as the strategy for Singapore's future development. The PAP, which won the election and has been in power since then, set in place such a strategy, oriented first (1960 to 1967) towards import substitution. Then the shock of the announcement in the 1960s of the withdrawal of the British military base, which accounted for some 20 per cent of employment (Tan and Hock 1982: 282), led to increased incentives for exporting and measures to increase the competitiveness of Singapore exports. Inward capital investment by foreign companies was strongly encouraged. The rate of growth doubled after 1967, and by 1973 manufacturing accounted for 22 per cent of GDP, compared with 13 per cent in 1960 (Tan and Hock 1982: 308). Growth was at this time largely extensive, with an expansion of relatively labour-intensive manufacturing industries, and little evidence of increased productivity via technical progress (Tsao 1985).

If such structural change causes an inverse-U Kuznets curve relationship between growth and inequality, with inequality first rising and then falling as a country develops, then it should be evident in a case where the transformation takes place so rapidly without major interruptions (such as wars). In Figure 5.7, the share of the top 1 per cent in Singapore for the period 1950 to 2003 is plotted against the level of GDP per capita measured in $1990 PPP terms (from the estimates of Maddison 2003 and website). There is no sign of an inverse-U. Indeed, as pointed out by earlier writers, such as Rao, the data 'indicate a U-shape for the past 25 years and not an inverted-U' (2000: 152). As noted at the outset, the Asian Development Bank when considering the distribution as a whole had found no evidence of a Kuznets curve.[8] The absence of any apparent Kuznets curve may reflect a narrow wage differential between the manufacturing and agricultural/domestic sectors. According to Fields (1984), the differential was of the order of 20 per cent, which he contrasts with other parts of the world where the differential could be 100 per cent or higher.[9] These conclusions relate to the overall distribution, but the same picture is shown by the top shares, which may be seen from Figure 5.7 to be highest at low levels of per capita income and at the recent high levels. The central period, when the economy was moving from

[7] These figures are from *International Financial Statistics* (January 1954), 32, and (January 1957), 36.

[8] Although Rao and Ramakrishnan suggest that the first part of the Kuznets curve could have started earlier: 'income inequality probably increased during the one hundred or more years of transition of Singapore from the fishing village to the entrepôt trade centre' (1980: 69).

[9] The differentials assumed by Kuznets (1955) in his numerical examples were 100% (smaller case) or 300% (larger case).

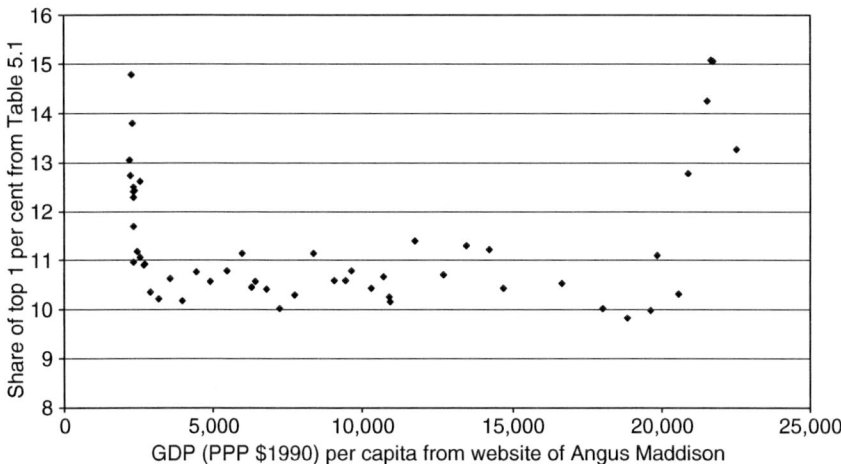

Figure 5.7 Share of top 1% plotted against GDP per capita Singapore, 1950–2003

$3,000 per head in 1966 to some $15,000 in 1991, is characterized by a long flat part of the U.

International Trade

As has been clearly identified by Rao, there are two evident reasons why Singapore has not exhibited the Kuznets inverse-U pattern: 'being an extremely open economy, wage incomes are in part determined by global influences, and in addition, government has used the wage as a policy instrument' (2000: 155). These are considered in turn.

The model underlying the Kuznets curve is that of an economy closed to international trade, whereas trade has been taken as one of the major drivers of trends in inequality. It has long been argued (for example, by Little, Scitovsky, and Scott 1970) that the adoption of a broadly based export promotion policy would increase the demand for unskilled labour in developing countries and hence reduce earnings inequality. This was spelled out by Wood in his book on north–south trade and inequality, where he supported, with qualifications, the view that 'expansion of manufactured exports raises the demand for—and hence the wages of—unskilled but literate (BAS-ED) labour relative to other sorts of labour. It thus tends to narrow the wage differential between BAS-EDs and the (higher-paid) skilled workers, reducing inequality' (1994: 13). Wood goes on to examine the time-series evidence for a number of countries, including Singapore, emphasizing that this evidence 'is by no means as clear-cut as is commonly supposed' (1994: 241). The forces described by Wood may well not have affected the top incomes covered by the income tax data, but we have seen that the CPF earnings data show a long period of stability during the period that Singapore was growing rapidly (the same data show the lower quartile also being stable as a percentage of the median between 1965 and the 1980s).

The broad stability of the earnings distribution is striking because it continued for much of the distribution after the introduction of the 'New Economic Policy' in 1979, which marked the switch away from labour-intensive low value-added industries to a growth strategy emphasizing skill formation. According to Islam and Kirkpatrick (1986: 125), this led to an adverse shift in earnings inequality. From Figure 5.5, we can see that there was indeed a rise for the top decile and top vintile, but the rise was not sustained. From Figure 5.6 we can see that throughout the 1970s and 1980s the upper percentiles remained within 5 per cent of their 1970 values.

Government Wages Policies

The structural change described above was heavily influenced by government policies, and these same policies were directly or indirectly redistributive. These are particularly important in the case of Singapore where there has been wide-ranging state intervention, notably in the determination of wages.

Early legislation was directed at securing export competitiveness, against a historical background of labour disputes. According to Tan and Hock, the 1968 employment legislation had two objectives: 'to give greater discretion to employers in their development of their work force. Decisions on promotions, internal transfer, hiring, and dismissal were to be taken without recourse to collective bargaining. The other aim was to reduce labour costs' (1982: 283). Subsequently, the National Wages Council (NWC) was set up in 1972, as a tripartite body with representatives of employers, employees, and the government. Its function was to recommend 'orderly' wage increases, providing guidelines to be applied in labour market relations (Lim 1999). According to Islam and Kirkpatrick, 'there is a general presumption that NWC recommendations have been closely adhered to by the private sector' (1986: 116 n.). In their evaluation of the phase of industrial restructuring (1973–84), Tan Yin Ying, Eng, and Robinson conclude that the NWC 'helped ensure wage stability at a time when pressures to increase wages were substantial' (2008: 16).

The role of wage policies in determining the success of export promotion policies has been emphasized by Fields, who argues that 'real wages barely grew in the 1970s because of the strong repressive hand of the Singaporean government in the labour market' (1994: 396). But this policy of wage repression was abandoned in the 1980s, during which period real wages grew by 80 per cent (GDP per capita grew by 78 per cent). The NWC policy had also a distributional dimension. According to Rao, the NWC wage guidelines 'had a moderating impact on income inequality' (1999: 1033). In the mid 1970s, the NWC recommended combinations of fixed amount and proportional increases that favoured lower-paid workers (Rao and Ramakrishnan 1980: 24). In 1979, the recommended increases were fixed amounts, which had an initial effect of narrowing differentials, as may be seen from Figure 5.5, but this was immediately followed by recommendations favouring performance. However, as we have seen, none of these changed the broad pattern of medium-run stability.

Progressive Income Taxation

The income tax has from the outset been charged at progressively graduated rates. For example, in 1952 (AR 1953: 3) there was a personal allowance (approximately 150 per cent of the mean income per adult for a single person), above which tax was charged at varying rates commencing at 3 per cent and rising to 30 per cent on income above $50,000 (or around 25 times mean income). These rates were increased over the colonial period to reach 50 per cent in 1959. The top rate increased to 55 per cent (on income above $100,000, or 50 times mean income) from 1 January 1961. During the Malaysia period, there was one year when the top rate was reduced to 50 per cent, but 55 per cent was maintained until the 1980s. For the income year 1977 the starting point for the 55 per cent rate was raised to $400,000 (reflecting the more than threefold increase in mean income) and for the year 1979 the starting point became $600,000 (some 50 times mean income).

For this important period of growth in Singapore, those with very high incomes—in excess of 50 times the mean—were paying marginal tax rates of 50 per cent or more. But tax policy changed, with top rates being reduced. At the end of the 1970s, the average tax rate being paid by the top income group was around 38 per cent; by the middle of the 1980s the average rate had fallen below 30 per cent. In 1987 income tax rates commenced at 3.5 per cent and reached a top rate of 33 per cent. Subsequently, they were reduced still further, the range being 2–28 per cent for income year 1996, 0–22 per cent from 2002, and 0–20 per cent from 2006. As a result, the income tax structure was still graduated but much less progressive.

As in many OECD countries, there has been a distinct shift in Singapore away from progressive income taxation. Examination of the impact on top income shares is complicated by the fact that the estimates for the 1980s are based on a shorter assessment period, but if we look at the more recent period it seems quite possible that the tax reductions since 1997 have contributed to the recent increase in top income shares. But top incomes may also have been affected by the financial crisis.

Asian Financial Crisis of 1997–1998

In their review of the distributive effect in East Asia of the financial crisis, Krongkaew and Ragayah Haji Mat Zin state that in the case of Singapore 'there has been a sharp rise in inequality since the crisis' (2006: 9). The results of

Statistics Singapore (Khee and Liong 2005: table 5) show that over the period 1998–2003 the top 20 per cent of households saw their income rise from 2.48 times the mean to 2.63 times the mean. We have seen that, even allowing for some reversal of the rise, top income shares in 2005 are well above their pre-1997 level. The fact that the crisis was associated, in Singapore, with a rise in measured top income shares may appear surprising, if one expects top shares normally to be pro-cyclical, as profit incomes, and capital incomes more generally, are adversely affected. Here the possibility should be recognized that the rise is, at least in part, a statistical artefact. To the extent that dividend payouts have increased, this would appear in the income tax data, whereas capital gains are not taxed. To the extent that more overseas capital income is now repatriated to Singapore, as a result of fiscal incentives, this may have caused an increase in the apparent top shares. On the other hand, there are reasons to expect a rise. It may be that the rich have preserved their position at a time when other groups in the population have lost, so that the gain is a relative one. It is also possible that, in a present-day financial crisis, the rich enjoy liquidity and favoured capital market access that allows them to acquire distressed income-earning assets at reduced prices.[10]

The rise in inequality after the financial crisis may be in part attributable to the liberalization packages introduced in 1998 and 2001. The UN Economic Commission for Asia and the Pacific commented in its 1998 Survey that 'the Singapore strategy of managing income inequality seems to convey the message that the market forces should not be tinkered with to alter income inequality, as it can have adverse consequences on growth. Instead, inequality should be managed through safety nets and targeted programmes for the benefit of the lower income groups' (1998: 132). It does indeed seem reasonable to consider separately the different parts of the distribution. At the same time, one cannot ignore what is happening to the top incomes on which we have focused here. They are important not least because of their impact on others, as through the formula that has linked the salaries of government ministers and senior civil servants to top wage earners in the private sector. Under the formula, 'the officials receive two-thirds of the median income of the top eight earners in six professions—bankers, lawyers, accountants, executives with multinational corporations, local manufacturing executives and engineers' (*Financial Times*, 10 May 2007). As this example illustrates, top incomes may be affected not only by global forces but also by pay norms and practices.

Summary

The evolution of the upper part of the income distribution in Singapore cannot be linked very directly to the rapid structural changes in its economy nor to the shifts in development policy nor to the different phases of real wage growth.

---

[10] I owe this suggestion to Salvatore Morelli.

It is remarkable that an economy whose labour market flexibility has been widely commended should have exhibited such a degree of distributional stability from the 1960s to the late 1980s. But the 1990s show a different picture, and the distributional consequences of the Asian financial crisis may have wider implications.

5.5 COMPARISON WITH TOP INCOME SHARES IN OTHER COUNTRIES

In 1947, Singapore was a British colony, administered by the Colonial Office in London. A natural first comparison therefore is with the distribution of income in the United Kingdom. I then turn to a comparison with other countries for which estimates of top income shares are available for the period since the Second World War, and end with specific comparisons with India and Indonesia.

Comparison with the United Kingdom

Ironically, at the time when the Singapore income tax data began to be recorded in 1947, the UK Inland Revenue did not publish annual distributions of income by income tax payers; the only available information being that limited to surtax payers. The data in the 1940s for Singapore are more extensive than those for the UK.[11] For this reason, I take the UK estimates for 1949, this being the first post-war quinquennial Survey of Personal Incomes. In the case of Singapore, I take the average of the estimates for 1947 to 1949. These show that the top income shares in Singapore and the UK were quite close: the share of the top 1 per cent was 10.4 per cent compared with 11.5 in the UK, which is comfortably within the 'confidence interval' shown in Figure 5.2 for Singapore. (Although it should be borne in mind that the Singapore calculations are on an adult individual basis rather than a tax unit basis, which may cause the share to be relatively overstated.) The shares of the top 0.5 per cent were 7.4 and 8.1 per cent, respectively. Given the uncertainty surrounding the control totals for income in Singapore at that time, it may be safer to take the Pareto–Lorenz coefficients: those based on the share of the top 0.1 per cent within the top 1 per cent (unless otherwise specified, the coefficients cited here are based on these two groups) are 2.05 in Singapore and 2.09 in the UK. On this basis, the top of the income distribution has a similar shape in Singapore and the UK.

We have seen that in Singapore top income shares fell over the 1950s but were then broadly stable for some thirty years. In contrast, in the UK top income shares fell for three decades from 1949. As a result, by 1979 the top income shares

---

[11] The surtax-based estimates for the UK only extend to the top 0.5% of tax units; the Singapore income tax data in 1947 cover 1.8% of the adult population.

in the UK were a great deal lower: the share of the top 0.1 per cent in the UK was under half that in Singapore. The share of the top 1 per cent in the UK was 5.9 per cent in 1979, compared with 11.2 per cent in Singapore. The Pareto–Lorenz coefficient had increased much more in the UK: to 2.96, compared with 2.46 in Singapore. This difference was however to disappear as top income shares in the UK rose again. By the early 1990s, top shares were higher in the UK. The post-Asian crisis rise in Singapore, even allowing for the subsequent decline, leaves the two countries in a not dissimilar position. Averaging the three years 2003–5, to reduce the impact of recent volatility, we find that the share of the top 1 per cent in Singapore was 13.7 per cent, which is close to the 13.1 per cent in the UK. Again the UK estimate is well within the confidence interval shown in Figure 5.2, although the Pareto–Lorenz coefficients (1.98 for Singapore and 1.81 for the UK) suggest that the top of the distribution is more concentrated in the UK.

On this basis, top incomes in colonial Singapore at the end of the 1940s appear to have been similarly distributed to those in the UK; the subsequent fall in top income shares was much less than in the UK, with top shares around 1979 about double those in the UK; the sharp rise in top shares after 1979 in the UK reversed this position, but, after the rise in top shares after the financial crisis in Singapore, the two countries find themselves again in rather similar positions.

Comparison with Other Countries

Top income shares in Singapore just after the Second World War were quite like those in the UK. If we look at the share of the top 1 per cent, then the same was true of a number of other countries. Of the fourteen countries shown in Table 5.2, all except three lie within the ±20 per cent interval (8.6 to 12.9 per cent) for Singapore averaging the results for 1947 to 1949. Singapore is in fact the median. Only Japan and New Zealand had a share less than 8.6 per cent (Sweden was close), and only Ireland had a share (just) in excess of 12.9 per cent. This degree of congruence may reflect the margin of uncertainty surrounding the estimates for Singapore, particularly in this early period. But if we take a narrower range of ±10 per cent, then we still find seven of the fourteen countries are within this range of Singapore. Overall, the shares of the top 1 per cent are close: if we drop the top two and the bottom two, the range is from 8.6 to 11.6 per cent.

It may be that the share of the top 1 per cent is unrepresentative: the distribution may 'pivot' about this value. The shares of the top 0.1 per cent are less similar, with only four of the fourteen lying within ±10 per cent. There is, to this extent, a difference in the shape of the top of the distribution in 1947–9. The difference is captured by the Pareto–Lorenz coefficients shown in Table 5.2, which also have the advantage of not being affected by the differences in the methods used to construct income totals. The degree of difference should not however be exaggerated: seven of the fourteen lie in a range of 1.9 to 2.2 surrounding the figure for Singapore.

Table 5.2 Comparative top income shares in fourteen countries

Row		Around 1947–9			Around 2003–5		
		Share of top 1%	Share of top 0.1%	Pareto–Lorenz coefficient	Share of top 1%	Share of top 0.1%	Pareto–Lorenz coefficient
1	Singapore	10.75	3.30	2.05	13.71	4.39	1.98
2	United Kingdom	11.47	3.45	2.09	13.09	4.66	1.81
3	France	9.22	2.59	2.23	8.04	2.10	2.39
4	The Netherlands	12.05	3.80	2.00	5.38	1.08	3.30
5	United States	10.95	3.24	2.12	16.12	6.84	1.59
6	Germany	11.60	3.90	1.90	11.10	4.40	1.67
7	Switzerland	9.88	3.23	1.94	7.76	2.67	1.86
8	Ireland	12.92	4.00	2.04	10.30		
9	Norway	9.10	2.83	2.03	11.20	5.14	1.51
10	Sweden	8.62	2.35	2.30	5.62	1.72	2.06
11	Canada	10.99	3.09	2.23	13.56	5.23	1.71
12	Australia	10.62	2.92	2.28	8.79	2.68	2.07
13	New Zealand	7.72	1.77	2.78	9.46	3.10	1.94
14	Japan	7.79	2.06	2.37	9.00	2.29	2.46
15	India	11.23	5.44	1.46	8.95	3.64	1.64

Notes: 1943 for Ireland, 1948 for Norway, 1949 for UK, 1950 for Germany. 1995 for Switzerland, 1998 for Germany, 1999 for Netherlands, 1999–2000 for India, 2000 for Canada and Ireland, 2002 for Australia, 2003 and 2004 for Norway and Sweden.

Sources: Rows 2–8 and 11–13 from Atkinson and Piketty (2007: volume 1 (updated); remainder from volume 2).

If we move to the end of the period—2003 to 2005—we find a rather different picture. The shares of the top 1 per cent in 2003–5 were within ±20 per cent of the Singapore estimate in only five of the fourteen cases, with nine being more than 20 per cent lower. Only Canada and the UK were within 10 per cent. Overall, the shares of the top 1 per cent are further apart than in 1947–9: if we drop the top two and the bottom two, the range is from 7.8 to 13.6 per cent. The central points of these ranges are not greatly different: 10.1 per cent in 1947–9 and 10.7 in 2003–5. In short, there is now more diversity in top income shares across the fourteen countries and Singapore is no longer close to the median. This applies particularly to the top 1 per cent. For the top 0.1 per cent, the share in Singapore is close to the median. The shape of the distribution (the Pareto–Lorenz coefficient) is less concentrated than in all except five of the countries shown.

Comparison with Other Asian Countries

The Pareto–Lorenz coefficient in Singapore (1.98 in 2003–5) contrasts with the much more concentrated 1.64 in India. It may appear absurd to compare Singapore, a prosperous country with a population less than 5 million, with India, a country with a population of over 1 billion, many of whom are living on less than $1 a day. At the same time, the comparison is interesting in the light of the differing growth trajectories and policies.[12] In their study of the income tax data in India, Banerjee and Piketty (see Chapter 1) find 'evidence of a substantial decline in the share of the elite during the years of socialist planning and a comparable recovery in the post-liberalisation era' (2005: 2). It is their estimates for India that underlie the points shown in Figure 5.4. It may be seen that the Pareto–Lorenz coefficient was higher in Singapore than in India from 1947, reflecting less concentration, and this was true even during the commodities boom. Although the shares of the top 1 per cent were similar, those of the top 0.1 per cent were higher in India. On the other hand, the coefficient steadily rose in India after Independence, indicating reduced concentration, and by 1981 the position was close to that in Singapore. There was then a reversal in India, with the degree of concentration rising again. The Indian series is volatile, but the share of the top 1 per cent broadly doubled between 1981 and 2000, and that of the top 0.1 per cent rose by a factor of 3. These are, relatively, bigger changes than those observed over the same period in Singapore. Both before and after 1981 the time paths are different.

The final comparison is with Indonesia. Here the colonial tax records have allowed Leigh and van der Eng (2009 and Chapter 4) to make estimates of the pre-war income shares up to 1939, which we may compare with those for Singapore immediately after the war (1947). Again such a comparison must be qualified, since the intervening Second World War had major consequences for both Singapore and Indonesia. Moreover, the estimates here relate to the adult population, whereas those for Indonesia relate to households. The top shares in Indonesia in 1939 were around double those in Singapore in 1947: the share of the top 1 per cent was 19.9, compared with 10.9, the share of the top 0.1 per cent was 7.0 compared with 3.3 per cent. (If we were to adjust the Singapore estimates by taking tax units rather than adults, the difference would be greater.) The larger estimated shares in Indonesia may be due to the impact of the war; they may also be due to differences in the control totals for income. If we eliminate the latter difference, by looking at the shares within shares, then the distributions look more similar: the Pareto–Lorenz coefficient in Indonesia is 1.82, compared with 2.06 in Singapore. But incomes in Indonesia—pre-war—were more concentrated.

5.6 CONCLUSIONS

This chapter has demonstrated that it is possible to study the evolution of the top of the income distribution in Singapore using income tax data combined with National Accounts and other external information. The series presented here cover the end of the colonial period and the subsequent political upheaval: self-government, union with Malaysia, and leaving the union. None of these appear to

[12] There are also historical links: Singapore, as part of the Straits Settlements, was initially under the control of British India.

be associated with changes in top shares. The series cover the period of fast economic growth, but the evolution of the upper part of the income distribution in Singapore cannot be linked very directly to the rapid structural changes in its economy nor to the shifts in development policy nor to the different phases of real wage growth. It is indeed remarkable that an economy whose labour market flexibility has been widely commended should have exhibited distributional stability from the 1960s to the late 1980s. There is a contrast with the UK, where, starting from similar top income shares, the UK has seen a much larger decline and then rise, and with India, where too there have been much larger distributional changes at the top. Since the Asian financial crisis of 1997–8, the situation appears to have changed, with top income shares rising by around a half. After 2002, these shares turned down, but in 2005 were still well above their 1997 levels. At 9.5 per cent in 2005, the share of the top 0.5 per cent was at a height comparable with that in the commodities boom at the start of the 1950s. As at that earlier time, the distribution of income in Singapore today may be influenced by global events, either directly through trade and technological change or indirectly via reduced progressivity of income taxation.

APPENDIX 5A: SOURCES FOR INCOME TAX DATA AND CONTROL TOTALS

The sources for the income tax data are shown in Table 5A.1. The control totals for the adult population and for total household income are shown in Table 5A.2. The sources of the wage distribution data are given in Table 5A.3.

Table 5A.1 Sources of Singapore income tax data

			actual year = year of assessment − 1	
Income year	Report of Income Tax Department		assessed to	SY
1947	IT 1948 and 1949	page 20	31-Dec-49	
1948	IT year ended 31 Dec 1950	Abstract E	31-Dec-50	
1949	IT year ended 31 Dec 1951	Abstract E	31-Dec-51	
1950	IT year ended 31 Dec 1952	Abstract E	31-Dec-52	
1951	IT year ended 31 Dec 1953	Abstract E	31-Dec-53	
1952	IT year ended 31 Dec 1954	Abstract E	31-Dec-54	
1953	IT year ended 31 Dec 1955	Abstract E	31-Dec-55	
1954	IT year ended 31 Dec 1956	Abstract E	31-Dec-56	
1955				
1956	IT AR 1958	Abstract E	31-Dec-58	
1957	IT AR 1959	Abstract E	31-Dec-59	
1958	IT AR 1960	Abstract E	31-Dec-60	
1959	IT AR 1961	Abstract E	31-Dec-61	
1960	IT AR 1962	Abstract E	31-Dec-62	
1961	IT AR 1963	Abstract E	31-Dec-63	
1962	IT AR 1964	Abstract E	31-Dec-64	
1963	IT AR 1965	Abstract E	31-Dec-65	
1964	IT AR 1966	Abstract E	31-Dec-66	
1965	IT AR 1967	Abstract E	31-Dec-67	SY 1968, identical Table 11.6
1966	IT AR 1968	Abstract E	31-Dec-68	
1967	IT AR 1969	Abstract E	31-Dec-69	
1968	IT AR 1970	Abstract E	31-Dec-70	
1969	IT AR 1971	Abstract E	31-Dec-71	
1970	IT AR 1972	Abstract E	31-Dec-72	
1971	IT AR 1973	Abstract E	31-Dec-73	
1972	IT AR 1974	Abstract E	31-Dec-74	
1973	IT AR 1975	Abstract E	31-Dec-75	
1974	IT AR 1976	Abstract E	31-Dec-76	
1975	IT AR 1977	Abstract E	31-Dec-77	
1976	IT AR 1978	Abstract E	31-Dec-78	
1977	IT AR 1979	Abstract E	31-Dec-79	
1978	IT AR 1980	Abstract E	31-Dec-80	

1979	IT AR 1981	Abstract E	31-Dec-81
1980	SY 1982/83	Table 12.12	31-Dec-81
1981	SY 1984/85	Table 13.11	31-Dec-82
1982	SY 1985/86	Table 13.11	31-Dec-83
1983	SY 1986	Table 13.11	31-Dec-84
1984	SY 1987	Table 13.8	31-Dec-85
1985	SY 1988	Table 13.8	31-Dec-86
1986	SY 1989	Table 13.8	31-Dec-87
1987	SY 1990	Table 13.8	31-Dec-89
1988	SY 1991	Table 13.9	31-Dec-90
1989	SY 1992	Table 13.9	31-Dec-91
1990	SY 1993	Table 13.9	31-Dec-92
1991	SY 1994	Table 13.9	31-Dec-93
1992			
1993	SY 1995	Table 16.9	31-Dec-94
1994	SY 1996	Table 16.9	
1995	SY 1997	Table 16.9	
1996	SY 1998	Table 16.11	
1997	SY 2000	Table 16.10	
1998	SY 2001	Table 18.11	
1999	SY 2002	Table 17.11	
2000	SY 2003	Table 17.11	
2001	IT AR 2002/03	App 5	31-Mar-03
2002	IT AR 2003/04	App 5	31-Mar-04
2003	IT AR 2004/05	App 5	31-Mar-05
2004	IT AR 2005/06	App 5	31-Mar-06
2005	IT AR 2006/07	App 5	31-Mar-07

Table 5A.2 Control totals for adult population and household income in Singapore

	Adult population thousands	Total indigenous national income $ million	Total household income $ million	Mean income per adult $
1947	502.5	902.3	834.6	1,661
1948	518.1	998.9	924.0	1,783
1949	533.8	1,104.8	1,022.0	1,914
1950	549.6	1,221.2	1,129.6	2,055
1951	575.1	1,295.5	1,198.3	2,084
1952	607.7	1,383.2	1,279.5	2,106
1953	643.6	1,485.0	1,373.6	2,134
1954	674.7	1,559.3	1,442.4	2,138
1955	707.0	1,657.3	1,533.0	2,168
1956	743.8	1,723.0	1,593.8	2,143
1957	784.9	1,818.9	1,664.3	2,120
1958	825.6	1,891.1	1,711.4	2,073
1959	863.7	1,882.9	1,685.2	1,951
1960	890.6	2,063.6	1,826.3	2,051
1961	920.8	2,235.9	1,956.4	2,125

(continued)

Table 5A.2 Continued

	Adult population thousands	Total indigenous national income $ million	Total household income $ million	Mean income per adult $
1962	946.9	2,413.2	2,087.4	2,205
1963	971.3	2,678.3	2,289.9	2,358
1964	997.2	2,606.0	2,202.1	2,208
1965	1,035.2	2,838.0	2,369.7	2,289
1966	1,062.6	3,189.8	2,631.6	2,476
1967	1,087.8	3,598.0	2,950.4	2,712
1968	1,108.2	3,922.0	3,196.4	2,884
1969	1,146.2	4,472.0	3,622.3	3,160
1970	1,205.3	4,990.0	4,017.0	3,333
1971	1,249.5	5,826.0	4,660.8	3,730
1972	1,295.1	6,884.0	5,472.8	4,226
1973	1,309.1	8,409.0	6,643.1	5,075
1974	1,391.0	9,966.0	7,823.3	5,624
1975	1,439.8	11,061.0	8,627.6	5,992
1976	1,487.3	12,073.0	9,356.6	6,291
1977	1,534.0	13,351.0	10,280.3	6,702
1978	1,580.3	14,126.0	10,806.4	6,838
1979	1,626.9	15,590.0	11,848.4	7,283
1980	1,671.5	19,039.0	14,374.4	8,600
1981	1,710.4	22,903.0	17,177.3	10,043
1982	1,748.7	26,224.0	19,668.0	11,247
1983	1,791.4	30,157.0	22,617.8	12,626
1984	1,830.5	33,232.0	24,924.0	13,616
1985	1,867.8	32,384.0	24,288.0	13,004
1986	1,907.0	32,898.8	24,674.1	12,939
1987	1,947.4	35,073.0	26,304.8	13,508
1988	1,991.1	40,776.0	30,582.0	15,359
1989	2,031.6	45,813.0	34,359.8	16,913
1990	2,050.1	51,512.0	38,634.0	18,845
1991	2,122.6	60,405.7	45,304.3	21,344
1992	2,167.8	68,367.6	51,275.7	23,653
1993	2,210.8	74,138.0	55,603.5	25,151
1994	2,255.3	86,279.0	64,709.3	28,692
1995	2,301.1	94,020.0	70,515.0	30,644
1996	2,349.8	102,007.0	76,505.3	32,558
1997	2,418.6	111,705.0	83,778.8	34,639
1998	2,451.9	110,306.0	82,729.5	33,741
1999	2,502.5	107,744.0	80,808.0	32,291
2000	2,553.1	119,099.0	89,324.3	34,987
2001	2,603.6	108,435.0	81,326.3	31,236
2002	2,654.2	109,351.0	82,013.3	30,899
2003	2,650.8	117,316.0	87,987.0	33,193
2004	2,710.6	131,182.0	98,386.5	36,297
2005	2,772.4	148,765.0	111,573.8	40,244

Note: Dollars are Singapore dollars.

Table 5A.3 Sources of Singapore wage distribution data

Year	Yearbook of Statistics Singapore (YSS)
1965	1974/75, Table 3.10
1966	1975/76, Table 3.11
1967	1975/76, Table 3.11
1968	1975/76, Table 3.11
1969	no data located
1970	1975/76, Table 3.11
1971	1980/81, Table 3.14
1972	1982/83, Table 3.14
1973	1982/83, Table 3.14
1974	1984/85, Table 3.14
1975	1984/85, Table 3.14
1976	1986, Table 3.13
1977	1987, Table 3.14
1978	1988, Table 3.14
1979	1988, Table 3.14
1980	1988, Table 3.14
1981	1988, Table 3.14
1982	1988, Table 3.14
1983	1988, Table 3.14
1984	1988, Table 3.14
1985	1988, Table 3.14
1986	1996, Table 4.13, 1992, Table 3.14 and 1988 Table 3.14
1987	1996, Table 4.13, 1992, Table 3.14 and 1988 Table 3.14
1988	1996, Table 4.13, 1992, Table 3.14 and 1988 Table 3.14
1989	1992, Table 3.14
1990	1992, Table 3.14
1991	1996, Table 4.13 and 1992, Table 3.14
1992	1996, Table 4.13 and 1992, Table 3.14
1993	1997, Table 4.13 and 1994, Table 3.14
1994	1997, Table 4.13 and 1994, Table 3.14
1995	1997, Table 4.13
1996	1997, Table 4.13
1997	1997, Table 4.13
1998	2000, Table 4.12
1999	2000, Table 4.12
2000	2001, Table 4.12
2001	2002, Table 4.12
2002	2008, Table 4.10
2003	2008, Table 4.10
2004	2008, Table 4.10
2005	2008, Table 4.10
2006	2008, Table 4.10
2007	2008, Table 4.10

Table 5A.4 Distribution of earnings in Singapore (and UK)

	Singapore				UK		
	Upper quartile	Upper quintile	Top decile	Top vintile	Upper quartile	Top decile	Top vintile
1965	155.7	172.0	264.8				
1966	157.0	173.5	267.2				
1967	156.4	171.0	265.1				
1968	157.6	175.0	269.3		135.0	174.4	207.6
1969							
1970	162.4	190.8			135.9	175.3	208.1
1971	162.4	191.4	281.3	402.5	134.4	173.3	206.4
1972	170.8	193.9	279.1	400.5	134.4	173.1	206.9
1973	164.2	190.3	279.5	391.3	133.5	171.0	203.3
1974	169.4	193.7	278.5	395.6	130.9	167.2	197.2
1975	171.1	194.5	283.7	399.6	131.6	167.5	196.5
1976	168.3	192.7	282.6	404.0	131.0	168.4	197.2
1977	167.1	193.4	281.4	403.0	130.8	166.9	195.1
1978	169.4	196.9	281.7	402.4	131.3	166.8	196.2
1979	169.9	191.7	278.5	397.7	131.6	168.1	196.2
1980	165.7	189.1	273.1	388.4	132.4	170.6	203.1
1981	168.1	189.8	278.5	379.6	134.0	175.8	208.6
1982	169.4	196.2	292.7	408.1	133.9	176.4	211.2
1983	166.5	190.9	284.2	392.2	133.4	176.9	211.5
1984	165.8	192.8	283.9	399.5	134.5	178.5	214.3
1985	166.8	191.8	288.3		134.6	179.2	215.3
1986	167.2	191.4	288.2	401.9	135.3	179.7	217.3
1987	170.6	197.5	296.9	418.7	135.3	182.3	221.4
1988	162.9	189.0	270.8	375.6	137.1	183.9	225.9
1989	164.6	188.8	271.1		137.5	183.6	226.5
1990	162.1	180.7	261.2		138.0	186.5	228.0
1991	157.4	179.1	257.7	356.7	139.2	186.1	
1992	154.4	176.8	252.2	343.9	139.1	186.3	
1993	156.2	174.9	249.1	347.3	139.8	187.5	
1994	156.1	176.6	248.7	342.5	138.9	187.3	
1995	153.1	173.7	243.0		139.8	188.3	
1996	155.3	174.5	248.0		140.1	190.1	
1997	156.1	176.0	244.5		139.4	187.9	
1998	156.1	176.8	251.6		140.0	190.4	
1999	156.6	176.3	250.5		140.6	191.7	
2000	158.2	179.1	253.9		140.0	191.9	
2001	158.0	179.6	256.8		141.2	195.6	
2002	158.3	180.0			141.3	197.3	
2003	158.6	180.4			141.8	196.1	
2004	159.5	182.0			140.7	195.7	
2005	160.4	182.9			142.0	198.7	
2006	161.4	183.9			141.4	199.5	
2007	168.0				141.5	199.2	

Sources: See Table 5A.3 and, for UK, Atkinson (2008: chapter S).

REFERENCES

Asian Development Bank (2007). 'Special Chapter, Inequality in Asia', in *Key Indicators 2007*. Manila: Asian Development Bank.

Atkinson, A. B. (2005). 'Top Incomes in the UK over the 20th Century', *Journal of the Royal Statistical Society*, 168(2): 325–43.

—— (2008). *The Changing Distribution of Earnings in OECD Countries*. Oxford: Oxford University Press.

—— and T. Piketty (eds.) (2007). *Top Incomes over the 20th Century*. Oxford: Oxford University Press.

Banerjee, A. and T. Piketty (2005). 'Top Indian Incomes, 1922–2000', *World Bank Economic Review*, 19: 1–20.

Benham, F. (1951). *The National Income of Malaya, 1947–49 (with a Note on 1950)*. Singapore: Government Printing Office.

—— (1959). *The National Income of Singapore, 1956*. Oxford: Chatham House Memoranda, Oxford University Press.

Chia Siow Yue and Chen Yen Yu (2003). 'Income Distribution in Singapore', unpublished paper.

Colony of Singapore (1959). *Report of the Commission of Inquiry into the $500,000 Bank Account of Mr Chew Swee Kee and the Income Tax Department Leakage in Connection therewith*. Singapore: Singapore Government Printing Office.

Commission on Growth and Development (chaired by M. Spence) (2008). *The Growth Report*. Washington, DC: World Bank.

Fields, G. S. (1984). 'Employment, Income Distribution and Economic Growth in Seven Small Open Economies', *Economic Journal*, 94: 74–83.

—— (1994). 'Changing Labour Market Conditions and Economic Development in Hong Kong, the Republic of Korea, Singapore, and Taiwan, China', *World Bank Economic Review*, 8: 395–414.

Gastwirth, J. L. (1972). 'The Estimation of the Lorenz Curve and Gini Index', *Review of Economics and Statistics*, 54: 306–16.

Islam, I. and C. Kirkpatrick (1986). 'Export-Led Development, Labour-Market Conditions and the Distribution of Income: The Case of Singapore', *Cambridge Journal of Economics*, 10: 113–27.

Khee, N. M. and Y. Y. Liong (2005). 'Trends in Household Income and Expenditure, 1993–2003', *Statistics Singapore Newsletter*, September.

Krongkaew, M. (1994). 'Income Distribution in East Asian Developing Countries: An Update', *Asia Pacific Economic Literature*, 8(2): 58–73.

—— and Ragayah Haji Mat Zin (2006). 'Income Distribution and Sustainable Economic Development in East Asia: A Comparative Analysis', paper presented at Conference on 'Economic Openness and Income Inequality', Shanghai, August.

Kuznets, S. (1955). 'Economic Growth and Income Inequality'. *American Economic Review*, 45: 1–28.

Leigh, A. and P. van der Eng (2009). 'Inequality in Indonesia: What Can We Learn from Top Incomes', *Journal of Public Economics*, 93: 209–12.

Lim, C.-Y. (1999). 'The National Wages Council: Targets and Goals', in C.-Y. Lim and R. Chew (eds.) *Wages and Wages Policies: Tripartism in Singapore*. Singapore: World Scientific.

Little, I. M. D., T. Scitovsky, and M. Fg. Scott (1970). *Industry and Trade in Some Developing Countries*. Oxford: Oxford University Press.

Maddison, A. (2003). *The World Economy: Historical Statistics*. Paris: Organization for Economic Cooperation and Development.

Okigbo, P. (1968). 'The Distribution of National Income in African Countries', in J. Marchal and B. Ducros (eds.) *The Distribution of National Income*. London: Macmillan.

Ragayah Haji Mat Zin (2002). 'The Impact of the Financial Crisis on Poverty and Inequality in Malaysia', in S. Khandker (ed.) *Impact of the East Asian Financial Crisis Revisited*. Washington, DC: The World Bank Institute.

—— (2003). 'Income Distribution in East Asian Developing Countries: Recent Trends', *Asian Pacific Economic Literature*, 8(2): 36–54.

Rao, V. V. Bhanoji (1996). 'Income Inequality in Singapore: Facts and Policies', in Lim Chong Yah (ed.) *Economic Policy Management in Singapore*. Singapore: Addison-Wesley.

—— (1999). 'East Asian Economies: Trends in Poverty and Income Inequality', *Economic and Political Weekly*, 34: 1029–39.

—— (2000). 'Income Distribution in Singapore: Trends and Issues', *Singapore Economic Review*, 35: 143–60.

—— D. S. Banerjee, and P. Mukhopadhaya (2003). 'Earnings Inequality in Singapore', *Journal of the Asia Pacific Economy*, 8: 210–28.

—— and N. Ramakrishnan (1980). *Income Inequality in Singapore*. Singapore: Singapore University Press.

Singapore Department of Statistics (2002). 'Income Distribution and Inequality Measures in Singapore', paper presented at conference at Hong Kong University of Science and Technology, June.

State of Singapore (1963). *Annual Report 1960*. London: HMSO.

Tan, A. H. H. and O. C. Hock (1982). 'Singapore', chapter 9 in B. Balassa et al. (eds.) *Development Strategies in Semi-Industrial Countries*. Baltimore: Johns Hopkins University Press.

Tan Yih Bin (1992). 'Wages Statistics', *Singapore Statistical News*, 15(2): 1–4.

Tan Yin Yang, A. Eng, and E. Robinson (2008). 'Perspectives on Growth: A Political Economy Framework. Lessons from the Singapore Experience', Working Paper No. 1, Commission on Growth and Development. Washington, DC: World Bank.

Tsao, Y. (1985). 'Growth without Productivity: Singapore Manufacturing in the 1970s', *Journal of Development Economics*, 19: 25–38.

United Nations (1968). *Economic Survey of Asia and the Far East 1967*. Bangkok: United Nations.

United Nations Economic Commission for Asia and the Pacific (1998). *Economic and Social Survey of Asia and the Pacific*. New York: United Nations.

Wood, A. (1994). *North–South Trade, Employment and Inequality*. Oxford: Clarendon Press.

6

The Rich in Argentina over the Twentieth Century, 1932–2004

Facundo Alvaredo

6.1 INTRODUCTION

This chapter presents series of top income shares in Argentina between 1932 and 2004. The use of long-run statistical information from the personal income tax, never exploited before in this country, allows us to cover a long time span and fill a gap in the analysis of the long-run dynamics of income concentration in Argentina. We find an increase in top income shares after the Great Depression, with maxima in 1942–4, and a substantial decline during the Peronist years. However, the limits of the Peronist redistributive policy are marked by the fact that in 1956 the top shares were, if lower than in 1945, still above the ones observed in the developed world; they were higher than in the United States, France, Australia, and even Spain. Since the mid 1990s, top income shares followed an increasing trend, similar to the pattern found in Anglo-Saxon economies.

The case of Argentina is special and consequently worth studying on several grounds.

1. So far, Banerjee and Piketty (2005) on India, Piketty and Qian (2009) on China, Leigh and van der Eng (2009) on Indonesia (Chapters 1, 2, and 4 in this volume), and this chapter on Argentina are the only works providing evidence for—currently—developing countries (see also Chapter 5 on Singapore). Argentina is the first case to be analysed in Latin America. To our knowledge, the statistical information on which these studies are built upon is not available in any other Latin American country over such a long period. Recently, the tax agencies of Brazil, Chile, and Ecuador have accepted to

I am grateful to Hildegart Ahumada, Tony Atkinson, Heber Camelo, Alfredo Canavese, Guillermo Cruces, Rafael Di Tella, Leonardo Gasparini, Daniel Heymann, Leandro Prados de la Escosura, Emmanuel Saez, José Antonio Sánchez Román, Walter Sosa Escudero, Analía Vasallo, anonymous referees, and seminar participants at PSE (Paris) and the 2006 World Bank Network of Income and Poverty Meeting for helpful comments. Special thanks go to Thomas Piketty for encouraging the work on Argentina.

produce (not always public) tabulations for a very limited number of years.[1] This reinforces the interest in looking at the Argentine experience.

2. Secondly, Argentina was once a relatively rich country that has consistently diverged from the industrial economies in the last fifty years; today it is indistinguishably a middle-income emerging economy. The deterioration of the country's position is one of the puzzling cases in the economics of development. Between 1870 and 1930 the economy displayed a growth process that changed its marginal position in the world and made many think that the country would play in South America the role the United States stood for in the north.[2] It enjoyed its own Belle Époque between 1900 and 1914. The formula of success has been widely analysed: a relatively literate and skilled population of immigrants, a seamless integration of domestic and world economies in trade through rail and shipping connections on land and sea financed with foreign investment, a large stock of fertile agricultural land, a considerable increase in the world demand for raw materials which translated into favourable terms of trade. In 1870, per capita income was only 60 per cent of the average per capita income of the world top ten economies.[3] Between 1875 and 1914 per capita GDP grew at an average rate above 4 per cent. During the fifty years following 1880 total population increased from 2.5 million to 11.9 million fostered by several immigration waves. Not only was per capita income high, but the growth rate was one of the highest in the world.[4] In 1913, Argentina's per capita income level ($4,519) was inferior to those of Great Britain ($5,855), the United States ($6,308), Canada ($5,290), Australia ($6,800), New Zealand ($6,130), Switzerland ($5,076), and Belgium ($5,021), but it surpassed the levels of other European economies, such as Germany, ($4,341), France ($4,147), Austria ($4,123), Denmark ($4,479), Finland ($2,512), Sweden ($3,684), Italy ($3,050), and Spain ($2,682).[5] These figures place Argentina's 1913 income level among or approaching the world's top ten. It was not a smooth process and the export-based growth model had its own limitations: high dependency rates, the need for external funding, a large but limited land stock.[6] Nevertheless, the circumstances helped create an

---

[1] The study of top incomes and personal income taxation in Latin America during recent years is part of an ongoing research project. In particular, we have recently found income tax tabulations (like the ones serving as primary data sources in this book) for Brazil, which cover several years of the second half of the twentieth century.

[2] To make reference to one of the multiple examples of this optimism, both the First Bank of Boston and the City of New York Bank (Citibank) opened their two major overseas branches in Buenos Aires as early as in the 1910s.

[3] We refer to the world top ten economies in terms of per capita income in 1870 according to Maddison (2001, 2003): Austria, Belgium, Denmark, France, the Netherlands, Switzerland, the United Kingdom, Australia, New Zealand, and the United States.

[4] See Diaz-Alejandro (1970).

[5] Comparative data from Maddison (2001, 2003) expressed in 2000 US dollars.

[6] For an analysis of these limitations, see Taylor (1992).

atmosphere of unlimited growth possibilities, which was mutually shared by the ruling class, the people, and the immigrants.

In contrast, the last fifty years are much more difficult to summarize. While Western countries (including Mexico and Brazil and especially Australia and New Zealand) experienced significant growth after the Second World War, Argentina stagnated and later declined. Political turmoil, institutional instability, macroeconomic volatility, income stagnation, high inflation, and two hyperinflations dominated the scenario. Cycles of poor economic performance and continuous political upheavals were associated with the conflict of interests between the landed gentry and the industrialist elite, and with the integration and final acceptance of the working classes into the social and political system. Between 1956 and 2004 per capita GDP only grew at an annual rate of less than 1 per cent; if we consider the figures in the aftermath of the 2001 macroeconomic crisis, the average income has virtually failed to grow in the last three decades while inequality has constantly increased (see Figures 6.1 and 6.10). By the end of 2002 the unemployment rate was well above 20 per cent; GDP sunk by 20 per cent and poverty skyrocketed, but recovery resumed rapidly, and the economy grew at annual rates of 7–9 per cent until 2007.

3. Thirdly, although the analysis presented in this chapter concerns only the very rich, little is known about the long-run evolution of the distribution of income in Argentina. The first study about inequality dates back to the research programme jointly conducted by the Economic Commission for Latin America and the Caribbean (ECLAC) and the National Development Council (CONADE) published in 1965.[7] This study attempted to measure the distribution of income in 1953, 1959, and 1961 using a variety of sources, including National Accounts, banking sector balance sheets, the 1963 income and expenditure survey, and tax statistics. It was not until 1972 that the National Bureau of Statistics began to conduct biannual household surveys. Before 1974, the survey was restricted to Greater Buenos Aires and it covered approximately 33 per cent of the population. Since then, other urban centres have progressively been incorporated so that today the fraction of represented households exceeds 60 per cent (70 per cent of urban population). Yet, micro-data displaying personal incomes are only available for 1980–2 and 1984–2006 with varying degree of detail. As a result, most studies about inequality and distribution are based on this survey, constrained to the analysis of the last twenty-five years and never focused on the top of the distribution.[8] In any case survey micro-data do not offer valuable information when targeting the top, as the rich are missing either for sampling reasons, low response rates, or ex post elimination of extreme values. Therefore, our study is also the first in looking at the upper part of the distribution in Argentina.

---

[7] CONADE (1965).
[8] Survey micro-data sets for 1972–3 and 1975–9 are not available.

4. Argentina has traditionally been identified as one of the economies with the lowest relative inequality in Latin America despite the recurrent macroeconomic crisis. It is indeed more egalitarian than Chile, Mexico, and Brazil.[9] A word of caution is in order, though. On the one side, Latin America is an area characterized by very high inequality levels when compared to Europe and Asia. On the other, during the last fifteen years, the increase in inequality in Argentina has outpaced Latin American averages. Finally, the periods of negative growth strongly hit the poor.[10] Notwithstanding this trend, Argentina's human development index has remained top in Latin America since its publication in 1975.

Income tax data suffer from serious drawbacks.[11] The definitions of taxable income and tax unit tend to change through time according to the tax laws. While there is a predisposition to under-reporting certain types of income, taxpayers also undertake a variety of avoidance responses, including planning, renaming, and retiming of activities to legally reduce the tax liability. Capital incomes and capital gains are taxed at different degrees across time. These elements, which are common to all countries at different degrees, become critical in developing economies. However, alternative sources such as household surveys are not free of problems regarding under-reporting, differential non-responses, unit design, and information at the top of the distribution. Therefore, even if results based on income tax statistics must be read with caution, especially in the case of developing economies with important levels of tax evasion, they can still be informative and remain a unique source to study the dynamics of income concentration during the first half of the twentieth century. The reader should also bear in mind that the degree of detail provided by tax statistics in Argentina, especially for recent years, is notoriously inferior to the one offered by many developed economies (see Piketty and Saez 2003 for the United States or Piketty 2001 for France). This is not surprising but poses serious limitations when trying to explain facts in an overall convincing way.

The chapter is organized as follows: section 6.2 describes the data and methodology. Section 6.3 presents the main findings. Section 6.4 is devoted to the conclusions. Details about data sources, methods, and adjustments are presented in Appendices 6A–E.

6.2 DATA, METHODOLOGICAL ISSUES, AND CONTEXT

At the start of the inter-war period customs on imports constituted the largest fraction of government revenue in Argentina. As public income depended heavily

---

[9] See Gasparini (2004) for an account of inequality levels in Latin America.

[10] See Gasparini, Gutiérrez, and Tornarolli (2007).

[11] The methodological issues around the use of tax data and aggregate income data to estimate top income shares have been well canvassed in Atkinson (2007).

on international trade, it was cyclically correlated with trade conditions. The consequences of the Great Depression exposed the country to the commodity lottery and the worsening of the terms of trade. In order to moderate the adverse effects of the crisis on public finances, the government followed a conservative fiscal policy and sought orthodox budget balance by replacing the lost customs revenues with a large increase in direct taxes on income and wealth. As part of this process, the first personal income tax was enforced in 1932 in Argentina as a policy response to the negative outcome that the world crisis had on the public budget. The legal evolution of the tax is briefly described in Appendix 6A.

Table 6.1 displays the composition of tax receipts between 1932 and 2004, while Table 6.2 shows tax collections as percentage of GDP. The growing importance of the personal income tax until the mid-1940s (it moved from 6 per cent of national government revenues in 1932 to 19 per cent in 1943) mirrored the decline of international trade-based taxes (which went down from 40 per cent in 1932 to 7 per cent in 1945).[12] The creation of the personal income tax in 1932 (initially established as an emergency and temporary tax for only two years) and its declining importance during the second half of the century (when Latin American countries developed a clear preference for non-personal taxation) shape the availability of data.

The tabulations of income tax returns published by the Argentine tax administration constitute the primary data source for this study. The data cover the years 1932 to 1954, 1956, 1958, 1970 to 1973, and 1997 to 2004.[13] Unfortunately, the continuity of the publication has been lost since the 1960s, altered by increasing macroeconomic volatility, growing inflation, and political instability. The tabulations report, by ranges of income, the number of taxpayers, total assessed income, taxable income, tax paid, and personal deductions.

As the right tail of the income distribution is well approximated by Pareto distributions, we use simple parametric interpolations methods to estimate the thresholds and average income levels for several fractiles. This method follows the classical study by Kuznets (1953) and has been used here as well as in many of the top income studies presented in Atkinson and Piketty (2007) and in this volume.[14]

The Argentine income tax is individually based. Consequently, the number of tax units (the number of individuals had everybody been required to file) is approximated by the number of persons in the population aged 20 and over from the national census. Throughout the chapter, 'tax units' always refer to individuals. Thus, our top groups are expressed in relation to the total number of adults.

We define income as gross income before all deductions and including all income items reported on personal tax returns: salaries and pensions, self-employment and

---

[12] Tables 6.1 and 6.2 consider all legislated taxes. It is worth stressing the importance that the inflation tax had in the public revenue in Argentina during the second half of the century (see Ahumada, Alvaredo, and Canavese 2000).

[13] Provisional tabulations exist for 1959, but they only include a fraction of total tax files.

[14] The Pareto interpolation can be done in different ways, yielding different results. Fortunately, with most data the choice does not matter much. The mean-split histogram method has been used to estimate top shares in the cases of the UK, the Netherlands, Australia, and New Zealand. For a discussion on interpolation methods, see Atkinson (2005).

Table 6.1 Structure of tax revenues, Argentina, 1932–2004

	% of national government tax receipts						
Personal income tax and corporate tax							
Personal income tax (1)	Corporate income tax (2)	Total (1) + (2) (3)	Social contributions (4)	Property taxes (5)	Sales tax (6)	International trade (7)	Other taxes (8)
1932 6.04	0.12	6.16	15.97	1.53	24.48	40.70	11.16
1933 5.97	2.31	8.28	14.99	1.42	25.01	40.35	9.95
1934 7.18	1.30	8.48	14.89	1.74	26.03	38.84	10.01
1935 6.74	2.64	9.38	14.08	1.67	30.89	35.22	8.76
1936 7.88	1.06	8.94	14.34	2.08	32.78	33.09	8.76
1937 8.17	2.01	10.18	12.92	1.55	31.91	36.58	6.86
1938 7.39	4.81	12.20	13.41	1.68	32.50	33.58	6.63
1939 8.08	4.90	12.98	14.13	1.66	34.72	29.39	7.12
1940 8.09	5.66	13.75	15.36	1.51	36.43	25.55	7.41
1941 11.10	2.85	13.95	16.05	2.15	39.17	20.88	7.79
1942 13.73	4.63	18.36	15.95	2.25	39.07	17.01	7.36
1943 19.33	11.01	30.34	15.54	2.31	35.70	9.78	6.33
1944 18.59	10.50	29.09	16.09	2.38	36.69	7.97	7.78
1945 15.96	8.64	24.60	27.39	1.63	31.84	7.50	7.05
1946 16.82	17.08	33.90	23.80	1.74	24.94	9.96	5.66
1947 15.78	12.57	28.35	32.38	1.07	20.31	13.30	4.60
1948 15.08	12.36	27.44	36.09	1.16	20.44	9.45	5.42
1949 13.92	10.80	24.72	38.08	0.90	26.98	4.55	4.77
1950 16.51	8.27	24.78	34.61	4.86	28.91	3.40	3.44
1951 15.08	9.67	24.75	31.98	3.20	31.78	5.19	3.09
1952 12.03	15.29	27.32	32.21	3.64	30.82	3.11	2.91
1953 11.74	10.61	22.35	35.33	4.49	32.49	1.78	3.56
1954 11.40	9.72	21.12	37.21	4.23	32.65	2.27	2.53
1955 10.91	10.50	21.41	37.54	3.64	31.40	2.75	3.26
1956 12.39	11.86	24.25	37.87	2.61	28.67	2.87	3.74
1957 15.78	8.53	24.31	33.32	1.78	31.53	3.42	5.65
1958 18.05	7.50	25.55	32.75	1.95	30.82	4.35	4.58
1959 16.06	10.44	26.50	34.05	1.48	27.37	6.51	4.11
1960 10.43	14.65	25.08	29.10	5.69	32.36	4.18	3.59
1961		23.28	31.66	4.30	33.59	3.58	3.59
1962		19.43	29.01	3.10	33.44	12.07	2.95
1963		17.84	28.42	2.39	34.67	13.64	3.03
1964		14.59	34.86	1.97	28.72	17.22	2.64
1965		19.95	30.89	1.89	29.41	14.67	3.20
1966		19.83	27.27	3.86	34.44	11.62	2.98
1967		17.54	30.83	5.34	28.27	15.28	2.74
1968		14.79	30.30	4.72	33.61	13.43	3.15
1969		15.23	28.86	4.88	34.16	13.34	3.52
1970 5.80	12.73	18.53	28.59	6.01	31.90	11.87	3.10
1971 6.00	8.15	14.14	32.19	5.59	32.50	12.74	2.84
1972 5.61	7.33	12.95	29.93	4.85	31.80	17.82	2.66
1973 4.70	9.04	13.74	33.84	5.08	29.28	15.11	2.95
1974		14.99	32.37	4.57	33.06	11.99	3.03
1975		8.21	39.36	0.51	35.35	13.83	2.73

1976			9.25	30.59	4.67	31.01	17.92	6.57
1977			11.80	24.07	6.07	38.76	10.51	8.80
1978			11.15	27.57	5.39	44.23	7.95	3.72
1979			7.83	31.16	4.89	44.12	8.97	3.03
1980			9.17	29.35	4.70	43.79	10.21	2.77
1981			10.62	15.77	5.12	54.75	11.51	2.23
1982			9.53	13.76	8.47	54.36	11.75	2.15
1983			7.49	14.84	7.08	49.69	16.62	4.28
1984			4.26	19.77	6.39	51.43	14.29	3.87
1985			6.00	22.33	6.92	43.80	18.40	2.56
1986			7.79	21.10	8.37	45.10	15.07	2.56
1987			9.84	24.51	8.42	41.03	12.09	4.12
1988			8.90	20.89	12.42	43.01	10.19	4.60
1989			10.39	14.76	12.56	34.16	22.86	5.27
1990			4.82	22.31	9.08	44.98	13.06	5.75
1991			4.54	23.76	12.16	46.62	6.43	6.50
1992			7.63	23.48	4.92	53.93	6.12	3.93
1993			11.15	24.34	1.78	52.86	6.41	3.47
1994			12.86	29.71	1.43	47.55	6.18	2.27
1995			14.62	27.45	1.21	49.94	4.42	2.36
1996			15.74	23.62	1.84	53.22	5.25	0.33
1997	3.60	13.52	17.12	21.78	1.26	53.92	5.77	0.14
1998	3.54	15.36	18.90	20.50	1.77	52.93	5.60	0.29
1999	3.41	17.40	20.81	19.29	2.10	52.04	4.84	0.91
2000	4.11	18.61	22.72	18.10	2.47	51.75	4.14	0.83
2001	3.40	19.87	23.27	17.76	8.25	46.27	3.64	0.82
2002	5.32	13.04	18.36	16.02	10.58	42.17	12.26	0.61
2003	5.24	16.65	21.89	13.41	10.36	38.62	15.35	0.38
2004	4.26	19.20	23.46	13.29	9.48	39.72	13.53	0.51

Sources: Dirección General de Impuestos a los Réditos, Memoria, several years; Dirección General Impositiva, Memoria, several years; Administración Federal de Ingresos Públicos, Estadísticas Tributarias, several years.

Table 6.2 Structure of tax revenues as % GDP, Argentina, 1932–2004

	National government tax receipts as % of GDP							
	Personal income tax and corporate tax							
	Personal income tax (1)	Corporate income tax (2)	Total (1) + (2) (3)	Social contributions (4)	Property taxes (5)	Sales tax (6)	International trade (7)	Other taxes (8)
1932	0.61	0.01	0.62	1.62	0.16	2.48	4.12	1.13
1933	0.58	0.22	0.80	1.46	0.14	2.43	3.92	0.97
1934	0.64	0.12	0.76	1.34	0.16	2.33	3.48	0.90
1935	0.68	0.27	0.94	1.42	0.17	3.11	3.54	0.88
1936	0.74	0.10	0.84	1.34	0.19	3.07	3.10	0.82
1937	0.77	0.19	0.96	1.22	0.15	3.00	3.44	0.65
1938	0.73	0.48	1.21	1.33	0.17	3.23	3.34	0.66
1939	0.76	0.46	1.22	1.33	0.16	3.26	2.76	0.67
1940	0.72	0.50	1.22	1.37	0.13	3.24	2.27	0.66
1941	0.88	0.23	1.11	1.28	0.17	3.11	1.66	0.62
1942	1.05	0.35	1.40	1.21	0.17	2.98	1.30	0.56

(*continued*)

Table 6.2 Continued

	National government tax receipts as % of GDP						
Personal income tax and corporate tax							
Personal income tax (1)	Corporate income tax (2)	Total (1) + (2) (3)	Social contributions (4)	Property taxes (5)	Sales tax (6)	International trade (7)	Other taxes (8)
1943	1.63	0.93	2.56	1.31	0.19	3.02	0.83	0.54
1944	1.58	0.89	2.47	1.37	0.20	3.12	0.68	0.66
1945	1.49	0.81	2.30	2.56	0.15	2.97	0.70	0.66
1946	1.87	1.90	3.77	2.65	0.19	2.77	1.11	0.63
1947	2.19	1.75	3.94	4.49	0.15	2.82	1.85	0.64
1948	2.24	1.84	4.08	5.37	0.17	3.04	1.41	0.81
1949	2.14	1.66	3.80	5.86	0.14	4.15	0.70	0.73
1950	2.85	1.43	4.27	5.97	0.84	4.99	0.59	0.59
1951	2.59	1.66	4.26	5.50	0.55	5.47	0.89	0.53
1952	1.90	2.41	4.30	5.07	0.57	4.85	0.49	0.46
1953	1.84	1.67	3.51	5.54	0.70	5.10	0.28	0.56
1954	1.91	1.63	3.54	6.23	0.71	5.47	0.38	0.42
1955	1.73	1.67	3.40	5.97	0.58	5.00	0.44	0.52
1956	1.98	1.89	3.87	6.04	0.42	4.58	0.46	0.60
1957	2.13	1.15	3.28	4.49	0.24	4.25	0.46	0.76
1958	2.20	0.91	3.11	3.98	0.24	3.75	0.53	0.56
1959	1.93	1.25	3.18	4.08	0.18	3.28	0.78	0.49
1960	1.25	1.76	3.01	3.49	0.68	3.88	0.50	0.43
1961			2.83	3.84	0.52	4.08	0.44	0.44
1962			2.12	3.17	0.34	3.65	1.32	0.32
1963			2.08	3.32	0.28	4.05	1.59	0.35
1964			1.54	3.68	0.21	3.03	1.82	0.28
1965			2.31	3.58	0.22	3.41	1.70	0.37
1966			2.50	3.43	0.49	4.33	1.46	0.37
1967			2.54	4.47	0.77	4.10	2.22	0.40
1968			1.99	4.08	0.64	4.53	1.81	0.42
1969			1.94	3.68	0.62	4.35	1.70	0.45
1970	0.92	2.02	2.94	4.54	0.95	5.07	1.89	0.49
1971	0.84	1.15	1.99	4.53	0.79	4.57	1.79	0.40
1972	0.70	0.91	1.61	3.73	0.60	3.96	2.22	0.33
1973	0.62	1.19	1.81	4.47	0.67	3.86	1.99	0.39
1974			2.35	5.08	0.72	5.19	1.88	0.48
1975			0.88	4.21	0.05	3.78	1.48	0.29
1976			1.18	3.90	0.59	3.95	2.28	0.84
1977			1.39	2.84	0.71	4.57	1.24	1.04
1978			1.31	3.24	0.63	5.19	0.93	0.44
1979			0.89	3.54	0.56	5.02	1.02	0.34
1980			1.16	3.72	0.60	5.55	1.29	0.35
1981			1.24	1.84	0.60	6.37	1.34	0.26
1982			0.95	1.37	0.84	5.40	1.17	0.21
1983			0.70	1.38	0.66	4.62	1.55	0.40
1984			0.40	1.84	0.59	4.78	1.33	0.36
1985			0.76	2.82	0.87	5.53	2.32	0.32
1986			0.95	2.58	1.02	5.51	1.84	0.31
1987			1.19	2.97	1.02	4.97	1.46	0.50
1988			0.94	2.21	1.31	4.54	1.08	0.49
1989			1.21	1.72	1.46	3.98	2.66	0.61

1990			0.51	2.38	0.97	4.80	1.39	0.61
1991			0.58	3.06	1.57	6.00	0.83	0.84
1992			1.14	3.51	0.74	8.07	0.92	0.59
1993			1.84	4.02	0.29	8.74	1.06	0.57
1994			2.30	5.30	0.25	8.49	1.10	0.40
1995			2.46	4.62	0.20	8.40	0.74	0.40
1996			2.54	3.82	0.30	8.60	0.85	0.05
1997	0.61	2.28	2.89	3.68	0.21	9.10	0.97	0.02
1998	0.60	2.61	3.21	3.48	0.30	8.98	0.95	0.05
1999	0.58	2.97	3.56	3.30	0.36	8.90	0.83	0.16
2000	0.72	3.25	3.97	3.17	0.43	9.05	0.72	0.14
2001	0.58	3.41	3.99	3.05	1.42	7.94	0.62	0.14
2002	0.88	2.16	3.05	2.66	1.76	6.99	2.03	0.10
2003	1.03	3.27	4.30	2.63	2.04	7.59	3.02	0.07
2004	0.96	4.31	5.27	2.98	2.13	8.92	3.04	0.11

Sources: Dirección General de Impuestos a los Réditos, Memoria, several years; Dirección General Impositiva, Memoria, several years; Administración Federal de Ingresos Públicos, Estadísticas Tributarias, several years.

unincorporated business net income, dividends, interest, other investment income, and other smaller income items. Realized capital gains are excluded. Our income definition is before personal income taxes and personal payroll taxes but after employers' payroll taxes and corporate income taxes. Appendices 6A–E complete the information about data sources.

Table 6.3 displays the reference totals for population and income. While the growing inflation (column 8) happening during the second half of the century could have implied a rise in the obligation to file (by reducing the significance of the taxable threshold), minimum non-taxable income and personal allowances were regularly revised so that exemption levels remained high. By necessity our analysis focuses on the very top of the distribution.

Table 6.4 gives thresholds and average incomes for top fractiles in 2000. There were 23.8 million tax units, with an average income of $7,871. Column 2 reports the income thresholds corresponding to each of the percentiles in column 1. For example, an annual income of at least $200,274 was required to belong to the top 0.1 per cent while the average income above the top 0.01 per cent was $1,547,033. Table 6.5 presents the top income shares between 1932 and 2004.

6.3 THE DYNAMICS OF TOP INCOMES

The Years 1932–1945

Figures 6.2 to 6.5 present the main findings. It is not the aim of this chapter to provide a detailed account of more than seventy years of economic history and economic policy. Nevertheless, to understand the evolution of top incomes, some historical landmarks are worth mentioning.

Table 6.3 Reference totals for population, income, and inflation, Argentina, 1932–2004

	Tax units and population				Total Income		Price Index	Inflation	Taxes
	(1)	(2)	(3)	(4)	(5)	(6)	(7)	(8)	(9)
	Population ('000s)	Tax units ('000s)	Number of tax returns ('000s)	(3)/(2)(%)	Total income (million 2000 Pesos)	Average income (2000 Pesos)	CPI (2000:100)	(%)	Top Marginal Tax Rate (%)
1932	11,570	6,372	113	1.8	28,520	4,476	1.51E-12	−10.3	12
1933	11,817	6,538	112	1.7	27,664	4,231	1.64E-12	8.2	12
1934	12,070	6,708	133	2.0	28,439	4,240	1.51E-12	−7.6	12
1935	12,328	6,883	142	2.1	30,199	4,387	1.60E-12	6.0	12
1936	12,592	7,063	150	2.1	31,026	4,393	1.74E-12	8.5	12
1937	12,861	7,247	151	2.1	31,283	4,317	1.78E-12	2.6	12
1938	13,137	7,436	145	2.0	33,550	4,512	1.77E-12	−0.6	12
1939	13,418	7,630	142	1.9	33,654	4,411	1.80E-12	1.5	12
1940	13,705	7,829	134	1.7	34,942	4,463	1.84E-12	2.2	12
1941	13,998	8,033	147	1.8	35,508	4,420	1.89E-12	2.6	12
1942	14,297	8,242	122	1.5	37,362	4,533	2.00E-12	5.7	12
1943	14,603	8,457	141	1.7	37,774	4,467	2.02E-12	1.1	25
1944	14,916	8,678	167	1.9	37,519	4,323	2.01E-12	−0.3	25
1945	15,235	8,904	180	2.0	41,744	4,688	2.41E-12	19.8	25
1946	15,561	9,136	189	2.1	40,403	4,422	2.83E-12	17.6	27
1947	15,894	9,375	221	2.4	44,014	4,695	3.22E-12	13.6	27
1948	16,178	9,562	250	2.6	48,906	5,115	3.64E-12	13.1	27
1949	16,468	9,754	255	2.6	51,588	5,289	4.77E-12	31.1	27
1950	16,762	9,949	365	3.7	50,917	5,118	5.99E-12	25.6	27
1951	17,062	10,148	386	3.8	51,534	5,078	8.19E-12	36.7	27
1952	17,367	10,352	476	4.6	53,542	5,172	1.14E-11	38.7	32
1953	17,678	10,559	558	5.3	50,846	4,815	1.18E-11	4.0	32
1954	17,994	10,770	545	5.1	53,539	4,971	1.23E-11	3.8	32
1955	18,316	10,986	n/a	n/a	55,750	5,075	1.38E-11	12.3	40

1956	18,644	11,206	587	5.2	59,689	5,327	1.56E-11	13.4	40
1957	18,977	11,430	n/a	n/a	61,346	5,367	1.95E-11	24.7	40
1958	19,317	11,659	605	5.2	64,523	5,534	2.56E-11	31.6	40
1959	19,662	11,893	491	4.1	68,464	5,757	5.47E-11	113.7	40
1960	20,014	12,131	n/a	n/a	64,040	5,279	6.93E-11	26.6	40
1961	20,326	12,343	n/a	n/a	69,079	5,597	7.88E-11	13.7	40
1970	23,362	14,438	591	4.1	98,567	6,827	4.76E-10	13.6	46
1971	23,785	14,686	551	3.8	103,869	7,073	6.41E-10	34.7	46
1972	24,215	14,939	532	3.6	108,836	7,285	1.02E-09	58.5	46
1973	24,653	15,196	494	3.3	112,235	7,386	1.63E-09	60.3	46
1997	34,756	22,403	1,259	5.6	172,927	7,719	101.20	0.5	33
1998	35,126	22,869	1,114	4.9	186,946	8,175	102.14	0.9	33
1999	35,500	23,346	819	3.5	194,148	8,316	100.95	-1.2	33
2000	35,878	23,833	786	3.3	187,578	7,871	100.00	-0.9	35
2001	36,260	24,329	674	2.8	179,303	7,370	98.93	-1.1	35
2002	36,646	24,836	728	2.9	159,769	6,433	124.53	25.9	35
2003	37,037	25,354	763	3.0	173,891	6,859	141.27	13.4	35
2004	37,431	25,882	748	2.9	189,539	7,323	147.49	4.4	35

Notes: Population and tax units estimates based on census. Tax units estimated as the number of adults aged 20 and over. The number of tax returns (column 3) excludes taxpayers with wage income only.

Table 6.4 Thresholds and average incomes in top income groups in Argentina in 2000

Percentile threshold (1)	Income threshold (2)	Income groups (3)	Number of adults (aged 20+) (4)	Average income in each group (5)
		Full adult population	23,833,000	$7,871
Top 1%	$41,115	Top 1–0.5%	119,165	$52,078
Top 0.5%	$70,855	Top 0.5–0.1%	95,332	$105,314
Top 0.1%	$200,274	Top 0.1–0.01%	21,450	$324,660
Top 0.01%	$779,223	Top 0.01%	2,383	$1,547,033

Notes: Computations based on income tax return statistics.
Amounts are expressed in 2000 US dollars.
Column (2) reports the income thresholds corresponding to each of the percentiles in column (1). For example, an annual income of at least $200,274 is required to belong to the top 0.1% tax units, etc.

Table 6.5 Top income shares in Argentina, 1932–2004

	Top 5% (2)	Top 1% (3)	Top 0.5%	Top 0.1% (5)	Top 0.01% (6)	Top 5–1% (8)	Top 1–0.5%	Top 0.5–0.1% (9)	Top 0.1–0.01% (11)	Top 0.01% (12)
1932		18.77	14.58	7.52	2.49		4.18	7.07	5.02	2.49
1933		17.18	13.35	6.80	2.39		3.83	6.55	4.41	2.39
1934		18.06	14.02	7.28	2.45		4.03	6.74	4.83	2.45
1935		18.44	14.32	7.41	2.49		4.12	6.91	4.92	2.49
1936		20.40	15.56	7.76	2.46		4.84	7.81	5.29	2.46
1937		20.44	15.84	8.11	2.60		4.60	7.73	5.51	2.60
1938		20.47	15.83	8.10	2.58		4.63	7.74	5.52	2.58
1939		20.88	16.23	8.34	2.72		4.66	7.89	5.62	2.72
1940		20.11	15.79	8.25	2.65		4.32	7.53	5.60	2.65
1941		22.43	17.85	9.44	3.09		4.58	8.41	6.35	3.09
1942		23.77	19.73	11.38	4.18		4.04	8.36	7.20	4.18
1943		25.96	20.90	11.62	4.16		5.06	9.27	7.46	4.16
1944		24.75	19.66	10.63	3.63		5.08	9.04	7.00	3.63
1945		23.39	18.34	9.76	3.31		5.04	8.59	6.45	3.31
1946		22.63	17.96	9.79	3.46		4.67	8.17	6.33	3.46
1947		24.02	19.06	10.51	3.72		4.96	8.54	6.80	3.72
1948		23.22	18.30	9.78	3.20		4.92	8.53	6.58	3.20
1949		19.34	15.11	7.87	2.40		4.23	7.24	5.48	2.40
1950		19.81	15.55	8.15	2.58		4.25	7.40	5.57	2.58
1951		16.96	13.25	6.85	2.14		3.70	6.41	4.70	2.14
1952		15.96	11.87	5.64	1.57		4.09	6.23	4.07	1.57
1953	29.07	15.35	11.21	5.12	1.42	13.71	4.15	6.09	3.70	1.42
1954	30.28	16.54	12.33	5.84	1.71	13.74	4.21	6.48	4.14	1.71
1956	28.96	15.66	11.66	5.42	1.54	13.31	4.00	6.23	3.89	1.54
1958		14.17	10.53	4.98	1.39		3.64	5.54	3.60	1.39
1959(a)	30.41	15.92	11.54	5.23	1.40	14.49	4.38	6.31	3.83	1.40
1961(a)	28.00	14.68	10.81	4.91	1.45	13.32	3.87	5.91	3.45	1.45

1970		12.18	7.66	2.60	0.51		4.52	5.06	2.09	0.51
1971		10.78	6.92	2.36	0.58		3.86	4.56	1.79	0.58
1972		9.44	6.06	2.15	0.55		3.37	3.91	1.60	0.55
1973		7.40	5.04	2.04	0.54		2.36	3.00	1.50	0.54
1997	22.45	12.39	9.02	4.27	1.39	10.07	3.37	4.74	2.88	1.39
1998		12.57	9.06	4.37	1.43		3.51	4.69	2.94	1.43
1999		13.53	10.32	5.22	1.78		3.22	5.10	3.44	1.78
2000		14.34	11.03	5.68	1.97		3.31	5.35	3.71	1.97
2001		12.91	10.03	5.22	1.82		2.88	4.81	3.40	1.82
2002		15.53	12.34	6.92	2.70		3.19	5.42	4.23	2.70
2003		16.85	13.41	7.40	2.79		3.44	6.01	4.61	2.79
2004		16.75	13.45	7.02	2.49		3.30	6.43	4.53	2.49

Notes: Taxpayers are ranked by gross income.
The table reports the percentage of total income accruing to each of the top groups. Top 1% denotes top percentile.
Income does not include capital gains.
(a) Results not based on income tax data but on CONADE (1965).

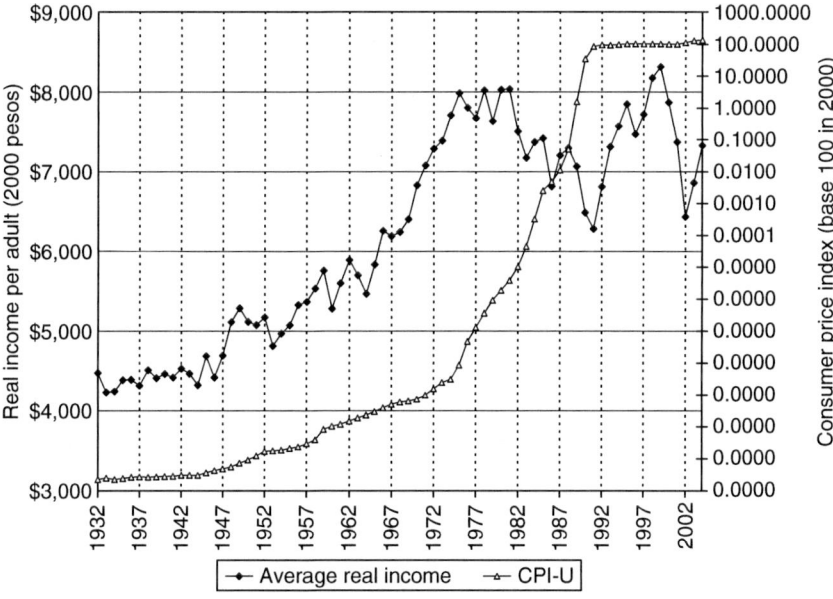

Figure 6.1 Average real income and consumer price index in Argentina, 1932–2004
Notes: Figure reports the average real income per adult (aged 20 and above), expressed in 2000 Pesos.
CPI index is equal to 100 in 2000 (logarithmic scale).
Source: Table 6.3.

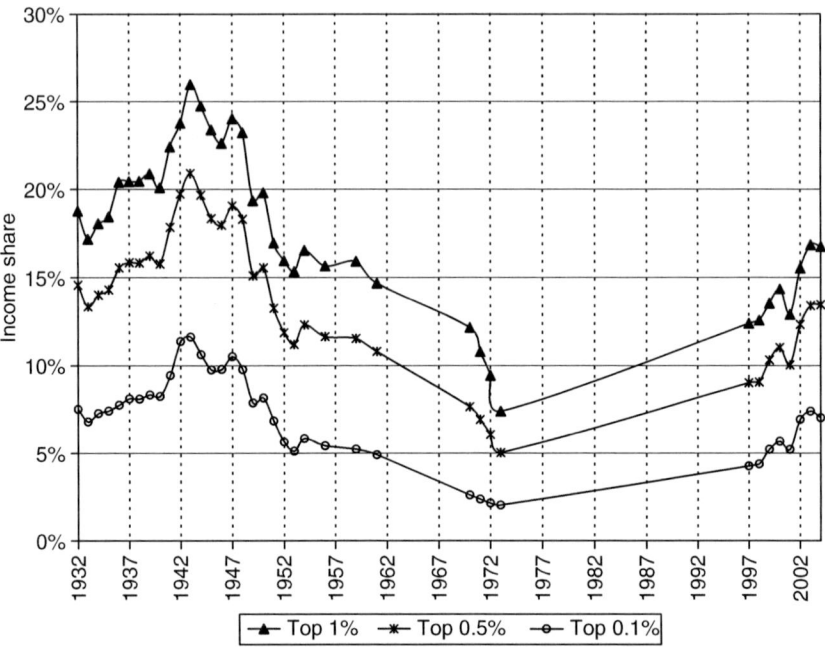

Figure 6.2 The top 1%, top 0.5%, and top 0.1% income shares in Argentina, 1932–2004

Note: Income excludes capital gains.

Source: Table 6.5.

The years between 1870 and 1930 (and more specifically between 1875 and 1914) were the golden period of the development process of the country. Falling transportation costs and the expansion of world trade made it possible for land-abundant countries to benefit from their strong comparative advantage in rural activities. Argentina was one of the prototypical examples. Together with the extension of the railway, all factors contributed to a striking increase in land prices so that many fortunes were made overnight.[15] The economy flourished, based on the exports of raw materials, mainly grains and chilled beef, but also wool, wood, and their derivatives, and the imports of manufactures from Europe (mainly from the UK) and the United States. The wealthy owners of the large *estancias* of the Pampas built urban palaces in Buenos Aires in the image and likeness of those they saw in Europe during their long-lasting trips. Many independent observers have extensively commented about the extreme wealth of the wealthy Argentineans of the beginning of the century.[16]

[15] See Sokoloff and Zolt (2007) for a general discussion on inequality and taxation in the Americas. Johnson and Frank (2006) analyse wealth inequality in Buenos Aires and Rio de Janeiro before 1860.

[16] For an account of the social life and customs of the wealthy Argentinean families in the beginning of the century, see Ocampo (1979), Luna (1958), Sebrelli (1985), Jauretche (1966).

Nevertheless, the source of the concentration of wealth has to be sought not only in the land ownership structure in the Pampas combined with the favourable and successful pattern of international insertion.[17] It was also the result of the not-so-peaceful construction process of the nation. By 1880, the political organization and the occupation of the territory had been achieved on the grounds of an alliance between the Buenos Aires elite and the provincial oligarchies: the Pampas-driven export-oriented economy granted, for the powerful regional groups, the protection of specific local products for domestic consumption. Thus, a rich sector devoted to the production of sugar cane developed in the north-west, a cotton-oriented sector in the north-east and a vine area in the centre-west. Consequently, all competition against them, either through imports or through local production in Buenos Aires, was deliberately blocked.[18]

By 1910, per capita income was among the world's top ten, the country attracted immigrants by the millions, and an atmosphere of unlimited growth possibilities was mutually shared by the ruling class, the people, and the immigrants. The pre-First World War migration waves responded elastically to the wage gap between the country and Europe. At the same time, Argentina was highly dependent on external finance. When British lending collapsed between 1914 and 1919, investment and capital formation rates declined markedly. It is likely that before 1930 the share of top incomes had been higher than the level of 1932 (18.7 per cent for the top 1 per cent) and probably even higher than the global maximum of 25.9 per cent in 1943.

In 1929, the Argentinean elite were suddenly shocked by the Great Depression and the dramatic downturn of conditions in the international sphere. The democratic government could not cope with the crisis, and was deposed by the first *coup d'état* that ended sixty-eight years of constitutional order. The inability of the elite to understand and adapt to the new situation within the constitution, the fear of anarchism and socialism, and the necessity to regain political control shaped the following thirteen years, 1930–43, known as the Conservative Restoration and the Infamous Decade. It was a period of electoral fraud, union conflicts, and the increasing importance of the army in political affairs.

Great Britain, the principal destination for exports, abandoned free trade practices and made preferential agreements with the ex-colonies during the Imperial Economic Conference celebrated in Ottawa in 1932 to promote trade within the limits of the empire. Argentina was set aside. The rich landowners pressured for a rapid accord with London to secure the exports to the United Kingdom. The result was the

[17] The occupation of the territory to the south, accomplished in 1880, was financed mainly by wealthy families, who eventually came into possession of large estates in the newly incorporated areas. For instance, General Roca, in charge of the expedition, received as compensation a 100-km-long property, which he named La Larga ('The Long One'); see Luna (1989). These methods of land occupation and distribution were not new: Rosas's Campaign to the Desert fifty years before had followed the same lines.

[18] For detailed studies on the economic development of Argentina in this period, see Diaz-Alejandro (1970), Cortés Conde and Gallo (1972), Cortés Conde (1979, 1997), Della Paolera and Taylor (2001, 2003), Rapoport (1980). For a sketch of the evolution of wealth concentration in Buenos Aires during the first half of the nineteenth century, see Johnson and Frank (2006).

Roca–Runciman agreement, signed between the Argentinean vice-president and the British minister of trade, which guaranteed Argentina a fixed share in the British meat market and eliminated tariffs on Argentine cereals. In return, Argentina agreed to restrictions with regard to trade and currency exchange, and preserved Britain's commercial interests in the country. From the macroeconomic point of view, the nature and consequences of this agreement and the true impact on the economic performance are still controversial. There are those who see the treaty as a sell-out to Britain, while others stress that the United Kingdom, by according privileges not given to any other country outside the empire, helped counter the recessionary situation. From the microeconomic side, it may be regarded as a successful mechanism to preserve the elite's (but also the state) sources of revenue. In any case, the Roca–Runciman agreement remains a historical landmark and the dynamics of top incomes reinforces the idea of the elite's favourable situation between 1933 and 1943.

Recovery began in 1933 after several years of negative growth.[19] By 1935, GDP had regained the 1928 level. The results of the current study coincide with the political and economic phase. The positive slope displayed by top income shares between 1933 and 1943 is consistent with the marked recuperation of the economy after the Great Depression. The top percentile increased from 17 per cent in 1933 to 25 per cent in 1943. Figure 6.3 provides the comparison of the top 1 per cent income share with several countries of 'new settlement', which are the subject of permanent comparison among scholars when trying to understand and explain the divergence of Argentina. The levels of income concentration in Argentina, Canada, New Zealand, and the United States—but not in Australia—were remarkably similar in the early 1930s. Such communality in levels was rapidly lost, and by the mid 1940s the top 1 per cent income share in Argentina more than doubled the observed shares in those other economies.[20]

Figure 6.5 displays the top 0.01 per cent income shares in Argentina, France, the United States, and Spain. At least two facts can be noticed. First, the level of top shares in Argentina in 1942 (4.1 per cent) is not very far from the one observed in the United States in 1916 (4.4 per cent). Secondly, the dynamics in Argentina between 1932 and 1951 seem to reproduce the shape of US top income shares between 1922 and 1940 but at higher levels, as if the Argentine cycle lagged around 10–13 years with respect to the United States. This reinforces the idea that the pre-1930 figures in Argentina could reasonably be higher than that observed in 1932, in parallel with the evolution in the USA, where the top 0.01 per cent share declined from 4.4 per cent in 1916 to 1.69 per cent in 1921. It is also possible that the higher top shares in Argentina as compared to the USA correspond to lower marginal tax rates.

Consequently, while top shares started a sustained decrease by the beginning of the Second World War in the developed world, they kept growing in Argentina,

[19] The 1929–32 crisis was, until 2002, the longest contraction experienced by the economy, while the deepest contraction occurred in 1914 as a result of both external and internal shocks (bad crops, capital outflows, and the beginning of the First World War).

[20] The results for the United States, Canada, Australia, and New Zealand are taken, respectively, from Piketty and Saez (2003), Saez and Veall (2005), and Atkinson and Leigh (2007a, 2007b).

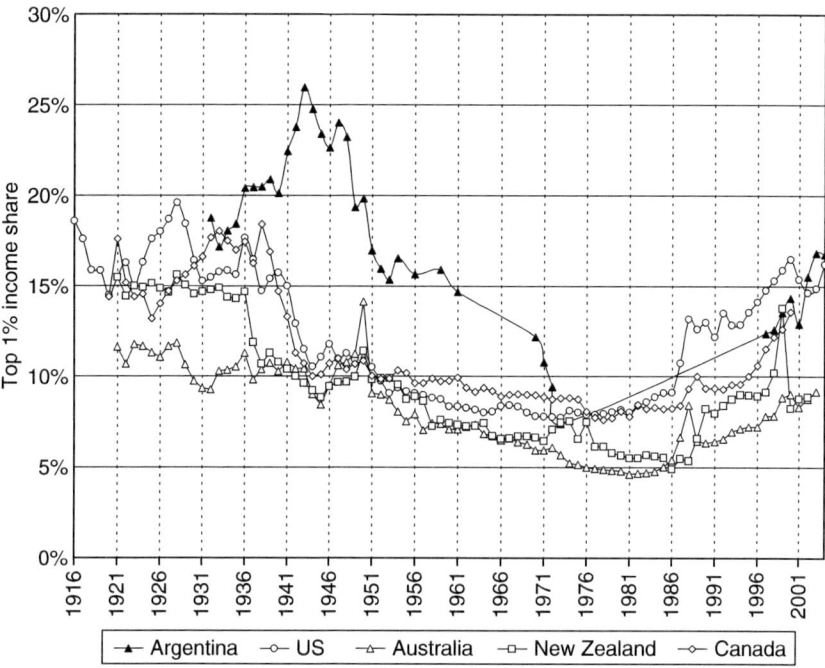

Figure 6.3 The top 1% income shares in Argentina, USA, Australia, New Zealand, and Canada

Sources: Argentina: Table 6.5; US: Piketty and Saez (2003); Australia: Atkinson and Leigh (2007a); New Zealand: Atkinson and Leigh (2007b); Canada: Saez and Veall (2005).

favoured by the export demand from Europe. The country was officially neutral during most of the war for several reasons. On the one hand, a relevant sector of the army showed a clear preference for the Axis. On the other, the British interests in Argentina encouraged neutrality, as it ensured the continuation of normal trade with Europe and mainly with the United Kingdom. Great Britain opposed all US proposals of economic sanctions against Argentina, based on the fact that Argentina's neutrality was crucial for ensuring the safe arrival of shipments to British ports.[21] In any case, the elite had been successful again: during the war, 40 per cent of the British meat and grain markets was supplied by Argentina (Rapoport 1980).

The strong connection between the relatively favourable world market conditions and the evolution of top incomes over this period can be seen from Figure 6.6, which displays the total real income reported by the top 1 per cent and top 0.1 per cent income earners along with total agricultural and livestock exports on a logarithmic scale from 1932 to 1956. The two series are highly correlated and

---

[21] For a detailed study on the conflict of interests in the triangular relationship between Argentina, the United Kingdom, and the United States during the Second World War, see Rapoport (1980, 1988).

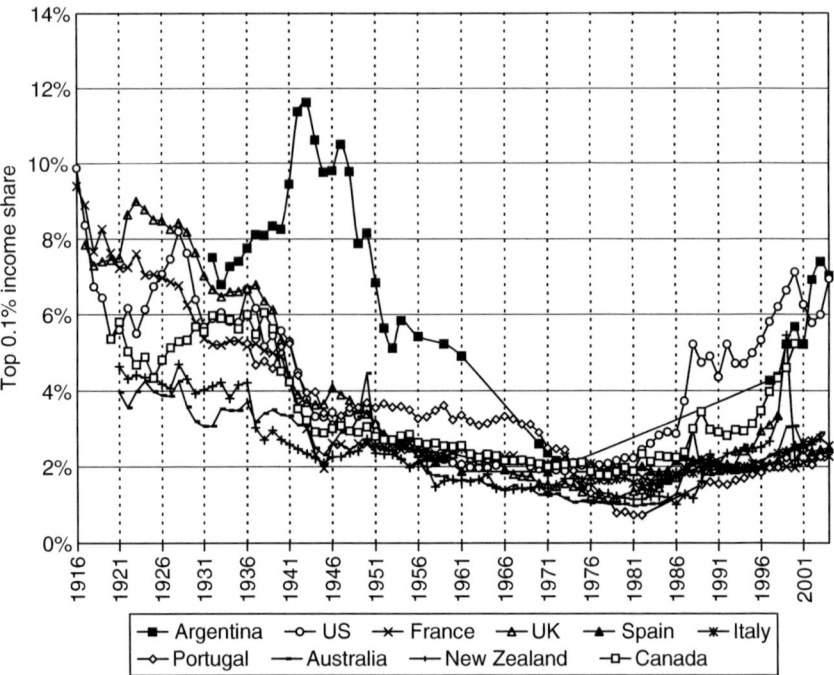

Figure 6.4 The top 0.1% income shares in Argentina, USA, France, Spain, Italy, Portugal, Canada, and UK

Sources: Argentina: Table 6.5; USA: Piketty and Saez (2003); France: Piketty (2001) and Landais (2007); UK: Atkinson (2007); Italy: Alvaredo and Pisano (2009) in Chapter 12; Portugal: Alvaredo (2009) and Chapter 11; Spain: Alvaredo and Saez (2009) and Chapter 10; Canada: Saez and Veall (2005); Australia: Atkinson and Leigh (2007a); New Zealand: Atkinson and Leigh (2007b).

show that when exports increased, high incomes got a disproportionate share of national income, explaining why top incomes followed exports cycles over this period.

As described in Atkinson and Piketty (2007), the drop in income concentration between 1914 and 1945 in Anglo-Saxon and continental Europe countries was primarily due to the fall in top capital incomes, as capital owners incurred severe shocks from destruction of infrastructure, inflation, bankruptcies, and fiscal policy for financing war debts. The reason why capital incomes did not recover during the second half of the century is still an open question; Piketty (2003) and Piketty and Saez (2006) suggest that the introduction of generalized progressive income and estate taxation made such a reversal impossible. For most of the period, the data for Argentina do not offer information about the composition of income by brackets. This is unfortunate, as economic mechanisms can be very different for the distribution of income from labour, capital, business, and rents, and limits the interpretation and comparison of results. Figure 6.7 displays the

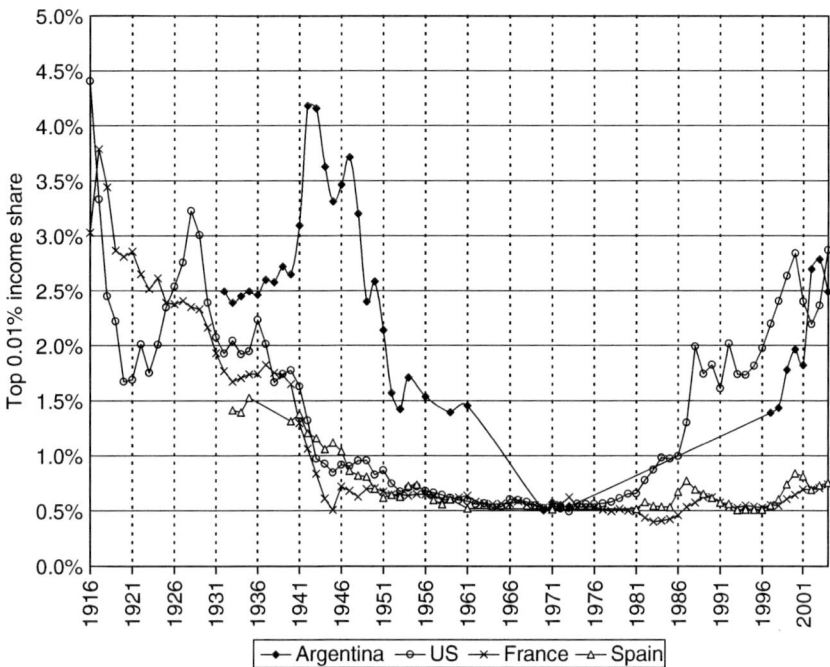

Figure 6.5 The top 0.01% income shares in Argentina, USA, Spain, and France

Sources: Argentina: Table 6.5; US: Piketty and Saez (2003); France: Piketty (2001) and Landais (2007); Spain: Alvaredo and Saez (2009) and Chapter 10.

evolution of the components of total assessed income between 1932 and 1958. For 1932–49, this covers the top 1.7–2.6 per cent of tax units, as shown in Table 6.3, column 4. In Argentina, the shares of wages, self-employment income, and capital income remained stable throughout this period, while the increase in business income (including agricultural activities), which moved from 30 per cent in 1932 to 60 per cent in 1949, was made at the expense of rural and urban rents.

Due in part to immigration, but also because of strong economic interests in the country, there was a substantial presence of foreign citizens among the top income earners. Table 6.6 shows the distribution of tax filers by country of origin between 1932 and 1946. On average, 40–5 per cent of individuals and reported income corresponded to foreigners. We can also get a rough idea of the relative distribution across nationalities within the top. In 1932, 2.25 per cent of tax filers were French and 1.61 per cent were British, while they both received income proportionally higher than their participation in the number of files (3.12 per cent of declared income each). In contrast, Spanish and Italian citizens represented 28.19 per cent of filers, with 22.38 per cent of assessed income.

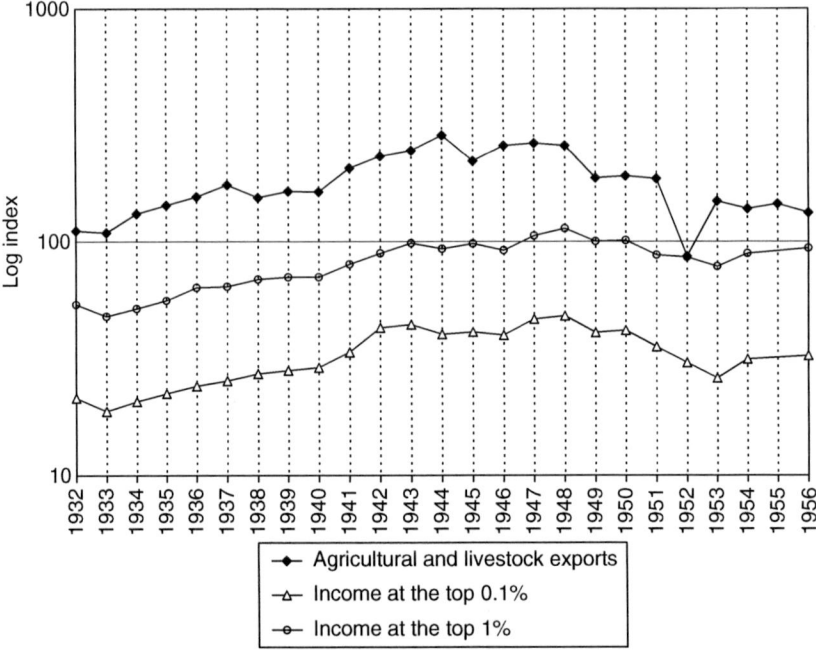

Figure 6.6 Agricultural and livestock exports and income at the top, Argentina, 1932–1956

Sources: Table 6.3 and 6.5 for income and Vazquez Presedo (1988) for exports. Income at the top 1% and 0.1% is the real amount of income reported by the top 1% and 0.1% income earners. Exports expressed as an index equal to 100 in 1930. The vertical axis is expressed in logarithmic scale.

The Years 1946–1955

The Perón years (1946–55) coincide with a clear decline in the share of the top percentile, which moved down to 15.3 per cent in 1953.[22] Mainly at the expense of rural rents and favoured by the accumulation of foreign reserves and the advantageous terms of trade in the world markets after the Second World War and the Korean War, the Peronist government deepened the industrialization process that had begun many years before, fostered by the impossibility of getting necessary imports from Europe during the war.[23] A deliberate inward-looking policy to

[22] Perón was also part of the de facto government in power between 1943 and 1946, first as secretary of labour and later as minister of war and vice-president.

[23] The true situation of Argentina's economy after 1945 should not be overstated. During the Second World War the country was under a United States blockade and cut off from continental Europe, while the United Kingdom had to devote all its resources to the war effort and could afford to sell very few industrial goods to Argentina. The trade surplus and the accumulation of foreign reserves achieved during the war were not due to the growth of exports but the result of a low level of exports and an even lower level of imports. As a result of the impossibility of purchasing new equipment, large amounts of international reserves reflected, then, an ageing capital stock.

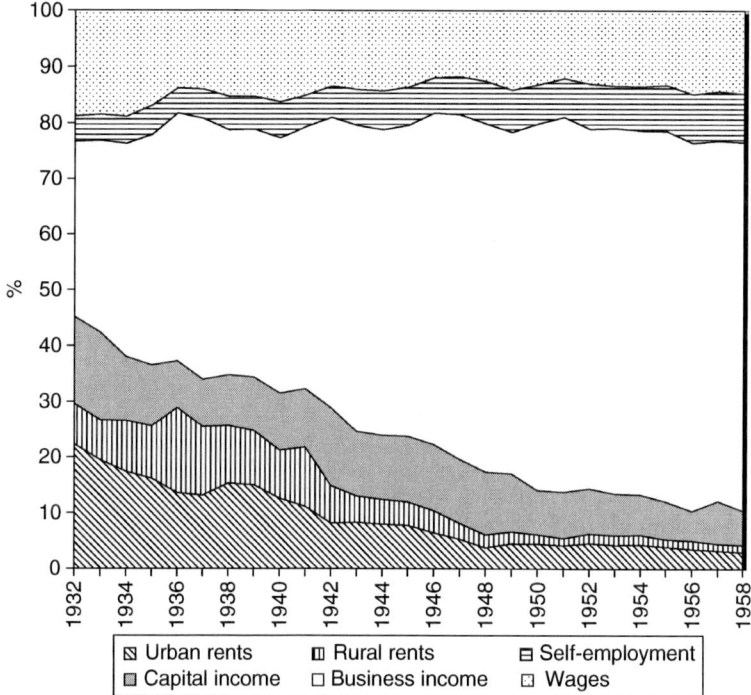

Figure 6.7 Composition of assessed income in Argentina, 1932–1958

Notes: The figure displays the composition of total assessed income. Thus, it covers 1.7%–2.6% of top income earners between 1932 and 1949, and 3.7%–5.2% between 1950 and 1958.

Source: Dirección Nacional de Impuestos a los Réditos, Memoria, several years.

finance industrialization and social improvements with rural rents was also to modify the structure of the wealthy sector. New industrial families appeared, but also the old names, traditionally attached to land wealth, diversified to industrial production. One important instrument of the Peronist policy was the IAPI, Institute for the Promotion of Trade, which established a state monopoly on exports and limited the gains of large estates proprietors.

Here it is worth noticing a striking contrast between Argentina and Australia. As Atkinson and Leigh (2007a) describe, the effect of the commodity price boom after the Second World War directly affected top shares in Australia, generating a clear spike in 1950, mainly due to the peak of wool prices which sheep farmers received in that year (Figures 6.3 and 6.4). The state management of exports in Argentina seems to have been a powerful tool in extracting a fraction of the surplus from exporters. The IAPI was disbanded as soon as Perón was deposed in 1955.

The government embarked upon a large redistributive policy during the three-year period between 1946 and 1949 and set the grounds for the welfare state and

Table 6.6 Country of origin of income tax payers, Argentina, 1932–1946

	Year													
	1932	1933	1934	1935	1936	1937	1938	1939	1940	1942	1943	1944	1945	1946
	Distribution of tax returns by nationality (%)													
Argentina	54.40	54.65	54.41	54.56	53.80	55.74	57.56	55.91	58.00	57.91	59.85	60.13	60.47	59.86
Germany	1.13	1.20	1.15	1.16	0.97	1.18	1.24	1.20	1.28	1.30	1.35	1.36	1.28	1.22
Belgium	0.17	0.17	0.17	0.15	0.13	0.14	0.14	0.14	0.17	0.15	0.18	0.15	0.16	0.13
Spain	14.27	14.36	14.39	14.58	14.90	15.53	14.63	14.56	14.68	13.86	12.51	12.59	12.69	11.79
United States	0.20	0.33	0.33	0.34	0.30	0.35	0.35	0.36	0.40	0.41	0.46	0.42	0.38	0.37
France	2.25	2.16	1.99	1.88	1.82	1.90	1.76	1.72	1.76	1.49	1.62	1.56	1.48	1.36
United Kingdom	1.61	1.73	1.52	1.49	1.29	1.44	1.41	1.39	1.55	1.37	1.53	1.42	1.34	1.25
Italy	13.92	13.42	13.40	12.86	14.61	13.65	13.10	11.01	11.41	9.79	9.57	9.37	9.20	10.70
URSS	0.95	0.99	1.02	1.04	1.03	1.17	1.13	1.12	1.15	1.22	1.18	1.22	1.21	1.23
Syria	1.04	1.05	1.20	1.30	1.34	1.34	1.33	1.32	1.37	1.39	1.34	1.31	1.30	1.15
Switzerland	0.53	0.54	0.49	0.48	0.48	0.52	0.53	0.48	0.52	0.47	0.52	0.51	0.48	0.46
Uruguay	1.23	1.19	1.14	1.09	1.01	1.10	1.04	1.05	1.07	1.03	1.10	1.04	0.99	0.88
Other	2.35	2.56	2.77	3.21	3.22	3.48	3.29	3.45	3.60	4.48	4.19	4.71	5.23	5.14
Not determined	5.94	5.65	6.03	5.87	5.11	2.44	2.50	6.28	3.04	5.12	4.59	4.21	3.80	4.46
	Distribution of assessed income by nationality (%)													
Argentina	57.51	56.90	56.74	57.94	55.51	58.55	60.31	58.30	59.64	58.15	59.63	60.27	62.69	60.62
Germany	1.13	1.41	1.35	1.34	1.21	1.42	1.46	1.30	1.49	1.25	1.32	1.38	1.23	1.07
Belgium	0.42	0.28	0.25	0.22	0.35	0.45	0.32	0.38	0.39	0.40	0.41	0.33	0.33	0.26
Spain	11.90	12.39	12.75	12.64	13.10	13.74	12.85	12.39	13.17	12.10	11.42	11.44	8.13	11.15
United States	0.57	0.85	0.86	0.89	0.69	0.67	0.81	0.84	0.94	0.95	1.00	0.88	0.74	0.68
France	3.12	3.10	2.70	2.57	2.60	2.69	2.83	2.37	2.59	2.10	1.96	2.13	2.13	1.88
United Kingdom	3.12	3.24	3.06	2.91	2.17	2.46	2.34	2.30	2.74	3.30	2.56	2.42	2.13	1.85
Italy	10.48	10.28	10.05	9.96	12.40	10.98	10.59	8.80	9.17	8.05	8.17	7.72	8.30	7.75
URSS	0.42	0.42	0.49	0.56	0.52	0.67	0.65	0.61	0.63	0.85	0.91	0.96	1.02	1.07
Syria	0.57	0.56	0.86	0.78	0.87	0.90	0.89	0.84	1.10	1.35	1.32	1.25	1.02	1.33
Switzerland	0.85	0.99	0.37	0.56	0.61	0.67	0.81	0.69	0.78	0.65	0.78	0.79	0.90	0.75
Uruguay	1.56	1.41	1.47	1.23	1.39	1.42	1.37	1.38	1.41	1.45	1.37	1.25	1.31	1.20
Other	1.84	2.11	2.45	1.90	2.78	2.99	2.59	2.83	3.29	4.40	4.84	5.05	5.80	5.51
Not determined	6.52	6.06	6.62	6.49	5.81	2.39	2.18	6.96	2.66	5.00	4.29	4.13	4.29	4.89

Note: information for 1941 missing.

Source: Dirección Nacional de Impuestos a los Réditos, Memoria, several years.

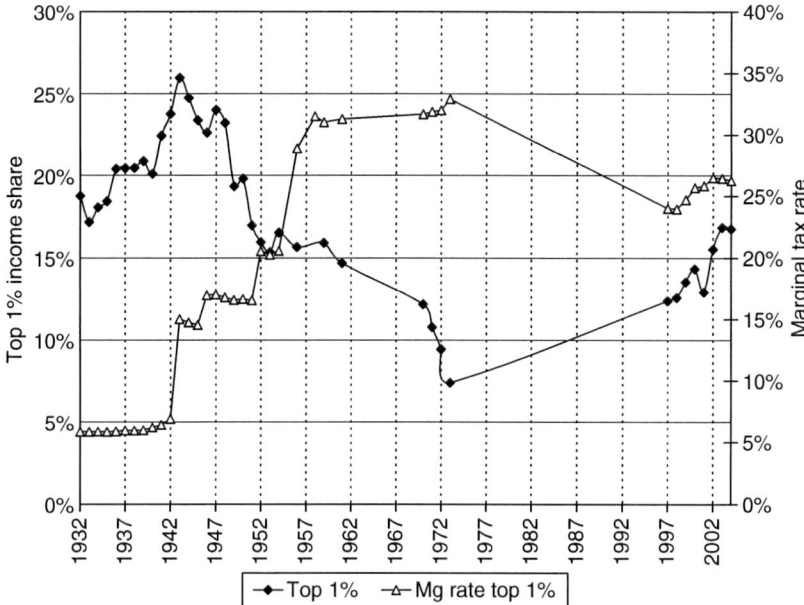

Figure 6.8 The top 1% income share in Argentina and income-weighted marginal tax rate.
Sources: Top 1% income share from Table 6.5. Top marginal tax rate from author's computations.

the development of the powerful middle class that characterized the country by
the end of the decade of 1960. It is this period that remained in the 'collective
memory' as the clearest expression of the economic policies of Peronism.[24] The
development of a progressive personal taxation system played a secondary role,
the redistribution being achieved by direct public assistance, subsidized interest
rate in the credit markets, price controls, minimum wage policy, and the state
management of exports.[25] Even if income tax rates steadily increased, the number
of taxpayers was kept low. On the eve of Perón's presidency, the top marginal rate
doubled, jumping from 12 per cent to 25 per cent between 1942 and 1943 and to
27 per cent in 1946 (similar to the levels found in Chile and Brazil). At the time of
the reform, in 1943, the authorities explicitly recognized that the top marginal

[24] Despite the negative remarks of an anonymous referee, I have decided to keep the expression
'collective memory', a concept developed by Maurice Halbwachs (Halbwachs 1950).
[25] Notwithstanding the secondary role in terms of redistribution, many changes were accomplished
in the tax policy arena: (i) the organization of a centralized tax agency (the Dirección General de
Impuestos a los Réditos and the Administración General de Impuestos Internos became the Dirección
General Impositiva); (ii) the creation of a new tax on profits (*beneficios extraordinarios*), aimed at
capping the increase in profits after the Second World War; (iii) the enforcement of a proportional tax
on capital gains in 1946 (*impuesto a las ganancias eventuales*). For an account of the evolution of
taxation during Perón's presidency, see Sánchez Román (2007).

rate and the tax scale as a whole were among the lowest in the world.[26] Figure 6.8 displays the income-weighted marginal tax rate for the top 1 per cent incomes. From 1952 to 1954, the highest incomes were affected by a top statutory marginal rate of 32 per cent, this rate being 40 per cent at the end of Perón's rule, in 1955.

Along with many other transformations, social and labour rights were enforced, unions gained in power, and the first national pension system was organized. The Peronist redistributive policy was successful and visible among the working class; this is a widely acknowledged phenomenon. The use of the income tax statistics let us numerically assess the magnitude of the losses experienced by the richest during the Peronist phase. The top percentile share moved down from 25.9 per cent in 1943 to 15.3 per cent in 1953. The most affected seem to have been the richest among the rich: the top 0.1 per cent decreased from 11.6 per cent to 5.1 per cent and the top 0.01 per cent declined from 4.1 per cent to 1.4 per cent in the same period. The reduction in income concentration was far from trivial. What is also new is the evidence showing the limited effect on the upper part of the distribution when compared to international standards: by 1954 the top percentile shares were still higher than those found in the United States, France, Canada, Australia, or Spain.

After the frantic expansion of the economy during the first three years (see Figure 6.1), a crisis in the external sector in 1949 forced major changes in the economic policy; initially the expansion of the public sector was held back while attempts were made to retain the policy of increasing wages. A new crisis took place in 1952 (negative trade balance, recession, and demonetization). The sharp reduction in agricultural and livestock exports is clearly depicted in Figure 6.6. Thereafter, redistribution and credit policies became more prudent and incentives were introduced to favour the agricultural sector (which would always be the main export sector and, as such, the main provider of foreign reserves), which explains the moderate impact of the drop in exports on top incomes shown in Figure 6.6 that year. Some recovery of top shares seems to have started even before the end of Perón's government.

Even if our data do not allow to go beyond searching for a detailed explanation of what was happening below the top 1 per cent, the drop in the top shares that took place until the middle of the decade of 1950 coincided with a general improvement in terms of income distribution, as indicated by the fact that the participation of wages in total income in National Accounts increased by 8 per cent between 1945 and 1954 (Altimir and Beccaria 1999). The ratio of wages to GDP reached a historical maximum of 50.8 per cent in 1954, one year before the military coup that deposed Perón (see Figure 6.9).[27]

---

[26] Preamble to Decree 18229 of 12/31/1943.

[27] In recent years, an increasing share of wages in aggregated income per se has ceased to be an indicator of diminishing income concentration, since the rise of top shares in English-speaking economies has been a driving force of the sharp increase in top wages.

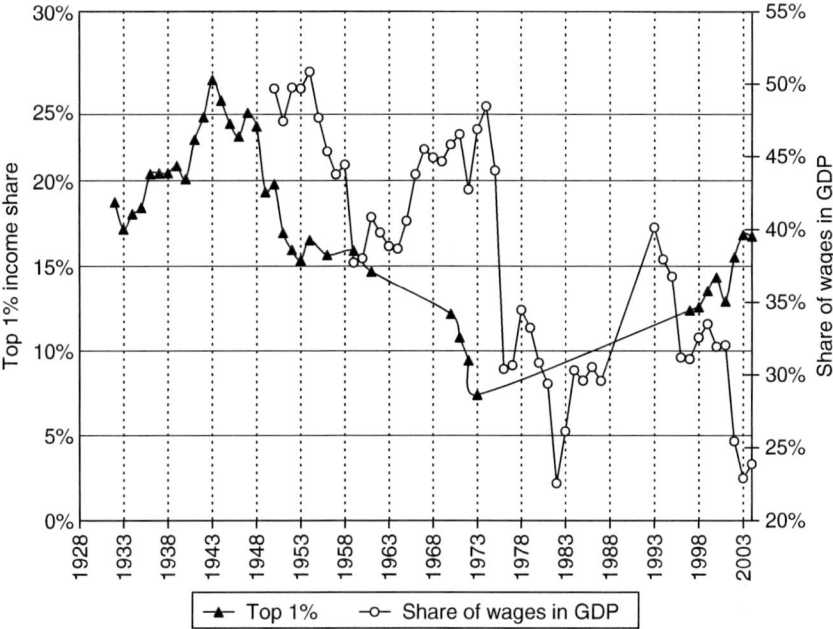

Figure 6.9 The top 1% income share in Argentina and share of wages in GDP, 1932–2004

Note: Income does not include capital gains.

Sources: Top 1% income share from Table 6.5. Share of wages in GDP from Lindemboim et al. (2005).

The Years 1956–2004

After 1955, the intrinsic limits of the import substitution industrialization strategy (which began to become apparent by the end of Perón's period) resulted in a sequence of oscillating economic policies with deep social and political implications during the following twenty years.[28] It became evident that neither the pro-industrialization sector nor the agricultural-based exporter sector (whose interests did not coincide) was powerful enough to permanently dominate the other. Repeated cycles of short expansions and contractions, increasing inflation, and institutional weakness dominated the period.

The agrarian activities were responsible for generating the surpluses to foster industry and finance the imports of inputs and capital goods demanded by the expanding manufacturing sector. The exchange rate was usually fixed, to help maintain low levels of inflation and high stability of import prices (denominated in local currency). At the same time, extensive and deliberate foreign trade

---

[28] Between 1955 and 1976 the country underwent four democratic governments (none of them completed the constitutional period), one military-controlled civilian government, and three military regimes.

protection secured the industry from external competition even in the face of the appreciation of the exchange rate. As exports were mainly based on food products, any devaluation implied a real loss for wage earners. Consequently, a fixed exchange rate, with a tendency to appreciation, favoured both workers and industrialists (protected from external competition) while it acted as a clear disincentive to landowners. The economic tensions translated to the political arena.

Under this scheme, any acceleration of the economy led to fewer exports (more exportable goods were demanded internally) and more imports of inputs and capital goods. Consuming more tradable goods, together with the discouragement of agriculture, generated recurrent balance of payment crises and output contractions. Sometimes the endogenous limits in this development strategy were reinforced by international conditions (drop in world prices of commodities) so that crises also occurred even if the economy was not growing rapidly. The way out of the crisis always implied a tightening of fiscal and monetary policies together with large devaluations that corrected the distortion in prices, favouring land-based activities again, drastically reducing the real value of wages, increasing exports, and regaining foreign reserves. Then the process could restart.

The 'stop-and-go' nature of economic policy, which eventually ended by the middle of the 1970s (to inaugurate a decade of stagnation and very high inflation), expressed therefore the limits to industrialization.[29] It was, nevertheless, a period of reasonable income growth *vis-à-vis* the poor performance that the economy displayed between 1981 and 1991.[30] The sudden movements of the nominal exchange rate ultimately led to violent redistributions between workers, the manufacturing sector, and the export-oriented agricultural sector.[31]

We only have observations for 1958, 1959, 1961, and 1970–3, a period in which top shares declined.[32] We cannot precisely assess which fraction of such a reduction is due to the increase in marginal rates, in tax evasion, or to other factors. This is a serious limitation and the results must be read with caution.

There was a marked increase in the shares at the top 0.1 per cent and top 0.01 per cent when 1973 and 2004 are compared. Between 1953 and 2004, the share of the top 0.01 per cent doubled. As it is not possible to fill the gap between 1973 and 1997 with a continuous series from income tax tabulations, we would like to read our results in perspective of the distribution based on household surveys, keeping in mind all the warnings about the use of survey-based data to study top incomes (see Appendix 6E). The Greater Buenos Aires is the only area that has been

---

[29] For an analytic approach to the 'stop-and-go' model, see Braun and Joy (1967).

[30] For an analysis of the political economy and the economic policy during the period, see Diaz-Alejandro (1970), Mallon and Sourrouille (1975), Di Tella and Dornbusch (1983), Di Tella and Zymelman (1967, 1973).

[31] The determination of the nominal exchange rate began to play a key and privileged role in all spheres of the economy. Di Tella (1987) has characterized the styled fact of the pendular policy: a 'repressed stage', when key prices were controlled to tame inflation, and a 'loosening state' when controls collapsed and inflation jumped.

[32] Top income shares for 1959 and 1961 are estimated from CONADE (1965), and not from tax statistics.

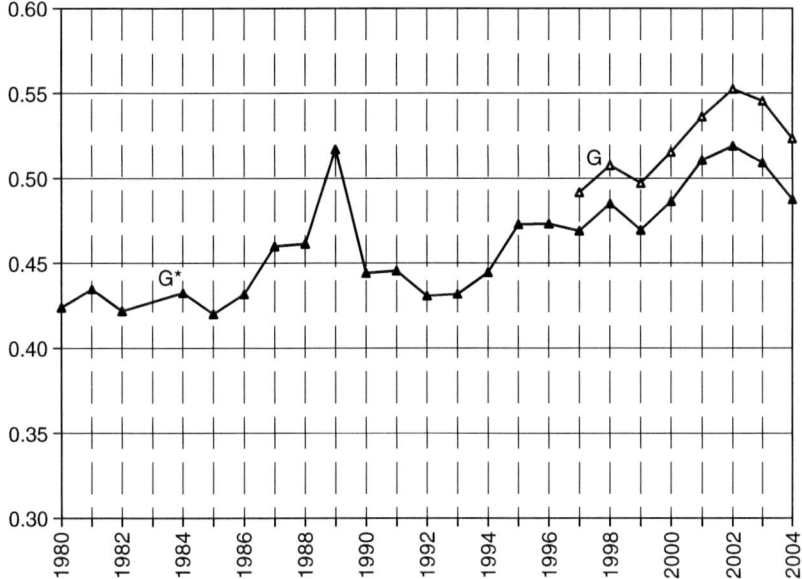

Figure 6.10 Gini coefficient 1980–2004 Greater Buenos Aires.

Notes: The black triangle denotes the Gini coefficient G* of individual income based on the Greater Buenos Aires household survey, own calculations. Database for 1983 is missing. All results correspond to October surveys, except for 2003 (May). Only income earners with positive income were considered and no further adjustments were applied. The white triangle denotes the Gini coefficient G = S+(1–S)G*, where S is the estimate of the top 0.1% income share (Table 6.5). See section 6.3 in the main text for details.

regularly covered by a survey since 1972. It has served as basis for multiple studies on inequality and, due to the geographical distribution of the population (highly concentrated in Buenos Aires) it has reflected well the dynamics of income distribution in the whole country.[33] Figure 6.10 depicts the evolution of the Gini coefficient between 1980 and 2004. Available statistical evidence shows a relative stability of inequality during the decade of 1960 and the first half of the decade of 1970, when per capita GDP growth exceeded 3 per cent per year.[34] On the contrary, between 1975 and 1980 income inequality experienced a sharp rise, and the growing trend continued, attaining a maximum in 1989 (hyperinflationary crisis). In terms of growth, the 1980s were the 'lost decade'.

With a half-century of inflationary experience, the country reached the highest inflation rates in the 1980s together with two hyperinflationary episodes in 1989 and 1990. Regrettably, available data do not allow us to examine the interesting potential effects of very high inflation on top incomes.[35] In 1991, Argentina put

---

[33] See Gasparini, Marchionnini, and Sosa Escudero (2001, 2004), Altimir (1986), Altimir and Beccaria (1999), González Rozada and Menéndez (2006).

[34] See Altimir and Beccaria (1999).

[35] Ahumada, Alvaredo, and Canavese (2000) analyse the redistributive effects of the inflationary tax in Argentina in the 1980s using household survey data.

its money supply under a dollar exchange standard, adopting a fixed exchange rate between the local currency and the United States dollar, and restricting the issue of money by the Central Bank. This rigorous monetary policy, together with a series of structural reforms (mass privatization of public services, trade openness, attempts to create a domestic capital market) started a decade of price stability and rapid growth until 1999. This policy was not neutral in terms of income distribution. Growth and stabilization only implied a temporary and mild improvement in inequality after 1990, and by 1995 the Gini coefficient was 12 per cent higher than in 1985. Overall inequality steadily grew in the last years, together with unemployment and poverty levels. The macroeconomic crisis of 2001–2 pushed those indicators to unprecedented levels.

The factors behind the constant increase in inequality during the last two decades have been broadly analysed and include both macroeconomic and microeconomic explanations. First, unemployment rates skyrocketed in the decade of 1990, and have remained high since then. Although there is a widespread belief that changes in labour market participation have been one of the main causes of the strong increase in inequality, Gasparini, Marchionnini, and Sosa Escudero (2004) suggest that these ideas should be scaled down. Even if the unemployment rate has been augmenting since 1992, the employment rate did not change much, so that there was a minor change in the number of individuals without earnings. Changes in the hours of work seem to have had more significant disequalizing effects, while the effect of unemployment translated into more inequality through the fall in the relative wages of the poorest. Secondly, changes in the returns to education and experience, the transformation of the educational structure of the population, and the fall in work hours among the low-income groups have all had important roles. Also relevant, an observed decrease in the wage gap between genders, a potential force for reducing inequality, has not induced any important change. Thirdly, there were the two dramatic crises of 1989 and 2002. As a result, inequality has been rising during positive growth years, and increasing even more during recessions.

Table 6.7 shows the top 10 per cent, top 1 per cent, and top 0.1 per cent income shares based on household surveys. The limited number of observations in the survey introduces large sample variability when focusing on the very top. Table 6.8 presents the composition of income by top groups between 2001 and 2004 from tax statistics. Income is divided into rents (urban and rural), capital income, business income, and wages. Between 1997 and 2004, top incomes again show (Table 6.5) an increasing trend with a drop in 2001 mainly due the reduction of capital and business income following the 2001 crash. However, with the rapid recovery of the economy since 2003, top shares soon regained and surpassed the pre-crisis levels, the top fractiles within the top 1 per cent being the most favoured by the process. While top 1 per cent share passed from 12.4 per cent in 1997 to 16.8 per cent in 2003, the top 0.01 per cent share doubled, going from 1.4 per cent to 2.8 per cent. It is not surprising that here again all sectors connected with exports have seen their relative income increase as long as the nominal exchange rate tripled during the crisis but the inflation rate between 2000 and 2004

Table 6.7 Income shares and composition in top Argentina income groups based on household survey, Greater Buenos Aires, 1982–2003

				Top 10%			Top 1%			Top 0.1%		
	Top 10%	Top 1%	Top 0.1%	Wage	Business	Capital + rents	Wage	Business	Capital + rents	Wage	Business	Capital + rents
1980												
1981												
1982	42.11	11.17	2.90	58.84	36.34	5.12	36.70	49.16	14.18	5.91	57.85	36.19
1983												
1984	44.24	13.90	4.81									
1985	43.49	10.37	2.55	59.90	36.98	3.28	51.20	42.90	5.88	68.89	30.93	0.00
1986	44.23	11.61	2.38	53.84	42.40	3.61	35.18	60.00	4.57	17.45	75.75	6.88
1987	46.07	11.77	2.21	81.59	35.12	3.19	81.59	35.12	3.19	57.28	37.71	5.08
1988	45.39	11.28	2.31	63.59	33.91	2.56	52.66	42.02	5.32	52.66	42.02	5.32
1989	46.37	12.68	3.21	61.61	34.45	3.98	47.14	44.19	8.77	39.52	38.36	22.47
1990	45.24	12.57	2.99	63.79	34.53	1.58	56.29	40.76	2.61	43.95	53.18	2.88
1991	45.95	13.44	4.32	60.92	35.97	2.88	45.69	47.41	6.87	20.54	63.75	15.80
1992	43.15	10.63	2.08	55.88	41.81	2.57	37.51	57.57	4.92	24.72	69.20	6.08
1993	42.53	10.14	2.11	56.76	41.14	2.08	51.70	45.12	3.17	37.55	58.62	3.85
1994	43.07	10.58	2.40	60.30	36.88	2.99	48.06	46.63	5.36	36.85	49.28	13.60
1995	41.83	11.96	2.44	81.27	36.62	2.11	57.30	41.04	1.66	65.20	34.80	0.00
1996	41.68	11.29	2.36	61.80	35.63	2.58	52.72	42.13	5.15	57.01	42.99	0.00
1997	42.15	9.61	2.30	63.08	33.89	3.03	56.61	37.47	5.92	56.33	35.00	8.67
1998	44.02	10.84	1.97	62.34	35.81	1.85	49.65	47.25	3.10	25.45	71.71	2.84
1999	42.45	9.79	2.01	67.59	30.15	2.26	52.75	42.47	4.78	45.03	54.97	0.00
2000	43.22	10.50	2.01	68.88	28.36	2.76	63.05	32.78	4.17	65.39	25.29	9.32
2001	47.12	10.62	1.98	72.22	25.46	2.33	57.01	39.84	3.15	61.86	38.14	0.00
2002	44.29	10.97	2.32	76.08	22.31	1.62	62.06	35.87	2.07	46.50	51.24	2.25
2003	42.59	10.81	2.20	71.68	26.23	2.09	56.61	38.06	3.33	41.18	52.74	8.08

Notes: Fractiles defined in terms of the number of tax units. Survey incomes with no adjustments.

Source: Household survey, Greater Buenos Aires (INDEC). October waves, except for 2003 (May).

Table 6.8 Composition in top income groups, Argentina, 2001–2004

	Top 1%				Top 0.5%				Top 0.1%				Top 0.01%			
	Rents	Capital	Business	Wages	Rents	Capital	Business	Wages	Rents	Capital	Business	Wages	Rents	Capital	Business	Wages
2001	6.2	10.0	34.7	49.2	5.0	8.5	39.7	46.8	2.5	6.7	54.9	35.9	0.9	7.5	64.8	26.8
2002	5.9	19.7	36.7	37.7	4.5	19.1	43.2	33.3	2.7	16.1	54.4	26.7	1.0	9.9	67.2	21.9
2003	5.3	19.6	41.4	33.6	4.5	19.1	45.2	31.2	2.2	14.9	59.1	23.7	0.7	9.4	69.5	20.4
2004	5.7	19.0	45.0	30.3	4.9	17.8	48.1	29.1	1.9	11.6	63.8	22.7	0.8	9.3	71.2	18.7

	Top 1–0.5%				Top 0.5–0.1%				Top 0.1–0.01%				Top 0.01%			
	Rents	Capital	Business	Wages	Rents	Capital	Business	Wages	Rents	Capital	Business	Wages	Rents	Capital	Business	Wages
2001	10.7	15.9	14.5	58.9	7.6	10.3	24.2	57.9	3.7	6.1	47.7	42.5	0.9	7.5	64.8	26.8
2002	10.8	21.8	14.3	53.1	7.4	24.0	24.3	44.4	3.5	18.9	48.8	28.8	1.0	9.9	67.2	21.9
2003	11.1	23.2	14.6	51.0	7.6	24.8	26.3	41.3	3.1	18.1	53.2	25.6	0.7	9.4	69.5	20.4
2004	13.2	29.1	16.7	40.9	8.8	25.8	28.5	36.9	2.8	13.5	57.8	25.9	0.8	9.3	71.2	18.7

Source: Computations based on income tax return statistics.

remained below 50 per cent. The crisis generated a massive redistribution in favour of the very rich, who have a significant portion of their income denominated in foreign currency due to the involvement in international trade.

Even when the number of well-off individuals may be regarded as very small when considering the whole economy, they cannot be neglected. If an infinitesimal (in term of members) richest group owns a finite share S of total income, then the Gini coefficient can be approximated as $G \approx S + (1-S) \ G^*$, where G^* is the Gini for the rest of the population.[36] The comparison between tax tabulations and household income surveys presented in Appendix 6E reveals that it is not an exaggeration to assume that the top 0.1 per cent earners' income is not considered in the survey. Under such an assumption, let G^* be the survey-based Gini.[37] Then, one can compute G by applying our estimates of top income shares to the approximation mentioned above. For instance, G^* was 0.469 in 1997 and 0.509 in 2003 (an increase of 8 per cent). Therefore G turned out to be 0.491 in 1997 and 0.545 in 2003 (an increase of 11 per cent).[38] In this case, the behaviour of top shares amplified the rise in survey-measured inequality. This means that when the participation of the rich in total income is important, changes in their income shares are potentially relevant in explaining changes in overall distribution. Figure 6.10 differentiates between G and G^* over the period 1997–2004.

6.4 CONCLUSIONS

This chapter has attempted to describe the evolution of top shares from a long-run perspective and to fill the gap in the analysis of the dynamics of income concentration in Argentina since 1932. So far, the only available source of information about distributive issues came from observations for 1953, 1959, 1961, and from the household surveys started in 1972. Until 1974 the survey was restricted to the Greater Buenos Aires area. Other urban centres have progressively been incorporated, so that today the fraction of represented individuals exceeds 70 per cent of the urban population (60 per cent of total population). Yet, micro-data showing personal income with some detail are only available for 1980–2 and 1984–2006. Despite the existence of survey data for recent years, they do not offer valuable information as the rich are missing either for sampling reasons, low response rates, or ex post elimination of 'extreme' values. Therefore, this study is the first in covering such a long span of years and in focusing on the upper part of the distribution. Since income tax statistics are the primary data source, the dynamic analysis has had to be restricted to the top 1 per cent.

[36] We borrow this explanation from Atkinson (2007).

[37] As shown in Cruces and Gasparini (2008), the Gini coefficients computed from the Greater Buenos Aires survey and from the all-urban-centre survey are almost identical.

[38] In 1997, the top 0.1% income share was 4.27% (Table 6.5). For G^* equal to 0.469 that year, then $G \approx 0.0427 + (1-0.0427) \ 0.469 = 0.491$.

The results suggest that income concentration was higher during the 1930s and first half of the 1940s than it is today. The recovery of the economy after the Great Depression and the visible effects of the Peronist policy between 1945 and 1955 generated an inverted U-shape in the dynamics of top shares. Any interpretation of this performance in terms of Kuznets's hypothesis (Kuznets 1955) would be, at best, difficult to accept in the light of inequality trends in the following years. Since then top shares seem to have followed a U-shape pattern, although several gaps in the data put a limit on the interpretation of such movements. Interestingly, the share of the top 1 per cent in 1954 was very similar to the level found in 2004, although they reflect two very different moments in history. The first corresponds to a period when the economy was on a path of improvement of social conditions and inequality, while the general belief that dominates the second is of a clear regression in these areas.

APPENDIX 6A: THE INCOME TAX

The Great Depression forced fundamental changes both in the economic policy and in the successful model of international insertion that Argentina had displayed since 1870. By December 1929 the current account imbalance was severe and the exchange rate was left to float after a two-year resumption of the gold standard. High public expenditures in 1928–30 were drastically reduced between 1931 and 1933. The government followed a conservative fiscal policy and sought orthodox budget balance by replacing the lost customs revenues with a large increase in direct taxes on income and wealth. In this context, the first personal income tax (*impuesto de emergencia a los réditos*) was established in 1932 (Law 1/19/1932) during the de facto presidency of José E. Uriburu, who had deposed President Yrigoyen two years before in the first military *coup d'état* against the constitutional order started in 1862.[39]

Taxable income was classified in four categories. The first category referred to rents and income obtained from agricultural and other rural activities when performed by the proprietor of the land. Total revenue from this source could not be lower than 5 per cent of the cadastral value established for local taxes. The second category included capital income, royalties, fixed claim asset income, dividends, annuities, and subsidies. The third category corresponded to self-employment and business income and farm income from rented land. The fourth category referred to wages, salaries, and pensions.[40]

Exemptions include income derived from patents, copyrights, and other intellectual property, profits from cooperatives, severance payments, local and federal treasury bonds interest, low-interest saving accounts (this exemption extended later to all saving accounts and time deposits), dividends, and severance payments. Capital gains, in practice, have always been exempted too. The initial tax structure was rather rudimentary: there was a flat rate for income in the first three categories, and a three-bracket progressive scale for wages, salaries, and pensions. Tax filing was strictly individual, but income under joint tenancy was allocated to the husband.

The exemption on local government bonds and national treasury bonds interest was eliminated in 1942 (Law 12808). The first major reform, motivated by the need of increasing fiscal revenues, was accomplished between 1943 and 1946 (Decree 18299 of 12/31/1943). The tax scale was radically modified, maintaining the existing rates on the lowest incomes and increasing them at the top. The top marginal rate more than doubled, jumping from 12 per cent to 25 per cent. The new top marginal rate was similar to those in force, at the time, in Chile (27 per cent) and Brazil (21.4 per cent) but considerably lower

---

[39] Several attempts to create a personal income tax between 1916 and 1930 (in 1917, 1920, 1922, 1924, and 1928) were systematically blocked in the senate, dominated by the Conservative party. For a detailed account on the political reasons for the failure of any fiscal reform concerning the income tax before 1932, see Sánchez Román (2008, 2009). Cf. the case of Spain (Alvaredo and Saez 2009 and Chapter 10), where the first personal income tax was enforced during the Second Republic.

[40] Throughout the years the classification of income in the four categories was a key element as each category is affected by different deductions.

than those in the United States, Canada, the UK, and France. Classification of income suffered some changes: professional income was transferred from the third to the fourth category while farm income—both from owned and rented land—was completely included in the third category (Decree 14338 of 5/20/1946).[41]

While the growing inflation started by the second half of the twentieth century could have implied a rise in the number of taxpayers (by reducing the significance of the minimum threshold), non-taxable income and family allowances were regularly updated. As only those with positive taxable income were obliged to file, the percentage of tax filers with respect to total tax filers remained low (see Table 6.3, column 4). At the same time, the brackets in the tax scale remained stable, whereas the rates were increased again in 1946, 1952, and1955 (Law 14393 of 12/31/1954) as shown in Table 6.3, column 9.

The tax scale was revised again in 1969 (Law 18527 of 12/31/1969), when marginal rates ranged from 12 per cent to 46 per cent, and in 1974, establishing a scale going from 7 per cent to 46 per cent (Law 20628 of 12/27/1973, which abolished the old *impuesto sobre los réditos personales* and created a new *impuesto a las ganancias de las personas físicas y de las sucesiones indivisas*). The maximum marginal tax rate moved down to 45 per cent in 1985 (Law 23260 of 9/25/1985).

By 1997, the top marginal rate had been reduced to 33 per cent and increased to 35 per cent again in 2000 (Decree 450 of 3/31/1986; Decree 2352 of 12/18/1986; Decree 649/97 of 8/6/1997; Law 25239 of 12/31/1999).

---

[41] Among the regulations that introduced important changes in the income tax during the first half of the twentieth century, the reader may refer to: Law 1/19/1932 (creation of the income tax); Law 11586 of 7/2/1932 (ordering of the tax); Law 11757 of 10/11/1933 (on the exemption on local government bonds and national treasury bonds); Law 11682 of 1/2/1933 and Decree 12578 of 5/4/1938 (classification of income and redefinition of the progressive tax scale); Decree 18299 of 12/31/1943 (change in tax scale); Decree 14338 of 5/20/1946 (reclassification of income).

APPENDIX 6B: REFERENCES ON DATA SOURCES

Tax Statistics

Statistical information covering the income tax for years 1932–50 has been regularly published between 1935 and 1950: Dirección General de Impuestos a los Réditos, *Memoria 1935, 1936, 1937, 1938, 1939, 1940, 1941, 1942, 1943, 1944, 1945, 1946*; Dirección General Impositiva, *Memoria 1947, 1948, 1949, 1950*. Tables display the distribution of taxpayers by brackets of income together with reported gross income, taxable income, family allowances, minimum exempted income, and tax paid. The continuity of the publication was lost between 1950 and 1997. Similar tabulations for 1951–4, 1956 1958, and 1959 were published in Dirección General Impositiva, *Boletín 1957, 1958, 1959, 1961, 1962 (April), 1962 (October)*.

The data for 1959 and 1961 were taken from Consejo Nacional de Desarrollo (1965), *Distribución del ingreso y cuentas nacionales en la Argentina: investigación conjunta CONADE-CEPAL*, volumes i–v, Buenos Aires.

The information for 1970, 1971, 1972, and 1973 was obtained from Dirección General Impositiva, Ministerio de Economía, *Estadísticas tributarias ejercicios 1972/73* and Departamento de Estudios, División Estadística, Ministerio de Economía, 1973, *Boletín estadístico número especial, aporte de la DGI a las III jornadas tributarias del Colegio de Graduados de Ciencias Económicas de Buenos Aires*.

More detailed data describe the evolution of the income tax and wealth tax between 1997 and 2004: Administración Federal de Ingresos Públicos, Ministerio de Economía, *Estadísticas tributarias 1998, 1999, 2000, 2001, 2002, 2003, 2004, 2005*.

Individuals with wages and salaries as the only income sources have never been obliged to fill a tax return, although they have been subject to income tax withholdings. They are not included in the tax tabulations. Cont and Susmel (2006) analyse this issue. Using administrative records from earnings, they estimate the distribution of wages and salaries for non-tax filers. Their results let us argue that the impact on our top income shares is small.

Total Number of Individuals and Tax Units

The income tax in Argentina has always been individually based. Consequently, the reference total for tax units, defined as the number of individuals had everybody been required to file, is computed as the number of persons in the Argentine population aged 20 and over. These series are based on census linear interpolations and reported in Table 6.3, column 2. National censuses were conducted in 1914, 1947, 1960, 1970, 1980, 1991, and 2001. Column 3 indicates the total number of tax returns actually filled. The fraction of the adult population filing a tax return is presented in column 4.

Comisión Nacional del Censo (1919), *Tercer Censo Nacional: levantado el 1 de junio de 1914, ordenado por la Ley no. 9108 bajo la presidencia del Dr. Roque Saenz Pena, ejecutado durante la presidencia del Dr. Victorino de la Plaza,* Buenos Aires; Dirección Nacional de Estadística y Censos (1951), *IV Censo General de Población 1947;* Dirección Nacional de Estadística y Censos (1965), *Censo General de Población 1960,* Buenos Aires; Instituto Nacional de Estadística y Censos (1993), *Censo Nacional de Población y Vivienda 1991: resultados definitivos, Total del País,* Serie B n° 25; Instituto Nacional de Estadística y Censos, *Censo Nacional de Población, Hogares y Vivienda 2001, resultados generales total del país,* Buenos Aires.

Income Denominator

To relate the amounts recorded in the tax tabulations to a comparable reference income, we build up the series of personal income from the National Accounts. Information comes from the National Accounts System 1993. Starting from total GDP, minus indirect and direct taxes not paid by families, minus depreciation, minus employers' social security contributions, minus imputed rents on owner-occupied houses, minus financial inter-mediation services consumed by the public sector, minus undistributed profits, plus social transfers, minus 33 per cent of unincorporated profits. This procedure generates a refer-ence income of about 60 per cent of GDP for recent years. The level of desegregation of information required to compute income is not available for most of the years. Conse-quently we applied the 60 per cent factor to the GDP in current prices taken from Administración Federal de Ingresos Públicos (2002), based on information from Secretaría de Política Económica, Banco Central de la República Argentina, and Instituto Nacional de Estadística y Censos.[42]

As pointed out in Atkinson (2005), given the increasing significance of items such as employers' contributions, non-household institutions such as pension funds, and public transfers, it is not evident that a constant percentage computed on recent information is appropriate to describe the situation during the first half of the century.

Prices

The first official consumer price index dates back to 1943. The CPI is published monthly by the Instituto Nacional de Estadística. The annual index was computed as the arithmetic average of monthly indices from 1943 to 2004. For 1935–42, the price index was taken from Vazquez Presedo (1971: column 1, table V-2.15); for 1932–1934 it comes from Della Paolera and Taylor (2001: chapter 13).

---

[42] In the case of Spain the reference total income also turns out to be roughly equal to 60% of GDP with deviations of less than 1% (see Alvaredo and Saez 2009).

APPENDIX 6C: ESTIMATING TOP SHARES

We follow the basic Pareto interpolation technique described in Chapter 10, Appendix 10D.

APPENDIX 6D: THE ISSUE OF TAX EVASION

In the developing world there is a generalized idea regarding the presence of important levels of tax evasion (fraudulent under-reporting or non-reporting) and tax elusion (the use of legal means to reduce tax liability through planning, renaming, or retiming of activities) that affect mainly the income and wealth taxes. On the one hand, legal responses to taxation cannot be neglected in either the developed or developing world. Slemrod (1992, 1995) and Auerbach and Slemrod (1997) have provided empirical evidence indicating the significance of avoidance responses to the major US tax changes of the 1980s and 1990s.[43] On the other hand, the tendency to hide certain types of income to evade taxes is a standard feature in developing countries, where a non-trivial fraction of transactions is carried out in the informal sector. In this sense how much to tax the rich has always been a critical matter, as one would like to limit their incentives both to pursue less socially productive activities (Slemrod 2000) and to carry out business in the shadow economy in order to avoid taxes.[44]

We are particularly concerned about tax evasion in Argentina. Because tax evasion means that we cannot observe the data, any quantitative assessment of its magnitude is very speculative. In any case we provide some elements for the analysis.

First, the official publications of the tax authority between 1932 and 1950 describe a rather extensive fiscal control; for instance, in 1939, 29,000 individuals were inspected out of a total of 144,923 files. This information, if relevant, is inconclusive as soon as one accepts that the number of tax files is endogenous and that the probability of being audited is the fraction of inspected individuals over the total number of potential (and not only observed) taxpayers. Notwithstanding this fact, an audit rate of 20 per cent is much higher than the ones observed today in countries such as Spain, as is discussed in Chapter 10. It is likely that audit rates were even higher for top taxpayers. The government seemed worried about the quantitative scope of evasion and elusion in the income tax by the end of the decade of 1950. Advice was requested from foreign experts (see Surrey and Oldman 1960). The Central Bank published a first report on the issue in the early 1960s (Banco Central de la República Argentina 1962). Nevertheless, a serious quantitative assessment of income tax evasion is missing in those publications.

Secondly, existing measures of the size of the underground economy in Argentina show that the level of unreported activities might have increased during the second half of the twentieth century.[45] These studies indicate that there is a positive relationship between tax burden, state regulations, and the incentive to hide transactions. In the first half of the

---

[43] For an analysis of the legal responses to taxation, from real substitution responses to avoidance responses, see Slemrod (2001) and Slemrod and Yitzhaki (2002).

[44] The changes in personal income tax rates and corporation income tax rates may generate a shifting of income both between the personal tax base and the corporate tax base (as described in Gordon and Slemrod 2000), and between the formal and informal sectors.

[45] See Ahumada et al. (2003) and Ahumada, Alvaredo, and Canavese (2007).

Table 6D.1 Under-reporting in income tax, Argentina, 1959

Income levels				
in 1959 m$n		in 2000 US dollars		un-reported income (% of reported income)
(from	to)	(from	to)	
	30,000		6,667	33
30,001	40,000	6,667	8,889	34
40,001	60,000	8,889	13,333	36
60,001	90,000	13,334	20,000	38
90,001	120,000	20,000	26,667	39
120,001	200,000	26,667	44,444	40
200,001	300,000	44,445	66,667	40
300,001	700,000	66,667	155,556	36
700,001	2,000,000	155,556	444,444	31
2,000,001		444,445		27

Note: m$n refers to 'pesos moneda nacional', the legal currency in 1959.

Source: Presidencia de la Nación (1967: volume v).

century the tax rates (mainly the top marginal rates) were far lower than those in European and North American countries, and slightly lower than in neighbouring countries such as Chile or Brazil. Finally, tax evasion is well connected with the environment of macroeconomic volatility and inflation distinctive of the post-1950 period. High inflation also provides strong incentives to postpone income reporting; even when this behavioural response is not strictly evasion, it can erode tax collections to a great extent.

A first comparison can be made between the results for 1953 from income tax data and those from CONADE (1965). This study is certainly not the absolute truth (in fact it contains many ad hoc adjustments) but provides some elements for judgement. Our estimates for the top shares in 1953 based on tax data (the top 1 per cent share being 15.3 per cent) are indeed slightly higher than those obtained from the cited study (the top 1 per cent being 12.8 per cent).

Using information from the 1962 tax amnesty (which attempted to uncover all income that had been evaded by taxpayers between 1956 and 1961), the authorities estimated evasion in 1959.[46] Results (very limited) are reproduced in Table 6D.1. The last column reports hidden income as percentage of declared income. Un-reporting, with values between 27 per cent and 40 per cent, described an inverse U pattern, with maxima for the brackets in the middle of the scale. This suggests that evasion, if important across all income levels, shows a lower impact at the bottom (where income from wage source dominates) and at the top of the tax scale (where inspections from the tax administration agency might be more frequent and enforcement through other taxes higher). However, these figures might exaggerate true evasion. On the one hand, it is not possible to know exactly how the authorities arrived at the figures in Table 6D.1: no data are available to replicate the computations. On the other hand, the notion of 'potential tax collection' (the tax collection had all income been declared) used by the tax agency contaminates the interpretation.

[46] Decree 6480/1962.

A new amnesty followed in 1970, for the tax evaded between 1964 and 1969.[47] Unfortunately, the tax authorities did not publish the results in detail either. Over a total of 589,000 taxpayers, 300,000 individuals declared 65 per cent of unreported income (with respect to reported income). Under the extreme assumption that those who did not have recourse to the amnesty had nothing to declare, then the average unreported income was 33 per cent ($0.65 \times 300/589$).[48]

It is difficult to provide better evidence for Argentina. However, it is unlikely that such high percentages of evasion represent the situation among top income earners. As also discussed in Chapter 10, the rich are very visible for tax authorities.

---

[47] The amnesty served primarily to close a temporary fiscal imbalance. This time, declaring net assets placed in foreign countries was not mandatory (Law 18529 of 12/31/1969). For a theoretical analysis of the efficiency and equity consequences of permanent and non-permanent tax amnesties, see Andreoni (1991).

[48] Ministerio de Economía (1973).

APPENDIX 6E: COMPARISON BETWEEN TAX TABULATIONS AND HOUSEHOLD SURVEYS

Household surveys are of little help when focusing on the very rich and do not offer valuable information when trying to get an idea of unreported income in tax data. The rich are missing from surveys either for sampling reasons or because they refuse to cooperate with the time-consuming task of completing or answering to a long form. When found, they are sometimes intentionally excluded so as to minimize bias problems generated by outliers. The practice of eliminating extreme observations, usually seen as data contamination, relies in many cases on expert judgement.[49] Groves and Couper (1998) report that the probability of response is negatively correlated with almost all measures of socio-economic status. They also report how, while survey interviewers in poor countries can usually collect data in very poor areas, penetrating the gated communities in which many rich people live is often impossible. Székely and Hilgert (1999) analyse a large number of Latin American surveys to confirm that the top reported incomes generally correspond to the prototype of highly educated professionals rather than capital owners.[50]

To get a sense of the mismatch, we quantified the gap between top incomes from Argentine household surveys and top incomes from tax tabulations. This was done by applying the statutory income tax schedule to the actual income of each individual in the survey, after subtracting exempted income, the main allowances, and family deductions and selecting those individuals with positive taxable income, as they are the ones present in the tax statistics. Household surveys correspond to Encuesta Permanente de Hogares (EPH), October, Instituto Nacional de Estadística y Censos.

We proceeded in the following way. We corrected the October 1997 survey weights so that the adult population covered by the survey matched our reference total for tax units. As survey income refers to monthly values, annual income was computed by upscaling labour income and pensions by a factor of 13 (twelve months plus a year-end bonus). Income from all other sources was multiplied by 12. Family deductions and allowances established by the tax schedule were calculated using the household composition information. Deduction for spouse was $2,400; deduction for each dependent child was $1,200. Personal allowance was $4,800. Since other allowances permitted by law vary according to personal characteristics, expenses, and sources of income, it is not possible to know exactly the individual amount to be deducted. We computed the ratio allowances/income by ranges of income from the tax tabulations, and applied those ratios to survey incomes. Finally, individuals were organized by levels of income so as to reproduce the tax tabulations.[51]

Table 6E.1 presents the results of the comparison for 1997. While there were 698 tax files with income above $1,000,000 and 26 tax files with income above $5,000,000, the survey's top 160 individuals only have income between $500,000 and $1,000,000.

---

[49] See Cowell and Victoria-Feser (1996).

[50] In ten cases, total income of the richest households in the survey is below the average salary of a manager.

[51] A similar procedure has been followed in Engel, Galetovic, and Raddatz (1999).

Table 6E.1 Income tax tabulation and household survey, Argentina, 1997

Income brackets in 1997 US dollars		Tax statistics		Survey statistics	
		#	th. US dollars	#	th. US dollars
	10,000	356,793	2,002,216	278,573	2,520,039
10,000	20,000	359,544	5,219,874	1,084,653	15,600,000
20,000	30,000	198,613	4,877,585	327,086	8,131,826
30,000	40,000	113,129	3,914,582	117,165	4,139,473
40,000	50,000	68,388	3,054,019	42,057	1,882,858
50,000	60,000	42,882	2,344,636	21,110	1,158,234
60,000	80,000	48,631	3,350,531	19,238	1,329,835
80,000	100,000	26,136	2,329,231	8,196	732,496
100,000	150,000	23,466	2,818,377	3,834	428,004
150,000	200,000	8,555	1,467,866	976	152,213
200,000	300,000	6,616	1,596,016		
300,000	500,000	3,849	1,455,500	1,345	487,354
500,000	1,000,000	1,895	1,259,405	160	115,200
1,000,000	1,500,000	411	488,769		
1,500,000	2,000,000	181	337,018		
2,000,000	3,000,000	31	85,207		
3,000,000	5,000,000	49	186,703		
5,000,000		26	226,908		
Total		1,259,195	37,014,443	1,904,393	36,677,531

Sources: AFIP, Estadísticas Tributarias 1998 and INDEC, Household survey, October 1997.

Survey information generally differs also from National Accounts data. However, a word of caution is necessary here. The fact that means of consumption and income from household surveys and National Accounts differ is not only because the rich might not be present in the surveys: the two sources of information are different and they measure different concepts. National Accounts track money and are more likely to capture large transactions, while surveys follow people and are less likely to include large transactors. In the developing world, surveys detect almost exclusively wages and pensions, self-employment income, and public transfers, while capital income is largely neglected. Deaton (2005) analyses the issue in detail and acknowledges that extensive prior adjustments of the National Accounts mean income (or consumption) are required before using them to upscaling survey estimates.[52] The Canberra Expert Group on Household Income Statistics, 2001 has also examined the relationships between the definition of income in National Accounts and the income appropriate for distribution analysis.

[52] Deaton (2005) has found that the ratio of survey to National Accounts consumption is generally higher in the poorest countries and lower in the richest. In general consumption measured from surveys frequently grows less rapidly than consumption measured from National Accounts. Additionally, there exists a negative relationship between the ratio of survey to National Accounts on the one hand, and the level of per capita GDP on the other. This relationship is steepest among the poorest countries, is flatter in the middle-income countries, and resumes its downward slope among the rich economies. One of the reasons is that consumption is easier to measure in surveys than is income in poorer countries where many people are self-employed, while the opposite is true in rich countries. Deaton's remarks are, however, mainly directed at the measurement of poverty. For example, the system of National Accounts recommends, in measuring production for own consumption, that the effort be made only when the amounts produced are likely to be quantitatively important in relation to the total supply of goods in the country. This rule makes little sense when we are worried about poor households.

REFERENCES

Administración Federal de Ingresos Públicos (2002). *Estadísticas tributarias*. Buenos Aires.

Ahumada, H., F. Alvaredo, and A. Canavese (2000). 'Un análisis comparativo del impacto distributivo del impuesto inflacionario y de un impuesto sobre el consumo', *Economica*, 46(2), July/December.

—— —— —— (2007). 'The Monetary Method and the Size of the Shadow Economy', *Review of Income and Wealth*, 53(2): 363–71.

—— —— —— and P. Canavese (2003). 'Estimación del tamaño de la economía oculta por medio de la demanda de circulante: una revisión de la metodología con una ilustración para Argentina', *Revista de análisis económico*, 18(1): 103–15.

Altimir, O. (1986). 'Estimaciones de la distribución del ingreso en la Argentina, 1953–1980', *Desarrollo económico*, 25(100): 521–66.

—— and L. Beccaria (1999). 'Distribución del ingreso en la Argentina', Serie Reformas Económicas, CEPAL.

Alvaredo, F. (2009). 'Top Incomes and Earnings in Portugal 1936–2005', *Explorations in Economic History*, 46(4): 404–17.

—— and E. Saez (2009). 'Income and Wealth Concentration in Spain from a Historical and Fiscal Perspective', *Journal of the European Economic Association*, 7(5): 1140–67.

Andreoni, J. (1991). 'The Desirability of a Permanent Tax Amnesty', *Journal of Public Economics*, 45(2): 143–59.

Atkinson, A. B. (2005). 'Top Incomes in the United Kingdom over the Twentieth Century', *Journal of the Real Statistical Society*, Series A, 168(2): 325–43.

—— (2007). 'Measuring Top Incomes: Methodological Issues', in Atkinson and Piketty (2007).

—— and A. Leigh (2007a). 'The Distribution of Top Incomes in Australia', in Atkinson and Piketty (2007).

—— —— (2007b). 'The Distribution of Top Incomes in New Zealand', in Atkinson and Piketty (2007).

—— and T. Piketty (2007). *Top Incomes over the Twentieth Century: A Contrast between European and English Speaking Countries*. Oxford: Oxford University Press.

Auerbach, A. and J. Slemrod (1997). 'The Economic Effects of the Tax Reform Act of 1986', *Journal of Economic Literature*, 35: 589–632.

Banco Central de la República Argentina (1962). *Boletín estadístico*, January.

Banerjee, A. and T. Piketty (2005). 'Top Indian Incomes 1922–2000', *World Bank Economic Review*, 19(1): 1–20.

Braun, O. and L. Joy (1967). 'A Model of Economic Stagnation: A Case Study of the Argentine Economy', *Economic Journal*, 78(312): 868–87.

Canberra Expert Group on Household Income Statistics (2001). *Final Report and Recommendations*. Ottawa.

CONADE-Consejo Nacional de Desarrollo and Comisión Económica para América Latina y el Caribe (1965). *Distribución del ingreso y cuentas nacionales en la Argentina*, 5 vols. Buenos Aires.

Cont, W. and N. Susmel (2006). 'Evasión impositiva en impuestos directos personales: ganancias de las personas y seguridad social', in Fundación de Investigaciones Latinoamericanas (ed.) *La presion tributaria sobre el sector formal de la economía*. Buenos Aires: chapter 8.

Cortés Conde, R. (1979). *El progreso argentino*. Buenos Aires: Editorial Sudamericana.

Cortés Conde, R. (1997). *La economía argentina en el largo plazo (siglos XIX y XX)*. Buenos Aires: Editorial Sudamericana.

—— and E. Gallo (1972). *La república conservadora*. Buenos Aires: Paidós.

Cowell, F. and M. Victoria-Feser (1996). 'Robustness Property of Inequality Measures', *Econometrica*, 64(1): 77–101.

Cruces, G. and L. Gasparini (2008). 'A Distribution in Motion: The Case of Argentina', Documento de Trabajo 78, Centro de Estudios Distributivos, Laborales y Sociales, Universidad de La Plata.

Deaton, A. (2005). 'Measuring Poverty in a Growing World (or Measuring Growth in a Poor World)', *Review of Economics and Statistics*, 87(1): 1–19.

Della Paolera, G. and Taylor, A. (2001). *Straining at the Anchor: The Argentine Currency Board and the Search for Macroeconomic Stability 1880–1935*. Chicago: University of Chicago Press.

—— —— (2003). *A New Economic History of Argentina*. Cambridge: Cambridge University Press.

Diaz-Alejandro, C. (1970). *Essays on the Economic History of the Argentine Republic*. New Haven: Yale University Press.

Di Tella, G. (1987). 'Argentina's Most Recent Inflationary Cycle, 1975–1987', in R. Thorp and L. Whitehead (eds.) *Latin American Debt and the Adjustment Crisis*. Pittsburgh: University of Pittsburgh Press: 162–207.

—— and R. Dornbusch (1983). *The Political Economy of Argentina 1946–1983*. Pittsburgh: University of Pittsburgh Press.

—— and M. Zymelman (1967). *Las etapas del desarrollo económico Argentino*. Buenos Aires: Editorial Universitaria de Buenos Aires.

—— —— (1973). *Los ciclos económicos argentinos*. Buenos Aires: Paidós.

Engel, E., A. Galetovic, and C. Raddatz (1999). 'Taxes and Income Distribution in Chile: Some Unpleasant Redistributive Arithmetic', *Journal of Development Economics*, 59(1): 155–92.

Gasparini, L. (1999). 'Incidencia distributiva del sistema impositivo Argentino', in Fundación de Investigaciones Latinoamericanas (ed.) *La reforma tributaria en la Argentina*. Buenos Aires.

—— (2004). 'Different Lives: Inequality in Latin America and the Caribbean', in D. Ferranti, G. Perry, and F. Ferreira (eds.) *Breaking with History? Inequality in Latin America and the Caribbean*. Washington, DC: World Bank: chapter 2.

—— F. Gutiérrez, and L. Tornarolli (2007). 'Growth and Income Poverty in Latin America and the Caribbean: Evidence from Household Surveys', *Review of Income and Wealth*, 53(2): 209–45.

—— M. Marchionnini and W. Sosa Escudero (2001). *La distribución del ingreso en la Argentina: perspectivas y efectos sobre el bienestar*. Buenos Aires: Fundación Arcor.

—— —— —— (2004). 'Characterization of Inequality Changes through Microeconometric Decompositions: The Case of Greater Buenos Aires', in F. Bourguignon, F. Ferreira, and N. Lustig (eds.) *The Microeconometrics of Income Distribution Dynamics in East Asia and Latin America*. New York: Oxford University Press.

—— and W. Sosa Escudero (2003). 'Implicit Rents from Own-Housing and Income Distribution: Econometric Estimates for Greater Buenos Aires', *Journal of Income Distribution*, 12.

González Rozada, M. and M. Menéndez (2006). 'Why have Poverty and Income Inequality Increased so Much? Argentina, 1991–2001', *Economic Development and Cultural Change*, 55(1): 109–38.

Gordon, R. and J. Slemrod (2000). 'Are "Real" Responses to Taxes Simply Income Shifting between Corporate and Personal Tax Bases?', in Slemrod (2000).

Groves, R. and M. Couper (1998). *Nonresponse in Household Interview Surveys*. New York: Wiley.

Halbwachs, M. (1950). *La Mémoire collective*. Paris: Les Presses Universitaires de France.

Jauretche, A. (1966). *El medio pelo en la sociedad Argentina*. Buenos Aires: A. Peña Lillo Editor.

Johnson, L. and Z. Frank (2006). 'Cities and Wealth in the South Atlantic: Buenos Aires and Rio de Janeiro before 1860', *Comparative Studies in Society and History*, 48: 634–68.

Kuznets, S. (1953). *Shares of Upper Income Groups in Income and Savings*. National Bureau of Economic Research.

—— (1955). 'Economic Growth and Income Inequality', *American Economic Review*, 45(1): 1–28.

Landais, C. (2007). 'Les Hauts Revenus en France (1998–2006): une explosion des inégalités?', Paris School of Economics, mimeo.

Leigh, A. and P. van der Eng (2009). 'Inequality in Indonesia: What Can We Learn from Top Incomes', *Journal of Public Economics*, 93: 209–12.

Lindemboim, J., J. Graña, and D. Kennedy (2005). 'Distribución funcional del ingreso en Argentina: ayer y hoy', Documentos de Trabajo, 4, Centro de Estudios sobre Población, Empleo y Desarrollo, Instituto de Investigaciones Económicas, Facultad de Ciencias Económicas, Universidad de Buenos Aires.

Luna, F. (1958). *Alvear*. Buenos Aires: Libros Argentinos.

—— (1989). *Soy Roca*. Buenos Aires: Sudamericana.

—— (2003). *The World Economy: Historical Statistics*. Paris: OECD.

Mallon, R. and J. Sourrouille (1975). *Economic Policymaking in a Conflict Society: The Argentine Case*. Cambridge, Mass.: Center for International Affairs, Harvard University Press.

Ministerio de Economía (1973). 'Boletín estadístico, número especial, aporte de la DGI a las III jornadas tributarias del Colegio de Graduados de Ciencias Económicas de Buenos Aires', Departamento de Estudios, División Estadística.

Ocampo, V. (1979–84). *Autobiografía*, 6 vols. Buenos Aires: Revista Sur.

Organización de Estados Americanos and Banco Interamericano de Desarrollo (1967). *Estudio sobre política fiscal en la Argentina*, 7 vols. Buenos Aires.

Piketty, T. (2001). *Les Hauts Revenus en France au 20ème siecle: inégalités et redistributions, 1901–1998*. Paris: Éditions Grasset.

—— (2003). 'Income Inequality in France 1901–1998', *Journal of Political Economy*, 111 (5): 1004–42.

—— and N. Qian (2009). 'Income Inequality and Progressive Income Taxation in China and India: 1986–2015' (forthcoming), *American Economic Journal: Applied Economics*.

—— and E. Saez (2003). 'Income Inequality in the United States, 1913–1998', *Quarterly Journal of Economics*, 118(1): 1–39.

—— —— (2006). 'The Evolution of Top Incomes: A Historical and International Perspective', *American Economic Review*, 96(2): 200–5.

Presidencia de la Nación República Argentina (1967). *Estudio de política fiscal en la Argentina, preparado por el programa conjunto de tributación OEA/BID, 1963*, 7 vols. Buenos Aires.

Rapoport, M. (1980). *1949–1945 Gran Bretaña, Estados Unidos y las clases dirigentes argentinas*. Buenos Aires: Editorial de Belgrano.

Rapoport, M. (1988). *Aliados o neutrales? La Argentina frente a la Segunda Guerra Mundial.* Buenos Aires: Editorial Universitaria de Buenos Aires.

Saez, E. and M. Veall (2005). 'The Evolution of Top Incomes in Northern America: Lessons from Canadian Evidence', *American Economic Review*, 95(3): 831–49.

Sánchez Román, J. (2007). 'Taxation and Peronism', mimeo.

—— (2008). 'Shaping Taxation: Economic Elites and Fiscal Decision-Making in Argentina, 1920–1945', *Journal of Latin American Studies*, 40(1): 83–108.

—— (2009). 'Economic Elites, Regional Cleavages and the First Attempts at Introducing the Income Tax in Argentina', *Hisparic American Historical Review*, 89(2): 253–83.

Sebrelli, J. (1985). *La Saga de los Anchorena.* Buenos Aires: Sudamericana.

Slemrod, J. (1992). 'Do Taxes Matter? Lessons from the 1980s', *American Economic Review*, 82(2): 250–6.

—— (1995). 'Income Creation or Income Shifting? Behavioral Responses to the Tax Reform Act of 1986', *American Economic Review*, 85(2): 175–80.

—— (2000). *Does Atlas Shrug? The Economic Consequences of Taxing the Rich.* Cambridge, Mass.: Harvard University Press.

—— (2001). 'A General Model of the Behavioral Response to Taxation', *International Tax and Public Finance*, 8(2): 119–28.

—— and S. Yitzhaki (2002). 'Tax Avoidance, Evasion, and Administration', in A. J. Auerbach and M. Feldstein (eds.) *Handbook of Public Economics.* Amsterdam: Elsevier: chapter 22.

Sokoloff, K. and E. Zolt (2007). 'Inequality and the Evolution of Institutions of Taxation in the Americas', in S. Edwards, G. Esquivel, and G. Marquez (eds.) *Growth, Institutions and Crises: Latin America from a Historic Perspective.* Chicago: University of Chicago Press: chapter 3.

Surrey, S. and O. Oldman (1960). *Examen preliminar del sistema impositivo de la República Argentina.* Buenos Aires: Dirección General Impositiva.

Székeley, M. and M. Hilgert (1999). 'What's Behind the Inequality We Measure: An Investigation Using Latin American Data', Research Department Working Paper 409, Inter-American Development Bank.

Taylor, A. (1992). 'External Dependence, Demographic Burdens and Argentine Economic Decline after the Belle Epoque', *Journal of Economic History*, 52(4): 907–36.

Vazquez Presedo, V. (1971). *Estadísticas históricas argentinas*, 2 vols. Buenos Aires: Ed. Macchi.

—— (1988). *Estadísticas históricas argentinas: compendio 1873–1973.* Buenos Aires: Academia Nacional de Ciencias Económicas.

7

Top Incomes in Sweden over the Twentieth Century

Jesper Roine and Daniel Waldenström

7.1 INTRODUCTION

The evolution of income inequality across different economic systems has received enormous attention. A key issue in the literature has been the possible trade-offs between egalitarian ambitions and incentive effects. It is not surprising, therefore, that Sweden, thanks to its tradition as an egalitarian society, has attracted disproportionate interest from inequality scholars. However, two important aspects have largely been overlooked. First, the lack of available micro-data has led to most studies not going further back than to 1968.[1] The lack of homogeneous, long-run series means that we cannot really put the developments over the past decades in historical perspective. We do not know, for example, to what extent the equal distribution of income in Sweden is mainly the outcome of the growth of the welfare state, or if Sweden perhaps has a history of being an egalitarian society. Second, the focus on welfare issues has resulted in most studies concentrating on general measures of the distribution, such as the Gini coefficient, or on the lower parts of it, but no attention has been paid to details of top incomes. This is potentially problematic as detailed knowledge about the top of

This chapter is an extended version of 'The Evolution of Top Incomes in an Egalitarian Society: Sweden, 1903–2004' published in *Journal of Public Economics*, 92(1): 366–87. Copyright Elsevier, February 2008. In particular, the extensive appendices published here contain detailed information about sources, the Swedish income data, as well as alternatives for constructing reference totals in the Swedish case.

[1] See Lindbeck (1997) for an overview of the Swedish welfare state; Gottschalk and Smeeding (1997) for Swedish income distribution in international perspective; and e.g. Björklund and Freeman (2006) for a recent overview of income equalization in Sweden. Examples of studies of income distribution before 1968 include Björklund and Palme (2000) who study the Swedish income distribution on decile level for four years between 1951 and 1973; Spånt's (1979) study of Census data for the period 1920–76, Lydall's (1968) for the period 1920–60; Gustafsson and Johansson (2003) who study tax returns for five separate years during the period 1925–58 (restricted to people living in the city of Gothenburg); Söderberg (1991) who studies salaries in various sectors between 1870 and 1950; Lindstrand (1949) studies the period 1935–47 and Quensel (1944) the period 1930–41, both using tax return data, etc. Bentzel's (1953) study of the period 1930–48 is closest to ours in methodology.

the distribution may be crucial for distinguishing between different explanations of what drives inequality (or the lack of it). For example, to differentiate between theories which, on the one hand, focus on changes in the relative wages of skilled and unskilled workers and, on the other hand, theories that stress the importance of savings and capital formation, we must have details about top incomes.

This chapter addresses these two shortcomings by providing new homogeneous series on top income shares in Sweden, starting at the time of the introduction of the modern tax system in 1902 and until today. We also propose ways of explaining these developments. In 1902 Sweden was largely agrarian, had not yet extended the franchise to all male citizens, and was still half a century away from the expansion of the welfare state. Our series, hence, allow us to study changes in income concentration over a period during which Swedish society has undergone major structural change and also allow us to add the historical perspective on income inequality in Sweden which previously has not been available. The fact that we can decompose income shares with respect to the source of income, as well as study smaller fractiles within the top of the distribution (from the top 10 per cent to the top 0.01 per cent), enables us to discriminate between the possible economic mechanisms that could explain our findings. As changes in wealth concentration and in particular wealth distribution by income class are important for understanding changes in top income shares we provide new series for these developments over the twentieth century.

This study can, of course, also be seen as a contribution to the recent work on long-run income inequality in which series of income concentration have been constructed using a common methodology.[2] These studies have given numerous new insights to changes in income concentration and in particular noted common developments for Anglo-Saxon countries, on the one hand, and continental European countries, on the other. As our study is concerned with one of the extremes of what Esping-Andersen (1990) denotes 'the different worlds of welfare capitalism', namely the *social democratic welfare state*, it is particularly interesting to compare our findings to the previous work.[3] It turns out that Sweden is indeed different from both the Anglo-Saxon as well as the continental European group of countries, although not entirely in ways which may have been expected.

---

[2] Following the first studies by Piketty (2001a, 2003) on France, Piketty and Saez (2003) on the USA, and Atkinson on the UK (2004), other recent studies include Australia (Atkinson and Leigh 2007a), Canada (Saez and Veall 2005), Germany (Dell 2005), Ireland (Nolan 2007), Japan (Moriguchi and Saez 2008), the Netherlands (Atkinson and Salverda 2005), New Zealand (Atkinson and Leigh 2007b), Spain (Alvaredo and Saez, Chapter 10 in this volume) and Switzerland (Dell, Piketty, and Saez 2007). Atkinson and Piketty (2007) collect much of this work. Lindert (2000) and Morrisson (2000) provide surveys of previous studies on long-run inequality developments.

[3] In his distinction between 'The Three Worlds of Welfare Capitalism', Esping-Andersen (1990) identifies three different types of welfare states; 'liberal welfare states' (e.g., the USA and the UK), the 'corporatist-conservative welfare states' (e.g., France, Germany, Italy), and the 'social democratic welfare states'. A similar distinction is often made between an Anglo-Saxon, a continental European, and a Scandinavian group of countries; see, e.g., Lindbeck (2006).

A number of broad facts stand out from our series. Over the first eighty years of the twentieth century top income shares in Sweden decreased. Most of this decrease happened during the first half of the century, that is, before the expansion of the welfare state, and most of it was due to large falls in the income share of the top percentile (P99–100). By contrast, the income share going to the lower half of the top decile (P90–P95), which consists mainly of wages, has been remarkably stable over the entire period. Between 1903 and 2006 this share has fluctuated between 9 and 11 per cent, while the top percentile has changed by a factor of four. This suggests that decomposing the top decile into smaller fractions is crucial for understanding the development. In terms of composition, most of the early decrease seems to have been driven by falls in capital income, but after around the mid 1930s wage compression also becomes important in explaining the decreasing top shares. The drops in capital shares fit well with sharp decreases in top wealth shares during the first half of the century, in particular in the early 1930s, but notably not during the Second World War, as was the case in many other countries. Between 1950 and 1980 the continued decrease in inequality was quite steady but smaller relative to the first half of the century. Over the past two decades the general picture turns out to depend crucially on how income from capital gains is treated.[4] If we include capital gains, Swedish income inequality has increased quite substantially; when excluding them, top income shares have increased much less. This indicates that while labour incomes have not diverged dramatically over the past decades, the gains from exceptionally large increases in asset prices (mainly increases in share prices) have been very unevenly distributed.[5] This, in turn, suggests that the Swedish case over the past decades is different from both the Anglo-Saxon case as well as from the continental European case previously identified in the literature.[6]

The remainder of the chapter is organized as follows: in section 7.2 we discuss the data and methodology used, in section 7.3 we present our main findings under four sub-headings; first we account for the evolution of top income shares in terms of gross income from all sources (separating series including and excluding capital gains), second we study the composition of these shares by source, third we analyse the effect of potential tax avoidance and evasion on our series, and fourth we study separate top income series when excluding taxable transfers giving us an income concept closer to market income.[7] Thereafter we

---

[4] It is important to note that throughout the chapter, whenever we refer to capital gains income, this means *realized* capital gains, which is what the tax data allow us to measure. In section 7.3 below we discuss possible implications of this distinction in more detail.

[5] Our data suggest that these capital gains have accrued to those who also have the highest wages, hence magnifying inequalities in the income distribution.

[6] See, e.g., Saez (2004) and Piketty and Saez (2006) for cross-country comparisons.

[7] For most other countries this distinction is not very important when studying top incomes, but in the Swedish context (taxable) social transfers are sufficiently large to have an effect on the top income shares, even if they do not make up any large part of top incomes, as including them affects the reference total for income (see, for example, Björklund and Freeman 2006 on the importance of transfers for income distribution in Sweden).

attempt to account for our results in section 7.4 by studying changes in factor shares, the wealth distribution, tax progressivity, and changes in asset prices. In section 7.5 we highlight differences and similarities in our results for Sweden with the findings in a number of other countries for which comparable data exist. Section 7.6 concludes. A number of appendices contain detailed information about data and various adjustments as well as sensitivity analysis of our main series.

7.2 METHODOLOGY AND DATA

In recent years, a methodology for studying income concentration using long time series of tax return data has been established following Piketty (2001a), who in turn builds on the seminal work by Kuznets (1953). The basic idea is to construct shares of total personal income received by different fractiles of the entire (tax) population, had everyone been required to file a tax return. Since historically only top income earners were taxed they are the only ones directly observed over the entire period. This in turn means that the reference totals for population and income, which are aimed at also including individuals who did not file a tax return and their incomes, must be constructed using aggregate sources from the population statistics and National Accounts. Top income shares are then computed by dividing the number of tax units in the top, and their incomes, by the reference tax population and reference total income.[8] Assuming that top incomes are approximately Pareto distributed, standard inter- and extrapolation techniques can be used to calculate the income shares for various top fractiles, such as the top 10 per cent (P90–100) or the top 0.01 per cent (P99.99–100).

Our data on income distribution come mainly from the income statistics published yearly by Statistics Sweden starting in 1943, and for the period before that from scattered public investigations.[9] These sources generally provide tabulations of

---

[8] There are, of course, a number of potential problems with using tax statistics data; they are collected as part of an administrative routine in which individuals have incentives to under-report income, they tell us nothing per se about the welfare of individuals, etc. Nevertheless, as long as we think that tax statistics, at least for the top income earners, approximate actual incomes, and as long as the problems with the statistics have not changed systematically over time, they are a useful source. Importantly, this is also the only available source for much of the twentieth century. Our general view in the case of Sweden is that the administrative process has, compared to most countries, been very thorough and Swedish tax data are quite reliable, at least for high-income groups. The estimates of tax avoidance and evasion that we have found suggest that the levels have not changed in any systematic way over the century (see further section 7.3 below).

[9] Data come from the Ministry of Finance in 1903 (only the very top), 1907, 1911, 1912, 1916, 1919, 1920, 1934, and 1941 and Statistics Sweden in the Censuses (*Folkräkningen*) of 1920, 1930, 1935, 1945, and 1950, and its annual publication of tax-based income statistics (*Skattetaxeringarna* and later titles) published from 1943 onwards (see Appendix 7A for a listing of these sources).

the number of taxpayers and their total assessed income for a large number of income brackets. Typically, these tables also include information on the different sources of income (e.g., wages and capital income), tax liabilities, and even data on net personal wealth in different income classes for some years.[10] To make these data comparable over time, a number of adjustments have been made as described in more detail in Table 7.1. Our preferred concept of income is *total (gross) income*, defined as income from all sources before taxes and transfers, but deducting deficits at source (mainly interest payments). Capital gains are included in this concept, but the structure of the data allows us to subtract them and construct series both with and without capital gains.[11] One specific aspect of the Swedish income statistics is that after 1974, new laws made several transfer-like, non-market incomes, such as unemployment compensation, family allowances, and sick pay, fully taxable. In our main series we have added these components before 1974 so as to get a total income concept that corresponds to today's definition of total income, but we have also done the opposite, i.e., deducted these non-market incomes after 1973 to get series which are closer to *market income*.[12]

To calculate the reference totals for income there are basically two ways in which to proceed: either starting from the total income reported on tax returns and then adding items not included in the tax base as well as income estimates of individuals not filing taxes (not including children), or starting from the National Accounts item 'Total Personal Sector Income' from which (estimates of) all that is not included in the preferred definition of income can be deducted. Thanks to the relative richness of Swedish historical tax data and National Accounts, we have been able to calculate our reference total for income in a number of ways and our final preferred series combine both ways of constructing the reference total for income.[13] When creating a series for the reference tax population, we must incorporate the fact that the Swedish tax law, and income statistics, changed

[10] Between 1910 and 1948 Sweden had a peculiar kind of wealth tax, which operated through an addition of a fraction (1/60 until 1938, thereafter 1/100) of taxable wealth to total income to get 'taxable income'. This creates problems in terms of having to adjust tax data to get actual incomes (without the wealth shares) but it also means that information on wealth distribution by income class is available.

[11] Data on taxable capital gains are available in 1945, 1951, and annually from 1967. In 1945 and 1951, the capital gains shares are very low in all fractiles. We use the 1945 shares as estimates for all prior years (see Appendix 7B for more details).

[12] For some years we have direct observations on the size of transfers by income class and this data supports the assumption that these transfers constitute very small shares of total income in the top of the distribution.

[13] Our main sources for calculating the reference income total are the new National Accounts data for Sweden compiled by Edvinsson (2005) and Swedish tax statistics (*Skattetaxeringen till inkomst och förmögenhet*, various years). For details see Appendix 7A–C where we also show that our findings are robust to alternative specifications of this reference total.

Table 7.1 Definitions and adjustments of the income data and reference totals in Sweden

Income years	Income concept appearing in data sources [Swedish term]	Adjustments	Reference total income	Reference total population
1903–1910	Taxable income [till statlig inkomstskatt taxerad inkomst]. Bascially 'Total income'.	–	Share of 'total personal sector income' (from National accounts) adding estimates of items not included in the preferred definition (1903–1942)	
1911–1942	Taxable amount [Taxerat belopp] = Taxable income (see above) + Wealth share (share of taxable personal net wealth) – Some taxes.	Removal of wealth shares and after 1920 addition of some municipal taxes		Adult population (>15 yrs) minus married women (–1950)
1943–1950	–	–	Tax statistics income plus estimates of non-taxed items included in preferred def. (mainly corrections for changed tax treatment of unemployment and sick pay insurance etc. before 1974) plus estimated incomes of 'non-filers' (1943–)	Adult population (>15 yrs) adj. for women being (partially) included in the income statistics (1951–1970)
1951–1970	Total income [Sammanräknad nettoinkomst] = Total (gross) income – Deficits at source	Age adjustment (excluding all <16 years old)		
1971–1990	Total (gross) income [Sammanräknad inkomst]	Subtracting deficits at source + Age adjustment		Adult population (>15 yrs) (1971–)
1991–2006	Total income [Summa förvärvs- och kapitalinkomst]	Age adjustment		

Note: All concepts are elaborated upon in Appendices 7A–C. No age-specific data were available for different income classes until 1951.

Table 7.2 Top income thresholds and average incomes in Sweden in 2004

Threshold	Income (incl. capital gains) in USD	Income (excl. capital gains) in USD	Fractiles	N tax units (individuals)	Ave. income (incl. capital gains) in USD	Ave. income (excl. capital gains) in USD
			Full tax pop.	7,395,545	27,875	26,801
P90	48,697	46,354	P90–95	369,777	55,021	51,625
P95	61,154	58,123	P95–99	295,822	72,943	73,665
P99	115,294	79,416	P99–99.9	66,560	156,915	118,619
P99.9	298,488	240,706	P99.9–99.99	6,656	497,511	344,027
P99.99	1,218,259	685,380	P99.99–100	740	3,336,038	1,554,507

Note: The calculations are based on income tax data, with income defined as total income (excluding and including capital gains, ranked in classes of total income *including* capital gains) before individual taxes expressed in 2004 USD converted from Swedish kronor (SEK) using the 2004 average exchange rate of 7.36SEK/USD.

from being household based to individual based between 1951 and 1971.[14] Our reference population total, hence, shifts from being the adult population (16 and above) minus married women, to the entire adult population (16 and above).[15] What effect this has on the top income shares is an open question. As shown by Atkinson and Leigh (2007b) it basically depends on how incomes were distributed among the married men and women.[16]

To get a sense of the size of the fractiles and what it takes in terms of income to be part of a particular income share today, Table 7.2 presents some descriptive statistics for 2004. As the incomes are highly dependent on whether capital gains are included or not we have included both in the table. The amounts have been converted into US-dollars using the average exchange rate in 2004.

7.3 THE BASIC FACTS

Figure 7.1 shows the evolution of the top decile income share in Sweden over the period 1903–2006. The broad trend is that this share has been divided by a factor of two over the first eighty years, from around 46 per cent of total income in the first years of the century, to 23 per cent in 1980. Approximately two-thirds of this decline took place before 1950, with large falls in the volatile years just after the two world wars. This means that most of the drop in pre-tax income inequality actually took place before the expansion of the welfare state. The decline thereafter is more stable with a new relatively sharp drop in the late 1960s and over the 1970s to a lowest point around 23 per cent in the early 1980s.[17] After the mid

[14] In 1951, the income statistics started being made based on a 10% individual sample (but with full coverage of high-income individuals) of the entire population, despite the fact that in the tax laws the shift to independent taxation did not come until 1966, when married couples could decide whether they wanted to file jointly or not, and finally in 1971 when individual assessment was made compulsory.

[15] The main source for our reference population series are Statistics Sweden, Population Statistics (*SCB, Programmet för befolkningsstatistik*)—see Appendix 7C. The shift from household based to independent taxation happened gradually between 1952 and 1970. We constructed a number of alternative reference totals to capture the possible variations across the different legal regimes, but found no significant effects on our basic findings. Moreover, we also changed the age cut-off of the adult population from 16 years to 20 years, which lowered top income shares by roughly 5% for the post-1951 period for which there are detailed age data.

[16] Using data on income distributions on both household (from public tax investigations) and individual (from censuses) for the years 1920, 1930, 1935, 1945, and 1950, we can get a rough idea of how the change in tax units affects our estimated top income shares. The individual income distribution seems to generate about 10% higher top income shares in 1920 and 1930 but the difference is almost insignificant (and even reversed) in the latter years. Overall, the two distributions are equal around the time of the actual shift (1951), but if one would account for the earlier effects the long-run decline in top income shares would be somewhat more pronounced.

[17] The period between 1951 and 1971 is potentially problematic because of the change in the definition of tax units from households to individuals. We have tried a number of different specifications for dealing with this gradual change, and while the levels may change over this period by as much as 10%, the trend and our qualitative results are not altered; see Appendix 7C.

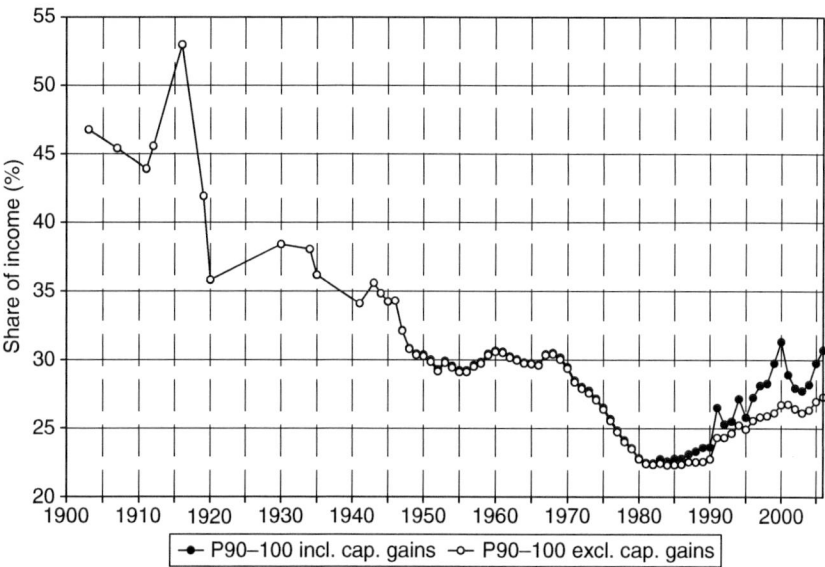

Figure 7.1 The top 10% income share in Sweden (with and without capital gains), 1903–2006

Source: Column 1 in Appendix Tables 7A.2 and 7A.3, respectively.

1980s the trend depends crucially on the treatment of capital gains incomes. When these are included, the income share for the top 10 per cent increases substantially, but when capital gains are excluded the top share remains quite stable, though it does increase slightly (we will analyse this in more detail below). The peaks in 1991 and 1994 in the series including capital gains are well-known effects of tax reforms which made it profitable to sell assets in these years.

Even though this development in itself reveals a number of interesting facts, it turns out that decomposing the top decile is crucial for understanding the development. Figure 7.2 shows the evolution of the income shares for P90–5, P95–9, and P99–100 respectively. Looking first at the decline over the first eighty years of the century, we see that virtually all of the fall in the top decile income share is due to a decrease in the very top of the distribution. The income share for the lower half of the top decile (P90–5) has been remarkably stable, hovering around 10 per cent over the entire period, while the P95–9 share declines gradually from about 15 per cent of total income in the beginning of the twentieth century to around 10 per cent in the early 1980s, with the sharpest drop over the 1970s. In contrast, the top percentile income share is divided by at least a factor of four, dropping from above 20 per cent in the early 1900s, to around 7 per cent in early 1950s, to a low of 4.7 per cent in the beginning of the 1980s. Over the past decades the pattern is similar; P90–5 is stable (whether including capital gains or not), P95–9 increases slightly as does P99–100 when

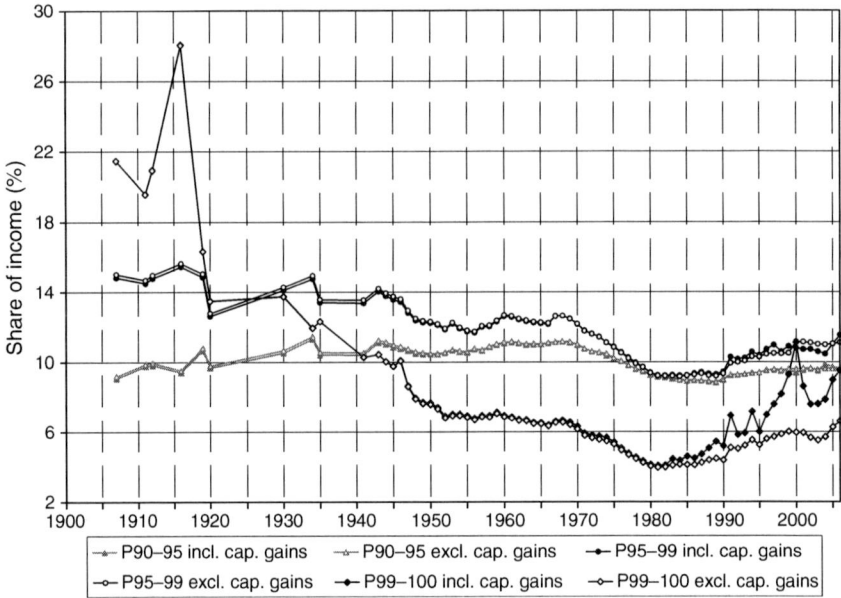

Figure 7.2 The P90–95, P95–99, and P99–100 (top 1%) income shares in Sweden (with and without capital gains), 1903–2006

Source: Columns 3, 8, and 9 in Appendix Tables 7A.2 and 7A.3, respectively.

excluding capital gains, but the major difference appears only when including capital gains for the top percentile. Over several years in the late 1990s the income share of the top percentile is about twice as large when including capital gains compared to excluding them.

The above patterns get even starker when considering higher fractiles within the top per cent. Figure 7.3 shows the income share of the top 0.01 per cent of the income distribution. This share was divided by a factor of about eight over the first half of the century, from above 3 per cent of income to around 0.4 per cent in the early 1950s. Given that most of the income in the very top consists of capital income it is interesting to note that the major falls take place during the financial crises after the First World War, in the early 1930s, and after the Second World War, but notably, not during the Second World War. This period (1939–45), which in many other countries was one of major cuts in top income shares, seems to have been a period of relative stability for the very top groups in Sweden. From the 1950s the P99.99–100 income share continues to decline steadily to their lowest points in the late 1970s after which it recovers, reaching new peaks at the time of the stock market boom around 2000 given that we include capital gains.

If we compare the incomes share for this top group when including and excluding capital gains respectively, the difference is a factor ten in order of

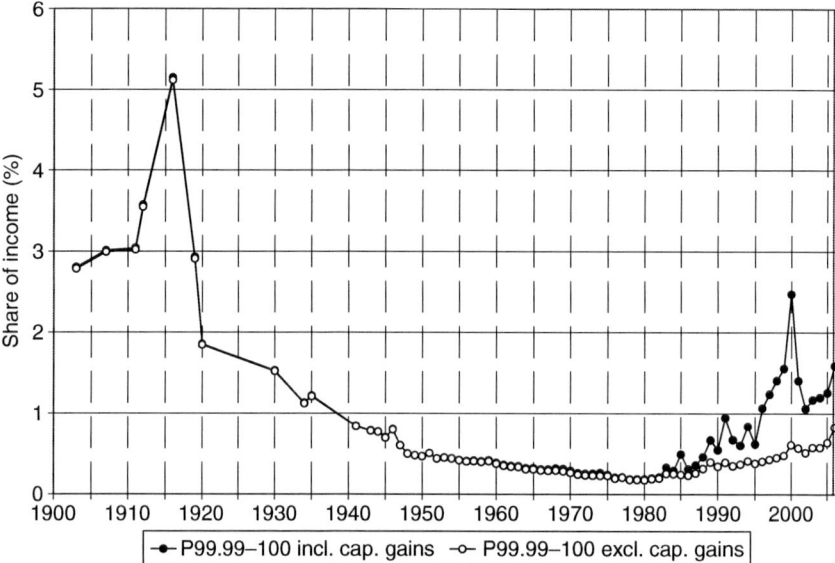

Figure 7.3 The top 0.01% income share in Sweden (with and without capital gains), 1903–2006

Source: Column 7 in Appendix Tables 7A.2 and 7A.3, respectively.

magnitude, which again highlights the impact of capital gains in Swedish top incomes. Expressing the incomes of the top 0.01 per cent group in multiples of average income, our data suggest that over the twentieth century their income has gone from being around 300 times the average income in the early 1900s, falling down to around 25 times average income in the 70s, and then rising to more than 100 times average income in the late 1990s (again when including capital gains).[18]

Composition of Top Incomes

Examining the composition of top incomes offers important hints to the understanding of the development of top income shares. For example, shocks to capital income during the First and Second World Wars explain much of the decline in French top incomes (Piketty 2003) while large increases in wage and salaries at the top has been the primary factor behind the increased income inequality in the USA during the 1980s and 1990s (Piketty and Saez 2003). The composition of

[18] It is worth pointing out that some internationally very visible super-rich Swedes are not driving these results. Incomes of individuals such as IKEA's owner Ingvar Kamprad, and the Rausing family, founders of Tetra Pak, all high up on the *Forbes* list of the world's wealthiest individuals, are not in our data as they do not reside in Sweden.

Table 7.3 Decomposition of changes in top income shares in Sweden into wage-, capital-, and other incomes over three sub-periods between 1912 and 1980

			Percentage change in		
				With contribution by	
		Total income shares	Wages	Capital income	Business income
1912–1935	P90–95	6.1	8.8	−1.2	−1.4
	P95–99	−9.4	−1.8	−6.3	−1.4
	P99–100	−41.1	−9.1	−23.8	−8.2
	P99.9–100	−53.0	−7.2	−35.2	−10.6
1935–1951	P90–95	0.3	−2.6	−4.6	7.5
	P95–99	−10.0	−9.9	−7.6	7.4
	P99–100	−38.6	−16.7	−19.4	−2.5
	P99.9–100	−56.2	−21.8	−27.0	−7.3
1951–1980	P90–95	−2.5	11.9	0.7	−15.1
	P95–99	−11.7	11.6	−1.5	−21.8
	P99–100	−36.1	−6.6	−4.9	−24.6
	P99.9–100	−49.5	−19.8	−5.0	−24.7

Notes: Calculations are based on tax returns data from 1945 onwards and Census data from 1920, 1930, 1935, and 1945, including estimates of returns to wealth. Business income is calculated as a residual prior to 1951.

Swedish top incomes also changes significantly during the twentieth century, and these changes hold important clues for explaining the general patterns.

Swedish tax laws distinguish four sources of income: labour (wages and salaries), capital (mainly interest earnings and dividends), business, and realized capital gains.[19] In Table 7.3, we decompose the decline in total top income shares (excluding capital gains) for various fractiles during three periods between 1912 and 1980.[20] In the period 1912–35, almost the entire decrease in total income shares is due to falls in capital income which explain about two-thirds of the drop of the top percentile. An interesting exception is the drop in 1916–20, which is mainly due to large earnings increases of the rest of the population (P0–90).[21]

[19] As described in Appendix 7A–C Swedish income statistics reported six different sources of incomes until 1990 and only three thereafter. Using available data we are however able to construct consistent and continuous series of the four above-mentioned sources for the entire post-war period. For the earlier periods we rely on data from the censuses (1920, 1930, 1935, and 1945) and estimates of returns to wealth to calculate approximate shares.

[20] These periods were chosen based on availability of data and to get one period pre-Second World War (1912–35), one period focusing on changes around the Second World War (1935–51), and one period stretching from the start of the expansion of the welfare state to the year when Swedish income equality peaked (1951–80). One could be concerned that increases in the capital income shares would mainly reflect compensation for high inflation. However, the level of inflation has been sufficiently constant over the century to rule out that adjustments for differences in inflation would significantly change our results.

[21] It is generally interesting to examine to what extent changes in top shares are driven mainly by relatively larger increases (or decreases) in the top fraction or in the denominator. It turns out that the 1910s is the only period where it is clearly one or the other that drives the change in the resulting top share, with the peak in 1916 being a consequence of much larger increases for the top fractiles, while the massive decline thereafter is due to an equally disproportionate increase for the P0–90 group.

During the period 1935–51, total income shares fall roughly as much as in 1912–35 (−9.4% compared to −12.9% for P95–9, −39.3% compared to −41.1% for P99–100), but this time about half of the decrease is attributed to a decreased wage share for top income earners. During 1950–80, total income shares continue to fall, but not because of falling capital or wage shares but falling top business income shares. Over this period business income goes from constituting approximately 20 per cent of total incomes in the top decile to being only a couple of per cent in 1980.[22]

To further illustrate the large differences both within the top decile as well as over time Figure 7.4 shows the income composition for different fractiles in the years 1945, 1978, and 2004 (where CG denotes a series including capital gains). The general pattern that capital income is more important higher up in the distribution is true for all of these years. However, between 1945 and 1978 the wage share at all levels of top incomes became more important, while the share of business income decreased at all levels. But in 2004 the pattern is back to that of 1945 in terms of the importance of capital, in particular when we include realized capital gains. In fact, at the very top of the income distribution, the share of capital income when including capital gains is larger today than it was in 1945.

The distribution of capital incomes and its development over the period 1912–2004 is illustrated in Figure 7.5. The upper panel shows the capital share of total income for fractiles in the top decile when excluding capital gains, while the lower panel includes realized capital gains.[23] Both figures show a similar pattern. Capital incomes become less important for all top groups over the first half of the century. Starting in the 1970s, however, the role of capital income for the top percentile becomes more important again and for the very top group the shares are even higher today than they were in the beginning of the period. When including realized capital income the recent increase is even more marked.[24]

The particular role of capital gains in the Swedish top income context, especially after 1980, is interesting. Capital gains are often excluded from studies of income inequality due to lack of data or due to their potentially problematic character (even though they constitute an indisputable part of income according to the classical Haig–Simons definition).[25] Ideally we would, of course, like to include *all* capital gains, but according to Swedish tax law only *realized* gains

---

[22] The drop in self-employment income should not be taken as evidence of decreased small-business activity, for per se, as self-employed individuals may choose to start a firm from which they pay themselves regular wages, etc.

[23] Observations for pre-Second World War shares are based on an assumed 4% rate of return of the net wealth of each top income fractile (which is available in the tax statistics) while the post-Second World War shares are directly observed in the income statistics.

[24] One should note, however, that it is likely that our estimates of realized capital gains in the first half of the century are underestimated, and consequently the shares including realized capital gains are likely to be higher before the Second World War.

[25] For example, the influential Luxemburg Income Study (LIS) does not contain capital gains at all. According to the Haig–Simons definition income should ideally be measured as the value of consumption plus any increase in real net wealth, that is, it should include all capital gains.

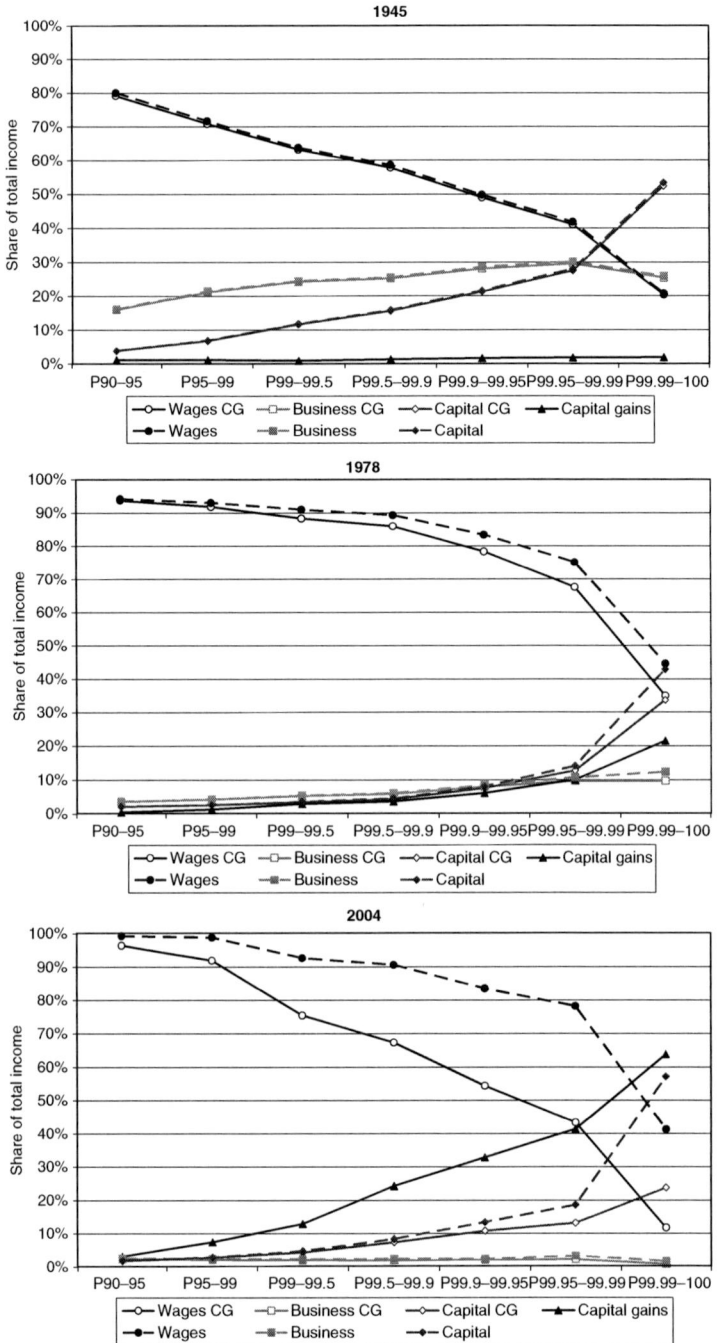

Figure 7.4 Income composition within the top decile in Sweden 1945, 1978, and 2004

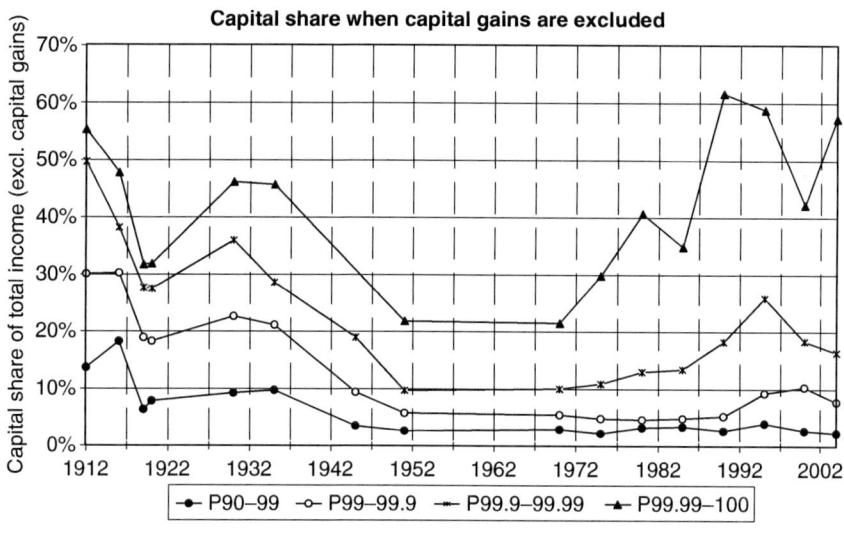

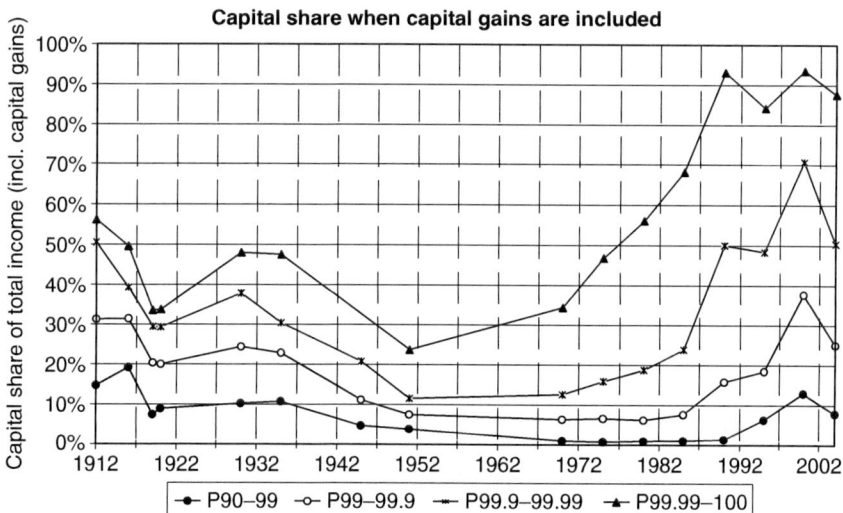

Figure 7.5 The evolution of capital income shares in Sweden (excluding and including capital gains) within the top decile, 1912–2004

constitute a taxable income and consequently this is what we can get information on. The main concern when realized capital gains are used in place of actual capital gains is the possibility that the realized gains actually represent increases over a longer period of time. This is problematic both in that such capital gains should be smoothed out over the years when they were made (but not realized) as well as in that it potentially introduces individuals in the top who are only there at the time of the sale of their asset. Furthermore it is, of course, somewhat arbitrary whether a real capital gain is realized at all. With respect to the first problem there is no doubt that we observe instances where, for example, changes in legislation made it more attractive to realize accumulated capital gains leading to likely overestimations of the top income shares for these years (the spikes in the series in 1991 and 1994 are traceable to sales being relatively attractive due to tax reasons). It is not likely, however, that the series including capital gains introduce 'new' individuals each year. Instead, it seems to be the case that the majority of capital gains are made by those with the highest earnings who year after year get additional income from capital gains (we come back to this in section 7.4 below).

Whether real capital gains that have not been realized would affect our shares depends on the distribution of such real gains. One may speculate that some assets are likely to be traded more frequently (such as financial assets) and therefore less likely to constitute large gains which have never appeared in tax records (not even in the form of realized gains possibly accumulated over several years) while others (such as housing) are more likely to fall into this category. If we think that real capital gains made by the top income groups are more likely to appear in the tax records (which could well be the case) we would risk overestimating their income share including capital gains when using realized capital gains. However, as Figure 7.5 above indicates, assets yielding interest and dividend are important in the top income groups (and have become increasingly so over the past decades) and given the very large increases in Swedish stock values (compared to housing, for example) we think that we would be making a more serious underestimation of the top income shares if we were to exclude capital gains altogether.

Tax Avoidance and Evasion

Problems with tax avoidance and evasion are present in all studies of income inequality based on data from personal tax returns.[26] In particular, if such activities change in systematic ways over time without being accounted for, changes in top income shares may just as well reflect changes in reported income as changes in actual income. Unfortunately there is only scattered evidence on the importance of tax avoidance and evasion in Sweden (see Appendix 7A–C for more details). The earliest official comment on the problem of tax evasion refers to 1919 when a special inquiry into the extent of evasion in the past five years was carried out (Statistics Sweden 1923: 13*). Information about how this special inquiry was conducted is sketchy and it is therefore difficult to say what conclusions can be drawn about evasion activities. According to the available information

---

[26] We will not emphasize the distinction between legal tax avoidance and illegal tax evasion as we are interested in all missing income. Based on the saying that the main difference between the two is a good tax lawyer we will call the activities in the top of the distribution tax avoidance without necessarily implying that all activities we discuss would be judged as being in accordance with the law.

it seems that evasion was concentrated in the top of the distribution but relatively small in relation to total income, but we do not know to what extent the top was targeted, nor the extent of the efforts to find evasion activities. Bentzel (1953) makes a more thorough calculation for the period 1930–48 suggesting that between 2 and 7 per cent of personal income may be missing due to under-reporting. Later studies such as Apel (1994), Löfqvist (2001), and Malmer and Persson (1994), variously using consumption equivalence scales and discrepancies in National Accounts arrive at similar estimates—between 4 and 6 per cent of all incomes—for years in the 1980s and 1990s.[27] Overall, these estimates suggest that there is no reason to believe that under-reporting has changed dramatically over time. A speculative reason for this may be that while the incentives to under-report have increased as tax rates have gone up over time the administrative control over tax compliance has also been improved. However, none of these studies focus on avoidance in the top of the distribution. As it is well known that the possibilities for high-income earners to avoid taxation on any wage income are small, the best source for attempting to study this is arguably the estimates of 'capital flight' since the early 1980s using unexplained residual capital flows ('net errors and omissions') published in official balance of payments statistics. In a recent survey of the Swedish household wealth concentration, Roine and Waldenström (2009) show that significant shares of wealth owned by the richest Swedes may be placed in offshore locations. They estimate that somewhere between 250 and 500 billion SEK has left the country without being accounted for.

To get a sense of the order of magnitude by which this 'missing wealth' would change our top income shares, we add all of the returns from this capital (the lower and upper bound estimates, respectively) first to the incomes of the top decile and then to the top percentile. The main results of this exercise are the following.[28] For the years before 1990, there is no effect on top income shares by adding income from offshore capital holdings since they are simply too small. However, after 1990, and especially after 1995, these incomes become sizeable. When adding all of them to the top decile, its income shares during 1995–2004 increase moderately (by approximately 3 per cent). When instead adding every-thing to the incomes of the top percentile, the income shares increase by about 25 per cent which is equivalent to an increased share from about 5.7 to 7.0 per cent. While this is a notable change, it does not raise Swedish top income shares over those in France (about 7.7 per cent in 1998), the UK (12.5 per cent in 1998), or the USA (15.3 per cent in 1998).

Overall, potential changes in under-reporting over the twentieth century probably play a marginal role in explaining the evolution of Swedish top income share series with the possible exception of the past decades. However, for the

---

[27] Apel (1994) mainly captures under-reporting among the self-employed, the study by Löfqvist (1991) estimates avoidance in the economy as a whole, while Malmer and Persson (1994) study the effects of the tax reform in 1991 on tax compliance.

[28] Details on the calculations are available from the authors upon request.

income shares to change much we must make the rather extreme assumption of attributing all of the missing capital income in recent years to the top percentile, and when doing so this only amplifies what we find without this adjustment.[29]

Total Income Shares vs. Market Income Shares—Excluding Taxable Transfers

In 1974 a number of work-related transfer programmes, such as unemployment insurance, sickness payments, and parental leave payments, became taxable. As such programmes have grown in importance over time it could be argued that our series of total gross (pre-tax) income shares have gone from being shares of market income (or even factor income) in the earlier parts of the century to being shares of a pre-tax income concept which includes substantial de facto transfers. To address the impact of these transfers on our income shares we have calculated series in which we exclude the most important transfer payments.[30] In our basic series above we added the total government outlays for the transfers that were made taxable in 1974 to the reference total for income for the period before 1974. Under the assumption that these transfers made up a negligible share of top incomes before 1974, this adjustment suffices to make the series conform to the current definition of gross pre-tax income. To exclude the transfers we basically do the opposite. Before 1974 we do not make any additions to the reference total for income, while we thereafter deduct total transfers from the reference total. However, we must now also take care of the fact that transfer incomes, while being small shares of top incomes, are not zero for everyone in the top decile. To correct our shares we rely on exact data on the size of these transfers by income class for the years 1974–7 and from 1991 and onwards, and estimations for the period in between.

Figure 7.6 displays the changes in the series for the top percentile when including these transfers in the income concept (*total income*, which is the same as our main series) and when excluding them (*market income*). The basic trend is that market income shares go from being relatively equal to total income shares in the 1950s, start to grow in the 1970s, and are about 20 per cent higher in the beginning of the twenty-first century. The marked recent increase is likely to be an effect of large increases in sickness payments. Overall the difference between total income and market income shares is insignificant and has no effect on the trend.

---

[29] Roine and Waldenström (2009) contains calculations of how this possibly missing wealth would affect wealth concentration.

[30] The most important transfers are unemployment insurance, sickness payments, and parental leave payments. Transfers which are not taxed (such as child benefits, housing benefits, study grants, etc.) never enter our series. See Appendices 7A–C for details.

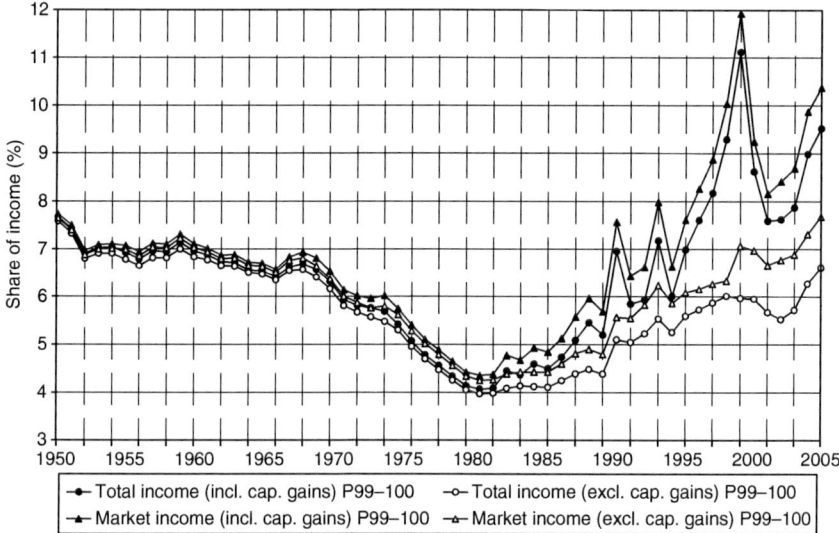

Figure 7.6 Total income shares vs. market income shares in Sweden of P99–100, 1950–2006

7.4 EXPLANATIONS OF THE EVOLUTION OF SWEDISH TOP INCOME SHARES

What accounts for the large declines of top income shares in the first half of the twentieth century, the steady decline during the expansion of the welfare state, the relatively sharp drops over the 1970s, and the increase in the recent decades (which is augmented when including capital gains)? This section discusses factors that can contribute to our understanding of the evolution of the top income shares presented above. First, we examine the roles of factor shares and wealth distribution, and their respective changes over time. In particular, the Swedish tax system before 1948 provides us with data on wealth by income class. Second, we study the evolution of the Swedish progressive income tax system and its effects on top income shares, and third, we account for the recent dramatic changes in asset prices, arguing that these are fundamental for understanding the particular Swedish experience with very large differences in top shares depending on whether capital gains are included or not.

The Roles of Factor Shares and the Wealth Distribution

According to David Ricardo, 'the principal problem of Political Economy... is to determine how...the produce of the earth...is divided between...the

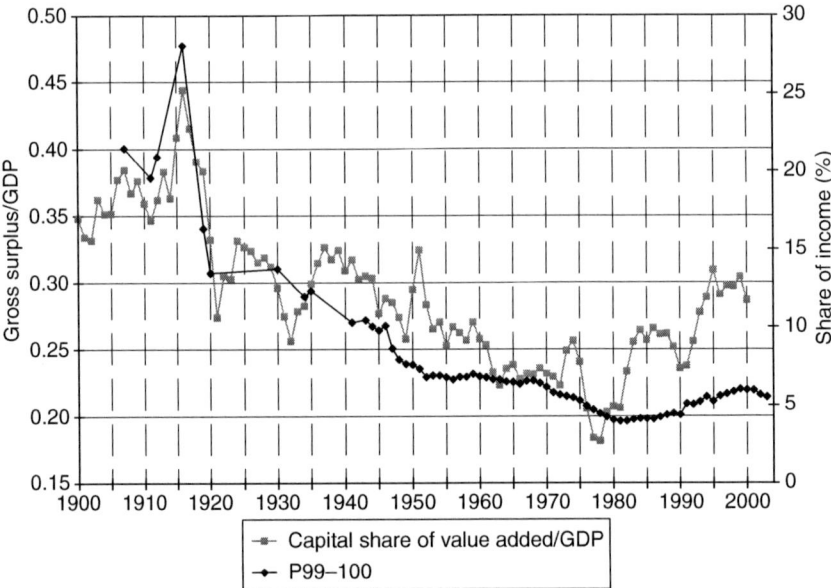

Figure 7.7 The capital share of value added as a share of GDP and the top 1% income share in Sweden, 1903–2003

Sources: Data on the capital share of value added and GDP by activity come from Edvinsson (2005). Top income percentile shares come from Appendix Table 7A.2, column 3.

proprietor of the land, the owner of the stock of capital needed for its cultivation, and the labourers by whose industry it is cultivated'.[31] If we were to assume that the very top of the income distribution consists mainly of wealth holders, while the rest of the population consists mainly of wage-earning workers, fluctuations in factor shares should also explain fluctuations in income shares. (We return to the question of how good an approximation this is below.) Figure 7.7 shows the changes in the capital share of value added (defined as GDP by activity, minus wages and salaries, minus imputed labour income of self-employed) as a share of GDP, and the evolution of the top 1 per cent income share.

The series are strongly correlated over the whole period (0.86) but with a clear difference between the first and second half of the century. Between 1907 and 1950 the correlation is 0.94, while it drops to 0.55 between 1951 and 2000. This indicates that, at least during the first fifty years, even short-term fluctuations of top incomes follow the fluctuations of the capital share of value added as a share of GDP. The figure also shows a downward trend in the capital share of value added over the first eighty years and a conservative reading would suggest a drop in this share from around 0.35 in the first decade, to approximately 0.25 in the

---

[31] Quoted in Atkinson (1975: 161).

1970s and 1980s.[32] If we take this share as a proxy for the share of GDP derived as a return to property it would translate directly to an equally large drop in the income share of property holders who, in turn, are found mainly among the top income earners. Of course, no income class consists of only wage earners or only property holders, and furthermore a number of institutions (such as firms and the government sector) stand between the productive sector and the personal sector whose income distribution we are concerned with. Nevertheless, such approximations give a sense of the magnitude by which the respective factors could have changed the income shares.[33]

To estimate the impact of returns to property on the top income shares we also need data on the property holdings of the top income groups. Typically such data are not available and as a substitute many studies have used wealth distribution estimates, assuming that the distributions of wealth and income overlap sufficiently. In the case of Sweden, however, there exist unusual data on individual wealth holdings by precisely those groups for which we also have income data. The reason is that between the years 1911 and 1948 Sweden had a peculiar form of joint income and wealth taxation in which taxes were levied on what was called the *taxable amount*, consisting of all income *plus* a share of net wealth holdings. For selected years, tabulations of incomes decomposed into actual income and wealth shares by income class are available.[34] Similar information is also available in the 1950 Census (for the year 1951) and for the years 1991–3. This allows us to calculate the *wealth shares held by top income groups*. Figure 7.8 shows changes in wealth shares by income class, together with our calculations of wealth shares (by wealth class) and income shares (by income class) for P99–100 and P90–9 of the respective distributions.[35] Not surprisingly, wealth shares by income class follow the fluctuations of income shares more closely than do wealth shares, but the

---

[32] The question of factor shares, to what extent they are relatively stable over time, and how 'relatively stable' should be interpreted, is of course a much debated question. See Atkinson (1975: chapter 9), for a good overview and a historical perspective, where it is also noted that the labour share seems to have been increasing at least since the 1930s up to the 1970s in a number of Western economies.

[33] Among the interesting details found by studying the development of the capital share of value added as share of GDP is that it is likely to explain the peak in the top income share in 1916. The first years of the First World War were a period during which industrial companies made huge profits while the majority of the population experienced substantial falls in real wages and trade restrictions that led to a food shortage (see Edvinsson 2005: 242, and references given there). The year 1916, which is the only year for which we have data during this period, was most probably the most extreme year. The average wage rate fell by 10% and the ratio between gross surplus and labour income jumped from about 50% in 1914–15, to around 70% in 1916–17 (after which it fell back down to 50% in 1918–19), indicating that 1916 was a year when the income share of capital owners was very high compared to the years immediately before and after.

[34] The taxable amount was equal to all income plus one-sixtieth of taxable wealth between 1910 and 1938 and thereafter all income plus one-hundredth of taxable wealth until 1948.

[35] Our series for wealth distribution are based on tax return data and are for the years 1920–75 similar to Spånt (1979) and for the years 1978–2002 to series calculated by Statistics Sweden (2002), rather than more recent estimates based on household panel data (such as Klevmarken 2004). In the present context these figures are most relevant as we are trying to estimate the impact of wealth concentration on income concentration rather than some measure of living standards.

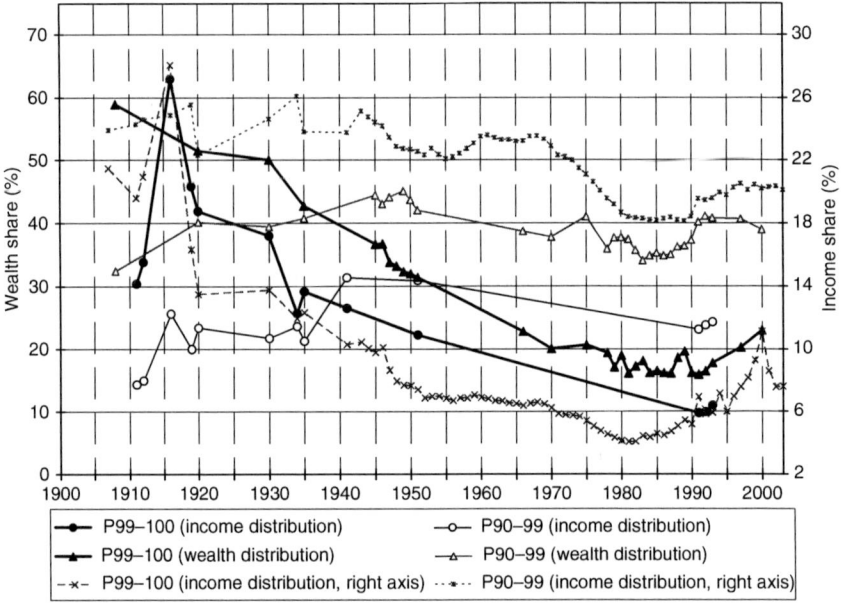

Figure 7.8 Wealth in top income and wealth fractiles in Sweden, 1908–2004

Source: Authors' own calculations.

Note: The circles relate to wealth shares (left-hand scale) of units ranked by income.

trends seem to be the same.[36] The wealth share of the top per cent among the income earners, as well as among wealth holders, decreases quite dramatically over the century with slight recoveries over the past decades.[37] The wealth shares for the P90–9 group, both in the income and in the wealth distribution, are instead increasing until around 1950. After that they fall slightly, to recover again after the mid 1980s. Once again this highlights the importance of distinguishing between different groups at the top to understand the trends.

What would be the joint impact of the changes in wealth concentration and the changes in factor shares on the income distribution? Following Meade (1964), we can make a simple approximation to get a sense of the magnitude of the effect. Let *a* and *b* be the share of all earnings and all returns to property, respectively, received by a certain income group. Then the total income share of this group is given by

[36] The exception is the first observations in the series. There could, however, be a problem in the data as the sources for 1911 and 1912 for wealth by income class are tax return data for the first two years when the wealth tax was implemented, which could underestimate the wealth in the top shares. The 1908 wealth data, on the other hand, are based on estates. By 1920 the system of joint income and wealth taxation was well established and wealth data were also collected for the Census, which leads us to think that these series are relatively reliable at least from that point on.

[37] The top per cent wealth share in the wealth distribution has increased over the past decades and assuming that the wealth of the top income earners has followed this is true for them as well. However, we only have data on the years between 1991 and 1993.

Table 7.4 Contribution of changes in the top income earners' wealth shares on their income shares in Sweden, 1911–1991

Period	Change in P99 income share[a] (percentage points)	Change resulting from changes in wealth (assuming factor share 0.3, percentage points)	Change resulting from changes in wealth (calculated factor shares, percentage points)
1911–12	1.36	0.52	0.92
1912–16	7.12	4.36	7.76
1916–19	−11.70	−2.57	−5.14
1919–20	−2.85	−0.59	−1.79
1920–30	0.26	−0.58	−1.29
1930–34	−1.80	−1.86	−2.01
1934–35	0.37	0.52	0.76
1935–41	−2.03	−0.39	−0.17
1941–51	−3.21	−0.64	−0.60
1951–91	−1.26	−1.87	−2.44

[a] Changes based on the series including capital gains. The calculated change in the P99–100 income share between 1951 and 1991 is based on an average of the share in 1990–2 as 1991 is an outlier in the series including capital gains (as discussed in section 7.3) due to the tax reform.

Sources: Own calculations based on income and wealth shares reported above.

$$a \cdot \text{(factor share of earnings)} + b \cdot \text{(factor share of property)}.$$

Setting the factor share of property to 0.3 or alternatively letting the factor share fluctuate and take on the yearly value displayed in Figure 7.7 above we can get a sense of the magnitude of the impact that changes in wealth concentration at the top of the income distribution has had between 1911 and 1991. Table 7.4 gives an example of such calculations for P99–100.

Table 7.4 suggests that the direction of change is correct for all intervals except for the period 1920–30 when the income share increases slightly for the top per cent of income earners but their wealth share drops. Between 1911 and 1920, however, the magnitudes are not right. The income share increases slightly more in 1911–16 and, in particular, drops much more in 1916–20 than can be explained by changes in wealth shares. However, this is exactly what we would expect given that most of the change in 1916–19/20 is due to increases in the incomes of the lower 90 per cent of the population.

Overall, the above suggests that an important reason for the substantial drop in the top 1 per cent income share—which is driving the decreased income share of the top 10 per cent—especially before 1950, is the decreased wealth share of the top income earners, which in turn decreased their share of returns to property. However, the question of why the top wealth share decreased so substantially has no obvious answer. Sweden did not take part in the world wars, and even though the country's economy was of course not unaffected by these wars, they did not cause the same direct destruction of capital in Sweden as they did in many other countries. If single events are to be pointed out, the effects of the Great Depression, which hit Sweden in 1931, and in particular the dramatic collapse of the industrial empire controlled by the Swedish industrialist Ivar Kreuger (the 'Kreuger-crash') in 1932, are probably most important.[38] Between 1930 and 1935 we observe a drop from 50 per cent to 43 per cent in the top per cent wealth share but an even larger drop in the wealth of the top 1 per cent of income earners, from 38 per cent in 1930 to 26 per cent in 1934 (see Figure 7.7 above). The Second World War, however, does not seem to have been a major shock to wealth holdings in Sweden. The top 1 per cent share does drop from 43 to 37 per cent between 1935 and 1945, but the drop just after the war is just as sharp continuing down to 32 per cent in 1950 (see section 7.5 for more on this point in international perspective).

By 1950 progressive taxation has started to play a major part and the most likely explanation for the continued decreasing top wealth share is that a larger share of new wealth was accumulated in the corporate and government sector and among the rest of the population, rather than in the wealthiest per cent. However, over the past decades wealth concentration has increased, and compared to many other countries Sweden today does have a surprisingly skewed wealth distribution.[39] A possible explanation for this is that the extensive welfare state takes away some of the typical reasons for, in particular, the middle class to accumulate capital (such as saving for (children's) higher education, healthcare, pension, etc.) since these things are provided by the state.[40] This in turn means that income from capital is likely to be skewed and, in particular at times when returns to capital increase, the gains will be concentrated at the top of the distribution (we will discuss this in more detail in section 4.3). As shown in Figure 7.5 above, the increasingly important role of capital for the very highest income earners seems consistent with such an explanation.

The Role of Taxation

Many previous studies have shown that top incomes are sensitive to changes in top marginal income tax rates, either through their direct effect on work incentives or through more subtle processes of tax arbitrage (see Saez 2004 for an overview of this literature). For example, Saez and Veall (2005) showed that Canadian top income shares were negatively correlated with Canadian marginal income tax rates, with elasticities of income with respect to the net-of-tax rates for the top percentile being about unity.

---

[38] In Sweden, the economic crisis in the early 1920s was in many ways more severe than the one ten years later which coincided with the 'Great Depression' in America.

[39] Much of the high wealth Gini figures in Sweden is due to a large part of the population having negative net wealth (rather than high concentration at the top) but also in terms of the wealth share held by the top per cent Sweden is second only to the USA in high wealth concentration according to the first comparable estimates in the LWS (Luxembourg Wealth Study) project (Sierminska, Brandolini, and Smeeding 2006).

[40] Domeij and Klein (2002) study to what extent the public pension system in Sweden can account for the high wealth inequality in data.

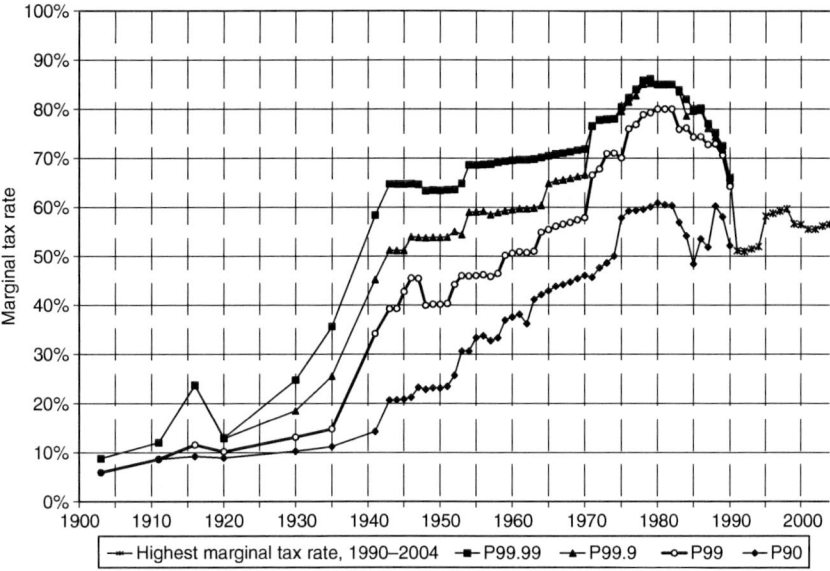

Figure 7.9 Top marginal tax rates in Sweden, 1903–2004

Source: Tax rates are computed for each top income level in Table 7A.4 using tax tables in Söderberg (1996) until 1990. After 1990, we show the 'highest marginal tax rate' (Swedish National Tax Board 2004), applying only to labour income (wages + business income).

In the case of Sweden, Figure 7.9 depicts the statutory marginal tax rates on incomes at the 90th, 99th, 99.9th, and 99.99th percentiles over the past century.[41] These rates more than doubled between the mid 1930s up to 1950, and then continued to rise until 1980 when they peaked. Thereafter the top marginal taxes were lowered, particularly in relation to the tax reform of 1990–1 which introduced separate taxation of capital incomes at a lower, flat rate.

To get a better picture of the role of taxation for Swedish top income shares, we estimate tax elasticities in several top income levels for the post-war period (1943–90).[42] In particular, we relate the incomes of the tax units exactly at the 90th, 99th, 99.9th, and 99.99th income percentiles to the marginal tax rates paid by precisely these tax units respectively. Although we employ a fairly standard approach towards estimating these tax responses (following Saez 2004), it should be noted that we only observe the product of the amount of hours worked and the per hour wage, at each income level, and any differential variation in these two as

[41] The presented marginal tax rates are the sum of the respective rates at the local (*kommunalskatt*) and state (*statlig skatt*) levels, calculated using tables in Söderberg (1996).

[42] Before 1943, there are no annual data and after the tax reform of 1990–1, wages and capital income are taxed at separate rates.

a response to changes in the marginal tax level is thereby missed.[43] However, since we confine the study to top and extreme top income earners, these variations may not be of first-order importance. Then log-linear regressions are estimated for each percentile separately:

$$\ln(S_P)_t = \beta_0 + \beta_1 \, (\ln(1-MTR_P)_t) + \beta_2 t + \beta_3 t^2 + u_t, \tag{1}$$

where S_P denotes income share for percentile P = P90, P99, P99.9, P99.99, $(1-MTR_P)$ the corresponding net-of-tax rate (one minus the marginal tax rate), t a linear time trend, and u_t a random error.[44] Since inflation may push incomes up in higher tax brackets ('bracket creep'), we may have a downward bias in the estimated tax elasticity $(\hat{\beta}_1)$. To control for this eventuality, we fit both OLS and two-stage least squares (2SLS) regressions using the log of one minus the highest statutory marginal tax rate as instrument. The results in Table 7.5 show that tax elasticities range from about 0.3 in the 90th (in the 2SLS case) and 99th percentiles, to 0.5–0.6 in the 99.9th percentile and 0.8–0.9 in the 99.99th percentile. The influence of bracket creep seems to be of minor importance as hinted by the similarity of the OLS and 2SLS results. Altogether, these results are well in line with previous findings from the estimated tax responses of US top income earners (Saez 2004). Progressive taxation hence seems to have been a major contributing factor in explaining the evolution of Swedish top incomes in the post-war period. However, given that much of the fall in top incomes happens before taxes reach extreme levels and largely as a result of decreasing income from wealth, an important effect of taxation in terms of top income shares has been to prevent the accumulation of new fortunes. To the extent that new fortunes were created they most probably remained outside the personal sector.[45]

The Role of Asset Prices

One aspect which stands out in our series over the past decades is the large difference in top income shares when realized capital gains are included or not. Whether capital gains should be included in the income concept is debatable and ultimately depends on the questions at hand.[46] When it comes to studying

[43] For example, if workers' bargaining strength *vis-à-vis* their employers increases with wages, a tax increase may imply that lower-wage workers have to accept constant pre-tax wages, and hence a real wage cut, whereas higher-wage workers may be able to threaten with reduced labour supply and thereby get a wage increase.

[44] Equation (1) uses Newey–West standard errors and is inspired by Saez (2004), but unlike him we use threshold incomes and corresponding marginal tax rates instead of average incomes in a group of income earners, say P99–100, and the corresponding weighted average marginal income tax for all the various income levels contained in the top percentile group.

[45] The particular structure of ownership via various tax exempt institutions for tax reasons is documented in Henrekson and Jakobsson (2005).

[46] In the case of Sweden the choice lies between excluding capital gains completely or using realized capital gains since data does not allow us to measure all capital gains. See for example Atkinson (1975: chapter 3), for a general discussion, and, in particular, Björklund, Palme, and Svensson (1995) for an estimation of real capital income using assumed real rates of return on net wealth.

Table 7.5 Marginal tax effects on top incomes in Sweden, 1943–1990

Fractile	Model	Constant ($\hat{\beta}_0$)	Elasticity ($\hat{\beta}_1$)	Trend ($\hat{\beta}_2$)	Trend² ($\hat{\beta}_3$)	R^2	Pr.>χ^2
				Coefficient estimates			
P90	OLS	3.51***	0.07	−0.01	−0.00	0.79	
		(0.06)	(0.13)	(0.01)	(0.00)		
	2SLS	3.53***	0.30***	−0.00	−0.00	0.77	0.00
		(0.04)	(0.11)	(0.00)	(0.00)		
P99	OLS	2.39***	0.27***	−0.02**	0.00**	0.88	
		(0.08)	(0.10)	(0.01)	(0.00)		
	2SLS	2.41***	0.32***	−0.02***	0.00***	0.88	0.98
		(0.05)	(0.06)	(0.00)	(0.00)		
P99.9	OLS	1.43***	0.53***	−0.04***	0.00***	0.92	
		(0.09)	(0.08)	(0.01)	(0.00)		
	2SLS	1.45***	0.58***	−0.04***	0.00***	0.92	0.87
		(0.07)	(0.07)	(0.00)	(0.00)		
P99.99	OLS	0.64***	0.81***	−0.07***	0.00***	0.91	
		(0.10)	(0.09)	(0.00)	(0.00)		
	2SLS	0.71***	0.89***	−0.06***	0.00***	0.91	0.19
		(0.13)	(0.13)	(0.00)	(0.00)		

Notes: OLS regressions use Newey–West standard errors (with 6 lags). The 2SLS instrument the net-of-tax rate with the ln(1 − Statutory top marginal tax rate). Tax rates are calculated using laws listed in Söderberg (1996). Pr.>χ^2 shows p-values from Hausman tests of a difference between OLS and 2SLS. All regressions have 48 observations. *, **, *** denote significance at the 10%, 5%, and 1% levels, respectively.

Swedish income inequality, and in particular the absolute top over recent decades, we argue that capital gains incomes are too important to be ignored. The main reason for this is the development of Swedish stock prices, which in comparison with many other Western countries is remarkable.[47] Figure 7.10 shows the evolution of the composite stock price index, in real terms, at the Stockholm Stock Exchange and the amount of capital gains earned by three top income fractiles since 1967 (which is the first year with separate capital gains figures for different total income classes). The realized capital gains and stock prices are significantly correlated over time (>0.9 in all cases), which suggests that the capital gains appearing in top incomes to a large extent stem from increased values of financial portfolios.[48]

One of the major concerns with including capital gains in the analysed total income concept is the possibility that some taxpayers in the top income fractiles

[47] Over the period 1980–2000, the real stock price index at the Stockholm Stock Exchange increased twenty times compared to four to six times in New York, London, and Paris.

[48] Compared to real estate prices, which have also increased substantially over the past decades (starting at 100 in 1981, the housing price index was 360 while the consumer price index was 250, in 2003) the gains from equities are much larger and also much more concentrated. However, it is likely that the increase in wealth holdings for the top 10% (even when excluding the top per cent) is largely due to the increases in owner-occupied housing prices.

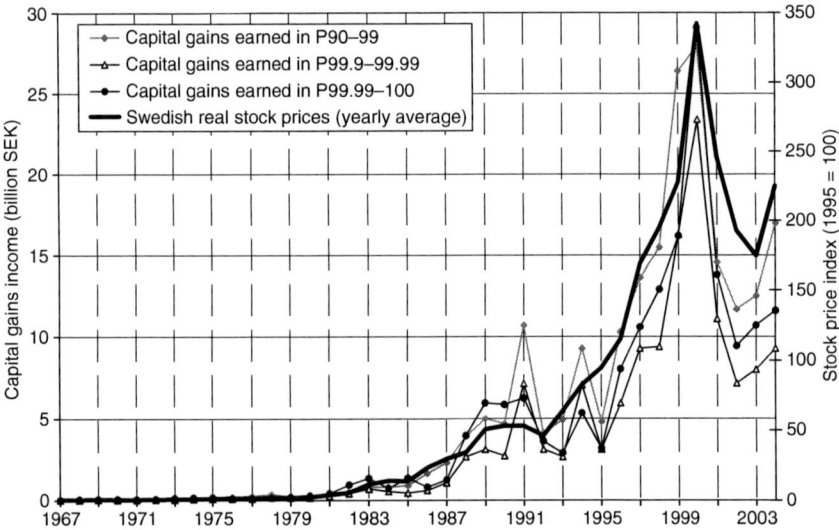

Figure 7.10 Capital gains in some top income fractiles and real stock prices in Sweden, 1967–2004

Note: Stock prices are yearly averages of end-of-month prices up to 1979 and daily closing prices thereafter of *Affärsvärldens Generalindex* (http://www.affarsvarlden.se), deflated with monthly CPI (monthly averages).

are there only because of recent realizations of gains that have been accumulated over a longer period of time. However, using tabulated income data listing capital gains in classes of labour income (which excludes capital gains), we can after 1990 confirm that this is not the case for the most part of our analysed capital gains incomes.[49] Furthermore, Magnusson (2004) uses panel data for the period 1991–2002 and shows that the top of the income distribution is not primarily represented by low-income earners with large one-time capital gains.[50] Altogether, our data suggest that the substantial increases in capital gains that drive much of the observed rise in top income shares in Sweden over the past decades are largely due to increased Swedish stock prices.

[49] Looking at the average realized capital gains over labour income classes, the overwhelmingly largest average capital gains in the entire period 1991–2004 accrue to those who already are positioned in the top of the income distribution.

[50] She studies two sub-periods, 1991–7 and 1996–2002, and shows that about one-fifth (19.1 and 19.2%, respectively) of those in the top 0.1 percentile in 1997 and 2002 when including capital gains belonged to the P0–90 group six years earlier. The same shares when excluding capital gains were about one-tenth (8.4 and 12.8%), which suggests that about one-tenth of top income earners were a relatively mobile group, and possibly low-wage earners with high one-time capital gains.

7.5 INTERNATIONAL COMPARISONS

In Figure 7.11 the long-run development of top percentile income shares in a number of Western countries is shown alongside that of Sweden.[51] Looking at the figure, three broad facts stand out. First, all countries experience a similar development with large decreases in top income shares between the beginning of the 1900s and the mid 1970s. The drop in Swedish top incomes over this period is the largest among all these countries, both in absolute and relative terms, but interestingly, much of the difference between Sweden and the other countries is established already by 1950. Second, the effect of the Second World War, which for all countries directly engaged in warfare turned out to be devastating for top incomes (see, e.g., Atkinson and Leigh 2005; Piketty and Saez 2006), is practically non-existent in Sweden. Table 7.6 shows this fact in more detail. During the war, the top income share for P99–100 decreased by between 13

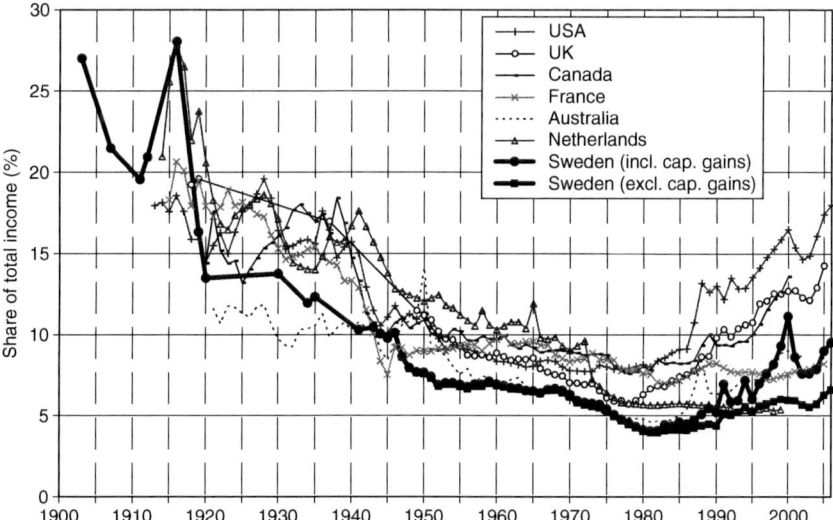

Figure 7.11 Income shares of the top percentile in Western countries, 1903–2006

Source: Atkinson and Piketty (2007) and this volume.

---

[51] The country-specific developments would be very similar for P90–100 and for P99.9–100. As always, the developments should be compared with some caution. Even if the series have been constructed using basically the same methodology there are still some differences such as the difference in the construction of reference totals which may understate the figures for the UK and the Netherlands compared to those for the USA and France. See Atkinson (2005b) for details.

Table 7.6 Percentage change in top percentile income shares in Sweden during the Second World War

Period:	Sweden	Australia	Canada	France	The Netherlands	UK	USA
			Percentage change in the top percentile income share in				
1939–1945	−4.6	−24.0	−40.1	−43.3	−12.7	−22.7	−25.5
1946–1951	−27.2	11.4	−0.9	19.4	−11.2	−15.2	−5.3

Note: For Sweden, we use 1941–5 since no data exist for 1939.

and 40 per cent in countries directly involved in warfare, but by less than 5 per cent in Sweden. By contrast, right after, the Swedish top shares dropped by one-quarter but elsewhere they decreased by much less or even increased.

The third fact that stands out in Figure 7.11 is the divergence after 1980 between one group of countries with significantly increasing top shares; Australia, Canada, UK, and the USA, and another group; France, the Netherlands, and Spain, where the top shares remain virtually constant.[52] This division between the 'Anglo-Saxon' and 'continental European' experience has received a lot of attention in the recent literature.[53] As can be seen in the figure, Sweden does not belong entirely to either one of these groups. More precisely, if capital gains are included Swedish top incomes shares have increased so much that the Swedish development resembles that of the Anglo-Saxon group. However, when capital gains are excluded, Sweden looks more like belonging to the continental European group. This difference in the series is unique to Sweden among the countries for which it has been possible to make this distinction.[54] Whether capital gains are included or not makes very little difference to the pattern of development in the USA, Canada, as well as Spain.[55]

The distinction between series including and excluding capital gains holds an important key to understanding the Swedish development in international comparison. Previous work on top incomes has pointed out that the main change over the twentieth century in Anglo-Saxon countries, and in particular in the USA, has been the replacement of the rentiers by the working rich in the top of the income distribution (see, e.g., Piketty and Saez 2006). To what extent this in turn depends on increased returns to education and skill-biased technological change is a much debated issue; however, the fact that so much of the increase in the top happens in the very top (top 1 per cent) has made many sceptical of a

---

[52] This division has previously been discussed in Saez (2004) and Atkinson and Leigh (2005), who also show that this division remains true when including New Zealand in the 'Anglo-Saxon' group.

[53] See, e.g., Piketty and Saez (2006).

[54] Besides Sweden, the construction of separate series including and excluding capital gains has been possible for the USA, Canada (after 1971), and Spain (Chapter 10).

[55] In the case of France this distinction is not very important, according to Piketty (2001b: 20 n.), as the capital gains share is very small even for the top income earners. The same relationship seems true for Germany (Dell 2005: 414 n. 2).

return-to-education story.[56] Our data for Sweden also seems to indicate that a skill-biased technological change story is not the most likely explanation for the observed changes. First, as was discussed above the movements for the lower part of the top decile P90–5 account for very little of the top decile income share. This is true both when including and excluding capital gains and, hence, suggests that to the extent that we think that high-skilled workers make up most of this group, their income share has not increased substantially over the past decades. Second, and more important, is the large difference in the development in the top depending on how capital gains are treated. The economic interpretation of this development rests on a distinction which we cannot entirely make based on our data. If we believe that much of the observed capital gains, in fact, stem from compensation for work made by, e.g., chief executives and other high-income individuals, then the Swedish development should be seen as resembling the Anglo-Saxon one, with working rich receiving an increasing share of all incomes over the past decades. What makes this interpretation plausible is the observed correlation between capital gains and wage incomes discussed in section 7.4, as well as the fact that Sweden has a dual tax system where capital incomes are taxed at lower rates than wage incomes. If, however, these capital gains do not stem directly from work but just from making investments with unusually large pay-offs over the past decades, then our data suggest that the key to becoming rich in Sweden over the past decades has been to invest wisely rather than to work hard.

7.5 SUMMARY AND CONCLUSIONS

In this chapter, we have studied the evolution of income concentration in Sweden over the twentieth century. We have presented new series on top income shares, their composition, as well as new data relevant for understanding their development. We have also tried to put our results into international perspective. Our findings suggest that top income shares in Sweden, as in many other Western countries, decreased significantly over the first eighty years of the century. They did so from levels indicating that Sweden was not more equal than other Western countries at the beginning of the twentieth century. Most of this decrease happened before 1950, that is, before the expansion of the Swedish welfare state. As in many other countries, most of the fall was due to decreasing shares in the very top of the distribution (the top 1 percent), while the income share of the lower half of the top decile (P90–P95) has been extraordinarily stable. Most of the fall is explained by decreased income from capital; however, it does not seem likely that this development in the case of Sweden is due only to shocks to capital holdings (which have been the suggested explanation in some other countries).

---

[56] Piketty and Saez (2003) are, for example, sceptical of the skill-biased technological change explanation for the USA. See also Dew-Becker and Gordon (2005).

Even though especially the financial crises in the early 1930s caused drops in both the wealth holdings and the income shares at the top of the income distribution, such shocks do not fully explain the decrease. In particular, we note that the major drop just after the First World War was mainly due to increased wages below the top decile. We also note that the Second World War had no obvious impact on Swedish top income shares. Instead a very significant drop takes place just after the war, at a time when marginal taxes for the top groups had just risen sharply. A closer look at the composition of the decrease in top income shares also suggests that wage compression was as important as decreased capital incomes between 1935 and 1951.

Even if the evolution of top income shares in Sweden in many ways resembles that in other Western countries over the first eighty years, there are some important differences. By 1950 top income shares had already dropped more in Sweden than in any other country (for which comparable data exist), and the further increases in marginal taxes as well as 'solidarity wage policies' caused them to drop even further in the 1970s. However, the most remarkably different aspect in the Swedish data appears over the past decades. During this period, when top income shares increased significantly in Anglo-Saxon countries, mainly due to wage increases, but remained virtually unchanged in continental Europe, the Swedish development depends largely on how realized capital gains are treated. If we include realized capital gains, Swedish top income shares look like the Anglo-Saxon ones; if we do not include them top shares have increased slightly but still resemble the continental European experience. Despite the potential problems with including realized capital gains in a study such as this, we believe there are good reasons to think that our data do capture a real development in terms of top incomes.

The picture of the Swedish income distribution that emerges from this study is in some ways quite different from that which is typically found in the literature. In some respects this is due to a different focus. Most previous studies have examined how the tax and transfer systems have achieved equalization of disposable income in relatively recent times, often focusing on the lower end of the distribution. We have instead been concerned mainly with gross income and its long-run concentration in the top of the distribution. This means that many of our findings, such as the large drop in income inequality before 1950, and the extent to which this is driven by the top percentile, are new findings complementing—rather than conflicting with—the previously emphasized achievements of the welfare state during the 1960s and 1970s. But when it comes to the development since 1980 our series do indicate that a revision of the standard view may be needed. Even though previous studies have pointed out that inequality has increased over the past decades, the important role that capital incomes have played for the top of the distribution has not been fully appreciated and, in particular, most studies have not included the further increase in inequality from including capital gains. Furthermore, as the focus has previously been on broader inequality measures it has not been noted how many of the recent developments are driven by the very top of the distribution. As such points may change not only our factual understanding about what has happened, but also our theories about the causes, further research is necessary to get a more complete view of income inequality in Sweden.

APPENDIX 7A: TABLES OF SOURCES
AND KEY RESULTS

The sources for total incomes and income composition, 1903–2003, are listed in Table 7A.1.

The key results on income shares are shown in Tables A7.2 (excluding capital gains) and A7.3 (including capital gains).

Table 7A.1 List of sources for total incomes and income composition in Sweden, 1903–2006

Year	Main source[a,b]	Tables	Pages	Series[c]
1903	Flodström (1906)		1, 3	FU
1907	Flodström (1909)		XI–XII	FU
1911	Flodström (1914)		11	FU
1912	Flodström (1915)		13*	FU
1916	Statistics Sweden (1921)	C, E	21*–27*	SOS
1919	Statistics Sweden (1923)	C	21*	SOS
1920	Statistics Sweden (1927)	21	558–9	SOS
1930	Statistics Sweden (1937)	11	268–9	SOS
1934	SOU 1936:18	10	47	SOS
1935	Statistics Sweden (1940)	21	88–9	SOS
1941	Quensel (1944)	VIII, IX	22–3, 28	SOS
1943	Skattetaxeringarna (1)…taxeringsåret 1944	L	31*	SOS
1944	Skattetaxeringarna (1)…taxeringsåret 1945	Q	43*	SOS
1945	Skattetaxeringarna (1)…taxeringsåret 1946	P	42*	SOS
	Statistics Sweden (1951), Census of 1945	4	2–3	SOS
1946	Skattetaxeringarna (1)…taxeringsåret 1947	R	47*	SOS
1947	Skattetaxeringarna (1)…taxeringsåret 1948	V	51*	SOS
1948	Skattetaxeringarna (1)…taxeringsåret 1949	Q	48*	SOS
1949	Skattetaxeringarna (2)…taxeringsåret 1950	R	48*	SOS
1950	Skattetaxeringarna (2)…taxeringsåret 1951	S	51*	SOS
1951	Skattetaxeringarna (2)…taxeringsåret 1952	Å, 8	63*, 26–7	SOS
	Statistics Sweden (1956), Census of 1950	7	20–1	SOS
1952	Skattetaxeringarna (2)…taxeringsåret 1953	Z, 8	53°, 26–7	SOS
1953	Skattetaxeringarna (2)…taxeringsåret 1954	Z, 8	49°, 26–7	SOS
1954	Skattetaxeringarna (2)…taxeringsåret 1955	Z, 8	47°, 26–7	SOS
1955	Skattetaxeringarna (2)…taxeringsåret 1956	Z, 8	46°, 28–9	SOS
1956	Skattetaxeringarna (2)…taxeringsåret 1957	Z, 8	47°, 28–9	SOS
1957	Skattetaxeringarna (2)…taxeringsåret 1958	Y, 8	47°, 28–9	SOS
1958	Skattetaxeringarna (2)…taxeringsåret 1959	Å, 8	50°, 34–5	SOS
1959	Skattetaxeringarna (2)…taxeringsåret 1960	J, 8	28°, 32–3	SOS
1960	Skattetaxeringarna (2)…taxeringsåret 1961	I, 10	28°, 32–3	SOS
1961	Skattetaxeringarna (3)…taxeringsåret 1962	I, 10	28°, 34–5	SOS
1962	Skattetaxeringarna (3)…taxeringsåret 1963	J, 10	29°, 34–5	SOS
1963	Skattetaxeringarna (3)…taxeringsåret 1964	J, 10	43°, 36–7	SOS

(continued)

Table 7A.1 Continued

Year	Main source[a, b]	Tables	Pages	Series[c]
1964	Skattetaxeringarna (3)...taxeringsåret 1965	K, 10	44°, 36–7	SOS
1965	Skattetaxeringarna (3)...taxeringsåret 1966	J, 10	43°, 116–17	SOS
1966	Skattetaxeringarna (3)...taxeringsåret 1967	L, 9	43°, 118–19	SOS
1967	Inkomst och förmögenhet 1967	2, 7	44–5, 58–61	SOS
1968	Inkomst och förmögenhet 1968	2, 7	50–1, 64–7	SOS
1969	Inkomst och förmögenhet 1969	2, 7	50–1, 64–7	SOS
1970	Inkomst och förmögenhet 1970	2, 7	48–9, 62–5	SOS
1971	Inkomst och förmögenhet 1971	3, 12	68–9, 90–3	SOS
1972	Inkomst och förmögenhet 1972	1, 3, 14	54–5, 70–1, 102–5	SOS
	Inkomst- och förmögenhetsfördelningen 1972	7	19	SM N 1973:94
1973	Inkomst och förmögenhet 1973	3, 14	68–9, 100–3	SOS
1974	Inkomst- och förmögenhetsfördelningen 1974	1, 7	11, 33	SM N 1976:4
1975	Inkomst- och förmögenhetsfördelningen 1975	1, 7	13, 35	SM N 1976:23
1976	Inkomst- och förmögenhetsfördelningen 1976	1, 7	18, 41, 43	SM N 1977:24
1977	Inkomst- och förmögenhetsfördelningen 1977	1, 7	22, 46–7	SM N 1978:22
1978	Inkomst- och förmögenhetsfördelningen 1978	1, 4.1, 4.2	29, 38, 41	SM N 1980:9
1979	Inkomst- och förmögenhetsfördelningen 1979	1, 4.1, 4.2	20, 27, 30	SM N 1981:9.1
1980	Inkomst- och förmögenhetsfördelningen 1980	1, 4.1, 4.2	7, 14, 17	SM N 1976:4
1981	Inkomst- och förmögenhetsfördelningen 1981	1, 4.1, 4.2	7, 14, 17	SM N 1976:4
1982	Inkomst- och förmögenhetsfördelningen 1982	1, 4.1, 4.2	14, 21, 24	SM Be 1984:6.1
1983	Inkomst- och förmögenhetsfördelningen 1983	1, 4.1, 4.2	14, 21, 24	Be 20 SM 8501
1984	Inkomst- och förmögenhetsfördelningen 1984	1, 3.1, 3.2	15, 19, 22	Be 20 SM 8601
1985	Inkomst- och förmögenhetsfördelningen 1985	1, 2.1, 2.2	15, 18, 21	Be 20 SM 8701
1986	Inkomst- och förmögenhetsfördelningen 1986	1, 2.1, 2.2	17, 20, 23	Be 20 SM 8801
1987	Inkomst- och förmögenhetsfördelningen 1987	1, 2.1, 2.2	17, 20, 23	Be 20 SM 8901
1988	Inkomst- och skattestatistik 1988	1, 2.1, 2.2	16, 19, 22	Be 20 SM 9001
1989	Inkomst- och skattestatistik 1989	1, 2.1, 2.2	16, 20, 23	Be 20 SM 9101
1990	Inkomst- och skattestatistik 1990	1, 2.1, 2.2	15, 20, 23	Be 20 SM 9201
1991–2006	Tables with grouped income distributions acquired directly from Statistics Sweden			

[a] Some publications titles are abbreviated. Skattetaxeringarna (1) = *Skattetaxeringarna samt inkomstfördelningen inom yrkesgrupper*, Skattetaxeringarna (2) = *Skattetaxeringarna samt fördelningen av inkomst och förmögenhet inom yrkesgrupper*, Skattetaxeringarna (3) = *Skattetaxeringarna samt fördelningen av inkomst och förmögenhet taxeringsåret*.

[b] The publications since 1982 also have the subtitle *Totalräknad statistik*.

[c] 'FU' denotes *Finansstatistiska utredningar* (Fiscal Surveys) and 'SOS' *Sveriges officiella statistik* (Swedish Official Statistics).

Table 7A.2 Total income shares (excluding capital gains) in Sweden, 1903–2006

	Shares (excl. capital gains income)						
Year	P90–100 (1)	P95–100 (2)	P99–100 (3)	P99.5–100 (4)	P99.9–100 (5)	P99.95–100 (6)	P99.99–100 (7)
1903	46.79	35.33	26.99	19.16	8.66	6.15	2.79
1904							
1905							
1906							
1907	45.42	36.33	21.46	16.57	8.72	6.47	2.99
1908							
1909							
1910							
1911	43.90	34.11	19.57	15.21	8.11	6.08	3.02
1912	45.59	35.75	20.92	16.29	8.99	6.84	3.55
1913							
1914							
1915							
1916	52.97	43.53	28.04	22.93	13.70	10.60	5.12
1917							
1918							
1919	41.91	31.23	16.33	11.70	7.33	5.55	2.91
1920	35.83	26.13	13.48	10.16	5.23	3.86	1.84
1921							
1922							
1923							
1924							
1925							
1926							
1927							
1928							
1929							
1930	38.41	27.87	13.74	10.15	4.82	3.45	1.52
1931							
1932							
1933							
1934	38.06	26.73	11.95	8.54	3.83	2.68	1.12
1935	36.18	25.74	12.32	8.98	4.22	2.99	1.21
1936							
1937							
1938							
1939							
1940							
1941	34.09	23.67	10.29	7.15	3.01	2.06	0.84
1942							
1943	35.61	24.48	10.44	7.19	2.99	2.01	0.78
1944	34.84	23.82	10.04	6.89	2.85	1.92	0.77
1945	34.23	23.36	9.77	6.69	2.72	1.82	0.70
1946	34.29	23.52	10.07	6.99	2.91	2.00	0.80
1947	32.09	21.43	8.62	5.85	2.35	1.59	0.60
1948	30.77	20.28	7.90	5.31	2.06	1.32	0.50
1949	30.35	19.89	7.64	5.09	1.96	1.29	0.48

(*continued*)

Table 7A.2 Continued

	Shares (excl. capital gains income)						
Year	P90–100 (1)	P95–100 (2)	P99–100 (3)	P99.5–100 (4)	P99.9–100 (5)	P99.95–100 (6)	P99.99–100 (7)
1950	30.25	19.80	7.59	5.06	1.94	1.28	0.47
1951	29.84	19.41	7.33	4.91	1.94	1.30	0.51
1952	29.08	18.60	6.80	4.49	1.73	1.15	0.44
1953	29.60	19.01	6.90	4.55	1.75	1.16	0.45
1954	29.21	18.71	6.90	4.57	1.75	1.15	0.44
1955	28.82	18.39	6.78	4.48	1.69	1.11	0.41
1956	28.83	18.20	6.65	4.38	1.64	1.07	0.40
1957	29.21	18.59	6.81	4.47	1.67	1.09	0.40
1958	29.52	18.75	6.81	4.45	1.65	1.07	0.40
1959	30.06	19.18	7.00	4.57	1.69	1.10	0.40
1960	30.35	19.34	6.83	4.41	1.60	1.03	0.37
1961	30.36	19.27	6.77	4.35	1.55	0.99	0.35
1962	30.08	19.03	6.65	4.25	1.50	0.96	0.34
1963	29.95	18.95	6.64	4.25	1.50	0.95	0.33
1964	29.80	18.77	6.50	4.14	1.43	0.90	0.31
1965	29.69	18.67	6.47	4.11	1.42	0.90	0.31
1966	29.58	18.50	6.35	4.02	1.37	0.86	0.29
1967	30.33	19.17	6.55	4.10	1.38	0.86	0.29
1968	30.39	19.21	6.57	4.11	1.39	0.87	0.29
1969	30.02	18.88	6.41	4.01	1.34	0.84	0.28
1970	29.36	18.34	6.16	3.83	1.28	0.79	0.26
1971	28.36	17.59	5.80	3.60	1.19	0.74	0.24
1972	27.89	17.27	5.67	3.51	1.15	0.71	0.23
1973	27.56	17.00	5.57	3.44	1.13	0.70	0.23
1974	27.07	16.58	5.47	3.39	1.12	0.69	0.23
1975	26.38	16.14	5.29	3.28	1.07	0.67	0.23
1976	25.55	15.48	4.95	3.04	0.96	0.59	0.19
1977	24.72	14.91	4.69	2.86	0.83	0.54	0.21
1978	23.99	14.38	4.47	2.70	0.83	0.50	0.18
1979	23.47	13.97	4.25	2.56	0.77	0.49	0.18
1980	22.73	13.44	4.05	2.42	0.74	0.47	0.17
1981	22.40	13.19	3.97	2.38	0.76	0.48	0.19
1982	22.33	13.18	3.98	2.40	0.77	0.49	0.19
1983	22.42	13.29	4.08	2.47	0.81	0.54	0.25
1984	22.30	13.31	4.13	2.52	0.82	0.57	0.25
1985	22.33	13.35	4.12	2.49	0.80	0.56	0.24
1986	22.35	13.39	4.11	2.47	0.77	0.54	0.23
1987	22.54	13.59	4.24	2.55	0.86	0.60	0.26
1988	22.53	13.62	4.38	2.72	0.99	0.70	0.31
1989	22.55	13.68	4.48	2.81	1.07	0.79	0.40
1990	22.75	13.73	4.38	2.72	1.02	0.73	0.34
1991	24.33	15.04	5.10	3.27	1.30	0.89	0.39
1992	24.33	15.04	5.04	3.19	1.22	0.82	0.35
1993	24.63	15.31	5.22	3.33	1.30	0.88	0.37
1994	25.23	15.85	5.53	3.61	1.45	1.00	0.41
1995	24.93	15.54	5.25	3.35	1.31	0.88	0.38
1996	25.56	16.05	5.59	3.69	1.41	0.98	0.40

1997	25.82	16.23	5.72	3.80	1.47	1.03	0.43
1998	25.91	16.35	5.87	3.91	1.57	1.09	0.45
1999	26.12	16.52	6.01	4.00	1.62	1.13	0.48
2000	26.72	17.12	5.97	4.43	1.93	1.37	0.61
2001	26.76	17.10	5.95	4.33	1.86	1.32	0.57
2002	26.43	16.77	5.67	4.07	1.69	1.18	0.51
2003	26.12	16.54	5.52	4.02	1.70	1.20	0.58
2004	26.34	16.71	5.72	4.09	1.73	1.22	0.58
2005	26.96	17.33	6.28	4.40	1.91	1.35	0.64
2006	27.30	17.73	6.61	4.73	2.21	1.63	0.83

Shares (excl. capital gains income)					
P90–95	P95–99	P99–99.5	P99.5–99.9	P99.9–99.95	P99.95–99.99

Year	P90–95 (1)	P95–99 (2)	P99–99.5 (3)	P99.5–99.9 (4)	P99.9–99.95 (5)	P99.95–99.99 (6)
1903	11.58	8.41	7.90	10.64	2.55	3.43
1904						
1905						
1906						
1907	9.19	15.03	4.92	7.94	2.29	3.54
1908						
1909						
1910						
1911	9.90	14.70	4.38	7.19	2.06	3.11
1912	9.95	14.99	4.66	7.39	2.18	3.36
1913						
1914						
1915						
1916	9.54	15.66	5.13	9.33	3.15	5.58
1917						
1918						
1919	10.81	15.06	4.67	4.42	1.81	2.68
1920	9.81	12.79	3.35	4.99	1.39	2.05
1921						
1922						
1923						
1924						
1925						
1926						
1927						
1928						
1929						
1930	10.66	14.28	3.62	5.40	1.40	1.96
1931						
1932						
1933						
1934	11.46	14.95	3.43	4.78	1.16	1.59
1935	10.56	13.58	3.36	4.82	1.25	1.81
1936						
1937						
1938						
1939						
1940						
1941	10.54	13.54	3.17	4.19	0.97	1.24
1942						
1943	11.25	14.20	3.28	4.26	0.99	1.25
1944	11.15	13.94	3.17	4.09	0.94	1.18

(*continued*)

Table 7A.2 Continued

	Shares (excl. capital gains income)					
Year	P90–95 (1)	P95–99 (2)	P99–99.5 (3)	P99.5–99.9 (4)	P99.9–99.95 (5)	P99.95–99.99 (6)
1945	10.99	13.75	3.11	4.02	0.92	1.14
1946	10.89	13.59	3.12	4.13	0.93	1.22
1947	10.76	12.94	2.81	3.56	0.77	1.00
1948	10.58	12.49	2.65	3.30	0.75	0.83
1949	10.54	12.35	2.61	3.18	0.68	0.82
1950	10.52	12.31	2.59	3.17	0.67	0.82
1951	10.49	12.17	2.50	3.01	0.65	0.79
1952	10.54	11.89	2.37	2.80	0.59	0.71
1953	10.65	12.19	2.42	2.84	0.59	0.72
1954	10.56	11.89	2.40	2.86	0.60	0.72
1955	10.48	11.69	2.35	2.83	0.59	0.70
1956	10.68	11.63	2.32	2.77	0.57	0.68
1957	10.68	11.85	2.39	2.84	0.59	0.69
1958	10.82	12.01	2.41	2.84	0.58	0.69
1959	10.92	12.26	2.47	2.92	0.60	0.71
1960	11.05	12.59	2.46	2.84	0.58	0.67
1961	11.13	12.58	2.46	2.84	0.56	0.65
1962	11.09	12.45	2.43	2.78	0.55	0.63
1963	11.04	12.38	2.42	2.78	0.55	0.63
1964	11.08	12.33	2.39	2.74	0.54	0.61
1965	11.05	12.26	2.38	2.72	0.53	0.60
1966	11.11	12.22	2.35	2.67	0.52	0.58
1967	11.16	12.63	2.45	2.72	0.52	0.57
1968	11.19	12.64	2.45	2.73	0.52	0.58
1969	11.14	12.47	2.40	2.66	0.50	0.56
1970	11.02	12.18	2.32	2.56	0.48	0.53
1971	10.78	11.78	2.21	2.41	0.45	0.49
1972	10.63	11.60	2.16	2.36	0.44	0.48
1973	10.56	11.43	2.12	2.31	0.43	0.47
1974	10.49	11.11	2.08	2.27	0.42	0.46
1975	10.23	10.85	2.01	2.21	0.40	0.45
1976	10.06	10.53	1.92	2.07	0.37	0.40
1977	9.82	10.21	1.84	2.03	0.28	0.34
1978	9.61	9.92	1.77	1.87	0.32	0.33
1979	9.51	9.72	1.69	1.79	0.28	0.31
1980	9.29	9.38	1.63	1.68	0.27	0.29
1981	9.21	9.22	1.59	1.63	0.28	0.29
1982	9.14	9.20	1.58	1.63	0.28	0.29
1983	9.13	9.21	1.61	1.67	0.27	0.29
1984	8.99	9.18	1.61	1.69	0.25	0.33
1985	8.98	9.23	1.63	1.70	0.24	0.32
1986	8.97	9.28	1.64	1.70	0.24	0.31
1987	8.95	9.35	1.69	1.68	0.26	0.34
1988	8.91	9.24	1.66	1.73	0.29	0.39
1989	8.87	9.21	1.66	1.75	0.28	0.40
1990	9.01	9.35	1.66	1.70	0.29	0.39
1991	9.29	9.95	1.82	1.97	0.41	0.50

1992	9.29	10.00	1.85	1.97	0.40	0.47
1993	9.33	10.08	1.90	2.03	0.42	0.51
1994	9.38	10.32	1.92	2.16	0.45	0.59
1995	9.39	10.29	1.90	2.05	0.42	0.51
1996	9.51	10.46	1.90	2.28	0.43	0.57
1997	9.59	10.51	1.92	2.33	0.43	0.61
1998	9.56	10.48	1.96	2.33	0.48	0.64
1999	9.60	10.51	2.02	2.37	0.50	0.65
2000	9.60	11.16	1.54	2.50	0.56	0.76
2001	9.65	11.15	1.62	2.48	0.54	0.75
2002	9.65	11.11	1.59	2.38	0.51	0.67
2003	9.58	11.02	1.50	2.32	0.50	0.63
2004	9.63	10.99	1.63	2.36	0.51	0.65
2005	9.64	11.05	1.87	2.50	0.56	0.71
2006	9.57	11.12	1.88	2.52	0.58	0.80

Notes: The shares 1903–66 are adjusted downwards by estimated capital gains shares.
In 1982, the gross total income (SRI) minus deficits at source (UF) and minus capital gains (CG) is negative, and therefore set to 0.

Table 7A.3 Total income shares (including capital gains) in Sweden, 1903–2006

	Shares (incl. social benefits, incl. capital gains)						
Year	P90–100 (1)	P95–100 (2)	P99–100 (3)	P99.5–100 (4)	P99.9–100 (5)	P99.95–100 (6)	P99.99–100 (7)
1903	46.76	35.32	27.01	19.21	8.71	6.19	2.81
1904							
1905							
1906							
1907	45.40	36.32	21.48	16.62	8.77	6.51	3.01
1908							
1909							
1910							
1911	43.88	34.10	19.58	15.25	8.15	6.12	3.04
1912	45.57	35.74	20.94	16.34	9.04	6.89	3.57
1913							
1914							
1915							
1916	52.94	43.52	28.06	22.99	13.78	10.67	5.15
1917							
1918							
1919	41.89	31.22	16.35	11.73	7.37	5.58	2.93
1920	35.81	26.12	13.49	10.19	5.25	3.88	1.85
1921							
1922							
1923							
1924							
1925							
1926							
1927							
1928							
1929							
1930	38.39	27.86	13.75	10.18	4.85	3.47	1.53

(continued)

Table 7A.3 Continued

	Shares (incl. social benefits, incl. capital gains)						
Year	P90–100 (1)	P95–100 (2)	P99–100 (3)	P99.5–100 (4)	P99.9–100 (5)	P99.95–100 (6)	P99.99–100 (7)
1931							
1932							
1933							
1934	38.04	26.72	11.95	8.56	3.85	2.70	1.13
1935	36.16	25.73	12.32	9.01	4.24	3.00	1.22
1936							
1937							
1938							
1939							
1940							
1941	34.08	23.67	10.30	7.16	3.02	2.07	0.84
1942							
1943	35.59	24.47	10.45	7.21	3.00	2.02	0.79
1944	34.83	23.81	10.05	6.91	2.87	1.94	0.77
1945	34.22	23.36	9.78	6.70	2.74	1.83	0.70
1946	34.31	23.54	10.10	7.01	2.93	2.01	0.80
1947	32.13	21.48	8.66	5.88	2.36	1.59	0.60
1948	30.84	20.34	7.96	5.33	2.06	1.32	0.50
1949	30.44	19.98	7.71	5.12	1.96	1.29	0.48
1950	30.37	19.91	7.67	5.10	1.94	1.28	0.47
1951	29.99	19.55	7.43	4.94	1.95	1.30	0.51
1952	29.22	18.73	6.89	4.53	1.74	1.15	0.44
1953	29.74	19.13	6.99	4.58	1.76	1.17	0.45
1954	29.34	18.83	6.99	4.61	1.76	1.16	0.44
1955	28.94	18.50	6.86	4.52	1.70	1.12	0.42
1956	28.94	18.31	6.73	4.42	1.66	1.09	0.41
1957	29.32	18.69	6.89	4.52	1.68	1.10	0.41
1958	29.62	18.85	6.89	4.50	1.67	1.09	0.40
1959	30.16	19.28	7.08	4.62	1.71	1.12	0.41
1960	30.45	19.44	6.91	4.46	1.63	1.05	0.38
1961	30.45	19.37	6.85	4.40	1.57	1.01	0.36
1962	30.16	19.12	6.72	4.30	1.53	0.98	0.35
1963	30.03	19.03	6.71	4.30	1.53	0.98	0.35
1964	29.88	18.84	6.57	4.19	1.46	0.93	0.32
1965	29.75	18.75	6.54	4.16	1.45	0.92	0.32
1966	29.64	18.58	6.41	4.07	1.41	0.89	0.31
1967	30.40	19.25	6.62	4.16	1.42	0.89	0.30
1968	30.49	19.32	6.69	4.22	1.46	0.92	0.32
1969	30.16	19.05	6.57	4.15	1.43	0.91	0.31
1970	29.47	18.49	6.32	3.97	1.35	0.85	0.29
1971	28.48	17.72	5.93	3.70	1.24	0.78	0.26
1972	28.03	17.43	5.81	3.62	1.21	0.76	0.25
1973	27.75	17.21	5.76	3.60	1.21	0.76	0.25
1974	27.17	16.80	5.68	3.58	1.23	0.77	0.26
1975	26.51	16.28	5.41	3.38	1.13	0.71	0.24
1976	25.69	15.63	5.07	3.13	1.02	0.63	0.21
1977	24.85	15.03	4.77	2.92	0.85	0.56	0.21
1978	24.13	14.53	4.56	2.76	0.87	0.53	0.19

1979	23.53	14.07	4.33	2.61	0.80	0.51	0.19
1980	22.82	13.55	4.13	2.50	0.79	0.50	0.19
1981	22.48	13.32	4.07	2.47	0.81	0.51	0.20
1982	22.44	13.32	4.08	2.49	0.83	0.53	0.21
1983	22.76	13.71	4.45	2.81	1.06	0.71	0.33
1984	22.59	13.59	4.36	2.72	0.96	0.67	0.29
1985	22.78	13.84	4.59	2.94	1.16	0.90	0.49
1986	22.79	13.84	4.49	2.83	1.04	0.72	0.31
1987	23.11	14.15	4.73	2.99	1.19	0.83	0.36
1988	23.30	14.42	5.08	3.34	1.44	1.02	0.46
1989	23.59	14.76	5.45	3.72	1.81	1.34	0.67
1990	23.62	14.63	5.20	3.47	1.62	1.17	0.55
1991	26.51	17.25	6.95	4.99	2.47	1.87	0.95
1992	25.30	16.02	5.84	4.02	1.79	1.33	0.67
1993	25.51	16.17	5.93	4.04	1.75	1.27	0.60
1994	27.14	17.77	7.18	4.99	2.43	1.78	0.84
1995	25.79	16.39	6.00	3.80	1.80	1.30	0.62
1996	27.26	17.71	6.99	4.76	2.50	1.93	1.06
1997	28.13	18.58	7.61	5.51	2.95	2.29	1.24
1998	28.27	18.78	8.17	5.69	3.15	2.48	1.41
1999	29.75	20.20	9.30	6.77	3.70	2.87	1.56
2000	31.31	21.93	11.12	8.54	5.21	4.20	2.47
2001	28.91	19.35	8.62	6.15	3.36	2.61	1.40
2002	27.94	18.32	7.59	5.20	2.62	2.00	1.06
2003	27.73	18.23	7.62	5.26	2.71	2.09	1.17
2004	28.21	18.34	7.87	5.52	2.80	2.15	1.20
2005	29.77	20.02	8.99	6.56	3.33	2.49	1.26
2006	30.72	21.07	9.53	6.92	3.77	2.91	1.59

Shares (incl. social benefits, incl. capital gains)

Year	P90–95 (1)	P95–99 (2)	P99–99.5 (3)	P99.5–99.9 (4)	P99.9–99.95 (5)	P99.95–99.99 (6)
1903	11.44	8.31	7.80	10.50	2.51	3.39
1904						
1905						
1906						
1907	9.08	14.85	4.86	7.85	2.26	3.50
1908						
1909						
1910						
1911	9.78	14.52	4.33	7.10	2.03	3.08
1912	9.83	14.80	4.60	7.30	2.15	3.31
1913						
1914						
1915						
1916	9.42	15.46	5.07	9.22	3.11	5.52
1917						
1918						
1919	10.67	14.87	4.61	4.37	1.79	2.65
1920	9.69	12.63	3.31	4.93	1.37	2.02
1921						
1922						
1923						
1924						

(*continued*)

Table 7A.3 Continued

Year	Shares (incl. social benefits, incl. capital gains)					
	P90–95 (1)	P95–99 (2)	P99–99.5 (3)	P99.5–99.9 (4)	P99.9–99.95 (5)	P99.95–99.99 (6)
1925						
1926						
1927						
1928						
1929						
1930	10.53	14.11	3.57	5.33	1.38	1.94
1931						
1932						
1933						
1934	11.32	14.77	3.39	4.72	1.15	1.57
1935	10.43	13.41	3.32	4.76	1.24	1.79
1936						
1937						
1938						
1939						
1940						
1941	10.41	13.37	3.13	4.14	0.95	1.22
1942						
1943	11.12	14.03	3.24	4.20	0.98	1.23
1944	11.02	13.77	3.13	4.04	0.93	1.16
1945	10.86	13.58	3.08	3.97	0.91	1.13
1946	10.77	13.44	3.09	4.08	0.92	1.21
1947	10.65	12.82	2.78	3.52	0.76	0.99
1948	10.50	12.38	2.63	3.27	0.74	0.82
1949	10.47	12.27	2.59	3.16	0.67	0.81
1950	10.46	12.24	2.57	3.15	0.67	0.81
1951	10.44	12.12	2.48	3.00	0.65	0.79
1952	10.50	11.84	2.36	2.79	0.59	0.71
1953	10.61	12.14	2.41	2.82	0.59	0.72
1954	10.51	11.84	2.39	2.85	0.60	0.72
1955	10.44	11.64	2.34	2.82	0.59	0.70
1956	10.63	11.58	2.31	2.76	0.57	0.68
1957	10.63	11.80	2.38	2.83	0.58	0.69
1958	10.77	11.96	2.40	2.83	0.58	0.68
1959	10.87	12.21	2.46	2.91	0.60	0.70
1960	11.00	12.53	2.45	2.83	0.57	0.67
1961	11.08	12.52	2.45	2.82	0.56	0.65
1962	11.05	12.40	2.42	2.77	0.55	0.63
1963	10.99	12.33	2.41	2.77	0.55	0.63
1964	11.03	12.27	2.38	2.73	0.53	0.60
1965	11.01	12.21	2.37	2.71	0.53	0.60
1966	11.07	12.17	2.34	2.66	0.52	0.58
1967	11.15	12.63	2.46	2.74	0.53	0.59
1968	11.17	12.64	2.46	2.76	0.54	0.60
1969	11.11	12.48	2.42	2.72	0.53	0.59
1970	10.98	12.18	2.34	2.62	0.50	0.56
1971	10.76	11.79	2.23	2.46	0.47	0.52
1972	10.61	11.62	2.19	2.41	0.46	0.50

1973	10.55	11.45	2.16	2.39	0.45	0.50
1974	10.37	11.12	2.10	2.35	0.45	0.51
1975	10.22	10.87	2.03	2.25	0.43	0.47
1976	10.06	10.57	1.94	2.11	0.39	0.43
1977	9.81	10.26	1.86	2.06	0.29	0.35
1978	9.60	9.97	1.79	1.89	0.34	0.34
1979	9.47	9.73	1.72	1.81	0.29	0.32
1980	9.27	9.41	1.64	1.71	0.29	0.32
1981	9.16	9.26	1.60	1.66	0.29	0.31
1982	9.12	9.24	1.60	1.66	0.30	0.32
1983	9.05	9.26	1.64	1.75	0.35	0.38
1984	9.00	9.23	1.64	1.76	0.29	0.38
1985	8.94	9.25	1.65	1.78	0.27	0.41
1986	8.95	9.34	1.67	1.79	0.32	0.41
1987	8.96	9.42	1.74	1.80	0.36	0.47
1988	8.88	9.34	1.74	1.90	0.42	0.56
1989	8.84	9.31	1.73	1.92	0.47	0.67
1990	8.99	9.44	1.72	1.85	0.45	0.62
1991	9.26	10.30	1.96	2.52	0.60	0.93
1992	9.28	10.18	1.83	2.22	0.46	0.66
1993	9.34	10.24	1.89	2.29	0.48	0.67
1994	9.37	10.59	2.19	2.56	0.65	0.94
1995	9.40	10.39	2.20	2.01	0.50	0.68
1996	9.55	10.72	2.22	2.26	0.57	0.87
1997	9.55	10.97	2.09	2.56	0.67	1.05
1998	9.50	10.60	2.48	2.54	0.67	1.07
1999	9.55	10.91	2.53	3.06	0.83	1.32
2000	9.39	10.81	2.58	3.33	1.01	1.73
2001	9.56	10.73	2.47	2.79	0.74	1.21
2002	9.62	10.73	2.39	2.58	0.63	0.94
2003	9.51	10.61	2.36	2.55	0.61	0.93
2004	9.87	10.47	2.35	2.72	0.65	0.95
2005	9.74	11.03	2.43	3.23	0.84	1.24
2006	9.65	11.54	2.61	3.15	0.85	1.33

APPENDIX 7B: DETAILS OF THE SWEDISH INCOME DATA

The Swedish income tax system contains several different concepts of income and deductions, and their basic relationships are shown in Table 7B.1. Apart from these, there have also been some additional changes that will be described below. In short, the most completely reported total incomes are those in 1971–2006, followed by those in 1943–70 when the tax authorities subtracted deficits in sources (mainly interest payments). Between 1903 and 1942, the incomes reported in the sources are incomes assessed for state taxation, meaning total net income *minus* municipal taxes paid and (from 1911) *plus* a share of taxable personal wealth. We have therefore deducted the wealth shares in all years when these are included and for the years after 1921 when municipal taxes were also progressive (flat rate taxes do not affect the top income shares and are therefore ignored), these are added to the incomes.

Concepts of Income in the Data, 1903–1942

In the years 1903 and 1907, the incomes reported in the tabulate tax returns data are incomes assessed to the progressive state income tax of 1902 (*till statlig inkomst- och förmögenhetsskatt taxerad inkomst*). This implies all income from labour and capital, and fixed rates of return from agricultural and other real estates, in order to capture the otherwise non-reported in-kind revenues from farming (see, e.g., Flodström 1909: p. viii). Deductions for deficits in sources of income (e.g. interest payments) were allowed, and thereby this income concept is a 'total net income'.[57]

In the years 1911, 1912, and 1916, the incomes reported in the statistical sources are amounts assessed for the state income and wealth tax, which means in practice 'total net income' plus a share, one-sixtieth in 1911–37 and one-hundredth in 1938–47, of taxable personal wealth. This income concept, 'total net income' plus a wealth share, was called 'centrally assessed amount' (*taxerat belopp*). We remove the wealth shares in the years 1911, 1912, and 1916, using data on the amount of wealth shares in each income class in the year 1912 (Flodström 1915: 47*–48*).

For 1919, the reported incomes are again assessed amounts, but this time we use the wealth shares in 1920 (Statistics Sweden 1929: 286–7) to remove the shares in 1919.

For 1920, we use another source of data: census material (reported in Statistics Sweden 1929). It reports incomes in the form of centrally assessed incomes, i.e. total net incomes not including wealth shares. However, the incomes used when reporting the taxes paid are based on the tax statistics and then using incomes in the form of 'assessed amounts', i.e. including the wealth shares. We use wealth share information from 1920 to remove the shares.

---

[57] In *Nordisk familjebok* (1910: 667) under the entry 'income tax' (*Inkomstskatt*) says that deductions are allowed for all costs that arise when earning the income and for interest payments.

For 1930, we use the census material in Statistics Sweden (1937), in which the income concept is the centrally assessed income. Although this implies that we do not need to remove any wealth shares, local taxes paid were from 1921 made deductible from the total net income before arriving at the centrally assessed income. This means that we have to add local taxes to the assessed income in order to arrive at a comparable income concept with earlier (and later) years. Since most local taxes are proportional and hence hit all types of income earners similarly, their effect on top income shares is limited. However, between 1921 and 1937 there were two *progressive* local taxes in place, called 'local progressive tax' (*kommunal progressivskatt*) and 'equalization tax' (*utjämningsskatt*). These must be added to the centrally assessed income for comparability reasons. For 1930, we add the progressive local taxes as they are described in Söderberg (1996: 76–7).

For 1934, the data come from a special inquiry made by the Ministry of Finance, based on a total collection of all tax filers reporting assessed amounts on SEK 8,000 income or above. For income earners with lower incomes, statistical calculations and spurious evidence were used (SOU 1936: 34 ff.). The income concept reported is hence centrally assessed amount, and we remove the wealth shares using information on wealth shares across income classes from the census of 1935/6 (Statistics Sweden 1940: 88–9). Furthermore, we add the progressive local taxes that are listed for each income class.

For 1935, the material is taken from the census of 1935/6 (Statistics Sweden 1940) and based on a 20 per cent individual-based sample of the population. The incomes collected are centrally assessed incomes, i.e. without including wealth shares. We add progressive local taxes based on their amounts listed for the income year of 1934 (see above).

For 1941, we use data from yet another special inquiry made by the Ministry of Finance based on all tax returns amounting to an assessed amount of SEK 8,000 or above (Quensel 1944: 28). Quensel makes corrections to make the incomes equivalent to centrally assessed incomes (called *korrigerat belopp*), i.e. including local taxes and without wealth shares.

Concepts of Income in the Data, 1943–2006

In the period 1943–70, Statistics Sweden introduced a new system for reporting the Swedish tax-based income distribution. Unlike the previous tabulations, however, a new official main concept of income was introduced: 'total net income' (*sammanräknad nettoinkomst*), defined as total income less deductions of deficit in any income source.

In 1971–90, Statistics Sweden changed main income concept to 'total income' (*sammanräknad inkomst*), which is defined as above but without deducting deficits in sources. A fairly important change in terms of the reported income statistics occurred in 1974, when the government decided to make all social benefits (e.g. unemployment insurance, social security transfers, state pensions) liable to taxation. This implied that incomes filed on tax returns, and hence also the official incomes used in the income statistics, now started to include social security transfers. Since our main focus is on the incomes at the top, where these benefits are relatively small and even insignificant, this rules-based change has limited bearing on this study. Therefore, we only make an adjustment on the reference total income by adding sums of social security transfers on the national level (published in the Statistical Yearbooks of Statistics Sweden) for all years before 1974 whenever such data were found (starting in the 1940s).

In 1991–2006, Statistics Sweden once again changed their main concept of income when producing their income statistics, now to *total earned income* (*sammanräknad förvärvsinkomst*), defined as the sum of labour and business income. Hence, capital income and capital gains were excluded. Fortunately, Statistics Sweden continued publishing a few summary tables in which they used total income (*summa förvärvs- och kapitalinkomst*) as concept of income, and these are series used by us.

Definitions of Sources of Income

As already mentioned above, the Swedish tax laws and income statistics define the sources of income that are to be specified on the tax returns. These definitions have been remarkably stable and the only major change came with the tax reform of 1991. Unfortunately, the published income statistics have not always reported compositional data across different income levels. In particular, before 1967, when such reports were made each year, these data are available only in two censuses: 1945 (Statistics Sweden 1951) and 1950 (Statistics Sweden 1956).

The sources of income used before 1991 were the following six:[58] labour income (*inkomst av tjänst*), mainly wages and salaries; capital income (*inkomst av kapital*), mainly interest earnings and dividends; entrepreneurial income (*inkomst av rörelse*), mainly firm profits and royalties; farm income (*inkomst av jordbruksfastighet*), mainly of sales of agricultural and forestry products and leases; real estate income (*inkomst av annan fastighet*), mainly rents and in-kind payments; and capital gains (*inkomst av tillfällig förvärvsverksamhet*) from sales of real estate and securities.[59]

After 1991, the number of income sources was reduced to three: labour (*inkomst av tjänst*), business (*inkomst av näringsverksamhet*), and capital (*inkomst av kapital (överskott)*). Compared with the earlier period, labour income was defined in basically the same way. Business income, however, included not only the previous entrepreneurial income, but also all of farm incomes and a small part of real estate income emanating from rental apartments. In the new concept of capital income, the previous capital income was included but also most of former real estate income coming from private rental and, notably, all forms of capital gains.

For analyses spanning the whole period, we use four main income sources primarily following the definitions of the post-1991 period (for computational reasons): wages, capital, business, and capital gains, defined in Table 7B.2.

Estimating the Share of Capital Income in Top Incomes, 1912–2006

Thanks to early wealth data in the tax statistics for income earners in different classes of total income, we are able to construct shares of capital income of total income as far back as 1912 and for some more years until the post-war period when we use the compositional sources described previously.

Specifically, the shares before 1945 are computed by assuming that capital income is a fixed rate of return flowing from the individuals' net wealth. Information about net wealth in different classes of income is available from the tax-based income statistics due to the fact that one-sixtieth of that wealth was to be added as taxable income until 1938 when the share was reduced to one-hundredth and 1943 when it was removed altogether (recall

---

[58] In the late 1960s, there was also a specific entry for income from partnerships (*inkomst av delägarskap i vanligt handelsbolag etc*), but this was included in entrepreneurial income from the 1970s onwards and we do this also for these years when it was reported separately.

[59] Detailed descriptions of the income sources are found in, e.g., Statistics Sweden (1945: 50–67) and Statistics Sweden (1975: 25–6).

Table 7.1). The approach was previously used by, e.g., Flodström (1915: 46–7) and Statistics Sweden (1927). Capital income is then computed as the annual rate of return from this wealth. We assume that the yield is flat and the same for all income earners disregarding the (unlikely) possibility of systematic differences in portfolios across income levels. The yields used are 5 per cent for the years 1912, 1916, and 1919, 5.5 per cent in 1920, 4.5 per cent in 1930, and 3 per cent in 1935. These are the same rates that Flodström and Statistics Sweden use (except for 1920 when they use 5 per cent).[60] Unlike them, however, we can also motivate our choice of these rates by referring to three other reference interest rates from the same particular years. Specifically, the yearly averages of the minimum lending rate (*diskontot*) set by the Swedish central bank, the average deposit rate at Swedish savings banks, and the effective Swedish government bond yield were in 1912: 4.81, 4.35, and 4.80; in 1916: 5.23, 4.76, and 5.09; in 1919: 6.38, 5.08, and 5.71; in 1920: 6.92, 5.16, and 7.00; in 1930: 3.71, 5.22, and 4.18; and in 1935: 2.50, 3.59 (in 1933), and 3.30 (*Svensk Sparbankstidskrift* 1934: 825). However, Östlind (1945: 261) shows numbers of effective yields of stock exchange-listed stocks during the First World War being somewhat lower than what we use (4.0 per cent for 1916). At the same time, Beije (1946: 64–87) shows the market yields of new corporate bond issues during 1912–20 more in line with the ones we use. Finally, the share of capital income of total income across the various top fractiles is computed using Pareto interpolation in the same way as in the rest of the compositional analysis.

Realized Capital Gains and the Identity of Top Income Earners, 1991–2006

One problem with using aggregate income statistics ordered in classes of total income is that we have problems assessing the true distributional effects of capital gains income. In short, we do not wish to have our top total income earners being populated by low-wage income earners selling their house or some old bonds and thereby jumping from the 50th to the 99th percentile.[61]

A simple way to at least rule out some of the ambiguity is to use the tabulations by Statistics Sweden of average gross capital gains income (i.e. before deductions against interest payments or capital losses) in classes of earned income, from 1991 onwards. Since the compositional analysis above showed that business income is only a minimal part of earned income during this period even for top total income earners, earned income in practice means wages and salaries. The results of this exercise are shown in Figure 7B.1, where the distributions of realized capital gains are plotted across classes of labour income for each year in 1991–2006. Apparently average capital gains are highest for those who also earn the most, i.e., at least for this late sub-period of the study we find no support for the hypothesis that realizations of capital gains create a large turnover of people in our income distribution and that a constantly significant share of top income earners is low-wage income earners.

Concepts of Tax Units

The Swedish income statistics have used two main definitions of tax units over the twentieth century. Before 1951, the tax unit is the *family,* meaning married couples or

---

[60] Unfortunately, no income data were collected in the census of 1940, so we have no information about wealth shares in different classes of income.

[61] This has previously been shown by Saez and Veall (2005) not to be the case among top income earners in Canada.

single households, both with any under-age resident children. After 1951, the tax unit is the *individual*. On top of these main types, there were some minor changes mainly during the latter period which are discussed in this section.

Income earners (tax units), 1903–50: Income earners in the Swedish income statistics refer to physical persons who lived in Sweden during the income year and who also filed a personal tax return.[62] The Swedish income statistics were family based until 1950, which meant that families with at least one income earner earning more than the lowest taxable income threshold should file one tax return. Married couples filed a joint tax return.

Income earners (tax units), 1951–2006: For the period 1951–2006, the Swedish income statistics changed to being individual based, meaning that individual tax returns form the basis for the income distribution data that we have used in this study. It should be noted that the definition of income earners according to published income statistics is typically, but not always, identical with the contemporaneous tax legislation. In particular, although the *income statistics* switched from using households to individuals in 1951, the Swedish *tax system* continued taxing families until 1971. But the transition was gradual between 1954 and 1971. Before 1954 the wife's income was automatically assessed as a part of her husband's income. Between 1954 and 1965 spouses filed separate tax returns after which their incomes were lumped together and taxed as one tax unit according to a specific rate of 'joint taxation' (*sambeskattning*). Between 1966 and 1970, the system was further adjusted so that married couples could choose whether to have their income taxed separately or as one couple according to a specific scale. Finally, in 1971 the Swedish tax system changed to being fully individual based and married couples were thereafter treated as two income earners.

In the period 1943–50 the income statistics followed the tax system by being household based, using the total number of filed tax returns as primary material. Due to processing constraints, however, only a few variables could be collected for each tax unit and therefore it was decided to switch to a sample-based system that allowed more background information to be collected and analysed. Because of this, Statistics Sweden decided to start using a nationally representative 10 per cent sample of the tax population as basis for its income statistics from the year 1951 onwards. This basically meant that the income statistics became individual based despite still having a family-based tax system since all persons with positive income had to file an individual tax return regardless of whether they were eventually taxed jointly with their spouses or parents.[63] The 10 per cent sample was drawn from the population of all adults aged 16 years or above and born on either the 5th, 15th, or 25th in each month.[64] To avoid sampling too few high-income earners, these groups were fully sampled.[65] This is, of course, important in the context of studying top incomes as it means that we do not have to worry about missing top income earners due to sampling in this period. The sample-based income statistics lasted until 1967 when

[62] Formally, unfinished death estates and family foundations are also counted as income earners, but they only represent about 1% of the total number of income earners.

[63] The switch to using a population sample followed the instructions of a governmental statute (*kungörelse den 21 december 1951*, No. 832).

[64] Having in fact 365.25 days per calendar year, the chosen sample was actually smaller than 10% of the population and instead of multiplying each income earner by 10 (for those jointly assessed 5) it should have been 10.146 (and 5.340). As noted by Statistics Sweden in *Inkomst och förmögenhet 1968*, p. 26 (see appendix sources), this could have some minor effects on the comparability of the data before and after 1967.

[65] The definition of high income was SEK 30,000 or above during 1951–9 and with income above and SEK 50,000 or above in 1960–6.

Statistics Sweden returned to basing the income statistics on the complete tax population with the help of new data-processing techniques.

Apart from these major changes in the income earner definitions, there have been several smaller adjustments and related changes that have affected the income earner concept. For example, in income years 1972 and 1973 all retirees receiving public pension only (*folkpensionärer*) were granted extra deductions so as to avoid paying taxes.[66] Another change happened in 1978 when both employers and employees were required to report all incomes paid and received, which in itself increased the tax-liable population by a couple of hundred thousand income earners who were most likely previously avoiding taxes altogether.

The main impact that these changes of tax units have in our study is on the choice of reference population and how to homogenize this over time. Details of how we do this are presented below.

Lowest Taxable Income Threshold

Sweden is an outlier internationally in terms of the large share of income earners that have been obliged to file taxes over the twentieth century. Figure 7B.2 shows the lowest income level obliging a tax return (in Swedish *deklarationspliktgräns* or '*skattestreck*'), which is negatively correlated with the number of people included in the tax population. During the first decade 1903–10, the level was relatively high, SEK 1,000, representing between one and two times the overall average income (reference total income divided by reference total population). Over time, the level was increased nominally, shown in the right scale in the figure. Already in 1920, only if one earned a fifth of the average income had one to file a personal tax return and since the 1950s the level has been lowered even further in relative terms.

It should be noted that although the fairly drastic discrete changes in the threshold in, e.g., 1911, 1919, 1952, 1962, and 1971 changed the number of tax filers by several percentage points, this does not affect our analysis since we always observe the absolute top income earners as well as the reference total population.[67]

---

[66] See, e.g., Statistics Sweden (1973: 15).

[67] The doubling of the threshold in 1962 was estimated to decrease the number of income earners by about 125,000, representing about 3% (Statistics Sweden, 1964: 21).

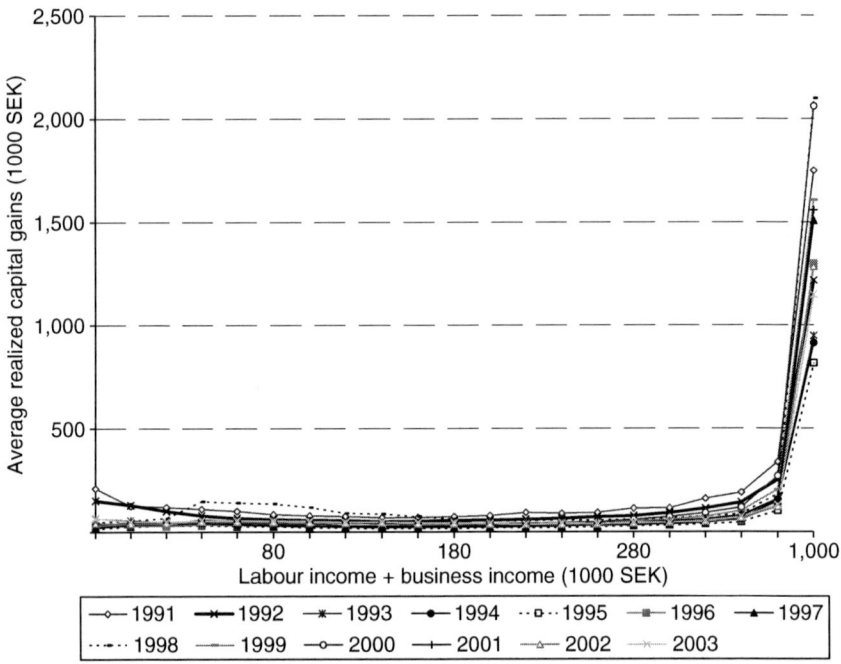

Figure 7B.1 Average gross capital gains income in classes of earned income in Sweden, 1991–2003

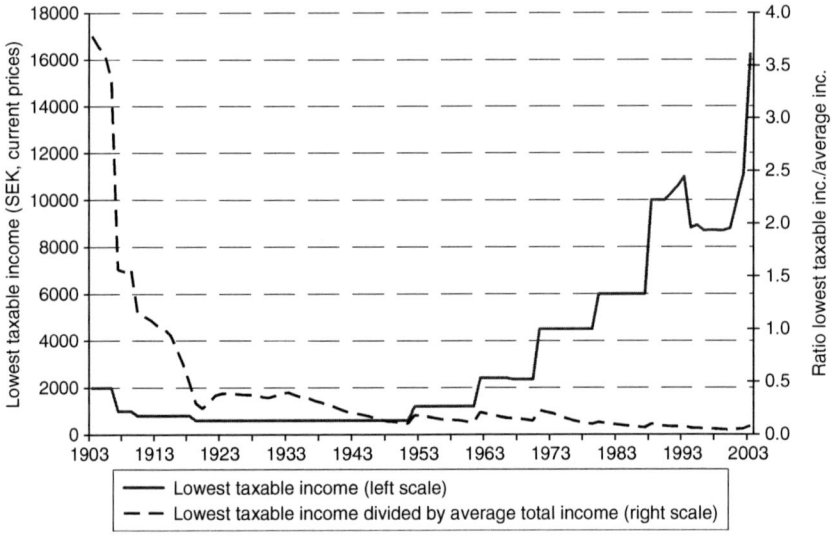

Figure 7B.2 Lowest taxable income and its share of average total income on Sweden, 1903–2003

Table 7B.1 Income concepts, deductions, and taxes and their interrelationships

Concept	Description and relationship with other concepts
SRI	*Total income* (Swedish term: *Sammanräknad inkomst*) from labour, capital, business, capital gains.
−UF	*Deficit in source of income* (*Underskott i förvärvskälla*), e.g., interest rate payments.
= SRNI	SRNI = SRI − UF: *Total net income* (*Sammanräknad nettoinkomst*). Main income concept in the Swedish income of Statistics Sweden during 1943–70. In this study used for the whole period.
−EA	*Basic deductions* for, e.g., state pension contributions (*folkpensionsavgift*, 1921–35), social security fees (*sjukförsäkringsavgift*, 1955–74), security charges (*egenavgifter*, 1993–).
= KTI	KTI = SRNI − EA: *Locally assessed income* (*Kommunalt taxerad inkomst*).
−KGA	*Local free allowance* (*Kommunala grundavdrag*). Since 1903, originally a regional adjustment for differences in cost of living (*kommunalt dyrortsavdrag*).
= KBI	KBI = KTI − KOA: *Locally taxable income* (*Kommunalt beskattningsbar inkomst*).
LTAX	LTAX = KBI∗(Local tax rate): *Local taxes paid* (*kommunala skatter*). These are mainly proportional, but during 1921–37 there were two local progressive taxes, municipal progressive tax (*Kommunal progressivskatt*) and equalization tax (*Utjämningsskatt*), which are added to the other taxes.
−AA	*Deduction for losses* (*Allmänna avdrag*): After 1920, this was mainly local taxes (LTAX). Other losses were state pension fees (*Folkpensionsavgifter*) and sick leave insurance fees (*Sjukförsäkringsavgifter*).
−LTAX	
= STI	STI = KTI − AA − LTAX: *Centrally assessed income* (*Statligt taxerad inkomst*). This is what we use in our series, but between 1911 and 1942 (except for the census material of 1920, 1930, and 1935), the tax laws defined STI as STB (see below).
or STB	STB = STI + 'Share of personal taxable wealth': *Centrally assessed amount* (*Statligt taxerat belopp*). During 1911–47. The wealth share added to STI was 1911–37 1/60 of taxable wealth and 1938–47 1/100. Note that the official income statistics used total net income as main concept from 1943, why STB did not appear in the data after 1942.
−SGA	*Central free allowance* (*Statligt grundavdrag*). Introduced in 1911 to mitigate effect from living in high-cost of living areas (*statligt dyrortsavdrag*, 1911–62), but also including deductions for wife (*hustruavdrag*, 1919–48) and children (*barnavdrag*, 1911–48). Moreover, additional allowances were possible in case of accident or long-term illness (*avdrag för särskilda förhållanden*),
= SBI	*Centrally taxable income* (*Statligt beskattningsbar inkomst*).
STAX	STAX = SBI∗(State income tax rate): *State income taxes paid* (*Statlig inkomstskatt*). There were several different kinds of central government income taxes.

Table 7B.2 The four income sources used in the compositional analysis in Sweden, 1912–2006

Income source	Description
Wages	Includes wages and salaries and is basically defined in the same way both before and after 1991.
Capital income	Includes interest earnings, dividends and real estate income. In the period before 1991, we add 'capital income' (interests and dividends) and 'real estate income' together.[a] After 1991, estimate capital income from the 'new capital income', which includes both the old concept and capital gains. Hence, we break out interest earnings and dividends (called *inkomst av ränta* in the income statistics), private rental income (*inkomst av uthyrning av privatbostad*), and special rental income (*inkomst av positiv räntefördelning*).
Business income	Includes mainly income from privately held firms. Before 1991, we add together 'entrepreneurial income' and 'farm income'. After 1991, we use 'business income'.
Capital gains	Includes net gains from sales of real estate and other assets.

[a] Formally, one part of the real estate income was also included in business income after 1991, namely income from public rental buildings. However, this only concerned so-called 'physical persons' (private individuals) and not 'judicial persons' (public and private companies) which instead had to report all of their income (including that from real estate) as entrepreneurial income and which was the largest part of the two incomes. Leif Johansson at Statistics Sweden (from a discussion on 25 June 2005) also would believe that the absolute majority of the real estate income before 1991 should refer to what would after 1991 have been included in capital income. For these reasons, we place all of real estate income in the capital income in our long-run series.

APPENDIX 7C: CONSTRUCTION
OF REFERENCE TOTAL

Here we explain in greater detail exactly how our reference totals have been constructed. The different reference totals are used to test the robustness of our series to the choice of reference total. The reference totals for tax units and income, 1903–2006, are shown in Table 7C.1.

Reference Total Population

As described above, there has been one major change in Swedish tax legislation in the twentieth century which has fundamentally changed the concept of tax unit, namely the 1970 tax reform shift from a family-based tax unit to an individually based concept. In terms of *tax statistics*, however, this change occurred (at least to some extent) already in 1951. Before this tax statistics were based on the entire tax population and figures referred to 'tax units', i.e. individuals as well as married couples counted as one income earner.[68] Before 1951 the obvious reference population is therefore the adult population (which we take to be everybody aged 16 or above) less married women (since a married woman formed one tax unit together with her husband). After 1951, however, statistics changed to being based on a representative sample (10 per cent) of the population with married couples, where both had income, now treated as two income earners in the statistics even though they were still *taxed* as one unit. The problem is that in cases where the woman did not work, or had low income, she was not necessarily counted. This means that income statistics between 1951 and 1971 when the individually based system was fully introduced (for labour income, tax on capital income remained family based) are a mix between a family based system and an individually based system including some women (those with substantial income) but not all. Starting 1971, the reference total is again relatively unambiguous, now obviously being the adult population.

Apart from the quantitatively more substantial decisions discussed above there are a number of smaller adjustments which can be considered. Over the course of a year individuals move in and out of the country, some die, some turn 16 after the population count but before taxes are filed, etc. Based on recent years when we believe that the coverage in the tax statistics is close to complete we have concluded that correcting for deaths is most important. The tax statistics before 1951 contain tax returns for those who died during the previous year (the income year), in the period 1951–73 these are not present in our data, but from 1974 and onwards they are again part of the statistics. We

---

[68] Note that this is the case for *tax statistics* before 1951 but not income figures in the census (*Folkräkningen*).

have therefore added deaths to our reference total for the population before 1951 and after 1973.[69] For these periods we therefore add the number of deaths during the year when calculating the reference total population.

In terms of choosing the appropriate reference population the period 1903–2006 can, hence, be divided into the following three periods: (1) 1903–50, the total population aged 16 or above minus married women, (2) 1951–70, the total population aged 16 or above minus women likely to be excluded in the statistics, (3) 1971–2006, the total population aged 16 or above.

For the period 1903–50 the reference total population is:

The population aged 16–	(from Statistics Sweden, Population statistics, *SCB Programmet för befolkningsstatistik*)
– married women	(from Statistics Sweden, Statistical Yearbook of Sweden, *Statistisk Årsbok,* various years)
+ deaths during the year	(from Statistics Sweden, Statistical Yearbook of Sweden, *Statistisk Årsbok,* various years)

For the period 1951–71 our preferred reference total population is:

The population aged 16–	(from Statistics Sweden, Population statistics, *SCB Programmet för befolkningsstatistik*)
– married women (no/low income)	Edvinsson (2005: 140) reports data on men and women in paid work and labels married women not in paid work 'housewives'. Part of this group does have income anyway so we subtract a declining share of 'housewives' in the period 1951–67 (based on smoothing shifts in the ratio between the number of tax returns and the reference population, as well as the income shares.[70] In 1967 (when individual taxation became voluntary) the deducted share shifts more drastically (as does the number of income earners in the statistics) and in the period 1967 to 1970 the remaining share of 'housewives' are subtracted.

For the period 1972–2006 the preferred reference total population is:

The population aged 16–	(from Statistics Sweden, Population statistics, *SCB Programmet för befolkningsstatistik*)

---

[69] To be precise, deaths are not in the statistics 1951–66 (though they are taxed) while they are separately accounted for in the period 1967–73 and hence we can exclude them from our tables. References for the treatment of deaths are e.g.: for the period before 1951, Statistics Sweden, *Inkomst och förmögenhet 1969,* p. 11, for the period 1951–66, Statistics Sweden, *Skattetaxeringarna ... 1966,* p. 32, for the period 1967–73 Statistics Sweden, *Inkomst och förmögenhet 1969,* pp. 13–15, 20–1, and after 1974 *Statistics Sweden,* SCB SM N 1976:4 (p. 2) and SCB OE 21 SM 0501.

[70] We start by subtracting 60% of married women (which is about 75% of the housewives) and then decrease this share with about 2 percentage points per year until 1967 (as this is about the rate at which the ratio of housewives to married women changes over this period) and then allow for a larger shift between 1966 and 1967 when (judging from the upward jump in the number of tax returns) the number of women with own reported income increased more.

+ deaths during the year   (added after 1973 since they reappear in the statistics in 1974, from Statistics Sweden, Statistical Yearbook of Sweden, *Statistisk Årsbok,* various years)

To check the robustness of our results we have calculated a number of alternatives which differ mainly in the period 1951–71. These are sometimes not 'alternatives' in the sense that we may know that they are clear over- or underestimations, but rather they serve the purpose of giving bounds to our estimates.[71] Figure 7C.1 shows the population aged 16 and above, the number of tax returns, and the different alternative specifications. The alternative specifications are the following:

Preferred series =   (Pop 16−) − Married W + deaths for 1903–50, (Pop 16−) − (Decreasing share of women 1951–71), and from 1967 − Pop 16−, subtracting declining share of housewives 1967–71 and adding deaths after 73 (1974−).
Tax units alt 1 =   (Pop 16−) − Married W for 1903–50, and (Pop 16−) from 1951.
Tax units alt 2 =   (Pop 16−) − Married W for 1903–50, (Pop 16−) − Housewives for 1951–66, and (Pop 16−) from 1967.
Tax units alt 3 =   (Pop 16−) − Married W + Deaths for 1903–50, (Pop 16−) − Housewives for 1951–66, (Pop 16−) − Declining share of housewives for 1967–73, (Pop 16−) + Deaths for 1974 onwards.

Looking at the behaviour of the ratio between the number of tax returns and our reference series, especially around the critical years when there are changes in the definition of tax unit, i.e. 1951, 1967, and 1971, indicates which series seem best. Put simply, we do not want there to be any sudden jumps in the ratio unless there are underlying real changes in the tax base. To exemplify, in 1919 the tax threshold was dropped from SEK 800 to SEK 600 leading to a real major expansion of the tax base. Here we expect the ratio to go up sharply. In 1951, however, the change was only in the type of statistics, not in the actual underlying number of tax-eligible individuals (units), so here we should not expect a break in the ratio. To the extent that the number of returns increase this should be compensated by an increase in the reference total. At the same time, we do not, of course, wish to make ad hoc adjustments to keep the ratio fixed, since there are also real changes in the number of tax filers. Figure 7C.2 shows the ratio between the number of tax returns and our preferred series with indications of critical breaks.

Reference Total Income

In constructing our reference total income we have used three basic approaches. The first two are based on that we can arrive at the 'Preferred Total Income Definition' either by (1) starting with 'Total Personal Sector Income' and deducting items not included in our preferred definition, or (2) starting from the 'Tax Statistics Income' and adding items not included in the tax base and income estimates for individuals not included in the tax statistics. The third—which is mainly included as a point of reference—is based on the assumption that our preferred income total can be approximated as a fixed share of GDP.

---

[71] Only Tax units 3 is really an alternative. Here we subtract all housewives in the period 1951–67.

Starting with the first approach, we need homogeneous estimates of 'Total Personal Sector Income' from which we want to deduct items not included in our preferred definition of total income. The best homogeneous National Accounts series which span the whole period which we study are those by Edvinsson (2005). These, however, contain only aggregate series for *Wages and salaries of employees* (*including social benefits*) and *Imputed labour income of self-employed* (*including social benefits*). To these we have added aggregate *capital income* and *property income* reported in the tax statistics giving us an estimate of 'Personal sector total income'.[72] This, hence, becomes:

Wages and salaries of employees (including social benefits) (from Edvinsson 2005)
+   Imputed labour income of self-employed (incl. social benefits)
     (from Edvinsson 2005)
+   individual capital income (from *Taxeringarna*..., 1922–88, and corresponding
     sources thereafter, and estimated before 1922)
+   individual property income (same as for capital income above)
=   Estimated 'Personal sector total income'

This estimate fluctuates around 0.7 times GDP (calculated from the expenditure side, reported in Edvinsson 2005) with a standard deviation of 0.03.

Starting from the tax statistics income we use the following method to get at our preferred reference total for income:

Tax statistics income (the aggregates from the same sources as the income statistics described above, sometimes corrected for wealth shares)
+   items not included in the tax base (we make the assumption that all important sources of income including certain social security benefits are included in the tax base after 1974 (hence abstracting from child allowances, *allmänt barnbidrag*, and study grants, *studiebidrag*, which are tax free) and add aggregate government expenditures for unemployment benefits (*arbetslöshetsersättning*), payments for sick leave (*sjukpenning*), and payments for mothers (*moderskapsförsäkring*, which in 1974 was replaced by 'parenthood insurance', *föräldrarförsäkring*, which was taxed) based on figures in the Statistical Yearbook of Sweden 1948– (before they are not listed but can be assumed to be a small share)
+   estimated income for 'non-filers' (in our preferred specification we take (reference population—tax filers) × (0.8 times the tax threshold). As an alternative specification we use 0.25 times the average income of tax filers)
=   'Preferred reference total' (starting from the tax statistics income)

Figure 7C.3 shows the alternative specifications over the whole period as shares of GDP, as well as in relation to 0.63 times GDP. What we can say with some certainty is that the estimate of 'Personal sector total income' is an overestimate of our preferred reference total. We can also say with some certainty that at least since 1974 the tax statistics income is relatively close to our preferred reference total since most people file taxes and everything we wish to include as income is included in the tax base. We can also note that in the period 1930–90 our 'Preferred reference total' calculated starting with the tax statistics income follows the estimated 'personal sector' total income very closely. In fact, taking 0.89 times the latter, yields numbers which follow the former with very small deviations.[73] We

---

[72] These are available from the aggregate taxation statistics *Taxering till inkomst- och förmögenhet* 1922–88, for the years before we add shares based on the observations 1922, and after 1988 we add the corresponding figures in the new tax statistics.

[73] The standard deviation is 0.02 and the maximum deviation is 0.05.

also note that for the early years (1903–20) imputing 0.8 times the threshold (or 0.25 times average income) clearly yields overestimates of reference income. This is to be expected since when most individuals are below the threshold small changes in assumptions about their average income make a big difference and at this point in time the average income amongst taxpayers was certainly much higher than later, implying that imputing similar shares to non-filers as later means overestimating their income a lot.

Given the behaviour of these series we have chosen to use 0.89 times our estimated 'personal sector total income' as our reference total for the period 1903–42 and then (as tax statistics become yearly) our calculated reference total income starting with tax statistics income. As with the reference total population we have calculated top income shares using a number of alternatives as well.

Sensitivity of Using Different Reference Totals

Using different reference totals can potentially have an important impact on the income shares. For some single years, such as the spike in top income shares in 1916, the difference can be up to five percentage points between the alternative that gives the lowest and highest estimate respectively. For some periods, such as in the 1950s when the treatment of women in the statistics is unclear, the variation can be up to 3 percentage points over some periods. Overall, however, the main trends in the results are robust to which alternative is chosen. Figure 7C.4 shows the variation in the P90–5 and P99–100 shares including alternatives which are likely to give upper and lower bounds for the series. The three first alternatives keep our preferred population total and varies the income total, while the following four alternatives change the population total but keep our preferred income total. As the figure shows, the beginning of the century, especially the peak in 1916, and the period 1951–71 when the treatment of working women is unclear in the statistics, are the periods with the broadest bands. Overall, however, the main trends in the results are robust to which alternative is chosen.

Sensitivity of Using Individuals or Households as Tax Units

Our income series are computed from the tax returns-based income statistics for most years, and as we described above this implies that we use two different concepts of income earners over the twentieth century. Before 1951, the income earner in our data is the *household* (or family), i.e., married couples with, or without, children, single men 16 years and older, and single women 16 years or older. From 1951 onwards, our income earner is the *individual*, meaning all men and women 16 years or older. Hence, while we in the first period count married couples as one income earner, they are counted as two income earners in the latter period.

This section offers some partial explorations of how this switch of income earner concept may influence the overall results of our study. As our historical data were chosen largely due to availability constraints, we cannot make a fully-fledged comparison as there are simply no parallel datasets based on tax data available. What we can do, however, is to compare our family-based series with the series in which individuals are the basis. This can be done from the years from which we use the *Census material* (the years 1920, 1930, 1935 (partial census), 1945 (partial census), and 1950) when the primary material is individual based but adjusted by us and others (especially Bentzel 1953) to be consistent with the family-based series from the years before 1920 and in between the other years (1934 and 1937).

Figure 7C.5 shows the income shares of the top fractiles (from top 10 per cent to the top 0.05 percent). Solid lines represent our main family-based income series used in our analysis (called 'Household') whereas the broken lines are the unadjusted, individual-based census series (called 'Individual'). Note that since we use different concepts of income earners in the two cases, we must also use two different reference total populations to calculate the correct population shares. In our family-based series, we use the adult population 16 years and above minus married women, and in the individual-based series the adult population 16 years and above is used. For this reason, the level of the shares may not fully correspond to each other although as Figure 7C.5 shows they do, as a matter of fact, to quite some extent. As for the changes in shares over the period, they pretty much coincide in all cases for all fractiles, and importantly there is no systematic tendency in some direction of either series. For example, whereas the individual-based series produce slightly larger declines between 1935 and 1950 for the top 10 per cent to top 0.5 per cent income earners, the family-based series do it for the top 0.1 to top 0.05 per cent fractiles. Altogether, we feel confident with our choice of income earner concepts and have not found any systematic biases when contrasting them with alternative definitions.

Age Adjustments and Effects of Censoring the Youngest Income Earners

Similar to previous studies of top incomes, we impose a lower age bound on the analysed tax population in order to ensure that we do not include under-age children in the analysis and that the series are conceptually consistent over the years. Specifically, we impose an age cut-off at 16 years, which means that we include all income earners aged 16 and above. We choose this age as it has long marked the beginning of a person's period in life after completing the compulsory Swedish secondary education. Furthermore, the 16-year-olds were the youngest ones sampled by Statistics Sweden in the income statistics during 1951–66, and ever since the late 1970s it has also been the lowest reported age in the published income statistics. For robustness purposes, however, we have also run our entire analysis using income earners aged 20 and older, but the results are qualitatively the same.[74] The finding that the exact choice of age cut-off is not important for the estimated trends in top income shares has also been found by Atkinson and Leigh (2007b).

In practice, our age cut-off means that we subtract the number of income earners aged 15 or less from our reference total population and from the main top income series but not from the reference income total. The reason is that we lack specific data on their incomes. However, it turns out that their incomes are quite marginal and leaving them in the reference income does not influence the results of our study.

In Figure 7C.6, we reinforce the aforementioned result that removing children between 0 and 15 years old from our analysed tax population makes no difference. In fact, the tax

---

[74] For some post-war years, Statistics Sweden used a different lowest age cut-off in its reported age-income distributions than 16. During 1957–66 it was 17 and during 1971–7 it was 18. We interpolate the shares of our (unobserved) 0–15 group based on the continuously observed 0–19 group. This bridging of the series appears to be of minor importance.

reform implemented changes which made almost all children with some bank holdings part of the tax population, so if we had made any such age adjustments we would have run into great difficulties. The figure shows that throughout the post-war period these youngsters had quite marginal incomes relative to the rest of the population, being about 0.1 per cent. Their share of the number of tax units in the tax population increased disproportionately, however, in 1978 and 1992. In 1978, new tax collection routines required employers to submit income statements (*kontrolluppgifter*) for all employees, which implied that a number of children working extra a few weeks during the summer holidays were included in the tax population. More importantly, after the tax reform in 1991 there was a drastic increase in the share of young income earners. This was directly related to new rules in the reform which stated that capital income over SEK 100 was made taxable. As a consequence, almost one million children, roughly one-ninth of the entire Swedish population, became tax units overnight.[75] In other words, by excluding the youngest income earners we avoid some unwarranted heterogeneity in the income earner shares caused by the tax reform of 1990–1.

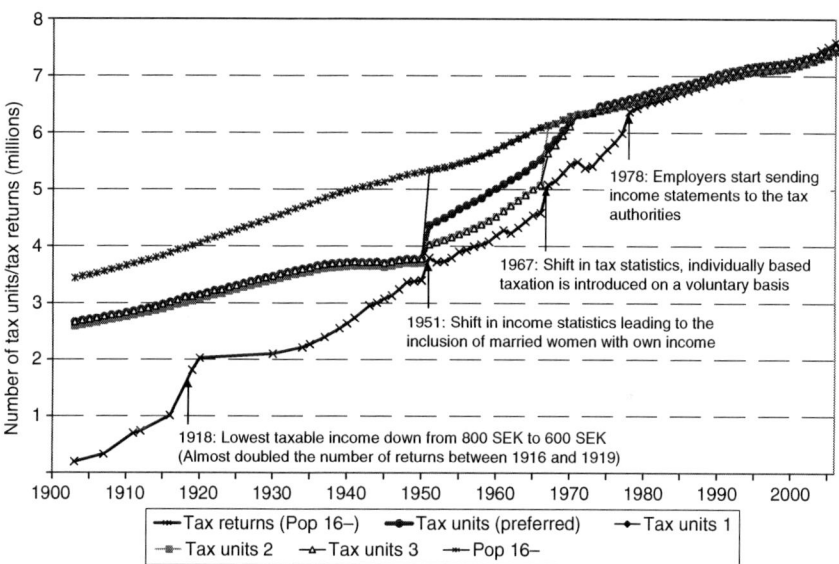

Figure 7C.1 Tax returns and alternative population totals in Sweden, 1903–2006

[75] Formally, the new rules were in practice already in 1991 but in that year's income statistics Statistics Sweden made an adjustment to exclude the new bulk of very young income earners. They excluded all income earners below 18 years of age with labour income less than SEK 12,000 (Statistics Sweden, *Inkomst- och skattestatistik 1991*, Be 20 SM 9301, p. 9).

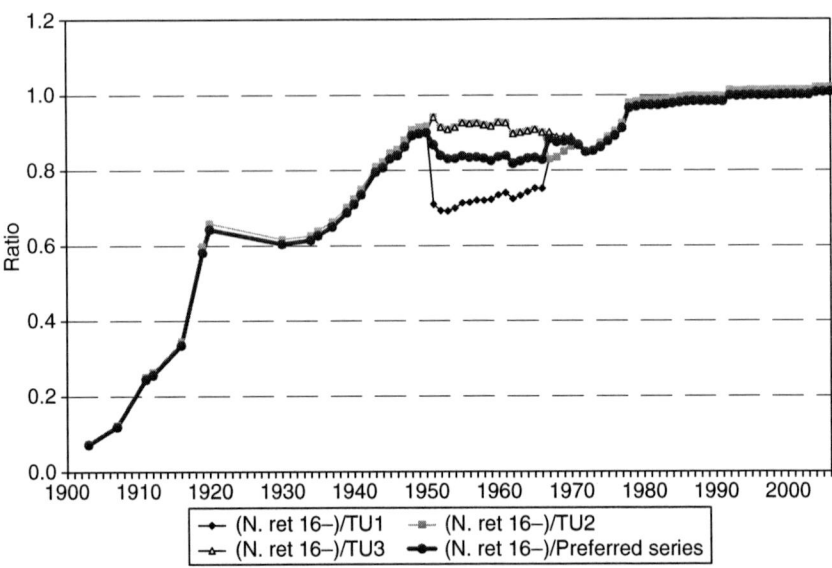

Figure 7C.2 Ratios between tax returns and alternative reference populations in Sweden, 1903–2006

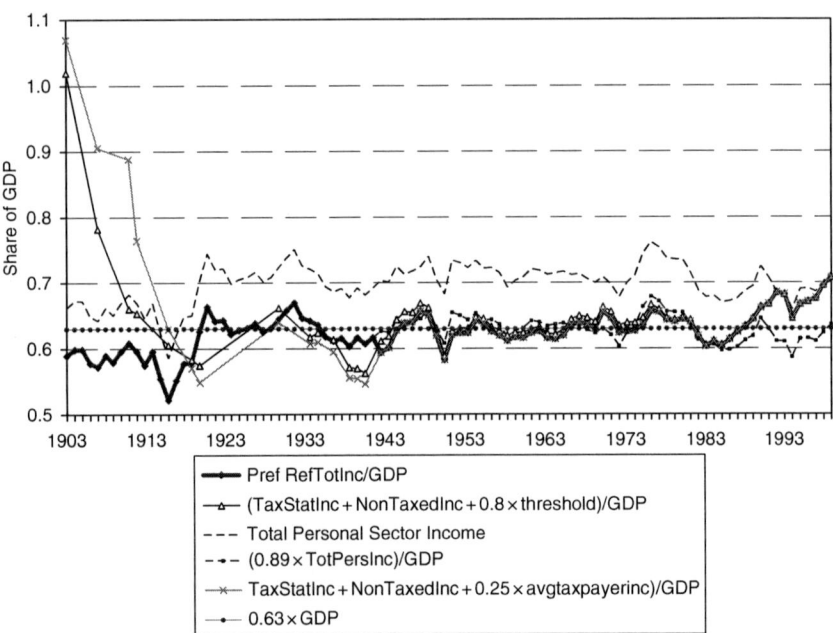

Figure 7C.3 Different reference totals for income as shares of GDP in Sweden, 1903–2004

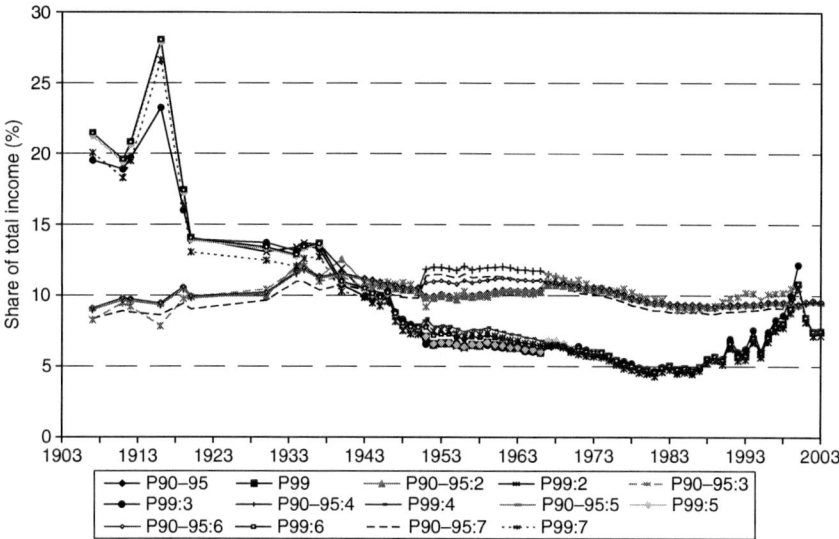

Figure 7C.4 P90–95 and P99 series in Sweden using different reference totals

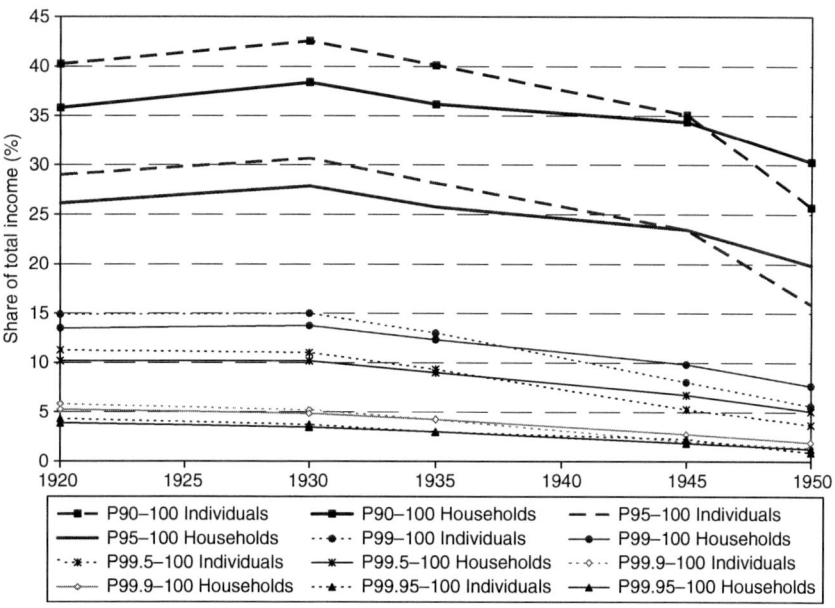

Figure 7C.5 Sensitivity of census-based top income shares in Sweden when switching tax unit definitions between individual and household

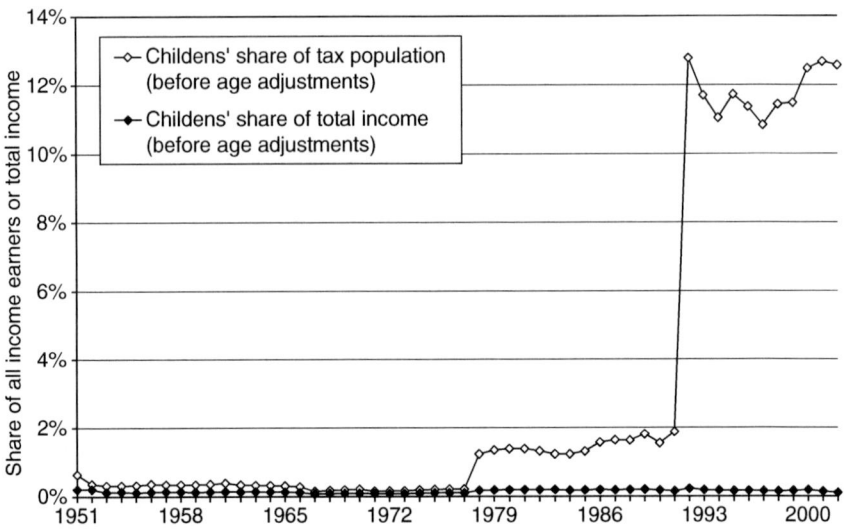

Figure 7C.6 Shares of population and total income of children under 16 years old in Sweden, 1951–2003

Table 7C.1 Reference totals for tax units and income in Sweden, 1903–2006

Year	Total tax units N (1)	Tax returns N (2)	Share (col. 2/1) % (3)	Income excl. capital gains		Income incl. capital gains	
				Total income Sum (TSEK) (4)	Ave. (col. 4/1) (5)	Total income Sum (TSEK) (8)	Ave. (col. 8/1) (9)
1903	2,659,911	191,515	7.2	1,389,293	522	1,406,589	529
1904	2,687,207			1,441,809	537	1,459,759	543
1905	2,706,379			1,483,502	548	1,501,971	555
1906	2,727,842			1,601,276	587	1,621,211	594
1907	2,756,634	328,992	11.9	1,743,376	632	1,765,080	640
1908	2,784,634			1,782,905	640	1,805,101	648
1909	2,799,518			1,755,932	627	1,777,792	635
1910	2,830,113			1,943,329	687	1,967,523	695
1911	2,856,711	700,954	24.5	2,013,619	705	2,038,688	714
1912	2,888,302	741,919	25.7	2,100,446	727	2,126,596	736
1913	2,908,770			2,222,844	764	2,250,518	774
1914	2,941,668			2,310,515	785	2,339,280	795
1915	2,976,466			2,482,713	834	2,513,622	844
1916	3,011,266	1,010,963	33.6	2,940,643	977	2,977,253	989
1917	3,051,956			3,623,331	1,187	3,668,441	1,202
1918	3,104,099			5,044,212	1,625	5,107,011	1,645
1919	3,117,303	1,813,876	58.2	6,298,162	2,020	6,376,572	2,046
1920	3,146,313	2,024,462	64.3	7,547,072	2,399	7,641,031	2,429
1921	3,178,804			6,159,471	1,938	6,236,155	1,962
1922	3,217,520			5,177,282	1,609	5,241,738	1,629
1923	3,233,086			4,953,887	1,532	5,015,562	1,551
1924	3,277,477			4,958,474	1,513	5,020,205	1,532
1925	3,310,033			5,101,173	1,541	5,164,681	1,560

(continued)

Table 7C.1 Continued

Year	Total tax units N (1)	Tax returns N (2)	Share (col. 2/1) % (3)	Income excl. capital gains — Total income Sum (TSEK) (4)	Ave. (col. 4/1) (5)	Income incl. capital gains — Total income Sum (TSEK) (8)	Ave. (col. 8/1) (9)
1926	3,344,617			5,237,633	1,566	5,302,840	1,585
1927	3,382,095			5,345,823	1,581	5,412,377	1,600
1928	3,411,417			5,420,466	1,589	5,487,949	1,609
1929	3,443,967			5,737,820	1,666	5,809,254	1,687
1930	3,471,440	2,100,000	60.5	5,900,304	1,700	5,973,761	1,721
1931	3,509,250			5,667,049	1,615	5,737,602	1,635
1932	3,540,812			5,395,869	1,524	5,463,046	1,543
1933	3,569,615			5,328,643	1,493	5,394,983	1,511
1934	3,596,654	2,213,000	61.5	5,725,887	1,592	5,797,172	1,612
1935	3,616,987	2,269,000	62.7	6,105,505	1,688	6,181,516	1,709
1936	3,659,455			6,327,644	1,729	6,406,421	1,751
1937	3,679,432	2,394,000	65.1	6,855,515	1,863	6,940,864	1,886
1938	3,691,394			7,255,456	1,966	7,345,784	1,990
1939	3,701,699	2,547,000	68.8	7,809,324	2,110	7,906,548	2,136
1940	3,712,732	2,637,000	71.0	8,512,235	2,293	8,618,210	2,321
1941	3,721,269	2,737,000	73.6	9,422,040	2,532	9,539,342	2,563
1942	3,713,351			10,520,534	2,833	10,651,511	2,868
1943	3,715,298	2,955,890	79.6	11,065,749	2,978	11,202,683	3,015
1944	3,720,658	3,003,973	80.7	11,709,195	3,147	11,854,193	3,186
1945	3,701,136	3,074,993	83.1	12,602,660	3,405	12,758,863	3,447
1946	3,727,199	3,131,168	84.0	14,591,812	3,915	14,753,058	3,958
1947	3,751,937	3,240,670	86.4	16,166,881	4,309	16,323,556	4,351
1948	3,770,950	3,367,806	89.3	18,014,723	4,777	18,165,108	4,817
1949	3,769,391	3,384,834	89.8	18,645,789	4,947	18,775,907	4,981
1950	3,777,033	3,401,393	90.1	19,563,440	5,180	19,673,224	5,209
1951	4,363,129	3,791,083	86.9	22,885,687	5,245	22,982,724	5,267
1952	4,413,809	3,721,611	84.3	26,577,977	6,022	26,690,383	6,047

Year							
1953	4,458,901	3,732,619	83.7	27,467,838	6,160	27,583,831	6,186
1954	4,514,116	3,795,327	84.1	29,242,354	6,478	29,365,586	6,505
1955	4,582,359	3,899,843	85.1	32,291,992	7,047	32,428,330	7,077
1956	4,644,564	3,934,072	84.7	34,888,533	7,512	35,035,633	7,543
1957	4,712,198	3,995,344	84.8	36,502,787	7,746	36,656,476	7,779
1958	4,789,073	4,029,342	84.1	38,167,789	7,970	38,328,210	8,003
1959	4,872,546	4,081,406	83.8	40,123,929	8,235	40,292,302	8,269
1960	4,959,080	4,190,155	84.5	44,245,603	8,922	44,430,805	8,959
1961	5,059,839	4,277,753	84.5	48,185,654	9,523	48,386,952	9,563
1962	5,152,249	4,229,111	82.1	53,165,500	10,319	53,387,066	10,362
1963	5,243,201	4,326,942	82.5	57,858,292	11,035	58,099,461	11,081
1964	5,341,505	4,431,848	83.0	63,604,263	11,908	63,868,889	11,957
1965	5,440,809	4,541,358	83.5	69,980,068	12,862	70,270,741	12,915
1966	5,529,968	4,579,902	82.8	76,798,500	13,888	77,117,129	13,945
1967	5,750,422	5,086,784	88.5	85,122,755	14,803	85,460,455	14,862
1968	5,876,561	5,148,562	87.6	90,676,471	15,430	91,003,771	15,486
1969	6,036,078	5,299,008	87.8	97,923,883	16,223	98,345,983	16,293
1970	6,194,967	5,441,976	87.8	108,654,568	17,539	109,060,268	17,605
1971	6,320,018	5,487,290	86.8	118,419,028	18,737	118,727,677	18,786
1972	6,333,098	5,377,931	84.9	128,282,502	20,256	128,660,770	20,316
1973	6,350,879	5,412,041	85.2	137,286,578	21,617	137,786,877	21,696
1974	6,464,266	5,574,282	86.2	157,524,389	24,368	158,216,541	24,476
1975	6,496,063	5,705,452	87.8	183,188,876	28,200	184,073,602	28,336
1976	6,526,143	5,826,869	89.3	207,853,848	31,849	208,966,808	32,020
1977	6,559,497	5,990,972	91.3	232,215,863	35,401	233,385,873	35,580
1978	6,592,278	6,372,054	96.7	259,385,859	39,347	260,946,683	39,584
1979	6,629,136	6,431,194	97.0	284,682,262	42,944	286,079,081	43,155
1980	6,670,790	6,494,749	97.4	318,496,317	47,745	319,844,679	47,947
1981	6,705,740	6,531,845	97.4	348,888,051	52,028	350,612,945	52,285
1982	6,740,072	6,565,341	97.4	377,085,887	55,947	379,852,901	56,357
1983	6,773,449	6,609,388	97.6	407,703,146	60,191	412,040,798	60,832
1984	6,803,684	6,657,145	97.8	445,966,952	65,548	449,501,558	66,067
1985	6,830,258	6,701,312	98.1	488,718,732	71,552	492,943,601	72,171
1986	6,856,978	6,742,286	98.3	529,142,905	77,169	534,778,674	77,990
1987	6,893,476	6,787,936	98.5	579,733,510	84,099	587,878,378	85,280
1988	6,936,033	6,826,256	98.4	630,089,899	90,843	647,227,486	93,314

(continued)

Table 7C.1 Continued

| | | | | Income excl. capital gains | | | Income incl. capital gains | | |
	Total tax units N (1)	Tax returns N (2)	Share (col. 2/1) % (3)	Total income Sum (TSEK) (4)	Ave. (col. 4/1) (5)		Total income Sum (TSEK) (8)	Ave. (col. 8/1) (9)
Year									
1989	6,984,652	6,874,984	98.4	700,291,628	100,261		722,610,112	103,457
1990	7,030,954	6,923,689	98.5	784,428,517	111,568		805,695,957	114,593
1991	7,060,631	7,087,528	100.4	856,232,513	121,269		893,271,977	126,514
1992	7,081,441	7,107,925	100.4	880,700,744	124,367		895,409,092	126,444
1993	7,109,685	7,139,138	100.4	912,094,785	128,289		926,303,618	130,288
1994	7,144,570	7,178,295	100.5	951,108,791	133,123		983,645,820	137,677
1995	7,163,497	7,201,488	100.5	990,246,452	138,235		1,006,748,895	140,539
1996	7,177,410	7,217,214	100.6	1,034,366,816	144,114		1,071,513,690	149,290
1997	7,187,081	7,232,695	100.6	1,076,806,119	149,825		1,130,844,902	157,344
1998	7,200,331	7,248,321	100.7	1,126,508,147	156,452		1,186,654,380	164,806
1999	7,215,231	7,262,257	100.7	1,188,708,879	164,750		1,286,073,700	178,244
2000	7,239,597	7,287,016	100.7	1,253,659,417	173,167		1,378,939,984	190,472
2001	7,273,123	7,321,060	100.7	1,312,767,595	180,496		1,371,991,000	188,638
2002	7,311,797	7,362,419	100.7	1,362,756,329	186,378		1,403,278,014	191,920
2003	7,350,260	7,405,489	100.8	1,414,031,516	192,378		1,459,078,346	198,507
2004	7,395,545	7,454,633	100.8	1,458,857,002	197,262		1,517,305,205	205,165
2005	7,448,581	7,513,754	100.9	1,515,189,510	203,420		1,606,753,012	215,713
2006	7,525,396	7,595,286	100.9	1,588,210,209	211,047		1,714,402,902	227,816

Total income has been adjusted so that it includes social benefits (unemployment insurance, sick-leave pay, etc which are taxable incomes after 1974) for the whole period.
Tax returns as share of total tax units exceed 100% after 1990 since that year's tax reform led to non-resident Swedes filing taxes in case they had some capital income. Setting a cap at 100% has a negligible effect on the reported shares (about 0.4%).

REFERENCES

Apel, M. (1994). 'An Expenditure-Based Study of Tax Evasion in Sweden', Tax Reform Evaluation Report No. 1. Stockholm: National Institute of Economic Research.

Atkinson, A. B. (1975). *The Economics of Inequality*. London: Oxford University Press.

—— (2004). 'Top Incomes in the UK over the Twentieth Century', *Journal of the Royal Statistical Society A*, 168: 325–43.

—— (2005a). 'Income Distribution and Structural Change in the Dual Economy', in S. Lahiri and P. Maiti (eds.) *Economic Theory in a Changing World: Policymaking for Growth*. New Delhi: Oxford University Press.

—— (2005b). 'Comparing the Distribution of Top Incomes across Countries', *Journal of the European Economic Association*, 3: 393–401.

—— and A. Leigh (2004). 'Understanding the Distribution of Top Incomes in Anglo-Saxon Countries over the Twentieth Century', Working Paper, Nuffield College, Oxford.

—— —— (2007a). 'The Distribution of Top Incomes in Australia', in Atkinson and Piketty (2007).

—— —— (2007b). 'The Distribution of Top Incomes in New Zealand', in Atkinson and Piketty (2007).

—— and Thomas Piketty (eds.) (2007). *Top Incomes over the Twentieth Century: A Contrast between European and English-Speaking Countries*. Oxford: Oxford University Press.

—— and W. Salverda (2005). 'Top Incomes in the Netherlands and the United Kingdom over the Twentieth Century', *Journal of the European Economic Association*, 3: 883–913.

Beije, R. (1946). *Medéns börshandbok, 1945–1946*. Stockholm: Medéns förlag.

Bentzel, R. (1953). *Inkomstfördelningen i Sverige*. Uppsala: Almqvist & Wiksell.

Björklund, A. and R. B. Freeman (2006). 'Generating Equality and Eliminating Poverty, the Swedish Way', in R. B. Freeman, R. Topel, and B. Swedenborg (eds.) *Reforming the Welfare State: Recovery and Beyond in Sweden*. Stockholm: SNS förlag.

—— and M. Palme (2000). 'The Evolution of Income Inequality during the Rise of the Swedish Welfare State 1951 to 1973', *Nordic Journal of Political Economy*, 26: 115–28.

—— —— and I. Svensson (1995). 'Tax Reforms and Income Distribution: An Assessment Using Different Income Concepts', *Swedish Economic Policy Review*, 2: 229–66.

Dell, F. (2005). 'Top Incomes in Germany and Switzerland over the Twentieth Century', *Journal of the European Economic Association*, 3: 412–21.

—— (2007). 'Top Incomes in Germany throughout the Twentieth Century', in Atkinson and Piketty (2007).

—— T. Piketty, and E. Saez (2007). 'Income and Wealth Concentration in Switzerland of the 20th Century', in Atkinson and Piketty (2007).

Dew-Becker, I. and R. J. Gordon (2005). 'Where did the Productivity Growth Go? Inflation Dynamics and the Distribution of Income', *Brookings Papers on Economic Activity*, 2: 67–150.

Domeij, D. and P. Klein (2002). 'Public Pensions: To What Extent Do They Account for Swedish Wealth Inequality?', *Review of Economic Dynamics*, 5: 503–34.

Edvinsson, R. (2005). *Growth, Accumulation, Crisis: With New Macroeconomic Data for Sweden, 1800–2000*. Stockholm: Almqvist & Wiksell International.

Esping-Andersen, G. (1990). *The Three Worlds of Welfare Capitalism*. Cambridge: Polity Press.

Flodström, I. (1906). *Redogörelse för statistisk utredning i och för utarbetande af förslag till förändrade bestämmelser dels angående bevillning af fast egendom dels ock om inkomstskatt*. Stockholm: Ministry of Finance.

Flodström, I. (1909). *Taxeringen till inkomstskatt år 1907 samt taxeringen till bevillning s. å. för inkomst under 1,000 kronor af kapital och arbete.* Stockholm: Ministry of Finance.

—— (1914). *Taxeringen till inkomst- och förmögenhetsskatt år 1912.* Stockholm: Ministry of Finance.

—— (1915). *Taxeringen till inkomst- och förmögenhetsskatt år 1913 jämte uppgifter om däri ingående förmögenhetsdelar.* Stockholm: Ministry of Finance.

Gottschalk, P. and T. M. Smeeding (1997). 'Empirical Evidence on Income Inequality in Industrialized Countries', in A. B. Atkinson and F. Bourgignon (eds.) *The Handbook of Income Distribution.* London: North Holland Press.

Gustafsson, B. and M. Johansson (2003). 'Steps Toward Equality: How and Why Income Inequality in Urban Sweden Changed during the Period 1925–1958', *European Review of Economic History,* 7: 191–211.

Hagstroem, K. G. (1944). 'Inkomstutjämningen i Sverige', *Skandinaviska Bankens Kvartalstidsskrift,* April: 35–40.

—— (1949). 'Inkomstinflation och inkomstnivellering i Sverige', *Skandinaviska Bankens Kvartalstidsskrift,* April: 39–41.

Henrekson, M. and U. Jakobsson (2005). 'The Swedish Model of Corporate Ownership and Control in Transition', in H. Huizinga and L. Jonung (eds.) *Who Will Own Europe? The Internationalisation of Asset Ownership in Europe.* Cambridge: Cambridge University Press.

Klevmarken, N. A. (2004). 'On the Wealth Dynamics of Swedish Families, 1984–98', *Review of Income and Wealth,* 50: 469–91.

Kuznets, S. (1953). *Shares of Upper Income Groups in Income and Savings.* New York: National Bureau of Economic Research.

—— (1955). 'Economic Growth and Economic Inequality', *American Economic Review,* 45: 1–28.

Lindbeck, A. (1997). 'The Swedish Experiment', *Journal of Economic Literature,* 25: 1273–319.

—— (2006). 'The Welfare State: Background, Achievements, Problems', *Palgrave Dictionary of Economics.* London: Palgrave Macmillan.

Lindert, P. H. (2000). 'Three Centuries of Inequality in Britain and America', in A. B. Atkinson and F. Bourguignon (eds.) *Handbook of Income Distribution,* vol. i. Amsterdam: North-Holland.

Lindstrand, M. (1949). *Inkomstfördelningen före och efter kriget.* Meddelande från Konjunkturinstitutet, Ser B:10. Stockholm.

Löfqvist, R. (1991). 'Tax Avoidance, Dividend Signaling and Shareholder Taxation in an Open Economy', Department of Economics, Uppsala University, Economic Studies 55.

Lydall, H. (1968). *The Structure of Earnings.* Oxford: Clarendon Press.

Magnusson, K. (2004). 'Utvecklingen av de högsta inkomsterna i Sverige, 1985–2002', *TCO granskar,* 13/04.

Malmer, H. and A. Persson (1994). 'Skattereformens effekter på skattesystemets driftskostnader, skatteplanering och skattefusk', in H. Malmer, A. Persson, and Å. Tengblad (eds.) *Århundradets skattereform.* Stockholm: Fritzes.

Meade, J. E. (1964). *Efficiency, Equality, and the Ownership of Property.* London: Allen & Unwin.

Moriguchi, C. and E. Saez (2008). 'The Evolution of Income Concentration in Japan, 1885–2002: Evidence from Income Tax Statistics', *Review of Economics and Statistics,* 90(4): 713–34.

Morrisson, C. (2000). 'Historical Perspectives on Income Distribution: The Case of Europe', in A. B. Atkinson and F. Bourguignon (eds.) *Handbook of Income Distribution,* vol. i. Amsterdam: North-Holland.

Nolan, B. (2007). 'Long Term Trends in Top Income Shares in Ireland', in Atkinson and Piketty (2007).

Nordisk familjebok (1910). Stockholm: Uggleupplagan.

Östlind, A. (1945). *Svensk samhällsekonomi 1914–1922: Med särskild hänsyn till industri, banker och penningväsen.* Stockholm: Svenska bankföreningen.

Piketty, T. (2001a). *Les Hauts Revenus en France au 20ème siècle.* Paris: Grasset.

—— (2001b). 'Income Inequality in France, 1900–98', CEPR Discussion Paper No. 2876.

—— (2003). 'Income Inequality in France, 1900–1998', *Journal of Political Economy,* 111: 1004–42.

—— and E. Saez (2003). 'Income Inequality in the United States, 1913–1998', *Quarterly Journal of Economics,* 118: 1–39.

—— —— (2006). 'The Evolution of Top Incomes: A Historical and International Perspective', *American Economic Review, Papers and Proceedings,* 96: 200–5.

Quensel, C.-E. (1944). *Inkomstfördelning och skattetryck.* Lund: Sveriges industriförbund.

Roine, J. and D. Waldenström (2008). 'The Evolution of Top Incomes in an Egalitarian Society: Sweden, 1903–2004', *Journal of Public Economics,* 9(1–2): 366–87.

—— —— (2009). 'Wealth Concentration over the Path of Development: Sweden, 1873–2006' (forthcoming), *Scandinavian Journal of Economics.*

Saez, E. (2004). 'Reported Incomes and Marginal Tax Rates, 1960–2000: Evidence and Policy Implications', in J. Poterba (ed.) *Tax Policy and the Economy* 18. Cambridge, Mass.: MIT Press.

—— and M. L. Veall (2005). 'The Evolution of High Incomes in Canada, 1920–2000', *American Economic Review,* 95: 831–49.

Sierminska, E., A. Brandolini, and T. M. Smeeding (2006). 'The Luxembourg Wealth Study: A Cross-Country Comparable Database for Household Wealth Research', *Journal of Economic Inequality,* 4: 375–83.

Söderberg, H. (1996). *Inkomstskattens utveckling under 1900-talet. En vägvisare för skatteberäkningar åren 1921–1996.* Skattebetalarnas förening. Stockholm.

Söderberg, J. (1991). 'Wage Differentials in Sweden, 1725–1950', in Y. S. Brenner, H. Kaelble, and M. Thomas (eds.) *Income Distribution in Historical Perspective.* Cambridge: Cambridge University Press.

SOU (1936). *Undersökningar rörande det samlade skattetrycket i Sverige och utlandet.* SOU 1936:18. Stockholm: Ministry of Finance.

—— (1949). *Betänkande angåendebeskattning av realisationsvinster, m.m. samt ackumulerade inkomster.* SOU 1949:9. Stockholm: Isaac Marcus.

—— (1951). *Betänkande angående den statliga direkta beskattningen.* SOU 1951:51. Stockholm: K. L. Beckmans.

—— (1975). *Beskattning av realisationsvinster: Betänkande avgivet av Realisationsskattekommittén.* SOU 1975:53. Stockholm: Liber.

—— (1986). *Reavinst, aktier och obligationer: Slutbetänkande av kapitalvinstkommittén.* SOU 1986:37. Stockholm: Gotab.

Spånt, R. (1979). *Den svenska inkomstfördelningens utveckling 1920–1976.* Background material to Långtidsutredningen 1979:4, Ds E 1979:4.

Statistics Sweden (1921). *Taxeringen till inkomst- och förmögenhetsskatt år 1917.* Stockholm: Ivar Häggströms AB.

—— (1923). *Taxeringen till inkomst- och förmögenhetsskatt år 1920.* Stockholm: Ivar Häggströms AB.

Statistics Sweden (1927). *Folkräkningen den 31 december 1920. V. Yrkesräkningen, 2: yrke, inkomst och förmögenhet kombinerade inbördes samt med kön, civilstånd och ålder.* Stockholm: P. A. Norstedt & Söner.

—— (1929). *Statistical Yearbook.* Stockholm.

—— (1937). *Folkräkningen den 31 december 1930. VII. Folkmängden efter yrke, inkomst och förmögenhet: 2 avd.* Stockholm: P. A. Norstedt & Söner.

—— (1938). *Folkräkningen den 31 december 1930. VIII. Folkmängden efter yrke, inkomst och förmögenhet: 3 avd.* Stockholm: P. A. Norstedt & Söner.

—— (1940). *Särskilda folkräkningen 1935/36. VIII. Partiella folkräkningen i mars 1936: Yrke. Yrkesväxling. Skol- och yrkesutbildning. Inkomst och förmögenhet.* Stockholm: P. A. Norstedt & Söner.

—— (1951). *Folkräkningen den 31 december 1945. VIII:1. Partiella undersökningar (bottensamplingen). Behandlar delar av statistiken över inkomst.* Sveriges Officiella Statistik: Folkmängden och dess förändringar. Stockholm: K. L. Beckmans Boktryckeri.

—— (1956). *Folkräkningen den 31 december 1950. VII. Urvalsundersökningar. Statistiken över inkomst.* Sveriges Officiella Statistik: Folkmängden och dess förändringar. Stockholm: Statistiska Centralbyrån.

—— (1964). *Skattetaxeringarna samt fördelningen av inkomst och förmögenhet taxeringsåret 1963.* Stockholm: Statistics Sweden.

—— (1973). *Inkomst och förmögenhet.* Stockholm: Statistics Sweden.

—— (1975). *Inkomst och förmögenhet.* Stockholm: Statistics Sweden.

—— (2001). *Reavinster och reaförluster 1999*, Rapport 2001. Statistics Sweden: Programmet för ekonomisk välfärdsstatistik.

—— (2002). *Rekordåret 2000. Reavinster och reaförluster. Förmögenhet*, Rapport 2002. Statistics Sweden: Programmet för ekonomisk välfärdsstatistik.

—— (2003). *Minskade vinster 2001. Kapitalvinster och kapitalförluster. Förmögenhet*, Rapport 2003. Statistics Sweden: Programmet för ekonomisk välfärdsstatistik.

Svensk Sparbankstidskrift (1934), 825.

Swedish National Tax Board (2004). *Skattestatistisk årsbok 2004.* Stockholm: Fritze.

8

Trends in Top Income Shares in Finland

M. Jäntti, M. Riihelä, R. Sullström, and M. Tuomala

8.1 INTRODUCTION

This chapter provides new evidence about the evolution of top incomes in Finland based both on tabulated income tax data for 1920–2003 and on micro-data over the period 1966–2004. The chapter shows how the proportion of income earned by the very richest 1 per cent has changed over time. We find a U-shaped pattern of the income share of top 1 per cent over the period from the beginning of 1960 to 2004. The results bring out clearly how the major equalization from the beginning of 1960 to the mid 1990s has been reversed, taking the shares of top income groups back to levels of inequality or even higher found over forty years ago.

There are a number of different ways of measuring inequality. Each provides a different kind of summary of the difference between the poor and the rich. The most commonly used summary measure of inequality is the Gini coefficient. The rapid growth in income inequality over the latter part of the 1990s in Finland is the most important feature of the changes in the Gini coefficient over the last forty years. Figure 8.1 shows that over the 1960s and 1970s the Gini coefficient declined, then remained almost constant until the turning point in the beginning of the 1990s. The rise in the Gini coefficient that started around the mid 1990s accelerated over the latter part of the 1990s. The increase has been the fastest income inequality growth in the modern Finnish economic history. These developments of the past ten or fifteen years have to be viewed in the light of the longer-run evolution of the income distribution in Finland.

The aim of this chapter is to document trends in income inequality in Finland over the period 1920–2004. We look more closely at changes in inequality by considering how income changes at the upper end of the income distribution have driven the rising movement in the Gini coefficient. In particular, we look at the share of total income held by groups at the upper ends of the distribution. This chapter also focuses on how far our income tax system has been responsible for changes in top income shares over the last ten years. How far are changes in top income shares a reflection of the rearrangement of income? How far are they associated with changes in redistribution of the tax system?

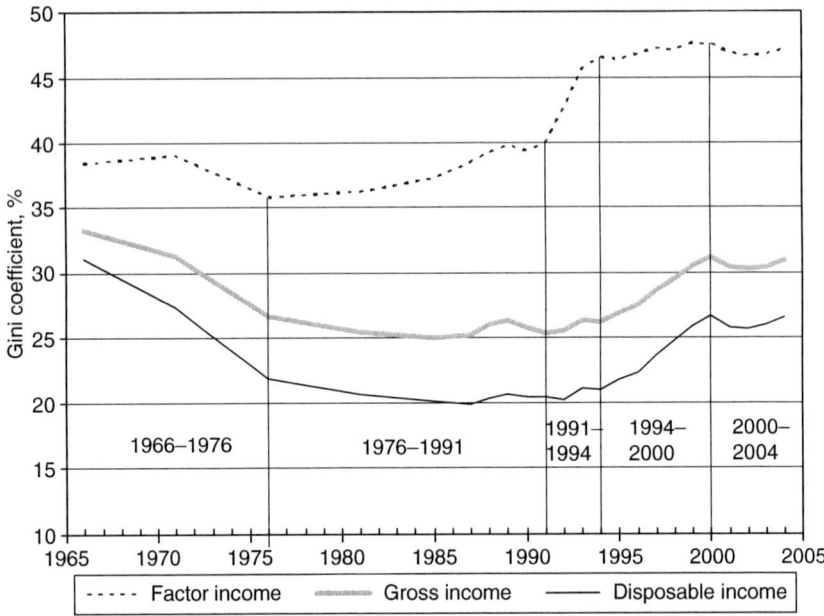

Figure 8.1 Gini coefficients in Finland, 1966–2004
Sources: Based on IDS data in 1987–2004 and HES data in 1966–85, Statistics Finland.

There has been among economists and other social scientists a recent upsurge of interest in advanced countries at the top of the income and wealth distribution. Recent studies, starting with Piketty (2003) for France, have used income tax statistics to examine long-run trends in top incomes in various countries—notably Atkinson (2002) for the UK, Atkinson and Salverda (2003) for the Netherlands, Piketty and Saez (2003) for the USA, Saez and Veall (2003) for Canada. Our estimated top shares in turn come both from tax data over the period 1920–2003 and from microeconomic surveys on income and expenditure from 1966 to 2004.

The structure of the chapter is as follows. Section 8.2 describes the data used in this study. Section 8.3 reports evidence on changes in income levels, its distribution, and top incomes 1920–2003. Section 8.4 summarizes the evidence about the top of the income distribution that can be derived from micro-data over the period 1966–2004, with a subsection devoted to summarizing changes in the composition of incomes, possible explanations of the observed changes in the distribution, and a subsection showing the impact of income tax system. In section 8.5, we discuss the role of income mobility. Section 8.6 concludes.

8.2 DATA AND METHODS

Tabulated Income Data from Tax Tables, 1920–2003

In this section, we describe the sources for the long series in income distribution starting in 1920 (see Table 8A.8). We focus on the definition of income, the tax system, and the compilation of the tables. Since the data cover a considerable period of time, we emphasize changes in the methods across time.

The data stem from Statistics of Income and Property, a publication series by Statistics Finland that started with the advent of the first modern law on income and wealth taxation in 1920 (Statistics Finland 1920–2003). Statistics of Income and Property contain on a semi-annual basis grouped data on the distribution of taxable income. The use of these in producing time series should be viewed with some caution. The statistics cover only those incomes and those units subject to taxation that the current laws stipulate. Changes in tax laws are likely to lead to changes in income distribution thus measured.

We present two sets of time series on income distribution after 1920, namely (a) *taxable income among the population of tax units* for 1920–92 and (b) *income subject to taxation among all adults* for 1949–2003. The sources from 1920 onward give *taxable income of taxed tax units*, from which we get the distribution among the population of tax units by augmenting the series with an estimate of the total number of tax units. 'Taxable income' consists of 'income subject to taxation' less income deductions. We thus have two time series of income distributions, defined with respect to the rules governing central government ('state') taxation at the time the data are gathered. The definition of what income is subject to *municipal taxation* and what deductions are allowed differs from central government taxation and varies across the years.

Definition of Income

The concept of income, both as defined and as included in the publications, has undergone substantial changes across the years. In 1920, only income that was taxed was reported in the published tables. Starting in 1949, the published tables included both the sum of all income sources and taxed income. This was further refined in 1969 when the modern concept of income subject to taxation was introduced (we have transformed data prior to that year to conform to this notion). *Income subject to taxation* is distinct from *taxable income*, the part of the income that is actually taxed. The difference consists of different exemptions. These include the basic deduction, i.e. the threshold at which tax units start paying taxes, and various other deductions, some for social reasons such as having dependent children.

The definition of income subject to taxation has undergone some change over time. In principle, the income concept includes all form of money income that accrues to the household during the tax year (which coincides with the calendar year throughout the period), except for some social transfers and a few other items. The concept includes in principle:

- labour income, consisting of wages and salaries fringe benefits, including lodging
- earnings-related pension income and other income
- agricultural and forest income
- self-employment income
- property income
- social transfer income (in part and during part of the period).

Major changes over the years are listed in Table 8.1. The overall tendency is for income subject to taxation to become more inclusive over time, in part by having

Table 8.1 Major changes to definition of income and taxation in Finland

1920	Inheritance and gifts exempted
	Income from abroad taxed in Finland
1924	Agricultural income assessments defined and standardized
1935	An additional tax of 20% on the tax amount on persons over 24 years old with no guardian obligations
1937–1942	An additional tax of 20% on the tax amount for defence purposes
1950	Bank deposits and their interest exempt from taxes
1957	Additional taxes on high incomes introduced
1958	Additional taxes on high incomes abolished
1964	An additional tax of 20% on the tax amount on income and sailor's tax introduced
1968	Changes in the assessment of property income, lower threshold considerably increased
1969	New law on taxation of assets from trade and profession, income and losses could be periodized over several years
1975	A forest premium was introduced
	The taxation of income and property was made more uniform
1976	Two separate progressive scales ('A' and 'B') abolished and a new single scale introduced
1980	The scale for property income lowered
1983	National pensions (base and addition) no longer exempted from income subject to taxation
1985	Other income sources brought within taxation: unemployment benefits, support for home care of children, social assistance for entrepreneurs, aid to students, sick pay, maternity allowance
1986	Sailors' income taxes as other persons'
1987	Other income source brought within taxation: pension and basic daily sick allowance, student aid to adults, certain other daily allowances and payments
1989	Fringe benefits and capital gains subject to taxation
	Agricultural income reformed, area subsidies subject to taxation
1992	Student aid to university students subject to taxation
	Strike pay subject to taxation
1993	Major reform of property income; capital gains taxed at same rate as other property income, imputed rents from owner-occupied housing exempted
1996	The property income tax rate raised from 25 to 28%

previously untaxed sources become subject to taxation and in part by new types of income becoming included when they become available. As some income sources in any given year are not included in the published tables, income levels in the statistics are too low. An important case in point is the national old-age pension, which was included in income subject to taxation in 1983. Some social transfers, such as child and housing allowances, are still not taxable. Other incomes exempted from taxation are scholarships and some pensions. For example pensions for war veterans are not subject to taxation. Even some types of factor income are not included in taxable income over most of the period, the main one being interest paid on deposit accounts.

The way in which a given income source is assessed for tax purposes has also changed across time. An important example prior to the Second World War is agricultural and forest income, which is widely believed to have been assessed at very low values. In part this is due to the low degree of monetization in the 1920s, in part because fringe benefits (which were hard to value) were a major part of agricultural labour income. The assessment of agricultural income underwent a substantial change in 1969 which increased the tax assessments of those incomes. Another case whose tax assessments may at times depart substantially from their true values is property, whose tax values tend always to be much lower than the market value but where this difference can vary quite substantially across time.

Deductions

The number of, reasons for, and amounts of tax deductions have changed a lot across the years. The following highlights some of these changes that are of particular distributional interest.

Prior to 1924, the tax law was not very specific about deductions except for the basic tax threshold. That year the tax code was amended to clarify a number of details. If both spouses were working, half of the income of the one earning less was deductible up to a limit of FIM 8,000. Income earners with dependent children (less than 15) could deduct FIM 2,500 per child. The deduction for dependent children has been subject to a very large number of changes across the years. For instance, from 1951 onwards, the deduction for the second and later children was doubled in size.

Other income exemptions for social reasons have been introduced. In 1956, an old-age deduction was enacted to apply at first for those aged 67 and older, and later extended to apply to those 65 and older. In 1957, the dependent child exemption was extended to unmarried persons (with children, of course). Another important deduction, the deduction for a spouse, has undergone many changes over the years, especially when separate taxation of married couples' income was introduced. In 1975, the spouse deduction could only be applied if the couple had children and it was abolished in 1989.

Exemptions and deductions based on household characteristics are by no means the only ones that applied. From 1926, tax units in areas determined to have high living costs were allowed to make deductions. Starting in 1947, interest income from some types of deposit accounts and bonds were exempted from taxable income. Starting in 1956, 15 per cent of all dividend income was exempted from taxation.

Other exemptions further include a so-called 'per cent deduction', which from 1957 allowed all persons with incomes from labour, property, agriculture, and/or forestry to make a 10 per cent deduction from taxes. This was later increased to 15 per cent for those with incomes below FIM 1,000,000.[1] From 1969, losses due to the practice of trade and profession could be deducted, and from 1975 also interest paid on some debts could be subtracted from income subject to taxation.

Many exemptions were abolished in 1989 as part of a major overhaul of tax laws. Those exemptions include exemptions due to having children in education, lone-parent exemptions, and a property tax deduction for entrepreneurs.

Tax Units

One major issue with the published data is that in the longest series, on tax units, the unit has undergone several changes. Finland introduced separate taxation of married couples in 1935. At that point, the data also take as the tax unit the person rather than the couple. Separate taxation was abolished in 1943, at which point the data revert to the use of couples as the unit. Separate taxation was reintroduced in 1976. Thus, married couples are treated as one tax unit from 1920 to 1934, as two units from 1935 to 1942 during the first period of separate taxation, and as one from 1943 to 1975, after which separate taxation was reintroduced.

However, in the tables of income subject to taxation per income recipient, married persons are counted individually from 1952 onwards. Joint taxation is only taken into account for taxable income per tax unit. On the other hand, tables for professional categories reported the incomes and taxes for men and women separately as early as in 1926.

Between 1947 and 1975, private persons can in the tables be either physical persons, persons who are jointly taxed, or undivided estates. Persons who are jointly taxed are so because they are jointly self-employed, such as those who jointly operate a farm. These should be distinguished from jointly taxed married spouses. The concept (i.e. jointly taxed) was introduced in 1921, and until 1947 such units were defined as belonging to the group corporations. After 1975, jointly taxed persons are no longer a single taxable unit and undivided estates are in turn defined as corporations.

Before 1949, only those whose taxable income exceeded the threshold for paying taxes were tabulated. At that time, all income earners who filed tax

[1] From 1963, the Finnish markka equalled 100 old markka and the old markka became penni. From 1999, the Finnish currency was linked to the euro, and from 2002 the markka and penni were replaced by the euro.

declarations were included in the published tables, except for those with only property income below the taxable threshold—they were included in the published tables in 1961. One consequence of not having untaxed units in the tables at all prior to 1949 is that variations in the rate of inflation generate substantial variation in the number of units taxed. When inflation is high, the tax schedules tend to creep up, making more units subject to taxation.

It is important to bear in mind, especially when considering the distribution in the whole population, that part of those with very low incomes worked only part time and especially during only part of the year. For instance, students who work only during the summer vacation tend to earn some income subject to taxation but typically not enough to pay taxes. The level of income inequality recorded is for this and other reasons substantially higher than when incomes are pooled within households, as is typically done in micro-data-based studies.

Other Changes in Statistics

Until 1945, almost the entire population liable to taxation is included in the material used for tabulations. That year, because of the increase in the number of units taxed, the tables were constructed on the basis of a statistical sample. Sampling was used until 1969 when the use of computers made it possible to return to tabulating the full population. This did not apply to the jointly taxed and undivided estates, as these were not included in the register, so these groups were sampled until 1975. At that time, as mentioned above, the jointly taxed ceased to be a single taxable unit and undivided real estates were defined to be corporations.

The sample was drawn in different ways, listed in Table 8.2, across the years. Note that during the period when a sample-based survey was made, spouses were jointly taxed and therefore considered as one unit. Tax return forms were used as the primary material before computerized registers became available. As to control the material, tax rolls were used. In 1969, a computerized register, based on the tax authority records, was taken into use.

The Population

An important complication is that for the data on taxable income among tax units, the total number of tax units is unknown. The distribution is truncated, as we only know the number of tax units whose income exceeds the lower limit of taxable income. The tax unit before the introduction of separate taxation in 1935 (and after it was abolished in 1943) was the family and each income earner during separate taxation. There are no census counts or survey information on the total number of families—which presumably could be used with the number of single persons to approximate the population of tax units—before the war. In principle,

Table 8.2 Changes in the construction of income statistics in Finland

1945	Helsinki was treated differently from rest of Finland. 20% of all private persons from Helsinki were in the sample. The rest of the sample was made by choosing some towns and districts in Finland as representatively as possible. 20% of the population outside Helsinki was included in the sample.
1947	
Income > 500,000 mk	all persons (under one percent of the whole population) included
Income < 500,000 mk	every tenth person included
1952	
Income > 900,000 mk	all persons included
300,000 mk–899,999 mk	every tenth person included
Income < 300,000 mk	every twentieth person included
1960	
Income > 2,000,000 mk	all persons included
800,000 mk–1,999,000 mk	every fifth person included
400,000 mk–799,000 mk	every tenth person included
1,000 mk–1,999,000 mk	every twentieth person included
1963	
Income > 29,999 mk	all persons (note the monetary reform in 1961)
10,000 mk–29,999 mk	every fifth person included
5,000 mk–9,999 mk	every tenth person included (applies to all persons with sailors' income)
1,000 mk–4,999 mk	every twentieth person included

it should be possible to approximate this population by taking the adult (defined, currently, as those 15 years and older) population and subtracting from it the number of married women. This, indeed, is what we resort to when estimating the statistics for the full population of tax units.

Summary

The changes to the published tables that underlie the series are large and whether or not they capture a real time series is open to debate. Many of the changes cannot be dealt with by adjustments of any sort. The one issue that is looked into below concerns changes in the proportion of the population that is covered by the tables. That is, different ways are used to try to look into the distribution of income among the whole adult population.

Estimation

The data used in this chapter are tabulations of *taxable income among taxed tax units* or *income subject to taxation among those declaring incomes*. The latter will for all practical purposes be treated as the whole population. In both cases, we know the class limits, the distribution of income-receiving units across those classes, as well as mean income within the class. There are three broad approaches to estimating income distribution functionals from grouped data. First, it is possible to estimate various income distribution functionals directly on the basis of the grouped data. Such an approach allows us to estimate for each year of data such things as means and variances, inequality indices, and even more detailed objects, such as Lorenz curves, albeit at a fairly coarse level. One can also think of the estimation first in terms of how to represent and estimate the distribution function for the data. A second approach is to estimate the distribution function non-parametrically, use that estimate to generate income quantiles. Third, given a suitable parametric distribution function, one can estimate the parameters and generate all functionals on the basis of those estimates. Each of these approaches is associated with advantages and disadvantages. In this chapter, we follow standard practice in the study of top incomes and use the grouped data approach (Atkinson 2007).

The simplest option to using the grouped data is to let the distribution be represented by the step function (Klugman, Panjer, and Willmot 1998):

$$F_n(x) = \frac{(b_j - x)F_n(a_j) + (x - a_j)F_n(b_j)}{b_j - a_j}, \ x \in [a_j, b_j), \ j = 0, 1, \dots, J, \quad (1)$$

with $F_n(x) = 0$, $x < a_0$ and $F_n(x) = 1$, $x > b_J$.

However, we have one additional piece of information to what is included above, namely the within-group average incomes. We therefore follow Cowell and Mehta (1982) and split each class into two pieces at the class mean, the so-called 'split histogram' approach. The split histogram takes a point in the interval $[a_j, b_j]$ and splits the distribution function in two at that point. As we use the class means, we force the histogram to pass through these points. The distribution function then becomes

$$F_n(x) = \begin{cases} \frac{(\bar{x}-x)F_n(a_j)+(x-a_j)F_n(\bar{x}_j)}{\bar{x}_j-a_j} & x \in (a_j, \bar{x}_j) \\ \frac{(b_j-x)F_n(a_j)+(x-\bar{x}_j)F_n(b_j)}{b_j-\bar{x}_j} & x \in (\bar{x}_j, b_j)j = 0, 1, \dots, J, \end{cases} \quad (2)$$

where $F_n(x) = 0$, $x < a_0$ and $F_n(x) = 1$, $x > b_j$ and where the value of the distribution function at $\bar{x}_j$ is

$$F_n(\bar{x}_j) = \frac{\bar{x}_j - a_j}{b_j - a_j}F(a_j) + \frac{b_j - \bar{x}_j}{b_j - a_j}F(b_j) \quad (3)$$

Using the split histogram approach gives a distribution function that consists of $2(J + 1)$ linear segments and is a simple way to combine information on both the within-class means and the distribution of units across all classes.

When we are working with the distribution of taxable income, we only know the number of tax units that had income above the threshold for taxable income. That is, we do not in fact know the number of units in the lowest class nor do we know what their average income is, i.e. n_0 and $\overline{x_0}$ are unknown to us. It follows that the true total number of tax units as well as total income is unknown. Our estimate of the total number of tax units is the adult population (defined as those who are more than 20 years old) less the number of married women. The number of untaxed tax units n_0 is estimated to be the difference between this estimated total and the number of taxed tax units $\hat{n} - \sum_{j=1}^{J} n_j$. We take the class midpoint in the lowest interval as our estimate of within-class average income. Our estimate of total taxable income is the sum total of the published table plus the estimated income of all untaxed units, which equals the number of untaxed units times their class midpoint.

The top interval in all years is open. We impute the highest income to be the 99th percentile of a fitted Pareto distribution in the top income class, using the lower bound and the mean in the top class to estimate the Pareto coefficient.

1966–2004 from Micro-Data

We use the Income Distribution Surveys (IDS) and Household Expenditure Surveys (HES) published by Statistics Finland. These surveys are representative national samples. The Household Survey is conducted for the purpose of computing the weights in consumer price index. We use HES sample data for 1966, 1971, 1976, 1981, and 1985. HES contain detailed information on households' incomes, expenditures, and characteristics. Personal income information of the Household Expenditure Surveys is collected from various registers, such as records of the tax boards and the social security administration. The IDS, from 1987 to 2004, in turn is a sample survey of around 9,000–12,000 households drawn from the private households in Finland (see Table 8A.10). The IDS contains information on personal incomes, taxes, and benefits together with various socio-economic characteristics of the Finnish households. Most of the information contained in the IDS has been collected from various administrative registers. Auxiliary information is collected through interviews. Each household is included in the sample for two consecutive years so that every year half of the total sample is based on a new panel. The following components of disposable income are used in this study:

  labour income (wages and salaries)
  + entrepreneurial income
  = earned income (primary income)
  + capital income (= dividends + interest income + rental income + imputed net rents of owner-occupied dwellings + realized capital gains)
  = factor income
  + current transfers received

= gross income
- current transfers paid (= state earned income tax + state capital income tax + property tax + other taxes + other current transfers paid incl. social security contributions)
= disposable income

Realized capital gains were only part taxable before the 1993 tax reform. Imputed rents of owner-occupied dwellings are not taxable. Therefore we checked the sensitivity of results to the exclusion of capital gains and imputed rents. All types of income used in this study concerning IDS and HES data are calculated on an annual basis. The OECD equivalence scale is used in order to make comparable income earners living in households with different size and composition.[2]

Indirect taxes, such as VAT and specific commodity taxes and the provision of public services, are not included in our data. This may have important consequences, because indirect taxes and public services tend to be regressive (see for example Sullström and Riihelä 1996; Suoniemi 1993; Jäntti 2004).

8.3 TRENDS IN TOP INCOMES: INCOME TAX TABLES 1920–2003

Changes in Real Income 1920–2003

We start by comparing the estimates from the tabulated data on taxable income and income subject to taxation to National Accounts data. There is, unfortunately, no consistent series of national income for the household sector that covers the period we are studying and even the gross domestic product (GDP) and gross national income (GNI) consistently cover only part of the period. The historical National Accounts series end in 1997. Panel A in Figure 8.2 shows the total income for the two series as a share of gross domestic product starting in 1920, and Panel B shows total income from the tax tables as a share of GNI starting in 1960, the first years of each National Accounts series. It is important to keep in mind that these National Accounts data are not limited to the household sector. While the National Accounts household sector covers some non-household units such as non-profit organizations, these data apply to the whole economy. This means that changes across time in total household taxed or taxable income relative to National Accounts aggregates reflect also changes in the sectoral distribution of income.[3]

---

[2] The OECD equivalence scale is calculated as follows. The first adult in each household has a weight of 1 and each additional adult a weight of 0.7. Each child under 18 years old gets a weight of 0.5.

[3] The United Nations Yearbooks of National Accounts provide estimates of the national income of the household sector starting in 1953, but not earlier. A comparison of the ratio of the tax data to those estimates yields qualitatively similar conclusions to those drawn here for the GDP comparison. The variability of the ratio is very large and largely coincides with the estimates shown here.

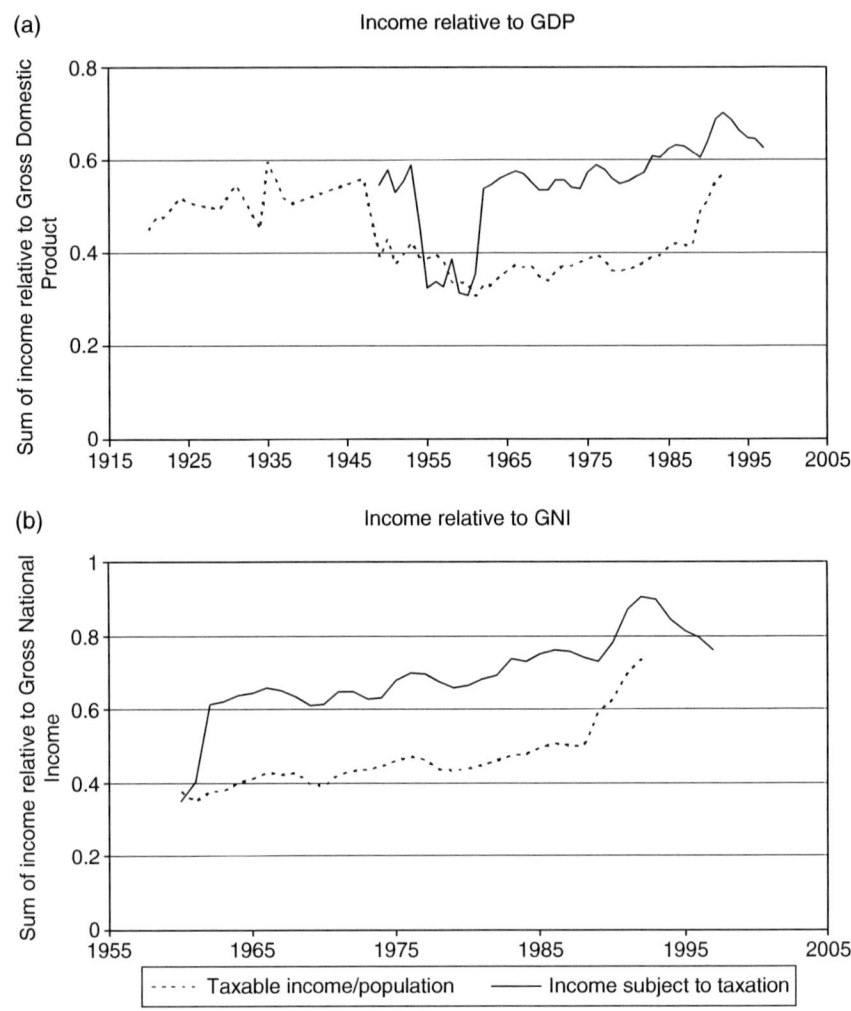

Figure 8.2 Total income from tables relative to national accounts aggregate in Finland

Taxable income was about 50 per cent of GDP between 1920 and 1939. Income subject to taxation drops suddenly in 1955 until 1962 by about 20 percentage points relative to GDP. It is not clear why this drop occurs and why it does not occur for taxable income. The late 1950s however were a very turbulent time in the Finnish economy and this divergence may be related to frequent industrial unrest (see, e.g., Jäntti, Saari, and Vartiainen 2006). After 1960, both Panels suggest total income increased as a share of GDP. The gap between total income subject to taxation and taxable income across tax units was quite substantial, being close to and above 20 per cent until the late 1980s when the gap became much narrower. Prior to 1960, the picture looks quite different.

The estimated proportion of tax units whose income is less than the minimum taxable amount, shown in Panel A of Figure 8.3, exhibits a sharp discontinuity around the time of the Second World War. In 1947, the first year after the Second World War, the threshold for taxable income had been lower so that virtually all tax units were brought into taxation and taxed income represented about 55 per cent of GDP. This large increase in the taxed population is driven both by the post-war resettlement of Karelian immigrants and by the need to finance both reconstruction and war reparations.

The proportion who were not taxed also varied considerably from year to year before the Second World War. Interestingly, the proportion that were not taxed increased substantially after the war, being around three-quarters of the population in 1960. After that the proportion of the population that was covered by taxes increased quite sharply. In 1992, the year our series on taxable income ends, about one in three tax units—at that point, persons—were not paying any taxes in state taxation (the threshold for municipal taxation tends to be lower, so many of these persons were probably paying municipal taxes). Panel B of Figure 8.3 shows how the real value of the threshold for taxable income and the proportion that is not taxed co-vary. The relationship is, as might be expected, steeply negative, but with large shifts from time to time.

Figure 8.4 compares the growth in GDP per capita (measured as the first differences in the ln of GDP per capita) with changes in estimated average income in each of the three series estimated from grouped data. The figure also shows a non-parametric smooth of the GDP per capita growth rate. While there are some quite substantial differences in the sets of series the correspondence is close enough to warrant some confidence. A notable exception is the period 1939–45, during which GDP per capita and personal income move in quite different directions. This is explained by the war economy, when much of GDP was diverted to military resources. For most of the period covered by the series, the income series follow changes in GDP per capita with a lag and perhaps a slightly smaller variability.

We show in Figures 8.5 and 8.6 the estimated average and median income for our two series. Taxable income among tax units is always higher than taxable income among the population (a gap which is of course sensitive to our assumption about mean income in the non-taxed part of the distribution). The growth rate in these two varies but is after the early 1960s reasonably stable. Income subject to taxation tracks taxed income among the population reasonably well and is of a similar magnitude. The difference between these two consists primarily of deductions, so one might expect them to be reasonably similar.

To conclude this discussion of changes in levels of real income and the relation of the tabulated income data to National Accounts aggregates, we note that deficiencies in the available data—in particular, the absence of reliable estimates of the total number of tax units, on the one hand, and the absence of household sector National Accounts aggregates, on the other—make it difficult to know

(a)

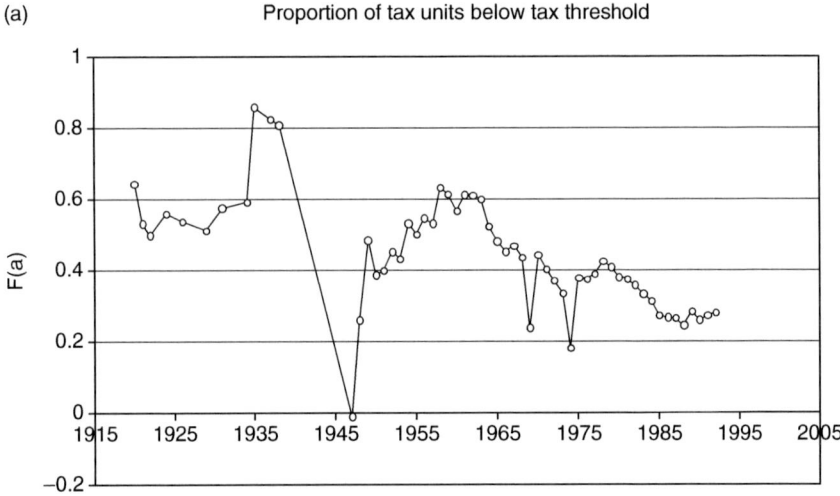

(b)

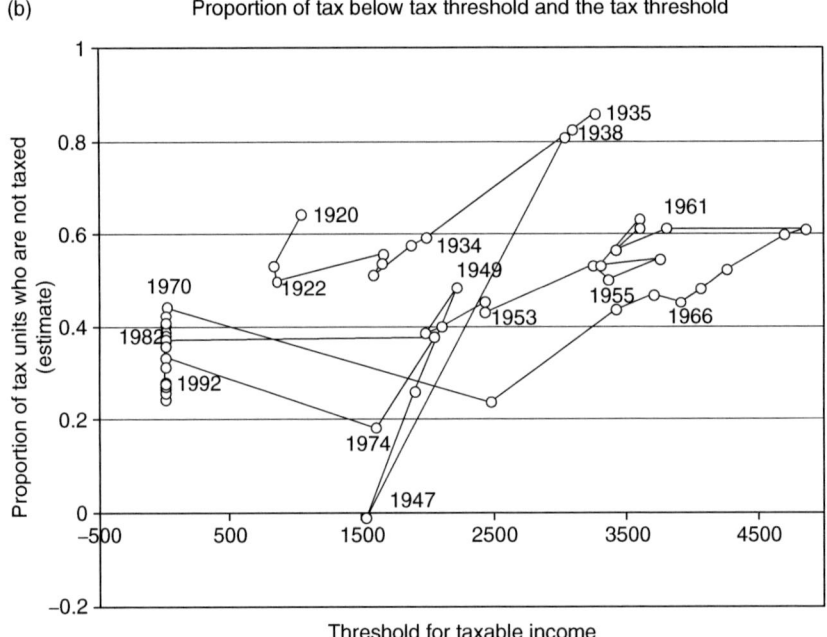

Figure 8.3 The estimated proportion of tax units not covered by tables for taxable income across time and the minimum threshold for taxation in Finland

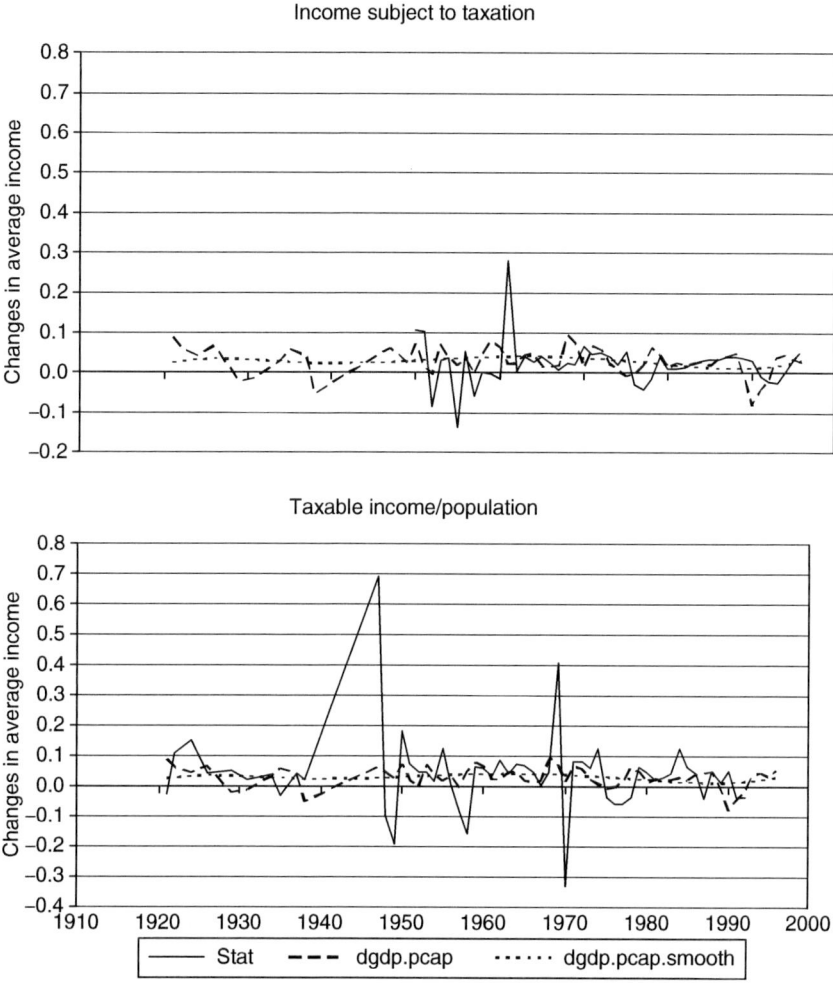

Figure 8.4 Growth in GDP per capita compared to growth in mean income in Finland

exactly how high quality our series are. The reasonable stability and similarity of series' mean and median income lend us confidence in the series.

Overall Inequality and Top Incomes

Figure 8.7 shows the Gini coefficients for our two series across time. The pattern across time in the Gini coefficients suggests roughly three phases in relative

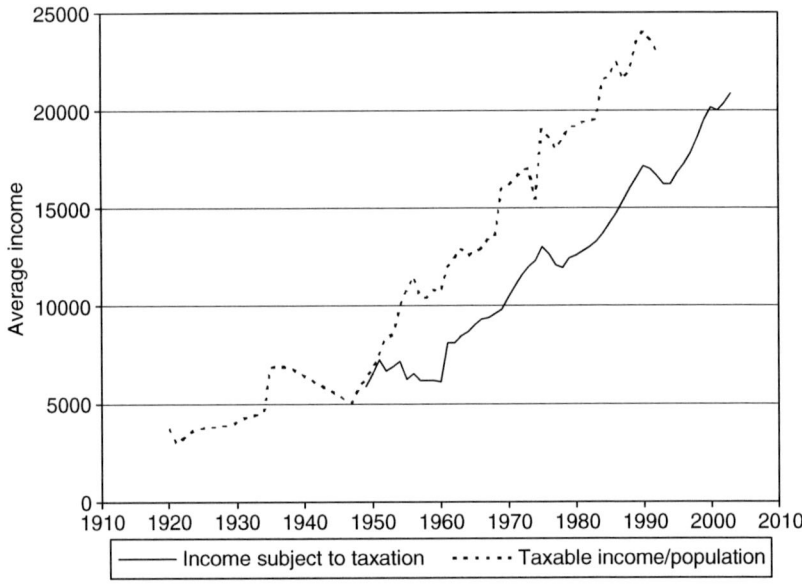

Figure 8.5 Average income: grouped data estimates in Finland

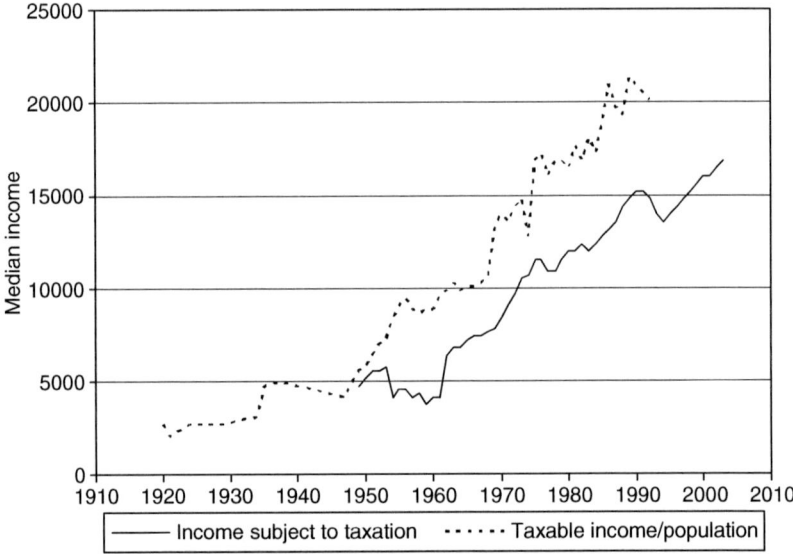

Figure 8.6 Median income: grouped data estimates in Finland

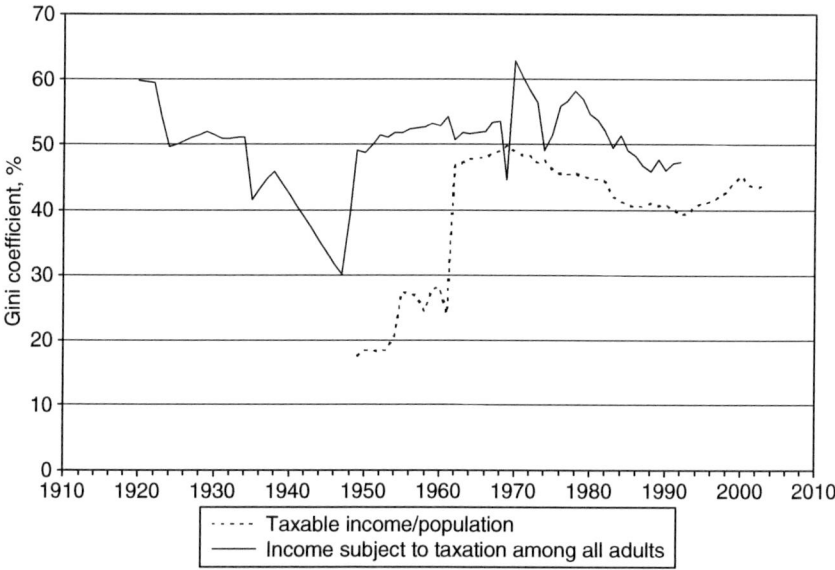

Figure 8.7 Gini coefficient: grouped data estimates in Finland

inequality (see also Table 8A.1). Before and just after the Second World War, inequality of taxed income among tax units and the population appears to have declined. After the late 1940s, inequality increased to levels experienced in the 1930s or above those. After the late 1960s, inequality started to decline until the early 1990s, after which it increased again. The level of the Gini coefficient of income subject to taxation is about the same level it was around 1980, which is substantially lower than the peak that was seen around 1960. Thus, relative inequality at the end of last century appears to be neither historically low nor historically high.

However, if we turn our attention to the top income groups, this conclusion appears premature. While the share of the top 5 per cent of earners of taxed income in the population—shown in Figure 8.8 and Table 8A.2—was more that 30 per cent in the early 1920s, it was about 15 per cent at its lowest around 1980. After this, the share (measured in income subject to taxation) increased quite rapidly and was in 2000 at least as high as in 1960, at around 20 per cent of total income. The share of the top 1 per cent of income earners—shown in Figure 8.9—also declined from around 15 per cent of taxed income among the population of tax units in 1920 to just over 6 per cent in the late 1940s to rapidly increase to about 10 per cent in the later 1950s. The top 1 per cent share then declines for almost thirty years until the early 1990s. The increase in this top share in the late 1990s is steep and brings it in 2000, when it peaked, to the same level as seen in the 1950s.

Figures 8.10 and 8.11 show the shares of the top 5 (1) per cent in the top 10 (5) per cent, respectively. These 'shares in shares' are not sensitive to having correct control totals of income. Both of the series suggest that the evolution of the

Figure 8.8 Share of top 5%: grouped data estimates in Finland

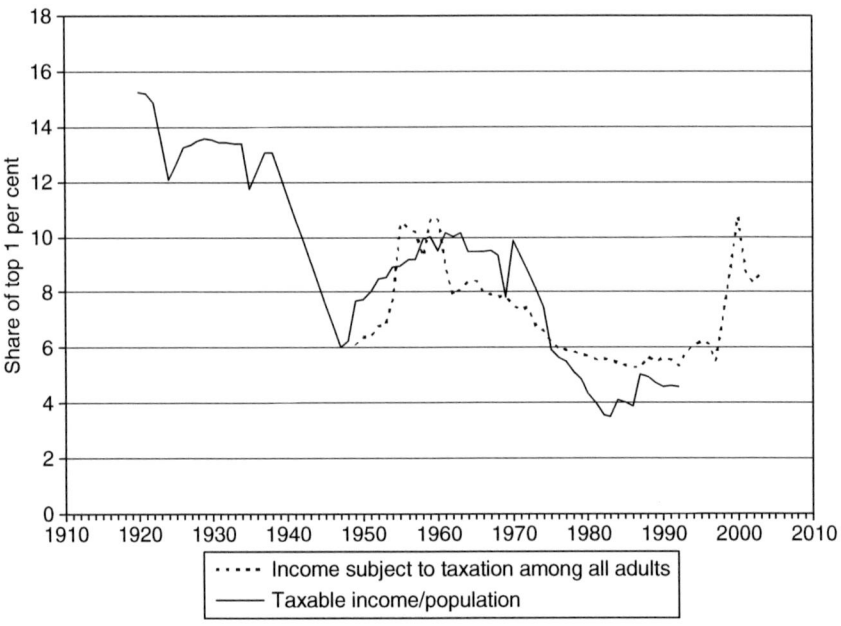

Figure 8.9 Share of top 1%: grouped data estimates in Finland

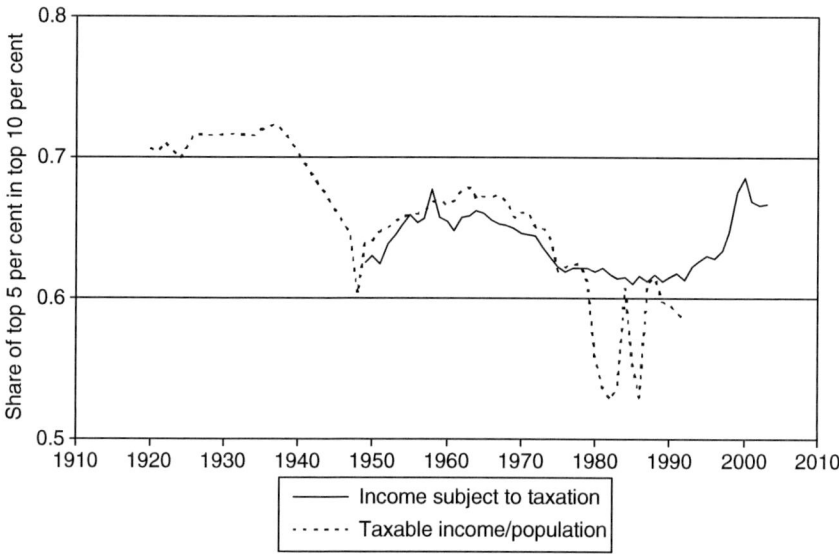

Figure 8.10 Share of top 5% in top 10% in Finland

Figure 8.11 Share of top 1% in top 5% in Finland

concentration of income at the top was relatively flat in the 1920s and 1930s, with about 70 per cent of the income in the top decile group going to the top 5 per cent and a little less than half of the total income of the top 5 per cent in turn accruing to the top 1 per cent. By 1949, concentration at the top had declined quite substantially. Roughly 62 and 34 per cent of the income of the top 10 and 5 per cent was received in that year by the top 5 and 1 per cent of those two groups, respectively. The concentration at the top increased after this to about the mid 1960s, when it starts to decline again. This slow decline in top income concentration is dramatically reversed in the late 1990s, when, for example, the share of the top 1 per cent in the top 5 per cent, for instance, increases by 13 percentage points from 35 per cent in 1996 to 48 per cent in 2000. Indeed, both shares in shares series suggest the increased concentration at the top in the late 1990s is by historical standards quite large.

Comparison with Other Countries

How does the concentration of income at the top of the distribution in Finland compare to that in other countries? As Atkinson and Piketty (2007) make clear in their discussion of the comparability of various countries' estimates, such comparisons need to be treated with caution. Indeed, as we saw in section 8.2 of this chapter, also the comparability of the estimates within countries need to be treated with care. It is, all the same, informative to compare Finnish estimates to those found in other countries, in particular the estimates gathered in Atkinson and Piketty (2007).

In 1920, the share of the top 1 per cent in Finland was about 15 per cent of total income. That share was higher in the Old World countries—the Netherlands had 21 per cent, 20 per cent in the United Kingdom, and 18 per cent in France. The Finnish share is higher, by contrast, than that in the New World countries—it was 15 per cent in the United States, 14 per cent in Canada, 12 per cent in Australia, and 11 per cent in New Zealand. By 1950, the top 1 per cent's share in all New World countries was higher than the 8 per cent share in Finland—in the United States and Canada it was 11 per cent, in Australia 14 per cent, and in New Zealand 9 per cent. By year 2000, the Finnish top 1 per cent's share is in the mid range of countries.

The share of the top 1 per cent in the top 5 per cent is relatively low in Finland, at 45 per cent in 1920. In the Netherlands this share in share is 57 per cent, the UK 62 per cent, France 57 per cent, the USA 53 per cent, and Australia 60 per cent. Only in Canada and New Zealand is it lower than in Finland, at 44 per cent. This contrasts with the year 2000, when Finland has one of the most highly concentrated top incomes measured in this way. The Finnish top 1 per cent's share of the top 5 per cent is in 2000 48 per cent and only in the USA (53 per cent) is it higher than this. The UK and Canada are close at 47 per cent, though.

It should, again, be emphasized that these country orderings may be quite sensitive to a large number of institutional and method differences. It is nonetheless instructive to note how country orderings of top income concentration can be sensitive to both the exact measure used and change across the years in perhaps unexpected ways.

8.4 TRENDS IN TOP INCOME SHARES: MICRO-DATA ESTIMATES FOR 1966–2004

General Trends in Top Income Shares, 1966–2004

In the latter part of the chapter we focus on micro-data. There are some advantages to using micro-data. We can use household as an income-receiving unit and adjust the income by an equivalence scale and then assign this value to each individual in the household. We can also now directly compute disposable income and tax rates from the data. The limitation of these data is that they are available for a much shorter period than tabulated income data from tax tables.

Figure 8.12 shows real average disposable income in different deciles and top 5 and 1 per cents in 1966–2004. Figure 8.13 in turn shows the rate of income growth at different points of the income distribution from 1990 to 2004. We see from Figure 8.13 that average income, as measured by the mean, increased by 29.7 per cent (2.1 per cent by when annualized). At the same time there were huge income gains at the very top. The top 1 per cent saw their real incomes roughly double over the less than ten-year period. Their incomes increased by 172.3 per cent over the period from 1990 to 2004 and 12.3 per cent on annualized basis. Hence a lion's share of that growth since the mid 1990s benefited those at the top of income distribution.

Table 8.3 and Figure 8.14 show the shares of the top incomes (0.1, 1, 5, and 10 per cents). These results are also striking. First, the share of the rich in total income is no longer trivial. As Table 8.3 and Figure 8.14 show, the top 1 per cent of the total income in our sample has taken an increasing share of total income since 1994, with sharp rise continuing over the latter part of the 1990s. In 2004 1 per cent of households—around the richest 50,000 people—receive 8.8 per cent of total factor income, compared with income shares of 4.4 per cent in 1990 and 3.9 per cent in 1981 (see Table 8.3). The top 1 per cent has 6.1 per cent of after-tax income (disposable income) in 2004. That share has doubled over the past fourteen years (2.9 per cent in 1990). That is a big shift to the top: as a matter of pure arithmetic, it must mean that the incomes of less-well-off individuals grew considerably more slowly than average income. And this just happened. Compared with the top 1 per cent group, the income shares of percentile groups within the rest of the 10 per cent have risen relatively modestly over the last ten years. The top 5 per cent have 10.4 per cent of total after-tax income in 1990. That share was 14.6 per cent in 2004. Hence most of the gains in the share of the top 10 per cent over last ten years were actually gains to the top 1 per cent, rather than the next 4 or 9 per cent. The share of income going to the top decile was

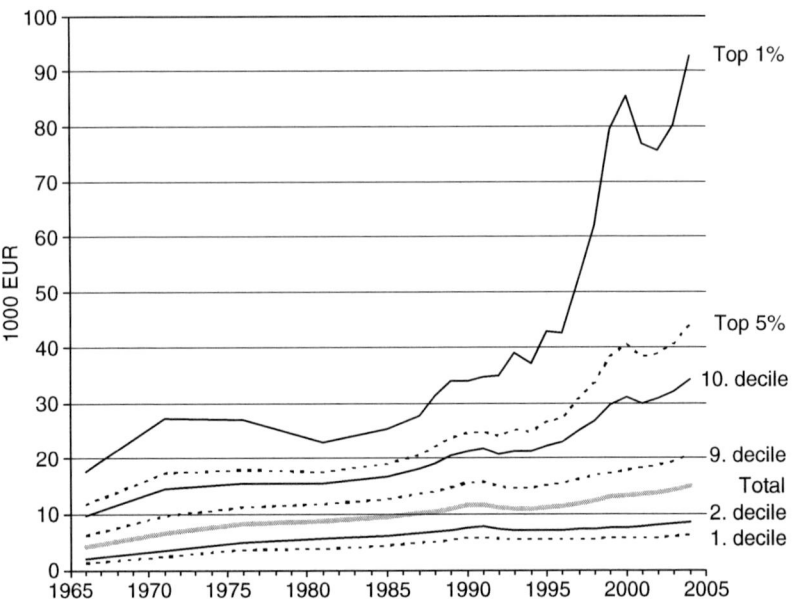

Figure 8.12 Real average disposable income, in deciles 1, 2, 9, and 10, total and in top 5% and 1% in Finland, 1966–2004

Source: Based on IDS data in 1987–2004 and HES data in 1966–85, Statistics Finland.

22.7 per cent, and it is now about as large as the share of the bottom 40 per cent of the population (24 per cent, see Table 8A.4).

As Figure 8.14 shows, top incomes shares display a U-shaped pattern over the period 1966–2004, with a drop during the period from 1966 to the beginning of the 1990s, followed by the sharp rise in the top shares until the beginning of the 2000s. Our series also shows that the level of inequality captured by the income shares of the rich is now much higher than in the mid 1990s.

One way to see how the gap between the rich and the median income is widening is to construct the ratio of top 1 per cent disposable income (evaluated at median and minimum) to median disposable income of the population. This is shown in Figure 8.15. This ratio also displays a U-shaped pattern. In the 1980s, the median income of the top 1 per cent was slightly less than three times as large as the median income of the population. In 2004, the ratio was almost five times.

Figure 8.16a displays the share of different income concepts (capital income, earnings, and disposable income) that goes to the top 1 per cent. For example, the uppermost curve shows that the 1 per cent of the population with the highest capital income received about 14 per cent of total capital income in 1971, about 20 per cent in the beginning of the 1990s, and 35 per cent in 2004. Figure 8.16a also shows that disposable income was more equally distributed than earnings

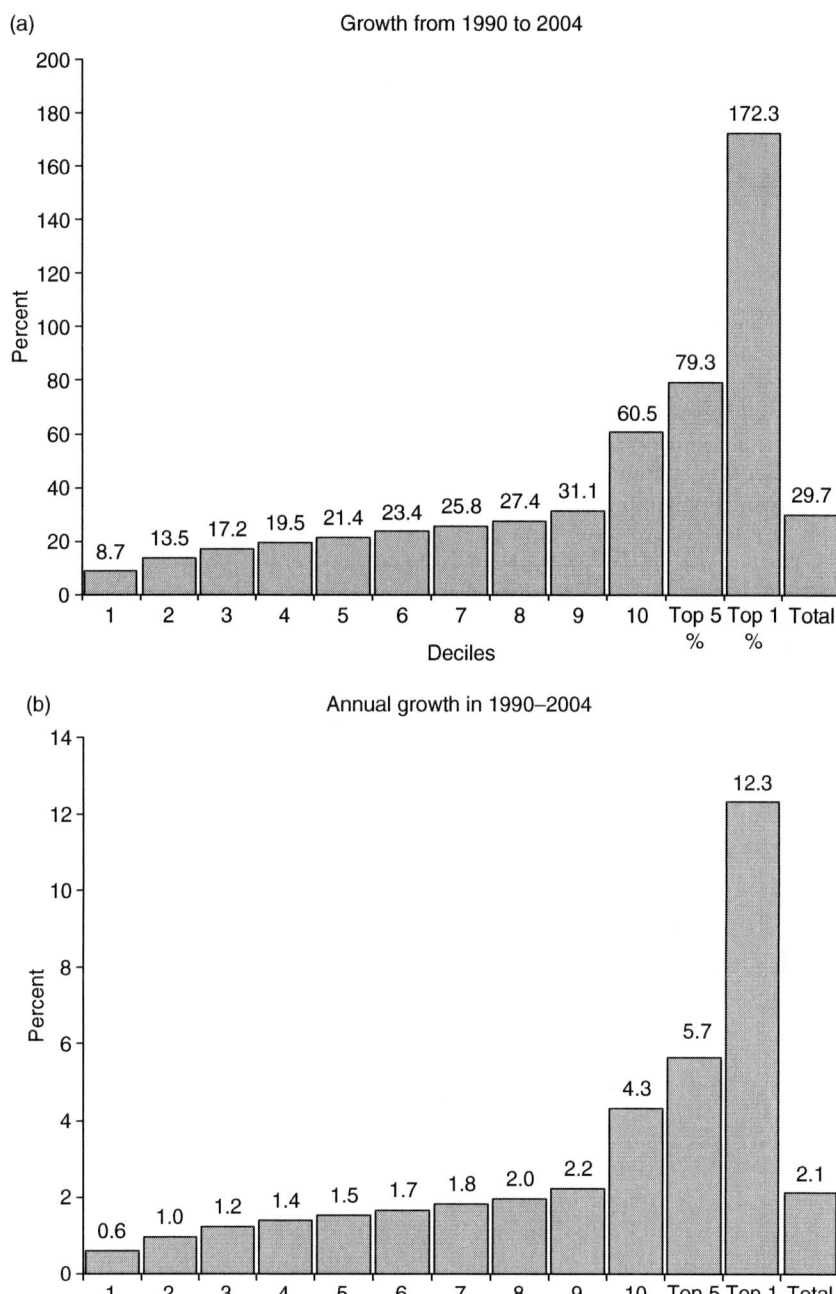

Figure 8.13 Real income growth by deciles, total and the top 5% and 1% in Finland

Source: Based on IDS data in 1990 and 2004, Statistics Finland.

Table 8.3 Top income shares (%) in Finland, 1966–2004

Year	Factor income					Gross income					Disposable income				
	50%	10%	5%	1%	0.10%	50%	10%	5%	1%	0.10%	50%	10%	5%	1%	0.10%
1966	76.54	26.79	16.40	4.98	0.91	72.89	25.06	15.26	4.57	0.83	71.42	23.70	14.23	4.27	0.76
1971	76.82	26.63	16.41	5.49	1.25	71.41	24.23	14.89	4.89	1.14	68.73	21.79	13.02	4.10	0.97
1976	74.93	23.69	14.16	4.42	1.08	68.44	21.15	12.67	3.95	0.93	65.22	18.74	10.91	3.27	0.82
1981	75.43	23.13	13.55	3.87	0.66	67.68	20.22	11.81	3.34	0.53	64.42	17.79	10.04	2.60	0.39
1985	76.17	23.67	13.76	3.75	0.60	67.36	20.33	11.84	3.31	0.53	63.97	17.85	10.09	2.71	0.38
1987	76.97	24.41	14.39	4.21	0.78	67.43	20.61	12.12	3.54	0.67	63.76	17.83	10.13	2.74	0.48
1988	77.42	25.11	14.99	4.53	0.84	67.85	21.31	12.73	3.87	0.74	64.04	18.32	10.56	3.00	0.52
1989	77.83	25.44	15.28	4.62	0.88	68.04	21.47	12.89	3.91	0.76	64.23	18.57	10.76	3.08	0.56
1990	77.58	25.21	14.95	4.48	0.85	67.73	21.08	12.50	3.72	0.68	64.11	18.44	10.62	2.95	0.48
1991	78.10	25.53	15.17	4.50	0.79	67.40	20.97	12.38	3.65	0.65	64.04	18.44	10.59	2.95	0.50
1992	80.05	26.83	16.08	4.73	0.79	67.51	21.20	12.66	3.77	0.66	63.86	18.53	10.77	3.11	0.58
1993	82.28	28.78	17.45	5.55	1.21	68.01	21.90	13.23	4.13	0.84	64.39	19.35	11.47	3.54	0.80
1994	82.97	28.96	17.40	5.26	1.03	67.85	21.82	13.01	3.88	0.70	64.27	19.31	11.35	3.39	0.64
1995	82.61	29.35	18.01	5.86	1.16	68.31	22.28	13.51	4.33	0.82	64.77	19.80	11.82	3.81	0.73
1996	83.10	29.33	17.91	5.70	0.99	68.81	22.43	13.63	4.29	0.64	65.20	19.93	11.92	3.73	0.60
1997	83.14	30.16	18.96	6.58	1.66	69.40	23.44	14.56	5.03	1.25	66.00	20.96	12.85	4.39	1.08
1998	82.80	30.45	19.44	7.35	2.22	69.93	24.02	15.16	5.68	1.63	66.64	21.60	13.47	4.98	1.52
1999	82.65	31.78	21.01	8.94	2.62	70.28	25.42	16.68	7.01	2.03	67.09	22.87	14.78	6.11	1.81
2000	82.64	31.84	21.24	9.13	3.34	70.73	25.76	17.00	7.23	2.62	67.58	23.37	15.23	6.48	2.31
2001	82.40	30.95	20.27	8.40	2.88	70.31	24.92	16.17	6.59	2.25	67.17	22.27	14.20	5.66	1.96
2002	82.09	30.98	20.26	8.29	2.44	70.18	24.94	16.15	6.47	1.88	67.12	22.28	14.06	5.49	1.53
2003	82.33	30.95	20.11	8.27	2.26	70.32	24.96	16.08	6.49	1.75	67.38	22.53	14.24	5.65	1.49
2004	82.42	31.21	20.59	8.98	3.43	70.59	25.26	16.53	7.08	2.65	67.64	22.83	14.68	6.17	2.42

Source: Based on IDS data in 1987–2004 and HES data in 1966–85, Statistics Finland.

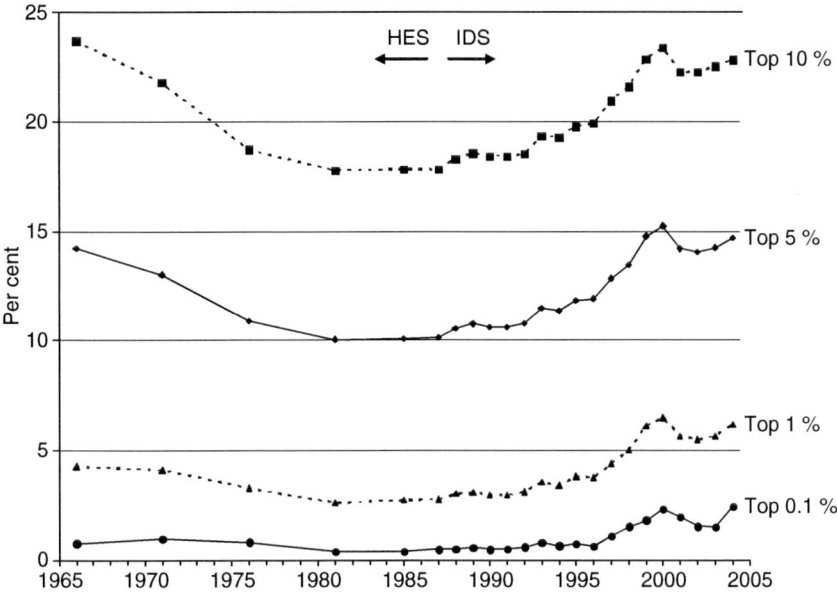

Figure 8.14 Top income shares in Finland, 1966–2004

Source: Based on IDs data in 1987–2004 and HES data in 1966–85, Statistics Finland.

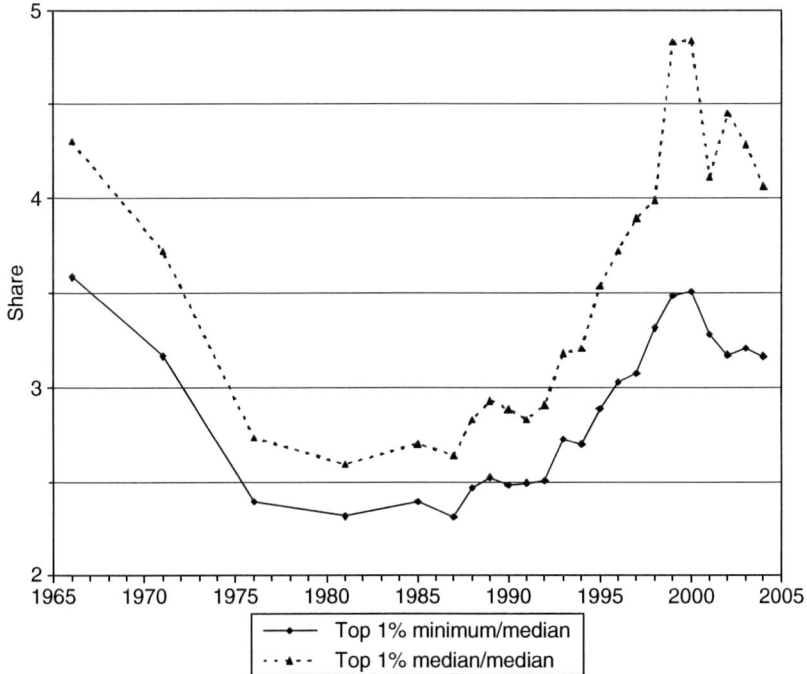

Figure 8.15 The ratio of top 1% disposable income (at median and minimum) to median disposable income in Finland, 1966–2004

Source: Based on IDS data in 1987–2004 and HES data in 1966–85, Statistics Finland.

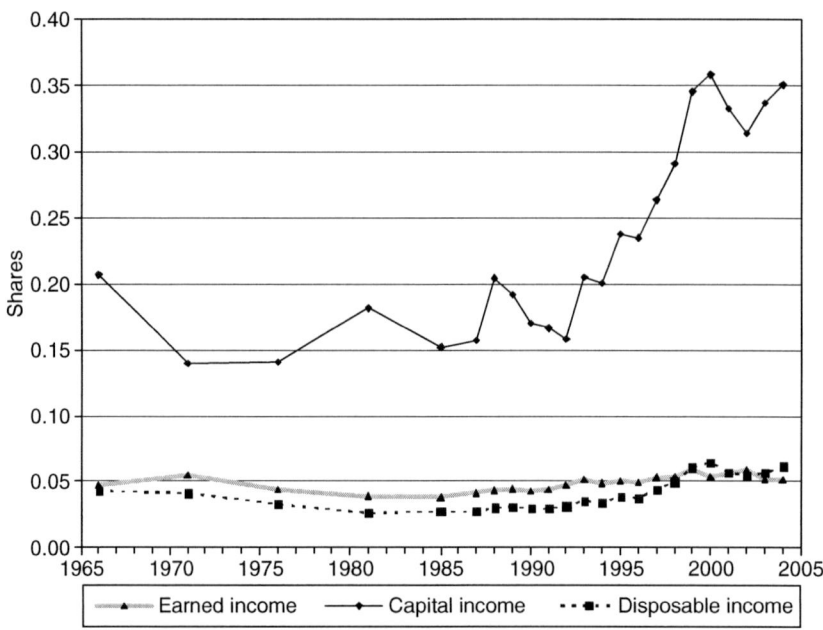

Figure 8.16a Top 1% shares in Finland, 1966–2004

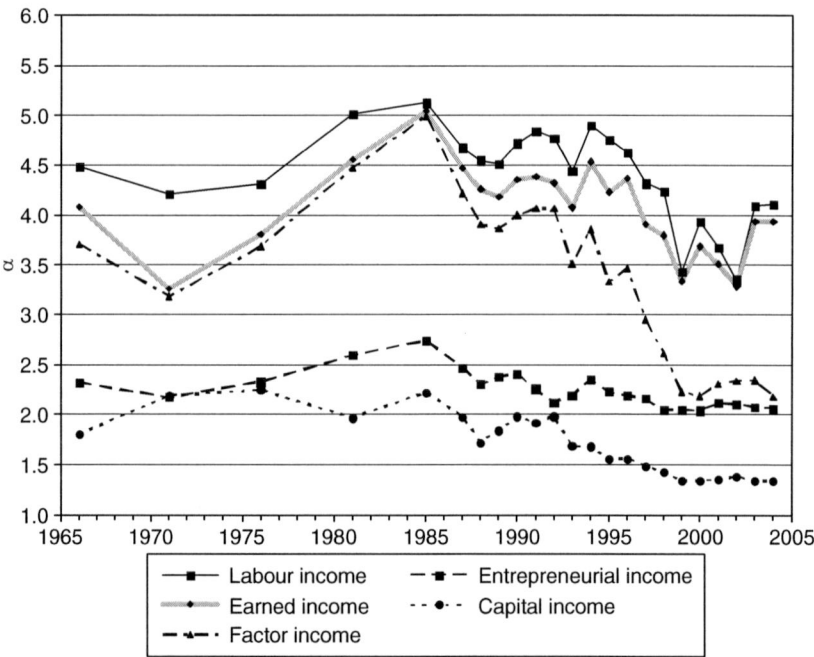

Figure 8.16b Pareto–Lorenz coefficients calculated from share of top 1% within top 10% in Finland, 1966–2004

until the end of the 1990s. Since then the share of top 1 per cent of disposable income and earnings has been roughly speaking the same.

Figure 8.16b provides estimates of Pareto–Lorenz coefficient,[4] a, for various income concepts (labour income, entrepreneurial income, earned income, capital income, and factor income) calculated from share of top 1 per cent within top 10 per cent in 1966–2004. To interpret Figure 8.16b, note that the larger the Pareto–Lorenz coefficient a, the smaller is the within-group share. The graph shows that inequality among top income people was high for earned income and factor income in the beginning of the 1970s, then decreased considerably until the mid 1990s, and then started to increase again. The line that is the lowest of all lines in the graph is the Pareto–Lorenz coefficient for capital income. It has a strong declining trend since the beginning of the 1970s. It fell from 2.2 in 1971 to 1.3 in 2004.

Some people argue that the inclusion of capital gains overstates the income of the top groups in several ways. Realized capital gains are not an annual flow of income and form a very volatile component of income depending on stock price variations. It is true that capital gains are not persistent income, but in any case asset sales must take place some time. Moreover, before 1993 capital gains were in part taxable. Therefore in order to assess the sensitivity of our results to the treatment of capital gains and imputed rents of homeowners we construct series excluding capital gains and imputed rents. The main conclusion from our sensitivity analysis is that excluding capital gains and imputed rents makes very little difference. The general U-shaped pattern over the period remains (see Figure 8.17, Table 8.3, and Table 8A.4).

With capital gains and imputed rents included, our calculations show the share of income accruing to the top 1 per cent rising from 3.0 to 6.2 per cent between 1990 and 2004 (see Figure 8.17 on the left). Without capital gains and imputed rents, the shift is from 2.9 to 5.4 per cent. Figure 8.17 on the right in turn displays the Gini coefficients for the same four different income concepts. As we see the general pattern remains rather similar, excluding the 'bubble' years 1999 and 2000 (see also Table 8A.3).

The Composition of Top Incomes 1966–2004

We saw that top income shares have increased drastically over the last ten years, and that this increase was concentrated within the top 1 per cent. How far are changes in top income shares associated with changes in the composition of top incomes? For different parts of the income distribution particular components of income are of more or less importance. The selected years 1966, 1987, 1994, and 2004 of Figure 8.18 show the importance of different sources of gross income (see more accurately Table 8A.5). For example the share of top 1 per cent depends on its share in total earnings and total capital income. In 2004 market incomes other than earnings i.e. capital income were around 6–12 per cent of income for all groups, apart from the

---

[4] See chapter 2 in Atkinson and Piketty (2007).

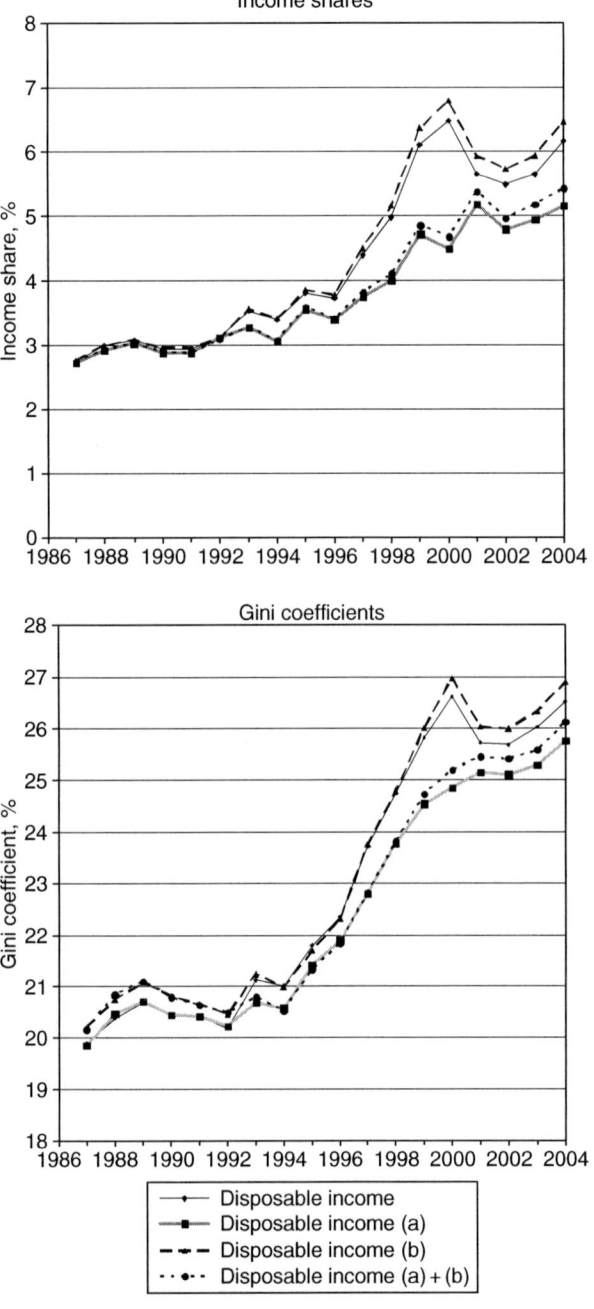

Figure 8.17 Income shares for top 1% and Gini coefficients in different income concepts in Finland, 1987–2004

Notes: (a) Disposable income without realized capital gains, (b) Disposable income without imputed net rents of owner-occupied dwellings, (a + b) Disposable income without realized capital gains and imputed net rents of owner-occupied dwellings.

Source: Based on IDS data in 1987–2004, Statistics Finland.

top decile for which they made up 30 per cent, resulting in earnings being a smaller share of the top decile than the rest of the top half. The differences in income composition mean that changes in relative values of different income sources have large effects on the overall distribution. As we expected very top incomes to be composed primarily of capital income, this suggests that a large increase in the share of the top 1 per cent is mainly driven by an increase in top capital incomes. At the same time, Figure 8.18 shows that the share of capital income has also increased dramatically within the top one group. Our series show that the sharply increasing pattern of capital income is entirely due to dividends. Our evidence confirms that the very large increase of top incomes observed during 1995–2004 was to a large extent a capital income phenomenon.

Figure 8.18 reports the composition of income in different deciles and in the top 1 per cent and top 5 per cent groups from 1966 and 2004. Figure 8.19 (and annually Table 8A.6) displays the composition of capital income respectively from 1987 to 2004. It shows that the share of dividends and interest income (in practice dividends) in total capital income has increased remarkably in the top 1 per cent group. It has increased from 53 per cent in 1987 to 66 per cent in 2004. The share of dividends in total gross income in the top 1 per cent group was 42 per cent in 2004 while the share of capital gains was 16 per cent. Figure 8.16a also shows that the share of capital income is not only increasing in income, but it is increasing now much more steeply than ten years ago.

Seeking Explanations for Increasing the Top Income Shares

The increasing share of the top 1 per cent in total income has been a notable feature of the changes in income inequality in the Anglo-Saxon countries, including USA, UK, Canada (see Atkinson 2002; Piketty and Saez 2003), while in Europe the Netherlands, France, and Switzerland display hardly any change in top income shares.[5]

What explains the growing income share of the top 1 per cent? What causal forces could have produced such dramatic changes in top income shares? How far has income taxation been responsible for this pattern of distributional change? Following Piketty (2003), most authors have argued that the dramatic increase in tax progressivity that has taken place in the inter-war period in many countries studied, and which remained in place at least until the recent decades, has been the main factor preventing top income shares from coming back to the very high levels observed at the beginning of the last century.[6]

Explaining the surge in top incomes in many advanced countries over the last ten to twenty years is more difficult. Economists have formulated several hypotheses about its causes. They are the shift from manufacturing to service

---

[5] The more recent estimates of Camille Landais (2007) show a rise in recent years in France.

[6] In fact Kuznets (1955) and Lampman (1962) also point out the role of progressive taxation as a central factor explaining the declined income and wealth inequality in the first half of the twentieth century.

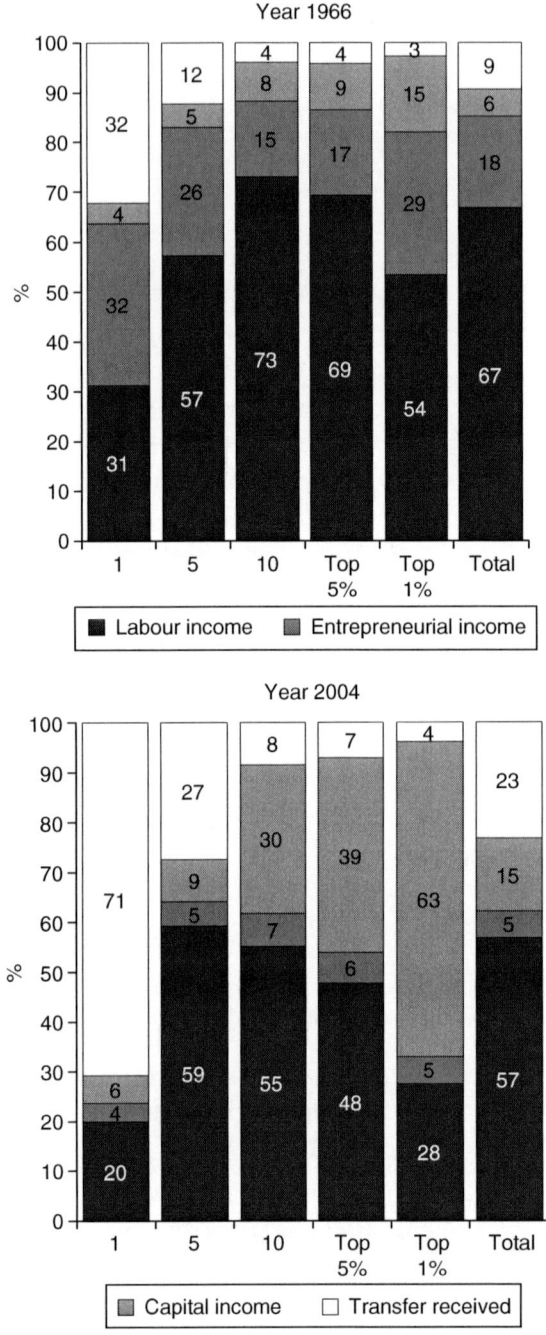

Figure 8.18 Gross income items in deciles and in top 5% and 1% in Finland

Source: Based on IDS data in 2004 and HES data in 1966, Statistics Finland.

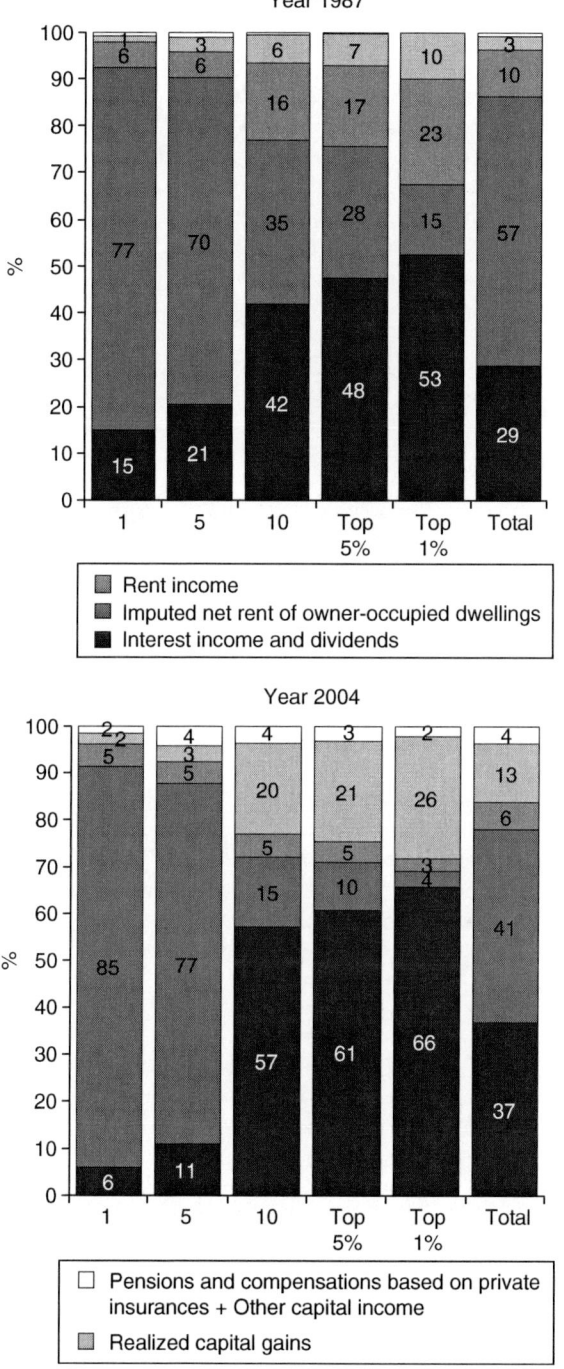

Figure 8.19 Capital income items in deciles and in top 5% and 1% in Finland
Source: Based on IDS data in 1987 and 2004, Statistics Finland.

production, technological changes, increased international trade, less progressive taxation, etc. Of these the most frequently cited explanation is that technological advances, particularly in the advent of computerized technologies, have created greater demand for higher-skilled and more educated workers and diminished demand for less-skilled and less-educated workers. By means of a simple application of supply and demand, this theory posits that skill-biased technological change has driven up the wages of the higher skilled and driven down those of the lower skilled. However, there is a growing group of economists who suggest it is not the sole explanation.[7] For example, Piketty and Saez (2003) challenge the skill-biased technological change thesis on the ground that the timing of the shifts in income differences does not support it in the USA. Similarly they contend that widening income differences cannot simply be a response to technical change or changes in the supply of educated workers, because the increase is highly concentrated among the very highest earners. The theory is not able to explain the rise of the working rich. Piketty and Saez (2003) instead argue that changing social norms are an important factor in explaining the recent increase in income inequality, particularly in the rise of mega-incomes for the very top earners. In the USA, according to Piketty and Saez (2003), 'the coupon-clipping rentiers have been overtaken by the working rich'.

In his book *The New Industrial State* J. K. Galbraith (1967) made important observations on the role of social norms in management. He writes: 'management does not go out ruthlessly to reward itself—a sound management is expected to exercise restraint...With the power of decision goes opportunity for making money...The corporation would be a chaos of competitive avarice. But these are not the sort of thing that a good company man does; a remarkably effective code bans such behaviour.'

The social norms have also changed in recent years in Finnish society. In Finland over the last ten-year period top incomes are composed more and more of dividend income (see Figures 8.16a and 8.19). In other words the coupon-clipping rentiers are back in Finland (Riihelä et al. 2005). Piketty and Saez (2003) give a central role to taxation, executive compensation, and shocks to capital returns. Our focus is the impact of taxation on top income shares in Finland.

The Role of Taxation

In order to explore the impact of taxation on underlying distribution, we need again to consider the composition of income. In particular the explanations are likely to be different for labour and capital income. On the basis of the composition of top incomes by source and how that evolved over time we can see that the remarkable rise in the share of the top incomes after the mid 1990s reflected a rise in income from capital, in particular in the form of dividends (see Figure 8.19).

[7] See, e.g., Atkinson (1999).

We attribute this directly to what happened to the tax system in 1993. The contribution of entrepreneurs to income inequality rose markedly during the latter part of the 1990s (see Riihelä et al. 2001). This is simply because capital income has become a more important income source for this group. Entrepreneurs have increased their share of total income in top income groups (see Figure 8.20). This share has increased from 16.1 per cent in 1987 to 33.3 per cent in 2004. At the same time capital income of entrepreneurs has become more unequally distributed amongst this group and has also steadily become more positively correlated with total income over the period. These three factors together explain the disequalizing effect of capital income for this group. The dramatic increase in the top 1 per cent is thus due to a sharp increase in capital income (dividends). As shown in Figure 8.18, the main factor that has driven up the top 1 per cent income share is an unprecedented increase in the fraction of capital income, which in 2004 represents about 63 per cent of incomes in the top 1 per cent group. It was 11 per cent in 1990. Therefore, as shown in Figure 8.18, the composition of high income at the end of the period considered is very different from those in earlier decades. It is important to note that the secular increase of top capital incomes is due to both an increased concentration of capital and an increase in the share of capital income in the Finnish economy as a whole. How can we explain the steep increase in capital income concentration?

The redistributive effects of income taxation depend on two things; on the legal definition of tax base and on the formal degree of progressivity. The Finnish tax reform in the latter part of the 1980s combined a reduction in the degree of progressivity with the broadening of the tax base. The major change took place in 1993, when the so-called dual income tax was introduced. It combines progressive taxation of earned income with a flat rate of tax on capital income (e.g. dividends, interest, and capital gains) and corporate profits. In the beginning the tax rate was 25 per cent and in recent years 29 per cent. A full imputation system has been applied to the taxation of distributed profits. In other words double taxation of dividends was completely eliminated by imputation. Under the dual income tax, capital income is taxed at a lower rate than the top marginal tax rate on labour income. Hence the taxpayer's total tax paid depends not only on his or her total income, but also on his or her income division.

The view that the 1993 tax reform is one of the key factors responsible for the increasing trend of the share of capital income (dividends) is also supported by the fact that the share of entrepreneurial income indicates a declining trend over the period. The dual income tax system requires a splitting of the income of the self-employed and the income of active owners of firms into a labour income component and a capital income component. Since the two components cannot be observed directly, this splitting gives rise to a number of practical problems. On the other hand, the dual income tax system created incentives for tax avoidance through the transformation of labour income subject to high marginal rates into capital income subject to low marginal rates. The Finnish scheme of taxing so-called closed corporations is not neutral in its impact on the allocation of capital to closely and widely held corporations (see Lindhe, Södersten, and

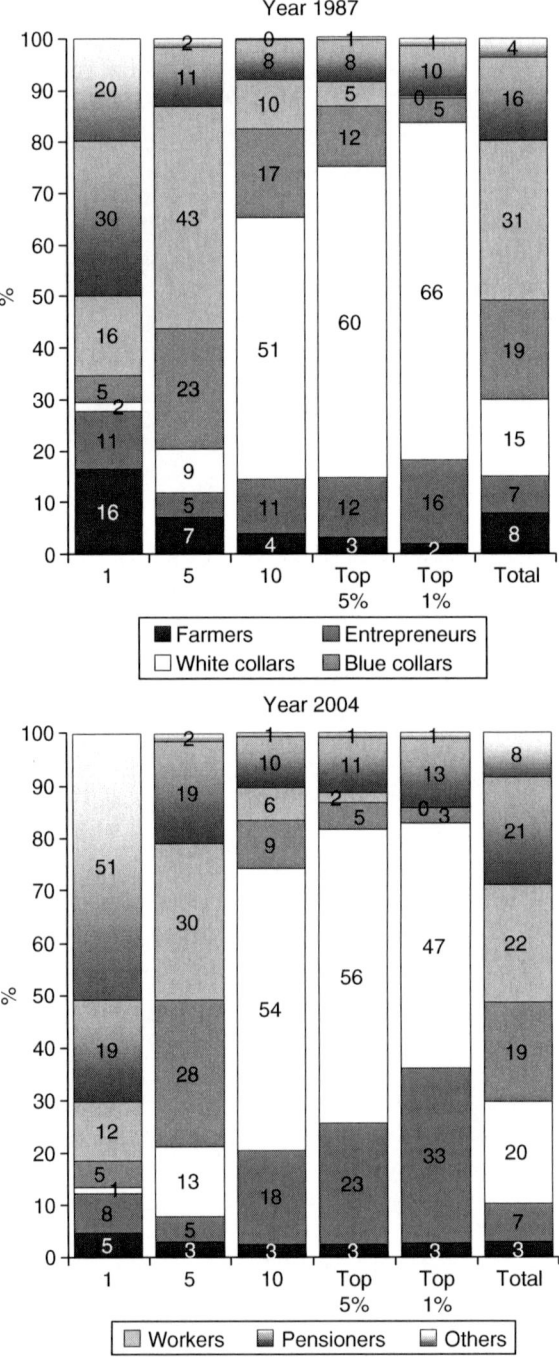

Figure 8.20 Gross income decomposed by seven socio-economic groups in Finland
Source: Based on IDS data in 1987 and 2004, Statistics Finland.

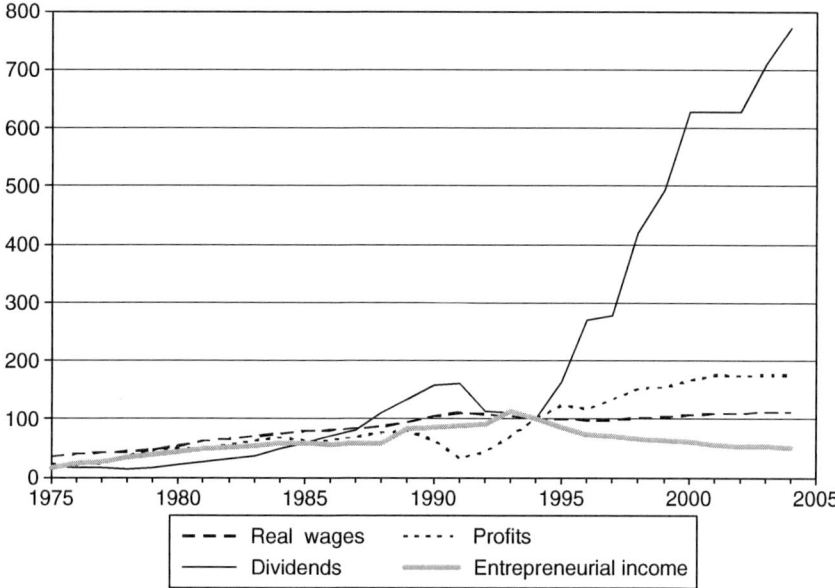

Figure 8.21 The growth rates of real wages, profits, dividends, and entrepreneurial income in Finland, 1975–2004; 1994 = '100'

Source: National Accounts, Statistics Finland.

Öberg 2002).[8] The net assets of the corporation form the basis for imputing income from capital. This increases the attractiveness of investing in closed corporations. It is obvious that this is the important reason why real dividends rose hugely over the latter part of the 1990s.

National income accounts series in Figure 8.21 show a sharp surge in real dividends following the 1993 reform. It is obvious that this huge growth was tax driven. Interestingly, at the same time real profits increased but much less than real dividends. Figure 8.21 shows also that wages rose only very modestly and the entrepreneurial incomes have declined since 1993.

The number of self-employed individuals decreased after 1993, while the total number of corporations increased at the same time. Figure 8.22 displays the increasing share of corporations of all firms and their increasing share of business income. Furthermore the business income of corporations doubled over the period 1993–2002. This can be interpreted as an indication of a tax-induced shift in organizational form and the choice of tax regime.

---

[8] 'The Finnish scheme for taxing owners in closed corporations is relatively simple, compared to corresponding tax laws in Norway and Sweden. However, the system seems to offer generous opportunities for tax-avoidance by transforming labor income into capital income. For example, retained corporate profits will increase the amount that is taxed as capital income, and capital gains on shares are only subject to capital income tax' (Lindhe, Södersten, and Öberg 2002: 6).

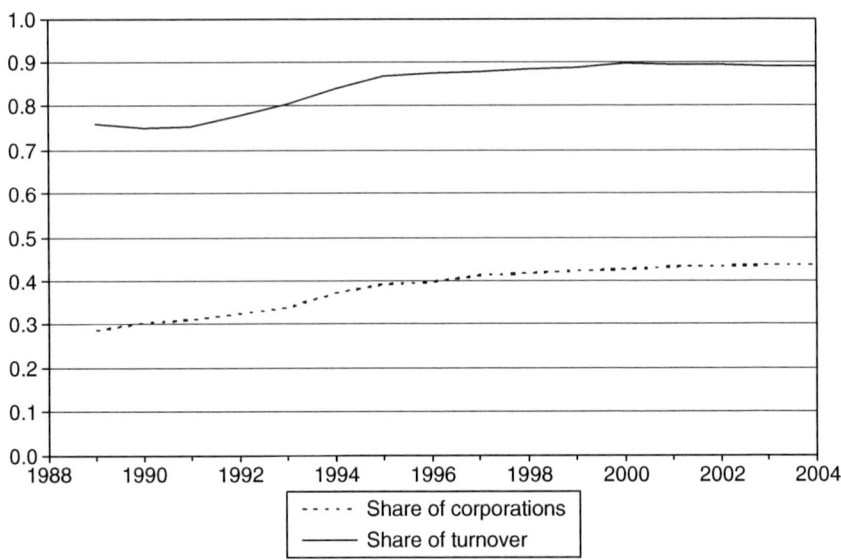

Figure 8.22 The share of corporations and their share of turnover in Finland, 1989–2004

Source: Statistics Finland.

Figure 8.23 gives one picture of the role of the tax system in the dramatic surge in top incomes. As seen in Figure 8.23 (and Table 8A.7) the composition of taxes has changed quite dramatically. The share of capital income taxes has increased in the top 1 per cent group. The share in 1994 was 14 per cent and in 2004 that share was 46 per cent. The share of earned income taxes (state-earned income tax + municipal tax) in turn has clearly declined over the last ten years from 68 per cent in 1994 to 44 per cent in 2004.

To get a sense of how the progressivity of the income tax system has changed Figure 8.24 shows how the average tax rates have changed at any given level of gross income. Figure 8.24 (left-hand side) shows the average tax rate of the individual whose tax burden is at the mean of tax burden of those in each decile. Figure 8.24 (right-hand side) in turn displays average tax rates for each percentile within the top decile. The average tax rate for the median was 22 per cent in 1987 and is slightly less in 2004 (21 per cent) The average tax rate for the richest 1 per cent has fallen about 44 per cent in 1987 to about 34 per cent in 2004. What is also interesting in Figure 8.24 is that the average tax rate schedule has been constant from 1994 onwards over the top 1 per cent (100–99). In other words it reflects the flat rate.

For a few reasons, the 34 per cent number paid by the top 1 per cent of taxpayers may be an inadequate measure of the average tax rate of this group. One important reason is that the person who nominally pays the tax (i.e. a

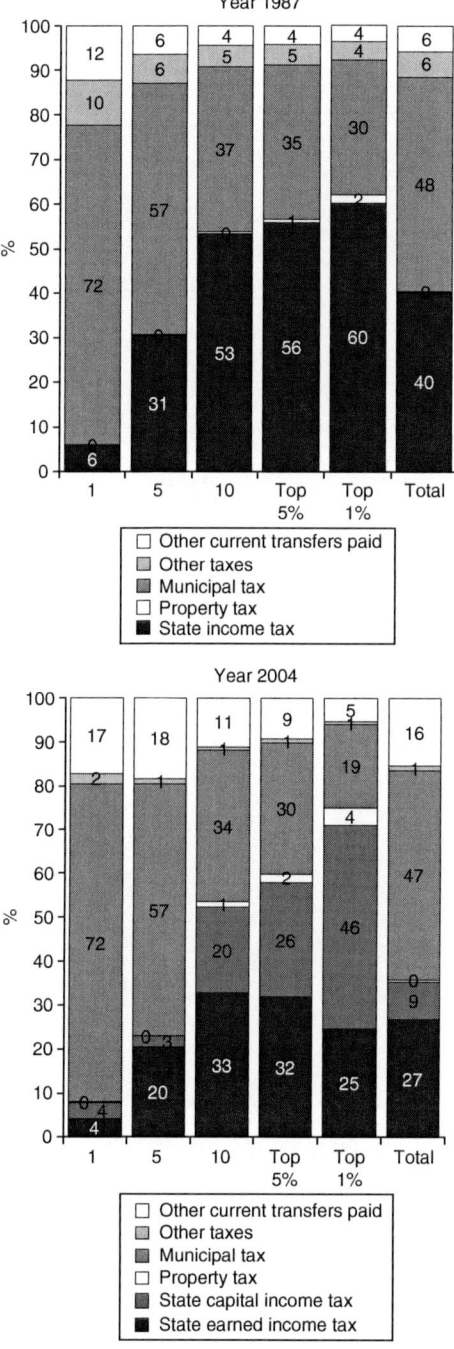

Figure 8.23 Tax items in deciles and in top 5% and 1% in Finland

Source: Based on IDS data in 1987 and 2004, Statistics Finland.

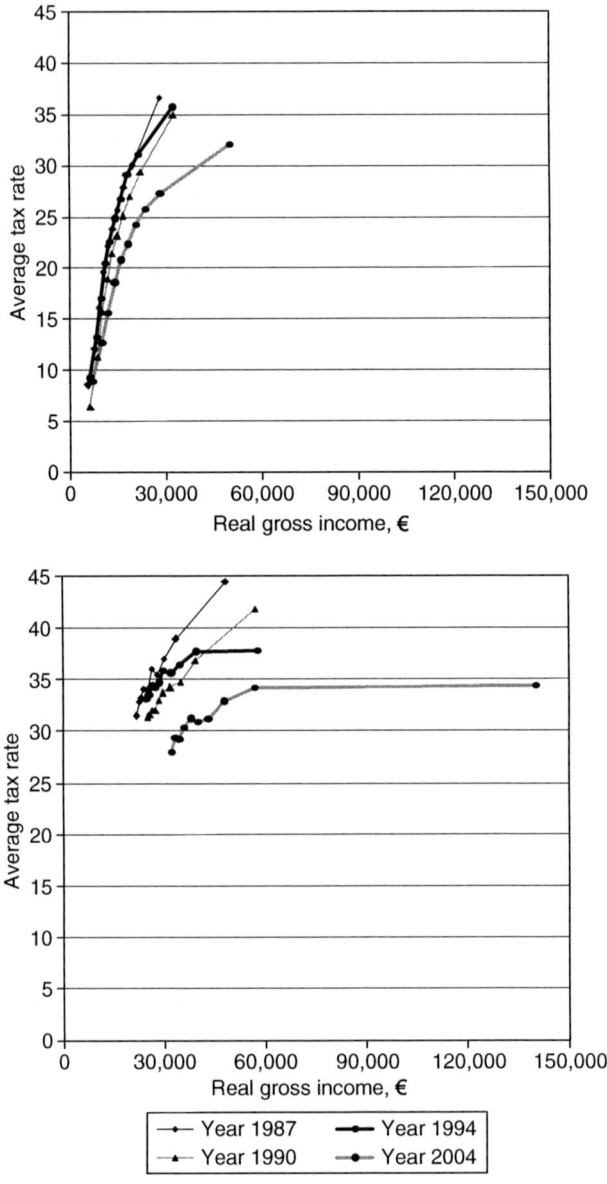

Figure 8.24 Average tax rates in the decile means and for percentiles in the top decile in Finland

Source: Based on IDS data in 1987, 1990, 1994, and 2004, Statistics Finland.

legal liability for a tax) is not necessarily the person who really pays the tax; the tax may be shifted onto someone else. How much shifting occurs depends on the supply and demand circumstances of the economy. This is a highly contro-versial issue among economists. Especially this is the case with the corporate income tax. For example, it is assumed by the IDS data that the shareholder pays the corporate income tax. So the IDS data overstate the tax rates of the top 1 per cent group.

A relevant question to ask is whether this increase in top incomes could have occurred had the income tax system remained the same as before 1993. It is plausible to think that the drastic reduction of top income tax rates, which started in 1993, opened the possibility of the dramatic increase in top incomes that started around the mid 1990s and accelerated in the end of the 1990s.

8.5 INCOME MOBILITY IN 1990–2001

All our evidence so far in this chapter has been based on a snapshot, or a series of snapshots, of the income distribution in Finland. The snapshot of the income distribution may be a misleading picture. People who have high income one year may have lower income the next and vice versa. In other words if the increased snapshot income concentration that we have documented in Finland has been associated with a substantial increase in income mobility, then the per-manent inequality has not necessarily changed much. In the IDS data each house-hold is included in the sample for two consecutive years, i.e. two-year rotation. Hence the IDS data allow us to provide some answers to questions such as whether individuals that belong to the top 1 per cent group, say, in 1997 would still have been in this group one year later. Hence we can analyse how income mobility at the top has evolved in the recent decades (see Riihelä and Sullström 2002 for a more detailed exposition on income mobility in Finland).

We constructed the mobility matrix for 1990 and 1991, 1994 and 1995, and 2001 and 2002. Let P be a matrix of $(n \times n)$ transitions, the ij[th] element of which, P_{ij}, is the percentage in the income class i (percentile) at time t_0 of those who at time t_1 were in class j. The advantage of the transition matrix is that it can nicely summarize mobility at various points in the distribution, which is harder to gauge from a single index. Figure 8.25 shows the percentage of those remaining in the same income group. In other words it is the diagonal of the mobility matrix. It is immediately evident that there is less mobility in the top and bottom than in the middle of the distribution. This is, however, unsurprising given that the top (bottom) can only stay in the same group or move down (up). Also the right-hand tail is particularly large, which is the reason why persistence in that group is particularly high.

Table 8.4 suggests that mobility at the top 1 per cent is quite modest. In fact mobility has decreased at this group from 1990/1 to 2001/2. It can be seen that 65

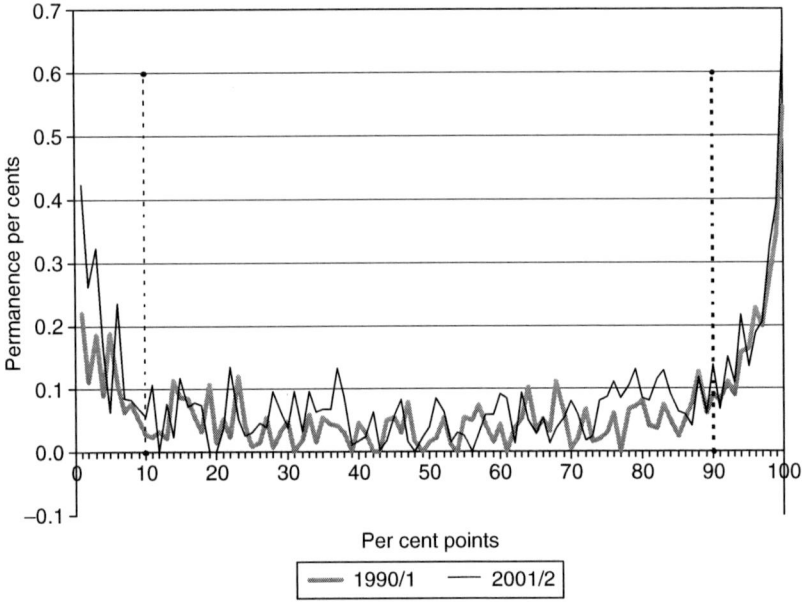

Figure 8.25 Permanence in the same percentiles in 1990/1 and 2001/2 in Finland
Source: Based on IDS data in 1990–2002, Statistics Finland.

(54) per cent were in the top 1 per cent in 2001/2 (1990/1). Those who moved their states in the top 1 per cent between (99–90) points (including the persistence) were 91 (85) per cent.

Hence the IDS data suggest that the increase in annual income concentration that we have documented in this report is associated with a similar increase in longer-term income concentration.

Table 8.4 Mobility and permanence in the top 1% in Finland, 1990/1, 1993/4, 1994/5, and 2001/2

	Per cent point	1990/1	1993/4	1994/5	2001/2
Mobility	0–49	5.23	5.98	5.65	0.39
	50–59	0.69	1.05	0.00	0.75
	60–69	0.90	2.17	0.00	0.95
	70–79	1.43	3.65	1.77	2.37
	80–89	7.02	0.00	6.14	3.96
	90–94	9.59	2.14	2.21	0.61
	95–98	20.65	32.87	27.63	25.87
Permanence	99–100	54.40	53.21	57.70	64.70

Source: Based on IDS data in 1990–2002, Statistics Finland.

8.6 CONCLUSIONS

This chapter provides new evidence about the evolution of top incomes in Finland based both on tabulated income tax data for 1920–2003 and on micro-data over the period 1966–2004. The chapter shows how the proportion of income earned by the very richest 1 per cent has changed over time. The total share of the highest earners fell consistently from the beginning of the 1960s to the mid 1990s but then began to rise. The results bring out clearly how the major equalization from the beginning of 1960 to the mid 1990s has been reversed, taking the shares of top income groups back to levels of inequality or even higher found over forty years ago.

The main factor that has driven up the top 1 per cent income share in Finland since the mid 1990s is an unprecedented increase in the fraction of capital income which is in 2004 63 per cent of incomes in the top 1 per cent group. Therefore the composition of high incomes at the end of the period considered is very different from those earlier years of this period. We argue in this chapter that the 1993 tax reform is one of the key factors responsible for this trend. Our results suggest that the decline in income progressivity since the mid 1990s is a central factor explaining the increase of top income shares in Finland.

APPENDIX 8A: BACKGROUND TABLES

This appendix contains background Tables 8A.1 to 8A.10.

Table 8A.1 Gini coefficients (%) in Finland from Statistics of Income and Property, 1920–2003

Year	Income subject to taxation among all adults	Taxable income/ population	Year	Income subject to taxation among all adults	Taxable income/ population
1920	-	59.77	1962	46.87	50.59
1921	-	59.57	1963	47.09	51.81
1922	-	59.45	1964	47.69	51.65
1923	-	54.50	1965	47.85	51.74
1924	-	49.53	1966	47.94	51.93
1925	-	50.03	1967	48.47	53.39
1926	-	50.52	1968	49.02	53.56
1927	-	50.98	1969	49.83	44.58
1928	-	51.45	1970	48.87	62.84
1929	-	51.91	1971	48.30	60.37
1930	-	51.40	1972	48.26	58.35
1931	-	50.88	1973	47.12	56.39
1932	-	50.92	1974	47.55	49.05
1933	-	50.95	1975	46.02	51.33
1934	-	50.99	1976	45.48	55.77
1935	-	41.52	1977	45.37	56.53
1936	-	43.15	1978	45.52	58.27
1937	-	44.79	1979	45.13	56.86
1938	-	45.87	1980	44.83	54.66
1939	-	44.11	1981	44.66	53.76
1940	-	42.35	1982	44.34	52.03
1941	-	40.59	1983	42.00	49.43
1942	-	38.83	1984	41.43	51.45
1943	-	37.07	1985	40.72	48.98
1944	-	35.30	1986	40.49	48.13
1945	-	33.55	1987	40.63	46.81
1946	-	31.79	1988	41.00	45.85
1947	-	30.03	1989	40.68	47.57
1948	-	39.30	1990	40.74	45.95
1949	39.29	48.99	1991	40.09	47.10
1950	40.88	48.66	1992	39.23	47.30
1951	42.20	49.89	1993	39.52	-

1952	40.86	51.37	1994	40.69	-
1953	40.97	51.03	1995	41.06	-
1954	47.78	51.71	1996	41.29	-
1955	49.60	51.67	1997	41.92	-
1956	53.07	52.24	1998	42.64	-
1957	53.99	52.48	1999	44.18	-
1958	50.14	52.62	2000	45.19	-
1959	55.65	53.11	2001	43.74	-
1960	53.96	52.88	2002	43.51	-
1961	55.97	54.18	2003	43.60	-

Source: Statistics of Income and Property, Statistics Finland.

Table 8A.2 Top income shares (%) in Finland from Statistics of Income and Property, 1920–2003

Year	Top 5% Income subject to taxation among all adults	Top 5% Taxable income/ population	Top 1% Income subject to taxation among all adults	Top 1% Taxable income/ population	Year	Top 5% Income subject to taxation among all adults	Top 5% Taxable income/ population	Top 1% Income subject to taxation among all adults	Top 1% Taxable income/ population
1920	-	33.55	-	15.27	1962	21.12	25.09	7.90	10.01
1921	-	32.26	-	15.20	1963	21.30	25.50	8.11	10.16
1922	-	31.98	-	14.85	1964	21.55	24.54	8.39	9.46
1923	-	29.53	-	13.46	1965	21.57	24.51	8.42	9.47
1924	-	27.07	-	12.07	1966	21.34	24.55	8.01	9.47
1925	-	27.78	-	12.64	1967	21.50	25.13	7.92	9.54
1926	-	28.50	-	13.22	1968	21.52	24.96	7.83	9.31
1927	-	28.75	-	13.34	1969	21.54	20.50	7.86	7.84
1928	-	29.00	-	13.45	1970	21.01	25.71	7.54	9.87
1929	-	29.26	-	13.57	1971	20.62	24.83	7.37	9.26
1930	-	29.36	-	13.50	1972	20.37	23.52	7.46	8.70
1931	-	29.47	-	13.43	1973	19.44	22.83	6.78	8.10
1932	-	29.43	-	13.41	1974	19.15	20.86	6.63	7.46
1933	-	29.38	-	13.40	1975	18.27	19.53	6.22	5.91
1934	-	29.33	-	13.38	1976	17.83	20.39	5.95	5.66
1935	-	25.11	-	11.74	1977	17.90	20.51	5.93	5.51
1936	-	26.16	-	12.39	1978	17.84	20.94	5.86	5.15
1937	-	27.21	-	13.04	1979	17.66	20.09	5.75	4.87
1938	-	27.57	-	13.04	1980	17.50	17.80	5.70	4.32
1939	-	26.32	-	12.26	1981	17.45	16.21	5.56	3.96
1940	-	25.07	-	11.47	1982	17.20	14.53	5.61	3.55
1941	-	23.82	-	10.69	1983	16.96	13.52	5.55	3.49
1942	-	22.57	-	9.91	1984	16.78	18.59	5.43	4.11
1943	-	21.33	-	9.13	1985	16.52	16.86	5.36	4.03

1944	-	20.08	-	8.35	1986	16.63	15.88	5.30	3.86
1945	-	18.83	-	7.57	1987	16.55	16.98	5.29	5.03
1946	-	17.58	-	6.79	1988	16.93	17.36	5.67	4.96
1947	-	16.33	-	6.01	1989	16.62	17.11	5.50	4.70
1948	-	17.05	-	6.23	1990	16.82	16.88	5.63	4.59
1949	17.57	20.73	6.11	7.71	1991	16.69	16.84	5.57	4.62
1950	18.34	20.72	6.39	7.75	1992	16.29	16.74	5.34	4.58
1951	18.51	21.29	6.39	8.03	1993	16.93	-	5.83	-
1952	18.19	22.18	6.80	8.48	1994	17.49	-	6.07	-
1953	18.47	22.23	6.83	8.51	1995	17.76	-	6.21	-
1954	20.58	23.16	7.79	8.91	1996	17.68	-	6.16	-
1955	27.45	23.03	10.52	8.94	1997	18.36	-	5.51	-
1956	27.14	23.74	10.36	9.20	1998	19.21	-	7.16	-
1957	26.77	23.68	10.18	9.18	1999	21.27	-	8.85	-
1958	24.41	25.12	9.30	9.92	2000	22.41	-	10.73	-
1959	27.78	25.19	10.66	10.01	2001	20.66	-	8.77	-
1960	28.13	24.37	10.64	9.50	2002	20.53	-	8.34	-
1961	23.99	25.93	8.86	10.16	2003	20.54	-	8.63	-

Source: Statistics of Income and Property, Statistics Finland.

Table 8A.3 Gini coefficients (%) with standard error in brackets in Finland, 1966–2004

Year	Factor income		Gross income		Disposable income		Disposable income					
							(a)		(b)		(a) + (b)	
	Gini	std	Gini	std	Gini	std	Gini	std	Gini	std	Gini	std
1966	38.45	0.61	33.22	0.57	31.06	0.53	–	–	–	–	–	–
1971	39.04	0.44	31.31	0.39	27.29	0.37	–	–	–	–	–	–
1976	35.81	0.39	26.64	0.33	21.94	0.31	–	–	–	–	–	–
1981	36.22	0.36	25.43	0.27	20.72	0.21	–	–	–	–	–	–
1985	37.25	0.35	25.03	0.26	20.15	0.20	–	–	–	–	–	–
1987	38.46	0.31	25.26	0.20	19.90	0.16	19.86	0.16	20.20	0.17	20.16	0.17
1988	39.24	0.30	25.99	0.20	20.37	0.17	20.47	0.18	20.74	0.17	20.85	0.18
1989	39.80	0.32	26.29	0.24	20.68	0.19	20.72	0.20	21.07	0.19	21.11	0.21
1990	39.40	0.31	25.76	0.22	20.45	0.17	20.45	0.18	20.81	0.18	20.80	0.18
1991	39.93	0.30	25.36	0.19	20.43	0.16	20.42	0.16	20.65	0.16	20.64	0.16
1992	42.54	0.33	25.48	0.21	20.18	0.19	20.22	0.19	20.45	0.19	20.49	0.19
1993	45.72	0.40	26.36	0.28	21.12	0.26	20.68	0.23	21.23	0.27	20.80	0.23
1994	46.53	0.41	26.18	0.27	21.02	0.25	20.58	0.24	20.98	0.26	20.53	0.24
1995	46.39	0.42	26.90	0.31	21.80	0.29	21.43	0.28	21.69	0.30	21.33	0.28
1996	46.79	0.42	27.53	0.28	22.35	0.26	21.90	0.23	22.30	0.27	21.85	0.23
1997	47.25	0.48	28.64	0.37	23.70	0.34	22.79	0.28	23.76	0.36	22.82	0.29
1998	47.09	0.55	29.54	0.46	24.73	0.45	23.78	0.35	24.79	0.48	23.82	0.38
1999	47.60	0.69	30.56	0.64	25.82	0.59	24.55	0.52	26.01	0.63	24.73	0.56
2000	47.57	0.79	31.22	0.75	26.61	0.72	24.86	0.49	26.97	0.77	25.20	0.52
2001	46.95	0.72	30.42	0.67	25.72	0.61	25.15	0.59	26.03	0.65	25.45	0.64
2002	46.65	0.63	30.32	0.58	25.68	0.53	25.11	0.48	25.99	0.57	25.41	0.50
2003	46.78	0.76	30.44	0.73	26.03	0.68	25.29	0.66	26.33	0.73	25.58	0.71
2004	47.16	0.82	30.91	0.79	26.51	0.76	25.76	0.67	26.89	0.82	26.13	0.73

Notes:
(a) Disposable income excluding realized capital income.
(b) Disposable income excluding imputed net rents of owner-occupied dwellings.
(a) + (b) Disposable income excluding realized capital income and imputed net rents of owner-occupied dwellings.

Source: Based on IDS data in 1987–2004 and HES data in 1966–1985, Statistics Finland.

Table 8A.4 Inverted Lorenz curve (100−Lorenz curve) in Finland, 1966–2004

Year	p-point%	Income concept			Income concept, excl. capital gain			Income concept, excl. imputed net rent			Income concept, excl. capital gain and imputed net rent		
		FI	GI	DI	FI	GI	DI	FI	GI	DI	FI	GI	DI
1966	0	100.00	100.00	100.00	-	-	-	-	-	-	-	-	-
	10	98.67	97.03	96.83	-	-	-	-	-	-	-	-	-
	20	95.14	92.61	92.10	-	-	-	-	-	-	-	-	-
	30	90.22	87.10	86.30	-	-	-	-	-	-	-	-	-
	40	84.04	80.59	79.45	-	-	-	-	-	-	-	-	-
	50	76.54	72.89	71.42	-	-	-	-	-	-	-	-	-
	60	67.35	63.76	62.08	-	-	-	-	-	-	-	-	-
	70	56.41	53.18	51.37	-	-	-	-	-	-	-	-	-
	80	43.23	40.54	38.90	-	-	-	-	-	-	-	-	-
	90	26.79	25.06	23.70	-	-	-	-	-	-	-	-	-
	95	16.40	15.26	14.23	-	-	-	-	-	-	-	-	-
	99	4.98	4.57	4.27	-	-	-	-	-	-	-	-	-
	99.9	0.91	0.83	0.76	-	-	-	-	-	-	-	-	-
1971	0	100.00	100.00	100.00	-	-	-	-	-	-	-	-	-
	10	99.16	96.79	96.33	-	-	-	-	-	-	-	-	-
	20	96.12	92.06	90.95	-	-	-	-	-	-	-	-	-
	30	91.25	86.23	84.49	-	-	-	-	-	-	-	-	-
	40	84.78	79.37	77.10	-	-	-	-	-	-	-	-	-
	50	76.82	71.41	68.73	-	-	-	-	-	-	-	-	-
	60	67.35	62.19	59.27	-	-	-	-	-	-	-	-	-
	70	56.18	51.60	48.60	-	-	-	-	-	-	-	-	-
	80	42.98	39.28	36.36	-	-	-	-	-	-	-	-	-
	90	26.63	24.23	21.79	-	-	-	-	-	-	-	-	-
	95	16.41	14.89	13.02	-	-	-	-	-	-	-	-	-
	99	5.49	4.89	4.10	-	-	-	-	-	-	-	-	-

(continued)

Table 8A.4 Continued

Year	p-point%	Income concept			Income concept, excl. capital gain			Income concept, excl. imputed net rent			Income concept, excl. capital gain and imputed net rent		
		FI	GI	DI	FI	GI	DI	FI	GI	DI	FI	GI	DI
1976	99.9	1.25	1.14	0.97	-	-	-	-	-	-	-	-	-
	0	100.00	100.00	100.00	-	-	-	-	-	-	-	-	-
	10	99.30	96.25	95.53	-	-	-	-	-	-	-	-	-
	20	96.02	90.93	89.39	-	-	-	-	-	-	-	-	-
	30	90.57	84.53	82.25	-	-	-	-	-	-	-	-	-
	40	83.47	77.03	74.21	-	-	-	-	-	-	-	-	-
	50	74.93	68.44	65.22	-	-	-	-	-	-	-	-	-
	60	64.88	58.77	55.33	-	-	-	-	-	-	-	-	-
	70	53.20	47.85	44.44	-	-	-	-	-	-	-	-	-
	80	39.67	35.49	32.39	-	-	-	-	-	-	-	-	-
	90	23.69	21.15	18.74	-	-	-	-	-	-	-	-	-
	95	14.16	12.67	10.91	-	-	-	-	-	-	-	-	-
	99	4.42	3.95	3.27	-	-	-	-	-	-	-	-	-
	99.9	1.08	0.93	0.82	-	-	-	-	-	-	-	-	-
1981	0	100.00	100.00	100.00	-	-	-	-	-	-	-	-	-
	10	99.51	96.24	95.58	-	-	-	-	-	-	-	-	-
	20	96.83	90.74	89.21	-	-	-	-	-	-	-	-	-
	30	91.46	84.10	81.82	-	-	-	-	-	-	-	-	-
	40	84.26	76.41	73.53	-	-	-	-	-	-	-	-	-
	50	75.43	67.68	64.42	-	-	-	-	-	-	-	-	-
	60	65.06	57.86	54.45	-	-	-	-	-	-	-	-	-
	70	53.10	46.91	43.48	-	-	-	-	-	-	-	-	-
	80	39.35	34.53	31.41	-	-	-	-	-	-	-	-	-
	90	23.13	20.22	17.79	-	-	-	-	-	-	-	-	-
	95	13.55	11.81	10.04	-	-	-	-	-	-	-	-	-

Year	%ile												
	99	3.87	3.34	2.60	–	–	–	–	–	–	–	–	–
	99.9	0.66	0.53	0.39	–	–	–	–	–	–	–	–	–
1985	0	100.00	100.00	100.00	–	–	–	–	–	–	–	–	–
	10	99.57	95.98	95.30	–	–	–	–	–	–	–	–	–
	20	97.18	90.39	88.78	–	–	–	–	–	–	–	–	–
	30	92.01	83.74	81.33	–	–	–	–	–	–	–	–	–
	40	84.93	76.08	73.06	–	–	–	–	–	–	–	–	–
	50	76.17	67.36	63.97	–	–	–	–	–	–	–	–	–
	60	65.82	57.60	54.05	–	–	–	–	–	–	–	–	–
	70	53.88	46.74	43.24	–	–	–	–	–	–	–	–	–
	80	40.08	34.53	31.30	–	–	–	–	–	–	–	–	–
	90	23.67	20.33	17.85	–	–	–	–	–	–	–	–	–
	95	13.76	11.84	10.09	–	–	–	–	–	–	–	–	–
	99	3.75	3.31	2.71	–	–	–	–	–	–	–	–	–
	99.9	0.60	0.53	0.38	–	–	–	–	–	–	–	–	–
1987	0	100.00	100.00	100.00	100.00	100.00	100.00	100.00	100.00	100.00	100.00	100.00	100.00
	10	99.59	96.10	95.22	99.59	96.10	95.24	99.96	96.27	95.40	99.96	96.27	95.40
	20	97.45	90.54	88.68	97.45	90.54	88.68	98.31	90.81	88.96	98.31	90.82	88.97
	30	92.52	83.83	81.21	92.53	83.83	81.20	93.52	84.15	81.53	93.52	84.15	81.52
	40	85.47	76.08	72.86	85.46	76.07	72.84	86.49	76.43	73.20	86.49	76.41	73.18
	50	76.68	67.33	63.69	76.67	67.32	63.66	77.69	67.68	64.00	77.68	67.66	63.98
	60	66.33	57.58	53.70	66.30	57.55	53.66	67.24	57.87	53.96	67.22	57.85	53.94
	70	54.31	46.70	42.82	54.29	46.67	42.78	55.10	46.98	43.06	55.07	46.93	43.02
	80	40.44	34.52	30.94	40.40	34.48	30.90	41.05	34.76	31.12	40.99	34.72	31.07
	90	24.02	20.37	17.57	23.97	20.33	17.53	24.41	20.53	17.67	24.37	20.48	17.64
	95	14.10	11.92	9.93	14.07	11.88	9.90	14.36	12.03	10.00	14.30	11.99	9.97
	99	4.07	3.44	2.67	4.04	3.40	2.64	4.16	3.48	2.69	4.11	3.44	2.67
	99.9	0.75	0.63	0.46	0.72	0.61	0.45	0.73	0.64	0.46	0.74	0.62	0.44
1988	0	100.00	100.00	100.00	100.00	100.00	100.00	100.00	100.00	100.00	100.00	100.00	100.00
	10	99.61	96.15	95.25	99.61	96.15	95.39	99.96	96.33	95.44	99.97	96.32	95.59
	20	97.55	90.66	88.75	97.55	90.63	88.89	98.46	90.98	89.10	98.47	90.95	89.24

(continued)

Table 8A.4 Continued

Year	p-point%	Income concept			Income concept, excl. capital gain			Income concept, excl. imputed net rent			Income concept, excl. capital gain and imputed net rent		
		FI	GI	DI	FI	GI	DI	FI	GI	DI	FI	GI	DI
	30	92.74	84.04	81.30	92.73	83.99	81.42	93.77	84.41	81.70	93.76	84.36	81.82
	40	85.79	76.37	73.01	85.76	76.31	73.10	86.83	76.75	73.40	86.81	76.69	73.52
	50	77.13	67.72	63.95	77.08	67.63	64.00	78.13	68.09	64.31	78.08	68.01	64.38
	60	66.87	58.08	54.06	66.78	57.98	54.10	67.78	58.40	54.38	67.69	58.30	54.42
	70	54.97	47.30	43.24	54.85	47.17	43.25	55.75	47.59	43.52	55.63	47.46	43.51
	80	41.15	35.16	31.41	40.98	35.00	31.36	41.73	35.41	31.61	41.55	35.24	31.56
	90	24.67	21.02	18.04	24.46	20.83	17.96	25.05	21.16	18.14	24.83	20.98	18.06
	95	14.67	12.52	10.35	14.47	12.35	10.25	14.93	12.62	10.41	14.72	12.44	10.31
	99	4.41	3.76	2.90	4.24	3.63	2.84	4.48	3.81	2.91	4.30	3.66	2.83
	99.9	0.81	0.70	0.53	0.73	0.64	0.50	0.82	0.69	0.53	0.73	0.63	0.51
1989	0	100.00	100.00	100.00	100.00	100.00	100.00	100.00	100.00	100.00	100.00	100.00	100.00
	10	99.63	96.16	95.23	99.63	96.15	95.34	99.99	96.36	95.46	99.99	96.35	95.57
	20	97.69	90.74	88.83	97.69	90.72	88.92	98.72	91.09	89.21	98.73	91.07	89.30
	30	92.97	84.19	81.42	92.96	84.14	81.50	94.13	84.58	81.85	94.13	84.55	81.94
	40	86.09	76.57	73.20	86.07	76.51	73.25	87.26	76.97	73.61	87.24	76.91	73.67
	50	77.48	67.94	64.14	77.43	67.85	64.17	78.57	68.33	64.52	78.52	68.25	64.56
	60	67.26	58.32	54.29	67.18	58.21	54.28	68.21	58.67	54.61	68.14	58.56	54.62
	70	55.38	47.56	43.53	55.27	47.45	43.49	56.20	47.87	43.80	56.08	47.74	43.76
	80	41.55	35.40	31.68	41.39	35.25	31.60	42.17	35.62	31.85	42.00	35.47	31.77
	90	24.99	21.19	18.29	24.80	21.01	18.19	25.37	21.35	18.37	25.16	21.16	18.27
	95	14.98	12.66	10.57	14.77	12.50	10.49	15.20	12.77	10.61	15.01	12.59	10.51
	99	4.47	3.78	2.99	4.36	3.69	2.95	4.55	3.84	2.99	4.41	3.72	2.95
	99.9	0.84	0.73	0.54	0.76	0.67	0.50	0.86	0.75	0.52	0.75	0.65	0.52

Year	Percentile												
1990	0	100.00	100.00	100.00	100.00	100.00	100.00	100.00	100.00	100.00	100.00	100.00	100.00
	10	99.55	96.09	99.55	95.15	96.08	95.22	99.99	96.30	95.38	99.99	96.30	95.44
	20	97.50	90.56	97.50	88.66	90.54	88.72	98.71	90.92	89.08	98.71	90.90	89.13
	30	92.76	83.90	92.74	81.24	83.86	81.29	94.07	84.34	81.73	94.06	84.30	81.77
	40	85.84	76.22	85.81	73.01	76.16	73.04	87.14	76.65	73.48	87.12	76.59	73.50
	50	77.23	67.59	77.17	64.00	67.51	64.00	78.43	67.99	64.39	78.38	67.91	64.38
	60	67.00	57.94	66.91	54.12	57.84	54.09	68.04	58.30	54.44	67.95	58.18	54.42
	70	55.10	47.15	54.99	43.36	47.03	43.30	55.96	47.46	43.62	55.83	47.32	43.56
	80	41.28	35.02	41.11	31.55	34.87	31.48	41.92	35.25	31.69	41.75	35.08	31.62
	90	24.73	20.80	24.54	18.12	20.64	18.05	25.08	20.92	18.20	24.88	20.76	18.11
	95	14.65	12.29	14.45	10.39	12.14	10.31	14.86	12.39	10.45	14.65	12.21	10.35
	99	4.36	3.63	4.20	2.89	3.52	2.81	4.43	3.66	2.90	4.25	3.52	2.83
	99.9	0.81	0.68	0.71	0.47	0.57	0.44	0.81	0.67	0.46	0.72	0.59	0.45
1991	0	100.00	100.00	100.00	100.00	100.00	100.00	100.00	100.00	100.00	100.00	100.00	100.00
	10	99.47	96.06	99.48	95.22	96.06	95.27	99.96	96.26	95.41	99.96	96.25	95.47
	20	97.39	90.41	97.40	88.67	90.41	88.72	98.69	90.76	89.01	98.70	90.76	89.06
	30	92.95	83.67	92.96	81.20	83.66	81.23	94.46	84.07	81.58	94.47	84.07	81.62
	40	86.29	75.93	86.30	72.92	75.90	72.92	87.83	76.34	73.28	87.85	76.31	73.30
	50	77.78	67.23	77.78	63.83	67.19	63.82	79.28	67.64	64.18	79.27	67.60	64.19
	60	67.60	57.57	67.58	54.00	57.52	53.97	68.94	57.94	54.30	68.93	57.89	54.27
	70	55.67	46.82	55.63	43.28	46.74	43.24	56.79	47.14	43.50	56.74	47.08	43.46
	80	41.78	34.76	41.71	31.49	34.67	31.42	42.61	34.98	31.61	42.53	34.88	31.54
	90	25.11	20.68	25.02	18.14	20.59	18.05	25.59	20.79	18.14	25.50	20.69	18.06
	95	14.89	12.18	14.79	10.38	12.08	10.29	15.18	12.26	10.39	15.05	12.15	10.30
	99	4.39	3.57	4.28	2.89	3.49	2.82	4.48	3.60	2.87	4.39	3.52	2.80
	99.9	0.77	0.63	0.71	0.50	0.59	0.46	0.79	0.64	0.47	0.73	0.59	0.45
1992	0	100.00	100.00	100.00	100.00	100.00	100.00	100.00	100.00	100.00	100.00	100.00	100.00
	10	99.64	95.98	99.64	95.09	95.98	95.11	99.99	96.19	95.30	99.99	96.20	95.33
	20	97.82	90.26	97.82	88.45	90.27	88.47	99.23	90.63	88.81	99.24	90.64	88.83
	30	94.05	83.54	94.06	80.92	83.55	80.95	95.91	83.96	81.34	95.92	83.97	81.37
	40	87.93	75.86	87.95	72.64	75.88	72.67	89.83	76.28	73.03	89.85	76.30	73.06
	50	79.82	67.27	79.84	63.64	67.29	63.66	81.67	67.66	63.99	81.69	67.69	64.02
	60	69.82	57.66	69.85	53.82	57.68	53.84	71.53	58.05	54.12	71.57	58.05	54.16

(continued)

Table 8A.4 Continued

Year	p-point%	Income concept			Income concept, excl. capital gain			Income concept, excl. imputed net rent			Income concept, excl. capital gain and imputed net rent		
		FI	GI	DI	FI	GI	DI	FI	GI	DI	FI	GI	DI
	70	57.84	46.97	43.15	57.86	46.98	43.17	59.30	47.33	43.40	59.33	47.32	43.41
	80	43.57	34.94	31.46	43.57	34.94	31.46	44.74	35.20	31.63	44.75	35.21	31.63
	90	26.37	20.90	18.21	26.38	20.89	18.21	27.06	21.06	18.29	27.05	21.06	18.29
	95	15.78	12.45	10.56	15.77	12.43	10.54	16.21	12.55	10.57	16.21	12.54	10.57
	99	4.62	3.65	3.01	4.60	3.65	3.01	4.73	3.69	3.01	4.73	3.68	3.00
	99.9	0.77	0.63	0.56	0.76	0.62	0.56	0.78	0.64	0.55	0.78	0.64	0.56
1993	0	100.00	100.00	100.00	100.00	100.00	100.00	100.00	100.00	100.00	100.00	100.00	100.00
	10	99.78	95.98	95.08	99.79	95.95	95.06	100.01	96.12	95.21	100.01	96.10	95.20
	20	98.30	90.35	88.53	98.30	90.28	88.46	99.52	90.56	88.72	99.54	90.51	88.66
	30	95.15	83.72	81.16	95.14	83.64	81.02	96.91	84.01	81.39	96.94	83.92	81.28
	40	89.67	76.23	73.05	89.64	76.09	72.87	91.53	76.52	73.28	91.54	76.39	73.10
	50	82.05	67.83	64.25	81.99	67.65	63.99	83.90	68.11	64.41	83.89	67.93	64.16
	60	72.44	58.42	54.62	72.33	58.20	54.31	74.21	58.69	54.78	74.14	58.47	54.45
	70	60.59	47.82	44.07	60.43	47.56	43.72	62.17	48.08	44.21	62.02	47.82	43.84
	80	46.19	35.79	32.41	45.96	35.52	32.02	47.46	36.03	32.53	47.26	35.73	32.12
	90	28.30	21.64	19.11	28.02	21.36	18.70	29.09	21.79	19.15	28.82	21.49	18.73
	95	17.12	13.02	11.29	16.83	12.75	10.92	17.62	13.13	11.33	17.32	12.85	10.95
	99	5.34	4.02	3.47	5.11	3.84	3.19	5.54	4.08	3.48	5.31	3.88	3.21
	99.9	1.10	0.84	0.76	0.95	0.78	0.65	1.18	0.85	0.78	0.99	0.76	0.66
1994	0	100.00	100.00	100.00	100.00	100.00	100.00	100.00	100.00	100.00	100.00	100.00	100.00
	10	99.88	95.98	95.07	99.89	95.95	95.08	100.01	96.09	95.12	100.01	96.06	95.15
	20	98.63	90.39	88.55	98.63	90.32	88.52	99.75	90.60	88.66	99.77	90.53	88.63
	30	95.84	83.78	81.17	95.88	83.68	81.07	97.65	84.04	81.32	97.74	83.94	81.25
	40	90.54	76.24	73.06	90.60	76.09	72.89	92.54	76.53	73.20	92.65	76.37	73.05

	50	82.85	67.78	64.21	82.87	67.57	63.97	84.86	68.07	64.31	84.94	67.86	64.09
	60	73.02	58.35	54.59	72.99	58.11	54.30	74.95	58.61	54.68	74.95	58.36	54.38
	70	61.04	47.81	44.09	60.94	47.52	43.74	62.71	48.05	44.16	62.64	47.75	43.80
	80	46.59	35.82	32.49	46.40	35.50	32.08	47.88	36.04	32.52	47.73	35.72	32.10
	90	28.49	21.56	19.11	28.21	21.22	18.65	29.33	21.72	19.13	29.04	21.39	18.69
	95	16.99	12.80	11.18	16.69	12.48	10.76	17.57	12.92	11.20	17.26	12.57	10.77
	99	5.06	3.77	3.29	4.80	3.54	3.00	5.28	3.78	3.32	4.98	3.59	2.99
	99.9	1.00	0.70	0.63	0.86	0.62	0.52	1.05	0.72	0.66	0.89	0.63	0.53
1995	0	100.00	100.00	100.00	100.00	100.00	100.00	100.00	100.00	100.00	100.00	100.00	100.00
	10	99.84	96.07	95.17	99.85	96.05	95.14	100.01	96.17	95.21	100.01	96.15	95.20
	20	98.53	90.59	88.76	98.54	90.53	88.70	99.73	90.79	88.84	99.75	90.74	88.79
	30	95.61	84.09	81.50	95.66	84.01	81.40	97.46	84.33	81.59	97.55	84.26	81.48
	40	90.15	76.66	73.48	90.23	76.56	73.34	92.12	76.90	73.55	92.25	76.80	73.41
	50	82.47	68.25	64.71	82.53	68.13	64.51	84.40	68.52	64.75	84.49	68.38	64.57
	60	72.76	58.83	55.10	72.79	58.68	54.87	74.62	59.10	55.14	74.67	58.95	54.91
	70	60.92	48.27	44.61	60.89	48.08	44.35	62.56	48.50	44.61	62.55	48.32	44.32
	80	46.58	36.22	32.95	46.48	36.02	32.62	47.84	36.42	32.95	47.74	36.19	32.62
	90	28.80	22.00	19.56	28.57	21.77	19.22	29.60	22.13	19.55	29.38	21.89	19.19
	95	17.67	13.33	11.66	17.37	13.10	11.35	18.20	13.46	11.70	17.92	13.22	11.36
	99	5.76	4.24	3.75	5.52	4.07	3.49	5.97	4.30	3.78	5.74	4.13	3.53
	99.9	1.12	0.78	0.84	1.08	0.79	0.80	1.21	0.81	0.87	1.17	0.81	0.83
1996	0	100.00	100.00	100.00	100.00	100.00	100.00	100.00	100.00	100.00	100.00	100.00	100.00
	10	99.85	96.19	95.30	99.85	96.16	95.31	100.01	96.26	95.32	100.01	96.24	95.36
	20	98.61	90.83	88.99	98.60	90.78	88.97	99.80	91.00	89.01	99.81	90.96	89.01
	30	95.87	84.45	81.79	95.88	84.34	81.69	97.66	84.64	81.83	97.71	84.54	81.76
	40	90.55	77.06	73.80	90.56	76.91	73.66	92.52	77.29	73.84	92.57	77.15	73.70
	50	82.88	68.68	65.02	82.84	68.49	64.81	84.87	68.96	65.09	84.88	68.77	64.86
	60	73.13	59.27	55.42	73.03	59.02	55.12	75.06	59.57	55.48	75.00	59.34	55.17
	70	61.20	48.66	44.92	61.04	48.37	44.53	62.90	48.97	44.97	62.75	48.67	44.59
	80	46.71	36.56	33.21	46.41	36.21	32.73	48.10	36.85	33.29	47.81	36.49	32.81
	90	28.85	22.22	19.74	28.41	21.83	19.20	29.75	22.43	19.80	29.31	22.02	19.25

(*continued*)

Table 8A.4 Continued

Year	p-point%	Income concept			Income concept, excl. capital gain			Income concept, excl. imputed net rent			Income concept, excl. capital gain and imputed net rent		
		FI	GI	DI	FI	GI	DI	FI	GI	DI	FI	GI	DI
	95	17.63	13.47	11.76	17.13	13.06	11.23	18.22	13.62	11.84	17.71	13.19	11.29
	99	5.63	4.29	3.71	5.22	3.95	3.30	5.86	4.34	3.75	5.43	4.01	3.33
	99.9	0.96	0.69	0.64	0.84	0.61	0.53	0.98	0.72	0.67	0.91	0.63	0.55
1997	0	100.00	100.00	100.00	100.00	100.00	100.00	100.00	100.00	100.00	100.00	100.00	100.00
	10	99.85	96.26	95.43	99.85	96.22	95.42	100.00	96.34	95.47	100.00	96.31	95.48
	20	98.59	91.05	89.30	98.59	90.93	89.19	99.81	91.18	89.34	99.83	91.08	89.26
	30	95.84	84.80	82.30	95.84	84.63	82.08	97.67	85.01	82.34	97.75	84.83	82.14
	40	90.50	77.56	74.51	90.48	77.29	74.19	92.51	77.81	74.53	92.58	77.52	74.21
	50	82.96	69.33	65.90	82.86	68.97	65.45	84.99	69.64	65.96	84.95	69.27	65.50
	60	73.31	60.04	56.42	73.09	59.57	55.84	75.28	60.37	56.51	75.10	59.91	55.91
	70	61.58	49.53	45.97	61.20	48.96	45.24	63.35	49.88	46.09	62.99	49.31	45.33
	80	47.38	37.50	34.27	46.78	36.83	33.40	48.88	37.87	34.43	48.31	37.16	33.52
	90	29.74	23.21	20.73	28.96	22.45	19.78	30.80	23.51	20.92	30.01	22.70	19.89
	95	18.66	14.39	12.69	17.85	13.66	11.76	19.38	14.62	12.88	18.51	13.86	11.87
	99	6.54	5.00	4.36	5.88	4.46	3.70	6.85	5.13	4.49	6.17	4.59	3.79
	99.9	1.66	1.23	1.07	1.36	1.00	0.85	1.77	1.32	1.14	1.44	1.04	0.90
1998	0	100.00	100.00	100.00	100.00	100.00	100.00	100.00	100.00	100.00	100.00	100.00	100.00
	10	99.86	96.41	95.59	99.86	96.35	95.71	100.01	96.48	95.61	100.01	96.42	95.77
	20	98.59	91.38	89.64	98.59	91.23	89.64	99.74	91.51	89.66	99.78	91.35	89.69
	30	95.69	85.28	82.82	95.68	85.03	82.67	97.43	85.46	82.84	97.50	85.20	82.71
	40	90.25	78.10	75.13	90.16	77.73	74.83	92.16	78.34	75.15	92.16	77.96	74.87
	50	82.61	69.89	66.58	82.40	69.40	66.11	84.51	70.18	66.63	84.41	69.68	66.18
	60	72.93	60.64	57.14	72.58	60.04	56.50	74.80	60.96	57.24	74.50	60.32	56.58
	70	61.34	50.12	46.65	60.78	49.36	45.84	63.01	50.46	46.79	62.49	49.69	45.95

80	47.30	38.04	34.94	46.50	37.16	33.94	48.75	38.41	35.11	47.95	37.48	34.08
90	30.02	23.81	21.40	28.95	22.80	20.26	31.02	24.10	21.62	29.92	23.06	20.38
95	19.16	15.04	13.38	18.00	14.00	12.18	19.86	15.29	13.57	18.62	14.20	12.27
99	7.29	5.66	5.00	6.18	4.77	4.00	7.66	5.84	5.18	6.47	4.90	4.13
99.9	2.23	1.70	1.55	1.53	1.19	1.02	2.37	1.78	1.64	1.65	1.22	1.07
1999												
0	100.00	100.00	100.00	100.00	100.00	100.00	100.00	100.00	100.00	100.00	100.00	100.00
10	99.81	96.44	95.64	99.82	96.35	95.91	100.00	96.52	95.67	100.01	96.42	96.01
20	98.53	91.44	89.80	98.52	91.23	89.89	99.71	91.58	89.81	99.77	91.36	89.96
30	95.48	85.35	83.07	95.47	85.01	82.96	97.18	85.57	83.11	97.29	85.21	83.05
40	89.95	78.32	75.50	89.83	77.80	75.16	91.76	78.60	75.57	91.77	78.07	75.27
50	82.46	70.27	67.07	82.16	69.57	66.48	84.33	70.62	67.21	84.11	69.91	66.63
60	73.09	61.17	57.79	72.51	60.28	56.93	74.89	61.59	57.96	74.40	60.66	57.13
70	61.72	50.90	47.49	60.85	49.80	46.36	63.40	51.33	47.72	62.59	50.19	46.58
80	48.04	39.15	35.96	46.80	37.80	34.55	49.48	39.56	36.22	48.21	38.18	34.77
90	31.36	25.23	22.70	29.69	23.68	21.02	32.43	25.62	22.97	30.69	23.98	21.20
95	20.79	16.58	14.71	18.98	15.01	13.00	21.60	16.91	15.01	19.69	15.25	13.16
99	8.94	7.03	6.14	7.35	5.73	4.71	9.41	7.29	6.40	7.66	5.89	4.87
99.9	2.56	1.97	1.85	2.09	1.56	1.30	2.77	2.07	2.01	2.24	1.63	1.37
2000												
0	100.00	100.00	100.00	100.00	100.00	100.00	100.00	100.00	100.00	100.00	100.00	100.00
10	99.80	96.52	95.72	99.80	96.40	96.03	100.00	96.59	95.73	100.01	96.47	96.14
20	98.47	91.62	90.00	98.43	91.35	90.09	99.66	91.80	90.07	99.71	91.52	90.23
30	95.44	85.69	83.37	95.38	85.22	83.17	97.14	85.92	83.51	97.21	85.49	83.38
40	89.96	78.68	75.89	89.78	78.00	75.40	91.78	79.06	76.10	91.71	78.37	75.64
50	82.44	70.69	67.56	81.99	69.79	66.74	84.30	71.11	67.81	83.97	70.18	67.01
60	73.03	61.61	58.29	72.25	60.44	57.13	74.86	62.09	58.57	74.15	60.88	57.41
70	61.62	51.37	48.02	60.41	49.92	46.52	63.29	51.84	48.36	62.13	50.34	46.78
80	48.06	39.61	36.54	46.40	37.87	34.65	49.50	40.09	36.92	47.81	38.29	34.94
90	31.44	25.58	23.18	29.28	23.64	21.03	32.53	26.05	23.60	30.28	24.02	21.29
95	20.94	16.86	15.12	18.57	14.86	12.90	21.83	17.26	15.52	19.32	15.15	13.14
99	9.06	7.20	6.44	6.85	5.44	4.52	9.57	7.46	6.74	7.24	5.62	4.68
99.9	3.20	2.50	2.32	1.94	1.50	1.25	3.42	2.64	2.49	2.08	1.57	1.34

(continued)

Table 8A.4 Continued

Year	p-point%	Income concept			Income concept, excl. capital gain			Income concept, excl. imputed net rent			Income concept, excl. capital gain and imputed net rent		
		FI	GI	DI	FI	GI	DI	FI	GI	DI	FI	GI	DI
2001	0	100.00	100.00	100.00	100.00	100.00	100.00	100.00	100.00	100.00	100.00	100.00	100.00
	10	99.78	96.54	95.77	99.79	96.50	95.83	99.71	96.60	95.80	100.00	96.57	95.88
	20	98.42	91.57	90.00	98.43	91.48	90.00	99.64	91.77	90.09	99.74	91.68	90.08
	30	95.38	85.52	83.26	95.41	85.39	83.16	97.18	85.81	83.39	97.28	85.66	83.30
	40	89.88	78.41	75.60	89.92	78.22	75.43	91.81	78.78	75.80	91.91	78.58	75.64
	50	82.21	70.28	67.13	82.17	70.01	66.85	84.19	70.70	67.35	84.22	70.44	67.08
	60	72.65	61.10	57.74	72.52	60.77	57.36	74.51	61.56	58.01	74.42	61.23	57.63
	70	61.15	50.72	47.30	60.91	50.31	46.83	62.84	51.19	47.64	62.64	50.78	47.15
	80	47.39	38.84	35.63	47.01	38.37	35.06	48.84	39.36	36.01	48.49	38.84	35.41
	90	30.54	24.76	22.11	29.99	24.19	21.44	31.65	25.21	22.47	31.11	24.62	21.77
	95	19.97	16.05	14.08	19.36	15.48	13.40	20.79	16.42	14.41	20.14	15.83	13.67
	99	8.26	6.52	5.65	7.71	6.08	5.14	8.69	6.75	5.90	8.12	6.27	5.36
	99.9	2.80	2.20	1.90	2.64	2.08	1.77	3.00	2.31	2.02	2.83	2.19	1.89
2002	0	100.00	100.00	100.00	100.00	100.00	100.00	100.00	100.00	100.00	100.00	100.00	100.00
	10	99.75	96.51	95.79	99.75	96.47	95.92	100.01	96.59	95.81	100.01	96.55	95.97
	20	98.32	91.52	89.99	98.32	91.41	90.04	99.62	91.69	90.05	99.65	91.59	90.14
	30	95.20	85.42	83.26	95.19	85.26	83.22	97.06	85.68	83.37	97.13	85.52	83.36
	40	89.59	78.30	75.58	89.54	78.07	75.45	91.56	78.68	75.79	91.58	78.45	75.67
	50	81.89	70.16	67.05	81.77	69.86	66.81	83.94	70.62	67.32	83.87	70.31	67.09
	60	72.31	60.97	57.63	72.08	60.58	57.26	74.25	61.43	57.92	74.05	61.03	57.54
	70	60.91	50.59	47.20	60.53	50.10	46.69	62.69	51.06	47.51	62.32	50.56	46.98
	80	47.28	38.78	35.55	46.72	38.18	34.89	48.79	39.25	35.89	48.24	38.63	35.19
	90	30.54	24.71	22.05	29.76	24.00	21.26	31.66	25.14	22.34	30.86	24.39	21.53
	95	19.97	16.03	13.94	19.13	15.28	13.12	20.81	16.38	14.24	19.90	15.60	13.37

	8.21 / 2.45	6.47 / 1.87	5.46 / 1.54	7.40 / 1.69	5.82 / 1.38	4.75 / 1.04	8.67 / 2.63	6.72 / 1.96	5.69 / 1.62	7.81 / 1.80	6.00 / 1.44	4.93 / 1.05
99												
99.9												
2003												
0	100.00	100.00	100.00	100.00	100.00	100.00	100.00	100.00	100.00	100.00	100.00	100.00
10	99.74	96.46	95.77	99.74	96.43	95.78	100.00	96.54	95.77	100.00	96.50	95.80
20	98.27	91.45	90.01	98.27	91.36	89.94	99.61	91.60	90.04	99.64	91.50	89.99
30	95.14	85.43	83.32	95.15	85.28	83.17	97.02	85.67	83.42	97.09	85.52	83.28
40	89.68	78.34	75.74	89.65	78.13	75.49	91.71	78.70	75.92	91.75	78.48	75.68
50	82.12	70.25	67.27	82.02	69.95	66.92	84.19	70.66	67.50	84.15	70.37	67.16
60	72.59	61.08	57.89	72.39	60.70	57.43	74.58	61.56	58.14	74.42	61.18	57.69
70	61.05	50.70	47.45	60.71	50.23	46.89	62.85	51.20	47.77	62.57	50.71	47.17
80	47.39	38.92	35.85	46.90	38.36	35.16	48.91	39.35	36.14	48.42	38.78	35.43
90	30.51	24.73	22.29	29.82	24.09	21.52	31.64	25.13	22.58	30.95	24.46	21.76
95	19.79	15.93	14.10	19.08	15.28	13.31	20.65	16.30	14.40	19.89	15.62	13.58
99	8.11	6.40	5.57	7.44	5.85	4.89	8.63	6.67	5.85	7.92	6.08	5.13
99.9	2.09	1.69	1.44	2.39	1.91	1.62	2.25	1.78	2.31	2.57	2.01	1.64
2004												
0	100.00	100.00	100.00	100.00	100.00	100.00	100.00	100.00	100.00	100.00	100.00	100.00
10	99.82	96.56	95.86	99.82	96.50	96.02	100.00	96.62	95.87	100.00	96.56	96.07
20	98.46	91.66	90.20	98.45	91.52	90.25	99.70	91.81	90.29	99.72	91.67	90.34
30	95.38	85.67	83.58	95.36	85.43	83.50	97.17	85.93	83.69	97.20	85.69	83.65
40	89.91	78.65	76.03	89.82	78.32	75.84	91.83	78.99	76.23	91.81	78.66	76.06
50	82.27	70.59	67.63	82.07	70.16	67.29	84.26	71.01	67.87	84.11	70.57	67.54
60	72.78	61.46	58.27	72.41	60.91	57.78	74.72	61.95	58.60	74.39	61.38	58.10
70	61.35	51.10	47.91	60.78	50.44	47.24	63.16	51.64	48.28	62.63	50.94	47.58
80	47.70	39.25	36.28	46.93	38.47	35.43	49.28	39.80	36.67	48.48	38.95	35.78
90	30.89	25.14	22.67	29.82	24.18	21.66	32.10	25.62	23.08	30.97	24.61	22.00
95	20.37	16.45	14.56	19.16	15.41	13.46	21.27	16.86	14.93	19.98	15.77	13.76
99	8.83	7.01	6.13	7.57	6.00	5.09	9.38	7.30	6.42	8.02	6.23	5.32
99.9	3.39	2.64	2.28	2.70	2.18	1.92	3.65	2.79	2.53	2.97	2.30	2.06

Notes: FI = Factor income, GI = Gross income, DI = Disposable income.

Source: Based on IDS data in 1987–2004, Statistics Finland.

Table 8A.5 Gross income items in deciles and in top 5%, 1%, and 0.1% in Finland, 1966–2004

Year	Deciles	Wages	Entrepreneurial income	Capital income	Transfers received	Gross income	Disposable income
1966	1	31.36	32.27	4.33	32.04	100	91.66
	5	57.39	25.55	4.72	12.34	100	88.21
	10	73.14	15.08	7.78	4.00	100	79.17
	Top 5%	69.25	17.26	9.29	4.19	100	77.78
	Top 1%	53.59	28.58	15.06	2.76	100	76.06
	Top 0.1%	-	-	-	-	-	-
	Total	66.82	18.38	5.54	9.26	100	84.34
1971	1	25.43	25.00	8.06	41.51	100	94.08
	5	62.35	18.24	5.13	14.27	100	84.50
	10	71.72	14.13	6.49	7.66	100	71.05
	Top 5%	67.97	16.74	6.94	8.35	100	68.61
	Top 1%	53.06	34.98	8.19	3.77	100	64.70
	Top 0.1%	32.30	51.03	14.50	2.17	100	61.86
	Total	66.68	14.16	5.96	13.20	100	80.33
1976	1	22.94	22.46	3.94	50.67	100	92.03
	5	67.47	12.82	4.04	15.67	100	78.84
	10	73.77	12.24	5.19	8.80	100	65.24
	Top 5%	69.33	15.06	5.86	9.75	100	62.71
	Top 1%	54.01	26.33	7.65	12.01	100	59.80
	Top 0.1%	55.65	39.62	3.02	1.71	100	60.81
	Total	68.82	11.43	4.30	15.45	100	75.02
1981	1	27.87	14.84	4.64	52.65	100	92.07
	5	68.31	11.83	2.71	17.15	100	80.53
	10	76.19	11.01	4.22	8.58	100	66.30
	Top 5%	73.87	12.80	4.98	8.35	100	63.32
	Top 1%	65.02	19.46	6.17	9.34	100	56.30
	Top 0.1%	36.23	42.48	7.06	14.24	100	51.69
	Total	69.72	10.29	3.24	16.75	100	76.66

Year							
1985	1	33.07	10.17	4.25	52.51	100	90.04
	5	68.54	8.73	3.05	19.68	100	77.00
	10	75.87	10.34	4.00	9.78	100	63.79
	Top 5%	72.70	11.16	4.67	11.46	100	61.47
	Top 1%	66.33	11.29	5.41	16.97	100	55.91
	Top 0.1%	53.88	10.16	7.13	28.82	100	49.03
	Total	68.91	8.73	3.35	19.01	100	73.98
1987	1	27.32	11.37	5.93	55.38	100	91.41
	5	68.82	6.20	3.57	21.41	100	77.79
	10	75.19	8.39	6.09	10.33	100	63.35
	Top 5%	73.19	8.74	7.11	10.97	100	60.88
	Top 1%	66.79	11.20	10.89	11.11	100	55.59
	Top 0.1%	51.76	13.81	21.65	12.79	100	51.64
	Total	68.29	6.98	4.58	20.15	100	74.22
1988	1	28.30	9.19	6.11	56.41	100	91.04
	5	68.74	6.28	3.64	21.33	100	76.94
	10	73.36	8.54	7.46	10.63	100	62.15
	Top 5%	69.66	9.95	9.07	11.31	100	59.62
	Top 1%	55.61	15.04	15.56	13.80	100	55.02
	Top 0.1%	39.20	13.95	28.35	18.51	100	47.36
	Total	67.83	6.93	4.89	20.35	100	73.18
1989	1	28.73	7.44	4.82	59.01	100	92.42
	5	65.87	7.25	4.17	22.71	100	77.75
	10	71.73	11.31	7.28	9.68	100	63.06
	Top 5%	68.52	13.28	8.81	9.39	100	60.91
	Top 1%	58.64	18.48	14.07	8.81	100	56.63
	Top 0.1%	33.92	26.47	28.26	11.36	100	52.16
	Total	67.11	7.85	4.86	20.17	100	73.75
1990	1	27.94	6.84	5.37	59.86	100	93.56
	5	65.99	7.00	3.91	23.10	100	78.58
	10	72.68	10.25	7.47	9.60	100	65.02
	Top 5%	70.29	11.90	8.66	9.15	100	62.98
	Top 1%	60.15	17.41	13.52	8.92	100	58.24
	Top 0.1%	51.26	22.36	24.26	2.12	100	51.14
	Total	66.79	7.37	5.10	20.73	100	75.06

(*continued*)

Table 8A.5 Continued

Year	Deciles	Wages	Entrepreneurial income	Capital income	Transfers received	Gross income	Disposable income
1991	1	28.00	8.30	5.53	58.17	100	93.18
	5	61.08	6.93	5.52	26.48	100	79.95
	10	69.68	8.84	9.91	11.58	100	66.71
	Top 5%	67.40	9.82	11.83	10.95	100	64.66
	Top 1%	53.64	15.64	17.96	12.76	100	61.06
	Top 0.1%	37.77	25.76	26.05	10.41	100	57.84
	Total	63.73	6.49	6.55	23.23	100	76.41
1992	1	22.20	6.97	6.21	64.62	100	92.05
	5	57.07	5.99	5.94	31.01	100	78.48
	10	66.55	9.52	9.51	14.43	100	64.52
	Top 5%	62.25	11.79	11.10	14.85	100	62.61
	Top 1%	47.62	17.58	16.99	17.81	100	60.66
	Top 0.1%	28.79	26.39	26.37	18.46	100	57.20
	Total	59.39	6.28	6.74	27.59	100	74.59
1993	1	19.31	7.52	5.73	67.44	100	92.96
	5	49.73	6.19	6.88	37.20	100	79.76
	10	63.80	8.06	13.69	14.45	100	65.65
	Top 5%	58.86	9.62	16.92	14.60	100	64.46
	Top 1%	48.99	12.54	24.49	13.97	100	62.56
	Top 0.1%	29.36	4.67	52.99	12.98	100	63.87
	Total	55.13	6.26	8.27	30.34	100	75.23
1994	1	13.56	4.49	4.82	77.13	100	90.73
	5	49.95	6.78	6.08	37.19	100	77.43
	10	62.44	9.98	13.04	14.54	100	64.30
	Top 5%	59.66	10.02	16.79	13.52	100	63.14
	Top 1%	45.55	15.21	27.20	12.03	100	62.23
	Top 0.1%	24.86	6.17	56.77	12.20	100	63.93
	Total	53.88	7.12	7.95	31.06	100	73.53

Year							
1995	1	14.17	6.00	5.01	74.82	100	90.38
	5	51.46	5.65	6.10	36.79	100	76.72
	10	61.04	10.03	14.77	14.16	100	64.25
	Top 5%	57.20	11.53	18.77	12.50	100	62.82
	Top 1%	41.58	13.48	36.23	8.72	100	63.11
	Top 0.1%	18.24	20.05	60.57	1.14	100	67.55
	Total	54.60	7.06	8.46	29.88	100	73.03
1996	1	17.76	5.08	5.09	72.07	100	90.11
	5	50.19	4.86	7.04	37.90	100	76.83
	10	63.09	7.82	16.18	12.91	100	64.05
	Top 5%	58.59	8.63	20.79	11.99	100	62.91
	Top 1%	43.08	9.71	36.76	10.45	100	62.12
	Top 0.1%	23.46	11.73	57.10	7.72	100	63.05
	Total	55.73	6.19	9.06	29.02	100	72.85
1997	1	18.60	5.20	5.64	70.55	100	90.55
	5	49.91	5.56	7.57	36.96	100	77.55
	10	59.99	9.00	19.56	11.44	100	65.48
	Top 5%	54.54	10.25	25.20	10.01	100	64.42
	Top 1%	38.22	12.19	41.94	7.65	100	63.45
	Top 0.1%	21.82	10.25	66.05	1.89	100	63.50
	Total	55.73	6.52	10.31	27.44	100	73.71
1998	1	16.70	4.73	5.04	73.54	100	91.04
	5	51.92	5.18	8.27	34.63	100	77.36
	10	59.22	9.20	21.20	10.38	100	65.60
	Top 5%	54.19	9.70	27.63	8.49	100	64.66
	Top 1%	33.59	10.45	49.59	6.37	100	64.03
	Top 0.1%	8.33	4.61	83.72	3.33	100	69.09
	Total	56.61	6.31	11.23	25.84	100	73.57
1999	1	16.23	4.63	5.64	73.50	100	90.90
	5	54.20	6.65	8.20	30.95	100	77.26
	10	56.60	8.20	26.30	8.90	100	65.83
	Top 5%	50.31	8.51	34.03	7.14	100	64.83
	Top 1%	32.83	5.42	56.62	5.13	100	63.22
	Top 0.1%	21.56	5.14	71.14	2.16	100	62.99
	Total	56.59	6.09	12.98	24.33	100	73.62
2000	1	18.97	4.71	5.44	70.88	100	90.70
	5	53.83	5.69	9.01	31.48	100	77.29

(continued)

Table 8A.5 Continued

Year	Deciles	Wages	Entrepreneurial income	Capital income	Transfers received	Gross income	Disposable income
	10	52.99	8.31	29.99	8.72	100	66.33
	Top 5%	46.00	8.71	38.86	6.43	100	65.47
	Top 1%	25.90	7.06	63.69	3.34	100	65.16
	Top 0.1%	6.37	8.26	83.99	1.38	100	65.44
	Total	56.45	6.08	14.24	23.24	100	73.63
2001	1	20.75	5.38	5.39	68.48	100	90.67
	5	55.32	6.04	8.20	30.44	100	78.25
	10	60.10	7.61	24.19	8.09	100	66.21
	Top 5%	54.28	7.90	31.53	6.28	100	64.87
	Top 1%	36.38	7.08	53.67	2.87	100	64.06
	Top 0.1%	15.80	4.11	78.44	1.66	100	63.65
	Total	58.44	5.87	12.33	23.36	100	74.54
2002	1	21.56	4.62	5.95	67.87	100	90.49
	5	56.80	4.25	8.44	30.51	100	78.67
	10	60.48	7.23	24.08	8.21	100	66.57
	Top 5%	55.42	7.79	30.66	6.13	100	64.76
	Top 1%	39.63	6.09	51.81	2.47	100	62.75
	Top 0.1%	28.97	1.77	68.63	0.64	100	61.16
	Total	58.35	5.79	12.53	23.33	100	74.94
2003	1	23.12	4.25	6.34	66.28	100	90.31
	5	54.78	5.58	9.07	30.56	100	79.48
	10	57.46	7.05	27.25	8.24	100	67.69
	Top 5%	51.02	6.49	35.39	7.10	100	66.25
	Top 1%	29.36	5.69	61.30	3.65	100	65.25
	Top 0.1%	8.42	2.18	88.64	0.76	100	66.42
	Total	57.38	5.53	13.57	23.52	100	75.54
2004	1	19.88	3.79	5.60	70.73	100	91.07
	5	59.24	4.87	8.65	27.24	100	79.18
	10	55.22	6.55	29.90	8.33	100	67.97
	Top 5%	47.71	6.31	38.98	7.01	100	66.72
	Top 1%	27.62	5.26	63.39	3.73	100	65.64
	Top 0.1%	5.33	0.08	93.99	0.60	100	67.73
	Total	56.95	5.33	14.58	23.14	100	75.65

Source: Based on IDS data in 1987–2004 and HES data in 1966–1985, Statistics Finland.

Table 8A.6 Capital income items in deciles and in top 5%, 1%, and 0.1% in Finland, 1987–2004

Year	Deciles	Interest income	Imputed net rents	Rental income	Realized capital gains	Other capital income	Total capital income
1987	1	14.88	77.48	5.52	1.29	0.83	100
	5	20.55	69.58	5.64	3.19	1.05	100
	10	41.93	35.11	16.43	5.86	0.67	100
	Top 5%	47.52	28.18	17.17	6.71	0.41	100
	Top 1%	52.73	14.64	22.72	9.88	0.04	100
	Top 0.1%	62.43	6.86	18.05	12.66	0.00	100
	Total	28.78	57.43	10.13	2.68	0.98	100
1988	1	18.11	72.66	5.38	2.04	1.80	100
	5	26.40	59.53	6.53	6.27	1.27	100
	10	35.34	25.60	15.56	22.48	1.02	100
	Top 5%	34.73	20.06	18.92	25.59	0.71	100
	Top 1%	32.28	12.33	20.00	35.27	0.13	100
	Top 0.1%	25.24	6.30	14.95	53.51	0.00	100
	Total	30.97	47.76	10.23	9.64	1.40	100
1989	1	18.79	75.47	2.58	1.38	1.78	100
	5	27.74	62.48	5.47	2.54	1.77	100
	10	35.01	28.79	12.31	18.97	4.91	100
	Top 5%	35.71	22.92	13.25	23.18	4.94	100
	Top 1%	34.79	13.35	14.34	31.48	6.05	100
	Top 0.1%	35.22	6.54	12.28	45.76	0.20	100
	Total	29.69	50.36	8.10	8.48	3.37	100
1990	1	19.72	72.24	2.80	1.02	4.21	100
	5	31.85	58.55	3.67	4.51	1.42	100
	10	35.59	33.71	11.53	17.39	1.78	100
	Top 5%	37.62	26.79	11.69	21.66	2.24	100
	Top 1%	34.20	13.76	10.89	37.85	3.30	100
	Top 0.1%	16.75	5.50	11.78	61.22	4.75	100
	Total	31.21	52.11	7.89	6.93	1.87	100
1991	1	24.94	68.48	3.95	1.42	1.20	100
	5	28.82	65.39	4.30	0.67	0.82	100
	10	42.90	34.08	12.14	8.23	2.65	100
	Top 5%	45.85	27.40	12.45	11.23	3.07	100
	Top 1%	46.04	18.16	11.24	20.33	4.23	100

(continued)

Table 8A.6 Continued

Year	Deciles	Interest income	Imputed net rents	Rental income	Realized capital gains	Other capital income	Total capital income
	Top 0.1%	41.66	10.78	5.08	31.15	11.33	100
	Total	33.78	53.00	7.47	3.60	2.15	100
1992	1	18.59	73.93	3.40	2.95	1.13	100
	5	21.49	68.61	3.56	3.67	2.68	100
	10	43.44	39.61	11.25	1.61	4.09	100
	Top 5%	47.27	32.67	13.17	2.01	4.88	100
	Top 1%	57.92	21.83	11.77	3.07	5.41	100
	Top 0.1%	56.01	11.94	21.12	0.00	10.93	100
	Total	29.80	59.22	7.13	1.20	2.65	100
1993	1	14.49	74.95	2.40	1.30	6.85	100
	5	19.13	67.52	5.17	5.31	2.88	100
	10	34.88	29.78	10.32	18.86	6.16	100
	Top 5%	36.90	23.28	11.09	21.55	7.19	100
	Top 1%	38.89	13.36	13.80	25.98	7.97	100
	Top 0.1%	36.00	5.31	20.22	33.32	5.14	100
	Total	25.18	52.92	7.59	10.09	4.22	100
1994	1	14.62	74.73	5.94	1.18	3.53	100
	5	10.06	76.76	6.67	2.80	3.71	100
	10	29.01	32.68	8.30	24.00	6.01	100
	Top 5%	32.31	24.89	8.04	27.81	6.96	100
	Top 1%	39.52	12.81	5.38	35.49	6.80	100
	Top 0.1%	45.17	4.53	1.39	44.89	4.02	100
	Total	18.13	57.90	7.84	12.02	4.11	100
1995	1	8.30	83.22	4.70	1.75	2.03	100
	5	7.88	79.10	7.37	2.69	2.96	100
	10	41.16	29.22	8.83	15.32	5.47	100
	Top 5%	48.45	22.44	7.83	15.21	6.07	100
	Top 1%	59.97	9.87	4.87	19.38	5.91	100
	Top 0.1%	78.07	3.39	1.10	15.86	1.59	100
	Total	23.14	54.86	8.36	9.47	4.17	100

Year							
1996	1	6.98	81.37	6.53	2.29	2.83	100
	5	11.35	76.77	5.70	3.42	2.77	100
	10	39.67	26.70	10.28	18.85	4.50	100
	Top 5%	44.22	20.29	9.45	21.34	4.69	100
	Top 1%	52.93	9.52	5.54	27.98	4.03	100
	Top 0.1%	47.76	3.21	2.42	42.15	4.46	100
	Total	22.38	55.24	8.38	10.29	3.70	100
1997	1	5.09	82.26	2.68	6.19	3.78	100
	5	6.03	81.06	4.66	4.77	3.47	100
	10	34.84	23.02	10.78	27.84	3.52	100
	Top 5%	39.13	16.48	10.22	30.96	3.22	100
	Top 1%	48.70	7.30	7.68	33.20	3.12	100
	Top 0.1%	62.97	2.02	0.76	33.49	0.77	100
	Total	20.64	52.52	8.38	15.24	3.22	100
1998	1	4.41	85.90	3.93	4.09	1.66	100
	5	8.18	76.75	4.52	6.57	3.97	100
	10	35.96	20.89	9.71	31.13	2.31	100
	Top 5%	38.88	14.79	9.29	35.12	1.93	100
	Top 1%	44.65	5.39	6.40	42.46	1.10	100
	Top 0.1%	38.86	1.35	5.29	54.21	0.29	100
	Total	22.57	48.05	8.20	18.10	3.08	100
1999	1	7.04	85.05	4.93	1.49	1.49	100
	5	7.75	77.51	6.59	5.73	2.43	100
	10	36.87	16.41	7.22	36.78	2.71	100
	Top 5%	39.57	11.30	6.68	39.77	2.68	100
	Top 1%	44.15	4.25	4.05	45.52	2.02	100
	Top 0.1%	50.98	1.37	6.17	40.94	0.53	100
	Total	24.55	42.73	6.79	23.16	2.77	100
2000	1	6.21	85.76	2.27	1.46	4.31	100
	5	11.40	72.31	5.08	6.55	4.66	100
	10	37.73	13.39	5.79	40.59	2.50	100
	Top 5%	40.13	8.86	5.26	43.38	2.37	100

(continued)

Table 8A.6 Continued

Year	Deciles	Interest income	Imputed net rents	Rental income	Realized capital gains	Other capital income	Total capital income
	Top 1%	43.33	3.17	2.85	48.90	1.76	100
	Top 0.1%	34.20	0.64	0.63	64.42	0.11	100
	Total	26.06	38.95	5.83	26.36	2.80	100
2001	1	8.34	78.91	5.82	3.14	3.79	100
	5	7.92	78.08	5.94	3.94	4.12	100
	10	54.70	16.76	7.58	17.24	3.71	100
	Top 5%	60.09	11.05	7.13	18.25	3.48	100
	Top 1%	69.06	4.27	5.07	18.53	3.07	100
	Top 0.1%	82.01	0.90	1.04	13.00	3.05	100
	Total	32.91	45.07	7.14	11.10	3.78	100
2002	1	14.62	80.09	2.20	1.36	1.72	100
	5	9.11	77.30	5.50	3.99	4.11	100
	10	50.79	18.63	6.93	19.01	4.64	100
	Top 5%	55.86	12.60	5.75	21.40	4.39	100
	Top 1%	63.90	4.50	3.73	24.93	2.94	100
	Top 0.1%	45.19	1.17	1.38	49.62	2.64	100
	Total	31.57	46.40	6.62	11.01	4.39	100
2003	1	6.49	81.81	6.41	3.50	1.79	100
	5	8.03	80.42	3.13	2.90	5.52	100
	10	56.19	17.56	6.06	16.11	4.08	100
	Top 5%	61.75	11.83	5.47	17.35	3.60	100
	Top 1%	69.52	3.58	4.39	19.53	2.99	100
	Top 0.1%	65.10	0.90	6.95	25.50	1.55	100
	Total	34.25	45.18	6.11	10.32	4.14	100
2004	1	6.05	85.20	4.78	2.35	1.63	100
	5	10.94	76.77	4.69	3.31	4.29	100
	10	57.05	14.88	4.94	19.50	3.63	100
	Top 5%	60.93	9.97	4.56	21.26	3.28	100
	Top 1%	65.65	3.52	2.67	25.95	2.20	100
	Top 0.1%	66.50	0.58	2.20	28.95	1.78	100
	Total	36.77	41.35	5.56	12.56	3.75	100

Source: Based on IDS data in 1987–2004, Statistics Finland.

Table 8A.7 Tax items in deciles and top 5%, 1%, and 0.1% in Finland, 1987–2004

Year	Decile	State earned income tax[1]	State capital income tax	Property tax	Municipal tax	Other taxes	Other current transfers paid	Total current transfers paid
1987	1	5.89	-	0.10	71.68	10.07	12.26	100
	5	30.50	-	0.02	56.63	6.45	6.40	100
	10	53.26	-	0.47	37.10	4.69	4.49	100
	Top 5%	55.81	-	0.69	34.69	4.52	4.28	100
	Top 1%	60.24	-	1.72	30.44	3.85	3.75	100
	Top 0.1%	63.47	-	3.65	26.19	3.27	3.42	100
	Total	40.37	-	0.15	48.05	5.72	5.71	100
1988	1	8.02	-	0.18	70.18	9.31	12.30	100
	5	32.84	-	0.01	54.78	6.01	6.35	100
	10	54.85	-	0.28	36.03	4.60	4.24	100
	Top 5%	57.54	-	0.38	33.77	4.35	3.95	100
	Top 1%	62.52	-	0.86	29.63	3.44	3.55	100
	Top 0.1%	66.15	-	2.03	25.85	2.74	3.23	100
	Total	42.18	-	0.10	46.78	5.47	5.47	100
1989	1	14.14	-	0.13	63.34	5.01	17.38	100
	5	32.85	-	0.01	55.48	0.74	10.92	100
	10	52.66	-	0.25	36.80	2.10	8.18	100
	Top 5%	54.55	-	0.34	34.49	2.83	7.78	100
	Top 1%	57.80	-	0.90	30.35	4.13	6.82	100
	Top 0.1%	56.87	-	2.49	25.14	9.62	5.88	100
	Total	41.68	-	0.10	46.90	1.28	10.03	100
1990	1	13.38	-	0.03	71.52	1.41	13.66	100
	5	31.17	-	0.04	57.10	0.97	10.72	100
	10	51.06	-	0.26	38.92	1.85	7.92	100
	Top 5%	53.16	-	0.35	36.49	2.32	7.69	100
	Top 1%	56.91	-	0.67	31.49	4.14	6.79	100
	Top 0.1%	60.03	-	0.97	27.22	5.23	6.55	100
	Total	40.06	-	0.10	49.15	1.12	9.57	100

(continued)

Table 8A.7 Continued

Year	Decile	State earned income tax[1]	State capital income tax	Property tax	Municipal tax	Other taxes	Other current transfers paid	Total current transfers paid
1991	1	10.21	–	0.11	73.01	4.22	12.45	100
	5	28.44	–	0.02	59.24	1.05	11.26	100
	10	47.42	–	0.28	40.87	2.07	9.36	100
	Top 5%	49.79	–	0.41	38.55	2.48	8.77	100
	Top 1%	53.03	–	0.91	33.35	4.29	8.42	100
	Top 0.1%	54.02	–	1.83	28.90	7.46	7.79	100
	Total	36.43	–	0.11	51.39	1.55	10.52	100
1992	1	9.34	–	0.08	68.19	2.31	20.07	100
	5	25.77	–	0.01	55.21	1.19	17.83	100
	10	43.24	–	0.23	38.15	3.84	14.53	100
	Top 5%	45.26	–	0.30	35.69	4.71	14.03	100
	Top 1%	47.27	–	0.61	31.49	7.70	12.94	100
	Top 0.1%	49.23	–	1.87	26.40	11.33	11.17	100
	Total	33.33	–	0.09	48.02	2.18	16.38	100
1993	1	5.47	4.61	0.21	61.85	3.99	23.86	100
	5	20.62	1.64	0.03	54.79	1.48	21.43	100
	10	39.27	4.42	0.43	37.28	1.62	16.97	100
	Top 5%	41.29	5.76	0.64	34.66	1.87	15.78	100
	Top 1%	44.09	9.17	1.17	29.97	2.22	13.38	100
	Top 0.1%	39.44	23.36	2.44	20.55	5.26	8.95	100
	Total	29.10	2.43	0.15	47.31	1.47	19.53	100
1994	1	2.46	3.45	0.07	75.04	2.20	16.78	100
	5	19.19	1.52	0.00	54.04	1.07	24.17	100
	10	37.13	5.61	0.42	36.65	1.12	19.06	100
	Top 5%	38.66	7.47	0.63	34.05	1.27	17.92	100
	Top 1%	39.07	14.47	1.46	28.47	1.93	14.60	100
	Top 0.1%	31.35	36.41	3.67	18.33	0.63	9.61	100
	Total	27.17	2.91	0.18	46.69	1.11	21.94	100
1995	1	3.63	3.10	0.00	73.72	2.03	17.52	100
	5	19.97	1.55	0.00	53.72	0.98	23.77	100

	10	37.71	6.05	0.41	36.05	1.10	18.68	100
	Top 5%	39.53	7.90	0.63	33.31	1.21	17.42	100
	Top 1%	38.69	17.59	1.32	27.02	1.55	13.83	100
	Top 0.1%	33.94	35.16	1.19	21.18	1.20	7.32	100
	Total	28.18	3.12	0.18	45.94	1.03	21.54	100
1996	1	4.52	3.77	0.02	70.21	2.12	19.37	100
	5	22.14	1.89	0.10	53.49	0.99	21.39	100
	10	37.96	7.52	0.70	35.29	1.18	17.35	100
	Top 5%	38.84	10.35	1.07	32.43	1.38	15.93	100
	Top 1%	35.81	20.98	2.58	25.42	2.25	12.96	100
	Top 0.1%	26.92	30.76	4.23	17.88	2.38	17.83	100
	Total	29.26	3.66	0.24	45.70	1.04	20.10	100
1997	1	3.58	4.93	0.06	68.62	1.68	21.14	100
	5	20.42	2.22	0.01	54.47	0.85	22.03	100
	10	36.31	10.74	0.95	34.48	0.95	16.57	100
	Top 5%	36.85	14.26	1.42	31.30	1.14	15.03	100
	Top 1%	33.33	25.38	3.51	22.95	1.95	12.89	100
	Top 0.1%	21.99	38.78	7.63	12.49	2.14	16.98	100
	Total	28.22	5.05	0.31	45.55	0.83	20.04	100
1998	1	3.71	5.02	0.42	70.53	1.98	18.33	100
	5	20.86	3.14	0.02	53.67	0.92	21.39	100
	10	36.58	12.62	1.03	34.10	1.29	14.38	100
	Top 5%	36.75	16.88	1.48	30.63	1.54	12.71	100
	Top 1%	32.45	31.87	3.15	21.93	2.67	7.92	100
	Top 0.1%	8.57	71.62	6.91	6.35	4.58	1.96	100
	Total	28.71	6.02	0.36	45.30	1.04	18.57	100
1999	1	3.73	4.15	0.00	71.94	2.03	18.15	100
	5	21.80	2.74	0.02	53.42	1.12	20.89	100
	10	35.48	16.84	1.80	32.26	0.93	12.68	100
	Top 5%	35.26	22.42	2.62	28.25	0.94	10.50	100
	Top 1%	31.48	37.98	4.65	19.47	1.04	5.36	100
	Top 0.1%	22.76	53.13	9.10	12.44	0.66	1.91	100
	Total	28.60	7.62	0.62	44.44	0.99	17.73	100
2000	1	5.15	3.97	0.09	70.30	1.91	18.58	100
	5	21.86	3.10	0.04	54.19	1.28	19.52	100

(continued)

Table 8A.7 Continued

Year	Decile	State earned income tax[1]	State capital income tax	Property tax	Municipal tax	Other taxes	Other current transfers paid	Total current transfers paid
	10	33.33	21.34	1.71	30.79	1.12	11.71	100
	Top 5%	31.96	28.15	2.47	26.42	1.21	9.79	100
	Top 1%	23.97	48.74	4.53	16.04	1.66	5.05	100
	Top 0.1%	14.89	68.18	6.80	8.26	0.30	1.57	100
	Total	28.43	9.15	0.62	43.94	1.15	16.72	100
2001	1	3.40	5.91	0.19	68.71	2.23	19.55	100
	5	19.64	2.76	0.02	57.05	1.36	19.18	100
	10	35.60	15.50	1.50	33.99	1.25	12.17	100
	Top 5%	35.54	20.62	2.16	29.82	1.42	10.44	100
	Top 1%	29.66	37.62	4.36	20.26	1.85	6.25	100
	Top 0.1%	18.95	56.90	9.34	10.61	2.00	2.21	100
	Total	27.94	7.11	0.54	46.73	1.20	16.48	100
2002	1	5.11	4.43	0.12	71.74	2.49	16.12	100
	5	20.60	2.40	0.00	57.47	1.22	18.31	100
	10	35.60	15.57	1.69	34.65	1.05	11.43	100
	Top 5%	36.03	20.34	2.45	30.49	1.09	9.61	100
	Top 1%	30.81	36.35	5.28	20.72	1.31	5.54	100
	Top 0.1%	24.29	48.17	9.90	13.54	1.99	2.11	100
	Total	27.94	7.19	0.59	47.61	1.15	15.52	100
2003	1	4.86	3.99	0.02	70.75	2.20	18.19	100
	5	19.34	2.46	0.01	59.02	1.36	17.80	100
	10	34.12	17.08	1.13	35.42	0.84	11.40	100
	Top 5%	33.95	22.60	1.64	31.36	0.86	9.60	100
	Top 1%	26.38	43.32	3.73	20.23	0.94	5.40	100
	Top 0.1%	10.91	72.16	8.18	6.70	0.62	1.43	100
	Total	27.01	7.69	0.39	48.36	1.07	15.47	100
2004	1	4.03	3.84	0.08	72.37	2.49	17.20	100
	5	20.37	2.56	0.03	57.39	1.22	18.43	100
	10	32.67	19.61	1.33	34.45	0.78	11.16	100
	Top 5%	31.76	26.21	1.94	29.90	0.78	9.42	100
	Top 1%	24.59	46.40	4.04	18.93	0.74	5.31	100
	Top 0.1%	6.79	79.77	7.14	4.83	0.39	1.09	100
	Total	26.71	8.74	0.48	47.42	1.11	15.54	100

[1] In 1987–1992 state income tax included earned and capital state income taxes.

Source: Based on IDS data in 1987–2004, Statistics Finland.

Table 8A.8 Income tax tables 1920–2003 in Finland

	Table number			Table number	
Year	Taxable income	Income subject to taxation	Year	Taxable income	Income subject to taxation
1920	1		1970	2	2
1921	1		1971	2	2
1922	2		1972	2	2
1924	2		1973	2	2
1926	2		1974	1a	1a
1929	2		1975	2a	2a
1931	2		1976	2	2
1934	2		1977	2	2
1935	2		1978	2	2
1937	2		1979	2	2
1938	3		1980	2	2
1942	5		1981	2	2
1943	1		1982	2	2
1945	6		1983	2	2
1947	8		1984	2	2
1948	7		1985	2	2
1949	7	4	1986	2	2
1950	7	4	1987	2	2
1951	8	4	1988	2	2
1952	8	5	1989	2	2
1953	9	5	1990	2	2
1954	9	5	1991	2	2
1955	7	5	1992	2	2
1956	7	5	1993		2
1957	6	5	1994		2
1958	7	5	1995		2
1959	10	9	1996		2
1960	11	10	1997		2
1961	11	6	1998		2
1962	11	6	1999		2
1963	11	6	2000		2
1964	11	6	2001		2
1965	11	6	2002		2
1966	11	6	2003		2
1967	11	6			
1968	11	6			
1969	2	2			

Note: Table number in Statistics on Income and Wealth, Statistics Finland, various years.

Table 8A.9 Reference totals for tax units and income, Finland, 1920–2003

Year	Taxable income among population				Income subject to taxation			Cost of living deflator
	Income (millions of 2005 €)	Number of filers	Total number of tax units	Average income (2005 €)	Income (millions of 2005 €)	Number of persons	Average income (2005 €)	
1920	2,133	457,573	1,281,900	1,664	n.a.	n.a.	n.a.	34.700
1921	2,123	611,317	1,307,530	1,624	n.a.	n.a.	n.a.	27.700
1922	2,406	667,258	1,333,160	1,805	n.a.	n.a.	n.a.	28.500
1924	2,906	611,642	1,384,420	2,099	n.a.	n.a.	n.a.	27.800
1926	3,140	662,377	1,435,680	2,187	n.a.	n.a.	n.a.	27.500
1929	3,476	737,280	1,512,570	2,298	n.a.	n.a.	n.a.	26.500
1931	3,649	659,087	1,554,124	2,348	n.a.	n.a.	n.a.	31.300
1934	3,912	653,257	1,601,895	2,442	n.a.	n.a.	n.a.	33.100
1935	5,349	316,956	2,261,100	2,366	n.a.	n.a.	n.a.	32.600
1937	5,707	400,188	2,308,300	2,472	n.a.	n.a.	n.a.	30.900
1938	5,907	445,825	2,333,600	2,531	n.a.	n.a.	n.a.	30.300
1947	8,490	1,706,867	1,690,077	5,024	n.a.	n.a.	n.a.	5.100
1948	7,423	1,252,203	1,691,563	4,388	n.a.	n.a.	n.a.	3.800
1949	6,433	872,459	1,696,629	3,791	8,975	1,529,125	5,869	3.700
1950	7,773	1,049,776	1,710,890	4,544	10,441	1,599,226	6,529	3.300
1951	8,413	1,030,161	1,717,720	4,898	11,845	1,632,914	7,254	2.800
1952	8,878	946,598	1,729,563	5,133	12,434	1,864,122	6,670	2.700
1953	9,338	987,635	1,736,697	5,377	13,015	1,891,062	6,882	2.700
1954	9,568	817,207	1,747,789	5,474	11,231	1,570,773	7,150	2.700
1955	10,901	876,373	1,759,951	6,194	9,144	1,466,865	6,234	2.800
1956	11,058	802,410	1,770,494	6,246	9,396	1,429,402	6,573	2.500
1957	10,321	832,576	1,781,626	5,793	8,823	1,424,124	6,195	2.200
1958	8,898	657,271	1,796,106	4,954	10,212	1,647,124	6,200	2.000
1959	9,582	699,958	1,811,603	5,289	8,913	1,440,294	6,188	2.000
1960	10,245	790,633	1,822,171	5,623	9,541	1,565,509	6,095	1.900
1961	10,735	716,650	1,847,922	5,809	12,381	1,532,967	8,077	1.900

1962	11,685	719,112	1,848,726	6,320	19,124	2,354,331	8,123	1.800
1963	12,303	747,933	1,864,877	6,597	20,294	2,399,575	8,457	1.741
1964	13,323	892,932	1,878,167	7,093	21,322	2,455,545	8,683	1.578
1965	14,475	987,757	1,905,038	7,598	22,779	2,515,268	9,056	1.505
1966	15,501	1,063,558	1,942,928	7,978	23,845	2,566,390	9,291	1.448
1967	15,843	1,054,175	1,981,445	7,996	24,507	2,617,451	9,363	1.371
1968	16,896	1,136,701	2,016,533	8,379	25,084	2,615,772	9,589	1.265
1969	17,625	1,551,585	2,036,393	8,655	27,156	2,770,455	9,802	1.237
1970	18,721	1,706,556	3,058,616	6,121	29,496	2,813,166	10,485	1.204
1971	20,676	1,852,697	3,108,174	6,652	31,777	2,890,141	10,995	1.131
1972	23,024	1,988,830	3,161,741	7,282	34,547	2,982,367	11,584	1.055
1973	25,160	2,138,503	3,211,988	7,833	36,464	3,023,149	12,062	0.945
1974	27,567	2,663,651	3,256,775	8,465	39,037	3,169,707	12,316	0.805
1975	27,298	2,048,762	3,294,356	8,286	40,385	3,104,684	13,008	0.683
1976	27,640	2,085,688	3,325,633	8,311	41,030	3,242,340	12,654	0.597
1977	26,149	2,052,695	3,356,855	7,790	39,462	3,252,133	12,134	0.530
1978	25,349	1,946,956	3,382,625	7,494	39,276	3,283,942	11,960	0.493
1979	27,464	2,016,986	3,411,893	8,049	41,862	3,357,647	12,468	0.459
1980	28,866	2,133,840	3,442,417	8,385	43,771	3,465,224	12,632	0.412
1981	29,570	2,178,882	3,477,810	8,502	45,105	3,526,145	12,792	0.368
1982	31,146	2,258,600	3,515,342	8,860	46,887	3,609,405	12,990	0.336
1983	32,996	2,371,934	3,552,029	9,289	51,275	3,847,970	13,325	0.310
1984	34,946	2,464,297	3,585,923	9,745	53,622	3,895,592	13,765	0.290
1985	37,559	2,626,728	3,613,751	10,393	56,763	3,984,295	14,247	0.274
1986	39,539	2,669,382	3,641,495	10,858	59,399	4,025,487	14,756	0.264
1987	41,154	2,693,191	3,667,634	11,221	62,321	4,058,427	15,356	0.255
1988	44,073	2,788,405	3,690,224	11,943	65,461	4,094,258	15,989	0.243
1989	54,250	2,665,914	3,710,830	14,619	67,236	4,044,684	16,623	0.228
1990	56,916	2,763,826	3,730,892	15,255	70,866	4,135,418	17,136	0.215
1991	55,996	2,733,584	3,753,724	14,917	69,712	4,100,940	16,999	0.206
1992	54,867	2,719,873	3,769,627	14,555	67,491	4,056,780	16,637	0.201
1993	n.a.	n.a.	n.a.	n.a.	65,309	4,029,339	16,208	0.197
1994	n.a.	n.a.	n.a.	n.a.	66,289	4,088,945	16,212	0.195
1995	n.a.	n.a.	n.a.	n.a.	69,075	4,110,790	16,803	0.193

(continued)

Table 8A.9 Continued

Year	Taxable income among population				Income subject to taxation			Cost of living deflator
	Income (millions of 2005 €)	Number of filers	Total number of tax units	Average income (2005 €)	Income (millions of 2005 €)	Number of persons	Average income (2005 €)	
1996	n.a.	n.a.	n.a.	n.a.	71,203	4,127,072	17,253	0.192
1997	n.a.	n.a.	n.a.	n.a.	73,887	4,152,349	17,794	0.189
1998	n.a.	n.a.	n.a.	n.a.	77,507	4,171,664	18,579	0.187
1999	n.a.	n.a.	n.a.	n.a.	82,248	4,208,467	19,544	1.100
2000	n.a.	n.a.	n.a.	n.a.	85,398	4,233,601	20,172	1.064
2001	n.a.	n.a.	n.a.	n.a.	85,091	4,253,151	20,007	1.035
2002	n.a.	n.a.	n.a.	n.a.	87,019	4,278,436	20,339	1.019
2003	n.a.	n.a.	n.a.	n.a.	89,609	4,296,696	20,855	1.010

Table 8A.10 Income sources in Finland, 1966–2004

Year	Income sources	Data	Sample		Population		OECD equivalence scale	Cost of living index 1951='100'
			Household	Member	Household 1000	Member 1000		
1966	Household Survey for 1966, Textvolume:1, Supplementary Tables:2, 1972	HES	3,259	13,048	1,383.8	4,625.0	2.40	185
1971	Household Survey 1971, Statistical Surveys, Nro 55, Volume II, 1977	HES	8,816	28,420	1,495.5	4,445.0	2.20	237
1976	Household Survey 1976, Statistical Surveys, Nro 62, Volume I, 1979	HES	7,971	23,327	1,635.7	4,535.8	2.09	449
1981	Household Survey 1981, Statistical Surveys, Nro 71, Volume I: 1–5, 1984	HES	7,368	22,792	1,919.4	4,727.3	1.90	729
1985	Household Survey 1985, Income and consumption, Quality descriptions, 1988	HES	8,200	26,804	2,045.2	4,833.3	1.85	980
1987	Income distribution statistics 1987, Income and consumption, 1989:5	IDS	11,863	34,122	2,082.3	4,884.3	1.83	1,052
1988	Income distribution statistics 1988, Income and consumption, 1990:4	IDS	12,192	34,297	2,102.3	4,872.1	1.81	1,104
1989	Income distribution statistics 1989, Income and consumption, 1992:4	IDS	11,971	32,800	2,149.2	4,931.6	1.80	1,177
1990	Income distribution statistics 1990, Income and consumption, 1992:15	IDS	11,445	31,471	2,170.6	4,974.4	1.79	1,248
1991	Income distribution statistics 1991, Income and consumption, 1993:8	IDS	11,749	32,412	2,200.2	5,000.2	1.78	1,300
1992	Income distribution statistics 1992, Income and consumption, 1994:7	IDS	10,417	28,763	2,218.0	5,021.8	1.77	1,333
1993	Income distribution statistics 1993, Income and consumption, 1995:10	IDS	9,176	25,354	2,243.1	5,015.1	1.76	1,361
1994	Income distribution statistics 1994, Income and consumption, 1996:10	IDS	8,964	24,774	2,270.0	5,035.0	1.75	1,376
1995	Income distribution statistics 1995, Income and consumption, 1997:12	IDS	9,262	25,229	2,290.1	5,053.1	1.74	1,390
1996	Income distribution statistics 1996, Income and consumption, 1998:14	IDS	9,349	25,358	2,310.0	5,063.4	1.73	1,398
1997	Income distribution statistics 1997, Income and consumption, 1999:15	IDS	10,010	26,902	2,326.0	5,076.5	1.73	1,415
1998	Income distribution statistics 1998, Income and consumption, 2000:15	IDS	9,345	25,010	2,355.0	5,086.1	1.71	1,435
1999	Income distribution statistics 1999, Income and consumption, 2001:11	IDS	9,590	25,646	2,365.1	5,096.7	1.71	1,452
2000	Income distribution statistics 2000, Income and consumption, 2002:14	IDS	10,423	27,841	2,373.0	5,096.7	1.71	1,501
2001	Income distribution statistics 2001, Income and consumption, 2003:13	IDS	10,736	28,303	2,381.5	5,120.0	1.71	1,539
2002	Income distribution statistics 2002, Income and consumption, 2004:14	IDS	10,843	28,201	2,397.5	5,131.8	1.71	1,563
2003	Income distribution statistics 2003, Income and consumption, 2005:11	IDS	11,200	29,070	2,405.0	5,145.2	1.71	1,577
2004	Income distribution statistics 2004, Income and consumption, 2006	IDS	11,229	29,112	2,415.0	5,160.8	1.70	1,580

Sources: The sources for the income data in Finland 1966–2004 are listed in Table 8A.10. The household based data are taken from the samples of the *Income Distribution Surveys* (IDS) 1987–2004 and of the *Household Expenditure Surveys* (HES) 1966, 1971, 1976, 1981, Statistics Finland.
The share of corporation and their shares of turnover in Figure 8.22 in Finland can be found in the *Corporate Enterprises and Personal Businesses in Finland* 1995, 2001 and 2006, Statistics Finland. The first one is published (1997) in Table 6, pp. 19–20, 1990–1995, the second one (2001) in Table 5, p. 19, 1994–2000 and the last one (2006) in Table 8, p, 20, 2001–2006.
The growth rates of real wages, profits, dividends and entrepreneurial income in Figure 8.21 are based on the *Finnish National Accounts 1974–2004* (2006) in Table 4.1 (Non-financial corporations, S111), Table 4.7 (National sectors total, S1) and Table 1.2 (Main aggregates, National income and disposable national income).

REFERENCES

Atkinson, A. B. (1999). 'Is Rising Income Inequality Inevitable? A Critique of the Transatlantic Consensus', *WIDER Annual Lectures*, 3.

—— (2002). 'Top Incomes in the United Kingdom over the 20th Century', Nuffield College, mimeo.

—— (2007). 'Measuring Top Incomes: Methodological Issues', in Atkinson and Piketty (2007: 18–42).

—— and T. Piketty (eds.) (2007). *Top Incomes over the 20th Century: A Contrast between Continental European and English-Speaking Countries*. Oxford: Oxford University Press.

—— and W. Salverda (2003). 'Top Incomes in the Netherlands and the United Kingdom over the 20th Century', Nuffield College, mimeo.

Cowell, F. A. and F. Mehta (1982). 'The Estimation and Interpolation of Inequality Measures', *Review of Economic Studies*, 49(2): 273–90.

Galbraith, J. K. (1967). *The New Industrial State*. Boston: Houghton Mifflin Co.

Jäntti, M. (2004). 'The Distribution of the Tax Burden in Finland 1985–2002', Åbo, mimeo.

—— J. Saari, and J. Vartiainen (2006). 'Growth and Equity in Finland', Discussion Paper 2006/06, UNU/WIDER, Helsinki.

Klugman, S. A., H. H. Panjer, and G. E. Willmot (1998). *Loss Models: From Data to Decisions*. Wiley Series in Probability and Statistics. New York: John Wiley & Sons.

Kuznets, S. (1955). 'Economic Growth and Income Inequality', *American Economic Review*, 49: 1–8.

Lampman, R. J. (1962). *The Share of Top Wealth-Holders in National Wealth, 1922–1956*. Princeton: Princeton University Press.

Landais, C. (2007). 'Les Hauts Revenus en France (1998–2006): une explosion des inégalitiés?' Paris School of Economics, Working Paper.

Lindhe, T., J. Södersten, and A. Öberg (2002). 'Economic Effects of Taxing Closed Corporations under a Dual Income Tax', *IFO Studien*, 4/2002.

Piketty, T. (2003). 'Income Inequality in France, 1901–1998', *Journal of Political Economy*, 111: 1004–42.

—— and E. Saez (2003). 'Income Inequality in the United States 1913–1998', *Quarterly Journal of Economics*, 118: 1–39.

Riihelä, M. and R. Sullström (2002). 'Käytettävissä olevien tulojen liikkuvuus vuosina 1990–1999', Government Institute for Economic Research, Discussion Papers 270 (in Finnish).

—— —— and M. Tuomala (2005). 'Kuponginleikkaajien paluu: ylimmät tulot ja niiden verotus', Labour Institute for Economic Research, *Talous & Yhteiskunta*, 1/2005 (in Finnish).

—— —— I. Suoniemi, and M. Tuomala (2001). 'Income Inequality in Finland during the 1990s', in J. Kalela, J. Kiander, M.-L. Kivikuru, H. A. Loikkanen, and J. Simpura (eds.) *Down from the Heavens, Up from the Ashes: The Finnish Economic Crisis of the 1990s in the Light of Economic and Social Research*. VATT Publications 27(6): 385–410.

Saez, E. and M. Veall (2003). 'The Evolution of High Incomes in Canada, 1920–2000', NBER Working Paper Series No. 9607.

Statistics Finland (1920–2002). *Statistics on Income and Property*, Income and Consumption. Helsinki: Statistics Finland.

Sullström, R. and M. Riihelä (1996). 'Indirect Taxes in the Finnish Tax System: An Analysis of the Effects of Taxes on the Households' Income Distribution in 1966–1990', Government Institute for Economic Research, Discussion Papers 120.

Suoniemi, I. (1993). 'Public Welfare Services and Inequality: Introduction to Methodology and Some Examples with the 1985 Finnish Household Expenditure Survey Data', Government Institute for Economic Research, Discussion Papers 45.

9

Top Incomes in Norway

R. Aaberge and A. B. Atkinson

9.1 INTRODUCTION

The shares of top incomes in Norway are of considerable intrinsic interest, since the series constructed in this chapter starts as far back as 1875. Based throughout on the same source—the municipal and central government income tax records—the series allows us to trace the evolution of the top of the income distribution over a period when Norway industrialized and then became oil-rich. The Norwegian experience is also of interest on a comparative basis. The studies in Atkinson and Piketty (2007) have shown how income inequality at the top of the distribution has increased in Anglo-Saxon countries, whereas the same rise in top income shares was not experienced by continental European countries—at least up to the late 1990s. It is therefore interesting to explore what has happened in Scandinavia. The present chapter examines the evidence for Norway, as well as making a comparison with other countries.

The chapter explores in detail the long-run changes at the top of the income distribution in Norway. It differs from a number of other analyses of income distribution in Norway (see for example, Aaberge et al. 2000, 2002; Aaberge and Langørgen 2006; Bojer 1987, 2008; Epland 1992, 1998; Ringen 1991) in that the chapter focuses on the top income groups. The concentration on the top groups means that we can produce a series extending much further back in time. While there are not data for all years, the results cover more than a century and a quarter.[1] The reader may wonder how far it is possible to construct a consistent series over time, and the results certainly need to be interpreted carefully in the light of changing economic and social circumstances, but there is continuity in the basic source: the data collected as part of administering the municipal and central government income tax.

We are most grateful to Erik Fjærli, Bård Lian, and Tom Wennemo for their assistance with the analysis of the micro-data, and Terje Skjerpen for careful proof-reading. We thank the Norwegian Research Council for financial support. We note that any opinions expressed in the chapter are solely those of the authors.

[1] In Denmark, the statistics go back further. Sørensen (1993) made estimates using the Danish income tax data 1870–1986. The first data for Sweden used by Roine and Waldenström (2008) relate to 1903.

The primary goal of the chapter is to provide a new data series and to spell out the issues involved in its construction. These issues are often taken for granted by economists, but it is essential to have an understanding of the origins of the data in order to interpret the evidence. The data sources and the methods applied, particularly the derivation of control totals for total population and total income, are set out in section 9.2. The results for Norway from 1875 to 2006 are set out in section 9.3. The next section (section 9.4) considers some of the factors that may explain the evolution of Norwegian top income shares over the period since 1875. Section 9.5 compares the top income shares in Norway with those in other countries for which the data begin in the last decade of the nineteenth century or in the first decade of the twentieth century. The conclusions of the chapter are summarized in section 9.6.

9.2 INCOME TAX DATA ON TOP INCOMES IN NORWAY

The use of income tax data for distributional analysis has long historical roots. In the UK, Bowley (1914) and Stamp (1916, 1936), among others, studied the tables of data resulting from the introduction of 'super-tax' in 1908. The work of Kuznets (1953) in the USA on the *Shares of Upper Income Groups in Income and Savings* was based on the tabulated federal income tax returns. In the Netherlands, Hartog and Veenbergen (1978) constructed a long time series of income distribution estimates from 1914 to 1972 using the published income tax statistical tables. Fresh impetus has however been given by the work of Piketty (2003) on top incomes for France, in which he employed both tabulations (as in the earlier studies) and individual tax data (micro-data).

The basic ingredients for the calculations of this chapter are the same as those used by Piketty. We use for the first part of the period (prior to 1967) tabulations of the distribution of income as assessed for tax purposes, giving the number of income recipients and total amount of income by ranges of assessed income. For the period since 1967, up to 2006, we use micro-data from the tax register files available to Statistics Norway.

In their tabulated form, the income tax statistics provide less rich information than the micro-data available for more recent years, but the tabulations for Norway often contain considerable detail on the classification of taxpayers by income ranges. For example, *Skattestatistikk for Budsjettåret 1951/52* contains information for the year 1950 giving 44 ranges of income, of which the top 6 apply to those with incomes of NOK 500,000 or more (NOK stands for Norwegian kroner) and contain respectively 5, 2, 2, 0, 1, and 10 income earners. There are published data for every year since 1948, apart from 1956 (on account of the changeover to PAYE (see Appendix 9A), which was introduced in the income year 1957). The income tax data have been supplemented by the Income Distribution Surveys (IDS). The IDS are sample surveys, covering a number of households; the sample size has varied, being 3,393 households and 9,582 people in 1987 and

14,679 households and 39,504 people in 1997. Most of the data in the IDS are collected from the income tax records, but household information is collected from household interview. Non-respondents to the survey are included, with information being substituted from the Central Population Register. The IDS have been conducted for 1958, 1962, 1967, 1973, 1976, 1979, 1982, and annually since 1984 (published in *Inntekts- og Formuesstatistikk*).

Prior to 1948, the data were assembled and published for only a small number of years, but they span a long period. The first tabulations of incomes for the tax were given in Kiær (1892–3) for 1859, but these cover only selected towns and cities. The first national data are those for 1875. Subsequently, income tabulations were published for 1888, 1896, 1902, 1906, 1910, 1913–14, 1929, and 1938. So, over a sixty-year period we have nine observations (for Sweden, Roine and Waldenström (2008 and Chapter 7) have ten observations for the pre-war period, but their series does not start until 1903). The first tabulations were made as part of parliamentary inquiries. The data for 1910 and 1929 were associated with the population census. The income information has been obtained from the tax register for municipal income tax in most of the earlier years (and for 1952–5), but the data for 1896, 1902, 1938, and 1948–51 relate to the central government income tax. (The data for 1938 are classified by taxable income, rather than assessed income.) Since 1957, the data have been drawn from the assessment of the central government income tax, but supplemented by data from the municipal tax assessments. Fuller information about the sources of the tabulations for 1875 to 1966 is given in Appendix 9A and Table 9A.1. Here we should simply note that the statistical tables are assembled from a variety of sources—including studies by individual authors and parliamentary inquiries, as well as official statistical yearbooks—and that they have not been easy to track down.

The basic limitation of the tax data is that they relate to the operation of the tax system. This affects the definition of income, so that this includes for example realized capital gains as defined for tax purposes, and we discuss later some of the consequences of changes in the tax law. Perhaps the most important shortcoming is that, for many years, they give only partial coverage of the population.[2] Here we follow two approaches, which we can associate with, respectively, Kuznets and Pareto. The approach of Kuznets (1953) was to compare the income tax data with countrywide estimates of the total population and of the total income. In the case of the Norwegian data for 1950, for example, the tax data cover some 1 million people with a total income of NOK 7.2 billion. We need to express these numbers as a percentage of the estimated total number and total amount in the economy as a whole. The key issue here is then the derivation of the control totals and these are discussed below. The second method focuses on the distribution *within the top group*. If we have a control total for numbers, we can calculate for example the share of the top 1 per cent within the top 10 per cent. This gives a measure of

---

[2] Although the tabulations for 1875, 1888, and 1906 included estimates of the number of persons not paying income tax.

the degree of inequality among the top incomes. Such an approach builds a bridge between Pareto and Lorenz.[3] For this reason, it is referred to below as the Pareto–Lorenz coefficient, since it is the Pareto coefficient derived from the Lorenz curve without resort to the income cut-off level.[4] By considering the share within the taxpaying population, we do not need to estimate the total income, although we still need a total for the population to locate the coefficients in the distribution.

Control Totals

The control totals are important in providing a degree of consistency over time and across countries. The first control total we are seeking is that for the population. Here we can apply either a total for the number of tax units, since there is joint taxation of the income of husband and wife, or we can apply a total for all adults, taken to be those aged 16 and over. The two series are plotted in Figure 9B.1, where we have estimated the number of tax units by subtracting the number of married women from total adults (see Appendix 9B for details). Although taxation is joint, separate filing has become increasingly prevalent as the number of two-earner couples has increased. As is clear from Figure 9B.1, the total recorded in the income tax statistics was in 1948 well below our calculated total tax units but began to exceed the total at the end of the 1970s, and approached the total adult population. Indeed, from 1998, Statistics Norway ceased to treat married couples with joint taxation as one personal taxpayer. This causes a break in comparability, but the two series were sufficiently close that the increase in the number of taxable units in 1998 was only some 200,000 (6 per cent). We have therefore taken as our control total the number of people aged 16+.[5]

The derivation of a control total for income is more difficult. As in studies for other countries, a point of departure is provided by the total household income series in the National Accounts. This series is a useful benchmark in view of the continuity in National Accounts and the fact that they provide a link across countries via the United Nations System of National Accounts (SNA). The sources for the household income totals are described in Appendix 9C, but

---

[3] Suppose that the upper tail of the distribution approaches the Pareto form: i.e. that the cumulative distribution F is such that $(1-F)$ is proportional to $y^{-\alpha}$, where y is income. If we assume that this holds exactly within the top income group, then this implies that the share of the top 1% within the top 10% is $(0.1)^{(1-1/\alpha)}$. For a specific α, the same value would be obtained if we took the share of the top 0.1% in the top 1%.

[4] It should be noted that where the distribution is not exactly Pareto, this method would yield a different value for the Pareto coefficient α from that reached, for example, by using the cut-off value of income and the cumulative frequency distribution, as is frequently done.

[5] It should be noted that no allowance is made for the existence in the tax data of part-year incomes. Part-year units may arise for several reasons. People reach the age of 16 in the course of the tax year; people die in the tax year; people may emigrate or immigrate.

in broad terms they include income from employment and self-employment, interest, rent and dividends, transfers from the government, and transfers from abroad. For the years from 1950, we have deducted employers' social security contributions. It should be noted that our totals include all public transfers, although certain of these are tax-free and are missing from the income tax statistics.

In all years, the household income total exceeds the total reported in the income tax tabulations. In 1950, for example, the household income total is NOK 13.1 million, whereas the total recorded in the tax statistics is NOK 7.2 million. In part this difference reflects the incomes of those not covered by the tax statistics; in part the difference reflects differences in definition or in the valuation of income. The second of these differences means that we cannot simply use the National Accounts household income totals. An alternative approach to the National Accounts is that which starts from the total recorded in the tax statistics and adds an estimate of the income of those not covered by the statistics ('non-filers'). The tabulations published by Kiær (1892–3) for 1875 and 1888 did indeed include estimates of the numbers and total income of those not covered, and in more recent years the same applies to the *Income Statistics* studies. As is noted in *Inntektsstatistikk 1970*, they provide 'estimates relating in principle to all personal income receivers and households, including persons with income and property under the taxation limits' (Statistisk Sentralbyrå 1973: 16). This alternative approach is discussed further in Appendix 9C, where we conclude that we need to combine the two approaches: a reasonable first approximation to an income concept that allows for those not covered, but is otherwise defined in the same way, is a fixed percentage (72 per cent) of the household income total. The remaining 28 per cent may be seen as corresponding to differences in definition (as with tax-free public transfers or imputed rent on owner-occupied housing) or to income missing from the tax statistics that is assumed to be distributed proportionately to recorded income. Finally, we should note the difference between 'gross' and 'assessed' income. The latter concept, used in the published tabulations and in the micro-data available to us, subtracts interest paid, premiums for pensions and life assurance, and certain other deductions. The subtractions do not include the special allowance for old age or those for seamen.

The use of income control totals allows us to incorporate, into a single series, data drawn from periods when there were differing proportions of taxpayers, but there are strong assumptions underlying their construction.

Interpolation

Since the basic data on which we are drawing prior to 1967 are in the form of grouped tabulations, and the intervals do not in general coincide with the percentage groups of the population with which we are concerned (such as the top 0.1 per cent), we have to interpolate in order to arrive at values for summary statistics such as the percentiles and shares of total income. Where there is information on both the number of persons and the total income in the range, we use the mean-split histogram. The rationale is as follows. Assuming, as seems reasonable in the case of top incomes, that the frequency distribution is non-increasing, then restricted upper and lower bounds can be calculated for the income shares (Gastwirth 1972). These bounds are limiting forms of the split histogram, with one of the two densities tending to zero or infinity—see Atkinson (2005) and the previous chapter. Guaranteed to lie between these is the histogram split at the interval mean with sections of positive density on either side. The mean-split histogram is used here. The ranges are in most cases sufficiently detailed that the bounds are close, and little extra precision is obtained by using more ranges.[6] In the case of 1929, where information is only given on frequencies, not total income per range, we use a simple Pareto interpolation fitted to the cumulative frequencies for each interval to identify the percentile cut-offs and to estimate the income shares.

9.3 RESULTS FOR TOP INCOMES IN NORWAY

Table 9.1 shows the results for Norway from 1875 to 2006 for the percentile shares covering the following six groups: top 10 per cent, 5 per cent, 1 per cent, 0.5 per cent, 0.1 per cent, and 0.05 per cent. The results relate to individuals (aged 16 and over) and to assessed (net) income before tax. The estimates from 1967 are based on micro-data; those up to 1967 are based on tabulated data. The shares of the top 5 per cent, 1 per cent, 0.5 per cent, 0.1 per cent, and 0.05 per cent are graphed in Figure 9.1.

For the post-war period, Table 9.1 and Figure 9.1 show the top income shares first falling and then rising sharply. In 1948, the share of the top 0.1 per cent was 2.8 per cent of total income: this group on average had 28 times their proportionate share. By the 1980s, the share of the top was less than 1 per cent. The share of the top 1 per cent in 1948 was 9 per cent; by the 1980s, it had more than halved. The decline in top income shares may have begun during the war years (we lack data for individual years between 1938 and 1948), but it continued after the Second World War. Apart from some recovery in the latter part of the 1950s, the top income shares in Norway declined for the best part of fifty years.

The change in direction may have been due to the liberalization of the capital markets in the 1980s, but the turning point in Figure 9.1 is clearly 1992. Since this coincides with the reform of income taxation, it creates interpretational difficulties, as evidenced by the volatility of the top income shares in recent years (for example, the share of the top 1 per cent in 2005 is twice that in 2006). These are discussed further below. Taken at face value, however, the upswing in top income shares was sharper than the preceding downward trend. The income share of the

---

[6] The tax statistics data typically have more ranges than those given in the publication *Historical Statistics*, but use of the more detailed data for 1948, for example, gave estimates of the shares that differed only in the second decimal place for the percentage shares.

Table 9.1 Top income shares, Norway, 1875–2006

	10%	5%	1%	0.50%	0.10%	0.05%
1875	40.00	31.74	18.37	14.37	7.89	5.86
1888	46.60	36.53	20.29	15.26	7.71	5.64
1896			19.80	15.46	8.79	
1902			15.21	11.71	6.59	5.13
1906	42.19	32.36	17.98	13.99	8.03	
1910	29.89	21.54	10.45	7.71		
1913	33.21	23.96	11.61	8.37		
1929	41.32	28.25	12.57	9.06	4.35	
1938		27.56	12.72	9.38	4.56	3.28
1948	34.38	22.46	9.10	6.36	2.83	2.00
1949	34.02	22.14	8.88	6.20	2.74	1.94
1950	34.10	22.09	8.76	6.06	2.63	1.84
1951	32.31	20.80	8.16	5.67	2.51	1.78
1952	31.39	19.57	6.93	4.59	1.87	1.29
1953	33.08	20.49	7.14	4.67	1.83	1.25
1954	31.79	19.79	6.86	4.46	1.70	1.15
1955	32.61	20.37	7.20	4.76	1.90	1.31
1956						
1957	32.72	20.94	7.88	5.35	2.35	1.70
1958	34.72	21.91	7.76	5.09	2.01	1.38
1959	34.20	21.51	7.39	4.73	1.77	1.19
1960	32.17	20.06	6.94	4.44	1.62	1.08
1961	31.77	19.78	6.76	4.29	1.53	1.01
1962	32.20	19.87	6.57	4.11	1.42	0.92
1963	32.03	19.67	6.43	3.98	1.35	0.87
1964	31.45	19.30	6.28	3.88	1.31	0.85
1965	30.65	18.65	5.99	3.69	1.23	0.79
1966	31.05	18.89	5.99	3.66	1.20	0.76
1967	31.25	19.01	5.92	3.58	1.16	0.74
1968	31.31	19.05	5.92	3.58	1.16	0.74
1969	31.46	19.21	6.03	3.67	1.21	0.77
1970	30.29	18.57	5.95	3.66	1.23	0.79
1971	30.81	18.85	5.99	3.68	1.23	0.79
1972	30.32	18.48	5.82	3.56	1.18	0.76
1973	29.60	18.07	5.72	3.50	1.15	0.74
1974	28.93	17.60	5.56	3.41	1.15	0.75
1975	29.41	17.73	5.49	3.33	1.09	0.69
1976	29.73	17.78	5.39	3.23	1.02	0.63
1977	30.09	18.00	5.45	3.28	1.05	0.67
1978	27.67	16.58	5.04	3.04	0.97	0.60
1979	27.01	16.22	5.03	3.09	1.05	0.67
1980	25.65	15.33	4.74	2.93	1.05	0.70
1981	25.00	14.93	4.57	2.79	0.98	0.65
1982	24.68	14.70	4.52	2.78	1.01	0.68
1983	24.32	14.56	4.51	2.79	1.02	0.68
1984	23.92	14.37	4.50	2.81	1.05	0.71
1985	24.02	14.48	4.59	2.88	1.08	0.73
1986	23.47	14.18	4.49	2.81	1.03	0.68
1987	23.44	14.18	4.52	2.83	1.05	0.70
1988	23.07	13.98	4.43	2.75	0.97	0.63

1989	22.22	13.44	4.24	2.64	0.94	0.61
1990	22.51	13.68	4.37	2.72	0.96	0.62
1991	22.56	13.80	4.45	2.78	0.96	0.62
1992	23.58	15.03	5.47	3.64	1.53	1.08
1993	25.91	17.15	7.09	5.05	2.44	1.79
1994	27.27	18.12	7.54	5.38	2.56	1.86
1995	27.22	18.08	7.48	5.34	2.61	1.94
1996	28.19	18.91	8.08	5.88	3.04	2.32
1997	29.49	20.00	8.75	6.42	3.33	2.51
1998	28.35	19.07	8.13	5.87	2.92	2.16
1999	28.65	19.43	8.49	6.21	3.15	2.35
2000	30.81	21.62	10.44	7.98	4.44	3.41
2001	27.21	18.18	7.48	5.28	2.50	1.82
2002	29.26	20.42	9.77	7.48	4.25	3.36
2003	30.27	21.43	10.58	8.18	4.68	3.67
2004	32.17	23.05	11.82	9.30	5.59	4.50
2005	37.67	28.61	16.78	13.71	8.41	6.75
2006	28.78	19.37	8.06	5.71	2.70	1.95

Note: The estimates for 1929 are based only on frequencies.

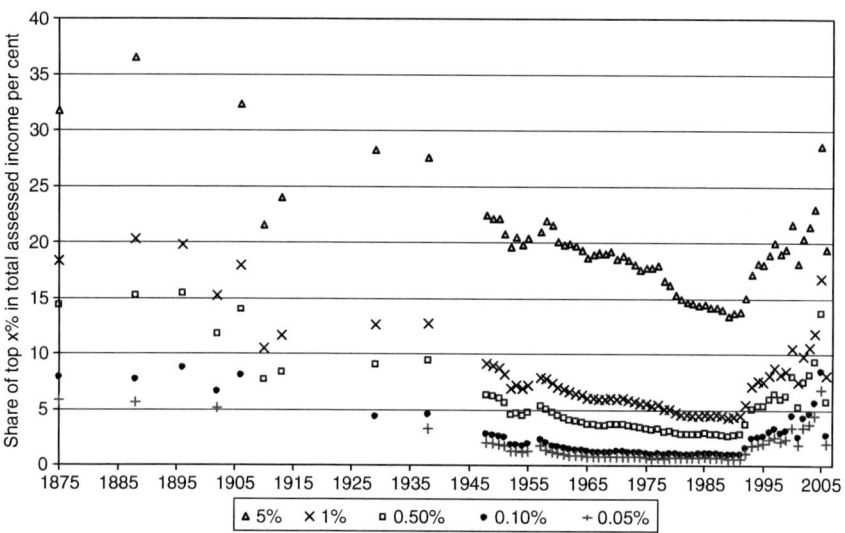

Figure 9.1 Share of top income groups in total assessed income, Norway, 1875–2006

top 1 per cent has more than doubled in fifteen years. The rise in top income shares since the end of the 1980s has reversed the decline of the previous forty years. Moreover, this increase has been largely confined to the top 1 per cent. Whereas the share of the top 1 per cent rose by some 7 percentage points between 1991 and 2004, the share of the next 4 per cent increased by only about 2 percentage points, and there was virtually no rise in the share of those in the top 10 per cent but not in the top 5 per cent.

The recent rise in top income shares is not surprising. Our main purpose here is to place the recent rise in historical perspective. What had happened before 1938? The estimates in Table 9.1 have to be qualified by the fact that they are drawn from a variety of sources, not a single regular series, and that the control totals are only approximate. But they suggest that the top income shares were high. The three estimates for the nineteenth century show the share of the top 1 per cent to be around 20 per cent and that of the top 0.5 per cent to be around 15 per cent. The latter group had some thirty times their proportionate share. To reduce these figures to the shares observed for 1948 would require the control totals to be out by a factor of 100 per cent, which seems implausible. Were the top shares rising or falling? Movements in fact occurred in both directions. There was a rise in the shares of the top 10 per cent, 5 per cent, and 1 per cent between 1875 and 1888. Between 1896 and 1902 there was a definite fall; there was some recovery in 1906, but then a further fall, with the share of the top 1 per cent losing 7.5 percentage points, and the share of the top 0.5 per cent falling to only a half of its 1896 value. After the First World War (in which Norway was not a combatant) there was some recovery in the top shares (although it should be noted that the 1929 figure is based only on frequencies).

Shares within Shares

The uncertainties surrounding the control totals for income can be avoided if we look at the 'shares within shares', as displayed in Figure 9.2. The within-group distribution is shown for the share of the top 1 per cent within the top 10 per cent, the share of the top 0.5 per cent within the top 5 per cent, and the share of the top 0.1 per cent within the top 1 per cent. These confirm that the nineteenth-century distribution was highly unequal: at the beginning of the period, the within-group shares were in excess of 40 per cent. A decline was then initiated after 1906 and the within-group shares were more like 30 per cent in 1948, and by the end of the 1960s under 20 per cent. The general U-shape is similar to that for the top shares, but with the difference that, while the rise in concentration was sharpest after 1991, it had already begun in the 1980s.

The similarity in the levels and movements of the shares within groups indicates that the upper tail of the distribution is close to Pareto in form. In 1906, the shares for the three groups were 42.6, 43.2, and 44.7 per cent. Translated into Pareto–Lorenz coefficients, these give values of 1.59, 1.57, and 1.54. The Pareto coefficients for 1875 and 1888 are similar. The values for all years are plotted in Figure 9.3, which shows the Pareto–Lorenz coefficients based on the share of the top 1 per cent within the top 10 per cent and the share of the top 0.5 per cent within the top 5 per cent. The rise in the coefficient—or fall in concentration at the top—began after 1906, but accelerated after 1948, when the coefficient was around 2.25, increasing to a point where it was close to 4 at the

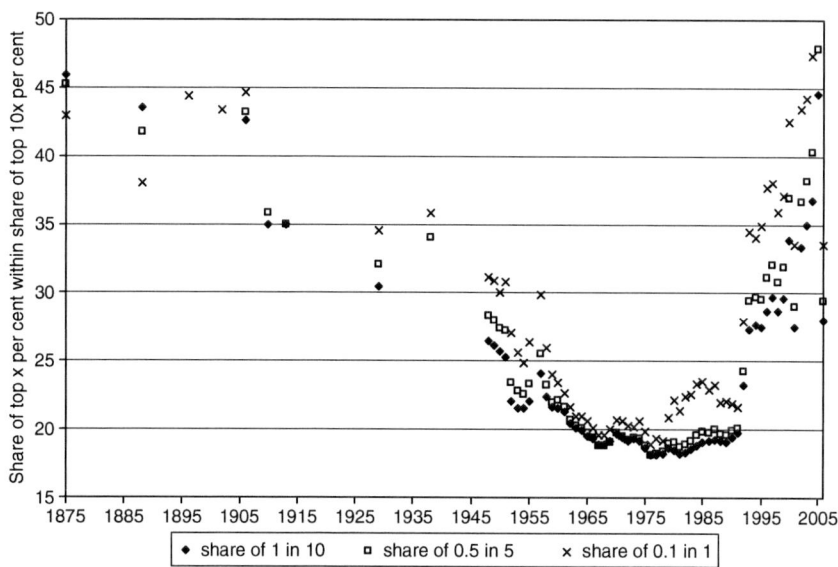

Figure 9.2 Shares within shares, Norway, 1875–2006

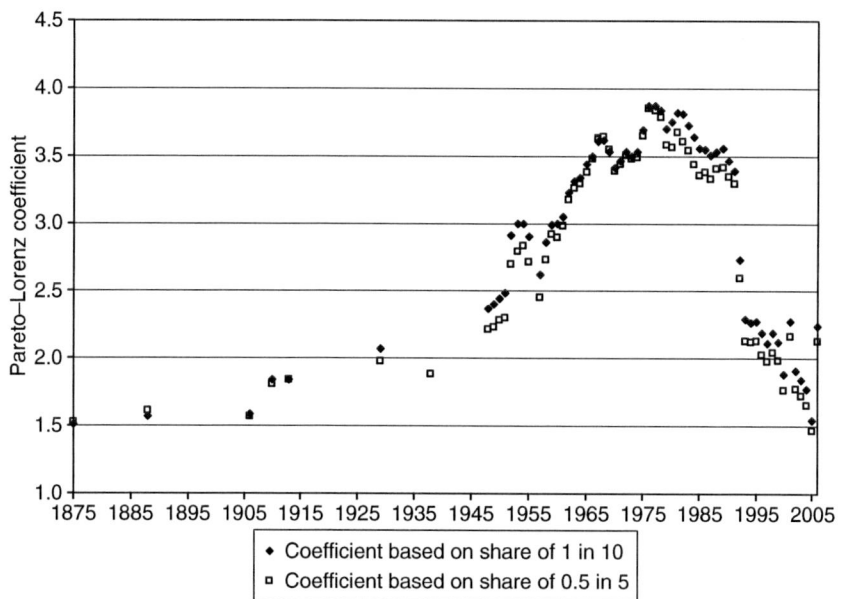

Figure 9.3 Pareto–Lorenz coefficients, Norway, 1875–2006

end of the 1970s. The Pareto coefficient then began to fall in the 1980s, at such a rate that for most years this century, it has been below 2.0. The shape of the distribution has changed in such a way that we have been through a complete cycle, of declining concentration followed by increasing concentration, with the increase taking place at a faster rate.

9.4 EXPLAINING THE OBSERVED EVOLUTION IN NORWAY

From being a pre-industrial society dominated by agricultural production Norway gradually developed into an industrial country during the second half of the nineteenth and first half of the twentieth century. The economic growth during this period was accompanied by a shift in population from rural to urban areas. In the late 1870s only one-seventh of the population lived in towns. Although Norway was in many respects a poor country by Western European standards around that time, it benefited from a large and effective shipping sector enjoying particularly favourable market conditions.[7] However, the high profits gained by the shipowners also partly explain why the share of the top 0.5 per cent approached 15 per cent in 1875, or 30 times their proportionate share. Except for a few years around 1880, the so-called Kristiania crash in 1899 with subsequent recession until 1904, and another recession around 1908–9, Norway experienced steady and relatively high economic growth until the recession in the late 1920s and early 1930s. Our estimates show that the top income shares increased from 1875 until 1896, but had been sharply reduced by 1902 due to the Kristiania crash.[8] Moreover, the recession around 1908–9 may explain the decline in the estimates of the top income shares in 1910 and 1913, compared with 1906. Overall, although there may have been an interregnum during the inter-war period, the long-term trend in top income shares in the first part of the period is strongly downward. For instance, the share of the top 0.1 per cent more or less halved from 1896 to 1938. As for most other European countries the Second World War had a major impact on the level as well as on the distribution of income. Our estimates show that the share of the top 0.5 per cent fell from 9.4 per cent in 1938 to 6.4 per cent in 1948.

It is interesting to compare these figures with the estimates of the concentration of capital in Norway constructed by Ohlsson, Roine, and Waldenström (2006). Their first observation is for 1789, but the relevant starting point here is 1868, when they estimate the share of the top 1 per cent in total wealth to be 36 per cent. Their next estimate, for 1912, is virtually identical at 37.2 per cent,

---

[7] Shipping as well as fish and timber accounted for 12% of GDP around 1870 (Sejersted 1992).
[8] The Kristiania crash meant a collapse in the financial and housing markets.

as is the third figure, for 1930, of 37.6 per cent. It was in the post-war period that the share of the top 1 per cent began to fall: from 34.6 per cent in 1948.

The early part of the post-war period was characterized by rather strict central planning of the economy, very progressive taxation, and gradual expansion of the welfare state. Over this period, the top income shares fell steadily and reached a turning point in the late 1980s/early 1990s. The share of the richest 0.5 per cent fell from 6.4 per cent in 1948 to 2.8 per cent in 1991. It should be noted that the turning point came some fifteen years after oil began to flow from the North Sea; by 1991 production had been at a high level for a number of years. Oil revenue may have been good for the public finances but did not spark off a rise in private top income shares. The recovery of the shares of top incomes that took place in the early 1990s is more likely to be related to a major reform of the financial markets from the mid 1980s that included abolishment of credit rationing and to a major tax reform in 1992 that included a significant reduction in taxes on capital incomes. As may be seen from Table 9.1, the financial deregulation initiated in 1984 did not lead immediately to a rise in top shares, but the subsequent events have to be interpreted in the light of the recession and the related Norwegian banking crisis of 1988 to 1992 (Gulbransen 2005, Vale 2005), which led to the nationalization of the three largest banks (share capital written down to zero, but no losses to depositors).

The implementation of the 1992 tax reform coincided not just with the end of the banking crisis, but with a change in the business cycles from a long period of recession with high unemployment and real interest rates to more favourable economic conditions with lower unemployment and interest rates. Moreover, a structural change from traditional manufacturing to services and technology took place in this period. Thus, all together the conditions for a rise in top income shares appear particularly favourable in the early 1990s. Indeed, our estimates show a sharp rise for the top income shares during the 1990s. This trend can be explained by a sharp increase in dividends and capital gains among the richest households after the 1992 tax reform.[9] Official Norwegian income statistics show a large increase in dividends received by households after the 1992 tax reform. The reported capital gains rose as well, but not as much as dividends. A government white paper[10] concluded that 'The increase in income from 1986 to 1996 has, in relative terms, been greatest for those with the highest incomes' and that 'The most important reason for the greater increase in high incomes is that capital incomes have been more unevenly distributed in the 1990s. This was due in particular to the sharp increase in dividend payments and gains from the sales of shares etc.' As demonstrated by Fjærli and Aaberge (2000), dividend receipts

---

[9] In the case of Sweden, Björklund, Palme, and Svensson (1995) report a jump in income inequality in Sweden from 1989 to 1991 due to realized capital gains that possibly can be explained by changes in the tax legislation.

[10] The Equitable Redistribution White Paper (the ER White Paper) on the distribution of income and living conditions in Norway, Ministry of Health and Social Affairs (1998–9).

Table 9.2 Share of top income groups in Norway: different income definitions, 1986–2005

	10%		1%		0.10%	
	Assessed	Hicksian	Assessed	Hicksian	Assessed	Hicksian
1986	22.45	23.37	3.97	4.50	0.65	0.95
1987	23.23	23.87	4.12	4.44	0.83	0.93
1988	23.26	24.20	4.56	5.04	1.01	1.25
1989	22.65	23.78	4.67	5.27	1.22	1.51
1990	22.29	23.38	4.44	5.06	0.96	1.20
1991	22.92	23.68	4.90	5.23	1.06	1.25
1992	23.31	23.27	5.21	5.19	1.15	1.13
1993	25.71	25.45	6.57	6.27	1.95	1.78
1994	27.10	26.49	7.52	6.88	2.42	2.08
1995	26.56	25.78	6.80	6.07	2.01	1.53
1996	28.21	27.52	8.33	7.72	3.27	2.91
1997	29.10	28.87	8.63	8.34	3.37	3.19
1998	27.70	26.79	7.54	6.95	2.29	2.11
1999	28.26	27.75	7.95	7.54	2.50	2.39
2000	30.19	28.25	9.86	8.23	3.32	2.57
2001	26.06	26.45	6.91	7.23	2.10	2.32
2002	28.64	25.01	9.43	6.29	3.79	1.86
2003	29.60	25.55	9.78	6.44	2.93	1.79
2004	31.26	26.47	11.13	6.89	5.05	1.90
2005	37.37	29.29	16.59	9.72	8.26	3.88

and capital gains received by the highest decile increased substantially soon after the implementation of the 1992 tax reform. However, this pattern might, as suggested by Fjærli and Aaberge (2000), partly be due to income shifting; i.e. actions taken by taxpayers to reclassify income. Moreover, a temporary tax on dividends explains the decline in top income shares in 2001, whereas the implementation of a permanent dividend tax from 2006 gave strong incentives for owner-managers of closely held firms to increase dividends in 2005. Thus, the sharp rise in top income shares in 2005 is a result of changes in dividends that are well above what might be considered as normal returns from shares.

To account for the interpretational difficulties related to reported dividends, it appears more relevant to use a measure derived from a Hicksian version of the definition of income. The 'Hicksian' measurement of the stock returns is less sensitive to changes in income-reporting behaviour than the conventional income definition and may thus provide a better basis for analysing the trend in top incomes during the pre- and post-reform period (1986–2004). To account for the effect of income shifting and strengthen the comparability of top incomes before and after the 1992 tax reform, we provide in Table 9.2 results of top incomes for the period 1986–2004 based on imputed returns from shares, which are assessed as the product of the estimated market value of the households' stocks[11] and the

[11] The procedure for estimation of the market values of non-quoted stocks is proposed by Fjærli and Aaberge (2000) and explained in Appendix 9D.

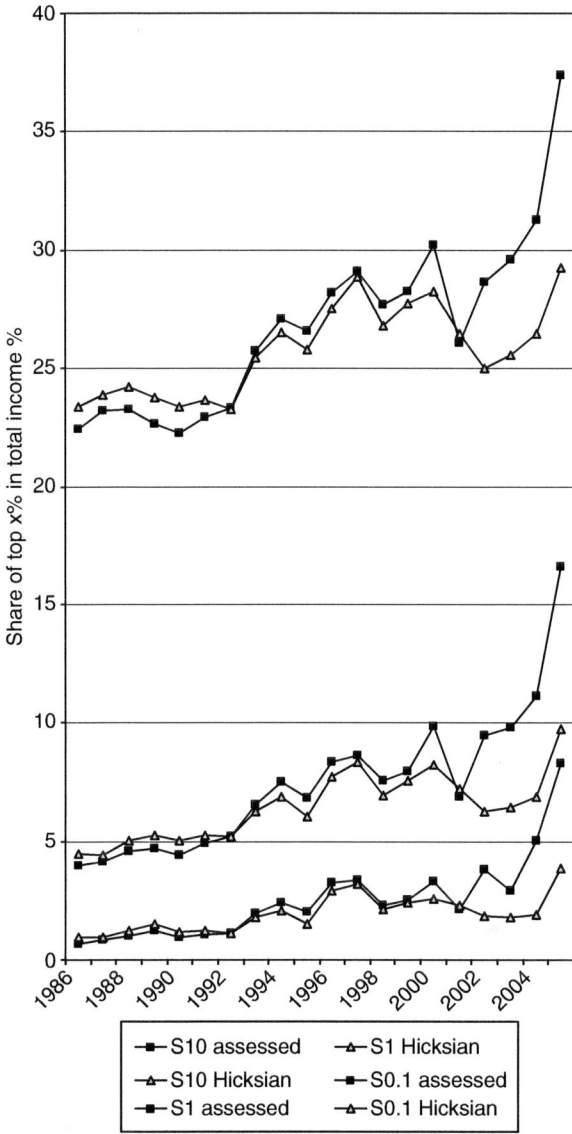

Figure 9.4 Share of top income groups in Norway: different income definitions, 1986–2005

long-run average rate of return (8.9 per cent) on the Oslo Stock Exchange (OSE).[12] Figure 9.4 illustrates the results with the different income concepts. The assessed income figures used in earlier graphs, for comparability with the

---

[12] The OSE index is a total return index that includes dividends.

results for earlier years, are shown by solid squares; and the imputed Hicksian measures are shown by shaded triangles.[13] The Hicksian series rises less fast, particularly after 2001, but still shows a definite increase: even leaving aside 2005, the share of the top 1 per cent rises by more than a half over the period.

9.5 COMPARISON WITH OTHER COUNTRIES

The Norwegian data are of particular interest in view of the long period covered. In this section we compare the top income shares with those in four other countries for which the data begin in the last decade of the nineteenth century or in the first decade of the twentieth century: Prussia/Germany, Sweden (from Chapter 7), and the UK. (The data for the United States do not commence until 1913.) Before doing so, we emphasize that the estimated top shares differ across countries in both sources and methods. The income tax is different and the differences inevitably affect the way in which income is measured. At the same time, the series are closer than is often the case for cross-country comparisons in that they are drawn from the same kind of source. We are not comparing household surveys in one country with register data in another. Figure 9.5

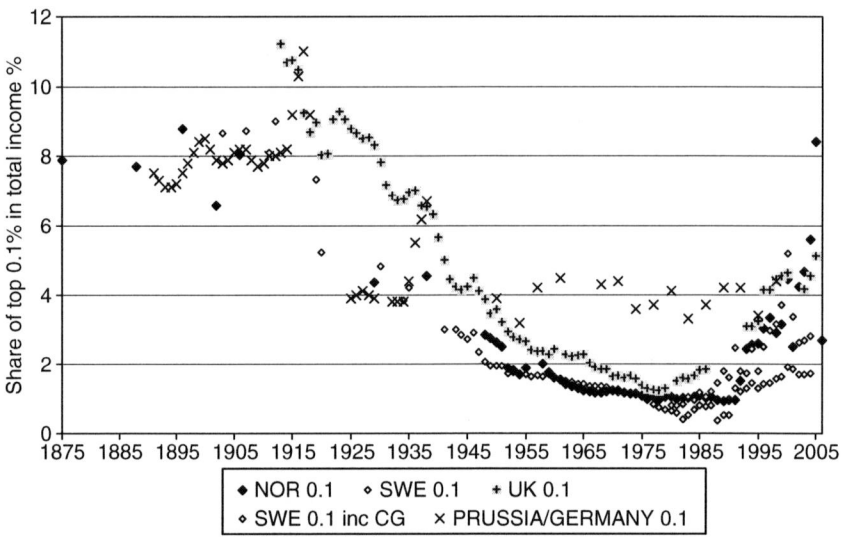

Figure 9.5 Comparison of share of top 0.1%, Norway, Prussia/Germany, Sweden, and the UK, 1875–2006

[13] These estimates are based on the Income Distribution Surveys, which are a sample, and hence may differ from the earlier results based on the tax registers. It should also be noted that we have used the same control totals as before, rather than construct new totals for each definition. Note, however,

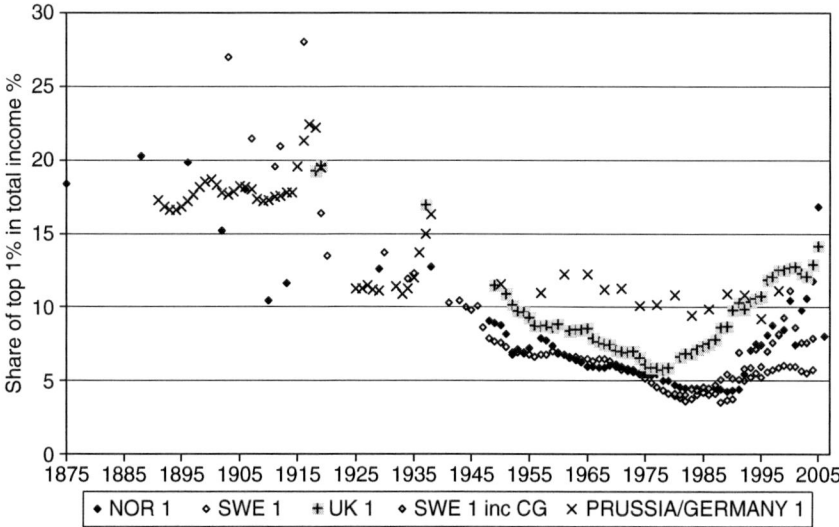

Figure 9.6 Comparison of share of top 1%, Norway, Prussia/Germany, Sweden, and the UK, 1875–2006

shows the shares of the top 0.1 per cent in each of the countries. It should be noted that the geographical boundaries have changed. This is particularly important for Germany, where the figures prior to the First World War (1918) relate to Prussia, those from 1925 to the Weimar Republic and the Third Reich, and those from 1950 to the Federal Republic, including from 1991 the former East Germany. The figures for the UK include the whole of Ireland up to 1920.

The first comparison is with Norway's neighbour: the dark diamonds are the estimates for Norway; the hollow diamonds are those for Sweden. As may be seen, with a few exceptions (such as the figure for Sweden for 1916 that is off the scale),[14] the two series follow each other closely until recent decades. For the period since 1980, we have shown the Swedish estimates with (light shading) and without (hollow diamonds) the inclusion of capital gains. The series with capital gains is closer in definition to that for Norway, and the series are indeed closer, but the rise in top shares is larger in the Norwegian case. The same is evident in Figure 9.6, which shows the shares of the top 1 per cent. Between 1980 and 2004, the share of the top 1 per cent more than doubled in Norway but rose less than a half in Sweden. The differential rise in Norway took place after 1990, long after oil production caused Norwegian GDP per capita to overtake that of Sweden.

---

that the estimates for top (assessed net) income shares based on data from sample surveys differ only slightly from the corresponding top income shares based on register data.

[14] The reasons for the high value in Sweden in 1916 are discussed by Roine and Waldenström in Chapter 7.

According to the estimates of Maddison (2003), Norwegian GDP per capita, purchasing power parity adjusted, was some 85 per cent of that in Sweden for much of the post-war period (having fallen during the Second World War), but began to rise in 1975, reaching 100 per cent around 1980 and continuing upwards.

Comparing Scandinavia with Germany, we can see that initially, in the 1890s and early 1900s, the top income shares in Prussia were similar to those in Scandinavia, and they show the same rise in the First World War as in Sweden. But the Weimar Republic was marked by stability in top shares, and they increased during the Nazi period: the share of the top 1 per cent increased from 11 per cent in 1933 to 16 per cent in 1938. (See the discussion in Dell 2002: 374–5.) Over the post-war period, there was no strong trend: the share of the top 1 per cent varied between 9 and 12 per cent. As such, it was, until recent years, well above the corresponding top share in Norway. The top shares in the UK followed a rather different pattern. Before the First World War, top shares were higher in the UK than in Scandinavia and Prussia, but the UK top shares fell during the First World War and from the 1930s. By the 1970s, the UK top shares had fallen to much the same level as those in Norway.

Pareto–Lorenz Coefficients

The comparison of the shares may be affected by the methods employed in each country to estimate control totals for income. Figure 9.7 shows the Pareto–Lorenz coefficients, which are not affected by the totals, and allow us to see the changing

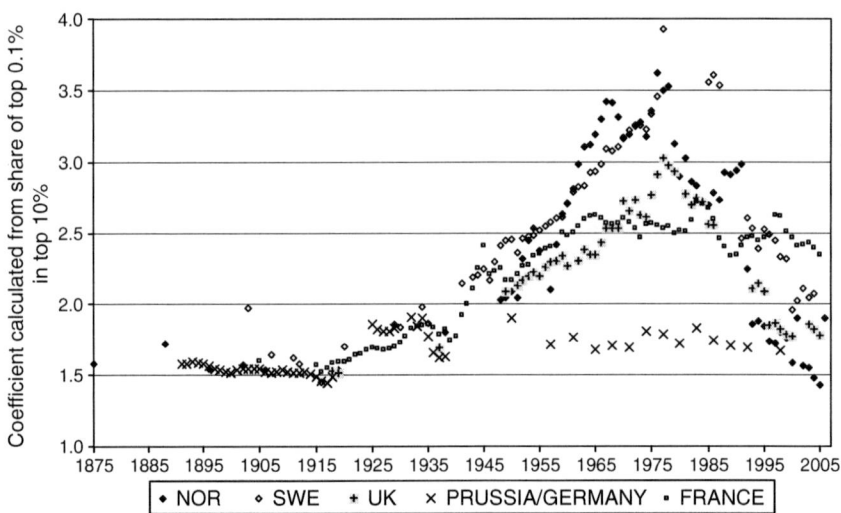

Figure 9.7 Pareto–Lorenz coefficients for Norway, France, Prussia/Germany, Sweden, and the UK, 1875–2006

shape of the top of the distribution. To the countries just considered, we add France, based on the estimates of Piketty (2000, 2003) and Landais (2007). We can see that at the time of Pareto, the coefficients were similar, and close to 1.55, in all five countries. The inter-war period saw the decline in concentration. In four of the five countries, there was an inverted V, but with differences in the height and location of the turning point. In France, the recent estimates of Landais (2007) show the Pareto–Lorenz coefficient as falling, but the turning point is less pronounced. It may be noted that the Pareto–Lorenz coefficient at its peak is close to 4 in the Nordic countries; in the UK the coefficient reaches 3.0, but in France the highest values are around 2.5. Perhaps the most striking feature is the relative stability of the Pareto–Lorenz coefficients in France and Germany in the post-war period compared with the Nordic countries and the UK.

9.6 CONCLUSIONS

Top incomes in Norway are of considerable interest since the series for their share in total income constructed in this chapter starts as far back as 1875, so that we have estimates covering 130 years, a period in which Norway first industrialized and then became an oil exporter.

The estimates of top income shares presented here must be qualified by the fact that they are drawn from a variety of sources, not a single regular series, and that the control totals are only approximate. But they suggest that the top income shares in the nineteenth century were high: the share of the top 1 per cent was around 20 per cent and that of the top 0.5 per cent around 15 per cent. The Pareto–Lorenz coefficients obtained by examining the shares within shares (that do not depend on the control totals for income) were around 1.55 for 1906 and earlier years. This indicates a high level of concentration: the top 1 per cent received more than 40 per cent of the total income of the top 10 per cent. Were the top shares rising or falling? Movements in fact occurred in both directions. There was a rise in the shares of the top 10 per cent, 5 per cent, and 1 per cent between 1875 and 1888. Between 1896 and 1902 there was a definite fall; there was some recovery in 1906, but then a further fall. The time-path can be interpreted in the light of events such as the Kristiania crash of 1899, followed by a recession, and the recession around 1908–9. After (and during) the First World War, there was some recovery in the top shares.

The early part of the post-Second World War period was characterized by central planning of the economy, very progressive taxation, and gradual expansion of the welfare state. Over this period, the top income shares fell steadily: the share of the richest 0.5 per cent fell from 6.4 per cent in 1948 to 2.8 per cent in 1991. The Pareto–Lorenz coefficient was around 2.25 in 1948, but rose close to 4 at the end of the 1970s. There was then, as in Sweden, the UK, and the USA, a turning point. The turning point for the Pareto–Lorenz coefficient came in the 1980s. The shape of the distribution has changed in such a way that we have been through a complete cycle, of declining concentration followed by increasing concentration, with the increase taking place at a faster rate. The turning point for the top income shares came at the start of the 1990s, rather later than in the UK and the USA, and some fifteen years after the start of substantial oil production. We have drawn attention to the role in increased top income shares of capital market reforms, but also emphasized the impact of changes in the tax system that distorted the statistical picture. In view of this, we have proposed an alternative set of estimates of 'Hicksian' income imputing a long-run return to capital. The Hicksian series rises less fast, particularly after 2001, but still shows a definite increase.

In sum, the Norwegian experience has been broadly similar over the twentieth century to that in the UK and in Sweden (but not Germany) in that top shares, and the concentration among top incomes, have first fallen and then risen. Note, however, that the top shares rose less sharply in Sweden than in Norway between 1990 and 2006. Moreover, the figures for Norway also—intriguingly—suggest that the nineteenth century may have been rather different.

APPENDIX 9A: SOURCES OF TABULATED INCOME TAX DATA FOR NORWAY FROM 1875

For the period 1875 to 1938, the sources are those described in the text and set out in detail in the first rows of Table 9A.1. As is clear, these early data have had to be assembled from a variety of sources, including a remarkable set of publications by A. N. Kiær, director of Det Statistiske Centralbureau (Central Bureau of Statistics of Norway) for many years, parliamentary papers, and analyses of the population censuses. In Table 9A.1, Oth. Prp stands for *Odelthings Proposition* and Sth. Prp stands for *Storthings Proposition*, both

Table 9A.1 Sources of Norwegian Income Tax Data (* before a source denotes more detailed)

Year	Source	Further source
1875	* Oth. Prp., number 11 for 1881, pages 20–5.	Kiær (1892–3), page 110.
1888	Kiær (1892–3), pages 99–101 and 105.	
1896	Sth. Prp., number 89 for 1898, pages 24–31.	
1902	Sth. Prp., number 10 for 1903–1904, pages 150–5 and 160–9.	
1906	Rygg (1910), pages 50 and 69.	
1910	Statistisk Sentralbyrå, 1915, page 61*.	Statistisk Sentralbyrå, 1915a, page 29*.
1913–14	Statistisk Sentralbyrå, 1915a, page 30*.	
1929 (frequencies only)	*Statistisk Årbok, 1936*, page 11.	
1938 (classified by taxable income)	*Statistiske Meddelelser, 1941*, No 11 and 12, page 333.	
1948	HS 1978, page 572.	
1949	HS 1978, page 572.	* Sk 1950/51, page 96.
1950	HS 1978, page 572.	* Sk 1951/52, page 204; SY 1953, page 275.
1951	HS 1978, page 572.	* Sk 1952/53, page 202; SY 1954, page 265.
1952	HS 1978, page 573.	
1953	HS 1978, page 573.	
1954	HS 1978, page 573.	
1955	HS 1978, page 573.	
1956		
1957	HS 1978, page 573.	

(*continued*)

Table 9A.1 Continued

Year	Source	Further source
1958	HS 1978, page 572.	Same figures in Sk 1958, page 40.
1959	HS 1978, page 572.	
1960	HS 1978, page 572.	
1961	HS 1978, page 572.	
1962	HS 1978, page 573.	
1963	* HS 1978, page 573.	SY 1966, page 181.
1964	* HS 1978, page 573.	SY 1967, page 184.
1965	* HS 1978, page 573.	SY 1968, page 189.
1966	* HS 1978, page 573.	SY 1969, page 185.
1967	* HS 1978, page 574.	
1968	* HS 1978, page 574.	SY 1971, page 206.
1969	* HS 1978, page 574.	SY 1972, page 214.
1970	HS 1978, page 574.	* SY 1973, page 216.
1971	HS 1978, page 574.	* SY 1974, page 230.
1972	HS 1978, page 574.	* SY 1975, page 290.
1973	HS 1978, page 574.	* SY 1976, page 294.
1974	HS 1978, page 574.	* SY 1977, page 298.
1975	SY 1978, page 298.	
1976	SY 1979, page 302.	
1977		Sk 1977, page 52.
1978	SY 1980, page 296.	
1979	SY 1981, page 296.	Sk 1980, page 55.
1980		Sk 1980, page 55.
1981		Sk 1982, page 50.
1982	SY 1985, page 335.	* Sk 1982, page 50.
1983	SY 1986, page 182.	
1984	SY 1987, page 174.	
1985	SY 1988, page 171.	
1986	SY 1989, page 168.	
1987	SY 1990, page 163.	
1988	SY 1991, page 163.	
1989	SY 1992, page 163.	
1990	SY 1993, page 160.	
1991	SY 1994, page 162.	
1992	SY 1995, page 135.	
1993		
1994	SY 1996, page 141.	
1995	SY 1997, page 161.	
1996	SY 1998, page 161.	
1997	SY 1999, Table 161.	
1998	First year that jointly taxed married couples not treated as 1 unit. SY 2000, Table 225.	
1999	SY 2001, Table 202.	
2000	SY 2002, Table 204.	
2001	SY 2003, Table 204	
2002	SY 2004, Table 205 (table dropped from 2005 edition)	

parliamentary papers. The income tax tabulations for the post-war period are published in a variety of places, as described in Table 9A.1, where HS denotes *Historisk Statistikk 1978* (Historical Statistics 1978); SY denotes the *Statistisk Årbok* (Statistical Yearbook); and Sk denotes *Skattestatistikk* (Tax Statistics). The tables in these publications show assessed income, after deductions such as those for interest paid but before subtracting the special allowances for age, disability, etc. In this sense, they are 'net' incomes (i.e. net of deductions) but more extensive than 'taxable income'. Since 1957, the assessment is for the central government income tax in the case of taxpayers paying central government income tax; for other taxpayers it is based on the municipal income tax assessment.

The results for the period 1967 to 2006 are based on the micro-data in the tax register files, but Table 9A.1 lists the sources for tabulations up to 2002. Statistics Norway have in the post-war period published analyses of the income distribution data in a series called *Inntektsstatistikk* (for example Statistisk Sentralbyrå 1971) and later called *Inntekts- og Formuesstatistikk*. There have been a number of studies by Statistics Norway of changes over time (for example, Statistisk Sentralbyr 1972a, which compares 1958, 1962, and 1967, Strøm, Wennemo, and Aaberge 1993, which covers 1973 to 1990, and Epland 1998, which covers 1986 to 1996).

APPENDIX 9B: SOURCES OF TOTAL POPULATION DATA FOR NORWAY

The starting point is the total population at 1 January each year taken from the Statistical Yearbook (2007: table 47) for years since 1900; figures for 1875, 1888, and 1896 from Statistisk Sentralbyrå (1949: Tabell 14), also in Maddison (2003: 37).

The population aged 16 and over for years from 1948 to 2006 was supplied by Statistics Norway. For years prior to 1948, data for 1 January (or 31 December of the previous year) are given for years ending in '1' or '6' up to 1991 in *Historisk statistikk* 1994 (Statistics Norway 1995): Tabell 3.5. The proportions were linearly interpolated between years when data were not available, and the interpolated percentages applied to the total population to give the figures in Table 9B.1.

Table 9B.1 Control total for population, Norway, 1875–2007

	Total tax units 000	Total adult population 000	Total recorded in tax statistics 000
1875	847	1,140	705
1888	919	1,241	790
1896	980	1,321	70
1902	1,062	1,426	69
1906	1,077	1,446	677
1910	1,115	1,496	520
1913	1,176	1,550	774
1929	1,451	1,917	895
1938	1,648	2,176	410
1948	1,734	2,404	955
1949	1,732	2,419	1,011
1950	1,727	2,429	1,047
1951	1,721	2,439	948
1952	1,720	2,452	1,413
1953	1,719	2,465	1,440
1954	1,720	2,479	1,425
1955	1,721	2,495	1,418
1956	1,724	2,514	
1957	1,729	2,526	1,397
1958	1,735	2,539	1,386
1959	1,745	2,557	1,372
1960	1,756	2,579	1,440
1961	1,771	2,605	1,456
1962	1,792	2,636	1,484
1963	1,816	2,671	1,478
1964	1,836	2,701	1,530
1965	1,854	2,729	1,504
1966	1,871	2,754	1,543
1967	1,888	2,779	1,698

1968	1,905	2,805	1,771
1969	1,922	2,830	1,816
1970	1,939	2,855	1,738
1971	1,953	2,876	1,788
1972	1,974	2,902	1,855
1973	1,995	2,930	1,902
1974	2,015	2,955	1,910
1975	2,035	2,981	1,947
1976	2,055	3,005	2,013
1977	2,078	3,029	2,074
1978	2,102	3,054	2,133
1979	2,124	3,078	2,199
1980	2,154	3,102	2,295
1981	2,185	3,128	2,286
1982	2,218	3,156	2,330
1983	2,252	3,186	2,318
1984	2,285	3,213	2,461
1985	2,319	3,241	2,545
1986	2,353	3,270	2,609
1987	2,387	3,297	2,788
1988	2,424	3,330	2,906
1989	2,458	3,357	2,917
1990	2,483	3,372	3,035
1991	2,504	3,387	3,072
1992	2,527	3,405	3,105
1993	2,549	3,422	
1994	2,569	3,436	3,182
1995	2,590	3,451	3,192
1996	2,607	3,463	3,227
1997	2,625	3,477	3,286
1998	2,643	3,492	3,465
1999	2,664	3,511	3,490
2000	2,684	3,531	3,503
2001	2,701	3,548	3,514
2002	2,719	3,563	3,536
2003	2,742	3,586	
2004	2,765	3,563	
2005	2,795	3,586	
2006	2,830	3,607	
2007	2,872	3,635	

Figures on the number of married women are given for a number of years up to 1991 in *Historisk statistikk* 1994 (Statistics Norway 1995): Tabell 3.7. The data on the number of married women for 1995 are from SY 1996: Tabell 37, for 1997 from SY 1997: Tabell 39, 1998 from SY 1998: Tabell 42, 1999 from SY 1999: Tabell 41, 2000 from SY 2000: Tabell 63; 2001 from SY 2001: Tabell 54; 2002 from SY 2002: Tabell 54; 2003 from SY 2003: Tabell 53; 2004 from SY 2004: Tabell 53, 2005 from SY 2005: Tabell 57, 2006 from SY 2006: Tabell 58, and 2007 from SY 2007: Tabell 59. The proportions are again linearly interpolated between years when data were not available, and the interpolated percentages applied to the total adult population. Total tax units are obtained by subtracting the calculated number of married women from the total adult population.

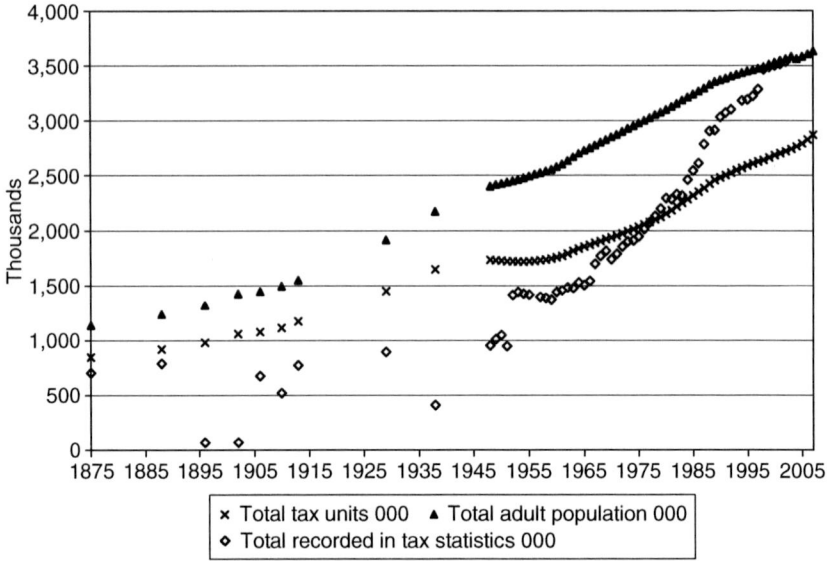

Figure 9B.1 Total taxpayers in tax data and control total, Norway, 1875–2007

The resulting control totals for total adults and total tax units are shown for the period since 1876 in Figure 9B.1, and compared with the totals in the tax data. The tax totals converge towards the control total, and are essentially identical from 1998 when independent taxation was introduced. It may be noted that the figures for the early years that included an estimate of the number of individuals not paying tax, such as 1876 and 1889, are closer to the control totals.

APPENDIX 9C: SOURCES OF TOTAL
INCOME DATA FOR NORWAY

The starting point is a series for total household income provided for 1978 to 2006 by Statistics Norway. Total household income is made up of (i) compensation of employees (not including employers' social security contributions), (ii) operating surplus of self-employed businesses, (iii) property income, (iv) transfers from government and from abroad, and (v) income not elsewhere classified. The estimate for 2006 is provisional.

In order to extrapolate this series backwards, we have made use of series that are as comparable as possible, given the available materials from *Historisk statistikk 1994* and earlier editions. In each case, the series have been linked at years where the estimates seem most comparable (for this reason we have started with 1979, rather than 1978). So that if the 1979 value from the Statistics Norway series is A_{1979}, and the first linked series is for 1975 to 1979, given by $B_{1975}, \ldots, B_{1979}$, then for 1978 we take the value of B_{1978}, multiplied by A_{1979}/B_{1979}.

Working backwards we have used the *Nasjonalregnskap 1968–1979*: Tabell 33, pp. 138–9 for the New Definition of Private Income for 1968 to 1978. For 1948 to 1968, we have used the Old Definition of Private Income from *Historisk statistikk 1978* (Statistics Norway 1978): Tabell 59 (p. 104) for 1965 to 1968 and from *Historisk statistikk 1968* (Statistics Norway 1968): Tabell 70 (pp. 110–11) for 1946, 1950 to 1964.[15] In each case employers' social security contributions were subtracted from the total of private income; these were taken from *Nasjonalregnskap 1969–1980*: Tabell 30 (for 1969 to 1974), *Nasjonalregnskap 1962–1978*: Tabell 29 (for 1962 to 1968), *Nasjonalregnskap 1953–1969*: Tabell 14 (for 1953 to 1961), and *Nasjonalregnskap 1968–1979*: Tabell 14 (for 1949 to 1952, with an estimate for 1946).

For years prior to 1946, we use the Old Definition of Private Income from *Historisk statistikk 1978* (Statistics Norway 1978): Tabell 59 (p. 104), where estimates are given at five-yearly intervals. The figures are linked to the estimate for 1950. The figures for intermediate years (such as 1902 and 1906) have been interpolated using the series for 'private gross income' from *Nasjonalregnskap 1900–1929*: Tabell 7. For the nineteenth century, annual estimates of the Old Definition of Private Income are given in *Langtidslinjer i Norsk Økonomi 1865–1960* (Statistics Norway 1966: Tabell VIII). It should be noted that employers' social security contributions are not deducted.

The resulting series for total household income is shown in Table 9C.1, together with the total income recorded in the tax statistics (up to 2002). The latter falls short of the total household income for two main reasons: (i) the omission of the income of those not covered by the tax statistics and (ii) the differences in income definitions, including the difference between total gross income and gross income as assessed for tax purposes. In our estimates, we wish to correct for the first of these, but not the second. This means that we

---

[15] 1948 has been extrapolated from 1946 using the household income series in *UN National Income Statistics 1938–1948* (1950: 130). 1949 has been extrapolated from 1948 using the GDP figures in *Historisk Statistikk 1994*: Tabell 22.1.

Table 9C.1 Control total for income, Norway, 1875–2006

	Total household income (national accounts) NOK million	Total income recorded in tax statistics NOK million	Control total used here for assessed income NOK million
1875	661	346	476
1888	614	389	442
1896	747		538
1902	906		652
1906	983	512	708
1910	1,202		866
1913	1,569	720	1,130
1929	3,688		2,656
1938	4,857	1,952	3,497
1948	11,402	5,930	8,209
1949	12,222	6,515	8,800
1950	13,143	7,152	9,463
1951	15,934	7,993	11,472
1952	17,438	10,227	12,556
1953	17,722	11,183	12,760
1954	19,521	11,670	14,055
1955	20,592	12,471	14,826
1956	23,195		16,701
1957	24,563	14,326	17,685
1958	24,029	14,976	17,301
1959	25,530	15,595	18,382
1960	27,223	16,435	19,601
1961	29,651	17,810	21,349
1962	31,939	19,732	22,996
1963	34,606	21,192	24,916
1964	38,284	23,590	27,564
1965	42,486	25,524	30,590
1966	45,621	28,058	32,847
1967	49,813	32,719	35,865
1968	53,156	35,188	38,272
1969	57,698	38,612	41,543
1970	65,298	42,164	47,014
1971	72,354	48,191	52,095
1972	79,767	53,195	57,432
1973	90,184	59,207	64,933
1974	103,615	66,984	74,603
1975	120,025	80,009	86,418
1976	136,588	95,168	98,343
1977	150,757	108,070	108,545
1978	178,788	121,173	128,727
1979	190,439	128,381	137,116
1980	217,588	144,882	156,663
1981	248,579	162,487	178,977
1982	279,463	181,161	201,213
1983	307,078	194,071	221,096
1984	339,380	211,376	244,354
1985	373,063	234,995	268,605
1986	421,492	261,425	303,474

1987	477,366	298,626	343,704
1988	515,143	320,907	370,903
1989	538,194	326,637	387,500
1990	567,289	347,545	408,448
1991	594,972	361,241	428,380
1992	624,043	351,941	449,311
1993	647,302		466,057
1994	660,718	397,216	475,717
1995	695,236	421,611	500,570
1996	730,657	456,163	526,073
1997	775,023	500,224	558,017
1998	850,023	550,394	612,017
1999	901,566	582,616	649,128
2000	968,408	627,174	697,254
2001	1,015,802	627,414	731,377
2002	1,096,054	682,206	789,159
2003	1,147,856		826,456
2004	1,182,727		851,563
2005	1,269,053		913,718
2006	1,253,443		902,479
2007	1,375,495		990,356

cannot simply take the total household income series.[16] Instead, we adjust the series making use of other information about the income of those not covered. As noted in the text, the earliest tabulations published by Kiær (1892–3) for 1876 and 1889 included estimates of the numbers and total income of those not covered. In 1889, the number of non-filers were estimated at 318,025 with an average income of NOK 262. The addition increased the total numbers from 51 per cent of total tax units to 86 per cent (it is of course a smaller percentage of total adults); it increased the total income from 49 per cent to 63 per cent of the calculated control total. If the remaining 14 per cent of tax units were to be allocated the same average income as the non-filers, this would bring the total income to 68 per cent of the calculated control total.

Moving on to the twentieth century, the study of the income distribution in 1958, 1962, and 1967 (Statistisk Sentralbyrå 1972: 13–14) included estimates of total *assessed* income, including those not covered by the tax statistics, which were, respectively, 66, 67, and 69 per cent of the National Accounts total household income figure. (It should be emphasized that one reason for the difference lies in the difference between assessed and gross income: for example, a number of deductions are made from gross income to arrive at assessed income.) From *Inntektsstatistikk* (*IS*), we can obtain estimates for 1970 of 67 per cent (*IS* 1970: 26–7), for 1973 of 66 per cent (*IS* 1973: 47), and for 1979 of 67 per cent (*IS* 1979: 55).

[16] In 1948 for example, the totals in the tax statistics are 0.955 million people and NOK 5,931 million. The control total for adults is 2.404 million, so that 1.449 million people are not covered. Total household income from our constructed series is NOK 11,480 million. If all the difference was to be allocated to those not covered, then they would have an average of NOK 3,829 each, which seems implausibly high.

Top Incomes in Norway

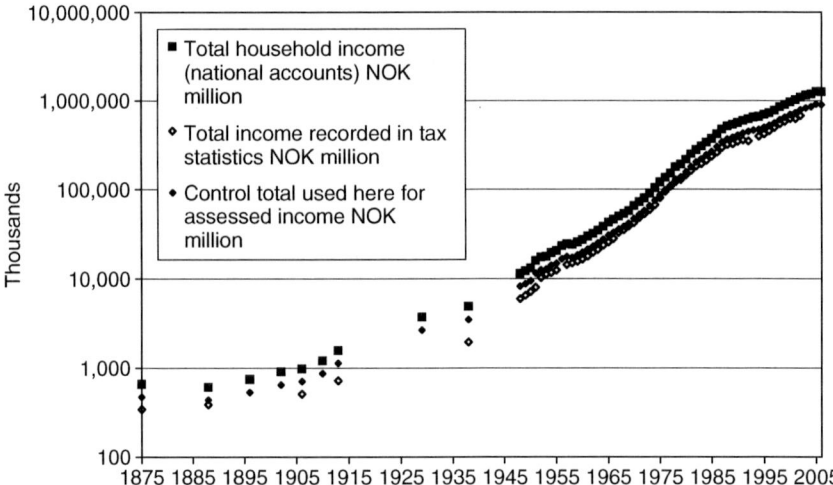

Figure 9C.1 Total income in tax data and control total income, Norway, 1875–2006

The highest percentage attained by the total recorded in the tax statistics is 72 per cent. More recently, over the period 1997 to 2002, total ordinary income 'allmenn intekt' in the tax return accounts varied between 62 and 66 per cent of the total household income figure (source: *Sjølvmeldingsstatistikk 2002*: 31). (Over the same period, gross income in the tax return statistics was around 85 per cent of the total household income figure.[17]) In the light of these findings covering a long span of years, we have decided, as a reasonable first approximation, to take as a control total a fixed percentage of our calculated total household income. This approach is close to that adopted for Sweden by Roine and Waldenström (2005, 2008), where they took a constant percentage of total personal income for the period 1943 to 2003, and not dissimilar to that applied in the UK (Atkinson 2007b), where the control totals varied around 80 per cent of total personal income (see Atkinson 2007a: figure 2.4). The percentage we have taken is 72 per cent, which is the maximum reached by the tax return statistics totals. To the extent that this percentage represents an upper bound, we shall be underestimating the top income shares. The resulting figures are shown in the third column of Table 9C.1 and are plotted in Figure 9C.1.

---

[17] The study of the income distribution in 1958, 1962, and 1967 (Statistisk Sentralbyrå 1972: 13–14) included estimates of total gross income, including those not covered by the tax statistics, which were, respectively, 82%, 87%, and 88% of the National Accounts total household income figure. From *Inntektsstatistikk* (*IS*), we can obtain estimates for 1970 of 85% (*IS* 1970: 26–7).

APPENDIX 9D: THE HICKSIAN APPROACH
FOR MEASURING INCOME

As indicated by Epland (1998) and Aaberge et al. (2000), the reported increase in income inequality in Norway during the 1990s was first and foremost due to a rising disequalizing contribution of capital income. However, since the rise in income inequality coincided with the implementation of a major tax reform which affected the financing incentives in the corporate sector and the income-shifting incentives in small enterprises, one might question whether it is meaningful to use yearly tax reported dividends and capital gains as measures of the returns from equities. Lack of comparability of tax reported dividends and capital gains motivated Fjærli and Aaberge (2000) to use a Hicksian version of the definition of income as a basis for studying the development of income inequality from 1986 to 1996. The Hicksian estimates displayed in Table 9.2 and Figure 9.4 are based on the procedure for estimation of market values of non-quoted stocks proposed by Fjærli and Aaberge (2000).

The tax return data from the Income Distribution Surveys contain information on financial assets and portfolio composition. Quoted stocks are reported in the tax returns at their true market value before 1992 and at 70 per cent of the true market value from 1992 to 2006, whilst the value of non-quoted stocks is 50 per cent (1991 and before) or 30 per cent (after 1991) of the technical liquidation value of the firm. Due to rather lenient valuation rules the tax-based estimated technical liquidation value is, as has been universally acknowledged, far below the market value of the firms' assets. As an alternative to the observed tax values for non-quoted stocks Fjærli and Aaberge (2000) proposed to use the following estimator of stocks (M_{it}) for household i in year t

$$M_{it} = \left[\left(\frac{1-A}{g_{Qt}} \right) + \left(\frac{A}{g_{Nt}} \right) \right] \cdot T_{it},$$

where T_{it} is the reported tax value of the stocks of household i in year t, g_{Qt} is the true ratio of tax value to market value for quoted stocks, g_{Nt} is the estimated ratio of tax value to market value for non-quoted stocks (approximately 0.25 from 1986 to 1991 and 0.30 from 1992 to 1998), and A is the estimated share of the reported tax value of stocks (T_{it}) that is held as non-quoted stocks.

Non-quoted firms are rarely traded; when traded, the prices are unobservable. So, the best one can do when it comes to approximation of market values for non-quoted firms is to base the valuation on ordinary (not tax-related) book values. However, the personal tax returns contain only stock value statements, and there is no link to the book value of the firm in question. However, by using data for 636 firms from a survey of closely held corporations and their owners in 1991, Fjærli and Aaberge (2000) found a weighted average ratio of tax-value to book value (g_N) equal to 0.25.

From 1992 to 2006 there have been several changes in the tax valuation rules for non-quoted shares. The most important was the change from separate to uniform reporting and moreover less favourable valuation of real assets, which caused liquidation values to increase. By contrast, the year-specific tax valuation changed, however, from 50 to 30 per cent of estimated liquidation value. By adjusting the 1991 tax values for the change in the year-specific tax valuation from 50 to 30 per cent and using the balance sheet data to add the effect of changes in the rules for calculation of liquidation values, an average estimate of the 1992 ratio of (approximated) tax value to the (observed) book value equal to 0.28 was obtained.

Since quoted and non-quoted stocks are not reported separately in the tax returns, Fjærli and Aaberge (2000) used the observed individual fractions of stocks reported as 'non-registered' as an approximation for each taxpayer's fraction of non-quoted stocks. From 1992 the stock values were reported separately depending on whether or not they were registered in the Norwegian Central Securities Depository. Before 1992, the fraction A is determined from aggregate data on the tax value of quoted and non-quoted stocks collected from official statistics,[18] assuming all investors held the same average fraction of quoted and non-quoted shares.[19]

REFERENCES

Aaberge, R. and A. Langørgen (2006). 'Measuring the Benefits from Public Services: The Effects of Local Government Spending on the Distribution of Income in Norway', *Review of Income and Wealth*, 52: 61–83.

—— A. Bjørklund, M. Jäntti, P. J. Pedersen, N. Smith, and T. Wennemo (2000). 'Unemployment Shocks and Income Distribution: How Did the Nordic Countries Fare During their Crises?', *Scandinavian Journal of Economics*, 102: 77–99.

—— —— —— M. Palme, P. J. Pedersen, N. Smith, and T. Wennemo (2002). 'Income Inequality and Income Mobility in the Scandinavian Countries Compared to the United States', *Review of Income and Wealth*, 48: 443–69.

Atkinson, A. B. (2005). 'Top Incomes in the UK over the 20th Century', *Journal of the Royal Statistical Society*, 168(2): 325–43.

—— (2007a). 'Measuring Top Incomes: Methodological Issues', in Atkinson and Piketty (2007).

—— (2007b). 'The Distribution of Top Incomes in the United Kingdom 1908–2000', in Atkinson and Piketty (2007).

—— and A. Leigh (2007). 'The Distribution of Top Incomes in Australia', *Economic Record*, 83: 247–61.

—— and T. Piketty (2007). *Top Incomes over the 20th Century*. Oxford: Oxford University Press.

—— and W. Salverda (2005). 'Top Incomes in the Netherlands and the United Kingdom over the Twentieth Century', *Journal of the European Economic Association*, 3: 883–913.

Björklund, A., M. Palme, and I. Svensson (1995). 'Tax Reforms and Income Distribution: An Assessment Using Different Income Concepts', *Swedish Economic Policy Review*, 2: 229–66.

---

[18] Statistical Yearbook of Norway (1993).

[19] Of course, if quoted and non-quoted firms attract different clienteles the use of a common average fraction could bias the results. However, ownership of quoted as well as non-quoted stocks seems to be highly concentrated in the upper part of the income distribution.

Bojer, H. (1987). 'Personlig inntektsfordeling i Norge 1970–1984', *Tidsskrift for Samfunnsforskning*, 28: 247–58.

—— (2008). 'Income Inequality and the Economic Position of Women in Norway 1970–2002', mimeo, Department of Economics, University of Oslo.

Bowley, A. L. (1914). 'The British Super-Tax and the Distribution of Income', *Quarterly Journal of Economics*, 28: 255–68.

Cowell, F. A. (1995). *Measuring Inequality*, 2nd edn. London: Prentice Hall.

Dell, F. (2002). *Inégalités de revenus et accumulation du capital sur longue période en Allemagne 1913–1959*. Paris: DELTA.

Epland, J. (1992). 'Inntektsfordelingen i 80-årene', *Økonomiske analyser*, 2. Olso: Statistisk Sentralbyrå: 17–26.

—— (1998). *Endringer i fordelingen av husholdningsinntekt 1986–1996* (Changes in the Distribution of Household Income: 1986–1996), Reports 98/17. Oslo: Statistisk Sentralbyrå.

Feinstein, C. H. (1972). *Statistical Tables of National Income, Expenditure and Output of the U.K. 1855–1965*. Cambridge: Cambridge University Press.

Fjærli, E. and R. Aaberge (2000). 'Tax Reforms, Dividend Policy and Trends in Income Inequality: Empirical Evidence based on Norwegian Data', Discussion Paper No. 284, Statistics Norway.

Gastwirth, J. L. (1972). 'The Estimation of the Lorenz Curve and Gini Index', *Review of Economics and Statistics*, 54: 306–16.

Gulbransen, K. (2005). 'A Norwegian Perspective on Banking Crisis Regulation', Norges Bank Conference on Banking Crisis Resolution, Oslo.

Hartog, J. and J. G. Veenbergen (1978). 'Long-Run Changes in Personal Income Distribution', *De Economist*, 126: 521–49.

Kiær, A. N. (1892–3). *Indtægtsforhold i Norge, Tillæg til Statsøkonomisk tidsskrift*, 1892 and 1893.

Kuznets, S. (1953). *Shares of Upper Income Groups in Income and Savings*. New York: National Bureau of Economic Research.

Landais, C. (2007). 'Les Hauts Revenus en France (1998–2006): une explosion des inégalités?', Paris School of Economics.

Macgregor, D. H. (1936). 'Pareto's Law', *Economic Journal*, 46: 80–7.

Maddison, A. (2003). *The World Economy: Historical Statistics*. Paris: OECD.

Ministry of Health and Social Affairs (1998–9), *The Equitable Redistribution White Paper on the Distribution of Income and Living Conditions in Norway*, White Paper No. 50.

Morrisson, C. (2000). 'Historical Perspectives on Income Distribution: The Case of Europe', in A. B. Atkinson and F. Bourguignon (eds.) *Handbook of Income Distribution*. Amsterdam: Elsevier.

NOU (1988). *Inntektsdannelsen i Norge, Forbruker- og administrasjonsdepartementet*.

Ohlsson, H., J. Roine, and D. Waldenström (2006). 'Long-Run Changes in the Concentration of Wealth', UNU-WIDER, Research Paper No. 2006/103.

Piketty, T. (2000). *Les Hauts Revenus en France au 20ème siècle*. Paris: Grasset.

—— (2003). 'Income Inequality in France, 1901–1998', *Journal of Political Economy*, 111: 1004–42.

—— and E. Saez (2003). 'Income Inequality in the United States', *Quarterly Journal of Economics*, 118: 1–39.

Ringen, S. (1991). 'Households, Standard of Living, and Inequality', *Review of Income and Wealth*, 37: 1–13.

Roine, J. and D. Waldenström (2005). 'Top Incomes in Sweden over the Twentieth Century', Working Paper, Stockholm School of Economics.

—— —— (2008). 'The Evolution of Top Incomes in an Egalitarian Society: Sweden, 1903–2004', *Journal of Public Economics*, 92: 366–87.

Rygg, N. (1910). *Skatternes fordeling efter indtægt og forsørgelsesbyrde*. Kristiania: Steen'ske boktrykkeri.

Saez, E. and M. Veall (2003). 'The Evolution of High Incomes in Canada, 1920–2000', NBER Discussion Paper.

Sejersted, F. (1992). 'A Theory of Economic and Technological Development in Norway in the Nineteenth Century', *Scandinavian Economic History Review*, 40(1): 40–75.

Soltow, L. (1965). *Toward Income Equality in Norway*. Madison: University of Wisconsin Press.

Sørensen, R. S. (1993). 'Changes in the Personal Income Distribution 1870–1986', in K. G. Persson (ed.) *The Economic Development of Denmark and Norway since 1870*. Cheltenham: Edward Elgar.

Stamp, J. C. (1916). *British Incomes and Property*. London: P. S. King.

—— (1936). 'The Influence of the Price Level on the Higher Incomes', *Journal of the Royal Statistical Society*, 99: 627–73.

Statistisk Sentralbyrå (Central Bureau of Statistics of Norway) (1915a). *Indtægts- og Formuesforhold efter Skatteligningen 1911 i forbindelse med Folketællingen 1910*, Norges Officielle Statistik (NOS) VI.24. Kristiania: Statistisk Sentralbyrå.

—— (1915b). *Indtægt, Formue og fordelingen av den kommunale skat ifølge Skatteligningen for 1913–14*, Norges Officielle Statistik (NOS) VI.57. Kristiania: Statistisk Sentralbyrå.

—— (1949). *Statistiske Oversikter 1948 (Statistical Surveys 1948)*. Oslo: Statistisk Sentralbyrå.

—— (1953). *Nasjonalregnskap 1900–1929 (National Accounts 1900–1929)*, Norges Officielle Statistik (NOS) XI.143. Oslo: Statistisk Sentralbyrå.

—— (1954). *Det norske skattesystems virkninger på den personliger inntektsfordeling*, SØS (Samfunnsøkonomiske Studier), No. 1. Oslo: Statistisk Sentralbyrå.

—— (1965). *Nasjonalregnskap 1865–1960 (National Accounts 1865–1960)*, Norges Officielle Statistik (NOS) XII.163. Oslo: Statistisk Sentralbyrå.

—— (1966). *Langtidslinjer i norsk økonomi* (Trends in Norwegian Economy) *1865–1960*, SØS (Samfunnsøkonomiske Studier), No. 16. Oslo: Statistisk Sentralbyrå.

—— (1969). *Historisk statistikk 1968* (Historical Statistics 1968) (NOS XII 245). Oslo: Statistisk Sentralbyrå.

—— (1971). *Inntektsstatistikk 1967* (Income Statistics 1967) (NOS A 391). Oslo: Statistisk Sentralbyrå.

—— (1972a). *Den personlige inntektsfordeling 1958, 1962 og 1967*, SA No. 2. Oslo: Statistisk Sentralbyrå.

—— (1972b). *Lavinntektsundersøkelsen 1967* (Survey of Low Income 1967), Statistical Analyses No. 4. Oslo: Statistisk Sentralbyrå.

—— (1973). *Inntektsstatistikk 1970* (NOS A 543). Oslo: Statistisk Sentralbyrå.

—— (1977). *Sosialt utsyn 1977*, Statistiske analyser (SA) No. 31. Oslo: Statistisk Sentralbyrå.

—— (1978). *Historisk statistikk 1978* (Historical Statistics 1978) (NOS XII 291). Oslo: Statistisk Sentralbyrå.

Statistisk Sentralbyrå (1993). *Inntekts- og Formuesstatistikk 1982, 1984–1990* (Income and Property Statistics 1982, 1984–1990). Oslo: Statistisk Sentralbyrå.

Statistisk Sentralbyrå (1995). *Historisk statistikk 1994* (Historical Statistics 1994) (NOS C 188). Oslo: Statistisk Sentralbyrå.

Strøm, S., T. Wennemo, and R. Aaberge (1993). *Inntektsulikheit i Norge 1973–1990* (Income Inequality in Norway 1973–1990), Rapporter 93/17. Oslo: Statistisk Sentralbyrå.

Utne, H. (2005). 'The Population and Housing Census Handbook 2001', Department of Social Statistics, Statistics Norway, Document 2005/2.

Vale, B. (2005). 'The Norwegian Banking Crisis 1988–1992', Bank of Slovenia Conference.

10

Income and Wealth Concentration in Spain in a Historical and Fiscal Perspective

Facundo Alvaredo and Emmanuel Saez

10.1 INTRODUCTION AND SUMMARY

The evolution of income and wealth inequality during the process of development has attracted much attention in the economics literature. Recent studies have constructed series for shares of income accruing to upper income groups for various countries using income tax statistics (Atkinson and Piketty 2007). The countries studied include Anglo-Saxon countries (United Kingdom, Ireland, United States, Canada, New Zealand, and Australia), continental European countries (Finland, France, Germany, the Netherlands, Sweden, and Switzerland), and large Asian countries (China, India, Indonesia, and Japan). This chapter focuses on the Spanish experience. Spain is an interesting country to analyse on several grounds.

First, there are very few studies on the evolution of inequality in Spain from a historical perspective. A number of studies have analysed the evolution of income, earnings, and expenditure inequality over the last three decades using survey data. Research has also been done using income tax data for recent years, but those studies focus on the effects of taxes on global inequality indices rather than top incomes as we do here.[1] Survey-based studies point to a reduction in income or expenditure inequality in the 1970s followed by relative stability in the

We thank Tony Atkinson, Orazio Attanasio, Luis Ayala, Olympia Bover, Samuel Calonge, Alfredo Canavese, Juan Carluccio, Francisco Comín, Carlos Gradín, Jorge Onrubia, Cesar Pérez, Thomas Piketty, Leandro Prados de la Escosura, Javier Ruiz-Castillo, Jesús Ruiz-Huerta, Mercedes Sastre, Rafael Vallejo Pousada, four anonymous referees, and many seminar participants at PSE, CREST (Paris), IEF, Carlos III, and Banco de España (Madrid) for helpful comments and discussions. Financial support from the Fundación Carolina (Facundo Alvaredo) and the Sloan Foundation and NSF Grant SES-0134946 (Emmanuel Saez) is thankfully acknowledged. A shorter version of this chapter was published as Facundo Alvaredo and Emmanuel Saez, 'Income and Wealth Concentration in Spain from a Historical and Fiscal Perspective', *Journal of the European Economic Association*, 7(5) (September 2009). © 2009 by the European Economic Association. Reprinted by permission.

[1] See Rodríguez and Salas (2006) for a recent example.

1980s and 1990s,[2] while tax-based results display a worsening in income inequality in 1982–91 and 1995–8.[3] More recently, Prados de la Escosura (2006a, 2008) has constructed long historical series on income inequality using macroeconomic series. Those series offer the best evidence to date on inequality trends in Spain from a historical perspective. Our study constructs long-run series of income concentration using primarily individual tax statistics, a source that has not been fully exploited by previous studies. Our series measure only top income (or wealth) concentration and hence are silent about changes in the lower and middle part of the distribution. As a result, our series can very well follow different patterns from broader and macro-based measures of inequality.

Second, up to the 1950s, Spain was still largely an agricultural economy with a GDP per capita around $4,000 (in dollars of today) similar to developing countries such as Pakistan or Egypt today.[4] Indeed, because of the civil war shock and the poor economic performance during the first decade of the Franco dictatorship, Spain GDP per capita did not reach the peak of 1929 before 1951. Starting in the 1950s and following economic liberalization and openness to trade, economic growth resumed at a very quick pace. Today, Spain's GDP per capita is only about 20 per cent lower than GDP per capita of the largest Western European economies such as France, Germany, or the United Kingdom. Therefore, it is quite interesting to analyse income concentration during the stagnation years and during the economic boom starting in the late 1950s to reassess the link between economic development and income concentration.

Third, Spain has undergone dramatic political changes since the 1930s. Spain was a republic from 1931 to 1939. A military coup led by General Franco in 1936, followed by a three-year civil war, transformed Spain into a dictatorship from 1939 till the death of Franco in 1975. Since then, Spain has returned to democracy and has implemented redistributive policies such as the development of progressive income and wealth taxation, and of a welfare state with universal health coverage. The study of top income and wealth shares in Spain can cast light on the effects of the political regime and economic policies on inequality and income concentration.

Our results show that income concentration was much higher during the 1930s than it is today. The top 0.01 per cent income share was twice higher in the 1930s than in recent decades. The top 0.01 per cent income share fell sharply during the first decade of the Franco dictatorship, and has increased slightly since the 1970s,

---

[2] Garde, Ruiz-Huerta, and Martínez (1995) provide a survey of the literature until 1995 and Ayala and Sastre (2005) present more recent findings. A summary of existing studies on inequality in Spain can be found in Appendix 10G.

[3] See Ayala and Onrubia (2001), Castañer (1991), and Lasheras, Rabadán, and Salas (1993).

[4] Prados de la Escosura (2003, 2006b, 2007) has constructed historical GDP and growth series for Spain. He emphasizes that, before the economic stagnation of the 1930–52 period, Spain had experienced significant economic growth since 1850, in particular from 1850 to 1883 and in the 1920s. Maddison (2001, 2003) also reproduces these historical series of real GDP per capita in Spain in his international compilation.

and especially since the mid 1990s. Interestingly, both the level and the time pattern of the top 0.01 per cent income share in Spain is fairly close to comparable estimates for the United States (Piketty and Saez 2003) and France (Piketty 2001, 2003) over the period 1933–71, especially the decades after the Second World War. These findings, along with a careful analysis of all published tax statistics as well as a re-evaluation of previous academic work on income tax evasion in Spain, leads us to conclude that income tax evasion in Spain before 1980 was much less prevalent than previously thought *at the top of the distribution.* Our analysis on the criteria required for successful income tax enforcement on top incomes shows that income tax statistics, even at an early stage of development such as Spain in the 1930s or 1940s, are a valuable primary data source for analysing income concentration. Our in-depth analysis of income tax enforcement also provides support to the reliability of top income studies gathered in Atkinson and Piketty (2007).

Although Spain had to wait till the return of democracy in 1975–7 to start implementing a modern welfare state and redistributive tax policies, our findings show that, perhaps contrary to previous views, income concentration in Spain was quite low from the early 1950s and this possibly played a role in the stability and longevity of the dictatorship regime.

Since 1981, top income shares have increased significantly due to an increase in top salaries and a surge in realized capital gains. The gains, however, have been concentrated in the top percentile (and especially the top fractiles within the top percentile) with little changes in income shares of upper income groups below the top percentile. Financial wealth concentration has also increased in the 1990s due to a surge in stock prices, which are held disproportionately by the wealthy. However, as real estate wealth is less concentrated than financial wealth and real estate prices have increased dramatically, netting these out, very top wealth shares (including both financial and real estate wealth) have declined during the period 1982–2005.

Our series can be fruitfully used to evaluate the effects of tax reforms on the economic behaviour and tax avoidance of the affluent. In particular, our series show that the wealth tax exemption of stocks for owner-managers introduced in 1994 has gradually and substantially eroded the wealth tax base, especially at the very top. Our empirical results, interpreted using a simple theoretical model of tax avoidance, show evidence of strong shifting effects whereby wealthy business owners were able to reorganize their business ownership and activities in order to take advantage of the reform. This implies that this tax reform, while reducing the redistributive power of the progressive wealth tax, also generated efficiency costs, as business owners were taking costly steps to qualify for the exemption.

The chapter is organized as follows. Section 10.2 describes our data sources, outlines our estimation methods, and discusses the issue of income tax evasion in Spain. In section 10.3 we present and analyse the trends in top income shares since 1933 as well as the composition of top incomes since 1981. Section 10.4 focuses on top wealth shares and composition since 1982. Section 10.5 uses the wealth series to analyse the efficiency costs of the wealth tax exemption of 1994. The complete details on our data and methods, as well as the complete sets of results are presented in the appendices.

10.2 DATA, METHODOLOGICAL ISSUES, AND CONTEXT

Data and Series Construction

Our estimates are from personal income and wealth tax return statistics compiled by the Spanish fiscal administration for a number of years from 1933 to 1971 and annually from 1981 on. The statistical data presented are much more detailed for the 1981–2005 period than for the older period. Because the received wisdom is that the individual income tax was poorly enforced, especially in the pre-1981 period, we will discuss in great detail this issue in section 10.2 and throughout the text in section 10.3. Complete details on the methodology are provided in the appendices.

Before 1981, because of very high exemption levels, only a very small fraction of individuals had to file individual tax returns, and therefore we must restrict our analysis to the top 0.1 per cent of the income distribution (and for 1933–47 even the top 0.01 per cent). From 1981 on, we can analyse the top 10 per cent of the income distribution. Spain has adopted an annual personal wealth tax since 1978. Detailed statistics on the 'new' income and wealth tax were first published in 1981 and 1982 respectively.[5] The progressive wealth tax has high exemption levels and only the top 2 per cent or 3 per cent wealthiest individuals file wealth tax returns. Thus, we limit our analysis of wealth concentration to the top 1 per cent and above, and for the period 1982 to 2005. For 1981 to the present, estimates are based on Spain excluding two autonomous regions, País Vasco and Navarra, because they manage the income and wealth taxes directly and hence are excluded from the statistics. Those two regions represent about 10 per cent of Spain in terms of population and income.[6]

Our top groups are defined relative to the total number of adults (aged 20 and above) from the Spanish census (not the number of tax returns actually filed). The Spanish income tax is individually based since 1988 (although joint filing remains possible, it is always advantageous to file separately when both spouses have incomes). Before 1988, the Spanish income tax was family based. We correct our estimates for 1981–7 using the micro-data (which allow us to compute both

---

[5] Official publication exists since 1979 for the income tax and since 1981 for the wealth tax. However, the statistical quality of the data for the first years is defective with obvious and large inconsistencies that make the data non-usable.

[6] In the old regime, from 1933 to 1935, estimates are based on all Spain; Navarra is excluded since 1937 and Alava (one of the three provinces in the País Vasco) since 1943.

family and individual income after the reform) in order to account for this change in law.[7]

We define income as gross income before all deductions and including all income items reported on personal tax returns: salaries and pensions, self-employment and unincorporated business net income, dividends, interest, other investment income, and other smaller income items. Realized capital gains are also included in the tax base since 1979 (but not before). In order to create comparable series before and after 1979, we also estimate series excluding capital gains for the period 1981–2005. Our income definition is before personal income taxes and personal payroll taxes but after the deduction of employers' payroll taxes and corporate income taxes.

The wealth tax is a progressive tax on the sum of all individual wealth components net of debts with a significant top rate of 2.5 per cent in the top bracket for very large wealth holdings.[8] In general, real estate wealth is not taxed according to its market value but according to its registry value for property tax purposes. Market prices are about three times as high as registry value on average. Real estate wealth is a very large component of wealth in Spain, especially after the surge in housing prices since 1995. Therefore, we use two definitions of wealth, one including real estate wealth evaluated at market prices and one excluding real estate wealth (and excluding also mortgage debt on the passive side) which we call financial wealth. Total wealth is clearly a better measure of wealth but is not directly measured in the wealth tax statistics and hence requires making large adjustments. Financial wealth is a more narrow definition of wealth but it is better measured in tax statistics.

Our main data consist of tables displaying the number of tax returns, the amounts reported, and the income or wealth composition for a large number of income brackets. As the top tail of the income distribution is very well approximated by Pareto distributions, we can use simple parametric interpolation methods to estimate the thresholds and average income levels for each fractile. This method follows the classical study by Kuznets (1953) and has been used in many of the top income studies presented in Atkinson and Piketty (2007).[9] In the case of Spain, income tax micro-data are available since 1982 allowing us to check the validity of our estimations based on published tax statistics. We find that our

---

[7] The old income tax was based on individual income from 1933 to 1939 and based on family income from 1940 on. We do not correct estimates for the 1940–71 period because, at the very top of the distribution, we expect spouses' incomes to be small during that period when very few married women worked.

[8] The wealth tax is individually based since 1988 and family based before. We correct for this discontinuity assuming that wealth shares from 1987 to 1988 grew at the average rate of 1986 to 1987 and 1988 to 1989 (see appendices). Our earlier draft did not correct for this change and Durán and Esteller (2007) pointed out to us this omission.

[9] The mean-split histogram method has been used to estimate top shares in the cases of Australia, Finland, the Netherlands, New Zealand, and the UK in Atkinson and Piketty 2007) and Norway (Chapter 9) and Singapore (Chapter 5) in this volume.

tabulations-based estimates are almost always very close (within 2 and 5 per cent) to the micro-data-based estimates, giving us confidence that the errors due to interpolation are fairly modest.[10]

In order to estimate shares of income, we need to divide the income amounts accruing to each fractile by an estimate of total personal income defined ideally as total personal income reported on income tax returns had everybody been required to file a tax return. Because only a fraction of individuals file a tax return (especially in the pre-1979 era), this total income denominator cannot be estimated using income tax statistics and needs to be estimated using National Accounts and the GDP series created by Prados de la Escosura (2003) for the pre-1979 period. For the recent period 1981–2005, we approximate the ideal income denominator as the sum of (1) total wages and salaries (net of social security contributions) from National Accounts, (2) 50 per cent of Social Transfers from National Accounts (as pensions, which represent about half of such transfers, are taxed under the income tax), (3) 66.6 per cent of unincorporated business income from National Accounts (as we estimate that about one-third of such business income is from the informal sector and hence escapes taxation), (4) all capital income reported on tax returns (as capital income is very concentrated, non-filers receive a negligible fraction of capital income). Our denominator for the 1981–2005 period is around 66 per cent of Spanish GDP (excluding País Vasco and Navarra) with small fluctuations across years, which is comparable to other studies in Atkinson and Piketty (2007). For the pre-1979 period, because of lack of personal income series in the National Accounts series, we define our denominator as 66 per cent of GDP.[11] Similarly we use estimates of aggregate financial net wealth and real estate wealth from the Bank of Spain statistics to compute wealth shares.

The Issue of Tax Avoidance and Evasion

Income tax data have hardly been used before to study income concentration, especially prior to 1979, because there is a widely held view that income tax evasion in Spain was very high, and that consequently, the income tax data vastly underestimate actual incomes.[12] A careful analysis of the income tax statistics

---

[10] We do not have micro-data in the case of the wealth tax to check the accuracy of our interpolation method. However, Durán and Esteller (2007) have constructed bounds on the top 1% average wealth and shown that those bounds are tight (within 3% in all years).

[11] We take into account the exclusion of Navarra since 1937 and that of Alava since 1943.

[12] Comín (1994) and Comín and Zafra Oteyza (1994) provide a historical account on the issues of fiscal fraud and tax amnesties over the last century in Spain. Díaz Fuentes (1994) focuses on the period 1940–90. For the view that income tax evasion was very high in the pre-1979 period, see Breña Cruz et al. (1974), Castillo López (1992), Instituto de Estudios Fiscales (1973), and Martí Basterrechea (1974).

shows that evasion and avoidance in Spain *at the very top of the distribution* during the first decades of existence of the tax was most likely not significantly higher than it was in other countries such as the United States or France. It is therefore critical to understand the roots of this widely held view, which is based on two main arguments.

First, very few individuals were paying income tax and the individual income tax was raising a very small amount of revenue relative to GDP. Second, the administration did not have the means to enforce the income tax, especially when the exemption thresholds were significantly reduced in the 1960s, and when tax filers could very easily exaggerate their deductions to avoid the tax.

The first argument is factually true as only about 1,500 individuals paid taxes in 1933—about 0.01 per cent of all adults—and throughout the 1950s and 1960s the number of taxpayers rarely exceeded 40,000—about 0.2 per cent of all adults—(Table 10D.3). Combined with relatively low tax rates (except at the very top brackets), it is therefore not surprising that the income tax was only raising between 0.03 per cent of GDP in 1933 and 0.22 per cent of GDP in 1978 (Table 10A.4). However, extremely high exemption levels can very well explain such facts even in the absence of tax evasion. Indeed, in 1933, the filing threshold was 100,000 pesetas, i.e. sixty-six times the average income per adult (equal to around 1,500 pesetas based on our estimated denominator described in section 10.2). Our series show that income concentration based on those tax statistics was very high in the 1930s (about twice as high as in recent decades), and actually not much lower than levels estimated for the United States or France. Therefore, the number of filers and income reported at the very top are not unreasonably low.

The second argument that enforcement was poor also needs to be qualified. It is undoubtedly true that the 1964–7 income tax reform that eliminated the high exemption levels failed to transform the income tax into a mass tax as the fiscal administration kept using de facto high exemption levels and did not try to make taxpayers with incomes below 200,000 or even 300,000 pesetas pay the tax (Martí Basterrechea 1974).

However, there are three main reasons to believe that enforcement *for very top taxpayers* was acceptable under the old income tax. First, historically, early comprehensive income tax systems always use very high exemption levels and therefore only a very small fraction of the population at the top was liable for the tax. The rationale for using income taxes on the very rich only is precisely because, at the early stages of economic development with substantial economic activity taking place in small businesses with no verifiable accounts, it is much easier to enforce a tax on a small number of easily identifiable individuals. The rich are identifiable because they are well known in each locality and they derive their incomes from large and modern businesses or financial institutions with verifiable accounts, or from highly paid (and verifiable) salaried positions, or property income from publicly known assets (such as large land estates with regular rental income).[13] Therefore, the Spanish income tax was small because it was a tax limited to the very rich and this should not be interpreted as the consequence of poor enforcement.[14] Indeed, official statistics show that the administration was able to audit a very significant fraction of individual tax returns in the pre-1960 period. The audit rates were on average around 10–20 per cent and hence significantly higher than today (Table 10A.2 and Table 10A.3). It is likely that audit rates were even higher for the top 2,000 income earners in the top 0.01 per cent.

Second, when the progressive income tax was started, Spain had already set in place schedular income taxes on wages and salaries, rents, corporate profits, business profits, and capital income.[15] As a result, most of the income components of the rich were already being taxed through these schedular taxes with a system of withholding at source,[16] which offered a robust way to verify the incomes of the rich.[17] Furthermore, like France, Spain also adopted and used presumptive income taxation based on external signs of wealth (ownership of cars, planes, vessels, and number of domestic workers) when the administration suspected tax evasion or avoidance.[18]

---

[13] Seligman (1911) is the classical reference on the history of early income taxes. The studies gathered in Atkinson and Piketty (2007) all show that the early income taxes in Western countries were limited to a small number of tax filers. All those studies show that income concentration measures derived from those early income tax statistics are always very high suggesting that enforcement of the income tax on the rich was acceptable. The case of Japan, which started an income tax in 1887, shows that a pre-industrial economy significantly less advanced than Spain in the 1930s could successfully enforce a tax on the rich (Moriguchi and Saez 2008 and Chapter 3 of this volume). The Spanish case follows this general pattern as well.

[14] In the discussions leading to the creation of the income tax during 1932, it was recognized that enforcement would be acceptable only if the exemption threshold chosen was high enough. The parliamentary debates show that, although some congressmen considered that the exemption level was too high, it was recognized that the tax authority lacked both the managerial capabilities and the necessary human resources to administer a broader income tax (Vallejo Pousada 1995). Most Western countries broadened their income tax during emergencies such as the world wars, and this required a very large administrative effort.

[15] The time series of the revenue raised by each of those schedule taxes are compiled and reported in Table 10A.4.

[16] For an account of the evolution of tax withholding at source for the different schedule income taxes, see García Caracuel (2004).

[17] Cross-checking of income tax returns with the schedule income tax returns did take place, as stated, for instance, in Albiñana et al. (1974) and Gota Losada (1966). Starting in 1933, the administration prepared personal listings with information from all schedule taxes in order to identify individuals with very high incomes. Along the same lines, in 1940 the government launched the *Registro de rentas y patrimonios* (Registry of Income and Wealth) in which information on personal wealth was gathered with the aim of assisting income tax audits. Additionally, the high level of land ownership concentration allowed local tax authorities to identify large estate proprietors and rents for rural rent tax purposes (see, for instance, Carrión 1972, 1973; and Alvarez Rey 2007).

[18] According to Albiñana et al. (1974), Castillo López (1992), and Martí Basterrechea (1974), extraordinary deductions were among the main sources for tax evasion after the reform of 1964–7. Tax statistics report the amount of extraordinary deductions, which are only around 5% of income in the late 1950s. Our series are estimated based on income *before* deductions and thus are not biased downwards due to excessive deductions.

Third, the administration also threatened to make public the list of taxpayers in order to shame prominent tax evaders (Albiñana 1969a). Such lists were published for tax years 1933 to 1935 in the official state bulletin and show that virtually all the largest aristocratic real estate owners among the *Grandes de España* (the highest nobility rank) were taxpayers, demonstrating that the traditional aristocracy could not evade the income tax.[19]

Contemporaneous observers (Albiñana 1969a, 1969b; Gota Losada 1970) suggest that enforcement deteriorated during the last decade of Franco's regime.[20] This view is based primarily on the fact that the 1964–7 reform virtually eliminated exemptions and legally transformed the income tax into a mass tax, linked to schedular taxes. In practice however, the income tax remained a tax on very high incomes only as the mass tax was not enforced. Therefore, a much more accurate statement is that the Spanish income tax could not become a mass tax (as this happened in most Western countries around the mid-twentieth century) without a significant administrative effort that the Franco regime never seriously attempted, hence giving the impression that the tax was primitive and poorly enforced relative to other countries.[21] However, this does not mean that the Spanish income tax was not properly enforced on very top incomes, and all the evidence that we have been able to gather points toward enforcement levels and techniques *for the very top of the distribution* that were comparable to those used in other countries.

Since the return to democracy, Spain has successfully extended the income tax, which now covers a large fraction of income earners (see Table 10C.2). Spain uses tax withholding at source for wages and pensions and has third party reporting requirements for most types of income (such as interest and dividends), making it very difficult to evade taxes on income paid through large businesses or

---

[19] In 1932, the list of all the *Grandes de España* (who were part of the land reform expropriation) was published in the Gaceta de Madrid (16 October 1932). Carrión (1973) provides details of the land area owned by the largest estate proprietors among them. By comparing these lists and the income tax lists it turns out that 100% of owners of more than 3,000 hectares were income taxpayers (36 people). Furthermore, 92% of proprietors with more than 1,000 hectares (60 out of 65 people) are present in the tax lists. Note that this does not imply that the missing 8% were necessarily evaders; in most cases their ascendants paid the income tax, which might reflect different timing between land ownership transfers and nobility title transfers. Additionally, inspection of the income tax lists shows that over one-tenth of *all taxpayers* in 1933–5 were either *Grandes* or close relatives.

[20] The economic historian Francisco Comín reported to us a well-known story: during the final period of the dictatorship, the commission in charge of redesigning the income tax examined the list of top taxpayers. Strikingly, the top of the list consisted of famous bullfighters and show business stars rather than bankers or large business owners. Unfortunately, there does not seem to be any written reference on this and it is possible that the story has been widely exaggerated as it was told and retold over time. As just discussed, the published lists of taxpayers in 1933–5 provide hard evidence that goes in the opposite direction.

[21] Fiscal inspectors were very competent, well compensated, and highly regarded. Many of them have extensively written on income tax issues, including Albiñana (1969a, 1969b), Albiñana et al. (1974), Breña Cruz et al. (1974), Gota Losada (1966, 1970), Martí Basterrachea (1974).

financial institutions.[22] As a result and as in most OECD countries, tax evasion is concentrated among the self-employed, especially in the informal sector where businesses do not use formal and verifiable accounts. Therefore, evasion within the top 10 per cent is expected to be relatively modest. The wealth tax is also systematically enforced using the official cadastral values for real estate and information from the income tax for financial assets. Strikingly, as we show in Appendix 10F, top wealth holders report substantially more wealth for wealth tax purposes than in the first wealth survey recently run by the Bank of Spain for year 2002.

10.3 TOP INCOME SHARES AND COMPOSITION

Top Income Shares

Figure 10.1 displays the average personal income per adult estimated from National Accounts that is used as the denominator for our top income shares estimations along with the price index for the period 1932 to 2005. As discussed

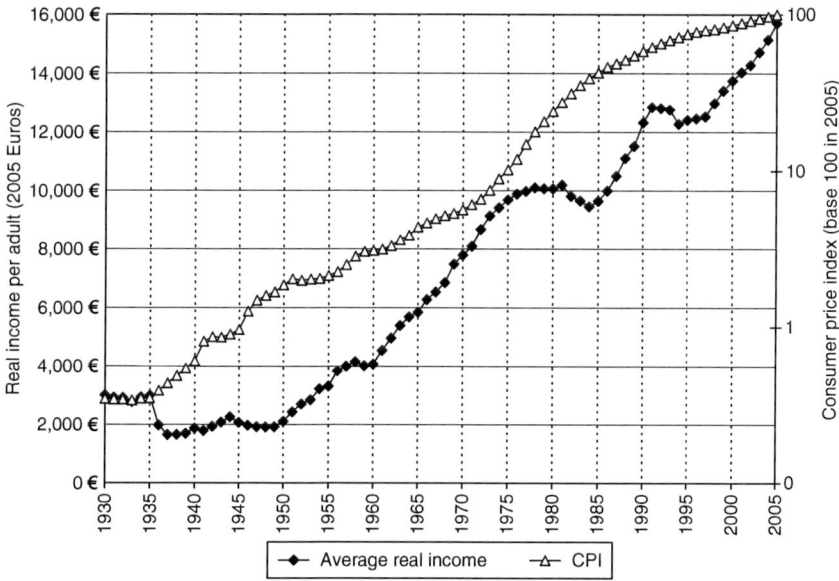

Figure 10.1 Average real income and consumer price index in Spain, 1930–2005

Notes: Figure reports the average real income per adult (aged 20 and above), expressed in real 2005 euros. CPI index is equal to 100 in 2005.

Source: Table 10C.2.

---

[22] For an account of the improvements in the third party reporting requirements over the last thirty years, especially on income from financial assets, see Castillo López (1992).

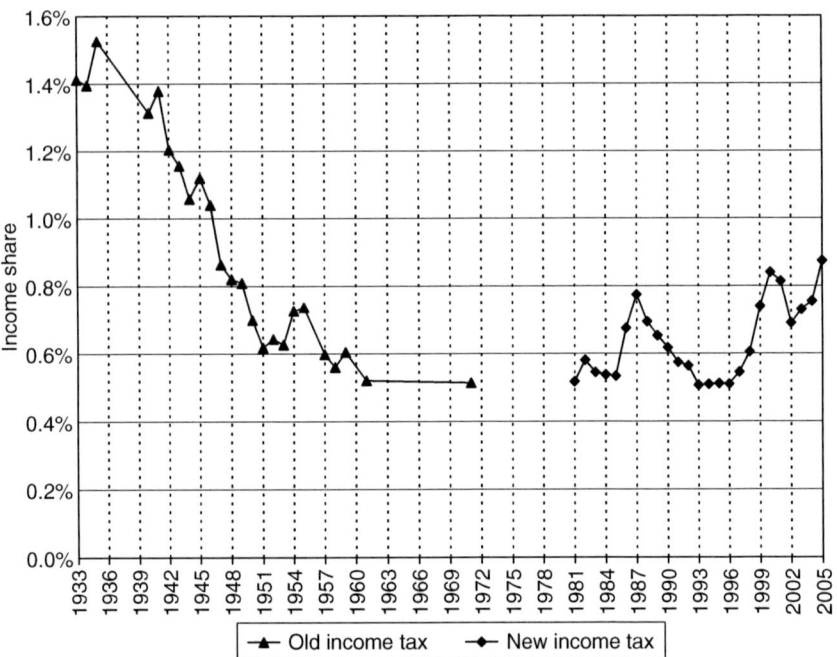

Figure 10.2 The top 0.01% income share in Spain, 1933–2005

Notes: For 1933 to 1971, estimates based on the old income tax statistics.

For 1981 to 2005, estimates based on income excluding realized capital gains (for homogeneity with old income tax.)

Sources: 1933–1971 from Table 10D.3 (column top 0.01%), 1981–2005 from Table 10D.2 (column top 0.01%).

in the introduction and as shown in Prados de la Escosura (2003, 2006b, 2007), real economic growth (per capita) was negative from 1930 to the early 1950s. Rapid economic growth started in the 1950s. Growth was fastest in the 1960s. Economic growth stalled during the transition period to democracy and in the first years of the democracy from 1975 to 1985, and then resumed again. Average income per adult in 2005 is around 15,700 euros. As discussed above, average income is estimated primarily from National Accounts and hence is largely independent of our tax statistics and not biased downwards because of tax evasion or avoidance. Average incomes are low because they include a large number of non-working adults (such as non-working wives or students) with either no or very small individual incomes who rely on other family members' income.

Figure 10.2 displays the top 0.01 per cent income share from 1933 to 2005. The break from 1971 to 1981 denotes the change from the old income tax to the new income tax. Four important findings emerge from this figure.

First, the highest income concentration occurs in the 1930s. The top 0.01 per cent share was around 1.5 per cent and about twice as high as in the recent period.

This finding is not surprising as Spain was a country with low average income and with high concentration of wealth and, in particular, land ownership.[23] However, lack of any statistics on income or wealth concentration made this claim impossible to establish rigorously. The use of the old income tax statistics demonstrates that Spanish income concentration was indeed much higher in the pre-civil war period than it is today.[24] Interestingly, tax statistics providing the composition of reported top incomes show that taxpayers in 1941 (representing the top 0.03 per cent) obtained about 20 per cent of their income from returns on real estate (rents), 35 per cent from returns on financial assets, 25 per cent from non-farm business income, 5 per cent from farm business income, and about 15 per cent from employment income (Table 10D.6). This suggests that, at the beginning of the Franco regime, only a minority of top income earners were passive landowners deriving all their income from rents (the traditional image of the agrarian aristocracy of the *Grandes de España*, mainly concentrated in the central and southern areas of the country). Top income earners were much more likely to be also owners of financial assets and non-farm businesses.

Second, the old income tax statistics display a large decrease in the top 0.01 per cent income share from 1.4 per cent in 1941 to 0.6 per cent in the early 1950s, during the first decade of the Franco dictatorship. We have argued in section 10.2 that there is no compelling hard evidence suggesting a deterioration of enforcement at the very top of the distribution and, therefore, we conclude that the poor economic management and the turn toward economic autarchy hit top incomes particularly hard and actually reduced income concentration in Spain. By 1953, the composition of top incomes had changed significantly relative to 1941: the fraction of non-farm business income has dropped from 26 per cent to 9 per cent while the fraction of farm business income has increased from less than 5 per cent to over 20 per cent.[25] This suggests that the closing of the Spanish economy in the 1940s led to a sharp reduction in successful non-farm business enterprises and, as a result, non-farm business owners were replaced by large farm business owners at the top of the distribution.

Third, top income concentration estimated with income tax statistics remains around 0.6 per cent from 1953 to 1971, the last year for which old income tax statistics are available, suggesting that the high economic growth starting in the 1950s did not bring a significant change in income concentration. Interestingly, the level of income concentration measured with the new income tax statistics in the early 1980s is quite similar to the level of 1971. Assuming again a constant level of enforcement from 1971 to 1981, this suggests that the transition from dictatorship to democracy was not associated with a significant change in income

---

[23] The land reform of the Second Republic was not successful in redistributing large land estates and was eventually abandoned (see Malefakis 1971 and Carrión 1973).

[24] If tax evasion at the very top was higher in the 1930s than today, then this reinforces our finding that income concentration was higher in the 1930s.

[25] The share of capital income from financial assets drops from 36% to 29% and the share of labour income increases from 13% to 19% from 1941 to 1953 (Table 10D.6).

concentration. Comparing the change in income composition in the top 0.05 per cent from 1961 to 1981 is interesting: in the capital income category, there is a dramatic shift away from real estate to financial assets and, in the business income category, there is a dramatic shift away from farm income toward non-farm business income. This shows that the very fast economic expansion from 1961 to 1981 made traditional land and farm owners fall behind other business owners at the top of the distribution. Our top income share series show, however, that such a shift took place with no change in overall income concentration.

Interestingly, our results display a striking asymmetry: the civil war shock and the subsequent economic mismanagement in the 1940s crippled the economy and reduced drastically the concentration of income. However, the fast economic growth after 1950 was not accompanied with a resurgence of income concentration. These findings are in line with the results from other countries (see Atkinson and Piketty 2007) suggesting that large but accidental shocks, rather than the natural economic growth process, are the main factors affecting top incomes. In the case of Spain, it is conceivable that the low level of income concentration since the 1950s contributed to the stability and longevity of the dictatorship.

Finally, Figure 10.2 shows that there are fluctuations in very top income concentration since 1981 with sharp increases in the late 1980s and since the late 1990s. The top 0.01 per cent income share in 2005 is the highest since 1946.

In light of our discussion in the introduction about the specific economic and political trajectory of Spain relative to other Western countries analysed previously, it is interesting to compare the trends in income concentration between Spain and other countries. Figure 10.3 displays the top 0.01 per cent income share in Spain, France (from Piketty 2001 and Landais 2007), and the United States (Piketty and Saez 2003). Two points are worth noting.

First, Spain starts with a level of income concentration in the 1930s that is slightly lower than France or the United States. However, income concentration in France and the United States falls more sharply than in Spain during the Second World War. Therefore, from the mid 1940s to 1971, income concentration across the three countries is actually strikingly close.[26] This shows that the number of high-income taxpayers is not inherently too low in Spain relative to other countries and supports our claim that enforcement at the top of the distribution was plausibly comparable across Spain and other Western countries. Second, although income concentration has increased in Spain in recent decades, this increase is very small relative to the surge experienced by top incomes in the United States. Thus, the Spanish experience is actually closer to that of continental Europe countries such as France than to Anglo-Saxon countries such as the United States.[27]

---

[26] The series are estimated using similar methodologies across countries although there are of course differences in the details. However, it is important to note that the denominator (as a fraction of GDP) is comparable across countries and around 60% to 65%. It is actually slightly higher in Spain (66% of GDP) than in France (around 60% of GDP on average).

[27] The studies gathered in Atkinson and Piketty (2007) show that Anglo-Saxon countries experienced a dramatic increase in income concentration in recent decades while continental European countries displayed either no or small increases in income concentration.

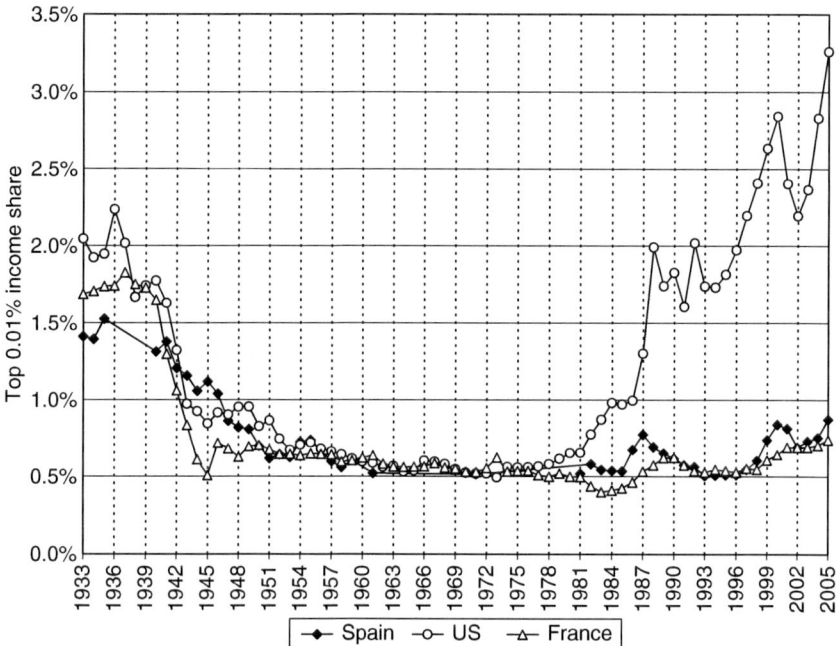

Figure 10.3 The top 0.01% income share in Spain, USA, and France, 1933–2005

Note: Top 0.01% income share excludes realized capital gains.

Sources: US: Piketty and Saez (2003); France: Piketty (2001) and Landais (2007); Spain: 1933–71 from Table 10D.3 (column top 0.01%), 1981–2005 from Table 10D.2 (column top 0.01%).

Detailed Analysis since 1981

The tax statistics since 1981 are much more detailed than the old income tax statistics. Thus, we can study larger income groups such as the top 10 per cent since 1981. Figure 10.4 displays top income shares for three groups within the top decile: the bottom half of the top decile (top 10–5 per cent), the next 4 per cent (top 5–1 per cent), and the top percentile. In contrast to Figure 10.2, we now include realized capital gains in the top income shares.[28] The figure shows that those top income shares have evolved quite differently: the top 1 per cent increased very significantly from 7.7 per cent in 1981 up to 11 per cent in 2005. In contrast, the top 10–5 per cent and the top 5–1 per cent shares actually slightly declined from 1981 and in 2005, with very modest fluctuations throughout the

---

[28] To a large extent, realized capital gains were not taxed (and hence not reported) under the old income tax. Therefore, for comparison purposes, we also excluded realized capital gains in Figures 10.2 and 10.3 for the period 1981–2005.

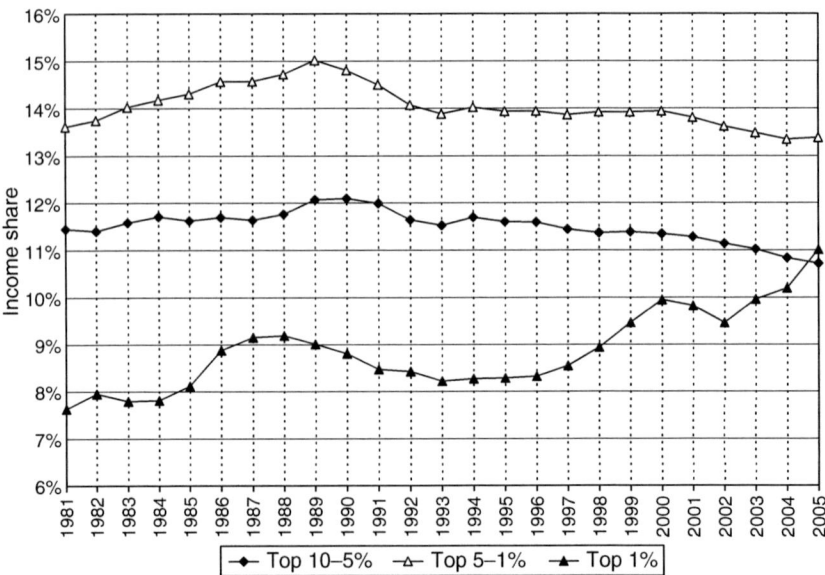

Figure 10.4 The top 10–5%, top 5–1%, and top 1% income share in Spain, 1981–2005

Note: Income includes realized capital gains.

Source: Table 10D.1, columns top 10–5%, top 5–1%, and top 1%.

period. Therefore the increase in income concentration which took place in Spain since 1981 has been a phenomenon concentrated within the top 1 per cent of the distribution. This result could not have been derived from survey data, which have too small samples and top coding issues to reliably study the top 1 per cent.

In order to understand the mechanisms behind this increase in income concentration at the top, which has been happening within the top percentile, we next turn to the analysis of the composition of top incomes. Figure 10.5 displays the share and composition of the top 0.1 per cent income fractile from 1981 to 2005. The figure shows that the top 0.1 per cent share more than doubled from 2 per cent in 1981 to 4.1 per cent in 2005. The figure also shows that the increase in the top 0.1 per cent income share is due solely to two components: realized capital gains noted K Gains) and wage income. The remaining two components, business income and capital income, have stayed about constant. The figure shows that the 1987, 2000, and 2005 spikes were primarily a capital gains phenomenon.[29] In contrast, the wage income increase has been a slow but persistent effect, which has taken place throughout the full period.

[29] Capital gains fluctuate from year to year as they follow closely the large stock market swings, explaining the peaks in 1987, 2000, and 2005 (Figure 10.11).

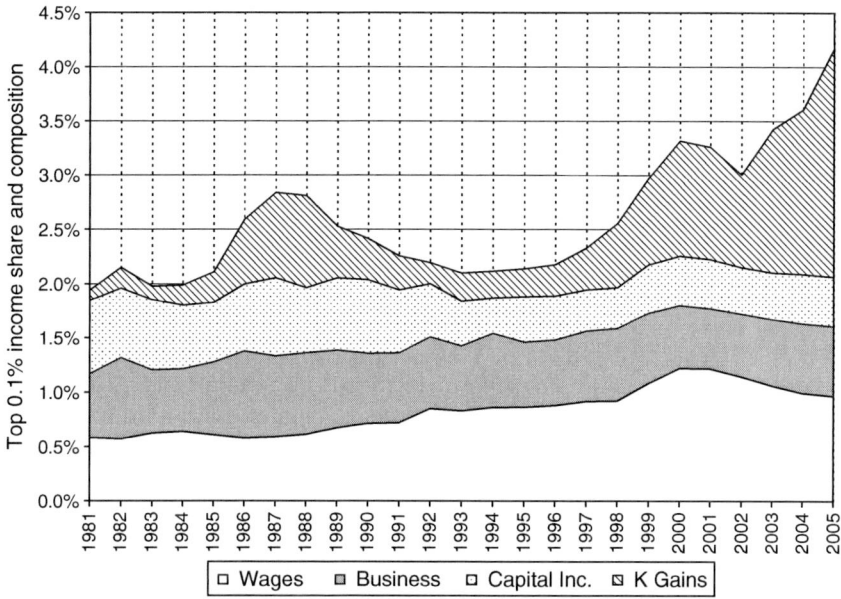

Figure 10.5 The top 0.1% income share and composition in Spain, 1981–2005

Notes: The figure displays the income share of the top 0.1% tax units, and how the top 0.1% incomes are divided into four income components: wages and salaries (including pensions), business and professional income, capital income (interest, dividends, and rents), and realized capital gains.

For example, in 1981, the top 0.1% was 1.95% of total income. Of those 1.95%, 0.55% were from wage income, 0.6% from business income, 0.7% from capital income, and 0.1% from capital gains.

Sources: Table 10D.1, top 0.1% income share and Table 10D.7, composition columns for top 0.1%.

10.4 TOP WEALTH SHARES AND COMPOSITION

In order to cast light on the capital income component of the income concentration series we discussed, we now turn to top wealth shares estimated from the wealth tax statistics. Figure 10.6 displays the evolution of average wealth (total net worth of the household sector divided by the total number of individuals aged 20 and above) and its composition from 1981 to 2005. These average wealth statistics come solely from National Accounts and are hence fully independent from wealth tax statistics.

Three elements should be noted. First, wealth has increased very quickly during that period, substantially faster than average income: average wealth in 2005 is 3.15 times higher than in 1982 while average income in 2005 is only 1.6 times higher than in 1982. Second, real estate is an extremely large fraction of total wealth. It represents about 80 per cent of total wealth on average over the period. Third and related, the growth in average wealth has been driven primarily by real estate price increases, and to a smaller degree by an increase in corporate stock prices. In contrast, fixed claim assets have grown little during the period.

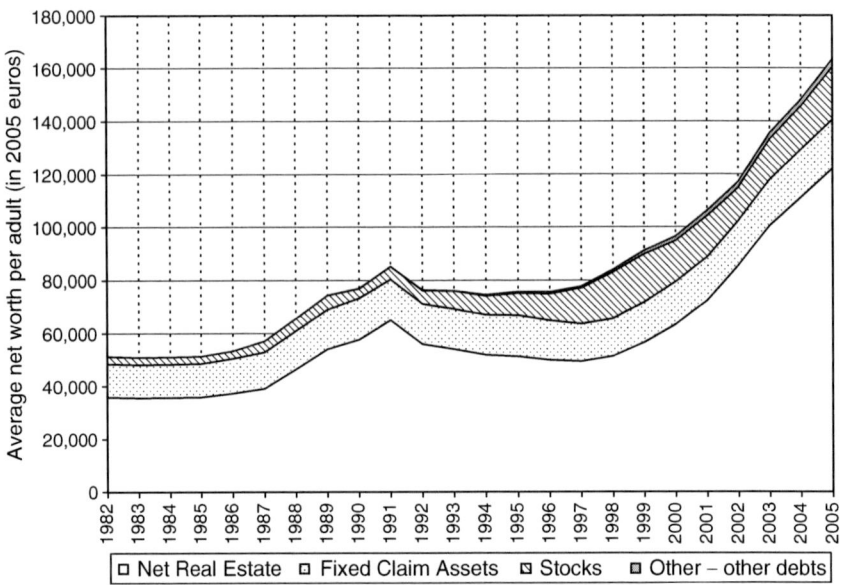

Figure 10.6 Average net worth and composition, Spain, 1982–2005

Notes: Net real estate is defined as total household real estate wealth net of mortgage debt.
Fixed claim assets are cash, deposits, and bonds.
Stocks include publicly traded and closely held stock, directly or indirectly held.

Source: Table 10C.1.

Figure 10.7 displays the composition of wealth in top fractiles of the wealth distribution in 1982 and 2005. As one would expect, the share of real estate is declining and the share of stocks is increasing as we move up the wealth distribution. It is notable that real estate still represents over 60 per cent of wealth for the bottom half of the top percentile. Thus, only the very rich hold a substantial share of their wealth in the form of stock holdings. The patterns in 1982 and 2005 are quite similar except that the level of stock ownership is higher across the board in 2005, a year with high stock market prices. Those compositional patterns suggest that an increase in real estate price will benefit relatively less the very top and should therefore reduce the very top wealth shares. In contrast, an increase in stock prices will benefit disproportionately the very rich and should increase the very top wealth shares.

Figure 10.8 displays the top 1 per cent wealth share (net worth including real estate wealth) along with the top 1 per cent financial wealth share (net worth excluding real estate wealth and mortgage debts). Unsurprisingly, the top financial wealth share is larger than the top wealth share because financial wealth is more concentrated than real estate wealth. Top financial wealth concentration is stable around 25 per cent from 1982 to 1990, decreases to about 21 per cent from

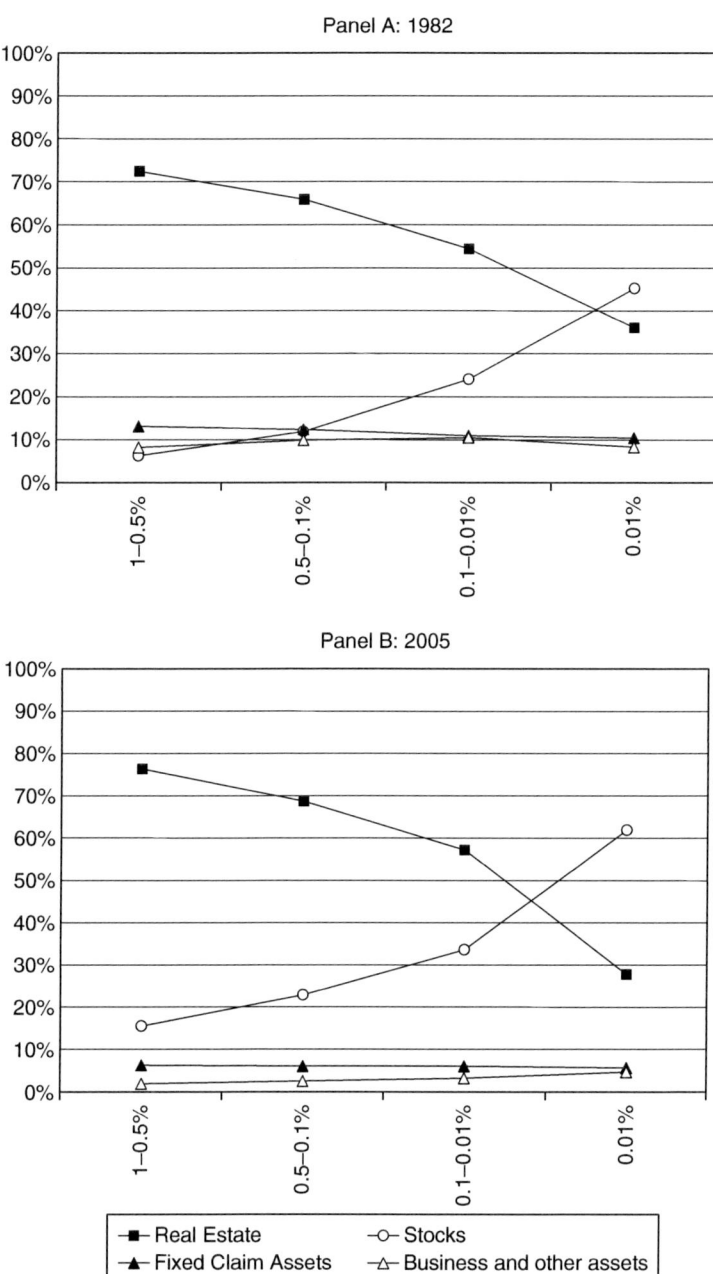

Figure 10.7 Wealth composition of top groups within the top decile in Spain in 1982 and 2005

Source: Table 10D.9, rows 1982 and 2005.

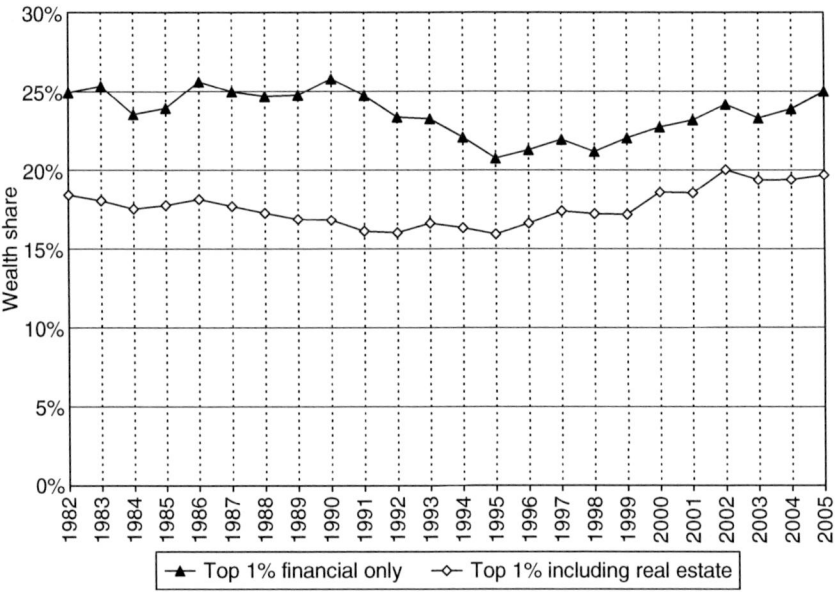

Figure 10.8 Top 1% wealth share in Spain, 1982–2005

Source: Table 10D.8, column top 1%.

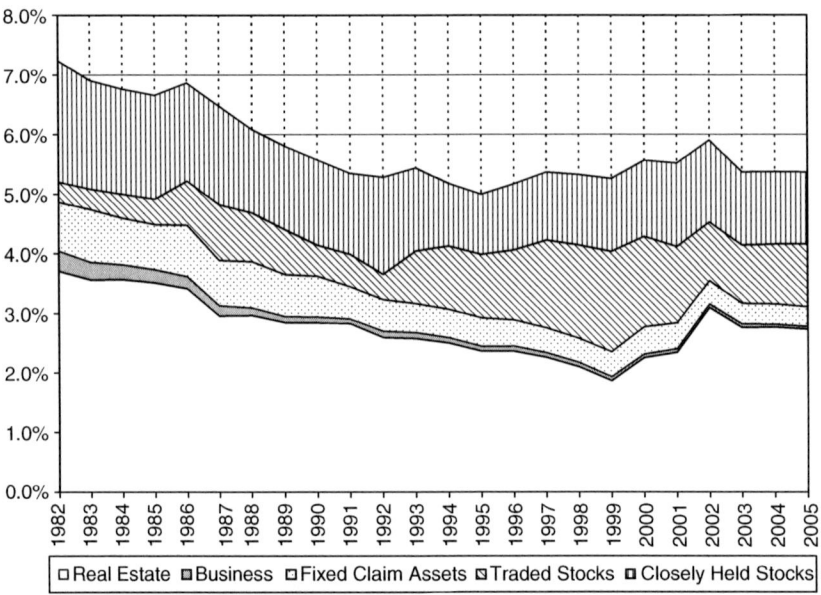

Figure 10.9 The top 0.1% wealth share and composition in Spain, 1982–2005

Notes: The figure displays the wealth share of the top 1% tax units, and how the top 0.1% wealth holdings are divided into five components: real estate, business assets, fixed claim assets (cash, deposits, bonds), and publicly traded stocks and closely held stocks.

Sources: Tables 10D.8 and 10D.9, column top 0.1%.

1990 to 1995, and then increases again to about 25 per cent by 2005. Top wealth concentration decreases from 19 per cent in 1982 to 16 per cent in 1992 and then increases to almost 20 per cent in 2005.

Figure 10.9 displays the wealth composition of top 0.1 per cent wealth holders from 1982 to 2005. In contrast to the top 1 per cent, it shows that the top 0.1 per cent has fallen substantially from over 7 per cent in 1982 to less than 5.5 per cent in 2005. Therefore, at the very top of the wealth distribution, the surge in stock prices has not been enough to compensate for the dramatic increase in real estate prices, which benefits upper (but not very top) wealth holders.

10.5 THE EROSION OF THE WEALTH TAX BASE

The series we have constructed and described in the previous sections can fruitfully be used to analyse the effects of tax reforms. In this section, we analyse the 1994 wealth tax reform, which introduced an exemption for business owners substantially involved in the management of their business. More precisely, stocks of corporations where the individual owns at least 15 per cent, or the individual and family own at least 20 per cent, and where the individual is substantially engaged in this business activity (getting over 50 per cent of his labour and business income from this activity) are exempted from the wealth tax. The value of those stocks still has to be reported to the fiscal administration and was included in our top wealth share series. Importantly for the empirical analysis below, the exemption criteria were relaxed for tax year 1995 (when the individual ownership requirement was lowered from 20 per cent to 15 per cent) and in tax year 1997 (when the 20 per cent family ownership criteria was introduced).[30]

In principle, the 1994 wealth tax reform could have two effects. First, the tax cut might spur business activity in the exempted sector—a supply side effect. Second, the tax cut for exempted business might induce some businesses, which did not originally meet the exemption criteria, to shift to the exempt sector in order to benefit from the tax cut—a shifting effect. For example, business owners could increase their share of stock in the company in order to meet the 15 per cent ownership threshold. Alternatively, they might become active managers in their businesses or drop other work activities outside the business. A business owner would be willing to shift to the exempt sector as long as the costs of shifting are less than the tax savings.

Figure 10.10 displays the composition and share of financial wealth held by the top 0.01 per cent wealth holders. Closely held stocks are now divided into two components: taxable and exempted. In 1994, the first year the exemption was introduced, exempted stock represents only about 15 per cent of total closely held stock reported by the top 0.01 per cent. By 2002, the fraction has grown to

---

[30] Starting in 2003, the individual ownership requirement was further reduced from 15 to 5%.

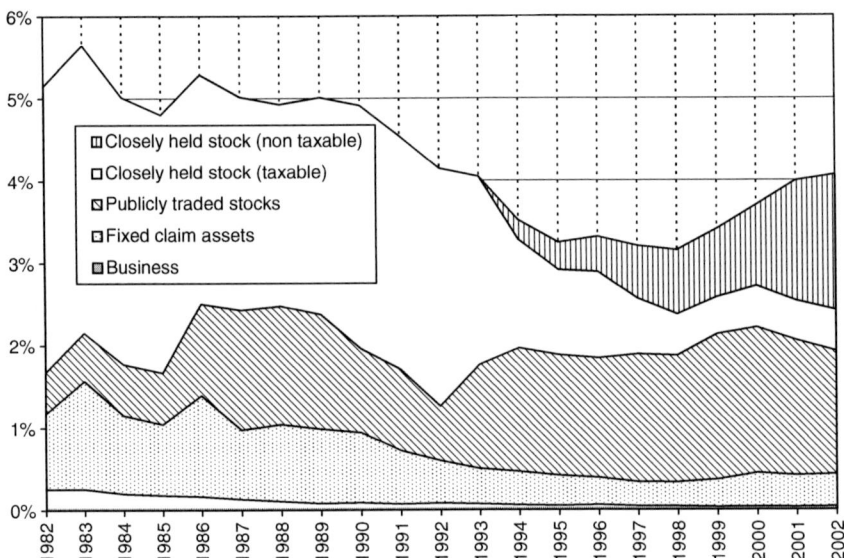

Figure 10.10 The top 0.01% financial wealth share and composition in Spain, 1982–2002

Notes: The figure displays the financial wealth share and composition of the top 0.01% tax units.
Stocks are broken down into three components: publicly traded stocks, taxable closely held stocks, and exempted closely held stocks.

Sources: Table 10D.8 and 10D.9, and direct computations based on wealth tax statistics.

77 per cent. Presumably, in 1994, individuals did not have time to reorganize substantially their business activity. Therefore, the 15 per cent fraction of closely held stock benefiting from the exemption in 1994 must be close or just slightly above the fraction of closely held stock which would benefit from the exemption absent any behavioural response to the introduction of the exemption.[31] The fraction of business exempt wealth grows enormously from 1994 to 2002, consistent either with a very large supply side effect or a significant shifting effect. However, the fraction of taxable closely held stocks shrinks significantly from 1994 to 2002 suggesting that the great increase in tax exempt wealth comes, at least in part, at the expense of taxable wealth through the shifting channel. We use our series to quantify the relative size of each effect. We first present a simple model to capture those two effects that we then estimate empirically.[32]

[31] Those would be businesses for which the cost of shifting q was zero because the businesses already met the criteria.

[32] To the best of our knowledge, such a model has not been presented before in the literature on the efficiency costs of taxation. It could be easily applied to other tax settings. For example, in the United States, the issue of shifting business profits from the corporate income tax base to the individual income tax base has received a lot of attention (see, e.g., Gordon and Slemrod 2000). Such shifting occurs because businesses meeting specific criteria (number of shareholders) can elect to be taxed directly at the individual level.

Conceptual Model

We assume that business owners have an objective function of the form $c - h(z)$ where z is pre-tax profits, c is net-of-tax profits, and $h(z)$ is an increasing and convex function representing the costs of earning profits. Those costs represent labour input costs (including the labour supply cost of the business owner if he is an active manager) and also capital input costs. The quasi-linear form of the objective function amounts to assuming away income effects or risk aversion effects, which simplifies the derivations and the welfare analysis.[33] We assume that the business owner can pay a cost $q \geq 0$ in order to meet the tax exemption status. Such costs represent for example the costs of increasing business owner-ship to 15 per cent or the opportunity costs of dropping outside work activities to meet the labour income requirement. Let $P(q)$ be the cumulated distribution of q. A fraction $P_0 = P(q = 0)$ of businesses meet those criteria even in the absence of the tax preference.

We assume that the tax rate on profits z in the taxed sector is τ_0 and that the tax rate in the exempt sector is τ_1 with of course $\tau_1 \leq \tau_0$. Note that τ_1 is not necessarily zero as the business also faces corporate and individual income taxes. It is also important to note that we convert the wealth tax rate t into a tax rate τ on profits using the standard formula $\tau = t/r$ where r is the normal annual return on assets. We denote by l the tax status of the business with $l = 0$ denoting the standard taxable status and $l = 1$ the exempt status. The manager solves the following maximization problem

$$\max_{l,\, z} \; z(1 - \tau_l) - h(z) - q \cdot l$$

This maximization problem can be decomposed into two stages. First, conditional on l, z maximizes $z(1 - \tau_l) - h(z)$ which generates the first-order condition $1 - \tau_l = h'(z)$. This equation captures the within sector supply side effect, as a decrease in τ_l leads to an increase in z_l with an elasticity $e_l = ((1 - \tau_l)/z_l)\partial z_l/\partial(1 - \tau_l) = h'(z)/\left(z_l h''(z_l)\right)$.

Second, the business chooses l. We denote by $V_l = \max_z [z(1 - \tau_l) - h(z)]$ the indirect utility in each taxable status $l = 0, 1$ (not including the cost q of becoming tax exempt). Therefore, if $q \leq V_1 - V_0$, then the exempt status $l = 1$ is optimal, while if $q > V_1 - V_0$, then $l = 0$ is optimal. As a result, a fraction $P^* = P(V_1 - V_0)$ of businesses chooses the exempt status. Using the envelope theorem, we have $\partial V_l/\partial \tau_l = -z_l$. Therefore, $\partial P^*/\partial \tau_0 = p(V_1 - V_0) \cdot z_0$ and $\partial P^*/\partial \tau_1 = -p(V_1 - V_0) \cdot z_1$, where $p(q)$ denotes the density of the distribution $P(q)$. Unsurprisingly, if there are firms on the margin between the tax exempt and taxable status, then increasing the tax τ_0 in the taxable sector generates a shift

---

[33] Including income effects would not change the qualitative nature of our findings but would complicate the presentation. In the case of wealthy business owners who actively work in their business, it seems plausible to assume that income effects are small (if income effects were large, those wealthy business owners would not be working).

toward the tax-exempt sector. Conversely, reducing the tax advantage of the exempt sector by increasing τ_1 reduces the number of firms in the tax-exempt sector.

We denote by $T = (1 - P^*)\,\tau_0 z_0 + P^* \tau_1 z_1$ the total tax revenue and by $W = (1 - P^*)\,V_0 + \int_0^{V_1 - V_0}(V_1 - q)dP(q)$ the private surplus in the economy. Social surplus is $SW = W + T$. Routine computations show that:

$$\frac{\partial T}{\partial \tau_0} = (1 - P^*)z_0 \left[1 - \frac{\tau_0}{1 - \tau_0} e_0 - \frac{p^*}{1 - P^*}(\tau_0 z_0 - \tau_1 z_1) \right] \qquad (1)$$

$$\frac{\partial T}{\partial \tau_1} = P^* z_1 \left[1 - \frac{\tau_1}{1 - \tau_1} e_1 + \frac{p^*}{P^*}(\tau_0 z_0 - \tau_1 z_1) \right] \qquad (2)$$

The first term (equal to one) inside the square brackets of (1) and (2) represents the mechanical increase in tax revenue in the absence of any behavioural response. The last two terms inside the square brackets represent the loss of tax revenue due to the supply side effect and the shifting effect respectively. The reduction in private surplus due to the tax change is equal to the mechanical tax increase (absent behavioural responses).[34] Therefore, the last two terms represent the net effect on social surplus SW of the tax increase or equivalently (minus) the marginal deadweight burden of increasing taxes. Absent shifting effects ($p^* = 0$), we obtain the standard Harberger formula showing that the marginal loss in tax revenue (per dollar) is proportional to the supply side elasticity e and the tax rate τ.

If the tax rate τ_0 in the taxable sector is below the Laffer rate maximizing tax revenue (when taking into account only supply side effects) then $\tau_0 z_0 > \tau_1 z_1$. Therefore, equation (1) shows that shifting effects increase the marginal deadweight burden of taxation in the taxable sector. In contrast, equation (2) shows that shifting effects decrease the marginal deadweight burden of taxation in the exempt sector. The economic intuition is transparent. Increasing the tax differential across the two sectors leads to more shifting: the marginal shifters spend q for a tax saving equal to q, which is pure deadweight burden. Strikingly, in the extreme case where $\tau_1 = 0$, $\partial SW/\partial \tau_1 = p^* \tau_0 z_0 / P^*$: social surplus increases with an increase in τ_1 no matter how large the supply side effect in the tax-exempt sector is.[35] Therefore, providing a wealth tax exemption for businesses meeting some specific set of criteria has two opposite effects on social surplus. First, it has a positive effect on social surplus through the standard supply side effect: exempt businesses face lower taxes and hence might expand their economic activity (with no effect in the taxable sector). This effect is measured through the supply side elasticity e. Second, however, the exemption might induce some businesses to shift to the exempt status and waste resources in doing so. This shifting effect leads to an increase in reported business wealth in

---

[34] This follows from $\partial V_l/\partial \tau_l = -z_l$, which is a direct consequence of the envelope theorem.

[35] As we discussed above, exempt business owners are exempt from the wealth tax, but still pay income taxes on the profits so that $\tau_1 > 0$.

the exempt sector coming at the expense of reported business wealth in the taxable sector. We propose an empirical estimation using our wealth composition series below.

Empirical Estimation

We propose a simple quantitative analysis using our estimated series and the model described above. Let us assume that, taking the tax or exempt status as fixed, business wealth is given by $z = \bar{z}(1 - \tau)^e$, where τ is the total tax rate (including income and wealth taxes) on profits, e is the supply side elasticity, and $\bar{z}$ is potential wealth absent any taxes. We assume that the fraction of businesses in the tax-exempt sector is given by $P = P(\tau_0, \tau_1)$. We use subscript b to denote before reform variables and subscript a to denote after reform variables. Hence P_b is the fraction of businesses meeting the exemption criteria just before the reform and P_a is the fraction of businesses meeting the exemption criteria after the reform. Hence $P_b - P_a$ captures the shifting effect (purged from the supply side effect).

For a given top wealth group (such as the top 1 per cent or the top 0.01 per cent), after the reform, we observe (1) exempt closely held stocks $P_a \bar{z}_a (1 - \tau_0)^e$ and (2) non-exempt closely held stock $(1 - P_a)\bar{z}_a(1 - \tau_1)^e$. Before the reform, we observe (3) the total closely held stocks held by the top group $P_b \bar{z}_b (1 - \tau_0)^e + (1 - P_b)\bar{z}_b(1 - \tau_0)^e$, as there is no distinction between taxable and exempt stock.

We estimate τ_0 and τ_1 as the sum of the income tax on profits and the wealth tax. We assume that the income tax on profits (corporate income tax if the business is incorporated or individual income tax if the business is unincorporated and taxed directly at the individual level) is 30 per cent for the top 1 per cent wealth holders and 40 per cent for top 0.01 per cent holders. We assume that the wealth tax rate (when the business is taxable) is 0.8 per cent of the value of assets for the top 1 per cent and 1.3 per cent for the top 0.01 per cent.[36] We convert wealth tax rates into an implicit tax on profits assuming a return rate on assets equal to 5 per cent. Therefore, the total tax rates on profits for non-exempt businesses are 46 per cent and 66 per cent for the top 1 per cent and top 0.01 per cent respectively. Although there is significant uncertainty about the exact tax rates, they only affect the estimation of e (and not P_a and P_b).

In order to estimate the three key parameters e, P_a, and P_b and the two auxiliary variables $\bar{z}_a$ and $\bar{z}_b$ from the three observed quantities, we need to make two important additional assumptions. First, we assume that the fraction of closely held stocks meeting the exemption criteria before the reform P_b is given by the observed fraction of stocks meeting the exemption the first year the reform is implemented. This assumption is reasonable if businesses do not have time to respond to the tax change in the first year after the reform. In any case, if businesses start responding in the first year, then we will overestimate P_b, hence

---

[36] Those estimates are based on the tabulated data. The wealth tax rates range from 0.2% up to 2.5% at the top but effective tax rates are substantially lower due to numerous exemptions.

underestimate the shifting effect $P_a - P_b$ and overestimate the supply side elasticity e.[37] In the empirical estimation, we need to take into account the fact that the wealth tax exemption criteria were relaxed in 1995 and in 1997. Therefore, we assume that the growth in the fraction exempt from 1994 to 1995 and from 1996 to 1997 is entirely due to the relaxation of the criteria (and hence that the fraction exempt would have stayed constant absent the relaxation). This is a very conservative estimate as the fraction exempt grows in every single year from 1994 to 2002. As a result, we assume that the fraction exempt (before the reform) is actually about twice as large as the fraction actually exempt in 1994. This conservative assumption leads to a conservative estimate of the shifting effect.

Second, we assume that, absent any tax change, total closely held stocks (taxable and non-taxable) would have grown at a rate g equal to the growth rate of other financial assets held by the top 1 per cent. In that case, $\bar{z}_a = (1 + g) \cdot \bar{z}_b$ where $1 + g$ is taken as the ratio of other financial assets held by the top 1 per cent after and before the reform. This is clearly a strong assumption. Using our pre-reform series, we show that it holds as a first approximation in the pre-reform period.[38] Panel A of Table 10.1 presents those key parameters for the top 1 per cent (left panel) and for the top 0.01 per cent (right panel) for various choices for the pre-reform base year and the post-reform year.

With those two assumptions, we can estimate the behavioural parameters e, P_a, and P_b, (Panel B) as well as evaluate the tax and efficiency consequences (Panel C). Three important results arise from this exercise. First and most important, all the estimates robustly suggest that there is a very large shifting effect: the two-thirds for the top 1 per cent. The shifting is even more extreme for the top 0.01 per cent and goes from 37 per cent exempt to over 80 per cent exempt. It is important to reiterate that this represents the pure shifting effect (controlling for the supply side effect).[39] Such a large shifting effect is not surprising in light of Figure 10.10 which showed a striking drop in taxable closely held wealth compensated by an increase in exempt closely held wealth. Second, the estimates for the supply side elasticity are sensitive to the choice of the comparison years and hence cannot be estimated precisely with our series.[40] However, the elasticity estimates are never extremely large and are often around zero (or even negative). This shows that the data series do not display consistent evidence of a very large

[37] A counter-argument could be that business owners did not know about the wealth tax exemption in the first year after the reform and hence failed to claim it even in cases where they were fully eligible. This argument is difficult to believe in the case of large wealth holders who use tax accountants to file their taxes. More broadly, the costs of learning about complex tax exemptions can be incorporated into the cost q of meeting the exemption criteria and our model and results would go through unchanged.

[38] For example from 1982 to 1993, among the top 1%, the (real) growth of other financial assets was 63% while the growth of closely held stocks was 44%. However from 1987 to 1993, closely held stock (in the top 1%) grew faster (36%) than other financial assets (16%).

[39] Such shifting effects are robust to assuming a rate of growth of closely held stock that is slower (absent any tax change) than other financial assets. For example, one would have to assume that closely held assets would have declined by 15% in real terms from 1993 to 2002 to make the shifting effects disappear for the top 1% group, which seems very unlikely given the growth that closely held stock experienced in the pre-tax reform period from 1982 to 1993.

[40] In contrast to shifting parameters, e is also sensitive to the assumption about the growth rate g of closely held assets absent the tax change.

supply side effect. Third and finally, Panel C shows that the combination of large shifting effects with moderate supply side elasticity implies that the actual tax loss due to the reform is much larger than the predicted tax loss of the reform absent any behavioural response. Even in the case of column 1 where the supply side elasticity *e* is largest and equal to 0.83, the actual loss in tax revenue from the top 1 per cent wealth holders is larger than the loss in tax revenue assuming no behavioural response. When the supply side elasticity estimate is smaller, the loss in tax revenue with behavioural responses can be three to four times larger than with no behavioural responses. As our theoretical model showed, the difference between actual changes in tax revenue and predicted changes in tax revenue (absent the behavioural response) are a measure of the efficiency costs of the tax change.[41] The last row in Table 10.1 displays such an estimated change in total surplus due to the tax change.

Therefore, our estimates suggest that the wealth tax exemption was an inefficient way to provide tax relief: the welfare gain to taxpayers was substantially smaller than the loss in tax revenue because taxpayers dissipate resources to meet the tax exemption criteria, creating deadweight burden.

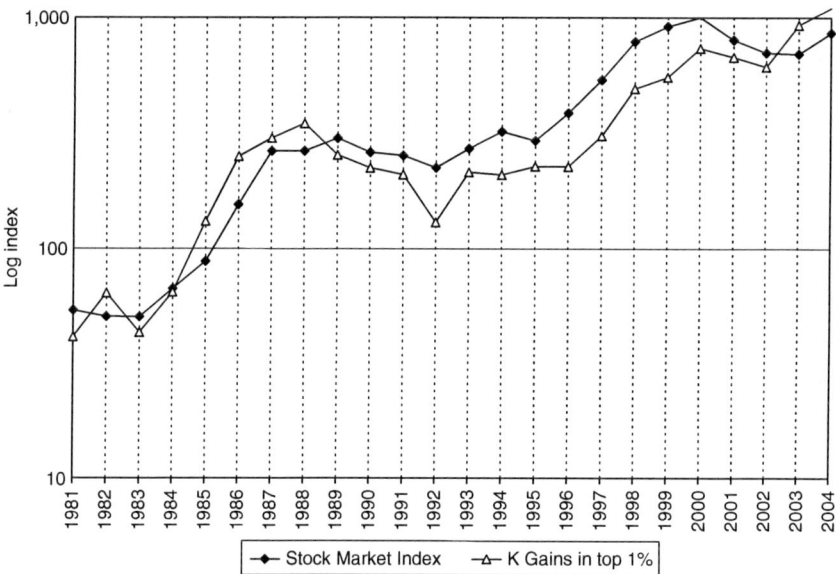

Figure 10.11 Madrid stock market index and capital gains at the top, Spain, 1981–2004

Notes: For each year, the mean of the low and high is reported.
Capital gains at the top 1% is the real amount of capital gains reported by the top 1% income earners.
The vertical axis measures the logarithm of the Madrid Stock Market Index and the logarithm of the top 1% capital gains.

Sources: Table 10C.2, Table 10D.7, and Madrid Stock Market Index from Globalfinance data and authors' computations.

[41] This is exactly true in the case of small tax changes. In the case of the relatively large change we are considering, this is only a first-order approximation.

Table 10.1 Estimating behavioural responses from the 1994 wealth tax exemption in Spain

	Top 1% wealth holders			Top 0.01% wealth holders		
	(1)	(2)	(3)	(4)	(5)	(6)
A. Observed variables and assumptions						
Before the reform (base year)	**1993**	**1993**	**1990**	**1993**	**1993**	**1990**
Imputed exempt closely held stock (E_b)	17,073	17,073	16,726	5,039	5,039	5,160
Imputed taxable closely held stock (T_b)	34,161	34,161	33,465	8,478	8,478	8,681
After the reform (post year)	**2002**	**2001**	**2002**	**2002**	**2001**	**2002**
Exempt closely held stock (E_a)	66,274	58,791	66,274	15,280	14,426	15,280
Taxable closely held stock (T_a)	26,942	27,668	26,942	4,615	4,753	4,615
Growth in other financial wealth from base year to post year (g)	56.9%	70.6%	73.1%	77.8%	102.0%	74.3%
Total tax rate on profits for non-exempt closely-held businesses (τ_0)	46%	46%	46%	66%	66%	66%
Total tax rate on profits for exempt closely-held businesses (τ_1)	30%	30%	30%	40%	40%	40%
B. Estimates of key behavioural parameters						
Fraction of closely held businesses exempt before tax change (P_b)	33.3%	33.3%	33.3%	37.3%	37.3%	37.3%
Fraction of closely held businesses exempt after tax change (P_a)	66.5%	68.4%	69.0%	80.8%	82.6%	80.9%
Supply side elasticity (e)	0.83	-0.06	0.39	-0.42	-0.79	-0.43
C. Tax and welfare implications of 1994 wealth tax reform						
Change in tax revenue assuming no behavioural responses	-183	-199	-198	-99	-113	-100
Change in tax revenue including behavioural responses	-201	-421	-328	-286	-389	-289
Estimated change in total social surplus	-18	-222	-130	-187	-276	-189

Notes: All amounts are in millions of 2005 euros. The tax rates are computed by adding the income tax rate on profits (30% for top 1% and 40% for top 0.01%) and the wealth tax. The wealth tax rate (0.8% for top 1% and 1.3% for top 0.01%) is converted into a profit tax rate assuming a return on assets of 5%.

APPENDIX 10A: THE INCOME AND WEALTH TAXES IN SPAIN

The 'Old' Income Tax

After six unsuccessful attempts since 1910, the first personal income tax (*Contribución general sobre la renta*) was established in all the territory of Spain, including Guipúzcoa and Vizcaya, in 1932 (Law 20/12/1932) during the Second Republic. Based on their historical autarky privileges, Navarra and Alava were excluded since 1937 and 1943 respectively.[42] Taxable income included income from real estate, capital, rural and mining activities, commercial and industrial business, labour, and pensions. Mainly due to the narrow managerial capabilities of the government, this first law determined a high taxable income threshold (100,000 pesetas lowered to 80,000 pesetas in 1936) together with low progressive rates, ranging from 1 per cent to 11 per cent (Table 10A.1). In 1933 there were only 1,446 tax returns and income tax collection represented 0.03 per cent of GDP and 0.35 per cent of total tax collections (Table 10A.2 and Table 10A.4). The income tax was based on individual income (as opposed to family income) from 1933 to 1939.

The fiscal reform of 1940 (Law 16/12/1940), which made changes in the whole tax system, was mainly motivated by the need to increase fiscal revenues to solve the post-civil war problems and to repay war debts. Consequently, the reform relied on the traditional schedule income and consumption taxes, which were much easier to collect. Concerning the *Contribución sobre la Renta*, it reduced the minimum taxable income to 70,000 pesetas and substantially increased the progressivity of the rates, with a top marginal tax rate of 40 per cent for incomes above 1,000,000 pesetas. It also raised the taxes on lower incomes, with the minimum tax rate jumping from 1 per cent to 7.5 per cent. It introduced family deductions and a supplementary 30 per cent surtax for single individuals. The new law applied to 1941 incomes. From 1940 on, the income tax was based on family income.

Tax rates were further increased in 1942 (Law 6/2/1943), when the minimum threshold was set to 60,000 pesetas. Two new reforms (Law 16/12/1953 and Law 26/12/1957) failed to generalize the coverage of the tax. The definition of 'unjustified wealth gains' (those which could not be explained by declared income flows) for audit purposes helped improve the inspection results, and had a positive impact on tax collection.

---

[42] The autarky regimes governing the territories of Navarra and País Vasco and their relationship with the central administration is not a new issue in the history of Spain. Those regimes date back to the fifteenth century. At the time of the second republic, Navarra's privileges were regulated by the *Ley Paccionada* (1841). The *Régimen de Concierto* was negotiated with Alava, Guipúzcoa, and Vizcaya in 1877, for which the provinces were responsible for the collection of national administration taxes while making lump sum transfers to Madrid. The 1936–9 civil war and Franco's policy towards 'traitor' local nationalisms changed the scenario. On the one hand, Alava and Navarra received a preferential treatment and kept their prerogatives after their contribution to the war on Franco's side. On the other, the autarky of Vizcaya and Guipúzcoa was abolished in 1937 (Decree Law 23/6/1937), even before the conflict had ended. Financial autonomy was recognized again during transition to democracy (Real Decreto-Ley 30/10/1976).

By the mid 1960s the *Contribución* had been pushed down in the fiscal agenda.[43] The stabilization plan of 1959 had been extremely successful in terms of government revenues so the tax reform of 1964 was not motivated by fiscal deficits but to promote growth and development. The Law 11/6/1964 and the Decree 27/11/1967 made the valuation of taxable income dependent on the system of schedule taxes.[44] Consequently, the personal income tax completely lost its autonomy. Theoretically there were no minimum thresholds to file; however, the usual obligation began at 200,000–300,000 pesetas. Tax rates ranged from 15 per cent to 61.4 per cent, with an average maximum rate of 50 per cent. The collection results were well below expectations again and the situation remained unchanged after the reforms of 1973 and 1975 (Decree Laws 12/1973 and 13/1975). The top marginal rate was reduced to 56.12 per cent with an average maximum rate of 40 per cent. Finally, and just before the introduction of the modern income tax in 1979, the Law 50/1977 offered a tax amnesty 1976; this was a success as 213,000 tax filers responded positively.

The Modern Income Tax

The modern income tax was established in 1979 (Law 44/1978), with two major reforms in 1991 and 1998. Albi Ibáñez (2006) provides a detailed description of the current system along with all the reforms from 1979 to date. From 1984 to 1987 the top marginal rate was 66 per cent; however the average tax rate could not exceed 46 per cent. In 1988 the tax scale was completely restructured downwards; the top marginal rate decreased from 66 per cent to 56 per cent, but the 46 per cent limit was eliminated (Table 10C.2, column 9).

The reform of 1991 did not modify either the tax rates or the main deductions. It updated the legislation in terms of individual and joint filing after the Constitutional Court decided in 1989 that the obligation to file jointly for married couples was thereafter unconstitutional. It also introduced changes in the taxation of capital gains, which we briefly describe below.

Since the reform of 1998 (Law 40/1998), the system was not supposed to tax overall but disposable income, after the deduction of a personal and family minimum income threshold (family-related reductions existed before, but they were applied to the amount of the tax and not to the income). The joint-filer tax scale disappeared, so that the same scale has applied to everybody since that year. The reform also provided a general rate reduction in the marginal rates. The drops ranged from 2 per cent (from 20 per cent to 18 per cent for the bottom bracket) to 8 per cent (from 56 per cent to 48 per cent for the top bracket). It also reduced the number of brackets from eight to six and eliminated the 0 per cent rate for the lowest income.

Concerning capital gains, the following facts are worth mentioning. Between 1978 and 1991, capital gains (excluding gratuitous *inter-vivos* and *mortis causa* transfers) were taxed as regular income, according to the tax rate scale. From 1992 to 2005, a distinction was made between short-run (or 'regular', meaning assets held less than one year) capital gains

---

[43] A result of this diminishing relevance is the non-existence of official detailed statistics about the individual income tax between 1961 and 1979.

[44] The powerful banking and industrial sectors, with strong influence in the dictatorship of Franco, seem to have been the source of a systematic attempt to block any generalization of the *Contribución sobre la Renta* and to sustain the status quo of the taxation scheme. See, for example, Albiñana (1969b) and Vallejo Pousada (1995), for details on how some private banks sketched income tax codes to be imposed to the government.

and long-run (or 'irregular') capital gains. Short-run capital gains are added to the main income and taxed according to the tax scale.

Since 1994, long-run capital gains from assets purchased before 1994 were first corrected downwards by a coefficient depending both on the nature of the asset and the number of years the asset had been held up to 1996 (real estate, −5.26 per cent per year; stock: −11.11 per cent per year; −7.14 per cent per year for other assets). Finally, the tax was computed as the maximum of (a) adding 50 per cent of irregular capital gains to the regular income and applying the tax scale to the result; and (b) applying the individual average tax rate to 100 per cent of the irregular gains. Since 1996 the average tax rate affecting irregular capital gains could not exceed 20 per cent.

From 1997 to 1998, long-run capital gains from assets held between one and two years continued to follow the rules described above. For those held more than two years, a 20 per cent rate was applied only to any amount beyond 200,000 pesetas. Since 1999 only gains for sales of assets held more than two years are considered 'irregular' and consequently taxed in a different way from the rest of income, at a 20 per cent rate (18 per cent for 2002 and 15 per cent since 2003). All capital gains (with the exception of the reductions mentioned above) are reported and thus included in our estimations, irrespective of whether they have been taxed based on the marginal tax scale or the flat tax rate.

We report in Table 10A.4 the revenue (as a share of GDP) of each tax source in Spain between 1930 and 2005, based on Comín (1985) and Instituto de Estudios Fiscales (BADESPE).

The Wealth Tax

The Law 50/1977 established a 'transitory' and 'exceptional' tax on net wealth, declared and paid annually at the same time as the income tax but on a separate form. Originally it was meant to serve as a control over the income tax, with limited redistributive goals. Tax filing was done on an individual basis, with the exception of married couples under joint tenancy. Since 1988, married couples can file individually.

Concerning taxable wealth and valuation rules: (a) urban real estate was valued at property registry values, corrected by coefficients which depended upon the year of construction; (b) rural real estate value was the result of capitalizing at 4 per cent the amount fixed by the local real estate tax; (c) chequing, savings accounts, and time deposits corresponded to the annual average balance, net of any amount used to purchase other components of wealth or to cancel debts; (d) life insurance corresponded to recovery value; (e) bonds and traded stock, at the monthly average price during the last quarter; (f) closely held stock, at liquidating value; (g) small personal goods, 3 per cent of wealth below 20 million pesetas and 5 per cent beyond; (h) other items, at market prices; and (i) debts at nominal value. Urban real estate declared historical monuments and art works involved in cultural activities were exempted.

Since 1992, a major reform by the Law 19/1991 put an end to the transitory and exceptional character of the tax. It established a strictly individual filing and introduced changes in some of the included components as well as in their valuation rules. In particular, (a) real estate is valued at the highest of (i) the property registry value, (ii) the purchasing price, (iii) the value determined for other taxes; (b) chequing, savings accounts, and time deposits, valued at the highest of the final balance or the fourth quarter average balance; (c) bonds and traded stock, at the average of market price during the fourth quarter; (d) closely held stock, at the theoretical value according to the last audited balance; if the audit is still pending the value is obtained from the highest of the last audited balance or the average of the last three annual profits capitalized at 12.5 per cent;[45] (e) life insurance at recovery value; (f) annuities at capitalization value; (g) art works and antiques, at market value; (h) intellectual and industrial property rights, exempted if belonging to the original author and valued at purchasing prices otherwise; (i) other items, at market prices; and (j) debts, at nominal value. Small personal items and pension funds were not taxed. The top marginal rate was set at 2 per cent in 1977 and raised to 2.5 per cent in 1991; however, the wealth tax plus the income tax should not exceed 70 per cent of the taxable income (60 per cent since 2003). The main residence was exempted up to 25 million pesetas (150,253.03 euros) since 2000 (Law 6/2000).

Of particular importance for section 10.5 in the main text, the Law 22/1993 introduced the following new exemptions, starting in 1994:

(a) Goods necessary for business activities constituting the main income source, performed in a direct and personal way by the individual.

(b) Closely held stocks of business corporations whenever all three of the following conditions were met:

  (i) the individual is substantially engaged in the business activity (he is the manager), getting over 50 per cent of his total labour, business, and professional income from it;

  (ii) the individual owns at least 20 per cent of the capital;

  (iii) the corporation is not involved in wealth management as main activity.

Since 1995 the minimum share requirement was reduced to 15 per cent (Law 42/1994) for the individual, and set to 20 per cent for the family in 1997 (Law 13/1996). In 1998, professional activities were also included in the exemption mentioned in (a) (Law 66/1997). In 2003, the individual ownership threshold was lowered to 5 per cent (Law 51/2002).[46]

As of 1 January 1997 the wealth tax revenues were transferred to the local governments (Law 46/1996).

[45] Capitalization rate was raised to 20% in 1999 (Law 50/1998).

[46] In 1994 the fiscal authorities found it difficult to predict the results of the new exemptions (Memoria de la Administración Tributaria 1994: 124).

Table 10A.1 Income tax rates, Spain, 1933–1973

Income level (pesetas) from	to	Tax rate (%)
1933–1935		
100,001	120,000	1.00
120,001	150,000	1.43
150,001	200,000	2.00
200,001	250,000	2.78
250,001	300,000	3.42
300,001	400,000	3.97
400,001	500,000	4.86
500,001	750,000	5.57
750,001	1,000,000	6.84
If income exceeds 1,000,000:		
first 1,000,000		7.70
excess		11.00
1936–1940		
80,001	100,000	1.00
100,001	120,000	1.50
120,001	150,000	1.93
150,001	200,000	2.50
200,001	250,000	3.28
250,001	300,000	3.92
300,001	400,000	4.47
400,001	500,000	5.36
500,001	750,000	6.07
750,001	1,000,000	7.34
If income exceeds 1,000,000:		
first 1,000,000		8.20
excess		11.00
1941		
70,001	100,000	7.50
100,001	250,000	18.00
250,001	500,000	25.00
500,001	1,000,000	30.00
over 1,000,000		40.00
1942–1953		
60,001	100,000	7.50
100,001	150,000	18.00
150,001	250,000	20.00
250,001	500,000	27.00
500,001	1,000,000	33.00
over 1,000,000		44.00

(*continued*)

Table 10A.1 Income tax rates, Spain, 1933–1973

Income level (pesetas) from	to	Tax rate (%)
1954–1956		
100,001	125,000	2.50
125,001	150,000	2.90
150,001	175,000	3.85
175,001	200,000	4.60
200,001	250,000	5.90
250,001	300,000	7.55
300,001	400,000	10.05
400,001	500,000	13.35
500,001	600,000	16.65
600,001	700,000	20.00
700,001	800,000	23.30
800,001	900,000	26.65
900,001	1,000,000	29.85
over 1,000,000		33.00
1957–1965		
100,001	125,000	2.50
125,001	175,000	3.85
175,001	200,000	4.60
200,001	250,000	5.90
250,001	300,000	7.55
300,001	400,000	10.05
400,001	500,000	13.35
500,001	600,000	16.65
600,001	700,000	20.00
700,001	800,000	23.30
800,001	900,000	26.65
900,001	1,000,000	29.85
1,000,001	2,000,000	33.00
2,000,001	3,000,000	35.65
3,000,001	4,000,000	37.75
4,000,001	5,000,000	39.30
5,000,001	6,000,000	42.00
over 6,000,000		44.00
1966–1973		
0	100,000	15.00
100,001	200,000	18.20
200,001	300,000	26.60
300,001	400,000	23.00
400,001	500,000	25.40
500,001	600,000	27.80
600,001	700,000	30.50
700,001	800,000	33.40
800,001	900,000	36.30
900,001	1,000,000	39.20
1,000,001	1,100,000	42.10
1,100,001	1,300,000	47.20
1,300,001	1,600,000	56.10
over 1,600,000		61.40

Table 10A.2 Total number of tax returns and inspections, Spain, 1933–1974

	# Tax returns (1)	# Tax returns with positive taxable income (2)	# Inspected files (3)
1933	1,446	1,446	
1934	1,792	1,792	
1935	2,880	2,880	
1936	3,507	3,507	
1937	1,542	1,542	
1938	1,978	1,978	
1939	2,289	2,289	
1940	3,840	3,840	
1941	4,495	4,495	
1942	5,123	5,123	
1943	5,538	5,538	
1944	12,312	5,849	1,147
1945	11,817	6,629	1,140
1946	13,189	8,223	2,096
1947	17,897	7,983	1,964
1948	16,649	9,067	2,933
1949	19,755	10,111	3,294
1950	22,930	12,419	3,403
1951	23,887	13,597	3,524
1952	26,373	15,427	2,772
1953	27,653	16,545	1,118
1954	89,460	21,332	2,638
1955	98,604	26,716	1,915
1956	109,026		1,074
1957	119,618	38,493	1,306
1958	175,172	35,581	1,794
1959	190,791	42,246	
1960	197,842		
1961	222,593	26,623	
1962	240,179		
1963	296,701		3,183
1964	323,223		3,231
1965	347,434		2,947
1966			2,536
1967			4,612
1968	199,592	5,777	6,595
1969	228,132	13,709	8,979
1970	263,181	20,072	7,813
1971	338,989	22,556	4,045
1972	350,761	29,329	
1973	498,663	36,663	
1974	1,318,313	28,236	

Sources: Income tax statistics published by the fiscal administration for years 1933 to 1971; Gota Losada (1966); Instituto de Estudios Fiscales (1973); Martí Basterrechea (1974).

Table 10A.3 Number of tax inspections, Spain, 1986–2002

	Income tax		Wealth tax	
	# Tax returns ('000s)	# Inspected files ('000s)	# Tax returns ('000s)	# Inspected files ('000s)
1986	7,896	34.90	781	
1987	8,028	33.75	887	9.34
1988	8,954	25.04	756	6.97
1989	9,845	16.45	855	5.40
1990	10,965	28.05	974	9.58
1991	11,584	21.31	1,033	7.04
1992	12,341	33.39	863	9.61
1993	12,794	31.93	928	7.46
1994	13,578	25.77	809	4.89
1995	14,119	21.28	783	3.26
1996	14,620	18.97	825	2.23
1997	15,000	15.34	892	1.73
1998	15,424	10.06	946	1.21
1999	13,797	10.90	981	1.14
2000	14,123	9.67	869	1.07
2001	14,734	8.34	874	0.99
2002	15,410	8.25	884	0.92

Sources: Agencia Tributaria, Memoria de Actividades, several years.

Table 10A.4 Structure of tax revenues, Spain, 1930–1979

National government tax receipts as % of GDP

| | Direct taxes | | | | | | | Indirect taxes | | | | | Total taxes |
	Rents (1)	Entrepreneurial income (2)	Capital income (3)	Wage income (4)	Personal income (5)	Corporate tax (6)	Gifts and estate (7)	Total (1)–(7) (8)	Customs (9)	Tax stamp (10)	Consumption (11)	Luxury (12)	Total (9)–(12) (13)	Direct plus indirect taxes (14)
1930	1.08	0.60	0.58	0.39		0.36	0.62	3.63	1.70	1.04	0.98		3.72	7.35
1931	1.12	0.60	0.62	0.40		0.40	0.64	3.77	1.51	0.99	1.03		3.53	7.30
1932	1.21	0.66	0.60	0.41		0.32	0.59	3.80	1.66	1.08	1.16		3.91	7.70
1933	1.31	0.69	0.65	0.43	0.03	0.37	0.64	4.12	1.50	1.19	1.08		3.76	7.88
1934	1.20	0.62	0.63	0.44	0.04	0.27	0.63	3.82	1.37	1.04	0.94		3.36	7.18
1935	1.22	0.61	0.63	0.47	0.04	0.31	0.62	3.91	1.32	1.11	0.94		3.37	7.28
1936														
1937														
1938														
1939														
1940	0.99	0.51	0.44	0.52	0.04	0.19	1.28	3.95	0.47	0.85	0.97		2.29	6.24
1941	1.12	0.82	0.50	0.62	0.06	0.61	0.98	4.71	0.48	0.93	1.44	0.79	3.64	8.34
1942	1.25	0.74	0.52	0.66	0.15	0.71	0.89	4.92	0.71	0.51	1.64	0.71	3.57	8.49
1943	1.19	0.71	0.46	0.75	0.17	0.75	0.88	4.91	1.01	0.94	2.10	0.81	4.85	9.76
1944	1.07	0.63	0.39	0.72	0.18	0.71	0.71	4.41	0.81	0.85	1.96	0.81	4.44	8.85
1945	1.15	0.67	0.47	0.81	0.19	0.85	0.79	4.92	0.53	0.83	1.82	0.88	4.06	8.98
1946	0.81	0.43	0.36	0.73	0.18	0.74	0.67	3.92	0.62	0.84	1.67	0.49	3.63	7.55
1947	0.86	0.44	0.44	0.77	0.17	0.80	0.78	4.26	0.68	0.91	1.76	0.43	3.77	8.04
1948	0.83	0.42	0.38	0.81	0.18	0.87	0.78	4.28	0.69	0.88	2.02	0.42	4.00	8.28
1949	0.81	0.40	0.60	0.86	0.19	1.01	0.67	4.53	0.54	0.89	2.73	0.41	4.56	9.09
1950	0.79	0.30	0.34	0.78	0.17	0.97	0.61	3.96	0.46	0.79	2.10	0.42	3.77	7.73
1951	0.65	0.34	0.34	0.73	0.13	0.88	0.59	3.67	0.37	0.72	1.89	0.41	3.39	7.06
1952	0.64	0.34	0.35	0.75	0.15	1.12	0.63	3.98	0.43	0.79	2.26	0.41	3.88	7.87
1953	0.68	0.35	0.36	0.87	0.18	1.34	0.61	4.38	0.45	0.79	2.30	0.44	3.98	8.36
1954	0.68	0.30	0.35	0.81	0.17	1.14	0.58	4.03	0.42	0.57	2.10	0.44	3.54	7.57
1955	0.72	0.30	0.42	0.71	0.10	1.21	0.63	4.10	0.44	0.59	2.20	0.49	3.72	7.81
1956	0.62	0.24	0.49	0.67	0.11	1.18	0.58	3.90	0.57	0.59	2.02	0.48	3.67	7.56

(continued)

Table 10A.4 Continued

National government tax receipts as % of GDP

| | Direct taxes | | | | | | | | Indirect taxes | | | | Total taxes | |
	Rents (1)	Entrepreneurial income (2)	Capital income (3)	Wage income (4)	Personal income (5)	Corporate tax (6)	Gifts and estate (7)	Total (1)–(7) (8)	Customs (9)	Tax stamp (10)	Consumption (11)	Luxury (12)	Total (9)–(12) (13)	Direct plus indirect taxes (14)
1957	0.54	0.22	0.50	0.78	0.13	1.20	0.59	3.95	0.35	0.71	2.09	0.46	3.60	7.55
1958	0.48	0.32	0.48	0.74	0.13	1.15	0.63	3.94	0.48	0.68	1.81	0.73	3.70	7.64
1959	0.44	0.40	0.37	0.76	0.17	1.24	0.67	4.06	0.51	0.72	1.84	0.93	4.00	8.05
1960	0.50	0.42	0.41	0.87	0.18	1.20	0.68	4.26	1.09	0.73	2.02	1.05	4.88	9.14
1961	0.42	0.39	0.39	0.82	0.16	1.15	0.66	3.99	1.64	0.71	1.80	1.03	5.18	9.17
1962	0.40	0.49	0.38	0.80	0.16	1.12	0.66	4.02	1.87	0.69	1.66	1.03	5.25	9.27
1963	0.35	0.46	0.32	0.76	0.16	0.97	0.65	3.67	1.89	0.71	1.54	1.04	5.18	8.85
1964	0.33	0.46	0.31	0.73	0.16	0.88	0.55	3.52	2.08	0.87	1.37	1.17	5.50	9.02
1965	0.31	0.47	0.38	0.66	0.15	0.92	0.56	3.43	2.26	1.18	0.91	1.29	5.64	9.08
1966	0.25	0.45	0.32	0.80	0.14	0.96	0.56	3.50	2.53	1.32	0.77	1.34	5.96	9.45
1967	0.25	0.47	0.33	0.83	0.15	0.98	0.60	3.59	2.19	1.41	0.88	1.43	5.91	9.50
1968	0.22	0.48	0.34	0.74	0.16	0.92	0.60	3.46	1.96	1.44	0.85	1.43	5.67	9.13
1969	0.23	0.45	0.34	0.79	0.15	1.05	0.64	3.67	2.07	1.53	0.86	1.55	6.01	9.67
1970	0.26	0.46	0.36	0.89	0.14	1.02	0.66	3.78	2.05	0.44	0.89	1.57	4.95	8.74
1971	0.28	0.47	0.39	1.01	0.17	1.05	0.70	4.07	1.83	1.66	0.91	0.56	4.96	9.03
1972	0.29	0.43	0.38	1.09	0.16	1.05	0.75	4.15	2.08	1.64	0.84	1.55	6.12	10.26
1973	0.28	0.39	0.38	1.28	0.17	1.06	0.84	4.41	2.16	1.68	0.76	1.61	6.21	10.62
1974	0.30	0.38	0.33	1.41	0.13	1.05	0.85	4.45	2.00	1.73	0.64	1.42	5.79	10.24
1975	0.28	0.42	0.45	1.60	0.14	1.10	0.79	4.78	1.96	1.47	0.54	1.39	5.36	10.13
1976	0.25	0.37	0.68	1.78	0.15	1.12	0.74	5.08	1.71	1.33	0.45	1.39	4.88	9.96
1977	0.23	0.36	0.68	2.09	0.13	1.05	0.72	5.26	1.82	1.31	0.38	1.43	4.94	10.20
1978	0.22	0.32	0.73	2.73	0.22	0.92	0.74	5.87	1.45	1.29	0.45	1.46	4.64	10.51
1979	0.03	0.20	0.31	1.14	2.52	1.16	0.73	6.08	1.41	1.37	0.37	1.55	4.70	10.78

Notes:

1930–957:

Tax on Rents: Contribución Rústica y Pecuaria, Contribución Urbana. Tax on Entrepreneurial Income: Contribución Industrial y de Comercio. Tax on Capital Income: Contribución sobre las Utilidades Procedentes del Capital. Tax on Wage Income: Contribución sobre las Utilidades del Trabajo Personal. Corporate Tax: Contribución sobre las Utilidades del Trabajo y del Capital. Personal Income Tax: Contribución General sobre la Renta (since 1932). Gift and Estate Tax: Contribución sobre Derechos Reales y Transmisión de Bienes.

1958–1979:

Tax on Rents: Contribución Rústica, Contribución Urbana. Tax on Entrepreneurial Income: Licencia Fiscal, Cuota de Beneficios. Tax on Capital Income: Impuesto sobre las Rentas del Capital. Tax on Wage Income: Impuesto sobre los Rendimientos del Trabajo Personal. Corporate Tax: Impuesto sobre las Sociedades; since 1975: Cuota sobre la Renta Global de las Sociedades. Personal Income Tax: Impuesto General sobre la Renta. Personal Income Tax: Impuesto General sobre la Renta. Gift and Estate Tax: Contribución sobre Derechos Reales y Transmisión de Bienes.

Source: Comín (1985).

Table 10A.4 (continued) Structure of tax revenues, Spain, 1980–2005

| | Direct taxes | | | | | | Indirect taxes | | | | | Total taxes |
| | National government tax receipts as % of GDP | | | | | | | | | | | |
	Personal income tax (1)	Wealth tax (2)	Corporate tax (3)	Gifts and estate (4)	Other taxes (5)	Total (1)–(5) (6)	Customs (7)	VAT (8)	Other taxes on consumption (9)	Other taxes (10)	Total (7)–(10) (11)	Direct plus indirect taxes (12)
1980	4.07	0.11	1.14	0.09	0.23	5.64	1.00	1.28	1.28	2.83	6.39	12.03
1981	4.34	0.08	1.12	0.11	0.17	5.82	1.00	1.61	1.61	3.11	7.33	13.15
1982	4.24	0.07	1.09	0.08	0.11	5.58	1.10	1.18	1.18	2.86	6.32	11.90
1983	4.56	0.06	1.24	0.09	0.11	6.06	1.16	1.27	1.27	3.51	7.22	13.28
1984	4.84	0.03	1.25	0.03	0.09	6.25	1.11	1.59	1.59	3.21	7.51	13.75
1985	4.98	0.03	1.37	0.02	0.09	6.49	1.22	1.52	1.52	3.52	7.78	14.27
1986	4.67	0.03	1.57	0.02	0.07	6.36	0.79	4.17	1.38	2.07	8.41	14.77
1987	6.43	0.03	1.77	0.02	0.05	8.31	0.94	4.81	1.91	0.88	8.54	16.85
1988	6.25	0.04	1.95	0.00	0.05	8.29	0.92	4.93	1.86	0.82	8.53	16.82
1989	7.07	0.03	2.71	0.04	0.00	9.85	0.81	5.00	1.82	0.49	8.12	17.97
1990	6.67	0.04	2.76	0.03	0.00	9.48	0.65	4.79	1.90	0.45	7.79	17.27
1991	7.18	0.04	2.40	−0.02	0.00	9.60	0.51	4.70	2.19	0.14	7.54	17.14
1992	7.54	0.04	2.05	0.00	0.00	9.62	0.34	5.07	2.35	0.22	7.98	17.60
1993	7.48	0.04	1.78	0.00	0.00	9.31	0.14	4.36	2.50	0.16	7.17	16.47
1994	7.25	0.04	1.61	0.00	0.00	8.91	0.14	4.73	2.68	0.15	7.70	16.61
1995	7.03	0.04	1.70	0.00	0.00	8.76	0.16	4.55	2.58	0.18	7.47	16.24
1996	6.68	0.04	1.75	0.00	0.00	8.47	0.13	4.60	2.62	0.14	7.48	15.95
1997	6.62	0.04	2.51	0.00	0.13	9.29	0.13	4.79	2.48	0.19	7.60	16.89
1998	5.57	0.04	2.59	0.00	0.00	8.21	0.15	4.86	2.67	0.24	7.93	16.13
1999	5.42	0.05	2.52	0.00	0.00	7.99	0.15	5.30	2.67	0.23	8.34	16.34
2000	5.27	0.05	2.73	0.00	0.00	8.05	0.15	5.30	2.56	0.23	8.24	16.29
2001	5.44	0.05	2.53	0.00	0.00	8.02	0.14	5.09	2.44	0.29	7.96	15.98
2002	4.57	0.00	2.94	0.00	0.00	7.51	0.13	4.76	2.22	0.24	7.35	14.87
2003	4.32	0.00	2.80	0.00	0.00	7.12	0.13	4.68	2.16	0.23	7.19	14.32
2004	3.79	0.00	3.10	0.00	0.00	6.89	0.15	4.68	2.09	0.22	7.14	14.03
2005	4.12	0.00	3.59	0.00	0.00	7.72	0.16	4.77	1.99	0.23	7.16	14.87

Note: Total tax receipts reduction in 2002 due to partial transfers of tax collections to Autonomous Regions.
Source: Instituto de Estudios Fiscales, BADESPE-Base de Datos Económicos del Sector Público Español.

APPENDIX 10B: REFERENCES ON DATA SOURCES FOR SPAIN

Tax Statistics

Income tax statistical information covering the 'old' income tax was published regularly between 1933 and 1961: Dirección General de Rentas Públicas, *Estadística de la contribución general sobre la renta 1933–1934*; Dirección General de Contribución sobre la Renta, *Estadística de la contribución sobre la renta, 1935–1940, 1941, 1942*; Dirección General de Contribución sobre la Renta, *Estadística de servicios 1943, 1944, 1945, 1946, 1947, 1948, 1949, 1950*; Ministerio de Hacienda, Dirección General de la Contribución sobre la Renta, *Estadística de servicios 1951, 1952, 1953, 1954, 1955*; Ministerio de Hacienda, Dirección General de Impuestos sobre la Renta, *Estadística de servicios de la contribución sobre la renta 1956, 1958, 1959, 1960, 1962*. Tables display the distribution of taxpayers by level of income together with taxable income and tax paid.

There are no official income tax statistics publications from 1962 to 1979. The Instituto de Estudios Fiscales (1973, 1974) has published a set of statistics covering total tax returns filed annually between 1963 and 1974 together with the distribution of tax returns by income brackets for 1971.

Much more detailed data describe the evolution of the income and wealth taxes between 1981 and 2005: Agencia Estatal de la Administración Tributaria, Departamento de Informática Tributaria, Madrid, *Estadísticas IRPF y patrimonio* 1990, 1991, 1992, 1993, 1994, 1995, 1996, 1997, 1998, 1999, 2000; Dirección General de Tributos, Subdirección General de Política Tributaria (2002), *El impuesto sobre la renta de las personas físicas y el impuesto sobre el patrimonio en 1999*; Ministerio de Economía y Hacienda, *Memoria de la administración tributaria*, 1982–3, 1984, 1985, 1986, 1987, 1988, 1989, 1990, 1991, 1992, 1993, 1994, 1995, 1996, 1997, 1998, 1999, 2000, 2001, 2002, 2003, 2004, 2005, 2006.

Wages and Salaries

Results displayed in Table 10D.12 are based on the panel of individual income tax returns 1982–98 (Instituto de Estudios Fiscales, *Panel IRPF-AEAT*) and the 2002 sample of income tax files (Instituto de Estudios Fiscales, *Muestra de declarantes de IRPF 2002*). Individual wage incomes are obtained from the corresponding box in the tax return. Therefore, Table 10D.12 includes civil servants. As for the denominator, total wages and salaries are defined as total employment income from National Accounts, net of social security, and excluding País Vasco and Navarra. Total number of employees is total salaried employment from National Accounts. As the wages of spouses are aggregated for income tax purposes until 1987, we corrected estimates for 1982–7 along the same lines as explained in Appendix 10A.

Table 10B.1 summarizes the references on data sources for Spain.

Table 10B.1 Data sources, Spain

Author	Title	Year (if applicable)
A. Income and wealth numerators		
Dirección General de Rentas Públicas	Estadística de la Contribución General sobre la Renta	1933–1934
Dirección General de Contribución sobre la Renta	Estadística de la Contribución sobre la Renta	1935–1940, 1941, 1942
Dirección General de Contribución sobre la Renta	Estadística de Servicios	1943, 1943, 1944, 1945, 1946, 1947, 1948, 1949, 1950
Ministerio de Hacienda, Dirección General de la Contribución sobre la Renta	Estadística de Servicios	1951, 1952, 1953, 1954, 1955
Ministerio de Hacienda, Dirección General de Impuestos sobre la Renta	Estadística de Servicios de la Contribución sobre la Renta	1956, 1958, 1959, 1960, 1962
Instituto de Estudios Fiscales (1973)	Informe sobre el Sistema Tributario Español	
Instituto de Estudios Fiscales, Hacienda Pública Española 1974, (30), pp. 473–89	Estadística	
Ministerio de Economía y Hacienda, Secretaría de Estado de Hacienda	Memoria de la Administración Tributaria	1982–1983, 1984, 1985, 1986, 1987 1988, 1989, 1990, 1991, 1992, 1993 1994, 1995, 1996, 1997, 1998, 1999 2000, 2001, 2002
Ministerio de Economía y Hacienda, Secretaría de Estado de Hacienda y Presupuestos	Memoria de la Administración Tributaria	2003, 2004, 2005, 2006
Agencia Estatal de la Administración Tributaria, Departamento de Informática Tributaria	Estadísticas IRPF y Patrimonio	1990, 1991, 1992, 1993, 1994, 1995 1996, 1997, 1998, 1999, 2000
Dirección General de Tributos, Subdirección General de Política Tributaria	El Impuesto sobre la Renta de las Personas Físicas y el Impuesto sobre el Patrimonio en 1999	1999

(continued)

Table 10B.1 Continued

Author	Title	Year (if applicable)
B. Income and Wealth Denominators		
Instituto Nacional de Estadística	Contabilidad Nacional de España Base 2000	
Instituto Nacional de Estadística	Contabilidad Nacional de España Base 1995	
Instituto Nacional de Estadística	Contabilidad Nacional de España Base 1986	
Presidencia del Consejo de Ministros, Dirección General del Instituto Geográfico Catastral	Censo de la Población de España	1930
Ministerio de Trabajo, Dirección General de Estadística	Censo de la Población de España	1940
Presidencia del Gobierno, Instituto Nacional de Estadística	Censo de la Población de España	1950
	Censo de la Población y las Viviendas de España	1960
	Censo de la Población de España	1970
Instituto Nacional de Estadística	Censo de Población y Viviendas	1980, 1991, 2001
Prados de la Escosura, Leandro (2003)	El Progreso Económico de España 1850–2000	
Banco de España (2004)	Cuentas Financieras de la Economía Española 1990–2005	
Banco de España (2004), Boletín Económico 11	Encuesta Financiera de las Familias: Descripción, Métodos y Resultados Preliminares	
Banco de España	Indicadores del Mercado de la Vivienda http://www.bde.es/infoest/sindi.htm	
Ministerio de Economía y Hacienda, Dirección General de Catastro	Estadísticas Catastrales 1990–2003 http://www.catastro.minhac.es/esp/estadisticas1.asp	
Caixa de Catalunya (2004), Informe sobre el Consumo y la Economía Familiar, Junio	Report Monográfico: El Crecimiento del Stock de Riqueza de las Familias Españolas y su Impacto sobre el Consumo en el Periodo 1995–2003: Una Versión Territorial	
Instituto de Estudios Fiscales (1976)	Datos Básicos para la Historia Financiera de España 1850–1975	

C. Other

Comín, Francisco (1985), Monografía n.40, Instituto de Estudios Fiscales	Fuentes Cuantitativas para el Estudio del Sector Público en España 1801–1980	
Instituto de Estudios Fiscales	Panel IRPF-AEAT 1982–1998	1982–1998
Instituto de Estudios Fiscales	Muestra de Declarantes de IRPF 2002	2002
Instituto de Estudios Fiscales	Base de Datos del Sector Público Español	
Ministerio de Economía y Hacienda, Dirección General de Inspección Financiera y Tributaria	Memoria de las Actuaciones de la Inspección de los Tributos durante 1987	1987
Secretaría de Estado de Hacienda, Dirección General de Inspección Financiera y Tributaria	Memoria de las Actuaciones de la Inspección de los Tributos	1988
Ministerio de Economía y Hacienda, Secretaría de Estado de Hacienda	Resultados de la Inspección de los Tributos	1989
Dirección General de Inpección Financiera y Tributaria	Memoria de la Dirección General de Inpección Financiera y Tributaria	1990, 1991
Agencia Tributaria, Departamento de Inspección Financiera y Tributaria	Memoria de Actividades	1992, 1993, 1994, 1995, 1996, 1997 1998, 1999, 2000, 2001, 2002
Instituto de Estudios Fiscales	Comisión para Evaluar el Fraude por el Impuesto sobre la Renta de las Personas Físicas	
Ministerio de Hacienda	Informe sobre Gestión Tributaria 1979–1981	
Boletín Oficial del Estado		
Gaceta de Madrid		
Global Find Data	http://www.globalfinddata.com	

APPENDIX 10C: WEALTH AND INCOME DENOMINATORS

Wealth Denominator

In order to compute wealth shares we need to estimate the total personal wealth. We have used two definitions of personal wealth: financial wealth (wealth excluding pension funds—which are not taxed—real estate, and mortgage debt) and total wealth (including real estate and mortgage debt but still excluding pension funds).

The wealth denominator relies on five statistical sources:

(a) Banco de España (2005), *Cuentas financieras de la economía española 1990–2005*. Table II.21, Hogares e Instituciones sin fines de Lucro al servicio de los Hogares.

(b) Banco de España (2004), *Encuesta financiera de las familias (EEF): descripción, métodos y resultados preliminares*, Boletín Económico 11/2004.

(c) Banco de España, *Indicadores del mercado de la vivienda*, www.bde.es/infoest/sindi.htm, Table sindi15. Data refer to averages in the fourth quarter between 1987 and 2005.

(d) Ministerio de Economía y Hacienda, Dirección General de Catastro, *Estadísticas catastrales 1990–2005*.

(e) Caixa de Catalunya (2004), *Report monográfico: el crecimiento del stock de riqueza de las familias españolas y su impacto sobre el consumo en el período 1995–2003: una version territorial*, in *Informe sobre el consumo y la economía familiar*, June.

Financial wealth: Financial wealth is defined as the sum of bank deposits, currency holdings, stocks and investment funds, other fixed claim assets, and insurance contracts on the asset side, minus commercial and other credit on the liability side. To match the definition of taxable wealth, we do not include pension funds. Also long-run loans are excluded as a proxy for mortgage debt. The data were selected from (a) and correspond to the fourth quarter, covering the period 1989–2005.

In order to estimate the financial wealth for the period 1982–8, we proceeded in the following way. The GDP shares of deposits and currency holdings, insurance contracts net of pensions, other fixed claim assets, and debts were rather stable for the first years for which data exist (1989–92); consequently we fixed the ratios for 1982–8 at the 1989 level. On the other hand, the stock and investment funds GDP share has displayed an increasing tendency during the decade of 1990, in parallel with the Madrid stock market index. Therefore, for 1986–8, we applied the 1989 stock and investment funds/GDP ratio corrected by the evolution of the stock market index during the fourth quarter (highest minus lowest values). For 1982–5 the share was set at the same level of 1986.

Real estate wealth: The consistency between valuation rules in the tax code and the data available posed several methodological problems to estimate this fraction of wealth. Between 1978 and 1992, urban real estate was mainly priced at cadastral values. Rural estate valuation formula required capitalizing at 4 per cent the amount fixed in the local estate tax. Since 1992, real estate, both urban and rural, must be valued at the highest of (a) the property registry value, (b) the purchasing price, (c) the value determined for other local taxes. Local real estate taxes are based on cadastral values, computed following an established formula with price coefficients defined for land surface, construction type, urban zone, etc., and which can be updated periodically by local authorities. Nevertheless, cadastral values are generally less than 50 per cent of market prices. This can be easily verified comparing the Bank of Spain statistics (based on market prices, source (c)) with the property registry statistics (source (d)). For instance, between 1990 and 2002 the ratio between both series ranged from 30 per cent to 45 per cent. This implies a gap difficult to correct between the numerator and the denominator. For this reason, we also studied separately the distribution of financial wealth (net of real estate) in the main text.

Real estate net wealth is the result of deducting mortgage loans from household real estate wealth. Real estate wealth is taken from Banco de España, *Indicadores del mercado de la vivienda*. Data correspond to the fourth quarter and cover years 1987 to 2005. These estimates are constructed upon the series of residential units, average surface, and average market prices. On the liability side, mortgage debts are approximated by long-run debts from *Cuentas financieras de la economía española* (source (a)). For the years 1982–6 we fixed the real estate wealth/GDP ratio at the 1987 level.

Wealth tax information excludes Navarra and Pais Vasco. To take this fact into account, we corrected total wealth as follows. We assumed that total wealth in those regions was roughly proportional to real estate wealth. The share of Navarra and País Vasco real estate wealth in Spain is taken from Caixa de Catalunya (2004) (source (e)), based on Ministerio de Fomento.

The numerator, that is, the real estate declared in the wealth tax files, was also adjusted to reflect market prices. The correction factor is the ratio between the market-priced wealth (source (c)) and the GDP from 1987 to 2002. Between 1982 and 1986 the factor was set to the 1987 value. This decision was based on the fact that the ratio (real estate wealth from source (c)/real estate wealth from property registry statistics source (d)) displays a very similar pattern but is available for a shorter period.

Results are displayed in Table 10C.1.

Total Number of Individuals

For the period 1933–71, the total number of adult individuals is computed as the number of individuals in the Spanish population aged 20 and above; this excludes Navarra and Alava since 1937 and 1943 respectively. These series are based on census interpolations provided by INE and reported in Table 10D.3, column 1. Column 2 indicates the total number of tax returns (with positive taxable income) actually filed and column 3 reports the fraction of adult population filling a tax return.

For the period 1982–2005, total individuals correspond to the number of adults aged 20 and over excluding País Vasco and Navarra. Again this series come from census interpolations and are reported in Table 10C.2, column 1. The census data have been taken from Presidencia del Consejo de Ministros, Dirección General del Instituto Geográfico Catastral, *Censo de la población de España 1930*; Ministerio de Trabajo, Dirección General de Estadística, *Censo de la población de España 1940*; Presidencia del Gobierno, Instituto Nacional de Estadística, *Censo de la población de España 1950*; *Censo de la población y las viviendas de España 1960*; *Censo de la población de España 1970*; Instituto Nacional de Estadística, *Censo de población y viviendas 1980, 1991, 2001*.

Total Income Denominator

For the period 1981–2005 total income is defined as wages and salaries from National Accounts net of social contributions plus 50 per cent of social transfers, plus 66.6 per cent of unincorporated business income (excluding Navarra and País Vasco), plus all non-business, non-labour income reported on tax returns (as capital income is very concentrated, non-filers receive a negligible fraction of it).[47] The total denominator series expressed in 2005 euros is reported in column 4 of Table 10C.2. The average income per adult is reported in column 7 while the CPI index (base 100 in year 2005) is reported in column 8.

For the period 1933–71, we use as denominator 66 per cent of the Spanish GDP from Prados de la Escosura (2003). The number 66 per cent is chosen to be consistent with our denominator for the recent period, which fluctuates between 63 per cent and 69 per cent of Spanish GDP (excluding País Vasco and Navarra). Our denominator for the 1933–71 period is reported in Table 10D.3, column 4, converted to euros 2005.

Table 10C.3 gives thresholds and average incomes for a selection of fractiles for Spain in 2005.

[47] For example, in 2002, the top 10% income earners (representing about one-fifth of all tax filers as only about half of adults file taxes) obtained 65% of total capital income reported on tax returns. Capital income in personal income in National Accounts is substantially different from capital income on tax returns because of imputed rents of homeowners, imputed interest to bank account holders, returns on (non-taxable) pension funds, etc. That is why we use capital income from tax returns to define our denominator. See, e.g., Park (2000) for a comprehensive comparison in the case of the United States where over 90% of adults file tax returns.

Table 10C.1 Aggregate net worth and composition, Spain, 1981–2005

	Wealth tax units and population			Total financial wealth		Total net wealth		Wealth composition						Inflation	Wealth tax
	(1)	(2)	(3)	(4)	(5)	(6)	(7)	(8)	(9)	(10)	(11)	(12)	(13)	(14)	(15)
		Number of wealth tax returns ('000s)		Total net financial wealth (millions 2005 euros)	Average (2005 euros)	Total net wealth (millions 2005 euros)	Average (2005 euros)			Fixed claim assets				CPI (2005 base)	Top marginal tax rate (%)
	Adults ('000s)		(2)/(1) (%)					Real estate	Mortgage debt		Stocks	Other	Other debts		
1981	22,857	509	2.2	355,939	15,572	1,185,193	51,853	78.8	−8.8	24.6	5.4	4.3	−4.3	27.520	2.5
1982	23,242	492	2.1	358,404	15,421	1,193,403	51,347	78.8	−8.8	24.6	5.4	4.3	−4.3	31.430	2.5
1983	23,635	541	2.3	361,581	15,299	1,203,985	50,941	78.8	−8.8	24.6	5.4	4.3	−4.3	35.478	2.5
1984	24,036	535	2.2	369,319	15,365	1,229,746	51,163	78.8	−8.8	24.6	5.4	4.3	−4.3	39.192	2.5
1985	24,445	675	2.8	377,370	15,438	1,256,554	51,403	78.8	−8.8	24.6	5.4	4.3	−4.3	42.619	2.5
1986	24,760	781	3.2	397,317	16,047	1,322,975	53,432	78.8	−8.8	24.6	5.4	4.3	−4.3	46.344	2.5
1987	25,082	887	3.5	451,211	17,989	1,434,261	57,183	77.2	−8.6	24.1	7.3	4.2	−4.3	48.797	2.5
1988	25,410	756	3.0	486,116	19,131	1,667,419	65,621	78.7	−7.9	22.0	7.2	3.9	−3.9	51.321	2.5
1989	25,745	855	3.3	522,796	20,307	1,913,817	74,337	79.9	−7.2	20.1	7.2	3.5	−3.6	54.733	2.5
1990	26,087	974	3.7	501,006	19,205	2,004,679	76,846	82.2	−7.1	20.4	4.8	3.5	−3.7	58.355	2.5
1991	26,335	1,033	3.9	533,012	20,240	2,245,462	85,265	83.0	−6.7	18.0	5.6	3.5	−3.4	61.885	2.5
1992	26,673	863	3.2	543,866	20,390	2,036,398	76,347	80.8	−7.5	20.0	6.6	4.0	−3.9	65.430	2.5
1993	27,015	928	3.4	594,877	22,020	2,054,749	76,060	78.5	−7.4	20.0	9.0	3.9	−3.9	68.554	2.5
1994	27,360	809	3.0	617,783	22,580	2,038,419	74,504	77.2	−7.5	20.2	9.6	4.3	−3.8	71.725	2.5
1995	27,710	783	2.8	676,783	24,423	2,099,024	75,750	75.2	−7.5	20.4	11.1	4.3	−3.6	74.849	2.5
1996	28,114	825	2.9	720,276	25,620	2,126,008	75,621	73.9	−7.8	19.6	13.4	4.3	−3.5	77.533	2.5
1997	28,523	892	3.1	806,550	28,277	2,216,794	77,720	72.0	−8.4	18.2	17.5	4.0	−3.3	79.380	2.5
1998	28,938	946	3.3	943,218	32,594	2,430,104	83,976	70.2	−9.0	16.8	20.9	4.1	−3.1	80.657	2.5
1999	29,359	981	3.3	1,016,100	34,609	2,675,884	91,144	71.6	−9.6	16.7	19.9	4.4	−3.0	82.549	2.5
2000	29,785	869	2.9	988,226	33,179	2,875,706	96,549	75.7	−10.1	16.6	16.0	4.6	−2.8	85.365	2.5
2001	30,016	874	2.9	1,014,583	33,801	3,185,046	106,112	78.1	−9.9	15.4	14.6	4.3	−2.5	88.093	2.5
2002	30,249	884	2.9	951,132	31,443	3,540,482	117,045	83.2	−10.0	14.3	10.7	4.2	−2.3	90.997	2.5
2003	30,482	896	2.9	1,067,223	35,012	4,131,688	135,545	84.1	−10.0	12.8	11.4	3.8	−2.1	93.726	2.5
2004	30,718	920	3.0	1,134,082	36,919	4,548,341	148,068	85.6	−10.5	12.2	11.0	3.6	−2.0	96.718	2.5
2005	30,956	957	3.1	1,260,976	40,734	5,057,193	163,367	86.0	−11.3	11.3	12.1	3.3	−1.5	100.000	2.5

Notes: Population and tax units estimates based on population census.
Tax units estimated as number of adults aged 20 and over in Spain (excluding País Vasco and Navarra).
Total wealth from flow of funds accounts and other sources (see Appendix 10C).
Consumer Price Index is the official CPI index.

Table 10C.2 Reference totals for population, income, and inflation, Spain, 1981–2005

| | Tax units and population | | | Total income | | | | Inflation | Taxes |
| | (1) | (2) | (3) | (4) | (5) | (6) | (7) | (8) | (9) |
	Adults ('000s)	Number of tax returns ('000s)	(2)/(1) (%)	Total income (millions 2005 euros)	Fraction income reported by tax filers (%)	Total income over GDP (%)	Average income (2005 euros)	CPI (2005 base)	Top marginal tax rate (%)
1981	22,857	6,296	27.5	233,100	57.8	66.6	10,198	27.520	65.09
1982	23,242	6,262	26.9	228,102	56.7	64.8	9,814	31.430	68.47
1983	23,635	6,397	27.1	228,265	57.1	64.2	9,658	35.478	65
1984	24,036	6,544	27.2	227,461	57.6	62.5	9,463	39.192	66
1985	24,445	7,081	29.0	235,919	59.6	63.3	9,651	42.619	66
1986	24,760	7,896	31.9	247,654	63.1	63.0	10,002	46.344	66
1987	25,082	8,028	32.0	263,460	62.9	62.8	10,504	48.797	66
1988	25,410	8,954	35.2	282,355	63.2	63.4	11,112	51.321	56
1989	25,745	9,845	38.2	296,630	66.4	63.4	11,522	54.733	56
1990	26,087	10,965	42.0	321,435	69.1	65.5	12,322	58.355	56
1991	26,335	11,584	44.0	338,398	69.3	66.7	12,850	61.885	56
1992	26,673	12,341	46.3	341,899	71.3	66.1	12,818	65.430	56
1993	27,015	12,794	47.4	344,919	70.8	67.6	12,768	68.554	56
1994	27,360	13,578	49.6	335,863	74.6	64.9	12,276	71.725	56
1995	27,710	14,119	51.0	344,003	74.8	64.2	12,414	74.849	56
1996	28,114	14,620	52.0	350,314	75.2	63.9	12,460	77.533	56
1997	28,523	15,000	52.6	357,467	75.0	62.7	12,533	79.380	56
1998	28,938	15,424	53.3	375,971	75.5	62.8	12,992	80.657	56
1999	29,359	13,797	47.0	393,751	71.5	62.8	13,412	82.549	48
2000	29,785	14,123	47.4	409,661	72.5	62.8	13,754	85.365	48
2001	30,016	14,734	49.1	421,513	73.6	62.4	14,043	88.093	48
2002	30,249	15,410	50.9	432,030	73.9	62.2	14,282	90.997	48
2003	30,482	15,978	52.4	448,816	74.6	61.7	14,724	93.726	45
2004	30,718	16,465	53.6	465,376	74.9	61.7	15,150	96.718	45
2005	30,956	17,105	55.3	486,108	76.2	62.0	15,703	100.000	45

Notes: Population and tax units estimates based on population census.

Tax units defined as number of adults aged 20 and over in Spain (excluding Pais Vasco and Navarra).

Total income defined as wages and salaries from National Accounts (net of social contributions) plus 50% of social transfers plus 66.6% of unincorporated business income (excluding Navarra and Pais Vasco), plus all non-business, non-labour income reported on tax returns.

Consumer Price Index is the official CPI index (see Appendix 10C for details).

Table 10C.3 Thresholds and average incomes in top income groups in Spain, 2005

Percentile threshold (1)	Income threshold (2)	Income groups (3)	Number of adults (aged 20+) (4)	Average income in each group (5)
A. Income including realized capital gains				
		Full Adult Population	30,956,000	15,703 €
Top 10%	29,471 €	Top 10–5%	1,547,800	33,666 €
Top 5%	39,576 €	Top 5–1%	1,238,240	52,561 €
Top 1%	79,609 €	Top 1–0.5%	154,780	91,951 €
Top 0.5%	109,520 €	Top 0.5–0.1%	123,824	153,837 €
Top 0.1%	261,709 €	Top 0.1–0.01%	27,860	446,709 €
Top 0.01%	1,063,140 €	Top 0.01%	3,096	2,528,354 €
B. Income excluding realized capital gains				
Top 10%	28,806 €	Top 10–5%	1,547,800	32,906 €
Top 5%	38,100 €	Top 5–1%	1,238,240	49,827 €
Top 1%	73,259 €	Top 1–0.5%	154,780	82,065 €
Top 0.5%	94,069 €	Top 0.5–0.1%	123,824	126,971 €
Top 0.1%	192,743 €	Top 0.1–0.01%	27,860	289,289 €
Top 0.01%	618,110 €	Top 0.01%	3,096	1,302,608 €

Notes: Computations based on income tax return statistics and National Accounts.

Income defined as annual gross income reported on tax returns including capital gains and before individual income taxes but net of all social contributions (employer and employee). Amounts are expressed in current 2005 euros.

Column (2) reports the income thresholds corresponding to each of the percentiles in column (1). For example, an annual income of at least 29,471 euros (including realized capital gains) is required to belong to the top 10% tax units, etc.

APPENDIX 10D: ESTIMATING TOP SHARES

Basic Pareto Interpolation

The general interpolation technique is based on the well-known empirical regularity that the top tail of the income distribution is very closely approximated by a Pareto distribution. A Pareto distribution has a cumulative distribution function of the form $F(y) = 1 - (k/y)^a$ where k and a are constants, and a is the Pareto parameter of the distribution. Such a distribution has the key property that the average income above a given threshold y is always exactly proportional to y. The coefficient of proportionality is equal to $b = a/(a-1)$.

The first step consists then in estimating the income thresholds corresponding to each of the percentiles P90, P95, P99, ..., P99.99 that define our top income groups. For each percentile p, we look first for the published income bracket $[s,t]$ containing the percentile p. We estimate then the parameters a and k of the Pareto distribution by solving the two equations: $k = s\,p^{(1/a)}$ and $k = t\,q^{(1/a)}$ where p is the fraction of tax returns above s and q the fraction of tax returns above t.[48] Note that the Pareto parameters k and a may vary from bracket to bracket. Once the density distribution on $[s,t]$ is estimated, it is straightforward to estimate the income threshold, say y_p, corresponding to percentile p.

The second step consists of estimating the amounts of income reported above income threshold y_p. We estimate the amount reported between income y_p and t (the upper bound of the published bracket $[s,t]$ containing y_p) using the estimated Pareto density with parameters a and k. We then add to that amount the amounts in all the published brackets above t.

Once the total amount above y_p is obtained, we obtain directly the mean income above percentile p by dividing the amount by the number of individuals above percentile p. Finally, the share of income accruing to individuals above percentile p is obtained by dividing the total amount above y_p by our income denominator series (Table 10C.2, column 4). Average incomes and income shares for intermediate fractiles (P90–5, P95–9, etc.) are obtained by subtraction.

Adjustments to Raw Pareto Interpolations

Period 1933–1971: In 1935 and 1940, the statistics also report tax filers from previous years who have been subject to an audit and a subsequent increase in reported income. Those audited tax filers are placed in the bracket where they belonged in the previous year but only the additional income uncovered by the audit is reported. As a result of those audited tax filers, the number of filers in each bracket is too high relative to income reported. In order to remove those audit taxpayers, we discard the information on the number of tax filers per bracket and we use only the total income per bracket. We recover the number of

---

[48] This is the standard method of Pareto interpolation used by Kuznets (1953) and Feenberg and Poterba (1993).

tax filers by assuming that, in each bracket, average income per current year taxpayer in 1935 and 1940 is the same as in 1934. Our estimates are slightly overestimated due to the additional income due to audits. However, additional income due to audits is probably small relative to regular reported income. Furthermore, income including audits is a closer approximation to real incomes than income before audits (although for 1935 and 1940, the additional income from audits corresponds to an earlier year).

For 1941, about 14 per cent of tax returns were reported separately and only in the aggregate. As the average income for those 14 per cent returns is extremely close to the average for remaining returns, we assume that those 14 per cent returns are distributed by brackets in the same way as the rest of returns. The same issue arises for 1957, 1958, 1961, where a significant fraction of returns were not processed in time for the regular publication and are only reported in aggregate in the subsequent publication year. In each case, we assume that those late returns are distributed as the regular returns. Because the average income of late returns is close to the average for regular returns, this seems an acceptable assumption.

From 1942, a deduction for dependent children was introduced and the tax returns are presented by size of income net of this dependent children exemption. The deduction is 3,000 pesetas for each child from 1942 to 1953, 10,000 pesetas from 1954 to 1960, and 25,000 pesetas in 1961. We add back those deductions to our income estimates in order to estimate shares based on income before those deductions. In most years, those deductions are reported by brackets. When they are only reported in aggregate, we impute the deductions in each bracket using years when this information is provided bracket by bracket. The average number of children is fairly stable over time and across brackets so this approximation is acceptable.

Two important additional deductions are introduced in 1954. The first deduction is deductions for extraordinary expenses and charitable contributions. The law allowed for deductible expenses without bounds, which were declared at the discretion of the tax-payers: wedding expenses, pharmacy purchases, transfers to family members in state of necessity (where the term necessity was fuzzily defined). Individuals could also make donations without limits (many of which were suspected of being de facto self-donations for high-income earners, when the individual himself managed the foundation, created with the sole purpose of attracting donations). The second deduction is a deduction for employment income equal to 33 per cent of labour income up to a maximum deduction of 100,000 pesetas. Those two deductions are reported by brackets for years 1958, 1959, and 1961, and are about 5 per cent of reported incomes each within the top 0.1 per cent. We assume that the level of deductions is the same as in 1958 in years 1954–7 when the information on deductions is not reported separately.

The 1971 tax statistics are reported by size of gross income equal to the sum of each component (capital income, business income, labour income, etc.) before the extraordinary deductions and the deductions for dependent children. However, the deduction for labour income has been netted out of the labour income component. Because there is no information of labour income by brackets, we assume that the fraction of labour income within the top 0.1 per cent is 20 per cent (which was the corresponding number in 1961, the closest year where this information is available). The labour income deduction is also about 5 per cent of total income in the top 0.1 per cent in 1971.

Period 1981–2005: Exclusions from the income tax: Statistics are presented by brackets of income net of the labour income deduction. The amount of those deductions is reported for each bracket in the tax statistics. Therefore, for each fractile, we compute the average amount of deductions and add those amounts to the raw estimates.

Series excluding capital gains: Since 1981, capital gains are included in taxable income (see Appendix 10A above). For series excluding capital gains, we need to subtract the capital gains component from the raw series. The amount of capital gains is also reported by brackets in the tax statistics. In order to compute our series from the raw series, one could simply deduct for each group the share of capital gains estimated from composition tables. The problem is that ranking according to the income including capital gains and ranking according to income excluding capital gains might be different, especially at the very top. For example, in the extreme case where very top incomes of the income tax statistics distributions consist only of capital gains, then the deduction of capital gains would lead to the conclusion that the very top incomes of the income (excluding capital gains) distribution are equal to zero. Therefore, deducting the full amount of capital gains would provide an underestimate of the income shares we would like to estimate. In order to correct for this re-ranking bias, we therefore need to subtract less than 100 per cent of capital gains.

Based on other studies such as Piketty and Saez (2003) for the United States and Saez and Veall (2005) for Canada, where not only similar tabulated tax statistics but also micro-data are available, a good approximation is to subtract 80 per cent of capital gains amounts instead of 100 per cent to obtain shares of income excluding capital gains. This is therefore the rule we follow in the case of Spain. Using the 2002 large sample of micro-tax returns, we have verified that this rule gives very accurate results: the estimates based on micro-data excluding capital gains for 2002 are extremely close to the results we obtain from the tabulated statistics published by the tax administration.

Shift from family to individual taxation in 1988: Before 1988, taxation was based on the family unit (as in the United States today). Starting in 1988, individual taxation became possible and is actually an advantageous option when the secondary earner has positive income. As we have discussed above, our top groups are defined relative to the total adult population and our series measure individual income concentration. For the period 1988 to 2005, income tax statistics measure individual incomes as married couples where both spouses have positive incomes have an incentive to file separately in order to reduce their tax burden.

Before 1988, however, income tax statistics measure family income as the incomes of spouses are aggregated for income tax purposes. Therefore, our basic methodology overstates income concentration (as spousal income is added to the income of top earners). Indeed, uncorrected series display a clearly visible discontinuity from 1987 to 1988. We use the micro tax panel data to make the correction for the 1981–7 period. Using the micro-data for 1988, we can compute top income shares at the household level and at the individual level (as the micro-data allows to reconstitute families). We can then compute adjustment factors as the ratio of the individual shares to the household shares. We then apply those factors to all years from 1981 to 1987 to obtain corrected estimates. This correction reduces raw income shares by about 10 per cent.

The estimates of top income shares between 1981 and 2005 are presented in Table 10D.1 (including capital gains) and Table 10D.2 (excluding capital gains). Table 10D.3 reports top shares between 1933 and 1971. Top income levels for a selection of fractiles between 1981 and 2005 are displayed in Table 10D.4 (including capital gains) and Table 10D.5 (excluding capital gains).

Top wealth shares estimation: Top wealth shares for the period 1982–2005 are also estimated using the same Pareto interpolation technique. The wealth tax has always been assessed at the individual level except for married couples with joint tenancy before 1988. There is no specific breakdown of amounts reported by each spouse on family tax returns. Therefore, we simply assume that the (log) growth of each top wealth share from 1987 to 1988 (when the law changes) is equal to the average (log) growth between 1986 to 1987 and 1988 to 1989. We then correct top income shares for each year from 1981 to 1987 by the same multiplicative factor.

As in the case of the income tax, we add back exempted items such as exempted businesses (after the 1994 reform) or the standard exemption for the main residence (after 2000), which are fortunately reported by wealth brackets in the published statistics. Our initial estimates did not correctly adjust for the real estate deduction since 2000. We thank Durán and Esteller (2007) for pointing out this mistake.

We estimate two top wealth shares series: series excluding real estate and series included market priced real estate. For series excluding real estates, we subtract the real estate (including the real estate exemption after 2000) from our raw estimates. For series including real estates, we inflate the value of real estate by a uniform multiplicative factor equal to total real estate from the Flow of Funds accounts divided by total cadastral value reported in aggregate real estate statistics, and we add back to our raw series the difference between the market price series and the cadastral value. Results are presented in Table 10D.8.

Estimation of wealth and income composition series: We have constructed income and wealth composition series for each of our top groups for the period 1981–2005 using tax statistics showing the breakdown of income and wealth into various components by income and wealth brackets.

The income composition series reported in Table 10D.7 indicate for each upper income group the fraction of total income (including capital gains) that comes from the various types of income. We consider four types of income: wage income; entrepreneurial income; capital income (excluding capital gains); and realized capital gains. Wage income includes wages and salaries (including the wage income deduction), as well as pensions. Entrepreneurial income includes self-employment income from professions such as doctors, lawyers, etc. Business income also includes income from sole proprietorships, partnership income, and farm income. Capital income includes dividends, interest income, rents, and other investment income. Capital gains include both long-term and short-term capital gains reported on tax returns. We have excluded from these composition series the other income category which never makes more than 5 per cent of the total income as this simplifies the reading of our composition series (the other income category was taken into account when computing top income levels and top income shares in total income).

The wealth composition series reported in Table 10D.9 indicate for each upper wealth group the fraction of total wealth (including the market value of real estate) that comes from the various types of assets. We consider six types of assets: real estate, business assets, fixed claim assets, stocks, other assets, and debts. Real estate includes the market value of real estate. It is estimated as reported real estate amount (including the deduction for primary residence since 2000) times the ratio of total market value of real estate in Spain divided by total cadastral value of real estate in Spain. Business assets include the value of unincorporated business assets. Fixed claim assets include cash, chequing and savings accounts, annualized wealth, life insurance, public and corporate bonds. Stocks include publicly traded and closely held corporate stock either directly owned or owned through investment funds. Other includes household goods, jewels, vehicles, intellectual property rights, non-exempted works of arts, and other assets. Debts include mortgage debts, consumer debts, and business debts.

The composition series are estimated from the published tables indicating for each income (or wealth) bracket not only the number of taxpayers and the total amount of their total income (or wealth) but also the separate amounts for each type of income (or wealth), as well as the deductions. The composition of income (or wealth) within each group was estimated from these tables using a simple linear interpolation method. Such a method is less satisfactory than the Pareto interpolation method used to estimate top income levels (no obvious law seems to fit composition patterns in a stable way). See Piketty and Saez (2007) for a more precise discussion of this method where it is systematically compared with direct estimates using micro-data.

Estimating Top Shares from Individual Income Tax Panel

We also computed top income shares with and without capital gains (Tables 10D.10 and 10D.11) and top wage shares (Table 10D.12) using the micro-data from the panel of income tax returns 1982–98 (*Panel IRPF-AEAT*) and the 2002 sample of income tax files (*Muestra de declarantes de IRPF 2002*). The panel is composed of approximately 2 per cent of total returns (the number of observations ranges from 123,599 in 1982 to 308,558 in 1998), while the 2002 sample has information for 907,399 out of 15,481,382 files and over-samples high incomes. The definition of individual income follows the same rules as in the tabulated data case. Total reference income and population is also the same.

As it was described above, before 1988 data available only identify family income as the income of spouses is aggregated in the tax file due to mandatory joint filing. We used the micro tax panel for 1988 to adjust for this.

For 2002, the results from the sample are very close to the results from the tax tabulations. The 2002 sample perfectly matches aggregates. On the other side, the panel shares display an overall similar pattern when compared to shares based on grouped data, but differences are somewhat larger. This is mainly due to sample size issues and sampling strategy problems in the panel.

Table 10D.1 Top income shares in Spain (including capital gains), 1981–2005

	Top 10% (1)	Top 5% (2)	Top 1% (3)	Top 0.5% (4)	Top 0.1% (5)	Top 0.01% (6)	Top 10–5% (7)	Top 5–1% (8)	Top 1–0.5% (9)	Top 0.5–0.1% (10)	Top 0.1–0.01% (11)	Top 0.01% (12)
1981	32.70	21.25	7.63	4.98	1.94	0.55	11.46	13.62	2.65	3.04	1.39	0.55
1982	33.11	21.70	7.95	5.27	2.15	0.66	11.41	13.75	2.69	3.11	1.50	0.66
1983	33.41	21.82	7.79	5.07	1.98	0.59	11.59	14.03	2.73	3.09	1.38	0.59
1984	33.71	21.99	7.81	5.07	1.99	0.62	11.72	14.18	2.74	3.08	1.37	0.62
1985	34.06	22.43	8.12	5.31	2.11	0.62	11.63	14.31	2.81	3.21	1.49	0.62
1986	35.15	23.45	8.88	5.97	2.59	0.93	11.70	14.57	2.91	3.38	1.67	0.93
1987	35.37	23.73	9.15	6.24	2.84	1.13	11.64	14.57	2.92	3.40	1.72	1.13
1988	35.68	23.91	9.19	6.24	2.81	1.08	11.77	14.72	2.95	3.43	1.72	1.08
1989	36.11	24.03	9.01	6.02	2.53	0.82	12.08	15.02	2.99	3.49	1.69	0.82
1990	35.71	23.61	8.80	5.85	2.42	0.73	12.10	14.81	2.96	3.43	1.69	0.73
1991	34.97	22.97	8.47	5.58	2.26	0.67	12.00	14.50	2.89	3.32	1.59	0.67
1992	34.15	22.50	8.42	5.54	2.20	0.62	11.65	14.08	2.89	3.34	1.58	0.62
1993	33.64	22.11	8.22	5.38	2.10	0.57	11.53	13.89	2.84	3.28	1.53	0.57
1994	34.00	22.30	8.27	5.41	2.12	0.58	11.70	14.03	2.86	3.30	1.54	0.58
1995	33.84	22.23	8.29	5.44	2.14	0.59	11.61	13.94	2.85	3.30	1.55	0.59
1996	33.87	22.27	8.32	5.49	2.18	0.60	11.60	13.95	2.83	3.32	1.58	0.60
1997	33.86	22.42	8.55	5.70	2.33	0.67	11.45	13.87	2.85	3.36	1.66	0.67
1998	34.24	22.86	8.94	6.04	2.56	0.81	11.37	13.92	2.90	3.48	1.75	0.81
1999	34.78	23.39	9.47	6.55	2.97	1.05	11.39	13.92	2.92	3.57	1.93	1.05
2000	35.25	23.90	9.95	7.00	3.32	1.25	11.35	13.94	2.95	3.68	2.07	1.25
2001	34.92	23.63	9.82	6.91	3.26	1.21	11.29	13.81	2.92	3.64	2.05	1.21
2002	34.23	23.08	9.46	6.59	3.01	1.01	11.15	13.63	2.87	3.58	2.00	1.01
2003	34.47	23.45	9.96	7.09	3.43	1.24	11.02	13.49	2.87	3.67	2.19	1.24
2004	34.39	23.55	10.20	7.33	3.61	1.30	10.84	13.35	2.87	3.73	2.31	1.30
2005	35.12	24.41	11.02	8.09	4.17	1.61	10.72	13.39	2.93	3.92	2.56	1.61

Notes: Computations by authors on tax return statistics. Taxpayers are ranked by gross income (including capital gains).
The table reports the percentage of total income accruing to each of the top groups. Top 10% denotes top decile, top 10–5% denotes the bottom half of the top decile, etc.

Table 10D.2 Top income shares in Spain (excluding capital gains), 1981–2005

	Top 10% (1)	Top 5% (2)	Top 1% (3)	Top 0.5% (4)	Top 0.1% (5)	Top 0.01% (6)	Top 10–5% (7)	Top 5–1% (8)	Top 1–0.5% (9)	Top 0.5–0.1% (10)	Top 0.1–0.01% (11)	Top 0.01% (12)
1981	32.61	21.12	7.50	4.87	1.87	0.52	11.48	13.62	2.63	3.01	1.35	0.52
1982	32.96	21.50	7.75	5.08	2.00	0.58	11.46	13.75	2.67	3.07	1.42	0.58
1983	33.29	21.67	7.65	4.94	1.88	0.55	11.62	14.02	2.71	3.06	1.33	0.55
1984	33.56	21.80	7.61	4.89	1.85	0.54	11.76	14.19	2.73	3.04	1.31	0.54
1985	33.72	22.03	7.75	4.99	1.90	0.53	11.69	14.28	2.76	3.09	1.37	0.53
1986	34.66	22.82	8.21	5.36	2.16	0.68	11.84	14.61	2.85	3.20	1.48	0.68
1987	34.85	23.05	8.40	5.52	2.26	0.77	11.80	14.65	2.88	3.26	1.48	0.77
1988	35.05	23.14	8.36	5.46	2.17	0.69	11.91	14.78	2.91	3.28	1.48	0.69
1989	35.67	23.49	8.47	5.52	2.19	0.65	12.18	15.02	2.95	3.33	1.53	0.65
1990	35.35	23.17	8.37	5.45	2.14	0.62	12.19	14.80	2.92	3.31	1.53	0.62
1991	34.58	22.53	8.08	5.23	2.03	0.57	12.06	14.45	2.84	3.20	1.46	0.57
1992	33.93	22.25	8.21	5.34	2.06	0.56	11.68	14.05	2.86	3.28	1.50	0.56
1993	33.19	21.61	7.83	5.06	1.92	0.51	11.58	13.78	2.77	3.14	1.41	0.51
1994	33.55	21.82	7.89	5.10	1.95	0.51	11.73	13.92	2.79	3.15	1.44	0.51
1995	33.38	21.71	7.89	5.12	1.96	0.51	11.66	13.83	2.77	3.16	1.45	0.51
1996	33.45	21.79	7.93	5.16	1.98	0.51	11.66	13.86	2.77	3.18	1.47	0.51
1997	33.29	21.77	8.03	5.25	2.07	0.55	11.52	13.75	2.77	3.19	1.52	0.55
1998	33.36	21.90	8.17	5.39	2.17	0.61	11.47	13.72	2.78	3.22	1.56	0.61
1999	33.95	22.45	8.62	5.78	2.41	0.74	11.50	13.83	2.84	3.37	1.68	0.74
2000	34.19	22.69	8.84	6.00	2.57	0.84	11.50	13.85	2.84	3.43	1.73	0.84
2001	34.03	22.60	8.80	5.95	2.51	0.81	11.44	13.80	2.84	3.44	1.70	0.81
2002	33.41	22.13	8.54	5.75	2.39	0.69	11.28	13.59	2.80	3.36	1.70	0.69
2003	33.30	22.07	8.59	5.82	2.45	0.73	11.22	13.48	2.77	3.37	1.72	0.73
2004	33.03	21.97	8.62	5.87	2.49	0.75	11.07	13.34	2.75	3.39	1.73	0.75
2005	33.21	22.17	8.79	6.03	2.62	0.87	11.05	13.38	2.76	3.41	1.75	0.87

Notes: Computations by authors on tax return statistics. Taxpayers are ranked by gross income (excluding capital gains).
The table reports the percentage of total income accruing to each of the top groups. Top 10% denotes top decile, top 10–5% denotes the bottom half of the top decile, etc.

Table 10D.3 Top income shares in Spain from older income tax statistics, 1933–1971

	Total number of tax units ('000s) (1)	Tax returns (2)	Fraction filing (%) (2)/(1) (3)	Total income (mns of 2005 euros) (4)	Fraction of income reported on tax returns (%) (5)	CPI (base 2005) (6)	Top 0.1% (7)	Top 0.05% (8)	Top 0.01% (9)	Top 0.1–0.05% (10)	Top 0.05–0.01% (11)	Top 0.01% (12)
1933	14,488	1,446	0.010	38,930	1.412	56.538			1.41			1.41
1934	14,652	1,792	0.012	41,731	1.539	58.117			1.40			1.40
1935	14,818	2,465	0.017	42,961	1.984	58.343			1.53			1.53
1940	15,677	3,222	0.021	33,423	1.823	101.037			1.31			1.31
1941	15,892	5,231	0.033	27,622	2.371	135.103			1.38			1.38
1942	16,110	5,123	0.032	30,314	2.013	144.440			1.21			1.21
1943	16,331	5,538	0.034	32,822	2.086	143.603			1.16			1.16
1944	16,555	5,849	0.035	36,296	1.943	149.978			1.06			1.06
1945	16,782	6,629	0.040	33,670	2.194	160.410			1.12			1.12
1946	17,012	8,223	0.048	32,459	2.233	210.510			1.04			1.04
1947	17,245	7,983	0.046	32,049	1.805	247.731			0.86			0.86
1948	17,481	9,067	0.052	32,411	1.864	264.410		1.83	0.82		1.01	0.82
1949	17,721	10,111	0.057	32,962	1.930	278.706		1.82	0.81		1.01	0.81
1950	17,964	12,419	0.069	36,689	1.886	308.971		1.63	0.70		0.93	0.70
1951	18,134	13,597	0.075	42,679	1.690	338.078		1.42	0.62		0.80	0.62
1952	18,307	15,427	0.084	47,876	1.820	331.381		1.45	0.64		0.81	0.64
1953	18,481	16,545	0.090	50,928	1.833	336.726		1.43	0.63		0.80	0.63
1954	18,657	21,332	0.114	58,189	2.812	340.912	2.63	1.82	0.73	0.81	1.09	0.73
1955	18,834	26,716	0.142	60,426	3.308	354.628	2.77	1.90	0.74	0.87	1.16	0.74
1957	19,194	41,637	0.217	74,399	3.460	415.869	2.27	1.53	0.60	0.73	0.94	0.60
1958	19,377	48,921	0.252	78,059	3.490	470.798	2.13	1.45	0.56	0.68	0.89	0.56
1959	19,561	54,143	0.277	76,158	3.805	505.572	2.23	1.52	0.60	0.71	0.92	0.60
1961	19,950	38,520	0.193	87,866	2.617	523.925	1.88	1.29	0.52	0.59	0.77	0.52
1971	22,129	338,989	1.532	173,630	7.200	1,018.48	1.86	1.24	0.51	0.62	0.73	0.51

Sources: Income tax statistics published by the fiscal administration for years 1933 to 1971.
Total number of tax units defined as the number of adults aged 20 and over.
CPI index: 100 euros in 2005 are equivalent to 56.538 Ptas in 1933,..., 1,018.48 Ptas in 1971.
Total income is defined as 66% of GDP (expressed in millions of 2005 euros). Navarra is excluded since 1937. Alava is excluded since 1943.

Table 10D.4 Top fractiles income levels (including capital gains) in Spain, 1981–2005 (fractiles are defined by total income including capital gains) (incomes are expressed in euros 2005)

	P90–100 (1)	P95–100 (2)	P99–100 (3)	P99.5–100 (4)	P99.9–100 (5)	P99.99–100 (6)	P90–95 (7)	P95–99 (8)	P99–99.5 (9)	P99.5–99.9 (10)	P99.9–99.99 (11)	P90 (12)	P95 (13)	P99 (14)	P99.5 (15)	P99.9 (16)	P99.99 (17)
1981	33,348	43,328	77,812	101,660	198,145	565,432	23,368	34,724	53,964	77,528	157,328	19,961	27,102	49,247	61,870	111,095	301,181
1982	32,489	42,605	78,058	103,357	211,073	642,896	22,392	33,732	52,759	76,432	163,095	19,199	26,274	48,150	60,637	111,044	334,528
1983	32,255	42,148	75,250	97,849	190,920	573,726	22,378	33,881	52,651	74,589	148,382	18,872	26,224	48,264	60,156	105,184	289,972
1984	31,897	41,619	73,930	95,997	188,145	589,140	22,174	33,553	51,863	72,964	143,582	18,663	25,947	47,661	59,070	102,192	278,698
1985	32,871	43,293	78,364	102,577	203,560	593,984	22,450	34,521	54,151	77,335	160,169	19,009	26,455	49,582	62,034	110,220	320,648
1986	35,157	46,907	88,808	119,478	259,200	925,649	23,408	36,428	58,125	84,554	185,151	19,725	27,791	52,924	66,956	124,017	383,270
1987	37,147	49,846	96,144	131,000	298,372	1,182,611	24,461	38,268	61,288	89,148	200,122	20,557	29,055	55,807	70,562	131,173	442,391
1988	39,641	53,132	102,084	138,669	312,283	1,198,996	26,150	40,894	65,499	95,268	213,759	22,262	31,397	58,508	74,997	141,749	473,424
1989	41,607	55,377	103,813	138,634	291,652	939,085	27,826	43,265	68,993	100,376	219,705	23,642	33,393	61,669	79,018	148,615	456,914
1990	43,999	58,181	108,462	144,097	297,711	900,178	29,816	45,616	72,837	105,691	230,766	25,501	35,502	65,133	83,249	156,559	469,606
1991	44,937	59,028	108,840	143,453	290,024	854,796	30,835	46,578	74,227	106,811	227,266	26,581	36,478	66,468	84,668	156,865	452,765
1992	43,769	57,686	107,949	141,899	281,557	792,809	29,853	45,110	74,008	106,985	224,753	26,105	34,823	66,182	84,599	157,349	435,866
1993	42,949	56,459	104,940	137,369	268,146	731,050	29,439	44,343	72,511	104,669	216,719	25,687	34,296	64,849	82,865	153,264	412,336
1994	41,738	54,743	101,525	132,855	259,736	708,788	28,733	43,045	70,194	101,131	209,845	25,147	33,392	62,820	80,216	147,377	416,716
1995	42,003	55,188	102,891	135,154	265,539	725,797	28,818	43,256	70,628	102,554	214,399	25,213	33,500	63,161	80,882	150,266	417,997
1996	42,200	55,495	103,703	136,895	271,271	750,111	28,906	43,441	70,502	103,299	218,071	25,209	33,673	63,239	81,036	152,050	428,856
1997	42,437	56,179	107,135	142,743	292,209	840,481	28,695	43,444	71,527	105,378	231,290	25,016	33,450	63,758	82,255	156,659	484,014
1998	44,478	59,403	116,123	156,868	332,081	1,049,915	29,552	45,223	75,379	113,068	252,320	25,722	34,537	66,959	87,115	170,757	523,501
1999	46,649	62,735	126,935	175,605	398,817	1,405,418	30,564	46,685	78,263	119,803	286,973	26,292	35,620	69,544	90,791	184,685	639,018
2000	48,480	65,735	136,893	192,673	456,747	1,718,116	31,225	47,946	81,115	126,653	316,596	26,888	36,474	71,685	95,015	198,734	728,415
2001	49,034	66,374	137,941	193,933	458,104	1,699,663	31,695	48,482	81,949	127,891	320,154	27,387	36,947	72,445	95,937	200,888	731,428
2002	48,890	65,940	135,101	188,170	429,702	1,447,815	31,840	48,651	82,031	127,787	316,579	27,571	37,123	72,508	95,842	200,843	707,321
2003	50,753	69,053	146,674	208,855	504,369	1,825,173	32,454	49,647	84,493	134,977	357,613	28,484	37,947	73,968	99,491	219,140	833,392
2004	52,100	71,354	154,504	222,194	546,431	1,962,813	32,846	50,567	86,814	141,134	389,056	28,836	38,477	75,818	102,719	233,586	903,130
2005	55,157	76,648	172,998	254,044	654,873	2,528,354	33,666	52,561	91,951	153,837	446,709	29,471	39,576	79,609	109,520	261,709	1,063,140

Notes: P99 denotes the income threshold required to belong to the top 1% of tax units; P99–100 is the average income of the top 1%; P99–99.5 denotes the average income in the bottom half of the top percentile.

Sources: Authors' computations based on tax statistics.

Table 10D.5 Top fractiles income levels (excluding capital gains) in Spain, 1981–2005 (fractiles are defined by total income excluding capital gains) (incomes are expressed in euros 2005)

	P90–100 (1)	P95–100 (2)	P99–100 (3)	P99.5–100 (4)	P99.9–100 (5)	P99.99–100 (6)	P90–95 (7)	P95–99 (8)	P99–99.5 (9)	P99.5–99.9 (10)	P99.9–99.99 (11)	P90 (12)	P95 (13)	P99 (14)	P99.5 (15)	P99.9 (16)	P99.99 (17)
1981	33,195	43,001	76,371	99,214	190,239	527,039	23,368	34,658	53,549	76,458	152,807	19,961	27,080	49,007	61,215	108,736	286,614
1982	32,279	42,108	75,878	99,398	196,158	569,256	22,431	33,655	52,376	75,189	154,700	19,237	26,274	47,921	59,930	107,296	306,762
1983	32,119	41,826	73,810	95,291	181,383	526,394	22,412	33,830	52,329	73,759	143,046	18,906	26,241	48,077	59,648	102,694	272,794
1984	31,651	41,128	71,798	92,194	174,144	506,852	22,174	33,461	51,418	71,706	137,187	18,663	25,916	47,400	58,319	99,033	253,012
1985	32,237	42,122	74,077	95,427	181,871	510,402	22,366	34,126	52,727	73,823	145,376	18,939	26,258	48,651	59,806	102,619	283,278
1986	34,094	44,910	80,819	105,459	212,034	664,464	23,291	35,923	56,166	78,822	161,768	19,621	27,532	51,666	63,558	111,970	304,992
1987	35,965	47,567	86,709	113,929	233,056	798,503	24,350	37,788	59,490	84,135	170,241	20,458	28,809	54,625	67,532	117,686	337,514
1988	38,224	50,474	91,181	118,994	236,970	756,137	25,963	40,297	63,368	89,495	179,282	22,110	31,057	57,137	71,507	126,021	347,813
1989	40,421	53,246	95,951	125,116	247,663	740,375	27,606	42,562	66,797	94,468	192,923	23,455	32,987	60,186	75,439	135,186	380,718
1990	42,958	56,306	101,644	132,459	260,335	749,891	29,610	44,977	70,818	100,490	205,934	25,326	35,131	63,783	80,046	144,283	405,143
1991	43,897	57,183	102,508	132,867	257,781	728,561	30,602	45,859	72,149	101,644	205,473	26,377	36,050	65,021	81,443	145,551	397,621
1992	43,016	56,427	104,018	135,423	261,560	715,044	29,605	44,532	72,603	103,889	211,177	25,885	34,446	65,126	82,569	150,322	401,328
1993	41,827	54,469	98,619	127,471	241,556	638,760	29,194	43,431	69,767	98,953	197,423	25,477	33,805	62,955	79,034	142,253	367,949
1994	40,573	52,765	95,450	123,403	235,604	616,531	28,381	42,090	67,496	95,349	193,271	24,837	32,814	60,918	76,378	137,338	373,151
1995	40,782	53,068	96,363	125,093	239,828	625,989	28,505	42,244	67,625	96,412	196,926	24,940	32,921	61,073	76,739	139,635	372,221
1996	41,053	53,487	97,292	126,555	242,520	627,153	28,612	42,541	68,021	97,563	199,785	24,953	33,146	61,463	77,362	141,453	375,726
1997	40,870	53,469	98,541	129,023	253,527	670,300	28,279	42,195	68,059	97,898	207,220	24,660	32,723	61,298	77,341	142,947	409,822
1998	41,914	55,021	102,673	135,452	272,179	759,383	28,815	43,107	69,894	101,272	218,044	25,082	33,300	62,957	79,395	150,251	415,514
1999	44,077	58,298	111,890	150,186	313,404	959,844	29,856	44,899	73,593	109,385	241,562	25,684	34,527	66,140	84,134	162,042	487,163
2000	45,323	60,152	117,145	159,002	340,265	1,113,476	30,493	45,905	75,287	113,684	254,365	26,258	35,271	67,585	86,738	169,027	528,656
2001	46,441	61,670	120,052	162,514	342,709	1,110,763	31,211	47,074	77,589	117,464	257,378	26,968	36,129	69,466	89,474	173,005	533,007
2002	46,497	61,604	118,912	160,006	332,102	960,654	31,389	47,277	77,818	116,981	262,254	27,181	36,336	69,622	89,329	175,119	527,634
2003	47,396	62,839	122,294	165,636	348,542	1,038,889	31,953	47,975	78,951	119,914	271,843	28,045	37,014	70,296	90,676	180,632	553,939
2004	48,182	64,076	125,767	171,305	362,629	1,099,961	32,289	48,653	80,230	123,476	280,712	28,347	37,422	71,508	92,398	186,448	578,871
2005	49,472	66,039	130,884	179,703	390,620	1,302,608	32,906	49,827	82,065	126,971	289,289	28,806	38,100	73,259	94,069	192,743	618,110

Notes: P99 denotes the income threshold required to belong to the top 1% of tax units; P99–100 is the average income of the top 1%; P99–99.5 denotes the average income in the bottom half of the top percentile.

Sources: Authors' computations based on tax statistics.

Table 10D.6 Composition of top incomes under old income tax, Spain

Year	Top income group fractile	Returns on real estate	Returns on financial assets	Business income (excluding farm)	Farm income	Employment income	Other
1941	Top 0.03%	19.92	35.81	26.43	4.43	12.54	0.87
1942	Top 0.03%	19.58	38.89	15.63	5.32	18.77	1.81
1943	Top 0.03%	19.96	37.79	10.95	6.88	21.77	2.66
1944	Top 0.04%	19.37	38.34	12.66	6.69	20.13	2.80
1945	Top 0.04%	19.34	36.60	12.87	7.51	19.21	4.47
1946	Top 0.05%	16.90	34.52	11.74	13.35	17.62	5.86
1947	Top 0.05%	17.96	32.14	12.14	13.42	19.04	5.30
1948	Top 0.05%	19.29	32.74	9.22	14.18	19.14	5.43
1949	Top 0.06%	19.45	32.94	8.08	13.44	19.90	6.18
1950	Top 0.07%	18.11	28.25	9.27	20.14	18.75	5.48
1951	Top 0.07%	17.34	28.26	9.18	20.48	19.29	5.45
1952	Top 0.08%	17.19	28.43	10.05	21.35	18.30	4.68
1953	Top 0.09%	17.43	28.88	9.20	20.24	18.41	5.84
1958	Top 0.05%	11.48	32.89	11.31	19.04	22.50	2.79
1959	Top 0.05%	11.65	33.26	9.51	18.71	24.10	2.76
1961	Top 0.05%	13.05	30.09	8.38	25.99	17.00	5.50
1981	Top 0.05%	5.00	34.70	34.30	0.40	25.60	

Notes: For years 1941–1953, the composition statistics are only available in aggregate.
As a result, the size of the corresponding top group varies across those years.
For 1958, 1959, 1961, and 1981, the composition data are available by brackets and are reported in the table for the top 0.05%.

Sources: Official income tax statistics.

Table 10D.7 Income composition in top income groups, Spain, 1981–2005

	Top 10%				Top 5%				Top 1%				Top 0.5%				Top 0.1%				Top 0.01%			
	Wage	Entrep.	Capital	K gains	Wage	Entrep.	Capital	K gains	Wage	Entrep.	Capital	K gains	Wage	Entrep.	Capital	K gains	Wage	Entrep.	Capital	K gains	Wage	Entrep.	Capital	K gains
1981	80.5	8.6	10.2	0.7	76.1	10.8	12.2	1.0	59.3	18.5	20.0	2.3	50.3	22.4	24.3	3.0	30.0	30.2	34.8	5.0	16.8	32.9	41.9	8.5
1982	79.7	9.8	9.6	0.9	74.9	12.1	11.6	1.5	57.3	20.5	18.6	3.5	47.7	25.1	22.4	4.9	26.6	34.6	29.9	8.9	15.1	37.1	33.5	14.3
1983	80.5	9.3	9.6	0.6	76.1	11.4	11.6	1.0	60.2	18.6	18.7	2.4	51.5	22.3	22.8	3.3	31.6	29.3	32.8	6.3	18.2	30.3	41.2	10.3
1984	79.0	10.9	9.1	1.0	75.0	12.7	10.8	1.6	59.9	19.5	17.0	3.6	51.5	22.9	20.6	5.0	32.2	28.8	29.6	9.4	18.2	27.8	36.5	17.5
1985	77.0	11.6	8.9	2.5	72.3	13.9	10.4	3.4	55.9	21.3	15.9	6.9	47.3	24.9	19.1	8.8	28.9	31.6	26.1	13.4	17.3	33.2	31.9	17.6
1986	73.5	13.5	9.1	3.9	68.0	15.8	10.7	5.5	49.2	23.0	16.4	11.4	39.8	26.2	19.1	14.8	22.4	30.7	23.9	23.0	13.3	26.8	24.6	35.3
1987	72.9	14.0	8.9	4.2	67.2	16.2	10.7	5.9	48.3	22.5	16.8	12.4	38.9	24.7	19.9	16.5	20.8	26.0	25.5	27.6	11.4	21.9	26.1	40.6
1988	72.6	14.3	8.6	4.5	66.9	16.9	10.0	6.3	47.0	24.4	15.2	13.4	37.9	26.7	17.7	17.7	21.8	26.6	21.4	30.2	11.8	21.3	20.7	46.2
1989	73.5	13.9	9.1	3.5	68.1	16.4	10.7	4.8	49.6	24.0	16.9	9.5	41.4	26.4	20.1	12.2	26.6	28.2	26.4	18.9	18.0	26.0	29.6	26.5
1990	73.6	13.2	10.3	3.0	68.4	15.6	12.0	4.0	51.2	22.5	18.4	7.9	43.7	24.5	21.7	10.1	29.5	26.7	28.1	15.7	21.5	26.5	31.1	20.9
1991	74.1	12.8	10.3	2.9	69.0	15.3	11.8	3.9	52.8	22.4	17.5	7.3	45.4	24.9	20.5	9.2	31.9	28.3	25.8	13.9	23.0	29.9	28.6	18.5
1992	73.1	14.3	10.5	2.1	68.4	16.7	12.3	2.7	56.6	22.7	16.3	4.5	50.7	25.3	18.4	5.7	38.7	30.0	22.5	8.9	29.0	33.6	25.1	12.3
1993	73.2	13.2	10.4	3.3	68.6	15.2	11.8	4.4	56.8	20.9	14.9	7.5	51.0	23.5	16.5	9.0	39.5	28.4	19.7	12.4	30.8	31.6	21.9	15.8
1994	74.8	13.3	8.4	3.5	70.2	15.6	9.6	4.5	58.2	22.4	11.9	7.5	52.4	25.6	13.2	8.9	40.7	32.2	15.5	11.6	25.6	39.6	18.6	16.3
1995	75.3	12.7	8.5	3.6	70.5	14.7	10.0	4.8	58.0	20.7	13.5	7.9	52.0	23.3	15.4	9.3	40.3	28.1	19.5	12.1	26.4	30.8	25.6	17.2
1996	76.3	11.8	8.5	3.4	71.7	13.8	10.0	4.5	59.0	20.0	13.3	7.7	52.9	22.6	15.1	9.4	40.4	27.7	18.7	13.3	25.8	30.9	22.8	20.5
1997	76.5	12.1	6.9	4.6	71.5	14.2	8.3	6.0	58.3	20.2	11.5	10.0	52.2	22.6	13.2	12.0	39.3	27.7	16.4	16.6	25.2	31.3	18.2	25.3
1998	74.6	12.0	6.2	7.2	69.0	14.1	7.6	9.3	54.8	19.7	10.9	14.6	48.6	21.7	12.4	17.3	36.0	26.1	14.8	23.1	27.5	22.7	15.3	34.6
1999	73.6	12.1	7.4	6.9	68.5	14.0	8.8	8.8	54.7	18.7	11.8	14.8	48.7	20.1	13.1	18.1	36.4	21.9	15.0	26.8	28.3	17.4	14.7	39.6
2000	73.0	11.2	7.7	8.2	67.6	12.8	9.0	10.6	53.5	16.5	11.9	18.1	48.0	17.2	12.9	21.9	36.8	17.5	13.7	32.0	29.7	13.5	12.8	44.0
2001	74.1	11.1	8.2	6.6	68.9	12.7	9.6	8.9	55.2	16.1	12.4	16.3	49.6	16.8	13.3	20.4	37.3	17.1	13.9	31.7	30.3	13.3	13.1	43.3
2002	74.6	11.2	8.1	6.1	69.4	13.0	9.4	8.2	55.7	17.0	12.3	15.0	49.8	18.2	13.3	18.7	38.0	19.4	14.2	28.4	29.7	16.0	12.2	42.1
2003	74.1	10.5	7.2	8.3	68.1	12.3	8.4	11.3	51.9	16.3	11.0	20.8	44.8	17.3	12.0	25.9	30.9	18.0	12.5	38.6	19.9	15.6	10.7	53.9
2004	72.8	10.4	7.5	9.4	66.4	12.1	8.7	12.8	49.2	16.0	11.5	23.3	42.0	17.0	12.4	28.6	27.5	17.8	12.7	42.1	17.9	16.7	10.4	55.0
2005	69.9	9.6	7.6	12.9	62.7	11.2	8.8	17.3	44.1	14.4	11.1	30.4	36.8	14.9	11.7	36.6	23.2	15.4	11.0	50.4	15.9	14.7	8.9	60.6

Notes: Fractiles defined by size of total income. For each fractile, the first four columns (summing to 100%) give the percentage of wage income (wages and salaries, pensions, other employment income), entrepreneurial income (self-employment income, farm income, and small business income), and capital income (dividends, interest, rents, foreign and other investment income), and capital gains in total income. Details on methodology are presented in Appendix 10D.

Sources: Computations based on tax return statistics.

Table 10D.7 (continued) Income composition in top income groups, Spain 1981–2005

	Top 10-5%				Top 5-1%				Top 1-0.5%				Top 0.5-0.1%				Top 0.1-0.01%				Top 0.01%			
	Wage	Entrep.	Capital	K gains	Wage	Entrep.	Capital	K gains	Wage	Entrep.	Capital	K gains	Wage	Entrep.	Capital	K gains	Wage	Entrep.	Capital	K gains	Wage	Entrep.	Capital	K gains
1981	89.3	4.3	6.5	-0.1	86.0	6.2	7.5	0.2	76.2	11.0	11.8	1.0	63.4	17.3	17.6	1.8	35.5	29.1	31.8	3.6	16.8	32.9	41.9	8.5
1982	89.5	5.2	5.6	-0.3	85.6	6.9	7.3	0.3	76.2	11.5	11.3	0.9	62.4	18.5	17.1	2.0	31.8	33.5	28.3	6.4	15.1	37.1	33.5	14.3
1983	89.3	5.3	5.7	-0.2	85.3	7.1	7.4	0.2	76.6	11.6	11.1	0.8	64.4	17.8	16.4	1.4	37.6	28.9	28.9	4.5	18.2	30.3	41.2	10.3
1984	87.1	7.2	5.7	0.0	83.7	8.8	7.1	0.3	75.6	13.2	10.2	1.1	64.0	19.1	14.8	2.2	38.9	29.3	26.2	5.6	17.3	27.8	36.5	17.5
1985	86.7	7.1	5.8	0.5	82.1	9.4	7.1	1.4	72.5	14.3	9.9	3.3	59.4	20.5	14.4	5.7	33.9	30.9	23.6	11.6	13.3	33.2	31.9	17.6
1986	85.3	8.7	5.5	0.6	80.0	11.2	7.1	1.7	68.7	16.4	10.6	4.2	53.4	22.7	15.5	8.5	27.7	33.0	23.5	15.8	13.3	26.8	24.6	35.3
1987	85.2	9.1	5.1	0.6	79.7	12.1	6.6	1.6	68.5	17.8	10.1	3.7	54.3	23.5	15.2	7.0	27.3	28.9	25.1	18.7	11.4	21.9	26.1	40.6
1988	84.3	9.1	5.7	0.9	79.3	12.2	6.7	1.8	66.4	19.7	9.9	4.1	51.1	26.8	14.6	7.6	28.1	29.9	21.8	20.2	11.8	21.3	20.7	46.2
1989	84.2	8.8	6.1	1.0	79.2	11.8	7.0	2.0	66.2	19.4	10.4	4.0	52.1	25.1	15.5	7.4	30.7	29.2	24.9	15.2	18.0	26.0	29.6	26.5
1990	83.7	8.4	7.1	0.9	78.5	11.6	8.2	1.8	66.2	18.4	11.9	3.5	53.7	23.1	17.1	6.2	33.0	26.7	26.8	13.5	21.5	26.5	31.1	20.9
1991	83.8	7.9	7.4	0.9	78.5	11.1	8.5	2.0	67.0	17.6	11.9	3.5	54.6	22.5	16.9	6.0	35.7	27.7	24.7	12.0	23.0	29.9	28.6	18.5
1992	81.8	10.0	7.2	1.1	75.3	13.2	9.9	1.6	67.6	17.7	12.3	2.4	58.3	22.3	15.8	3.6	42.5	28.5	21.4	7.6	29.0	33.6	25.1	12.3
1993	82.1	9.3	7.5	1.0	75.5	11.8	10.1	2.6	67.6	15.8	11.8	4.7	58.4	20.4	14.4	6.8	42.8	27.2	18.9	11.1	30.8	31.6	21.9	15.8
1994	83.5	8.9	6.1	1.5	77.3	11.7	8.3	2.8	69.3	16.3	9.7	4.8	59.9	21.3	11.6	7.2	46.3	29.5	14.4	9.9	25.6	39.6	18.6	16.3
1995	84.3	8.7	5.6	1.4	78.0	11.1	7.9	2.9	69.3	15.6	9.8	5.3	59.6	20.2	12.7	7.5	45.5	27.0	17.3	10.2	26.4	30.8	25.6	17.2
1996	85.1	7.8	5.8	1.3	79.3	10.1	8.0	2.6	70.9	14.8	9.9	4.4	61.1	19.3	12.7	6.9	46.0	26.5	17.1	10.5	25.8	30.9	22.8	20.5
1997	86.2	7.9	4.1	1.8	79.7	10.5	6.2	3.6	70.4	15.3	8.3	6.1	61.2	19.0	10.9	8.9	45.0	26.3	15.7	13.0	25.2	31.3	18.2	25.3
1998	85.9	7.6	3.4	3.1	78.2	10.5	5.5	5.9	67.7	15.6	7.7	9.1	57.8	18.6	10.6	13.0	40.4	28.0	14.7	17.0	27.5	22.7	15.3	34.6
1999	84.2	8.2	4.7	2.9	77.8	10.8	6.7	4.8	68.2	15.4	9.0	7.5	59.0	18.6	11.5	10.9	40.8	24.3	15.2	19.8	28.3	17.4	14.7	39.6
2000	84.6	7.7	4.8	2.9	77.6	10.2	6.9	5.3	66.7	14.7	9.7	9.0	58.1	17.0	12.1	12.8	40.9	20.1	14.4	24.6	29.7	13.5	12.8	44.0
2001	84.9	7.7	5.4	1.9	78.5	10.3	7.6	3.6	68.6	14.5	10.3	6.7	60.6	16.5	12.7	10.2	41.4	19.5	14.6	24.5	30.3	13.3	13.1	43.3
2002	85.2	7.7	5.4	1.8	78.9	10.2	7.4	3.5	69.3	14.3	10.0	6.4	59.7	17.1	12.6	10.6	42.2	21.1	15.3	21.5	29.7	16.0	12.2	42.1
2003	86.8	6.7	4.6	1.9	80.1	9.3	6.4	4.2	69.4	13.7	8.7	8.2	57.8	16.8	11.5	14.0	37.2	19.3	13.6	30.0	19.9	15.6	10.7	53.9
2004	86.7	6.5	4.7	2.1	79.5	9.2	6.6	4.7	67.8	13.5	9.2	9.5	55.9	16.3	12.2	15.6	32.9	18.4	13.9	34.8	17.9	16.7	10.4	55.0
2005	86.3	6.0	4.9	2.8	78.0	8.6	6.9	6.5	64.1	12.8	9.7	13.4	51.3	14.4	12.4	21.8	27.8	15.9	12.3	44.1	15.9	14.7	8.9	60.6

Notes: Fractiles defined by size of total income. For each fractile, the first first columns (summing to 100%) give the percentage of wage income (wages and salaries, pensions, other employment income), entrepreneurial income (self-employment income, farm income, and small business income), and capital income (dividends, interest, rents, foreign and other investment income), and capital gains in total income. Details on methodology are presented in Appendix 10D.

Sources: Computations based on tax return statistics.

Table 10D.8 Top wealth shares in Spain, 1982–2005

	Top 1% (1)	Top 0.5% (2)	Top 0.1% (3)	Top 0.01% (4)	Top 1–0.5% (5)	Top 0.5–0.1% (6)	Top 0.1–0.01% (7)	Top 0.01% (8)
A. Top wealth shares including real estate								
1982	18.43	14.37	7.48	2.48	4.06	6.89	5.01	2.48
1983	18.07	14.00	7.39	2.57	4.08	6.61	4.82	2.57
1984	17.54	13.55	7.07	2.36	3.99	6.48	4.71	2.36
1985	17.78	13.58	6.95	2.27	4.20	6.63	4.67	2.27
1986	18.16	13.83	7.10	2.44	4.33	6.74	4.65	2.44
1987	17.71	13.38	6.71	2.21	4.33	6.67	4.50	2.21
1988	17.28	12.98	6.36	2.04	4.30	6.62	4.32	2.04
1989	16.88	12.62	6.04	1.92	4.26	6.58	4.11	1.92
1990	16.82	12.38	5.79	1.78	4.44	6.60	4.01	1.78
1991	16.12	11.73	5.39	1.59	4.39	6.34	3.79	1.59
1992	16.02	11.63	5.32	1.60	4.39	6.32	3.72	1.60
1993	16.62	11.84	5.46	1.66	4.78	6.38	3.80	1.66
1994	16.33	11.50	5.18	1.53	4.83	6.32	3.66	1.53
1995	15.93	11.20	5.00	1.47	4.73	6.20	3.52	1.47
1996	16.62	11.75	5.25	1.56	4.88	6.50	3.69	1.56
1997	17.39	12.17	5.39	1.59	5.23	6.78	3.81	1.59
1998	17.22	12.03	5.36	1.61	5.19	6.67	3.74	1.61
1999	17.17	12.26	5.31	1.58	4.92	6.95	3.73	1.58
2000	18.58	13.21	5.64	1.62	5.38	7.57	4.02	1.62
2001	18.54	13.12	5.59	1.64	5.42	7.54	3.95	1.64
2002	20.02	14.20	5.97	1.62	5.82	8.23	4.35	1.62
2003	19.37	13.37	5.42	1.47	5.99	7.95	3.96	1.47
2004	19.39	13.37	5.43	1.47	6.02	7.94	3.96	1.47
2005	19.68	13.51	5.41	1.41	6.17	8.10	4.00	1.41
B. Top financial wealth shares (excluding real estate)								
1982	24.95	21.12	12.43	5.15	3.82	8.70	7.28	5.15
1983	25.34	21.11	12.59	5.65	4.23	8.51	6.95	5.65
1984	23.53	19.50	11.52	5.02	4.03	7.98	6.51	5.02
1985	23.92	19.56	11.30	4.80	4.36	8.26	6.50	4.80
1986	25.61	20.85	12.10	5.29	4.76	8.75	6.81	5.29
1987	24.97	20.26	11.78	5.02	4.70	8.48	6.76	5.02
1988	24.68	20.06	11.64	4.93	4.62	8.43	6.71	4.93
1989	24.76	20.24	11.66	5.01	4.52	8.58	6.64	5.01
1990	25.78	20.92	11.77	4.91	4.86	9.15	6.85	4.91
1991	24.74	19.98	11.09	4.54	4.76	8.89	6.55	4.54
1992	23.35	18.72	10.19	4.15	4.64	8.53	6.04	4.15
1993	23.25	18.18	9.97	4.05	5.07	8.21	5.92	4.05
1994	22.08	17.03	9.02	3.52	5.06	8.01	5.50	3.52
1995	20.77	15.85	8.37	3.25	4.92	7.48	5.12	3.25
1996	21.28	16.16	8.59	3.32	5.12	7.57	5.28	3.32
1997	21.94	16.32	8.63	3.20	5.62	7.69	5.42	3.20
1998	21.17	15.64	8.39	3.15	5.53	7.25	5.24	3.15
1999	22.04	17.27	9.07	3.41	4.78	8.20	5.66	3.41
2000	22.72	18.07	9.72	3.70	4.65	8.35	6.02	3.70
2001	23.17	18.45	10.05	3.99	4.72	8.40	6.05	3.99
2002	24.17	19.31	10.48	4.07	4.86	8.83	6.41	4.07
2003	23.30	18.74	10.16	3.95	4.55	8.58	6.21	3.95
2004	23.88	19.24	10.51	4.19	4.64	8.73	6.32	4.19
2005	24.98	19.95	10.60	4.03	5.04	9.35	6.57	4.03

Sources: Computations by authors on wealth tax return statistics. See details in Appendix 10D.

Table 10D.9 Composition in top wealth groups, Spain, 1982–2005

	Top 1–0.5%						Top 0.5–0.1%						Top 0.1–0.01%						Top 0.01%					
	Real estate	Busi-ness	Fixed claim	Stock	Other	Debts	Real estate	Busi-ness	Fixed claim	Stock	Other	Debts	Real estate	Busi-ness	Fixed claim	Stock	Other	Debts	Real estate	Busi-ness	Fixed claim	Stock	Other	Debts
1982	75.3	4.9	13.6	6.5	3.6	−3.9	67.6	5.6	12.7	12.2	4.5	−2.6	55.8	5.2	11.3	24.7	5.6	−2.5	36.8	2.9	10.7	46.2	5.6	−2.2
1983	73.2	5.1	14.5	7.0	3.6	−3.4	67.2	5.4	12.9	12.8	4.6	−2.9	56.3	4.8	11.6	23.8	5.7	−2.2	33.0	2.5	12.8	39.6	13.3	−1.1
1984	73.9	4.6	14.0	7.1	3.5	−3.1	68.7	4.8	12.2	12.5	4.6	−2.7	58.2	4.1	11.0	23.3	5.6	−2.1	35.0	2.3	11.2	45.4	7.1	−1.1
1985	73.2	4.3	14.2	7.7	3.7	−3.2	68.3	4.4	12.2	13.2	4.6	−2.7	57.9	3.7	11.0	24.1	5.5	−2.1	35.5	2.2	10.6	46.0	6.8	−1.1
1986	71.6	4.2	14.0	9.5	3.9	−3.2	66.9	4.1	12.1	15.0	4.8	−2.8	55.7	3.3	10.8	27.1	5.7	−2.5	33.9	2.0	14.6	46.2	5.6	−2.3
1987	70.6	4.1	13.9	10.7	4.2	−3.5	66.1	3.9	12.3	15.9	4.9	−3.1	52.3	2.9	11.1	30.4	6.0	−2.8	27.5	1.8	11.5	55.2	6.6	−2.6
1988	68.7	3.3	13.3	12.9	4.7	−2.8	62.9	2.7	12.3	19.2	5.5	−2.6	54.8	2.3	12.0	27.2	6.3	−2.5	29.7	1.4	12.3	50.9	8.7	−3.0
1989	71.0	2.9	12.9	11.8	4.2	−2.8	64.4	2.4	11.7	19.1	5.1	−2.6	55.9	1.9	11.4	27.4	5.9	−2.5	28.8	1.1	12.0	53.3	7.5	−2.7
1990	72.6	2.6	13.9	9.5	4.0	−2.7	65.3	2.3	12.4	17.6	5.0	−2.5	57.3	1.9	12.1	25.6	5.8	−2.5	31.0	1.2	11.2	52.1	7.3	−2.8
1991	74.3	2.3	12.8	9.8	3.4	−2.6	67.9	2.0	10.8	18.8	3.1	−2.5	60.4	1.8	10.3	27.0	3.2	−2.6	33.6	1.1	9.4	55.3	3.5	−2.8
1992	71.9	2.9	15.1	10.8	2.1	−2.8	63.9	2.6	11.4	21.9	2.9	−2.7	56.7	2.2	10.7	29.9	3.3	−2.7	30.6	1.4	8.5	58.6	4.0	−3.1
1993	69.4	2.7	14.1	14.3	2.2	−2.7	62.7	2.5	10.7	23.8	2.8	−2.6	54.9	2.1	9.7	32.9	3.1	−2.7	29.5	1.2	7.4	61.5	3.4	−3.0
1994	68.7	2.4	14.1	15.4	2.1	−2.7	62.3	2.2	10.9	24.4	2.8	−2.6	55.5	1.9	9.9	32.6	3.0	−2.8	30.9	1.1	7.9	59.9	3.4	−3.3
1995	66.8	2.2	14.6	16.8	2.1	−2.6	61.6	2.2	11.5	24.6	2.7	−2.5	54.4	1.9	10.2	33.4	2.9	−2.8	30.2	1.1	7.9	60.7	3.3	−3.1
1996	64.7	2.1	12.8	20.6	2.2	−2.3	60.8	2.0	10.5	26.2	2.5	−2.1	52.0	1.8	9.0	36.1	2.9	−1.8	28.5	1.2	6.8	60.6	3.9	−1.0
1997	60.9	2.1	10.4	26.8	2.2	−2.3	58.7	2.1	9.4	29.7	2.4	−2.2	48.2	1.7	8.2	41.4	2.7	−2.3	26.7	1.0	6.5	64.9	3.5	−2.7
1998	58.6	1.9	9.2	30.3	2.3	−2.3	57.8	1.9	8.9	31.3	2.3	−2.2	45.7	1.5	7.9	44.4	2.8	−2.3	24.2	1.0	6.9	67.1	3.5	−2.7
1999	63.1	1.8	10.5	25.0	1.9	−2.3	55.2	1.7	8.9	33.9	2.4	−2.1	42.4	1.4	8.0	47.5	3.0	−2.3	18.3	0.8	7.8	71.4	4.4	−2.6
2000	67.6	1.5	10.0	21.0	1.6	−1.7	60.2	1.5	8.8	29.1	2.2	−1.8	47.5	1.2	8.0	42.3	3.0	−2.0	21.2	0.7	8.5	67.5	4.9	−2.8
2001	69.7	1.4	9.9	19.1	1.5	−1.6	62.7	1.5	8.7	26.6	2.1	−1.7	50.1	1.3	8.0	39.7	2.9	−2.0	22.3	0.6	7.2	67.9	4.3	−2.4
2002	74.9	1.2	8.7	15.3	1.3	−1.4	69.3	1.2	7.5	21.7	1.8	−1.5	59.1	1.1	6.7	32.3	2.4	−1.6	32.4	0.7	6.3	59.0	3.6	−2.0
2003	77.7	1.1	7.3	14.2	1.1	−1.4	70.4	1.2	6.8	21.5	1.7	−1.5	58.6	1.1	6.5	32.9	2.4	−1.7	30.1	0.6	5.6	61.8	3.7	−1.8
2004	78.3	1.0	6.9	14.1	1.1	−1.4	70.9	1.1	6.6	21.3	1.6	−1.5	59.2	1.0	6.4	32.7	2.4	−1.8	28.7	0.5	5.7	63.3	3.8	−2.0
2005	77.5	0.9	6.3	15.7	1.1	−1.4	69.8	1.0	6.1	23.2	1.6	−1.4	58.3	0.9	6.1	34.2	2.4	−1.6	28.5	0.5	5.8	63.6	4.2	−2.6

Notes: Fractiles defined by size of total wealth. For each fractile, the six columns (summing to 100%) give the percentage of real estate, business assets, fixed claim assets (cash, deposits, bonds), other (insurance, annuities, and other small items) in total wealth. Details on methodology are presented in Appendix 10D.

Sources: Computations based on wealth tax return statistics.

Table 10D.10 Top income shares in Spain (including capital gains) from income tax panel, 1982–1998, and survey, 2002

	Top 10% (1)	Top 5% (2)	Top 1% (3)	Top 0.5% (4)	Top 0.1% (5)	Top 0.01% (6)	Top 10–5% (7)	Top 5–1% (8)	Top 1–0.5% (9)	Top 0.5–0.1% (10)	Top 0.1–0.01% (11)	Top 0.01% (12)
1982	32.37	20.38	7.03	4.53	1.72	0.46	11.98	13.35	2.50	2.81	1.26	0.46
1983	32.50	20.44	6.96	4.42	1.61	0.38	12.05	13.48	2.54	2.80	1.23	0.38
1984	32.38	20.78	7.09	4.52	1.69	0.46	11.60	13.68	2.58	2.82	1.24	0.46
1985	32.13	20.70	7.06	4.48	1.66	0.47	11.42	13.64	2.58	2.82	1.19	0.47
1986	32.69	21.21	7.38	4.72	1.77	0.48	11.48	13.83	2.66	2.94	1.29	0.48
1987	33.23	21.69	7.72	5.02	1.99	0.57	11.54	13.97	2.70	3.03	1.42	0.57
1988	34.58	22.76	8.29	5.43	2.18	0.60	11.82	14.47	2.85	3.25	1.58	0.60
1989	35.16	23.13	8.47	5.59	2.32	0.76	12.03	14.66	2.88	3.27	1.56	0.76
1990	34.97	22.82	8.28	5.44	2.21	0.68	12.15	14.53	2.85	3.23	1.53	0.68
1991	34.43	22.32	7.95	5.13	1.95	0.52	12.11	14.37	2.82	3.18	1.43	0.52
1992	33.58	21.93	8.05	5.23	2.00	0.52	11.65	13.88	2.81	3.23	1.48	0.52
1993	33.24	21.70	7.99	5.21	2.05	0.64	11.54	13.71	2.78	3.17	1.41	0.64
1994	33.87	22.11	8.17	5.36	2.12	0.64	11.77	13.94	2.81	3.24	1.47	0.64
1995	33.53	21.89	8.10	5.30	2.09	0.64	11.64	13.79	2.80	3.21	1.45	0.64
1996	33.09	21.74	8.16	5.42	2.23	0.78	11.35	13.58	2.74	3.18	1.46	0.78
1997	33.33	22.01	8.36	5.58	2.29	0.71	11.32	13.65	2.79	3.28	1.58	0.71
1998	33.88	22.60	8.82	5.98	2.57	0.82	11.28	13.78	2.84	3.40	1.75	0.82
2002	34.32	23.16	9.51	6.64	3.05	1.04	11.17	13.64	2.88	3.59	2.01	1.04

Sources: Computations based on income tax panel (IEF, Panel IRPF IEF–AEAT 1982–1998) and income tax survey (IEF, Muestra de Declarantes IRPF 2002).

Table 10D.11 Top income shares in Spain (excluding capital gains) from income tax panel, 1982–1998, and survey, 2002

	Top 10% (1)	Top 5% (2)	Top 1% (3)	Top 0.5% (4)	Top 0.1% (5)	Top 0.01% (6)	Top 10–5% (7)	Top 5–1% (8)	Top 1–0.5% (9)	Top 0.5–0.1% (10)	Top 0.1–0.01% (11)	Top 0.01% (12)
1982	32.18	20.19	6.86	4.39	1.63	0.43	11.99	13.33	2.47	2.75	1.21	0.43
1983	32.34	20.28	6.83	4.31	1.56	0.38	12.06	13.45	2.52	2.75	1.17	0.38
1984	32.15	20.54	6.91	4.35	1.59	0.41	11.60	13.64	2.55	2.77	1.18	0.41
1985	31.90	20.48	6.88	4.32	1.56	0.41	11.43	13.60	2.55	2.76	1.15	0.41
1986	32.30	20.81	7.06	4.46	1.61	0.41	11.49	13.75	2.61	2.84	1.21	0.41
1987	32.79	21.25	7.36	4.71	1.78	0.48	11.55	13.89	2.65	2.93	1.30	0.48
1988	33.67	22.20	7.86	5.07	1.96	0.52	11.48	14.34	2.78	3.11	1.44	0.52
1989	34.11	22.58	7.96	5.14	1.99	0.54	11.53	14.61	2.82	3.15	1.45	0.54
1990	34.00	22.33	7.83	5.02	1.89	0.49	11.67	14.50	2.81	3.13	1.40	0.49
1991	33.65	21.94	7.66	4.89	1.80	0.46	11.70	14.28	2.77	3.10	1.34	0.46
1992	32.76	21.49	7.76	5.01	1.88	0.49	11.27	13.73	2.75	3.13	1.40	0.49
1993	32.36	21.25	7.71	5.00	1.93	0.59	11.10	13.54	2.71	3.07	1.34	0.59
1994	32.80	21.59	7.80	5.05	1.91	0.52	11.21	13.79	2.75	3.14	1.39	0.52
1995	32.49	21.41	7.80	5.06	1.96	0.57	11.08	13.62	2.73	3.10	1.39	0.57
1996	32.05	21.19	7.75	5.07	1.99	0.60	10.86	13.43	2.69	3.08	1.38	0.60
1997	32.02	21.39	7.94	5.23	2.10	0.64	10.64	13.45	2.71	3.13	1.46	0.64
1998	31.79	21.61	8.13	5.40	2.20	0.65	10.18	13.48	2.73	3.20	1.56	0.65
2002	33.25	22.03	8.53	5.75	2.41	0.73	11.23	13.50	2.78	3.34	1.69	0.73

Sources: Computations based on income tax panel (IEF, Panel IRPF IEF–AEAT 1982–98) and income tax survey (IEF, Muestra de Declarantes IRPF 2002).

Table 10D.12 Top wage income shares in Spain from panel of tax returns, 1982–2002

	Total number of employees ('000s) (1)	Total wages (millions of 2005 euros) (2)	CPI (base 2005) (3)	Top 10% (4)	Top 5% (5)	Top 1% (6)	Top 0.5% (7)	Top 0.1% (8)	Top 10–5% (9)	Top 5–1% (10)	Top 1–0.5% (11)	Top 0.5–0.1% (11)
1982	8,614	152,951	31.430	22.47	13.58	4.08	2.45	0.78	8.88	9.51	1.63	1.67
1983	8,558	152,282	35.478	22.63	13.70	4.06	2.41	0.75	8.93	9.64	1.65	1.66
1984	8,305	147,104	39.192	22.96	13.91	4.12	2.46	0.78	9.06	9.78	1.66	1.68
1985	8,370	149,880	42.619	23.00	13.92	4.11	2.45	0.79	9.08	9.81	1.66	1.67
1986	8,645	154,863	46.344	23.52	14.26	4.24	2.53	0.79	9.27	10.02	1.71	1.74
1987	9,060	164,974	48.797	24.29	14.81	4.46	2.69	0.87	9.48	10.34	1.77	1.82
1988	9,440	176,904	51.321	25.26	15.44	4.73	2.86	0.96	9.83	10.71	1.86	1.90
1989	9,964	186,380	54.733	26.41	16.16	4.99	3.02	1.01	10.26	11.17	1.97	2.01
1990	10,441	201,381	58.355	26.94	16.51	5.17	3.18	1.07	10.43	11.34	2.00	2.11
1991	10,653	211,634	61.885	26.82	16.46	5.18	3.20	1.09	10.37	11.28	1.98	2.11
1992	10,425	213,433	65.430	25.76	16.06	5.29	3.32	1.19	9.70	10.77	1.98	2.13
1993	10,138	210,600	68.554	25.67	16.06	5.40	3.44	1.35	9.61	10.66	1.96	2.09
1994	10,102	205,616	71.725	25.92	16.13	5.35	3.38	1.23	9.79	10.78	1.98	2.14
1995	10,346	210,696	74.849	25.91	16.14	5.36	3.39	1.24	9.77	10.77	1.97	2.15
1996	10,480	214,001	77.533	25.92	16.16	5.43	3.45	1.31	9.76	10.74	1.97	2.14
1997	10,889	222,952	79.380	26.11	16.35	5.51	3.55	1.34	9.76	10.84	1.96	2.20
1998	11,348	235,791	80.657	26.25	16.48	5.59	3.60	1.37	9.77	10.89	1.99	2.23
2002	12,998	270,415	90.997	27.33	17.54	6.41	4.25	1.73	9.79	11.13	2.16	2.52

Sources: Computations based on income tax panel (IEF, Panel IRPF IEF–AEAT 1982–98) and income tax survey (IEF, Muestra de Declarantes IRPF 2002). See Appendix 10D for details.

APPENDIX 10E: COMPUTING MARGINAL TAX RATES

Marginal tax rates displayed in Table 10E.1 were computed using the panel of individual income tax returns 1982–98 and the 2002 sample of income tax files. For each individual we computed the taxable income following the tax code, as the sum of taxable sources excluding elements taxed by average or flat rates and not subject to the progressive tax scale (capital gains, irregular income, and income adjustments from previous years). Then we applied the tax scale to identify the marginal rate that affects each individual.

We also computed total gross income as the sum of taxable sources, capital gains, and irregular income (but excluding adjustments from previous years) plus labour income deductions. We ranked individuals by gross income (as done for our estimates based on grouped data) and computed the average marginal tax rates for top percentiles weighted by gross income. This procedure explains the fact that in some cases the marginal tax rate is lower for the top 0.01 per cent than for the top 0.1 per cent. The reason is the following: consider two individuals in the top 0.01 per cent; the first one has no capital gains and no irregular income; consequently she faces the maximum marginal rate; the second individual has only capital gains; therefore she faces a zero marginal rate according to the progressive tax scale, while she still belongs to the top group. As the proportion of capital gains in total income increases with income (see Table 10D.7), it is then possible to find more people at the top subject to relatively smaller marginal rates.

Table 10E.1 Marginal tax rates by income groups, Spain, 1982–2002

	Top 10% (1)	Top 5% (2)	Top 1% (3)	Top 0.5% (4)	Top 0.1% (5)	Top 0.01% (6)	Top 10–5% (7)	Top 5–1% (8)	Top 1–0.5% (9)	Top 0.5–0.1% (10)	Top 0.1–0.01% (11)	Top 0.01% (12)
1982	26.38	29.21	38.04	42.96	56.29	65.74	21.01	24.34	29.25	35.12	52.75	65.74
1983	27.94	31.01	40.20	44.99	56.66	63.68	22.15	26.07	32.00	38.52	54.39	63.68
1984	30.03	33.50	43.52	48.63	60.41	65.39	23.46	28.12	34.70	41.83	58.51	65.39
1985	31.00	34.67	45.27	50.49	61.35	63.03	23.95	28.98	36.32	44.33	60.65	63.03
1986	33.14	37.38	49.02	54.32	63.48	64.72	24.87	30.94	39.75	49.01	63.00	64.72
1987	34.36	38.84	51.00	56.35	63.60	65.25	25.45	31.87	41.19	51.79	62.92	65.25
1988	34.88	38.41	48.24	52.11	54.84	55.67	28.13	32.84	40.94	50.30	54.52	55.67
1989	35.93	39.65	49.38	52.60	54.51	53.73	28.80	34.10	43.18	51.80	54.80	53.73
1990	37.07	41.03	51.19	54.27	55.45	55.95	29.69	35.29	45.36	53.48	55.23	55.95
1991	37.58	41.56	51.71	54.49	55.19	55.76	30.30	35.99	46.68	54.07	54.99	55.76
1992	36.80	40.95	50.80	53.86	54.93	55.23	29.23	35.38	45.18	53.20	54.82	55.23
1993	37.80	41.89	51.67	54.33	55.45	55.91	30.35	36.33	46.72	53.61	55.25	55.91
1994	38.06	42.13	51.83	54.33	55.33	55.66	30.65	36.59	47.11	53.69	55.19	55.66
1995	38.20	42.26	51.83	54.29	55.14	55.47	30.77	36.77	47.24	53.73	55.00	55.47
1996	37.95	42.08	51.57	54.17	55.09	55.03	30.27	36.52	46.50	53.53	55.12	55.03
1997	37.64	41.88	51.68	54.08	54.85	54.87	29.63	36.01	46.95	53.54	54.85	54.87
1998	38.84	42.91	52.08	53.69	54.00	53.75	30.92	37.18	48.72	53.46	54.12	53.75
2002	37.39	41.36	45.59	45.89	45.24	44.72	29.15	38.41	44.89	46.44	45.51	44.72

Sources: Computations based on income tax panel (IEF, Panel IRPF IEF–AEAT 1982–98) and income tax survey (IEF, Muestra de Declarantes IRPF 2002). Individuals are ranked according to gross income. The average marginal tax rate is weighted by gross income. See Appendix 10E for details.

APPENDIX 10F: ESTIMATING NET WORTH SHARES AND COMPOSITION FROM THE WEALTH SURVEY

In 2002 the Bank of Spain conducted a household wealth survey whose preliminary results are presented in Bover (2004). It is instructive to compare the wealth reported on wealth tax returns with the wealth reported in the survey (Table 10F.1).

To be consistent with our tax estimates we defined net financial wealth as the sum of: chequing accounts, bank deposits, jewellery, antiques, artworks, life insurance, mutual funds, fixed income securities, business assets, and other household claims net of debts different from mortgage debts. Total net wealth is net financial wealth as described plus the declared price for the main residence plus other real estate minus mortgage debts. We do not consider pension funds, which are not taxed.

As the survey data are based on household information while our results refer to the individual distribution, we compute the top shares under two extreme scenarios. In the first one, we assume that all wealth belongs to the head of the household (panels C and D in Table 10F.1). For the second scenario, we assume that every spouse owns 50 per cent of the household wealth (panels E and F in Table 10F.1). The reference total for the population is the number of adults aged 20 and over in all Spain, this time including País Vasco and Navarra.

Three important findings emerge. First, we find that wealth reported on wealth tax statistics for top income groups such as the top 1 per cent is higher than the wealth reported on the survey by the top 1 per cent, even under the assumption that all the household wealth belongs to the head of household. For example, including real estate, the average top 1 per cent wealth from tax returns is 1.8 million euros while it is only 1.2 million in the survey. This shows that, in contrast to popular belief, it is not clear that tax evasion for the wealth tax is pervasive, as wealthy individuals report more wealth for tax purposes than for the survey purposes.

Second, the total wealth reported in the survey (and especially financial wealth) is substantially lower than the aggregates from National Accounts that we use as the denominator. For example, the survey reports total wealth of about 2,000 billion euros while National Accounts report total wealth of about 3,000 billion euros. This suggests that households are under-reporting their wealth in the survey or that the survey might not have been sampled adequately to reflect a fully representative cross-section of Spanish households.

Finally, because the gap in the aggregate between the survey and National Accounts and the gap for top groups between the survey and the wealth tax data are of comparable magnitude, our top wealth shares computed using wealth tax statistics and National Accounts for the denominator are relatively close to the top wealth shares computed internally from the survey (using as denominator total survey wealth).

Table 10F:1 Aggregate net worth and composition, households wealth survey in Spain, 2002, vs. tax statistics

	Units	Total financial wealth		Total wealth		Top shares (%)	Wealth composition					
	Adults ('000s)	Total Net financial wealth (millions 2005 euros)	Average (2005 euros)	Total net wealth (millions 2005 euros)	Average (2005 euros)		Real estate (%)	Fixed claim assets (%)	Stocks (%)	Business (%)	Other (%)	Debts (%)
Total from tax stats	30,249	951,132	31,443	3,540,482	117,045							
Total from survey	32,339	453,836	14,034	2,317,025	71,649		88.07	6.60	5.39	8.52	0.96	−9.55
A. Including real estate. Individual distribution from tax returns												
top 1%	302			708,734	2,342,999	20.02	65.77	7.57	25.10	1.16	1.93	−1.53
top 0.5%	151			502,642	3,323,364	14.20	61.98	7.12	29.16	1.13	2.18	−1.57
top 0.1%	30			211,331	6,986,392	5.97	51.87	6.61	39.48	0.98	2.76	−1.70
top 1–0.5%				206,091		5.82						
top 0.5–0.1%				291,311		8.23						
top 0.1%				211,331		5.97						
B. Excluding real estate. Individual distribution from tax returns												
top 1%	302	216,116	714,457			22.72						
top 0.5%	151	171,879	1,136,428			18.07						
top 0.1%	30	92,421	3,055,357			9.72						
top 1–0.5%		44,237				4.65						
top 0.5–0.1%		79,458				8.35						
top 0.1%		92,421				9.72						

(continued)

Table 10F.1 Continued

Units	Total financial wealth		Total wealth			Wealth composition						
Adults ('000s)	Total Net financial wealth (millions 2005 euros)	Average (2005 euros)	Total net wealth (millions 2005 euros)	Average (2005 euros)	Top shares (%)	Real estate (%)	Fixed claim assets (%)	Stocks (%)	Business (%)	Other (%)	Debts (%)

C. Including real estate. Individual distribution from the survey assuming that all wealth belongs to the head of household

top 10%	3,234	380,335	117,610	1,467,767	453,874	63.35	78.06	6.03	7.67	11.96	1.14	−4.86
top 5%	1,617	325,817	201,503	1,057,739	654,165	45.65	72.93	5.65	9.80	14.69	1.42	−4.49
top 1%	323	206,324	638,011	470,728	1,455,622	20.32	58.55	4.76	16.80	20.62	2.22	−2.94
top 0.5%	162	169,285	1,046,955	343,075	2,121,763	14.81	52.70	4.59	20.29	22.33	2.62	−2.53
top 0.1%	32	106,334	3,288,127	161,192	4,984,513	6.96	35.19	3.40	30.65	31.18	1.02	−1.44
top 10–5%		54,518		410,028		17.70						
top 5–1%		119,493		587,011		25.33						
top 1–0.5%		37,039		127,654		5.51						
top 0.5–0.1%		62,952		181,882		7.85						
top 0.1%		106,334		161,192		6.96						

D. Excluding real estate. Individual distribution from the survey assuming that all wealth belongs to the head of household

top 10%	3,234	432,492	133,739			95.30						
top 5%	1,617	379,267	234,560			83.57						
top 1%	323	244,464	755,949			53.87						
top 0.5%	162	194,058	1,200,163			42.76						
top 0.1%	32	119,630	3,699,288			26.36						
top 10–5%		53,225				11.73						
top 5–1%		134,804				29.70						
top 1–0.5%		50,405				11.11						
top 0.5–0.1%		74,428				16.40						
top 0.1%		119,630				26.36						

E. Including real estate. Individual distribution based on the survey assuming that wealth is divided equally between spouses

top 10%	3,234	342,343	105,862	1,179,340	364,685	50.90	74.88	5.96	8.91	13.66	1.39	−4.79
top 5%	1,617	286,344	177,091	839,270	519,051	36.22	69.26	5.70	11.33	16.19	1.55	−4.03
top 1%	323	177,808	549,833	384,911	1,190,251	16.61	56.70	4.52	18.15	21.23	2.74	−3.35
top 0.5%	162	153,051	946,553	275,135	1,701,585	11.87	46.75	4.29	22.99	25.65	3.12	−2.80
top 0.1%	32	93,905	2,903,806	127,948	3,956,495	5.52	27.86	3.04	32.87	36.65	1.11	−1.53
top 10–5%		55,999		340,071		14.68						
top 5–1%		108,535		454,359		19.61						
top 1–0.5%		24,757		109,776		4.74						
top 0.5–0.1%		59,146		147,187		6.35						
top 0.1%		93,905		127,948		5.52						

F. Excluding real estate. Individual distribution based on the survey assuming that wealth is divided equally between spouses

top 10%	3,234	397,257	122,843	87.53
top 5%	1,617	337,907	208,981	74.46
top 1%	323	208,676	645,285	45.98
top 0.5%	162	167,632	1,036,727	36.94
top 0.1%	32	101,545	3,140,048	22.37
top 10–5%		59,350		13.08
top 5–1%		129,231		28.48
top 1–0.5%		41,045		9.04
top 0.5–0.1%		66,087		14.56
top 0.1%		101,545		22.37

Notes: The number of total adults for the tax-based statistics (30.249 million) is smaller than the number of total adults for the survey-based statistics (32.339 million) because the former excludes País Vasco and Navarra.

Sources: Computations based on tax returns and Bank of Spain, Encuesta Financiera de las Familias 2002.

APPENDIX 10G: PREVIOUS WORK
ON INEQUALITY IN SPAIN

Until the beginning of the decade of 1970 the studies on inequality and income distribution in Spain are very scarce, due mainly to the lack of data. The Instituto de Estudios Agrosociales (1958) ran a study on the distribution of expenditure in 1956, as an assignment for the FAO, while the Spanish statistics bureau (INE) conducted a households' consumption survey in 1958 (Información Comercial Española 1962).

The first households' budget surveys (*Encuesta de Presupuestos Familiares, EPF*) were carried out in 1964/5, 1966/7, 1969/70, 1973/4, and 1980/1. The results were somewhat deficient, and many ad hoc assumptions were made for consistency with the National Accounts, including corrections for under-reporting by income size and income source, as well as adjustments to a Pareto distribution. In fact, the ability of these surveys to approximate a comparable total personal income from National Accounts was extremely limited.[49] They generated the first distribution series to be comparable in time (Alcaide Inchausti 1967, 1974; Alcaide and Alcaide 1974, 1977, 1983). According to their estimates, the top 10 per cent received 36.8 per cent, 41.3 per cent, 40.7 per cent, 39.5 per cent, and 29.2 per cent of income respectively, stressing a decrease in inequality levels from 1973/4 to 1980/1.[50]

In 1963 the INE launched the publication *Salarios*, based on an annual employers' survey for workers legally employed by any firm employing at least ten individuals. The survey covered most of the industrial sector, construction, and some services, but excluded the agricultural sector, non-road transportation, leisure, and civil service. Respondents were about 2,400 establishments that reported on the number of workers and their average salary by wage intervals. The survey had important methodological revisions in 1976 and 1981. Albi Ibáñez (1975) computed Gini coefficients from this wage survey between 1963 and 1972, finding an increasing trend in earnings inequality; Cordero, Melis, and Quesada (1988) compared the 1982 and 1986 wage surveys and also found a growing level of wage concentration.[51]

Between 1964 and 1980, the INE published an annual report on national income and distribution (Instituto Nacional de Estadística 1965–70 and 1971–80), but the information was extremely limited and focused not on the personal but on the functional distribution of aggregate income from National Accounts; it also included a summary of the main results from the wage survey mentioned above.

---

[49] The differences between National Accounts and household surveys regarding income measurement have been analysed in Deaton (2005) and the Canberra Expert Group on Household Income Statistics (2001).

[50] As an example, the magnitude of the corrections applied by these studies can be seen from the fact that, according to the 1980/1 survey, the top 10% received 25.4% of income before any correction was made.

[51] See Cordero, Melis, and Quesada (1988) for an account of the limitations of the wage survey since 1981.

Based on the 1980/1 households' budget survey, Ruiz-Castillo (1987) studied inequality using the information about expenditure and not income. Bosch, Escribano, and Sánchez (1989) applied the same methodology to compare the 1973/4 and 1980/1 surveys. A new comparison between the 1973/4 and 1980/1 surveys is presented in Ruiz-Castillo (1998). Ruiz-Castillo and Sastre (1999) added the comparison with the 1990/1 survey. The authors find a considerable drop in inequality between 1973/4 and 1980/1; given the increase of per capita expenditure, they conclude that a rise in welfare took place. For the 1980s decade, they observe an increase in the average expenditure but a stop in the pattern of reduction in inequality that took place during the previous decade. These studies have been extended in Del Rio and Ruiz-Castillo (2001a, 2001b). Gradín (2000, 2002) has used the EPFs to analyse polarization and inequality from 1973 to 1991.[52]

Notwithstanding the different levels reported in inequality indexes and the different variable analysed (income, expenditure), the studies based on households' surveys show a decrease in inequality during the 1970s.

Research has also been done on the basis of the European Community Household Panel (ECHP). See, for example, Pascual and Sarabia (2004) for an analysis of the period 1993–2000 (they find a drop in inequality in 1993–4, a sustained increase in 1994–6, and a new decrease in 1997–2000; overall inequality measured by the Gini coefficient seems to display a small overall reduction), and Ayala and Sastre (2005) for mobility issues between 1994 and 1998. Budría and Díaz-Giménez (2007) analyse in detail the 1998 ECHP wave, as well as income mobility between 1994 and 1998.

Starting in 1985, the INE developed a continuous households' survey. Oliver, Ramos, and Raymond (2001) have used this source between 1985 and 1996 and document an improvement in income distribution for the whole period according to several indicators; nevertheless, the reported Gini coefficient for 1996 is statistically equal to that of 1987.

More recently, researchers have used income tax data to assess inequality, providing a different picture when compared to results from households' surveys. Castañer (1991) and Lasheras, Rabadán, and Salas (1993) analyse the redistributive power of the income tax; the authors show that several inequality indicators grew steadily between 1982 and 1990. Ayala and Onrubia (2001) use the income tax panel between 1982 and 1994 and income tax tabulations between 1995 and 1998 to compute Gini indices. They do not consider capital gains. They observe an increasing inequality trend between 1982 and 1991, followed by a relative stability until 1994, and a new increasing trend after 1995, which the authors attribute to a growing inequality in the wage distribution. Rodríguez and Salas (2006) use the income tax panel to analyse the redistributive consequences of the income tax reforms between 1982 and 1995.

Finally, both survey and tax sources have been used to study tax reforms, as in Díaz and Sebastián (2004) and González-Torrabadella and Pijoan-Mas (2006), among others.

REFERENCES

Albi Ibáñez, E. (1975). 'La distribución de la renta personal en España (1964–1967–1970)', *Hacienda pública española*, 32: 53–66.

—— (2006). *Sistema fiscal español*, 21st edn. Barcelona: Ariel.

---

[52] Other studies include Medel, Molina, and Sánchez (1988), Escribano (1990), Ayala, Martínez, and Ruiz-Huerta (1993), Alvarez et al. (1996).

Albiñana, C. (1969a). 'La contribución general sobre la renta en los años 1953–1954', *Revista española de economía política*, 51–2: 7–58.

—— (1969b). 'Evolución histórico-normativa de la contribución general sobre la renta', *Revista española de economía política*, 51–2: 327–72.

—— J. Cañada, J. Fernández, J. Martínez, E. Sanz, and R. Villegas (1974). 'La inspección del impuesto sobre la renta de las personas físicas', *Hacienda pública española*, 30: 269–89.

Alcaide, A. and J. Alcaide (1974). 'Metodología para la estimación de la distribución personal de la renta en España en 1970', *Hacienda pública española*, 26: 55–63.

—— —— (1977). 'Distribución personal de la renta en España y otros países de la OECD', *Hacienda pública española*, 47: 17–57.

—— —— (1983). 'Distribución personal de la renta española en 1980', *Hacienda pública española*, 85: 485–509.

Alcaide Inchausti, J. (1967). 'La renta nacional en España y su distribución', *Revista sindical de estadística*, 68: 2–49.

—— (1974). 'Así se distribuye la riqueza y la renta en la sociedad española', *Revista sindical de estadística*, 116(29): 2–32.

—— (1999). 'Distribución sectorial, factorial y personal de la renta', in J. L. García Delgado (ed.) *España, economía: ante el siglo XXI*. Madrid: Espasa: 457–81.

Alvaredo, F. and E. Saez (2009). 'Income and Wealth Concentration in Spain from a Historical and Fiscal Perspective', *Journal of the European Economic Association*, 7(5): 1140–67.

Alvarez, C., L. Ayala, I. Oriondo, R. Martínez, R. Palacio, and J. Ruiz-Huerta (1996). 'La distribución funcional y personal de la renta en España', Colección Estudios 30. Madrid: Consejo Económico y Social.

Alvarez Rey, L. (2007). 'Reforma y contrareforma agraria durante la Segunda República: Carmona 1931–1936', *Carel, revista de estudios locales*, 5(5): 194–245.

Atkinson, A. B. and T. Piketty (2007). *Top Incomes over the Twentieth Century: A Contrast between European and English Speaking Countries*. Oxford: Oxford University Press.

Ayala, L., R. Martínez, and J. Ruiz-Huerta (1993). 'La distribución de la renta en España en los años ochenta: una perspectiva comparada', in L. Gutiérrez and J. Almunia (eds.) *La distribución de la renta*, vol. ii. Madrid: Fundación Argentaria.

—— and J. Onrubia (2001). 'La distribución de la renta en España según datos fiscales', *Papeles de economía española*, 88: 89–125.

—— and M. Sastre (2005). 'La movilidad de ingresos en España', *Revista de economía aplicada*, 38: 123–58.

Bosch, A., C. Escribano, and I. Sánchez (1989). *Evolución de la desigualdad y la pobreza en España: estudio basado en las encuestas de presupuestos familiares 1973/1974 y 1980/1981*. Madrid: INE.

Bover, O. (2004). 'Encuesta financiera de las familias españolas (EFF): descripción y métodos de la encuesta de 2002', Banco de España, Documentos Ocasionales No. 0409.

Breña Cruz, F., J. Cortés, R. Drake, J. Fernández, A. Gota, and D. Sáenz (1974). 'La administración del impuesto general sobre la renta', *Hacienda pública española*, 30: 231–67.

Budría, S. and J. Díaz-Giménez (2007). 'Economic Inequality in Spain: The European Community Household Panel Dataset', *Spanish Economic Review*, 1: 1–38.

Canberra Expert Group on Household Income Statistics (2001). *Final Report and Recommendations*. Ottawa.

Carrión, P. (1972). *Los latifundios en España: su importancia, origen, consecuencias y solución*. Barcelona: Ariel.

—— (1973). *La reforma agraria de la Segunda República y la situación actual de la agricultura española*. Barcelona: Ariel.

Castañer, J. M. (1991). 'El efecto redistributivo del IRPF 1982–1988', *Hacienda pública española*, Monográfico 2.

Castillo López, J. (1992). *El fraude fiscal en España*. Granada: Editorial Comares.

Comín, F. (1985). *Fuentes cuantitativas para el estudio del sector público en España 1801–1980*. Monografía 40, Instituto de Estudios Fiscales.

—— (1994). 'El fraude fiscal en la historia: un planteamiento de sus fases', in *Hacienda pública española*, Monografías 1/1994: 31–46, Madrid.

—— and J. Zafra Oteyza (1994). *El fraude fiscal en la historia de España*. Madrid: Instituto de Estudios Fiscales.

Cordero, M. F. Melis and J. Quesada (1988). 'La distribución personal de los salarios en 1982 y 1986', *Boletín trimestral de Coyuntura*, INE, 28: 51, 68.

Deaton, A. (2005). 'Measuring Poverty in a Growing World (or Measuring Growth in a Poor World)', *Review of Economic and Statistics*, 87(1): 1–19.

Del Río, Coral and J. Ruiz-Castillo (2001a). 'Intermediate Inequality and Welfare: The Case of Spain, 1980–81 to 1990–91', *Review of Income and Wealth*, 47(2): 221–38.

—— —— (2001b). 'Accounting for the Decline in Spanish Household Expenditures Inequality during the 1980s', *Spanish Review of Economics*, 3: 151–75.

Díaz, M. and M. Sebastián (2004). 'Ideas para una reforma fiscal en España', in J. Perez, C. Sebastián, and P. Tedde (eds.) *Políticas, mercados e instituciones económicas: estudios en homenaje a Luis Angel Rojo*, vol i. Madrid: Editorial Complutense.

Díaz Fuentes, D. (1994). 'Fraude y amnistías fiscales en la España contemporánea, 1940–1990', in Comín and Zafra Oteyza (1994).

Durán, J. and A. Esteller (2007). 'An Empirical Analysis of Wealth Taxation: Equity vs. Tax Compliance', Institut d'Economia de Barcelona Working Paper 1/2007.

Escribano, C. (1990). 'Evolución de la pobreza y la desigualdad en España 1973–1987', *Información comercial española*, 686: 81–108.

Febrer, A. and J. Mora (2005). 'Wage Distribution in Spain, 1994–1999: An Application of a Flexible Estimator of Conditional Distributions', IVIE Working Papers, EC-2005–04.

Feenberg, D. and J. Poterba (1993). 'Income Inequality and the Incomes of Very High Income Taxpayers: Evidence from Tax Returns', in J. Poterba (ed.) *Tax Policy and the Economy*, vol. vii. Cambridge, Mass.: MIT Press: 145–77.

Feldstein, M. (1999). 'Tax Avoidance and the Deadweight Loss of the Income Tax', *Review of Economics and Statistics*, 81(4): 674–80.

García Caracuel, M. (2004). 'Las prestaciones tributarias a cuenta: perspectivas de Reforma', Departamento de Derecho Financiero y Tributario. Granada: Universidad de Granada.

Garde, J., J. Ruiz-Huerta, and R. Martínez (1995). 'Los estudios sobre distribución de la renta en España: fuentes, resultados, perspectivas de futuro', Instituto de Estudios Fiscales, Papeles de Trabajo No. 18.

Goerlich, F. and M. Mas (2001). 'Inequality in Spain 1973–91: Contribution to a Regional Database', *Review of Income and Wealth*, 47(3): 361–78.

—— —— (2004). 'Distribución personal de la renta en España. 1973–2001', *Papeles de economía española*, 100: 50–8.

González-Torrabadella, M. and J. Pijoan-Mas (2006). 'Flat Tax Reforms: A General Equilibrium Evaluation for Spain', *Investigaciones económicas*, 30(2): 317–51.

Gordon, R. and J. Slemrod (2000). 'Are Real Responses to Taxes Simply Income Shifting between Corporate and Personal Tax Bases?', in J. Slemrod (ed.) *Does Atlas Shrug? The Economic Consequences of Taxing the Rich*. Cambridge: Cambridge University Press.

Gota Losada, A. (1966). 'La política fiscal y la agilidad de gestión en los impuestos generales sobre la renta en España', Conferencia Pronunciada en la Asamblea Annual de la Mutualidad del Cuerpo de Inspectores Diplomados de los Tributos, Madrid.

—— (1970). 'La realidad de la imposición personal sobre la renta', *Hacienda pública española*, 3: 17–42.

Gradín, C. (2000). 'Polarization by Sub-populations in Spain, 1973–91', *Review of Income and Wealth*, 46(4): 457–74.

—— (2002). 'Polarization and Inequality in Spain: 1973–91', *Journal of Income Distribution*, 11(1–2): 34–52.

Información Comercial Española (1962). *Monográfico sobre la distribución de la renta en España*, No. 352.

Instituto de Estudios Agro-Sociales (1958). *Proyecto de fomento para la región Mediterránea*. Madrid: Ministerio de Agricultura.

Instituto de Estudios Fiscales (1973). *Informe sobre el sistema tributario español*. Madrid.

—— (1974). Estadística, *Hacienda pública española*, 30: 473–89.

—— (n.d.). *BADESPE: Base de datos económicos del sector público español*.

Instituto Nacional de Estadística (1965–70). *Informe sobre la distribución de las rentas*. Madrid.

—— (1971–80). *La renta nacional y su distribución*. Madrid.

Kuznets, S. (1953). *Shares of Upper Income Groups in Income and Savings*. New York: National Bureau of Economic Research.

Landais, C. (2007). 'Les Hauts Revenus en France (1998–2006): une explosion des inégalités?', Paris School of Economics Working Paper, June.

Lasheras, M., I. Rabadán, and R. Salas (1993). 'Política redistributiva en el IRPF entre 1982 y 1990', *Actas del I Simposio sobre Igualdad y Distribución de la Renta y la Riqueza*. Madrid: viii. 7–24.

Maddison, A. (2001). *The World Economy: A Millennial Perspective*. Paris: OECD.

—— (2003). *The World Economy: Historical Statistics*. Paris: OECD.

Malefakis, E. (1971). *Reforma agraria y revolución campesina en la España del siglo XX*. Barcelona: Ariel.

Martí Basterrechea, J. (1974). 'El impuesto general sobre la renta de las personas físicas', *Hacienda pública española*, 30: 75–89.

Martín-Guzmán, P., M. Toledo, N. Bellido, J. López, and N. Jano (1996). *Encuesta de presupuestos familiares, desigualdad y pobreza en España: estudio basado en las Encuestas de Presupuestos Familiares de 1973–74, 1980–81 y 1990–91*. Instituto Nacional de Estadística and Universidad Autónoma de Madrid.

Medel, B., A. Molina, and J. Sánchez (1988). 'Los efectos del gasto público en España', Documentos de Trabajo de la Fundación FIES, 28.

Moriguchi, C. and E. Saez (2008) 'The Evolution of Income Concentration in Japan, 1886–2005: Evidence from Income Tax Statistics', *Review of Economics and Statistics*, 90(4): 713–34.

Oliver I Alonso, J., X. Ramos Morilla, and J. L. Raymond Bara (2001). 'Anatomía de la distribución de la renta en España, 1985–1996: la continuidad de la mejora', *Papeles de economía española*, 88: 67–87.

Park, T. S. (2000). 'Comparison of BEA Estimates of Personal Income and IRS Estimates of Adjusted Gross Income', *Survey of Current Business*, November: 7–13.

Pascual, M. and J. M. Sarabia (2004). 'Factores determinantes de la distribución personal de la renta: un estudio empírico a partir del PHOGHE', Instituto de Estudios Fiscales.

Piketty, T. (2001). *Les Hauts Revenus en France au 20ème siècle: inégalités et redistributions, 1901–1998*. Paris: Éditions Grasset.

—— (2003). 'Income Inequality in France 1901–1998', *Journal of Political Economy*, 111 (5): 1004–42.

—— and E. Saez (2003). 'Income Inequality in the United States, 1913–1998', *Quarterly Journal of Economics*, 118(1): 1–39.

—— —— (2007). 'Income Inequality in the United States, 1913–2002', in Atkinson and Piketty (2007).

Prados De La Escosura, L. (2003). *El progreso económico de España, 1850–2000*. Madrid: Fundación BBVA.

—— (2006a). 'Growth, Inequality, and Poverty in Spain, 1850–2000: Evidence and Speculation', Working Papers in Economic History wp 06–04, Universidad Carlos III.

—— (2006b). 'Growth and Structural Change in Spain, 1850–2000', Working Papers in Economic History wp 06–05, Universidad Carlos III.

—— (2007). 'Growth and Structural Change in Spain, 1850–2000: A European Perspective', *Revista de historia económica/Journal of Iberian and Latin American Economic History*, 25(1): 147–81.

—— (2008). 'Inequality, Poverty, and the Kuznets Curve in Spain, 1850–2000', *European Review of Economic History*, 12(3): 287–324.

Rodríguez, J. G. and R. Salas (2006). 'The Spanish Progressive Income Taxation Evidence', Universidad Complutense de Madrid, mimeo.

Ruiz-Castillo, J. (1987). 'La medición de la pobreza y la desigualdad en España', Servicio de Estudios del Banco de España, Estudios Económicos, No. 42, Madrid.

—— (1998). 'A Simplified Model for Social Welfare Analysis: An Application to Spain, 1973–74 to 1980–81', *Review of Income and Wealth*, 44: 123–41.

—— and M. Sastre (1999). 'Desigualdad y bienestar en España en términos reales: 1973–74, 1980–81 y 1990–91', in *Dimensiones de la desigualdad: Tercer Simposio sobre Igualdad y Distribución de la Renta y la Riqueza*, vol. i. Madrid: Fundación Argentaria, Colección Igualdad: 345–66.

Saez, E. (2004). 'Reported Incomes and Marginal Tax Rates, 1960–2000: Evidence and Policy Implications', in J. Poterba (ed.) *Tax Policy and the Economy*, 18. Cambridge, Mass.: MIT Press.

—— and M. R. Veall (2005). 'The Evolution of Top Incomes in Northern America: Lessons from Canadian Evidence', *American Economic Review*, 95(3): 831–49.

Seligman, E. R. A. (1911). *The Income Tax*. New York: Macmillan.

Slemrod, J. (1995). 'Income Creation or Income Shifting? Behavioral Responses to the Tax Reform Act of 1986', *American Economic Review*, 85(2): 175–80.

—— (1996). 'High Income Families and the Tax Changes of the 1980s: The Anatomy of Behavioral Response', in M. Feldstein and J. Poterba (eds.) *Empirical Foundations of Household Taxation*. Chicago: University of Chicago Press.

Vallejo Pousada, R. (1995). 'El impuesto sobre la renta en España: antecedentes y evolución hasta 1978', in F. Comín (ed.) *La práctica fiscal en la España contemporánea: una historia de la administración tributaria (1800–1990)*. Madrid: Instituto de Estudios Fiscales.

11

Top Incomes and Earnings in Portugal, 1936–2005

Facundo Alvaredo

11.1 INTRODUCTION

This chapter analyses the evolution of income and wage concentration in Portugal between 1936 and 2005 using tax statistics and administrative records on individual earnings. Together with the chapters on Italy and Spain, this completes the study of top income shares in three southern European countries for which tax data are available. The case of Portugal is interesting and worth studying on several grounds.

First, Portugal has undergone important changes in the political arena since the beginning of the twentieth century. After the decline and final collapse of the constitutional monarchy, the First Republic was established in 1910. The parliamentary regime was turbulent and unstable, with eight presidents, thirty-eight prime ministers, and a brief monarchy restoration over a seventeen-year period.[1] Participation in the First World War on the Entente side, large government deficits, rapid monetary expansion, and high inflation dominated the scenario. The First Republic was ended in 1926 by a military coup, which installed an authoritarian republic followed by seven years of institutional change. There was no apocalyptic civil war as in Spain and the ultimate leader of the new regime was not a general, but a university professor, António Salazar, who believed that neither English parliamentarism nor English democracy were adaptable to every European country.[2] The Second Republic evolved to a right-wing dictatorship under the form of a single party corporative regime. In the absence of the clear polarization of Spanish society, the authoritarian system developed in a framework of institutional continuity. In 1928 Salazar was appointed minister of

This chapter is a longer version of 'Top Incomes and Earnings in Portugal, 1936-2005' (Alvaredo 2009). I thank Jose Albuquerque, Tony Atkinson, Santiago Budría, Ana Rute Cardoso, Jordi Guilera, Manoel João, Pedro Lains, Alfredo Pereira, Thomas Piketty, Leandro Prados de la Escosura Carlos Farinha Rodrigues, Emmanuel Saez, and three anonymous referees for comments and discussions. Special acknowledgements go to António Manuel Sá Santos and the staff of the Centro de Estudos Fiscais at the Direcçao-Geral dos Impostos and the Instituto Nacional de Estatística of Portugal.

[1] For an account of the history of Portugal until the late 1960s, see Payne (1972). See also Robinson (1979) and Gallaher (1983).

[2] Salazar (1939).

finance, and in 1933 he became prime minister, remaining in power until 1968. From the early 1930s to the end of the 1950s, Portugal followed a policy of relative isolationism under a corporatist socio-economic system (extensive state regulation and private ownership of means of production). In the late 1950s, the regime shifted towards a moderately outward-looking policy, which inaugurated a period of rapid growth until the beginning of the 1970s. Like Spain, Portugal remained neutral during the Second World War, but unlike Spain, it was accepted into the Marshall plan in 1947 and NATO in 1949. In 1974 a left-wing military coup (known as the Carnation Revolution) put an end to the dictatorship. The revolutionary government granted independence to the Portuguese colonies in Africa and Asia, set out on a course of land expropriation and sweeping nationalization (banks, basic industries, utilities, insurance companies, newspapers), and followed a policy of freezing prices and raising wages. The process has been described as a successful challenge to capitalist property.[3] In 1975 the country held its first free multi-party elections since 1926. By the beginning of the 1980s most of the reforms of the revolutionary period started to be reversed, one of the motivating factors being Portugal joining the European Communities, which happened in 1986. The country adopted the euro in 2002. The study of top incomes in Portugal provides new insights on the relationships between the political regimes and the evolution of income concentration.

Second, from the economic point of view, Portugal underwent dramatic changes over the last hundred years. During the first half of the twentieth century, the country was an agricultural-based economy in which wine accounted for one-third of total agrarian output.[4] In 1950, Portugal GDP per capita was 15 per cent lower than in Spain, 60 per cent lower than in France, and 70 per cent lower than in the United Kingdom.[5] Between the 1950s and the beginning of the 1970s the government shifted towards mild liberalization policies and imposed a strategy aimed at economic development and structural change; economic growth resumed at a quicker pace. However, the growth rates of per capita income in those years should be read with caution in the light of massive emigration flows between 1950 and the early 1980s.[6] In the 1970s growth came to a halt, affected by the revolution of 1974, the nationalization spree, and the less favourable international conditions. Since the mid 1980s, the privatization of major financial and industrial conglomerates and the fiscal and monetary policies followed to join the European Union have started a period of considerable modernization and growth. Today, Portugal's GDP per capita is about 30–5 per cent lower than

---

[3] Bermeo (1997).

[4] Lains (2003a, 2003b) argues that, despite its backwardness, the Portuguese economy had a good performance during the first half of the twentieth century if compared to the previous fifty years. The economy expanded slowly under favourable external conditions before 1913, and expanded more rapidly when international economic conditions were less favourable after the First World War. Nevertheless, improvements were poor by Western European standards. See also Lains (2003c).

[5] Comparative data from Maddison (2001, 2003).

[6] The debate around the dynamic or stagnating features of the *Estado Novo* economic policy can be seen in Baklanoff (1992), Hudson (1989), ILO (1979), and Wheeler (1990).

the GDP per capita of the largest Western European economies such as France, Germany, or the United Kingdom, and about 20 per cent lower than the GDP per capita of Spain.[7] As in the case of Spain, it is important to analyse income concentration during the growth and stagnation years in order to reassess the link between economic development and income distribution.

Third, Portugal (as well as Spain) provides new evidence on the relationship between economic integration and income concentration. As mentioned above, the country joined the European Union in 1986, after seven years of gradual reforms for the dismantling of barriers to trade, capital, and labour mobility.

Finally, there are no studies on the evolution of inequality in Portugal from a long-run historical perspective. Therefore, this study can be seen as the first serious attempt at compiling systematic time series of income concentration using primarily individual tax statistics, which have been completely ignored by previous studies.[8]

A number of researchers have analysed the evolution of income, earnings, and expenditure inequality during the *last thirty years* in Portugal based on two types of sources: survey data and administrative records on wages and salaries. In the following paragraphs I summarize the main findings.[9]

Using micro-data from the 1980/1 and 1990/1 households' surveys, Rodrigues (1993, 1994, 1996) and Gouveia and Tavares (1995) detect an unambiguous decline in income inequality during the 1980s.[10] In particular, Rodrigues (1994) finds that wages and capital income inequality rose, but their effects were nonetheless offset by the evolution of self-employees' income and pensions. On the contrary, Gouveia and Tavares (1995) argue that the reduction in inequality during the 1980s could have been the result of the trade–earnings argument acting in reverse in Portugal: increased trade with Europe might have reinforced the country's specialization in low-skilled activities and therefore increased wages of unskilled workers. Nevertheless, the returns to education augmented substantially during the years after joining the European Union, as shown in Machado and Mata (2001) and Hartog, Pereira, and Vieira (2001).[11]

----

[7] For an account of the economic evolution of Portugal during the twentieth century, see Lains (1995), Lopes (1994, 1996), Nunes, Mata, and Valério (1989), and Valério (2001).

[8] During the completion of this chapter there came to my attention the work by Guilera (2008), which uses tax statistics to study income concentration in Portugal.

[9] The first two households' budget surveys were conducted in 1967/8 and 1973/4. As is usually the case, their primary purpose was to collect information on expenditures, required as input to the construction of the consumer price index. As a result, the 1967/8 survey did not contain income information. The 1973/4 survey did inquire about incomes. Descriptive results from these two first surveys can be found in Castinheira and Ribeiro (1977), Rodrigues (1988), and Silva (1971). However, the micro-data have not survived. Since the 1980/1 survey, information has been collected on household income, household composition, and other socio-economic characteristics.

[10] This conclusion relies on the comparison of both surveys, implying that it is not possible to rigorously establish the evolution of income inequality in the intermediate years.

[11] Murray and Steedman (1998) analyse the evolution of workers' skills in France, Germany, the Netherlands, Portugal, Sweden, and the United Kingdom and show that the greatest change in the qualification of the young has taken place in Portugal. Batista (2002) finds, however, that the skill premium in Portugal has fallen since the mid 1990s.

Based on the employees' administrative records that I also use as a data source in this chapter, Cardoso (1998a) analyses the years 1983–92 and finds that rising inequality characterized the evolution of labour returns over the whole period, the upper part of the earnings distribution playing a major role in shaping both the level and the trend of inequality. One feature stands out: a stretched top, where dispersion increased remarkably. The same trend has been described in OECD (1992) and Ministério do Emprego (1992), which reports a 10 per cent rise in the Gini index for earnings from 1982 to 1989.[12]

Research has also been done on the basis of the European Community Household Panel (ECHP). Rodrigues (1999) compares the 1994/5 households' survey with the 1995 ECHP. Budría (2007) analyses in detail the ECHP between 1994 and 2001 and documents a reduction in earnings and income inequality as well as a rise in the concentration of capital income during that period.

The series presented in this chapter measure only top income (and wage) concentration and hence are silent about changes in the lower and middle parts of the distribution. Therefore, they can very well follow different patterns when compared to global inequality measures such as Gini coefficients or macro-based estimates. Additionally, it is worth remembering that the rich are usually missing from surveys either for sampling reasons or because they refuse to cooperate with the time-consuming task of completing or answering a long form. This explains the fact that the dynamics of top income shares estimated from tax statistics may not resemble those deriving from survey data. In particular, high-income earners in this study are much richer than those described in Budría (2007), whose results are based on the ECHP.[13]

My results show that income concentration was much higher during the 1930s and 1940s than it is today. Top income shares stayed relatively stable between the end of the Second World War and the end of the 1960s, followed by a large drop that began to be reversed at the beginning of the 1980s. Over the last fifteen years top income shares have increased steadily, and the rise in wage concentration contributed to the process to a great extent.

The chapter is organized as follows. Section 11.2 describes the data sources and outlines the estimation methods. Section 11.3 presents and analyses the evolution

---

[12] Other studies on income and earnings inequality in Portugal over the last three decades include Albuquerque and Gouveia (1994), Budría and Nunes (2005), Budría and Pereira (2007, 2008), Cantó, Cardoso, and Jimeno (2002), Cardoso (1994, 1998b, 1999, 2006), Carneiro (2008), Castanheira and Carvalho (1997), Costa (1994), Ferreira (1992), Gouveia and Rodrigues (2002), Hartog, Pereira, and Vieira (1999), Jimeno et al. (2000), Martins and Pereira (2004), Rodrigues (2008), Rodrigues and Albuquerque (2000), Santos (1983), Teekens (1990), Vieira (1999), Viera, Couto, and Tiago (2006). Cardoso and Cunha (2005) estimate aggregate wealth owned by Portuguese households between 1980 and 2004; however the authors do not deal with the distribution of wealth. Bover, García-Perea, and Portugal (1998) study the Portuguese and the Spanish labour markets from a comparative perspective.

[13] According to the results presented in Budría (2007), an income of at least 73,330 (in 2005 euros) was required in 2001 to belong to the top 1%, which had an average income of 88,660. My estimations of top fractile income levels show that the top 1% had an average income of 142,500, while an income of 73,330 only qualified as top 5–1%; see Table 11D.2. Budría's unit of analysis is the household; mine is the tax unit defined as the married couple or single adult.

of top incomes between 1936 and 2005. Section 11.4 focuses on earnings concentration. Finally, section 11.5 offers a brief conclusion. The details on data
sources and methods together with the complete set of results are presented in the
appendices to this chapter.

11.2 DATA AND METHODOLOGICAL ISSUES

I study top income shares and wage concentration based on three data sources:
statistics from the personal income tax, information from schedule taxes on
wages and salaries, and micro-data from administrative records on earnings.

Income

The estimates of top income shares are based on personal income tax return
statistics compiled by the Bureau of Statistics and the tax agency of Portugal from
1936 to 1982 and between 1989 and 2005. Before 1976, because of high exemption levels, only a small fraction of individuals had to file a tax return; consequently I must restrict the analysis to the top 0.1 per cent of the income
distribution. From 1976 onwards, I can analyse the top 10 per cent.

Top groups are defined relative to the total number of tax units had everyone
been required to file a tax return. The unit to which the tax data relate is the
married couple, or single adult, or single minor with income in his or her own
right above a given threshold. The reference total for tax units takes this fact into
account. Consequently the total number of tax units is defined as the number of
all adult males and females (aged 20 and over) less the number of married
females.[14] For example, in 2005, there are 8,387,000 adults in the Portuguese
population, 5,759,000 tax units, and 4,294,000 tax files. The top 1 per cent
represents the top 57,590 tax filers.

I define income as gross income before all deductions and including all income
items reported on personal tax returns: salaries and pensions, self-employment
and unincorporated business net income, dividends, other investment income,
rents, and other smaller income items. Interest income (taxed at the source) is not
included. Capital gains were almost completely untaxed before 1989; only a
fraction of them is included in the tax base since 1989, and it is easy to satisfy
the conditions for capital gains to go untaxed (and not reported). In particular,
gains from public debt bonds are exempted, as well as gains from stocks if kept for
more than twelve months. Capital gains from real estate are also untaxed when
they come from the main residence or when their proceeds are used to purchase
real estate property again. No information is available about the distribution of

---

[14] I am implicitly assuming that the number of single people aged less than 20 years old with
enough income to file a tax return is negligible.

Table 11.1 Thresholds and average incomes in top income groups in Portugal in 2005

Percentile threshold (1)	Income threshold (2)	Income groups (3)	Number of tax units (4)	Average income in each group (5)
		Full number of tax units	5,758,946	14,611 €
Top 10%	29,504 €	Top 10–5%	287,947	35,776 €
Top 5%	43,885 €	Top 5–1%	230,358	59,323 €
Top 1%	87,054 €	Top 1–0.5%	28,795	97,812 €
Top 0.5%	113,979 €	Top 0.5–0.1%	23,036	144,044 €
Top 0.1%	206,538 €	Top 0.1–0.01%	5,183	289,503 €
Top 0.01%	557,582 €	Top 0.01%	576	1,012,397 €

Notes: Computations based on income tax return statistics and National Accounts.
Income defined as annual gross income reported on tax returns, before individual income taxes but net of all social contributions.
Amounts are expressed in 2005 euros.
Column (2) reports the income thresholds corresponding to each of the percentiles in column (1). For example, an annual income of at least 29,504 euros is required to belong to the top 10% tax units, etc.

reported capital gains. They are presumably very small. The income definition is before personal income taxes and personal payroll taxes but after employers' payroll taxes and corporate income taxes.[15]

The main data consist of tables displaying the number of tax returns and the amounts reported (gross income, taxable income, tax paid) for a large number of income brackets. As the top tail of the income distribution is very well approximated by Pareto distributions, I use simple parametric interpolation methods to estimate the thresholds and average income levels for each fractile. Details of the estimation technique and the adjustments made to the raw series are provided in the appendices. I then estimate shares of income by dividing the income amounts accruing to each fractile by the series of personal income, defined ideally as total personal income reported on income tax returns, had everybody been required to file a tax return.[16] The total income denominator, described in the appendix, is based on National Accounts statistics. The fact that only a small fraction of tax units file a tax return (especially until 1988) implies that the income denominator cannot be approximated by using income tax statistics only.[17]

Table 11.1 gives thresholds and average incomes for a selection of fractiles in Portugal in 2005.

[15] A description of the evolution of the income tax in Portugal between 1936 and 2005 concerning exemption thresholds, family allowances, main tax deductions, and marginal rates is provided in Appendix Tables 11A.1 and 11A.2.

[16] This methodology follows the same steps as a number of chapters in this volume, and is based on the classical study of Kuznets (1953) as well as on several studies presented in Atkinson and Piketty (2007).

[17] The methodology of using tax returns to compute the level of top incomes, and using national accounts to compute the total income denominator, is standard in historical studies of income inequality. However, it differs from Feenberg and Poterba (1993), who use total income reported on tax returns as their denominator and the total adult population as the number of tax units.

Wages

The estimates of top wage shares are based on two types of sources: (i) tax statistics (the schedule tax on wages until 1982 and the withholding tax at the source on wage income for the modern income tax since 1989) and (ii) micro-data from administrative records (*quadros de pessoal*, 1985–2004).

The tabulations from the schedule tax have essentially the same structure as the one described above for the income tax. They have been compiled by the Portuguese Bureau of Statistics between 1936 and 1982 and display the number of taxed workers and the tax collection for a number of brackets. However, several changes in the tax code, modifications in the coverage of the tax, and the way statistics are presented imply that I can only provide homogeneous estimates for 1964–82. The tabulations based on withholding from wages for the income tax cover the period 1989–2000. I also assume a Pareto distribution to estimate top wage shares. In this case, the top groups are defined relative to the total number of workers while the shares of top wages are defined relative to the total wage bill from National Accounts, net of employer social security contributions.

I also provide estimates of shares of top wages based on micro-data from administrative records, which are available between 1985 and 2004 (1990 and 2001 are missing). Every year, employers are required by law to provide information about the firm and their employees. Civil service and domestic workers are excluded. State-owned companies are included. Agricultural workers are included, although in practice the level of coverage is very low. Top groups are defined in terms of the total number of workers present in the records and the top shares are defined relative to the aggregate wages and salaries in the database.

11.3 TOP INCOME SHARES

Figure 11.1 displays the average personal income per adult and per tax unit along with the consumer price index for the period 1936 to 2005. As Portugal stayed neutral during the Second World War, the impact of the conflict in terms of per capita GDP was relatively small; after the end of the war and up to 1950 growth was positive but low. The gap with the European core began to be partially abridged, though part of the recovery was due more to the negative effects of the war in the rest of the countries rather than to the improvements in Portugal. Rapid growth started in the 1950s and lasted until the beginning of the 1970s. The slowing down of economic growth that followed is generally attributed to the oil shock and to the aftermath of the revolution that ended the dictatorship in 1974. The country experienced a severe economic crisis in the first half of the 1980s, but growth resumed again after Portugal's accession to the European Union in 1986, starting a period in which GDP per capita grew faster than the EU average;

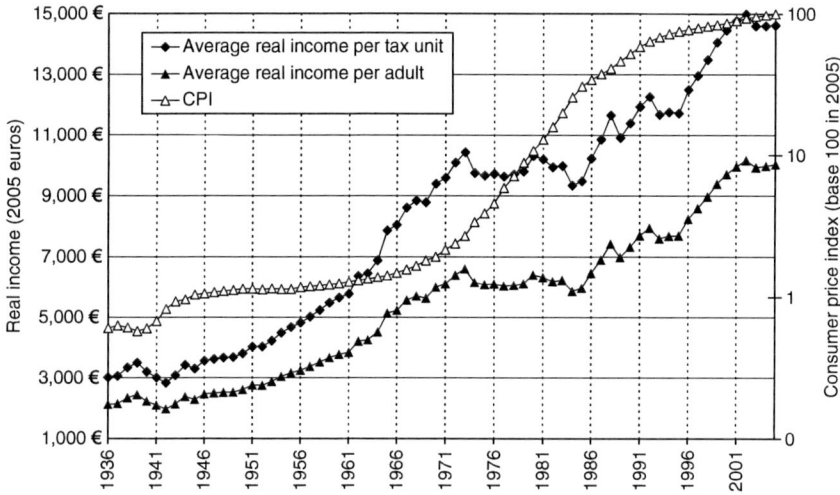

Figure 11.1 Average real income and consumer price index in Portugal, 1936–2005

Notes: Figure reports the average real income per adult (aged 20 and above) and per tax unit, expressed in real 2005 euros. CPI index is equal to 100 in 2005.

Source: Table 11C.1.

however, since 1999 the economy has slowed down and in early 2002 entered a recession.

Figure 11.2 displays the top 0.01 per cent and the top 0.1 per cent income shares between 1936 and 2005. The break between 1982 and 1989 reflects the unavailability of tax data during the five years before the change from the old to the new income tax. A number of important conclusions become apparent. First, the highest income concentration occurred in the 1930s and early 1940s. The top 0.1 per cent share was above 4.5 per cent in 1936, 1941, and 1942 (almost twice as high as in the recent period). This strongly suggests that income concentration in Portugal in the 1930s was substantially higher than it is today. This pattern, also found in the case of Spain and in many of the studies gathered in Atkinson and Piketty (2007) and in this book, should not be unexpected, as Portugal displayed a low average income and a high concentration of wealth.

Second, the old income tax statistics displayed a large decrease in top shares in the first half of the 1940s. This coincided with the Second World War and with a sharp increase in the statutory marginal tax rates: the top rate moved from 8.5 per cent in 1945 to 30 per cent in 1946. However, the income-weighted marginal rates augmented only from 5 per cent to around 9 per cent. If such a drop in the top 0.1 per cent income share were solely due to an increase in the tax evasion/avoidance following the increase in the marginal rate, then the elasticity of high incomes with respect to one minus the marginal tax rate would have been exaggeratedly high.

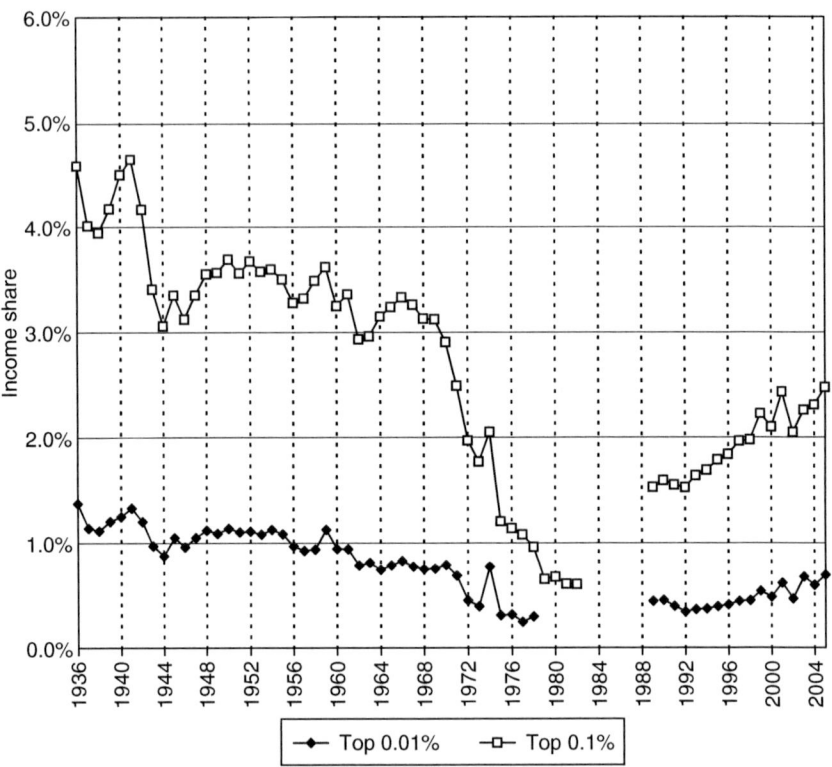

Figure 11.2 The top 0.01% and 0.1% income shares in Portugal, 1936–2005
Source: Table 11D.1, column Top 0.01% and column Top 0.1%.

Third, top income shares recovered partially after the end of the war, this improvement being concentrated in the top 0.1–0.01 per cent. However, such a recovery was small and almost non-existent for the top 0.01 per cent: after 1946 top 0.01 per cent shares hardly attained the values displayed before. Tax statistics providing the composition of reported top incomes show that taxpayers in 1946 (representing the top 0.3 per cent) obtained about 37 per cent of their income from returns on real estate and farm income, 7 per cent from returns on financial assets, 26 per cent from non-farm business income, and about 30 per cent from employment income.[18] This suggests that a significant portion of the very rich were actually passive landowners deriving income from rents and farm business. Such facts are not astonishing in the light of the agricultural-based nature of the Portuguese economy by the middle of the twentieth century; however, they stand in contrast with Spain, where top income earners at that time were much more

---

[18] See Table 11D.3 in Appendix 11D.

likely to be owners of financial assets and non-farm businesses, as shown in Chapter 10 and in Alvaredo and Saez (2009).[19]

Fourth, income concentration remained around 1.0–1.1 per cent for the top 0.01 per cent and around 3.5 per cent for the top 0.1 per cent from 1946 to 1960, suggesting that the high income growth started at the beginning of the 1950s did not produce important changes on income concentration until the beginning of the following decade. Top 0.01 per cent shares in 1962–71 were again stable but slightly lower than the levels observed in 1946–61. It can be concluded that the mild liberalization policies adopted by the government during the third quarter of the twentieth century, and which are usually associated with the increase in growth rates, did not impact on the concentration of income to a great extent.[20] By 1963 the composition of top incomes had not changed in a significant way compared to 1946 either.[21] This reflects the slow changes in the economic structure of the country. The published statistics show that the participation of capital income lost some ground in favour of employment and business income.[22]

Finally, a drastic jump downwards in top shares happened after 1970, and specially after 1974. This coincided with the final period of the dictatorship and could be attributed to the loss of the African colonies and to the leftward movement of the revolutionary government after 1974, when a process of nationalizations broke up the concentration of economic power in the hands of the financial-industrial groups. Banks and insurance companies were nationalized, basic industries became the property of the state, and officials began to call for a

[19] Harsgor (1976) argues that under the old regime, Portugal's private sector was dominated by forty great families. The industrial dynasties were allied by marriage with the large traditional landowning families of the nobility. The top ten families owned all the important commercial banks.

[20] The results in Guilera (2008) show a large rise in top shares in 1964 and 1965, years of the first income assessments under the rules of the 1963 tax reform. The adjustments to the raw data explain the discrepancy between his estimates and mine. Published tabulations provide information on gross incomes until 1963 and on taxable incomes between 1964 and 1982. Gross income equals taxable income plus allowances (mainly fixed amounts for family circumstances, and a fraction of wages up to a cap), which are only reported in the aggregate. For 1964–82 I assumed that each tax filer was entitled to the same allowance. Guilera allocated only a fraction of allowances equally among tax units, and imputed the remaining proportionally to taxable income, generating a jump. Both adjustments are debatable; however, the seeming increase in top shares in Guilera's estimates is due more to changes in the tax regulations and to the treatment of the data than to true economic forces.

[21] It should be noted that the changes in the composition of income shown in Table 11D.3 are affected by the group considered: as composition statistics are only available in the aggregate, they describe the top 0.3% of tax units in 1946 and the top 1.2% of tax units in 1963.

[22] In 1965 a survey of 306 heads (chief executives, presidents) of manufacturing and service enterprises in Portugal's six most industrialized districts (Aveiro, Braga, Lisbon, Oporto, Santarem, and Setúbal) was conducted. The survey included questions pertaining to the socio-economic origins, career patterns, self-image, and opinions of the industrial elite. With the rapid advance of the industry and the growth of cities, new channels of upward mobility seemed to have opened. Makler (1969) reveals that the typical businessman was drawn from a middle-class background. See also Makler (1976).

major programme of large-scale land expropriation.[23] Individuals who had compromised with the old regime were ejected from their posts in universities and government agencies. As described in Bermeo (1987), faced with the real possibility of expropriation or loss of employment, large groups of the Portuguese upper classes simply left the country. Presumably the spike in top shares observed specifically in 1974 was related to a more strict government control over the wealthy (or the fear of it). Consequently, the transition from dictatorship to democracy was associated with a significant drop in top shares.

Top Incomes in the Last Three Decades

The number of tax files has augmented considerably since the mid 1970s; therefore I can analyse the top 10 per cent of the distribution between 1976 and 2005. Figure 11.3 displays top income shares for three groups within the top decile: the bottom half of the top decile (top 10–5 per cent), the next 4 per cent (top 5–1 per cent), and the top percentile. Three elements are worth noticing. First, the decrease in income concentration, started at the beginning of the 1970s and accelerated since 1974, reversed in the early 1980s. Second, although I cannot rigorously establish what happened between 1983 and 1988, the level of income concentration measured with the new income tax statistics in 1989 was noticeably higher than in 1982. Indeed, top shares in the early 1990s were similar to the levels of 1976. This contrasts with the results, obtained from survey data, which point to a relative stable income distribution during the 1980s. Finally, since 1989, the increase in top shares has been higher, the higher the fractile considered.

Figure 11.4 investigates the concentration pattern further by splitting the top 1 per cent into three groups: the top 1–0.5 per cent, the top 0.5–0.1 per cent, and the top 0.1 per cent. Again, the higher the fractile, the higher the increase in the share from 1989 to 2005: the top 1–0.5 per cent increased 30 per cent from 2.5 per cent to 3.3 per cent while the top 0.1 per cent increased over 65 per cent from 1.5 per cent to 2.5 per cent. This pattern has also been found in the cases of Spain (Chapter 10) and Italy (Chapter 12). Alvaredo and Saez (2009) have shown that the increase in income concentration that took place in Spain since 1981 has

---

[23] Between 1974 and 1975 more than 1,300 industrial companies were nationalized; for a detailed account of nationalizations in the industrial sector see Martins and Chaves Rosa (1979). In less than six months 1.2 million hectares were expropriated in the southern and central provinces south of the Tagus river, that is, 13% of the country's surface and 25% of total agricultural land. The occupation of large estates had begun even before a governmental decision gave it legal status through Decree-Law 203C/1975 and Decree-Law 207/1975 (see Barreto 1983, 1987, and 1988). Two thousand houses were seized in the two weeks following the fall of the dictatorship, and only in February 1975 2,500 apartments were occupied in Lisbon alone (see Downs 1983). A decollectivization process started modestly by the end of the 1970s and culminated with the reformed agrarian law enacted in 1988 (Law 109/1988 of 26/9/1988) and with the final setting of monetary compensations for original proprietors (Law 199/1988 of 31/5/1988). By the mid 1990s only one-tenth of the expropriated estates was still in possession of collective farms.

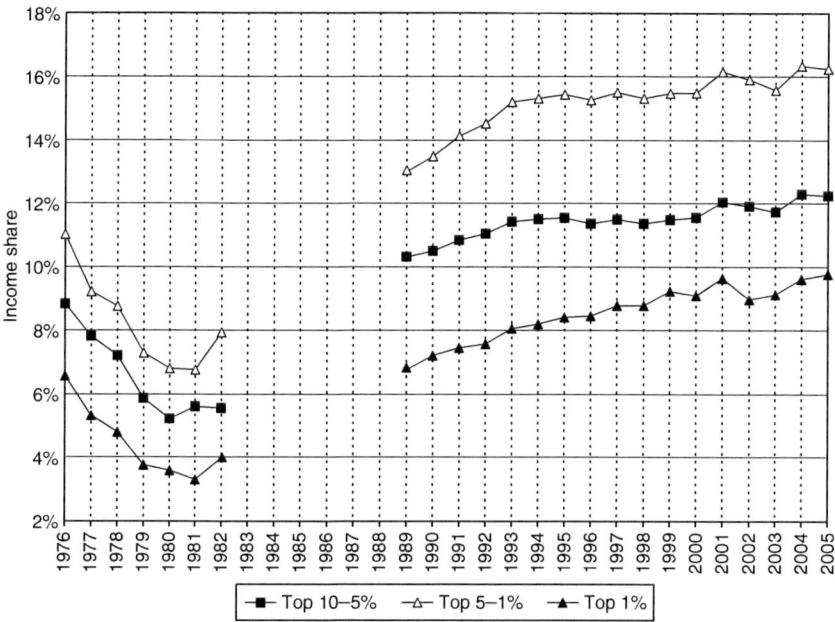

Figure 11.3 The top 10–5%, top 5–1%, and top 1% income shares in Portugal, 1976–2005
Source: Table 11D.1, columns Top 10–5%, Top 5–1%, and Top 1%.

been a phenomenon concentrated within the top 1 per cent of the distribution and in particular within the top 0.1 per cent; the top 10–5 per cent share declined. In Portugal all groups within the top decile displayed important increases.

The break in the series between 1982 and 1989 hides the effects of key changes to the tax structure. Between those years, the top statutory marginal rates came down from 70 per cent (80 per cent for single individuals) to 40 per cent. In 1988 the schedule tax on wages (with a top marginal rate of 22 per cent) was removed. Figure 11.4 displays such a drop. The income-weighted marginal rate for the top 0.1 per cent group dropped from around 62 per cent in 1979 to 40 per cent in 1989. The experience since 1989, when constant top marginal rates coexisted with an increasing trend in top shares, suggest that the level of marginal tax rates at the top cannot be a primary determinant of the level of top reported incomes.

International Comparison

How does Portugal stand in relationship with other countries? Figure 11.5 displays the top 0.1 per cent income shares in Portugal in comparison with a number of economies: Spain (from Chapter 10 and Alvaredo and Saez 2009), Italy (Chapter 12), France (Piketty 2001, Landais 2007), the United States

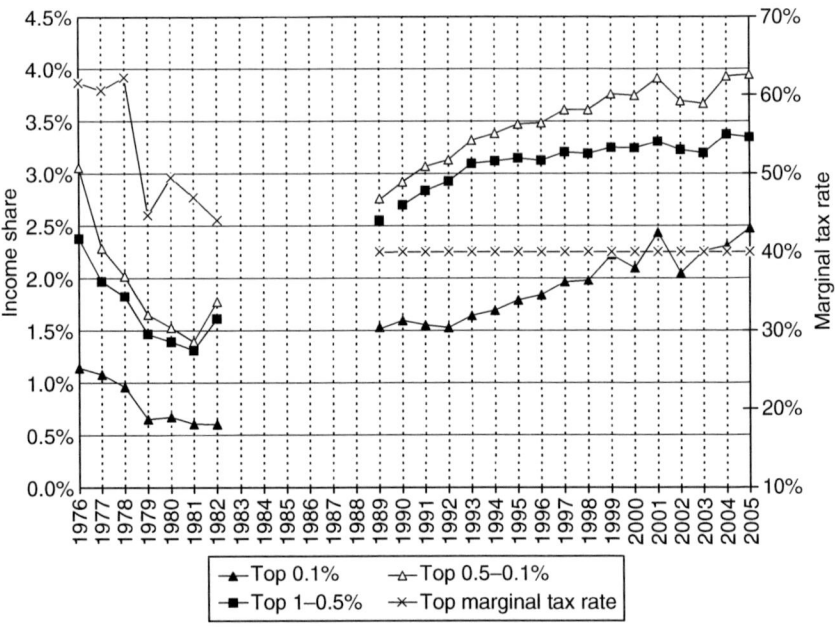

Figure 11.4 The top 1–0.5%, top 0.5–0.1%, and top 0.1% income shares and income-weighted top marginal tax rate in Portugal, 1976–2005

Source: Table 11D.1, columns Top 1–0.5%, Top 0.5–0.1%, and Top 0.1%.

(Piketty and Saez 2003), Switzerland (Dell, Piketty, and Saez 2007), and the United Kingdom (Atkinson 2007). In the early 1940s, Portugal had a level of income concentration that was very similar to that of all the countries shown. Nevertheless, top shares in France and the United States fell more sharply than in Portugal after the Second World War. As a consequence, the level of concentration in Portugal between 1950 and 1970 remained high relative to the other countries, with one exception: between 1945 and the early 1960s the levels of concentration in Portugal and Switzerland were comparable. Between 1960 and the first half of the 1970s, top income shares in Switzerland were higher, but the distance to Portugal narrows if the emigration flows (analysed in the next section) are taken into account. The large drop in top shares since the beginning of the 1970s is noticeable not only in terms of the evolution of concentration in Portugal, but also from a comparative perspective. Nevertheless, it is clear that not all the drop should be attributed to the political turmoil or the economic policies of the revolutionary period: top shares in the UK and Switzerland also experienced important reductions in 1970–5, even when the change in Portugal was definitely more radical. Finally, as in the cases of Spain and Italy, the increase in income concentration in the last years was small compared to the upsurge observed in the United States and other Anglo-Saxon countries; Portugal's experience was closer to those of continental Europe.

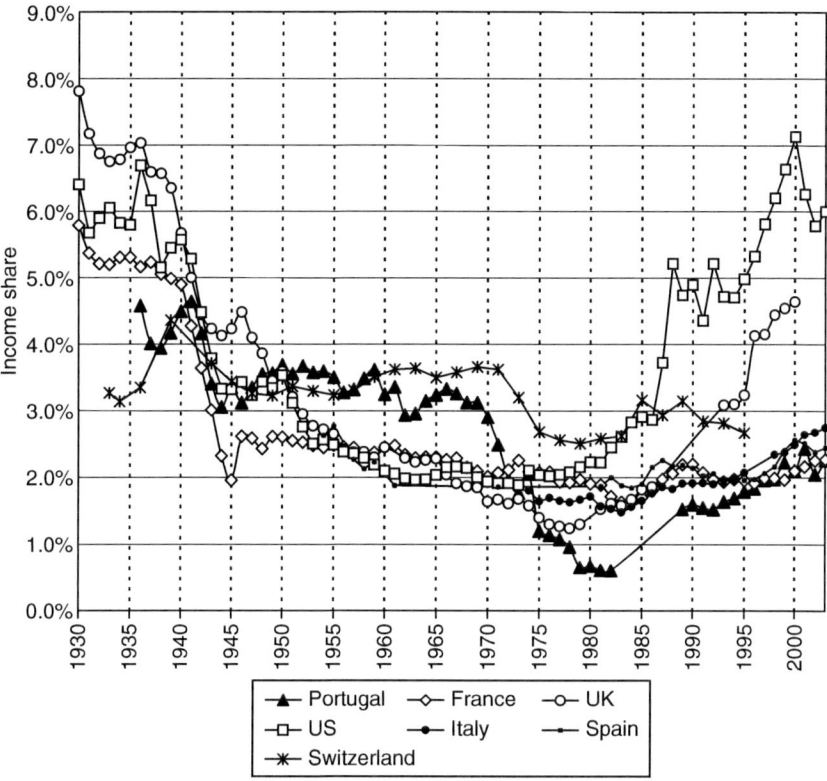

Figure 11.5 Top 0.1% shares in Portugal, UK, Italy, France, Switzerland, United States, and Spain

Sources: US: Piketty and Saez (2003); France: Piketty (2001) and Landais (2007); Spain: Chapter 10 and Alvaredo and Saez (2009): Italy: Chapter 12; UK: Atkinson (2007); Switzerland: Dell, Piketty, and Saez (2007); Portugal: Table 11D.1.

Emigration Flows and Sensitivity of the Results

Emigration has been one of the main features of the Portuguese socio-economic situation in Portugal during the twentieth century. It has provided a safety valve for open and disguised unemployment. According to official estimates, 1.8 million individuals left the country between 1950 and 1975, which is a significant number for a population that only grew from 8.5 million to 9.3 million between those years.[24] I would like to assess the effects of such large-scale migrations on the top shares estimates. Other things equal, adding up all emigrants each year to

[24] Valério (2001).

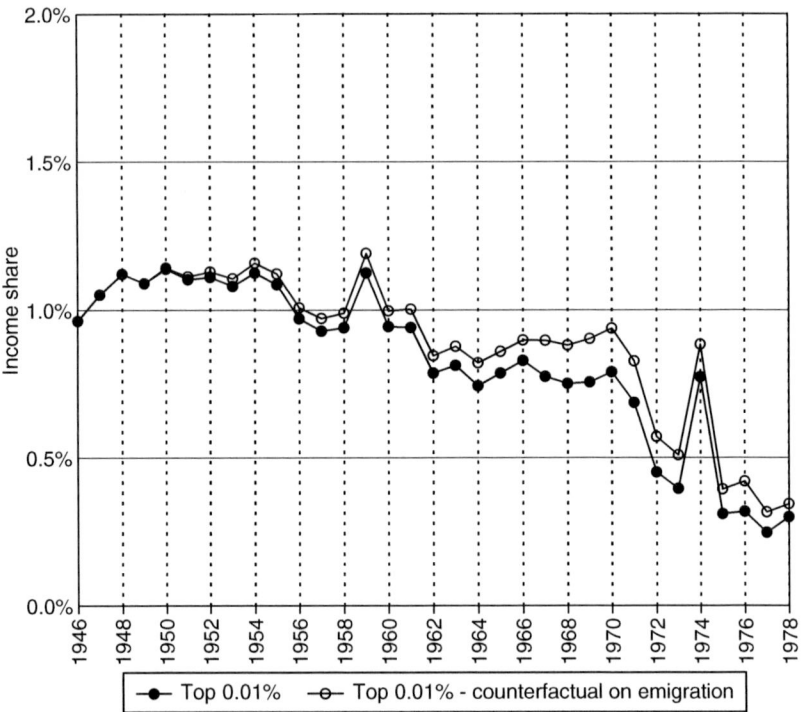

Figure 11.6 The top 0.01% income share in Portugal and counterfactual effects of emigration

the population control provides an *upper bound* for top shares.[25] Such a change increases estimates in 1970 by 19 per cent for the top 0.01 per cent and by 22 per cent for the top 0.1 per cent (meaning that the share of the top 0.01 per cent became 0.94 per cent in place of 0.79 per cent and the share of the top 0.1 per cent became 3.54 per cent in place of 2.91 per cent). The results are presented in Figure 11.6 for the top 0.01 per cent income share between 1946 and 1978 together with the counterfactual estimates. The main results are not altered. Consequently, one of the findings presented in the previous section—that the top 0.01 per cent share remained fairly stable between 1946 and 1961 and also stable between 1962 and 1971 at a slightly lower level—was not driven by the dynamics of migrant flows.

[25] Adding up all emigrants to the population control amounts to assuming that all of them can be considered as tax units, that they are alive throughout the period, and that they would have had little income if they had stayed in Portugal. Therefore it is necessary to go further down in the distribution to locate the top x%. Statistics show that migrants were mostly young males, as described in Conim (1976). Assuming the same growth rate of tax units since 1950 for Portugal as in Spain or France gives very similar results.

11.4 WAGE CONCENTRATION

Unfortunately, tax statistics do not allow for a dynamic analysis of income composition at the top because the Portuguese tax tabulations do not provide information on the composition of top incomes. Notwithstanding this short-coming, I can get more direct evidence on changes in inequality from wage statistics available on an annual homogeneous basis.

As done for overall personal income, Figure 11.7 displays top wage shares between 1964 and 2000 for three groups within the top decile: the bottom half of the top decile (top 10–5 per cent), the next 4 per cent (top 5–1 per cent), and the top percentile; while Figure 11.8 splits the top percentile in three groups: the top 1–0.5 per cent, the top 0.5–0.1 per cent, and the top 0.1 per cent. The information suggests that wage concentration (top 1 per cent and above) fell significantly during the last years of the authoritarian regime and the transition. Unlike the case of total income, the sharp decrease in top wages between 1970 and 1976 was a phenomenon concentrated in the top 1 per cent, and especially in the top fractiles within the top 1 per cent. Interestingly, despite important movements over the period, the level of concentration within the top 1 per cent by the end of the 1990s was comparable to the level of 1970 and slightly lower than the levels in 1964–9.

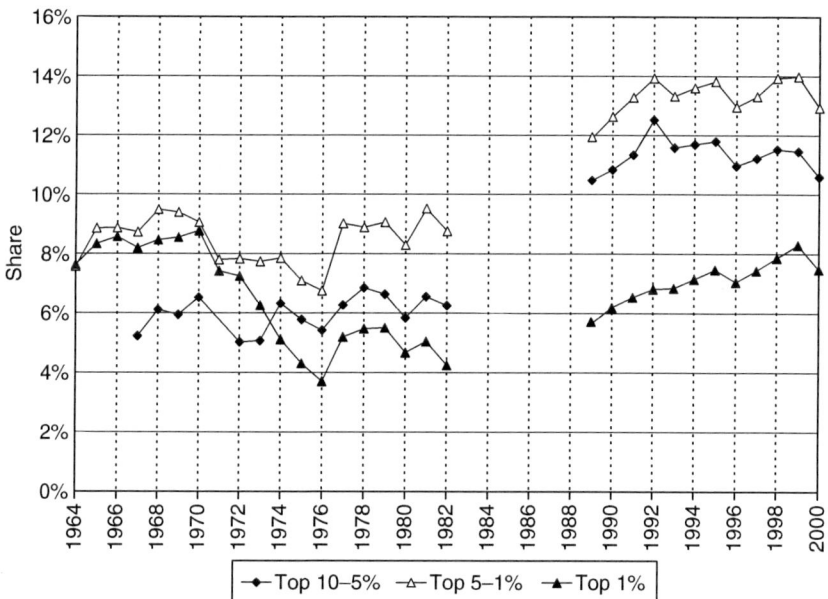

Figure 11.7 Top wage shares in Portugal from tax statistics, 1964–2000

Note: Civil service is excluded.

Source: Table 11D.4, columns Top 10–5%, Top 5–1%, Top 1%.

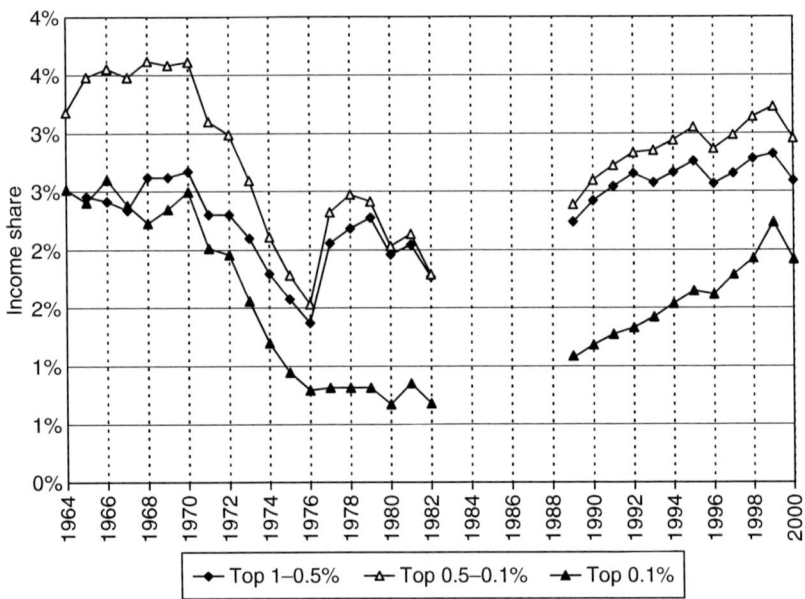

Figure 11.8 Top wage shares in Portugal, 1964–2000

Note: Civil service is excluded.

Source: Table 11D.4, columns Top 1–0.5%, Top 0.5–0.1%, Top 0.1%.

This suggests that the increase in overall income concentration over the last years in Portugal has also been extremely influenced by the evolution of top wages.

Figures 11.9 and 11.10 show the same shares but their results come from the micro-data from administrative records from 1985 to 2004. Two periods seem to be clearly identifiable: (i) until 1993 the increase in earnings concentration was mostly condensed in the top 5–0.1 per cent; the top 0.1 per cent was stable or even declined between 1985 and 1986; (ii) since 1994 the increase in concentration was mainly happening in the top 0.1 per cent, which augmented considerably from 1.4 per cent in 1994 to 2.4 per cent in 2004, that is, around 70 per cent.

These conclusions do not depend on the subset of workers included in the administrative records. Figure 11.11 compares the top 1–0.5 per cent, the top 0.5–0.1 per cent, and the top 0.1 per cent wage shares from the *quadros de pessoal* (already presented in Figure 11.10) with the series computed from income tax statistics (in which all workers filing a return are included, without distinction of sector of activity). Both sets of series follow the same pattern, and the income tax statistics display even larger increases. Figure 11.12 compares the shares within shares according to both sources. The similarity is not surprising, given that the data are not independent: wages reported by employers to the *quadros de pessoal* are subject to withholding tax.

Together with the estimates in Table 11D.6, the presented evidence suggests that the patterns are not only coincident with the findings of Cardoso (1998) for

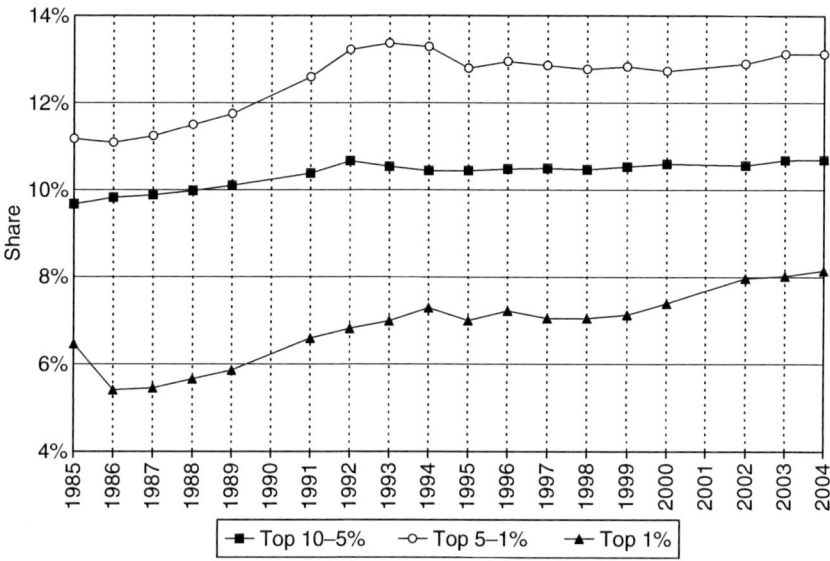

Figure 11.9 The top 10–5%, top 5–1%, and top 1% wage shares in Portugal, 1985–2004 from administrative records (*quadros de pessoal*)

Source: Table 11D.6, columns Top 10–5%, Top 5–1%, and Top 1%.

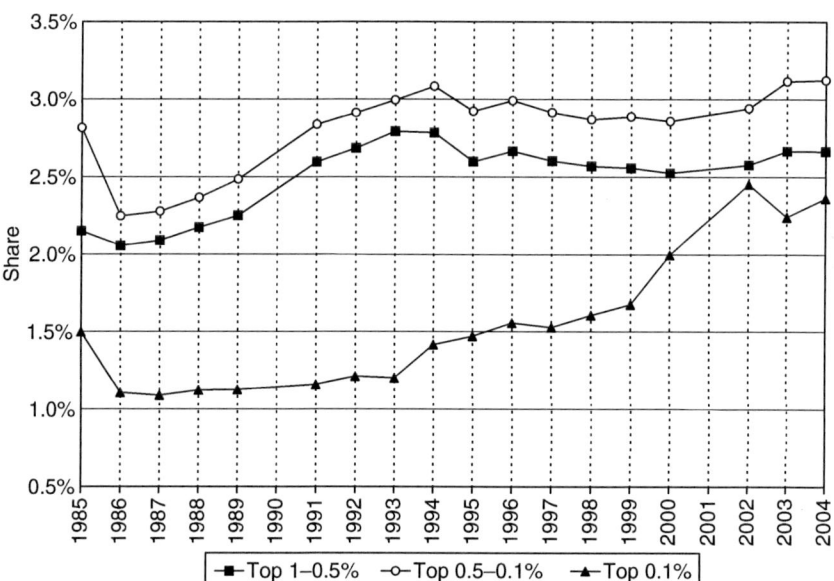

Figure 11.10 The top 1–0.5%, top 0.5–0.1%, and top 0.1% wage shares in Portugal, 1985–2004 from administrative records (*quadros de pessoal*)

Source: Table 11D.6, columns Top 1–0.5%, Top 0.5–0.1%, and Top 0.1%.

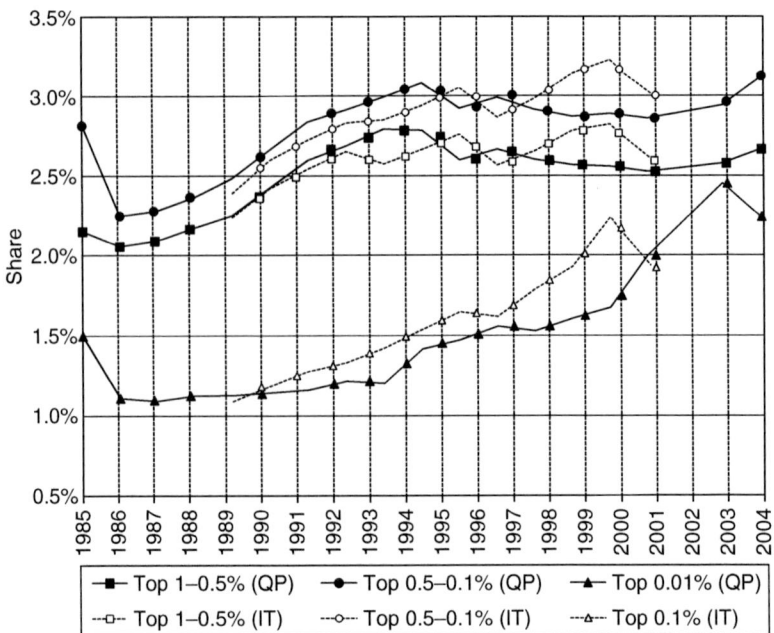

Figure 11.11 The top 1–0.5%, top 0.5–0.1%, and top 0.1% earnings shares in Portugal, 1985–2004: comparison between administrative records (*quadros de pessoal*) and income tax statistics

Notes: QP denotes results based on *quadros de pessoal*; IT denotes results based on income tax statistics.

Sources: Table 11D.4 and Table 11D.6, columns Top 1–0.5%, Top 0.5–0.1%, and Top 0.1%.

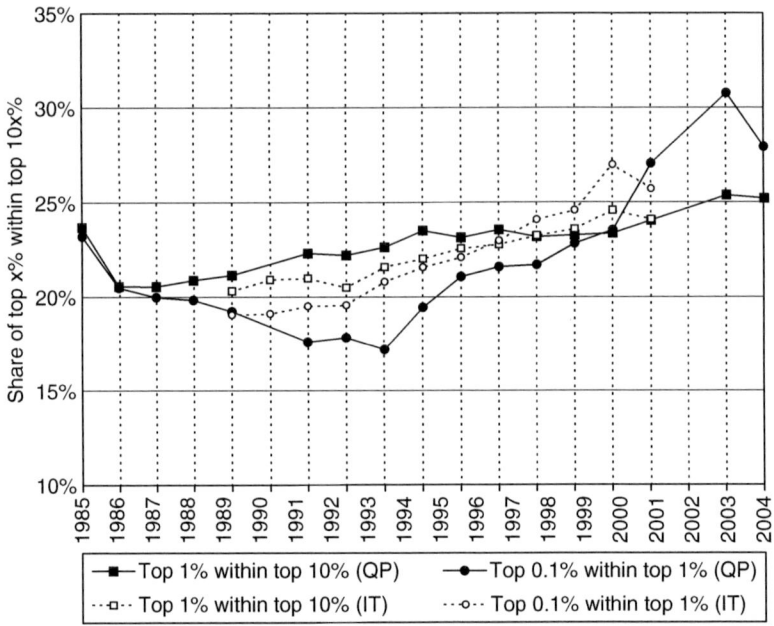

Figure 11.12 Shares within shares in Portugal 1985–2004: comparison between administrative records (*quadros de pessoal*) and income tax statistics

Notes: QP denotes results based on *quadros de pessoal*; IT denotes results based on income tax statistics.

Sources: Table 11D.4 and Table 11D.6.

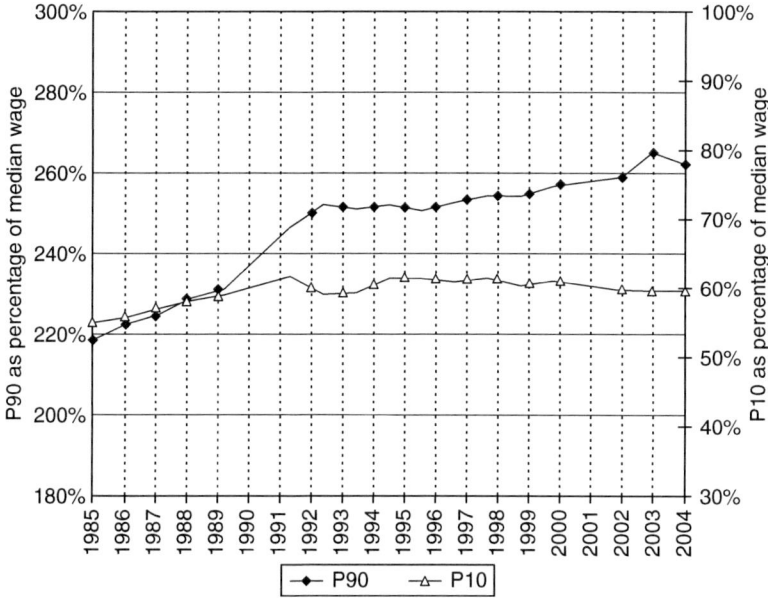

Figure 11.13 P10 and P90 earnings levels as percentage of median wage in Portugal, 1985–2004

Source: Table 11D.7.

the period 1983–92 but also that they have been reinforced between 1992 and 2004: a relatively compressed bottom and a stretched top can be highlighted as the main characteristics of the Portuguese earnings distribution. The high degree of inequality prevailing in the country's labour market is essentially due to the fact that high wages are very high relative to the rest of the distribution, and the gap has kept growing. Figure 11.13 plots the P90 and P10 fractile wage levels as a percentage of the median wage from 1985 to 2004 as another way of looking at the widening gap.

11.5 CONCLUSION

This chapter has attempted to analyse income and earnings concentration in Portugal from a long-run perspective using the best available statistical evidence. My results suggest that income concentration was much higher during the 1930s and early 1940s (at levels comparable to other countries such as France, Spain, or the United States) than it is today. Top income shares estimated from reported incomes deteriorated during the Second World War, even if Portugal did not take active participation in the conflict. However, the magnitude of the drop was less important than in other European countries. The level of concentration between 1950 and 1970 remained relatively high compared to countries such as Spain, France, the UK, or the United States. The decrease in income concentration, started in 1970–1 and accelerating after the revolution of 1974, began to be reversed in the early 1980s. During the last fifteen years the shares above the top 10 per cent have augmented steadily. The increase has been higher, the higher the fractile considered.

The evidence since 1989 suggests that the level of marginal tax rates at the top has not been a primary determinant of the level of top reported incomes. Marginal rates have stayed constant in a context of growing top shares.

The dynamics of top incomes have been partially driven by the behaviour of top wages. Between 1985 and 1994 the increase in earnings concentration was mostly condensed in the top 5–0.1 per cent. Since then, the increase in concentration has been happening mainly in the top 0.1 per cent of the wage distribution.

APPENDIX 11A: THE TAXES ON INCOME AND WAGES IN PORTUGAL

The 'Old' Income Tax

In Portugal, income taxation was enforced for the first time in 1641 as a 10 per cent flat rate on rents, capital incomes, and business incomes (*décima militar*); in its origins it was a source to finance the restoration wars. During the nineteenth century, the system evolved towards the scheme of independent schedule taxes: *contribução predial, contribução industrial, décima de juros*. With modifications, the schedule taxes survived until 1988.

Table 11A.1 summarizes the main features of the evolution of the personal income tax in Portugal between 1922 and 2005. The first *personal* income tax (*imposto pessoal do rendimento*) was enforced in 1922 (Law 1368/1922). It was defined as a tax levied on top incomes in addition to the traditional schedule taxes (at the time: *contribuçao industrial* on wages, business income, and self-employment income, *contribuçao predial* on rents, *imposto sobre a aplicação de capitais* on capital income); no provisions were made regarding capital gains. It was a truly independent personal overall income tax. However, several difficulties on its applicability, a high non-compliance rate, and the turbulent macroeconomic environment of the First Republic forced its rapid replacement.

In 1928, the government replaced the *imposto pessoal do rendimento* with a new income tax, the *imposto complementar* (Law 15290/1928 and Decree 16731/1929), affecting the taxable income defined for the schedule taxes (at the time: *contribuçao industrial* for business income, *imposto profissional* for wages and self-employment income, *contribuçao predial* for rents, *imposto sobre a aplicação de capitais* for capital income). For many of the income components, presumptive and not actual revenues were in fact taxed. The *imposto complementar*, with two major reforms in 1946 and 1963, remained in existence until 1988.

Between 1950 and 1963 those individuals accumulating two or more civil servant positions, jobs in the private sector, or independent professions were subject also to a supplementary tax (*adicionamento*, Decree-Law 37771 of 28/2/1950). This tax affected a very small number of individuals and only a fraction of the income assessed for the *imposto complementar*: in 1951, for instance, only 537 individuals paid the *adicionamento*, out of 25,362 who filed for the *imposto complementar*.

The 'Modern' Income Tax

The modern personal income tax (*imposto sobre o rendimento das pessoas singulares, IRS*) was established in 1989 (Decree-Law 442A/1988), when the *imposto complementar* and all the schedule taxes were abolished. Taxable income covers (i) wages and salaries (*Categoria A*), (ii) self-employment income (*Categoria B*), (iii) business income (*Categoria C*), (iv) farm income (*Categoria D*), (v) capital income (*Categoria E*), (vi) urban and rural real estate rents (*Categoria F*), (vii) capital gains (*Categoria G*), (viii) pensions (*Categoria H*), and (ix) other smaller income items (*Categoria I*). Concerning the *Categoria G*, capital gains from public debt bonds are untaxed and not reported, as well as gains from stocks if kept for more than one year. Capital gains from real estate are also untaxed if the proceeds are used to purchase new real estate. Interest income and other capital income items are taxed at the source at flat rates and generally not reported. Consequently, the income definition excludes most capital gains and a fraction of capital incomes.

Between 1989 and 2005 the top marginal tax rate was stable at 40 per cent, while the bottom rate declined from 16 per cent in 1989–90, to 15 per cent in 1991–8, 14 per cent in 1999–2000, 12 per cent in 2001–4, and finally 10.5 per cent in 2005. Contrary to the worldwide trend of reducing the number of brackets of the statutory tax scale, Portugal moved first from a five-bracket to a four-bracket scale between 1990 and 1991, but then went back to five brackets in 1999 and to six brackets in 2002. Taxation is based on the family unit. To take the taxpayer's family status into account, the use of an income-splitting system to ascertain taxable income is applied. In particular, income of married couples is divided by two in order to determine the marginal tax rate to be applied according to the statutory tax scales shown in Table 11A.2.

For a comprehensive description of the modern income tax in Portugal, see Direcçao-Geral dos Impostos (1998a, 1998b, 2005).

Schedule Tax on Wages

In 1929 the government created the *imposto profissional*, a schedule tax on wages and salaries (including agriculture) and self-employed liberal professionals; civil servants were excluded (Decree 16731 of 14/4/1929 and Decree 19359 of 19/2/1931).[26] Initially there was a progressive tax scale with marginal tax rates from 2 per cent to 8 per cent affecting wage income, while self-employees were taxed with lump sums (variable across professions). Several reforms modified the scope of the tax, the exemption thresholds, and the tax scales (Decree 19359 of 16/2/1931, Law 1952 of 10/3/1937, Decree-Law 33735 of 26/6/1944, Decree-Law 34353 of 30/12/1944). A detailed description of the first fifteen years of the *imposto profissional* can be found in Mouteira Guerreiro (1947). After the fiscal reform of 1962–4 (Decree-Laws 44305 of 27/4/1962, 45400 of 30/11/1963, 45676 of 24/4/1964, 45977 of 19/10/1964), statutory top marginal tax rates were successively increased to 15 per cent in 1964–1972, 20 per cent in 1973–5, and 22 per cent in 1976–88. The number of tax brackets also rose considerably. The tax was abolished in 1988 with the introduction of the *imposto sobre o rendimento das pessoas singulares*.

---

[26] Before 1929, a fraction of wage earners was already taxed under the *contribuïçao industrial*.

Table 11A.1 The income tax in Portugal, 1922–2005

Tax denomination	Period	Exempted income (escudos until 2001, euros since 2002)	Main allowances from gross income (escudos until 2001, euros since 2002)	Main deductions from tax (escudos until 2001, euros since 2002)	Joint filing
Imposto Pessoal do Rendimiento	1922–1926 Lei 1368/1922	3,600	30% on wage income spouse: 1,200 dependant child (up to 4): 600 dependant child (above 4): 1,000 other dependants: 500	none	mandatory
Imposto Complementar	1927–1928 Decreto 15.290/1928	7,000	none	none	mandatory
	1929–1932 Decreto 16.731/1929	10,000	none	none	mandatory
	1933–1945 Decreto-Lei 22.541/1933	10,500	none	none	mandatory
	1946–1963 Decreto 35.595/1946	50,000	Civil Service income, pensions	allowances for spouse and dependents	mandatory
	1964–1972 Decreto-Lei 45.399 30/11/1963 Decreto-Lei 49.483/1969	60,000	20% on wage income up to 20,000 spouse: 20,000 dependant <8 yo: 2,500 dependant aged 8–11 yo: 5,000 dependant aged 12–16 yo: 7,500 dependant aged 16–21 yo: 10,000 non-residents: 40,000	none	mandatory

(continued)

Table 11A.1 Continued

Tax denomination / Period	Exempted income (escudos until 2001, euros since 2002)	Main allowances from gross income (escudos until 2001, euros since 2002)	Main deductions from tax (escudos until 2001, euros since 2002)	Joint filing
1973–1978 Decreto-lei 375/1974 Decreto-lei 667/1976	60,000	20% on wage income up to 25,000 spouse: 20,000 dependant <7 yo: 4,000 dependant aged 8–11 yo: 8,000 dependant aged 12–16 yo: 12,000 dependant aged 16–21 yo: 16,000 non-residents: 40,000	none	mandatory
1979–1980 Decreto-lei 183F/1980	80,000	20% on wage income up to 30,000 spouse: 40,000 dependant <11 yo: 10,000 dependant aged 11–21 yo: 20,000 non-residents: 40,000	none	mandatory
1981 Decreto-lei 196/1982	80,000	30% on wage income up to 50,000 spouse: 40,000 dependant <11 yo: 10,000 dependant aged 11–18 yo: 20,000 dependant aged 19–24 yo in undergraduate studies: 20,000 non-residents: 40,000	none	mandatory
1982 Decreto-lei 119j/1983	120,000	30% on wage income up to 50,000 spouse: 40,000 dependant <11 yo: 20,000 dependant aged 11–18 yo: 30,000	none	mandatory

Year / Decree	Amount	Description		
		dependant aged 19–24 yo in undergraduate studies: 30,000 non-residents: 40,000	none	mandatory
1983 Decreto-lei 192/1984	120,000	30% on wage income up to 50,000 spouse: 120,000 dependant <11 yo: 25,000 dependant aged 11–18 yo: 40,000 dependant aged 19–24 yo in undergraduate studies: 40,000 non-residents: 40,000	none	mandatory
1984 Decreto-lei 115d/1985	150,000	30% on wage income up to 65,000 spouse: 150,000 dependant <11 yo: 30,000 dependant aged 11–18 yo: 50,000 dependant aged 19–24 yo in undergraduate studies: 50,000 non-residents: 40,000	none	mandatory
1985 Decreto-lei 112/1986	180,000	30% on wage income up to 105,000 spouse: 180,000 dependant <11 yo: 40,000 dependant aged 11–18 yo: 60,000 dependant aged 19–24 yo in undergraduate studies: 60,000 dependant aged 19–24 yo unemployed: 60,000 non-residents: 40,000	none	mandatory
1986–1987 Decreto 135/1987	295,000	30% on wage income up to 155,000 spouse: 205,000	none	mandatory

(continued)

Table 11A.1 Continued

Tax denomination	Period	Exempted income (escudos until 2001, euros since 2002)	Main allowances from gross income (escudos until 2001, euros since 2002)	Main deductions from tax (escudos until 2001, euros since 2002)	Joint filing
			dependant <11 yo: 60,000 dependant aged 11–18 yo: 70,000 dependant aged 19–24 yo in undergraduate studies: 70,000 dependant aged 19–24 yo unemployed: 70,000 non-residents: 70,000		
	1988 Decreto-lei 66/1989	1,000,000	30% on wage income up to 155,000 spouse: 200,000 dependant <11 yo: 60,000 dependant aged 11–18 yo: 70,000 dependant aged 19–24 yo in undergraduate studies: 70,000 dependant aged 19–24 yo unemployed: 70,000 non-residents: 70,000	none	mandatory
Imposto sobre a Rendas das Pessoas Físicas	1989 Decreto-Lei 442A/1988	after-tax wage income cannot be below the national minimum wage	65% on wage income up to 250,000 mortgage interests to purchase main residence education expenses, life and other insurances pension up to 1000,000	single: 20,000 married: 15,000 × 2 dependant: 10,000	mandatory splitting
	1990	after-tax wage income cannot be below the national minimum wage	65% on wage income up to 300,000 mortgage interests to purchase main residence education expenses, life and other insurances pension up to 1,250,000	single: 23,000 married: 17,000 × 2 dependant: 12,000	mandatory splitting

Year				
1991	after-tax wage income cannot be below the national minimum wage	65% on wage income up to 340,000 mortgage interests to purchase main residence education expenses, life and other insurances pension up to 1,400,000	single: 25,500 married: 19,000 × 2 dependant: 14,000	mandatory splitting
1992	after-tax wage income cannot be below the national minimum wage	65% on wage income up to 378,000 mortgage interests to purchase main residence education expenses, life and other insurances pension up to 1,512,000	single: 27,500 married: 20,500 × 2 dependant: 15,100	mandatory splitting
1993	after-tax wage income cannot be below the national minimum wage	65% on wage income up to 400,000 mortgage interests to purchase main residence education expenses, life and other insurances pension up to 1,600,000	single: 29,000 married: 22,000 × 2 dependant: 16,000	mandatory splitting
1994	after-tax wage income cannot be below the national minimum wage	65% on wage income up to 416,000 mortgage interests to purchase main residence education expenses, life and other insurances pension up to 1,200,000	single: 31,000 married: 22,800 × 2 dependant: 16,500	mandatory splitting
1995	after-tax wage income cannot be below the national minimum wage	65% on wage income up to 440,000 mortgage interests to purchase main residence education expenses, life and other insurances pension up to 1,272,000	single: 32,000 married: 24,000 × 2 dependant: 17,500	mandatory splitting

(continued)

Table 11A.1 Continued

Tax denomination	Period	Exempted income (escudos until 2001, euros since 2002)	Main allowances from gross income (escudos until 2001, euros since 2002)	Main deductions from tax (escudos until 2001, euros since 2002)	Joint filing
	1996	after-tax wage income cannot be below the national minimum wage	highest of (a) 70% on wage income up 465,000 or (b) 71% of the highest minimum wage mortgage interests to purchase main residence education expenses, life and other insurances pension up to 1,350,000	single: 33,000 married: 25,000 × 2 dependant: 18,500	mandatory splitting
	1997	after-tax wage income cannot be below 120% of the highest national minimum wage	highest of (a) 70% on wage income up 484,000 or (b) 71% of the highest minimum wage mortgage interests to purchase main residence education expenses, life and other insurances pension up to 1,385,000	single: 34,500 married: 26,300 × 2 dependant: 19,000 (1st.), 19,210 (2nd.), 19,430 (3rd.), 19,550 (+4th.)	mandatory splitting
	1998	after-tax wage income cannot be below 120% of the highest national minimum wage	highest of (a) 70% on wage income up 498,000 or (b) 71% of the highest minimum wage mortgage interests to purchase main residence education expenses, life and other insurances pension up to 1,415,000	single: 35,200 married: 26,800 × 2 dependant: 19,400 (1st.), 19,620 (2nd.), 19,840 (3rd.), 19,860 (+4th.)	mandatory splitting
	1999	after-tax wage income cannot be below 120% of the highest national minimum wage	highest of (a) 70% on wage income up to 522,000 or (b) 72% of the highest minimum	single: 36,000 married: 27,400 × 2 dependant: 19,800 (1st.),	mandatory splitting

Year				
		wage mortgage interests to purchase main residence education expenses, life and other insurances pension up to 1,445,000	20,025 (2nd.), 20,250 (3rd.), 20,375 (+4th.)	mandatory splitting
2000	after-tax wage income cannot be below 120% of the highest national minimum wage	highest of (a) 70% on wage income up to 535,000 or (b) 72% of the highest minimum wage mortgage interests to purchase main residence education expenses, life and other insurances pension up to 1,482,000	single: 36,720 married: 27,950 × 2 dependant: 20,200 (1st.), 20,430 (2nd.), 21,070 (3rd.), 21,47 (+4th.)	mandatory splitting
2001	after-tax wage income cannot be below 120% of the highest national minimum wage	highest of (a) 70% on wage income up to 550,000 or (b) 72% of the highest minimum wage mortgage interests to purchase main residence education expenses, life and other insurances pension up to 1,523,000	single: 40,200 married: 33,500 × 2 dependant: 26,800 each	mandatory splitting
2002	after-tax wage income cannot be below 120% of the highest national minimum wage	72% of the highest minimum wage mortgage interests to purchase main residence education expenses, life and other insurances pension up to 7,805.60	single: 60% of monthly minimum wage married: 50% of monthly minimum wage × 2 dependant: 40% of monthly minimum wage each	mandatory splitting

(continued)

Table 11A.1 Continued

Tax denomination	Period	Exempted income (escudos until 2001, euros since 2002)	Main allowances from gross income (escudos until 2001, euros since 2002)	Main deductions from tax (escudos until 2001, euros since 2002)	Joint filing
	2003	after-tax wage income cannot be below 120% of the highest national minimum wage	72% of the highest minimum wage mortgage interests to purchase main residence education expenses, life and other insurances pension up to 7,961.71	single: 60% of monthly minimum wage married: 50% of monthly minimum wage × 2 dependant: 40% of monthly minimum wage each	mandatory splitting
	2004	after-tax wage income cannot be below 120% of the highest national minimum wage	72% of the highest minimum wage mortgage interests to purchase main residence education expenses, life and other insurances pension up to 7,778.74	single: 60% of monthly minimum wage married: 50% of monthly minimum wage × 2 dependant: 40% of monthly minimum wage each	mandatory splitting
	2005	after-tax wage income cannot be below 120% of the highest national minimum wage	72% of the highest minimum wage mortgage interests to purchase main residence education expenses, life and other insurances pension up to 7,778.74	single: 60% of monthly minimum wage married: 50% of monthly minimum wage × 2 dependant: 40% of monthly minimum wage each	mandatory splitting

Table 11A.2 Tax scales: income taxes in Portugal, 1922–1932

Imposto pessoal do rendimento 1922–1926			Imposto complementar 1927–1932		
Range of taxable income (escudos)		Rate (%)	Range of taxable income (escudos)		Rate (%)
	5,000	0.50	7,000	15,000	2.00
5,000	10,000	1.00	15,000	30,000	2.50
10,000	15,000	1.50	30,000	45,000	3.00
15,000	20,000	2.00	45,000	60,000	3.50
20,000	25,000	2.50	60,000	75,000	4.00
25,000	30,000	3.25	75,000	90,000	4.50
30,000	35,000	4.00	90,000	105,000	5.00
35,000	40,000	4.75	105,000	120,000	5.50
40,000	45,000	5.50	120,000	135,000	6.00
45,000	50,000	6.25	135,000	150,000	6.50
50,000	55,000	7.00	150,000	165,000	7.00
			165,000	180,000	7.50
beyond 55,000 escudos, rate increases 1% per			180,000	200,000	8.00
each additional 5,000 escudos up to a maximum			200,000		8.50
marginal rate of 30%					

Table 11A.2 Tax scale Imposto Complementar. Portugal 1933–1945

Range of Taxable Income (escudos)		Rate (%)	Range of Taxable Income (escudos)		Rate (%)	Range of Taxable Income (escudos)		Rate (%)	Range of Taxable Income (escudos)		Rate (%)
10,000	11,000	0.18	61,000	62,000	2.14	112,000	113,000	3.46	163,000	164,000	4.36
11,000	12,000	0.33	62,000	63,000	2.49	113,000	114,000	3.48	164,000	165,000	4.38
12,000	13,000	0.46	63,000	64,000	2.52	114,000	115,000	3.50	165,000	166,000	4.40
13,000	14,000	0.57	64,000	65,000	2.54	115,000	116,000	3.52	166,000	167,000	4.42
14,000	15,000	0.67	65,000	66,000	2.56	116,000	117,000	3.53	167,000	168,000	4.43
15,000	16,000	0.78	66,000	67,000	2.58	117,000	118,000	3.55	168,000	169,000	4.45
16,000	17,000	0.88	67,000	68,000	2.60	118,000	119,000	3.57	169,000	170,000	4.47
17,000	18,000	0.97	68,000	69,000	2.62	119,000	120,000	3.58	170,000	171,000	4.49
18,000	19,000	1.05	69,000	70,000	2.64	120,000	121,000	3.60	171,000	172,000	4.51
19,000	20,000	1.12	70,000	71,000	2.66	121,000	122,000	3.62	172,000	173,000	4.52
20,000	21,000	1.19	71,000	72,000	2.68	122,000	123,000	3.64	173,000	174,000	4.54
21,000	22,000	1.25	72,000	73,000	2.70	123,000	124,000	3.66	174,000	175,000	4.56
22,000	23,000	1.30	73,000	74,000	2.72	124,000	125,000	3.68	175,000	176,000	4.57
23,000	24,000	1.35	74,000	75,000	2.73	125,000	126,000	3.70	176,000	177,000	4.59
24,000	25,000	1.40	75,000	76,000	2.76	126,000	127,000	3.72	177,000	178,000	4.61
25,000	26,000	1.44	76,000	77,000	2.78	127,000	128,000	3.73	178,000	179,000	4.62
26,000	27,000	1.48	77,000	78,000	2.80	128,000	129,000	3.75	179,000	180,000	4.64
27,000	28,000	1.52	78,000	79,000	2.82	129,000	130,000	3.77	180,000	181,000	4.66
28,000	29,000	1.55	79,000	80,000	2.84	130,000	131,000	3.79	181,000	182,000	4.68
29,000	30,000	1.58	80,000	81,000	2.86	131,000	132,000	3.80	182,000	183,000	4.69
30,000	31,000	1.63	81,000	82,000	2.88	132,000	133,000	3.82	183,000	184,000	4.71
31,000	32,000	1.67	82,000	83,000	2.90	133,000	134,000	3.84	184,000	185,000	4.73
32,000	33,000	1.71	83,000	84,000	2.92	134,000	135,000	3.85	185,000	186,000	4.75
33,000	34,000	1.75	84,000	85,000	2.94	135,000	136,000	3.87	186,000	187,000	4.76
34,000	35,000	1.79	85,000	86,000	2.96	136,000	137,000	3.89	187,000	188,000	4.78
35,000	36,000	1.82	86,000	87,000	2.98	137,000	138,000	3.91	188,000	189,000	4.80
36,000	37,000	1.85	87,000	88,000	2.99	138,000	139,000	3.93	189,000	190,000	4.82
37,000	38,000	1.88	88,000	89,000	3.01	139,000	140,000	3.95	190,000	191,000	4.83
38,000	39,000	1.91	89,000	90,000	3.03	140,000	141,000	3.96	191,000	192,000	4.85
39,000	40,000	1.94	90,000	91,000	3.05	141,000	142,000	3.98	192,000	193,000	4.86

From	To	Rate	From	To	Rate	From	To	Rate	From	To	Rate
40,000	41,000	1.96	91,000	92,000	3.07	142,000	143,000	4.00	193,000	194,000	4.88
41,000	42,000	1.99	92,000	93,000	3.09	143,000	144,000	4.02	194,000	195,000	4.90
42,000	43,000	2.01	93,000	94,000	3.11	144,000	145,000	4.03	195,000	196,000	4.91
43,000	44,000	2.03	94,000	95,000	3.13	145,000	146,000	4.05	196,000	197,000	4.93
44,000	45,000	2.06	95,000	96,000	3.15	146,000	147,000	4.07	197,000	198,000	4.94
45,000	46,000	2.09	96,000	97,000	3.17	147,000	148,000	4.08	198,000	199,000	4.96
46,000	47,000	2.12	97,000	98,000	3.19	148,000	149,000	4.10	199,000	200,000	4.97
47,000	48,000	2.15	98,000	99,000	3.21	149,000	150,000	4.12			
48,000	49,000	2.17	99,000	100,000	3.22	150,000	151,000	4.14			
49,000	50,000	2.20	100,000	101,000	3.24	151,000	152,000	4.15			
50,000	51,000	2.23	101,000	102,000	3.26	152,000	153,000	4.17			
51,000	52,000	2.25	102,000	103,000	3.28	153,000	154,000	4.19			
52,000	53,000	2.27	103,000	104,000	3.29	154,000	155,000	4.21			
53,000	54,000	2.30	104,000	105,000	3.31	155,000	156,000	4.23			
54,000	55,000	2.32	105,000	106,000	3.33	156,000	157,000	4.24			
55,000	56,000	2.34	106,000	107,000	3.35	157,000	158,000	4.26			
56,000	57,000	2.36	107,000	108,000	3.37	158,000	159,000	4.28			
57,000	58,000	2.38	108,000	109,000	3.39	159,000	160,000	4.30			
58,000	59,000	2.40	109,000	110,000	3.41	160,000	161,000	4.31			
59,000	60,000	2.42	110,000	111,000	3.43	161,000	162,000	4.33			
60,000	61,000	2.44	111,000	112,000	3.45	162,000	163,000	4.35			

For income above 200,000 escudos
the tax rate = 8.5-705/(income/1,000)

Table 11A.2 Tax scale Imposto Complementar. Portugal 1946–1978

1946–1963 Range of Taxable Income (escudos)		Rate (%)	1964–1968 Range of Taxable Income (escudos)		Rate (%)	1969–1972 Range of Taxable Income (escudos)		Rate (%)	1973–1974 Range of Taxable Income (escudos)		Rate (%)	1975–1978 Range of Taxable Income (escudos)		Rate (%)
—	50,000	3.0	—	50,000	3.0	—	50,000	3.0	—	50,000	3.0	—	50,000	4.0
50,000	100,000	4.0	50,000	100,000	4.0	50,000	100,000	4.0	50,000	100,000	4.5	50,000	100,000	6.0
100,000	150,000	5.0	100,000	150,000	5.0	100,000	150,000	5.0	100,000	150,000	6.0	100,000	200,000	8.0
150,000	200,000	6.0	150,000	200,000	6.0	150,000	200,000	6.0	150,000	200,000	8.0	200,000	300,000	14.0
200,000	250,000	7.0	200,000	250,000	7.0	200,000	250,000	7.0	200,000	250,000	10.0	300,000	400,000	20.0
250,000	300,000	8.0	250,000	300,000	8.0	250,000	300,000	8.5	250,000	300,000	12.0	400,000	500,000	26.0
300,000	350,000	9.0	300,000	350,000	9.0	300,000	350,000	10.0	300,000	350,000	14.0	500,000	600,000	34.0
350,000	400,000	10.0	350,000	400,000	10.0	350,000	400,000	11.5	350,000	400,000	17.0	600,000	700,000	42.0
400,000	450,000	11.0	400,000	450,000	11.0	400,000	450,000	13.0	400,000	450,000	20.0	700,000	800,000	50.0
450,000	500,000	12.0	450,000	500,000	12.0	450,000	500,000	14.5	450,000	500,000	23.0	800,000	900,000	60.0
500,000	550,000	13.0	500,000	550,000	13.0	500,000	550,000	16.0	500,000	550,000	26.0	900,000	1,000,000	70.0
550,000	600,000	14.0	550,000	600,000	14.0	550,000	600,000	17.5	550,000	600,000	29.0	1,000,000	—	80.0
600,000	650,000	15.0	600,000	650,000	15.0	600,000	650,000	19.0	600,000	650,000	32.0			
650,000	700,000	16.0	650,000	700,000	16.0	650,000	700,000	21.0	650,000	700,000	35.0			
700,000	750,000	17.0	700,000	750,000	17.0	700,000	750,000	23.0	700,000	750,000	38.0			
750,000	800,000	18.0	750,000	800,000	18.0	750,000	800,000	25.0	750,000	800,000	41.0			
800,000	850,000	19.0	800,000	850,000	19.0	800,000	850,000	27.0	800,000	850,000	44.0			
850,000	900,000	20.0	850,000	900,000	20.0	850,000	900,000	29.0	850,000	900,000	48.0			
900,000	950,000	21.0	900,000	950,000	21.0	900,000	950,000	31.0	900,000	950,000	52.0			
950,000	1,000,000	22.0	950,000	1,000,000	22.0	950,000	1,000,000	33.0	950,000	1,000,000	56.0			
1,000,000	1,050,000	23.0	1,000,000	1,050,000	23.0	1,000,000	1,050,000	35.0	1,000,000	1,050,000	60.0			
1,050,000	1,100,000	24.0	1,050,000	1,100,000	24.0	1,050,000	1,100,000	37.0	1,050,000	1,100,000	64.0			
1,100,000	1,150,000	25.0	1,100,000	1,150,000	25.0	1,100,000	1,150,000	39.0	1,100,000	1,150,000	68.0			
1,150,000	1,200,000	26.0	1,150,000	1,200,000	26.0	1,150,000	1,200,000	41.0	1,150,000	1,200,000	72.0			
1,200,000	1,250,000	27.0	1,200,000	1,250,000	27.0	1,200,000	1,250,000	43.0	1,200,000	1,250,000	76.0			
1,250,000	1,300,000	28.0	1,250,000	1,300,000	28.0	1,250,000	1,300,000	45.0	1,250,000	1,300,000	80.0			

1,350,000	1,400,000	29.0		
1,400,000		30.0		

1,400,000	1,500,000	29.0
1,500,000	1,600,000	30.0
1,600,000	1,700,000	31.0
1,700,000	1,800,000	32.0
1,800,000	1,900,000	33.0
1,900,000	2,000,000	34.0
2,000,000	2,100,000	35.0
2,100,000	2,200,000	36.0
2,200,000	2,300,000	37.0
2,300,000	2,400,000	38.0
2,400,000	2,500,000	39.0
2,500,000	2,600,000	40.0
2,600,000	2,700,000	41.0
2,700,000	2,800,000	42.0
2,800,000	2,900,000	43.0
2,900,000	3,000,000	44.0
3,000,000		45.0

1,300,000	1,350,000	47.0
1,350,000	1,400,000	49.0
1,400,000	1,450,000	51.0
1,450,000	1,500,000	53.0
1,500,000		55.0

Table 11A.2 (continued) Tax scale Imposto Complementar. Portugal 1979–1982

1979–1980 Range of Taxable Income (escudos)		1981 Range of Taxable Income (escudos)		1982 Range of Taxable Income (escudos)		Rates married (%)	Rates single (%)
	100,000		150,000		180,000	4.0	4.8
100,000	200,000	150,000	300,000	180,000	360,000	6.0	7.2
200,000	350,000	300,000	500,000	360,000	600,000	8.0	9.6
350,000	500,000	500,000	700,000	600,000	840,000	14.0	16.8
500,000	650,000	700,000	900,000	840,000	1,080,000	20.0	24.0
650,000	800,000	900,000	1,100,000	1,080,000	1,320,000	26.0	31.2
800,000	950,000	1,100,000	1,300,000	1,320,000	1,560,000	34.0	40.8
950,000	1,100,000	1,300,000	1,500,000	1,560,000	1,800,000	42.0	50.4
1,100,000	1,250,000	1,500,000	1,700,000	1,800,000	2,040,000	50.0	60.0
1,250,000	1,400,000	1,700,000	1,900,000	2,040,000	2,280,000	60.0	72.0
1,400,000		1,900,000		2,280,000		70.0	80.0

Table 11A.2 (continued) Tax scale Imposto Complementar. Portugal 1983–1988

for married couples

1983 Range of Taxable Income (escudos)		Rates (%)	1984 Range of Taxable Income (escudos)		Rates (%)	1985 Range of Taxable Income (escudos)		1986–1987 Range of Taxable Income (escudos)		1988 Range of Taxable Income (escudos)		Rates (%)
	220,000	4.0		280,000	4.0		320,000		350,000		375,000	4.0
220,000	440,000	6.0	280,000	550,000	6.0	320,000	630,000	350,000	690,000	375,000	740,000	6.0
440,000	720,000	8.0	550,000	900,000	8.0	630,000	1,040,000	690,000	1,140,000	740,000	1,220,000	8.0
720,000	1,080,000	14.0	900,000	1,350,000	14.0	1,040,000	1,550,000	1,140,000	1,700,000	1,220,000	1,820,000	12.0
1,080,000	1,300,000	20.0	1,350,000	1,650,000	20.0	1,550,000	1,900,000	1,700,000	2,070,000	1,820,000	2,215,000	18.0
1,300,000	1,900,000	26.0	1,650,000	2,350,000	26.0	1,900,000	2,700,000	2,070,000	2,950,000	2,215,000	3,160,000	24.0
1,900,000	2,500,000	34.0	2,350,000	3,100,000	34.0	2,700,000	3,530,000	2,950,000	3,850,000	3,160,000	4,120,000	30.0
2,500,000	3,100,000	42.0	3,100,000	3,900,000	42.0	3,530,000	4,450,000	3,850,000	4,850,000	4,120,000	5,190,000	36.0
3,100,000	3,700,000	50.0	3,900,000	4,600,000	50.0	4,450,000	5,250,000	4,850,000	5,720,000	5,190,000	6,120,000	42.0
3,700,000	4,300,000	60.0	4,600,000	5,300,000	60.0	5,250,000	6,050,000	5,720,000	6,590,000	6,120,000	7,050,000	48.0
4,300,000	–	70.0	5,300,000	–	70.0	6,050,000	–	6,590,000	–	7,050,000		50.0

for single individuals

1983 Range of Taxable Income (escudos)		Rates (%)	1984 Range of Taxable Income (escudos)		Rates (%)	1985 Range of Taxable Income (escudos)		1986–1987 Range of Taxable Income (escudos)		1988 Range of Taxable Income (escudos)		Rates (%)
	180,000	4.8		230,000	4.8		270,000		295,000		315,000	4.8
180,000	360,000	7.2	230,000	450,000	7.2	270,000	520,000	295,000	570,000	315,000	610,000	7.2
360,000	600,000	9.6	450,000	750,000	9.6	520,000	870,000	570,000	950,000	610,000	1,015,000	9.6
600,000	840,000	14.4	750,000	1,050,000	14.4	870,000	1,210,000	950,000	1,320,000	1,015,000	1,415,000	14.4
840,000	1,080,000	21.6	1,050,000	1,350,000	21.6	1,210,000	1,560,000	1,320,000	1,700,000	1,415,000	1,820,000	21.6
1,080,000	1,580,000	31.2	1,350,000	1,950,000	31.2	1,560,000	2,240,000	1,700,000	2,440,000	1,820,000	2,610,000	28.8
1,580,000	2,080,000	40.8	1,950,000	2,600,000	40.8	2,240,000	2,960,000	2,440,000	3,230,000	2,610,000	3,465,000	36.0
2,080,000	2,580,000	50.4	2,600,000	3,200,000	50.4	2,960,000	3,650,000	3,230,000	3,980,000	3,465,000	4,260,000	43.2
2,580,000	3,080,000	60.0	3,200,000	3,850,000	60.0	3,650,000	4,400,000	3,980,000	4,800,000	4,260,000	5,135,000	50.4
3,080,000	3,580,000	72.0	3,850,000	4,450,000	64.8	4,400,000	5,000,000	4,800,000	5,450,000	5,135,000	5,830,000	57.6
3,580,000	–	80.0	4,450,000	–	70.0	5,000,000	–	5,450,000	–	5,830,000		60.0

Table 11A.2 (continued) Tax scale Imposto sobre a Renda das Pessoas Físicas. Portugal 1989–2005

1989

Range of Taxable Income (escudos)	
0	450,000
450,000	850,000
850,000	1,250,000
1,250,000	3,000,000
3,000,000	

1990

Range of Taxable Income (escudos)		Rates (%)
0	540,000	16.0
540,000	1,020,000	20.0
1,020,000	1,500,000	27.5
1,500,000	3,600,000	35.0
3,600,000		40.0

1991

Range of Taxable Income (escudos)	
0	750,000
750,000	1,750,000
1,750,000	4,500,000
4,500,000	

1992

Range of Taxable Income (escudos)	
0	810,000
810,000	1,890,000
1,890,000	4,860,000
4,860,000	

1993

Range of Taxable Income (escudos)	
0	880,000
880,000	2,010,000
2,010,000	5,160,000
5,160,000	

1994

Range of Taxable Income (escudos)		Rates (%)
0	930,000	15.0
930,000	2,170,000	25.0
2,170,000	5,570,000	35.0
5,570,000		40.0

1995

Range of Taxable Income (escudos)	
0	970,000
970,000	2,260,000
2,260,000	5,790,000
5,790,000	

1996

Range of Taxable Income (escudos)	
0	1,010,000
1,010,000	2,350,000
2,350,000	6,000,000
6,000,000	

1997

Range of Taxable Income (escudos)	
0	1,050,000
1,050,000	2,435,000
2,435,000	6,150,000
6,150,000	

1998

Range of Taxable Income (euros)		Rates (%)
0	5,387.02	15.0
5,387.02	12,469.95	25.0
12,469.95	31,324.51	35.0
31,324.51		40.0

1999

Range of Taxable Income (euros)	
0	3,491.59
3,491.59	5,511.72
5,511.72	13,716.64
13,716.64	31,948.01
31,948.01	

2000

Range of Taxable Income (euros)		Rates (%)
0	3,641.22	14.0
3,641.22	5,371.19	15.0
5,371.19	14,165.86	25.0
14,165.86	32,825.89	35.0
32,825.89		40.0

2001

Range of Taxable Income (euros)	
0	3,990.38
3,990.38	6,035.45
6,035.45	14,963.94
14,963.94	34,417.05
34,417.05	49,879.79
49,879.79	

2002

Range of Taxable Income (euros)	
0	4,100.12
4,100.12	6,201.42
6,201.42	15,375.45
15,375.45	35,363.52
35,363.52	51,251.48
51,251.48	

2003

Range of Taxable Income (euros)	
0	4,182.12
4,182.12	6,325.45
6,325.45	15,682.96
15,682.96	36,070.79
36,070.79	52,276.51
52,276.51	

2004

Range of Taxable Income (euros)		Rates (%)
0	4,266.00	12.0
4,266.00	6,452.00	14.0
6,452.00	15,997.00	24.0
15,997.00	36,792.00	34.0
36,792.00	53,322.00	38.0
53,322.00	-	40.0

2005

Range of Taxable Income (euros)		Rates (%)
0	4,351.00	10.5
4,351.00	6,581.00	13.0
6,581.00	16,317.00	23.5
16,317.00	37,528.00	34.0
37,528.00	54,388.00	36.5
54,388.00		40.0

APPENDIX 11B: REFERENCES ON DATA SOURCES FOR PORTUGAL

Income Tax Statistics

Available statistical information about the *imposto pessoal do rendimento* appears in República Portuguesa, Ministério das Finanças, Direcção Geral de Estatística, Ia. Reparti-çao, *Estatística das contribuïções e impostos, liquidaçaõ e cobrança nas gerências de 1922–1923 a 1924–1925*, and República Portuguesa, Ministério das Finanças, Direcção Geral de Estatística, Ia. Repartiçao, *Liquidaçaõ e cobrança na gerência de 1925–1926*. However, these publications only display total tax collections with no data about the distribution of income or tax paid by brackets. Therefore, this information, if interesting from the historical point of view, has not been used in the estimations.

Statistical information has been published regularly since 1936 with increasing degree of detail.

1936–45: The published tables show the distribution of the number of taxpayers by ranges of tax collection. Instituto Nacional de Estatística, *Anuário estatístico das contribuï-ções e impostos 1936, 1937, 1938, 1939, 1940, 1941, 1942, 1943, 1944, 1945*.

1946–63: The published tabulations display (i) the number of taxpayers and the gross assessed income organized by ranges of total before tax income, (ii) the number of taxpayers and the taxable income by ranges of taxable income, and (iii) the number of taxpayers and tax paid by ranges of tax paid. Instituto Nacional de Estatística, *Anuário estatístico das contribuïções e impostos, 1946, 1947, 1948, 1949, 1950, 1951, 1952, 1953, 1954, 1955, 1956, 1957, 1958, 1959, 1960, 1961, 1962, 1963*.

1963–82: The published statistics are organized by range of taxable income (gross income net of allowances), and they provide the distribution of the number of taxpayers and taxable income by brackets. The data also provide information on total allowances. Instituto Nacional de Estatística, *Anuário estatístico das contribuïções e impostos, 1964, 1965, 1966*, and *Portugal, Instituto Nacional de Estatística, Estatísticas das contribuïções e impostos, continente e ilhas adjacentes, 1967, 1968, 1969, 1970, 1971, 1972, 1973, 1974, 1975, 1976, 1977, 1978, 1979, 1980, 1981, 1982*.

1983–8: During the transition period from the *imposto complementar* to the new *imposto sobre o rendimento das pessoas singolares*, no usable tabulations by income or tax brackets are available. Only aggregated information about total assessed income, total taxable income, and total tax collection appears in Instituto Nacional de Estatística, *Estatísticas das contribuïções e impostos, continente e ilhas adjacentes, 1983–1988*. Consequently the series have a gap in those years.

1989–2005: Finally, the fiscal reform of 1988 and the increasing managerial capabilities of the tax agency implied an improvement in the amount and quality of available information on individuals' income. Since then, the published statistics, by brackets of gross income, display taxable income, gross income, tax paid, and a thorough detail of allowances and deductions. No information is provided about the composition of income. Individuals are classified in two groups: those having income from wages and pension only, on the one side, and those having income also from other sources. Portugal, Instituto Nacional de Estatística, *Estatísticas das receitas fiscais, 1989–1992, 1993–1995, 1996, 1997,*

1998, 1999, 2000. Tabulations for 2001, 2002, and 2003 were provided by the tax agency of Portugal, based on internal reports. Tabulations for 2004 and 2005 come from Direcção de Serviços do IRS, *Estatísticas do IRS (declaração modelo 3), exercícios de 2004 e 2005.*

Statistics on Wages and Salaries

The information on earnings is obtained from the tabulations of the schedule tax on wages and salaries, the *imposto profissional* (1936–82), the income tax (1989–2000), and the micro-data from the *quadros de pessoal* (1985–9 (1990 missing), 1991–2000 (2001 missing), and 2002–4).

1936–82: The tabulations from the *imposto profissional* are organized by intervals of tax collections, and they display the number of taxed workers and the total tax paid by brackets. The published information covers 1936–82; however, homogeneous estimates can only be produced for the period 1964–82. I used the tax code to recover the brackets of gross earnings from the brackets of tax paid, and the earnings by brackets from the tax collections by brackets. Instituto Nacional de Estatística, *Anuário estatístico das contribuï-ções e impostos, 1936, 1937, 1938, 1939, 1940, 1941, 1942, 1943, 1944, 1945*; Instituto Nacional de Estatística, *Anuário estatístico das contribuïções e impostos, 1946, 1947, 1948, 1949, 1950, 1951, 1952, 1953, 1954, 1955, 1956, 1957, 1958, 1959, 1960, 1961, 1962, 1963*; Instituto Nacional de Estatística, *Anuário estatístico das contribuïções e impostos, 1964, 1965, 1966*; Portugal, Instituto Nacional de Estatística, *Estatísticas das contribuições e impostos, continente e ilhas adjacentes, 1967, 1968, 1969, 1970, 1971, 1972, 1973, 1974, 1975, 1976, 1977, 1978, 1979, 1980, 1981, 1982, 1983–1988.*

1989–2000: For the period 1989–2000, the information on earnings comes from the tabulations of the income tax. The published statistics, based on withholdings at source and organized by ranges of gross earnings, display the number of workers and the gross wages. The information corresponds to the individual and not to the family as in the income tax statistics. Portugal, Instituto Nacional de Estatística, *Estatísticas das receitas fiscais, 1989–1992, 1993–1995, 1996, 1997, 1998, 1999, 2000.* No usable information on earnings is available from the tax statistics since 2001.

Administrative Records on Wages:
Quadros de Pessoal

Every year, employers are required by law to provide information about the firm (location, economic activity, employment, sales, legal setting) and their employees (individual basic wages, overtime, bonuses, gender, level of education, skills, duration of work (full-time/part-time), date of latest promotion, tenure). The information corresponds to March for years 1985–93, and October for years 1994–2004. Civil service and domestic work are excluded. State-owned companies are included. Agriculture workers are included, although in practice the level of coverage is very low. For manufacturing, a thorough evaluation of the coverage of the *quadros de pessoal* can be made, since a census of manufacturing is available. As argued in Cardoso (1998a), comparison of the two sets reveals that the *quadros de pessoal* cover more workers than the census itself, despite the fact that the census includes very small productive units (mainly firms with no wage earners) that are not a part of the population covered by the *quadros de pessoal* (mainly firms with no wage earners). The Direcçao-Geral de Estudos, Estatística e Planeamento (DGEEP) publishes regularly a report with the main results, *Estatísticas em síntese* (available online). The data were first collected in 1982 but micro-data start in 1985. All results based on the *quadros de pessoal* were computed from the micro-data for 1985–9 (1990 missing), 1991–2000 (2001 missing), and 2002–4.

APPENDIX 11C: CONTROL TOTALS
FOR INDIVIDUALS,
INCOME, AND WAGES

Total Number of Individuals and Tax Units

As mentioned before, joint filing for married couples has always been mandatory in Portugal. Thus, the unit to which the income tax data relate is the married couple, or single adult, or single minor with income in his or her own right above a given threshold. The reference total for tax units takes this fact into account. Consequently the total number of tax units is defined as the total number of adult males and females (aged 20 years old and over) less the number of married females. I assume that the number of minors with enough income to file separately is negligible. Information is obtained from the national census: *Recenseamento geral da população e da habitação, 1930, 1940, 1950, 1960, 1970, 1981, 1991, 2001.* Intermediate years have been linearly interpolated. The information is also available in Instituto Nacional de Estatística, *Anuário estatístico de Portugal,* several years, Instituto Nacional de Estatística, 1985, *Portugal 50 anos, 1935–1985,* and Valério (2001). Table 11C.1 reports the number of adults (column 1), the number of tax units (column 2), and the number of tax returns actually filed (column 3).

Total Number of Employees

The number of employees comes from (a) Banco de Portugal, *Séries longas para a economia portuguesa: pós II Guerra Mundial,* vols. i and ii (1953–95); (b) Instituto Nacional de Estatística, 2003, *Contas nacionais anuais definitivas base 1995,* and Instituto Nacional de Estatística, 2005, *Contas nacionais anuais definitivas base 2000* (1996–2004); and (c) the national census of 1930, 1940, and 1950; missing years have been linearly interpolated (1936–52).

The number of civil servants was obtained from (d) the national census of 1930, 1940, and 1950 (1936–52); (e) Banco de Portugal, *Séries longas para a economia portuguesa: pós II Guerra Mundial,* vols. i and ii (1953–67); and (f) International Labor Organization Database. Between 1964 and 1982 the control total for employees excludes civil servants, as most of them were not subject to the *imposto profissional* and were excluded from the published statistics.

Total Income Denominator

The National Accounts income series between 1953 and 1995 was obtained from Banco de Portugal, *Séries longas para a economia portuguesa. pós II Guerra Mundial,* vols. i and ii. For the years following 1996, the information comes from Instituto Nacional de Estatística, 2003, *Contas nacionais base 1995* and Instituto Nacional de Estatística, 2006, *Contas nacionais anuais definitivas base 2000.* For 1936–52 the previously described series were extended backwards using the information from Batista et al. (1997).

For the period 1989–2005, total income is defined as wages and salaries from National Accounts net of effective social security contributions, plus 50 per cent of social transfers, plus 66 per cent of unincorporated business income plus all non-business, non-labour income reported on tax returns. This methodology generates an income denominator that fluctuates around 55–60 per cent of Portuguese GDP, which is similar to that used for France (Piketty 2001) and Spain (Alvaredo and Saez 2009). For the period 1936–83, I use as denominator 60 per cent of the Portuguese GDP from the sources listed above. The total income denominator series expressed in 2005 euros is reported in Table 11C.1, column 5. The average income per adult is reported in column 6 while the average income per tax unit is displayed in column 7.

Total Wage Denominator

Total wages are defined as wages and salaries from national accounts net of effective social contributions. The information for 1953–95 has been taken from Banco de Portugal, *Séries longas para a economia portuguesa: pós II Guerra Mundial,* vols. i and ii (series Remunerações do Trabalho no Território, Ordenados e Salários and Contribuições Sociais Efectivas dos Empregadores). For the years following 1996, the information comes from Instituto Nacional de Estatística, 2003, *Contas nacionais anuais definitivas base 1995* and Instituto Nacional de Estatística, 2005, *Contas nacionais anuais definitivas base 2000.* The wage denominator excludes civil service between 1964 and 1982.

Prices

The price index is based on the following sources: (a) for the period 1936–45: Instituto Nacional de Estatística, *Anuário estatístico, 1936, 1937, 1938, 1939, 1940, 1941, 1942, 1943, 1944, 1945,* Indices de Preços de Retalho, base 1914 = 100; (b) for the period 1946–51, Instituto Nacional de Estatística, 1985, *Portugal 50 anos 1935–1985;* (c) for the years following 1951, Consumer Price Index from Instituto Nacional de Estatística, *Anuário Estatístico, years 1952–1975* and Instituto Nacional de Estatística, Divisão de Estatísticas da Distribuçao e Serviços, *Indicadores da actividade económica: indices de precios do consumidor,* several years. Table 11C.1, column 8, shows the CPI index (base 100 in year 2005).

Data on Emigration Flows

The number of emigrants from Portugal, used for the results shown in Figure 11.7, was obtained from Valério (2001), which builds on Baganha (1990, 1991, 1993, 1994) and Pereira (1993).

Table 11C.1 Reference totals for population, income, and inflation, Portugal, 1936–2005

	Tax units				Total income			Inflation	Taxes
	(1)	(2)	(3)	(4)	(5)	(6)	(7)	(8)	(9)
	Adults ('000s)	Tax units ('000s)	Number of tax returns ('000s)	(3)/(2) (%)	Total income (millions) (2005 euros)	Average income per adult (2005 euros)	Average income per tax unit (2005 euros)	CPI (base 2005)	Top marginal tax rate (%)
1936	4,298	3,025	43	1.44	9,155	2,130	3,026	0.61	8.5
1937	4,357	3,062	45	1.47	9,405	2,158	3,072	0.63	8.5
1938	4,418	3,099	48	1.53	10,364	2,346	3,344	0.61	8.5
1939	4,479	3,136	50	1.60	10,979	2,451	3,501	0.57	8.5
1940	4,541	3,174	54	1.72	10,167	2,239	3,203	0.60	8.5
1941	4,604	3,213	58	1.81	9,689	2,105	3,016	0.68	8.5
1942	4,668	3,252	62	1.91	9,221	1,975	2,836	0.83	8.5
1943	4,732	3,291	67	2.05	10,150	2,145	3,084	0.93	8.5
1944	4,798	3,331	74	2.21	11,433	2,383	3,432	0.96	8.5
1945	4,865	3,372	97	2.88	11,146	2,291	3,306	1.04	8.5
1946	4,932	3,412	11	0.34	12,176	2,469	3,568	1.06	30
1947	5,000	3,454	14	0.42	12,515	2,503	3,624	1.08	30
1948	5,070	3,496	16	0.45	12,811	2,527	3,665	1.10	30
1949	5,140	3,538	18	0.52	13,039	2,537	3,685	1.12	30
1950	5,211	3,581	22	0.62	13,632	2,616	3,807	1.14	30
1951	5,254	3,600	25	0.70	14,498	2,760	4,027	1.14	30
1952	5,296	3,619	25	0.68	14,604	2,757	4,035	1.14	30
1953	5,339	3,638	27	0.75	15,383	2,881	4,228	1.15	30
1954	5,383	3,658	28	0.76	16,427	3,052	4,491	1.14	30
1955	5,426	3,677	29	0.79	17,201	3,170	4,678	1.14	30
1956	5,470	3,697	35	0.94	17,819	3,257	4,820	1.17	30
1957	5,515	3,716	38	1.01	18,648	3,381	5,018	1.19	30
1958	5,560	3,736	40	1.08	19,574	3,521	5,240	1.21	30
1959	5,605	3,756	35	0.93	20,563	3,669	5,475	1.22	30
1960	5,650	3,776	34	0.90	21,342	3,777	5,653	1.25	30

1961	5,633	3,747	34	0.92	21,647	3,843	1.28	5,777	30
1962	5,616	3,718	37	0.99	23,672	4,215	1.31	6,366	30
1963	5,599	3,690	44	1.19	23,829	4,256	1.35	6,457	45
1964	5,582	3,662	29	0.80	25,202	4,515	1.38	6,882	45
1965	5,565	3,634	44	1.22	28,565	5,133	1.42	7,860	45
1966	5,548	3,607	45	1.25	29,023	5,231	1.49	8,047	45
1967	5,531	3,579	53	1.48	30,812	5,571	1.58	8,608	45
1968	5,514	3,552	58	1.63	31,415	5,697	1.67	8,844	45
1969	5,497	3,525	64	1.81	30,973	5,634	1.82	8,787	55
1970	5,480	3,498	75	2.13	32,856	5,995	1.93	9,392	55
1971	5,565	3,543	87	2.47	33,966	6,104	2.17	9,587	55
1972	5,650	3,588	106	2.97	36,187	6,404	2.40	10,085	55
1973	5,737	3,634	125	3.45	37,893	6,605	2.71	10,428	80
1974	5,825	3,680	149	4.04	35,858	6,155	3.39	9,743	80
1975	5,915	3,727	128	3.43	36,020	6,090	3.90	9,664	80
1976	6,006	3,775	684	18.13	36,693	6,109	4.58	9,721	80
1977	6,098	3,823	559	14.62	36,844	6,042	5.87	9,638	80
1978	6,192	3,872	548	14.15	37,537	6,062	7.12	9,696	80
1979	6,287	3,921	702	17.90	38,430	6,112	8.85	9,801	80
1980	6,384	3,971	837	21.07	40,945	6,414	10.79	10,311	70(married) 80 (single)
1981	6,482	4,022	1,112	27.65	41,010	6,327	12.94	10,197	70(married) 80 (single)
1982	6,548	4,078	1,333	32.68	40,522	6,189	15.84	9,936	70(married) 80 (single)
1983	6,614	4,135	1,389	33.58	41,246	6,236	19.88	9,974	70(married) 80 (single)
1984	6,681	4,194	1,385	33.03	39,170	5,863	25.71	9,341	70
1985	6,749	4,252	1,189	27.95	40,295	5,971	30.68	9,476	50(married) 60 (single)
1986	6,817	4,312	1,259	29.20	44,099	6,469	34.26	10,227	50(married) 60 (single)
1987	6,886	4,373	1,436	32.84	47,495	6,897	37.48	10,861	50(married) 60 (single)
1988	6,956	4,434	542	12.22	51,692	7,431	41.11	11,657	50(married) 60 (single)
1989	7,027	4,497	2,104	46.79	49,094	6,987	46.31	10,918	40
1990	7,098	4,560	2,606	57.15	51,994	7,325	52.16	11,403	40
1991	7,170	4,624	2,642	57.14	55,177	7,696	58.48	11,933	40
1992	7,251	4,697	2,781	59.21	57,619	7,947	64.00	12,267	40

(continued)

Table 11C.1 Continued

	Tax units				Total income			Inflation	Taxes
	(1) Adults ('000s)	(2) Tax units ('000s)	(3) Number of tax returns ('000s)	(4) (3)/(2) (%)	(5) Total income (millions) (2005 euros)	(6) Average income per adult (2005 euros)	(7) Average income per tax unit (2005 euros)	(8) CPI (base 2005)	(9) Top marginal tax rate (%)
1993	7,332	4,771	2,734	57.31	55,712	7,598	11,677	68.35	40
1994	7,415	4,847	2,897	59.78	56,966	7,683	11,754	71.99	40
1995	7,498	4,923	2,882	58.54	57,690	7,694	11,718	74.99	40
1996	7,583	5,001	3,046	60.90	62,480	8,240	12,494	77.29	40
1997	7,668	5,080	3,215	63.29	65,845	8,587	12,962	79.11	40
1998	7,754	5,160	3,312	64.18	69,577	8,972	13,483	81.32	40
1999	7,842	5,242	3,425	65.35	73,667	9,394	14,054	83.20	40
2000	7,930	5,325	3,662	68.78	76,963	9,705	14,454	85.58	40
2001	8,019	5,409	3,869	71.53	79,871	9,960	14,767	89.30	40
2002	8,110	5,494	3,969	72.24	82,384	10,159	14,994	92.51	40
2003	8,201	5,581	3,979	71.29	81,433	9,930	14,591	95.53	40
2004	8,293	5,669	4,244	74.86	82,743	9,977	14,595	97.78	40
2005	8,387	5,759	4,294	74.57	84,143	10,033	14,611	100.00	40

APPENDIX 11D: ESTIMATING TOP SHARES

Pareto Interpolation

We follow the basic Pareto interpolation technique described in Chapter 10, Appendix 10D.

Adjustments to Raw Pareto Interpolations for Income

1936–45: Statistics are organized by ranges of tax paid and they only display the number of tax files. I estimated the ranges of gross income by means of the statutory tax scale and the taxable thresholds given in Tables 11A.1 and 11A.2. Only the ranges of gross income, the number of tax units, and the assumption of a Pareto distribution were used to estimate top fractiles and top shares in this period.

1964–82: Statistics are organized by ranges of taxable income, and they provide information on taxable income and tax files. Total income equals taxable income plus family allowances (which were introduced in 1964) plus other allowances (their evolution is described in Table 11A.1). As allowances are reported only in aggregate, I imputed them to each bracket by assuming that on average each tax filer is entitled to the same amount. This implies assuming that no re-ranking takes place in the gross and taxable income distributions.

The estimates of top income shares between 1936 and 2005 are presented in Table 11D.1, while top fractile income series 1989–2005 are reported in Table 11D.2. Table 11D.3 describes the composition of top incomes under the old income tax between 1946 and 1963; as composition data are only available in aggregates, the size of top groups varies across those years.

Adjustments to Raw Pareto Interpolations for Wages

1964–82: Statistics are organized by ranges of tax paid and they display the amounts of tax collections and the number of workers taxed. I estimated the ranges of gross wages by means of the statutory tax scale of the *imposto profissional* between those years.

The estimates of top earnings shares between 1964 and 2000 are presented in Table 11D.4, while selected fractiles for 1989–2005 are reported in Table 11D.5.

Estimating Top Shares from Administrative
Records on Earnings

We also computed shares of top wages using micro-data from the *quadros de pessoal* between 1985 and 2004 (1990 and 2001 missing). The number of observations ranges from 1,898,675 in 1985 to 2,912,304 in 2004. However, not all of them refer to workers.

Table 11D.1 Top income shares in Portugal, 1936–2005

	Top 10% (3)	Top 5% (4)	Top 1% (5)	Top 0.5% (6)	Top 0.1% (7)	Top 0.01% (8)	Top 10–5% (11)	Top 5–1% (12)	Top 1–0.5% (13)	Top 0.5–0.1% (14)	Top 0.1–0.01% (15)	Top 0.01% (16)
1936					4.58	1.37					3.21	1.37
1937					4.01	1.14					2.87	1.14
1938					3.94	1.12					2.83	1.12
1939					4.17	1.21					2.97	1.21
1940					4.49	1.25					3.24	1.25
1941					4.64	1.33					3.31	1.33
1942					4.16	1.20					2.96	1.20
1943					3.41	0.97					2.44	0.97
1944					3.06	0.88					2.18	0.88
1945					3.35	1.05					2.30	1.05
1946					3.12	0.96					2.16	0.96
1947					3.35	1.05					2.30	1.05
1948					3.55	1.12					2.43	1.12
1949					3.57	1.09					2.48	1.09
1950					3.69	1.14					2.55	1.14
1951					3.56	1.10					2.46	1.10
1952					3.67	1.11					2.56	1.11
1953					3.58	1.08					2.50	1.08
1954					3.60	1.13					2.47	1.13
1955					3.50	1.09					2.42	1.09
1956					3.28	0.97					2.31	0.97
1957					3.32	0.93					2.39	0.93
1958					3.49	0.94					2.55	0.94
1959					3.62	1.13					2.49	1.13
1960					3.25	0.94					2.30	0.94
1961					3.36	0.94					2.42	0.94
1962					2.93	0.79					2.15	0.79
1963					2.96	0.81					2.15	0.81

Year											
1964				3.15	0.74					2.41	0.74
1965				3.24	0.79					2.45	0.79
1966				3.33	0.83					2.50	0.83
1967				3.26	0.78					2.48	0.78
1968				3.13	0.75					2.38	0.75
1969				3.12	0.76					2.37	0.76
1970				2.91	0.79					2.12	0.79
1971				2.49	0.69					1.80	0.69
1972				1.97	0.45					1.52	0.45
1973				1.77	0.40					1.38	0.40
1974				2.05	0.77					1.28	0.77
1975				1.21	0.31					0.90	0.31
1976	26.43	6.58	4.20	1.14	0.32	8.83	11.02	2.38	3.06	0.82	0.32
1977	22.36	5.34	3.37	1.08	0.25	7.82	9.21	1.97	2.29	0.83	0.25
1978	20.77	4.81	2.98	0.96	0.30	7.21	8.76	1.83	2.02	0.66	0.30
1979	16.94	3.77	2.30	0.65		5.87	7.30	1.47	1.65		
1980	15.64	3.60	2.20	0.68		5.23	6.82	1.39	1.53		
1981	15.70	3.31	2.00	0.61		5.62	6.77	1.31	1.39		
1982	17.49	4.00	2.38	0.61		5.56	7.94	1.61	1.78		
1983											
1984											
1985											
1986											
1987											
1988											
1989	30.20	6.84	4.29	1.53	0.45	10.31	13.05	2.55	2.76	1.08	0.45
1990	31.19	7.21	4.52	1.60	0.45	10.49	13.49	2.70	2.92	1.14	0.45
1991	32.43	7.46	4.62	1.55	0.40	10.85	14.13	2.84	3.07	1.16	0.40
1992	33.15	7.58	4.66	1.53	0.35	11.04	14.53	2.93	3.13	1.18	0.35
1993	34.68	8.06	4.96	1.64	0.37	11.42	15.20	3.10	3.32	1.27	0.37
1994	35.02	8.19	5.08	1.69	0.37	11.50	15.32	3.12	3.39	1.32	0.37
1995	35.38	8.41	5.26	1.79	0.39	11.54	15.43	3.14	3.47	1.40	0.39

(continued)

Table 11D.1 Continued

	Top 10% (3)	Top 5% (4)	Top 1% (5)	Top 0.5% (6)	Top 0.1% (7)	Top 0.01% (8)	Top 10–5% (11)	Top 5–1% (12)	Top 1–0.5% (13)	Top 0.5–0.1% (14)	Top 0.1–0.01% (15)	Top 0.01% (16)
1996	35.07	23.71	8.45	5.33	1.84	0.41	11.36	15.26	3.12	3.49	1.43	0.41
1997	35.76	24.27	8.78	5.57	1.97	0.45	11.49	15.50	3.20	3.61	1.52	0.45
1998	35.45	24.09	8.78	5.59	1.98	0.45	11.35	15.32	3.19	3.61	1.53	0.45
1999	36.18	24.71	9.23	5.98	2.23	0.54	11.48	15.48	3.25	3.76	1.68	0.54
2000	36.13	24.58	9.09	5.85	2.10	0.49	11.55	15.49	3.24	3.75	1.61	0.49
2001	37.84	25.80	9.65	6.35	2.43	0.62	12.04	16.15	3.30	3.91	1.82	0.62
2002	36.77	24.87	8.97	5.74	2.05	0.47	11.90	15.90	3.23	3.70	1.58	0.47
2003	36.41	24.69	9.13	5.93	2.26	0.68	11.72	15.57	3.19	3.67	1.59	0.68
2004	38.24	25.95	9.62	6.24	2.31	0.60	12.29	16.33	3.38	3.93	1.71	0.60
2005	38.25	26.01	9.77	6.42	2.48	0.69	12.24	16.24	3.35	3.94	1.78	0.69

Table 11D.2 Top fractiles income levels in Portugal, 1989–2005 (amounts in 2005 euros)

	P90–100 (1)	P95–100 (2)	P99–100 (3)	P99.5–100 (4)	P99.9–100 (5)	P99.99–100 (6)	P90–95 (7)	P95–99 (8)	P99–99.5 (9)	P99.5–99.9 (10)	P99.9–99.99 (11)	P90 (12)	P95 (13)	P99 (14)	P99.5 (15)	P99.9 (16)	P99.99 (17)
1989	32,973	43,430	74,706	93,636	166,926	486,837	22,517	35,611	55,776	75,314	131,380	18,938	27,227	50,613	62,678	100,938	228,592
1990	35,567	47,202	82,255	103,003	182,001	517,899	23,931	38,439	61,507	83,254	144,679	20,104	29,083	55,558	69,274	111,456	264,214
1991	38,700	51,518	88,984	110,264	185,240	472,006	25,882	42,151	67,703	91,521	153,377	21,600	31,714	61,200	76,345	120,245	271,061
1992	40,671	54,254	93,033	114,247	187,320	423,047	27,089	44,559	71,819	95,979	161,128	22,535	33,307	64,688	80,402	126,516	270,660
1993	40,495	54,316	94,057	115,832	191,620	428,325	26,675	44,380	72,282	96,885	165,319	22,048	32,998	64,939	80,593	128,192	277,753
1994	41,154	55,269	96,309	119,329	198,846	437,141	27,040	45,009	73,288	99,450	172,369	22,358	33,395	65,826	82,089	132,084	287,484
1995	41,461	55,874	98,519	123,354	209,753	461,657	27,048	45,212	73,685	101,754	181,764	22,384	33,363	66,541	83,386	137,889	303,488
1996	43,817	59,245	105,557	133,058	229,853	514,411	28,388	47,667	78,056	108,859	198,236	23,430	35,222	70,062	88,959	149,437	334,440
1997	46,347	62,920	113,766	144,491	254,682	578,442	29,774	50,209	83,042	116,943	218,709	24,523	36,978	74,034	95,012	163,949	372,366
1998	47,795	64,974	118,342	150,674	266,757	606,514	30,616	51,632	86,010	121,653	229,006	25,176	38,055	76,350	98,149	171,598	390,156
1999	50,848	69,445	129,759	168,194	312,620	760,393	32,251	54,367	91,323	132,088	262,867	26,502	40,091	80,938	104,437	191,942	466,865
2000	52,214	71,048	131,329	168,950	303,434	701,367	33,379	55,978	93,708	135,329	259,219	27,527	41,458	83,524	107,593	193,020	446,153
2001	55,868	76,185	142,500	187,402	359,427	912,555	35,551	59,606	97,598	144,396	297,968	29,218	43,772	87,340	111,621	213,985	543,291
2002	55,142	74,592	134,489	172,261	307,326	703,541	35,693	59,618	96,718	138,495	263,302	29,316	43,812	86,824	110,301	196,784	450,485
2003	53,131	72,055	133,142	173,093	329,955	985,525	34,207	56,783	93,191	133,878	257,114	28,237	42,152	84,103	107,571	187,866	504,655
2004	55,810	75,736	140,341	182,130	337,258	871,103	35,884	59,584	98,551	143,348	277,942	29,609	44,038	87,489	114,276	203,406	509,836
2005	55,887	75,999	142,703	187,594	361,793	1,012,397	35,776	59,323	97,812	144,044	289,503	29,504	43,885	87,054	113,979	206,538	557,582

Notes: P99 denotes the income threshold required to belong to the top 1% of tax units; P99–100 is the average income of the top 1%; P99–99.5 denotes the average income in the bottom half of the top percentile. Fractiles are defined by total income.

Source: Computations based on tax statistics.

Table 11D.3 Composition of top incomes under old income tax, Portugal, 1946–1963

Year	Top income group fractile	Composition (%)			
		Returns from real estate and farm income	Returns from capital	Business income (excluding farm)	Employment income
1946	Top 0.3 %	37.30	7.17	25.61	29.92
1947	Top 0.4 %	34.16	6.92	29.77	29.14
1948	Top 0.5 %	32.25	7.33	31.20	29.22
1949	Top 0.5 %	33.01	7.53	30.84	28.62
1950	Top 0.6 %	34.75	7.04	28.23	29.98
1951	Top 0.7 %	35.02	7.09	28.00	29.90
1952	Top 0.7 %	34.65	7.19	27.26	30.89
1953	Top 0.8 %	35.52	6.77	26.82	30.90
1954	Top 0.8 %	36.75	6.67	26.01	30.57
1955	Top 0.8 %	36.58	6.40	25.88	31.14
1956	Top 0.9 %	37.16	6.10	26.11	30.63
1957	Top 1.0 %	34.32	5.26	26.38	34.05
1958	Top 1.1 %	37.39	4.87	25.07	32.67
1959	Top 0.9 %	38.41	4.86	24.55	32.17
1960	Top 0.9 %	39.32	4.61	22.69	33.39
1961	Top 0.9 %	39.97	4.75	22.28	33.00
1962	Top 1.0 %	39.65	4.45	22.56	33.33
1963	Top 1.2 %	38.47	4.38	22.90	34.25

Note: The composition statistics are only available in aggregate. As a result, the size of the corresponding top group varies across those years.

Source: Income tax statistics.

Table 11D.4 Top earnings shares from tax statistics in Portugal, 1964–2000

	Top 10% (1)	Top 5% (2)	Top 1% (3)	Top 0.5% (4)	Top 0.1% (5)	Top 0.01% (6)	Top 10–5% (7)	Top 5–1% (8)	Top 1–0.5% (9)	Top 0.5–0.1% (10)	Top 0.1–0.01% (11)	Top 0.01% (12)
1964		15.20	7.63	5.69	2.51	0.69		7.57	1.94	3.18	1.83	0.69
1965		17.19	8.34	5.88	2.40	0.62		8.85	2.46	3.48	1.78	0.62
1966		17.43	8.57	6.15	2.60	0.72		8.87	2.41	3.55	1.88	0.72
1967	22.15	16.93	8.20	5.86	2.38	0.63	5.22	8.74	2.34	3.48	1.75	0.63
1968	24.06	17.95	8.46	5.85	2.23	0.55	6.11	9.49	2.62	3.62	1.67	0.55
1969	23.87	17.94	8.55	5.93	2.35	0.62	5.93	9.39	2.62	3.58	1.73	0.62
1970	24.36	17.83	8.78	6.11	2.50	0.69	6.52	9.06	2.67	3.61	1.80	0.69
1971		15.22	7.41	5.11	2.01	0.53		7.81	2.30	3.10	1.48	0.53
1972	20.11	15.09	7.25	4.95	1.96	0.52	5.02	7.84	2.30	2.99	1.44	0.52
1973	19.05	14.00	6.25	4.15	1.56	0.38	5.06	7.74	2.10	2.59	1.18	0.38
1974	19.28	12.96	5.10	3.31	1.20	0.28	6.32	7.86	1.80	2.11	0.92	0.28
1975	17.18	11.40	4.31	2.73	0.95	0.21	5.78	7.10	1.58	1.78	0.74	0.21
1976	15.88	10.46	3.70	2.33	0.80	0.17	5.42	6.76	1.37	1.53	0.63	0.17
1977	20.49	14.21	5.20	3.14	0.82		6.27	9.02	2.06	2.32		
1978	21.21	14.36	5.47	3.29	0.82		6.85	8.89	2.18	2.47		
1979	21.21	14.56	5.50	3.23	0.82		6.64	9.06	2.28	2.41		
1980	18.80	12.96	4.67	2.71	0.67		5.83	8.30	1.96	2.03		
1981	21.12	14.56	5.04	2.99	0.85		6.56	9.52	2.05	2.14		
1982	19.26	13.00	4.24	2.47	0.68		6.26	8.76	1.77	1.79		
1983												
1984												
1985												
1986												
1987												
1988												
1989	28.15	17.66	5.72	3.48	1.09	0.23	10.48	11.95	2.24	2.39	0.86	0.23
1990	29.67	18.83	6.20	3.78	1.18	0.24	10.84	12.63	2.42	2.60	0.94	0.24
1991	31.16	19.82	6.54	4.00	1.28	0.28	11.34	13.28	2.54	2.72	1.00	0.28

(continued)

Table 11D.4 Continued

	Top 10% (1)	Top 5% (2)	Top 1% (3)	Top 0.5% (4)	Top 0.1% (5)	Top 0.01% (6)	Top 10–5% (7)	Top 5–1% (8)	Top 1–0.5% (9)	Top 0.5–0.1% (10)	Top 0.1–0.01% (11)	Top 0.01% (12)
1992	33.27	20.74	6.81	4.16	1.33	0.28	12.52	13.93	2.65	2.83	1.05	0.28
1993	31.76	20.17	6.85	4.27	1.42	0.31	11.59	13.32	2.57	2.85	1.12	0.31
1994	32.44	20.74	7.14	4.48	1.54	0.36	11.70	13.60	2.66	2.94	1.18	0.36
1995	33.07	21.27	7.46	4.70	1.65	0.38	11.80	13.82	2.76	3.05	1.27	0.38
1996	30.98	20.01	7.05	4.48	1.62	0.41	10.97	12.96	2.57	2.87	1.21	0.41
1997	31.97	20.75	7.43	4.77	1.79	0.46	11.22	13.32	2.65	2.99	1.33	0.46
1998	33.32	21.79	7.86	5.07	1.93	0.52	11.53	13.93	2.78	3.14	1.42	0.52
1999	33.74	22.28	8.29	5.47	2.24	0.66	11.46	13.99	2.82	3.23	1.58	0.66
2000	31.00	20.41	7.47	4.88	1.92	0.53	10.59	12.94	2.59	2.96	1.40	0.53

Notes: Wage information taken from tabulations of the Imposto Profissional 1964–82, and from tabulations of the Imposto sobre o Rendimento das Pessoas Singulares 1989–2000. The results for 1964–82 exclude civil servants.

Table 11D.5 Fractiles of earnings from tax statistics in Portugal, 1989–2000 (amounts in 2005 euros)

	P90 (2)	P95 (3)	P99 (4)	P99.5 (5)	P99.9 (6)	P99.99 (7)	P90–100 (8)	P95–100 (9)	P99–100 (10)	P99.5–100 (11)	P99.9–100 (12)	P99.99–100 (13)	P90–95 (14)	P95–99 (15)	P99–99.5 (16)	P99.5–99.9 (17)	P99.9–99.99 (18)
1989	15,559	20,539	34,853	42,530	66,156	125,522	23,946	30,056	48,643	59,161	92,648	191,329	17,836	25,409	38,126	50,789	81,684
1990	16,886	22,213	39,199	48,560	75,070	137,629	26,447	33,575	55,255	67,366	105,568	216,159	19,319	28,155	43,144	57,816	93,280
1991	18,524	24,858	43,239	53,292	82,781	167,502	29,262	37,227	61,392	75,062	119,700	260,357	21,297	31,185	47,723	63,902	104,071
1992	19,579	26,229	45,642	56,703	90,566	184,846	32,578	40,627	66,729	81,543	130,455	278,173	24,530	34,101	51,914	69,315	114,042
1993	20,006	26,421	46,667	58,167	94,073	198,363	30,905	39,257	66,636	83,169	138,451	298,496	22,554	32,412	50,104	69,348	120,668
1994	19,880	26,241	46,857	58,928	96,581	220,725	31,621	40,434	69,613	87,300	150,037	348,346	22,808	33,139	51,925	71,616	128,003
1995	20,143	26,846	48,011	60,557	101,083	234,326	31,975	41,132	72,103	90,880	159,221	369,099	22,818	33,390	53,325	73,795	135,902
1996	20,558	27,561	49,587	62,727	105,862	260,430	33,090	42,740	75,301	95,794	172,969	440,362	23,439	34,599	54,808	76,500	143,258
1997	21,264	28,731	51,773	65,899	115,919	297,638	35,038	45,478	81,405	104,638	195,942	507,686	24,598	36,497	58,173	81,811	161,304
1998	21,122	28,919	52,801	67,425	118,783	315,470	35,571	46,530	83,870	108,329	206,035	550,260	24,612	37,195	59,410	83,902	167,788
1999	22,028	30,298	56,190	71,938	132,884	393,095	37,869	50,010	93,041	122,719	251,210	743,125	25,729	39,252	63,362	90,596	196,553
2000	22,804	31,603	57,718	73,722	135,545	371,287	38,880	51,192	93,667	122,311	241,023	660,214	26,568	40,574	65,024	92,633	194,446

Table 11D.6 Top earnings shares from administrative records in Portugal, 1985–2004

	Top 10% (1)	Top 5% (2)	Top 1% (3)	Top 0.5% (4)	Top 0.1% (5)	Top 0.01% (6)	Top 10–5% (7)	Top 5–1% (8)	Top 1–0.5% (9)	Top 0.5–0.1% (10)	Top 0.1–0.01% (11)	Top 0.01% (12)
1985	27.32	17.64	6.46	4.31	1.50	0.25	9.68	11.18	2.15	2.81	1.25	0.25
1986	26.32	16.50	5.41	3.35	1.11	0.22	9.82	11.09	2.06	2.25	0.89	0.22
1987	26.58	16.69	5.46	3.37	1.09	0.20	9.88	11.24	2.09	2.28	0.89	0.20
1988	27.15	17.17	5.66	3.49	1.12	0.20	9.98	11.50	2.17	2.37	0.92	0.20
1989	27.72	17.61	5.86	3.61	1.13	0.19	10.11	11.75	2.25	2.48	0.94	0.19
1990												
1991	29.56	19.18	6.59	4.00	1.16	0.19	10.38	12.59	2.59	2.84	0.97	0.19
1992	30.70	20.03	6.81	4.13	1.21	0.23	10.66	13.22	2.68	2.91	0.98	0.23
1993	30.90	20.35	6.99	4.20	1.20	0.22	10.54	13.37	2.79	2.99	0.98	0.22
1994	31.01	20.57	7.28	4.50	1.42	0.35	10.44	13.29	2.78	3.08	1.07	0.35
1995	30.22	19.78	6.99	4.39	1.47	0.30	10.43	12.79	2.60	2.92	1.17	0.30
1996	30.65	20.17	7.21	4.55	1.56	0.31	10.48	12.95	2.66	2.99	1.24	0.31
1997	30.40	19.90	7.04	4.44	1.53	0.31	10.49	12.86	2.60	2.91	1.21	0.31
1998	30.28	19.82	7.04	4.48	1.61	0.37	10.47	12.77	2.57	2.87	1.23	0.37
1999	30.48	19.95	7.12	4.56	1.67	0.44	10.53	12.83	2.56	2.89	1.23	0.44
2000	30.70	20.11	7.38	4.86	2.00	0.77	10.59	12.73	2.52	2.86	1.23	0.77
2001												
2002	31.42	20.87	7.97	5.39	2.45	1.06	10.56	12.90	2.58	2.94	1.39	1.06
2003	31.82	21.14	8.02	5.36	2.24	0.78	10.68	13.12	2.66	3.12	1.46	0.78
2004	31.95	21.26	8.15	5.48	2.36	0.90	10.69	13.12	2.66	3.12	1.46	0.90

Source: Own computations based on micro-data from *quadros de pessoal*.

Table 11D.6 (continued) Top earnings shares from administrative records in Portugal, 1985–2004

	Top 90% (1)	Top 80% (2)	Top 70% (3)	Top 60% (4)	Top 50% (5)	Top 40% (6)	Top 30% (8)	Top 20% (9)	Top 10% (10)	Top 100-90% (11)	Top 90-80% (12)	Top 80-70% (13)	Top 70-60% (14)	Top 60-50% (15)	Top 50-40% (16)	Top 40-30% (17)	Top 30-20% (18)	Top 20-10% (19)	Top 10% (20)
1985	97.08	91.94	86.04	79.43	71.98	63.57	53.90	42.21	27.32	2.92	5.14	5.90	6.61	7.45	8.41	9.67	11.69	14.90	27.32
1986	96.98	91.72	85.70	79.03	71.54	63.11	53.39	41.53	26.32	3.02	5.26	6.02	6.67	7.48	8.44	9.72	11.86	15.21	26.32
1987	96.94	91.71	85.73	79.10	71.69	63.33	53.69	41.84	26.58	3.06	5.23	5.98	6.62	7.42	8.36	9.64	11.85	15.26	26.58
1988	96.84	91.70	85.83	79.31	71.98	63.72	54.16	42.41	27.15	3.16	5.14	5.88	6.52	7.33	8.26	9.56	11.75	15.26	27.15
1989	96.80	91.73	85.95	79.54	72.31	64.10	54.55	42.87	27.72	3.20	5.07	5.78	6.41	7.23	8.21	9.55	11.68	15.16	27.72
1990																			
1991	96.80	91.90	86.43	80.30	73.39	65.49	56.19	44.69	29.56	3.20	4.90	5.48	6.13	6.91	7.90	9.30	11.51	15.12	29.56
1992	96.84	92.15	86.85	80.87	74.14	66.38	57.24	45.86	30.70	3.16	4.69	5.30	5.98	6.73	7.76	9.14	11.38	15.16	30.70
1993	96.86	92.27	87.01	81.07	74.33	66.60	57.42	46.03	30.90	3.14	4.59	5.26	5.94	6.74	7.74	9.17	11.39	15.14	30.90
1994	96.84	92.26	86.99	81.06	74.33	66.62	57.53	46.17	31.01	3.16	4.58	5.27	5.93	6.73	7.70	9.10	11.36	15.16	31.01
1995	96.68	92.01	86.64	80.64	73.84	66.08	56.93	45.50	30.22	3.32	4.67	5.37	6.00	6.80	7.76	9.15	11.43	15.28	30.22
1996	96.65	92.03	86.67	80.72	73.97	66.28	57.21	45.88	30.65	3.35	4.63	5.35	5.96	6.74	7.69	9.07	11.33	15.23	30.65
1997	96.74	92.07	86.70	80.70	73.94	66.22	57.11	45.72	30.40	3.26	4.66	5.37	6.00	6.76	7.71	9.11	11.39	15.32	30.40
1998	96.59	91.89	86.53	80.55	73.80	66.10	56.98	45.55	30.28	3.41	4.69	5.36	5.98	6.76	7.70	9.12	11.42	15.27	30.28
1999	96.51	91.81	86.45	80.48	73.73	66.05	56.98	45.68	30.48	3.49	4.69	5.36	5.97	6.74	7.69	9.07	11.29	15.20	30.48
2000	96.67	91.98	86.67	80.73	74.02	66.34	57.27	46.01	30.70	3.33	4.69	5.31	5.94	6.71	7.68	9.07	11.26	15.31	30.70
2001																			
2002	96.86	92.28	87.02	81.14	74.50	66.87	57.84	46.62	31.42	3.14	4.59	5.26	5.88	6.64	7.63	9.03	11.22	15.19	31.42
2003	97.06	92.51	87.28	81.42	74.80	67.20	58.22	47.05	31.82	2.94	4.54	5.24	5.85	6.62	7.60	8.98	11.17	15.23	31.82
2004	97.08	92.55	87.36	81.54	74.94	67.33	58.34	47.17	31.95	2.92	4.53	5.19	5.82	6.60	7.61	8.99	11.17	15.22	31.95

Source: Own computations based on micro-data from *quadros de pessoal.*

Table 11D.7 Fractiles of earnings from administrative records in Portugal, 1985–2004 (amounts in 2005 euros)

	Median Wage (1)	P90 (2)	P95 (3)	P99 (4)	P99.5 (5)	P99.9 (6)	P99.99 (7)	P90–100 (8)	P95–100 (9)	P99–100 (10)	P99.5–100 (11)	P99.9–100 (12)	P99.99–100 (13)	P90–95 (14)	P95–99 (15)	P99–99.5 (16)	P99.5–99.9 (17)	P99.9–99.99 (18)
1985	6,158	13,462	17,351	30,195	38,451	90,681	163,533	21,304	32,150	58,899	78,593	136,519	229,303	15,077	21,765	33,516	54,797	107,927
1986	6,456	14,364	18,359	30,587	37,503	62,260	134,220	21,466	26,911	44,118	54,710	90,310	179,374	16,035	22,636	33,566	45,866	80,542
1987	6,756	15,186	19,509	32,771	40,437	65,864	137,378	22,864	28,722	46,947	57,938	93,783	175,280	16,995	24,149	35,932	48,946	84,672
1988	6,795	15,554	20,182	34,530	42,696	70,076	141,124	23,771	30,066	49,602	61,125	98,348	174,849	17,491	25,204	38,115	51,858	90,018
1989	6,785	15,680	20,559	35,859	44,863	73,371	133,540	24,340	30,934	51,455	63,399	98,916	166,057	17,754	25,814	39,531	54,546	91,507
1990																		
1991	7,165	17,668	23,884	45,380	57,346	89,501	146,171	28,933	37,553	64,515	78,207	113,469	184,464	20,315	30,804	50,772	69,377	105,590
1992	7,529	18,986	26,624	50,412	63,157	97,833	158,504	31,960	41,715	70,900	85,911	126,341	244,212	22,208	34,426	55,901	75,810	113,254
1993	7,663	19,237	26,897	53,078	67,303	99,669	157,139	32,858	43,294	74,304	89,243	127,780	239,191	22,412	35,525	59,337	79,571	115,387
1994	7,789	19,634	27,094	54,137	69,095	108,636	187,612	33,740	44,767	79,249	97,924	154,062	378,943	22,804	36,294	60,824	84,221	129,631
1995	7,889	19,775	26,764	50,584	64,634	108,683	230,402	32,858	43,024	76,005	95,549	160,059	324,866	22,684	34,766	56,441	79,395	141,635
1996	8,104	20,482	27,942	53,716	68,669	115,457	258,357	34,508	45,413	81,241	102,420	175,281	354,659	23,510	36,321	59,773	83,869	154,893
1997	8,141	20,707	27,926	52,936	66,909	113,073	259,803	34,355	44,992	79,598	100,404	172,691	354,908	23,709	36,328	58,768	82,304	152,427
1998	8,381	21,306	28,769	53,807	68,198	114,592	295,954	35,329	46,239	82,173	104,446	187,482	437,290	24,490	37,364	60,062	83,939	160,205
1999	8,427	21,636	29,378	54,466	68,524	118,462	291,706	36,024	47,159	84,146	107,850	197,970	523,842	24,936	37,959	60,532	85,451	162,142
2000	8,642	22,392	30,061	54,912	69,361	122,401	319,950	37,220	48,757	89,487	117,965	242,973	931,921	25,664	38,549	61,157	86,594	165,763
2001																		
2002	8,836	22,851	31,145	57,775	73,370	130,077	492,789	39,220	52,083	99,458	134,621	306,051	1,327,662	26,302	40,156	64,167	91,583	192,343
2003	8,772	23,003	31,349	59,133	75,853	141,257	392,081	39,530	52,521	99,639	133,111	278,449	972,375	26,477	40,647	66,028	96,537	201,191
2004	8,771	23,040	31,513	59,223	76,333	141,174	424,320	39,871	53,063	101,661	136,863	294,690	1,127,089	26,681	40,917	66,462	97,410	202,354

Note: Original information refers to monthly earnings. Amounts have been annualized by considering 14 monthly pays per year.

Source: Own computations based on micro-data from *quadros de pessoal*.

Table 11D.7 (continued) Fractiles of earnings from administrative records in Portugal, 1985–2004 (amounts in 2005 euros)

	Median Wage (1)	P10 (2)	P20 (3)	P30 (4)	P40 (5)	P50 (6)	P60 (7)	P70 (8)	P80 (9)	P90 (10)	P10–100 (11)	P20–100 (12)	P30–100 (13)	P40–100 (14)	P50–100 (15)	P60–100 (16)	P70–100 (17)	P80–100 (18)	P90–100 (19)	P10–20 (20)	P20–30 (21)	P30–40 (22)	P40–50 (23)	P50–60 (24)	P60–70 (25)	P70–80 (26)	P80–90 (27)
1985	6,158	3,386	4,370	4,837	5,462	6,158	6,958	8,225	10,135	13,462	8,413	8,964	9,587	10,325	11,227	12,395	14,012	16,461	21,304	4,005	4,593	5,150	5,807	6,549	7,533	9,104	11,606
1986	6,456	3,598	4,586	5,116	5,768	6,457	7,338	8,662	10,780	14,364	8,786	9,349	9,983	10,740	11,668	12,865	14,512	16,933	21,466	4,294	4,912	5,445	6,110	6,888	7,931	9,682	12,416
1987	6,756	3,853	4,788	5,440	6,022	6,756	7,642	9,118	11,424	15,186	9,267	9,863	10,536	11,342	12,335	13,621	15,398	17,998	22,864	4,499	5,145	5,696	6,376	7,186	8,284	10,192	13,123
1988	6,795	3,952	4,790	5,436	6,026	6,795	7,697	9,173	11,577	15,554	9,423	10,038	10,737	11,575	12,607	13,950	15,810	18,568	23,771	4,504	5,150	5,714	6,423	7,238	8,378	10,300	13,377
1989	6,785	4,002	4,735	5,315	6,016	6,785	7,682	9,150	11,468	15,680	9,445	10,069	10,782	11,641	12,699	14,071	15,968	18,824	24,340	4,457	5,078	5,634	6,352	7,211	8,385	10,259	13,314
1990																											
1991	7,165	4,419	5,051	5,675	6,329	7,165	8,352	10,031	12,659	17,668	10,526	11,242	12,083	13,098	14,365	16,023	18,331	21,865	28,933	4,792	5,358	5,995	6,760	7,729	9,100	11,258	14,795
1992	7,529	4,449	5,185	5,861	6,547	7,529	8,729	10,530	13,396	18,986	11,202	11,993	12,917	14,035	15,438	17,280	19,864	23,871	31,960	4,881	5,521	6,229	7,002	8,080	9,520	11,851	15,785
1993	7,663	4,547	5,211	5,967	6,700	7,663	8,889	10,728	13,737	19,237	11,448	12,267	13,220	14,371	15,812	17,707	20,359	24,478	32,858	4,880	5,593	6,312	7,166	8,223	9,752	12,109	16,090
1994	7,789	4,782	5,353	6,091	6,823	7,789	9,027	10,922	14,097	19,634	11,710	12,549	13,523	14,701	16,176	18,125	20,867	25,118	33,740	5,001	5,756	6,481	7,356	8,414	9,939	12,414	16,564
1995	7,889	4,842	5,503	6,155	6,927	7,889	9,099	10,988	14,151	19,775	11,683	12,507	13,459	14,614	16,059	17,964	20,635	24,737	32,858	5,076	5,838	6,526	7,386	8,435	9,950	12,424	16,609
1996	8,104	4,933	5,661	6,325	7,129	8,104	9,311	11,287	14,538	20,482	12,096	12,952	13,942	15,147	16,659	18,657	21,472	25,827	34,508	5,191	6,003	6,681	7,563	8,628	10,174	12,712	17,079
1997	8,141	5,005	5,738	6,402	7,163	8,141	9,379	11,368	14,707	20,707	12,152	13,009	13,999	15,202	16,714	18,712	21,518	25,838	34,355	5,268	6,073	6,776	7,643	8,716	10,292	12,874	17,314
1998	8,381	5,058	5,927	6,599	7,402	8,381	9,702	11,765	15,153	21,306	12,522	13,400	14,421	15,662	17,217	19,277	22,156	26,571	35,329	5,492	6,273	6,993	7,907	9,006	10,669	13,365	17,865
1999	8,427	5,145	5,987	6,685	7,500	8,427	9,812	11,785	15,192	21,636	12,678	13,563	14,596	15,852	17,428	19,514	22,446	26,995	36,024	5,557	6,345	7,069	7,982	9,097	10,737	13,367	17,994
2000	8,642	5,206	6,120	6,797	7,653	8,642	10,017	12,114	15,561	22,392	13,024	13,940	15,010	16,312	17,947	20,106	23,145	27,889	37,220	5,677	6,437	7,196	8,133	9,301	10,984	13,647	18,547
2001																											
2002	8,836	5,267	6,205	6,930	7,774	8,836	10,296	12,408	15,945	22,851	13,434	14,396	15,515	16,878	18,596	20,866	24,064	29,091	39,220	5,711	6,548	7,319	8,271	9,500	11,248	13,980	18,924
2003	8,772	5,226	6,140	6,875	7,702	8,772	10,234	12,281	15,830	23,003	13,400	14,367	15,490	16,860	18,586	20,872	24,109	29,224	39,530	5,633	6,491	7,255	8,209	9,420	11,136	13,846	18,874
2004	8,771	5,235	6,114	6,841	7,732	8,771	10,266	12,321	15,866	23,040	13,461	14,436	15,572	16,957	18,702	21,003	24,264	29,428	39,871	5,647	6,480	7,264	8,234	9,496	11,219	13,937	18,987

Note: Original information refers to monthly earnings. Amounts have been annualized by considering 14 monthly pays per year.

Source: Own computations based on micro-data from *quadros de pessoal*.

Individuals are classified as employers, family employees with no salary, employees, and cooperative workers. In the estimations I only consider individuals with non-zero wages in the last two groups. Shares of top wages are presented in Table 11D.6, where I also provide estimations for the left part of the distribution. Original amounts reflect monthly earnings. Table 11D.7 shows income levels of selected fractiles, where I annualized the amounts by upscaling monthly earnings by a factor of 14 (to take into account two annual bonuses).

REFERENCES

Albuquerque, R. and M. Gouveia (1994). 'Distribuição dos salarios em Portugal 1980 e 1990', in Banco de Portugal, *Relatório anual*.

Alvaredo, F. (2009). 'Top Incomes and Earnings in Portugal 1936–2005', *Explorations in Economic History*, 46(4): 404–17.

—— and E. Saez (2009). 'Income and Wealth Concentration in Spain from a Historical and Fiscal Perspective', *Journal of the European Economic Association*, 7(5): 1140–67. Longer version in Chapter 10 of this volume.

Atkinson, A. B. (2007). 'The Distribution of Top Incomes in the United Kingdom 1908–2000', in Atkinson and Piketty (2007).

—— and T. Piketty (2007). *Top Incomes over the Twentieth Century: A Contrast between European and English Speaking Countries*. Oxford: Oxford University Press.

Baganha, M. (1990). *Portuguese Emigration to the United States 1820–1930*. New York: Garland Publishing Inc.

—— (1991). 'Uma imagem desfocada: a emigração portuguesa e as fontes sobre a emigração', *Análise social*, 26(3–4): 723–39.

—— (1993). 'Principais características e tendências da emigração portuguesa', in APS, *Estructuras Sociais e Desenvolvimento*. Lisbon: Fragmentos.

—— (1994). 'As correntes emigratórias portuguesas no século XX e o seu impacto na economia nacional', *Análise social*, 29(4): 959–80.

Baklanoff, E. (1992). 'The Political Economy of Portugal's Later Estado Novo: A Critique of the Stagnation Thesis', *Luso-Brazilian Review*, 29(1): 1–17.

Barreto, A. (1983). *Memórias da reforma agrária*. Lisbon: Publicações Europa-América.

—— (1987). *Anatomia de uma revoluçao*. Lisbon: Publicações Europa-América.

—— (1988). 'Reforma agraria y revolución en Portugal, 1974–76', *Revista de estudios políticos (nueva epoca)*, 60–1: 413–29.

Batista, C. (2002). 'Skill Premium in Portugal: Some Evidence on the Capital–Skill Complementarity Hypothesis', mimeo.

Batista, D., C. Martins, M. Pinheiro, and J. Reis (1997). 'New Estimates for Portugal's GDP 1910–1958', *História económica*, 7, Banco de Portugal.

Bermeo, N. (1997). 'Myths of Moderation: Confrontation and Conflict during Democratic Transitions', *Comparative Politics*, 29(3): 305–22.

Bover, O., P. García-Perea, and P. Portugal (1998). 'A Comparative Study of the Portuguese and Spanish Labor Markets', Bank of Spain Working Paper 9807.

Budría, S. (2007). 'Economic Inequality in Portugal: A Picture in the Beginnings of the 21st Century', Munich Personal RePEc Archive Working Paper No. 1784.

—— and C. Nunes (2005). 'Education and Wage Inequality in Portugal', in R. Asplund and E. Barth (eds.) *Education and Wage Inequality in Europe: A Literature Review.* ETLA, Series B209, Helsinki.

—— and P. Pereira (2007). 'The Wage Effects of Training in Portugal: Differences across Skill Groups, Genders, Sectors, and Training Types', *Applied Economics*, 39(6): 787–807.

—— —— (2008). 'Education and Wage Dispersion: New Evidence for Europe', in P. Dolton, R. Asplund, and E. Barth (eds.) *Education and Inequality across Europe.* Cheltenham: Edward Elgar.

Cantó, O., A. Cardoso, and J. Jimeno (2002). 'Earnings Inequality in Portugal and Spain: Contrasts and Similarities', in D. Cohen, T. Piketty, and G. Saint-Paul (eds.) *The Economics of Rising Inequalities.* Oxford: Oxford University Press: 55–73.

Cardoso, A. (1994). 'Regional Wage Inequality in Portugal', *Estudos de economia*, 14(4): 429–50.

—— (1998a). 'Earnings Inequality in Portugal: High and Rising?', *Review of Income and Wealth*, 44(3): 325–43.

—— (1998b). 'Workers or Employers: Who is Shaping Wage Inequality?' *Oxford Bulletin of Economics and Statistics*, 59(4): 523–47.

—— (1999). 'Firms' Wage Policies and the Rise in Labor Market Inequality: The Case of Portugal', *Industrial and Labor Relations Review*, 53(1): 87–102.

—— (2006). 'Wage Mobility: Do Institutions Make a Difference? A Replication Study Comparing Portugal and the UK', *Labour Economics*, 13(3): 387–404.

Cardoso. F. and V. Cunha (2005). 'Household Wealth in Portugal: 1980–2004', Banco de Portugal Working Paper 4.

Carneiro, P. (2008). 'Equality of Opportunity and Educational Achievement in Portugal', *Portuguese Economic Journal*, 7(1): 17–41.

Castanheira, M. and M. Carvalho (1997). 'Desigualdade na distribução do rendimento e disparidades regionais', *Prospectiva e planeamento*, 3–4: 267–78.

—— and M. Ribeiro (1977). 'A repartição pessoal do rendimento em Portugal', *Análise social*, 13(3): 727–39.

Conim, C. (1976). 'Algumas considerações sobre a situação demográfica portuguesa de 1960 a 1975', in Instituto Nacional de Estatística, *Revista do centro de estudos demográficos*, 22: 171–239.

Costa, A. (1994). 'The Measurement of Poverty in Portugal', *Journal of the European Social Policy*, 4(2): 95–115.

Dell, F., T. Piketty, and E. Saez (2007). 'Income and Wealth Concentration in Switzerland over the Twentieth Century', in Atkinson and Piketty (2007).

Direcçao-Geral dos Impostos (1998a). *Sistema fiscal português*, Centro de Estudos Fiscais. Lisbon: Editora Rei dos Livros.

—— (1998b). *Relatório da comissão para o desenvolvimento da reforma fiscal*, chapter 13.

—— (2005). 'Simplificação do sistema fiscal português: relatório do grupo de trabalho criado por despacho do Ministro de Estado e das Finanças', *Cadernos ciência e técnica fiscal*, 201.

Downs, C. (1983). 'Residents' Commissions and Urban Struggles in Revolutionary Portugal', in L. Graham and D. Wheeler (eds.) *In Search of Modern Portugal: The Revolution and its Consequences.* Madison: University of Wisconsin Press: 151–79.

Feenberg, D. and J. Poterba (1993). 'Income Inequality and the Incomes of Very High Income Taxpayers: Evidence from Tax Returns', in J. Poterba (ed.) *Tax Policy and the Economy*, vol. vii. Cambridge, Mass.: MIT Press: 145–77.

Ferreira, L. (1992). 'Pobreza em Portugal: variação e decomposição de medidas de pobreza a partir dos orçamentos familiares de 1980–1981 e 1989–1990', *Estudos de economia*, 12(4): 377–93.

Gallaher, T. (1983). *Portugal: A Twentieth-Century Interpretation*. Manchester: Manchester University Press.

Gouveia, M. and C. Rodrigues (2002). 'The Impact of Guaranteed Minimum Income Program in Portugal', *Public Finance and Management*, 2(2).

—— and J. Tavares (1995). 'The Distribution of Household Income and Expenditure in Portugal: 1980 and 1990', *Review of Income and Wealth*, 41(1): 1–17.

Guilera, J. (2008). 'Top Income Shares in Portugal over the Twentieth Century', Documents de Treball de la Facultat de Ciències Econòmiques I Empresarials, E08/195, Universitat de Barcelona.

Harsgor, M. (1976). 'Portugal in Revolution', The Washington Papers, 3, No. 33, Beverly Hills, Calif.: Sage Publications.

Hartog, J., P. Pereira, and J. Vieira (1999). 'Inter-Industry Wage Dispersion in Portugal: High but Falling', IZA Discussion Paper No. 53.

—— —— —— (2001). 'Changing Returns to Education in Portugal during the 1980s and the early 1990s: OLS and Quantile Regression Estimators', *Applied Economics*, 33(8): 1021–37.

Hudson, M. (1989). 'Portugal to 1993: Investing in a European Future'. London: The Economist Intelligence Unit, Special Report 1157.

ILO (International Labor Organization) (1979). *Employment and Basic Needs in Portugal*, Annex I: 'The Economic and Social Development of Portugal to 1975'. Geneva.

Jimeno, J., O. Cantó, A. Rute, M. Izquierdo, and C. Rodrigues (2000). 'Integration and Inequality: Lessons from the Accessions of Portugal and Spain to the EU'. Madrid: FEDEA.

Kuznets, S. (1953). *Shares of Upper Income Groups in Income and Savings*. New York: National Bureau of Economic Research.

Lains, P. (1995). *A economia portuguesa no século XIX: crescimento económico e comércio externo*. Lisbon: Imprensa Nacional.

—— (2003a). 'Catching Up to the European Core: Portuguese Economic Growth, 1910–1990', *Explorations in Economic History*, 40(4): 369–86.

—— (2003b). 'Portugal's Growth Paradox 1870–1950', Working Paper No. 135, Faculdade de Economia, Universidade do Porto.

—— (2003c). 'New Wine in Old Bottles: Output and Productivity Trends in Portuguese Agriculture 1850–1950', *European Review of Economic History*, 7(1): 1–30.

Landais, C. (2007). 'Les Hauts Revenus en France (1998–2006): une explosion des inégalités?', Paris School of Economics, mimeo.

Lopes, L. (1994). 'Manufacturing Productivity in Portugal in a Comparative Perspective', *Notas económicas*, 4: 55–76.

—— (1996). *A economia Portuguesa desde 1960*. Lisbon: Gradiva.

Machado, J. and J. Mata (2001). 'Earnings Functions in Portugal 1982–1994: Evidence from Quantile Regressions', *Empirical Economics*, 26(1): 115–34.

Maddison, A. (2001). *The World Economy. A Millennial Perspective*. Paris: OECD.

—— (2003). *The World Economy. Historical Statistics*. Paris: OECD.

Makler, H. (1969). *A 'elite' industrial portuguesa*. Lisbon: Instituto Gulbenkian de Ciencia.

—— (1976). 'The Portuguese Industrial Elite and its Corporative Relations: A Study of Compartmentalization in an Authoritarian Regime', *Economic Development and Cultural Change*, 24(3): 495–526.

Martins, M. and J. Chaves Rosa (1979). *O grupo estado: anàlise e listagem completa das sociedades de sector publico empresarial.* Lisbon: Edições Journal Expresso.

Martins, P. and P. Pereira (2004). 'Does Education Reduce Wage Inequality? Quantile Regressions Evidence from Sixteen European Countries', *Labour Economics*, 11(3): 355–71.

Ministério do Emprego e da Segurança Social (1992). *Relatório de cojuntura anual de 1989: relatórios e análises*, 44, Departamento de Estudos e Planeamento.

Mouteira Guerreiro, A. (1947). *Imposto profissional.* Biblioteca Fiscal Atlântida. Coimbra: Livraria Editora Lda.

Murray, A. and H. Steedman (1998). 'Growing Skills in Europe: The Changing Skills Profiles of France, Germany, the Netherlands, Portugal, Sweden and the UK', CEP Discussion Paper No. 399, London School of Economics.

Nunes, A., E. Mata, and N. Valério (1989). 'Portuguese Economic Growth 1833–1985', *Journal of European Economic History*, 18(3): 291–300.

OECD (Organization for Economic Cooperation and Development) (1992). 'Earnings Inequality: Changes in the 1980s', *Employment Outlook*, July: 157–84.

Payne, S. (1972). *A History of Spain and Portugal.* Madison: University of Wisconsin Press.

Pereira, M. (1993). 'Liberdade e contenção na emigração portuguesa 1850–1930', in M. Silva (ed.) *Emigração/imigração.* Lisbon: Fragmentos.

Piketty, T. (2001). *Les Hauts Revenus en France au 20ème siècle: inégalités et redistributions, 1901–1998.* Paris: Éditions Grasset.

——— and E. Saez (2003). 'Income Inequality in the United States, 1913–1998', *Quarterly Journal of Economics*, 118(1): 1–39. Longer version in Atkinson and Piketty (2007).

Robinson, R. (1979). *Contemporary Portugal.* London: George Allen & Unwin.

Rodrigues, C. (1988). 'Estudo comparativo da desigualdade das famílias portuguesas 1973/74–1980/81', CISEP Working Paper, Instituto Superior de Economia e Gestão, Lisbon.

——— (1993). 'The Measurement and Decomposition of Inequality in Portugal 1980/1981–1989/1990', Microsimulation Unit Discussion Paper MU9302, Department of Applied Economics, Cambridge University.

——— (1994). 'Repartição do rendimento e disigualade: Portugal nos anos 80', *Estudos de economia*, 14(4): 399–427.

——— (1996). 'Medição e decomposição da desigualdade em Portugal 1980–1990', *Revista de estatística*, 3(1): 47–70.

——— (1999). 'Income Distribution and Poverty in Portugal 1994/1995: A Comparison between the European Community Household Panel and the Household Budget Survey', Working Paper CISEP, ISEG/Universidade Técnica de Lisboa, June. Portuguese version: 'Repartição do rendimento e pobreza em Portugal 1994/1995: uma comparação entre o painel dos agregados familiares e o inquérito aos orçamentos familiares', *Revista de estatística*, 5(1): 117–42.

——— (2008). *Distribuição do rendimento, desigualdade e pobreza: Portugal nos anos 90.* Coimbra: Editora Almedina.

——— and J. Albuquerque (2000). 'Pobreza e exclusão social: percursos e perspectivas da investigação em Portugal', in *Actas do Seminário Pobreza e Exclusão Social: Percursos e Perspectivas da Investigação em Portugal.* Lisbon: CESIS.

Salazar, A. (1939). *Doctrine and Action: Internal and Foreign Policy of the New Portugal 1928–1939.* London: Faber & Faber Ltd.

Santos, J. (1983). 'A distribuçao lognormal: sua aplicação a dados portugueses de distribução do rendimento', *Estudos de economia*, 3(2): 201–18.

Silva, M. (1971). 'O nível das receitas das famílias portuguesas', Monografias. Porto: Brotéria.

Teekens, R. (1990). 'Inequality and Poverty: Portugal Compared with Greece, Ireland and Spain', *Estudos de economia*, 10(2): 111–42.

Valério, N. (2001). *Estatísticas históricas portuguesas*. Lisbon: Instituto Nacional de Estatística.

Vieira, J. (1999). 'The Evolution of Wage Structure in Portugal 1982–1992', Ph.D. Thesis, Tinbergen Institute, Amsterdam.

—— J. Couto, and M. Tiago (2006). 'Inter-regional Wage Dispersion in Portugal, Regional and Sectoral Economic Studies', *Regional and Sectoral Economic Studies, Euro-American Association of Economic Development*, 6(1): 85–106.

Wheeler, D. (1990). 'Review of Portugal to 1993', *Portuguese Studies Newsletter*, 22: 44–5.

12

Top Incomes in Italy, 1974–2004

Facundo Alvaredo and Elena Pisano

12.1 INTRODUCTION

Italy was the home of Vilfredo Pareto, and under his influence the debate about the shape of the income and wealth distributions was very active nationwide during the first half of the twentieth century.[1] However, little could be done in practical terms at that moment to know the actual distributions, mainly due to the unavailability of data. The first household survey was conducted in 1947/8.[2] Since then, the study of income distribution has gained new interest and growing relevance in the public and academic debates. Brandolini and Sestito (1994) and Brandolini (1999, 2000, 2004) provide a comprehensive description of the dynamics of inequality in Italy during the second half of the twentieth century based on survey information.[3] Their estimates offer the best evidence to date in Italy from a historical perspective. The main features can be summarized as follows. First, the level of inequality did not significantly change between 1948 and 1968, the years of the 'Italian economic miracle'. As no comparable data are available for the intermediate years, it is not possible to rigorously establish whether this was

We thank Tony Atkinson, Aldo Barba, Luigi Bernardi, Marco Bartolich, Andrea Brandolini, Riccardo Capocaccia, Piero Cipollone, Cinzia Fortuzzi, Maurizio Franzini, Francesca Gastaldi, Daniela Monacelli, Michele Raitano, Giacomo Rondina, Antonio Pedone, Thomas Piketty, Romeo Pisano, Emmanuel Saez, Simone Tedeschi, Stefano Toso, and Giulio Zanella. Special acknowledgements go to Maria Teresa Pandolfi, the staff of the Bank of Italy library in Rome, SOGEI, and the Dipartimento delle Politiche Fiscali del Ministero dell'Economia e delle Finanze.

[1] Pareto was born in Paris in 1848, during his family's self-imposed exile. They moved back to Italy *c.*1858. He died in Geneva in 1923.

[2] Brandolini (1999) gives a detailed account of the development of household surveys in Italy. A private agency (Istituto Doxa) conducted the 1947/8 survey sponsored by public funds. The Italian statistics bureau (ISTAT) organized the first official surveys in 1953/4 and 1963/4. The Bank of Italy has conducted an annual survey of income and wealth between 1965 and 1987 (except for 1985) and every two years between 1989 and 1995 and since 1998 (IBFI, *Indagine sui bilanci delle famiglie italiane*, or SHIW, Survey of Households' Income and Wealth).

[3] An extensive list of works based on the Survey of Households' Income and Wealth can be found in Banca d'Italia (2008). Studies about income and wealth distributions in Italy include, among others, Albertini (2003, 2004), Baldini (1996), Biancotti, D'Alessio, and Neri (2008), Bottiroli Civardi and Targetti Lenti (2001), Brandolini and Cannari (1994), Brandolini et al. (2004), Brandolini, Cipollone, and Sestito (2001), Cannari and D'Alessio (1994, 2006), Clementi and Gallegati (2005), D'Alessio and Signorini (2000), Fiorio (2006), and Roberti (1971).

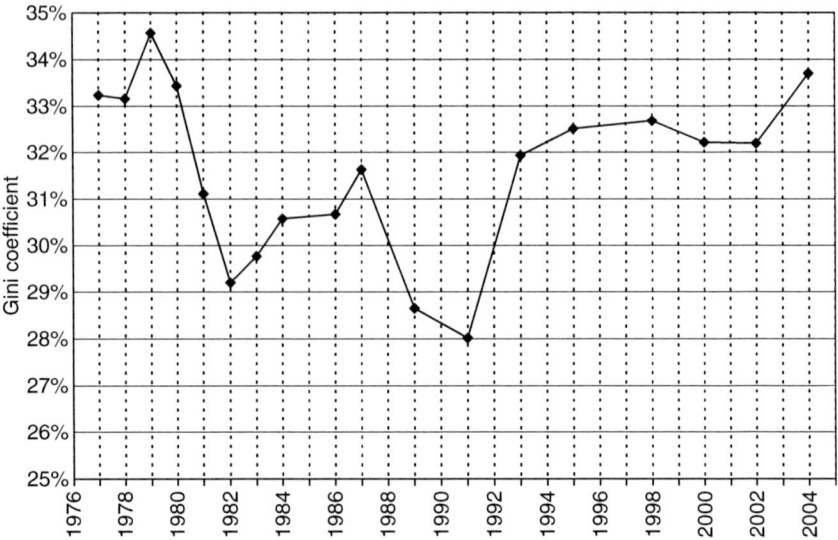

Figure 12.1 Gini coefficient in Italy, 1977–2004

Note: Gini coefficient of household disposable income.

Source: Own calculations based on Survey of Households' Income and Wealth-Historical Archive (SHIW-HA).

the result of a relative stability or, rather, of movements that eventually balanced each other. Second, income distribution markedly improved during the following decade 1968–77. Third, the Gini coefficient has displayed a W-shaped dynamics since the end of the 1970s, with valleys in 1982 and 1991 and peaks in 1979, 1987, and 1995.[4] Fourth, inequality remained fairly stable between 1995 and 2002; an increase was observed in 2004. Estimates of the Gini coefficient from the Bank of Italy's Survey of Households' Income and Wealth between 1977 and 2004 are shown in Figure 12.1. In terms of levels, the inequality of equivalent disposable income in Italy is one of the highest in the European Union, as shown in Smeeding (2000) and the Luxembourg Income Study comparative indicators, but it is still similar to those of Spain and Portugal.[5]

Despite the stability of relative measures of inequality (and the improvement of absolute ones) between 1995 and 2002, Italian households seem to have developed a feeling of impoverishment. Their perceptions about financial hardship and housing conditions had deteriorated since the mid 1990s and, more recently,

---

[4] Atkinson (2003) gives the same description.

[5] According to the Luxembourg Income Study for years 1999 and 2000 (depending on the country), Italy displayed a Gini index of 0.33, equal to that of Germany, above those of Denmark (0.22), Finland, Norway, the Netherlands, Slovenia, and Sweden (0.25), Austria and Luxembourg (0.26), Switzerland (0.28), Poland, Hungary (0.29), Belgium, France (0.28), Canada (0.30), Ireland (0.31), but below those of the United States (0.37), the United Kingdom, and Spain (0.34). Boeri and Brandolini (2004) give the following values for the Gini of disposable income in 1998: Italy, 0.34, Spain, 0.33, Portugal, 0.35.

their expectations about economic prospects (both personal and of their country) got significantly worse than in other European Union economies. Boeri and Brandolini (2004) discuss several potential explanations for this apparent contradiction between perceptions and facts. A first explanation points to expectations. The strong deceleration of growth since 1993 with respect to the previous two decades, the concerns about the long-term sustainability of the public budget (a Ricardian equivalence argument), and the belief of a weakening of the country competitiveness due to the European monetary policy could have led Italians to drastically revise downwards their expectations of future consumption growth.[6] A second explanation points to possible measurement problems with the data, which the authors rule out by comparing different sources. A third possible cause has to do with the observed widening gap between the incomes of employees and self-employees, suggesting that offsetting movements lie behind the stability of aggregate inequality indices. A final tentative reason is associated to the increased job precariousness: under stagnating incomes and risk aversion, greater uncertainty would reduce the well-being of individuals.

The feeling among the middle class that the rich are progressively becoming even richer can be hypothesized as an additional element to explain the sense of impoverishment among Italian households. In 2003 the Italian tax agency published the names of the top 500 income recipients in tax year 2000, together with their income.[7] First in the list, a businessman with annual revenue of 265 million euros, followed by ten other entrepreneurs and one CEO. In the twelfth place, a soccer player, getting 11.8 million euros, mostly in the form of wages. Close inspection of the list shows that 20 per cent of the individuals (85 people) in the top 0.001 per cent (457 people) were either soccer players or soccer coaches. Such facts seem to follow the 'superstar' theory of Rosen (1981), according to which the expansion of scale associated with globalization and with increased communication opportunities has disproportionately raised the rents of those with the very highest abilities. This pattern could have direct effects on the process of wealth accumulation, as the period of life over which these 'stars' are active and getting fantastic contracts can be (and usually is) very short. As noted in Atkinson (2003) the explanation for income inequality at the top goes well beyond the static picture of earned income.

In this chapter we analyse the performance of the very high-income recipients and describe the evolution of top income shares in Italy between 1974 and 2004. We provide systematic and homogeneous time series of income concentration based on tax records. Tax statistics have hardly been used before to study income concentration in Italy.[8] This is mainly due to the usual limitations of tax-based

[6] Real GDP grew at a rate of 2.3% per year between 1983 and 1992, at 1.7% per year between 1994 and 2003, and at 0.3% per year between 2004 and 2005.

[7] Agenzia delle Entrate (2003). Only 33 out of the 500 individuals in the list are women, that is, less than 7%.

[8] Exceptions are Brandolini (2000, 2004) and ISAE (2002). Income tax statistics have been extensively used for the analysis of fiscal reforms and to predict tax receipts, as in Giarda (2003), and Pellegrino (2006, 2007). The limitations of tax-based data are not exclusive to the Italian case.

data: the definitions of income and the income unit follow those of the changing tax legislation; capital gains are mostly untaxed; capital incomes are recorded to different degrees along time; tax data are affected by tax evasion and avoidance.

Unfortunately, we cannot build a secular evolution of top income shares; records based on tax returns are only available since 1974, following the introduction of the modern income tax. In 1923 the government established the *imposta complementare*, which was a surtax (additional to the traditional schedule taxes) levied on high incomes with a progressive tax scale; in 1951 the authorities imposed the requirement of a unique annual tax file detailing all taxable income and schedule taxes paid.[9] The *imposta complementare* remained in existence until 1972 and could have provided information on top incomes, but, to our knowledge, there are no published tabulations showing incomes assessed to it.

Together with the cases of Spain (Alvaredo and Saez 2009 and Chapter 10) and Portugal (Alvaredo 2009 and Chapter 11), the experience of Italy provides new information to compare the evolution of income concentration in Mediterranean Europe. We find a persistent increasing pattern in top income shares since the mid 1980s, mainly driven by top wages and self-employment income. From a new perspective, we confirm that the late 1980s and early 1990s were years of unequal growth (Brandolini and Sestito 1994), and also find that the years that followed combined rising income concentration with a lower growth rate. Notwithstanding the increasing trend, the rise in Italian top shares has been small relative to the surge experienced by top incomes in the United States and other Anglo-Saxon developed economies, as documented in Atkinson and Piketty (2007). Thus, the Italian case is also closer to that of continental Europe countries.

The chapter is structured as follows. Section 12.2 describes our data, sources, and methods, and discusses the issue of tax evasion. Section 12.3 presents and analyses the trends in top income shares between 1974 and 2004. Section 12.4 briefly discusses the role of marginal tax rates on top shares. Section 12.5 offers a conclusion. Details on data sources and methods are presented in the appendices.

12.2 DATA AND METHODOLOGICAL ISSUES

Data and Series Construction

Our estimates are based on personal income tax return statistics compiled by SOGEI and the Italian tax administration annually from 1974 to 2004.[10] The published tabulations, structured by range of total before tax income, provide

---

[9] In essence, the structure of the Italian tax system before 1973 (schedule taxes and a surtax) was similar to that in place in the UK by the first decade of the twentieth century.

[10] SOGEI (Società Generale d'Informatica) is the company established in 1976 to create the tax registry and to help the tax administration implement the complex reform of 1973. Since then it has been in charge of collecting and processing tax data.

information of total income assessed, number of taxpayers, taxable income, deductions, allowances, composition, and tax paid. As far as we can document, no tabulation exists before 1974. Consequently, our analysis is focused by necessity on the thirty years following 1974.

Our top groups are defined relative to the total number of adults (aged 20 and above) from the Italian census (not the number of tax returns actually filed). For example, in 2004, there were 46,811,000 adults in Italy, so the top 1 per cent represents the top 468,110 tax filers. The Italian income tax is individually based since 1976 (in contrast to many countries where joint filing remains optional, in Italy individual filing is mandatory). Until 1975, it was family based. As tax returns statistics for 1974 and 1975 were elaborated after the code change, fortunately published statistics provide both the individual and the family distributions separately. The former are used in our estimations so that no ad hoc corrections are necessary to account for the shift from the family to the individual.

We define income as gross income before all deductions and including all income items reported on personal tax returns: salaries and pensions, self-employment and unincorporated business net income, dividends, farm income, real estate income, and other smaller income items. Interest income is not included, as it is subject to a flat tax withheld at the source without further requirement of reporting. Realized capital gains went mostly untaxed and not reported until 1998; since then, gains from qualified equities have been reported at varying degrees. Consequently, income covers capital income incompletely and excludes most capital gains.[11] We apply several adjustments to make the series consistent along time. Our income definition is before personal income taxes but after corporate income taxes. Details can be found in Appendix 12A.

As the top tail of the income distribution is very well approximated by Pareto distributions, we apply simple parametric interpolation methods to estimate the thresholds and average income levels for each fractile. This method follows the classical study by Kuznets (1953) and has been used in many of the top income studies presented in Atkinson and Piketty (2007) and in this volume.[12] In the case of Italy, there is no public micro-data of tax returns that would allow us to check the validity of our estimations based on the published tax statistics. However, Piketty (2001), Piketty and Saez (2003), and Alvaredo and Saez (2009) (and Chapter 10 in this volume) have validated this method by comparing the results obtained using micro-data available for recent years in France, the United States, and Spain.[13]

In order to estimate shares of income, we need to divide the income amounts accruing to each fractile by an estimate of total personal income ideally defined as total personal income fully reported on income tax returns had everybody been

[11] The treatment of capital incomes and capital gains is a matter of utter importance, given the relevance of those components among top income earners. We warn about the limitations of the Italian data in this respect and refer the reader to the general discussion in Chapter 13.

[12] The mean-split histogram method has also been used to estimate top income shares in some of the chapters of Atkinson and Piketty (2007) and in this volume.

[13] These authors find that tabulation-based estimates are always very close to the micro-data-based estimates (within 2–5%), giving confidence that the errors due to interpolation are fairly modest.

Table 12.1 Thresholds and average incomes in top income groups in Italy, 2000 and 2004

Percentile threshold (1)	Income threshold (2)	Income groups (3)	Number of adults (aged 20 +) (4)	Average income in each group (5)
A. 2004				
		Full adult population	46,811,000	15,860 €
Top 10%	28,815 €	Top 10–5%	2,340,550	32,778 €
Top 5%	38,626 €	Top 5–1%	1,872,440	52,883 €
Top 1%	81,280 €	Top 1–0.5%	234,055	93,268 €
Top 0.5%	108,129 €	Top 0.5–0.1%	187,244	142,993 €
Top 0.1%	216,238 €	Top 0.1–0.01%	42,130	325,946 €
Top 0.01%	670,397 €	Top 0.01%	4,681	1,318,121 €
B. 2000				
		Full adult population	45,710,000	15,104 €
Top 10%	27,582 €	Top 10–5%	2,285,500	31,360 €
Top 5%	37,223 €	Top 5–1%	1,828,400	50,863 €
Top 1%	79,016 €	Top 1–0.5%	228,550	89,878 €
Top 0.5%	104,910 €	Top 0.5–0.1%	182,840	136,914 €
Top 0.1%	207,304 €	Top 0.1–0.01%	41,139	300,100 €
Top 0.01%	582,907 €	Top 0.01–0.001%	4,114	845,737 €
Top 0.001%	1,973,571 €	Top 0.001%	457	4,160,256 €

Notes: Computations based on income tax return statistics and National Accounts. Income defined as annual gross income reported on tax returns, before individual income taxes but net of social contributions, and excluding interest income and most capital gains. Amounts are expressed in current 2004 euros. Column (2) reports the income thresholds corresponding to each of the percentiles in column (1). For example, an annual income of at least 28,815 euros is required to belong to the top 10% tax units in 2004, etc.

required to file a tax return. We approximate the ideal income denominator as the sum of (1) total wages and salaries from National Accounts net of social security contributions, (2) old-age and disability pensions from the Social Security Administration, (3) 50 per cent of unincorporated business income from National Accounts (we assume that the rest is from the informal sector an escapes taxation), (4) all non-business, non-labour income reported on tax returns (as capital income is very concentrated, non-filers receive a negligible fraction of capital income).[14]

Table 12.1 gives thresholds and average incomes for a selection of top fractiles in Italy in 2000 and 2004. For 2000, in particular, we use the cited list of the top 500 income earners to provide estimates up to the top 0.001 per cent. Tables with remaining information are presented in the appendix to this chapter: Table 12A.1

[14] The control total for income (Table 12A.1, column 4) is thus lower than the ideal economy income as it excludes 50% of unincorporated business revenue. Atkinson (2007a) makes explicit reference to the challenges and difficulties in the definition of the income denominator.

shows reference totals for population, income, and inflation used in our computations; Tables 12A.2 and 12A.3 present the results of shares and incomes for top groups.

Published tabulations also provide information about the composition of income by brackets (composition being available at the individual level since 1976), allowing for an analysis of income sources within each fractile. As no obvious hypothesis on the distribution function of income components within each fractile can be made, we use a simple linear interpolation method to decompose the amount of income for each fractile into real estate rents, employment income, entrepreneurial income, self-employment, business income, and capital income. Table 12A.4 displays the composition results.

The Issues of Tax Avoidance and Evasion

There is a generalized view of tax evasion being extremely high in Italy, and much higher than in other OECD countries. Audits and subsequent scandals involving show business people, well-known fashion designers, and sport stars help support this idea among the general public, even when they also provide evidence about the fact that top income earners are very visible for the tax administration. The publication of the top 500 income earners, probably motivated by a strategy to shame prominent evaders (as done in Spain in the 1930s, see Chapter 10), is an example of such visibility.[15] It is thus necessary to qualify the effect of income tax evasion for our estimates as well as for their comparability. We make reference to three key elements: the level of incomes reported in the tax returns, the existent estimations of income tax evasion, and the amounts evaded through tax havens.

First, it is usually claimed that the average income reported in Italian tax files is excessively low compared to the amounts declared in similar countries (ISAE 2006). However, inspection of published tabulations, of our computations, and of the results in Alvaredo and Saez (2009) show that income thresholds and average incomes corresponding to the *top percentiles* are significantly higher in Italy than in Spain, for example. In 2004, an income of at least 69,191 euros was required to belong to the top 1 per cent in Spain (excluding capital gains), this figure being 81,280 euros in Italy. This represents a 17.5 per cent difference, which more than doubles the gap between average incomes in both countries.[16] The situation seems different at the bottom half of the distribution: also in 2004, the bottom 50 per cent of Italian tax filers had incomes below 13,000 euros, while their Spanish counterparts had incomes below 15,500 euros. However, this last type of comparison, which usually appears in the media and in scholarly papers as supportive evidence of scandalous levels of evasion, is misleading. In Spain, in 2004, only 53 per cent of adults filed a tax return; in Italy 86 per cent of adults did

---

[15] In 2008 the tax agency published the complete list of taxpayers for tax year 2005 online. Considered a threat to privacy rights, the information was available only for a few hours.

[16] According to the income definition for the purposes of this paper, average income was 15,860 euros in Italy and 14,652 euros in Spain in 2004 (an 8% difference).

so.[17] This means that the bottom 50 per cent of Italian tax filers is not necessarily comparable to the bottom 50 per cent of their Spanish counterparts.

Secondly, existent estimates of tax evasion in Italy over this period agree on the following facts. First, evasion decreases with true income (D'Amuri and Fiorio 2005). Second, as in other OECD countries, it is low for wages, salaries, and pensions at the *top of the distribution*: there is little room for evading those income components that must be reported independently by employers or payers. Third, evasion is important among small businesses and self-employees (traditionally numerous in Italy), for whom there is no double reporting. D'Amuri and Fiorio (2005) compare the incomes from the Bank of Italy survey with a representative sample of 250,000 anonymous tax returns in 2000, taking the discrepancy as a proxy of under-reporting. They find that evasion from wages is virtually zero in the top 10 per cent, while it is 63 per cent in the first decile. For self-employment income, these authors estimate evasion rates of 8 per cent and 70 per cent in the tenth and first deciles, respectively.[18] In any case, estimations must be read with caution due to the various ad hoc assumptions required: they can only be taken as rough approximations.[19]

Finally, recent events have put back in the spotlight the issue of tax havens. The very rich are generally thought to be able to evade tax on important fractions of their incomes through fiscal paradises. In their study of top incomes in Switzerland, Dell, Piketty, and Saez (2007) have addressed this issue. Even when there are many tax haven jurisdictions which are actively used to evade taxes on capital income, their estimates for Switzerland dissipate the myth that the sums earned through secret Swiss accounts are gigantic and capable of modifying the top share estimates in a significant way.[20]

[17] This is due to different exemption thresholds, dissimilar reporting rules, and different taxation unit (mandatory individual filing in Italy and optional family filing in Spain).

[18] Bernardi and Bernasconi (1996) and Bernardi (1996) analyse the issue for the years 1991 and 1996 by comparing reported incomes with national accounts information; they estimate the following under-reporting rates: 26% for overall income, 8.5% for wages, and 58.7% for self-employment income. Other studies providing similar results include Bernasconi, Marenzi, and Pozzi (1992), Bernasconi and Marenzi (1997) (who obtain an overall evasion rate of 15% for 1991, 11% for wages, 30% for professionals' income, and 53% for other self-employees' income), Cannari, Ceriani, and D'Alessio (1997), Cannari and Violi (1990), Marè (1996), SOGEI (1999). Brosio, Cassone, and Ricciuti (2002) analyse geographical differences and unsurprisingly argue that non-compliance is more important in the south. ISAE (2006) and Monacelli (1996) provide a review of the literature applied to Italy.

[19] When the estimations of evasion are based on the comparison of tax statistics with National Accounts, the researcher always faces the problem of the mismatch between income definitions. When the estimations are based on the comparison with incomes reported to households' surveys, re-ranking issues and under-reporting in the survey come into play (see Deaton 2005 and Canberra Expert Group on Household Income Statistics 2001 for an examination of the theoretical relation between the definition of income in National Accounts and the control total for income appropriate for income distribution analysis). The noticeable difficulties in comparing individual incomes from tax statistics and incomes from the Bank of Italy household survey have been analysed in Marenzi (1989), Marino and Rapallini (2003), Pellegrino (2006, 2007).

[20] Dell, Piketty, and Saez (2007) compare a measure of capital income evaded by non-Swiss nationals through Swiss accounts with the income reported by top income groups in France. They show that evaded capital income is small relative to the top 1% or even the top 0.1%, although it is comparable in magnitude to total incomes reported by the top 0.01%. If all this evaded capital income (which belongs, noteworthily, also to non-French nationals) were added back to the top 0.01% French incomes, the top 0.01% share would double in recent years, still resulting, however, in a very modest figure compared to top income concentration in the United States.

Our top income shares would indeed be underestimated if many high-income individuals were evader self-employees and small business owners. In section 12.3 we conduct some experiments to assess the impact of evasion on our results. Nevertheless, if tax evasion has not changed significantly over the period considered, then our series reflect income concentration dynamics in a proper way. Equivalently, whenever the level of evasion is similar among the top groups, then under-reporting does not affect our estimates of shares within shares.

12.3 THE DYNAMICS OF TOP INCOME SHARES IN ITALY

Figure 12.2 displays the average personal income per adult that is used as the denominator for our top income shares estimations, along with the price index for the years 1974 to 2004. After a period of expansion between 1975 and 1992, the 1992 crisis (linked to a record level of public debt and to the exchange rate crisis, which forced Italy to abandon the fixed exchange rate regime) was followed by important oscillations in real economic growth, resulting in an average income in 2004 that was only 5 per cent higher than in 1992.

Figure 12.3 shows the share of total personal income owned by the top decile divided into three subgroups: the bottom half of the top decile (top 10–5 per cent), the following 4 per cent (top 5–1 per cent), and the top percentile.

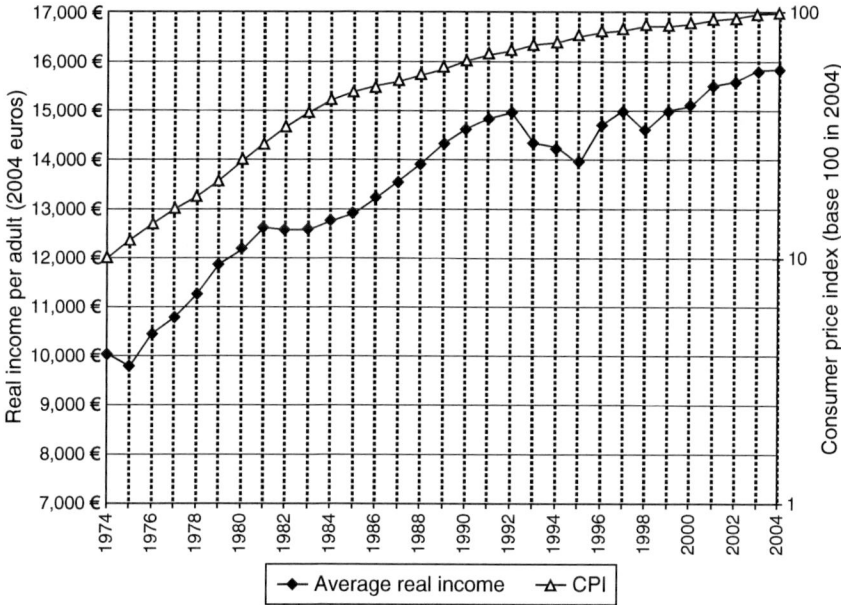

Figure 12.2 Average real income and consumer price index in Italy, 1974–2004

Notes: Figure reports the average real income per adult (aged 20 and above), expressed in real 2004 euros. CPI index is equal to 100 in 2004.

Source: Table 12A.1.

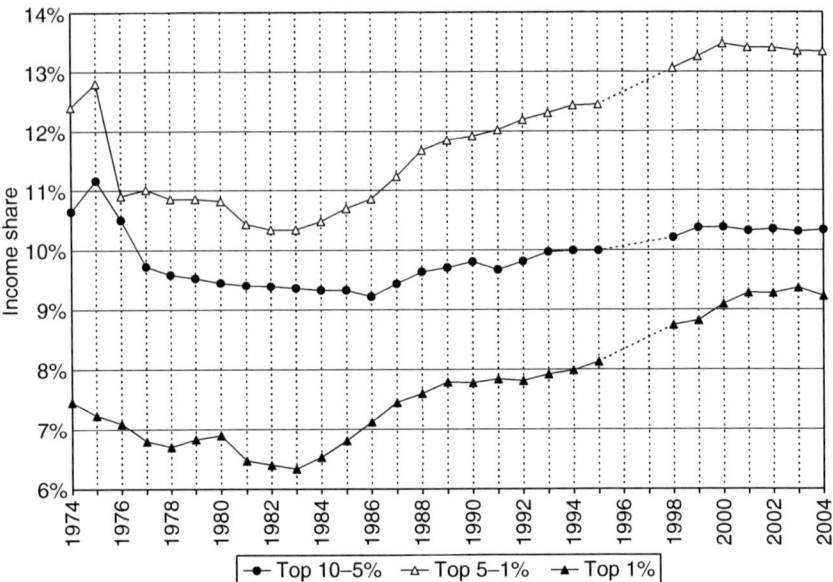

Figure 12.3 The top 10–5%, top 5–1%, and top 1% income shares in Italy, 1974–2004

Note: Income excludes interest and most realized capital gains. See Appendix 12A for details.

Source: Table 12A.2, columns top 10–5%, top 5–1%, and top 1%.

The three series respond to two different patterns. The top 10–5 per cent share has displayed modest fluctuations throughout the period. The top 5–1 per cent and the top 1 per cent have displayed first a U-shaped pattern, with a reduction in income concentration until the mid 1980s, followed later by a rising trend; the top 1 per cent share increased from 6.3 per cent in 1983 to 9.3 per cent in 2003. Consequently, the increase in income concentration which took place in Italy from the mid 1980s has been a phenomenon happening within the top 5 per cent of the distribution, and mainly within the top 1 per cent.[21]

Figure 12.4 analyses concentration further by splitting the top 1 per cent into three groups: the top 1–0.5 per cent, the top 0.5–0.1 per cent, and the top 0.1 per cent. The richer the group considered, the higher the increase in the share from the mid 1980s: the top 1–0.5 per cent increased from 2.2 per cent to 2.9 per cent between 1982 and 2004, while the top 0.1 per cent increased sharply by over 80 per cent from 1.5 per cent in 1983 to 2.7 per cent in 2003.

The presented estimations depend both on the definition of the income denominator and the control total for the number of tax units. The broad conclusions are not likely to be affected by errors in the control totals. However, the more detailed year-by-year changes may *be* sensitive, as may comparison across countries at a point in time. We therefore follow Atkinson (2007b), in

---

[21] As described in Chapter 10, the increase in income concentration that has taken place in Spain since 1981 has been a phenomenon concentrated within the top 1% of the distribution.

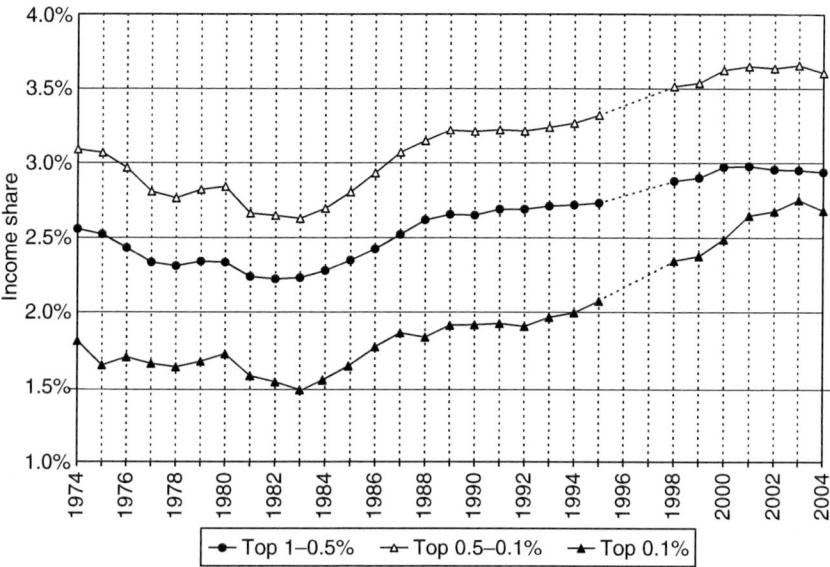

Figure 12.4 The top 1–0.5%, top 0.5–0.1%, and top 0.1% income shares in Italy, 1974–2004

Note: Income excludes interest and most realized capital gains. See Appendix 12A for details.

Source: Table 12A.2, columns top 1–0.5%, top 0.5–0.1%, and top 0.1%.

considering the distribution within the top groups. Figure 12.5 shows the share of the top 1 per cent within the share of the top 10 per cent, the share of the top 0.1 per cent within the share of the top 1 per cent, and the share of the top 0.01 per cent within the share of the top 0.1 per cent. The relative distribution does not depend on the control for total income. This demonstrates in another way the rise of income concentration within the top groups. The fact that figures for shares within shares are so close suggests that the Pareto distribution is a good fit.

To understand the mechanisms of this increase in income concentration at the top we move on now to the analysis of the composition of incomes. Figures 12.6, 12.7, and 12.8 display the share and composition of the top 0.01 per cent, top 0.1 per cent, and top 10 per cent income fractiles from 1976 to 2004. They show that the increase in top shares is mainly due to two components: wage income and self-employment income. The importance of top wages (especially top executive compensation) to explain the rise in top income shares during the last quarter of the twentieth century is not new and has been a standard result in all the studies analysing concentration in Anglo-Saxon countries. However, top wages did not surge in continental Europe or Japan to the same extent and even the results for Italy are very modest compared to the existent estimations for North America (see Piketty and Saez 2003; Saez and Veall 2005).

The published list of taxpayers cited in the introduction seems to support the 'superstars' theory, as mentioned in the introduction. Nevertheless, Italy also has

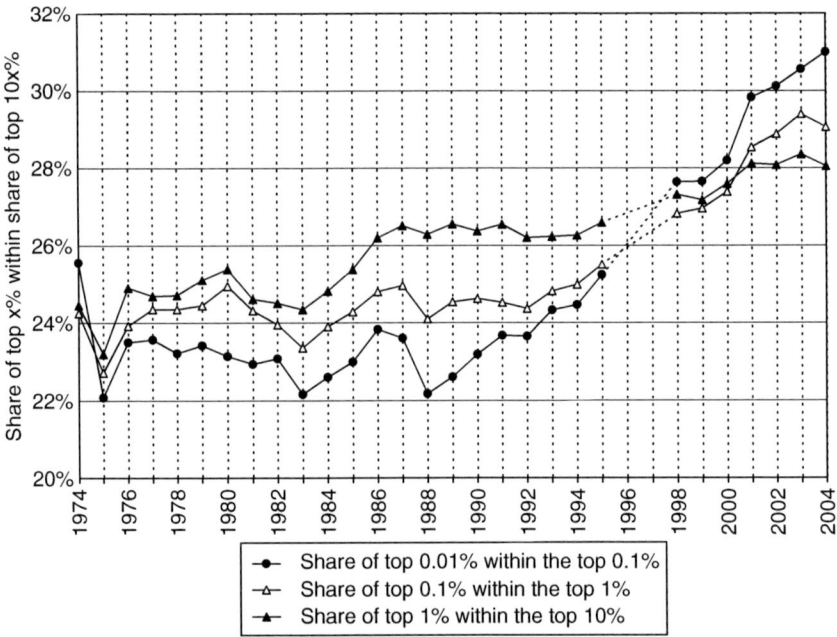

Figure 12.5 Shares within shares in Italy, 1974–2004

Note: Income excludes interest and most realized capital gains. See Appendix 12A for details.

Source: Table 12A.2, columns top 10%, top 1%, top 0.1%, and top 0.01%.

other specificities. It has been argued that the drop in earnings inequality during the 1970s was in fact the result of labour market institutions created in that decade. The *Scala Mobile* was a wage indexation mechanism granting the same absolute wage increase to all employees as prices rose. More specifically, it provided a fixed increment in nominal wages according to a special price index (*Indice Sindacale*). By granting the same absolute (as opposed to the same percentage) wage increase to every worker, this institution tended to compress the wage distribution and played a key role in the reduction of earnings inequality between the mid 1970s and the mid 1980s, years of harsh social conflict. Manacorda (2004) claims that when the *Scala Mobile* was abandoned, the subsequent rise in inequality was largely a reaction to the compression differentials generated before.[22] The impact of such a mechanism on top wages and executive compensation was presumably

---

[22] In the early 1980s the equalizing power of the *Scala Mobile* started to decline both due to the drop in inflation and to the weakening of unions' power. In 1980, 40,000 white-collar workers demonstrated against the equalizing effects of the *Scala* in front of the FIAT headquarters in Turin. The growing dissatisfaction forced the government to progressively lower the scope of the *Scala Mobile* until its total abolition in 1992, when a system of proportional wage increases contingent on expected inflation was established. A phase of moderation in wage adjustments (*Concertazione*) started in 1993. See also Erickson and Ichino (1995) and Signorini and Visco (2002).

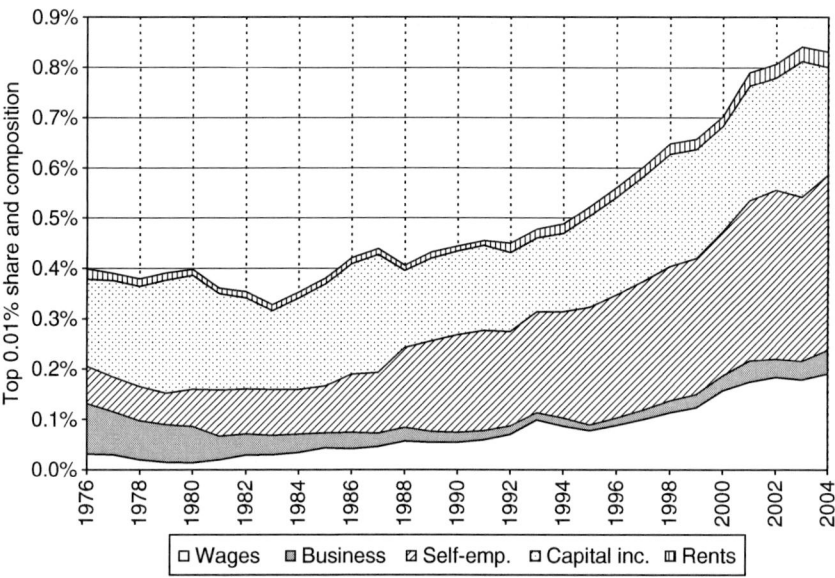

Figure 12.6 The top 0.01% income share and composition in Italy, 1976–2004

Notes: The figure displays the income share of the top 0.01% tax units, and how the top 0.01% incomes are divided into the following income components: wages and salaries (including pensions), business income, self-employment income, capital income (mainly dividends), and rents. Income excludes interest and most realized capital gains. See Appendix 12A for details.

Sources: Table 12A.2, top 0.01% income share, and Table 12A.4, composition columns for top 0.01%.

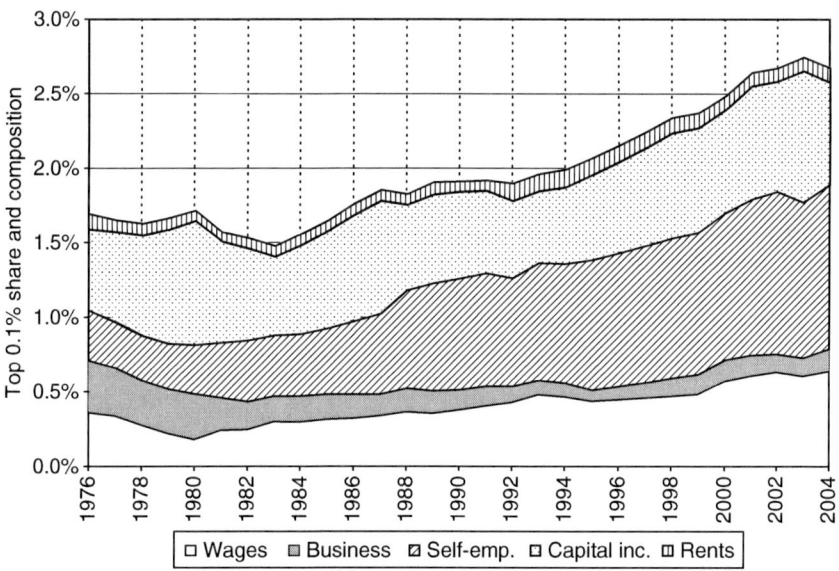

Figure 12.7 The top 0.1% income share and composition in Italy, 1976–2004

Notes: The figure displays the income share of the top 0.1% tax units, and how the top 0.1% incomes are divided into the following income components: wages and salaries (including pensions), business income, self-employment income, capital income (mainly dividends), and rents. Income excludes interest and most realized capital gains. See Appendix 12A for details.

Sources: Table 12A.2, top 0.1% income share, and Table 12A.4, composition columns for top 0.1%.

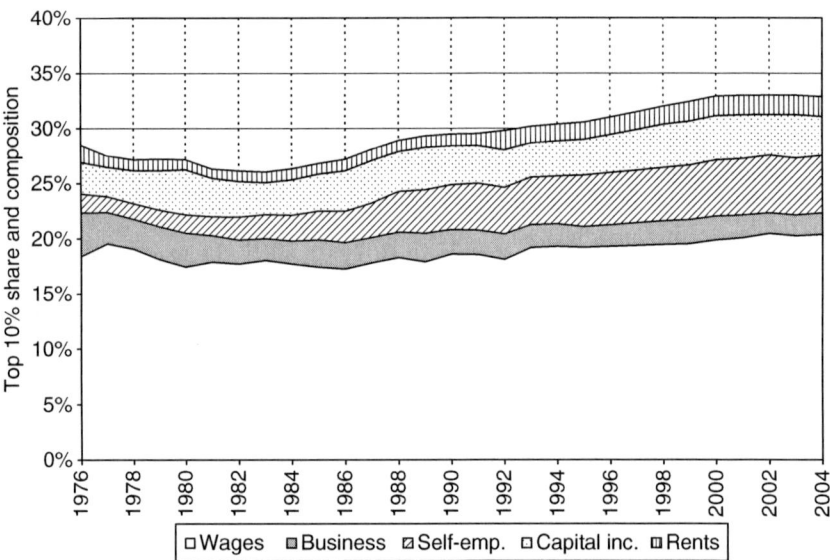

Figure 12.8 The top 10% income share and composition in Italy, 1976–2004

Notes: The figure displays the income share of the top 10% tax units, and how the top 10% incomes are divided into the following income components: wages and salaries (including pensions), business income, self-employment income, capital income (mainly dividends), and rents. Income excludes interest and most realized capital gains. See Appendix 12A for details.

Sources: Table 12A.2, top 10% income share, and Table 12A.4, composition columns for top 10%.

very limited, but the decline in top shares in the late 1970s and their subsequent rise since the first half of the 1980s matches the evolution of the Gini coefficient (based on survey data) between 1982 and 1987.

It is instructive to compare the trends in income concentration between Italy and other countries. Figure 12.9 shows the top 0.01 per cent income share in Italy, Spain, France, and the United States. As in the case of Spain, although income concentration has increased in Italy during the last twenty years, the change is very small relative to the surge experienced by top incomes in the United States. Thus, the Italian experience is also closer to continental Europe countries. Figure 12.10 plots the same variables but excluding the United States. The top 0.01 per cent income share in Italy is initially below those of Spain and France, but approaches and eventually surpasses them.[23]

The behaviour of the shares within shares can be expressed in terms of the Pareto coefficient. Comparing distributions relative to the mean, a higher Pareto coefficient denotes less concentration. The Pareto coefficients computed from the share of the top 0.1 per cent within the top 1 per cent in Spain, Italy, France, the

---

[23] Given the large number of adjustments made in raw data, it is not obvious how to rigorously establish whether the values presented in Figure 12.10 are statistically different. It should be noted, however, that income tax information refers to the universe of taxpayers and not to a sample.

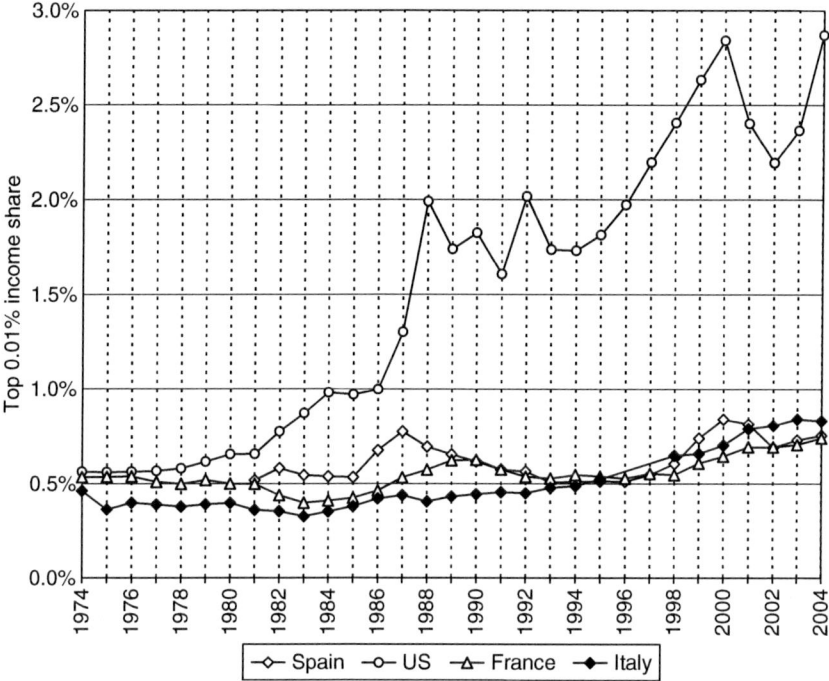

Figure 12.9 The top 0.01% income share in Italy, Spain, USA, and France, 1974–2004

Note: Income excludes most realized capital gains (and interest income in the case of Italy).

Sources: US: Piketty and Saez (2003); France: Piketty (2001) and Landais (2007); Spain: Alvaredo and Saez (2009) and Chapter 10; Italy: Table 12A.2.

UK, and the USA are shown in Figure 12.11, which reproduces the patterns observed in Figure 12.10 but unaffected by the income denominator: commonality between continental Europe countries, and marked increase in concentration in the UK and the USA. For instance, the Pareto exponent fell from 3.02 in 1977 to 1.77 in 2000 in the UK, while in Italy it moved from 2.81 in 1975 to 2.14 in 2003.

Sensitivity of Results

Given the comparisons with other European countries presented in the previous section, and the concern about the effects of evasion and non-compliance on our estimates, it is reasonable to ask how sensitive these results are to changes in the personal income numerator and denominator. Reducing the income denominator to 90 per cent of the series used (Table 12.A, column 4) would mean that the share of the top 0.01 per cent in 1988 became 0.45 per cent in place of 0.41 per cent and that the share of the top 0.1 per cent became 2.0 per cent in place

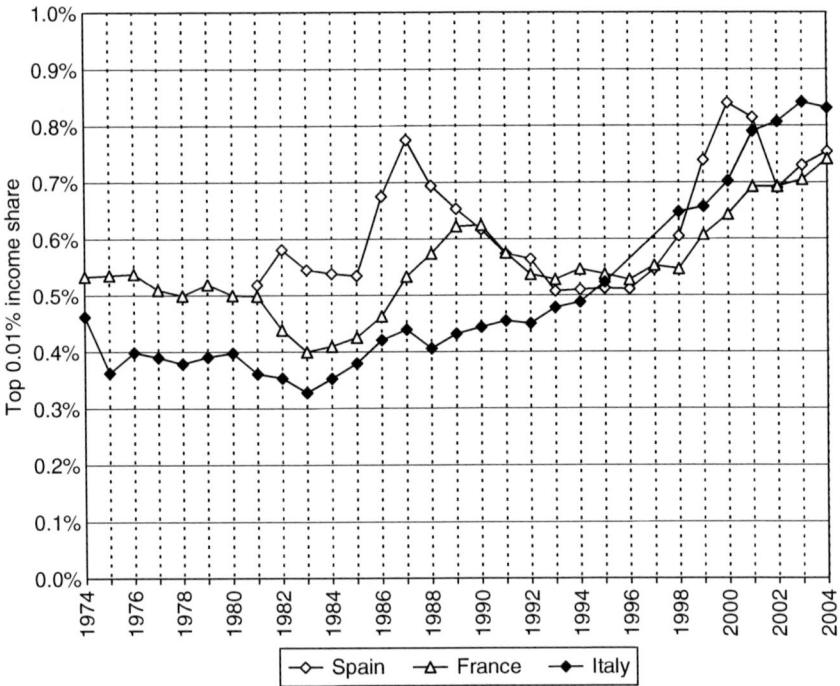

Figure 12.10 The top 0.01% income share in Italy, Spain, and France, 1974–2004

Note: Income excludes most realized capital gains (and interest income in the case of Italy).

Sources: France: Piketty (2001) and Landais (2007); Spain: Alvaredo and Saez (2009) and Chapter 10; Italy: Table 12A.2.

of 1.83 per cent. These changes would not affect the comparisons presented in Figures 12.9 and 12.10.

A second important question refers to the impact of tax evasion and, in particular, of evasion from self-employment income, on our top share estimates. Which is the effect of a 10 per cent under-reporting rate in self-employment income among high-income earners? Such a change would mean that the share of the top 10 per cent is adjusted upwards by 1 per cent *on average* (not 1 percentage point); for example, the top 10 per cent share in 1995 becomes 31 per cent instead of 30.5 per cent. Along the same lines, the share of the top 0.1 per cent is increased by 2.7 per cent *on average* (not 2.7 percentage points): the top 0.1 per cent share in 1995 becomes 2.15 per cent in place of 2.07 per cent. Full results for this exercise are shown in Table 12A.5.

These magnitudes seem to suggest that evasion from self-employment and small business income is unlikely to account for the gap in top incomes between Italy and Anglo-Saxon countries. Evasion would not imply either that true income concentration in Italy is much higher than in other European countries.

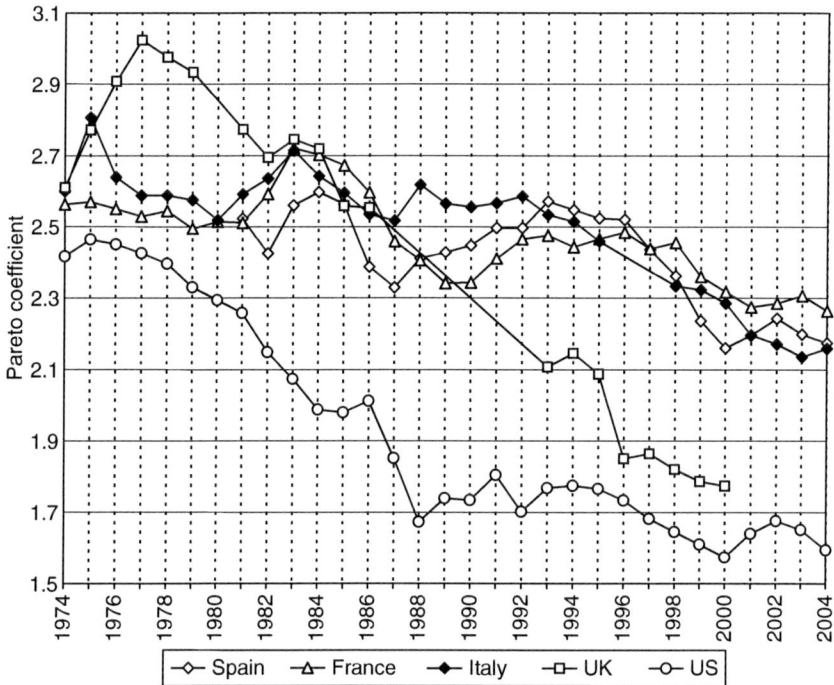

Figure 12.11 The Pareto coefficients in Italy, Spain, France, UK, and USA, 1974–2004

Note: Based on the share of the top 0.1% within the share of the top 1%.

Sources: France: Piketty (2001) and Landais (2007); UK: Atkinson (2007); USA: Piketty and Saez (2003); Spain: Alvaredo and Saez (2009) and Chapter 10; Italy: Table 12A.2.

12.4 THE EFFECTS OF MARGINAL TAX RATES ON REPORTED TOP INCOMES

The literature on behavioural responses to taxation stresses the important role that income taxes can have on incomes reported for tax purposes. At least until the beginning of the 1980s, the income tax in Italy had a very progressive structure with many brackets and a very high statutory top marginal rate (82 per cent in 1974). However, few taxpayers had enough income to be in the top bracket. In the last thirty years the system has evolved to a much smaller number of brackets with a lower top statutory rate (Table 12B.1).[24]

---

[24] This has been a common pattern of personal income tax systems in most developed countries. Top statutory marginal tax rates were reduced in 1975 (from 82% to 72%), 1983 (from 72% to 65%), 1989 (from 62% to 50%), in 1998 (from 51% to 46%), in 2000 (from 46% to 45.5%), and in 2001 (from 45.5% to 45%).

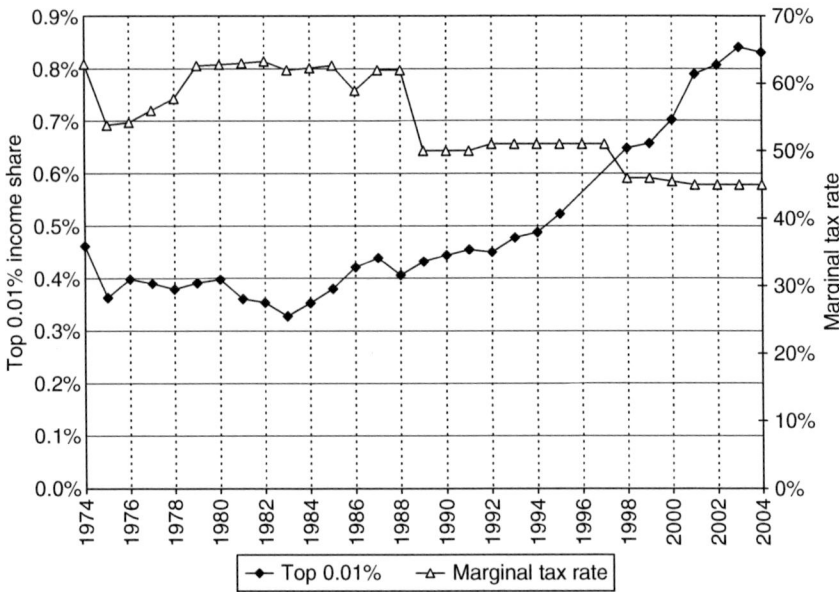

Figure 12.12 The top 0.01% income share in Italy and marginal tax rate, 1974–2004

Sources: Top 0.01% income share 1974–2004 from Table 12A.2 (column top 0.01%). Marginal tax rate: Own computations. Details in Appendix 12B.

We computed the average marginal tax rate (weighted by income) for the top 0.01 per cent group and plot it in Figure 12.12 together with the top 0.01 per cent income share.[25] Several elements are worth noticing. First, the tax rate cut of 1975 is associated with a decrease in the top income share from 1974 to 1975. Second, the relative stability of the top 0.01 per cent income share between 1976 and 1988 happens in a period of stable (or increasing in 1976–9) marginal rates. Finally, the rising trend of top shares started by the end of the 1980s is associated with a non-trivial reduction in tax rates (the statutory top marginal rate goes down 17 percentage points from 62 per cent in 1988 to 45 per cent in 2001–4). The inherent noise in top income shares from year to year, however, would make it difficult to detect systematic effects unless the elasticity of response is very large. New research and better data are required to analyse whether the elasticity of reported income with respect to tax rates is not an intrinsic parameter but might vary with the degree of enforcement and the ability of taxpayers to avoid and evade taxes, as proposed by Slemrod (1995).

---

[25] Details about the estimation of the income-weighted marginal tax rates are given in Appendix 12B.

12.5 FINAL REMARKS

This chapter has analysed income concentration in Italy between 1974 and 2004 using income tax statistics. Unfortunately, as tax returns tabulations are only available since 1974, it is not feasible to provide an account of the long-run evolution of top shares. Despite their limited time scope, tax records provide interesting insights on income concentration for the last three decades, which are not adequately caught by existent survey data. Top income shares have increased steadily since the mid 1980s, a phenomenon happening within the top 5 per cent of the distribution, and mainly within the top 1 per cent; a large fraction of the increase is due to the growing importance of top wages and self-employment income. Notwithstanding this trend, the rise is much smaller than the one that took place in Anglo-Saxon countries. Consequently, the Italian case, together with the results obtained for Spain in Chapter 10 and Portugal in Chapter 11, shows that Mediterranean Europe has evolved closer to the trends observed in continental Europe. Our series measure only top income concentration and hence are silent about changes in the lower and middle part of the distribution. As a result, our series follow different patterns from broader measures of inequality such as Gini coefficients or macro-based estimates.

APPENDIX 12A: TOP INCOME SHARE SERIES

The Income Tax in Italy

Between 1864 and 1877 Italy reorganized the different taxes already in place in the pre-unification states into a new tax system, which emulated that of the Kingdom of Piemonte and Sardegna (Law 1830 of 14/7/1864 and Royal Decree 4021 of 24/8/1877). The reform relied on the traditional schedule taxes on salaries, rents, corporate profits, business profits, self-employment and capital income, estate and gifts (*imposta sul reddito dominicale dei terreni, imposta sul reddito dei fabbricati, imposta sul reddito agrario, imposta sui redditi di ricchezza mobile* (wages, salaries, pensions, business income, capital income, self-employment income), *imposta fondiaria*). Under such a complicated system, with withholdings at the source and different schedules covering different sources of income, the authorities did not know the total income of individuals, which were the subject of different assessments.

The *Progetto Meda* and the *Riforma De Stefani* (Royal Decree 3062 of 30/12/1923) introduced a surtax (*imposta complementare*), which was an additional income tax levied on personal incomes, with a progressive tax scale, the bottom marginal rate being 2 per cent and the top marginal rate evolving from 65 per cent (1923–50) to 50 per cent (1951–73). Only in 1951 (Law 25 of 11/1/1951, *Riforma Vanoni*) did the authorities impose the requirement of a unique annual tax return per taxpayer detailing all taxable income and schedule taxes paid. The *imposta complementare* remained in existence until 1972. Even if it could have provided information on top incomes, to our knowledge there are no published tabulations by ranges of income covering the income assessed to the *imposta complementare* over this period.

Local governments imposed an additional personal income tax, the *imposta di famiglia*, with progressive rates ranging from 2 per cent to 12 per cent (Law 4513/1868; abolished by Presidential Decree DPR 597 of 29/9/1973). For an account of the facts around the main tax reforms between 1950 and 1970, see Botarelli (2004).

After almost a decade of studies on tax reforms,[26] the modern personal income tax (*imposta sui redditi delle persone fisiche, IRPEF*) was introduced by the Law 10/9/1971. It fully came into force in the year 1974 and since then, detailed official tax statistics began to be recorded on a yearly basis. The reform caused a shift from a limited overall income tax system with 2.2 million returns for the *imposta complementare* in 1972 to a mass tax with more than 15 million family-based tax returns or 23.3 million individual-based tax returns in 1974 (Table 12A.1, column 2).

Initially, taxation was based on the family unit, but in 1976 the Constitutional Court decided that the obligation to file jointly for married couples was thereafter unconstitutional (Court Decision 179/1976), joint filing interfering with the choice of creating or dissolving a conjugal tie. Published tabulations by range of income provide both the individual and the family distributions separately both for 1974 and 1975.

Taxable income covers (a) urban and rural rents, (b) wages and salaries, (c) pensions, (d) self-employment income, (e) farm income, (f) business income, (g) capital income,

---

[26] On the work done by the ad hoc commission on the tax reform, see Cosciani (1964).

and (h) other income (a small fraction of non-financial capital gains, copyrights, income from games of chance).[27]

Despite the original intentions to create a true comprehensive income tax, several components of capital incomes were excluded from the tax base, being subject to 'substitutive' tax regimes usually at flat rates. This is the case of the tax on interest income, withheld at the source. The choice to leave a fraction of capital incomes under a separate and proportional regime was mainly motivated by the fear of capital flight abroad.

Dividends are included in the tax base. A distinct treatment was introduced in 1998 for dividends from qualified shares (completely included until 2003; only 40 per cent of them have to be reported to the income tax since 2004) and from non-qualified shares (until 2003, subject to the option of applying a flat tax of 12.5 per cent or including them in the tax base; the flat tax becoming compulsory in 2004).

As a practical matter, capital gains were mostly exempted (and not reported) until 1998. In principle, gains on equities were subject to the income tax if the relevant transactions were undertaken with speculative intent. Since the definition of speculative intent was not objective and the burden of proof lay with the tax revenue service, gains were not reported. The speculative intent was presumed for shares held for less than five years and only in some exceptional cases (until 1984, the sale of unlisted shares of real estate companies; between 1984 and 1990, the sale of more than 2 per cent of the value of listed companies, more than 10 per cent (5 per cent after 1987) of unlisted companies, and more than 25 per cent (15 per cent between 1987 and 1992 and 10 per cent after 1993) of unincorporated companies).[28] Between 1999 and 2003, capital gains from qualified equities, although subject to separate taxation, had to be fully reported, while only 40 per cent of them had to be reported in 2004. Since 1998 capital gains from non-qualified equities are not included in the income tax base. For an account of the changes in capital income and capital gains taxation, see Ricotti and Sanelli (2005), Baldini and Bosi (2002), Visco (1995), and Bosi and Guerra (2008, and previous editions).

Tax tabulations do not offer separate information about capital gains; their revenues are added to other small income components, making a very small amount relative to total assessed income. Consequently, our income definition excludes interest and most realized capital gains.

In 1974 tax rates ranged from 10 per cent to 82 per cent with thirty-two brackets; a ten-point reduction in top marginal rates followed in 1975, the number of brackets being fairly stable up to 1982 (see Table 12A.1). In 2004 there were only five brackets with a top marginal tax rate of 45 per cent. As pointed out in Saez and Veall (2005), the evolution of many brackets extending very far into the distribution of incomes and a high nominal top rate toward a much smaller number of brackets with a lower top rate is a common pattern of personal income tax systems of developed countries. However, the top marginal rate is a very defective measure of tax burden: in 1974 very few taxpayers had enough income to be in the top bracket and taxed at 82 per cent. Fixed bracket limits along time together with a positive inflation rate implied an increase in effective marginal rates between 1975 and 1979 (Figure 12.12) even when there were no changes in the statutory schedule.

Despite the frequent changes in the tax code, the fundamentals of the Italian personal income tax have not changed in a radical way since the introduction of the *IRPEF*. A detailed description of the evolution of the *IRPEF* between 1974 and 1998 can be

---

[27] Non-financial capital gains mainly refer to capital gains from real estate sold within five years after purchase, if not used as main dwelling.

[28] See, for example, Law 853 of 19/12/1984 and Law 17 of 17/2/1985.

found in Herr (2002). For a general view of the Italian taxation structure, see Bernardi (1996, 2002, 2005) and Bosi and Guerra (2008 and previous editions).

References on Data Sources for Italy

Following the requirement of a unique annual tax file per taxpayer established in 1951, the tax agency launched an annual publication detailing the number of tax files and total assessed income, disaggregated by provinces, which appeared annually from 1951 to 1973: Ministero delle Finanze, Direzione Generale delle Imposte Dirette, *Dichiarazione unica dei redditi presentata nell'anno* 1950, 1951, 1952, 1953, 1954, 1955, 1956, 1957, 1958, 1959, 1960, 1961, 1962, 1963, 1964, 1965, 1966, 1967, 1968, 1969, 1970, 1971, 1972, 1973, Rome: Istituto Poligrafico dello Stato. Unfortunately no tabulations by range of income are provided; the only information available displays total assessed income and total number of tax returns. We report these references for bibliographical purposes.

Much more detailed data describe the evolution of the income tax between 1974 and 2004. Income tax statistics are published by the Ministry of Finance every year since 1974, when a taxpayers' register was organized and an information system for recording and processing tax returns was set up in order to deal with the large number of tax files.

1974: Ministero delle Finanze, Anagrafe Tributaria, *Analisi delle dichiarazioni dei redditi delle persone fisiche presentate nel 1975*. Table DU-74–12–01: Distribuzione del reddito individuale comprensivo del reddito da lavoro dipendente dichiarato col modello 101 rispetto al reddito complessivo individuale. Two previous preliminary publications exist: Ministero delle Finanze, Anagrafe Tributaria, *Elaborazioni statistiche sulle dichiarazioni delle persone fisiche (modello 740) relative ai redditi del 1974*; and Ministero delle Finanze, Direzione Generale delle Imposte Dirette, Centro Informativo, *Elaborazioni statistiche generali sulle dichiarazioni dei redditi delle persone fisiche (modello 740) presentate nel 1975*.

1975: Ministero delle Finanze, Anagrafe Tributaria, *Le dichiarazioni dei redditi delle persone fisiche presentate nel 1976*. Table DU-75–12–01: Distribuzione del reddito individuale comprensivo del reddito da lavoro dipendente dichiarato col modello 101 rispetto al reddito complessivo individuale.

1976: Ministero delle Finanze, Anagrafe Tributaria, *Le dichiarazioni dei redditi delle persone fisiche presentate nel 1977*. Table 3.2.2: Composizione dell'Ammontare dei Tipi di Redditi per Classi di Reddito Complessivo and Table 3.4.1: Riepilogo Generale delle Dichiarazioni per Classi di Reddito Complessivo.

1977: Ministero delle Finanze, Anagrafe Tributaria, Centro Informativo delle Imposte Dirette, *Analisi delle dichiarazioni dei redditi delle persone fisiche presentate nel 1978*. Table 3.2.2: Distribuzione dell'ammontare dei redditi del totale percettori in relazione al reddito complessivo; Table 3.4.1: Distribuzione del numero complessivo dei dichiaranti e degli ammontari di redditi, deduzioni, detrazioni e imposte individuali rispetto al reddito complessivo.

1978–91: Ministero delle Finanze, Direzione Generale delle Imposte Dirette, *Analisi delle dichiarazioni dei redditi delle persone fisiche presentate nel 1979, 1980, 1981, 1982, 1983, 1984, 1985, 1986, 1987, 1988, 1989, 1990, 1991, 1992*. Table 3.2.2: Distribuzione dell'ammontare dei redditi del totale dichiaranti in relazione al reddito complessivo; Table 3.4.1: Distribuzione del numero complessivo dei dichiaranti e degli ammontari di redditi, deduzioni, detrazioni e imposte individuali rispetto al reddito complessivo.

1992–5: Ministero delle Finanze, *Analisi delle dichiarazioni dei redditi delle persone fisiche presentate nel 1993, 1994, 1995*. Table 2.2: Distribuzione dell'ammontare dei redditi del totale dichiaranti in relazione al reddito complessivo.

1996–7: No tax statistics available.

1998–2004: Ministero dell'Economia e delle Finanze. Dipartimento per le Politiche Fiscali. Ufficio Studi e Politiche Economico-Fiscali. Sistema Statistico Nazionale. *Le dichiarazioni in cifre. Analisi statistiche anno d'imposta 1998, 1999, 2000, 2001, 2002, 2003, 2004. Persone fisiche* (electronic publication). Table 1.2.2. Distribuzione dell'ammontare dei redditi per classi di reddito complessivo.

Additional information in: Ministero delle Finanze. Direzione Generale delle Imposte Dirette. Ufficio di Statistica. *Analisi dei redditi delle persone fisiche suddivisi per categorie omogenee di contribuenti. Dichiarazioni presentate nel 1982, 1983, 1984, 1985, 1986, 1987, 1989, 1990, 1991, 1992, 1993.*

Tax statistics are affected by the evolution of the different individual tax forms as well as by the changes in the requirements to file. Form 740 (valid over the whole period 1974–2004) is the general form. Form 730 (introduced in 1992) is reserved for employees and pensioners receiving also real estate income and partnership income, and benefiting from specific deductions. Form 101 (Form 201 after 1984) corresponds to employees and pensioners with no other sources of income beyond wages, salaries, and pensions.

Since 1980 pensioners with no other income source were exempted from filing Form 101 (Law 119 of 31/3/1981). Since 1991 employees receiving only wages and salaries and not benefiting from specific deductions have also been exempted from filing tax returns through Form 101. This fact affects tax statistics only in 1991 and 1992 and not in a relevant way for our top income shares estimates. First, because many individuals kept sending the Form 101 even if it was not required (Herr 2002). Secondly, because employers as well as the social security administration (INPS, INPDAP) must report individuals' incomes to the tax agency through Form 770 since 1993; the information in Form 770 is then matched with tax returns (Forms 740 and 730) in order to add the incomes of exempted (from reporting) employees and pensioners to tax statistics. Thirdly, because the reduction in the number of tax files in 1991 and 1992 due to the mentioned exemption unsurprisingly occurred at the lower part of the distribution.

Control Total for Individuals

For the period 1974–2004, the total number of tax units is computed as the number of individuals in the Italian population aged 20 and above. Figures are reported in Table 12A.1, column 1. Column 2 indicates the total number of tax returns actually filled and column 3 the fraction of the adult population filing a tax return.

For 1974–80 the data are taken from Capocaccia and Caselli (1990) *Popolazione residente per età e sesso nelle province italiane: anni 1971–1981*, Università degli Studi di Roma La Sapienza, Dipartimento di Scienze Demografiche, Fonti e Strumenti, No. 2. For 1981–2004 the series are obtained from ISTAT-Istituto Nazionale di Statistica, *Ricostruzione intercensuaria della popolazione al 1° gennaio 1982–1991*; ISTAT-Istituto Nazionale di Statistica, *Ricostruzione intercensuaria della popolazione al 1° gennaio 1992–2001* and ISTAT-Istituto Nazionale di Statistica, *Popolazione totale per singolo anno di età 2002, 2003, 2004.*

Control Total for Income

Total income is defined as: (i) wages and salaries from National Accounts net of effective social security contributions (paid by employers and employees) plus (ii) old-age and disability pensions (which have to be reported) plus (iii) half of unincorporated business income plus (iv) all capital income (all non-business non-labour income) reported on tax returns: we follow this strategy because capital income in National Accounts is substantially different from capital income on tax returns due to imputed rents of homeowners, imputed interest to bank account holders, returns on (non-taxable) pension funds, etc.; this amounts to assuming that non-filers receive a negligible fraction of capital income (for example, in 2004, the top 10 per cent income earners obtained 62 per cent of total reported capital income). See Park (2000) for a comprehensive comparison in the case of the United States, where over 90 per cent of adults file tax returns.

Regarding the estimation of the unincorporated business income in the denominator, business income in National Accounts statistics includes an estimation of the black market economy. This is captured by a very large unincorporated business sector, which is disproportionately larger than business income assessed in income tax returns. We estimate that about half of such business income is from the informal sector and hence escapes taxation (see Chapter 10 on Spain, where the control total for income includes two-thirds of unincorporated business income from National Accounts).

Wages from National Accounts also include an estimation of under-reporting. Not correcting them may be seen as introducing an inconsistency between numerator and denominator. However, we assume that the bulk of wage under-reporting takes place at the left of the income distribution. Under this assumption, adjusting the denominator by subtracting an estimation of aggregated non-declared wages would cause an overestimation of top income shares. Consequently, our control total for income includes the total amount of wages.

The income denominator relies, thus, on the following statistical sources:

GDP, wages, and salaries:

(a) Istituto Nazionale di Statistica (ISTAT), *Contabilità nazionale: conti economici nazionali 1970–2005.* For real GDP 1974–2004: Produzione a prezzi base (Reference year 2000). For nominal GDP 1974–2004: Conto della produzione a prezzi correnti. For wages and salaries 1974–2004: Conto dell'attribuzione dei redditi primari (current values).

Prices:

(b) Istituto Nazionale di Statistica (ISTAT), Consumer Price Index 1974–2004 (also in OECD, Statistical Compendium, 2007.1).

Social security contributions:

(c) Istituto Nazionale di Statistica (ISTAT), *Conti e aggregati economici delle amministrazioni pubbliche 1980–2006,* Table 1: Conto Economico Consolidato delle Amministrazioni Pubbliche for effective social security contributions 1980–2004 and Table 20: Contributi Sociali Prelevati dalle Amministrazioni Pubbliche per tipo 1980–2006. For the effective social security contributions for 1974–9 we assumed that their ratio to GDP was equal to the ratio observed in 1980.

Pensions:

(e) Istituto Nazionale di Statistica (ISTAT), *Le prestazioni pensionistiche in Italia dal 1975 al 2000.* For pensions 1975–2000: Table 2: Spesa pensionistica totale per tipo, settore, ente erogatore, categoria, gestione e ripartizione territoriale, al 31 dicembre.

(f) Istituto Nazionale di Statistica (ISTAT), *Annuario statistico italiano 2001,* chapter 4 Assistenza e previdenza sociale, Table 4.9: Pensioni e relativo importo annuo per comparto, ente erogatore e tipo—Anno 2001.

(g) Istituto Nazionale di Statistica (ISTAT), *Le prestazioni pensionistiche in Italia 2002, 2003, 2004*. Table. 1.1 and Table 2.1: Spesa pensionistica IVS e pensioni indennitarie per tipo, settore, ente erogatore, categoria, gestione e ripartizione territoriale, al 31 dicembre.

Unincorporated profits:

(h) Istituto Nazionale di Statistica (ISTAT), *Conti nazionali per settore istituzionale*, Table 4: Ripartizione del reddito primario, Quota di reddito misto trasferita alle famiglie consumatrici, 1990–2002.

(i) OECD, Statistical Compendium, 2007#1. Simplified Accounts for Households and Non Profit Institutions Serving Households (NPISH) and for Corporation. Mixed income, Gross, Current prices. This series was used to extrapolate the series from source (h) to 1974–89 and to 2003–4.

   The total denominator series expressed in 2000 euros is reported in Table 12A.1, column 4. The average income per adult (not per income earner) is reported in column 5, and the CPI index (base 100 in year 2000) is presented in column 6.

Basic Pareto Interpolation

We follow the basic Pareto interpolation technique described in Chapter 10, Appendix 10D.

Adjustments to Raw Pareto Interpolations

Shift from family to individual taxation in 1976: Until 1975, taxation was based on the family unit (as in the United States today). Starting in 1976, individual filing became compulsory. Since tax returns statistics for 1974 and 1975 were elaborated after the tax code change, fortunately published tabulations by range of income provide both the individual and the family distributions separately. The former are used in our estimations so that no ad hoc corrections were necessary to account for the shift.

Changes in reporting rules for capital income: Until 2003, dividends from qualified shares were completely reported and included in the tax base. Since 2004 only 40 per cent of them has to be reported to the income tax. Also until 2003, dividends from non-qualified shares were subject, at the taxpayer's option, either to the income tax (by adding them to the taxable income) or to a flat tax of 12.5 per cent. In 2004 the flat tax became compulsory. These changes created a clear discontinuity in the amounts reported as capital income between 2003 and 2004. We applied an ad hoc adjustment of 1/0.40 to capital incomes in 2004.

   Results of top income shares are presented in Table 12A.2 while top fractile income series are reported in Table 12A.3.

Estimation of Income Composition Series

Besides the number of taxpayers and total income for each income bracket, income tax tabulations also indicate the separated amounts for each type of income, as well as the deductions and the tax paid. This information has been exploited in order to show the breakdown of income into the various components.

   The composition of income within each top group was estimated from these tables using linear interpolations. Such a method is less satisfactory than the Pareto interpolation used to estimate top income thresholds; however no obvious law seems to fit composition patterns in a stable way. Estimates perform satisfactorily when compared to micro-data (see, e.g., Piketty and Saez 2003 for a more precise discussion of this method and Alvaredo and Saez 2009 and Chapter 10 for the comparison between tax data and micro-data in the case of Spain).

Tax records provide income composition (individual distribution) between 1976 and 2004. We consider five types of income: rents, wage income, self-employment income, entrepreneurial income, and capital income. Rents include income from rural and urban real estate. Wage income includes wages, salaries, and pensions, net of social security contributions. Self-employment income is income from professionals (such as dentists, lawyers, etc.) and independent workers, while entrepreneurial income includes small business income (income from sole proprietorship, partnerships income) and farm income. Finally, capital income includes mainly dividends and a small portion of capital gains. Discrepancies between total assessed income and the sum of components are usually very small until 1998; larger discrepancies are recorded for some of the last years, and they have been added to business income to correct for evident discontinuities in that component.

Results are presented in Table 12A.4.

Adjustments to Raw Composition Series

Changes in composition due to changes in the tax code: Starting in 2001 income from the *Collaborazioni Coordinate e Continuative* (Co.Co.Co.) had to be reported under the form of wages and salaries (Law 342 of 21/11/2000). Before, it was considered self-employment income for tax purposes. As this is an important source of income among top taxpayers, the shift generates a spurious and visible change in the raw compositional patterns of top fractiles from self-employment towards wage income since 2001. To correct this for 2001–2, we assumed that the distribution between wages and self-employment income remained at the level of 2000. Consequently, Co.Co.Co. income is always included in self-employment income in our composition series.

Table 12A.1 Reference totals for population, income, and inflation, Italy, 1974–2004

	Tax units and population			Total income		Inflation	Taxes
	(1)	(2)	(3)	(4)	(5)	(6)	(7)
	Adults ('000s)	Number of tax returns ('000s)	(2)/(1) (%)	Total income (millions 2000 euros)	Average income (2000 euros)	CPI (2000 base)	Top marginal tax rate (%)
1974	37,867	23,293	61.5	343,478	9,071	11.07	82
1975	38,120	21,924	57.5	336,299	8,822	12.95	72
1976	38,367	15,654	40.8	362,894	9,459	15.10	72
1977	38,634	21,126	54.7	376,395	9,743	17.69	72
1978	38,896	22,468	57.8	395,196	10,160	19.82	72
1979	39,177	23,639	60.3	420,998	10,746	22.76	72
1980	39,466	24,005	60.8	434,611	11,012	27.55	72
1981	39,778	23,477	59.0	454,220	11,419	32.50	72
1982	39,778	23,850	60.0	453,458	11,400	37.86	72
1983	40,091	24,387	60.8	456,103	11,377	43.41	65
1984	40,415	24,822	61.4	466,040	11,531	48.09	65
1985	40,829	25,226	61.8	476,673	11,675	52.52	65
1986	41,218	25,886	62.8	491,815	11,932	55.58	62
1987	41,616	26,437	63.5	509,851	12,251	58.21	62
1988	42,004	27,373	65.2	528,140	12,574	61.16	62
1989	42,387	27,857	65.7	549,360	12,961	64.99	50
1990	42,796	28,604	66.8	566,417	13,235	69.18	50
1991	43,178	24,586	56.9	580,747	13,450	73.51	50
1992	43,821	26,422	60.3	594,647	13,570	77.38	51
1993	44,154	28,625	64.8	572,170	12,959	80.96	51
1994	44,473	29,110	65.5	571,741	12,856	84.24	51
1995	44,781	29,290	65.4	564,876	12,614	88.65	51
1996	45,049			599,041	13,298	92.21	51
1997	45,276			613,384	13,548	94.09	51
1998	45,458	30,960	68.1	600,490	13,210	95.93	46
1999	45,599	38,315	84.0	618,449	13,563	97.53	46
2000	45,710	38,504	84.2	624,709	13,667	100.00	45.5
2001	45,825	38,794	84.7	643,259	14,037	102.79	45
2002	45,935	39,939	86.9	648,493	14,118	105.32	45
2003	46,282	40,582	87.7	661,345	14,289	108.13	45
2004	46,811	40,492	86.5	671,760	14,350	110.52	45

Notes: Population and tax units estimates based on populations census.

Tax units estimated as number of adults aged 20 and over in Italy. Total income defined as wages and salaries from National Accounts (net of social contributions) plus pensions plus 50% of unincorporated business income, plus all non-business, non-labour income reported on tax returns.

Consumer Price Index is the official CPI index (see Appendix 12A for details).

The total number of tax returns in 1976 does not include individuals filing Form 101; the actual number of taxpayers was not very different from that observed in 1975 and 1977.

Table 12A.2 Top income shares in Italy (excluding capital gains), 1974–2004

	Top 10% (2)	Top 5% (3)	Top 1% (4)	Top 0.5% (5)	Top 0.1% (6)	Top 0.01% (7)	Top 10–5% (10)	Top 5–1% (11)	Top 1–0.5% (12)	Top 0.5–0.1% (13)	Top 0.1–.01% (14)	Top 0.01% (7)
1974	30.50	19.86	7.46	4.90	1.81	0.46	10.64	12.40	2.56	3.09	1.35	0.46
1975	31.20	20.04	7.24	4.71	1.64	0.36	11.16	12.80	2.52	3.07	1.28	0.36
1976	28.50	18.00	7.10	4.67	1.70	0.40	10.50	10.90	2.43	2.97	1.30	0.40
1977	27.53	17.81	6.80	4.47	1.66	0.39	9.72	11.01	2.33	2.81	1.27	0.39
1978	27.15	17.56	6.71	4.40	1.63	0.38	9.58	10.86	2.31	2.77	1.25	0.38
1979	27.21	17.69	6.83	4.49	1.67	0.39	9.53	10.86	2.34	2.82	1.28	0.39
1980	27.17	17.72	6.90	4.56	1.72	0.40	9.45	10.82	2.33	2.84	1.32	0.40
1981	26.31	16.91	6.47	4.24	1.57	0.36	9.40	10.43	2.24	2.66	1.21	0.36
1982	26.14	16.75	6.40	4.18	1.53	0.35	9.39	10.34	2.22	2.65	1.18	0.35
1983	26.04	16.68	6.34	4.11	1.48	0.33	9.36	10.34	2.23	2.63	1.15	0.33
1984	26.34	17.01	6.54	4.26	1.56	0.35	9.32	10.48	2.28	2.70	1.21	0.35
1985	26.83	17.50	6.81	4.46	1.65	0.38	9.32	10.70	2.35	2.81	1.27	0.38
1986	27.20	17.98	7.13	4.70	1.77	0.42	9.22	10.86	2.42	2.93	1.35	0.42
1987	28.12	18.68	7.45	4.93	1.86	0.44	9.43	11.23	2.52	3.07	1.42	0.44
1988	28.91	19.27	7.60	4.98	1.83	0.41	9.64	11.67	2.62	3.15	1.43	0.41
1989	29.34	19.64	7.79	5.13	1.91	0.43	9.70	11.85	2.66	3.22	1.48	0.43
1990	29.50	19.69	7.78	5.13	1.92	0.44	9.80	11.91	2.65	3.21	1.47	0.44
1991	29.53	19.86	7.84	5.15	1.92	0.46	9.67	12.02	2.69	3.22	1.47	0.46
1992	29.81	20.00	7.81	5.12	1.90	0.45	9.81	12.19	2.69	3.22	1.45	0.45
1993	30.19	20.23	7.92	5.21	1.97	0.48	9.97	12.31	2.71	3.24	1.49	0.48
1994	30.41	20.42	7.99	5.26	2.00	0.49	9.99	12.43	2.72	3.27	1.51	0.49
1995	30.57	20.58	8.13	5.40	2.07	0.52	9.99	12.45	2.73	3.32	1.55	0.52
1996												
1997												
1998	32.01	21.80	8.74	5.86	2.35	0.65	10.21	13.06	2.88	3.52	1.70	0.65
1999	32.44	22.07	8.82	5.91	2.38	0.66	10.37	13.25	2.90	3.54	1.72	0.66
2000	32.94	22.56	9.09	6.12	2.49	0.70	10.38	13.47	2.98	3.63	1.79	0.70
2001	33.00	22.68	9.28	6.30	2.65	0.79	10.32	13.40	2.98	3.65	1.86	0.79
2002	33.03	22.68	9.28	6.32	2.68	0.81	10.35	13.40	2.96	3.64	1.87	0.81
2003	33.02	22.71	9.36	6.41	2.75	0.84	10.31	13.35	2.95	3.66	1.91	0.84
2004	32.90	22.56	9.23	6.29	2.68	0.83	10.33	13.34	2.94	3.61	1.85	0.83

Notes: Computations based on tax return statistics. Taxpayers are ranked by gross income (excluding capital gains). The table reports the percentage of total income accruing to each of the top groups. Top 10% denotes top decile, top 10–5% denotes the bottom half of the top decile, etc. The income definition excludes interest income as well as most capital gains (see Appendix 12A for details).

Table 12A.3 Top fractiles income levels (excluding capital gains) in Italy, 1974–2004 (fractiles defined by total income (excluding capital gains); incomes expressed in 2000 euros)

	P90–100 (1)	P95–100 (2)	P99–100 (3)	P99.5–100 (4)	P99.9–100 (5)	P99.99–100 (6)	P90–95 (7)	P95–99 (8)	P99–99.5 (9)	P99.5–99.9 (10)	P99.9–99.99 (11)	P90 (12)	P95 (13)	P99 (14)	P99.5 (15)	P99.9 (16)	P99.99 (17)
1974	27,668	36,032	67,656	88,887	164,020	418,960	19,305	28,125	46,425	70,103	135,693	17,043	22,339	41,531	54,441	100,384	243,745
1975	27,524	35,358	63,843	83,157	145,045	319,796	19,690	28,236	44,530	67,684	125,611	17,577	22,573	38,955	52,834	95,188	214,655
1976	26,957	34,054	67,139	88,263	160,571	377,626	19,859	25,783	46,015	70,186	136,454	17,480	19,465	39,429	54,609	100,291	242,046
1977	26,826	34,704	66,230	87,005	161,257	379,796	18,948	26,822	45,455	68,442	136,975	17,221	21,405	39,429	53,497	99,066	244,081
1978	27,582	35,689	68,153	89,409	165,925	385,207	19,474	27,573	46,896	70,280	141,561	17,650	22,012	40,624	55,064	102,218	249,653
1979	29,244	38,012	73,410	96,545	179,506	420,381	20,477	29,162	50,275	75,805	152,742	18,601	23,168	43,682	58,947	110,531	273,394
1980	29,915	39,018	75,946	100,491	189,415	438,050	20,811	29,787	51,400	78,261	161,789	18,927	23,521	44,778	60,314	115,975	290,242
1981	30,044	38,611	73,927	96,778	179,789	411,953	21,476	29,782	51,077	76,026	153,993	19,691	23,910	44,478	59,510	111,497	274,990
1982	29,794	38,178	73,004	95,371	174,909	403,882	21,411	29,472	50,638	75,486	149,468	19,638	23,783	44,139	59,071	108,880	262,921
1983	29,621	37,944	72,095	93,496	168,390	372,923	21,297	29,406	50,695	74,773	145,664	19,559	23,715	44,144	59,174	107,141	249,743
1984	30,369	39,237	75,361	98,225	180,091	407,132	21,502	30,206	52,497	77,758	154,864	19,675	24,023	45,789	61,159	113,016	280,307
1985	31,317	40,869	79,482	104,115	192,929	443,672	21,765	31,216	54,848	81,912	165,069	19,815	24,474	47,800	63,913	120,326	287,902
1986	32,454	42,912	85,012	112,174	210,849	502,933	21,997	32,387	57,849	87,506	178,395	19,953	25,008	50,324	67,642	129,397	315,323
1987	34,445	45,781	91,306	120,859	227,926	538,122	23,109	34,399	61,753	94,092	193,460	20,885	26,280	53,813	72,643	139,619	342,912
1988	36,347	48,463	95,553	125,220	230,243	510,598	24,231	36,690	65,886	98,964	199,093	21,827	27,767	57,389	76,975	145,488	340,608
1989	38,025	50,897	100,953	133,046	247,624	559,899	25,152	38,383	68,860	104,402	212,927	22,602	28,834	60,063	80,528	154,902	370,833
1990	39,040	52,128	102,951	135,732	253,462	587,785	25,952	39,422	70,170	106,299	216,316	23,348	29,669	61,367	82,141	157,330	378,719
1991	39,712	53,418	105,421	138,428	258,554	612,002	26,007	40,417	72,413	108,397	219,282	23,177	30,184	63,315	84,383	159,208	387,369
1992	40,456	54,282	105,997	138,940	258,296	611,198	26,631	41,353	73,053	109,101	219,085	23,661	31,038	64,074	85,055	159,681	386,043
1993	39,123	52,418	102,612	134,912	254,683	619,638	25,829	39,869	70,311	104,969	214,133	23,039	29,995	61,693	81,738	154,732	386,285
1994	39,090	52,499	102,659	135,340	256,458	627,640	25,681	39,959	69,978	105,061	215,215	22,822	29,899	61,589	81,437	155,247	386,441
1995	38,558	51,920	102,540	136,137	261,499	659,561	25,195	39,265	68,942	104,797	217,270	22,292	29,425	60,461	80,559	155,884	396,395
1996																	
1997																	
1998	42,281	57,597	115,478	154,859	309,739	856,100	26,965	43,126	76,097	116,139	249,032	23,698	31,748	66,824	88,977	174,618	476,707
1999	43,997	59,861	119,556	160,427	322,244	891,101	28,133	44,938	78,685	119,973	259,038	24,834	33,176	69,117	91,965	180,583	496,828
2000	45,020	61,666	124,243	167,162	340,284	959,032	28,375	46,021	81,323	123,882	271,535	24,956	33,680	71,495	94,924	187,571	527,422
2001	46,328	63,679	130,256	176,839	371,742	1,109,433	28,976	47,035	83,673	128,113	289,776	25,512	34,129	73,530	97,773	195,217	582,608
2002	46,627	64,035	130,934	178,353	378,207	1,139,208	29,219	47,310	83,516	128,389	293,651	25,704	34,518	73,328	97,702	197,094	593,671
2003	47,180	64,904	133,780	183,197	393,208	1,201,830	29,456	47,686	84,362	130,695	303,361	25,928	34,809	73,974	99,033	202,415	618,677
2004	47,210	64,763	132,417	180,444	384,693	1,192,654	29,658	47,849	84,390	129,382	294,920	26,072	34,950	73,543	97,837	195,655	606,584

Notes: P99 denotes the income threshold required to belong to the top 1% of tax units; P99–100 is the average income of the top 1%; P99–99.5 denotes the average income in the bottom half of the top percentile. The income definition excludes interest income as well as most capital gains (see Appendix 12A for details).

Source: Computations based on tax statistics.

Table 12A.4 Income composition in top income groups, Italy, 1976–2004

	Top 10%					Top 5%					Top 1%					Top 0.5%					Top 0.1%					Top 0.01%				
	Rents	Wage	Self-Empl.	Business	Capital	Rents	Wage	Self-Empl.	Business	Capital	Rents	Wage	Self-Empl.	Business	Capital	Rents	Wage	Self-Empl.	Business	Capital	Rents	Wage	Self-Empl.	Business	Capital	Rents	Wage	Self-Empl.	Business	Capital
1976	5.6	64.6	6.0	13.9	10.0	6.0	58.2	8.2	15.1	12.5	6.5	43.6	15.2	16.1	18.6	6.4	37.3	18.2	16.6	21.5	6.4	21.1	19.9	20.7	31.9	5.3	7.8	18.5	25.3	43.2
1977	3.8	71.0	5.1	10.3	9.7	4.5	62.5	7.4	12.7	13.0	5.4	42.4	14.5	16.1	21.7	5.3	35.8	17.0	16.6	25.3	5.0	20.4	18.6	19.5	36.6	3.7	7.6	17.5	22.0	49.1
1978	3.6	70.2	5.2	10.0	11.0	4.3	61.3	7.5	12.2	14.8	5.1	40.7	14.2	15.4	24.6	5.1	34.0	16.2	15.9	28.8	5.0	16.8	18.5	18.4	41.3	3.8	5.2	17.9	20.5	52.5
1979	3.8	66.6	5.6	10.9	13.1	4.5	56.7	8.0	13.3	17.6	5.1	35.2	15.0	16.1	28.6	5.1	27.9	17.4	16.4	33.3	4.8	13.2	18.3	17.9	45.9	3.6	3.8	15.9	19.2	57.5
1980	3.4	64.3	6.2	11.2	14.9	4.0	53.2	8.8	13.9	20.2	4.5	30.6	15.8	16.9	32.2	4.5	23.2	18.0	17.3	37.1	4.1	10.4	19.1	17.9	48.6	3.0	3.5	18.6	18.2	56.7
1981	3.2	68.1	6.6	9.0	13.2	3.8	57.3	9.6	11.3	18.0	4.4	37.2	17.0	13.4	28.0	4.4	30.4	19.3	13.6	32.3	4.1	15.3	23.5	13.9	43.1	3.1	5.5	25.5	13.0	53.0
1982	3.7	67.8	7.9	8.3	12.3	4.4	57.2	11.6	10.2	16.7	5.0	36.7	21.2	11.8	25.3	5.1	29.6	24.5	11.9	28.9	4.7	16.0	26.8	12.4	40.2	3.6	8.2	25.2	11.9	51.1
1983	3.7	69.3	8.4	7.6	11.1	4.4	59.3	12.2	9.3	14.8	5.1	40.5	21.8	10.7	22.0	5.1	34.0	24.9	10.9	25.2	4.9	20.2	27.6	11.7	35.7	3.6	9.7	27.8	11.8	47.7
1984	3.8	67.3	8.8	8.0	12.1	4.5	56.9	12.7	9.7	16.1	5.2	39.0	21.6	10.8	23.6	5.2	32.8	23.8	11.0	27.2	4.9	19.0	26.7	11.2	38.2	3.5	9.7	25.2	10.3	51.3
1985	3.7	65.0	9.6	9.2	12.5	4.3	54.8	13.7	10.9	16.4	4.8	38.6	21.9	10.8	24.0	4.8	33.1	23.3	10.8	28.0	4.4	19.0	26.6	10.3	39.6	2.9	11.4	24.6	7.8	53.2
1986	3.9	63.6	10.4	8.8	13.4	4.5	53.7	14.5	10.0	17.3	4.8	38.0	22.1	10.0	25.1	4.8	32.3	23.7	10.0	29.3	4.3	18.2	27.7	9.3	40.5	2.9	9.9	27.5	7.7	52.1
1987	3.7	63.5	11.1	8.1	13.6	4.2	53.4	15.4	9.3	17.6	4.5	37.7	23.4	8.9	25.5	4.5	31.9	25.2	8.8	29.6	4.0	18.2	29.0	7.8	40.9	2.7	10.5	27.5	6.1	53.3
1988	3.5	63.3	12.7	8.0	12.5	4.0	53.5	17.5	9.1	15.9	4.3	37.6	27.4	9.0	21.7	4.3	31.8	30.0	9.2	24.7	4.1	19.9	35.8	8.7	31.5	2.6	14.0	39.2	6.7	37.5
1989	3.7	61.1	13.3	8.8	13.1	4.2	50.6	18.4	10.1	16.7	4.6	35.2	28.1	9.7	22.4	4.6	29.6	31.0	9.5	25.2	4.5	18.5	37.8	8.0	31.3	2.8	12.6	41.7	5.1	37.8
1990	3.7	63.1	13.7	7.6	12.0	4.1	53.1	18.9	8.6	15.2	4.3	37.6	29.1	8.3	20.9	4.2	31.0	32.1	8.2	23.7	3.7	19.7	39.0	7.2	30.5	2.2	12.3	43.8	4.4	37.2
1991	3.8	62.9	14.3	7.5	11.5	4.1	54.2	19.4	8.1	14.1	4.2	39.0	30.4	7.6	18.9	4.2	33.1	33.3	7.7	21.8	3.6	21.0	39.3	7.0	29.0	3.1	13.1	43.8	4.0	37.1
1992	6.0	60.8	14.1	7.7	11.4	6.5	53.3	18.8	7.9	13.5	6.9	40.2	28.3	6.9	17.7	6.9	34.6	31.4	6.8	20.3	6.3	22.5	38.2	5.7	27.4	4.2	15.7	41.7	3.7	34.7
1993	5.1	63.6	14.2	6.9	10.3	5.7	55.8	19.1	7.1	12.2	6.3	41.9	29.5	6.2	16.0	6.4	36.3	32.8	6.1	18.4	5.9	24.4	40.1	4.9	24.7	3.7	20.7	42.0	3.1	30.6
1994	5.2	63.5	14.2	6.7	10.5	5.9	55.4	19.2	7.0	12.5	6.5	41.2	29.5	6.1	16.8	6.6	35.5	32.7	5.9	19.3	6.0	23.3	40.1	4.7	25.9	3.9	17.8	43.3	3.3	31.7
1995	5.2	62.9	15.2	6.1	10.6	5.8	54.3	20.5	6.4	13.0	6.4	38.6	31.5	5.5	18.0	6.4	32.7	35.0	5.2	20.8	5.6	21.0	42.1	3.7	27.7	3.5	14.8	44.7	2.3	34.7
1996																														
1997																														
1998	5.1	60.8	15.0	6.7	12.4	5.6	52.1	20.0	7.3	15.1	5.8	36.0	30.1	7.2	20.9	5.7	29.9	33.5	7.1	23.8	4.5	20.0	40.1	5.3	30.1	3.1	17.6	41.1	3.7	34.5
1999	5.5	60.3	15.2	6.7	12.3	5.9	51.7	20.0	7.3	15.0	5.9	35.6	30.0	7.6	20.9	5.7	29.5	33.5	7.6	23.7	4.3	20.3	40.1	5.7	29.7	3.0	18.8	41.1	4.0	33.1
2000	5.4	60.4	15.4	6.6	12.2	5.7	52.6	20.1	7.1	14.7	5.2	37.7	29.5	7.3	20.1	5.2	31.5	33.1	7.4	22.9	3.8	23.0	39.6	5.8	27.9	2.8	22.4	40.8	4.2	29.8
2001	5.4	60.8	15.5	6.2	12.1	5.6	52.9	20.1	6.7	14.7	5.3	38.1	29.8	6.7	20.1	4.9	31.8	33.4	6.9	23.1	3.5	22.9	39.5	5.3	28.8	3.5	22.1	40.3	5.3	28.8
2002	5.4	62.0	15.8	5.7	11.2	5.6	54.3	20.6	6.0	13.5	5.2	39.3	30.7	5.8	19.0	4.9	32.9	34.6	5.8	21.9	3.4	23.6	40.7	4.6	27.7	3.4	22.8	41.6	4.6	27.7
2003	5.4	61.4	15.6	5.7	11.9	5.6	53.5	20.3	6.0	14.6	5.3	38.0	29.7	5.8	21.3	4.8	31.5	33.2	5.7	24.9	3.4	22.0	38.0	4.4	32.1	3.4	21.3	38.8	4.4	32.1
2004	5.5	62.0	15.8	5.9	10.8	5.7	54.3	20.6	6.3	13.1	5.4	39.2	30.6	6.5	18.3	5.0	32.9	34.6	6.5	20.9	3.7	23.8	41.1	5.7	25.8	3.7	23.0	41.9	5.7	25.8

Notes: Fractiles defined by size of total income. For each fractile, the first five columns (summing to 100%) give the percentage of wage income (wages and salaries, pensions, other employment income), self-employment income, entrepreneurial income (farm income and small business income), capital income (dividends) and rents. The income definition excludes interest income as well as most capital gains.
Details on methodology are presented in Appendix 12A.

Source: Computations based on tax return statistics.

Table 12A.4 (continued) Income composition in top income groups, Italy 1976–2004

	Top 10–5%					Top 5–1%					Top 1–0.5%					Top 0.5–0.1%					Top 0.1–0.01%					Top 0.01%				
	Rents	Wage	Self-Empl.	Business	Capital	Rents	Wage	Self-Empl.	Business	Capital	Rents	Wage	Self-Empl.	Business	Capital	Rents	Wage	Self-Empl.	Business	Capital	Rents	Wage	Self-Empl.	Business	Capital	Rents	Wage	Self-Empl.	Business	Capital
1976	4.7	77.6	1.4	11.4	4.9	5.7	67.8	3.7	14.4	8.5	6.6	55.7	9.5	15.1	13.0	6.7	46.6	17.2	14.3	15.5	6.4	25.2	20.3	19.4	28.5	5.3	7.8	18.5	25.3	43.2
1977	2.7	86.7	1.1	6.0	3.9	3.9	74.9	3.0	10.5	7.7	5.5	55.1	9.6	15.0	14.9	5.4	44.9	16.1	14.9	18.6	5.4	24.3	18.9	18.7	32.7	3.7	7.6	17.5	22.0	49.1
1978	2.4	86.7	1.0	5.9	3.8	3.8	74.0	3.3	10.3	8.7	5.2	53.4	10.4	14.5	16.6	5.2	44.1	14.9	14.5	21.3	5.3	20.3	18.6	17.8	38.0	3.8	5.2	17.9	20.5	52.5
1979	2.7	85.2	1.0	6.4	4.0	4.0	70.2	3.6	11.5	10.7	5.2	49.2	10.4	15.5	19.6	5.3	36.6	16.9	15.4	25.8	5.1	16.0	19.0	17.5	42.4	3.6	3.8	15.9	19.2	57.5
1980	2.3	85.2	1.2	6.2	3.6	3.6	67.5	4.4	12.0	12.5	4.6	45.1	11.6	16.1	22.7	4.7	31.0	17.3	16.9	30.2	4.7	12.5	18.9	17.8	46.1	3.0	3.5	18.6	18.2	56.7
1981	2.0	87.5	1.2	4.9	3.4	3.4	69.7	5.0	10.1	11.8	4.4	50.0	12.6	12.9	20.0	4.6	39.3	16.8	13.4	25.9	4.6	18.3	22.7	14.2	40.2	3.1	5.5	25.5	13.0	53.0
1982	2.4	86.8	1.5	4.8	4.0	4.0	69.8	5.6	9.2	11.3	5.0	50.1	14.9	11.6	18.4	5.2	37.5	23.2	11.7	22.4	5.2	18.4	27.0	12.5	36.9	3.6	8.2	25.2	11.9	51.1
1983	2.4	87.2	1.6	4.5	4.0	4.0	70.9	6.3	8.5	10.4	5.0	52.5	16.0	10.3	16.2	5.2	37.5	23.4	10.4	23.5	5.3	21.8	29.0	11.7	32.2	3.6	9.1	27.8	11.8	47.7
1984	2.5	86.2	1.7	4.7	4.2	4.2	68.2	7.3	9.1	11.4	5.1	50.5	17.3	10.3	16.8	5.4	41.8	22.2	10.9	19.7	5.3	21.3	27.6	11.4	34.4	3.5	9.7	25.2	10.3	51.3
1985	2.5	84.3	2.0	6.2	4.0	4.0	65.2	8.5	10.9	11.5	4.8	48.9	19.1	10.8	16.4	5.3	40.7	21.4	11.1	21.5	5.0	20.7	27.3	11.4	35.6	3.0	11.4	24.6	7.8	53.2
1986	2.7	82.7	2.5	6.3	4.2	4.2	64.1	9.5	10.1	12.2	4.9	49.1	18.9	9.9	17.2	5.1	41.4	21.3	10.4	21.8	4.8	20.6	26.6	11.1	36.9	2.9	9.9	27.5	7.7	52.1
1987	2.6	83.3	2.6	5.8	4.0	4.0	63.9	10.1	9.6	12.4	4.6	49.2	19.9	9.0	17.4	4.8	40.8	22.9	9.4	22.1	4.4	21.6	27.1	9.8	37.1	2.7	10.5	27.5	6.1	53.3
1988	2.5	82.9	3.0	5.9	3.8	3.8	63.9	11.1	9.1	12.1	4.2	48.5	22.6	8.7	16.0	4.5	40.1	26.6	9.4	19.4	4.5	20.3	37.0	8.4	29.8	2.6	14.0	39.2	6.7	37.5
1989	2.7	82.2	3.1	6.2	4.0	4.0	60.8	12.0	10.4	12.9	4.4	46.1	22.4	10.2	17.0	4.9	38.8	27.0	10.4	18.9	4.9	21.9	34.6	9.3	29.3	2.8	12.6	41.7	5.1	37.8
1990	2.8	83.1	3.2	5.4	4.1	4.1	63.3	12.3	8.8	11.6	4.4	48.7	23.2	8.3	15.4	4.5	36.2	28.0	8.9	22.4	4.2	23.5	35.0	8.8	28.5	2.2	12.3	43.8	4.4	37.2
1991	3.2	80.8	3.9	6.2	4.1	4.1	64.2	12.3	8.4	11.0	4.2	50.2	24.7	7.4	13.4	4.5	39.1	29.8	8.1	18.5	4.1	24.6	36.8	8.0	26.5	2.0	13.1	43.8	4.0	37.1
1992	5.0	76.2	4.5	7.2	6.3	6.3	61.7	12.6	8.6	10.8	6.8	50.7	22.6	7.3	12.6	7.3	40.2	27.3	7.4	17.8	4.2	25.6	37.2	7.9	25.1	4.2	15.7	41.7	3.7	34.7
1993	3.7	79.5	4.2	6.3	5.4	5.4	64.7	12.4	7.7	9.8	6.2	52.8	23.1	6.6	11.4	7.4	41.9	28.4	6.7	15.6	3.7	25.1	42.1	6.3	22.8	3.7	20.7	42.0	3.1	30.6
1994	3.7	80.0	4.1	6.0	5.4	5.4	64.6	12.6	7.6	9.8	6.3	52.2	23.2	6.5	11.8	7.0	43.5	28.1	6.7	14.7	3.9	23.1	43.5	5.5	24.0	3.9	17.8	43.3	3.3	31.7
1995	3.8	80.6	4.3	5.5	5.8	5.4	64.6	13.3	7.0	9.7	6.4	50.3	24.6	6.3	12.5	6.9	42.9	30.5	6.1	13.6	3.5	23.1	43.0	5.1	25.3	3.5	14.8	44.7	2.3	34.7
1996																														
1997																														
1998	4.0	79.5	4.5	5.5	6.5	5.5	62.9	13.2	7.3	11.2	6.2	48.4	23.1	7.5	14.9	8.3	36.6	29.1	7.5	18.5	5.1	20.9	39.6	5.9	28.5	3.1	17.6	41.1	3.7	34.5
1999	4.7	78.4	4.9	5.4	6.6	5.9	62.5	13.4	7.2	11.1	6.4	47.9	22.9	7.7	15.1	8.8	35.7	29.1	7.7	18.7	4.8	20.9	39.5	6.4	28.4	3.0	18.8	41.1	4.0	33.1
2000	4.9	77.3	5.4	5.5	6.8	5.8	62.6	13.6	6.9	11.1	6.2	50.5	22.0	7.2	14.4	8.5	37.3	28.6	7.2	18.4	4.1	23.2	39.1	6.4	27.2	2.8	22.4	40.8	4.2	29.8
2001	4.8	78.3	5.4	5.2	6.3	5.9	62.9	13.6	6.7	10.9	5.9	51.4	22.3	6.5	13.9	8.0	38.0	29.1	6.7	18.2	3.5	23.2	39.2	5.3	28.8	3.5	22.1	40.3	5.3	28.8
2002	4.8	78.8	5.5	5.0	6.0	5.9	64.3	13.9	6.1	9.8	6.0	52.5	22.8	5.9	12.8	6.7	39.5	30.3	5.8	17.7	3.4	23.9	40.4	4.6	27.7	3.4	22.8	41.6	4.6	27.7
2003	4.8	78.9	5.5	5.0	5.9	5.9	64.1	13.9	6.1	10.0	6.2	51.8	22.6	6.1	13.5	6.6	38.6	29.6	6.1	19.1	3.4	22.3	37.8	4.4	32.1	3.4	21.3	38.8	4.4	32.1
2004	5.0	78.7	5.5	5.0	5.8	5.9	64.4	14.0	6.2	9.5	6.2	52.1	22.6	6.3	12.8	7.2	39.4	30.2	6.3	16.9	3.7	24.1	40.7	5.7	25.8	3.7	23.0	41.9	5.7	25.8

Notes: Fractiles defined by size of total income. For each fractile, the first five columns (summing to 100%) give the percentage of wage income (wages and salaries, pensions, other employment income), self-employment income, entrepreneurial income (farm income and small business income), capital income (dividends) and rents. The income definition excludes interest income as well as most capital gains. Details on methodology are presented in Appendix 12A.

Source: Computations based on tax return statistics.

Table 12A.5 Effect of 10% under-reporting in self-employment income on top income shares, Italy, 1976–2004

	Top 10%		Top 1%		Top 0.1%		Top 0.01%	
	Original incomes as reported	Original incomes + 10% of reported self-employment income	Original incomes as reported	Original incomes + 10% of reported self-employment income	Original incomes as reported	Original incomes + 10% of reported self-employment income	Original incomes as reported	Original incomes + 10% of reported self-employment income
1976	28.50	28.65	7.10	7.20	1.70	1.73	0.40	0.41
1977	27.53	27.68	6.80	6.89	1.66	1.68	0.39	0.39
1978	27.15	27.28	6.71	6.80	1.63	1.66	0.38	0.39
1979	27.21	27.36	6.83	6.92	1.67	1.70	0.39	0.40
1980	27.17	27.33	6.90	7.00	1.72	1.74	0.40	0.40
1981	26.31	26.48	6.47	6.58	1.57	1.61	0.36	0.37
1982	26.14	26.34	6.40	6.53	1.53	1.58	0.35	0.36
1983	26.04	26.25	6.34	6.47	1.48	1.52	0.33	0.33
1984	26.34	26.57	6.54	6.66	1.56	1.59	0.35	0.36
1985	26.83	27.08	6.81	6.95	1.65	1.70	0.38	0.39
1986	27.20	27.48	7.13	7.27	1.77	1.81	0.42	0.43
1987	28.12	28.42	7.45	7.58	1.86	1.91	0.44	0.45
1988	28.91	29.26	7.60	7.78	1.83	1.90	0.41	0.42
1989	29.34	29.73	7.79	8.00	1.91	1.98	0.43	0.45
1990	29.50	29.89	7.78	7.96	1.92	1.97	0.44	0.46
1991	29.53	29.94	7.84	8.05	1.92	1.99	0.46	0.48
1992	29.81	30.22	7.81	8.02	1.90	1.97	0.45	0.47
1993	30.19	30.61	7.92	8.15	1.97	2.04	0.48	0.50
1994	30.41	30.83	7.99	8.17	2.00	2.06	0.49	0.51
1995	30.57	31.03	8.13	8.34	2.07	2.15	0.52	0.55
1996								
1997								
1998	32.01	32.47	8.74	9.00	2.35	2.43	0.65	0.69
1999	32.44	32.92	8.82	9.04	2.38	2.47	0.66	0.70
2000	32.94	33.44	9.09	9.34	2.49	2.58	0.70	0.75
2001	33.00	33.28	9.28	9.42	2.65	2.70	0.79	0.83
2002	33.03	33.32	9.28	9.43	2.68	2.74	0.81	0.85
2003	33.02	33.31	9.36	9.52	2.75	2.81	0.84	0.88
2004	32.90	33.21	9.23	9.38	2.68	2.75	0.83	0.88

Notes: Fractiles defined by size of total income. For each fractile, the first column ('original incomes as reported') reproduces the top income share estimates from Table 12A.2. The second column ('original incomes + 10% of reported self-employment income') assumes that under-reporting in self-employment income is 10%, this amount being added to the raw statistics.

Source: Computations based on tax return statistics.

APPENDIX 12B: ESTIMATING MARGINAL TAX RATES

Average marginal tax rates (income weighted) used in Figure 12.12 have been computed as follows. We consider each of the income thresholds P99, P99.9, etc. estimated from the interpolation methods described above. We subtracted from the raw income the average level of income allowances (for example, for the income threshold P99, we identify the bracket in the tax tabulations to which this level of income belongs and subtract the average income allowance in that bracket). This gives the net taxable income. Tax liability is obtained from taxable income from the tax schedules in Table 12B.1 from which the marginal tax rate for any taxable income can be obtained.

We estimate the income-weighted marginal tax rate for the top 0.01 per cent as:

[Share P99.99 − 99.999 × MTR 99.995 + Share 99.999 − 100 × (MTR 99.999
+ MTR 99.9999)/2]/[Share P99.99 − 99.999 + Share P99.999 − 100]

where Share P99.99–99.999 denotes the income share of group P99.99–99.999 and MTR 99.995 denotes the marginal tax rate at percentile 99.995.

Table 12B.1 Income tax rates in Italy, 1974–2004

1974			1975			1976–1982		
Income (million lire) from	to	Tax rate (%)	Income (million lire)		Tax rate (%)	Income (million lire)		Tax rate (%)
0	2	10	0	2	10	0	3	10
2	3	13	2	3	13	3	4	13
3	4	16	3	4	16	4	5	16
4	5	19	4	5	19	5	6	19
5	6	22	5	6	22	6	7.5	22
6	7	25	6	7	25	7.5	9	25
7	8	27	7	8	27	9	11	27
8	9	29	8	9	29	11	13	29
9	10	31	9	10	31	13	15	31
10	12	37	10	12	32	15	17	32
12	14	38	12	14	33	17	19	33
14	16	44	14	16	34	19	22	34
16	18	45	16	18	35	22	25	35
18	20	46	18	20	36	25	30	36
20	25	48	20	25	38	30	35	38
25	30	50	25	30	40	35	40	40
30	40	52	30	40	42	40	50	42
40	50	54	40	50	44	50	60	44
50	60	56	50	60	46	60	80	46
60	80	58	60	80	48	80	100	48
80	100	60	80	100	50	100	125	50
100	125	62	100	125	52	125	150	52
125	150	64	125	150	54	150	175	54
150	175	66	150	175	56	175	200	56
175	200	68	175	200	58	200	250	58
200	250	70	200	250	60	250	300	60
250	300	72	250	300	62	300	350	62
300	350	74	300	350	64	350	400	64
350	400	76	350	400	66	400	450	66
400	450	78	400	450	68	450	500	68

1983–1985

from	to	Tax rate (%)
0	11	18
11	24	27
24	30	35
30	38	37
38	60	41
60	120	47
120	250	56
250	500	62
500		65
450	500	80
500		82

1986–1988

from	to	Tax rate (%)
0	6	12
6	11	22
11	28	27
28	50	34
50	100	41
100	150	48
150	300	53
300	600	58
600		62
450	500	70
500		72

1989

from	to	Tax rate (%)
0	6	10
6	12	22
12	30	26
30	60	33
60	150	40
150	300	45
300	500	50
500	550	70
550		72

1990

from	to	Tax rate (%)
0	6.4	10
6.4	12.7	22
12.7	31.8	26
31.8	63.7	33
63.7	159.1	40
159.1	318.3	45
318.3		50

1991

from	to	Tax rate (%)
0	6.8	10
6.8	13.5	22
13.5	33.7	26
33.7	67.6	33
67.6	168.8	40
168.8	337.7	45
337.7		50

1992–1997

from	to	Tax rate (%)
0	7.2	10
7.2	14.4	22
14.4	30	27
30	60	34
60	150	41
150	300	46
300		51

1998–1999

from	to	Tax rate (%)
0	15	18.5
15	30	26.5
30	60	33.5
60	135	39.5
135		45.5

2000

from	to	Tax rate (%)
0	20	18.5
20	30	25.5
30	60	33.45
60	135	39.5
135		45.5

2001

from	to	Tax rate (%)
0	20	18
20	30	24
30	60	32
60	135	39
135		45

2002

Income (euros) from	to	Tax rate (%)
0.00	10,329.14	18
10,329.14	15,493.71	24
15,493.71	30,987.68	32
30,987.68	69,721.68	39
69,721.68		45

2003–2004

Income (euros) from	to	Tax rate (%)
0.00	15,000.00	23
15,000.00	29,000.00	29
29,000.00	32,600.00	31
32,600.00	70,000.00	39
70,000.00		45

APPENDIX 12C: RESULTS BASED ON THE SURVEY OF HOUSEHOLDS' INCOME AND WEALTH

Results presented in Figure 12.1 are based on micro-data from the Bank of Italy's Survey of Households' Income and Wealth-Historical Database between 1977 and 2004. Over the years, the survey questionnaire has undergone several modifications, including changes in the components of households' disposable income (mainly concerning capital income). Dividends and interest were recorded in 1973–5; interest on bank accounts and government bonds was also recorded in 1982–4; since 1986 these items have been calculated by multiplying the household's holdings of each financial asset by the relevant average market return. All income is recorded net of payment of taxes and social security contributions. A summary of the components that formed the household disposable income can be found in Brandolini (2000).

In order to enhance comparison over time, our household income definition from the survey includes wages, social transfers, self-employment income, business income, imputed rents for owner-occupied houses, and excludes income from financial assets (variable *Y1* in the Historical Archive).

REFERENCES

Agenzia delle Entrate (2003). 'Paperoni d'Italia, il 37 per cento in Lombardia: quasi uno su tre vive a Milano', *Fisco oggi*, 17 January.

Albertini, M. (2003). 'The Impact of Changes in Household Forms on Income Inequality: The Case of Italy 1977–2000', EUI Working Paper No. 19, European University Institute.

—— (2004). 'Who Were and Who Are the Poorest and the Richest People in Italy: The Changing Household's Characteristics of the People at the Bottom and at the Top of the Income Distribution', Quaderni del Dipartimento di Sociologia e Ricerca Sociale No. 31, Università degli Studi di Trento.

Alvaredo, F. (2009). 'Top Incomes and Earnings in Portugal 1936–2005', *Explorations in Economic History*, 46(4): 404–17. Longer version in Chapter 11 of this volume.

—— and E. Saez (2009). 'Income and Wealth Concentration in Spain from a Historical and Fiscal Perspective', *Journal of the European Economic Association*, 7(5): 1140–67. Longer version in Chapter 10 of this volume.

Atkinson, A. B. (2003). 'Income Inequality in OECD Countries: Data and Explanations', CESifo Working Paper No. 881.

—— (2007a). 'Measuring Top Incomes: Methodological Issues', in Atkinson and Piketty (2007).

—— (2007b). 'The Distribution of Top Incomes in the United Kingdom 1908–2000', in Atkinson and Piketty (2007).

—— and T. Piketty (2007). *Top Incomes over the Twentieth Century: A Contrast between European and English Speaking Countries.* Oxford: Oxford University Press.

Baldini, M. (1996). 'Inequality Decomposition by Income Source in Italy, 1987–1993', Materiali di Discussione del Dipartimento di Economia Politica dell'Università di Modena, No. 143.

—— and P. Bosi (2002). 'La riforma dell'imposta sul reddito: aspetti di equità e di efficienza', *Politica economica*, 3: 303–40.

Banca d'Italia (2008). 'Bibliografia dei lavori basati sull'indagine dei bilanci delle famiglie italiane', mimeo. Update of 13 February 2008.

Bernardi, L. (1996). 'L'Irpef: un'introduzione al dibattito', in A. Fossati and S. Giannini (eds.) *I nuovi sistemi tributari.* Milan: Franco Angeli: 17–48.

—— (2002). 'Tax System and Reforms in Europe: Italy', Società Italiana di Economia Pubblica Working Papers, No. 183.

—— (2005). 'Tax Reforms in Italy and in Europe: An Introduction', *Giornale degli economisti*, 64(2/3): 133–52.

—— and M. Bernasconi (1996). 'L'evasione fiscale in Italia: evidenze empiriche', *Il fisco*, 38: 19–35.

Bernasconi, M. and A. Marenzi (1997). 'Gli effetti redistributivi dell'evasione fiscale in Italia', Ricerche Quantitative per la Politica Economica, Banca d'Italia, Roma.

—— —— and F. Pozzi (1992). 'L'analisi di microsimulazione delle imposte dirette e dei contributi sociale a carico delle famiglie: modello e risultati', in P. Bosi and S. Lugaresi (eds.) *Bilancio pubblico e redistribuzione: teorie, modelli, riforme.* Bologna: Il Mulino: 129–75.

Biancotti, C., G. D'Alessio, and A. Neri (2008). 'Measurement Errors in the Bank of Italy's Survey of Household Income and Wealth', *Review of Income and Wealth*, 54(3): 466–93.

Boeri, T. and A. Brandolini (2004). 'The Age of Discontent: Italian Households at the Beginning of the Decade', *Giornale degli economisti e annali di economia*, 63(3/4): 449–87.

Bosi, P. and M. Guerra (2008). *I tributi nell'economia italiana.* Bologna: Il Mulino, and previous editions.

Botarelli, S. (2004). 'Tra riforme mancate e riforme attenuate: da Vanoni alla riforma degli anni '70', Università degli Studi di Siena, Quaderni del Dipartimento di Economia Politica, No. 434.

Bottiroli Civardi, M. and R. Targetti Lenti (2001). 'Profili reddituali, livello di istruzione e disuguaglianza nella distribuzione personale dei redditi in Italia', Quaderni del Dipartimento di Economia Pubblica e Territoriale, Università degli Studi di Pavia, No. 1.

Brandolini, A. (1999). 'The Distribution of Personal Income in Post-War Italy: Source Description, Data Quality, and the Time Pattern of Income Inequality', *Giornale degli economisti e annali di economia*, 58(2): 183–239.

—— (2000). 'Appunti per una storia della distribuzione del reddito in Italia nel secondo dopoguerra', *Rivista di storia economica*, 16(2): 215–30.

—— (2004). 'Income Inequality and Poverty in Italy: A Statistical Compendium', Banca d'Italia, mimeo.

—— and L. Cannari (1994). 'Methodological Appendix: The Bank of Italy's Survey of Household Income and Wealth', in A. Ando, L. Guiso, and I. Visco (eds.) *Savings and the Accumulation of Wealth.* Cambridge: Cambridge University Press: 369–86.

—— P. Cipollone, and P. Sestito (2001). 'Earnings Dispersion, Low Pay and Household Poverty in Italy, 1977–1998', Banca d'Italia, Temi di Discussione No. 427.

—— and P. Sestito (1994). 'La distribuzione dei redditi familiari in Italia: 1977–1991', in Rossi (1994: 335–82).

Brandolini, A., L. Cannari, G. D'Alessio, and I. Faiella (2004). 'Household Wealth Distribution in Italy in the 1990s', Banca d'Italia, Temi di Discussione No. 530.

Brosio, G., A. Cassone, and R. Ricciuti (2002). 'Tax Evasion across Italy: Rational Noncompliance or Inadequate Civic Concern?', *Public Choice*, 112(3–4): 259–73.

Canberra Expert Group on Household Income Statistics (2001). *Final Report and Recommendations*. Ottawa.

Cannari, L., V. Ceriani, and G. D'Alessio (1997). 'Il recupero degli imponibili sottratti a tassazione', *Ricerche quantitative per la politica economica*. Banca d'Italia: 493–589.

—— and G. D'Alessio (1994). 'Composizione e distribuzione della ricchezza delle famiglie', in Rossi (1994: 245–77).

—— —— (2006). *La ricchezza degli italiani*. Bologna: Il Mulino.

—— and R. Violi (1990). 'Effetti redistributivi dell'imposta personale sul reddito: il caso italiano e l'ipotesi di tassazione secondo il reddito normale', in M. Leccisotti (ed.) *Per un'imposta sul reddito normale*. Bologna: Il Mulino: 105–22.

Capocaccia, R. and G. Caselli (1990). 'Popolazione residente per età e sesso nelle province italiane: anni 1971–1981', Università degli Studi di Roma 'La Sapienza', Dipartimento di Scienze Demografiche, Fonti e Strumenti, No. 2.

Clementi, F. and M. Gallegati (2005). 'Power Law Tails in the Italian Personal Income Distribution', *Physica A: Statistical Mechanics and its Applications*, 350(2–4): 427–38.

Cosciani, C. (1964). *Stato dei lavori della commissione per lo studio della riforma tributaria*. Milan: Giuffrè.

D'Alessio, G. and L. Signorini (2000). 'Disuguaglianza dei redditi individuali e ruolo della famiglia in Italia', Banca d'Italia, Temi di Discussione No. 390.

D'Amuri, F. and C. Fiorio (2005). 'Workers' Tax Evasion in Italy', *Giornale degli economisti*, 64(2/3): 247–70.

Deaton, A. (2005). 'Measuring Poverty in a Growing World (or Measuring Growth in a Poor World)', *Review of Economics and Statistics*, 87(1): 1–19.

Dell, F., T. Piketty, and E. Saez (2007). 'Income and Wealth Concentration in Switzerland over the Twentieth Century', in Atkinson and Piketty (2007).

Erickson, C. and A. Ichino (1995). 'Wage Differentials in Italy: Market Forces, Institutions and Inflation', in R. Freeman and L. Katz (eds.) *Differences and Changes in the Wage Structure*. National Bureau of Economic Research, Comparative Labor Market Series. Chicago: University of Chicago Press: 265–305.

Fiorio, C. (2006). 'Understanding Inequality Trends: A Microsimulation Decomposition for Italy', STICERD—Distributional Analysis Research Programme Papers 78, London School of Economics.

Giarda, E. (2003). 'Distribuzione dei redditi dichiarati: stime e previsioni del gettito IRPEF', Dipartimento di Economia Pubblica e Territoriale, Università di Pavia, Società Italiana di Economia Pubblica.

Herr, U. (2002). 'L'evoluzione della struttura dell'IRPEF: un'analisi attraverso le dichiarazioni', in E. Longobardi (ed.) *I centogiorni e oltre: verso una rifondazione del rapporto fisco-economia?* Rome: De Agostini Professionale-Il Fisco: 381–401.

ISAE (Istituto di Studi e Analisi Economica) (2002). 'Evoluzione ventennale della distribuzione del reddito in Italia: un'analisi dei dati fiscali a partire dal 1974', Rapporto Trimestrale, 11: 189–208.

—— (2006), 'L'evasione dell'imposta personale sul reddito delle persone fisiche: rilevanza e problemi', in *Rapporto finanza pubblica e redistribuzione*: 51–108.

Kuznets, S. (1953). *Shares of Upper Income Groups in Income and Savings*. New York: National Bureau of Economic Research.

Landais, C. (2007). 'Les Hauts Revenus en France (1998–2006): une explosion des inégalités?', Paris School of Economics, mimeo.

Manacorda, M. (2004). 'Can the Scala Mobile Explain the Fall and the Rise of Earnings Inequality in Italy? A Semiparametric Analysis 1977–93', *Journal of Labor Economics*, 22 (3): 585–613.

Marè, M. (1996). 'L'evasione in Italia e nei paesi OCSE: evidenze, determinanti, ed effetti economici', *Moneta e credito*, 49(195): 393–443.

Marenzi, A. (1989). 'La distribuzione del carico fiscale in Italia: un modello di microsimulazione'. Pavia: Dipartimento di Economia Pubblica e Territoriale.

Marino, M. and C. Rapallini (2003). 'La composizione familiare dell'imposta sul reddito delle persone fisiche: un'analisi degli effetti redistributivi e alcune considerazioni sul benessere sociale', Banca d'Italia, Temi di Discussione, No. 477.

Monacelli, D. (1996). 'Problemi di stima dell'evasione fiscale: una rassegna dei metodi e degli studi effettuati per l'Italia', *Economia pubblica*, 6: 103–25.

Park, T. (2000). 'Comparison of BEA Estimates of Personal Income and IRS Estimates of Adjusted Gross Income', *Survey of Current Business*, November: 7–13.

Pellegrino, S. (2006). 'La lordizzazione dei redditi netti IRPEF: strumenti per la microsimulazione sul 2005', Dipartimento di Economia Pubblica e Territoriale, Università di Pavia, Società Italiana di Economia Pubblica, Working Paper No. 478.

—— (2007). 'Il modello di microsimulazione IRPEF 2004', Dipartimento di Economia Pubblica e Territoriale, Università di Pavia, Società Italiana di Economia Pubblica, Working Paper No. 583.

Piketty, T. (2001). *Les Hauts Revenus en France au 20ème siècle: inégalités et redistributions, 1901–1998*. Paris: Éditions Grasset.

—— and E. Saez, E. (2003). 'Income Inequality in the United States, 1913–1998', *Quarterly Journal of Economics*, 118(1): 1–39. Longer version in Atkinson and Piketty (2007).

Ricotti, G. and A. Sanelli (2005). 'Conti finanziari e fiscalità: un'analisi storica', presented at the congress 'I Conti Finanziari: La Storia, I Metodi, l'Italia, I Confronti Internazionali', SADIBA, Banca d'Italia, Perugia 1–2 December.

Roberti, P. (1971). 'Le variazioni nella distribuzione personale del reddito in Italia: 1948–1966', *Rassegna economica*, 35(4): 801–32.

Rosen, S. (1981). 'The Economics of Superstars', *American Economic Review*, 71(5): 845–58.

Rossi, N. (1994). *La transizione equa 1992–1993: secondo rapporto Consiglio Nazionale dell'Economia e del Lavoro sulla Distribuzione e Redistribuzione del Reddito in Italia*. Bologna: Il Mulino.

Saez, E. and M. Veall (2005). 'The Evolution of Top Incomes in Northern America: Lessons from Canadian Evidence', *American Economic Review*, 95(3): 831–49.

Signorini, L. and I. Visco (2002). *L'economia italiana*. Bologna: Il Mulino.

Slemrod, J. (1995). 'Income Creation or Income Shifting? Behavioral Responses to the Tax Reform Act of 1986', *American Economic Review*, 85(2): 175–80.

Smeeding, T. (2000). 'Changing Income Inequality in OECD Countries: Updated Results from the Luxembourg Income Study (LIS)', in R. Hauser and I. Becker (eds.) *The Personal Distribution of Income in an International Perspective*. Berlin: Springer-Verlag: 205–24.

SOGEI (Società Generale d'Informatica) (1999). *Confronto tra dati fiscali e dati di contabilità nazionale*, vols. i and ii. Rome.

Visco, V. (1995). 'Alcune note sulla evoluzione della legislazione fiscale in materia di redditi di capitale', in G. Muraro and N. Sartor (eds.) *La tassazione delle attività finanziarie*. Milan: Franco Angeli.

13

Top Incomes in the Long Run of History

A. B. Atkinson, Thomas Piketty,
and Emmanuel Saez

13.1 INTRODUCTION

In this book, and Volume I (Atkinson and Piketty 2007), we have assembled evidence on top incomes in 22 countries, covering periods that range from 15 years (China) and 30 years (Italy) to 120 years (Japan) and 132 years (Norway). The coverage by countries and years is shown in Figure 13.1. For 7 of the 22 countries, the series start before the First World War (1914), and for all but 3 we have observations from before the Second World War. The median number of observations per country is 67.5. To avoid any possible misunderstanding, we should make clear that is not a rectangular data set: there are many missing years (if any reader can help fill the gaps, we should be pleased to hear from them). In fact, the total number of country/year observations is 1,454.

By the standards of economics, these are a rich set of time series. The results for top income shares for the twenty-two countries are summarized in the Appendix Tables 13A.1 to 13A.22. Estimates of the Pareto–Lorenz coefficients (and the inverse coefficients) characterizing the upper tail of the distribution in these twenty-two countries are provided in Appendix Tables 13A.23 and 13A.24. In the case of the ten countries covered in the first volume, we have been able to extend the series in some cases. We have also incorporated (under Germany) the results for Prussia for the period 1891 to 1919 (see Dell 2008). The estimates reported in these appendix tables are those excluding capital gains (where these can be excluded), an aspect discussed below in section 13.2, and they relate to gross incomes, typically after transfers but before the deduction of income tax. It should be noted that we focus in this chapter on the studies of top incomes published in these two volumes, but there have been other important recent contributions, including those by Merz, Hirschel, and Zwick (2005) and by Bach, Corneo, and Steiner (2008) of Germany, by Gustafsson and Jansson (2007) of Sweden, and by Guilera (2008) of Portugal. The reader is also referred to the valuable survey by Leigh (2009).

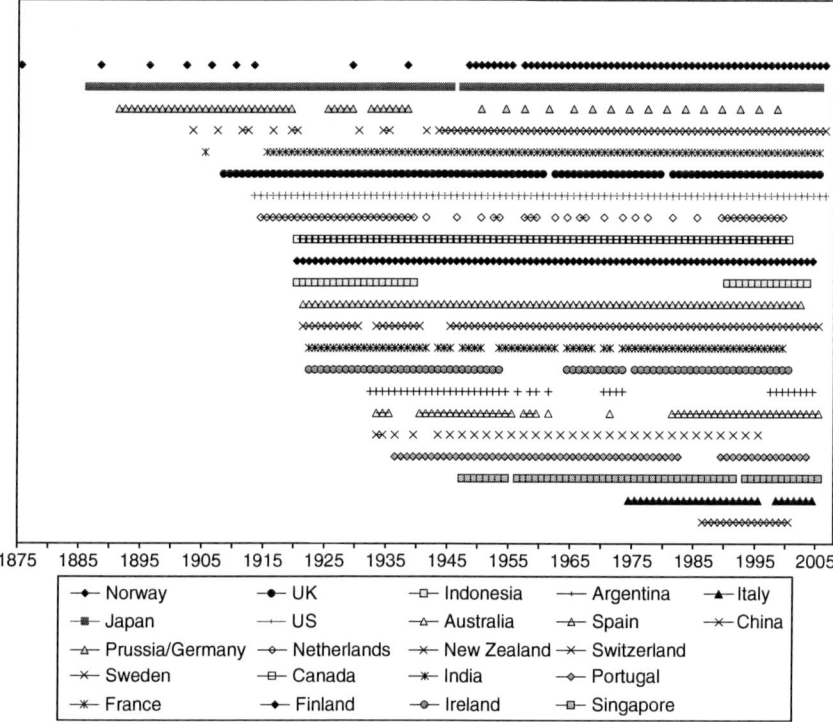

Figure 13.1 Coverage of countries and years

In this chapter, we summarize the main findings from the two volumes, and consider the range of possible explanations. We first, in section 13.2, discuss the quality and comparability of the data. How far can the results from different chapters be treated as comparable? What are the limitations of income tax data as a source? The qualifications set out in this section are essential reading before making use of the results on top income shares, presented in summary form in section 13.3. Our summary starts with the sixty years since the Second World War, taking 1949 as a point of departure, before turning to the lessons from the years before 1949. We ask how far there are common patterns of change. We ask whether top incomes are different. In the final part of the chapter (sections 13.4 and 13.5), we turn to possible explanations for the changes in top shares over time. In section 13.4, we consider how the behaviour and functional form of top income shares can be modelled—theoretically and empirically. In section 13.5, we examine some of the main forces that have been evoked in the individual chapter histories in both this and the previous volume. These include the impact of progressive taxation, globalization, and political change. The final section 13.6 concludes.

In considering the twenty-two countries, it is natural to look for groupings. In the first volume, we contrasted the English-speaking countries and continental Europe. In the present volume, we have added three Nordic countries. Are they part-way between being Anglo-Saxon and continental? We have added three southern European countries. Do they have common features? We have added five Asian countries, two with high GDP per capita, and three less developed but rapidly growing. Are top income shares rising with fast economic growth? Or does the behaviour of their top shares reflect a global pattern? These questions are discussed in more detail below, but in Table 13.1 we summarize in words the main findings from the country chapters in this volume.

Table 13.1 Summary of main findings from Chapters 1 to 12

Country	Main findings
1. India	The shares of the top 0.01%, the top 0.1%, and the top 1% shrank substantially from the 1950s until the early to mid 1980s but then went back up again, so that today these shares are only slightly below the level of the 1920s–1930s. This U-shaped pattern is broadly consistent with the evolution of economic policy in India: the period from the 1950s to the early to mid 1980s was also the period of 'socialist' policies in India, while the subsequent period saw a gradual shift towards more pro-business policies.
2. China	Income inequality in urban China has increased at a high rate between 1986 and 2003, with the share of the top 10% increasing by more than 60%. The share of the top 1% more than doubled.
3. Japan	Income concentration was extremely high throughout the pre-Second World War period during which the nation underwent rapid industrialization; a drastic de-concentration of income at the top took place in 1938–45; income concentration remained low during the rest of the century but shows some sign of increase in the last decade; and top income composition in Japan has shifted dramatically from capital income to employment income over the course of the twentieth century.
4. Indonesia	Top income shares grew during the 1920s and 1930s, but fell in the post-war era. In more recent decades, there was a sharp rise in top income shares during the late 1990s, coinciding with the 1997–8 economic crisis, and some evidence that top income shares fell in the early 2000s.
5. Singapore	During the time Singapore was a colony, top income shares rose to a peak in 1951 and then declined over the 1950s. Following independence there followed 25 years of broad stability at the very top. The 1990s saw a fall in top shares, but after the Asian financial crisis they rose by around a half, and they remain above earlier levels.
6. Argentina	There was an increase in top income shares after the Great Depression, with maxima in 1942–4, and a substantial decline during the Peronist years. However, the limits of the Peronist redistributive policy are marked by the fact that in 1956, if lower than in 1945, the top shares were still above the ones observed in the developed world; they were higher than in the United States, France, Australia, and even Spain. Since the mid 1990s, top income shares followed an increasing trend, similar to the pattern found in Anglo-Saxon economies.
7. Sweden	Starting from levels of inequality approximately equal to those in other Western countries at the time, the income share of the Swedish top decile dropped sharply over the first 80 years of the twentieth century. Most of the decrease takes place before the expansion of the welfare state and by 1950 Swedish top income shares were already lower than in other countries. The fall is almost entirely due to a dramatic drop in the top percentile explained mostly by decreases in capital income, while the lower half of the top decile—consisting mainly of wage earners—experienced virtually no change

over this period. In the past decades top income shares evolve very differently depending on whether capital gains are included or not. With capital gains included, Sweden's experience resembles that in the USA, with sharp increases in top incomes; excluding capital gains, Sweden looks more like the continental European countries.

8. Finland	The share of the top 1% of income earners declined from around 15% of taxed income among the population of tax units in 1920 to just over 6% in the late 1940s to rapidly increase to about 10% in the later 1950s. The top 1% share then declines for almost thirty years until the early 1990s. The increase in this top share in the late 1990s is steep and brings it in 2000, when it peaked, to the same level as seen in the 1950s. The total share of the highest earners fell consistently from the beginning of the 1960s to the mid 1990s but then began to rise. The results bring out clearly how the major equalization from the beginning of 1960 to the mid 1990s has been reversed, taking the shares of top income groups back to levels of inequality or even higher than those found over forty years ago.
9. Norway	Top income shares in the nineteenth century were high: the share of the top 1% was around 20% and that of the top 0.5% around 15%. There was a rise in the shares of the top 10%, 5%, and 1% between 1875 and 1888. Between 1896 and 1902 there was a definite fall; there was some recovery in 1906, but then a further fall. After (and during) the First World War, there was some recovery in the top shares. There was a sharp drop between the 1930s and the late 1940s. Over the early part of the post-Second World War period, top income shares fell steadily: the share of the richest 0.5% fell from 6.4% in 1948 to 2.8% in 1991. There was then, as in Sweden, the UK, and the USA, a turning point, which came at the start of the 1990s, rather later than in the UK and the USA.
10. Spain	Income concentration was much higher during the 1930s than it is today. The top 0.01% income share was twice higher in the 1930s than in recent decades. The top 0.01% income share fell sharply during the first decade of the Franco dictatorship, and has increased slightly since the 1970s, and especially since the mid-1990s. Both the level and the time pattern of the top 0.01% income share in Spain are fairly close to comparable estimates for the US and France over the period 1933–71, especially the decades after the Second World War.
11. Portugal	Income concentration was, as in Spain, much higher during the 1930s and 1940s than it is today. Top income shares stayed relatively stable between the end of the Second World War and the end of the 1960s, followed by a large drop. The drop began to be reversed at the beginning of the 1980s. Over the last fifteen years top income shares have increased steadily, with a considerable contribution from the rise in wage dispersion.
12. Italy	There has been a persistent increasing pattern in top income shares since the mid 1980s, mainly driven by top wages and self-employment income. Notwithstanding the increasing trend, the rise in Italian top shares has been small relative to the surge experienced by top incomes in the United States and other Anglo-Saxon developed economies.

13.2 QUALITY AND COMPARABILITY OF THE DATA

The evidence presented in this, and the preceding, volume comes almost exclusively from tax and other administrative returns in different countries. The use of tax data is often regarded by economists with considerable disbelief. The index to

Morgenstern's book *On the Accuracy of Economic Observations* (1963) contains the entry 'income tax, as reason for lying', and this summarizes well the general—if not very specific—scepticism. In the UK, Richard Titmuss wrote around the same date a book-length critique of the income tax-based statistics on distribution, concluding, 'we are expecting too much from the crumbs that fall from the conventional tables' (1962: 191). More recently, compilers of databases on income inequality have tended to rely on household survey data, dismissing income tax data as unrepresentative.

These doubts are well justified for at least two reasons. The first is that tax data are collected as part of an administrative process, which is not tailored to our needs, so that the definition of income, of income unit, etc. are not necessarily those that we would have chosen. This causes particular difficulties for comparisons across countries, but also for time-series analysis where there have been substantial changes in the tax system, such as the moves to and from the joint taxation of couples. Secondly, it is obvious that those paying tax have a financial incentive to present their affairs in a way that reduces tax liabilities. There is tax avoidance and tax evasion. The rich, in particular, have a strong incentive to understate their taxable incomes. Those with wealth take steps to ensure that the return comes in the form of asset appreciation, typically taxed at lower rates or not at all. Those with high salaries seek to ensure that part of their remuneration comes in forms, such as fringe benefits or stock options, that receive favourable tax treatment. Both groups may make use of tax havens that allow income to be moved beyond the reach of the national tax net.

These shortcomings limit what can be said from tax data, but this does not mean that the data are worthless. Like all economic data they measure with error the 'true' variable in which we are interested. As with all data, there are potential sources of bias, but, as in other cases, we can say something about the possible direction and magnitude of the bias. Moreover, we can compensate for some of the shortcomings of the income tax data. It is true that income tax data cover only the taxpaying population, which, in the early years of income tax, was typically only a small fraction of the total population. However, following the pioneering contribution of Kuznets (1953), we can combine the tax data with external estimates of the total population and the total income. These control totals are typically based on censuses of population and on National Accounts estimates of the total income of persons. The control totals require a number of adjustments and are surrounded by a margin of error, but the important point is that when we refer to the top 1 per cent having x per cent of income, this means the top 1 per cent of the total population and x per cent of the total income. It is *not* the top 1 per cent of taxpayers. Nor is the total of income limited to that accruing to taxpayers. We may not be able to describe the whole distribution, but we can estimate the upper part of the Lorenz curve.

But why not use household surveys, which cover the whole (non-institutional) population? Why use income tax data? There are two main answers. The first is that household surveys themselves are not without shortcomings. These include sampling error, which may be sizeable with the typical sample sizes for surveys, whereas tax data drawn from administrative records are based on very much larger samples. Indeed, in many cases the tax statistics relate to the whole universe of taxpayers, in which case traditional confidence intervals do not apply. Household surveys suffer from differential non-response and incomplete response (these two being the survey counterpart of tax evasion). Such problems particularly affect the top income ranges, as is recognized in studies that combine household survey data with information on upper income ranges from tax sources (see, for example, in the UK, Brewer et al. 2008). The second answer is that household surveys are a fairly recent innovation. Household surveys only became regular in most countries in the 1970s or later, and in a number of cases they are held at intervals rather than annually. We are interested here in covering the whole post-war period, and indeed in going back further. This is what the income tax data allow us to do. The beauty of income tax evidence is that it is available for long runs of years, typically on an annual basis, and that it is available for wide variety of countries.

Comparability of Methods

Although the authors of individual chapters in this volume and in Volume I have modelled their research on Piketty (2001), they have in some cases been unable to follow exactly the same methods and in other cases they have chosen a different approach. Some of these differences in methodology are unlikely to affect the broad conclusions drawn, as has been shown by sensitivity analysis in individual chapters. This applies to the choice of interpolation method, which, at least within intervals (as opposed to extrapolation of an open interval), is not going to have a major impact (see Appendix 9C in Volume I). The same applies to the choice of age cut-off for the adult population. The studies for Australia, Finland, New Zealand, Singapore, and the UK use persons aged 15 and over, while those for Argentina, Canada, Italy, Japan, Portugal, and the USA use persons aged 20 and over, which means that the former may give a higher estimate of the share of the top x per cent (since they are including more people from the tax returns). However, the effect is small: Atkinson and Leigh (chapter 7 in Volume I) find for Australia that using persons aged 20 and over would reduce the share of the top 1 per cent by approximately a twentieth.

Other differences are quantitatively more important. Three of the differences seem to us to be of particular significance. The first is the difference in the unit of analysis. For Argentina, Australia, Canada, China, and Italy (in the period covered), the unit is the individual. In a number of other countries, including France, Germany, Ireland, the Netherlands, Portugal, Switzerland, and the USA, the unit of analysis is the 'tax unit' combining the incomes of husbands and wives. In India, the unit is the individual or the Hindu undivided family. In the case of China and Indonesia, the estimates relate to households. The differences between these units of analysis affect the comparability of the estimates in a way that depends on the joint distribution of income. The difference could go in either direction (see Atkinson, chapter 2 in Volume I). The unit may also change over time, as in Japan (with adjustments made in Chapter 3 to the pre-1950 data), New Zealand (since 1953), Spain (with adjustments made in Chapter 10), and the UK (since 1990).

The differences in unit cannot be treated simply as a fixed effect. The growth of female labour force participation means that the joint distribution of earned incomes is now of much greater significance. The ageing of the population means that there are more single elderly persons in the distribution. On the other hand, we can learn from the cases where there was a change. In the case of the USA, Piketty and Saez (chapter 5 in Volume I) increase the recorded income shares by 'about 2.5 per cent' for the earlier period 1913–47 when there was a degree of separate filing (Piketty and Saez 2001: 35 n.).[1] In the case of the United Kingdom, the introduction of independent taxation in 1990 was associated with (chapter 4 in Volume I) a rise in the share of the top 1 per cent of around an eighth. In the case of New Zealand (chapter 8 in Volume I), the introduction of individual taxation in 1953 was associated with an upward jump of around a quarter in the share of the top 1 per cent. Not all of this change can necessarily be attributed to the introduction of independent taxation, but it suggests that the difference between individual and tax unit bases needs to be taken into account in interpreting the series for the different countries.

The second significant difference is in the derivation of control totals for income. As described in Chapter 2, there are two main approaches. These are illustrated by those applied in the USA at different dates. Piketty and Saez (chapter 5 in Volume I) for the second half of the period (from 1944) extrapolate from the recorded incomes, imputing to non-filers a fixed fraction of filers' average income, to arrive at a total (tax-defined) income for all individuals. They note that the resulting total series is a broadly constant percentage (between 77 per cent and 83 per cent) of total personal income recorded in the National Accounts if transfers are excluded. They therefore take for the earlier period 1913–43 a control total equal to a constant percentage (80 per cent) of total personal income less transfers. (The estimates for Switzerland involve a similar combination of the two approaches.) These two methods—estimates of the income of non-filers, and National Accounts-based totals—are used to differing degrees in different countries. In the UK (chapter 4 in Volume I), the total income of non-filers is constructed from estimates of the different elements of income missing from the tax returns. The resulting total declines from around 95 per cent to around 85 per cent of total personal income minus transfers recorded in the National Accounts. In the Netherlands, a similar approach is followed, with similar implications for the relationship between the control total and total personal income in the National Accounts. In their estimates for Sweden (Chapter 7), Roine and Waldenström compare the two methods. They make estimates of total personal income from the categories in the National Accounts (the total varies around 70 per cent of GDP); they make estimates by adding to the total in

---

[1] It should be noted that they use throughout a control total based on tax units, so that separate filing will definitely cause the top share to be understated.

tax returns amounts for income not included and estimates of the income of non-filers. They argue that the latter gives too high a figure in the early years of the twentieth century, but that from 1930 it is close to 89 per cent of the personal income total. They therefore use throughout a figure of 89 per cent of personal income, which is around 63 per cent of GDP. The approach followed in Norway (Chapter 9) is similar, with a lower percentage (72 per cent) to correspond to the concept of assessed income in the tax data.

Most of the estimates are based on the second approach, applied in varying degrees of detail. In Canada, Saez and Veall (chapter 6 in Volume I) use throughout (1920 to 2000) a constant percentage (80 per cent), applied to 'total personal income less transfers'. The estimates for Ireland (chapter 12 in Volume I) follow the same method. For Japan (Chapter 3), Moriguchi and Saez construct a personal income total from the National Accounts, deducting items that do not appear in taxable income such as employer social contributions and imputed rents on owner-occupied homes. For Spain (Chapter 10), Alvaredo and Saez add for 1981–2004 the National Accounts figures for wages and salaries (not including social contributions), plus 50 per cent of transfers, plus two-thirds of unincorporated business income, plus all non-labour non-business income reported on tax returns. This yields a figure around 66 per cent of GDP and they apply this percentage in the earlier years 1933–71. For Portugal (Chapter 11) in 1989–2003 and Italy (Chapter 12) the procedure is similar. For Portugal, the percentage of GDP is 60 per cent, and this is assumed to apply to the earlier period 1936–83.

In considering the control totals for income, we need to bear in mind that the present volume covers countries where national accounting has been more recently developed and where historical data are hard to obtain. As we saw in Chapter 5, the national income figures for the 1940s and 1950s in Singapore involved 'a considerable amount of guesswork'. This has meant adopting more approximate methods. The control totals for India (Chapter 1) are taken as 70 per cent of national income. In the case of Singapore, allowance has to be made for the international position of the economy, and the estimates are based on figures for indigenous GDP, taking a variable percentage to represent household income. The Indonesian estimates of Leigh and van der Eng (Chapter 4) make use of input output data.

The differences in method are greatest in the area of income totals, and the resulting estimates of top income shares need to be treated with caution. If, for example, the appropriate income total were considered to be 60 per cent rather than 70 per cent of GDP, the top share would be increased by more than 15 per cent. At the same time, we should note that the estimates of shares-within-shares, and the (inverse) Pareto–Lorenz coefficients, are not affected by differences in the income totals, since they are measures of the *shape* of the upper part of the distribution.

The Definition of Taxable Income

Taxes affect the *substance* of the income distribution, and we return to this in section 13.3, but they also affect the *form* of the income distribution statistics. In all cases, the estimates follow the tax law, rather than a 'preferred' definition of income. The latter income concept may seek to approximate the Haig–Simons comprehensive definition, including such items as imputed rent, in kind employment benefits, capital gains and losses, and transfer payments.[2] For a single country study, it may be reasonable to assume that taxable income is a concept well understood in that context. Alternatively, one may assume that all taxable incomes differ from the preferred definition by the same percentage. Neither of these assumptions, however, seems particularly satisfactory, and use of taxable income may well affect the conclusions drawn about changes over time. When we come to a cross-country comparison, there seems an even stronger case for adopting a definition of income that is common across countries and that does not depend on the specificities of the tax law in each country.

Approaching a common definition of income does however pose considerable problems, as illustrated by the treatment of transfers (which have grown very considerably in importance over the century), by capital gains, by the interrelation with the corporate tax system, and by tax deductions. The studies for the USA and Canada subtract social security transfers on the grounds that they are either partially or totally exempt from tax. In other countries, such as Australia, New Zealand, Norway, and the UK, the tax treatment of transfers differs, with typically more transfers being brought into taxation over time.

Perhaps the most important aspect that affects the comparability of series over time within each country has been the erosion of capital income from the progressive income tax base. Early progressive income tax systems included a much larger fraction of capital income than the present progressive income tax systems. Indeed, over time, many sources of capital income, such as interest income, or returns on pension funds, have been either taxed separately at flat rates or fully exempted, and hence have disappeared from the tax base. Some early income tax systems (such as France from 1914 to 1964) also included imputed rents of homeowners in the tax base, but today imputed rents are typically excluded. As a result of this imputed rent exclusion and the development of numerous other forms of legally tax-exempt capital income, the share of capital income that is reportable on income tax returns, and hence included in the series presented, has significantly decreased over time. To the extent that such excluded capital income accrues disproportionately to top income groups, this will lead to an underestimation of top income shares. Ideally, one would want to impute excluded capital income back to each income group. Because of lack of data, such an imputation is very difficult to fully carry out. Some of the studies discuss whether the exclusion of capital income affects the series. For example, Moriguchi and Saez, in the case of Japan, use survey data to try to estimate how interest

---

[2] In principle, transfers from the government should be not be included in pre-fisc incomes as they are part of the government redistributive schemes which tax pre-fisc incomes and provide transfers. In practice, the largest cash transfer payments are public pensions which are often related to social security contributions during the work life and hence can be considered as deferred earnings. Means-tested transfer programmes are in general non-taxable and excluded from the estimates presented.

income—today almost completely excluded from the comprehensive income tax base—is distributed across income groups. In the case of France, Piketty has shown that the long-run decline of top income shares was robust, in the sense that even an upper bound imputation of today's tax-exempt capital incomes to today's reported top incomes would be largely insufficient to undo the observed fall. We should make clear however that there was no systematic attempt to impute full capital income on a comparable basis over time and across countries. We view this as one of the main shortcomings—probably the main shortcoming—of our data set. As we shall see in sections 13.4 and 13.5 below, this puts strong limitations on the extent to which one can use our data set to rigorously test the theoretical economic mechanisms at play.

The treatment of capital gains and losses also differs across time and across countries. In the USA, 'the tax treatment of capital gains and losses has undergone several sweeping revisions since 1913' (Goode 1964: 184). Capital gains have been regarded as within the purview of the income tax, but with different treatments regarding the deductibility of losses and the rates of taxation. In Volume I, chapters 5 and 6 present series for the USA and Canada both excluding and including realized capital gains, and the same procedure has been followed here for Japan (Chapter 3), Sweden (Chapter 7), Finland (Chapter 8), and Spain (Chapter 10). The effects of the inclusion of capital gains on the share of the top 1 per cent in the period since 1949 are shown in Figure 13.2 for five of these

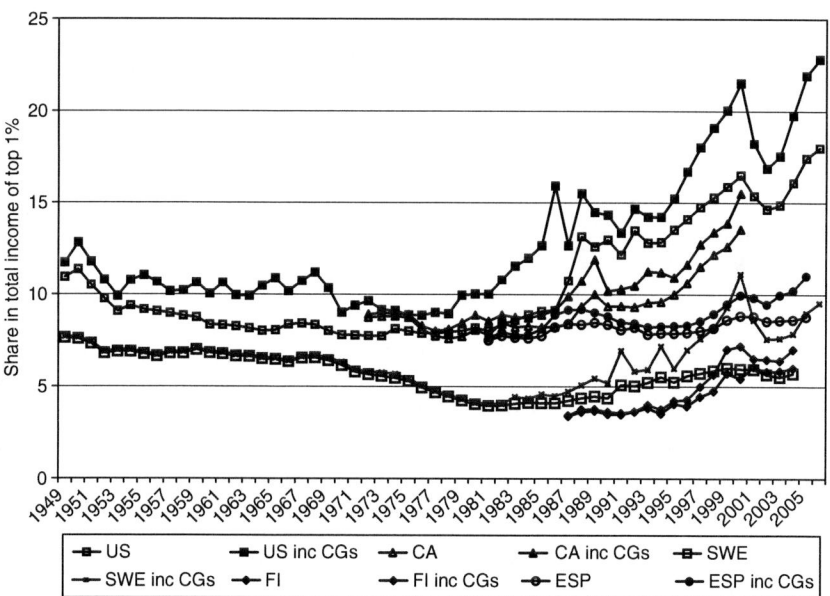

Figure 13.2 Effect of capital gains on share of top 1%

countries (data are given in Chapter 3 for Japan but only for the top 0.1 per cent). The adjustments have been important in the USA throughout the period but have increased in recent years. In 1949, the exclusion of capital gains reduced the share of the top 1 per cent by about a tenth; fifty years later, in 1999, it reduced the share by about a fifth. In the case of Sweden, Roine and Waldenström note that 'over the past two decades the general picture turns out to depend crucially on how income from capital gains is treated. If we include capital gains, Swedish income inequality has increased quite substantially; when excluding them, top income shares have increased much less' (Chapter 7). The estimates for Spain (Chapter 10) show the share of the top 1 per cent rising between 1982 and 2002 from 7.8 to 8.5 per cent before capital gains but from 8.0 to 9.5 per cent when capital gains are included.

Income tax systems differ in the extent of their provisions allowing the deduction of such items as interest paid, depreciation, pension contributions, alimony payments, and charitable contributions. Income from which these de-ductions have been subtracted is often referred to as 'net income'. (We are not referring here to personal exemptions.) The aim is in general to measure gross income before deductions, but this is not always possible. The French estimates (chapter 3 in Volume I) show income after deducting employee social security contributions. In a number of countries, the earlier income tax distributions refer to income after these deductions, but the later distributions refer to gross income. In the USA, the income tax returns prior to 1944 showed the distribution by net income, after deductions. Piketty and Saez (chapter 5 in Volume I) apply adjust-ment factors to the threshold levels and mean incomes for the years 1913–43 (see Piketty and Saez 2001: 40). In Canada, the tax returns for 1920 to 1945 relate to net income. Deductions were smaller, and Saez and Veall (chapter 6 in Volume I) make no adjustment prior to 1929 and for 1929 to 1945 increase all amounts by 2 per cent. In Australia (chapter 7 in Volume I), estimates for 1921–44 are based on taxable rather than total income by ranges of taxable income, while the estimates from 1947–57 are based on the distribution of taxable income by ranges of actual income. Using estimates from overlapping years, adjustments are made to ac-count for these changes. The estimates for Norway in Chapter 9 relate to 'assessed' income after deduction of interest paid and certain other deductions.

The areas highlighted above—transfers, tax-exempt capital income, capital gains, and deductions—may all give rise to cross-country differences and to lack of comparability over time in the income tax data. Any user needs to take them into account. The same applies to tax evasion, to which we devote the next sub-section.

Tax Avoidance and Tax Evasion

As highlighted by the quotation from Morgenstern, the standard objection to use of income tax data to study the distribution of income is that tax returns are largely works of fiction, as taxpayers seek to avoid and evade being taxed. The under-reporting of income can affect cross-country comparisons where there are differences in prevalence of evasion and can affect measurement of trends where the extent of evasion has changed over time.

It is not a coincidence that the development of income taxation follows a very similar path across the countries studied in these volumes. All countries start with progressive taxes on comprehensive income using high exemption levels which limits the tax to only a small group at the top of the distribution. Indeed, at an early stage of industrial development, when a substantial fraction of economic activity takes place in small informal businesses, it is just not possible for the government to enforce a comprehensive income tax on a wide share of the population.[3] However, even in early stages of economic development, Alvaredo and Saez note 'the incomes of high income individuals are identifiable because they derive their incomes from large and modern businesses or financial institutions with verifiable accounts, or from highly paid (and verifiable) salaried positions, or property income from publicly known assets (such as large land estates with regular rental income)'.[4] Comprehensive income taxes are extended to larger groups only when economic development has reduced the number of untaxable informal income earners to a reasonably small fraction of the population. Therefore, it is conceivable that the early progressive income taxes, upon which statistics those studies are based, captured reasonably well most components of top incomes.

The extent of contemporary tax evasion is considered specifically in a number of the country chapters. In the case of Sweden, Roine and Waldenström (Chapter 7) conclude that overall evasion is modest (around 5 per cent of all incomes) and that there is no reason to believe that under-reporting has changed dramatically over time. A speculative reason for this may be that while the incentives to under-report have increased as tax rates have gone up over time the administrative control over tax compliance has also been improved. The Nordic countries may well be different. In the case of Spain (Chapter 10), Alvaredo and Saez note the widely held view that income tax evasion in Spain is (and was) very high, and that consequently, the income tax data vastly underestimate actual incomes. They go on to examine the evidence for this view. Of course, such evidence is hard to come by, and may only be partial, but it does exist. For instance, the Spanish tax administration made public the list of taxpayers for tax years 1933 to 1935, and from this it can be seen that virtually all the largest aristocratic real estate owners were taxpayers. More generally, a careful analysis of the income tax statistics shows that evasion and avoidance in Spain *at the very top of the distribution* during the first decades of existence of the tax was most likely not significantly higher than it was in other countries such as the United States or France. In the case of Italy, Alvaredo and Pisano note the

---

[3] Even today in the most advanced economies, small informal businesses can escape the individual income taxes.

[4] Indeed, before comprehensive taxation starts, most countries had already adopted schedular separate taxes on specific income sources such as wages and salaries, profits from large businesses, rental income from large estates. Such taxes emerge when economic development makes enforcement feasible.

widespread view of tax evasion being much higher than in other OECD countries. Audits and subsequent scandals involving show business people, well-known fashion designers, and sport stars help support this idea among the general public, even when they also provide evidence about the fact that top income earners are very visible for the tax administration. The evidence for Italy does indeed suggest that evasion is important among small businesses and the self-employed (traditionally numerous in Italy), for whom there is no double reporting, but that for wages, salaries, and pensions at the *top of the distribution* there is little room for evading those income components that must be reported independently by employers or the paying authorities. They conclude that the evasion from self-employment and small business income is unlikely to account for the gap in top incomes between Italy and Anglo-Saxon countries.

Another source of evidence is provided by tax amnesties, and Alvaredo discusses the results for Argentina (Chapter 6). Information from the 1962 tax amnesty (which attempted to uncover all income that had been evaded by taxpayers between 1956 and 1961) suggested under-reporting of between 27 and 40 per cent. However, it varied with income. Evasion shows a lower impact at the bottom (where income from wage source dominates) and at the top of the tax scale (where inspections from the tax administration agency might be more frequent and enforcement through other taxes higher). The evidence may be indirect. In the case of India, Banerjee and Piketty (Chapter 1) note the innovations in tax collection that may have affected the prevalence of filing. They investigate the impact by considering the evolution of wage income, where taxes are typically deducted at source, so that no change would be observed if all that was happening was improved collection. They conclude that there was a 'real' increase in top incomes. As in other studies (such as that for Australia in Volume I, chapter 7), this is corroborated by independent evidence about what happened to top salaries.

It is important to remember that, while taxpayers may have a strong incentive to evade, the taxing authorities have a strong incentive to enforce collection. This takes the form of both sticks and carrots. For example, the Inland Revenue Authority of Singapore devotes considerable resources to enforcing tax collection, but also provides positive encouragement to tax compliance through emphasizing the role of taxes in financing key government services such as schools. The resources allocated to tax administration have been substantial: for example, in Spain in the pre-1960 period the administration was able to audit a very significant fraction (10–20 per cent) of individual tax returns. The tax authorities may also be expected to target their enforcement activities on those with higher potential liabilities. The scope for evasion may therefore be less for the very top incomes than for those close to the tax threshold, as Leigh and van Eng note to be the case in Indonesia (Chapter 4).

One important route to avoiding personal income tax is for income to be sheltered in companies. The extent to which this is possible depends on the *personal* tax law and on the taxation of *corporations*. One key feature is the extent to which there is an imputation system, under which part of any corporation tax paid is treated as a pre-payment of personal income tax. Payment of dividends can be made more attractive by the introduction of an imputation system, as in the UK in 1973, Australia in 1987, and New Zealand in 1989, in place of a 'classical' system where dividends are subject to both corporation and personal income tax. Insofar as capital gains are missing from the estimates (as discussed above) but dividends are covered, a switch towards (away from) dividend payment will increase (reduce) the apparent top income shares. This needs to be taken into account when interpreting the results. That is why estimating series including realized capital gains is valuable in order to assess the contribution of retained profits of corporations on top individual incomes. When realized capital gains are untaxed and hence not observed, it is important to assess the effects of attributing retained profits to top income. For example, in the UK, Atkinson (chapter 4 in Volume I) examined the consequences of the large increase after the Second World War in the proportion of profits retained by companies. The attribution of the retained profits to top income groups would have reduced the magnitude of the fall in the share of the top 1 per cent between 1937 and 1957 but still left a very considerable reduction.

The reported shares of top incomes can also be affected by the move between incorporated and non-incorporated activities. This has been modelled by Gordon and Slemrod (2000) and others. The potential impact is particularly marked in the case of the dual income tax introduced in Nordic countries. The tax reform in Finland in 1993 combined progressive taxation of earned income with a flat rate of tax on capital income and corporate profits, with a full imputation system applied to the taxation of distributed profits. Under the dual income tax, capital income is taxed at a lower rate than the top marginal tax rate on labour income. As discussed in Chapter 8, the 1993 tax reform led to an increasing trend of the share of capital income (dividends) and declining share of entrepreneurial income. This can be interpreted as an indication of a tax-induced shift in organizational form and the choice of tax regime. In Chapter 10, Alvaredo and Saez provide a model of the incentive to adopt a (wealth tax) exempt organizational form and examine the effect of the wealth tax reform undertaken in Spain. Their empirical estimates suggest that there is a very large shifting effect: the fraction of businesses benefiting from the exemption jumps from one-third to about two-thirds for the top 1 per cent.

An extreme form of adjustment to income taxation is to leave the country. In their study of Switzerland (chapter 11 in Volume I), Dell, Piketty, and Saez investigated the issue of tax evasion by foreigners relocating to that country or through Swiss bank accounts. They found that the fraction of taxpayers in Switzerland with income abroad or non-resident taxpayers had increased in recent years but remains below 20 per cent even at the very top of the distribution, suggesting that the migration to Switzerland of the very wealthy is a limited phenomenon. They similarly conclude that the amount of capital income earned through Swiss accounts and not reported is small in relation to the total incomes of top income recipients in other countries. In the case of Sweden, Roine and Waldenström (Chapter 7) make estimates of 'capital flight' since the early 1980s using unexplained residual capital flows ('net errors and omissions') published in official balance of payments statistics. They estimate that somewhere between 250 and 500 billion SEK has left the country without being accounted for. To get a sense of the order of magnitude by which this 'missing wealth' would change top income shares in Sweden, they add all of the returns from this capital first to the incomes of the top decile and then to the top percentile. For the years before 1990, there is no effect on top income shares by adding income from offshore capital holdings since they are simply too small. However, after 1990, and especially after 1995, when adding all of them to the top decile, income shares increase moderately (by approximately 3 per cent). When instead adding everything to the incomes of the top percentile, the income shares increase by about 25 per cent which is equivalent to an increased share from about 5.7 to 7.0 per cent. While this is a notable change, it does not raise Swedish top income shares above those in France (about 7.7 per cent in 1998), the UK (12.5 per cent in 1998), or the USA (15.3 per cent in 1998).

To sum up, the different pieces of evidence indicate that tax evasion and tax avoidance need to be taken seriously and can quantitatively affect the conclusions drawn. They need to be borne in mind when considering the results, but they are not so large as to mean that the tax data should be rejected out of hand. Our view is that legally tax-exempt capital income poses more serious problems than tax evasion and tax avoidance per se.

Summary

The data are rich but need to be used with due circumspection, particularly with respect to incomes from capital. In drawing conclusions, users need to ask themselves whether their findings could be reversed by taking into account the inherent limitations of fiscal data, of the breaks in continuity over time, and of the differences in methods that remain. Put differently, there is a wide confidence interval surrounding the estimates, reflecting not sampling error (since in many cases the statistics cover the universe) but non-sampling error. In concrete terms, the different considerations described above suggest that an error margin of ± 20 per cent is not unreasonable, although it could well be exceeded if the different errors cumulate in the same direction. In what follows, we take ± 20 per cent as a yardstick.

13.3 A SUMMARY OF THE MAIN FINDINGS

Our summary of the evidence begins in the middle of the twentieth century. The first columns in Table 13.2 show the position in 1949 (1950).[5] We take this year as one for which we have estimates for all except four of the twenty-two countries (for Indonesia we have taken the 1939 estimate and for Ireland that for 1943), and

---

[5] In the case of New Zealand, we have used the estimates of Atkinson and Leigh (2008: table 1) that adjust for the change in the tax unit in 1953.

as one when most countries had begun to return to normality after the Second World War (for Germany and the Netherlands we take 1950). Moreover, it was before the 1950–1 commodity price boom that affected top shares in Australia, New Zealand, and Singapore.

If we start with the top 1 per cent—the group on which attention is commonly focused—then we can see from Table 13.2 that the shares of total gross income are strikingly similar when we take account of the possible margins of error. There are 18 countries for which we have estimates. If we take 10 per cent as the central value (the median is in fact around 10.8), then 12 of the 18 lie within the range 8 to 12 per cent (i.e. with an error margin of ±20 per cent). In countries as diverse as India, Norway, France, New Zealand, and the USA, the top 1 per cent had on

Table 13.2 Comparative top income shares

	Around 1949			Around 2005		
	Share of top 1%	Share of top 0.1%	β coefficient	Share of top 1%	Share of top 0.1%	β coefficient
Indonesia	19.87	7.03	2.22		1.34	2.94
Argentina	19.34	7.87	2.56	16.75	7.02	2.65
Ireland	12.92	4.00	1.96	10.30		2.00
Netherlands	12.05	3.80	2.00	5.38	1.08	1.43
India	12.00	5.24	2.78	8.95	3.64	2.56
Germany	11.60	3.90	2.11	11.10	4.40	2.49
United Kingdom	11.47	3.45	1.92	14.25	5.19	2.28
Australia	11.26	3.31	1.88	8.79	2.68	1.94
United States	10.95	3.34	1.94	17.42	7.70	2.82
Canada	10.69	2.91	1.77	13.56	5.23	2.42
Singapore	10.38	3.24	1.98	13.28	4.29	2.04
New Zealand	9.98	2.42	1.63	8.76	2.51	1.84
Switzerland	9.88	3.23	2.06	7.76	2.67	2.16
France	9.01	2.61	1.86	8.20	2.19	1.74
Norway	8.88	2.74	1.96	11.82	5.59	3.08
Japan	7.89	1.82	1.57	9.20	2.40	1.71
Finland	7.71		1.63	7.08	2.65	2.34
Sweden	7.64	1.96	1.69	6.28	1.91	1.93
Spain			1.99	8.79	2.62	1.90
Portugal		3.57	1.94	9.13	2.26	1.65
Italy				9.03	2.55	1.82
China				5.87	1.20	1.45

Notes: 1939 for Indonesia, 1943 for Ireland, 1950 for Germany and the Netherlands, 1954 for Spain. 1995 for Switzerland, 1998 for Germany, 1999 for the Netherlands, 1999–2000 for India, 2000 for Canada and Ireland, 2002 for Australia, 2003 for Indonesia and Portugal, 2004 for Argentina, Italy, Norway and Sweden.

β coefficients are calculated using share of top 0.1% in top 1% (see Tables 13A.23 and 13A.24), with the following exceptions:
  (i) β coefficient for Finland in 1949 calculated using share of top 1% in top 5%
  (ii) β coefficient for Spain in 1949 calculated using share of top 0.01% in top 0.05%
  (iii) β coefficient for Portugal in 1949 calculated using share of top 0.01% in top 0.1%
  (iv) β coefficient for Ireland in 2000 calculated using share of top 0.5% in top 1%
  (v) β coefficient for Indonesia in 2003 calculated using share of top 0.01% in top 0.1%.

Table 13.2B Pareto–Lorenz a coefficients vs. inverted-Pareto–Lorenz β coefficients

a	$\beta = a/(a-1)$	β	$a = \beta/(\beta-1)$
1.10	11.00	1.50	3.00
1.30	4.33	1.60	2.67
1.50	3.00	1.70	2.43
1.70	2.43	1.80	2.25
1.90	2.11	1.90	2.11
2.00	2.00	2.00	2.00
2.10	1.91	2.10	1.91
2.30	1.77	2.20	1.83
2.50	1.67	2.30	1.77
3.00	1.50	2.40	1.71
4.00	1.33	2.50	1.67
5.00	1.25	3.00	1.50
10.00	1.11	3.50	1.40

Notes: The 'a' coefficient is the standard Pareto–Lorenz coefficient commonly used in power-law distribution formulas: $1 - F(y) = (A/y)^a$ and $f(y) = aA^a/y^{1+a}$ ($A > 0$, $a > 1$, $f(y)$ = density function, $F(y)$ = distribution function, $1 - F(y)$ = proportion of population with income above y). A higher coefficient a means a faster convergence of the density towards zero, i.e. a less fat upper tail.

The 'β' coefficient is defined as the ratio $y^*(y)/y$, i.e. the ratio between the average income $y^*(y)$ of individuals with income above threshold y and the threshold y. The characteristic property of power laws is that this ratio is a constant, i.e. does not depend on the threshold y. Simple computations show that $\beta = y^*(y)/y = a/(a-1)$, and conversely $a = \beta/(\beta-1)$.

average between 8 to 12 times average income. Three countries were only just below 8 per cent: Japan, Finland, and Sweden. The countries above the range were Ireland, Argentina, and (colonial) Indonesia. The top 1 per cent is of course just one point on the distribution. If we look at the top 0.1 per cent, shown in Table 13.2 for 18 countries (Portugal replacing Finland), then we find that again 12 lie within a (± 20 per cent) range around 3.25 per cent from 2.6 to 3.9 per cent. Leaving out the three outliers at each end, the top 0.1 per cent had between 26 and 39 times the average income.

We also report in Table 13.2 the inverse Pareto–Lorenz coefficients associated to the upper tail of the observed distribution in the various countries in 1949 and 2005. In this table, and throughout this chapter, we choose to focus the attention upon the inverted-Pareto–Lorenz 'β' coefficient rather than the standard Pareto–Lorenz 'a' coefficient. Note that there exists a one-to-one, monotonically decreasing relationship between the a and β coefficients, i.e. $\beta = a/(a-1)$ and $a = \beta/(\beta-1)$ (see the notes to Table 13.2B). The reasons for using the β coefficient are twofold. First, as was noted by Piketty (chapter 1 in Volume I), the β coefficient has arguably greater economic appeal, in that it measures the average income of people above y, relative to y. It provides a direct intuitive measure of the fatness of the upper tail of the distribution. Next, a higher β coefficient means larger top income shares and higher top income inequality (while the reverse is true with the more commonly used a coefficient), which facilitates the presentation and discussion of the results. In practice, we shall see that the β coefficient typically varies between 1.5 and 2.5: values around 1.5 or below indicate low top income inequality, while values around 2.5 or below indicate high top income inequality. A value of 1.5 means that people above a specified level have on average 50 per cent more income; a value of 2.5 means that they have 150 per cent more income.

Coming back to 1949, we find that 10 of the 20 countries for which β coefficient values are shown in Table 13.2 lie between 1.88 and 2.00 in 1949. Countries as different as Spain, Norway, the USA, and (colonial) Singapore had Pareto coefficients that differed only in the second decimal place. As of 1949, the only countries with β coefficients above 2.5 were Argentina and India.

1949 is of interest not just for being mid-century, but also because later years did not exhibit the degree of similarity described above. The right-hand part of Table 13.2 assembles estimates for 2005 (or a close year). The central value for the share of the top 1 per cent is not too different from that in 1949: 9 per cent. But we now find more dispersion. For the top 1 per cent, 9 out of 21 countries lie outside the range of ± 20 per cent. Leaving out the two outliers at each end, the top 0.1 per cent had between 13 and 56 times the average income (in 1949 these figures had been 20 and 52). In terms of the β coefficients only 4 of the 22 countries had values between 1.88 and 2.00. Of the countries present in 1949, five now have values of β in excess of 2.5.

The Post-War Picture

There was in fact considerable diversity of experience over the period from 1949 to the beginning of the twenty-first century. If we ask in how many cases the share of the top 1 per cent rose or fell by more than 2 percentage points between 1949 and 2005 (bearing in mind that two-thirds were in the range 8 to 12 per cent in 1949), then we find the 17 countries more or less evenly divided: 6 had a fall of 2 points or more, 5 had a rise of 2 points or more, and 6 had a smaller or no change. If we ask in how many cases the inverted-Pareto–Lorenz β coefficient changed by more than 0.1, then this was true of 15 out of 20 countries in Table 13.2, with 12 showing a rise (a move to greater concentration). Examination of the annual data for individual countries in Tables 13A.1 to 13A.22 confirms that during the 50+ years since 1949 individual countries followed different time paths.

Can we nonetheless draw any common conclusions? Is it for example the case that all were following a U-shape, and that the differences when comparing 2005 and 1949 arise simply because some countries are further advanced? Is the USA leading the way, with other countries lagging? In Table 13.3, we summarize the time paths from 1949 to 2005 for the sixteen countries for which we have fairly complete data over this period for the share of the top 1 per cent and top 0.1 per cent. In focusing on change, we are not interested in small differences after the decimal points. The criterion applied in the case of the share of the top 1 per cent is that used above: a change of 2 percentage points or more. For the share of the top 0.1 per cent, we apply a criterion of 0.65 percentage points (i.e. scaled by 3.25/10). In applying this, we consider only *sustained* changes. This means that we

Table 13.3 Summary of changes in shares of top 1% and 0.1% between 1949 and 2005

Country	Share of top 1%	Share of top 0.1%
France	No change. Rose 1 point between 1998 and 2005.	Fell 1 point between 1949 and early 1980s. Rose 0.4 point between 1998 and 2005.
UK	Fell 6; rose 7½ points.	Fell 2; rose 3 points.
USA	Fell 3; rose 10 points.	Fell 1; rose 6 points.
Canada	Fell 3; rose 6 points (up to 2000).	Fell 1; rose 3½ points (up to 2000).
Australia	Fell 7; rose 4 points.	Fell 2; rose 1½ points.
New Zealand	Fell 3; rose 4 points.	Fell 1; rose 1½ points.
Germany	No sustained change.	No sustained change.
The Netherlands	Fell 6½ points (up to 1999).	Fell 3 points (up to 1999).
Switzerland	No sustained change.	No sustained change.
India	Fell 7½; rose 4½ points (up to 1999).	Fell 4; rose 2½ points (up to 1999).
Japan	No sustained change up to 1999; rose 1½ points between 1999 and 2005.	No sustained change up to 1999; rose 1 point between 1999 and 2005.
Singapore	No sustained change from 1960 to 1998; rose 2 points between 1998 and 2005.	No sustained change from 1960 to 1990s; rose 2 points between 1990s and 2005.
Argentina	Fell 12; rose 4 points.	Fell 5½; rose 3 points.
Sweden	Fell 3½; rose 2 points.	Fell 1¼; rose 1¼ points.
Finland	Rose 2 points up to early 1960s; fell 6 points; rose 3½ points.	
Norway	Fell 4½; rose 8 points.	Fell 1; rose 4½ points.

Notes: 'No change' means change less than 2 percentage points for top 1%; less than 0.65 percentage point for top 0.1%.
Data coverage incomplete for part of the period for Argentina.

do not recognize changes due to tax reforms that distort the figures, as in the case of Norway (Chapter 9) or New Zealand (see Volume I, chapter 8), those due to the commodity price boom of the early 1950s, as for Australia, New Zealand, and Singapore, or other changes that are not maintained for several years.

Applying this criterion, there is just one case—Finland—where there is a pattern of rise/fall/rise. The share of the top 1 per cent in Finland rose from below 8 per cent in 1949 (it has been lower before then) to around 10 per cent in the early 1960s. Of the remaining 15 countries, one can distinguish a group of 6 'flat' countries (France, Germany, Switzerland, the Netherlands, Japan, Singapore), and a group of 9 'U-shaped' countries (UK, USA, Canada, Australia, New Zealand, India, Argentina, Sweden, Norway). Broadly the same story is revealed by the β coefficients plotted in Figures 13.3 and 13.4 for both groups of countries.

The ten countries belonging to the second group appear to fit, to varying degrees, the U-shape hypothesis that top shares have first fallen and then risen over the post-war period. In most countries, the initial fall was of limited size, with β coefficients declining from about 1.7 in 1949 to about 1.5 during the 1970s, before climbing towards 2–2.5–3 during the 1990s–2000s. In Argentina

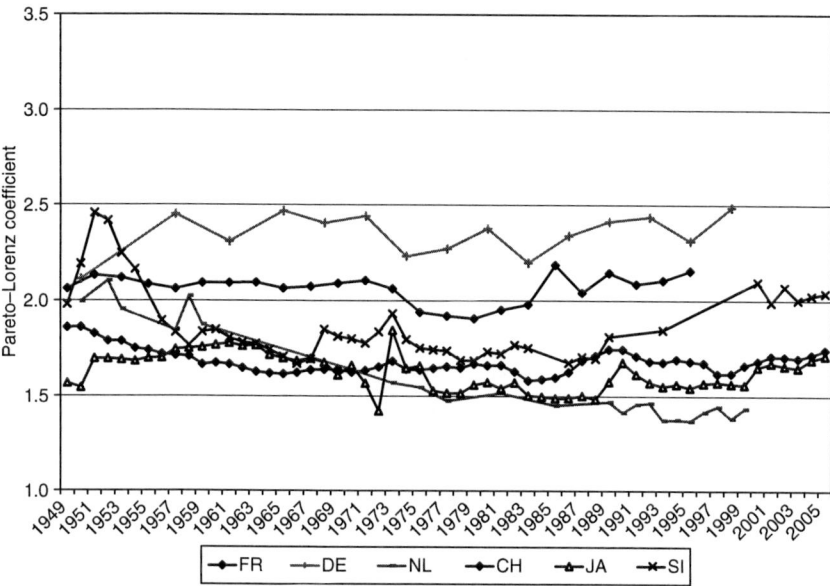

Figure 13.3 Inverted-Pareto–Lorenz β coefficients, 1949–2005: 'flat' countries

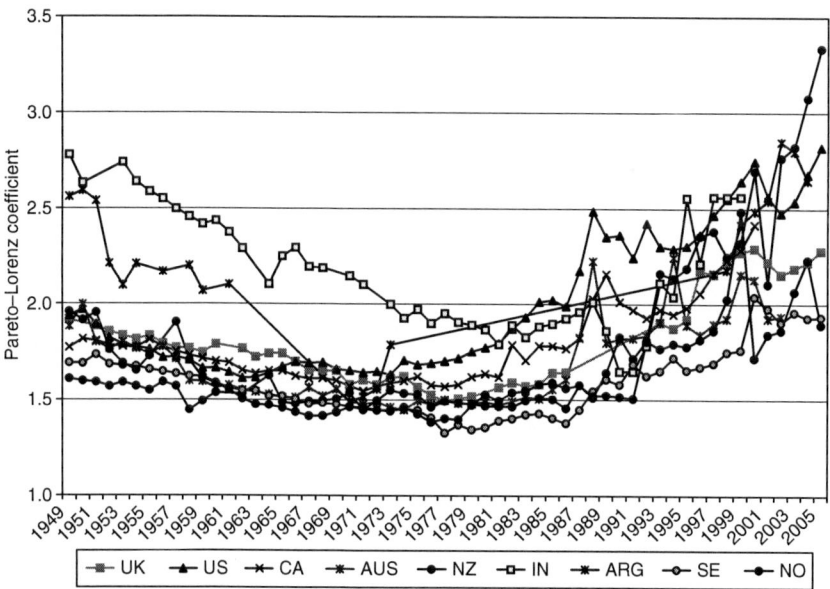

Figure 13.4 Inverted-Pareto–Lorenz β coefficients, 1949–2005: 'U-shape' countries

and India, there was higher concentration to start with (β coefficients above 2.5 in 1949), and the declining part of the U-curve was more marked (see Figure 13.4). The individual country patterns differ in other respects as well. As may be seen from Table 13.3, the initial falls in top shares were less marked in the USA, Canada, and New Zealand than in the UK, Australia, and India. The share of the top 1 per cent was much the same in the USA and UK in 1949 but in the UK the share then halved over the next quarter century, whereas in the USA it fell by only a little over a quarter. From Figure 13.4 we can see that the decline in the β coefficient reached 1.7 in the USA in 1969, the same value as in the UK, but the latter went on to decline to about 1.5 by the late 1970s. Norway and Sweden reached values as low as 1.3–1.4.

The frontier between the U-shaped countries and the flat countries is somewhat arbitrary and should not be overstressed. In France, after an initial reduction in concentration, the coefficient hovered around 1.7 from 1960 to the late 1990s, but has begun to rise since the late 1990s. In Japan and Singapore, the rebound in recent years is even more pronounced (see Figure 13.3 and the top income shares series in the appendix tables). The only three countries with no sign of a rise in income concentration during the most recent period, namely Switzerland, Germany, and the Netherlands, are countries where our series stop in the late 1990s. There exists some reasonable presumption that when data become available for the 2000s, these countries might also display an upward trend. Finally, note that Switzerland and especially Germany have always been characterized by significantly larger concentration at the top than other continental European countries.

What about countries for which we have only a shorter time series? The time series for China is indeed short, but there too the top of the distribution is heading for greater concentration. For instance, β coefficients have gradually risen from about 1.2 in 1986 to about 1.5 in 2003 (see Tables 13A.23 and 13A.24). These are still very small β coefficients by international and historical standards, but the trend is strong (and the levels might be underestimated due to the nature of the available Chinese data, see Chapter 2). China has a way to go, but the degree of concentration is heading in the direction of the values in OECD countries. Regarding the other countries with limited time coverage (Spain, Portugal, and Italy), one also observes a significant rise in income concentration during the most recent period.

Before 1949

What happened in our twenty-two countries before 1949 may appear like pre-history to some readers, but the experience may be relevant for several reasons. The behaviour of the income distribution in today's rich countries may provide a guide as to what can be expected in today's fast-growing economies. We can learn from nineteenth-century data, such as those for Norway, that cover the period of industrialization. Events in today's world economy may resemble those in the past. If we are concerned as to the distributional impact of recession, then there may be lessons to be learned from the 1930s.

The data assembled here provide evidence about the inter-war period for 19 of the 22 countries; and for 5 of the countries we have more than one observation before the First World War. In Table 13.4 we have assembled the changes in the shares of the top 1 per cent and top 0.1 per cent for certain key periods, such as the world wars, and the crash of 1929–32, as well as for the whole period up to 1949.

The first striking conclusion is that the top shares in 1949 were much lower than thirty years earlier (1919) in the great majority of countries. Of the 18 countries for which we can make the comparison with 1919 (or in some cases with the early 1920s), no fewer than 13 showed a strong decline in top income shares. In only 1 case (Indonesia) was there an increase in the top shares. In half of the countries, the fall caused the shares to be at least halved between 1919 and 1949. For countries where one can compare 1949 with 1913–14, the fall generally seems at least as large.

Table 13.4 Summary of changes in shares of top 1% and 0.1% before 1949

Country	Share of top 1%	Share of top 0.1%
France	1928–31: lose 2 points	1928–31: lose a fifth
	WW2: lose 4 points	WW2: halved
	1949 = half of 1914	1949 = a third of 1919
UK	-	WW1: lose a fifth
	-	1928–31: lose a fifth
	-	WW2: lose 30 per cent
	1949 = half of 1914	1949 = 40 per cent of 1919
		Pre-WW1: *no obvious trend*
USA	WW1: lose 3 points	WW1: lose a third
	1928–31: lose 4 points	1928–31: lose a third
	WW2: lose 3 points	WW2: lose a third
	1949 = 70 per cent of 1919	1949 = half of 1919
Canada	1928–31: gain 1 point	1928–31: no change
	WW2: lose 6 points	WW2: halved
	1949 = 3/4 of 1920	1949 = half of 1920
Australia	1928–31: lose 2½ points	1928–31: lose a quarter
	WW2: lose 1 point	WW2: lose a quarter
	1949 same as 1921	1949 = 85 per cent of 1921
New Zealand	1928–30: lose 1 point	1928–30: lose a fifth
	WW2: lose 2 points	WW2: lose a quarter
	1949 = 2/3 of 1921	1949 = half of 1921
Germany	1928–32: no change	1928–32: no change
	1933–38: gain 5 points	1933–38: gain 3 points
	1950 = 2/3 of 1938	1950 = half of 1938
	Prussia: 1914 unchanged relative to 1881	*Prussia: 1914 unchanged relative to 1881*
	(Germany 1925 = 60% of Prussia 1914)	*(Germany 1925 = half of Prussia 1914)*

(continued)

Table 13.4 Continued

Country	Share of top 1%	Share of top 0.1%
The Netherlands	WW1: gain 3 points	WW1: gain a quarter
	1928–32: lose 4 points	1928–32: lose a third
	WW2: lose 5 points	WW2: lose a third
	1950 = 60 per cent of 1914	1950 = 45 per cent of 1914
Switzerland	WW2: lose 1 point	WW2: lose a fifth
	1949 is unchanged relative to 1933	1949 is unchanged relative to 1933
Ireland	28–32: gain 40 per cent	WW2: lose a fifth
		1949 same as 1922
India	28–31: gain 2 points	28–31: gain a fifth
	WW2: lose 5 points	WW2: lose a quarter
	1949 is unchanged relative to 1922	1949 is unchanged relative to 1922
Japan	WW1: lose 3 points	WW1: lose a tenth
	28–31: lose 1 point	28–31: lose a tenth
	WW2: lose 9 points	WW2: lose two-thirds
	1949 = 40 per cent of 1914	1949 = quarter of 1914
	1914 is unchanged relative to 1886	*1914 is unchanged relative to 1886*
Indonesia	28–32: gain 5 points	28–32: gain 15 per cent
	1939 = 8 points higher than 1921	1939 = quarter higher than 1921
Argentina	WW2: gain of 2 points	WW2: gain of fifth
	1949 is unchanged relative to 1932	1949 is unchanged relative to 1932
Sweden	1949 is a third of 1912	1949 is a fifth of 1912
	1912 = 3/4 of 1903	*1912 unchanged relative to 1903*
Finland	28–30: no change	
	WW2: loss of 5 points	
	1949 = half 1920	
Norway	WW2: lose 4 points	WW2: lose 40 per cent
	1949 = 3/4 of 1913	
	1913 = 2/3 of 1875	
Spain		1949 = 60 per cent of 1933
Portugal		1949 = 3/4 of 1936

Notes: WW1 denotes the First World War; WW2 denotes the Second World War. 'No change' means change less than
2 percentage points for top 1%; less than 0.65 percentage point for top 0.1%.
Data coverage incomplete for part of the period for Argentina.

What happened before 1914? In five cases, shown in italics, we have data for
a number of years before the First World War. Naturally the evidence has to
be treated with caution and has evident limitations: for example, the German
figures relate only to Prussia (see Dell 2008 for estimates for Baden, Hesse, Sachsen,
and Württemberg). But it is interesting that in the two Nordic countries (Sweden
and Norway) the top shares seem to have fallen somewhat at the very beginning
of the twentieth century, a period when they might have been in the upward part
of the Kuznets inverted-U. As is noted in Chapters 7 and 9, at that time Norway
and Sweden were largely agrarian economies. In neither Japan nor the UK is
there evidence of a trend in top shares. (For the German states the picture is less

clear and varies across states—see Dell 2008.) Given the scarcity of reliable income data for the pre-1914 period, using wealth data is probably the most promising way to go in order to put the First World War shocks into a long-run historical perspective. Using large samples of Parisian and national estate tax returns over the 1807–1994 period, Piketty, Postel-Vinay, and Rosenthal (2006) have found that wealth concentration rose continuously during the 1807–1914 period (with an acceleration of the trend in the last three to four decades prior to 1914), and that the downturn did not start until the First World War. Due to the lack of similar wealth series for other countries, it is difficult to know whether this is a general pattern. But for all countries where some pre-1914 evidence does exist, available information suggests that the sharp decline in wealth concentration did not start before 1914—or at least that the trend was much more moderate prior to the First World War.

Are Top Incomes Different?

In Volume I, we emphasized the differences between the very top of the distribution, the top 1 per cent, and the adjacent income recipients. In Table 13.5 we assemble the findings for the 'next 4 per cent' (those in the second to fifth percentile groups) and the 'second vingtile group' (those in the sixth to tenth percentile groups). The values are shown for three of the dates we have highlighted: around 1919 (or at the eve of the First World War, when available), 1949, and 2005. We have added, in the final column, text comments about these groups. In three cases, the data do not allow us to estimate shares below that of the top 1 per cent, so that there are 19 countries shown.

In many cases—15 out of 19—the top 1 per cent *are* different, in the sense that the changes in income concentration have particularly affected this group. For some countries, the 'next 4 per cent' exhibit some of the same features as the top 1 per cent (as in the UK in recent decades), so that it would be fairer to talk of concentration among the top 5 per cent, but typically the second vingtile group does not share the same experience. In other cases, like China, it is a matter of degree. But this is not universal, and in Table 13.5 we have shown in italics the four cases (Germany, Japan, Singapore, and Portugal) where there have been changes in the next 4 per cent and below.

Being in the top 1 per cent does not necessarily imply being rich, and there are also marked differences within this group. The very rich are different from the rich. We have earlier considered the top 0.1 per cent (in Table 13.2), and a number of the chapters examine the top 0.01 per cent. In Chapter 1, Banerjee and Piketty show that in India in the 1990s it was only the top 0.1 per cent who enjoyed a growth rate of income faster than that of GDP per capita, in contrast to the situation in the 1980s when there was faster growth for the whole top percentile.

Table 13.5 Summary of changes in shares of top 'next 4%' and 'second vintile'

Country	'Next 4%'	'Second vintile'	Text comments
France	1919 14.3	1919 8.4	'The secular decline of the top decile income share is almost entirely due to very high incomes' (i. 48).
	1949 12.7	1949 10.5	
	2005 13.0	2005 11.0	
UK	1919 11.9	1919 7.2	'This highlights the "localized nature of redistribution"' (i. 96).
	1949 11.9	1949 8.9	
	1978 11.4	1978 10.7	
	2005 14.5	2005 11.2	
USA	1919 13.5	1919 10.2	The next 4% and the second vintile 'account for a relatively small fraction of the total fluctuation of the top decile income share' (i. 146).
	1949 12.5	1949 10.3	
	2005 15.2	2005 11.8	
Canada	1920 18.2		The 'upturn during the last two decades is concentrated in the top percentile' (i. 232).
	1949 14.7	1949 12.8	
	2000 15.4	2000 13.3	
Australia	1921 7.8		After 1958, 'the downward trend continued for the next 4% but not for the second vintile' (i. 320).
	1949 12.4	1949 9.1	
	2002 11.2	2002 10.4	
New Zealand	1921 14.1		After 1953, 'the share of the [second] vintile was not much reduced' (i. 343).
	1949 12.3	1949 9.2	
	2005 12.7	2005 10.8	
Germany	1950 13.3	1950 9.5	*'The bottom part of the top decile does not exhibit the same stability as the upper part.…From the early 1960s… the share of the bottom 9% of the top decile has been constantly growing'* (i. 377).
	1998 13.1	1998 11.2	
The Netherlands	1919 15.7	1919 10.1	'Most of the inter-war decline of the top 10% is restricted to the top 1%, while its post-war decline is broader and covers the upper vintile as a whole' (i. 444).
	1950 14.1	1950 10.6	
	1999 11.7	1999 11.0	
Switzerland	1949 12.3	1949 10.1	'The two bottom groups [the next 4% and the second vintile] are remarkably stable over the period' (i. 488).
	1995 11.5	1995 9.9	
Ireland (next 9%)	1943 30.3	-	'a much sharper rise [from 1990 to 2000] the higher one goes up the distribution' (i. 515).
	2000 25.8	-	
China	1986 7.2	1986 7.6	'the rise in income inequality was so much concentrated within top incomes in both countries [China and India]' (p. 47).
	2003 11.9	2003 10.2	

Japan	1919 9.6	-	'*the income de-concentration phenomenon that took place during the Second World War was limited to within the top 1%... [From 1992 to 2005 there has been] a sharp increase [in the share of the next 4%]*' (p. 88).
	1949 13.8	-	
	2005 16.1	-	
Singapore	1974 12.3	1974 7.9	'*Over a thirty year period there was broad stability of the very top income shares. At the same time there was some change lower down the distribution*' (p. 230).
	2005 14.6	2005 9.5	
Sweden	1919 14.9	1919 10.7	'Looking first at the decline over the first eighty years of the century, we see that virtually all of the fall in the top decile income share is due to a decrease in the very top of the distribution. The income share for the lower half of the top decile (P90–95) has been remarkably stable' (p. 307).
	1949 12.3	1949 10.5	
	2005 11.1	2005 9.6	
Finland	1920 18.3	-	'Compared with top one per cent group, the income shares of percentile groups within the rest of the 10 per cent has risen relatively modestly over the last ten years' (p. 391).
	1949 13.0	-	
	1992 12.1	-	
	1965 10.7	1965 9.8	
	2004 9.5	2004 8.7	
Norway	1913 12.4	1913 9.3	'Whereas the share of the top 1 per cent rose by some 7 percentage points between 1991 and 2004, the share of the next 4 per cent increased by only about 2 percentage points, and there was virtually no rise in the share of those in the [second vintile]' (pp. 455–6).
	1949 13.2	1949 11.9	
	2005 11.3	2005 9.4	
Spain	1981 13.6	1981 11.5	'the increase in income concentration which took place in Spain since 1981 has been a phenomenon concentrated within the top 1% of the distribution' (p. 497).
	2005 13.4	2005 11.0	
Portugal	1976 11.0	1976 8.8	'*in Portugal, all groups within the top decile display important increases*' (p. 571).
	2003 15.6	2003 11.7	
Italy	1974 12.4	1974 10.6	'the increase in income concentration which took place in Italy since the mid 1980s has been a phenomenon happening within the top 5% of the distribution' (p. 634).
	2004 12.3	2004 10.3	

Composition of Top Incomes

In their study of the United States, Piketty and Saez found that the 'rise in top incomes is due not to the revival of top capital incomes, but rather to the very large increases in top wages (especially top executive compensation). As a consequence, top executives (the "working rich") replaced top capital owners (the "rentiers") at the top of the income hierarchy during the twentieth century' (2006: 204). In France (Piketty 2003), the top capital incomes had not been able to recover from a succession of adverse shocks over the period 1914 to 1945; progressive income and inheritance taxation had prevented the re-establishment of large fortunes.

Data on the composition of top incomes are only available for around half of the countries studied here, but a number record the decline of capital incomes and the rise of top earnings. The Japanese data show that 'the dramatic fall in income concentration at the top was primarily due to the collapse of capital income during the Second World War' (Moriguchi and Saez, Chapter 3, p. 78). In the Netherlands, 'capital and wage incomes have traded places within the top shares [although] the increased role of the latter has not been able to prevent the decline or the stability of the top shares' (Salverda and Atkinson, chapter 10 in Volume I, p. 452). In Canada, 'the income composition pattern has changed significantly from 1946 to 2000. . . . the share of wage income has increased for all groups, and this increase is larger at the very top. . . . The share of capital income [excluding capital gains] has fallen very significantly for the very top groups' (Saez and Veall, chapter 6 in Volume I, p. 239). The Italian data (Chapter 12) only start in 1974 and the rise in top shares is modest: the share of the top 1 per cent rose from around 7 per cent in the mid 1970s to around 9 per cent in 2004. But the Italian data show a rise in the role of wage income in the very top groups. In 1976, earnings accounted for less than 10 per cent of the income of the top 0.01 per cent, but by 2004 this had increased to over 20 per cent. Over the same period, the share of capital income more or less halved (Table 12A.4). In Spain, a similar calculation (from figures that omit capital gains) shows that in 1981, earnings accounted for less than 20 per cent of the income of the top 0.01 per cent, but by 2004 this had increased to 40 per cent.

Further evidence can be obtained from other sources for some of the countries without evidence on the composition of incomes in the income tax data. In the case of Portugal, for example, the administrative records on earnings show that the share of the very top earners increased: between 1991 and 2004 the share of the top 0.1 per cent doubled (Table 11D.6).

At the same time, the picture is not totally uniform. A major difference between the Nordic countries and the USA is the continuing importance in the former of capital income. In Sweden, Roine and Waldenström find that 'between 1945 and 1978 the wage share at all levels of top incomes became more important...But in 2004 the pattern is back to that of 1945 in terms of the importance of capital, in particular when we include realized capital gains' (Chapter 7, p. 311). The conclusions reached regarding Finland stress that 'the main factor that has driven up the top 1 per cent income share in Finland after the mid 1990s is an unprecedented increase in the fraction of capital income' (Chapter 8, p. 403). This may reflect differences in reporting behaviour following tax reforms, but it is not totally a difference between Nordic countries and the Anglo-Saxons. In Australia, Atkinson and Leigh found that 'the proportion of salary and wage income for top income groups in 2000 was quite similar to the proportion in 1980' (chapter 7 in Volume I, p. 322). In the UK, it is true that the major themes have been the fall in capital incomes over the first three-quarters of the twentieth century and the subsequent rise in top earnings, but minor themes have been an earlier fall on the share of top earners and a partial restoration of capital incomes since 1979.

Summary

It is not easy to summarize a summary, not least because to almost every statement there is a counterexample among the twenty-two countries we have been studying.

- At the middle of the twentieth century, the top of the income distribution looked similar in many of the different countries for which we have data: for two-thirds the top 1 per cent had on average between 8 and 12 times average income. Countries as different as Spain, Norway, the USA, and (colonial) Singapore had inverse Pareto coefficients that differed only in the second decimal place.
- This was to change: from 1950 to the present, countries followed different paths, and there is now greater diversity. Out of 17 countries we can track from 1949 to 2005, 6 had over the period as a whole a fall of 2 points or more in the share of the top 1 per cent, 5 had a rise of 2 points or more, and 6 had a smaller or no change.
- Within the period, the majority of countries appear to fit, to varying degrees, the U-shape hypothesis that top shares have first fallen and then risen over the post-war period. This was not universal: a number exhibited either no change or a limited recent rise in top shares.
- The post-war fall in top shares (where it happened) may be seen as continuing the pattern of the first half of the century, but the 1900–45 period was particularly affected by events, including, for both combatants and non-combatants, the two world wars, and the Great Crash of 1929.

- In most countries, the changes, and particularly the recent increases, have been concentrated at the very top.
- The decline in top income shares over the first three-quarters of the twentieth century was largely associated with a decline in top capital incomes; the recent rise in top shares in a number of countries has been particularly associated with increased top earnings, but this is not universal and in the Nordic countries the rise was associated largely with capital income.

One way to summarize our findings over the entire 1900–2005 period is again to plot separately top income shares and β coefficients for the two groups of countries defined above, which now become the 'L-shape' group and the 'U-shape' group—keeping in mind that the frontier between both groups is fuzzy, and that L-shape countries seem to be gradually shifting towards the U-shape pattern (see Figures 13.5, 13.6, 13.7, and 13.8).

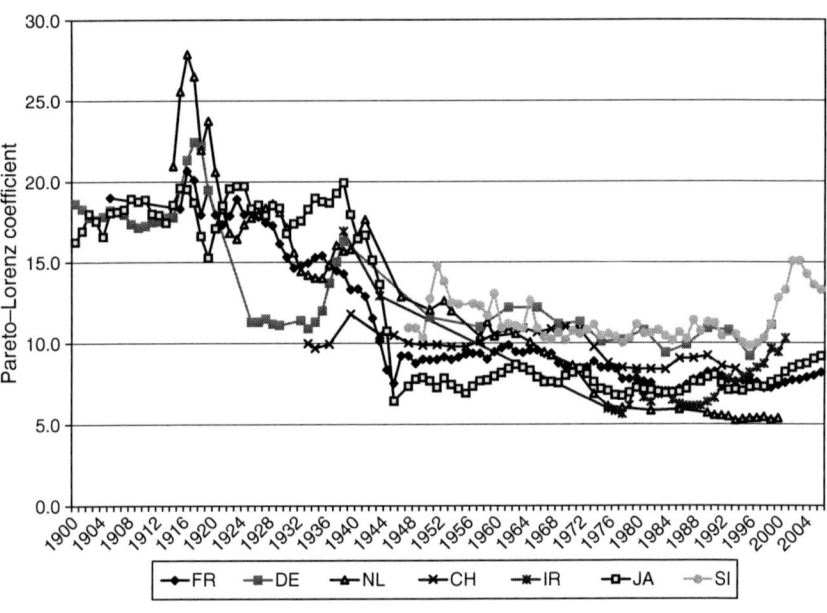

Figure 13.5 Top 1% income shares, 1900–2005: 'L-shape' countries

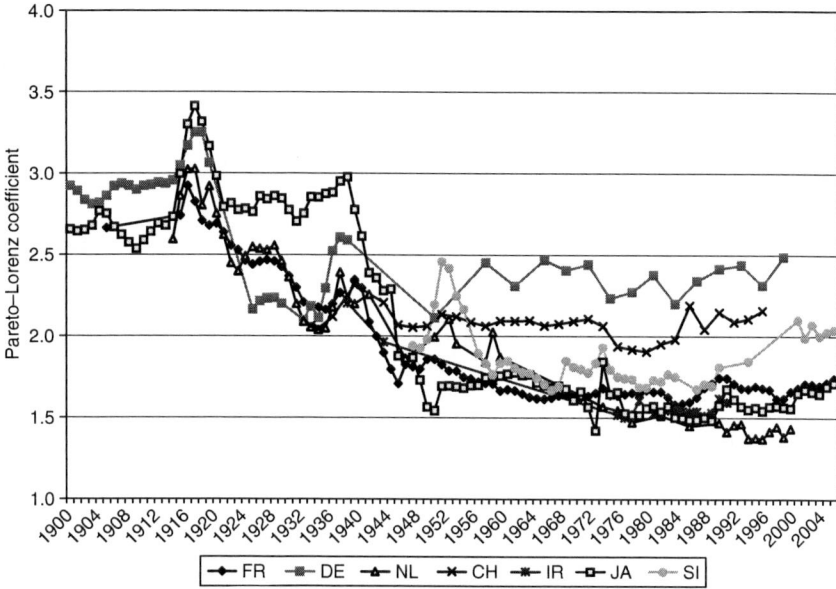

Figure 13.6 Inverted-Pareto–Lorenz β coefficients, 1900–2005: 'L-shape' countries

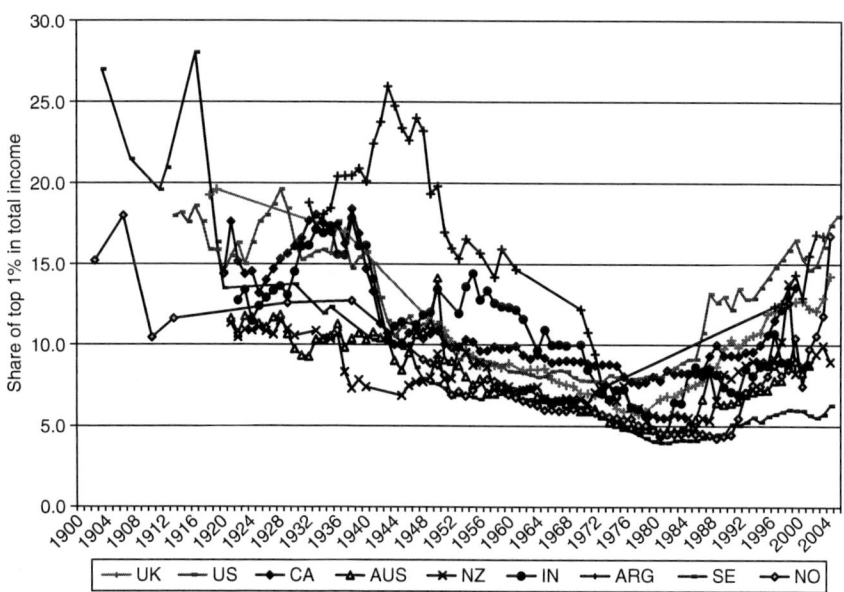

Figure 13.7 Top 1% income shares, 1900–2005: 'U-shape' countries

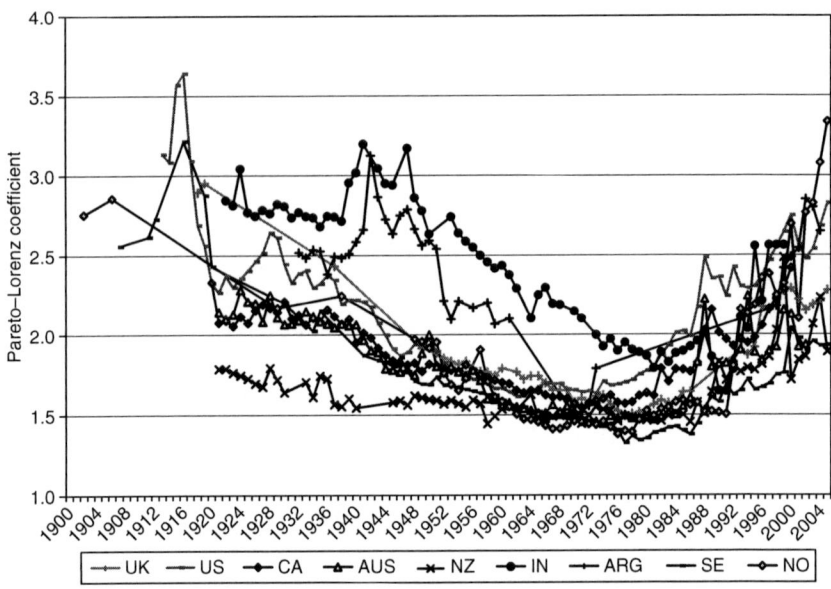

Figure 13.8 Inverted-Pareto–Lorenz β coefficients, 1900–2005: 'U-shape' countries

13.4 SEEKING POSSIBLE EXPLANATIONS: EMPIRICAL
AND THEORETICAL MODELS

From the data on the changes in the upper part of the income distribution assembled in these two volumes certain possible explanations stand out. We have drawn attention to the falls in top income shares in countries fighting in the First and Second World Wars (and that some, but not all, non-combatant countries, were less strongly hit, or even saw an increase in top shares). According to Moriguchi and Saez, 'the defining event for the evolution of income concentration in Japan was a historical accident, namely the Second World War' (Chapter 3, p. 000). Much less momentous, but still distinctive as an event, was the commodity price boom of 1950, which saw a rise in top shares in Australia, New Zealand, and Singapore. In these cases, a single event is sufficiently large for us to be content with a single variable analysis. Moreover, there is unlikely to be reverse causality, with the fall or rise in shares causing the wars or the commodity boom. The slump in commodity prices in the Great Depression may also be such an event—see the discussion of Indonesia by Leigh and van der Eng in Chapter 4—but the wider economic circumstances were also highly relevant.

Indeed, in general, explanations are likely to be multivariate, and we are confronted with the task of seeking to separate different influences. In the introductory chapter to Volume I, Piketty suggested that the database constructed here could be exploited as a cross-country panel, and this approach has already been adopted by Roine, Vlachos, and Waldenström (2008) and Atkinson and Leigh (2007). The former authors find, for example, that growth in GDP per head is associated with increases in top income shares and that financial development is pro-rich in the early stages of a country's development.

Multivariate statistical analysis may help us disentangle some of the factors at work. For example, a number of the chapters, following Piketty (2001, 2003), highlight the role of progressive income taxation. In the UK, for example, the period of falling top income shares was one of high marginal rates of tax, and the shares began to rise again when the tax rates were sharply reduced in the 1980s. But how can we be sure that there is a causal path from progressive taxation to reduced top income shares? In the UK, high top rates of income tax were first introduced during the First World War. Could these tax rates, and the reduction in top shares, not be seen as both *resulting* from third factors associated with the war and its aftermath, such as the loss of overseas income? Statistical analysis seeks to separate out the independent variation in different variables. For example, the UK was a combatant in the First World War but the Netherlands (also a colonial power) was not. It may therefore be informative to compare the two countries, both of which had progressive income taxes. At the same time, there are possible third factors. Both the UK and the Netherlands faced similar global economic conditions that may have independently affected top shares. In the same way, the tax cuts of the 1980s took place under Reagan and Thatcher, just as the First World War increases in the UK had been initiated by Liberal governments. These governments pursued other policies apart from income taxation, such as the measures to prevent profiteering in the First World War, or the liberalization of the capital markets and privatization in the 1980s, which may have affected the top income shares. There is also the possibility of reverse causality. The increases in top incomes as a result of changed executive remuneration policies may have increased political pressure for cutting top taxes. We need therefore a simultaneous, as well as multivariate, model.

Statistical analysis can help us identify independent variation, but it rarely proves fully conclusive. The conclusions that we draw inevitably involve elements of judgement. Judgement in turn is likely to be influenced by a range of considerations. Here we consider two: historical narrative and economic theory (on which we particularly focus).

The conclusion regarding the role of progressive income taxation in France was reached by Piketty after an extensive discussion of the economic history of France over the twentieth century. While it would be reinforced by regression analysis in which the relevant tax rate variable had a highly (statistically) significant coefficient of a plausible magnitude, the conclusion was based on a reading of the events of the period. In the same way, the individual chapters in these two volumes provide each a historical narrative that in itself is part of the evidence. The narrative typically draws on a variety of evidence. A number of chapters, such as that on Japan, contain evidence from a range of sources: income tax data, wealth data, estate data, and wage data. In combining these disparate sets of information, the authors are not carrying out a mechanical operation, but exercising judgement about the strengths and weaknesses of different sources. These narratives are of course subjective, reflecting the standpoints of the authors, and there will no doubt be disagreement about the interpretation of history. Again they cannot be definitive. But equally they cannot be dismissed out of hand, and they play a significant role in our summary of major mechanisms in the next section.

Theoretical Models

The judgement concerning the importance of progressive taxation in France was also reached on the basis of theoretical considerations, notably simulation models of capital accumulation. This brings us to the question of the relation between theoretical models of income distribution and the specification of statistical relationships. How closely are these to be linked? In the theory of consumer demand, if a consumer maximizes a logarithmic utility function (of the consumption of each good plus a constant as in the Stone–Geary form) subject to a linear budget constraint, we can derive the predicted demands as linear functions of income. This straight line curve can be fitted to expenditure data, and since the days of Engel this has provided a valuable framework for understanding how consumer spending is likely to change over time. The coefficient on income is interpreted as the marginal propensity to consume, and the specified functional form allows inferences to be drawn about the response to price changes. There is in this case a tight link between the theoretical model and the empirical implementation.

In contrast, the income inequality literature has typically a looser connection (see Atkinson and Brandolini 2006 for a survey). Theoretical models are invoked, but to produce a list of explanatory variables rather than to generate an estimating equation. The functional form is not specified, so that it is not clear how the explanatory variables should enter the estimating equation. Should the model be linear? Should the explanatory variables interact? There is no guide to the form of the variable to be explained. Should the left-hand side be the top income share? Should it be a transformation? Should it be the (inverse) Pareto coefficient?

Modelling Sectoral Shifts

Building a link between theory and empirical specification is not straightforward, as may be illustrated by reference to the most popular model in the income distribution literature: the Kuznets inverse-U curve. This curve is based on the structural change that takes place in an economy as it is transformed from largely agricultural (traditional) to industrial (modern). We should note, before using this model, that its popularity seems to far exceed its demonstrated empirical relevance. As stressed by Piketty (2001, 2003), in the first post-Kuznets study of top incomes, the inverse-U has little purchase in explaining top income shares; indeed, he argues that we should look instead at those sections of Kuznets's (1955) article where he emphasizes the factors counteracting the concentration of savings, notably the impact of progressive taxation—to which we return below.

If we take the Kuznets model of structural change, what does it imply for top income shares? With his numerical assumptions, the top income group is the top decile of those in the higher-paid industrial sector. They initially constitute, when the agricultural sector employs 80 per cent of the population, 2 per cent of the population. Half their share (that of the top 1 per cent) in the Kuznets numerical example is either 2.4 per cent (moderately unequal) or 3.2 per cent (more unequal) of total income. As the industrial sector grows, this share falls: with the agricultural sector employing 70 per cent of the population, the shares become 2.2 and 2.9 per cent. With a linear top section of the Lorenz curve (as assumed in Kuznets's example), the share of the top 1 per cent, S_1, is simply a constant divided by mean income (and hence is strictly decreasing with mean income). (More realistic would be an assumption that the upper tail of incomes in the industrial sector follows some distribution such as the Pareto.)

The basic problem with the Kuznets model as far as top shares are concerned is that it focuses essentially on labour income, whereas it is clear that we need to consider both labour and capital income, and their changing roles. Indeed it is with capital incomes that we start, since historically they accounted for the bulk of top incomes.

Modelling Capital Incomes

In the first part of his Presidential Address, Kuznets (1955) evokes *two* 'groups of forces in the long-term operation of developed counties [that] make for *widening* inequality in the distribution of income' (1955: 7). The first of these is the concentration of savings in the upper income brackets and the cumulative effect on asset holding. Subsequently, Meade (1964) developed a theory of individual wealth holding, allowing for accumulation and transmission of wealth via inheritance, and this model has been analysed in a general equilibrium setting by Stiglitz (1969). With equal division of estates at death, a linear savings process, and persistent differences in earnings across generations, in the long run the steady-state distribution of wealth simply mirrors the distribution of earnings (Atkinson and Harrison 1978: 211). If the society starts with a more unequal distribution of capital than steady-state level, then the top shares will fall in the approach to this equilibrium (and conversely if it starts below steady-state levels, say if earnings inequality increased for some exogenous reason). But to explain the extent of inequality we have to have appeal to explanations of the distribution of earnings.

Alternative assumptions about bequests can however generate long-run equilibria where there is inequality of wealth even where earnings are equal. Stiglitz shows how the operation of primogeniture (leaving all wealth to one child) can lead in equilibrium to a stable distribution with a Pareto upper tail, with the Pareto coefficient

$$a = \log[1+n]/\log[1+sr(1-t)] \tag{1}$$

where $sr(1-t)$ is the rate of accumulation out of wealth, s being the savings rate, r being the rate of return, t the tax rate, and n is the rate of population growth (Atkinson and Harrison 1978: 213). For stability, the population growth rate has to exceed the rate of accumulation by the wealthy, so it follows that a is greater than 1. The faster the rate of accumulation, the closer a is to 1. Equation (1) provides a—deceptively—simple answer to the questions concerning specification. Approximating $\log(1+x)$ by x, we should regress $1/a$ (or $1/\beta$) on sr $(1-t)/n$. This provides a natural way of testing the impact of progressive income taxation. However, this is indeed deceptive, since it assumes that the parameters are constant over time, and that the primogeniture assumption is remotely plausible. The first of these concerns might be met by using a moving average of past tax rates. In countries such as the UK where the top tax rate was cut from 98 per cent to 40 per cent in the first half of the 1980s, there would then be a continuing rise in top shares until the new equilibrium was approached.

Wealth is not typically concentrated in a single line of descent. Primogeniture may have applied in aristocratic England, but it was not legally permissible in most European countries (and, after 1947, Japan) and it never became widely established in the United States. With equal division of inheritance, which seems a more reasonable assumption, Vaughan (1993) has shown that the equation for the equilibrium value of a is given by the implicit form:

$$a[sr(1-t) - 1/2\sigma^2 r^2(1-t)^2] + 1/2\sigma^2 r^2(1-t)^2 a^2$$
$$= (\delta + n)[1 - (1 + n/\delta)^{-a}] \tag{2}$$

where δ is the rate of mortality. In this model, Vaughan has also introduced a random element in the return to capital (and for the underlying portfolio choice), where σ^2 is the variance of the white noise stochastic process. If there is no randomness, and n = 0, so that the population is not growing (so primogeniture is the same as equal division), then we have $(1/a) = sr(1-t)/\delta$, similar to the earlier estimating equation. If n is small relative to δ, we can approximate the power on the right hand side of (2) and solve for a as a decreasing linear function of the net rate of return, $r(1-t)$, and which falls with the contribution of the stochastic term, $\sigma^2 r^2(1-t)^2$.

The models of top incomes described above relate to capital income; we need now to consider possible explanations in terms of earned incomes.

Modelling Top Earnings

Referees of a number of the papers in these two volumes, when they were submitted for journal publication in an earlier form, took the authors to task for not paying sufficient attention to the dominant paradigm in labour economics, which explains rising wage dispersion in terms of skill-biased technical change. Or, as it had earlier been put by Tinbergen (1975), there is a race between the expansion of education and the increased demand for educated labour as a result of technological change. While we agree that this literature offers important insights, we do not feel that it has a great deal to say about what is happening at the very top of the earnings distribution. Empirically, labour economists have discussed the top decile as a proportion of the median, but we are interested in what happens to the top percentile and within the top percentile group. The skill-bias explanation has highlighted the premium to college education (see, for example, Katz and Autor 1999), but that has little to say directly about why the top percentile has increased relative to the top decile. The recent 'polarization' thesis of Autor, Katz, and Kearney (2006) has specifically focused on the impact of technical change in replacing routine manual jobs, which only indirectly affects top earners.

There are in fact a number of earlier theories that are directly relevant to top earnings. One such set of theories is those dealing with executive remuneration in a hierarchical structure. The model advanced by Simon (1957) and Lydall (1959) generates an approximately Pareto tail to the earnings distribution, with a Pareto exponent given by

$$a = \log [\text{span of managerial control}] / \log [1 + \text{increment with promotion}] \tag{3}$$

In this form, the model is purely mechanical, but it provides a vehicle by which we may introduce a number of explanatory variables, including technological change, taxation, and changes in the size distribution of firms and other organizations. Tournament theory (Lazear and Rosen 1981), for example, has provided an explanation of the size of the necessary increment. If one considers the position of people at a particular level in an organization, deciding whether or not to be a candidate for promotion to the next rank, then they are comparing the certainty of their present position with the risk of taking a new position in which they may fail, and lose their job. The higher-rank job also involves greater effort. In the very simplest case, the worker weighs the mean gain against the risk. There are two competing effects. On the one hand, the tax reduces the financial gain from promotion and more is needed to compensate for the increased effort. On the other hand, the tax reduces the risk of the new job: the government shares part of the risk.

A second explanation of the rise in top earnings shares in a number of countries in the second half of the post-war period is provided by the 'superstar' theory of Rosen (1981). The expansion of scale associated with globalization and with increased communication opportunities has raised the rents of those with the very highest abilities. Where the 'reach' of the top performer is extended by technical changes such as those in Information and Communications Technologies (ICT), and by the removal of trade barriers, then the earnings gradient becomes steeper. Moreover, Frank and Cook (1995) argue that the winner-take-all pay-off structure has spread beyond fields like sport and entertainment: 'it is fair to say that virtually all top-decile earners in the United States are participants in labour markets in which rewards depend heavily on relative performance' (Frank 2000: 497). This could explain the fall in the Pareto α coefficient (and the rise in the β coefficient) in the past quarter century. Indeed Rosen made precisely this prediction in 1981, referring back to Marshall's *Principles*, where Marshall identifies 'the development of new facilities for communication, by which men, who have once attained a commanding position, are enabled to apply their constructive or speculative genius to undertakings vaster, and extending over a wider area, than ever before' (1920: 685). As captured in the title of the book by Frank and Cook (1995), it is a *Winner-Take-All Society*, and this suggests that it can usefully be modelled as an extreme value process. The distribution of earnings in this case is given by the maximum values generated by the results of many separate 'competitions'. If we limit attention to those values exceeding some specified threshold, then for a sufficiently high threshold the distribution function takes on the generalized Pareto form (Embrechts, Klüppelberg, and Mikosch 1997: 164 or Coles 2001: 75), which has a Pareto upper tail.

Finally, considerable attention has been devoted to the effects of marginal tax rates—and especially top marginal tax rate—on the earnings distribution. Higher top marginal tax rates can reduce top reported earnings through three main channels. First, top earners may work less and hence earn less—the classical supply side channel. Second, top earners may substitute taxable cash compensation with other forms of compensation such as non-taxable fringe benefits, deferred stock-option or pension compensation—the tax-shifting channel.[6] Third, because the marginal productivity of top earners, such as top executives, is not perfectly observed, top earners might be able to increase their pay by exerting effort to influence corporate boards. High top tax rates might discourage such efforts aimed at extracting higher compensation.[7]

The central concept capturing all those behavioural responses to taxation is the elasticity of reported earnings with respect to the net-of-tax rate (defined as one minus the marginal tax rate). There is a large literature (surveyed in Saez,

---

[6] The taxation of stock options varies substantially across countries, In the United States, profits from stock-option exercises are included in wages and salaries for tax purposes and hence captured in the estimates. In other countries, such as France, profits from stock options are taxed separately and hence are not included in the estimates.

[7] The welfare consequences of taxation differ widely across the three channels. The first channel creates pure tax distortions. In the second channel, the tax distortion is reduced by 'fiscal externalities' as tax shifting might generate deferred tax revenue as well. In the third channel, taxes can actually correct a negative externality if the contract between the executive and the board does not take into account the best interests of shareholders and other wage earners.

Slemrod, and Giertz 2009) which attempts to estimate this elasticity. In general, the literature estimates this elasticity based on the sum of labour and capital income although, as we discussed above, the effects of tax rates on capital income might have a fairly long lag.

With a constant and uniform elasticity e, and a marginal tax rate t, by definition, reported earnings will be: $z = z^0(1 - t)^e$, where z^0 is reported income when the marginal tax rate is zero. Therefore, the top income share will be proportional to $(1 - t_T)^e/(1 - t_M)^e$, where t_T is the top group marginal tax rate on earnings and t_M is the average marginal tax rate on earnings. Therefore, top income shares, combined with information on marginal tax rates by income groups, can be used to test this theory and estimate the elasticity e with a log-form regression specification of the form:

$$log(Top\ Income\ Share) = a + e\ log(1 - t_T) + \epsilon.$$

As discussed below, Saez (2004) proposes such an exercise with US data from 1960 to 2000. Atkinson and Leigh (2007) and Roine, Vlachos, and Waldenström (2008) combine data from several countries (and include several other variables) to test this relationship. In all those studies, top marginal tax rates do seem to negatively affect top income shares, although causality is difficult to establish. The main limiting factor to extend such an analysis is the absence of systematic series on marginal tax rates by income groups.[8]

Combining Capital and Earned Income

In order to explain the shifting mix of capital and earned income, we need to bring the two income sources together in a single model. This crucially depends on their joint distribution. Are those with large capital incomes also those with high salaries, accumulating assets over their careers? Or are there, as assumed in classical distribution theories, separate classes of 'workers' and 'capitalists'?

The latter case, with two distinct groups with high incomes, is the easier to handle. We can consider the upper tail of the income distribution being formed as a mixture of the two upper tails. For example, if the upper tail of earnings, for reasons we have just discussed, has a Pareto relative cumulative distribution with exponent a_l, and capital income is distributed according to a Pareto distribution with exponent a_k, then the overall distribution could be seen as a combination of the two: a simple mixture. The shape of the cumulative distribution depends on

---

[8] Top marginal income tax rates may not approximate well effective marginal tax rates in upper income groups because of various exemptions, special provisions, the presence of other taxes such as social security contributions, or local income taxes. When top tax rates were extremely high, the fraction of taxpayers in the top bracket was often extremely small as well so that the marginal tax rate in the top 1% was substantially lower than the top marginal tax rate.

the relative weight on the two distributions, and in this way we can introduce the overall shares of wage and capital income (factor shares). If the exponent is assumed to be less for capital income than for earnings (i.e. $a_k < a_l$), then those with capital income become increasingly dominant as we move up the income scale.

Where people receive both earned and capital income, we have to make assumptions about their correlation. Where they are independent, we have the convolution of the two distributions. This again introduces the relative shares of earned and capital income in total income. However, this approach does not offer any obvious simple functional forms (since we are adding not multiplying the two components). Moreover, it seems more realistic to assume some positive degree of correlation. In the extreme case where people are ranked the same in the two distributions, we can form the combined distribution by inverting the cumulative distribution. Expressing y as a function of $(1 - F)$, we have in the case of the Pareto distribution, $y = [A/(1 - F)]^{1/a}$. So that, if we add earned and capital income, we have total income as

$$[A/(1 - F)]^{1/al} + [B/(1 - F)]^{1/ak} \qquad (4)$$

Where $a_k < a_l$, the ratio of capital to earned income rises as we move up the distribution. Again the relative weight of capital and labour income enters via the constants A and B.

The different elements may be brought together in a simple decomposition. Taking for illustration the share of the top 1%, this can be broken down as follows:

Share of top 1% = Proportion of earned income
    × Share of top 1% of earners
    × Alignment coefficient for earnings
    + Proportion of capital income
    × Share of top 1% with capital income
    × Alignment coefficient for capital income   (5)

The 'alignment coefficient' for earnings (capital income) is the share in earnings (capital income) of the top 1 per cent of income recipients divided by the share of top 1 per cent of earners (capital income recipients). Since the top 1 per cent of earners (capital income recipients) are not necessarily in the top 1 per cent of income recipients, the alignment coefficient is by definition less than or equal to 1. It is equal to 1 in the case discussed at the end of the previous paragraph, but in a class model where no workers are in the top 1 per cent the coefficient is zero. Evidence about the degree of alignment in the case of Sweden is provided in Chapter 7, which shows the distribution of wealth both ranked by wealth and by total income. As may be seen from Figure 7.8, the share in total wealth of the top 1 per cent is some 5 to 10 percentage points lower when ranked by total income, but the two series move closely together over time.

Summary

The above examples give some idea of the strength of assumptions that is necessary to bridge the gap between theoretical models and empirical specification. For some readers the assumptions required may indeed be a bridge too far, and proof that we have simply to accept ad hoc specifications. Other readers however may see the formulation as solid ground in shifting sands, even if some way removed from where we would like to be. Our view is that micro-based models, in particular micro-based formulae for (inverse) Pareto coefficients, probably provide the most promising strategy to develop convincing empirical tests of the determinants and consequences of income and wealth concentration—probably more promising than standard cross-country regressions. However our data set, especially because of its lack of systematic decomposition between labour income and capital income components, and of systematic series on labour and capital tax rates, is unfortunately insufficient to do this in a fully satisfactory manner at this stage.

13.5 SEEKING POSSIBLE EXPLANATIONS: MAJOR THEMES

In this section we consider some of the major explanatory factors suggested by the theoretical models described in the previous section and by the country accounts given in this volume and in Volume I.

Politics and Political Economy

The periods covered by our top income data have seen great changes in the political landscape. In 1900, all but 4 of the 22 countries studied here were (or were ruled by) monarchies (the exceptions were Argentina, France, Switzerland, and the USA). Before the First World War, a quarter of the world's population lived as part of the British Empire. When the League of Nations was founded in 1920, there were just forty-two member countries. Of the twenty-two countries studied, six gained their independence since 1900. Many of the countries saw significant changes in their boundaries, such as the partition of India, and the division and reunification of Germany. Most of the countries were combatants in either the First or Second World

Table 13.6 Summary of major political changes over period covered for countries in Volumes I and II

Country	Main events
(first observation)	*Volume 1*
France 1905	Combatant in First World War 1914–18. Occupied during Second World War.
UK 1908	Combatant in First World War 1914–18. Combatant in Second World War 1939–45.
US 1913	Combatant in First World War 1917–18. Combatant in Second World War 1941–5.
Canada 1920	Combatant in First World War 1914–18. Combatant in Second World War 1939–45.
Australia 1921	Combatant in First World War 1914–18. Combatant in Second World War 1939–45.
New Zealand 1921	Combatant in First World War 1914–18. Combatant in Second World War 1939–45.
Germany 1896 (Prussia)	Combatant in First World War 1914–18. Republic 1918 with reduced territory. Hitler Chancellor 1933. Combatant in Second World War 1939–45. Occupied and Federal Republic 1949. Re-unified 1990.
Netherlands 1914	Occupied in Second World War.
Switzerland 1933	
Ireland 1922	Irish Free State 1922. Neutral in Second World War.
	Volume 2
India 1922	Combatant in First World War 1914–18. Combatant in Second World War 1939–45. Partition and independence in 1947.
China 1986	
Japan 1886	Combatant in First World War 1914–18. Combatant in Second World War 1941–5. Occupied until 1952.
Indonesia 1920	Dutch colony. Occupied during Second World War. Independence in 1945. Military rule (Suharto) 1966–98.
Singapore 1947	British colony. Internal self-government 1959. Joined Malaysia 1963. Expelled from Malaysia and fully independent from 1965.
Argentina 1932	Neutral in Second World War. Peron Presidency 1946, deposed in 1955 (brief return in 1974). Military *coups d'état* in 1930, 1943, 1955, 1962, 1966, and 1976.
Sweden 1903	Neutral in both world wars.
Finland 1920	After declaration of independence from Russia and civil war, Finland became a republic in 1919. Engaged in Winter War 1939–40, Continuation War 1941–4, and Lapland War 1944–5. Ceded around 10% of territory to Russia in treaty of 1947.
Norway 1875	Separated from Sweden in 1905. Neutral in First World War. Occupied in Second World War.
Spain 1933	Spanish Civil War 1936–9. Franco dictatorship. Neutral in Second World War. Democracy restored in 1976.
Portugal 1936	Salazar dictatorship. Neutral in Second World War. Democracy restored in 1974 following the peaceful 'Carnation' revolution.
Italy 1974	

Wars, and all were affected by these wars. The countries studied here include four of the six that founded the European Union, and ten are current members of the EU. In Table 13.6, we have summarized some of the main events that affected the twenty-two countries during the period covered by the series used here.

The most momentous events were the world wars, and for most countries these were associated with falls in the top income shares. Starting with the Second World War, for fourteen countries we can observe the shares before and after entry into the war. Of these, one showed an increase: Argentina, where the top income shares were buoyed by expanded food exports to combatant countries (see Chapter 6). The remaining thirteen all saw the top shares fall (for Germany no comparison is possible). The falls were again large: the share of the top 0.1 per cent fell by a third or more in France, the USA, Canada, the Netherlands, Japan, and Norway. For the First World War, we have fewer observations. The top shares rose in the Netherlands, which was a non-combatant, but they fell in all of the three combatants in Table 13.4 for whom data exist: Japan, the UK, and the USA.

What caused the falls in top shares during world wars? Two forces seem to have been in operation. The first, and probably much the most important, was the loss of capital income. For France, Piketty stresses that 'the physical destructions induced by both World Wars were truly enormous in France.... about one-third of the capital stock was destroyed during the First World War, and about two-thirds during the Second World War' (Volume I, p. 56). This was followed in 1945 by nationalization and a capital levy. The UK lost during the wars much of its capital income from abroad. In 1910 UK net property income from abroad represented 8 per cent of GNP; by 1920 it had fallen to 4.5 per cent; in 1938 it was close to 4 per cent, but by 1948 it had fallen to under 2 per cent (Feinstein 1972: table 1). In the case of Japan, Moriguchi and Saez attribute the precipitous fall in income concentration during the Second World War primarily to the collapse of capital income due to wartime regulations, inflation, and wartime destruction. They go on to argue that the change in the institutional structure under the Allied occupational reforms made the one-time income de-concentration difficult to reverse. The reductions in capital incomes also reflected the rise in corporate taxes during the wars and the restrictions on the payment of dividends.

The second mechanism by which world wars led to falls in top shares is via an equalization of earned incomes. In the USA, Goldin and Margo (1992) have applied the term 'the Great Compression' to the narrowing in the United States wage structure in the 1940s: 'when the United States emerged from war and depression, it had not only a considerably lower rate of unemployment, it also had a wage structure more egalitarian than at any time since' (1992: 2). The war economy imposed wage controls, under the National War Labor Board, as described by Piketty and Saez in chapter 5 of Volume I. Saez and Veall find that a compression also took place in Canada during the war years (chapter 6 in Volume I). In Japan, the share in total wages of the top 5 per cent fell from 19 per cent in 1939 to 9 per cent in 1944 (Table 3C.2).

Along with wars went changes in political regimes, either as a consequence or as a cause. The countries studied include five that were governed by dictatorships/military rule during the period covered by our data: Argentina, Germany, Indonesia, Portugal, and Spain. It is not possible in all cases to use the top income series to investigate their distributional impact, since the dictatorship coincided with the virtual absence of data (Argentina and Indonesia). But for some countries conclusions can be drawn. Of Germany, Dell writes: 'when the Nazis came to power in 1933, the top decile had been thoroughly equalized... The effect of Nazi economic administration changed radically this outcome... In a period of time of only five years, the pre-First World War shares were nearly recovered' (chapter 9 in Volume I, p. 374). In contrast, in the case of Spain, Alvaredo and Saez (Chapter 10) find that the top income shares fell during the first decade of the Franco dictatorship. They also conclude that the transition from dictatorship to democracy was not associated with a significant change in top shares. This latter finding in turn may be contrasted with that for Portugal, where Alvaredo finds a downward jump in top shares after 1970, and particularly 1974. He notes that this 'coincided with the final period of the dictatorship and could be attributed to the loss of the African colonies and to the leftward movement of the revolutionary government after 1974, when a process of nationalizations broke up the concentration of economic power in the hands of the financial-industrial groups' (Chapter 11, p. 000).

Within democracies, the top shares may be affected by changes over time in political partisanship—whether Clinton or a Bush was in the White House. It is naturally tempting to relate the observed changes over time to political variables. Scheve and Stasavage (2009) use a panel of top income data for thirteen countries, but cannot find any strong effect of partisanship. This will doubtless be further explored. Political variables may be more relevant to explaining differences across countries, reflecting political climate and traditions. As is noted by Roine and Waldenström in Chapter 7, a distinction is often drawn between liberal (Anglo-Saxon) welfare states, corporatist-conservative (continental European) welfare states, and social democratic (Scandinavian) welfare states. This makes it interesting to compare top income shares in Sweden and Norway with those in the USA/UK and in France and Germany.

Finally, a major change in political regime is the end of colonial rule. The twenty-two countries include three for which we have data before and after independence. In the case of Indonesia, however, there is too large a gap in time to draw conclusions. In India, as with Indonesia, independence coincided with the end of the Second World War, so that it is hard to distinguish the effect of independence per se. Only for Singapore do we have observations for a post-war colonial period. Here, as shown in Chapter 5, there is little evidence of a decisive break in the top income series with self-government.

Macroeconomics and Financial Crises

Today there is much interest in looking back to the Great Depression. What were the distributional consequences of major recession? Was it bad for top income shares? Among the thirteen countries for which we have data, the period 1928–31 (2) saw a rise in top shares in Canada (top 1 per cent), India, Indonesia, and Ireland, and no change in Finland and Germany. The remaining seven all saw top shares reduced. The top 0.1 per cent lost a fifth or more of their income share in Australia, France, the Netherlands, New Zealand, the UK, and the USA. In many countries, therefore, the depression reduced inequality at the top.

How far is this borne out by the historical accounts for individual countries? For the USA, Piketty and Saez (chapter 5 in Volume I) find that the share of the top 0.01 per cent fell sharply from 1929 to 1932, in the sense that their average income went from 300 times the mean to 200 times. In the UK the same group saw their average income fall from 300 to 230 times. In the Netherlands, the top 0.05 per cent saw their share fall from 5.6 to 3.4 per cent. In contrast, the fall in Japan in top shares was much smaller. In the case of Sweden, Roine and Waldenström draw attention to the depression hitting Sweden later in 1931 (although they note that the depression of the 1920s was more severe), and in particular the dramatic collapse of the industrial empire controlled by the Swedish industrialist Ivar Kreuger in 1932. They show that between 1930 and 1935 there was a drop from 50 per cent to 43 per cent in the top percentile wealth share but an even larger drop in the wealth of the top one percent of income earners, from 38 per cent in 1930 to 26 per cent in 1934.

1929, like 2008, combined the onset of a wide recession with a financial crisis. What can we say about the latter from other episodes of financial crisis? In the case of Norway, there are grounds for believing that the Kristiania crash in 1899 led to a fall in top income shares (Chapter 9). Much more recently, however, the Norwegian banking crisis of 1988–92 does not appear to have led to a fall in top shares, although it may have postponed the increases associated with financial market liberalization. It is possible that today's financial crises are different from those in the past in their distributional consequences. In the case of Singapore, top income shares rose following the Asian financial crisis of 1997, even if they have fallen back to some extent subsequently. In Indonesia (Chapter 4), there are some similarities.

Turning to the wider macroeconomic determinants of top shares, we saw in our discussion of the theoretical models that an important role is potentially played by the relative shares of earned and capital income. These are related to, but not identical to, factor shares in GNP. As is shown by Piketty for France (Figure 3.4 in Volume I), the capital share in household income follows a different path from the corporate share in value added. The same is demonstrated for the US by Piketty and Saez (chapter 5 in Volume I, Figure 5.6). The two shares are not the same, because the distributional figures concern households. Between households and the total economy stand various institutions, including the company sector (which retains profits), pension funds (which own shares), and the government (which levies taxes and receives profit income). The dividends paid to pension funds, for example, generate the income which is then paid to pensioners, in whose hands it is treated as deferred earnings, so that—in these statistics—it does not appear as unearned income. It is nonetheless interesting to examine the relation between factor shares and top incomes.

The separation of national and household income is one reason why the decline of top capital incomes may have taken place even if the factor share of capital has remained unchanged. This point is made forcefully for France by Piketty (chapter 3 in Volume I). Profits may be retained within the company sector and rents may be accruing to owner-occupiers or public authorities rather than to private landlords. (These are, of course, a reminder of the incompleteness of the measure of income in the income tax data.) On the other hand, in some other countries there is a correlation. Roine and Waldenström plot for Sweden the changes in the capital share of value added and the evolution of the top 1 per cent income share. The series are strongly correlated over the whole period, but with a clear difference between the first and second half of the century. Between 1907 and 1950 the correlation is 0.94, while it drops to 0.55 between 1951 and 2000. This indicates that, at least during the first fifty years, even short-term fluctuations of top incomes follow the fluctuations of the capital share of value added as a share of GDP. They also find a downward trend in the capital share of value added over the first eighty years.

Global Forces

While popular theories of income distribution concentrate on a closed economy, top income shares are undoubtedly influenced by international movements of capital and labour. The extent of mobility has differed over time, and our observations span a wide variety of periods, including the previous globalization of the nineteenth century and the protectionism of the inter-war years.

It would clearly be interesting to use the data contained in the two volumes covering twenty-two countries, with much of the data on a near-annual basis, to explore the common economic influences on the evolution of top shares and possible interdependencies. Important among the common forces are the degree of integration of capital markets and the movements in major commodity prices.

One line of approach is to contrast the time variation of different income groups. A common feature to most of the chapters has been the difference between the time paths of the very top groups and the paths followed by those just below the top. The top 1 per cent, and certainly the top 0.1 per cent, are different from the next 9 per cent (9.9 per cent). It is indeed interesting to ask whether the top 0.1 per cent are more like their counterparts in other countries than they are like the next 9.9 per cent in their own country.

If we consider possible explanatory variables, then the most obvious candidates are the rate of return, movements in commodity prices (to which we have already made references), and, in recent years, the international market for managers and for superstars.

In addition to global correlations, there are other cross-country commonalities. Saez and Veall (chapter 6 in Volume I) use the top income share in the USA as an explanatory variable in a regression explaining the top income share in Canada. Leigh and van der Eng (Chapter 4) show the correlation between the top income share in Indonesia and those in other countries. They conclude that the correlation is highest with another developing country—India—but note that the correlation with Argentina is negative.

Progressive Taxation

In the study of France that initiated this project, Piketty (2001, 2003) highlighted the role of progressive income taxation: 'how can one account for the fact that large fortunes never recovered from the 1914–45 shocks, while smaller fortunes did recover perfectly well? The most natural and plausible candidate for an explanation seems to be the creation and development of the progressive income tax' (chapter 3 in Volume I, p. 61). It should be stressed here that this conclusion refers to the impact on the distribution of *gross* income: i.e. income before the deduction of income tax. (See Table 4.2 on the UK in Volume I for one of the few tables that relate to the distribution of income after tax.)

Evidence about the impact of taxation is discussed in many of the chapters. In the case of Sweden, Roine and Waldenström conclude that 'Progressive taxation hence seems to have been a major contributing factor in explaining the evolution of Swedish top incomes in the post-war period. However, given that much of the fall in top incomes happens before taxes reach extreme levels and largely as a result of decreasing income from wealth, an important effect of taxation in terms of top income shares has been to prevent the accumulation of new fortunes' (Chapter 7, p. 324). In the case of Finland, Jäntti, Riihelä, Sullström, and Tuomala conclude that the decline in income tax progressivity since the mid 1990s is a central factor explaining the increase of top income shares in Finland. In the case of Switzerland, a country that has never imposed very high rates of taxation, Dell, Piketty, and Saez (chapter 11 in Volume I) conclude that the observed stability of top shares is consistent with the explanation of trends elsewhere in terms of tax effects.

Outside Europe, Moriguchi and Saez recall in the case of Japan 'that the enormous fortunes that generated the high top 1 per cent income share in the pre-Second World War period had been accumulated at the time when progressive income tax hardly existed and capitalists could reinvest almost all of their incomes for further capital accumulation' (Chapter 3, p. 104). They go on to say that the fiscal environment faced by Japanese capitalists after the Second World War was vastly different: the top statutory marginal tax rate for individual income tax stayed at 60–75 per cent from 1950 until the 1988 tax reform. Progressive taxation hindered the re-accumulation of large wealth, resulting in more equal distribution of capital income. This is the same mechanism that Piketty had earlier identified in France, and was highlighted in the case of the USA by Piketty and Saez (chapter 5 in Volume I). Noting that 'it is difficult to prove in a rigorous way that the dynamic effects of progressive taxation on capital accumulation and pre-tax inequality have the right quantitative magnitude and account for the observed facts' (Volume I, p. 157), they conclude that the interpretation seems reasonable on a priori grounds.

On the other hand, there are different findings in some countries. Saez and Veall devote a whole section of their study of Canada (chapter 6 in Volume I) to the role of taxation and the consequences of the drop in marginal tax rates since the 1960s. They conclude that 'the concentration of the surge in the last decade and among only the very top income shares suggests that tax changes in Canada cannot be the sole cause' (chapter 6 in Volume I, p. 257). Their econometric analysis finds that 'Canadian top income changes are much more strongly associated with similar US changes than with Canadian tax developments' (chapter 6 in Volume I, p. 257). The econometric research of Leigh and van der Eng for Indonesia (Chapter 4) does not find conclusive evidence of a link with marginal tax rates. In the chapter on Portugal, Alvaredo notes the top tax rate has been constant (Figure 11.4) at a new lower rate for a long period, during which top shares continued to rise. The same is true for the UK (chapter 4 in Volume I), where top shares rose steadily over the twenty years since the top rate of income tax was reduced to 40 per cent. As noted by Saez, 'in contrast to the United States...the increase in top share has been relatively smooth since 1979 with no break around the tax changes' (2004: 33).

As these latter cases bring out, a key element in assessing the effect of taxation concerns the *timing* of the impact. Is the current income share a function of the current tax rate or of the past tax rates? The answer depends on how we envisage the underlying behavioural model. The models used by Saez (2004) to examine the relation between marginal tax rates and reported incomes are based on current tax rates. In Chapter 10, Alvaredo and Saez examine the response of business organization to taxation using a model that relates current incomes to current tax rates. On the other hand, models of wealth accumulation typically treat the *change* in wealth as a function of the current tax rate. In this case, the present top income shares may reflect a weighted average of past tax rates. Piketty (2001, 2003) provides numerical simulations with a fixed saving rate model, which indicate that substantial capital taxes are a serious obstacle to the recovery of wealth holdings from negative shocks, and that the barriers would be further raised if the reduction in the rate of return were to reduce the propensity to save.

Summary

We have sketched in this section some of the major mechanisms influencing the development of top income shares. Understanding the relative importance of these different factors is important in the design of public policy. Concern about the rise in top shares in a number of countries has led to a range of proposals. Some countries have already announced increases in top income tax rates; others are considering limits on remuneration. These are being implemented at a time of recession, which may also lead to a decline in top shares.

13.6 ENVOI

The subtitle of this volume—A Global Perspective—is an exaggeration. Major countries are missing, such as Brazil and Russia; we have no evidence for Africa; and Latin America is represented only by Argentina. At the same time, the twenty-two countries covered in the two volumes contain more than half (54 per cent) of the world's population. Our data cover much of the twentieth century, including the Great Depression, the Golden Age, and the Roaring Nineties. In some cases, the data reach back before the First World War and into the nineteenth century. We hope that the data will provide a rich source for future researchers.

Table 13A.1 Shares in total before tax income, France

	Top 10%	Top 5%	Top 1%	Top 0.5%	Top 0.1%	Top 0.05%	Top 0.01%
1905	45.00	34.00	19.00	15.00	8.00		3.00
1906							
1907							
1908							
1909							
1910							
1911							
1912							
1913							
1914							
1915			18.31		7.90		3.03
1916			20.65		9.39		3.79
1917			20.09		8.89		3.44
1918			17.95		7.67		2.87
1919	42.25	33.84	19.50		8.26		2.81
1920	39.59	31.41	17.95		7.63		2.86
1921	39.70	31.04	17.32		7.23		2.65
1922	41.54	32.50	17.87		7.26		2.51
1923	43.54	34.15	18.91		7.61		2.61
1924	42.14	32.27	17.96		7.05		2.39
1925	44.07	33.63	18.16		7.07		2.38
1926	42.06	32.34	17.82		6.98		2.41
1927	42.95	32.47	17.45		6.87		2.35
1928	42.75	32.19	17.27		6.77		2.33
1929	41.59	30.90	16.15		6.25		2.16
1930	41.08	30.14	15.31		5.79		1.93

(*continued*)

Table 13A.1 Continued

	Top 10%	Top 5%	Top 1%	Top 0.5%	Top 0.1%	Top 0.05%	Top 0.01%
1931	41.12	29.67	14.63		5.37		1.77
1932	43.44	31.06	14.80		5.22		1.67
1933	44.87	31.95	14.95		5.20		1.69
1934	46.01	32.68	15.28		5.31		1.71
1935	46.61	33.10	15.40		5.31		1.74
1936	44.10	31.58	14.74		5.17		1.74
1937	42.90	30.21	14.46		5.24		1.83
1938	42.52	29.79	14.27		5.05		1.75
1939	38.24	27.21	13.30		4.99		1.73
1940	39.11	27.85	13.35		4.90		1.65
1941	38.70	27.37	12.88		4.27		1.30
1942	35.04	24.90	11.53		3.64		1.06
1943	32.26	22.68	10.13		3.01		0.84
1944	29.42	20.18	8.37		2.32		0.61
1945	29.70	19.58	7.54		1.96		0.51
1946	32.87	22.34	9.22		2.61		0.72
1947	33.20	23.05	9.22		2.59		0.68
1948	32.35	21.46	8.75		2.43		0.63
1949	32.20	21.70	9.01		2.61		0.70
1950	31.97	21.62	8.98		2.60		0.70
1951	32.93	22.06	9.00		2.55		0.68
1952	33.19	22.35	9.16		2.53		0.65
1953	32.89	22.10	9.00		2.48		0.65
1954	33.53	22.55	9.14		2.45		0.64
1955	34.42	23.16	9.33		2.48		0.65
1956	34.36	23.11	9.37		2.46		0.65
1957	34.74	23.38	9.37		2.44		0.64
1958	34.05	22.76	9.01		2.34		0.60
1959	35.88	24.14	9.46		2.37		0.60
1960	36.11	24.40	9.71		2.45		0.62
1961	36.82	24.92	9.88		2.48		0.64
1962	35.88	24.16	9.46		2.34		0.58
1963	36.41	24.43	9.43		2.29		0.56
1964	36.84	24.75	9.56		2.30		0.56
1965	37.15	24.94	9.58		2.30		0.56
1966	36.46	24.41	9.36		2.26		0.57
1967	36.21	24.27	9.36		2.29		0.59
1968	34.80	23.08	8.77		2.15		0.56
1969	33.96	22.48	8.55		2.09		0.55
1970	33.14	21.95	8.33		2.02		0.53
1971	33.35	22.10	8.47		2.07		0.53
1972	33.03	21.97	8.52		2.11		0.55
1973	33.90	22.61	8.87		2.26		0.62
1974	33.33	22.09	8.50		2.09		0.53
1975	33.41	22.06	8.48		2.08		0.54
1976	33.19	21.91	8.44		2.08		0.54
1977	31.68	20.71	7.79		1.94		0.51
1978	31.38	20.56	7.80		1.93		0.50
1979	31.03	20.42	7.82		1.97		0.52
1980	30.69	20.11	7.63		1.91		0.50
1981	30.73	20.04	7.55		1.89		0.50
1982	29.93	19.37	7.07		1.72		0.44

1983	30.43	19.53	6.99	1.63	0.40
1984	30.52	19.57	7.03	1.65	0.41
1985	31.05	19.96	7.20	1.70	0.43
1986	31.39	20.30	7.44	1.81	0.46
1987	31.73	20.66	7.75	1.98	0.53
1988	32.09	20.90	7.92	2.06	0.57
1989	32.42	21.31	8.21	2.20	0.62
1990	32.64	21.45	8.23	2.20	0.62
1991	32.44	21.18	7.97	2.07	0.57
1992	32.23	20.90	7.75	1.97	0.54
1993	32.22	20.81	7.65	1.94	0.53
1994	32.37	20.90	7.71	1.98	0.55
1995	32.41	20.93	7.70	1.96	0.54
1996	32.25	20.79	7.59	1.92	0.53
1997	31.38	20.16	7.24	1.74	0.66
1998	31.40	20.20	7.27	1.75	0.55
1999	31.52	20.34	7.43	1.86	0.65
2000	31.60	20.48	7.57	1.93	0.64
2001	31.71	20.66	7.73	2.01	0.67
2002	31.72	20.68	7.76	2.01	0.66
2003	32.02	20.94	7.89	2.03	0.66
2004	32.15	21.08	8.02	2.10	0.66
2005	32.24	21.24	8.20	2.19	0.75

Notes: Figure for 1905 is for 1900–10 averaged.

Source: Table 3A.1 in volume I and Landais (2007).

Table 13A.2 Shares in total before tax income, UK

	Top 10%	Top 5%	Top 1%	Top 0.5%	Top 0.1%	Top 0.05%	Top 0.01%
1908						8.22	4.04
1909						8.31	4.12
1910						8.37	4.18
1911						8.38	4.19
1912						8.38	4.15
1913					11.24	8.53	4.25
1914					10.71	8.11	4.04
1915					10.77	8.17	4.07
1916					10.47	7.97	4.00
1917					9.26	7.06	3.52
1918	37.03	30.35	19.24	15.46	8.68	6.58	3.21
1919	38.73	31.48	19.59	15.69	8.98	6.79	3.32
1920					8.03	6.06	2.94
1921					8.08	6.04	2.90
1922					9.07	6.78	3.23
1923					9.29	6.95	3.34
1924					9.05	6.74	3.23
1925					8.79	6.53	3.13
1926					8.67	6.42	3.07
1927					8.49	6.28	3.01
1928					8.54	6.34	3.04

(continued)

Table 13A.2 Continued

	Top 10%	Top 5%	Top 1%	Top 0.5%	Top 0.1%	Top 0.05%	Top 0.01%
1929					8.33	6.15	2.93
1930					7.81	5.74	2.71
1931					7.17	5.24	2.44
1932					6.87	5.00	2.32
1933					6.75	4.91	2.24
1934					6.78	4.92	2.23
1935					6.96	5.08	2.35
1936					7.03	5.12	2.35
1937	38.37	29.75	16.98	13.07	6.59	4.78	2.18
1938					6.57	4.79	2.21
1939					6.35	4.61	2.13
1940					5.67	4.09	1.84
1941					5.00	3.57	1.57
1942					4.44	3.15	1.37
1943				9.04	4.23	2.98	1.28
1944				8.97	4.13	2.90	1.22
1945				9.38	4.23	2.95	1.23
1946				10.00	4.48	3.10	1.27
1947				9.38	4.10	2.81	1.14
1948				8.88	3.86	2.63	1.05
1949	32.25	23.39	11.47	8.12	3.45	2.34	0.94
1950				8.51	3.59	2.42	0.96
1951			10.89	7.69	3.21	2.15	0.85
1952			10.20	7.15	2.95	1.97	0.77
1953			9.72	6.78	2.77	1.84	0.70
1954	30.63	21.22	9.67	6.71	2.72	1.80	0.67
1955			9.30	6.48	2.65	1.77	0.68
1956			8.75	6.03	2.42	1.60	0.61
1957			8.70	5.96	2.37	1.57	0.59
1958			8.76	5.98	2.38	1.57	0.60
1959	29.96	20.26	8.60	5.85	2.30	1.52	0.60
1960			8.87	6.08	2.45	1.63	0.63
1961							
1962	29.37	19.72	8.43	5.76	2.29	1.52	0.58
1963	29.94	20.10	8.49	5.76	2.23	1.47	0.57
1964	29.91	20.07	8.48	5.77	2.26	1.49	0.58
1965	29.88	20.10	8.55	5.79	2.28	1.52	0.62
1966	28.94	19.22	7.92	5.32	2.04	1.37	0.52
1967	28.78	18.99	7.69	5.11	1.91	1.25	0.51
1968	28.55	18.76	7.54	5.00	1.87	1.21	0.47
1969	28.72	18.86	7.46	4.96	1.85	1.22	0.47
1970	28.82	18.65	7.05	4.59	1.64	1.05	0.42
1971	29.29	18.81	7.02	4.56	1.67	1.09	0.40
1972	28.90	18.48	6.94	4.52	1.61	1.04	0.37
1973	28.31	18.18	6.99	4.59	1.68	1.08	0.40
1974	28.10	17.77	6.54	4.29	1.58	1.02	0.37
1975	27.82	17.40	6.10	3.92	1.40	0.91	0.31
1976	27.89	17.33	5.89	3.75	1.30	0.86	0.30
1977	27.96	17.33	5.93	3.75	1.27	0.82	0.28
1978	27.78	17.11	5.72	3.60	1.24	0.79	0.28
1979	28.37	17.57	5.93	3.76	1.30	0.83	0.31

1980						
1981	31.03	19.45	6.67	4.27	1.53	0.99
1982	31.23	19.65	6.85	4.40	1.61	1.07
1983	31.76	19.98	6.83	4.36	1.58	1.04
1984	32.52	20.67	7.16	4.59	1.67	1.10
1985	32.65	20.75	7.40	4.83	1.82	
1986	32.94	21.04	7.55	4.92	1.86	
1987	33.27	21.38	7.78	5.04		
1988	34.21	22.37	8.63	5.80		
1989	34.15	22.51	8.67	5.90		
1990	36.90	24.43	9.80	6.72		
1991	37.65	25.13	10.32	7.18		
1992	37.64	24.89	9.86	6.74		
1993	38.34	25.51	10.36	7.20	3.09	
1994	38.33	25.62	10.60	7.36	3.10	
1995	38.51	25.80	10.75	7.49	3.24	2.28
1996	39.30	26.85	11.90	8.59	4.13	3.03
1997	38.94	26.78	12.07	8.72	4.15	3.02
1998	39.47	27.42	12.53	9.11	4.44	3.27
1999	38.97	27.18	12.51	9.15	4.54	3.35
2000	38.43	27.04	12.67	9.33	4.64	3.37
2001	39.33	27.53	12.71	9.28	4.51	3.25
2002	38.69	26.96	12.27	8.87	4.22	3.02
2003	37.75	26.39	12.12	8.79	4.23	3.06
2004	39.54	27.66	12.89	9.40	4.57	3.33
2005	41.62	29.57	14.25	10.49	5.19	3.80

Notes: Up to 1920 includes what is now the Republic of Ireland.
From 1975, estimates relate to 'total income'; prior to 1975 estimates relate to income net of certain deductions.
From 1990, estimates relate to individuals; prior to 1990 estimates relate to tax units.

Source: Table 4.1 in Volume I, updated.

Table 13A.3 Shares in total before tax income, USA

	Top 10%	Top 5%	Top 1%	Top 0.5%	Top 0.1%	Top 0.05%	Top 0.01%
1913			17.96	14.73	8.62		2.76
1914			18.16	15.08	8.60		2.73
1915			17.58	14.58	9.22		4.36
1916			18.57	15.60	9.87		4.40
1917	40.29	30.33	17.60	14.23	8.36		3.33
1918	39.90	29.30	15.88	12.39	6.74		2.45
1919	39.48	29.31	15.87	12.23	6.45		2.22
1920	38.10	27.47	14.46	10.95	5.37		1.67
1921	42.86	30.46	15.47	11.60	5.60		1.69
1922	42.95	31.05	16.29	12.38	6.17		2.01
1923	40.59	28.95	14.99	11.32	5.50		1.75
1924	43.26	30.93	16.32	12.42	6.14		2.01
1925	44.17	32.47	17.60	13.41	6.75		2.35
1926	44.07	32.75	18.01	13.75	7.07		2.54
1927	44.67	33.43	18.68	14.33	7.47		2.76
1928	46.09	34.77	19.60	15.17	8.19		3.23

(*continued*)

Table 13A.3 Continued

	Top 10%	Top 5%	Top 1%	Top 0.5%	Top 0.1%	Top 0.05%	Top 0.01%
1929	43.76	33.05	18.42	14.21	7.62		3.01
1930	43.07	31.18	16.42	12.42	6.40		2.39
1931	44.40	31.01	15.27	11.32	5.68		2.07
1932	46.30	32.59	15.48	11.55	5.90		1.93
1933	45.03	32.49	15.77	11.78	6.05		2.04
1934	45.16	32.99	15.87	11.80	5.82		1.92
1935	43.39	30.99	15.63	11.67	5.80		1.95
1936	44.77	32.65	17.64	13.37	6.69		2.23
1937	43.35	31.38	16.45	12.42	6.16		2.02
1938	43.00	30.18	14.73	10.82	5.16		1.67
1939	44.57	31.29	15.39	11.37	5.45		1.74
1940	44.43	31.29	15.73	11.66	5.57		1.77
1941	41.02	29.02	15.01	11.15	5.29		1.63
1942	35.49	25.11	12.91	9.60	4.48		1.32
1943	32.67	23.02	11.48	8.43	3.78		0.97
1944	31.55	21.76	10.54	7.60	3.33		0.92
1945	32.64	22.90	11.07	7.87	3.32		0.84
1946	34.62	24.66	11.76	8.28	3.43		0.92
1947	33.02	23.30	10.95	7.71	3.24		0.90
1948	33.72	23.70	11.27	8.03	3.44		0.95
1949	33.76	23.46	10.95	7.77	3.34		0.95
1950	33.87	23.87	11.36	8.14	3.53		0.83
1951	32.82	22.67	10.52	7.41	3.12		0.87
1952	32.07	21.85	9.76	6.81	2.76		0.75
1953	31.38	21.01	9.08	6.26	2.51		0.67
1954	32.12	21.56	9.39	6.47	2.57		0.71
1955	31.77	21.38	9.18	6.28	2.49		0.72
1956	31.81	21.35	9.09	6.14	2.38		0.68
1957	31.69	21.17	8.98	6.08	2.36		0.66
1958	32.11	21.26	8.83	5.94	2.29		0.64
1959	32.03	21.02	8.75	5.90	2.19		0.62
1960	31.66	20.51	8.36	5.52	2.10		0.60
1961	31.90	20.91	8.34	5.41	2.05		0.59
1962	32.04	20.94	8.27	5.40	1.98		0.56
1963	32.01	20.90	8.16	5.33	1.96		0.57
1964	31.64	20.62	8.02	5.33	1.97		0.53
1965	31.52	20.70	8.07	5.42	2.04		0.54
1966	31.98	20.99	8.37	5.59	2.15		0.60
1967	32.05	21.07	8.43	5.63	2.16		0.60
1968	31.98	20.98	8.35	5.58	2.15		0.58
1969	31.82	20.68	8.02	5.30	2.00		0.55
1970	31.51	20.39	7.80	5.16	1.94		0.53
1971	31.75	20.50	7.79	5.12	1.91		0.52
1972	31.62	20.37	7.75	5.10	1.92		0.52
1973	31.85	20.57	7.74	5.07	1.89		0.50
1974	32.36	21.04	8.12	5.41	2.11		0.56
1975	32.62	21.03	8.01	5.31	2.04		0.56
1976	32.42	20.85	7.89	5.23	2.02		0.56
1977	32.43	20.83	7.90	5.25	2.04		0.57
1978	32.44	20.86	7.95	5.30	2.08		0.58

1979	32.35	20.83	8.03	5.38	2.16	0.62
1980	32.87	21.17	8.18	5.51	2.23	0.65
1981	32.72	20.97	8.03	5.42	2.23	0.66
1982	33.22	21.40	8.39	5.73	2.45	0.77
1983	33.69	21.79	8.59	5.94	2.61	0.87
1984	33.95	22.10	8.89	6.22	2.83	0.98
1985	34.25	22.38	9.09	6.39	2.91	0.97
1986	34.57	22.59	9.13	6.38	2.87	1.00
1987	36.48	24.49	10.75	7.76	3.73	1.30
1988	38.63	26.95	13.17	9.96	5.21	1.99
1989	38.47	26.66	12.61	9.37	4.74	1.74
1990	38.84	27.05	12.98	9.71	4.90	1.83
1991	38.38	26.43	12.17	8.90	4.36	1.61
1992	39.82	27.88	13.48	10.11	5.21	2.02
1993	39.48	27.41	12.82	9.45	4.72	1.74
1994	39.60	27.50	12.85	9.45	4.70	1.73
1995	40.54	28.46	13.53	9.99	4.98	1.82
1996	41.16	29.16	14.11	10.49	5.33	1.97
1997	41.73	29.85	14.77	11.12	5.81	2.20
1998	42.12	30.36	15.29	11.61	6.20	2.41
1999	42.67	30.97	15.87	12.16	6.64	2.63
2000	43.11	31.51	16.49	12.78	7.13	2.84
2001	42.23	30.40	15.37	11.71	6.26	2.40
2002	41.67	29.66	14.64	11.06	5.78	2.19
2003	42.04	29.95	14.87	11.29	6.00	2.37
2004	43.11	31.20	16.08	12.33	6.81	2.83
2005	44.36	32.59	17.42	13.59	7.70	3.26
2006	45.26	33.32	17.98	14.07	7.97	3.35

Note: Estimates excluding capital gains.

Source: Website of Emmanuel Saez, November 2008, Table A1.

Table 13A.4 Shares in total before tax income, Canada

	Top 10%	Top 5%	Top 1%	Top 0.5%	Top 0.1%	Top 0.05%	Top 0.01%
1920		32.60	14.40	10.49	5.36		2.10
1921		40.58	17.60	12.55	5.81		1.70
1922		34.34	15.17	10.74	5.04		1.63
1923		30.15	14.38	10.22	4.69		1.53
1924		30.65	14.53	10.39	4.89		1.63
1925		29.76	13.18	9.48	4.34		1.32
1926		30.15	14.01	10.22	4.81		1.57
1927		30.70	14.69	10.78	5.13		1.74
1928		31.31	15.32	11.23	5.29		1.75
1929		31.73	15.64	11.47	5.34		1.71
1930		32.74	16.10	11.86	5.68		1.84
1931		36.03	16.60	12.00	5.55		1.72
1932		39.42	17.67	12.72	5.98		1.90
1933		40.88	18.03	12.89	5.91		1.73
1934		39.11	17.50	12.59	5.86		1.84

(*continued*)

Table 13A.4 Continued

	Top 10%	Top 5%	Top 1%	Top 0.5%	Top 0.1%	Top 0.05%	Top 0.01%
1935		38.09	16.99	12.19	5.63		1.72
1936		38.35	17.45	12.67	6.00		1.91
1937		35.81	16.26	11.79	5.48		1.54
1938		39.55	18.41	13.31	6.05		1.87
1939		37.23	16.88	12.23	5.63		1.67
1940		33.68	14.71	10.35	4.52		1.53
1941	45.31	30.74	13.30	9.46	4.24		1.29
1942	39.56	26.42	11.30	8.01	3.53		1.06
1943	39.29	25.84	10.72	7.51	3.23		0.92
1944	37.38	24.49	10.01	6.95	2.92		0.82
1945	37.27	24.63	10.12	6.99	2.89		0.78
1946	37.75	25.30	10.72	7.42	3.02		0.79
1947	38.14	25.66	10.99	7.61	3.09		0.82
1948	36.68	24.49	10.39	7.20	2.94		0.71
1949	38.22	25.37	10.69	7.38	2.91		0.69
1950	38.24	25.45	10.88	7.58	3.06		0.74
1951	36.31	23.96	10.03	6.94	2.80		0.65
1952	36.44	23.91	9.85	6.75	2.71		0.67
1953	37.36	24.37	9.88	6.75	2.70		0.66
1954	38.68	25.29	10.33	7.10	2.82		0.71
1955	38.08	24.90	10.19	7.00	2.86		0.75
1956	37.22	24.19	9.63	6.57	2.63		0.65
1957	37.76	24.50	9.64	6.54	2.59		0.64
1958	38.39	25.00	9.89	6.68	2.62		0.64
1959	38.44	24.94	9.74	6.55	2.54		0.61
1960	38.78	25.13	9.77	6.56	2.52		0.61
1961	39.35	25.53	9.93	6.63	2.55		0.63
1962	37.77	24.42	9.37	6.23	2.33		0.54
1963	37.37	24.11	9.14	6.06	2.24		0.51
1964	37.77	24.43	9.38	6.24	2.33		0.54
1965	37.23	24.04	9.20	6.12	2.28		0.54
1966	36.76	23.70	8.91	5.88	2.16		0.49
1967	37.06	23.91	9.00	5.93	2.15		0.47
1968	37.31	24.02	9.04	5.96	2.17		0.47
1969	37.34	24.01	9.01	5.91	2.13		0.46
1970	37.92	24.22	8.97	5.87	2.07		0.43
1971	37.83	24.08	8.87	5.79	2.00		0.40
1972	37.55	23.84	8.75	5.74	2.02		0.43
1973	37.02	23.65	8.80	5.78	2.06		0.46
1974	37.38	23.82	8.81	5.76	2.09		0.48
1975	37.28	23.71	8.74	5.73	2.11		0.51
1976	36.74	22.99	8.08	5.21	1.88		0.44
1977	36.18	22.43	7.74	4.98	1.79		0.43
1978	35.77	22.17	7.60	4.90	1.77		0.44
1979	35.57	22.11	7.72	5.06	1.86		0.48
1980	36.23	22.68	8.06	5.27	1.97		0.53
1981	35.39	22.10	7.80	5.08	1.88		0.50
1982	36.24	22.92	8.46	5.66	2.33		0.68
1983	36.19	22.71	8.21	5.44	2.13		0.57
1984	35.78	22.48	8.29	5.55	2.28		0.68

1985	35.25	22.20	8.21	5.51	2.26		0.67
1986	35.22	22.22	8.24	5.52	2.24		0.64
1987	35.05	22.22	8.40	5.69	2.38		0.70
1988	35.66	23.11	9.34	6.54	3.00		1.01
1989	36.36	23.83	10.01	7.15	3.44		1.29
1990	35.54	23.08	9.35	6.55	2.98		1.01
1991	36.31	23.47	9.37	6.51	2.91		0.99
1992	36.72	23.60	9.31	6.44	2.82		0.94
1993	37.31	24.03	9.56	6.64	2.97		0.99
1994	37.49	24.16	9.59	6.65	2.94		0.95
1995	37.85	24.65	10.00	6.99	3.13		1.03
1996	38.77	25.48	10.62	7.53	3.47		1.14
1997	39.78	26.51	11.52	8.32	3.97		1.33
1998	40.61	27.35	12.18	8.87	4.34		1.48
1999	41.17	27.89	12.62	9.25	4.61		1.68
2000	42.34	29.01	13.56	10.11	5.23		1.89
2001							
2002							

Note: Estimates excluding capital gains.
Source: Table 6B.1 in Volume I.

Table 13A.5 Shares in total before tax income, Australia

	Top 10%	Top 5%	Top 1%	Top 0.5%	Top 0.1%	Top 0.05%	Top 0.01%
1921		19.43	11.63	8.55	3.97	2.80	1.24
1922		17.65	10.68	7.91	3.57	2.45	
1923			11.76	9.08	3.98	2.80	
1924			11.67	8.84	4.25		
1925			11.31	8.58	3.99	2.81	
1926			11.07	8.42	3.88	2.72	
1927			11.68	8.56	3.86	2.64	
1928			11.85	8.92	4.26	3.16	
1929			10.67	7.91	3.58	2.50	
1930			9.75	7.15	3.20	2.22	
1931			9.34	6.93	3.07	2.11	0.85
1932			9.27	6.91	3.08	2.14	0.90
1933			10.32	7.73	3.53	2.46	
1934			10.36	7.79	3.49	2.44	
1935			10.54	7.77	3.49	2.42	
1936			11.28	8.25	3.71	2.56	
1937			9.83	7.17	3.19	2.20	0.89
1938			10.39	7.61	3.41	2.36	0.97
1939		20.71	10.73	7.81	3.50	2.44	1.04
1940		20.57	10.30	7.48	3.37	2.35	0.99
1941	34.61	23.67	10.78	7.68	3.34	2.32	0.94
1942	34.12	23.26	10.43	7.34	3.11	2.12	0.85
1943	34.23	23.42	10.45	7.32	3.09	2.12	0.86
1944	31.25	21.09	9.03	6.22	2.49	1.66	0.64
1945	28.75	19.56	8.44	5.79	2.31	1.55	0.62
1946	31.61	21.76	9.51	6.52	2.59	1.72	0.66
1947	33.10	23.41	10.62	7.31	2.92	1.94	0.73

(continued)

Table 13A.5 Continued

	Top 10%	Top 5%	Top 1%	Top 0.5%	Top 0.1%	Top 0.05%	Top 0.01%
1948	32.77	23.35	10.80	7.40	2.89	1.96	0.73
1949	32.82	23.66	11.26	7.89	3.31	2.23	
1950	31.53	25.56	14.13	10.22	4.47		
1951	26.65	18.87	9.08	6.23	2.53	1.67	
1952	26.31	19.51	8.99	6.11	2.44	1.57	0.55
1953	26.10	18.70	8.71	5.97	2.43	1.58	0.58
1954	25.77	18.10	8.06	5.48	2.19	1.42	0.52
1955	25.53	17.49	7.54	5.10	2.01	1.29	0.48
1956	25.69	17.84	7.91	5.42	2.16	1.39	0.51
1957	23.99	16.33	7.04	4.75	1.84	1.19	0.43
1958	29.77	19.41	7.44	4.86	1.76	1.14	0.41
1959	29.85	19.44	7.39	4.82	1.75	1.12	0.41
1960	29.60	19.14	7.09	4.58	1.62	1.04	0.37
1961	29.71	19.20	7.10	4.58	1.65	1.06	0.40
1962	30.22	19.62	7.23	4.64	1.64	1.04	0.38
1963	30.35	19.84	7.36	4.72	1.65	1.05	0.37
1964	29.45	18.95	6.84	4.37	1.52	0.96	0.34
1965	29.22	18.68	6.69	4.27	1.46	0.92	0.31
1966	28.51	18.19	6.47	4.12	1.41	0.89	0.31
1967	28.66	18.29	6.58	4.23	1.51	0.98	0.38
1968	28.36	17.99	6.38	4.06	1.40	0.89	0.32
1969	27.85	17.61	6.25	4.00	1.42	0.92	0.36
1970	27.65	17.30	5.92	3.74	1.26	0.79	0.27
1971	28.24	17.59	5.92	3.70	1.25	0.78	0.27
1972	27.80	17.50	6.06	3.81	1.29	0.81	0.28
1973	26.74	16.73	5.67	3.54	1.17	0.73	0.24
1974	25.87	15.87	5.22	3.24	1.06	0.65	0.21
1975	25.54	15.65	5.13	3.22	1.10	0.68	0.23
1976	25.20	15.35	4.99	3.11	1.05	0.65	0.21
1977	25.15	15.25	4.92	3.08	1.06	0.67	
1978	25.01	15.14	4.87	3.02	1.03	0.65	
1979	25.17	15.20	4.83	2.97	1.02	0.65	
1980	25.39	15.31	4.79	2.95	1.02	0.66	
1981	25.31	15.15	4.61	2.83	0.96	0.62	
1982	25.82	15.44	4.67	2.87	1.00	0.63	
1983	25.32	15.16	4.68	2.89	1.02	0.66	
1984	25.50	15.25	4.75	2.96	1.03		
1985	25.93	15.63	5.02	3.19	1.14	0.75	0.35
1986	26.61	16.17	5.39	3.48	1.29	0.85	0.36
1987	28.66	17.94	6.67	4.53	1.89	1.41	0.60
1988	30.28	19.84	8.41	6.04	2.99	2.13	0.98
1989	27.64	17.46	6.43	4.29	1.79	1.31	0.51
1990	27.66	17.37	6.34	4.24	1.79	1.33	0.55
1991	28.22	17.70	6.41	4.28	1.81	1.35	0.57
1992	28.52	17.95	6.55	4.38	1.87	1.37	0.57
1993	29.40	18.66	6.96	4.69	2.08	1.46	0.61
1994	29.42	18.87	7.13	5.10	2.56	1.65	0.71
1995	29.13	18.76	7.23	4.95	2.14	1.52	0.73
1996	29.16	18.77	7.24	4.93	2.07	1.44	0.65
1997	30.41	19.73	7.81	5.38	2.32	1.64	0.75

1998	30.11	19.63	7.84	5.43	2.37	1.67	0.76
1999	31.48	20.95	8.84	6.29	3.04	2.15	
2000	31.28	20.98	9.03	6.44	3.06	2.24	
2001	30.61	20.33	8.31	5.75	2.51	1.75	
2002	31.34	20.90	8.79	6.11	2.68	1.87	

Source: Table 7.1 in Volume I.

Table 13A.6 Shares in total before tax income, New Zealand

	Top 10%	Top 5%	Top 1%	Top 0.5%	Top 0.1%	Top 0.05%	Top 0.01%
1921		25.39	11.34	7.82	3.13		
1922		23.84	10.47	7.22	2.89		
1923		24.72	10.94	7.54	2.96		
1924	33.73	24.47	10.89	7.51	2.91		
1925	34.97	25.16	11.08	7.60	2.92		
1926	35.73	25.18	10.84	7.36	2.79		
1927	35.69	24.99	10.64	7.20	2.69		
1928	35.85	25.42	11.47	7.98	3.17		
1929	36.54	25.48	10.99	7.48	2.88		
1930	38.38	26.17	10.57	7.06	2.60		
1931							
1932							
1933	38.13	25.99	10.86	7.39	2.81		
1934	37.97	25.64	10.42	6.96	2.49		
1935		24.65	10.36	6.93	2.77		
1936	34.49	24.15	10.66	7.28	2.81		
1937	30.36	20.51	8.33	5.48	1.91		
1938	27.64	18.47	7.32	4.79	1.66		
1939	29.72	19.92	7.85	5.15	1.86		
1940	28.67	19.16	7.42	4.83	1.67		
1941							
1942							
1943							
1944							
1945	25.26	17.08	6.88	4.49	1.60		
1946	27.10	18.54	7.50	4.90	1.76		
1947	28.44	19.54	7.72	5.03	1.77		
1948	28.80	19.67	7.74	5.09	1.87		
1949	29.56	20.32	8.02	5.26	1.92		
1950	31.32	22.59	9.44	6.17	2.23		
1951	29.32	20.11	7.88	5.11	1.85		
1952	30.14	20.59	7.94	5.11	1.83		
1953	35.93	24.83	9.90	6.41	2.33		
1954	35.40	24.29	9.54	6.15	2.20		
1955	34.13	22.89	8.76	5.61	1.98		
1956	35.04	23.53	8.91	5.74	2.10		
1957	33.94	22.69	8.65	5.61	2.00		
1958	31.93	20.66	7.26	4.51	1.48		
1959	32.65	21.37	7.60	4.77	1.63		
1960	32.17	20.93	7.44	4.71	1.66		
1961							

(continued)

Table 13A.6 Continued

	Top 10%	Top 5%	Top 1%	Top 0.5%	Top 0.1%	Top 0.05%	Top 0.01%
1962	31.97	20.59	7.25	4.60	1.61		
1963	31.98	20.67	7.29	4.63			
1964	32.32	20.85	7.42	4.82	1.80		
1965	31.06	19.69	6.72	4.23	1.43		
1966	30.72	19.30	6.56	4.12	1.38		
1967	30.91	19.39	6.59	4.14	1.41		
1968	31.15	19.59	6.72	4.23	1.44		
1969	31.02	19.47	6.70	4.23	1.45		
1970	30.76	19.11	6.64	4.21	1.48		
1971	30.66	19.01	6.43	4.00	1.31		
1972	31.29	19.90	7.08	4.47	1.52		
1973	31.84	20.35	7.47	4.79	1.69		
1974	32.02	20.38	7.55	4.95	1.68		
1975	29.98	18.70	6.56	4.20	1.45		
1976	31.10	20.36	7.48	4.74	1.55		
1977	28.86	17.89	6.13	3.86	1.31		
1978	29.10	17.99	6.12	3.85	1.29		
1979	28.22	17.29	5.77	3.62	1.21		
1980	28.83	17.51	5.65	3.52	1.18		
1981	28.48	17.15	5.50	3.44	1.14		
1982	28.70	17.24	5.49	3.41	1.14		
1983	28.92	17.52	5.68	3.56	1.22		
1984	28.19	17.09	5.60	3.53	1.22		
1985	27.57	16.74	5.51	3.48	1.19		
1986	26.51	15.85	4.88	3.01	1.00		
1987	26.61	16.29	5.48	3.52	1.27		
1988	26.26	16.08	5.35	3.38	1.16		
1989	28.34	17.97	6.59	4.33	1.62		
1990	31.12	20.41	8.21	5.66	2.33		
1991	31.48	20.53	7.96	5.37	2.08		
1992	32.49	21.32	8.40	5.71	2.35		
1993	32.99	21.86	8.76	5.94	2.38		
1994	32.86	22.06	9.00	6.12	2.49		
1995	32.62	21.97	8.98	6.11	2.46		
1996	32.18	21.69	8.92	6.12	2.51		
1997	32.57	22.03	9.16	6.32	2.66		
1998	34.39	23.58	10.21	7.23	3.28		
1999	38.68	27.74	13.77		5.45		
2000	32.26	21.20	8.25	5.50	2.16		
2001	32.79	21.76	8.76	5.98	2.51		
2002	32.52	21.56	8.78	6.09	2.55		
2003	33.01	22.17	9.45		3.10		
2004	33.55	22.71	9.96		3.55		
2005	32.45	21.69	8.98		2.66		

Notes: The series up to 1940 relates to assessable income; thereafter it relates to total income. The series up to 1952 relates to tax units; thereafter it relates to individuals.

Source: Table 8.1 in Volume I.

Table 13A.7 Shares in total before tax income, Prussia/Germany

	Top 10%	Top 5%	Top 1%	Top 0.5%	Top 0.1%	Top 0.05%	Top 0.01%
1891	37.92	29.95	17.28	13.56	7.44		2.79
1892	37.47	29.45	16.81	13.15	7.18		2.67
1893	37.21	29.21	16.59	12.95	7.04		2.61
1894	37.13	29.18	16.59	12.98	7.10		2.66
1895	37.18	29.29	16.77	13.15	7.22		2.69
1896	37.54	29.68	17.16	13.50	7.48		2.82
1897	38.19	30.27	17.64	13.94	7.80		3.00
1898	38.72	30.84	18.11	14.38	8.09		3.16
1899	38.97	31.13	18.49	14.75	8.39		3.34
1900	39.13	31.29	18.63	14.88	8.47		3.39
1901	38.99	31.04	18.29	14.56	8.25		3.29
1902	38.59	30.52	17.78	14.08	7.89		3.10
1903	38.52	30.42	17.63	13.93	7.77		3.03
1904	38.60	30.55	17.81	14.10	7.86		3.06
1905	38.91	30.95	18.22	14.51	8.15		3.19
1906	38.20	30.49	18.14	14.52	8.24		3.27
1907	37.78	30.14	17.96	14.40	8.19		3.28
1908	37.26	29.55	17.36	13.85	7.90		3.14
1909	37.84	29.69	17.15	13.65	7.75		3.08
1910	38.01	29.84	17.24	13.75	7.84		3.13
1911	37.77	29.57	17.48	13.96	7.96		3.16
1912	37.73	29.55	17.52	14.01	8.01		3.18
1913	38.52	30.40	17.77	14.41	8.11		3.13
1914	38.10	30.24	17.78	14.44	8.16		3.15
1915	39.31	31.90	19.53	15.91	9.18		3.66
1916	40.75	32.84	21.32	17.70	10.31		4.10
1917	41.98	33.55	22.42	18.72	11.04		4.52
1918	41.52	33.21	22.20	18.52	10.93		4.49
1919	37.92	30.02	19.47	15.96	9.18		3.71
1920							
1921							
1922							
1923							
1924							
1925			11.30	8.20	3.90		1.20
1926	32.50	22.10	11.30	8.30	4.00		1.40
1927			11.50	8.50	4.10		1.40
1928	32.20	22.60	11.20	8.20	4.00		1.30
1929			11.10	8.10	3.90		1.30
1930							
1931							
1932	38.40	26.60	11.40	8.30	3.80		1.20
1933			10.90	8.20	3.80		1.20
1934	36.30	25.30	11.30	8.20	3.80		1.30
1935			12.00	8.90	4.40		1.60
1936	37.30	27.00	13.70	10.40	5.50		2.20
1937			15.00	11.50	6.20		2.50
1938			16.30	12.60	6.70		2.60
1939							

(continued)

Table 13A.7 Continued

	Top 10%	Top 5%	Top 1%	Top 0.5%	Top 0.1%	Top 0.05%	Top 0.01%
1940							
1941							
1942							
1943							
1944							
1945							
1946							
1947							
1948							
1949							
1950	34.40	24.90	11.60	8.20	3.90		1.50
1951							
1952							
1953							
1954				6.90	3.20		1.00
1955							
1956							
1957			11.00	7.00	4.30		1.40
1958							
1959							
1960							
1961	31.40	23.40	12.20	9.10	4.50		1.30
1962							
1963							
1964							
1965	31.30	23.10	12.20	9.30	4.80		1.80
1966							
1967							
1968	30.30	21.90	11.20	8.40	4.30		1.60
1969							
1970							
1971	31.80	22.10	11.30	8.50	4.40		1.70
1972							
1973							
1974	30.80	21.60	10.10	7.40	3.60		1.30
1975							
1976							
1977	31.50	21.50	10.20	7.50	3.70		1.30
1978							
1979							
1980	32.80	22.60	10.80	8.10	4.10		1.50
1981							
1982							
1983	31.80	21.30	9.40	6.90	3.30		1.00
1984							
1985							
1986	32.20	21.80	9.90	7.40	3.70		1.30
1987							
1988							
1989	33.90	23.30	10.90	8.20	4.20		1.60
1990							
1991							
1992	34.60	23.60	10.80	8.00	4.20		1.60

	Top 10%	Top 5%	Top 1%	Top 0.5%	Top 0.1%		Top 0.01%
1993							
1994							
1995	32.70	21.70	9.20	6.70	3.40		1.40
1996							
1997							
1998	35.40	24.20	11.10	8.30	4.40		1.60

Note: Excluding capital gains apart from 1925–38.

Source: Table 9I.6 in Volume I.

Table 13A.8 Shares in total before tax income, the Netherlands

	Top 10%	Top 5%	Top 1%	Top 0.5%	Top 0.1%	Top 0.05%	Top 0.01%
1914	45.87	36.51	20.96	16.34	8.63	6.34	
1915	51.21	42.07	25.58	20.31	11.44	8.58	
1916	53.31	44.18	27.88	22.53	13.02	9.84	
1917	52.47	42.78	26.51	21.34	12.39	9.53	
1918	48.50	38.20	21.95	17.18	9.65	7.40	
1919	49.48	39.34	23.74	19.07	10.79	8.17	
1920	46.23	35.92	20.59	16.30	8.92	6.65	
1921	44.03	33.35	18.29	14.23	7.60	5.65	
1922	43.19	32.13	16.82	12.79	6.57	4.83	
1923	43.08	31.93	16.45	12.40	6.30	4.61	
1924	43.84	32.84	17.34	13.22	6.88	5.09	
1925	43.87	33.04	17.75	13.64	7.19	5.37	
1926	43.87	33.18	17.99	13.82	7.26	5.39	
1927	44.33	33.72	18.37	14.13	7.39	5.47	
1928	44.58	34.01	18.63	14.38	7.57	5.64	
1929	43.85	33.34	18.09	13.86	7.10	5.21	
1930	43.02	32.41	17.15	12.97	6.47	4.69	2.09
1931	42.18	31.11	15.59	11.51	5.47	3.90	1.70
1932	41.33	30.04	14.43	10.46	4.79	3.37	1.44
1933	41.19	29.91	14.20	10.24	4.63	3.24	1.38
1934	40.82	29.62	14.02	10.09	4.53	3.17	1.34
1935	40.69	29.54	14.00	10.10	4.55	3.18	1.33
1936	41.10	30.18	14.83	10.89	5.15	3.70	1.68
1937	41.92	31.23	16.05	12.06	6.13	4.57	2.41
1938	41.60	30.93	15.68	11.63	5.60	4.02	1.81
1939	42.02	31.28	15.79	11.64	5.54	3.93	1.71
1940							
1941	45.07	34.25	17.64	13.06	6.36	4.55	
1942							
1943							
1944							
1945							
1946	40.82	29.08	12.86	8.93	3.74	2.56	1.03
1947							
1948							
1949							
1950	36.74	26.16	12.05	8.59	3.80	2.65	
1951							
1952	36.95	26.45	12.61	9.13	4.22	2.94	
1953	36.76	26.14	11.99	8.44	3.69	2.57	

(*continued*)

Table 13A.8 Continued

	Top 10%	Top 5%	Top 1%	Top 0.5%	Top 0.1%	Top 0.05%	Top 0.01%
1954							
1955							
1956							
1957	33.98	23.75	10.39	7.20	2.98		
1958	34.88	24.61	11.29	8.03	3.62		
1959	34.20	23.89	10.43	7.23	3.05		
1960							
1961							
1962	34.12	23.93	10.58	7.39			
1963							
1964	33.25	23.13	10.07	7.00			
1965							
1966	33.05	22.69	9.46	6.44			
1967	32.64	22.30	9.26	6.29			
1968							
1969							
1970	31.34	21.25	8.64	5.76	2.12	1.39	0.57
1971							
1972							
1973	28.37	18.40	6.90	4.48	1.59	1.02	0.36
1974							
1975	27.47	17.40	6.12	3.95	1.38	0.88	0.33
1976							
1977	27.81	17.35	6.01	3.81	1.26	0.77	
1978							
1979							
1980							
1981	28.46	17.57	5.85	3.66	1.28	0.81	
1982							
1983							
1984							
1985	29.10	18.00	5.92	3.65	1.21	0.77	
1986							
1987							
1988							
1989	28.48	17.62	5.70	3.52	1.19	0.78	
1990	28.20	17.33	5.56	3.42	1.09	0.68	
1991	28.11	17.25	5.54	3.41	1.14	0.73	
1992	27.99	17.13	5.50	3.39	1.14	0.73	
1993	27.96	16.97	5.24	3.15	0.98	0.60	
1994	28.28	17.18	5.33	3.21	1.00	0.63	
1995	28.45	17.32	5.37	3.23	1.00	0.61	
1996	28.24	17.22	5.39	3.28	1.06	0.69	
1997	28.21	17.23	5.46	3.34	1.11	0.72	
1998	28.03	17.06	5.29	3.21	1.00	0.61	
1999	28.09	17.13	5.38	3.28	1.08	0.69	
2000							

Notes: Series up to 1946 based on tabulated income tax data.
Series from 1950 to 1975 based on tabulated data produced by Central Bureau of Statistics.
Series from 1977 based on micro-data Income Panel Survey using tax and other administrative data.

Source: Table 11.2 in Volume I.

Table 13A.9 Shares in total before tax income, Switzerland

	Top 10%	Top 5%	Top 1%	Top 0.5%	Top 0.1%	Top 0.05%	Top 0.01%
1933	31.16	21.92	9.98	7.19	3.27		0.94
1934	30.92	21.59	9.69	6.94	3.14		0.91
1935							
1936	30.47	21.46	9.94	7.21	3.35		0.98
1937							
1938							
1939	32.94	23.77	11.78	8.78	4.36		1.52
1940							
1941							
1942							
1943	32.59	22.70	10.54	7.67	3.71		1.43
1944							
1945	33.24	23.36	10.49	7.50	3.44		1.10
1946							
1947	31.58	21.95	10.01	7.15	3.26		1.03
1948							
1949	32.29	22.22	9.88	7.13	3.23		0.96
1950							
1951	31.29	21.65	9.91	7.18	3.37		1.07
1952							
1953	30.33	21.16	9.78	7.08	3.30		1.05
1954							
1955	29.72	20.92	9.78	7.06	3.24		0.97
1956							
1957	30.99	21.79	10.11	7.24	3.31		1.03
1958							
1959	31.47	22.35	10.54	7.58	3.51		1.09
1960							
1961	31.56	22.70	10.87	7.85	3.62		1.06
1962							
1963	31.72	22.83	10.91	7.88	3.64		1.12
1964							
1965	31.60	22.60	10.67	7.67	3.50		1.05
1966							
1967	32.29	23.01	10.86	7.81	3.58		1.08
1968							
1969	32.70	23.32	11.00	7.92	3.66		1.14
1970							
1971	32.49	23.03	10.81	7.79	3.62		1.14
1972							
1973	30.96	21.51	9.77	6.98	3.20		1.04
1974							
1975	30.29	20.47	8.79	6.15	2.68		0.83
1976							
1977	29.93	20.12	8.49	5.90	2.56		0.79
1978							
1979	29.89	20.06	8.40	5.82	2.51		0.76
1980							
1981	29.87	20.02	8.40	5.85	2.58		0.84

(continued)

Table 13A.9 Continued

	Top 10%	Top 5%	Top 1%	Top 0.5%	Top 0.1%	Top 0.05%	Top 0.01%
1982							
1983	29.88	20.00	8.39	5.85	2.62		0.86
1984							
1985	30.35	20.64	9.05	6.48	3.16		1.25
1986							
1987	30.78	20.93	9.07	6.41	2.94		0.96
1988							
1989	30.78	20.96	9.22	6.59	3.15		1.15
1990							
1991	29.99	20.14	8.60	6.09	2.85		1.00
1992							
1993	29.65	19.87	8.42	6.01	2.82		0.98
1994							
1995	29.22	19.27	7.76	5.67	2.67		0.87

Notes: For all except 1933, the estimates relate to income averaged over the year shown and the following year.
Source: Table 11.2 in Volume I.

Table 13A.10 Shares in total before tax income, Ireland

	Top 10%	Top 5%	Top 1%	Top 0.5%	Top 0.1%	Top 0.05%	Top 0.01%
1922					4.64		
1923					5.25		
1924					4.77		
1925					5.07		
1926					4.72		
1927					4.83		
1928					4.80		
1929					4.94		
1930					5.21		
1931					7.78		
1932					6.71		
1933					6.74		
1934					6.61		
1935					6.77		
1936					6.31		
1937					6.32		
1938	47.61		16.93	12.38	5.95		
1939					5.46		
1940					4.93		
1941					4.93		
1942					4.61		
1943	35.68		12.92	9.36	4.00		
1944					4.56		
1945					4.56		
1946					4.73		
1947					4.80		
1948					4.48		
1949					4.35		

1950				4.21	1951	3.65
1952				3.31		
1953				2.98		
1954						
1955						
1956						
1957						
1958						
1959						
1960						
1961						
1962						
1963						
1964				2.09		
1965			5.46	2.11		
1966			5.57	2.11		
1967				2.02		
1968				1.87		
1969				1.78		
1970				1.73		
1971				1.52		
1972				1.33		
1973			3.51	1.27		
1974						
1975	28.62	5.96	3.76	1.31		
1976	27.96	5.83	3.66	1.26		
1977	27.29	5.64	3.56	1.24		
1978	28.20	6.16	3.98	1.47		
1979	31.32	8.03	5.68	2.65		
1980	31.50	6.65	4.21	1.47		
1981	30.85	6.37	4.02	1.40		
1982	32.57	6.87	4.36	1.55		
1983	33.29	7.05	4.48	1.60		
1984	31.57	6.50	4.10	1.46		
1985	31.28	6.27	3.93	1.40		
1986	31.03	6.15	3.83	1.38		
1987	31.16	6.14	3.81	1.34		
1988	30.51	6.15	3.85	1.37		
1989	30.52	6.38	4.10	1.54		
1990	31.05	6.64	4.28	1.57		
1991	32.46	7.30	4.82			
1992	34.00	7.83	5.09			
1993	33.39	7.55	4.85			
1994	34.84	7.93	5.10			
1995	35.33	8.19	5.39			
1996	35.55	8.48	5.65			
1997	35.51	8.73	5.90			
1998	35.89	9.67	6.75			
1999	34.93	9.44	6.60			
2000	36.07	10.30	7.28			

Notes: Estimates for 1938 and 1943 based on Table 12.2 rather than surtax returns.
Estimates from 1975 based on income tax returns.

Source: Table 12.5 in Volume I.

Table 13A.11 Shares in total before tax income, India

	Top 10%	Top 5%	Top 1%	Top 0.5%	Top 0.1%	Top 0.05%	Top 0.01%
1922			12.72	9.97	5.66		2.00
1923			13.39	10.47	5.91		2.07
1924			11.46	9.18	5.37		1.84
1925			12.38	9.64	5.39		1.84
1926			12.89	10.02	5.57		1.87
1927			13.32	10.39	5.82		1.98
1928			13.62	10.61	5.92		1.98
1929			13.07	10.25	5.77		1.90
1930			14.53	11.40	6.39		2.11
1931			16.09	12.55	6.94		2.26
1932			16.14	12.64	7.03		2.32
1933			17.11	13.37	7.39		2.45
1934			16.90	13.17	7.28		2.41
1935			17.33	13.42	7.34		2.42
1936			15.58	12.13	6.73		2.31
1937			15.54	12.09	6.71		2.32
1938			17.82	13.80	7.63		2.90
1939			16.11	12.74	7.38		2.88
1940			16.15	12.83	7.53		2.98
1941			14.06	11.32	6.85		2.73
1942							
1943			10.32	8.22	4.84		1.87
1944			11.13	8.80	5.10		2.00
1945			11.41	9.01	5.21		2.03
1946							
1947			11.23	9.05	5.44		2.27
1948			11.84	9.29	5.29		2.15
1949			12.00	9.35	5.24		2.10
1950			13.42	10.37	5.60		2.07
1951							
1952							
1953			11.92	9.41	5.15		1.85
1954			13.58	10.55	5.68		2.01
1955			14.41	11.15	5.92		2.01
1956			12.77	9.85	5.18		1.69
1957			13.34	10.26	5.31		1.68
1958			12.56	9.64	4.92		1.51
1959			12.36	9.44	4.77		1.44
1960			12.31	9.45	4.79		1.47
1961			12.15	9.29	4.61		1.38
1962			11.58	8.75	4.24		1.27
1963							
1964			9.65	6.99	3.23		1.04
1965			10.92	8.23	3.93		1.21
1966			9.99	7.57	3.66		1.16
1967			10.01	7.59	3.51		1.03
1968			9.95	7.52	3.48		1.01
1969							
1970			10.02	7.74	3.43		1.03
1971			8.47	6.31	2.83		0.88
1972							
1973			7.02	5.24	2.22		0.64

1974	6.65	4.77	2.01	0.54
1975	7.24	5.30	2.25	0.62
1976	7.27	5.19	2.16	0.62
1977	6.18	4.55	1.90	0.51
1978	6.05	4.33	1.81	0.51
1979	5.61	3.90	1.66	0.46
1980	4.78	3.30	1.39	0.40
1981	4.39	3.00	1.21	0.30
1982	4.51	3.13	1.33	0.34
1983	6.46	4.35	1.83	0.48
1984	6.39	4.48	1.88	0.50
1985	8.24	5.98	2.45	0.66
1986	8.64	6.43	2.61	0.70
1987	8.12	6.13	2.51	0.63
1988	8.52	6.38	2.71	0.83
1989	8.19	6.17	2.38	0.78
1990	7.42	5.16	1.84	0.64
1991	7.12	4.85	1.76	0.57
1992	6.96	4.81	1.91	0.59
1993	8.53	6.02	2.86	1.15
1994	8.09	5.82	2.61	1.07
1995	8.67	6.61	3.52	2.05
1996	8.72	6.47	3.08	1.54
1997	10.70	8.40	4.36	1.88
1998	8.95	7.02	3.64	1.57
1999	8.95	7.02	3.64	1.57

Source: Table 1A.5.

Table 13A.12 Shares in total before tax income, China

	Top 10%	Top 5%	Top 1%	Top 0.5%	Top 0.1%	Top 0.05%	Top 0.01%
1986	17.37	9.80	2.65	1.51	0.47		
1987	17.80	9.97	2.67	1.49	0.46		
1988	19.20	11.09	3.34	2.02	0.62		
1989	19.74	11.71	3.45	2.03	0.56		
1990	19.34	11.35	3.33	1.95	0.57		
1991	19.50	11.56	3.38	1.98	0.61		
1992	20.63	12.52	3.96	2.39	0.75		
1993	22.65	13.83	4.34	2.58	0.75		
1994	23.57	14.39	4.42	2.61	0.77		
1995	23.30	14.26	4.38	2.56	0.70		
1996	23.98	14.78	4.69	2.82	0.86		
1997	24.78	15.31	4.89	2.94	0.90		
1998	24.72	15.24	4.84	2.89	0.87		
1999	24.94	15.35	4.77	2.84	0.85		
2000	25.53	15.85	5.04	3.06	0.96		
2001	25.91	16.08	5.05	3.06	0.95		
2002	26.70	16.71	5.32	3.24	1.03		
2003	27.94	17.75	5.87	3.64	1.20		

Note: Individuals.

Source: Table 2A.6.

Table 13A.13 Shares in total before tax income, Japan

	Top 10%	Top 5%	Top 1%	Top 0.5%	Top 0.1%	Top 0.05%	Top 0.01%
1886			19.14	14.19	7.22		2.98
1887			19.89	14.52	7.24		3.03
1888			17.67	13.16	6.78		2.95
1889			16.07	12.03	6.30		2.68
1890			14.33	10.76	5.63		2.44
1891			13.19	9.92	5.19		2.22
1892			14.45	10.96	5.79		2.43
1893			14.27	10.94	5.87		2.44
1894			13.40	10.37	5.69		2.40
1895			12.82	10.03	5.59		2.38
1896			13.23	10.39	5.80		2.47
1897			12.16	9.55	5.21		2.15
1898			13.57	10.46	5.58		2.02
1899			15.72	12.27	6.72		2.51
1900			16.26	12.63	6.83		2.51
1901			16.93	13.14	7.09		2.62
1902			17.99	13.97	7.55		2.80
1903			17.55	13.66	7.43		2.74
1904			16.58	13.01	7.21		2.74
1905			18.07	14.13	7.82		2.97
1906			18.12	14.08	7.64		2.83
1907		32.25	18.26	14.12	7.58		2.76
1908		33.82	18.93	14.62	7.74		2.79
1909		33.71	18.74	14.43	7.56		2.68
1910		33.54	18.88	14.61	7.75		2.81
1911		31.40	17.99	13.98	7.52		2.77
1912		31.48	17.91	13.93	7.61		2.83
1913		30.56	17.45	13.56	7.38		2.73
1914		32.53	18.55	14.49	7.98		2.92
1915		32.79	19.60	15.63	9.09		3.70
1916		30.87	19.52	15.87	9.72		4.38
1917		28.98	18.68	15.32	9.52		4.31
1918		25.55	16.62	13.54	8.30		3.68
1919		24.83	15.25	12.24	7.37		3.12
1920		28.12	17.09	13.62	7.90		3.23
1921		31.47	18.48	14.51	8.10		3.15
1922		32.96	19.55	15.38	8.63		3.40
1923		33.58	19.72	15.45	8.60		3.37
1924		33.60	19.72	15.45	8.62		3.43
1925			18.32	14.34	7.96		3.16
1926			18.55	14.64	8.29		3.39
1927			17.89	14.12	7.96		3.22
1928			18.51	14.64	8.28		3.37
1929			18.35	14.51	8.17		3.33
1930			16.78	13.21	7.32		2.95
1931			17.38	13.62	7.42		2.92
1932			17.56	13.81	7.61		3.03
1933			18.28	14.48	8.16		3.40
1934			18.96	15.01	8.46		3.49
1935			18.74	14.83	8.41		3.49
1936			18.68	14.76	8.40		3.57
1937		31.34	19.26	15.33	8.83		3.80
1938		31.81	19.92	15.90	9.19		3.81

1939		17.95	14.16	7.83	3.10
1940		16.45	12.82	6.82	2.59
1941		16.67	12.58	6.36	2.31
1942		15.11	11.28	5.69	2.07
1943		13.63	10.04	4.96	1.78
1944		10.74	7.91	3.93	1.40
1945		6.43	4.42	1.89	0.56
1946					
1947	18.50	7.36	5.16	2.15	0.61
1948	20.37	7.79	5.24	2.06	0.55
1949	21.67	7.89	4.97	1.82	0.46
1950	20.96	7.69	4.90	1.73	0.42
1951	19.90	7.28	4.77	1.87	0.53
1952	21.19	7.85	5.18	2.02	0.55
1953	20.17	7.46	4.94	1.91	0.49
1954	19.73	7.20	4.76	1.83	0.47
1955	18.87	6.91	4.59	1.78	0.46
1956	19.55	7.37	4.94	1.90	0.49
1957	20.15	7.69	5.20	2.05	0.54
1958	20.17	7.74	5.23	2.08	0.54
1959	20.48	7.97	5.44	2.15	0.54
1960	20.75	8.17	5.51	2.22	0.58
1961	20.68	8.44	5.79	2.31	0.60
1962	21.19	8.68	5.91	2.35	0.61
1963	21.03	8.50	5.74	2.31	0.60
1964	20.62	8.33	5.59	2.18	0.56
1965	20.04	7.91	5.26	2.04	0.52
1966	19.47	7.62	5.07	1.94	0.49
1967	19.86	7.63	5.11	1.96	0.49
1968	19.45	7.56	5.05	1.91	0.46
1969	20.38	8.01	5.27	1.91	0.47
1970	21.13	8.19	5.50	2.05	0.57
1971	21.67	8.42	5.49	1.94	0.63
1972	21.49	8.10	5.14	1.60	0.44
1973	21.01	7.62	5.02	2.18	0.86
1974	19.93	7.20	4.61	1.78	0.57
1975	19.58	7.08	4.60	1.77	0.61
1976	19.52	6.81	4.28	1.51	0.34
1977	19.45	6.77	4.26	1.48	0.34
1978	19.74	6.96	4.39	1.52	0.35
1979	20.23	7.25	4.68	1.65	0.38
1980	20.10	7.16	4.65	1.65	0.38
1981	20.07	7.11	4.61	1.59	0.36
1982	19.99	7.02	4.60	1.62	0.40
1983	20.03	6.94	4.46	1.50	0.34
1984	20.09	6.95	4.48	1.49	0.35
1985	20.25	7.03	4.50	1.50	0.35
1986	20.60	7.21	4.59	1.54	0.40
1987	21.42	7.66	4.88	1.65	0.51
1988	21.52	7.63	4.79	1.62	0.53
1989	21.70	7.90	5.07	1.83	0.72
1990	21.78	8.05	5.22	2.04	0.86
1991	21.16	7.54	4.84	1.81	0.73
1992	20.58	7.12	4.60	1.65	0.50

(*continued*)

Table 13A.13 Continued

	Top 10%	Top 5%	Top 1%	Top 0.5%	Top 0.1%	Top 0.05%	Top 0.01%
1993		20.72	7.15	4.61	1.62		0.49
1994		20.93	7.07	4.50	1.62		0.49
1995		21.47	7.30	4.68	1.64		0.47
1996		21.61	7.36	4.71	1.69		0.50
1997		21.72	7.32	4.66	1.69		0.45
1998		22.30	7.59	4.85	1.74		0.45
1999		22.77	7.76	4.93	1.77		0.47
2000		23.52	8.22	5.32	2.04		0.57
2001		24.16	8.49	5.55	2.14		0.60
2002		24.60	8.65	5.64	2.16		0.58
2003		24.96	8.75	5.70	2.16		0.60
2004		25.29	9.04	5.92	2.32		0.69
2005		25.33	9.20	6.07	2.40		0.80

Source: Table 3A.2.

Table 13A.14 Shares in total before tax income, Indonesia

	Top 10%	Top 5%	Top 1%	Top 0.5%	Top 0.1%	Top 0.05%	Top 0.01%
1920				6.92	3.70	2.73	1.39
1921			11.82	10.08	5.54	4.15	2.21
1922			14.28	11.53	5.35	3.72	1.69
1923			14.81	11.99	5.69	4.04	1.93
1924			14.42	11.62	5.67	4.06	1.97
1925			14.19	11.42	5.65	4.01	1.91
1926			15.00	12.08	5.97	4.30	2.04
1927			15.52	12.41	5.98	4.24	1.94
1928			16.38	13.04	6.14	4.30	1.93
1929			16.71	13.31	6.32	4.45	1.92
1930			16.64	13.08	5.87	4.02	1.67
1931		30.57	20.03	15.65	6.77	4.53	1.78
1932		32.62	21.13	16.57	7.02	4.62	1.74
1933		32.83	21.55	17.01	7.18	4.68	1.72
1934		31.82	21.51	17.02	7.22	4.69	1.68
1935				15.82	6.81	4.45	1.60
1936				15.99	6.93	4.52	1.63
1937				14.64	6.56	4.38	1.69
1938			19.80	15.84	7.24	4.90	2.00
1939			19.87	15.83	7.03	4.68	1.83
1940							
1941							
1942							
1943							
1944							
1945							
1946							
1947							
1948							
1949							
1950							

1951			
1952			
1953			
1954			
1955			
1956			
1957			
1958			
1959			
1960			
1961			
1962			
1963			
1964			
1965			
1966			
1967			
1968			
1969			
1970			
1971			
1972			
1973			
1974			
1975			
1976			
1977			
1978			
1979			
1980			
1981			
1982			
1983			
1984			
1985			
1986			
1987			
1988			
1989			
1990		1.01	0.69
1991		0.90	0.58
1992		1.04	0.69
1993		1.02	0.66
1994		1.02	0.67
1995		0.89	0.55
1996		0.91	0.56
1997		0.94	0.59
1998		0.80	0.54
1999		0.84	0.58
2000		1.05	0.78
2001		1.20	0.81
2002	1.47	1.26	0.75
2003	1.34	1.10	0.61

Source: Table 4.1.

Table 13A.15 Shares in total before tax income, Singapore

	Top 10%	Top 5%	Top 1%	Top 0.5%	Top 0.1%	Top 0.05%	Top 0.01%
1947			10.94	7.72	3.34	2.31	0.99
1948			10.93	7.69	3.31	2.31	0.99
1949			10.38	7.40	3.24	2.26	0.92
1950			12.74	9.39	4.46	3.13	1.32
1951			14.79	11.21	5.79	4.28	2.12
1952			13.80	10.32	5.32	4.00	2.04
1953			12.49	9.17	4.48	3.32	1.68
1954			12.39	8.98	4.28	3.15	1.63
1955							
1956			12.42	8.72	3.68	2.49	0.98
1957			12.29	8.57	3.50	2.33	0.83
1958			11.70	8.06	3.17	2.07	0.74
1959			13.05	9.15	3.72	2.44	0.87
1960			10.97	7.72	3.15	2.12	0.80
1961			11.19	7.86	3.12	2.05	0.74
1962			11.07	7.69	3.04	1.99	0.75
1963			10.93	7.58	2.98	1.94	0.71
1964			12.62	8.65	3.37	2.20	0.84
1965			10.91	7.50	2.83	1.80	0.64
1966			10.36	7.06	2.61	1.63	0.55
1967			10.23	6.99	2.62	1.67	0.59
1968			10.63	7.44	3.06	2.09	0.92
1969		21.79	10.18	7.12	2.86	1.91	0.75
1970		22.87	10.77	7.51	2.99	2.01	0.82
1971		22.60	10.57	7.32	2.89	1.92	0.74
1972		23.22	10.80	7.50	3.08	2.07	0.85
1973		23.26	11.15	7.87	3.38	2.34	
1974	30.69	22.77	10.46	7.22	2.90	1.92	
1975	31.40	23.26	10.57	7.24	2.84	1.85	
1976	31.39	23.13	10.41	7.14	2.78	1.81	
1977	30.58	22.43	10.02	6.83	2.66	1.76	
1978	31.97	23.29	10.30	6.97	2.63	1.71	
1979	34.46	25.15	11.15	7.53	2.84	1.87	
1980	32.07	23.63	10.59	7.21	2.80	1.84	
1981	32.14	23.62	10.60	7.27	2.78		
1982	33.22	24.28	10.79	7.41	2.93		
1983	32.12	23.55	10.45	7.12	2.81		
1984	31.74	23.10	10.17	6.90			
1985	33.80	24.54	10.67	7.22			
1986	32.76	23.91	10.26	6.86	2.60		
1987	36.01	26.06	11.41	7.69	2.96		
1988	33.95	24.57	10.72	7.24	2.76		
1989	34.67	25.29	11.30	7.79	3.17		1.05
1990	35.04	25.50	11.22	7.65			0.79
1991	33.09	24.01	10.43	7.03			0.72
1992							
1993	32.37	23.59	10.53	7.16	3.03	2.13	
1994	30.41	22.16	10.02	6.87			
1995	30.18	21.93	9.84	6.67			
1996	30.91	22.47	9.99	6.76			

1997	30.79	22.64	10.31	7.06		2.15
1998	32.64	24.11	11.10	7.62		2.34
1999	36.28	27.01	12.78	8.94		2.88
2000	38.06	28.28	13.26		4.43	
2001	43.87	32.50	15.07	10.58	4.74	3.34
2002	43.53	32.19	15.06	10.70	4.95	3.56
2003	41.36	30.63	14.24	10.02	4.51	
2004	38.92	28.91	13.60	9.63	4.36	
2005	37.36	27.92	13.28	9.46	4.29	

Source: Table 5.1.

Table 13A.16 Shares in total before tax income, Argentina

	Top 10%	Top 5%	Top 1%	Top 0.5%	Top 0.1%	Top 0.05%	Top 0.01%
1932			18.77	14.58	7.52		2.49
1933			17.18	13.35	6.80		2.39
1934			18.06	14.02	7.28		2.45
1935			18.44	14.32	7.41		2.49
1936			20.40	15.56	7.76		2.46
1937			20.44	15.84	8.11		2.60
1938			20.47	15.83	8.10		2.58
1939			20.88	16.23	8.34		2.72
1940			20.11	15.79	8.25		2.65
1941			22.43	17.85	9.44		3.09
1942			23.77	19.73	11.38		4.18
1943			25.96	20.90	11.62		4.16
1944			24.75	19.66	10.63		3.63
1945			23.39	18.34	9.76		3.31
1946			22.63	17.96	9.79		3.46
1947			24.02	19.06	10.51		3.72
1948			23.22	18.30	9.78		3.20
1949			19.34	15.11	7.87		2.40
1950			19.81	15.55	8.15		2.58
1951			16.96	13.25	6.85		2.14
1952			15.96	11.87	5.64		1.57
1953		29.07	15.35	11.21	5.12		1.42
1954		30.28	16.54	12.33	5.84		1.71
1955							
1956		28.96	15.66	11.66	5.42		1.54
1957							
1958			14.17	10.53	4.98		1.39
1959		30.41	15.92	11.54	5.23		1.40
1960							
1961		28.00	14.68	10.81	4.91		1.45
1962							
1963							
1964							
1965							
1966							
1967							
1968							

(*continued*)

Table 13A.16 Continued

	Top 10%	Top 5%	Top 1%	Top 0.5%	Top 0.1%	Top 0.05%	Top 0.01%
1969							
1970			12.18	7.66	2.60		0.51
1971			10.78	6.92	2.36		0.58
1972			9.44	6.06	2.15		0.55
1973			7.40	5.04	2.04		0.54
1974							
1975							
1976							
1977							
1978							
1979							
1980							
1981							
1982							
1983							
1984							
1985							
1986							
1987							
1988							
1989							
1990							
1991							
1992							
1993							
1994							
1995							
1996							
1997		22.45	12.39	9.02	4.27		1.39
1998			12.57	9.06	4.37		1.43
1999			13.53	10.32	5.22		1.78
2000			14.34	11.03	5.68		1.97
2001			12.91	10.03	5.22		1.82
2002			15.53	12.34	6.92		2.70
2003			16.85	13.41	7.40		2.79
2004			16.75	13.45	7.02		2.49

Source: Table 6.5.

Table 13A.17 Shares in total before tax income, Sweden

	Top 10%	Top 5%	Top 1%	Top 0.5%	Top 0.1%	Top 0.05%	Top 0.01%
1903	46.79	35.33	26.99	19.16	8.66	6.15	2.79
1904							
1905							
1906							
1907	45.42	36.33	21.46	16.57	8.72	6.47	2.99
1908							

1909							
1910							
1911	43.90	34.11	19.57	15.21	8.11	6.08	3.02
1912	45.59	35.75	20.92	16.29	8.99	6.84	3.55
1913							
1914							
1915							
1916	52.97	43.53	28.04	22.93	13.70	10.60	5.12
1917							
1918							
1919	41.91	31.23	16.33	11.70	7.33	5.55	2.91
1920	35.83	26.13	13.48	10.16	5.23	3.86	1.84
1921							
1922							
1923							
1924							
1925							
1926							
1927							
1928							
1929							
1930	38.41	27.87	13.74	10.15	4.82	3.45	1.52
1931							
1932							
1933							
1934	38.06	26.73	11.95	8.54	3.83	2.68	1.12
1935	36.18	25.74	12.32	8.98	4.22	2.99	1.21
1936							
1937							
1938							
1939							
1940							
1941	34.09	23.67	10.29	7.15	3.01	2.06	0.84
1942							
1943	35.61	24.48	10.44	7.19	2.99	2.01	0.78
1944	34.84	23.82	10.04	6.89	2.85	1.92	0.77
1945	34.23	23.36	9.77	6.69	2.72	1.82	0.70
1946	34.29	23.52	10.07	6.99	2.91	2.00	0.80
1947	32.09	21.43	8.62	5.85	2.35	1.59	0.60
1948	30.77	20.28	7.90	5.31	2.06	1.32	0.50
1949	30.35	19.89	7.64	5.09	1.96	1.29	0.48
1950	30.25	19.80	7.59	5.06	1.94	1.28	0.47
1951	29.84	19.41	7.33	4.91	1.94	1.30	0.51
1952	29.08	18.60	6.80	4.49	1.73	1.15	0.44
1953	29.60	19.01	6.90	4.55	1.75	1.16	0.45
1954	29.21	18.71	6.90	4.57	1.75	1.15	0.44
1955	28.82	18.39	6.78	4.48	1.69	1.11	0.41
1956	28.83	18.20	6.65	4.38	1.64	1.07	0.40
1957	29.21	18.59	6.81	4.47	1.67	1.09	0.40
1958	29.52	18.75	6.81	4.45	1.65	1.07	0.40
1959	30.06	19.18	7.00	4.57	1.69	1.10	0.40
1960	30.35	19.34	6.83	4.41	1.60	1.03	0.37
1961	30.36	19.27	6.77	4.35	1.55	0.99	0.35
1962	30.08	19.03	6.65	4.25	1.50	0.96	0.34

(*continued*)

Table 13A.17 Continued

	Top 10%	Top 5%	Top 1%	Top 0.5%	Top 0.1%	Top 0.05%	Top 0.01%
1963	29.95	18.95	6.64	4.25	1.50	0.95	0.33
1964	29.80	18.77	6.50	4.14	1.43	0.90	0.31
1965	29.69	18.67	6.47	4.11	1.42	0.90	0.31
1966	29.58	18.50	6.35	4.02	1.37	0.86	0.29
1967	30.33	19.17	6.55	4.10	1.38	0.86	0.29
1968	30.39	19.21	6.57	4.11	1.39	0.87	0.29
1969	30.02	18.88	6.41	4.01	1.34	0.84	0.28
1970	29.36	18.34	6.16	3.83	1.28	0.79	0.26
1971	28.36	17.59	5.80	3.60	1.19	0.74	0.24
1972	27.89	17.27	5.67	3.51	1.15	0.71	0.23
1973	27.56	17.00	5.57	3.44	1.13	0.70	0.23
1974	27.07	16.58	5.47	3.39	1.12	0.69	0.23
1975	26.38	16.14	5.29	3.28	1.07	0.67	0.23
1976	25.55	15.48	4.95	3.04	0.96	0.59	0.19
1977	24.72	14.91	4.69	2.86	0.83	0.54	0.21
1978	23.99	14.38	4.47	2.70	0.83	0.50	0.18
1979	23.47	13.97	4.25	2.56	0.77	0.49	0.18
1980	22.73	13.44	4.05	2.42	0.74	0.47	0.17
1981	22.40	13.19	3.97	2.38	0.76	0.48	0.19
1982	22.33	13.18	3.98	2.40	0.77	0.49	0.19
1983	22.42	13.29	4.08	2.47	0.81	0.54	0.25
1984	22.30	13.31	4.13	2.52	0.82	0.57	0.25
1985	22.33	13.35	4.12	2.49	0.80	0.56	0.24
1986	22.35	13.39	4.11	2.47	0.77	0.54	0.23
1987	22.54	13.59	4.24	2.55	0.86	0.60	0.26
1988	22.53	13.62	4.38	2.72	0.99	0.70	0.31
1989	22.55	13.68	4.48	2.81	1.07	0.79	0.40
1990	22.75	13.73	4.38	2.72	1.02	0.73	0.34
1991	24.33	15.04	5.10	3.27	1.30	0.89	0.39
1992	24.33	15.04	5.04	3.19	1.22	0.82	0.35
1993	24.63	15.31	5.22	3.33	1.30	0.88	0.37
1994	25.23	15.85	5.53	3.61	1.45	1.00	0.41
1995	24.93	15.54	5.25	3.35	1.31	0.88	0.38
1996	25.56	16.05	5.59	3.69	1.41	0.98	0.40
1997	25.82	16.23	5.72	3.80	1.47	1.03	0.43
1998	25.91	16.35	5.87	3.91	1.57	1.09	0.45
1999	26.12	16.52	6.01	4.00	1.62	1.13	0.48
2000	26.72	17.12	5.97	4.43	1.93	1.37	0.61
2001	26.76	17.10	5.95	4.33	1.86	1.32	0.57
2002	26.43	16.77	5.67	4.07	1.69	1.18	0.51
2003	26.12	16.54	5.52	4.02	1.70	1.20	0.58
2004	26.34	16.71	5.72	4.09	1.73	1.22	0.58
2005	26.96	17.33	6.28	4.40	1.91	1.35	0.64
2006	27.30	17.73	6.61	4.73	2.21	1.63	0.83

Note: Estimates excluding capital gains.

Source: Table 7A.2.

Table 13A.18 Shares in total before tax income, Finland

	Top 10% HES/IDS	Top 5%	Top 5% HES/IDS	Top 1%	Top 1% HES/IDS	Top 0.5%	Top 0.1% HES/IDS	Top 0.05%	Top 0.01%
1920		33.55		15.27					
1921		32.26		15.20					
1922		31.98		14.85					
1923		29.53		13.46					
1924		27.07		12.07					
1925		27.78		12.64					
1926		28.50		13.22					
1927		28.75		13.34					
1928		29.00		13.45					
1929		29.26		13.57					
1930		29.36		13.50					
1931		29.47		13.43					
1932		29.43		13.41					
1933		29.38		13.40					
1934		29.33		13.38					
1935		25.11		11.74					
1936		26.16		12.39					
1937		27.21		13.04					
1938		27.57		13.04					
1939		26.32		12.26					
1940		25.07		11.47					
1941		23.82		10.69					
1942		22.57		9.91					
1943		21.33		9.13					
1944		20.08		8.35					
1945		18.83		7.57					
1946		17.58		6.79					
1947		16.33		6.01					
1948		17.05		6.23					
1949		20.73		7.71					
1950		20.72		7.75					
1951		21.29		8.03					
1952		22.18		8.48					
1953		22.23		8.51					
1954		23.16		8.91					
1955		23.03		8.94					
1956		23.74		9.20					
1957		23.68		9.18					
1958		25.12		9.92					
1959		25.19		10.01					
1960		24.37		9.50					
1961		25.93		10.16					
1962		25.09		10.01					
1963		25.50		10.16					
1964		24.54		9.46					
1965		24.51		9.47					
1966	*25.06*	24.55	*15.26*	9.47	*4.57*		*0.83*		
1967		25.13		9.54					

(*continued*)

Table 13A.18 Continued

	Top 10% HES/IDS	Top 5%	*Top 5% HES/IDS*	Top 1%	*Top 1% HES/IDS*	Top 0.5%	*Top 0.1% HES/IDS*	Top 0.05%	Top 0.01%
1968		24.96		9.31					
1969		20.50		7.84					
1970		25.71		9.87					
1971	*24.23*	24.83	*14.89*	9.26	*4.89*		*1.14*		
1972		23.52		8.70					
1973		22.83		8.10					
1974		20.86		7.46					
1975		19.53		5.91					
1976	*21.15*	20.39	*12.67*	5.66	*3.95*		*0.93*		
1977		20.51		5.51					
1978		20.94		5.15					
1979		20.09		4.87					
1980		17.80		4.32					
1981	*20.22*	16.21	*11.81*	3.96	*3.34*		*0.53*		
1982		14.53		3.55					
1983		13.52		3.49					
1984		18.59		4.11					
1985	*20.33*	16.86	*11.84*	4.03	*3.31*		*0.53*		
1986		15.88		3.86					
1987	*20.61*	16.98	*12.12*	5.03	*3.54*		*0.67*		
1988	*21.31*	17.36	*12.73*	4.96	*3.87*		*0.74*		
1989	*21.47*	17.11	*12.89*	4.70	*3.91*		*0.76*		
1990	*21.08*	16.88	*12.50*	4.59	*3.72*		*0.68*		
1991	*20.97*	16.84	*12.38*	4.62	*3.65*		*0.65*		
1992	*21.20*	16.74	*12.66*	4.58	*3.77*		*0.66*		
1993	*21.90*		*13.23*		*4.13*		*0.84*		
1994	*21.82*		*13.01*		*3.88*		*0.70*		
1995	*22.28*		*13.51*		*4.33*		*0.82*		
1996	*22.43*		*13.63*		*4.29*		*0.64*		
1997	*23.44*		*14.56*		*5.03*		*1.25*		
1998	*24.02*		*15.16*		*5.68*		*1.63*		
1999	*25.42*		*16.68*		*7.01*		*2.03*		
2000	*25.76*		*17.00*		*7.23*		*2.62*		
2001	*24.92*		*16.17*		*6.59*		*2.25*		
2002	*24.94*		*16.15*		*6.47*		*1.88*		
2003	*24.96*		*16.08*		*6.49*		*1.75*		
2004	*25.26*		*16.53*		*7.08*		*2.65*		

Source: Tables 8A.2 and 8.3.

Table 13A.19 Shares in total before tax income, Norway

	Top 10%	Top 5%	Top 1%	Top 0.5%	Top 0.1%	Top 0.05%	Top 0.01%
1875	40.00	31.74	18.37	14.37	7.89	5.86	
1876							
1877							
1878							

1879						
1880						
1881						
1882						
1883						
1884						
1885						
1886						
1887						
1888	46.60	36.53	20.29	15.26	7.71	5.64
1889						
1890						
1891						
1892						
1893						
1894						
1895						
1896			19.80	15.46	8.79	
1897						
1898						
1899						
1900						
1901						
1902			15.21	11.71	6.59	5.13
1903						
1904						
1905						
1906	42.19	32.36	17.98	13.99	8.03	
1907						
1908						
1909						
1910	29.89	21.54	10.45	7.71		
1911						
1912						
1913	33.21	23.96	11.61	8.37		
1914						
1915						
1916						
1917						
1918						
1919						
1920						
1921						
1922						
1923						
1924						
1925						
1926						
1927						
1928						
1929	41.32	28.25	12.57	9.06	4.35	
1930						
1931						
1932						
1933						

(*continued*)

Table 13A.19 Continued

	Top 10%	Top 5%	Top 1%	Top 0.5%	Top 0.1%	Top 0.05%	Top 0.01%
1934							
1935							
1936							
1937							
1938		27.56	12.72	9.38	4.56	3.28	
1939							
1940							
1941							
1942							
1943							
1944							
1945							
1946							
1947							
1948	34.38	22.46	9.10	6.36	2.83	2.00	
1949	34.02	22.14	8.88	6.20	2.74	1.94	
1950	34.10	22.09	8.76	6.06	2.63	1.84	
1951	32.31	20.80	8.16	5.67	2.51	1.78	
1952	31.39	19.57	6.93	4.59	1.87	1.29	
1953	33.08	20.49	7.14	4.67	1.83	1.25	
1954	31.79	19.79	6.86	4.46	1.70	1.15	
1955	32.61	20.37	7.20	4.76	1.90	1.31	
1956							
1957	32.72	20.94	7.88	5.35	2.35	1.70	
1958	34.72	21.91	7.76	5.09	2.01	1.38	
1959	34.20	21.51	7.39	4.73	1.77	1.19	
1960	32.17	20.06	6.94	4.44	1.62	1.08	
1961	31.77	19.78	6.76	4.29	1.53	1.01	
1962	32.20	19.87	6.57	4.11	1.42	0.92	
1963	32.03	19.67	6.43	3.98	1.35	0.87	
1964	31.45	19.30	6.28	3.88	1.31	0.85	
1965	30.65	18.65	5.99	3.69	1.23	0.79	
1966	31.05	18.89	5.99	3.66	1.20	0.76	
1967	31.25	19.01	5.92	3.58	1.16	0.74	
1968	31.31	19.05	5.92	3.58	1.16	0.74	
1969	31.46	19.21	6.03	3.67	1.21	0.77	
1970	30.29	18.57	5.95	3.66	1.23	0.79	
1971	30.81	18.85	5.99	3.68	1.23	0.79	
1972	30.32	18.48	5.82	3.56	1.18	0.76	
1973	29.60	18.07	5.72	3.50	1.15	0.74	
1974	28.93	17.60	5.56	3.41	1.15	0.75	
1975	29.41	17.73	5.49	3.33	1.09	0.69	
1976	29.73	17.78	5.39	3.23	1.02	0.63	
1977	30.09	18.00	5.45	3.28	1.05	0.67	
1978	27.67	16.58	5.04	3.04	0.97	0.60	
1979	27.01	16.22	5.03	3.09	1.05	0.67	
1980	25.65	15.33	4.74	2.93	1.05	0.70	
1981	25.00	14.93	4.57	2.79	0.98	0.65	
1982	24.68	14.70	4.52	2.78	1.01	0.68	
1983	24.32	14.56	4.51	2.79	1.02	0.68	
1984	23.92	14.37	4.50	2.81	1.05	0.71	

1985	24.02	14.48	4.59	2.88	1.08	0.73
1986	23.47	14.18	4.49	2.81	1.03	0.68
1987	23.44	14.18	4.52	2.83	1.05	0.70
1988	23.07	13.98	4.43	2.75	0.97	0.63
1989	22.22	13.44	4.24	2.64	0.94	0.61
1990	22.51	13.68	4.37	2.72	0.96	0.62
1991	22.56	13.80	4.45	2.78	0.96	0.62
1992	23.58	15.03	5.47	3.64	1.53	1.08
1993	25.91	17.15	7.09	5.05	2.44	1.79
1994	27.27	18.12	7.54	5.38	2.56	1.86
1995	27.22	18.08	7.48	5.34	2.61	1.94
1996	28.19	18.91	8.08	5.88	3.04	2.32
1997	29.49	20.00	8.75	6.42	3.33	2.51
1998	28.35	19.07	8.13	5.87	2.92	2.16
1999	28.65	19.43	8.49	6.21	3.15	2.35
2000	30.81	21.62	10.44	7.98	4.44	3.41
2001	27.21	18.18	7.48	5.28	2.50	1.82
2002	29.26	20.42	9.77	7.48	4.25	3.36
2003	30.27	21.43	10.58	8.18	4.68	3.67
2004	32.17	23.05	11.82	9.30	5.59	4.50
2005	37.67	28.61	16.78	13.71	8.41	6.75
2006	28.78	19.37	8.06	5.71	2.70	1.95

Source: Table 9.1.

Table 13A.20 Shares in total before tax income, Spain

	Top 10%	Top 5%	Top 1%	Top 0.5%	Top 0.1%	Top 0.05%	Top 0.01%
1933							1.41
1934							1.40
1935							1.53
1936							
1937							
1938							
1939							
1940							1.31
1941							1.38
1942							1.21
1943							1.16
1944							1.06
1945							1.12
1946							1.04
1947							0.86
1948						1.83	0.82
1949						1.82	0.81
1950						1.63	0.70
1951						1.42	0.62
1952						1.45	0.64
1953						1.43	0.63
1954					2.63	1.82	0.73
1955					2.77	1.90	0.74

(*continued*)

Table 13A.20 Continued

	Top 10%	Top 5%	Top 1%	Top 0.5%	Top 0.1%	Top 0.05%	Top 0.01%
1956							
1957					2.27	1.53	0.60
1958					2.13	1.45	0.56
1959					2.23	1.52	0.60
1960							
1961					1.88	1.29	0.52
1962							
1963							
1964							
1965							
1966							
1967							
1968							
1969							
1970							
1971					1.86	1.24	0.51
1972							
1973							
1974							
1975							
1976							
1977							
1978							
1979							
1980							
1981	32.61	21.12	7.50	4.87	1.87		0.52
1982	32.96	21.50	7.75	5.08	2.00		0.58
1983	33.29	21.67	7.65	4.94	1.88		0.55
1984	33.56	21.80	7.61	4.89	1.85		0.54
1985	33.72	22.03	7.75	4.99	1.90		0.53
1986	34.66	22.82	8.21	5.36	2.16		0.68
1987	34.85	23.05	8.40	5.52	2.26		0.77
1988	35.05	23.14	8.36	5.46	2.17		0.69
1989	35.67	23.49	8.47	5.52	2.19		0.65
1990	35.35	23.17	8.37	5.45	2.14		0.62
1991	34.58	22.53	8.08	5.23	2.03		0.57
1992	33.93	22.25	8.21	5.34	2.06		0.56
1993	33.19	21.61	7.83	5.06	1.92		0.51
1994	33.55	21.82	7.89	5.10	1.95		0.51
1995	33.38	21.71	7.89	5.12	1.96		0.51
1996	33.45	21.79	7.93	5.16	1.98		0.51
1997	33.29	21.77	8.03	5.25	2.07		0.55
1998	33.36	21.90	8.17	5.39	2.17		0.61
1999	33.95	22.45	8.62	5.78	2.41		0.74
2000	34.19	22.69	8.84	6.00	2.57		0.84
2001	34.03	22.60	8.80	5.95	2.51		0.81
2002	33.41	22.13	8.54	5.75	2.39		0.69
2003	33.30	22.07	8.59	5.82	2.45		0.73
2004	33.03	21.97	8.62	5.87	2.49		0.75
2005	33.21	22.17	8.79	6.03	2.62		0.87

Note: Estimates excluding capital gains.

Sources: Tables 10D.2 and 10D.3.

Table 13A.21 Shares in total before tax income, Portugal

	Top 10%	Top 5%	Top 1%	Top 0.5%	Top 0.1%	Top 0.05%	Top 0.01%
1936					4.58		1.37
1937					4.01		1.14
1938					3.94		1.12
1939					4.17		1.21
1940					4.49		1.25
1941					4.64		1.33
1942					4.16		1.20
1943					3.41		0.97
1944					3.06		0.88
1945					3.35		1.05
1946					3.12		0.96
1947					3.35		1.05
1948					3.55		1.12
1949					3.57		1.09
1950					3.69		1.14
1951					3.56		1.10
1952					3.67		1.11
1953					3.58		1.08
1954					3.60		1.13
1955					3.50		1.09
1956					3.28		0.97
1957					3.32		0.93
1958					3.49		0.94
1959					3.62		1.13
1960					3.25		0.94
1961					3.36		0.94
1962					2.93		0.79
1963					2.96		0.81
1964					3.15		0.74
1965					3.24		0.79
1966					3.33		0.83
1967					3.26		0.78
1968					3.13		0.75
1969					3.12		0.76
1970					2.91		0.79
1971					2.49		0.69
1972					1.97		0.45
1973					1.77		0.40
1974					2.05		0.77
1975					1.21		0.31
1976	26.43	17.60	6.58	4.20	1.14		0.32
1977	22.36	14.55	5.34	3.37	1.08		0.25
1978	20.77	13.56	4.81	2.98	0.96		0.30
1979	16.94	11.07	3.77	2.30	0.65		
1980	15.64	10.41	3.60	2.20	0.68		
1981	15.70	10.08	3.31	2.00	0.61		
1982	17.49	11.93	4.00	2.38	0.61		
1983							
1984							
1985							

(continued)

Table 13A.21 Continued

	Top 10%	Top 5%	Top 1%	Top 0.5%	Top 0.1%	Top 0.05%	Top 0.01%
1986							
1987							
1988							
1989	30.20	19.89	6.84	4.29	1.53		0.45
1990	31.19	20.70	7.21	4.52	1.60		0.45
1991	32.43	21.59	7.46	4.62	1.55		0.40
1992	33.15	22.11	7.58	4.66	1.53		0.35
1993	34.68	23.26	8.06	4.96	1.64		0.37
1994	35.02	23.51	8.19	5.08	1.69		0.37
1995	35.38	23.84	8.41	5.26	1.79		0.39
1996	35.07	23.71	8.45	5.33	1.84		0.41
1997	35.76	24.27	8.78	5.57	1.97		0.45
1998	35.45	24.09	8.78	5.59	1.98		0.45
1999	36.18	24.71	9.23	5.98	2.23		0.54
2000	36.13	24.58	9.09	5.85	2.10		0.49
2001	37.84	25.80	9.65	6.35	2.43		0.62
2002	36.77	24.87	8.97	5.74	2.05		0.47
2003	36.41	24.69	9.13	5.93	2.26		0.68
2004	38.24	25.95	9.62	6.24	2.31		0.60
2005	38.25	26.01	9.77	6.42	2.48		0.69

Source: Table 11D.1.

Table 13A.22 Shares in total before tax income, Italy

	Top 10%	Top 5%	Top 1%	Top 0.5%	Top 0.1%	Top 0.05%	Top 0.01%
1974	30.50	19.86	7.46	4.90	1.81		0.46
1975	31.20	20.04	7.24	4.71	1.64		0.36
1976	29.75	18.00	7.10	4.67	1.70		0.40
1977	27.53	17.81	6.80	4.47	1.66		0.39
1978	27.15	17.56	6.71	4.40	1.63		0.38
1979	27.21	17.69	6.83	4.49	1.67		0.39
1980	27.17	17.72	6.90	4.56	1.72		0.40
1981	26.31	16.91	6.47	4.24	1.57		0.36
1982	26.14	16.75	6.40	4.18	1.53		0.35
1983	26.04	16.68	6.34	4.11	1.48		0.33
1984	26.40	17.01	6.54	4.26	1.56		0.35
1985	26.83	17.50	6.81	4.46	1.65		0.38
1986	27.20	17.98	7.13	4.70	1.77		0.42
1987	28.12	18.68	7.45	4.93	1.86		0.44
1988	28.91	19.27	7.60	4.98	1.83		0.41
1989	29.34	19.64	7.79	5.13	1.91		0.43
1990	29.50	19.69	7.78	5.13	1.92		0.44
1991	29.53	19.86	7.84	5.15	1.92		0.46
1992	29.81	20.00	7.81	5.12	1.90		0.45
1993	30.19	20.23	7.92	5.21	1.97		0.48
1994	30.41	20.42	7.99	5.26	2.00		0.49
1995	30.57	20.58	8.13	5.40	2.07		0.52

1996						
1997						
1998	32.01	21.80	8.74	5.86	2.35	0.65
1999	32.44	22.07	8.82	5.91	2.38	0.66
2000	32.94	22.56	9.09	6.12	2.49	0.70
2001	33.00	22.68	9.28	6.30	2.65	0.79
2002	33.03	22.68	9.28	6.32	2.68	0.81
2003	33.02	22.71	9.36	6.41	2.75	0.84
2004	32.64	22.32	9.03	6.12	2.55	0.75
2005	32.90	22.56	9.23	6.29	2.68	0.83

Source: Table 12A.2.

Table 13A.23 Pareto–Lorenz α coefficients

	FR	UK	US	CA	AUS	NZ	DE	NL	CH	IR	IN	CHI	JA	IND	SI	ARG	SE	FI	NO	SP	PO	IT
1900							1.52						1.60									
1901							1.53						1.61									
1902							1.55						1.61						1.57			
1903							1.55						1.60				1.98					
1904							1.55						1.57									
1905	1.60						1.54						1.57									
1906							1.52						1.60						1.54			
1907							1.52						1.62				1.64					
1908							1.52						1.64									
1909							1.53						1.65									
1910							1.52						1.63									
1911							1.52						1.61				1.62					
1912							1.52						1.59				1.58					
1913			1.47				1.52						1.60									
1914			1.48				1.51						1.58									
1915	1.57		1.39				1.49	1.63					1.50									
1916	1.52		1.38				1.46	1.54					1.43				1.45					
1917	1.55		1.48				1.44	1.49					1.41									
1918	1.59	1.53	1.59				1.44	1.49					1.43				1.53					
1919	1.60	1.51	1.64				1.48	1.55					1.46									
1920	1.59		1.75	1.75				1.52					1.50				1.70					
1921	1.61		1.79	1.93	1.88	2.27		1.57					1.56	1.49								
1922	1.64		1.73	1.92	1.91	2.27		1.62			1.54		1.55	1.74								
1923	1.65		1.77	1.95	1.89	2.31		1.69			1.55		1.56	1.71								
1924	1.68		1.74	1.90	1.78	2.34		1.71			1.49		1.56	1.68								
1925	1.69		1.71	1.93	1.83	2.38	1.86	1.67			1.57		1.57	1.67								
1926	1.69		1.68	1.87	1.83	2.44	1.82	1.65			1.57		1.54	1.67								
1927	1.68		1.66	1.84	1.92	2.48	1.81	1.65			1.56		1.54	1.71								
1928	1.69		1.61	1.86	1.80	2.26	1.81	1.65			1.57		1.54	1.74								
1929	1.70		1.62	1.88	1.90	2.39	1.83	1.64			1.55		1.54	1.73					1.86			
1930	1.73		1.69	1.83	1.94	2.56		1.73			1.55		1.56	1.83			1.83					
1931	1.77		1.75	1.91	1.93			1.83			1.58		1.59	1.89								

Year	C1	C2	C3	C4	C5	C6	C7	C8	C9	C10	C11	C12	C13	C14	C15	C16
1932	1.83		1.72	1.89	1.92	2.42	1.91	1.92	1.94	1.57	1.57	1.92		1.66		
1933	1.85		1.71	1.94	1.87	2.64	1.84	1.95	1.96	1.57	1.54	1.91		1.67		
1934	1.85		1.77	1.90	1.90	2.35	1.90	1.96		1.58	1.54	1.90		1.65	1.98	
1935	1.86		1.76	1.92	1.92	2.38	1.77	1.95		1.60	1.53			1.66	1.87	
1936	1.84		1.73	1.86	1.94	2.77	1.66	1.85	1.90	1.57	1.53			1.72		
1937	1.79	1.70	1.74	1.90	1.96	2.81	1.62	1.72		1.57	1.51			1.67		
1938	1.82		1.84	1.94	1.94	2.66	1.63	1.81		1.58	1.51	1.78		1.67		
1939	1.74		1.82	1.91	1.95	2.83		1.83	1.76	1.51	1.56	1.82		1.66		
1940	1.77		1.82	2.05	1.94					1.50	1.62			1.63		
1941	1.92		1.83	1.99	2.03			1.80		1.45	1.72			1.60	2.15	1.80
1942	2.00		1.85	2.02	2.11						1.74			1.47		
1943	2.11		1.93	2.09	2.12				1.83	1.49	1.78			1.54	2.19	
1944	2.25		2.00	2.15	2.27					1.51	1.78			1.58	2.21	
1945	2.41		2.10	2.19	2.28	2.73			1.94	1.52	2.14			1.61	2.25	
1946	2.21		2.15	2.23	2.30	2.70		2.16						1.57	2.17	
1947	2.23		2.13	2.23	2.28	2.78			1.95	1.46	2.15		2.06	1.56	2.30	
1948	2.25		2.06	2.21	2.34	2.61				1.54	2.37		2.08	1.60	2.41	2.03
1949	2.16	2.09	2.07	2.30	2.13	2.64			1.94	1.56	2.77		2.02	1.64	2.45	2.04
1950	2.16		2.03	2.23	2.00	2.67	1.90	2.00		1.61	2.84		1.84	1.63	2.45	2.09
1951	2.21	2.13	2.12	2.24	2.25	2.69			1.88		2.44		1.69	1.65	2.36	2.05
1952	2.27	2.17	2.22	2.28	2.31	2.76		1.91		1.57	2.45		1.71	1.82	2.46	2.32
1953	2.27	2.20	2.27	2.29	2.25	2.69		2.05	1.89	1.61	2.47		1.80	1.91	2.47	2.45
1954	2.34	2.23	2.29	2.30	2.30	2.75				1.63	2.43		1.86	1.83	2.48	2.53
1955	2.35	2.20	2.31	2.23	2.35	2.82			1.92	1.65	2.43				2.52	2.37
1956	2.39	2.26	2.39	2.29	2.29	2.69	1.69	2.19	1.94	1.67	2.34		2.12	1.85	2.55	
1957	2.40	2.30	2.38	2.33	2.40	2.75		1.98		1.69	2.33		2.20		2.57	2.10
1958	2.41	2.30	2.41	2.37	2.67	3.24		2.15		1.71	2.32		2.31	1.83	2.60	2.42
1959	2.50	2.34	2.51	2.40	2.68	3.03			1.92	1.70	2.30		2.20	1.94	2.61	2.63
1960	2.48	2.27	2.50	2.43	2.78	2.86	1.76			1.73	2.29		2.18		2.70	2.71
1961	2.50		2.55	2.44	2.74				1.92	1.77	2.31		2.24	1.91	2.79	2.81
1962	2.55	2.30	2.63	2.53	2.82	2.89					2.31		2.28		2.82	2.98
1963	2.59	2.38	2.62	2.57	2.85				1.91		2.40		2.29		2.83	3.11
1964	2.62	2.35	2.56	2.53	2.89	2.60				1.91	2.43		2.35		2.92	3.12
1965	2.63	2.35	2.48	2.54	2.96	3.05	1.68		1.94	1.80			2.42		2.93	3.19

(continued)

	FR	UK	US	CA	AUS	NZ	DE	NL	CH	IR	IN	CHI	JA	IND	SI	ARG	SE	FI	NO	SP	PO	IT
1966	2.61	2.43	2.44	2.60	2.95	3.09					1.77		2.46		2.50		2.99	3.86	3.30			
1967	2.57	2.53	2.45	2.64	2.78	3.04			1.93		1.84		2.44		2.44		3.09		3.42			
1968	2.56	2.54	2.44	2.63	2.93	3.02	1.71				1.84		2.48		2.18		3.08		3.42			
1969	2.57	2.54	2.52	2.67	2.81	2.99			1.92				2.64		2.23		3.11		3.31			
1970	2.60	2.73	2.53	2.75	3.04	2.87		2.57			1.87		2.52		2.25		3.16		3.17			
1971	2.58	2.66	2.56	2.83	3.10	3.25	1.69		1.90		1.91		2.76		2.29	3.04	3.22	2.72	3.19			
1972	2.53	2.74	2.55	2.75	3.06	3.02							3.38		2.20	2.94	3.25		3.25			
1973	2.47	2.63	2.59	2.70	3.18	2.82		2.76	1.94		2.00		2.19		2.07	2.80	3.26		3.28			2.60
1974	2.56	2.61	2.42	2.67	3.24	2.88	1.81				2.08		2.55		2.26	2.27	3.22		3.18			2.82
1975	2.57	2.77	2.46	2.61	3.03	2.90			2.07	2.92	2.03		2.52		2.33		3.25		3.36			
1976	2.55	2.91	2.45	2.73	3.11	3.17				2.99	2.11		2.90		2.35		3.47	2.69	3.62		4.61	2.64
1977	2.53	3.02	2.42	2.76	3.00	3.03	1.79	3.11	2.09	2.92	2.05		2.94		2.36		4.07		3.50		3.25	2.58
1978	2.54	2.98	2.40	2.73	3.08	3.07				2.65	2.10		2.94		2.46		3.72		3.53		3.34	2.59
1979	2.49	2.93	2.33	2.61	3.10	3.10			2.10	1.93	2.12		2.79		2.46		3.92		3.13		4.22	2.58
1980	2.51		2.29	2.57	3.05	3.14	1.73			2.90	2.15		2.75		2.37		3.82		2.90		3.66	2.52
1981	2.51	2.77	2.26	2.62	3.12	3.15		2.94	2.05	2.92	2.27		2.85		2.39		3.58		3.02	2.52	3.78	2.60
1982	2.59	2.69	2.15	2.27	3.04	3.16				2.83	2.12		2.75		2.30		3.50		2.86	2.42	5.46	2.64
1983	2.72	2.75	2.07	2.41	2.95	3.02	1.83		2.02	2.81	2.21		2.99		2.33		3.37		2.83	2.56		2.72
1984	2.70	2.72	1.99	2.28	2.99	2.96				2.85	2.13		3.01				3.34		2.72	2.60		2.65
1985	2.67	2.56	1.98	2.28	2.80	2.99		3.22		2.87	2.11		3.05				3.48		2.69	2.56		2.60
1986	2.60	2.55	2.01	2.30	2.65	3.20	1.75		1.84	2.85	2.08	5.46	3.05		2.48		3.65	3.61	2.78	2.39		2.53
1987	2.46		1.85	2.21	2.21	2.73				2.95	2.04	5.70	3.00		2.42		3.24	3.55	2.73	2.33		2.52
1988	2.41		1.67	1.97	1.82	2.96			1.96	2.87	1.99	4.15	3.07		2.44		2.83		2.93	2.41		2.62
1989	2.34		1.74	1.86	2.25	2.56	1.71	3.13	1.87	2.61	2.16	4.13	2.74	1.31	2.23		2.65	3.46	2.91	2.43	2.86	2.57
1990	2.34		1.73	1.99	2.22	2.21		3.42		2.68	2.54	4.24	2.48	1.38			2.72	3.82	2.94	2.45	2.89	2.55
1991	2.41		1.81	2.03	2.22	2.40		3.19	1.92		2.54	4.18	2.63	1.34			2.46	3.99	2.98	2.50	3.15	2.57
1992	2.47		1.70	2.08	2.20	2.24	1.70	3.16			2.28	3.53	2.75	1.37			2.60		2.24	2.50	3.28	2.59
1993	2.48	2.11	1.77	2.03	2.10	2.30		3.68	1.90		1.90	3.54	2.82		2.18		2.54	3.24	1.86	2.57	3.24	2.53
1994	2.44	2.15	1.77	2.06	1.80	2.26		3.66			1.96	3.67	2.78	1.36			2.39	3.90	1.88	2.55	3.18	2.51
1995	2.47	2.09	1.77	2.02	2.12	2.28	1.76	3.70	1.86		1.64	3.65	2.84	1.42			2.53	3.61	1.84	2.52	3.05	2.47

1996	2.48	1.85	1.73	1.95	2.19	2.23		3.40	1.82	3.43	2.76	1.42			2.49		1.74	2.52	2.96	
1997	2.62	1.86	1.68	1.86	2.11	2.16		3.25	1.64	3.39	2.75	1.40		1.86	2.45	2.53	1.72	2.44	2.85	
1998	2.62	1.82	1.64	1.81	2.08	1.97	1.67	3.62	1.64	3.42	2.77	1.32		1.85	2.34	2.18	1.80	2.36	2.83	2.33
1999	2.51	1.79	1.61	1.78	1.87	1.67		3.30	1.64	3.55	2.79	1.29		1.71	2.32	2.17	1.76	2.24	2.61	2.32
2000	2.47	1.77	1.57	1.71	1.89	2.39				3.38	2.53	1.23	1.91	1.67	1.96	1.79	1.59	2.16	2.75	2.29
2001	2.41	1.82	1.64		2.08	2.19				3.45	2.49	1.33	2.01	1.65	2.02	1.88	1.90	2.20	2.49	2.19
2002	2.42	1.87	1.68		2.07	2.16				3.34	2.52	1.46	1.93	1.54	2.11	2.16	1.57	2.24	2.79	2.17
2003	2.43	1.84	1.65			1.94				3.10	2.54	1.57	2.00	1.56	2.04	2.32	1.55	2.20	2.54	2.14
2004	2.40	1.82	1.60			1.81					2.44		1.98	1.61	2.08	1.74	1.48	2.17		2.22
2005	2.35	1.78	1.55			2.12					2.40		1.96		2.07		1.43	2.11		

Note: The Pareto–Lorenz α coefficients reported in these tables were computed using the top shares series reported in Tables 13A.1 to 13A.22. As a rule we estimated α from the top 0.1% share within top 1% share: $\alpha = 1/[1 - \log(S_{1\%}/S_{0.1\%})/\log(10)]$. When the top 0.1% and top 1% shares were not available we used the closest substitutes.

Table 13A.24 Pareto–Lorenz β coefficients

	FR	UK	US	CA	AUS	NZ	DE	NL	CH	IR	IN	CHI	JA	IND	SI	ARG	SE	FI	NO	SP	PO	IT
1900													2.65									
1901													2.64									
1902													2.65						2.75			
1903													2.68									
1904													2.77									
1905	2.66												2.75									
1906													2.67						2.86			
1907													2.62				2.56					
1908													2.57									
1909													2.53									
1910													2.59									
1911													2.64				2.61					
1912													2.69				2.73					
1913			3.14										2.68									
1914			3.08										2.73									
1915	2.74		3.57										3.00				3.22					
1916	2.92		3.64				3.17	3.02					3.30									
1917	2.82		3.09				3.25	3.03					3.41									
1918	2.71	2.89	2.69				3.25	2.80					3.32				2.87					
1919	2.68	2.95	2.56				3.06	2.92					3.17				2.43					
1920	2.69		2.33	2.33				2.75					2.98									
1921	2.64		2.27	2.08	2.14	1.79		2.62					2.79	3.04								
1922	2.56		2.37	2.09	2.10	1.79		2.45			2.84		2.82	2.34								
1923	2.53		2.30	2.06	2.13	1.76		2.40			2.81		2.77	2.41								
1924	2.46		2.36	2.11	2.28	1.75		2.49			3.04		2.78	2.47								
1925	2.44		2.40	2.07	2.21	1.73	2.16	2.55			2.77		2.76	2.50								
1926	2.46		2.46	2.15	2.20	1.69	2.22	2.54			2.75		2.86	2.50								
1927	2.47		2.51	2.19	2.08	1.68	2.23	2.53			2.78		2.84	2.42								
1928	2.46		2.64	2.17	2.25	1.79	2.24	2.56			2.76		2.86	2.35								
1929	2.43		2.61	2.14	2.11	1.72	2.20	2.46			2.82		2.85	2.37					2.17			
1930	2.37		2.44	2.21	2.07	1.64		2.36			2.81		2.77	2.21			2.20					
1931	2.30		2.33	2.10	2.07			2.20			2.74		2.70	2.12								

Year																	
1932	2.21		2.39	2.12	2.09		2.10	2.09			2.77	2.75	2.09		2.52		
1933	2.18		2.41	2.06	2.15		2.19	2.05	2.06		2.74	2.86	2.09		2.48		
1934	2.18		2.30	2.11	2.12		2.11	2.04	2.05		2.74	2.85	2.11		2.53	2.02	
1935	2.16		2.32	2.08	2.08	1.70	2.30	2.05			2.68	2.88			2.53	2.15	
1936	2.20		2.37	2.16	2.07	1.61	2.52	2.18			2.74	2.88			2.38		
1937	2.27	2.43	2.34	2.12	2.05	1.74	2.61	2.39	2.12		2.74	2.95			2.49		
1938	2.22		2.19	2.07	2.07	1.73	2.59	2.24		2.20	2.71	2.98	2.29		2.48		2.24
1939	2.35		2.22	2.10	2.06	1.57		2.20	2.32		2.95	2.78	2.22		2.51		
1940	2.30		2.22	1.95	2.06	1.55					3.02	2.61			2.58		
1941	2.09		2.21	2.01	1.97	1.60		2.26			3.20	2.39			2.66	1.87	
1942	2.00		2.17	1.98	1.90	1.55						2.36			3.13		
1943	1.90		2.07	1.92	1.89				2.21	1.96	3.05	2.28			2.86	1.84	1.97
1944	1.80		2.00	1.87	1.79	1.58					2.95	2.29			2.72	1.83	1.96
1945	1.71		1.91	1.84	1.78	1.59			2.07		2.94	1.88			2.63	1.80	1.92
1946	1.83		1.87	1.82	1.77	1.56		1.86							2.75	1.86	1.95
1947	1.81		1.89	1.81	1.78	1.62			2.05		3.17	1.87		1.94	2.79	1.77	1.76
1948	1.80		1.94	1.82	1.75	1.61					2.86	1.73		1.93	2.66	1.71	1.69
1949	1.86	1.92	1.94	1.77	1.88	1.60			2.06		2.78	1.57		1.98	2.56	1.69	1.69
1950	1.86		1.97	1.82	2.00	1.59	2.11	2.00			2.63	1.54		2.19	2.59	1.69	1.65
1951	1.83	1.88	1.89	1.81	1.80	1.57			2.13			1.70		2.46	2.54	1.73	1.73
1952	1.79	1.86	1.82	1.78	1.76	1.59		2.10			2.74	1.70		2.42	2.21	1.68	
1953	1.79	1.83	1.79	1.78	1.80	1.57		1.95	2.12		2.64	1.69		2.25	2.10	1.68	
1954	1.75	1.82	1.78	1.77	1.77	1.55					2.59	1.68		2.16	2.21	1.67	
1955	1.74	1.83	1.76	1.81	1.74	1.59			2.09		2.55	1.70				1.66	
1956	1.72	1.79	1.72	1.78	1.78	1.57	2.45	1.84			2.50	1.70		1.89	2.17	1.65	
1957	1.71	1.77	1.72	1.75	1.71	1.45		2.02	2.06		2.46	1.74		1.83		1.64	1.91
1958	1.71	1.77	1.71	1.73	1.60	1.49		1.87			2.42	1.75		1.76	2.20	1.62	1.71
1959	1.67	1.75	1.66	1.71	1.59	1.54			2.09		2.44	1.76		1.84	2.07	1.62	1.61
1960	1.67	1.79	1.67	1.70	1.56			2.09			2.38	1.77		1.85		1.59	1.58
1961	1.67		1.64	1.69	1.58	1.53	2.31		2.09		2.29	1.78		1.80	2.10	1.56	1.55
1962	1.65	1.77	1.61	1.65	1.55			2.10				1.76		1.78		1.55	1.50
1963	1.63	1.72	1.62	1.64	1.54	1.63			2.10		2.10	1.76		1.77		1.55	1.47
1964	1.62	1.74	1.64	1.65	1.53			2.06				1.72		1.74		1.52	1.47
1965	1.62	1.74	1.67	1.65	1.51	1.49	2.47		2.06		2.25	1.70		1.71		1.52	1.46

(continued)

Table 13A.24. Continued

	FR	UK	US	CA	AUS	NZ	DE	NL	CH	IR	IN	CHI	JA	IND	SI	ARG	SE	FI	NO	SP	PO	IT
1966	1.62	1.70	1.70	1.62	1.51	1.48					2.30		1.68		1.67		1.50	1.35	1.43			
1967	1.64	1.65	1.69	1.61	1.56	1.49					2.19		1.70		1.69		1.48		1.41			
1968	1.64	1.65	1.69	1.61	1.52	1.49	2.41		2.07		2.19		1.68		1.85		1.48		1.41			
1969	1.64	1.65	1.66	1.60	1.55	1.50		1.64	2.09				1.61		1.81		1.47		1.43			
1970	1.62	1.58	1.65	1.57	1.49	1.53					2.15		1.66		1.80	1.49	1.46	1.58	1.46			
1971	1.63	1.60	1.64	1.55	1.48	1.45	2.44		2.11		2.10		1.57		1.78	1.52	1.45		1.46			
1972	1.65	1.58	1.65	1.57	1.49	1.50							1.42		1.84	1.56	1.44		1.44			
1973	1.68	1.62	1.63	1.59	1.46	1.55	2.23	1.57	2.06		2.00		1.84		1.93	1.79	1.44		1.44			
1974	1.64	1.62	1.71	1.60	1.45	1.53					1.93		1.64		1.80		1.45		1.46			1.63
1975	1.64	1.56	1.68	1.62	1.49	1.53		1.55	1.94	1.52	1.97		1.66		1.75		1.44		1.42			1.55
1976	1.64	1.52	1.69	1.58	1.47	1.46				1.50	1.90		1.53		1.74		1.40	1.59	1.38		1.28	1.61
1977	1.65	1.49	1.70	1.57	1.50	1.49	2.27	1.47	1.92	1.52	1.95		1.52		1.74		1.33		1.40		1.44	1.63
1978	1.65	1.51	1.72	1.58	1.48	1.48				1.61	1.91		1.51		1.69		1.37		1.40		1.43	1.63
1979	1.67	1.52	1.75	1.62	1.48	1.48			1.91		1.89		1.56		1.69		1.34		1.47		1.31	1.63
1980	1.66		1.77	1.63	1.49	1.47	2.38			1.53	1.87		1.57		1.73		1.35		1.53		1.38	1.66
1981	1.66	1.56	1.79	1.62	1.47	1.46		1.52	1.95	1.52	1.79		1.54		1.72		1.39		1.49	1.66	1.36	1.63
1982	1.63	1.59	1.87	1.79	1.49	1.46				1.55	1.89		1.57		1.77		1.40		1.54	1.70	1.22	1.61
1983	1.58	1.57	1.93	1.71	1.51	1.50	2.20		1.98	1.55	1.83		1.50		1.75		1.42		1.55	1.64		1.58
1984	1.59	1.58	2.01	1.78	1.50	1.51		1.45		1.54	1.88		1.50				1.43		1.58	1.63		1.61
1985	1.60	1.64	2.02	1.78	1.56	1.50			2.19	1.54	1.90		1.49		1.68		1.40		1.59	1.64		1.62
1986	1.63	1.64	1.99	1.77	1.61	1.45	2.34			1.54	1.92	1.22	1.49		1.70		1.38	1.38	1.56	1.72		1.65
1987	1.69		2.17	1.82	1.83	1.58			2.04	1.51	1.96	1.21	1.50		1.70		1.45	1.39	1.58	1.75		1.66
1988	1.71		2.49	2.03	2.23	1.51				1.53	2.01	1.32	1.48		1.81		1.55	1.41	1.52	1.71		1.62
1989	1.75		2.35	2.16	1.80	1.64	2.41	1.47	2.15	1.62	1.86	1.32	1.58	4.25			1.61	1.35	1.52	1.70	1.54	1.64
1990	1.74		2.36	2.01	1.82	1.83		1.41		1.60	1.65	1.31	1.68	3.65			1.58	1.33	1.51	1.69	1.53	1.65
1991	1.71		2.24	1.97	1.82	1.72		1.46	2.09		1.65	1.31	1.61	3.96			1.69		1.50	1.67	1.47	1.64
1992	1.68		2.42	1.93	1.84	1.81	2.44	1.46			1.78	1.40	1.57				1.62		1.80	1.67	1.44	1.63
1993	1.68	1.90	2.30	1.97	1.91	1.77		1.37	2.11		2.11	1.39	1.55	3.69	1.85		1.65	1.45	2.16	1.64	1.45	1.65
1994	1.69	1.87	2.29	1.95	2.24	1.79		1.38			2.04	1.37	1.56	3.75			1.72	1.34	2.13	1.65	1.46	1.66
1995	1.68	1.92	2.30	1.98	1.89	1.78	2.31	1.37	2.16		2.55	1.38	1.54	3.41			1.65	1.38	2.19	1.66	1.49	1.68

1996	1.67	2.18	2.37	2.06	1.84	1.82		1.42	2.21	1.41	1.57	3.36			1.67		2.36	1.66	1.51	
1997	1.62	2.16	2.47	2.16	1.90	1.86		1.45	2.56	1.42	1.57	3.53		2.16	1.69	1.65	2.38	1.70	1.54	
1998	1.62	2.22	2.55	2.23	1.92	2.03	2.49	1.38	2.56	1.41	1.56	4.14		2.18	1.75	1.84	2.25	1.73	1.55	1.75
1999	1.66	2.27	2.64	2.29	2.16	2.48		1.43	2.56	1.39	1.56	4.44		2.42	1.76	1.86	2.32	1.81	1.62	1.76
2000	1.68	2.29	2.75	2.42	2.13	1.72				1.42	1.65	5.31	2.10	2.49	2.04	2.27	2.69	1.86	1.57	1.78
2001	1.71	2.22	2.56		1.92	1.84				1.41	1.67	4.05	1.99	2.54	1.98	2.14	2.11	1.84	1.67	1.84
2002	1.70	2.15	2.48		1.94	1.86				1.43	1.66	3.16	2.07	2.85	1.90	1.86	2.76	1.81	1.56	1.85
2003	1.70	2.19	2.54			2.07				1.48	1.65	2.74	2.00	2.80	1.96	1.76	2.82	1.83	1.65	1.88
2004	1.72	2.22	2.68			2.23					1.69		2.02	2.65	1.93	2.34	3.08	1.85		1.82
2005	1.74	2.28	2.82			1.89					1.71		2.04		1.93		3.34	1.90		

Note: The β coefficients reported in this table were computed from the α coefficients reported in Table 13A.23 using the formula: $\beta = \alpha/(\alpha - 1)$. Alternatively they can be computed by using directly the top income shares series and the formula: $\beta = 1/[\log(S_{1\%}/S_{0.1\%})/\log(10)]$.

REFERENCES

Atkinson, A. B. and A. Brandolini (2006). 'The Panel-of-Countries Approach to Explaining Income Inequality', in S. L. Morgan, D. B. Grusky, and G. S. Fields (eds.) *Mobility and Inequality*. Stanford, Calif.: Stanford University Press.

—— and A. J. Harrison (1978). *The Distribution of Personal Wealth in Britain*. Cambridge: Cambridge University Press.

—— and A. Leigh (2007). 'The Distribution of Top Incomes in Five Anglo-Saxon Countries over the Twentieth Century'. Canberra: Australian National University, mimeo.

—— —— (2008). 'Top Incomes in New Zealand 1921–2005: Understanding the Effects of Marginal Tax Rates, Migration Threat, and the Macroeconomy', *Review of Income and Wealth*, 54(2): 149–65.

—— and T. Piketty (2007). *Top Incomes over the Twentieth Century: A Contrast between Continental European and English-Speaking Countries*. Oxford: Oxford University Press.

Autor, D. H., L. F. Katz, and M. S. Kearney (2006). 'The Polarization of the U.S. Labour Market', *American Economic Review, Papers and Proceedings*, 96: 189–94.

Bach, S., G. Corneo, and V. Steiner (2008). 'Effective Taxation of Top Incomes in Germany, 1992–2002', DIW Discussion Paper 767, Berlin.

Brewer, M., A. Muriel, D. Phillips, and L. Sibieta (2008). *Poverty and Inequality in the UK: 2008*. London: Institute for Fiscal Studies.

Coles, S. (2001). *An Introduction to Statistical Modeling of Extreme Values*. London: Springer Verlag.

Dell, F. (2008). 'L'Allemagne inégale', Ph.D. thesis, Paris School of Economics.

Embrechts, P., C. Klüppelberg, and T. Mikosch (1997). *Modelling Extremal Events*. Berlin: Springer Verlag.

Feinstein, C. H. (1972). *Statistical Tables of National Income, Expenditure and Output of the U.K. 1855–1965*. Cambridge: Cambridge University Press.

Frank, R. H. (2000). 'Progressive Taxation and the Incentive Problem', in J. B. Slemrod (ed.) *Does Atlas Shrug?* New York: Russell Sage Foundation: 490-507.

—— and P. J. Cook (1995). *The Winner Take-All Society*. New York: Free Press.

Goldin, C. and R. Margo (1992). 'The Great Compression: The Wage Structure in the United States at Mid-Century', *Quarterly Journal of Economics*, 107: 1–34.

Goode, R. (1964). *The Individual Income Tax*. Washington, DC: Brookings Institution.

Gordon, R. and J. Slemrod (2000). 'Are Real Responses to Taxes Simply Income Shifting between Corporate and Personal Tax Bases?', in J. Slemrod (ed.) *Does Atlas Shrug? The Economic Consequences of Taxing the Rich*. Cambridge: Cambridge University Press.

Guilera, J. (2008). 'Top Income Shares in Portugal over the Twentieth Century', Documents de Treball de la Facultat de Ciències Econòmiques I Empresarials, E08/195, Universitat de Barcelona.

Gustafsson, B. and B. Jansson (2007). 'Top Incomes in Sweden during Three-Quarters of a Century: A Micro-Data Approach', IZA Discussion Paper 2672, IZA Bonn.

Katz, L. F. and D. H. Autor (1999). 'Changes in the Wage Structure and Earnings Inequality', in O. Ashenfelter and D. Card (eds.) *Handbook of Labor Economics*, volume 3A. Amsterdam: North-Holland.

Kuznets, S. (1953). *Shares of Upper Income Groups in Income and Savings*. New York: National Bureau of Economic Research.

—— (1955). 'Economic Growth and Income Inequality', *American Economic Review*, 45: 1–28.

Landais, C. (2007). 'Les Hauts Revenus en France 1998–2006: une explosion des inégalités?', Paris School of Economics Working Paper.

Lazear, E. P. and S. Rosen (1981). 'Rank-Order Tournaments as Optimum Labor Contracts', *Journal of Political Economy*, 89: 841–64.

Leigh, A. (2007). 'How Closely do Top Income Shares Track Other Measures of Inequality?', *Economic Journal*, 117: F619–F633.

—— (2009). 'Top Incomes', in W. Salverda, B. Nolan, and T. Smeeding (eds.) *The Oxford Handbook of Economic Inequality*. Oxford: Oxford University Press .

Lydall, H. F. (1959). 'The Distribution of Employment Incomes', *Econometrica*, 27: 110–15.

Marshall, A. (1920). *Principles of Economics*, 8th edn. London: Macmillan.

Meade, J. E. (1964). *Efficiency, Equality and the Ownership of Property*. London: Allen & Unwin.

Merz, J., D. Hirschel, and M. Zwick (2005). 'Struktur und Verteilung hoher Einkommen: Mikroanalysen auf der Basis der Einkommensteuerstatistik', Beitrag zum zweiten Armuts- und Reichtumsbericht 2004 der Bundesregierung.

Morgenstern, O. (1963). *On the Accuracy of Economic Observations*, 2nd edn. Princeton: Princeton University Press.

Piketty, T. (2001). *Les Hauts Revenus en France au 20ème siècle*. Paris: Grasset.

—— (2003). 'Income Inequality in France, 1901–1998', *Journal of Political Economy*, 111: 1004–42.

—— G. Postel-Vinay, and J. L. Rosenthal (2006). 'Wealth Concentration in a Developing Economy: Paris and France, 1807–1994', *American Economic Review*.

—— and Saez, E. (2001). 'Income Inequality in the United States, 1913–1998', NBER Working Paper 8467.

—— —— (2006). 'The Evolution of Top Incomes: A Historical and International Perspective', *American Economic Review, Papers and Proceedings*, 96: 200–5.

Roine, J., J. Vlachos, and D. Waldenström (2008). 'The Long-Run Determinants of Inequality: What Can we Learn from Top Income Data?', Discussion Paper.

Rosen, S. (1981). 'The Economics of Superstars', *American Economic Review*, 71: 845–58.

Saez, E. (2004). 'Reported Incomes and Marginal Tax Rates, 1960–2000: Evidence and Policy Implications', in J. Poterba (ed.) *Tax Policy and the Economy*, 18. Cambridge, Mass.: MIT Press.

—— J. Slemrod, and S. Giertz (2009). 'The Elasticity of Taxable Income with Respect to Marginal Tax Rates: A Critical Review', working paper, February, in preparation for the *Journal of Economic Literature*.

Scheve, K. and D. Stasavage (2009). 'Institutions, Partisanship, and Inequality in the Long Run', *World Politics*, 61.

Simon, H. (1957). 'The Compensation of Executives', *Sociometry*, 20: 32–5.

Stiglitz, J. E. (1969). 'Distribution of Income and Wealth among Individuals', *Econometrica*, 37: 382–97.

Tinbergen, J. (1975). *Income Distribution: Analysis and Policies*. Amsterdam: North-Holland.

Titmuss, R. M. (1962). *Income Distribution and Social Change*. London: Allen & Unwin.

Vaughan, R. N. (1993). 'On the Microfoundations of Wealth Distribution Functions', in E. N. Wolff (ed.) *Research on Economic Inequality*, iv: *Studies in the Distribution of Household Wealth*. Greenwich, Conn.: JAI Press.

Index